Pocket
Thesaurus

Pocket
Thesaurus

HarperResource
An Imprint of HarperCollinsPublishers

first edition 2002

© **HarperCollins Publishers 2002**

www.collinsdictionaries.com

Bank of English® is a registered trademark
of HarperCollins Publishers Limited

HarperResource is an imprint
of HarperCollins Publishers

HarperCollins Publishers, Inc.
10 East 53rd Street, New York, NY 10022

ISBN 0-06-008569-X

www.harpercollins.com

Library of Congress Cataloging-in-Publication Data
has been applied for

HarperCollins books may be purchased for educational, business,
or sales promotional use. For information, please write to:
Special Markets Department, HarperCollins Publishers Inc.
10 East 53rd Street, New York, NY 10022

Computing support and typesetting by Stewart C Russell
and John Podbielski

Editorial Staff

US Editor
Jennifer Sagala

Editor
Lorna Gilmour

Publishing Manager
Elaine Higgleton

Series Editor
Lorna Sinclair Knight

BANK *of* ENGLISH

This book has been compiled by referring to the Bank of English, a unique database of the English language with examples of over 450 million words taken from a very wide range of American and international books, newspapers, magazines, radio, TV, letters and talks, reflecting the whole spectrum of English today. This database enables Collins lexicographers to analyze how American English is actually used today and how it is changing.

The Bank of English was set up as a joint initiative by HarperCollins Publishers and Birmingham University to be a resource for language research and lexicography. Its size and range make it an unequalled source of information and the purpose-built software for its analysis is unique to Collins English Dictionaries.

This ensures that Collins Dictionaries accurately reflect English as it is used today in a way that is most helpful to the user, as well as including the full range of rarer and historical words and meanings.

Foreword

The American edition of the **HarperCollins Pocket Thesaurus**, which was first published in 1990, has proved to be an immensely popular language resource. It allows you to look up a word and find a useful selection of alternatives that can replace it. It is, therefore, tremendously helpful when you are trying to find different ways of expressing yourself, as well as being an invaluable aid for crosswords and puzzles.

Collins thesauruses are designed to give the user as much help as possible in finding the right word for any occasion. Because the **Pocket Thesaurus** has its main entry words arranged in A-Z form, you can go straight to the word you want without having to resort to an index, just as if you were looking it up in a dictionary. In this new edition, the number of main entry words has been increased, giving you an even greater chance of finding the word you want. At the same time, the list of alternative words (synonyms) for each main entry has been reviewed so that the most helpful alternatives are included in each case. The new edition also takes account of recent changes in the language, with terms like *gridlock, dweeb,* and *Internet* included as main entry words for the first time, and words like *twenty-four-seven, phat, wannabe,* and *scuzzbucket* being found among the synonyms.

This new edition further demonstrates Collins' commitment to helping the user. As part of an innovative design, key synonyms have been put in capital letters and placed first in each list. This layout enables you to see at once which sense of the word is being referred to, which is particularly helpful when a main entry word has a number of different senses. It also gives you an idea of which synonym is the closest alternative to the word you have looked up.

These innovations mean that the American edition of the **HarperCollins Pocket Thesaurus** continues to provide the user with a treasury of useful words arranged in the most helpful format possible.

Guide to the Text

Headword

Synonyms
words, listed in
alphabetical order,
that can be used in
place of the headword

Part of speech labels

Labels
a label in brackets
applies only to the word
preceding it

Key Synonyms
given first and
highlighted

abnormality *noun* ODDITY,
deformity, exception,
irregularity, peculiarity,
singularity, strangeness

abode *noun* HOME, domicile,
dwelling, habitat, habitation,
house, lodging, pad (*slang,
dated*), quarters, residence

abolish *verb* DO AWAY WITH,
annul, cancel, destroy,
eliminate, end, eradicate, put
an end to, quash, rescind,
revoke, stamp out

abolition *noun* ENDING,
cancellation, destruction,
elimination, end,
extermination, termination,
wiping out

abominable *adjective* TERRIBLE,
despicable, detestable,
disgusting, hateful, horrible,
horrid, lousy (*slang*), repulsive,
revolting, scuzzy (*slang*), vile

abort *verb* **1** TERMINATE (*a
pregnancy*), miscarry **2** STOP,
arrest, ax (*informal*), call off,
check, end, fail, halt, terminate

abortion *noun* TERMINATION,
deliberate miscarriage,
miscarriage

abortive *adjective* FAILED,
fruitless, futile, ineffectual,
miscarried, unsuccessful,
useless, vain

abound *verb* BE PLENTIFUL,
flourish, proliferate, swarm,
swell, teem, thrive

abounding *adjective* PLENTIFUL,
abundant, bountiful, copious,
full, profuse, prolific, rich

about *preposition* **1** REGARDING, as
regards, concerning, dealing

Guide to the Text

with, on, referring to, relating
to **2** NEAR, adjacent to, beside,
circa (*used with dates*), close to,
nearby ►*adverb* **3** NEARLY,
almost, approaching,
approximately, around, close
to, more or less, roughly

above *preposition* OVER, beyond,
exceeding, higher than, on top
of, upon

above board *adjective* HONEST,
fair, genuine, legitimate,
square, straight

abrasion *noun Medical* GRAZE,
chafe, scrape, scratch, scuff,
surface injury

abrasive *adjective* **1** UNPLEASANT,
caustic, cutting, galling,
grating, irritating, rough, sharp
2 ROUGH, chafing, grating,
scraping, scratchy

abreast *adjective* **1** ALONGSIDE,
beside, side by side **2 abreast
of** INFORMED ABOUT, acquainted
with, *au courant* with, *au fait*
with, conversant with, familiar
with, in the picture about, in
touch with, keeping one's
finger on the pulse of,
knowledgeable about, up to
date with, up to speed with

abridge *verb* SHORTEN,
abbreviate, condense, cut,
decrease, reduce, summarize

abroad *adverb* OVERSEAS, in
foreign lands, out of the
country

abrupt *adjective* **1** SUDDEN,
precipitate, quick, surprising,
unexpected **2** CURT, brusque,
gruff, impatient, rude, short,
terse

Labels
a label which is
not in brackets
relates to the
whole of that
particular sense

**Foreign words
and phrases**

**Phrases and
idioms**

Sense Numbers
synonyms divided
according to
meaning to help
you find the
sense you want

A a

abandon *verb* 1 LEAVE, desert, forsake, strand 2 GIVE UP, relinquish, surrender, yield
▶ *noun* 3 WILDNESS, recklessness

abandonment *noun* LEAVING, dereliction, desertion, forsaking

abashed *adjective* EMBARRASSED, ashamed, chagrined, disconcerted, dismayed, humiliated, mortified, shamefaced, taken aback

abate *verb* DECREASE, decline, diminish, dwindle, fade, lessen, let up, moderate, relax, slacken, subside, weaken

abbey *noun* MONASTERY, convent, friary, nunnery, priory

abbreviate *verb* SHORTEN, abridge, compress, condense, contract, cut, reduce, summarize

abbreviation *noun* SHORTENING, abridgment, contraction, reduction, summary, synopsis

abdicate *verb* GIVE UP, abandon, quit, relinquish, renounce, resign, step down (*informal*)

abdication *noun* GIVING UP, abandonment, quitting, renunciation, resignation, retirement, surrender

abduct *verb* KIDNAP, carry off, seize, snatch (*slang*)

abduction *noun* KIDNAPING, carrying off, seizure

aberration *noun* ODDITY, abnormality, anomaly, defect, irregularity, lapse, peculiarity, quirk

abet *verb* HELP, aid, assist, connive at, support

abeyance *noun* **in abeyance** SHELVED, hanging fire, on ice (*informal*), pending, suspended

abhor *verb* HATE, abominate, detest, loathe, shrink from, shudder at

abhorrent *adjective* HATEFUL, abominable, disgusting, distasteful, hated, horrid, loathsome, offensive, repulsive, scuzzy (*slang*)

abide *verb* TOLERATE, accept, bear, endure, put up with, stand, suffer

abide by *verb* OBEY, agree to, comply with, conform to, follow, observe, submit to

abiding *adjective* EVERLASTING, continuing, enduring, lasting, permanent, persistent, unchanging

ability *noun* SKILL, aptitude, capability, competence, expertise, proficiency, talent

abject *adjective* 1 MISERABLE, deplorable, forlorn, hopeless, pitiable, wretched 2 SERVILE, cringing, degraded, fawning, grovelling, submissive

ablaze *adjective* ON FIRE, aflame, alight, blazing, burning, fiery, flaming, ignited, lighted

able *adjective* CAPABLE, accomplished, competent, efficient, proficient, qualified, skillful

able-bodied *adjective* STRONG, fit, healthy, robust, sound, sturdy

abnormal *adjective* UNUSUAL,

atypical, exceptional, extraordinary, irregular, odd, peculiar, strange, uncommon

abnormality *noun* ODDITY, deformity, exception, irregularity, peculiarity, singularity, strangeness

abode *noun* HOME, domicile, dwelling, habitat, habitation, house, lodging, pad (*slang, dated*), quarters, residence

abolish *verb* DO AWAY WITH, annul, cancel, destroy, eliminate, end, eradicate, put an end to, quash, rescind, revoke, stamp out

abolition *noun* ENDING, cancellation, destruction, elimination, end, extermination, termination, wiping out

abominable *adjective* TERRIBLE, despicable, detestable, disgusting, hateful, horrible, horrid, lousy (*slang*), repulsive, revolting, scuzzy (*slang*), vile

abort *verb* 1 TERMINATE (*a pregnancy*), miscarry 2 STOP, arrest, ax (*informal*), call off, check, end, fail, halt, terminate

abortion *noun* TERMINATION, deliberate miscarriage, miscarriage

abortive *adjective* FAILED, fruitless, futile, ineffectual, miscarried, unsuccessful, useless, vain

abound *verb* BE PLENTIFUL, flourish, proliferate, swarm, swell, teem, thrive

abounding *adjective* PLENTIFUL, abundant, bountiful, copious, full, profuse, prolific, rich

about *preposition* 1 REGARDING, as regards, concerning, dealing with, on, referring to, relating to 2 NEAR, adjacent to, beside, circa (*used with dates*), close to, nearby ▸ *adverb* 3 NEARLY, almost, approaching, approximately, around, close to, more or less, roughly

above *preposition* OVER, beyond, exceeding, higher than, on top of, upon

above board *adjective* HONEST, fair, genuine, legitimate, square, straight

abrasion *noun Medical* GRAZE, chafe, scrape, scratch, scuff, surface injury

abrasive *adjective* 1 UNPLEASANT, caustic, cutting, galling, grating, irritating, rough, sharp 2 ROUGH, chafing, grating, scraping, scratchy

abreast *adjective* 1 ALONGSIDE, beside, side by side 2 **abreast of** INFORMED ABOUT, acquainted with, *au courant* with, *au fait* with, conversant with, familiar with, in the picture about, in touch with, keeping one's finger on the pulse of, knowledgeable about, up to date with, up to speed with

abridge *verb* SHORTEN, abbreviate, condense, cut, decrease, reduce, summarize

abroad *adverb* OVERSEAS, in foreign lands, out of the country

abrupt *adjective* 1 SUDDEN, precipitate, quick, surprising, unexpected 2 CURT, brusque, gruff, impatient, rude, short, terse

abscond *verb* FLEE, clear out, disappear, escape, make off, run off, steal away

absence *noun* **1** NONATTENDANCE, absenteeism, truancy **2** LACK, deficiency, need, omission, unavailability, want

absent *adjective* **1** MISSING, away, elsewhere, gone, nonexistent, out, unavailable **2** ABSENT-MINDED, blank, distracted, inattentive, oblivious, preoccupied, vacant, vague ▶ *verb* **3 absent oneself** STAY AWAY, keep away, play truant, withdraw

absent-minded *adjective* VAGUE, distracted, dreaming, forgetful, inattentive, preoccupied, unaware

absolute *adjective* **1** TOTAL, complete, outright, perfect, pure, sheer, thorough, utter **2** SUPREME, full, sovereign, unbounded, unconditional, unlimited, unrestricted

absolutely *adverb* TOTALLY, completely, entirely, fully, one hundred per cent, perfectly, utterly, wholly

absolution *noun* FORGIVENESS, deliverance, exculpation, exoneration, mercy, pardon, release

absolve *verb* FORGIVE, deliver, exculpate, excuse, let off, pardon, release, set free

absorb *verb* **1** SOAK UP, consume, digest, imbibe, incorporate, receive, suck up, take in **2** PREOCCUPY, captivate, engage, engross, fascinate, rivet

absorbed *adjective* **1** PREOCCUPIED, captivated, engrossed, fascinated, immersed, involved, lost, rapt, riveted, wrapped up **2** DIGESTED, assimilated, incorporated, received, soaked up

absorbent *adjective* PERMEABLE, porous, receptive, spongy

absorbing *adjective* FASCINATING, captivating, engrossing, gripping, interesting, intriguing, riveting, spellbinding

absorption *noun* **1** SOAKING UP, assimilation, consumption, digestion, incorporation, sucking up **2** CONCENTRATION, fascination, immersion, intentness, involvement, preoccupation

abstain *verb* REFRAIN, avoid, decline, deny (oneself), desist, fast, forbear, forgo, give up, keep from

abstemious *adjective* SELF-DENYING, ascetic, austere, frugal, moderate, sober, temperate

abstention *noun* REFUSAL, abstaining, abstinence, avoidance, forbearance, refraining, self-control, self-denial, self-restraint

abstinence *noun* SELF-DENIAL, abstemiousness, avoidance, forbearance, moderation, self-restraint, soberness, teetotalism, temperance

abstinent *adjective* SELF-DENYING, abstaining, abstemious, forbearing, moderate, self-controlled, sober, temperate

abstract *adjective* **1** THEORETICAL, abstruse, general, hypothetical, indefinite, notional, recondite ▶ *noun* **2** SUMMARY, abridgment, digest, epitome, outline, précis, résumé, synopsis ▶ *verb* **3** SUMMARIZE, abbreviate, abridge, condense, digest, epitomize, outline, précis, shorten 4 REMOVE, detach, extract, isolate, separate, take away, take out, withdraw

abstraction noun 1 IDEA, concept, formula, generalization, hypothesis, notion, theorem, theory, thought 2 ABSENT-MINDEDNESS, absence, dreaminess, inattention, pensiveness, preoccupation, remoteness, woolgathering

abstruse adjective OBSCURE, arcane, complex, deep, enigmatic, esoteric, recondite, unfathomable, vague

absurd adjective RIDICULOUS, crazy (informal), farcical, foolish, idiotic, illogical, inane, incongruous, irrational, ludicrous, nonsensical, preposterous, senseless, silly, stupid, unreasonable

absurdity noun RIDICULOUSNESS, farce, folly, foolishness, incongruity, joke, nonsense, silliness, stupidity

abundance noun PLENTY, affluence, bounty, copiousness, exuberance, fullness, profusion

abundant adjective PLENTIFUL, ample, bountiful, copious, exuberant, filled, full, luxuriant, profuse, rich, teeming

abuse noun 1 ILL-TREATMENT, damage, exploitation, harm, hurt, injury, maltreatment, manhandling 2 INSULTS, blame, castigation, censure, defamation, derision, disparagement, invective, reproach, scolding, vilification 3 MISUSE, misapplication ▶verb 4 ILL-TREAT, damage, exploit, harm, hurt, injure, maltreat, misuse, take advantage of 5 INSULT, castigate, curse, defame, disparage, malign, scold, vilify

abusive adjective 1 INSULTING, censorious, defamatory, disparaging, libelous, offensive, reproachful, rude, scathing 2 HARMFUL, brutal, cruel, destructive, hurtful, injurious, rough

abysmal adjective TERRIBLE, appalling, awful, bad, dire, dreadful

abyss noun PIT, chasm, crevasse, fissure, gorge, gulf, void

academic adjective 1 SCHOLARLY, bookish, erudite, highbrow, learned, literary, studious 2 HYPOTHETICAL, abstract, conjectural, impractical, notional, speculative, theoretical ▶noun 3 SCHOLAR, academician, don, fellow, lecturer, master, professor, tutor

accede verb 1 AGREE, accept, acquiesce, admit, assent, comply, concede, concur, consent, endorse, grant 2 INHERIT, assume, attain, come to, enter upon, succeed, succeed to (as heir)

accelerate verb SPEED UP, advance, expedite, further, hasten, hurry, quicken

acceleration noun SPEEDING UP, hastening, hurrying, quickening, stepping up (informal)

accent noun 1 PRONUNCIATION, articulation, brogue, enunciation, inflection, intonation, modulation, tone 2 EMPHASIS, beat, cadence, force, pitch, rhythm, stress, timbre ▶*verb* 3 EMPHASIZE, accentuate, stress, underline, underscore

accentuate *verb* EMPHASIZE, accent, draw attention to, foreground, highlight, stress, underline, underscore

accept *verb* 1 RECEIVE, acquire, gain, get, obtain, secure, take 2 AGREE TO, admit, approve, believe, concur with, consent to, cooperate with, recognize

acceptable *adjective* SATISFACTORY, adequate, admissible, all right, fair, moderate, passable, tolerable

acceptance *noun* 1 ACCEPTING, acquiring, gaining, getting, obtaining, receipt, securing, taking 2 AGREEMENT, acknowledgment, acquiescence, admission, adoption, approval, assent, concurrence, consent, cooperation, recognition

accepted *adjective* AGREED, acknowledged, approved, common, conventional, customary, established, normal, recognized, traditional

access *noun* ENTRANCE, admission, admittance, approach, entry, passage, path, road

accessibility *noun* 1 HANDINESS, availability, nearness, possibility, readiness 2 APPROACHABILITY, affability, cordiality, friendliness, informality 3 OPENNESS, susceptibility

accessible *adjective* 1 HANDY, achievable, at hand, attainable, available, near, nearby, obtainable, reachable

2 APPROACHABLE, affable, available, cordial, friendly, informal 3 OPEN, exposed, liable, susceptible, vulnerable, wide-open

accessory *noun* 1 ADDITION, accompaniment, adjunct, adornment, appendage, attachment, decoration, extra, supplement, trimming 2 ACCOMPLICE, abettor, assistant, associate (*in crime*), colleague, confederate, helper, partner

accident *noun* 1 MISFORTUNE, calamity, collision, crash, disaster, misadventure, mishap 2 CHANCE, fate, fluke, fortuity, fortune, hazard, luck

accidental *adjective* UNINTENTIONAL, casual, chance, fortuitous, haphazard, inadvertent, incidental, random, unexpected, unforeseen, unlooked-for, unplanned

accidentally *adverb* UNINTENTIONALLY, by accident, by chance, fortuitously, haphazardly, inadvertently, incidentally, randomly, unwittingly

acclaim *verb* 1 PRAISE, applaud, approve, celebrate, cheer, clap, commend, exalt, hail, honor, salute ▶*noun* 2 PRAISE, acclamation, applause, approval, celebration, commendation, honor, kudos

acclamation *noun* PRAISE, acclaim, adulation, approval, ovation, plaudit, tribute

acclimatization *noun* ADAPTATION, adjustment, habituation, inurement, naturalization

acclimatize verb ADAPT,
accommodate, accustom,
adjust, get used to, habituate,
inure, naturalize

accolade noun PRAISE, acclaim,
applause, approval,
commendation, compliment,
ovation, recognition, tribute

accommodate verb 1 HOUSE,
cater for, entertain, lodge, put
up, shelter 2 HELP, aid, assist,
oblige, serve 3 ADAPT, adjust,
comply, conform, fit,
harmonize, modify, reconcile,
settle

accommodating adjective
HELPFUL, considerate,
cooperative, friendly,
hospitable, kind, obliging,
polite, unselfish, willing

accommodation noun HOUSING,
board, house, lodging(s),
quarters, shelter

accompaniment noun
1 SUPPLEMENT, accessory,
companion, complement
2 BACKING MUSIC, backing

accompany verb 1 GO WITH,
attend, chaperon, conduct,
convoy, escort, hold
(someone's) hand 2 OCCUR
WITH, belong to, come with,
follow, go together with,
supplement

accompanying adjective
ADDITIONAL, associated,
attached, attendant,
complementary, related,
supplementary

accomplice noun HELPER,
abettor, accessory, ally,
assistant, associate,
collaborator, colleague,
henchman, partner

accomplish verb DO, achieve,
attain, bring about, carry out,
complete, effect, execute,
finish, fulfill, manage, perform,
produce

accomplished adjective SKILLED,
expert, gifted, masterly,
polished, practiced, proficient,
talented

accomplishment noun
1 COMPLETION, bringing about,
carrying out, conclusion,
execution, finishing, fulfillment,
performance 2 ACHIEVEMENT, act,
coup, deed, exploit, feat,
stroke, triumph

accord noun 1 AGREEMENT,
conformity, correspondence,
harmony, rapport, sympathy,
unison ▶ verb 2 FIT, agree,
conform, correspond,
harmonize, match, suit, tally

accordingly adverb
1 APPROPRIATELY, correspondingly,
fitly, properly, suitably
2 CONSEQUENTLY, as a result,
ergo, hence, in consequence,
so, therefore, thus

according to adverb 1 AS STATED
BY, as believed by, as
maintained by, in the light of,
on the authority of, on the
report of 2 IN KEEPING WITH,
after, after the manner of,
consistent with, in accordance
with, in compliance with, in
line with, in the manner of

accost verb APPROACH,
buttonhole, confront, greet, hail

account noun 1 DESCRIPTION,
explanation, narrative, report,
statement, story, tale, version
2 Commerce STATEMENT, balance,
bill, books, charge, invoice,
reckoning, register, score, tally
3 IMPORTANCE, consequence,

honor, note, significance, standing, value, worth ▸ *verb* 4 CONSIDER, count, estimate, judge, rate, reckon, regard, think, value

accountability *noun* RESPONSIBILITY, answerability, chargeability, culpability, liability

accountable *adjective* RESPONSIBLE, amenable, answerable, charged with, liable, obligated, obliged

accountant *noun* AUDITOR, bean counter (*informal*), book-keeper

account for *verb* EXPLAIN, answer for, clarify, clear up, elucidate, illuminate, justify, rationalize

accredited *adjective* AUTHORIZED, appointed, certified, empowered, endorsed, guaranteed, licensed, official, recognized

accrue *verb* INCREASE, accumulate, amass, arise, be added, build up, collect, enlarge, flow, follow, grow

accumulate *verb* COLLECT, accrue, amass, build up, gather, hoard, increase, pile up, store

accumulation *noun* COLLECTION, build-up, gathering, heap, hoard, increase, mass, pile, stack, stock, stockpile, store

accuracy *noun* EXACTNESS, accurateness, authenticity, carefulness, closeness, correctness, fidelity, precision, strictness, truthfulness, veracity

accurate *adjective* EXACT, authentic, close, correct, faithful, precise, scrupulous, strict, true, unerring

accurately *adverb* EXACTLY,

authentically, closely, correctly, faithfully, precisely, scrupulously, strictly, to the letter, truly, unerringly

accursed *adjective* 1 CURSED, bewitched, condemned, damned, doomed, hopeless, ill-fated, ill-omened, jinxed, unfortunate, unlucky, wretched 2 HATEFUL, abominable, despicable, detestable, execrable, hellish, horrible, lousy (*slang*), scuzzy (*slang*)

accusation *noun* CHARGE, allegation, complaint, denunciation, incrimination, indictment, recrimination

accuse *verb* CHARGE, blame, censure, denounce, impeach, impute, incriminate, indict

accustom *verb* ADAPT, acclimatize, acquaint, discipline, exercise, familiarize, train

accustomed *adjective* 1 USUAL, common, conventional, customary, established, everyday, expected, habitual, normal, ordinary, regular, traditional 2 USED, acclimatized, acquainted, adapted, familiar, familiarized, given to, in the habit of, trained

ace *noun* 1 *Cards, dice, etc.* ONE, single point 2 *Informal* EXPERT, champion, master, star, virtuoso, wizard (*informal*)

ache *verb* 1 HURT, pain, pound, smart, suffer, throb, twinge ▸ *noun* 2 PAIN, hurt, pang, pounding, soreness, suffering, throbbing

achieve *verb* ATTAIN, accomplish, acquire, bring about, carry out, complete, do, execute, fulfill, gain, get, obtain, perform

achievement noun
ACCOMPLISHMENT, act, deed, effort, exploit, feat, feather in one's cap, stroke

acid adjective **1** SOUR, acerbic, acrid, pungent, tart, vinegary **2** SHARP, biting, bitter, caustic, cutting, harsh, trenchant, vitriolic

acidity noun **1** SOURNESS, acerbity, pungency, tartness **2** SHARPNESS, bitterness, harshness

acknowledge verb **1** ACCEPT, admit, allow, concede, confess, declare, grant, own, profess, recognize, yield **2** GREET, address, hail, notice, recognize, salute **3** REPLY TO, answer, notice, react to, recognize, respond to, return

acknowledged adjective
ACCEPTED, accredited, approved, confessed, declared, professed, recognized, returned

acknowledgment noun
1 ACCEPTANCE, admission, allowing, confession, declaration, profession, realization, yielding **2** GREETING, addressing, hail, hailing, notice, recognition, salutation, salute **3** APPRECIATION, answer, credit, gratitude, kudos, reaction, recognition, reply, response, return, thanks

acquaint verb TELL, disclose, divulge, enlighten, familiarize, inform, let (someone) know, notify, reveal

acquaintance noun **1** ASSOCIATE, colleague, contact **2** KNOWLEDGE, awareness, experience, familiarity,

fellowship, relationship, understanding

acquainted with adjective
FAMILIAR WITH, alive to, apprised of, au fait with, aware of, conscious of, experienced in, informed of, knowledgeable about, versed in

acquiesce verb AGREE, accede, accept, allow, approve, assent, comply, concur, conform, consent, give in, go along with, submit, yield

acquiescence noun AGREEMENT, acceptance, approval, assent, compliance, conformity, consent, giving in, obedience, submission, yielding

acquire verb GET, amass, attain, buy, collect, earn, gain, gather, obtain, receive, secure, win

acquisition noun **1** POSSESSION, buy, gain, prize, property, purchase **2** ACQUIRING, attainment, gaining, procurement

acquisitive adjective GREEDY, avaricious, avid, covetous, grabbing, grasping, predatory, rapacious

acquit verb **1** CLEAR, discharge, free, liberate, release, vindicate **2** BEHAVE, bear, comport, conduct, perform

acquittal noun CLEARANCE, absolution, deliverance, discharge, exoneration, liberation, release, relief, vindication

acrid adjective PUNGENT, bitter, caustic, harsh, sharp, vitriolic

acrimonious adjective BITTER, caustic, irascible, petulant, rancorous, spiteful, splenetic, testy

acrimony *noun* BITTERNESS, harshness, ill will, irascibility, rancor, virulence

act *noun* **1** DEED, accomplishment, achievement, action, exploit, feat, performance, undertaking **2** LAW, bill, decree, edict, enactment, measure, ordinance, resolution, statute **3** PERFORMANCE, routine, show, sketch, turn **4** PRETENSE, affectation, attitude, front, performance, pose, posture, show ▶ *verb* **5** DO, carry out, enact, execute, function, operate, perform, take effect, work **6** PERFORM, act out, impersonate, mimic, play, play or take the part of, portray, represent

act for *verb* STAND IN FOR, cover for, deputize for, fill in for, replace, represent, substitute for, take the place of

acting *noun* **1** PERFORMANCE, characterization, impersonation, performing, playing, portrayal, stagecraft, theater ▶ *adjective* **2** TEMPORARY, interim, pro tem, provisional, substitute, surrogate

action *noun* **1** DEED, accomplishment, achievement, act, exploit, feat, performance **2** LAWSUIT, case, litigation, proceeding, prosecution, suit **3** ENERGY, activity, force, liveliness, spirit, vigor, vim, vitality **4** MOVEMENT, activity, functioning, motion, operation, process, working **5** BATTLE, clash, combat, conflict, contest, encounter, engagement, fight, skirmish, sortie

activate *verb* START, arouse, energize, galvanize, initiate, mobilize, move, rouse, set in motion, stir

active *adjective* **1** BUSY, bustling, hard-working, involved, occupied, on the go (*informal*), on the move, strenuous **2** ENERGETIC, alert, animated, industrious, lively, quick, sprightly, spry, vigorous **3** IN OPERATION, acting, at work, effectual, in action, in force, operative, working

activist *noun* MILITANT, organizer, partisan

activity *noun* **1** ACTION, animation, bustle, exercise, exertion, hustle, labor, motion, movement **2** PURSUIT, hobby, interest, pastime, project, scheme

actor *noun* PERFORMER, actress, player, Thespian

actress *noun* PERFORMER, actor, leading lady, player, starlet, Thespian

actual *adjective* DEFINITE, concrete, factual, physical, positive, real, substantial, tangible

actually *adverb* REALLY, as a matter of fact, indeed, in fact, in point of fact, in reality, in truth, literally, truly

act up *verb Informal* MAKE A FUSS, have a fit, horse around, misbehave, raise Cain, raise hell

acumen *noun* JUDGMENT, astuteness, cleverness, ingenuity, insight, intelligence, perspicacity, shrewdness

acute *adjective* **1** SERIOUS, critical, crucial, dangerous, grave, important, severe, urgent

2 SHARP, excruciating, fierce, intense, piercing, powerful, severe, shooting, violent
3 PERCEPTIVE, astute, clever, insightful, keen, observant, sensitive, sharp, smart

acuteness noun 1 SERIOUSNESS, gravity, importance, severity, urgency 2 PERCEPTIVENESS, astuteness, cleverness, discrimination, insight, perspicacity, sharpness

adamant adjective DETERMINED, firm, fixed, obdurate, resolute, stubborn, unbending, uncompromising

adapt verb ADJUST, acclimatize, accommodate, alter, change, conform, convert, modify, remodel, tailor

adaptability noun FLEXIBILITY, changeability, resilience, versatility

adaptable adjective FLEXIBLE, adjustable, changeable, compliant, easy-going, plastic, pliant, resilient, versatile

adaptation noun 1 ACCLIMATIZATION, familiarization, naturalization 2 CONVERSION, adjustment, alteration, change, modification, transformation, variation, version

add verb 1 COUNT UP, add up, compute, reckon, total, tot up 2 INCLUDE, adjoin, affix, append, attach, augment, supplement

addendum noun ADDITION, appendage, appendix, attachment, extension, extra, postscript, supplement

addict noun 1 JUNKIE (informal), fiend (informal), freak (informal)

2 FAN, adherent, buff (informal), devotee, enthusiast, follower, nut (slang)

addicted adjective HOOKED (slang), absorbed, accustomed, dedicated, dependent, devoted, habituated

addiction noun DEPENDENCE, craving, enslavement, habit, obsession

addition noun 1 INCLUSION, adding, amplification, attachment, augmentation, enlargement, extension, increasing 2 EXTRA, addendum, additive, appendage, appendix, extension, gain, increase, increment, supplement 3 COUNTING UP, adding up, computation, totalling, totting up 4 **in addition (to)** AS WELL (AS), additionally, also, besides, into the bargain, moreover, over and above, to boot, too

additional adjective EXTRA, added, fresh, further, new, other, spare, supplementary

address noun 1 LOCATION, abode, dwelling, home, house, residence, situation, whereabouts 2 SPEECH, discourse, dissertation, lecture, oration, sermon, talk ▶ verb 3 SPEAK TO, approach, greet, hail, talk to 4 **address (oneself) to** CONCENTRATE ON, apply (oneself) to, attend to, devote (oneself) to, engage in, focus on, take care of

add up verb COUNT UP, add, compute, count, reckon, total, tot up

adept adjective 1 SKILFUL, able, accomplished, adroit, expert, practiced, proficient, skilled, versed ▶ *noun* **2** EXPERT, genius, hotshot (*informal*), master

adequacy *noun* SUFFICIENCY, capability, competence, fairness, suitability, tolerability

adequate *adjective* ENOUGH, competent, fair, satisfactory, sufficient, tolerable, up to scratch (*informal*)

adhere *verb* STICK, attach, cleave, cling, fasten, fix, glue, hold fast, paste

adherent *noun* SUPPORTER, admirer, devotee, disciple, fan, follower, upholder

adhesive *adjective* **1** STICKY, clinging, cohesive, gluey, glutinous, tenacious ▶ *noun* **2** GLUE, cement, gum, paste

adieu *noun* GOOD-BYE, farewell, leave-taking, parting, valediction

adjacent *adjective* NEXT, adjoining, beside, bordering, cheek by jowl, close, near, neighboring, next door, touching

adjoin *verb* CONNECT, border, join, link, touch

adjoining *adjective* CONNECTING, abutting, adjacent, bordering, neighboring, next door, touching

adjourn *verb* POSTPONE, defer, delay, discontinue, interrupt, put off, suspend

adjournment *noun* POSTPONEMENT, delay, discontinuation, interruption, putting off, recess, suspension

adjudicate *verb* JUDGE, adjudge, arbitrate, decide, determine, mediate, referee, settle, umpire

adjudication *noun* JUDGMENT, arbitration, conclusion, decision, finding, pronouncement, ruling, settlement, verdict

adjust *verb* ALTER, accustom, adapt, make conform, modify

adjustable *adjective* ALTERABLE, adaptable, flexible, malleable, modifiable, movable

adjustment *noun* **1** ALTERATION, adaptation, modification, redress, regulation, tuning **2** ACCLIMATIZATION, orientation, settling in

ad-lib *verb* IMPROVISE, busk, extemporize, make up, speak off the cuff, wing it (*informal*)

administer *verb* **1** MANAGE, conduct, control, direct, govern, handle, oversee, run, supervise **2** GIVE, apply, dispense, impose, mete out, perform, provide

administration *noun* MANAGEMENT, application, conduct, control, direction, government, running, supervision

administrative *adjective* MANAGERIAL, directorial, executive, governmental, organizational, regulatory, supervisory

administrator *noun* MANAGER, bureaucrat, executive, official, organizer, supervisor

admirable *adjective* EXCELLENT, commendable, exquisite, fine, laudable, praiseworthy, wonderful, worthy

admiration *noun* REGARD, amazement, appreciation, approval, esteem, praise, respect, wonder

admire *verb* **1** RESPECT,

appreciate, approve, esteem, look up to, praise, prize, think highly of, value **2** MARVEL AT, appreciate, delight in, take pleasure in, wonder at

admirer noun **1** SUITOR, beau, boyfriend, lover, sweetheart, wooer **2** FAN, devotee, disciple, enthusiast, follower, partisan, supporter

admissible adjective PERMISSIBLE, acceptable, allowable, passable, tolerable

admission noun **1** ENTRANCE, acceptance, access, admittance, entrée, entry, initiation, introduction **2** CONFESSION, acknowledgment, allowance, declaration, disclosure, divulgence, revelation

admit verb **1** CONFESS, acknowledge, declare, disclose, divulge, fess up (informal), own, reveal **2** ALLOW, agree, grant, let, permit, recognize **3** LET IN, accept, allow, give access, initiate, introduce, receive, take in

admonish verb REPRIMAND, berate, chide, rebuke, scold, slap on the wrist, tell off (informal)

adolescence noun **1** YOUTH, boyhood, girlhood, minority, teens **2** YOUTHFULNESS, childishness, immaturity

adolescent adjective **1** YOUNG, boyish, girlish, immature, juvenile, puerile, teenage, youthful ▶ noun **2** YOUTH, juvenile, minor, teenager, youngster

adopt verb **1** FOSTER, take in **2** CHOOSE, assume, espouse, follow, maintain, take up

adoption noun **1** FOSTERING, adopting, taking in **2** CHOICE, appropriation, assumption, embracing, endorsement, espousal, selection, taking up

adorable adjective LOVABLE, appealing, attractive, charming, cute, dear, delightful, fetching, pleasing

adore verb LOVE, admire, cherish, dote on, esteem, exalt, glorify, honor, idolize, put on a pedestal (informal), revere, worship

adoring adjective LOVING, admiring, affectionate, devoted, doting, fond

adorn verb DECORATE, array, embellish, festoon

adornment noun DECORATION, accessory, embellishment, festoon, frill, frippery, ornament, supplement, trimming

adrift adjective **1** DRIFTING, afloat, unanchored, unmoored **2** AIMLESS, directionless, goalless, purposeless ▶ adverb **3** WRONG, amiss, astray, off course

adroit adjective SKILLFUL, adept, clever, deft, dexterous, expert, masterful, neat, proficient, skilled

adulation noun WORSHIP, fawning, fulsome praise, servile flattery, sycophancy

adult noun **1** GROWN-UP, grown or grown-up person (man or woman), person of mature age ▶ adjective **2** FULLY GROWN, full grown, fully developed, grown-up, mature, of age, ripe

advance verb **1** PROGRESS, come

forward, go on, hasten, make inroads, proceed, speed 2 BENEFIT, further, improve, prosper 3 SUGGEST, offer, present, proffer, put forward, submit 4 LEND, pay beforehand, supply on credit ▶ noun 5 PROGRESS, advancement, development, forward movement, headway, inroads, onward movement 6 IMPROVEMENT, breakthrough, gain, growth, progress, promotion, step 7 LOAN, credit, deposit, down payment, prepayment, retainer 8 **advances** OVERTURES, approach, approaches, moves, proposals, proposition ▶ adjective 9 PRIOR, beforehand, early, forward, in front 10 **in advance** BEFOREHAND, ahead, earlier, previously

advanced adjective FOREMOST, ahead, avant-garde, forward, higher, leading, precocious, progressive

advancement noun PROMOTION, betterment, gain, improvement, preferment, progress, rise

advantage noun BENEFIT, ascendancy, dominance, good, help, lead, precedence, profit, superiority, sway

advantageous adjective 1 BENEFICIAL, convenient, expedient, helpful, of service, profitable, useful, valuable, worthwhile 2 SUPERIOR, dominant, dominating, favorable, win-win (informal)

adventure noun ESCAPADE, enterprise, experience, exploit, incident, occurrence, undertaking, venture

adventurer noun 1 MERCENARY, charlatan, fortune-hunter, gambler, opportunist, rogue, speculator 2 HERO, daredevil, heroine, knight-errant, traveler, voyager

adventurous adjective DARING, bold, daredevil, enterprising, intrepid, reckless

adversary noun OPPONENT, antagonist, competitor, contestant, enemy, foe, rival

adverse adjective UNFAVORABLE, contrary, detrimental, hostile, inopportune, negative, opposing

adversity noun HARDSHIP, affliction, bad luck, disaster, distress, hard times, misfortune, reverse, trouble

advertise verb PUBLICIZE, announce, inform, make known, notify, plug (informal), promote, tout

advertisement noun NOTICE, ad (informal), announcement, blurb, circular, commercial, plug (informal), poster

advice noun GUIDANCE, counsel, help, opinion, recommendation, suggestion

advisability noun WISDOM, appropriateness, aptness, desirability, expediency, fitness, propriety, prudence, suitability

advisable adjective WISE, appropriate, desirable, expedient, fitting, politic, prudent, recommended, seemly, sensible

advise verb 1 RECOMMEND, admonish, caution, commend, counsel, prescribe, suggest, urge 2 NOTIFY, acquaint, apprise, inform, make known, report, tell, warn

adviser noun GUIDE, aide, confidant or (fem.) confidante, consultant, counselor, helper, mentor, right-hand man

advisory adjective ADVISING, consultative, counseling, helping, recommending

advocate verb 1 RECOMMEND, advise, argue for, campaign for, champion, commend, encourage, promote, propose, support, uphold ▸noun 2 SUPPORTER, campaigner, champion, counselor, defender, promoter, proponent, spokesman, upholder 3 Law LAWYER, attorney, barrister, counsel

affable adjective FRIENDLY, amiable, amicable, approachable, congenial, cordial, courteous, genial, pleasant, sociable, urbane

affair noun 1 EVENT, activity, business, episode, happening, incident, matter, occurrence 2 RELATIONSHIP, amour, intrigue, liaison, romance

affect[1] verb 1 INFLUENCE, act on, alter, bear upon, change, concern, impinge upon, relate to 2 MOVE, disturb, overcome, perturb, stir, touch, upset

affect[2] verb PUT ON, adopt, aspire to, assume, contrive, feign, imitate, pretend, simulate

affectation noun PRETENSE, act, artificiality, assumed manners, façade, insincerity, pose, pretentiousness, show

affected adjective PRETENDED, artificial, contrived, feigned, insincere, mannered, phoney or phony (informal), put-on,

unnatural

affecting adjective MOVING, pathetic, pitiful, poignant, sad, touching

affection noun FONDNESS, attachment, care, feeling, goodwill, kindness, liking, love, tenderness, warmth

affectionate adjective FOND, attached, caring, devoted, doting, friendly, kind, loving, tender, warm-hearted

affiliate verb JOIN, ally, amalgamate, associate, band together, combine, incorporate, link, unite

affinity noun 1 ATTRACTION, fondness, inclination, leaning, liking, partiality, rapport, sympathy 2 SIMILARITY, analogy, closeness, connection, correspondence, kinship, likeness, relationship, resemblance

affirm verb DECLARE, assert, certify, confirm, maintain, pronounce, state, swear, testify

affirmation noun DECLARATION, assertion, certification, confirmation, oath, pronouncement, statement, testimony

affirmative adjective AGREEING, approving, assenting, concurring, confirming, consenting, corroborative, favorable, positive

afflict verb TORMENT, distress, grieve, harass, hurt, oppress, pain, plague, trouble

affliction noun SUFFERING, adversity, curse, disease, hardship, misfortune, ordeal, plague, scourge, torment, trial, trouble, woe

affluence noun WEALTH, abundance, fortune, opulence, plenty, prosperity, riches

affluent adjective WEALTHY, loaded (slang), moneyed, opulent, prosperous, rich, well-heeled (informal), well-off, well-to-do

afford verb 1 As in **can afford** SPARE, bear, manage, stand, sustain 2 GIVE, offer, produce, provide, render, supply, yield

affordable adjective INEXPENSIVE, cheap, economical, low-cost, moderate, modest, reasonable

affront noun 1 INSULT, offense, outrage, provocation, slap in the face (informal), slight, slur ▸ verb 2 OFFEND, anger, annoy, displease, insult, outrage, provoke, slight

aflame adjective BURNING, ablaze, alight, blazing, fiery, flaming, lit, on fire

afoot adverb GOING ON, abroad, brewing, current, happening, in preparation, in progress, on the go (informal), up (informal)

afraid adjective 1 SCARED, apprehensive, cowardly, faint-hearted, fearful, frightened, nervous, wired (slang) 2 SORRY, regretful, unhappy

afresh adverb AGAIN, anew, newly, once again, once more, over again

after adverb FOLLOWING, afterwards, behind, below, later, subsequently, succeeding, thereafter

aftermath noun EFFECTS, aftereffects, consequences, end result, outcome, results, sequel, upshot, wake

again adverb 1 ONCE MORE, afresh, anew, another time 2 ALSO, besides, furthermore, in addition, moreover

against preposition 1 BESIDE, abutting, facing, in contact with, on, opposite to, touching, upon 2 OPPOSED TO, anti (informal), averse to, hostile to, in defiance of, in opposition to, resisting, versus 3 IN PREPARATION FOR, in anticipation of, in expectation of, in provision for

age noun 1 TIME, date, day(s), duration, epoch, era, generation, lifetime, period, span 2 OLD AGE, advancing years, decline (of life), majority, maturity, senescence, senility, seniority ▸ verb 3 GROW OLD, decline, deteriorate, mature, mellow, ripen

aged adjective OLD, ancient, antiquated, antique, elderly, getting on, gray

agency noun 1 BUSINESS, bureau, department, office, organization 2 Old-fashioned MEDIUM, activity, means, mechanism

agenda noun LIST, calendar, diary, plan, program, schedule, timetable

agent noun 1 REPRESENTATIVE, envoy, go-between, negotiator, rep (informal), surrogate 2 WORKER, author, doer, mover, operator, performer 3 FORCE, agency, cause, instrument, means, power, vehicle

aggravate verb 1 MAKE WORSE, exacerbate, exaggerate, increase, inflame, intensify, magnify, worsen 2 Informal

ANNOY, bother, get on one's nerves (*informal*), irritate, nettle, provoke

aggravation *noun* 1 WORSENING, exacerbation, exaggeration, heightening, increase, inflaming, intensification, magnification 2 *Informal* ANNOYANCE, exasperation, gall, grief (*informal*), hassle (*informal*), irritation, provocation

aggregate *noun* 1 TOTAL, accumulation, amount, body, bulk, collection, combination, mass, pile, sum, whole ▶ *adjective* 2 TOTAL, accumulated, collected, combined, composite, cumulative, mixed ▶ *verb* 3 COMBINE, accumulate, amass, assemble, collect, heap, mix, pile

aggression *noun* 1 HOSTILITY, antagonism, belligerence, destructiveness, pugnacity 2 ATTACK, assault, injury, invasion, offensive, onslaught, raid

aggressive *adjective* 1 HOSTILE, belligerent, destructive, offensive, pugnacious, quarrelsome 2 FORCEFUL, assertive, bold, dynamic, energetic, enterprising, militant, pushy (*informal*), vigorous

aggressor *noun* ATTACKER, assailant, assaulter, invader

aggrieved *adjective* HURT, afflicted, distressed, disturbed, harmed, injured, unhappy, wronged

aghast *adjective* HORRIFIED, amazed, appalled, astonished, astounded, awestruck, confounded, shocked, startled, stunned

agile *adjective* 1 NIMBLE, active, brisk, lithe, quick, sprightly, spry, supple, swift 2 ACUTE, alert, bright (*informal*), clever, lively, quick-witted, sharp

agility *noun* NIMBLENESS, litheness, liveliness, quickness, suppleness, swiftness

agitate *verb* 1 UPSET, disconcert, distract, excite, fluster, perturb, trouble, unnerve, worry 2 STIR, beat, convulse, disturb, rouse, shake, toss

agitation *noun* 1 TURMOIL, clamor, commotion, confusion, disturbance, excitement, ferment, trouble, upheaval 2 TURBULENCE, convulsion, disturbance, shaking, stirring, tossing

agitator *noun* TROUBLEMAKER, agent provocateur, firebrand, instigator, rabble-rouser, revolutionary, stirrer (*informal*)

agog *adjective* EAGER, avid, curious, enthralled, enthusiastic, excited, expectant, impatient, in suspense, wired (*slang*)

agonize *verb* SUFFER, be distressed, be in agony, be in anguish, go through the mill, labor, strain, struggle, worry

agony *noun* SUFFERING, anguish, distress, misery, pain, throes, torment, torture

agree *verb* 1 CONSENT, assent, be of the same opinion, comply, concur, see eye to eye 2 GET ON (TOGETHER), coincide, conform, correspond, match, tally

agreeable *adjective* 1 PLEASANT,

delightful, enjoyable, gratifying, likable *or* likeable, pleasing, satisfying, to one's taste **2** CONSENTING, amenable, approving, complying, concurring, in accord, onside (*informal*), sympathetic, well-disposed, willing

agreement noun **1** ASSENT, agreeing, compliance, concord, concurrence, consent, harmony, union, unison **2** CORRESPONDENCE, compatibility, conformity, congruity, consistency, similarity **3** CONTRACT, arrangement, bargain, covenant, deal (*informal*), pact, settlement, treaty, understanding

agricultural adjective FARMING, agrarian, country, rural, rustic

agriculture noun FARMING, cultivation, culture, husbandry, tillage

aground adverb BEACHED, ashore, foundered, grounded, high and dry, on the rocks, stranded, stuck

ahead adverb IN FRONT, at an advantage, at the head, before, in advance, in the lead, leading, to the fore, winning

aid noun **1** HELP, assistance, benefit, encouragement, favor, promotion, relief, service, support ▶verb **2** HELP, assist, encourage, favor, promote, serve, subsidize, support, sustain

aide noun ASSISTANT, attendant, helper, right-hand man, second, supporter

ailing adjective ILL, indisposed, infirm, poorly, sick, under the weather (*informal*), unwell, weak

ailment noun ILLNESS, affliction, complaint, disease, disorder, infirmity, malady, sickness

aim verb **1** INTEND, attempt, endeavor, mean, plan, point, propose, seek, set one's sights on, strive, try ▶noun **2** INTENTION, ambition, aspiration, desire, goal, objective, plan, purpose, target

aimless adjective PURPOSELESS, directionless, pointless, random, stray

air noun **1** ATMOSPHERE, heavens, sky **2** WIND, breeze, draft, zephyr **3** MANNER, appearance, atmosphere, aura, demeanor, impression, look, mood **4** TUNE, aria, lay, melody, song ▶verb **5** PUBLICIZE, circulate, display, exhibit, express, give vent to, make known, make public, reveal, voice **6** VENTILATE, aerate, expose, freshen

airborne adjective FLYING, floating, gliding, hovering, in flight, in the air, on the wing

airing noun **1** VENTILATION, aeration, drying, freshening **2** EXPOSURE, circulation, display, dissemination, expression, publicity, utterance, vent

airless adjective STUFFY, close, heavy, muggy, oppressive, stifling, suffocating, sultry

airs plural noun AFFECTATION, arrogance, haughtiness, hauteur, pomposity, pretensions, superciliousness

airy adjective **1** WELL-VENTILATED, fresh, light, open, spacious, uncluttered **2** LIGHT-HEARTED, blithe, cheerful, high-spirited, jaunty, lively, sprightly

aisle noun PASSAGEWAY, alley, corridor, gangway, lane, passage, path

alacrity noun EAGERNESS, alertness, enthusiasm, promptness, quickness, readiness, speed, willingness, zeal

alarm noun 1 FEAR, anxiety, apprehension, consternation, fright, nervousness, panic, scare, trepidation 2 DANGER SIGNAL, alarm bell, alert, bell, distress signal, hooter, siren, warning ▶ verb 3 FRIGHTEN, daunt, dismay, distress, give (someone) a fright (*informal*), panic, scare, startle, unnerve

alarming adjective FRIGHTENING, daunting, distressing, disturbing, scaring, shocking, startling, unnerving

alcoholic noun 1 DRUNKARD, dipsomaniac, drinker, drunk, inebriate, tippler, toper, wino (*informal*) ▶ adjective 2 INTOXICATING, brewed, distilled, fermented, hard, strong

alcove noun RECESS, bay, compartment, corner, cubbyhole, cubicle, niche, nook

alert adjective 1 WATCHFUL, attentive, awake, circumspect, heedful, observant, on guard, on one's toes, on the lookout, vigilant, wide-awake ▶ noun 2 WARNING, alarm, signal, siren ▶ verb 3 WARN, alarm, forewarn, inform, notify, signal

alertness noun WATCHFULNESS, attentiveness, heedfulness, liveliness, vigilance

alias adverb 1 ALSO KNOWN AS, also called, otherwise,

otherwise known as ▶ noun 2 PSEUDONYM, assumed name, nom de guerre, nom de plume, pen name, stage name

alibi noun EXCUSE, defense, explanation, justification, plea, pretext, reason

alien adjective 1 FOREIGN, exotic, incongruous, strange, unfamiliar ▶ noun 2 FOREIGNER, newcomer, outsider, stranger

alienate verb SET AGAINST, disaffect, estrange, make unfriendly, shut out, turn away

alienation noun SETTING AGAINST, disaffection, estrangement, remoteness, separation, turning away

alight[1] verb 1 GET OFF, descend, disembark, dismount, get down 2 LAND, come down, come to rest, descend, light, perch, settle, touch down

alight[2] adjective 1 ON FIRE, ablaze, aflame, blazing, burning, fiery, flaming, lighted, lit 2 LIT UP, bright, brilliant, illuminated, shining

align verb 1 ALLY, affiliate, agree, associate, cooperate, join, side, sympathize 2 LINE UP, even up, order, range, regulate, straighten

alignment noun 1 ALLIANCE, affiliation, agreement, association, cooperation, sympathy, union 2 LINING UP, adjustment, arrangement, evening up, order, straightening up

alike adjective 1 SIMILAR, akin, analogous, corresponding, identical, of a piece, parallel, resembling, the same ▶ adverb 2 SIMILARLY, analogously, correspondingly, equally, evenly, identically, uniformly

alive *adjective* **1** LIVING, animate, breathing, in the land of the living (*informal*), subsisting **2** IN EXISTENCE, active, existing, extant, functioning, in force, operative **3** LIVELY, active, alert, animated, energetic, full of life, vital, vivacious

all *adjective* **1** THE WHOLE OF, every bit of, the complete, the entire, the sum of, the totality of, the total of **2** EVERY, each, each and every, every one of, every single **3** COMPLETE, entire, full, greatest, perfect, total, utter ▶ *adverb* **4** COMPLETELY, altogether, entirely, fully, totally, utterly, wholly ▶ *noun* **5** WHOLE AMOUNT, aggregate, entirety, everything, sum total, total, totality, utmost

allegation *noun* CLAIM, accusation, affirmation, assertion, charge, declaration, statement

allege *verb* CLAIM, affirm, assert, charge, declare, maintain, state

alleged *adjective* **1** STATED, affirmed, asserted, declared, described, designated **2** SUPPOSED, doubtful, dubious, ostensible, professed, purported, so-called, unproved

allegiance *noun* LOYALTY, constancy, devotion, faithfulness, fidelity, obedience

allegorical *adjective* SYMBOLIC, emblematic, figurative, symbolizing

allegory *noun* SYMBOL, fable, myth, parable, story, symbolism, tale

allergic *adjective* SENSITIVE,

affected by, hypersensitive, susceptible

allergy *noun* SENSITIVITY, antipathy, hypersensitivity, susceptibility

alleviate *verb* EASE, allay, lessen, lighten, moderate, reduce, relieve, soothe

alley *noun* PASSAGE, alleyway, backstreet, lane, passageway, pathway, walk

alliance *noun* UNION, affiliation, agreement, association, coalition, combination, confederation, connection, federation, league, marriage, pact, partnership, treaty

allied *adjective* UNITED, affiliated, associated, combined, connected, in league, linked, related

allocate *verb* ASSIGN, allot, allow, apportion, budget, designate, earmark, mete, set aside, share out

allocation *noun* ASSIGNMENT, allotment, allowance, lot, portion, quota, ration, share

allot *verb* ASSIGN, allocate, apportion, budget, designate, earmark, mete, set aside, share out

allotment *noun* **1** PLOT, kitchen garden, patch, tract **2** ASSIGNMENT, allocation, allowance, grant, portion, quota, ration, share, stint

all-out *adjective* TOTAL, complete, exhaustive, full, full-scale, maximum, thoroughgoing, undivided, unremitting, unrestrained

allow *verb* **1** PERMIT, approve, authorize, enable, endure, let, sanction, stand, suffer, tolerate

2 GIVE, allocate, allot, assign, grant, provide, set aside, spare **3** ACKNOWLEDGE, admit, concede, confess, grant, own

allowable *adjective* PERMISSIBLE, acceptable, admissible, all right, appropriate, suitable, tolerable

allowance *noun* **1** PORTION, allocation, amount, grant, lot, quota, ration, share, stint **2** CONCESSION, deduction, discount, rebate, reduction

allow for *verb* TAKE INTO ACCOUNT, consider, make allowances for, make concessions for, make provision for, plan for, provide for, take into consideration

alloy *noun* **1** MIXTURE, admixture, amalgam, blend, combination, composite, compound, hybrid ▶*verb* **2** MIX, amalgamate, blend, combine, compound, fuse

all right *adjective* **1** SATISFACTORY, acceptable, adequate, average, fair, O.K. *or* okay (*informal*), standard, up to scratch (*informal*) **2** O.K. *or* OKAY (*informal*), healthy, safe, sound, unharmed, uninjured, well, whole

allude *verb* REFER, hint, imply, intimate, mention, suggest, touch upon

allure *noun* **1** ATTRACTIVENESS, appeal, attraction, charm, enchantment, enticement, glamour, lure, persuasion, seductiveness, temptation ▶*verb* **2** ATTRACT, captivate, charm, enchant, entice, lure, persuade, seduce, tempt, win over

alluring *adjective* ATTRACTIVE, beguiling, captivating, come-hither, fetching, glamorous, seductive, tempting

allusion *noun* REFERENCE, casual remark, hint, implication, innuendo, insinuation, intimation, mention, suggestion

ally *noun* **1** PARTNER, accomplice, associate, collaborator, colleague, friend, helper, homeboy (*slang*), homegirl (*slang*) ▶*verb* **2** UNITE, associate, collaborate, combine, join, join forces, unify

almighty *adjective* **1** ALL-POWERFUL, absolute, invincible, omnipotent, supreme, unlimited **2** *Informal* GREAT, enormous, excessive, intense, loud, severe, terrible

almost *adverb* NEARLY, about, approximately, close to, just about, not quite, on the brink of, practically, virtually

alone *adjective* BY ONESELF, apart, detached, isolated, lonely, only, separate, single, solitary, unaccompanied

aloof *adjective* DISTANT, detached, haughty, remote, standoffish, supercilious, unapproachable, unfriendly

aloud *adverb* OUT LOUD, audibly, clearly, distinctly, intelligibly, plainly

already *adverb* BEFORE NOW, at present, before, by now, by then, even now, heretofore, just now, previously

also *adverb* TOO, additionally, and, as well, besides, further, furthermore, in addition, into the bargain, moreover, to boot

alter *verb* CHANGE, adapt, adjust,

amend, convert, modify, reform, revise, transform, turn, vary

alteration noun CHANGE, adaptation, adjustment, amendment, conversion, difference, modification, reformation, revision, transformation, variation

alternate verb 1 CHANGE, act reciprocally, fluctuate, interchange, oscillate, rotate, substitute, take turns ▸ adjective 2 EVERY OTHER, alternating, every second, interchanging, rotating

alternative noun 1 CHOICE, option, other (of two), preference, recourse, selection, substitute ▸ adjective 2 DIFFERENT, alternate, another, other, second, substitute

alternatively adverb OR, as an alternative, if not, instead, on the other hand, otherwise

although conjunction THOUGH, albeit, despite the fact that, even if, even though, notwithstanding, while

altogether adverb 1 COMPLETELY, absolutely, fully, perfectly, quite, thoroughly, totally, utterly, wholly 2 ON THE WHOLE, all in all, all things considered, as a whole, collectively, generally, in general 3 IN TOTAL, all told, everything included, in all, in sum, taken together

altruistic adjective SELFLESS, benevolent, charitable, generous, humanitarian, philanthropic, public-spirited, self-sacrificing, unselfish

always adverb CONTINUALLY, consistently, constantly, eternally, evermore, every

time, forever, invariably, perpetually, repeatedly, twenty-four-seven (slang), without exception

amalgamate verb COMBINE, ally, blend, fuse, incorporate, integrate, merge, mingle, unite

amalgamation noun COMBINATION, blend, coalition, compound, fusion, joining, merger, mixture, union

amass verb COLLECT, accumulate, assemble, compile, gather, hoard, pile up

amateur noun NONPROFESSIONAL, dabbler, dilettante, layman

amateurish adjective UNPROFESSIONAL, amateur, bungling, clumsy, crude, inexpert, unaccomplished

amaze verb ASTONISH, alarm, astound, bewilder, dumbfound, shock, stagger, startle, stun, surprise

amazement noun ASTONISHMENT, admiration, bewilderment, confusion, perplexity, shock, surprise, wonder

amazing adjective ASTONISHING, astounding, breathtaking, eye-opening, overwhelming, staggering, startling, stunning, surprising

ambassador noun REPRESENTATIVE, agent, consul, deputy, diplomat, envoy, legate, minister

ambiguity noun VAGUENESS, doubt, dubiousness, equivocation, obscurity, uncertainty

ambiguous adjective UNCLEAR, dubious, enigmatic, equivocal, inconclusive, indefinite, indeterminate, obscure, vague

ambition *noun* **1** ENTERPRISE, aspiration, desire, drive, eagerness, longing, striving, yearning, zeal **2** GOAL, aim, aspiration, desire, dream, hope, intent, objective, purpose, wish

ambitious *adjective* ENTERPRISING, aspiring, avid, eager, hopeful, intent, purposeful, striving, zealous

ambivalent *adjective* UNDECIDED, contradictory, doubtful, equivocal, in two minds, uncertain, wavering

amble *verb* STROLL, dawdle, meander, mosey (*informal*), ramble, saunter, walk, wander

ambush *noun* **1** TRAP, lying in wait, waylaying ▶*verb* **2** TRAP, attack, bushwhack (*U.S.*), ensnare, surprise, waylay

amenable *adjective* RECEPTIVE, able to be influenced, acquiescent, agreeable, open, persuadable, responsive, susceptible

amend *verb* CHANGE, alter, correct, fix, improve, mend, modify, reform, remedy, repair, revise

amendment *noun* **1** CHANGE, alteration, correction, emendation, improvement, modification, reform, remedy, repair, revision **2** ALTERATION, addendum, addition, attachment, clarification

amends *plural noun* As in **make amends for** COMPENSATION, atonement, recompense, redress, reparation, restitution, satisfaction

amenity *noun* FACILITY, advantage, comfort, convenience, service

amiable *adjective* PLEASANT, affable, agreeable, charming, congenial, engaging, friendly, genial, likable *or* likeable, lovable

amicable *adjective* FRIENDLY, amiable, civil, cordial, courteous, harmonious, neighborly, peaceful, sociable

amid, amidst *preposition* IN THE MIDDLE OF, among, amongst, in the midst of, in the thick of, surrounded by

amiss *adverb* **1** WRONGLY, erroneously, improperly, inappropriately, incorrectly, mistakenly, unsuitably **2** As in **take (something) amiss** AS AN INSULT, as offensive, out of turn, wrongly ▶*adjective* **3** WRONG, awry, faulty, incorrect, mistaken, untoward

ammunition *noun* MUNITIONS, armaments, explosives, powder, rounds, shells, shot

amnesty *noun* GENERAL PARDON, absolution, dispensation, forgiveness, immunity, remission (*of penalty*), reprieve

amok, amuck *adverb* As in **run amok** MADLY, berserk, destructively, ferociously, in a frenzy, murderously, savagely, uncontrollably, violently, wildly

among, amongst *preposition* **1** IN THE MIDST OF, amid, amidst, in the middle of, in the thick of, surrounded by, together with, with **2** IN THE GROUP OF, in the class of, in the company of, in the number of, out of **3** TO EACH OF, between

amorous *adjective* LOVING, erotic, impassioned, in love, lustful, passionate, tender

amount *noun* QUANTITY, expanse, extent, magnitude, mass, measure, number, supply, volume

amount to *verb* ADD UP TO, become, come to, develop into, equal, mean, total

ample *adjective* PLENTY, abundant, bountiful, copious, expansive, extensive, full, generous, lavish, plentiful, profuse

amplify *verb* 1 EXPLAIN, develop, elaborate, enlarge, expand, flesh out, go into detail 2 INCREASE, enlarge, expand, extend, heighten, intensify, magnify, strengthen, widen

amply *adverb* FULLY, abundantly, completely, copiously, generously, profusely, richly

amputate *verb* CUT OFF, curtail, lop, remove, separate, sever, truncate

amuck see AMOK

amuse *verb* ENTERTAIN, charm, cheer, delight, interest, please, tickle

amusement *noun* 1 ENTERTAINMENT, cheer, enjoyment, fun, merriment, mirth, pleasure 2 ENTERTAINMENT, diversion, game, hobby, joke, pastime, recreation, sport

amusing *adjective* FUNNY, comical, droll, enjoyable, entertaining, humorous, interesting, witty

analogy *noun* SIMILARITY, comparison, correlation, correspondence, likeness, parallel, relation, resemblance

analysis *noun* EXAMINATION, breakdown, dissection, inquiry,

investigation, perusal, scrutiny, sifting, test

analytic, analytical *adjective* RATIONAL, inquiring, inquisitive, investigative, logical, organized, problem-solving, systematic

analyze *verb* 1 EXAMINE, evaluate, investigate, research, test, work over 2 BREAK DOWN, dissect, divide, resolve, separate, think through

anarchic *adjective* LAWLESS, chaotic, disorganized, rebellious, riotous, ungoverned

anarchist *noun* REVOLUTIONARY, insurgent, nihilist, rebel, terrorist

anarchy *noun* LAWLESSNESS, chaos, confusion, disorder, disorganization, revolution, riot

anatomy *noun* 1 EXAMINATION, analysis, dissection, division, inquiry, investigation, study 2 STRUCTURE, build, composition, frame, framework, make-up

ancestor *noun* FOREFATHER, forebear, forerunner, precursor, predecessor

ancient *adjective* OLD, aged, antique, archaic, old-fashioned, primeval, primordial, timeworn

ancillary *adjective* SUPPLEMENTARY, additional, auxiliary, extra, secondary, subordinate, subsidiary, supporting

and *conjunction* ALSO, along with, as well as, furthermore, in addition to, including, moreover, plus, together with

anecdote *noun* STORY, reminiscence, short story, sketch, tale, urban legend, yarn

anemic *adjective* PALE, ashen, colorless, feeble, pallid, sickly, wan, weak

anesthetic noun 1 PAINKILLER, analgesic, anodyne, narcotic, opiate, sedative, soporific ▶ adjective 2 PAIN-KILLING, analgesic, anodyne, deadening, dulling, numbing, sedative, soporific

angel noun 1 DIVINE MESSENGER, archangel, cherub, seraph 2 Informal DEAR, beauty, darling, gem, jewel, paragon, saint, treasure

angelic adjective 1 PURE, adorable, beautiful, entrancing, lovely, saintly, virtuous 2 HEAVENLY, celestial, cherubic, ethereal, seraphic

anger noun 1 RAGE, annoyance, displeasure, exasperation, fury, ire, outrage, resentment, temper, wrath ▶ verb 2 MADDEN, annoy, displease, enrage, exasperate, gall, incense, infuriate, outrage, rile, vex

angle¹ noun 1 INTERSECTION, bend, corner, crook, edge, elbow, nook, point 2 POINT OF VIEW, approach, aspect, outlook, perspective, position, side, slant, standpoint, viewpoint

angle² verb FISH, cast

angry adjective FURIOUS, annoyed, cross, displeased, enraged, exasperated, incensed, infuriated, irate, mad, outraged, resentful

angst noun ANXIETY, apprehension, unease, worry

anguish noun SUFFERING, agony, distress, grief, heartache, misery, pain, sorrow, torment, woe

animal noun 1 CREATURE, beast, brute 2 Applied to a person BRUTE, barbarian, beast, monster, savage, wild man ▶ adjective 3 PHYSICAL, bestial, bodily, brutish, carnal, gross, sensual

animate verb 1 ENLIVEN, energize, excite, fire, inspire, invigorate, kindle, move, stimulate ▶ adjective 2 LIVING, alive, alive and kicking, breathing, live, moving

animated adjective LIVELY, ebullient, energetic, enthusiastic, excited, passionate, spirited, vivacious, wired (slang)

animation noun LIVELINESS, ebullience, energy, enthusiasm, excitement, fervor, passion, spirit, verve, vivacity, zest

animosity noun HOSTILITY, acrimony, antipathy, bitterness, enmity, hatred, ill will, malevolence, malice, rancor, resentment

annals plural noun RECORDS, accounts, archives, chronicles, history

annex verb 1 SEIZE, acquire, appropriate, conquer, occupy, take over 2 JOIN, add, adjoin, attach, connect, fasten

annihilate verb DESTROY, abolish, decimate, eradicate, exterminate, extinguish, obliterate, wipe out

announce verb MAKE KNOWN, advertise, broadcast, declare, disclose, proclaim, report, reveal, tell

announcement noun STATEMENT, advertisement, broadcast, bulletin, communiqué, declaration, proclamation, report, revelation

announcer noun PRESENTER, broadcaster, commentator, master of ceremonies, newscaster, newsreader, reporter

annoy verb IRRITATE, anger, bother, displease, disturb, exasperate, get on one's nerves (*informal*), hassle (*informal*), madden, molest, pester, plague, trouble, vex

annoyance noun 1 IRRITATION, anger, bother, hassle (*informal*), nuisance, trouble 2 NUISANCE, bore, bother, drag (*informal*), pain (*informal*)

annoying adjective IRRITATING, disturbing, exasperating, maddening, troublesome

annual adjective YEARLY, once a year, yearlong

annually adverb YEARLY, by the year, once a year, per annum, per year

annul verb INVALIDATE, abolish, cancel, declare or render null and void, negate, nullify, repeal, retract

anoint verb CONSECRATE, bless, hallow, sanctify

anomalous adjective UNUSUAL, abnormal, eccentric, exceptional, incongruous, inconsistent, irregular, odd, peculiar

anomaly noun IRREGULARITY, abnormality, eccentricity, exception, incongruity, inconsistency, oddity, peculiarity

anonymous adjective UNNAMED, incognito, nameless, unacknowledged, uncredited, unidentified, unknown,

unsigned

answer verb 1 REPLY, explain, react, resolve, respond, retort, return, solve ▶noun 2 REPLY, comeback, defense, explanation, reaction, rejoinder, response, retort, return, riposte, solution

answerable adjective (usually with *for* or *to*) RESPONSIBLE, accountable, amenable, chargeable, liable, subject, to blame

answer for verb BE RESPONSIBLE FOR, be accountable for, be answerable for, be chargeable for, be liable for, be to blame for

antagonism noun HOSTILITY, antipathy, conflict, discord, dissension, friction, opposition, rivalry

antagonist noun OPPONENT, adversary, competitor, contender, enemy, foe, rival

antagonistic adjective HOSTILE, at odds, at variance, conflicting, incompatible, in dispute, opposed, unfriendly

antagonize verb ANNOY, anger, get on one's nerves (*informal*), hassle (*informal*), irritate, offend

anthem noun 1 HYMN, canticle, carol, chant, chorale, psalm 2 SONG OF PRAISE, paean

anthology noun COLLECTION, compendium, compilation, miscellany, selection, treasury

anticipate verb EXPECT, await, foresee, foretell, hope for, look forward to, predict, prepare for

anticipation noun EXPECTATION, expectancy, foresight, forethought, premonition, prescience

anticlimax noun DISAPPOINTMENT, bathos, comedown (*informal*), letdown

antics plural noun CLOWNING, escapades, horseplay, mischief, playfulness, pranks, tomfoolery, tricks

antidote noun CURE, countermeasure, remedy

antipathy noun HOSTILITY, aversion, bad blood, dislike, enmity, hatred, ill will

antiquated adjective OBSOLETE, antique, archaic, dated, old-fashioned, out-of-date, passé

antique noun 1 PERIOD PIECE, bygone, heirloom, relic ▶ adjective 2 VINTAGE, antiquarian, classic, olden 3 OLD-FASHIONED, archaic, obsolete, outdated

antiquity noun 1 OLD AGE, age, ancientness, elderliness, oldness 2 DISTANT PAST, ancient times, olden days, time immemorial

antiseptic adjective 1 HYGIENIC, clean, germ-free, pure, sanitary, sterile, uncontaminated ▶ noun 2 DISINFECTANT, germicide, purifier

antisocial adjective 1 UNSOCIABLE, alienated, misanthropic, reserved, retiring, uncommunicative, unfriendly, withdrawn 2 DISRUPTIVE, antagonistic, belligerent, disorderly, hostile, menacing, rebellious, uncooperative

antithesis noun OPPOSITE, contrary, contrast, converse, inverse, reverse

anxiety noun UNEASINESS, angst, apprehension, concern, foreboding, misgiving, nervousness, tension, trepidation, worry

anxious adjective 1 UNEASY, apprehensive, concerned, fearful, in suspense, nervous, on tenterhooks, tense, troubled, wired (*slang*), worried 2 EAGER, desirous, impatient, intent, keen, yearning

apart adverb 1 TO PIECES, asunder, in bits, in pieces, to bits 2 SEPARATE, alone, aside, away, by oneself, isolated, to one side 3 **apart from** EXCEPT FOR, aside from, besides, but, excluding, not counting, other than, save

apartment noun ROOM, accommodation, flat, living quarters, penthouse, quarters, rooms, suite

apathetic adjective UNINTERESTED, cool, indifferent, passive, phlegmatic, unconcerned

apathy noun LACK OF INTEREST, coolness, indifference, inertia, nonchalance, passivity, torpor, unconcern

apex noun HIGHEST POINT, crest, crown, culmination, peak, pinnacle, point, summit, top

apiece adverb EACH, for each, from each, individually, respectively, separately, to each

aplomb noun SELF-POSSESSION, calmness, composure, confidence, level-headedness, poise, sang-froid, self-assurance, self-confidence

apocryphal adjective DUBIOUS, doubtful, legendary, mythical, questionable, unauthenticated, unsubstantiated

apologetic *adjective* REGRETFUL, contrite, penitent, remorseful, rueful, sorry

apologize *verb* SAY SORRY, ask forgiveness, beg pardon, express regret

apology *noun* 1 DEFENSE, acknowledgment, confession, excuse, explanation, justification, plea 2 *As in* **an apology for** MOCKERY, caricature, excuse, imitation, travesty

apostle *noun* 1 EVANGELIST, herald, messenger, missionary, preacher 2 SUPPORTER, advocate, champion, pioneer, propagandist, proponent

apotheosis *noun* DEIFICATION, elevation, exaltation, glorification, idealization, idolization

appall *verb* HORRIFY, alarm, daunt, dishearten, dismay, frighten, outrage, shock, unnerve

appalling *adjective* HORRIFYING, alarming, awful, daunting, dreadful, fearful, frightful, horrible, shocking, terrifying

apparatus *noun* 1 EQUIPMENT, appliance, contraption (*informal*), device, gear, machinery, mechanism, tackle, tools 2 ORGANIZATION, bureaucracy, chain of command, hierarchy, network, setup (*informal*), structure, system

apparent *adjective* 1 OBVIOUS, discernible, distinct, evident, manifest, marked, unmistakable, visible 2 SEEMING, ostensible, outward, superficial

apparently *adverb* IT APPEARS THAT, it seems that, on the face of it, ostensibly, outwardly, seemingly, superficially

apparition *noun* GHOST, chimera, phantom, specter, spirit, wraith

appeal *verb* 1 PLEAD, ask, beg, call upon, entreat, pray, request 2 ATTRACT, allure, charm, entice, fascinate, interest, please, tempt ▸ *noun* 3 PLEA, application, entreaty, petition, prayer, request, supplication 4 ATTRACTION, allure, beauty, charm, fascination

appealing *adjective* ATTRACTIVE, alluring, charming, desirable, engaging, winsome

appear *verb* 1 COME INTO VIEW, be present, come out, come to light, crop up (*informal*), emerge, occur, show up (*informal*), surface, turn up 2 LOOK (LIKE *or* AS IF), occur, seem, strike one as

appearance *noun* 1 ARRIVAL, coming, emergence, introduction, presence 2 LOOK, demeanor, expression, figure, form, looks, manner, mien (*literary*) 3 IMPRESSION, front, guise, illusion, image, outward show, pretense, semblance

appease *verb* 1 PACIFY, calm, conciliate, mollify, placate, quiet, satisfy, soothe 2 EASE, allay, alleviate, calm, relieve, soothe

appeasement *noun* 1 PACIFICATION, accommodation, compromise, concession, conciliation, mollification, placation 2 EASING, alleviation, lessening, relieving, soothing

appendage noun ATTACHMENT, accessory, addition, supplement

appendix noun SUPPLEMENT, addendum, addition, adjunct, appendage, postscript

appetite noun DESIRE, craving, demand, hunger, liking, longing, passion, relish, stomach, taste, yearning

appetizing adjective DELICIOUS, appealing, inviting, mouthwatering, palatable, succulent, tasty, tempting, yummy (*informal*)

applaud verb CLAP, acclaim, approve, cheer, commend, compliment, encourage, extol, praise

applause noun OVATION, accolade, approval, big hand, cheers, clapping, hand, praise

appliance noun DEVICE, apparatus, gadget, implement, instrument, machine, mechanism, tool

applicable adjective APPROPRIATE, apt, fitting, pertinent, relevant, suitable, useful

applicant noun CANDIDATE, claimant, inquirer

application noun 1 REQUEST, appeal, claim, inquiry, petition, requisition 2 EFFORT, commitment, dedication, diligence, hard work, industry, perseverance

apply verb 1 REQUEST, appeal, claim, inquire, petition, put in, requisition 2 USE, bring to bear, carry out, employ, exercise, exert, implement, practice, utilize 3 PUT ON, cover with, lay on, paint, place, smear, spread on 4 BE RELEVANT, be applicable, be appropriate, bear upon, be

fitting, fit, pertain, refer, relate 5 **apply oneself** TRY, be diligent, buckle down (*informal*), commit oneself, concentrate, dedicate oneself, devote oneself, persevere, work hard

appoint verb 1 ASSIGN, choose, commission, delegate, elect, name, nominate, select 2 DECIDE, allot, arrange, assign, choose, designate, establish, fix, set 3 EQUIP, fit out, furnish, provide, supply

appointed adjective 1 ASSIGNED, chosen, delegated, elected, named, nominated, selected 2 DECIDED, allotted, arranged, assigned, chosen, designated, established, fixed, set 3 EQUIPPED, fitted out, furnished, provided, supplied

appointment noun 1 MEETING, arrangement, assignation, date, engagement, interview, rendezvous 2 SELECTION, assignment, choice, election, naming, nomination 3 JOB, assignment, office, place, position, post, situation 4 **appointments** FITTINGS, fixtures, furnishings, gear, outfit, paraphernalia, trappings

apportion verb DIVIDE, allocate, allot, assign, dispense, distribute, dole out, ration out, share

apportionment noun DIVISION, allocation, allotment, assignment, dispensing, distribution, doling out, rationing out, sharing

apposite adjective APPROPRIATE, applicable, apt, fitting, pertinent, relevant, suitable, to the point

appraisal *noun* ASSESSMENT, estimate, estimation, evaluation, judgment, opinion

appraise *verb* ASSESS, estimate, evaluate, gauge, judge, rate, review, value

appreciable *adjective* SIGNIFICANT, considerable, definite, discernible, evident, marked, noticeable, obvious, pronounced, substantial

appreciate *verb* 1 VALUE, admire, enjoy, like, prize, rate highly, respect, treasure 2 BE AWARE OF, perceive, realize, recognize, sympathize with, take account of, understand 3 BE GRATEFUL FOR, be appreciative, be indebted, be obliged, be thankful for, give thanks for 4 INCREASE, enhance, gain, grow, improve, rise

appreciation *noun* 1 GRATITUDE, acknowledgment, gratefulness, indebtedness, obligation, thankfulness, thanks 2 AWARENESS, admiration, comprehension, enjoyment, perception, realization, recognition, sensitivity, sympathy, understanding 3 INCREASE, enhancement, gain, growth, improvement, rise

appreciative *adjective* 1 GRATEFUL, beholden, indebted, obliged, thankful 2 AWARE, admiring, enthusiastic, respectful, responsive, sensitive, sympathetic, understanding

apprehend *verb* 1 ARREST, capture, catch, seize, take prisoner 2 UNDERSTAND, comprehend, conceive, get the picture, grasp, perceive, realize, recognize

apprehension *noun* 1 ANXIETY, alarm, concern, dread, fear, foreboding, suspicion, trepidation, worry 2 ARREST, capture, catching, seizure, taking 3 AWARENESS, comprehension, grasp, perception, understanding

apprehensive *adjective* ANXIOUS, concerned, foreboding, nervous, uneasy, wired (*slang*), worried

apprentice *noun* TRAINEE, beginner, learner, novice, probationer, pupil, student

approach *verb* 1 MOVE TOWARDS, come close, come near, draw near, near, reach 2 MAKE A PROPOSAL TO, appeal to, apply to, make overtures to, sound out 3 SET ABOUT, begin work on, commence, embark on, enter upon, make a start, undertake ▶*noun* 4 COMING, advance, arrival, drawing near, nearing 5 (often plural) PROPOSAL, advance, appeal, application, invitation, offer, overture, proposition 6 ACCESS, avenue, entrance, passage, road, way 7 WAY, manner, means, method, style, technique 8 LIKENESS, approximation, semblance

approachable *adjective* 1 FRIENDLY, affable, congenial, cordial, open, sociable 2 ACCESSIBLE, attainable, reachable

appropriate *adjective* 1 SUITABLE, apt, befitting, fitting, pertinent, relevant, to the point, well-suited ▶*verb* 2 SEIZE, commandeer, confiscate, impound, take possession of, usurp 3 STEAL, embezzle, filch,

misappropriate, pilfer, pocket
4 SET ASIDE, allocate, allot,
apportion, assign, devote,
earmark

approval noun **1** CONSENT,
agreement, assent,
authorization, blessing,
endorsement, permission,
recommendation, sanction
2 FAVOR, acclaim, admiration,
applause, appreciation, esteem,
good opinion, praise, respect

approve verb **1** FAVOR, admire,
commend, have a good
opinion of, like, praise, regard
highly, respect **2** AGREE TO,
allow, assent to, authorize,
consent to, endorse, pass,
permit, ratify, recommend,
sanction

approximate adjective **1** CLOSE,
near **2** ROUGH, estimated,
inexact, loose ▶ verb **3** COME
CLOSE, approach, border on,
come near, reach, resemble,
touch, verge on

approximately adverb ALMOST,
about, around, circa (used with
dates), close to, in the region
of, just about, more or less,
nearly, roughly

approximation noun GUESS,
conjecture, estimate,
estimation, guesswork, rough
calculation, rough idea

apron noun PINAFORE

apt adjective **1** INCLINED,
disposed, given, liable, likely,
of a mind, prone, ready
2 APPROPRIATE, fitting, pertinent,
relevant, suitable, to the point
3 GIFTED, clever, quick, sharp,
smart, talented

aptitude noun **1** TENDENCY,
inclination, leaning,

predilection, proclivity,
propensity **2** GIFT, ability,
capability, faculty, intelligence,
proficiency, talent

arable adjective PRODUCTIVE,
farmable, fertile, fruitful

arbiter noun **1** JUDGE,
adjudicator, arbitrator, referee,
umpire **2** AUTHORITY, controller,
dictator, expert, governor,
lord, master, pundit, ruler

arbitrary adjective RANDOM,
capricious, chance, erratic,
inconsistent, personal,
subjective, whimsical

arbitrate verb SETTLE, adjudicate,
decide, determine, judge,
mediate, pass judgment,
referee, umpire

arbitration noun SETTLEMENT,
adjudication, decision,
determination, judgment

arbitrator noun JUDGE,
adjudicator, arbiter, referee,
umpire

arc noun CURVE, arch, bend,
bow, crescent, half-moon

arcade noun GALLERY, cloister,
colonnade, portico

arcane adjective MYSTERIOUS,
esoteric, hidden, occult,
recondite, secret

arch¹ noun **1** CURVE, archway,
dome, span, vault **2** CURVE, arc,
bend, bow, hump, semicircle
▶ verb **3** CURVE, arc, bend, bow,
bridge, span

arch² adjective PLAYFUL,
frolicsome, mischievous, pert,
roguish, saucy, sly, waggish

archaic adjective **1** OLD, ancient,
antique, bygone, olden
(archaic), primitive
2 OLD-FASHIONED, antiquated,
behind the times, obsolete,

outmoded, out of date, passé

archetypal *adjective* 1 TYPICAL, classic, ideal, model, standard 2 ORIGINAL, prototypic *or* prototypical

archetype *noun* 1 STANDARD, model, paradigm, pattern, prime example 2 ORIGINAL, prototype

architect *noun* DESIGNER, master builder, planner

architecture *noun* 1 DESIGN, building, construction, planning 2 STRUCTURE, construction, design, framework, make-up, style

archive *noun* 1 RECORD OFFICE, museum, registry, repository 2 **archives** RECORDS, annals, chronicles, documents, papers, rolls

arctic *adjective Informal* FREEZING, chilly, cold, frigid, frozen, glacial, icy

Arctic *adjective* POLAR, far-northern, hyperborean

ardent *adjective* 1 PASSIONATE, amorous, hot-blooded, impassioned, intense, lusty 2 ENTHUSIASTIC, avid, eager, keen, zealous

ardor *noun* 1 PASSION, fervor, intensity, spirit, vehemence, warmth 2 ENTHUSIASM, avidity, eagerness, keenness, zeal

arduous *adjective* DIFFICULT, exhausting, fatiguing, grueling, laborious, onerous, punishing, rigorous, strenuous, taxing, tiring

area *noun* 1 REGION, district, locality, neighborhood, zone 2 PART, portion, section, sector 3 FIELD, department, domain, province, realm, sphere,

territory

arena *noun* 1 RING, amphitheater, bowl, enclosure, field, ground, stadium 2 SPHERE, area, domain, field, province, realm, sector, territory

argue *verb* 1 DISCUSS, assert, claim, debate, dispute, maintain, reason, remonstrate 2 QUARREL, bicker, disagree, dispute, fall out (*informal*), fight, squabble

argument *noun* 1 QUARREL, clash, controversy, disagreement, dispute, feud, fight, row, squabble 2 DISCUSSION, assertion, claim, debate, dispute, plea, questioning, remonstration 3 REASON, argumentation, case, defense, dialectic, ground(s), line of reasoning, logic, polemic, reasoning

argumentative *adjective* QUARRELSOME, belligerent, combative, contentious, contrary, disputatious, litigious, opinionated

arid *adjective* 1 DRY, barren, desert, parched, sterile, torrid, waterless 2 BORING, dreary, dry, dull, tedious, tiresome, uninspired, uninteresting

arise *verb* 1 HAPPEN, begin, emerge, ensue, follow, occur, result, start, stem 2 GET UP, get to one's feet, go up, rise, stand up, wake up

aristocracy *noun* UPPER CLASS, elite, gentry, nobility, patricians, peerage, ruling class

aristocrat *adjective* NOBLE, grandee, lady, lord, patrician, peer, peeress

aristocratic *noun* UPPER-CLASS,

blue-blooded, elite,
gentlemanly, lordly, noble,
patrician, titled

arm[1] *noun* UPPER LIMB,
appendage, limb

arm[2] *verb Especially with
weapons* EQUIP, accouter, array,
deck out, furnish, issue with,
provide, supply

armada *noun* FLEET, flotilla, navy,
squadron

armaments *plural noun*
WEAPONS, ammunition, arms,
guns, materiel, munitions,
ordnance, weaponry

armed *adjective* CARRYING
WEAPONS, equipped, fitted out,
primed, protected

armistice *noun* TRUCE, ceasefire,
peace, suspension of hostilities

armor *noun* PROTECTION, armor
plate, covering, sheathing,
shield

armored *adjective* PROTECTED,
armor-plated, bombproof,
bulletproof, ironclad, mailed,
steel-plated

arms *plural noun* 1 WEAPONS,
armaments, firearms, guns,
instruments of war, ordnance,
weaponry 2 HERALDRY, blazonry,
crest, escutcheon, insignia

army *noun* 1 SOLDIERS, armed
force, legions, military, military
force, soldiery, troops 2 VAST
NUMBER, array, horde, host,
multitude, pack, swarm, throng

aroma *noun* SCENT, bouquet,
fragrance, odor, perfume,
redolence, savor, smell

aromatic *adjective* FRAGRANT,
balmy, perfumed, pungent,
redolent, savory, spicy,
sweet-scented, sweet-smelling

around *preposition*

1 SURROUNDING, about,
encircling, enclosing,
encompassing, on all sides of,
on every side of
2 APPROXIMATELY, about, circa
(*used with dates*), roughly
▶ *adverb* 3 EVERYWHERE, about, all
over, here and there, in all
directions, on all sides,
throughout, to and fro 4 NEAR,
at hand, close, close at hand,
nearby, nigh (*archaic or dialect*)

arouse *verb* 1 STIMULATE, excite,
incite, instigate, provoke, spur,
stir up, summon up, whip up
2 AWAKEN, rouse, waken, wake
up

arrange *verb* 1 PLAN, construct,
contrive, devise, fix up,
organize, prepare 2 AGREE,
adjust, come to terms,
compromise, determine, settle
3 PUT IN ORDER, classify, group,
line up, order, organize,
position, sort 4 ADAPT,
instrument, orchestrate, score

arrangement *noun* 1 (often
plural) PLAN, organization,
planning, preparation,
provision, schedule
2 AGREEMENT, adjustment,
compact, compromise, deal,
settlement, terms 3 ORDER,
alignment, classification, form,
organization, structure, system
4 ADAPTATION, instrumentation,
interpretation, orchestration,
score, version

array *noun* 1 ARRANGEMENT,
collection, display, exhibition,
formation, line-up, parade,
show, supply 2 *Poetic* CLOTHING,
apparel, attire, clothes, dress,
finery, garments, regalia ▶ *verb*
3 ARRANGE, display, exhibit,
group, parade, range, show

4 DRESS, adorn, attire, clothe, deck, decorate, festoon

arrest verb **1** CAPTURE, apprehend, catch, detain, seize, take prisoner **2** STOP, block, delay, end, inhibit, interrupt, obstruct, slow, suppress **3** GRIP, absorb, engage, engross, fascinate, hold, intrigue, occupy ▶ noun **4** CAPTURE, bust (informal), detention, seizure **5** STOPPING, blockage, delay, end, hindrance, interruption, obstruction, suppression

arresting adjective STRIKING, cool (informal), engaging, impressive, noticeable, outstanding, phat (slang), remarkable, stunning, surprising

arrival noun **1** COMING, advent, appearance, arriving, entrance, happening, occurrence, taking place **2** NEWCOMER, caller, entrant, incomer, visitor

arrive verb **1** COME, appear, enter, get to, reach, show up (informal), turn up **2** Informal SUCCEED, become famous, make good, make it (informal), make the grade (informal)

arrogance noun CONCEIT, disdainfulness, haughtiness, high-handedness, insolence, pride, superciliousness, swagger

arrogant adjective CONCEITED, disdainful, haughty, high-handed, overbearing, proud, scornful, supercilious

arrow noun **1** DART, bolt, flight, quarrel, shaft (archaic) **2** POINTER, indicator

arsenal noun ARMORY, ammunition dump, arms depot, ordnance depot,

stockpile, store, storehouse, supply

art noun SKILL, craft, expertise, ingenuity, mastery, virtuosity

artful adjective CUNNING, clever, crafty, shrewd, sly, smart, wily

article noun **1** PIECE, composition, discourse, essay, feature, item, paper, story, treatise **2** THING, commodity, item, object, piece, substance, unit **3** CLAUSE, item, paragraph, part, passage, point, portion, section

articulate adjective **1** EXPRESSIVE, clear, coherent, eloquent, fluent, lucid, well-spoken ▶ verb **2** EXPRESS, enunciate, pronounce, say, speak, state, talk, utter, voice

artifice noun **1** TRICK, contrivance, device, machination, maneuver, stratagem, subterfuge, tactic **2** CLEVERNESS, ingenuity, inventiveness, skill

artificial adjective **1** SYNTHETIC, man-made, manufactured, non-natural, plastic **2** FAKE, bogus, counterfeit, imitation, mock, sham, simulated **3** INSINCERE, affected, contrived, false, feigned, forced, phoney or phony (informal), unnatural

artillery noun BIG GUNS, battery, cannon, cannonry, gunnery, ordnance

artisan noun CRAFTSMAN, journeyman, mechanic, skilled workman, technician

artistic adjective CREATIVE, aesthetic, beautiful, cultured, elegant, refined, sophisticated, stylish, tasteful

artistry noun SKILL, brilliance,

craftsmanship, creativity, finesse, mastery, proficiency, virtuosity

artless *adjective*
1 STRAIGHTFORWARD, frank, guileless, open, plain **2** NATURAL, homely, plain, pure, simple, unadorned, unaffected, unpretentious

as *conjunction* **1** WHEN, at the time that, during the time that, just as, while **2** IN THE WAY THAT, in the manner that, like **3** WHAT, that which **4** SINCE, because, considering that, seeing that **5** FOR INSTANCE, like, such as ▶*preposition* **6** BEING, in the character of, in the role of, under the name of

ascend *verb* MOVE UP, climb, go up, mount, scale

ascent *noun* **1** RISE, ascending, ascension, climb, mounting, rising, scaling, upward movement **2** UPWARD SLOPE, gradient, incline, ramp, rise, rising ground

ascertain *verb* FIND OUT, confirm, determine, discover, establish, learn

ascetic *noun* **1** MONK, abstainer, hermit, nun, recluse ▶*adjective* **2** SELF-DENYING, abstinent, austere, celibate, frugal, puritanical, self-disciplined

ascribe *verb* ATTRIBUTE, assign, charge, credit, impute, put down, refer, set down

ashamed *adjective* EMBARRASSED, distressed, guilty, humiliated, mortified, remorseful, shamefaced, sheepish, sorry

ashen *adjective* PALE, colorless, gray, leaden, like death warmed over (*informal*), pallid,

wan, white

ashore *adverb* ON LAND, aground, landwards, on dry land, on the beach, on the shore, shorewards, to the shore

aside *adverb* **1** TO ONE SIDE, apart, beside, on one side, out of the way, privately, separately, to the side ▶*noun* **2** INTERPOLATION, parenthesis

asinine *adjective* STUPID, fatuous, foolish, idiotic, imbecilic, moronic, senseless

ask *verb* **1** INQUIRE, interrogate, query, question, quiz **2** REQUEST, appeal, beg, demand, plead, seek **3** INVITE, bid, summon

askew *adverb* **1** CROOKEDLY, aslant, awry, obliquely, off-center, to one side ▶*adjective* **2** CROOKED, awry, cockeyed (*informal*), lopsided, oblique, off-center

asleep *adjective* SLEEPING, dormant, dozing, fast asleep, napping, slumbering, snoozing (*informal*), sound asleep

aspect *noun* **1** FEATURE, angle, facet, side **2** POSITION, outlook, point of view, prospect, scene, situation, view **3** APPEARANCE, air, attitude, bearing, condition, demeanor, expression, look, manner

asphyxiate *verb* SUFFOCATE, choke, smother, stifle, strangle, strangulate, throttle

aspiration *noun* AIM, ambition, desire, dream, goal, hope, objective, wish

aspire *verb* AIM, desire, dream, hope, long, seek, set one's heart on, wish

aspiring *adjective* HOPEFUL, ambitious, eager, longing, wannabe (*informal*), would-be

ass *noun* **1** DONKEY **2** FOOL, blockhead, dork (*slang*), halfwit, idiot, jackass, oaf, schmuck (*slang*)

assail *verb* ATTACK, assault, fall upon, set upon

assailant *noun* ATTACKER, aggressor, assailer, assaulter, invader

assassin *noun* MURDERER, executioner, hatchet man (*slang*), hit man (*slang*), killer, liquidator, slayer

assassinate *verb* MURDER, eliminate (*slang*), hit (*slang*), kill, liquidate, slay, take out (*slang*)

assault *noun* **1** ATTACK, charge, invasion, offensive, onslaught ▶*verb* **2** ATTACK, beset, fall upon, set about, set upon, strike at

assemble *verb* **1** GATHER, amass, bring together, call together, collect, come together, congregate, meet, muster, rally **2** PUT TOGETHER, build up, connect, construct, fabricate, fit together, join, piece together, set up

assembly *noun* **1** GATHERING, collection, company, conference, congress, council, crowd, group, mass, meeting **2** PUTTING TOGETHER, building up, connecting, construction, piecing together, setting up

assent *noun* **1** AGREEMENT, acceptance, approval, compliance, concurrence, consent, permission, sanction ▶*verb* **2** AGREE, allow, approve, consent, grant, permit

assert *verb* **1** STATE, affirm, declare, maintain, profess,

pronounce, swear **2** INSIST UPON, claim, defend, press, put forward, stand up for, stress, uphold **3** **assert oneself** BE FORCEFUL, exert one's influence, make one's presence felt, put oneself forward, put one's foot down (*informal*)

assertion *noun* **1** STATEMENT, claim, declaration, pronouncement **2** INSISTENCE, maintenance, stressing

assertive *adjective* CONFIDENT, aggressive, domineering, emphatic, feisty (*informal*), forceful, insistent, positive, pushy (*informal*), strong-willed

assess *verb* **1** JUDGE, appraise, estimate, evaluate, rate, size up (*informal*), value, weigh **2** EVALUATE, fix, impose, levy, rate, tax, value

assessment *noun* **1** JUDGMENT, appraisal, estimate, evaluation, rating, valuation **2** EVALUATION, charge, fee, levy, rating, toll, valuation

asset *noun* **1** BENEFIT, advantage, aid, blessing, boon, feather in one's cap, help, resource, service **2** **assets** PROPERTY, capital, estate, funds, goods, money, possessions, resources, wealth

assiduous *adjective* DILIGENT, hard-working, indefatigable, industrious, persevering, persistent, unflagging

assign *verb* **1** SELECT, appoint, choose, delegate, designate, name, nominate **2** GIVE, allocate, allot, apportion, consign, distribute, give out, grant **3** ATTRIBUTE, accredit, ascribe, put down

assignation *noun* 1 SECRET MEETING, clandestine meeting, illicit meeting, rendezvous, tryst 2 SELECTION, appointment, assignment, choice, delegation, designation, nomination

assignment *noun* TASK, appointment, commission, duty, job, mission, position, post, responsibility

assimilate *verb* 1 LEARN, absorb, digest, incorporate, take in 2 ADJUST, adapt, blend in, mingle

assist *verb* HELP, abet, aid, cooperate, lend a helping hand, serve, support

assistance *noun* HELP, aid, backing, cooperation, helping hand, support

assistant *noun* HELPER, accomplice, aide, ally, colleague, right-hand man, second, supporter

associate *verb* 1 CONNECT, ally, combine, identify, join, link, lump together 2 MIX, accompany, consort, hobnob, mingle, socialize ▶ *noun* 3 PARTNER, collaborator, colleague, confederate, co-worker 4 FRIEND, ally, companion, comrade, homeboy (*slang*), homegirl (*slang*)

association *noun* 1 GROUP, alliance, band, club, coalition, federation, league, organization, society 2 CONNECTION, blend, combination, joining, juxtaposition, mixture, pairing, union

assorted *adjective* VARIOUS, different, diverse, miscellaneous, mixed, motley, sundry, varied

assortment *noun* VARIETY, array, choice, collection, jumble, medley, mixture, selection

assume *verb* 1 TAKE FOR GRANTED, believe, expect, fancy, imagine, infer, presume, suppose, surmise, think 2 TAKE ON, accept, enter upon, put on, shoulder, take over 3 PUT ON, adopt, affect, feign, imitate, impersonate, mimic, pretend to, simulate

assumed *adjective* 1 FALSE, bogus, counterfeit, fake, fictitious, made-up, make-believe 2 TAKEN FOR GRANTED, accepted, expected, hypothetical, presumed, presupposed, supposed, surmised

assumption *noun* 1 PRESUMPTION, belief, conjecture, guess, hypothesis, inference, supposition, surmise 2 TAKING ON, acceptance, acquisition, adoption, entering upon, putting on, shouldering, takeover, taking up 3 TAKING, acquisition, appropriation, seizure, takeover

assurance *noun* 1 ASSERTION, declaration, guarantee, oath, pledge, promise, statement, vow, word 2 CONFIDENCE, boldness, certainty, conviction, faith, nerve, poise, self-confidence

assure *verb* 1 PROMISE, certify, confirm, declare confidently, give one's word to, guarantee, pledge, swear, vow 2 CONVINCE, comfort, embolden, encourage, hearten, persuade, reassure 3 MAKE CERTAIN, clinch, complete, confirm, ensure, guarantee, make sure, seal, secure

assured *adjective* **1** CONFIDENT, certain, poised, positive, self-assured, self-confident, sure of oneself **2** CERTAIN, beyond doubt, confirmed, ensured, fixed, guaranteed, in the bag (*slang*), secure, settled, sure

astonish *verb* AMAZE, astound, bewilder, confound, daze, dumbfound, stagger, stun, surprise

astonishing *adjective* AMAZING, astounding, bewildering, breathtaking, brilliant, sensational (*informal*), staggering, stunning, surprising

astonishment *noun* AMAZEMENT, awe, bewilderment, confusion, consternation, surprise, wonder, wonderment

astounding *adjective* AMAZING, astonishing, bewildering, breathtaking, brilliant, cool (*informal*), impressive, phat (*slang*), sensational (*informal*), staggering, stunning, surprising

astray *adjective, adverb* OFF THE RIGHT TRACK, adrift, amiss, lost, off, off course, off the mark, off the subject

astute *adjective* INTELLIGENT, canny, clever, crafty, cunning, perceptive, sagacious, sharp, shrewd, subtle

asylum *noun* **1** REFUGE, harbor, haven, preserve, retreat, safety, sanctuary, shelter
2 *Old-fashioned* MENTAL HOSPITAL, funny farm (*slang*), hospital, institution, madhouse (*informal*), psychiatric hospital, psychiatric ward

atheism *noun* NONBELIEF, disbelief, godlessness, heathenism, infidelity, irreligion, paganism, skepticism, unbelief

atheist *noun* NONBELIEVER, disbeliever, heathen, infidel, pagan, skeptic, unbeliever

athlete *noun* SPORTSPERSON, competitor, contestant, gymnast, player, runner, sportsman, sportswoman

athletic *adjective* FIT, active, energetic, muscular, powerful, strapping, strong, sturdy

athletics *plural noun* SPORTS, contests, exercises, gymnastics, races, track and field events

atmosphere *noun* **1** AIR, aerosphere, heavens, sky
2 FEELING, ambience, character, climate, environment, mood, spirit, surroundings, tone

atom *noun* PARTICLE, bit, dot, molecule, speck, spot, trace

atone *verb* (usually with *for*) MAKE AMENDS, compensate, do penance, make redress, make reparation, make up for, pay for, recompense, redress

atonement *noun* AMENDS, compensation, penance, recompense, redress, reparation, restitution

atrocious *adjective* **1** CRUEL, barbaric, brutal, fiendish, infernal, monstrous, savage, vicious, wicked **2** *Informal* SHOCKING, appalling, detestable, grievous, horrible, horrifying, terrible

atrocity *noun* **1** CRUELTY, barbarity, brutality, fiendishness, horror, savagery, viciousness, wickedness **2** ACT

OF CRUELTY, abomination, crime, evil, horror, outrage

attach verb 1 CONNECT, add, couple, fasten, fix, join, link, secure, stick, tie 2 PUT, ascribe, assign, associate, attribute, connect

attached adjective 1 SPOKEN FOR, accompanied, engaged, married, partnered 2 **attached to** FOND OF, affectionate towards, devoted to, full of regard for

attachment noun 1 FONDNESS, affection, affinity, attraction, liking, regard 2 ACCESSORY, accouterment, extension, extra, fitting, fixture, supplement

attack verb 1 ASSAULT, invade, raid, set upon, storm, strike (at) 2 CRITICIZE, abuse, blame, censure, put down, vilify ▶noun 3 ASSAULT, campaign, charge, foray, incursion, invasion, offensive, onslaught, raid, strike 4 CRITICISM, abuse, blame, censure, denigration, stick (slang), vilification 5 BOUT, convulsion, fit, paroxysm, seizure, spasm, stroke

attacker noun ASSAILANT, aggressor, assaulter, intruder, invader, raider

attain verb ACHIEVE, accomplish, acquire, complete, fulfill, gain, get, obtain, reach

attainment noun ACHIEVEMENT, accomplishment, completion, feat

attempt verb 1 TRY, endeavor, seek, strive, undertake, venture ▶noun 2 TRY, bid, crack (informal), effort, go (informal), shot (informal), stab (informal), trial

attend verb 1 BE PRESENT, appear, frequent, go to, haunt, put in an appearance, show oneself, turn up, visit 2 LOOK AFTER, care for, mind, minister to, nurse, take care of, tend 3 PAY ATTENTION, hear, heed, listen, mark, note, observe, pay heed 4 **attend to** APPLY ONESELF TO, concentrate on, devote oneself to, get to work on, look after, occupy oneself with, see to, take care of

attendance noun 1 PRESENCE, appearance, attending, being there 2 TURNOUT, audience, crowd, gate, house, number present

attendant noun 1 ASSISTANT, aide, companion, escort, follower, guard, helper, servant ▶adjective 2 ACCOMPANYING, accessory, associated, concomitant, consequent, related

attention noun 1 CONCENTRATION, deliberation, heed, intentness, mind, scrutiny, thinking, thought 2 NOTICE, awareness, consciousness, consideration, observation, recognition, regard 3 CARE, concern, looking after, ministration, treatment

attentive adjective 1 INTENT, alert, awake, careful, concentrating, heedful, mindful, observant, studious, watchful 2 CONSIDERATE, courteous, helpful, kind, obliging, polite, respectful, thoughtful

attic noun LOFT, garret

attire noun CLOTHES, apparel, costume, dress, garb, garments, outfit, robes, wear

attitude noun **1** DISPOSITION, approach, frame of mind, mood, opinion, outlook, perspective, point of view, position, stance **2** POSITION, pose, posture, stance

attract verb APPEAL TO, allure, charm, draw, enchant, entice, lure, pull (*informal*), tempt

attraction noun APPEAL, allure, charm, enticement, fascination, lure, magnetism, pull (*informal*), temptation

attractive adjective APPEALING, alluring, charming, fair, fetching, good-looking, handsome, inviting, lovely, pleasant, pretty, tempting

attribute verb **1** ASCRIBE, assign, charge, credit, put down to, refer, set down to, trace to ▶noun **2** QUALITY, aspect, character, characteristic, facet, feature, peculiarity, property, trait

attune verb ACCUSTOM, adapt, adjust, familiarize, harmonize, regulate

audacious adjective **1** DARING, bold, brave, courageous, fearless, intrepid, rash, reckless **2** CHEEKY, brazen, defiant, impertinent, impudent, insolent, presumptuous, shameless

audacity noun **1** DARING, boldness, bravery, courage, fearlessness, nerve, rashness, recklessness **2** CHEEK, chutzpah (*informal*), effrontery, impertinence, impudence, insolence, nerve

audible adjective CLEAR, detectable, discernible, distinct, hearable, perceptible

audience noun **1** SPECTATORS, assembly, crowd, gallery, gathering, listeners, onlookers, turnout, viewers **2** INTERVIEW, consultation, hearing, meeting, reception

aura noun AIR, ambience, atmosphere, feeling, mood, quality, tone

auspicious adjective FAVORABLE, bright, encouraging, felicitous, hopeful, promising

austere adjective **1** STERN, forbidding, formal, serious, severe, solemn, strict **2** ASCETIC, abstemious, puritanical, self-disciplined, sober, solemn, strait-laced, strict **3** PLAIN, bleak, harsh, homely, simple, spare, Spartan, stark

austerity noun **1** STERNNESS, formality, inflexibility, rigor, seriousness, severity, solemnity, stiffness, strictness **2** ASCETICISM, puritanism, self-denial, self-discipline, sobriety **3** PLAINNESS, simplicity, starkness

authentic adjective GENUINE, actual, authoritative, bona fide, legitimate, pure, real, true-to-life, valid

authenticity noun GENUINENESS, accuracy, certainty, faithfulness, legitimacy, purity, truthfulness, validity

author noun **1** WRITER, composer, creator **2** CREATOR, architect, designer, father, founder, inventor, originator, producer

authoritarian adjective **1** STRICT, autocratic, dictatorial, doctrinaire, dogmatic, severe, tyrannical ▶noun **2** DISCIPLINARIAN, absolutist, autocrat, despot, dictator, tyrant

authoritative *adjective*
1 RELIABLE, accurate, authentic, definitive, dependable, trustworthy, valid
2 COMMANDING, assertive, imperious, imposing, masterly, self-assured

authority *noun* 1 POWER, command, control, direction, influence, supremacy, sway, weight 2 (usually plural) POWERS THAT BE, administration, government, management, officialdom, police, the Establishment 3 EXPERT, connoisseur, judge, master, professional, specialist

authorization *noun* PERMISSION, a blank check, approval, leave, license, permit, warrant

authorize *verb* 1 EMPOWER, accredit, commission, enable, entitle, give authority 2 PERMIT, allow, approve, give authority for, license, sanction, warrant

autocracy *noun* DICTATORSHIP, absolutism, despotism, tyranny

autocrat *noun* DICTATOR, absolutist, despot, tyrant

autocratic *adjective* DICTATORIAL, absolute, all-powerful, despotic, domineering, imperious, tyrannical

automatic *adjective*
1 MECHANICAL, automated, mechanized, push-button, self-propelling 2 INVOLUNTARY, instinctive, mechanical, natural, reflex, spontaneous, unconscious, unwilled

autonomous *adjective*
SELF-RULING, free, independent, self-determining,

self-governing, sovereign

autonomy *noun* INDEPENDENCE, freedom, home rule, self-determination, self-government, self-rule, sovereignty

auxiliary *adjective*
1 SUPPLEMENTARY, back-up, emergency, fall-back, reserve, secondary, subsidiary, substitute 2 SUPPORTING, accessory, aiding, ancillary, assisting, helping ▶ *noun*
3 BACKUP, reserve 4 HELPER, assistant, associate, companion, subordinate, supporter

avail *verb* 1 BENEFIT, aid, assist, be of advantage, be useful, help, profit ▶ *noun* 2 BENEFIT, advantage, aid, good, help, profit, use

availability *noun* ACCESSIBILITY, attainability, handiness, readiness

available *adjective* ACCESSIBLE, at hand, at one's disposal, free, handy, on tap, ready, to hand

avalanche *noun* 1 SNOW-SLIDE, landslide, landslip 2 FLOOD, barrage, deluge, inundation, torrent

avant-garde *adjective*
PROGRESSIVE, experimental, ground-breaking, innovative, pioneering, unconventional

avarice *noun* GREED, covetousness, meanness, miserliness, niggardliness, parsimony, stinginess

avaricious *adjective* GRASPING, covetous, greedy, mean, miserly, niggardly, parsimonious, stingy

avenge *verb* GET REVENGE FOR, get

even for (*informal*), hit back, punish, repay, retaliate

avenue *noun* STREET, approach, boulevard, course, drive, passage, path, road, route, way

average *noun* 1 USUAL, mean, medium, midpoint, norm, normal, par, standard 2 **on average** USUALLY, as a rule, for the most part, generally, normally, typically ▸ *adjective* 3 USUAL, commonplace, fair, general, normal, ordinary, regular, standard, typical 4 MEAN, intermediate, median, medium, middle ▸ *verb* 5 MAKE ON AVERAGE, balance out to, be on average, do on average, even out to

averse *adjective* OPPOSED, disinclined, hostile, ill-disposed, loath, reluctant, unwilling

aversion *noun* HATRED, animosity, antipathy, disinclination, dislike, hostility, revulsion, unwillingness

avert *verb* 1 TURN AWAY, turn aside 2 WARD OFF, avoid, fend off, forestall, frustrate, preclude, prevent, stave off

aviator *noun* PILOT, aeronaut, airman, flyer

avid *adjective* 1 ENTHUSIASTIC, ardent, devoted, eager, fanatical, intense, keen, passionate, zealous 2 INSATIABLE, grasping, greedy, hungry, rapacious, ravenous, thirsty, voracious

avoid *verb* 1 REFRAIN FROM, dodge, duck (out of) (*informal*), eschew, fight shy of, shirk 2 PREVENT, avert 3 KEEP AWAY FROM, bypass, dodge, elude, escape, evade, shun,

steer clear of

avoidance *noun* EVASION, dodging, eluding, escape, keeping away, shunning, steering clear

avowed *adjective* 1 DECLARED, open, professed, self-proclaimed, sworn 2 CONFESSED, acknowledged, admitted

await *verb* 1 WAIT FOR, abide, anticipate, expect, look for, look forward to, stay for 2 BE IN STORE FOR, attend, be in readiness for, be prepared for, be ready for, wait for

awake *adjective* 1 NOT SLEEPING, aroused, awakened, aware, conscious, wakeful, wide-awake 2 ALERT, alive, attentive, aware, heedful, observant, on the lookout, vigilant, watchful ▸ *verb* 3 WAKE UP, awaken, rouse, wake 4 ALERT, arouse, kindle, provoke, revive, stimulate, stir up

awaken *verb* 1 AWAKE, arouse, revive, rouse, wake 2 ALERT, kindle, provoke, stimulate, stir up

awakening *noun* WAKING UP, arousal, revival, rousing, stimulation, stirring up

award *verb* 1 GIVE, bestow, confer, endow, grant, hand out, present ▸ *noun* 2 PRIZE, decoration, gift, grant, trophy

aware *adjective* 1 **aware of** KNOWING ABOUT, acquainted with, conscious of, conversant with, familiar with, mindful of 2 INFORMED, enlightened, in the picture, knowledgeable

awareness *noun* KNOWLEDGE, consciousness, familiarity,

perception, realization, recognition, understanding

away *adverb* **1** OFF, abroad, elsewhere, from here, from home, hence **2** AT A DISTANCE, apart, far, remote **3** ASIDE, out of the way, to one side **4** CONTINUOUSLY, incessantly, interminably, relentlessly, repeatedly, uninterruptedly, unremittingly ▸ *adjective* **5** NOT PRESENT, abroad, absent, elsewhere, gone, not at home, not here, out

awe *noun* **1** WONDER, admiration, amazement, astonishment, dread, fear, horror, respect, reverence, terror ▸ *verb* **2** IMPRESS, amaze, astonish, frighten, horrify, intimidate, stun, terrify

awesome *adjective* **1** AWE-INSPIRING, amazing, astonishing, breathtaking, cool (*informal*), formidable, impressive, intimidating, phat (*slang*), stunning **2** *Informal* FIRST-CLASS, choice, elite, excellent, first-rate, hand-picked, superior, world-class

awful *adjective* TERRIBLE, abysmal, appalling, deplorable, dreadful, frightful, ghastly, horrendous

awfully *adverb* **1** BADLY, disgracefully, dreadfully, reprehensibly, unforgivably, unpleasantly, woefully, wretchedly **2** *Informal* VERY, dreadfully, exceedingly, exceptionally, extremely, greatly, immensely, terribly

awkward *adjective* **1** CLUMSY, gauche, gawky, inelegant, lumbering, uncoordinated, ungainly **2** UNMANAGEABLE,

clunky (*informal*), cumbersome, difficult, inconvenient, troublesome, unwieldy **3** EMBARRASSING, delicate, difficult, ill at ease, inconvenient, uncomfortable

awkwardness *noun* **1** CLUMSINESS, gawkiness, inelegance, ungainliness **2** UNWIELDINESS, difficulty, inconvenience **3** EMBARRASSMENT, delicacy, difficulty, inconvenience

ax *noun* **1** HATCHET, adz, chopper **2 the ax** *Informal* DISMISSAL, termination, the boot (*slang*), the chop (*slang*) ▸ *verb* **3** *Informal* CUT BACK, cancel, dismiss, dispense with, eliminate, fire (*informal*), get rid of, remove, sack (*informal*)

axiom *noun* PRINCIPLE, adage, aphorism, dictum, maxim, precept, truism

axiomatic *adjective* SELF-EVIDENT, accepted, assumed, certain, given, granted, manifest, understood

axis *noun* PIVOT, axle, center line, shaft, spindle

axle *noun* SHAFT, axis, pin, pivot, rod, spindle

B b

babble *verb* **1** GABBLE, burble, chatter, jabber, prattle **2** GIBBER, gurgle ▸ *noun* **3** GABBLE, burble, drivel, gibberish

baby *noun* **1** INFANT, babe, babe in arms, child, newborn child ▸ *adjective* **2** SMALL, little, mini,

miniature, minute,
teeny-weeny, tiny, wee

babyish adjective CHILDISH,
foolish, immature, infantile,
juvenile, puerile, sissy, spoiled

back noun 1 REAR, end, far end,
hind part, hindquarters,
reverse, stern, tail end
2 **behind one's back** SECRETLY,
covertly, deceitfully, sneakily,
surreptitiously ▶ verb 3 MOVE
BACK, back off, backtrack, go
back, retire, retreat, reverse,
turn tail, withdraw 4 SUPPORT,
advocate, assist, champion,
endorse, promote, sponsor
▶ adjective 5 REAR, end, hind,
hindmost, posterior, tail
6 PREVIOUS, delayed, earlier,
elapsed, former, overdue, past

backbiting noun SLANDER,
bitchiness (slang), cattiness
(informal), defamation,
disparagement, gossip, malice,
scandalmongering, spitefulness

backbone noun 1 Medical SPINAL
COLUMN, spine, vertebrae,
vertebral column 2 STRENGTH OF
CHARACTER, character, courage,
determination, fortitude, grit,
nerve, pluck, resolution

backbreaking adjective
EXHAUSTING, arduous, crushing,
grueling, hard, laborious,
punishing, strenuous

back down verb GIVE IN, accede,
admit defeat, back-pedal,
concede, surrender, withdraw,
yield

backer noun SUPPORTER,
advocate, angel (informal),
benefactor, patron, promoter,
second, sponsor, subscriber

backfire verb FAIL, boomerang,
disappoint, flop (informal),

miscarry, rebound, recoil

background noun HISTORY,
circumstances, culture,
education, environment,
grounding, tradition,
upbringing

backing noun SUPPORT, aid,
assistance, encouragement,
endorsement, moral support,
patronage, sponsorship

backlash noun REACTION,
counteraction, recoil,
repercussion, resistance,
response, retaliation

backlog noun BUILD-UP,
accumulation, excess, hoard,
reserve, stock, supply

back out verb (often with of)
WITHDRAW, abandon, cancel,
excuse oneself, give up, go
back on, quit, resign, retreat,
wimp out (slang)

backslide verb RELAPSE, go
astray, go wrong, lapse, revert,
slip, stray, weaken

backslider noun RELAPSER,
apostate, deserter, recidivist,
recreant, renegade, turncoat

back up verb SUPPORT, aid, assist,
bolster, confirm, corroborate,
reinforce, second, stand by,
substantiate

backward adjective SLOW,
behind, dull, retarded,
subnormal, underdeveloped,
undeveloped

backwards, backward adverb
TOWARDS THE REAR, behind, in
reverse, rearward

bacteria plural noun
MICROORGANISMS, bacilli, bugs
(slang), germs, microbes,
pathogens, viruses

bad adjective 1 INFERIOR,
defective, faulty, imperfect,

inadequate, lousy (*slang*), poor, substandard, unsatisfactory **2** HARMFUL, damaging, dangerous, deleterious, detrimental, hurtful, ruinous, unhealthy **3** EVIL, corrupt, criminal, immoral, mean, sinful, wicked, wrong **4** NAUGHTY, disobedient, mischievous, unruly **5** ROTTEN, decayed, moldy, putrid, rancid, sour, spoiled **6** UNFAVORABLE, adverse, distressing, gloomy, grim, troubled, unfortunate, unpleasant

badge *noun* MARK, brand, device, emblem, identification, insignia, sign, stamp, token

badger *verb* PESTER, bully, goad, harass, hound, importune, nag, plague, torment

badinage *noun* WORDPLAY, banter, mockery, pleasantry, repartee, teasing

badly *adverb* **1** POORLY, carelessly, imperfectly, inadequately, incorrectly, ineptly, wrongly **2** UNFAVORABLY, unfortunately, unsuccessfully **3** SEVERELY, deeply, desperately, exceedingly, extremely, greatly, intensely, seriously

bad-mouth *verb Slang* CRITICIZE, abuse, deride, insult, malign, mock, slander

baffle *verb* PUZZLE, bewilder, confound, confuse, flummox, mystify, nonplus, perplex, stump

bag *noun* **1** CONTAINER, receptacle, sac, sack ▶*verb* **2** CATCH, acquire, capture, kill, land, shoot, trap

baggage *noun* LUGGAGE, accouterments, bags,

belongings, equipment, gear, paraphernalia, suitcases, things

baggy *adjective* LOOSE, bulging, droopy, floppy, ill-fitting, oversize, roomy, sagging, slack

bail *noun Law* SECURITY, bond, guarantee, pledge, surety, warranty

bail out *verb* **1** HELP, aid, relieve, rescue, save (someone's) bacon (*informal*) **2** ESCAPE, quit, retreat, withdraw

bait *noun* **1** LURE, allurement, attraction, decoy, enticement, incentive, inducement, snare, temptation ▶*verb* **2** TEASE, annoy, bother, harass, hassle (*informal*), hound, irritate, persecute, torment

baked *adjective* DRY, arid, desiccated, parched, scorched, seared, sun-baked, torrid

balance *noun* **1** STABILITY, composure, equanimity, poise, self-control, self-possession, steadiness **2** EQUILIBRIUM, correspondence, equity, equivalence, evenness, parity, symmetry **3** REMAINDER, difference, residue, rest, surplus ▶*verb* **4** STABILIZE, level, match, parallel, steady **5** COMPARE, assess, consider, deliberate, estimate, evaluate, weigh **6** *Accounting* CALCULATE, compute, settle, square, tally, total

balcony *noun* **1** TERRACE, veranda **2** UPPER CIRCLE, gallery, gods

bald *adjective* **1** HAIRLESS, baldheaded, depilated **2** PLAIN, blunt, direct, forthright, straightforward, unadorned, unvarnished

balderdash noun NONSENSE, claptrap (*informal*), drivel, garbage (*informal*), gibberish, hogwash, hot air (*informal*), rubbish

baldness noun 1 HAIRLESSNESS, alopecia (*Pathology*), baldheadedness 2 PLAINNESS, austerity, bluntness, severity, simplicity

balk verb 1 RECOIL, evade, flinch, hesitate, jib, refuse, resist, shirk, shrink from 2 FOIL, check, counteract, defeat, frustrate, hinder, obstruct, prevent, thwart

ball noun SPHERE, drop, globe, globule, orb, pellet, spheroid

ballast noun COUNTERBALANCE, balance, counterweight, equilibrium, sandbag, stability, stabilizer, weight

balloon verb SWELL, billow, blow up, dilate, distend, expand, grow rapidly, inflate, puff out

ballot noun VOTE, election, poll, polling, voting

ballyhoo noun FUSS, babble, commotion, hubbub, hue and cry, hullabaloo, noise, racket, to-do

balm noun 1 OINTMENT, balsam, cream, embrocation, emollient, lotion, salve, unguent 2 COMFORT, anodyne, consolation, curative, palliative, restorative, solace

balmy adjective MILD, clement, pleasant, summery, temperate

baloney noun Informal NONSENSE, claptrap (*informal*), crap (*slang*), drivel, garbage, hogwash, poppycock (*informal*), rubbish, stuff and nonsense, trash, tripe (*informal*)

bamboozle verb Informal 1 CHEAT, con (*informal*), deceive, dupe, fool, hoodwink, swindle, trick 2 PUZZLE, baffle, befuddle, confound, confuse, mystify, perplex, stump

ban verb 1 PROHIBIT, banish, bar, block, boycott, disallow, disqualify, exclude, forbid, outlaw ▶noun 2 PROHIBITION, boycott, disqualification, embargo, restriction, taboo

banal adjective UNORIGINAL, hackneyed, humdrum, mundane, pedestrian, stale, stereotyped, trite, unimaginative

band[1] noun 1 ENSEMBLE, combo, group, orchestra 2 GANG, body, company, group, party, posse (*informal*)

band[2] noun STRIP, belt, bond, chain, cord, ribbon, strap

bandage noun 1 DRESSING, compress, gauze, plaster ▶verb 2 DRESS, bind, cover, swathe

bandit noun ROBBER, desperado, highwayman, marauder, outlaw, thief

bane noun PLAGUE, bête noire, curse, nuisance, pest, ruin, scourge, torment

bang noun 1 EXPLOSION, clang, clap, clash, pop, slam, thud, thump 2 BLOW, bump, cuff, knock, punch, smack, stroke, whack ▶verb 3 HIT, belt (*informal*), clatter, knock, slam, strike, thump 4 EXPLODE, boom, clang, resound, thump, thunder ▶adverb 5 HARD, abruptly, headlong, noisily, suddenly 6 STRAIGHT, precisely, slap, smack

banish verb 1 EXPEL, deport,

eject, evict, exile, outlaw **2** GET
RID OF, ban, cast out, discard,
dismiss, oust, remove

banishment *noun* EXPULSION,
deportation, exile, expatriation,
transportation

banisters *plural noun* RAILING,
balusters, balustrade, handrail,
rail

bank[1] *noun* **1** STOREHOUSE,
depository, repository **2** STORE,
accumulation, fund, hoard,
reserve, reservoir, savings,
stock, stockpile ▸ *verb* **3** SAVE,
deposit, keep

bank[2] *noun* **1** MOUND, banking,
embankment, heap, mass, pile,
ridge **2** SIDE, brink, edge,
margin, shore ▸ *verb* **3** PILE,
amass, heap, mass, mound,
stack **4** TILT, camber, cant, heel,
incline, pitch, slant, slope, tip

bank[3] *noun* ROW, array, file,
group, line, rank, sequence,
series, succession

bankrupt *adjective* INSOLVENT,
broke (*informal*), destitute,
impoverished, in queer street,
in the red, ruined, wiped out
(*informal*)

bankruptcy *noun* INSOLVENCY,
disaster, failure, liquidation, ruin

banner *noun* FLAG, colors,
ensign, pennant, placard,
standard, streamer

banquet *noun* FEAST, dinner,
meal, repast, revel, treat

banter *verb* **1** JOKE, jest, kid
(*informal*), rib (*informal*), taunt,
tease ▸ *noun* **2** JOKING,
badinage, jesting, kidding
(*informal*), repartee, teasing,
wordplay

baptism *noun Christianity*
CHRISTENING, immersion,

purification, sprinkling

baptize *verb Christianity* PURIFY,
cleanse, immerse

bar *noun* **1** ROD, paling,
palisade, pole, rail, shaft, stake,
stick **2** OBSTACLE, barricade,
barrier, block, deterrent,
hindrance, impediment,
obstruction, stop **3** PUBLIC
HOUSE, canteen, counter, inn,
saloon, tavern, watering hole
(*facetious slang*) ▸ *verb* **4** FASTEN,
barricade, bolt, latch, lock,
secure **5** OBSTRUCT, hinder,
prevent, restrain **6** EXCLUDE,
ban, black, blackball, forbid,
keep out, prohibit

Bar *noun* **the Bar** *Law* BARRISTERS,
body of lawyers, counsel,
court, judgment, tribunal

barb *noun* **1** DIG, affront, cut,
gibe, insult, sarcasm, scoff,
sneer **2** POINT, bristle, prickle,
prong, quill, spike, spur, thorn

barbarian *noun* **1** SAVAGE, brute,
yahoo **2** LOUT, bigot, boor,
philistine

barbaric *adjective* **1** UNCIVILIZED,
primitive, rude, wild **2** BRUTAL,
barbarous, coarse, crude, cruel,
fierce, inhuman, savage

barbarism *noun* SAVAGERY,
coarseness, crudity

barbarous *adjective*
1 UNCIVILIZED, barbarian, brutish,
primitive, rough, rude, savage,
uncouth, wild **2** BRUTAL,
barbaric, cruel, ferocious,
heartless, inhuman, monstrous,
ruthless, vicious

barbed *adjective* **1** CUTTING,
critical, hostile, hurtful, nasty,
pointed, scathing, unkind
2 SPIKED, hooked, jagged,
prickly, spiny, thorny

bare *adjective* 1 NAKED, nude, stripped, unclad, unclothed, uncovered, undressed, without a stitch on (*informal*) 2 PLAIN, bald, basic, sheer, simple, stark, unembellished 3 SIMPLE, austere, homely, spare, spartan, unadorned, unembellished

barefaced *adjective* 1 OBVIOUS, blatant, flagrant, open, transparent, unconcealed 2 SHAMELESS, audacious, bold, brash, brazen, impudent, insolent

barely *adverb* ONLY JUST, almost, at a push, by the skin of one's teeth, hardly, just, scarcely

barf *verb Slang* VOMIT, heave, puke (*slang*), retch, spew, throw up (*informal*), toss one's cookies (*slang*) ▶ *noun* VOMIT, puke, sick

bargain *noun* 1 AGREEMENT, arrangement, contract, pact, pledge, promise 2 GOOD BUY, (cheap) purchase, discount, giveaway, good deal, reduction, steal (*informal*) ▶ *verb* 3 NEGOTIATE, agree, contract, covenant, promise, stipulate, transact

barge *noun* CANAL BOAT, flatboat, lighter, narrow boat

bark[1] *noun, verb* YAP, bay, growl, howl, snarl, woof, yelp

bark[2] *noun* COVERING, casing, cortex (*Anatomy, botany*), crust, husk, rind, skin

barracks *plural noun* CAMP, billet, encampment, garrison, quarters

barrage *noun* 1 TORRENT, burst, deluge, hail, mass, onslaught, plethora, stream 2 *Military* BOMBARDMENT, battery, cannonade, fusillade, gunfire, salvo, shelling, volley

barren *adjective* 1 INFERTILE, childless, sterile 2 UNPRODUCTIVE, arid, desert, desolate, dry, empty, unfruitful, waste

barricade *noun* 1 BARRIER, blockade, bulwark, fence, obstruction, palisade, rampart, stockade ▶ *verb* 2 BAR, block, blockade, defend, fortify, obstruct, protect, shut in

barrier *noun* 1 BARRICADE, bar, blockade, boundary, fence, obstacle, obstruction, wall 2 HINDRANCE, difficulty, drawback, handicap, hurdle, obstacle, restriction, stumbling block

barter *verb* TRADE, bargain, drive a hard bargain, exchange, haggle, sell, swap, traffic

base[1] *noun* 1 BOTTOM, bed, foot, foundation, pedestal, rest, stand, support 2 BASIS, core, essence, heart, key, origin, root, source 3 CENTER, camp, headquarters, home, post, settlement, starting point, station ▶ *verb* 4 FOUND, build, construct, depend, derive, establish, ground, hinge 5 PLACE, locate, post, station

base[2] *adjective* 1 DISHONORABLE, contemptible, despicable, disreputable, evil, immoral, lousy (*slang*), scuzzy (*slang*), shameful, sordid, wicked 2 COUNTERFEIT, alloyed, debased, fake, forged, fraudulent, impure

baseless *adjective* UNFOUNDED, groundless, unconfirmed, uncorroborated, ungrounded, unjustified, unsubstantiated, unsupported

bash verb Informal HIT, belt (informal), smash, sock (slang), strike, wallop (informal)

bashful adjective SHY, blushing, coy, diffident, reserved, reticent, retiring, timid

basic adjective ESSENTIAL, elementary, fundamental, key, necessary, primary, vital

basically adverb ESSENTIALLY, at heart, fundamentally, inherently, in substance, intrinsically, mostly, primarily

basics plural noun ESSENTIALS, ABCs, brass tacks (informal), fundamentals, nitty-gritty (informal), nuts and bolts (informal), principles, rudiments

basis noun FOUNDATION, base, bottom, footing, ground, groundwork, support

bask verb LIE IN, laze, loll, lounge, relax, sunbathe, swim in

bass adjective DEEP, deep-toned, low, low-pitched, resonant, sonorous

bastard noun 1 Informal, offensive ROGUE, miscreant, reprobate, scoundrel, villain, wretch 2 ILLEGITIMATE CHILD, love child, natural child

bastion noun STRONGHOLD, bulwark, citadel, defense, fortress, mainstay, prop, rock, support, tower of strength

bat noun, verb HIT, bang, smack, strike, swat, thump, wallop (informal), whack

batch noun GROUP, amount, assemblage, bunch, collection, crowd, lot, pack, quantity, set

bath noun 1 WASH, cleansing, douche, scrubbing, shower,

soak, tub ▶ verb 2 WASH, bathe, clean, douse, scrub down, shower, soak

bathe verb 1 WASH, cleanse, rinse, soak 2 COVER, flood, immerse, steep, suffuse

baton noun STICK, club, crook, mace, rod, scepter, staff, truncheon, wand

batten verb (usually with down) FASTEN, board up, clamp down, cover up, fix, nail down, secure, tighten

batter verb BEAT, buffet, clobber (slang), pelt, pound, pummel, thrash, wallop (informal)

battery noun ARTILLERY, cannon, cannonry, gun emplacements, guns

battle noun 1 FIGHT, action, attack, combat, encounter, engagement, hostilities, skirmish 2 CONFLICT, campaign, contest, crusade, dispute, struggle ▶ verb 3 STRUGGLE, argue, clamor, dispute, fight, lock horns, strive, war

battlefield noun BATTLEGROUND, combat zone, field, field of battle, front

battleship noun WARSHIP, gunboat, man-of-war

batty adjective CRAZY, absent-minded, bonkers (informal), daft (informal), eccentric, mad, odd, peculiar

bauble noun TRINKET, bagatelle, gewgaw, gimcrack, knick-knack, plaything, toy, trifle

baulk see BALK

bawdy adjective RUDE, coarse, dirty, indecent, lascivious, lecherous, lewd, ribald, salacious, smutty

bawl *verb* **1** CRY, blubber, sob, wail, weep **2** SHOUT, bellow, call, clamor, howl, roar, yell

bay[1] *noun* INLET, bight, cove, gulf, natural harbor, sound

bay[2] *noun* RECESS, alcove, compartment, niche, nook, opening

bay[3] *verb* HOWL, bark, clamor, cry, growl, yelp

bazaar *noun* **1** FAIR, bring-and-buy, fête, sale of work **2** MARKET, exchange, marketplace

be *verb* EXIST, be alive, breathe, inhabit, live

beach *noun* SHORE, coast, sands, seashore, seaside, water's edge

beached *adjective* STRANDED, abandoned, aground, ashore, deserted, grounded, high and dry, marooned, wrecked

beacon *noun* SIGNAL, beam, bonfire, flare, lighthouse, sign, watchtower

bead *noun* DROP, blob, bubble, dot, droplet, globule, pellet, pill

beady *adjective* BRIGHT, gleaming, glinting, glittering, sharp, shining

beak *noun* BILL, mandible, neb (*archaic or dialect*), nib

beam *noun* **1** SMILE, grin **2** RAY, gleam, glimmer, glint, glow, shaft, streak, stream **3** RAFTER, girder, joist, plank, spar, support, timber ▶ *verb* **4** SMILE, grin **5** RADIATE, glare, gleam, glitter, glow, shine **6** SEND OUT, broadcast, emit, transmit

bear *verb* **1** SUPPORT, have, hold, maintain, possess, shoulder, sustain, uphold **2** CARRY, bring, convey, move, take, transport **3** PRODUCE, beget, breed, bring forth, engender, generate, give birth to, yield **4** TOLERATE, abide, allow, brook, endure, permit, put up with (*informal*), stomach, suffer

bearable *adjective* TOLERABLE, admissible, endurable, manageable, passable, sufferable, supportable, sustainable

bearer *noun* CARRIER, agent, conveyor, messenger, porter, runner, servant

bearing *noun* **1** (usually with *on* or *upon*) RELEVANCE, application, connection, import, pertinence, reference, relation, significance **2** MANNER, air, aspect, attitude, behavior, demeanor, deportment, posture

bearings *plural noun* POSITION, aim, course, direction, location, orientation, situation, track, way, whereabouts

bear out *verb* SUPPORT, confirm, corroborate, endorse, justify, prove, substantiate, uphold, vindicate

beast *noun* **1** ANIMAL, brute, creature **2** BRUTE, barbarian, fiend, monster, ogre, sadist, savage, swine

beastly *adjective* UNPLEASANT, awful, disagreeable, horrid, mean, nasty, rotten

beat *verb* **1** HIT, bang, batter, buffet, knock, pound, strike, thrash **2** FLAP, flutter **3** THROB, palpitate, pound, pulsate, quake, thump, vibrate **4** DEFEAT, conquer, outdo, overcome, overwhelm, surpass, vanquish ▶ *noun* **5** THROB, palpitation, pulsation, pulse **6** ROUTE, circuit, course, path, rounds, way **7** RHYTHM, accent, cadence, meter, stress, time

beaten adjective **1** STIRRED, blended, foamy, frothy, mixed, whipped, whisked **2** DEFEATED, cowed, overcome, overwhelmed, thwarted, vanquished

beat up verb Informal ASSAULT, attack, batter, beat the living daylights out of (informal), knock about or around, pound, pulverize, thrash

beau noun **1** Old-fashioned BOYFRIEND, admirer, fiancé, lover, suitor, sweetheart **2** DANDY, coxcomb, fop, gallant, ladies' man

beautiful adjective ATTRACTIVE, charming, delightful, exquisite, fair, fine, gorgeous, handsome, lovely, pleasing

beautify verb MAKE BEAUTIFUL, adorn, decorate, embellish, festoon, garnish, glamorize, ornament

beauty noun **1** ATTRACTIVENESS, charm, comeliness, elegance, exquisiteness, glamour, grace, handsomeness, loveliness **2** BELLE, good-looker, lovely (slang), stunner (informal)

becalmed adjective STILL, motionless, settled, stranded, stuck

because conjunction SINCE, as, by reason of, in that, on account of, owing to, thanks to

beckon verb GESTURE, bid, gesticulate, motion, nod, signal, summon, wave at

become verb **1** COME TO BE, alter to, be transformed into, change into, develop into, grow into, mature into, ripen into **2** SUIT, embellish, enhance, fit, flatter, set off

becoming adjective **1** APPROPRIATE, compatible, fitting, in keeping, proper, seemly, suitable, worthy **2** FLATTERING, attractive, comely, enhancing, graceful, neat, pretty, tasteful

bed noun **1** BEDSTEAD, berth, bunk, cot, couch, divan **2** PLOT, area, border, garden, patch, row, strip **3** BOTTOM, base, foundation, groundwork

bedevil verb **1** TORMENT, afflict, distress, harass, plague, trouble, vex, worry **2** CONFUSE, confound

bedlam noun PANDEMONIUM, chaos, commotion, confusion, furor, tumult, turmoil, uproar

bedraggled adjective MESSY, dirty, dishevelled, disordered, muddied, scuzzy (slang), unkempt, untidy

bedridden adjective CONFINED TO BED, confined, flat on one's back, incapacitated, laid up (informal)

bedrock noun **1** BOTTOM, bed, foundation, rock bottom, substratum, substructure **2** BASICS, basis, core, essentials, fundamentals, nuts and bolts (informal), roots

beefy adjective Informal BRAWNY, bulky, hulking, muscular, stocky, strapping, sturdy, thickset

befall verb HAPPEN, chance, come to pass, fall, occur, take place, transpire (informal)

befitting adjective APPROPRIATE, apposite, becoming, fit, fitting, proper, right, seemly, suitable

before *preposition* **1** AHEAD OF, in advance of, in front of **2** EARLIER THAN, in advance of, prior to **3** IN THE PRESENCE OF, in front of ▶*adverb* **4** PREVIOUSLY, ahead, earlier, formerly, in advance, sooner **5** IN FRONT, ahead

beforehand *adverb* IN ADVANCE, ahead of time, already, before, earlier, in anticipation, previously, sooner

befriend *verb* HELP, aid, assist, back, encourage, side with, stand by, support, welcome

beg *verb* **1** SCROUNGE, cadge, seek charity, solicit charity, sponge on **2** IMPLORE, beseech, entreat, petition, plead, request, solicit

beggar *noun* TRAMP, bag lady, bum (*informal*), down-and-out, pauper, vagrant

beggarly *adjective* POOR, destitute, impoverished, indigent, needy, poverty-stricken

begin *verb* **1** START, commence, embark on, initiate, instigate, institute, prepare, set about **2** HAPPEN, appear, arise, come into being, emerge, originate, start

beginner *noun* NOVICE, amateur, apprentice, learner, neophyte, rookie (*informal*), starter, trainee, tyro

beginning *noun* **1** START, birth, commencement, inauguration, inception, initiation, onset, opening, origin, outset **2** SEED, fount, germ, root

begrudge *verb* RESENT, be jealous, be reluctant, be stingy, envy, grudge

beguile *verb* **1** FOOL, cheat, deceive, delude, dupe, hoodwink, mislead, take for a ride (*informal*), trick **2** CHARM, amuse, distract, divert, engross, entertain, occupy

beguiling *adjective* CHARMING, alluring, attractive, bewitching, captivating, enchanting, enthralling, intriguing

behave *verb* **1** ACT, function, operate, perform, run, work **2** CONDUCT ONESELF PROPERLY, act correctly, keep one's nose clean, mind one's manners

behavior *noun* **1** CONDUCT, actions, bearing, demeanor, deportment, manner, manners, ways **2** ACTION, functioning, operation, performance

behind *preposition* **1** AFTER, at the back of, at the heels of, at the rear of, following, later than **2** CAUSING, at the bottom of, initiating, instigating, responsible for **3** SUPPORTING, backing, for, in agreement, on the side of ▶*adverb* **4** AFTER, afterwards, following, in the wake (of), next, subsequently **5** OVERDUE, behindhand, in arrears, in debt ▶*noun* **6** *Informal* BOTTOM, butt (*informal*), buttocks, posterior

behold *verb* LOOK AT, observe, perceive, regard, survey, view, watch, witness

beholden *adjective* INDEBTED, bound, grateful, obliged, owing, under obligation

being *noun* **1** EXISTENCE, life, reality **2** NATURE, entity, essence, soul, spirit, substance **3** CREATURE, human being, individual, living thing

belated *adjective* LATE,

behindhand, behind time, delayed, late in the day, overdue, tardy

belch verb 1 BURP (informal), hiccup 2 EMIT, discharge, disgorge, erupt, give off, spew forth, vent

beleaguered adjective 1 HARASSED, badgered, hassled (informal), persecuted, pestered, plagued, put upon, vexed 2 BESIEGED, assailed, beset, blockaded, hemmed in, surrounded

belief noun 1 TRUST, assurance, confidence, conviction, feeling, impression, judgment, notion, opinion 2 FAITH, credo, creed, doctrine, dogma, ideology, principles, tenet

believable adjective CREDIBLE, authentic, imaginable, likely, plausible, possible, probable, trustworthy

believe verb 1 ACCEPT, be certain of, be convinced of, credit, depend on, have faith in, rely on, swear by, trust 2 THINK, assume, gather, imagine, judge, presume, reckon, speculate, suppose

believer noun FOLLOWER, adherent, convert, devotee, disciple, supporter, upholder, zealot

belittle verb DISPARAGE, decry, denigrate, deprecate, deride, scoff at, scorn, sneer at

belligerent adjective 1 AGGRESSIVE, bellicose, combative, hostile, pugnacious, unfriendly, warlike, warring ► noun 2 FIGHTER, combatant, warring nation

bellow noun, verb SHOUT, bawl, clamor, cry, howl, roar, scream, shriek, yell

belly noun 1 STOMACH, abdomen, gut, insides (informal), paunch, potbelly, tummy ► verb 2 SWELL OUT, billow, bulge, fill, spread, swell

bellyful noun SURFEIT, enough, excess, glut, plateful, plenty, satiety, too much

belonging noun RELATIONSHIP, acceptance, affinity, association, attachment, fellowship, inclusion, loyalty, rapport

belongings plural noun POSSESSIONS, accouterments, chattels, effects, gear, goods, paraphernalia, personal property, stuff, things

belong to verb 1 BE THE PROPERTY OF, be at the disposal of, be held by, be owned by 2 BE A MEMBER OF, be affiliated to, be allied to, be associated with, be included in

beloved adjective DEAR, admired, adored, darling, loved, pet, precious, prized, treasured, worshipped

below preposition 1 LESSER, inferior, subject, subordinate 2 LESS THAN, lower than ► adverb 3 LOWER, beneath, down, under, underneath

belt noun 1 WAISTBAND, band, cummerbund, girdle, girth, sash 2 Geography ZONE, area, district, layer, region, stretch, strip, tract

bemoan verb LAMENT, bewail, deplore, grieve for, mourn, regret, rue, weep for

bemused adjective PUZZLED, at sea, bewildered, confused, flummoxed, muddled, nonplussed, perplexed

bench noun 1 SEAT, form, pew, settle, stall 2 WORKTABLE, board, counter, table, trestle table, workbench 3 **the bench** COURT, courtroom, judges, judiciary, magistrates, tribunal

benchmark noun REFERENCE POINT, criterion, gauge, level, measure, model, norm, par, standard, yardstick

bend verb 1 CURVE, arc, arch, bow, lean, turn, twist, veer ▶ noun 2 CURVE, angle, arc, arch, bow, corner, loop, turn, twist

beneath preposition 1 UNDER, below, lower than, underneath 2 INFERIOR TO, below, less than 3 UNWORTHY OF, unbefitting ▶ adverb 4 UNDERNEATH, below, in a lower place

benefactor noun SUPPORTER, backer, donor, helper, patron, philanthropist, sponsor, well-wisher

beneficial adjective HELPFUL, advantageous, benign, favorable, profitable, useful, valuable, wholesome, win-win (informal)

beneficiary noun RECIPIENT, heir, inheritor, payee, receiver

benefit noun 1 HELP, advantage, aid, asset, assistance, favor, good, profit ▶ verb 2 HELP, aid, assist, avail, enhance, further, improve, profit

benevolent adjective KIND, altruistic, benign, caring, charitable, generous, philanthropic

benign adjective 1 KINDLY, amiable, friendly, genial, kind, obliging, sympathetic

2 Medical HARMLESS, curable, remediable

bent adjective 1 CURVED, angled, arched, bowed, crooked, hunched, stooped, twisted 2 **bent on** DETERMINED TO, disposed to, fixed on, inclined to, insistent on, predisposed to, resolved on, set on ▶ noun 3 INCLINATION, ability, aptitude, leaning, penchant, preference, propensity, tendency

bequeath verb LEAVE, bestow, endow, entrust, give, grant, hand down, impart, pass on, will

bequest noun LEGACY, bestowal, endowment, estate, gift, inheritance, settlement

berate verb SCOLD, castigate, censure, chide, criticize, harangue, rebuke, reprimand, reprove, tell off (informal), upbraid

bereavement noun LOSS, affliction, death, deprivation, misfortune, tribulation

bereft adjective DEPRIVED, devoid, lacking, parted from, robbed of, wanting

berserk adverb CRAZY, amok, enraged, frantic, frenzied, mad, raging, wild

berth noun 1 BUNK, bed, billet, hammock 2 Nautical ANCHORAGE, dock, harbor, haven, pier, port, quay, wharf ▶ verb 3 Nautical ANCHOR, dock, drop anchor, land, moor, tie up

beseech verb BEG, ask, call upon, entreat, implore, plead, pray, solicit

beset verb PLAGUE, bedevil, harass, pester, trouble

beside preposition 1 NEXT TO,

abreast of, adjacent to, alongside, at the side of, close to, near, nearby, neighboring **2 beside oneself** DISTRAUGHT, apoplectic, at the end of one's tether, demented, desperate, frantic, frenzied, out of one's mind, unhinged

besides adverb **1** TOO, also, as well, further, furthermore, in addition, into the bargain, moreover, otherwise, what's more ▶preposition **2** APART FROM, barring, excepting, excluding, in addition to, other than, over and above, without

besiege verb **1** SURROUND, blockade, encircle, hem in, lay siege to, shut in **2** HARASS, badger, harry, hassle (informal), hound, nag, pester, plague

besotted adjective INFATUATED, doting, hypnotized, smitten, spellbound

best adjective **1** FINEST, foremost, leading, most excellent, outstanding, pre-eminent, principal, supreme, unsurpassed ▶adverb **2** MOST HIGHLY, extremely, greatly, most deeply, most fully ▶noun **3** FINEST, cream, crème de la crème, elite, flower, pick, prime, top

bestial adjective BRUTAL, barbaric, beastly, brutish, inhuman, savage, sordid

bestow verb PRESENT, award, commit, give, grant, hand out, impart, lavish

bet noun **1** GAMBLE, long shot, risk, speculation, stake, venture, wager ▶verb **2** GAMBLE, chance, hazard, risk, speculate, stake, venture, wager

betoken verb INDICATE, bode, denote, promise, represent, signify, suggest

betray verb **1** BE DISLOYAL, be treacherous, be unfaithful, break one's promise, double-cross (informal), inform on or against, sell out (informal), stab in the back **2** GIVE AWAY, disclose, divulge, expose, let slip, reveal, uncover, unmask

betrayal noun **1** DISLOYALTY, deception, double-cross (informal), sell-out (informal), treachery, treason, trickery **2** GIVING AWAY, disclosure, divulgence, revelation

better adjective **1** SUPERIOR, excelling, finer, greater, higher-quality, more desirable, preferable, surpassing **2** WELL, cured, fully recovered, on the mend (informal), recovering, stronger ▶adverb **3** IN A MORE EXCELLENT MANNER, in a superior way, more advantageously, more attractively, more competently, more effectively **4** TO A GREATER DEGREE, more completely, more thoroughly ▶verb **5** IMPROVE, enhance, further, raise

between preposition AMIDST, among, betwixt, in the middle of, mid

beverage noun DRINK, liquid, liquor, refreshment

bevy noun GROUP, band, bunch (informal), collection, company, crowd, gathering, pack, troupe

bewail verb LAMENT, bemoan, cry over, deplore, grieve for, moan, mourn, regret

beware verb BE CAREFUL, be

cautious, be wary, guard against, heed, look out, mind, take heed, watch out

bewilder verb CONFOUND, baffle, bemuse, confuse, flummox, mystify, nonplus, perplex, puzzle

bewildered adjective CONFUSED, at a loss, at sea, baffled, flummoxed, mystified, nonplussed, perplexed, puzzled

bewitch verb ENCHANT, beguile, captivate, charm, enrapture, entrance, fascinate, hypnotize

bewitched adjective ENCHANTED, charmed, entranced, fascinated, mesmerized, spellbound, under a spell

beyond preposition 1 PAST, above, apart from, at a distance, away from, over 2 EXCEEDING, out of reach of, superior to, surpassing

bias noun 1 PREJUDICE, favoritism, inclination, leaning, partiality, tendency ▸ verb 2 PREJUDICE, distort, influence, predispose, slant, sway, twist, warp, weight

biased adjective PREJUDICED, distorted, one-sided, partial, slanted, weighted

bicker verb QUARREL, argue, disagree, dispute, fight, squabble, wrangle

bid verb 1 OFFER, proffer, propose, submit, tender 2 SAY, call, greet, tell, wish 3 TELL, ask, command, direct, instruct, order, require ▸ noun 4 OFFER, advance, amount, price, proposal, sum, tender 5 ATTEMPT, crack (informal), effort, go (informal), stab (informal), try

bidding noun ORDER, beck and

call, command, direction, instruction, request, summons

big adjective 1 LARGE, enormous, extensive, great, huge, immense, massive, substantial, vast 2 IMPORTANT, eminent, influential, leading, main, powerful, prominent, significant 3 GROWN-UP, adult, elder, grown, mature 4 GENEROUS, altruistic, benevolent, gracious, magnanimous, noble, unselfish

big cheese noun Informal MANAGER, boss (informal), bossman (slang), foreman, head honcho (slang), overseer, superintendent, supervisor

bighead noun Informal BOASTER, braggart, know-all (informal)

bigheaded adjective BOASTFUL, arrogant, cocky, conceited, egotistic, immodest, overconfident, swollen-headed

bigot noun FANATIC, racist, sectarian, zealot

bigoted adjective INTOLERANT, biased, dogmatic, narrow-minded, opinionated, prejudiced, sectarian

bigotry noun INTOLERANCE, bias, discrimination, dogmatism, fanaticism, narrow-mindedness, prejudice, sectarianism

bill[1] noun 1 CHARGES, account, invoice, reckoning, score, statement, tally 2 PROPOSAL, measure, piece of legislation, projected law 3 ADVERTISEMENT, bulletin, circular, handbill, handout, leaflet, notice, placard, poster 4 LIST, agenda, card, catalog, inventory, listing, program, roster, schedule ▸ verb 5 CHARGE, debit, invoice

6 ADVERTISE, announce, give advance notice of, post

bill² noun BEAK, mandible, neb (archaic or dialect), nib

billet verb 1 QUARTER, accommodate, berth, station ▶ noun 2 QUARTERS, accommodation, barracks, lodging

billow noun 1 WAVE, breaker, crest, roller, surge, swell, tide ▶ verb 2 SURGE, balloon, belly, puff up, rise up, roll, swell

bind verb 1 SECURE, fasten, hitch, lash, strap, tie 2 OBLIGE, compel, constrain, engage, force, necessitate, require ▶ noun Informal 3 NUISANCE, bore, drag (informal), pain in the neck (informal), 4 DIFFICULTY, dilemma, quandary, spot (informal)

binding adjective COMPULSORY, indissoluble, irrevocable, mandatory, necessary, obligatory, unalterable

binge noun Informal BOUT, feast, fling, orgy, spree

biography noun LIFE STORY, account, curriculum vitae, CV, life, memoir, profile, record

birth noun 1 CHILDBIRTH, delivery, nativity, parturition 2 ANCESTRY, background, blood, breeding, lineage, parentage, pedigree, stock

bisect verb CUT IN TWO, cross, cut across, divide in two, halve, intersect, separate, split

bit¹ noun PIECE, crumb, fragment, grain, morsel, part, scrap, speck

bit² noun CURB, brake, check, restraint, snaffle

bitch noun 1 Informal COMPLAINT,

gripe (informal), grouse, grumble, objection, protest ▶ verb 2 Informal COMPLAIN, bemoan, gripe (informal), grouse, grumble, lament, object

bitchy adjective Informal SPITEFUL, backbiting, catty (informal), mean, nasty, snide, vindictive

bite verb 1 CUT, chew, gnaw, nip, pierce, pinch, snap, tear, wound ▶ noun 2 WOUND, nip, pinch, prick, smarting, sting, tooth marks 3 SNACK, food, light meal, morsel, mouthful, piece, refreshment, taste

biting adjective 1 PIERCING, bitter, cutting, harsh, penetrating, sharp 2 SARCASTIC, caustic, cutting, incisive, mordant, scathing, stinging, trenchant, vitriolic

bitter adjective 1 SOUR, acid, acrid, astringent, harsh, sharp, tart, unsweetened, vinegary 2 RESENTFUL, acrimonious, begrudging, hostile, sore, sour, sullen 3 FREEZING, biting, fierce, intense, severe, stinging

bitterness noun 1 SOURNESS, acerbity, acidity, sharpness, tartness 2 RESENTMENT, acrimony, animosity, asperity, grudge, hostility, rancor, sarcasm

bizarre adjective STRANGE, eccentric, extraordinary, fantastic, freakish, ludicrous, outlandish, peculiar, unusual, weird, zany

blab verb TELL, blurt out, disclose, divulge, give away, let slip, let the cat out of the bag, reveal, spill the beans (informal)

black adjective 1 DARK, dusky, ebony, jet, raven, sable,

swarthy 2 HOPELESS, depressing,
dismal, foreboding, gloomy,
ominous, sad, somber 3 ANGRY,
furious, hostile, menacing,
resentful, sullen, threatening
4 WICKED, bad, evil, iniquitous,
nefarious, villainous ▶verb
5 BOYCOTT, ban, bar, blacklist

blacken verb 1 DARKEN, befoul,
begrime, cloud, dirty, make
black, smudge, soil 2 DISCREDIT,
defame, denigrate, malign,
slander, smear, smirch, vilify

blacklist verb EXCLUDE, ban, bar,
boycott, debar, expel, reject,
snub

black magic noun WITCHCRAFT,
black art, diabolism,
necromancy, sorcery, voodoo,
wizardry

blackmail noun 1 THREAT,
extortion, hush money (slang),
intimidation, ransom ▶verb
2 THREATEN, coerce, compel,
demand, extort, hold to
ransom, intimidate, squeeze

blackness noun DARKNESS,
duskiness, gloom, murkiness,
swarthiness

blackout noun
1 UNCONSCIOUSNESS, coma, faint,
loss of consciousness, oblivion,
swoon 2 NONCOMMUNICATION,
censorship, radio silence,
secrecy, suppression,
withholding news

blame verb 1 HOLD RESPONSIBLE,
accuse, censure, chide,
condemn, criticize, find fault
with, reproach ▶noun
2 RESPONSIBILITY, accountability,
culpability, fault, guilt, liability,
onus

blameless adjective INNOCENT,
above suspicion, clean,

faultless, guiltless, immaculate,
impeccable, irreproachable,
perfect, unblemished, virtuous

blameworthy adjective
REPREHENSIBLE, discreditable,
disreputable, indefensible,
inexcusable, iniquitous,
reproachable, shameful

bland adjective DULL, boring,
flat, humdrum, insipid,
tasteless, unexciting,
uninspiring, vapid

blank adjective 1 UNMARKED,
bare, clean, clear, empty,
plain, void, white
2 EXPRESSIONLESS, deadpan,
empty, impassive, poker-faced
(informal), vacant, vague ▶noun
3 EMPTY SPACE, emptiness, gap,
nothingness, space, vacancy,
vacuum, void

blanket noun 1 COVER, coverlet,
rug 2 COVERING, carpet, cloak,
coat, layer, mantle, sheet ▶verb
3 COVER, cloak, coat, conceal,
hide, mask, obscure, suppress

blare verb SOUND OUT, blast,
clamor, clang, resound, roar,
scream, trumpet

blasé adjective INDIFFERENT,
apathetic, lukewarm,
nonchalant, offhand,
unconcerned

blaspheme verb CURSE, abuse,
damn, desecrate, execrate,
profane, revile, swear

blasphemous adjective
IRREVERENT, godless, impious,
irreligious, profane,
sacrilegious, ungodly

blasphemy noun IRREVERENCE,
cursing, desecration,
execration, impiety, profanity,
sacrilege, swearing

blast noun 1 EXPLOSION, bang,

burst, crash, detonation, discharge, eruption, outburst, salvo, volley **2** GUST, gale, squall, storm, strong breeze, tempest **3** BLARE, blow, clang, honk, peal, scream, toot, wail ▶ *verb* **4** BLOW UP, break up, burst, demolish, destroy, explode, put paid to, ruin, shatter

blatant *adjective* OBVIOUS, brazen, conspicuous, flagrant, glaring, obtrusive, ostentatious, overt

blaze *noun* **1** FIRE, bonfire, conflagration, flames **2** GLARE, beam, brilliance, flare, flash, gleam, glitter, glow, light, radiance ▶ *verb* **3** BURN, fire, flame **4** SHINE, beam, flare, flash, glare, gleam, glow

bleach *verb* WHITEN, blanch, fade, grow pale, lighten, wash out

bleak *adjective* **1** EXPOSED, bare, barren, desolate, unsheltered, weather-beaten, windswept **2** DISMAL, cheerless, depressing, discouraging, dreary, gloomy, grim, hopeless, joyless, somber

bleary *adjective* DIM, blurred, blurry, foggy, fuzzy, hazy, indistinct, misty, murky

bleed *verb* **1** LOSE BLOOD, flow, gush, ooze, run, shed blood, spurt **2** DRAW *or* TAKE BLOOD, extract, leech **3** *Informal* EXTORT, drain, exhaust, fleece, milk, squeeze

blemish *noun* **1** MARK, blot, defect, disfigurement, fault, flaw, imperfection, smudge, stain, taint ▶ *verb* **2** STAIN, damage, disfigure, impair, injure, mar, mark, spoil, sully,

taint, tarnish

blend *verb* **1** MIX, amalgamate, combine, compound, merge, mingle, unite **2** GO WELL, complement, fit, go with, harmonize, suit ▶ *noun* **3** MIXTURE, alloy, amalgamation, combination, compound, concoction, mix, synthesis, union

bless *verb* **1** SANCTIFY, anoint, consecrate, dedicate, exalt, hallow, ordain **2** GRANT, bestow, favor, give, grace, provide

blessed *adjective* HOLY, adored, beatified, divine, hallowed, revered, sacred, sanctified

blessing *noun* **1** BENEDICTION, benison, commendation, consecration, dedication, grace, invocation, thanksgiving **2** APPROVAL, backing, consent, favor, good wishes, leave, permission, sanction, support **3** BENEFIT, favor, gift, godsend, good fortune, help, kindness, service, windfall

blight *noun* **1** CURSE, affliction, bane, contamination, corruption, evil, plague, pollution, scourge, woe **2** DISEASE, canker, decay, fungus, infestation, mildew, pest, pestilence, rot ▶ *verb* **3** FRUSTRATE, crush, dash, disappoint, mar, ruin, spoil, undo, wreck

blind *adjective* **1** SIGHTLESS, eyeless, unseeing, unsighted, visionless **2** UNAWARE OF, careless, heedless, ignorant, inattentive, inconsiderate, indifferent, insensitive, oblivious, unconscious of **3** UNREASONING, indiscriminate, prejudiced ▶ *noun* 4 COVER, camouflage, cloak, façade, feint, front, mask, masquerade, screen, smoke screen

blindly *adverb* 1 THOUGHTLESSLY, carelessly, heedlessly, inconsiderately, recklessly, senselessly 2 AIMLESSLY, at random, indiscriminately, instinctively

blink *verb* 1 WINK, bat, flutter 2 FLICKER, flash, gleam, glimmer, shine, twinkle, wink ▶ *noun* 3 **on the blink** Slang NOT WORKING (PROPERLY), faulty, malfunctioning, out of action, out of order, playing up

bliss *noun* JOY, beatitude, blessedness, blissfulness, ecstasy, euphoria, felicity, gladness, happiness, heaven, nirvana, paradise, rapture

blissful *adjective* JOYFUL, ecstatic, elated, enraptured, euphoric, happy, heavenly (*informal*), rapturous

blister *noun* SORE, abscess, boil, carbuncle, cyst, pimple, pustule, swelling

blithe *adjective* HEEDLESS, careless, casual, indifferent, nonchalant, thoughtless, unconcerned, untroubled

blitz *noun* ATTACK, assault, blitzkrieg, bombardment, campaign, offensive, onslaught, raid, strike

blizzard *noun* SNOWSTORM, blast, gale, squall, storm, tempest

bloat *verb* PUFF UP, balloon, blow up, dilate, distend, enlarge, expand, inflate, swell

blob *noun* DROP, ball, bead, bubble, dab, droplet, globule, lump, mass

bloc *noun* GROUP, alliance, axis, coalition, faction, league, union

block *noun* 1 PIECE, bar, brick, chunk, hunk, ingot, lump, mass 2 OBSTRUCTION, bar, barrier, blockage, hindrance, impediment, jam, obstacle ▶ *verb* 3 OBSTRUCT, choke, clog, close, plug, stem the flow, stop up 4 STOP, bar, check, halt, hinder, impede, obstruct, thwart

blockade *noun* STOPPAGE, barricade, barrier, block, hindrance, impediment, obstacle, obstruction, restriction, siege

blockage *noun* OBSTRUCTION, block, impediment, occlusion, stoppage

blockhead *noun* IDIOT, chump (*informal*), dork (*slang*), dunce, fool, nitwit, schmuck (*slang*), thickhead

blond, blonde *adjective* FAIR, fair-haired, fair-skinned, flaxen, golden-haired, light, tow-headed

blood *noun* 1 LIFEBLOOD, gore, vital fluid 2 FAMILY, ancestry, birth, descent, extraction, kinship, lineage, relations

bloodcurdling *adjective* TERRIFYING, appalling, chilling, dreadful, fearful, frightening, hair-raising, horrendous, horrifying, scaring, spine-chilling

bloodshed *noun* KILLING, blood bath, blood-letting, butchery, carnage, gore, massacre, murder, slaughter, slaying

bloodthirsty *adjective* CRUEL, barbarous, brutal, cut-throat, ferocious, gory, murderous, savage, vicious, warlike

bloody *adjective* 1 BLOODSTAINED, bleeding, blood-soaked, blood-spattered, gaping, raw 2 CRUEL, ferocious, fierce, sanguinary, savage

bloom *noun* 1 FLOWER, blossom, blossoming, bud, efflorescence, opening (*of flowers*) 2 PRIME, beauty, flourishing, freshness, glow, health, heyday, luster, radiance, vigor ▶ *verb* 3 BLOSSOM, blow, bud, burgeon, open, sprout 4 FLOURISH, develop, fare well, grow, prosper, succeed, thrive, wax

blossom *noun* 1 FLOWER, bloom, bud, floret, flowers ▶ *verb* 2 FLOWER, bloom, burgeon 3 GROW, bloom, develop, flourish, mature, progress, prosper, thrive

blot *noun* 1 SPOT, blotch, mark, patch, smear, smudge, speck, splodge 2 STAIN, blemish, defect, fault, flaw, scar, spot, taint ▶ *verb* 3 STAIN, disgrace, mark, smirch, smudge, spoil, spot, sully, tarnish 4 SOAK UP, absorb, dry, take up 5 **blot out: a** OBLITERATE, darken, destroy, eclipse, efface, obscure, shadow **b** ERASE, cancel, expunge

blow¹ *verb* 1 CARRY, buffet, drive, fling, flutter, move, sweep, waft 2 EXHALE, breathe, pant, puff 3 PLAY, blare, mouth, pipe, sound, toot, trumpet, vibrate

blow² *noun* 1 KNOCK, bang, clout (*informal*), punch, smack, sock (*slang*), stroke, thump, wallop (*informal*), whack 2 SETBACK, bombshell, calamity,

catastrophe, disappointment, disaster, misfortune, reverse, shock

blow out *verb* 1 PUT OUT, extinguish, snuff 2 BURST, erupt, explode, rupture, shatter

blow up *verb* 1 EXPLODE, blast, blow sky-high, bomb, burst, detonate, rupture, shatter 2 INFLATE, bloat, distend, enlarge, expand, fill, puff up, pump up, swell 3 *Informal* LOSE ONE'S TEMPER, become angry, erupt, fly off the handle (*informal*), hit the roof (*informal*), rage, see red (*informal*)

bludgeon *noun* 1 CLUB, cudgel, truncheon ▶ *verb* 2 CLUB, beat up, cudgel, knock down, strike 3 BULLY, bulldoze (*informal*), coerce, force, railroad (*informal*), steamroller

blue *adjective* 1 AZURE, cerulean, cobalt, cyan, navy, sapphire, sky-colored, ultramarine 2 DEPRESSED, dejected, despondent, downcast, low, melancholy, sad, unhappy 3 SMUTTY, indecent, lewd, obscene, risqué, X-rated (*informal*)

blueprint *noun* PLAN, design, draft, outline, pattern, pilot scheme, prototype, sketch

blues *plural noun* DEPRESSION, doldrums, dumps (*informal*), gloom, low spirits, melancholy, unhappiness

bluff¹ *verb* 1 DECEIVE, con, delude, fake, feign, mislead, pretend, pull the wool over someone's eyes ▶ *noun* 2 DECEPTION, bluster, bravado, deceit, fraud, humbug, pretense, sham, subterfuge

bluff[2] noun 1 PRECIPICE, bank, cliff, crag, escarpment, headland, peak, promontory, ridge ▶adjective 2 HEARTY, blunt, blustering, genial, good-natured, open, outspoken, plain-spoken

blunder noun 1 MISTAKE, bloomer (informal), faux pas, foul-up (slang), indiscretion 2 ERROR, fault, inaccuracy, mistake, oversight, slip, slip-up (informal) ▶verb 3 MAKE A MISTAKE, botch, bungle, err, foul up (slang), slip up (informal) 4 STUMBLE, bumble, flounder

blunt adjective 1 DULL, dulled, edgeless, pointless, rounded, unsharpened 2 FORTHRIGHT, bluff, brusque, frank, outspoken, plain-spoken, rude, straightforward, tactless ▶verb 3 DULL, dampen, deaden, numb, soften, take the edge off, water down, weaken

blur verb 1 MAKE INDISTINCT, cloud, darken, make hazy, make vague, mask, obscure ▶noun 2 INDISTINCTNESS, confusion, fog, haze, obscurity

blurt out verb EXCLAIM, disclose, let the cat out of the bag, reveal, spill the beans (informal), tell all, utter suddenly

blush verb 1 TURN RED, color, flush, go red (as a beetroot), redden, turn scarlet ▶noun 2 REDDENING, color, flush, glow, pink tinge, rosiness, rosy tint, ruddiness

bluster verb 1 ROAR, bully, domineer, hector, rant, storm ▶noun 2 HOT AIR (informal), bluff, bombast, bravado

blustery adjective GUSTY, boisterous, inclement, squally, stormy, tempestuous, violent, wild, windy

board noun 1 PLANK, panel, piece of timber, slat, timber 2 DIRECTORS, advisers, committee, conclave, council, panel, trustees 3 MEALS, daily meals, provisions, victuals ▶verb 4 GET ON, embark, enter, mount 5 LODGE, put up, quarter, room

boast verb 1 BRAG, blow one's own trumpet, crow, strut, swagger, talk big (slang), vaunt 2 POSSESS, be proud of, congratulate oneself on, exhibit, flatter oneself, pride oneself on, show off ▶noun 3 BRAG, avowal

boastful adjective BRAGGING, cocky, conceited, crowing, egotistical, full of oneself, swaggering, swollen-headed, vaunting

bob verb DUCK, bounce, hop, nod, oscillate, wiggle, wobble

bode verb PORTEND, augur, be an omen of, forebode, foretell, predict, signify, threaten

bodily adjective PHYSICAL, actual, carnal, corporal, corporeal, material, substantial, tangible

body noun 1 PHYSIQUE, build, figure, form, frame, shape 2 TORSO, trunk 3 CORPSE, cadaver, carcass, dead body, remains, stiff (slang) 4 ORGANIZATION, association, band, bloc, collection, company, confederation, congress, corporation, society 5 MAIN PART, bulk, essence, mass, material, matter, substance

bog *noun* MARSH, fen, mire, morass, quagmire, slough, swamp, wetlands

bogey *noun* BUGBEAR, bête noire, bugaboo, nightmare

bogus *adjective* FAKE, artificial, counterfeit, false, forged, fraudulent, imitation, phoney *or* phony (*informal*), sham

bohemian *adjective*
1 UNCONVENTIONAL, alternative, artistic, arty (*informal*), left bank, nonconformist, offbeat, unorthodox ▶ *noun*
2 NONCONFORMIST, beatnik, dropout, hippie, iconoclast

boil¹ *verb* BUBBLE, effervesce, fizz, foam, froth, seethe

boil² *noun* PUSTULE, blister, carbuncle, gathering, swelling, tumor, ulcer

boisterous *adjective* UNRULY, disorderly, loud, noisy, riotous, rollicking, rowdy, unrestrained, vociferous, wild

bold *adjective* **1** FEARLESS, adventurous, audacious, brave, courageous, daring, enterprising, heroic, intrepid, valiant **2** IMPUDENT, barefaced, brazen, cheeky, confident, forward, insolent, rude, shameless

bolster *verb* SUPPORT, augment, boost, help, reinforce, shore up, strengthen

bolt *noun* **1** BAR, catch, fastener, latch, lock, sliding bar **2** PIN, peg, rivet, rod ▶ *verb* **3** RUN AWAY, abscond, dash, escape, flee, fly, make a break (for it), run for it **4** LOCK, bar, fasten, latch, secure **5** GOBBLE, cram, devour, gorge, gulp, guzzle,

stuff, swallow whole, wolf

bomb *noun* **1** EXPLOSIVE, device, grenade, mine, missile, projectile, rocket, shell, torpedo ▶ *verb* **2** BLOW UP, attack, blow sky-high, bombard, destroy, shell, strafe, torpedo

bombard *verb* **1** BOMB, assault, blitz, fire upon, open fire, pound, shell, strafe **2** ATTACK, assail, beset, besiege, harass, hound, pester

bombardment *noun* BOMBING, assault, attack, barrage, blitz, fusillade, shelling

bombastic *adjective* GRANDILOQUENT, grandiose, high-flown, inflated, pompous, verbose, wordy

bona fide *adjective* GENUINE, actual, authentic, honest, kosher (*informal*), legitimate, real, true

bond *noun* **1** FASTENING, chain, cord, fetter, ligature, manacle, shackle, tie **2** TIE, affiliation, affinity, attachment, connection, link, relation, union **3** AGREEMENT, contract, covenant, guarantee, obligation, pledge, promise, word ▶ *verb* **4** HOLD TOGETHER, bind, connect, fasten, fix together, glue, paste

bondage *noun* SLAVERY, captivity, confinement, enslavement, imprisonment, subjugation

bonus *noun* EXTRA, dividend, gift, icing on the cake, plus, premium, prize, reward

bony *adjective* THIN, emaciated, gaunt, lean, scrawny, skin and bone, skinny

book *noun* **1** WORK, publication,

title, tome, tract, volume
2 NOTEBOOK, album, diary,
exercise book, jotter, pad ▸ *verb*
3 RESERVE, arrange for, charter,
engage, make reservations,
organize, program, schedule
4 NOTE, enter, list, log, mark
down, put down, record,
register, write down

booklet *noun* BROCHURE, leaflet,
pamphlet

boom *verb* 1 BANG, blast, crash,
explode, resound, reverberate,
roar, roll, rumble, thunder
2 FLOURISH, develop, expand,
grow, increase, intensify,
prosper, strengthen, swell,
thrive ▸ *noun* 3 BANG, blast,
burst, clap, crash, explosion,
roar, rumble, thunder
4 EXPANSION, boost,
development, growth,
improvement, increase, jump,
upsurge, upswing, upturn

boon *noun* BENEFIT, advantage,
blessing, favor, gift, godsend,
manna from heaven, windfall

boorish *adjective* LOUTISH,
churlish, coarse, crude, oafish,
uncivilized, uncouth, vulgar

boost *noun* 1 HELP,
encouragement, praise,
promotion 2 RISE, addition,
expansion, improvement,
increase, increment, jump
▸ *verb* 3 INCREASE, add to,
amplify, develop, enlarge,
expand, heighten, raise
4 ADVERTISE, encourage, foster,
further, hype, plug (*informal*),
praise, promote

boot *verb* KICK, drive, drop-kick,
knock, punt, shove

booty *noun* PLUNDER, gains, haul,
loot, prey, spoils, swag (*slang*),

takings, winnings

border *noun* 1 FRONTIER,
borderline, boundary, line,
march 2 EDGE, bounds, brink,
limits, margin, rim, verge ▸ *verb*
3 EDGE, bind, decorate, fringe,
hem, rim, trim

bore¹ *verb* DRILL, burrow, gouge
out, mine, penetrate,
perforate, pierce, sink, tunnel

bore² *verb* 1 TIRE, be tedious,
fatigue, jade, pall on, send to
sleep, wear out, weary ▸ *noun*
2 NUISANCE, geek (*slang*), pain
(*informal*) 3 PAIN (*informal*),
yawn (*informal*)

bored *adjective* FED UP, listless,
tired, uninterested, wearied

boredom *noun* TEDIUM, apathy,
ennui, flatness, monotony,
sameness, tediousness,
weariness, world-weariness

boring *adjective* UNINTERESTING,
dull, flat, humdrum,
mind-numbing, monotonous,
tedious, tiresome

borrow *verb* 1 TAKE ON LOAN,
cadge, scrounge (*informal*), use
temporarily 2 STEAL, adopt,
copy, obtain, plagiarize, take,
usurp

bosom *noun* 1 BREAST, bust,
chest ▸ *adjective* 2 INTIMATE,
boon, cherished, close,
confidential, dear, very dear

boss¹ *noun Informal* HEAD, chief,
director, employer, leader,
manager, master, supervisor

boss² *noun* STUD, knob, point,
protuberance, tip

boss around *verb Informal*
DOMINEER, bully, dominate,
oppress, order, push around
(*slang*)

bossy *adjective* DOMINEERING,

arrogant, authoritarian, autocratic, dictatorial, hectoring, high-handed, imperious, overbearing, tyrannical

botch *verb* 1 SPOIL, blunder, bungle, foul up (*slang*), mar, mess up, screw up (*informal*) ▶*noun* 2 MESS, blunder, bungle, failure

bother *verb* 1 TROUBLE, alarm, concern, disturb, harass, hassle (*informal*), inconvenience, pester, plague, worry ▶*noun* 2 TROUBLE, difficulty, fuss, hassle (*informal*), inconvenience, irritation, nuisance, problem, worry

bottleneck *noun* HOLD-UP, block, blockage, congestion, impediment, jam, obstacle, obstruction

bottle up *verb* SUPPRESS, check, contain, curb, keep back, restrict, shut in, trap

bottom *noun* 1 LOWEST PART, base, bed, depths, floor, foot, foundation 2 UNDERSIDE, lower side, sole, underneath 3 BUTTOCKS, backside, behind (*informal*), posterior, rear, rump, seat, tush (*slang*) ▶*adjective* 4 LOWEST, last

bottomless *adjective* UNLIMITED, boundless, deep, fathomless, immeasurable, inexhaustible, infinite, unfathomable

bounce *verb* 1 REBOUND, bob, bound, jump, leap, recoil, ricochet, spring ▶*noun* 2 *Informal* LIFE, dynamism, energy, go (*informal*), liveliness, vigor, vivacity, zip (*informal*) 3 SPRINGINESS, elasticity, give, recoil, resilience, spring

bound¹ *adjective* 1 TIED, cased, fastened, fixed, pinioned, secured, tied up 2 CERTAIN, destined, doomed, fated, sure 3 OBLIGED, beholden, committed, compelled, constrained, duty-bound, forced, pledged, required

bound² *verb* LIMIT, confine, demarcate, encircle, enclose, hem in, restrain, restrict, surround

bound³ *verb, noun* LEAP, bob, bounce, gambol, hurdle, jump, skip, spring, vault

boundary *noun* LIMITS, barrier, border, borderline, brink, edge, extremity, fringe, frontier, margin

boundless *adjective* UNLIMITED, endless, immense, incalculable, inexhaustible, infinite, unconfined, untold, vast

bounds *plural noun* BOUNDARY, border, confine, edge, extremity, limit, rim, verge

bountiful *adjective Literary* 1 PLENTIFUL, abundant, ample, bounteous, copious, exuberant, lavish, luxuriant, prolific 2 GENEROUS, liberal, magnanimous, open-handed, prodigal, unstinting

bounty *noun Literary* 1 GENEROSITY, benevolence, charity, kindness, largesse *or* largess, liberality, philanthropy 2 REWARD, bonus, gift, present

bouquet *noun* 1 BUNCH OF FLOWERS, buttonhole, corsage, garland, nosegay, posy, spray, wreath 2 AROMA, fragrance, perfume, redolence, savor, scent

bourgeois *adjective* MIDDLE-CLASS,

conventional, hidebound, materialistic, traditional

bout noun 1 PERIOD, fit, spell, stint, term, turn 2 FIGHT, boxing match, competition, contest, encounter, engagement, match, set-to, struggle

bow¹ verb 1 BEND, bob, droop, genuflect, nod, stoop 2 GIVE IN, acquiesce, comply, concede, defer, kowtow, relent, submit, succumb, surrender, yield ▸ noun 3 BENDING, bob, genuflexion, kowtow, nod, obeisance

bow² noun Nautical PROW, beak, fore, head, stem

bowels plural noun 1 GUTS, entrails, innards (informal), insides (informal), intestines, viscera, vitals 2 DEPTHS, belly, core, deep, hold, inside, interior

bowl¹ noun BASIN, dish, vessel

bowl² verb THROW, fling, hurl, pitch

box¹ noun 1 CONTAINER, carton, case, casket, chest, pack, package, receptacle, trunk ▸ verb 2 PACK, package, wrap

box² verb FIGHT, exchange blows, spar

boxer noun FIGHTER, prizefighter, pugilist, sparring partner

boy noun LAD, fellow, junior, schoolboy, stripling, youngster, youth

boycott verb EMBARGO, ban, bar, black, exclude, outlaw, prohibit, refuse, reject

boyfriend noun SWEETHEART, admirer, beau, date, lover, man, suitor

boyish adjective YOUTHFUL, adolescent, childish, immature,

juvenile, puerile, young

brace noun 1 SUPPORT, bolster, bracket, buttress, prop, reinforcement, stay, strut, truss ▸ verb 2 SUPPORT, bolster, buttress, fortify, reinforce, steady, strengthen

bracing adjective REFRESHING, brisk, crisp, exhilarating, fresh, invigorating, stimulating

brag verb BOAST, blow one's own trumpet, bluster, crow, swagger, talk big (slang), vaunt

braggart noun BOASTER, bigmouth (slang), bragger, show-off (informal)

braid verb INTERWEAVE, entwine, interlace, intertwine, lace, plait, twine, weave

brainless adjective STUPID, foolish, idiotic, inane, mindless, senseless, thoughtless, witless

brains plural noun INTELLIGENCE, intellect, sense, understanding

brainy adjective Informal INTELLIGENT, bright, brilliant, clever, smart

brake noun 1 CONTROL, check, constraint, curb, rein, restraint ▸ verb 2 SLOW, check, decelerate, halt, moderate, reduce speed, slacken, stop

branch noun 1 BOUGH, arm, limb, offshoot, shoot, spray, sprig 2 DIVISION, chapter, department, office, part, section, subdivision, wing

brand noun 1 LABEL, emblem, hallmark, logo, mark, marker, sign, stamp, symbol, trademark 2 KIND, cast, class, grade, make, quality, sort, species, type, variety ▸ verb 3 MARK, burn, burn in, label, scar, stamp 4 STIGMATIZE, censure, denounce, discredit, disgrace, expose, mark

brandish verb WAVE, display, exhibit, flaunt, flourish, parade, raise, shake, swing, wield

brash adjective BOLD, brazen, cocky, impertinent, impudent, insolent, pushy (informal), rude

bravado noun SWAGGER, bluster, boastfulness, boasting, bombast, swashbuckling, vaunting

brave adjective 1 COURAGEOUS, bold, daring, fearless, heroic, intrepid, plucky, resolute, valiant ▶ verb 2 CONFRONT, defy, endure, face, stand up to, suffer, tackle, withstand

bravery noun COURAGE, boldness, daring, fearlessness, fortitude, heroism, intrepidity, mettle, pluck, spirit, valor

brawl noun 1 FIGHT, affray (Law), altercation, clash, dispute, fracas, fray, melee or mêlée, rumpus, scuffle, skirmish ▶ verb 2 FIGHT, scrap (informal), scuffle, tussle, wrestle

brawn noun MUSCLE, beef (informal), might, muscles, power, strength, vigor

brawny adjective MUSCULAR, beefy (informal), hefty (informal), lusty, powerful, strapping, strong, sturdy, well-built

brazen adjective BOLD, audacious, barefaced, brash, defiant, impudent, insolent, shameless, unabashed, unashamed

breach noun 1 NONOBSERVANCE, contravention, infraction, infringement, noncompliance, transgression, trespass, violation 2 CRACK, cleft, fissure, gap, opening, rift, rupture, split

bread noun 1 FOOD, fare, nourishment, sustenance 2 Slang MONEY, cash, dough (slang)

breadth noun 1 WIDTH, broadness, latitude, span, spread, wideness 2 EXTENT, compass, expanse, range, scale, scope

break verb 1 SEPARATE, burst, crack, destroy, disintegrate, fracture, fragment, shatter, smash, snap, split, tear 2 DISOBEY, breach, contravene, disregard, infringe, renege on, transgress, violate 3 REVEAL, announce, disclose, divulge, impart, inform, let out, make public, proclaim, tell 4 STOP, abandon, cut, discontinue, give up, interrupt, pause, rest, suspend 5 WEAKEN, demoralize, dispirit, subdue, tame, undermine 6 Of a record, etc. BEAT, better, exceed, excel, go beyond, outdo, outstrip, surpass, top ▶ noun 7 DIVISION, crack, fissure, fracture, gap, hole, opening, split, tear 8 REST, breather (informal), hiatus, interlude, intermission, interruption, interval, let-up (informal), lull, pause, respite 9 Informal STROKE OF LUCK, advantage, chance, fortune, opening, opportunity

breakable adjective FRAGILE, brittle, crumbly, delicate, flimsy, frail, frangible, friable

breakdown noun COLLAPSE, disintegration, disruption, failure, mishap, stoppage

break down verb 1 COLLAPSE,

come unstuck, fail, seize up, stop, stop working **2** BE OVERCOME, crack up (*informal*), go to pieces

break-in *noun* BURGLARY, breaking and entering, robbery

break off *verb* **1** DETACH, divide, part, pull off, separate, sever, snap off, splinter **2** STOP, cease, desist, discontinue, end, finish, halt, pull the plug on, suspend, terminate

break out *verb* BEGIN, appear, arise, commence, emerge, happen, occur, set in, spring up, start

breakthrough *noun* DEVELOPMENT, advance, discovery, find, invention, leap, progress, quantum leap, step forward

break up *verb* **1** SEPARATE, dissolve, divide, divorce, part, scatter, sever, split **2** STOP, adjourn, disband, dismantle, end, suspend, terminate

breast *noun* BOSOM, bust, chest, front, teat, udder

breath *noun* RESPIRATION, breathing, exhalation, gasp, gulp, inhalation, pant, wheeze

breathe *verb* **1** INHALE AND EXHALE, draw in, gasp, gulp, pant, puff, respire, wheeze **2** WHISPER, murmur, sigh

breather *noun Informal* REST, break, breathing space, halt, pause, recess, respite

breathless *adjective* **1** OUT OF BREATH, gasping, gulping, panting, short-winded, spent, wheezing **2** EXCITED, eager, on tenterhooks, open-mouthed, wired (*slang*), with bated breath

breathtaking *adjective* AMAZING, astonishing, awe-inspiring, cool (*informal*), exciting, impressive, magnificent, phat (*slang*), sensational, stunning (*informal*), thrilling

breed *verb* **1** REPRODUCE, bear, bring forth, hatch, multiply, procreate, produce, propagate **2** BRING UP, cultivate, develop, nourish, nurture, raise, rear **3** PRODUCE, arouse, bring about, cause, create, generate, give rise to, stir up ▶ *noun* **4** VARIETY, pedigree, race, species, stock, strain, type **5** KIND, brand, sort, stamp, type, variety

breeding *noun* **1** UPBRINGING, ancestry, cultivation, development, lineage, nurture, raising, rearing, reproduction, training **2** REFINEMENT, conduct, courtesy, cultivation, culture, polish, sophistication, urbanity

breeze *noun* **1** LIGHT WIND, air, breath of wind, current of air, draft, gust, waft, zephyr ▶ *verb* **2** MOVE BRISKLY, flit, glide, hurry, pass, sail, sweep

breezy *adjective* **1** WINDY, airy, blowy, blustery, fresh, gusty, squally **2** CAREFREE, blithe, casual, easy-going, free and easy, jaunty, light-hearted, lively, sprightly

brevity *noun* **1** SHORTNESS, briefness, impermanence, transience, transitoriness **2** CONCISENESS, crispness, curtness, economy, pithiness, succinctness, terseness

brew *verb* **1** MAKE (*beer*), boil, ferment, infuse (*tea*), soak, steep, stew **2** DEVELOP, foment, form, gather, start, stir up ▶ *noun* **3** DRINK, beverage, blend, concoction, infusion, liquor, mixture, preparation

bribe *verb* 1 BUY OFF, corrupt, grease the palm *or* hand of (*slang*), pay off (*informal*), reward, suborn ▶ *noun* 2 INDUCEMENT, allurement, backhander (*slang*), enticement, kickback, pay-off (*informal*), sweetener (*slang*)

bribery *noun* BUYING OFF, corruption, inducement, palm-greasing (*slang*), payola (*informal*)

bric-a-brac *noun* KNICK-KNACKS, baubles, curios, ornaments, trinkets

bridal *adjective* MATRIMONIAL, conjugal, connubial, marital, marriage, nuptial, wedding

bridge *noun* 1 ARCH, flyover, overpass, span, viaduct ▶ *verb* 2 CONNECT, join, link, span

bridle *noun* 1 CURB, check, control, rein, restraint ▶ *verb* 2 GET ANGRY, be indignant, bristle, draw (oneself) up, get one's back up, raise one's hackles, rear up

brief *adjective* 1 SHORT, ephemeral, fleeting, momentary, quick, short-lived, swift, transitory ▶ *noun* 2 SUMMARY, abridgment, abstract, digest, epitome, outline, précis, sketch, synopsis ▶ *verb* 3 INFORM, advise, explain, fill in (*informal*), instruct, keep posted, prepare, prime, put (someone) in the picture (*informal*)

briefing *noun* INSTRUCTIONS, conference, directions, guidance, information, preparation, priming, rundown

briefly *adverb* SHORTLY, concisely,

hastily, hurriedly, in a nutshell, in brief, momentarily, quickly

brigade *noun* GROUP, band, company, corps, force, organization, outfit, squad, team, troop, unit

bright *adjective* 1 SHINING, brilliant, dazzling, gleaming, glowing, luminous, lustrous, radiant, shimmering, vivid 2 INTELLIGENT, astute, aware, clever, inventive, quick-witted, sharp, smart, wide-awake 3 SUNNY, clear, cloudless, fair, limpid, lucid, pleasant, translucent, transparent, unclouded

brighten *verb* MAKE BRIGHTER, gleam, glow, illuminate, lighten, light up, shine

brightness *noun* 1 SHINE, brilliance, glare, incandescence, intensity, light, luminosity, radiance, vividness 2 INTELLIGENCE, acuity, cleverness, quickness, sharpness, smartness

brilliance *noun* 1 BRIGHTNESS, dazzle, intensity, luminosity, luster, radiance, sparkle, vividness 2 TALENT, cleverness, distinction, excellence, genius, greatness, inventiveness, wisdom 3 SPLENDOR, éclat, glamour, grandeur, illustriousness, magnificence

brilliant *adjective* 1 SHINING, bright, dazzling, glittering, intense, luminous, radiant, sparkling, vivid 2 SPLENDID, celebrated, famous, glorious, illustrious, magnificent, notable, outstanding, superb 3 INTELLIGENT, clever, expert, gifted, intellectual, inventive, masterly, penetrating, profound, talented

brim noun 1 RIM, border, brink, edge, lip, margin, skirt, verge ▶ verb 2 BE FULL, fill, fill up, hold no more, overflow, run over, spill, well over

bring verb 1 TAKE, bear, carry, conduct, convey, deliver, escort, fetch, guide, lead, transfer, transport 2 CAUSE, contribute to, create, effect, inflict, occasion, produce, result in, wreak

bring about verb CAUSE, accomplish, achieve, create, effect, generate, give rise to, make happen, produce

bring off verb ACCOMPLISH, achieve, carry off, execute, perform, pull off, succeed

bring up verb 1 REAR, breed, develop, educate, form, nurture, raise, support, teach, train 2 MENTION, allude to, broach, introduce, move, propose, put forward, raise

brink noun EDGE, border, boundary, brim, fringe, frontier, limit, lip, margin, rim, skirt, threshold, verge

brisk adjective LIVELY, active, bustling, busy, energetic, quick, sprightly, spry, vigorous

briskly adverb QUICKLY, actively, apace, efficiently, energetically, promptly, rapidly, readily, smartly

bristle noun 1 HAIR, barb, prickle, spine, stubble, thorn, whisker ▶ verb 2 STAND UP, rise, stand on end 3 BE ANGRY, bridle, flare up, rage, see red, seethe

bristly adjective HAIRY, prickly, rough, stubbly

brittle adjective FRAGILE, breakable, crisp, crumbling, crumbly, delicate, frail, frangible, friable

broach verb 1 BRING UP, introduce, mention, open up, propose, raise the subject, speak of, suggest, talk of, touch on 2 OPEN, crack, draw off, pierce, puncture, start, tap, uncork

broad adjective 1 WIDE, ample, expansive, extensive, generous, large, roomy, spacious, vast, voluminous, widespread 2 GENERAL, all-embracing, comprehensive, encyclopedic, inclusive, sweeping, wide, wide-ranging

broadcast noun 1 TRANSMISSION, program, show, telecast ▶ verb 2 TRANSMIT, air, beam, cable, put on the air, radio, relay, show, televise 3 MAKE PUBLIC, advertise, announce, circulate, proclaim, publish, report, spread

broaden verb EXPAND, develop, enlarge, extend, increase, spread, stretch, supplement, swell, widen

broad-minded adjective TOLERANT, free-thinking, indulgent, liberal, open-minded, permissive, unbiased, unbigoted, unprejudiced

broadside noun ATTACK, assault, battering, bombardment, censure, criticism, denunciation, diatribe

brochure noun BOOKLET, advertisement, circular, folder, handbill, hand-out, leaflet, mailshot, pamphlet

broke *adjective Informal* PENNILESS, bankrupt, bust (*informal*), down and out, down on one's luck (*informal*), impoverished, insolvent, in the red, ruined, short

broken *adjective* 1 SMASHED, burst, fractured, fragmented, ruptured, separated, severed, shattered 2 INTERRUPTED, discontinuous, erratic, fragmentary, incomplete, intermittent, spasmodic 3 NOT WORKING, defective, imperfect, kaput (*informal*), on the blink (*slang*), out of order 4 IMPERFECT, disjointed, halting, hesitating, stammering

brokenhearted *adjective* HEARTBROKEN, desolate, devastated, disconsolate, grief-stricken, inconsolable, miserable, sorrowful, wretched

broker *noun* DEALER, agent, factor, go-between, intermediary, middleman, negotiator

bronze *adjective* REDDISH-BROWN, brownish, chestnut, copper, rust, tan

brood *noun* 1 OFFSPRING, clutch, family, issue, litter, progeny ▶*verb* 2 THINK UPON, agonize, dwell upon, mope, mull over, muse, ponder, ruminate

brook *noun* STREAM, beck, rill, rivulet, watercourse

brother *noun* 1 SIBLING, blood brother, kin, kinsman, relation, relative 2 MONK, cleric, friar

brotherhood *noun* 1 FELLOWSHIP, brotherliness, camaraderie, companionship, comradeship, friendliness, kinship 2 ASSOCIATION, alliance, community, fraternity, guild, league, order, society, union

brotherly *adjective* KIND, affectionate, altruistic, amicable, benevolent, cordial, fraternal, friendly, neighborly, philanthropic, sympathetic

browbeat *verb* BULLY, badger, coerce, dragoon, hector, intimidate, ride roughshod over, threaten, tyrannize

brown *adjective* 1 BRUNETTE, auburn, bay, bronze, chestnut, chocolate, coffee, dun, hazel, sunburned, tan, tanned, tawny, umber ▶*verb* 2 FRY, cook, grill, sauté, seal, sear

browse *verb* 1 SKIM, dip into, examine cursorily, flip through, glance at, leaf through, look round, look through, peruse, scan, survey 2 GRAZE, chow down (*slang*), eat, feed, nibble

bruise *verb* 1 DISCOLOR, damage, injure, mar, mark, pound ▶*noun* 2 DISCOLORATION, black mark, blemish, contusion, injury, mark, swelling

brunt *noun* FULL FORCE, burden, force, impact, pressure, shock, strain, stress, thrust, violence

brush[1] *noun* 1 BROOM, besom, sweeper 2 ENCOUNTER, clash, conflict, confrontation, skirmish, tussle ▶*verb* 3 CLEAN, buff, paint, polish, sweep, wash 4 TOUCH, flick, glance, graze, kiss, scrape, stroke, sweep

brush[2] *noun* SHRUBS, brushwood, bushes, copse, scrub, thicket, undergrowth

brush off *verb Slang* IGNORE, blow off (*slang*), disdain, dismiss, disregard, reject, repudiate, scorn, snub, spurn

brush up verb REVISE, bone up (informal), cram, go over, polish up, read up, refresh one's memory, relearn, study

brusque adjective CURT, abrupt, discourteous, gruff, impolite, sharp, short, surly, terse

brutal adjective 1 CRUEL, bloodthirsty, heartless, inhuman, ruthless, savage, uncivilized, vicious 2 HARSH, callous, gruff, impolite, insensitive, rough, rude, severe

brutality noun CRUELTY, atrocity, barbarism, bloodthirstiness, ferocity, inhumanity, ruthlessness, savagery, viciousness

brute noun 1 SAVAGE, barbarian, beast, devil, fiend, monster, sadist, swine 2 ANIMAL, beast, creature, wild animal ▶adjective 3 MINDLESS, bodily, carnal, fleshly, instinctive, physical, senseless, unthinking

bubble noun 1 AIR BALL, bead, blister, blob, drop, droplet, globule ▶verb 2 FOAM, boil, effervesce, fizz, froth, percolate, seethe, sparkle 3 GURGLE, babble, burble, murmur, ripple, trickle

bubbly adjective 1 LIVELY, animated, bouncy, elated, excited, happy, merry, sparky, wired (slang) 2 FROTHY, carbonated, effervescent, fizzy, foamy, sparkling

buccaneer noun PIRATE, corsair, freebooter, privateer, sea-rover

buckle noun 1 FASTENER, catch, clasp, clip, hasp ▶verb 2 FASTEN, clasp, close, hook, secure 3 DISTORT, bend, bulge, cave in,

collapse, contort, crumple, fold, twist, warp

bud noun 1 SHOOT, embryo, germ, sprout ▶verb 2 DEVELOP, burgeon, burst forth, grow, shoot, sprout

budding adjective DEVELOPING, beginning, burgeoning, embryonic, fledgling, growing, incipient, nascent, potential, promising

budge verb MOVE, dislodge, push, shift, stir

budget noun 1 ALLOWANCE, allocation, cost, finances, funds, means, resources ▶verb 2 PLAN, allocate, apportion, cost, estimate, ration

buff[1] adjective 1 YELLOWISH-BROWN, sandy, straw, tan, yellowish ▶verb 2 POLISH, brush, burnish, rub, shine, smooth

buff[2] noun Informal EXPERT, addict, admirer, aficionado, connoisseur, devotee, enthusiast, fan

buffer noun SAFEGUARD, bulwark, bumper, cushion, fender, intermediary, screen, shield, shock absorber

buffet[1] noun SNACK BAR, brasserie, café, cafeteria, refreshment counter, sideboard

buffet[2] verb BATTER, beat, bump, knock, pound, pummel, strike, thump, wallop (informal)

buffoon noun CLOWN, comedian, comic, fool, harlequin, jester, joker, wag

bug noun 1 Informal ILLNESS, disease, infection, virus 2 FAULT, defect, error, flaw, glitch, gremlin ▶verb 3 Informal ANNOY, bother, disturb, get on one's nerves (*informal*), hassle (*informal*), irritate, pester, vex **4** TAP, eavesdrop, listen in, spy

bugbear *noun* PET HATE, bane, bête noire, bogey, dread, horror, nightmare

build *verb* **1** CONSTRUCT, assemble, erect, fabricate, form, make, put up, raise ▶ *noun* **2** PHYSIQUE, body, figure, form, frame, shape, structure

building *noun* STRUCTURE, domicile, dwelling, edifice, house

build-up *noun* INCREASE, accumulation, development, enlargement, escalation, expansion, gain, growth

bulbous *adjective* BULGING, bloated, convex, rounded, swelling, swollen

bulge *noun* **1** SWELLING, bump, hump, lump, projection, protrusion, protuberance **2** INCREASE, boost, intensification, rise, surge ▶ *verb* **3** SWELL OUT, dilate, distend, expand, project, protrude, puff out, stick out

bulk *noun* **1** SIZE, dimensions, immensity, largeness, magnitude, substance, volume, weight **2** MAIN PART, better part, body, lion's share, majority, mass, most, nearly all, preponderance

bulky *adjective* LARGE, big, cumbersome, heavy, hulking, massive, substantial, unwieldy, voluminous, weighty

bulldoze *verb* DEMOLISH, flatten, level, raze

bullet *noun* PROJECTILE, ball, missile, pellet, shot, slug

bulletin *noun* ANNOUNCEMENT, account, communication, communiqué, dispatch, message, news flash, notification, report, statement

bully *noun* **1** PERSECUTOR, browbeater, bully boy, coercer, intimidator, oppressor, ruffian, tormentor, tough ▶ *verb* **2** PERSECUTE, browbeat, coerce, domineer, hector, intimidate, oppress, push around (*slang*), terrorize, tyrannize

bulwark *noun* **1** FORTIFICATION, bastion, buttress, defense, embankment, partition, rampart **2** DEFENSE, buffer, guard, mainstay, safeguard, security, support

bumbling *adjective* CLUMSY, awkward, blundering, bungling, incompetent, inefficient, inept, maladroit, muddled

bump *verb* **1** KNOCK, bang, collide (with), crash, hit, slam, smash into, strike **2** JERK, bounce, jolt, rattle, shake ▶ *noun* **3** KNOCK, bang, blow, collision, crash, impact, jolt, thud, thump **4** LUMP, bulge, contusion, hump, nodule, protuberance, swelling

bumper *adjective* EXCEPTIONAL, abundant, bountiful, excellent, jumbo (*informal*), massive, whopping (*informal*)

bumpkin *noun* YOKEL, country bumpkin, hick (*informal*), hillbilly, peasant, redneck (*slang*), rustic

bumptious *adjective* COCKY, arrogant, brash, conceited, forward, full of oneself, overconfident, pushy (*informal*), self-assertive

bumpy *adjective* ROUGH, bouncy, choppy, jarring, jerky, jolting, rutted, uneven

bunch *noun* 1 NUMBER, assortment, batch, bundle, clump, cluster, collection, heap, lot, mass, pile 2 GROUP, band, crowd, flock, gang, gathering, party, team ▸*verb* 3 GROUP, assemble, bundle, cluster, collect, huddle, mass, pack

bundle *noun* 1 BUNCH, assortment, batch, collection, group, heap, mass, pile, stack ▸*verb* 2 (with *out, off, into,* etc.) PUSH, hurry, hustle, rush, shove, throw, thrust

bundle up *verb* WRAP UP, swathe

bungle *verb* MESS UP, blow (*slang*), blunder, botch, foul up, make a mess of, muff, ruin, spoil

bungling *adjective* INCOMPETENT, blundering, clumsy, inept, maladroit

bunk, bunkum *noun Informal* NONSENSE, balderdash, baloney (*informal*), garbage (*informal*), hogwash, hot air (*informal*), moonshine, poppycock (*informal*), rubbish, stuff and nonsense, twaddle

buoy *noun* 1 MARKER, beacon, float, guide, signal ▸*verb* 2 **buoy up** ENCOURAGE, boost, cheer, cheer up, hearten, keep afloat, lift, raise, support, sustain

buoyancy *noun* 1 LIGHTNESS, weightlessness 2 CHEERFULNESS, animation, bounce (*informal*), good humor, high spirits, liveliness

buoyant *adjective* 1 FLOATING, afloat, light, weightless 2 CHEERFUL, carefree, chirpy (*informal*), happy, jaunty, light-hearted, upbeat (*informal*)

burden *noun* 1 LOAD, encumbrance, weight 2 TROUBLE, affliction, millstone, onus, responsibility, strain, weight, worry ▸*verb* 3 WEIGH DOWN, bother, handicap, load, oppress, saddle with, tax, worry

bureau *noun* 1 OFFICE, agency, branch, department, division, service 2 DESK, writing desk

bureaucracy *noun* 1 GOVERNMENT, administration, authorities, civil service, corridors of power, officials, the system 2 RED TAPE, officialdom, regulations

bureaucrat *noun* OFFICIAL, administrator, civil servant, functionary, mandarin, officer, public servant

burglar *noun* HOUSEBREAKER, cat burglar, filcher, pilferer, robber, sneak thief, thief

burglary *noun* BREAKING AND ENTERING, break-in, housebreaking, larceny, robbery, stealing, theft, thieving

burial *noun* INTERMENT, entombment, exequies, funeral, obsequies

buried *adjective* 1 INTERRED, entombed, laid to rest 2 HIDDEN, concealed, private, sequestered, tucked away

burlesque *noun* 1 PARODY, caricature, mockery, satire, spoof (*informal*), travesty ▸*verb* 2 SATIRIZE, ape, caricature, exaggerate, imitate, lampoon, make a monkey out of, make fun of, mock, parody, ridicule, spoof (*informal*), travesty

burly *adjective* BRAWNY, beefy (*informal*), big, bulky, hefty, hulking, stocky, stout, sturdy, thickset, well-built

burn *verb* 1 BE ON FIRE, be ablaze, blaze, flame, flare, glow, go up in flames, smoke 2 SET ON FIRE, char, ignite, incinerate, kindle, light, parch, scorch, sear, singe, toast 3 BE PASSIONATE, be angry, be aroused, be inflamed, fume, seethe, simmer, smolder

burning *adjective* 1 INTENSE, ardent, eager, fervent, impassioned, passionate, vehement 2 CRUCIAL, acute, compelling, critical, essential, important, pressing, significant, urgent, vital 3 BLAZING, fiery, flaming, flashing, gleaming, glowing, illuminated, scorching, smoldering

burnish *verb* POLISH, brighten, buff, furbish, glaze, rub up, shine, smooth

burrow *noun* 1 HOLE, den, lair, retreat, shelter, tunnel ▸ *verb* 2 DIG, delve, excavate, hollow out, scoop out, tunnel

burst *verb* 1 EXPLODE, blow up, break, crack, puncture, rupture, shatter, split, tear apart 2 RUSH, barge, break, break out, erupt, gush forth, run, spout ▸ *noun* 3 EXPLOSION, bang, blast, blowout, break, crack, discharge, rupture, split 4 RUSH, gush, gust, outbreak, outburst, outpouring, spate, spurt, surge, torrent ▸ *adjective* 5 RUPTURED, flat, punctured, rent, split

bury *verb* 1 INTER, consign to the grave, entomb, inhume, lay to rest 2 EMBED, engulf, submerge 3 HIDE, conceal, cover, enshroud, secrete, stow away

bush *noun* 1 SHRUB, hedge, plant, shrubbery, thicket 2 **the bush** THE WILD, backwoods, brush, scrub, scrubland, woodland

bushy *adjective* THICK, bristling, fluffy, fuzzy, luxuriant, rough, shaggy, unruly

busily *adverb* ACTIVELY, assiduously, briskly, diligently, energetically, industriously, purposefully, speedily, strenuously

business *noun* 1 TRADE, bargaining, commerce, dealings, industry, manufacturing, selling, transaction 2 ESTABLISHMENT, company, concern, corporation, enterprise, firm, organization, venture 3 PROFESSION, career, employment, function, job, line, occupation, trade, vocation, work 4 CONCERN, affair, assignment, duty, problem, responsibility, task

businesslike *adjective* EFFICIENT, methodical, orderly, organized, practical, professional, systematic, thorough, well-ordered

businessman *noun* EXECUTIVE, capitalist, employer, entrepreneur, financier, industrialist, merchant, tradesman, tycoon

bust[1] *noun* BOSOM, breast, chest, front, torso

bust[2] *Informal* ▸ *verb* 1 BREAK,

burst, fracture, rupture
2 ARREST, catch, raid, search
▶ *adjective* **3 go bust** GO
BANKRUPT, become insolvent, be
ruined, fail

bustle *verb* **1** HURRY, fuss,
hasten, rush, scamper, scurry,
scuttle ▶ *noun* **2** ACTIVITY, ado,
commotion, excitement, flurry,
fuss, hurly-burly, stir, to-do

bustling *adjective* BUSY, active,
buzzing, crowded, full,
humming, lively, swarming,
teeming

busy *adjective* **1** OCCUPIED,
active, employed, engaged,
hard at work, industrious, on
duty, rushed off one's feet,
working **2** LIVELY, energetic,
exacting, full, hectic, hustling
▶ *verb* **3** OCCUPY, absorb,
employ, engage, engross,
immerse, interest

busybody *noun* NOSY ROSY (*U.S.
informal*), gossip, meddler,
snooper, stirrer (*informal*),
troublemaker

but *conjunction* **1** HOWEVER,
further, moreover,
nevertheless, on the contrary,
on the other hand, still, yet
▶ *preposition* **2** EXCEPT, bar,
barring, excepting, excluding,
notwithstanding, save, with
the exception of ▶ *adverb*
3 ONLY, just, merely, simply,
singly, solely

butcher *noun* **1** MURDERER,
destroyer, killer, slaughterer,
slayer ▶ *verb* **2** SLAUGHTER, carve,
clean, cut, cut up, dress, joint,
prepare **3** KILL, assassinate, cut
down, destroy, exterminate,
liquidate, massacre, put to the
sword, slaughter, slay

butt¹ *noun* **1** END, haft, handle,
hilt, shaft, shank, stock **2** STUB,
cigarette end, leftover, tip
3 *Informal* BUTTOCKS, behind
(*informal*), bottom, *derrière*
(*euphemistic*), rump (*informal*),
tush (*slang*)

butt² *noun* TARGET, dupe,
laughing stock, victim

butt³ *verb, noun* **1** *With or of
the head or horns* KNOCK, bump,
poke, prod, push, ram, shove,
thrust ▶ *verb* **2 butt in** INTERFERE,
chip in (*informal*), cut in,
interrupt, intrude, meddle, put
one's oar in, stick one's nose in

butt⁴ *noun* CASK, barrel

buttonhole *verb* DETAIN, accost,
bore, catch, grab, importune,
take aside, waylay

buttress *noun* **1** SUPPORT, brace,
mainstay, prop, reinforcement,
stanchion, strut ▶ *verb*
2 SUPPORT, back up, bolster,
prop up, reinforce, shore up,
strengthen, sustain, uphold

buxom *adjective* PLUMP, ample,
bosomy, busty, curvaceous,
healthy, voluptuous,
well-rounded

buy *verb* **1** PURCHASE, acquire,
get, invest in, obtain, pay for,
procure, shop for ▶ *noun*
2 PURCHASE, acquisition,
bargain, deal

by *preposition* **1** VIA, by way of,
over **2** THROUGH, through the
agency of **3** NEAR, along,
beside, close to, next to, past
▶ *adverb* **4** NEAR, at hand, close,
handy, in reach **5** PAST, aside,
away, to one side

bygone *adjective* PAST,
antiquated, extinct, forgotten,
former, lost, of old, olden

bypass verb GO ROUND, avoid, circumvent, depart from, detour round, deviate from, get round, give a wide berth to, pass round

bystander noun ONLOOKER, eyewitness, looker-on, observer, passer-by, spectator, viewer, watcher, witness

byword noun SAYING, adage, maxim, motto, precept, proverb, slogan

C c

cab noun TAXI, hackney carriage, minicab, taxicab

cabal noun 1 CLIQUE, caucus, conclave, faction, league, party, set 2 PLOT, conspiracy, intrigue, machination, scheme

cabin noun 1 ROOM, berth, compartment, quarters 2 HUT, chalet, cottage, lodge, shack, shanty, shed

cabinet noun CUPBOARD, case, chiffonier, closet, commode, dresser, escritoire, locker

Cabinet noun COUNCIL, administration, assembly, counselors, ministry

caddish adjective UNGENTLEMANLY, despicable, ill-bred, lousy (slang), low, scuzzy (slang), unmannerly

café noun SNACK BAR, brasserie, cafeteria, coffee bar, coffee shop, lunchroom, restaurant, tearoom

cage noun ENCLOSURE, pen, pound

cagey adjective Informal WARY, careful, cautious, chary, discreet, guarded, noncommittal, shrewd, wily

cajole verb PERSUADE, brown-nose (slang), coax, flatter, seduce, sweet-talk (informal), wheedle

cake noun 1 BLOCK, bar, cube, loaf, lump, mass, slab ►verb 2 ENCRUST, bake, coagulate, congeal, solidify

calamitous adjective DISASTROUS, cataclysmic, catastrophic, deadly, devastating, dire, fatal, ruinous, tragic

calamity noun DISASTER, cataclysm, catastrophe, misadventure, misfortune, mishap, ruin, tragedy, tribulation

calculate verb 1 WORK OUT, compute, count, determine, enumerate, estimate, figure, reckon 2 PLAN, aim, design, intend

calculated adjective DELIBERATE, considered, intended, intentional, planned, premeditated, purposeful

calculating adjective SCHEMING, crafty, cunning, devious, Machiavellian, manipulative, sharp, shrewd, sly

calculation noun 1 WORKING OUT, answer, computation, estimate, forecast, judgment, reckoning, result 2 PLANNING, contrivance, deliberation, discretion, foresight, forethought, precaution

caliber noun 1 WORTH, ability, capacity, distinction, merit, quality, stature, talent 2 DIAMETER, bore, gauge, measure

call verb 1 NAME, christen,

describe as, designate, dub, entitle, label, style, term **2** CRY, arouse, hail, rouse, shout, yell **3** PHONE, telephone **4** SUMMON, assemble, convene, gather, muster, rally ▶*noun* **5** CRY, hail, scream, shout, signal, whoop, yell **6** SUMMONS, appeal, command, demand, invitation, notice, order, plea, request **7** NEED, cause, excuse, grounds, justification, occasion, reason

call for *verb* **1** REQUIRE, demand, entail, involve, necessitate, need, occasion, suggest **2** FETCH, collect, pick up

calling *noun* PROFESSION, career, life's work, mission, trade, vocation

call on *verb* VISIT, drop in on, look in on, look up, see

callous *adjective* HEARTLESS, cold, hard-boiled, hardened, hardhearted, insensitive, uncaring, unfeeling

callow *adjective* INEXPERIENCED, green, guileless, immature, naive, raw, unsophisticated

calm *adjective* **1** COOL, collected, composed, dispassionate, relaxed, sedate, self-possessed, unemotional **2** STILL, balmy, mild, quiet, serene, smooth, tranquil, windless ▶*noun* **3** PEACEFULNESS, hush, peace, quiet, repose, serenity, stillness ▶*verb* **4** QUIETEN, hush, mollify, placate, relax, soothe

calmness *noun* **1** COOLNESS, composure, cool (*slang*), equanimity, impassivity, poise, sang-froid, self-possession **2** PEACEFULNESS, calm, hush, quiet, repose, restfulness, serenity, stillness, tranquillity

camouflage *noun* **1** DISGUISE, blind, cloak, concealment, cover, mask, masquerade, screen, subterfuge ▶*verb* **2** DISGUISE, cloak, conceal, cover, hide, mask, obfuscate, obscure, screen, veil

camp[1] *noun* CAMP SITE, bivouac, camping ground, encampment, tents

camp[2] *adjective Informal* EFFEMINATE, affected, artificial, mannered, ostentatious, posturing

campaign *noun* OPERATION, attack, crusade, drive, expedition, movement, offensive, push

canal *noun* WATERWAY, channel, conduit, duct, passage, watercourse

cancel *verb* **1** CALL OFF, abolish, abort, annul, delete, do away with, eliminate, erase, expunge, obliterate, repeal, revoke **2 cancel out** MAKE UP FOR, balance out, compensate for, counterbalance, neutralize, nullify, offset

cancellation *noun* ABANDONMENT, abolition, annulment, deletion, elimination, repeal, revocation

cancer *noun* GROWTH, corruption, malignancy, pestilence, sickness, tumor

candid *adjective* HONEST, blunt, forthright, frank, open, outspoken, plain, straightforward, truthful

candidate *noun* CONTENDER, applicant, claimant, competitor, contestant, entrant, nominee, runner

candor *noun* HONESTY, directness, forthrightness,

frankness, openness, outspokenness, straightforwardness, truthfulness

canker *noun* DISEASE, bane, blight, cancer, corruption, infection, rot, scourge, sore, ulcer

cannon *noun* GUN, big gun, field gun, mortar

canny *adjective* SHREWD, astute, careful, cautious, clever, judicious, prudent, wise

canon *noun* 1 RULE, criterion, dictate, formula, precept, principle, regulation, standard, statute, yardstick 2 LIST, catalog, roll

canopy *noun* AWNING, covering, shade, sunshade

cant[1] *noun* 1 HYPOCRISY, humbug, insincerity, lip service, pretense, pretentiousness, sanctimoniousness 2 JARGON, argot, lingo, patter, slang, vernacular

cant[2] *verb* TILT, angle, bevel, incline, rise, slant, slope

cantankerous *adjective* BAD-TEMPERED, choleric, contrary, disagreeable, grumpy, irascible, irritable, testy, waspish

canter *noun* 1 JOG, amble, dogtrot, lope ▸ *verb* 2 JOG, amble, lope

canvass *verb* 1 CAMPAIGN, electioneer, solicit, solicit votes 2 POLL, examine, inspect, investigate, scrutinize, study ▸ *noun* 3 POLL, examination, investigation, scrutiny, survey, tally

cap *verb* BEAT, better, crown, eclipse, exceed, outdo, outstrip, surpass, top, transcend

capability *noun* ABILITY, capacity, competence, means, potential, power, proficiency, qualification(s), wherewithal

capable *adjective* ABLE, accomplished, competent, efficient, gifted, proficient, qualified, talented

capacious *adjective* SPACIOUS, broad, commodious, expansive, extensive, roomy, sizable *or* sizeable, substantial, vast, voluminous, wide

capacity *noun* 1 SIZE, amplitude, compass, dimensions, extent, magnitude, range, room, scope, space, volume 2 ABILITY, aptitude, aptness, capability, competence, facility, genius, gift 3 FUNCTION, office, position, post, province, role, sphere

cape *noun* HEADLAND, head, peninsula, point, promontory

caper *noun* 1 ESCAPADE, antic, high jinks, jape, lark (*informal*), mischief, practical joke, prank, stunt ▸ *verb* 2 DANCE, bound, cavort, frolic, gambol, jump, skip, spring, trip

capital *noun* 1 MONEY, assets, cash, finances, funds, investment(s), means, principal, resources, wealth, wherewithal ▸ *adjective* 2 PRINCIPAL, cardinal, major, prime, vital 3 *Old-fashioned* FIRST-RATE, excellent, fine, splendid, sterling, superb

capitalism *noun* PRIVATE ENTERPRISE, free enterprise, laissez faire *or* laisser faire, private ownership

capitalize on *verb* TAKE ADVANTAGE OF, benefit from, cash in on (*informal*), exploit, gain from, make the most of, profit from

capitulate *verb* GIVE IN, come to terms, give up, relent, submit, succumb, surrender, yield

caprice *noun* WHIM, fad, fancy, fickleness, impulse, inconstancy, notion, whimsy

capricious *adjective* UNPREDICTABLE, changeful, erratic, fickle, fitful, impulsive, inconsistent, inconstant, mercurial, variable, wayward, whimsical

capsize *verb* OVERTURN, invert, keel over, tip over, turn over, turn turtle, upset

capsule *noun* 1 PILL, lozenge, tablet 2 *Botany* POD, case, receptacle, seed case, sheath, shell, vessel

captain *noun* LEADER, boss (*informal*), chief, commander, head, master, skipper

captivate *verb* CHARM, allure, attract, beguile, bewitch, enchant, enrapture, enthrall, entrance, fascinate, infatuate, mesmerize

captive *noun* 1 PRISONER, convict, detainee, hostage, internee, prisoner of war, slave ▶ *adjective* 2 CONFINED, caged, enslaved, ensnared, imprisoned, incarcerated, locked up, penned, restricted, subjugated

captivity *noun* CONFINEMENT, bondage, custody, detention, imprisonment, incarceration, internment, slavery

capture *verb* 1 CATCH, apprehend, arrest, bag, collar (*informal*), secure, seize, take,

take prisoner ▶ *noun* 2 CATCHING, apprehension, arrest, imprisonment, seizure, taking, taking captive, trapping

car *noun* 1 VEHICLE, auto, automobile, clunker (*informal*), jalopy (*informal*), machine, motor, motorcar, wheels (*informal*) 2 (RAILWAY) CARRIAGE, buffet car, cable car, coach, dining car, sleeping car, van

carcass *noun* BODY, cadaver (*Medical*), corpse, dead body, framework, hulk, remains, shell, skeleton

cardinal *adjective* PRINCIPAL, capital, central, chief, essential, first, fundamental, key, leading, main, paramount, primary

care *verb* 1 BE CONCERNED, be bothered, be interested, mind ▶ *noun* 2 CAUTION, attention, carefulness, consideration, forethought, heed, management, pains, prudence, vigilance, watchfulness 3 PROTECTION, charge, control, custody, guardianship, keeping, management, supervision 4 WORRY, anxiety, concern, disquiet, perplexity, pressure, responsibility, stress, trouble

career *noun* 1 OCCUPATION, calling, employment, life's work, livelihood, pursuit, vocation ▶ *verb* 2 RUSH, barrel (along) (*informal*), bolt, dash, hurtle, race, speed, tear

care for *verb* 1 LOOK AFTER, attend, foster, mind, minister to, nurse, protect, provide for, tend, watch over 2 LIKE, be fond of, desire, enjoy, love, prize, take to, want

carefree *adjective* UNTROUBLED, blithe, breezy, cheerful, easy-going, halcyon, happy-go-lucky, light-hearted

careful *adjective* **1** CAUTIOUS, chary, circumspect, discreet, prudent, scrupulous, thoughtful, thrifty **2** THOROUGH, conscientious, meticulous, painstaking, particular, precise

careless *adjective* **1** SLAPDASH, cavalier, inaccurate, irresponsible, lackadaisical, neglectful, offhand, slipshod, sloppy (*informal*) **2** NEGLIGENT, absent-minded, forgetful, hasty, remiss, thoughtless, unthinking **3** NONCHALANT, artless, casual, unstudied

carelessness *noun* NEGLIGENCE, indiscretion, irresponsibility, laxity, neglect, omission, slackness, sloppiness (*informal*), thoughtlessness

caress *verb* **1** STROKE, cuddle, embrace, fondle, hug, kiss, make out (*informal*), neck (*informal*), nuzzle, pet ▶*noun* **2** STROKE, cuddle, embrace, fondling, hug, kiss, pat

caretaker *noun* WARDEN, concierge, curator, custodian, janitor, keeper, porter, superintendent, watchman

cargo *noun* LOAD, baggage, consignment, contents, freight, goods, merchandise, shipment

caricature *noun* **1** PARODY, burlesque, cartoon, distortion, farce, lampoon, satire, travesty ▶*verb* **2** PARODY, burlesque, distort, lampoon, mimic, mock, ridicule, satirize

carnage *noun* SLAUGHTER, blood bath, bloodshed, butchery, havoc, holocaust, massacre, mass murder, murder, shambles

carnal *adjective* SEXUAL, erotic, fleshly, lascivious, lewd, libidinous, lustful, sensual

carnival *noun* FESTIVAL, celebration, fair, fête, fiesta, gala, holiday, jamboree, jubilee, merrymaking, revelry

carol *noun* SONG, chorus, ditty, hymn, lay

carp *verb* FIND FAULT, cavil, complain, criticize, pick holes, quibble, reproach

carpenter *noun* JOINER, cabinet-maker, woodworker

carriage *noun* **1** VEHICLE, cab, coach, conveyance **2** BEARING, air, behavior, comportment, conduct, demeanor, deportment, gait, manner, posture

carry *verb* **1** TRANSPORT, bear, bring, conduct, convey, fetch, haul, lug, move, relay, take, transfer **2** WIN, accomplish, capture, effect, gain, secure

carry on *verb* CONTINUE, endure, keep going, last, maintain, perpetuate, persevere, persist

carry out *verb* PERFORM, accomplish, achieve, carry through, effect, execute, fulfill, implement, realize

carton *noun* BOX, case, container, pack, package, packet

cartoon *noun* **1** DRAWING, caricature, comic strip, lampoon, parody, satire, sketch **2** ANIMATION, animated cartoon, animated film

cartridge *noun* **1** SHELL, charge, round **2** CONTAINER, capsule, case, cassette, cylinder, magazine

carve *verb* CUT, chip, chisel, engrave, etch, hew, mold, sculpt, slice, whittle

cascade *noun* 1 WATERFALL, avalanche, cataract, deluge, downpour, falls, flood, fountain, outpouring, shower, torrent ▶ *verb* 2 FLOW, descend, fall, flood, gush, overflow, pitch, plunge, pour, spill, surge, teem, tumble

case[1] *noun* 1 INSTANCE, example, illustration, occasion, occurrence, specimen 2 SITUATION, circumstance(s), condition, context, contingency, event, position, state 3 *Law* LAWSUIT, action, dispute, proceedings, suit, trial

case[2] *noun* 1 CONTAINER, box, canister, carton, casket, chest, crate, holder, receptacle, suitcase, tray 2 COVERING, capsule, casing, envelope, jacket, sheath, shell, wrapper

cash *noun* MONEY, coinage, currency, dough (*slang*), funds, notes, ready money, silver

cashier[1] *noun* TELLER, bank clerk, banker, bursar, clerk, purser, treasurer

cashier[2] *verb* DISMISS, discard, discharge, drum out, expel, give the boot to (*slang*)

casket *noun* BOX, case, chest, coffer, jewel box

cast *noun* 1 ACTORS, characters, company, dramatis personae, players, troupe 2 TYPE, complexion, manner, stamp, style ▶ *verb* 3 CHOOSE, allot, appoint, assign, name, pick, select 4 GIVE OUT, bestow, deposit, diffuse, distribute, emit, radiate, scatter, shed, spread 5 FORM, found, model, mold, set, shape 6 THROW, fling, hurl, launch, pitch, sling, thrust, toss

caste *noun* CLASS, estate, grade, order, rank, social order, status, stratum

castigate *verb* REPRIMAND, berate, censure, chastise, criticize, lambast(e), rebuke, scold

cast-iron *adjective* CERTAIN, copper-bottomed, definite, established, fixed, guaranteed, settled

castle *noun* FORTRESS, chateau, citadel, keep, palace, stronghold, tower

cast-off *adjective* 1 UNWANTED, discarded, rejected, scrapped, surplus to requirements, unneeded, useless ▶ *noun* 2 REJECT, discard, failure, outcast, second

castrate *verb* NEUTER, emasculate, geld

casual *adjective* 1 CARELESS, blasé, cursory, lackadaisical, nonchalant, offhand, relaxed, unconcerned 2 OCCASIONAL, accidental, chance, incidental, irregular, random, unexpected 3 INFORMAL, non-dressy, sporty

casualty *noun* VICTIM, death, fatality, loss, sufferer, wounded

cat *noun* FELINE, kitty (*informal*), puss (*informal*), pussy (*informal*), tabby

catacombs *plural noun* VAULT, crypt, tomb

catalog *noun* 1 LIST, directory, gazetteer, index, inventory, record, register, roll, roster, schedule ▶ *verb* 2 LIST, accession, alphabetize, classify, file, index, inventory, register, tabulate

catapult noun 1 SLING, slingshot (U.S.) ▶verb 2 SHOOT, heave, hurl, pitch, plunge, propel

catastrophe noun DISASTER, adversity, calamity, cataclysm, fiasco, misfortune, tragedy, trouble

catcall noun JEER, boo, gibe, hiss, raspberry, whistle

catch verb 1 SEIZE, clutch, get, grab, grasp, grip, lay hold of, snatch, take 2 CAPTURE, apprehend, arrest, ensnare, entrap, snare 3 DISCOVER, catch in the act, detect, expose, find out, surprise, take unawares, unmask 4 CONTRACT, develop, get, go down with, incur, succumb to, suffer from 5 MAKE OUT, comprehend, discern, get, grasp, hear, perceive, recognize, sense, take in ▶noun 6 FASTENER, bolt, clasp, clip, latch 7 DRAWBACK, disadvantage, fly in the ointment, hitch, snag, stumbling block, trap, trick

catching adjective INFECTIOUS, communicable, contagious, transferable, transmittable

catch on verb UNDERSTAND, comprehend, find out, get the picture, grasp, see, see through

catchword noun SLOGAN, byword, motto, password, watchword

catchy adjective MEMORABLE, captivating, haunting, popular

categorical adjective ABSOLUTE, downright, emphatic, explicit, express, positive, unambiguous, unconditional, unequivocal, unqualified, unreserved

category noun CLASS, classification, department, division, grade, grouping, heading, section, sort, type

cater verb PROVIDE, furnish, outfit, purvey, supply

cattle plural noun COWS, beasts, bovines, livestock, stock

catty adjective SPITEFUL, backbiting, bitchy (informal), malevolent, malicious, rancorous, shrewish, snide, venomous

cause noun 1 ORIGIN, agent, beginning, creator, genesis, mainspring, maker, producer, root, source, spring 2 REASON, basis, grounds, incentive, inducement, justification, motivation, motive, purpose 3 AIM, belief, conviction, enterprise, ideal, movement, principle ▶verb 4 PRODUCE, bring about, create, generate, give rise to, incite, induce, lead to, result in

caustic adjective 1 BURNING, acrid, astringent, biting, corroding, corrosive, mordant, vitriolic 2 SARCASTIC, acrimonious, cutting, pungent, scathing, stinging, trenchant, virulent, vitriolic

caution noun 1 CARE, alertness, carefulness, circumspection, deliberation, discretion, forethought, heed, prudence, vigilance, watchfulness 2 WARNING, admonition, advice, counsel, injunction ▶verb 3 WARN, admonish, advise, tip off, urge

cautious adjective CAREFUL, cagey

(*informal*), chary, circumspect, guarded, judicious, prudent, tentative, wary

cavalcade *noun* PARADE, array, march-past, procession, spectacle, train

cavalier *adjective* HAUGHTY, arrogant, disdainful, lofty, lordly, offhand, scornful, supercilious

cavalry *noun* HORSEMEN, horse, mounted troops

cave *noun* HOLLOW, cavern, cavity, den, grotto

cavern *noun* CAVE, hollow, pothole

cavernous *adjective* DEEP, hollow, sunken, yawning

cavity *noun* HOLLOW, crater, dent, gap, hole, pit

cease *verb* STOP, break off, conclude, discontinue, end, finish, halt, leave off, refrain, terminate

ceaseless *adjective* CONTINUAL, constant, endless, eternal, everlasting, incessant, interminable, never-ending, nonstop, perpetual, twenty-four-seven (*slang*), unremitting

cede *verb* SURRENDER, concede, hand over, make over, relinquish, renounce, resign, transfer, yield

celebrate *verb* 1 REJOICE, commemorate, drink to, keep, kill the fatted calf, observe, put the flags out, toast 2 PERFORM, bless, honor, solemnize

celebrated *adjective* WELL-KNOWN, acclaimed, distinguished, eminent, famous, illustrious, notable, popular, prominent, renowned

celebration *noun* 1 PARTY, festival, festivity, gala, jubilee, merrymaking, red-letter day, revelry 2 PERFORMANCE, anniversary, commemoration, honoring, observance, remembrance, solemnization

celebrity *noun* 1 PERSONALITY, big name, big shot (*informal*), dignitary, luminary, star, superstar, V.I.P. 2 FAME, distinction, notability, prestige, prominence, renown, reputation, repute, stardom

celestial *adjective* HEAVENLY, angelic, astral, divine, ethereal, spiritual, sublime, supernatural

celibacy *noun* CHASTITY, continence, purity, virginity

cell *noun* 1 ROOM, cavity, chamber, compartment, cubicle, dungeon, stall 2 UNIT, caucus, core, coterie, group, nucleus

cement *noun* 1 MORTAR, adhesive, glue, gum, paste, plaster, sealant ▶*verb* 2 STICK TOGETHER, attach, bind, bond, combine, glue, join, plaster, seal, unite, weld

cemetery *noun* GRAVEYARD, burial ground, churchyard, God's acre, necropolis

censor *verb* CUT, blue-pencil, bowdlerize, expurgate

censorious *adjective* CRITICAL, captious, carping, cavilling, condemnatory, disapproving, disparaging, fault-finding, hypercritical, scathing, severe

censure *noun* 1 DISAPPROVAL, blame, condemnation, criticism, obloquy, rebuke, reprimand, reproach, reproof, stick (*slang*) ▶*verb* 2 CRITICIZE, blame, castigate, condemn, denounce, rap over the knuckles, rebuke, reprimand, reproach, scold, slap on the wrist

center noun 1 MIDDLE, core, focus, heart, hub, kernel, midpoint, nucleus, pivot ▶ verb 2 FOCUS, cluster, concentrate, converge, revolve

central adjective 1 MIDDLE, inner, interior, mean, median, mid 2 MAIN, chief, essential, focal, fundamental, key, primary, principal

centralize verb UNIFY, concentrate, condense, incorporate, rationalize, streamline

ceremonial adjective 1 RITUAL, formal, liturgical, ritualistic, solemn, stately ▶ noun 2 RITUAL, ceremony, formality, rite, solemnity

ceremonious adjective FORMAL, civil, courteous, deferential, dignified, punctilious, solemn, stately, stiff

ceremony noun 1 RITUAL, commemoration, function, observance, parade, rite, service, show, solemnities 2 FORMALITY, ceremonial, decorum, etiquette, niceties, pomp, propriety, protocol

certain adjective 1 SURE, assured, confident, convinced, positive, satisfied 2 KNOWN, conclusive, incontrovertible, irrefutable, true, undeniable, unequivocal 3 INEVITABLE, bound, definite, destined, fated, inescapable, sure 4 FIXED, decided, definite, established, settled

certainly adverb DEFINITELY,

assuredly, indisputably, indubitably, surely, truly, undeniably, undoubtedly, without doubt

certainty noun 1 SURENESS, assurance, confidence, conviction, faith, positiveness, trust, validity 2 FACT, reality, sure thing (informal), truth

certificate noun DOCUMENT, authorization, credential(s), diploma, license, testimonial, voucher, warrant

certify verb CONFIRM, assure, attest, authenticate, declare, guarantee, testify, validate, verify

chafe verb 1 RUB, abrade, rasp, scrape, scratch 2 BE ANNOYED, be impatient, fret, fume, rage, worry

chaff¹ noun WASTE, dregs, husks, refuse, remains, rubbish, trash

chaff² verb TEASE, mock, rib (informal), ridicule, scoff, taunt

chain noun 1 LINK, bond, coupling, fetter, manacle, shackle 2 SERIES, progression, sequence, set, string, succession, train ▶ verb 3 BIND, confine, enslave, fetter, handcuff, manacle, restrain, shackle, tether

chairman noun DIRECTOR, chairperson, chairwoman, master of ceremonies, president, speaker, spokesman

challenge noun 1 TEST, confrontation, provocation, question, trial, ultimatum ▶ verb 2 TEST, confront, defy, dispute, object to, question, tackle, throw down the gauntlet

chamber noun 1 ROOM, apartment, bedroom,

compartment, cubicle, enclosure, hall **2** COUNCIL, assembly, legislative body, legislature

champion noun **1** WINNER, conqueror, hero, title holder, victor **2** DEFENDER, backer, guardian, patron, protector, upholder ▶verb **3** SUPPORT, advocate, back, commend, defend, encourage, espouse, fight for, promote, uphold

chance noun **1** PROBABILITY, likelihood, odds, possibility, prospect **2** OPPORTUNITY, occasion, opening, time **3** LUCK, accident, coincidence, destiny, fate, fortune, providence **4** RISK, gamble, hazard, jeopardy, speculation, uncertainty ▶verb **5** RISK, endanger, gamble, hazard, jeopardize, stake, try, venture, wager

chancy adjective Slang DANGEROUS, difficult, hazardous, perilous, risky

change noun **1** ALTERATION, difference, innovation, metamorphosis, modification, mutation, revolution, transformation, transition **2** VARIETY, break (informal), departure, diversion, novelty, variation **3** EXCHANGE, conversion, interchange, substitution, swap, trade ▶verb **4** ALTER, convert, modify, mutate, reform, reorganize, restyle, shift, transform, vary **5** EXCHANGE, barter, convert, interchange, replace, substitute, swap, trade

changeable adjective VARIABLE, erratic, fickle, inconstant, irregular, mobile, mutable,

protean, shifting, unsettled, unstable, volatile, wavering

channel noun **1** ROUTE, approach, artery, avenue, course, means, medium, path, way **2** PASSAGE, canal, conduit, duct, furrow, groove, gutter, route, strait ▶verb **3** DIRECT, conduct, convey, guide, transmit

chant verb **1** SING, carol, chorus, descant, intone, recite, warble ▶noun **2** SONG, carol, chorus, melody, psalm

chaos noun DISORDER, anarchy, bedlam, confusion, disorganization, lawlessness, mayhem, pandemonium, tumult

chaotic adjective DISORDERED, anarchic, confused, deranged, disorganized, lawless, riotous, topsy-turvy, tumultuous, uncontrolled

chap noun Informal FELLOW, character, guy (informal), individual, man, person

chaperone noun **1** ESCORT, companion ▶verb **2** ESCORT, accompany, attend, protect, safeguard, shepherd, watch over

chapter noun SECTION, clause, division, episode, part, period, phase, stage, topic

character noun **1** NATURE, attributes, caliber, complexion, disposition, personality, quality, temperament, type **2** REPUTATION, honor, integrity, rectitude, strength, uprightness **3** ROLE, part, persona, portrayal **4** ECCENTRIC, card (informal), oddball (informal), original **5** SYMBOL, device, figure, hieroglyph, letter, mark, rune, sign

characteristic *noun* 1 FEATURE, attribute, faculty, idiosyncrasy, mark, peculiarity, property, quality, quirk, trait ▶ *adjective* 2 TYPICAL, distinctive, distinguishing, idiosyncratic, individual, peculiar, representative, singular, special, symbolic, symptomatic

characterize *verb* IDENTIFY, brand, distinguish, indicate, mark, represent, stamp, typify

charade *noun* PRETENSE, fake, farce, pantomime, parody, travesty

charge *verb* 1 ACCUSE, arraign, blame, impeach, incriminate, indict 2 RUSH, assail, assault, attack, stampede, storm 3 FILL, load 4 COMMAND, bid, commit, demand, entrust, instruct, order, require ▶ *noun* 5 PRICE, amount, cost, expenditure, expense, outlay, payment, rate, toll 6 ACCUSATION, allegation, imputation, indictment 7 RUSH, assault, attack, onset, onslaught, sortie, stampede 8 CARE, custody, duty, office, responsibility, safekeeping, trust 9 WARD 10 INSTRUCTION, command, demand, direction, injunction, mandate, order, precept

charisma *noun* CHARM, allure, attraction, lure, magnetism, personality

charismatic *adjective* CHARMING, alluring, attractive, enticing, influential, magnetic

charitable *adjective* 1 TOLERANT, considerate, favorable, forgiving, humane, indulgent,

kindly, lenient, magnanimous, sympathetic, understanding 2 GENEROUS, beneficent, benevolent, bountiful, kind, lavish, liberal, philanthropic

charity *noun* 1 DONATIONS, assistance, benefaction, contributions, endowment, fund, gift, hand-out, help, largesse *or* largess, philanthropy, relief 2 KINDNESS, altruism, benevolence, compassion, fellow feeling, generosity, goodwill, humanity, indulgence

charlatan *noun* FRAUD, cheat, con man (*informal*), fake, impostor, phoney *or* phony (*informal*), pretender, quack, sham, swindler

charm *noun* 1 ATTRACTION, allure, appeal, fascination, magnetism 2 SPELL, enchantment, magic, sorcery 3 TALISMAN, amulet, fetish, trinket ▶ *verb* 4 ATTRACT, allure, beguile, bewitch, captivate, delight, enchant, enrapture, entrance, fascinate, mesmerize, win over

charming *adjective* ATTRACTIVE, appealing, captivating, cute, delightful, fetching, likable *or* likeable, pleasing, seductive, winsome

chart *noun* 1 TABLE, blueprint, diagram, graph, map, plan ▶ *verb* 2 PLOT, delineate, draft, map out, outline, shape, sketch

charter *noun* 1 DOCUMENT, contract, deed, license, permit, prerogative ▶ *verb* 2 HIRE, commission, employ, lease, rent 3 AUTHORIZE, sanction

chase *verb* 1 PURSUE, course, follow, hunt, run after, stalk, track **2** DRIVE AWAY, drive, expel, hound, put to flight ▶*noun* **3** PURSUIT, hunt, hunting, race

chasm *noun* GULF, abyss, crater, crevasse, fissure, gap, gorge, ravine

chaste *adjective* PURE, immaculate, innocent, modest, simple, unaffected, undefiled, virtuous

chasten *verb* SUBDUE, chastise, correct, discipline, humble, humiliate, put in one's place, tame

chastise *verb* **1** SCOLD, berate, castigate, censure, correct, discipline, upbraid **2** *Old-fashioned* BEAT, flog, lash, lick (*informal*), punish, scourge, whip

chastity *noun* PURITY, celibacy, continence, innocence, maidenhood, modesty, virginity, virtue

chat *noun* **1** TALK, chatter, conversation, gossip, heart-to-heart, natter, tête-à-tête ▶*verb* **2** TALK, chatter, chew the fat (*slang*), gossip, jaw (*slang*), natter

chatter *noun* **1** PRATTLE, babble, blather, chat, gab (*informal*), gossip ▶*verb* **2** PRATTLE, babble, blather, chat, chew the fat (*slang*), gab (*informal*), gossip, schmooze (*slang*)

cheap *adjective* **1** INEXPENSIVE, bargain, cut-price, economical, keen, low-cost, low-priced, reasonable, reduced **2** INFERIOR, common, poor, second-rate, shoddy, tatty, tawdry, two a penny, worthless

cheapen *verb* DEGRADE, belittle, debase, demean, denigrate,

depreciate, devalue, discredit, disparage, lower

cheat *verb* **1** DECEIVE, beguile, con (*informal*), defraud, double-cross (*informal*), dupe, fleece, fool, mislead, rip off (*slang*), swindle, trick ▶*noun* **2** DECEIVER, charlatan, con man (*informal*), double-crosser (*informal*), shark, sharper, swindler, trickster **3** DECEPTION, deceit, fraud, rip-off (*slang*), scam (*slang*), swindle, trickery

check *verb* **1** EXAMINE, inquire into, inspect, investigate, look at, make sure, monitor, research, scrutinize, study, test, vet **2** STOP, delay, halt, hinder, impede, inhibit, limit, obstruct, restrain, retard ▶*noun* **3** EXAMINATION, inspection, investigation, once-over (*informal*), research, scrutiny, test **4** STOPPAGE, constraint, control, curb, damper, hindrance, impediment, limitation, obstacle, obstruction, restraint

cheeky *adjective* IMPUDENT, audacious, disrespectful, forward, impertinent, insolent, insulting, pert, saucy

cheer *verb* **1** APPLAUD, acclaim, clap, hail **2** CHEER UP, brighten, buoy up, comfort, encourage, gladden, hearten, uplift ▶*noun* **3** APPLAUSE, acclamation, ovation, plaudits

cheerful *adjective* HAPPY, buoyant, cheery, chirpy (*informal*), enthusiastic, jaunty, jolly, light-hearted, merry, optimistic, upbeat (*informal*)

cheerfulness *noun* HAPPINESS, buoyancy, exuberance, gaiety, geniality, good cheer, good humor, high spirits, jauntiness, light-heartedness

cheerless adjective GLOOMY, bleak, desolate, dismal, drab, dreary, forlorn, miserable, somber, woeful

cheer up verb 1 COMFORT, encourage, enliven, gladden, hearten 2 TAKE HEART, buck up (informal), perk up, rally

cheery adjective CHEERFUL, breezy, carefree, chirpy (informal), genial, good-humored, happy, jovial, upbeat (informal)

chemist noun PHARMACIST, apothecary (obsolete), dispenser

cherish verb 1 CLING TO, cleave to, encourage, entertain, foster, harbor, hold dear, nurture, prize, sustain, treasure 2 CARE FOR, comfort, hold dear, love, nurse, shelter, support

chest noun BOX, case, casket, coffer, crate, strongbox, trunk

chew verb BITE, champ, chomp, crunch, gnaw, grind, masticate, munch

chewy adjective TOUGH, as tough as old boots, leathery

chic adjective STYLISH, cool (informal), elegant, fashionable, phat (slang), smart, trendy (informal)

chide verb Old-fashioned SCOLD, admonish, berate, censure, criticize, lecture, rebuke, reprimand, reproach, reprove, tell off (informal)

chief noun 1 HEAD, boss (informal), captain, commander, director, governor, leader, manager, master, principal, ruler ▶ adjective 2 PRIMARY, foremost,

highest, key, leading, main, predominant, pre-eminent, premier, prime, principal, supreme, uppermost

chiefly adverb 1 ESPECIALLY, above all, essentially, primarily, principally 2 MAINLY, in general, in the main, largely, mostly, on the whole, predominantly, usually

child noun YOUNGSTER, babe, baby, juvenile, kid (informal), minor, offspring, toddler, tot

childbirth noun CHILD-BEARING, confinement, delivery, labor, lying-in, parturition, travail

childhood noun YOUTH, boyhood or girlhood, immaturity, infancy, minority, schooldays

childish adjective IMMATURE, boyish or girlish, foolish, infantile, juvenile, puerile, young

childlike adjective INNOCENT, artless, guileless, ingenuous, naive, simple, trusting

chill noun 1 COLD, bite, coldness, coolness, crispness, frigidity, nip, rawness, sharpness ▶ verb 2 COOL, freeze, refrigerate 3 DISHEARTEN, dampen, deject, depress, discourage, dismay ▶ adjective 4 COLD, biting, bleak, chilly, freezing, frigid, raw, sharp, wintry

chilly adjective 1 COOL, brisk, crisp, drafty, fresh, nippy, penetrating, sharp 2 UNFRIENDLY, frigid, hostile, unresponsive, unsympathetic, unwelcoming

chime verb, noun RING, clang, jingle, peal, sound, tinkle, toll

china noun POTTERY, ceramics,

crockery, porcelain, service, tableware, ware

chink noun OPENING, aperture, cleft, crack, cranny, crevice, fissure, gap

chip noun 1 SCRATCH, fragment, nick, notch, shard, shaving, sliver, wafer ▶ verb 2 NICK, chisel, damage, gash, whittle

chirp verb CHIRRUP, cheep, peep, pipe, tweet, twitter, warble

chivalrous adjective COURTEOUS, bold, brave, courageous, gallant, gentlemanly, honorable, valiant

chivalry noun COURTESY, courage, gallantry, gentlemanliness, knight-errantry, knighthood, politeness

choice noun 1 OPTION, alternative, pick, preference, say 2 SELECTION, range, variety ▶ adjective 3 BEST, elite, excellent, exclusive, prime, rare, select

choke verb 1 STRANGLE, asphyxiate, gag, overpower, smother, stifle, suffocate, suppress, throttle 2 BLOCK, bar, bung, clog, congest, constrict, obstruct, stop

choose verb PICK, adopt, designate, elect, opt for, prefer, select, settle upon

choosy adjective FUSSY, discriminating, faddy, fastidious, finicky, particular, picky (informal), selective

chop verb CUT, cleave, fell, hack, hew, lop, sever

chore noun TASK, burden, duty, errand, job

chortle verb, noun CHUCKLE, cackle, crow, guffaw

chorus noun 1 CHOIR, choristers, ensemble, singers, vocalists 2 REFRAIN, burden, response, strain 3 UNISON, accord, concert, harmony

christen verb 1 BAPTIZE 2 NAME, call, designate, dub, style, term, title

Christmas noun FESTIVE SEASON, Noel, Xmas, Yule, Yuletide

chronicle noun 1 RECORD, account, annals, diary, history, journal, narrative, register, story ▶ verb 2 RECORD, enter, narrate, put on record, recount, register, relate, report, set down, tell

chubby adjective PLUMP, buxom, flabby, portly, rotund, round, stout, tubby

chuckle verb LAUGH, chortle, crow, exult, giggle, snigger, titter

chum noun Informal FRIEND, companion, comrade, crony, homeboy (slang), homegirl (slang), pal (informal)

chunk noun PIECE, block, dollop (informal), hunk, lump, mass, nugget, portion, slab

churlish adjective RUDE, brusque, harsh, ill-tempered, impolite, sullen, surly, uncivil

churn verb STIR UP, agitate, beat, convulse, swirl, toss

cinema noun FILMS, big screen (informal), flicks (slang), motion pictures, movies, pictures

cipher noun 1 CODE, cryptograph 2 NOBODY, nonentity

circle noun 1 RING, disc, globe, orb, sphere 2 GROUP, clique, club, company, coterie, set, society ▶ verb 3 GO ROUND, circumnavigate, circumscribe, encircle, enclose, envelop, ring, surround

circuit *noun* COURSE, journey, lap, orbit, revolution, route, tour, track

circuitous *adjective* INDIRECT, labyrinthine, meandering, oblique, rambling, roundabout, tortuous, winding

circular *adjective* 1 ROUND, ring-shaped, rotund, spherical 2 ORBITAL, circuitous, cyclical ▶ *noun* 3 ADVERTISEMENT, notice

circulate *verb* 1 SPREAD, broadcast, disseminate, distribute, issue, make known, promulgate, publicize, publish 2 FLOW, gyrate, radiate, revolve, rotate

circulation *noun* 1 BLOODSTREAM 2 FLOW, circling, motion, rotation 3 DISTRIBUTION, currency, dissemination, spread, transmission

circumference *noun* BOUNDARY, border, edge, extremity, limits, outline, perimeter, periphery, rim

circumstance *noun* EVENT, accident, condition, contingency, happening, incident, occurrence, particular, respect, situation

circumstances *plural noun* SITUATION, means, position, state, state of affairs, station, status

cistern *noun* TANK, basin, reservoir, sink, vat

citadel *noun* FORTRESS, bastion, fortification, keep, stronghold, tower

cite *verb* QUOTE, adduce, advance, allude to, enumerate, extract, mention, name, specify

citizen *noun* INHABITANT, denizen, dweller, resident, subject, townsman

city *noun* TOWN, conurbation, metropolis, municipality

civic *adjective* PUBLIC, communal, local, municipal

civil *adjective* 1 CIVIC, domestic, municipal, political 2 POLITE, affable, courteous, obliging, refined, urbane, well-mannered

civilization *noun* 1 CULTURE, advancement, cultivation, development, education, enlightenment, progress, refinement, sophistication 2 SOCIETY, community, nation, people, polity

civilize *verb* CULTIVATE, educate, enlighten, refine, sophisticate, tame

civilized *adjective* CULTURED, educated, enlightened, humane, polite, sophisticated, tolerant, urbane

claim *verb* 1 ASSERT, allege, challenge, insist, maintain, profess, uphold 2 DEMAND, ask, call for, insist, need, require ▶ *noun* 3 ASSERTION, affirmation, allegation, pretension, privilege, protestation 4 DEMAND, application, call, petition, request, requirement 5 RIGHT, title

clairvoyant *noun* 1 PSYCHIC, diviner, fortune-teller, visionary ▶ *adjective* 2 PSYCHIC, extrasensory, second-sighted, telepathic, visionary

clamber *verb* CLIMB, claw, scale, scrabble, scramble, shin

clammy *adjective* MOIST, close, damp, dank, sticky, sweaty

clamor *noun* NOISE, commotion,

din, hubbub, outcry, racket, shouting, uproar

clamp *noun* **1** VICE, bracket, fastener, grip, press ▶*verb* **2** FASTEN, brace, fix, make fast, secure

clan *noun* FAMILY, brotherhood, faction, fraternity, group, society, tribe

clandestine *adjective* SECRET, cloak-and-dagger, concealed, covert, furtive, private, stealthy, surreptitious, underground

clap *verb* APPLAUD, acclaim, cheer

clarification *noun* EXPLANATION, elucidation, exposition, illumination, interpretation, simplification

clarify *verb* EXPLAIN, clear up, elucidate, illuminate, interpret, make plain, simplify, throw *or* shed light on

clarity *noun* CLEARNESS, definition, limpidity, lucidity, precision, simplicity, transparency

clash *verb* **1** CONFLICT, cross swords, feud, grapple, lock horns, quarrel, war, wrangle **2** CRASH, bang, clang, clank, clatter, jangle, jar, rattle ▶*noun* **3** CONFLICT, brush, collision, confrontation, difference of opinion, disagreement, fight, showdown (*informal*)

clasp *noun* **1** FASTENING, brooch, buckle, catch, clip, fastener, grip, hook, pin **2** GRASP, embrace, grip, hold, hug ▶*verb* **3** GRASP, clutch, embrace, grip, hold, hug, press, seize, squeeze **4** FASTEN, connect

class *noun* **1** GROUP, category, division, genre, kind, set, sort, type ▶*verb* **2** CLASSIFY, brand,

categorize, designate, grade, group, label, rank, rate

classic *adjective* **1** DEFINITIVE, archetypal, exemplary, ideal, model, quintessential, standard **2** TYPICAL, characteristic, regular, standard, time-honored, usual **3** BEST, consummate, finest, first-rate, masterly, world-class **4** LASTING, abiding, ageless, deathless, enduring, immortal, undying ▶*noun* **5** STANDARD, exemplar, masterpiece, model, paradigm, prototype **6** comical *Informal* HILARIOUS, hysterical, ludicrous, uproarious

classical *adjective* PURE, elegant, harmonious, refined, restrained, symmetrical, understated, well-proportioned

classification *noun* CATEGORIZATION, analysis, arrangement, grading, sorting, taxonomy

classify *verb* CATEGORIZE, arrange, catalog, grade, pigeonhole, rank, sort, systematize, tabulate

classy *adjective Informal* HIGH-CLASS, elegant, exclusive, ritzy, stylish, superior, swanky, top-drawer, up-market

clause *noun* SECTION, article, chapter, condition, paragraph, part, passage

claw *noun* **1** NAIL, pincer, talon, tentacle ▶*verb* **2** SCRATCH, dig, lacerate, maul, rip, scrape, tear

clean *adjective* **1** PURE, flawless, fresh, immaculate, impeccable, spotless, unblemished, unsullied **2** HYGIENIC, antiseptic, decontaminated, purified, sterile, sterilized, uncontaminated, unpolluted **3** MORAL, chaste, decent, good, honorable, innocent, pure, respectable, upright, virtuous **4** COMPLETE, conclusive, decisive, entire, final, perfect, thorough, total, unimpaired, whole ▶ *verb* **5** CLEANSE, disinfect, launder, purge, purify, rinse, sanitize, scour, scrub, wash

cleanse *verb* CLEAN, absolve, clear, purge, purify, rinse, scour, scrub, wash

cleanser *noun* DETERGENT, disinfectant, purifier, scourer, soap, solvent

clear *adjective* **1** CERTAIN, convinced, decided, definite, positive, resolved, satisfied, sure **2** OBVIOUS, apparent, blatant, comprehensible, conspicuous, distinct, evident, manifest, palpable, plain, pronounced, recognizable, unmistakable **3** TRANSPARENT, crystalline, glassy, limpid, pellucid, see-through, translucent **4** BRIGHT, cloudless, fair, fine, light, luminous, shining, sunny, unclouded **5** UNOBSTRUCTED, empty, free, open, smooth, unhindered, unimpeded **6** UNBLEMISHED, clean, immaculate, innocent, pure, untarnished ▶ *verb* **7** UNBLOCK, disentangle, extricate, free, loosen, open, rid, unload **8** PASS OVER, jump, leap, miss, vault **9** BRIGHTEN, break up, lighten **10** CLEAN, cleanse, erase, purify, refine, sweep away, tidy (up), wipe **11** ABSOLVE, acquit, excuse, exonerate, justify, vindicate **12** GAIN, acquire, earn, make, reap, secure

clear-cut *adjective*

STRAIGHTFORWARD, black-and-white, cut-and-dried (*informal*), definite, explicit, plain, precise, specific, unambiguous, unequivocal

clearly *adverb* OBVIOUSLY, beyond doubt, distinctly, evidently, markedly, openly, overtly, undeniably, undoubtedly

clergy *noun* PRIESTHOOD, churchmen, clergymen, clerics, holy orders, ministry, the cloth

clergyman *noun* MINISTER, chaplain, cleric, man of God, man of the cloth, padre, parson, pastor, priest, vicar

clever *adjective* INTELLIGENT, bright, gifted, ingenious, knowledgeable, quick-witted, resourceful, shrewd, smart, talented

cleverness *noun* INTELLIGENCE, ability, brains, ingenuity, quick wits, resourcefulness, shrewdness, smartness

cliché *noun* PLATITUDE, banality, commonplace, hackneyed phrase, stereotype, truism

client *noun* CUSTOMER, applicant, buyer, consumer, patient, patron, shopper

clientele *noun* CUSTOMERS, business, clients, following, market, patronage, regulars, trade

cliff *noun* ROCK FACE, bluff, crag, escarpment, overhang, precipice, scar, scarp

climactic *adjective* CRUCIAL, critical, decisive, paramount, peak

climate *noun* WEATHER, temperature

climax *noun* CULMINATION, height, highlight, high point, peak, summit, top, zenith

climb *verb* ASCEND, clamber, mount, rise, scale, shin up, soar, top

climb down *verb* 1 DESCEND, dismount 2 BACK DOWN, eat one's words, retract, retreat

clinch *verb* SETTLE, conclude, confirm, decide, determine, seal, secure, set the seal on, sew up (*informal*)

cling *verb* STICK, adhere, clasp, clutch, embrace, grasp, grip, hug

clinical *adjective* UNEMOTIONAL, analytic, cold, detached, dispassionate, impersonal, objective, scientific

clip¹ *verb* 1 TRIM, crop, curtail, cut, pare, prune, shear, shorten, snip ▶ *noun, verb* 2 *Informal* SMACK, clout (*informal*), cuff, knock, punch, strike, thump, wallop (*informal*), whack

clip² *verb* ATTACH, fasten, fix, hold, pin, staple

clique *noun* GROUP, cabal, circle, coterie, faction, gang, set

cloak *noun* 1 CAPE, coat, mantle, wrap ▶ *verb* 2 COVER, camouflage, conceal, disguise, hide, mask, obscure, screen, veil

clog *verb* OBSTRUCT, block, congest, hinder, impede, jam

close¹ *verb* 1 SHUT, bar, block, lock, plug, seal, secure, stop up 2 END, cease, complete, conclude, finish, shut down, terminate, wind up 3 CONNECT, come together, couple, fuse, join, unite ▶ *noun* 4 END, completion, conclusion, culmination, denouement, ending, finale, finish

close² *adjective* 1 NEAR, adjacent, adjoining, at hand, cheek by jowl, handy, impending, nearby, neighboring, nigh 2 INTIMATE, attached, confidential, dear, devoted, familiar, inseparable, loving 3 CAREFUL, detailed, intense, minute, painstaking, rigorous, thorough 4 COMPACT, congested, crowded, dense, impenetrable, jam-packed, packed, tight 5 STIFLING, airless, heavy, humid, muggy, oppressive, stuffy, suffocating, sweltering 6 SECRETIVE, private, reticent, secret, taciturn, uncommunicative 7 MEAN, miserly, stingy

closed *adjective* 1 SHUT, fastened, locked, out of service, sealed 2 EXCLUSIVE, restricted 3 FINISHED, concluded, decided, ended, over, resolved, settled, terminated

cloth *noun* FABRIC, material, textiles

clothe *verb* DRESS, array, attire, cover, drape, equip, fit out, garb, robe, swathe

clothes *plural noun* CLOTHING, apparel, attire, costume, dress, garb, garments, gear (*informal*), outfit, wardrobe, wear

clothing *noun* CLOTHES, apparel, attire, costume, dress, garb, garments, gear (*informal*), outfit, wardrobe, wear

cloud *noun* 1 MIST, gloom, haze, murk, vapor ▶ *verb* 2 OBSCURE, becloud, darken, dim, eclipse, obfuscate, overshadow, shade, shadow, veil 3 CONFUSE, disorient, distort, impair, muddle, muddy the waters

cloudy *adjective* 1 DULL, dim, gloomy, leaden, louring *or* lowering, overcast, somber, sunless 2 OPAQUE, muddy, murky

clout *Informal* ▶ *noun* 1 INFLUENCE, authority, power, prestige, pull, weight ▶ *verb* 2 HIT, clobber (*slang*), punch, sock (*slang*), strike, thump, wallop (*informal*)

clown *noun* 1 COMEDIAN, buffoon, comic, fool, harlequin, jester, joker, prankster ▶ *verb* 2 PLAY THE FOOL, act the fool, jest, mess about

club *noun* 1 ASSOCIATION, company, fraternity, group, guild, lodge, set, society, union 2 STICK, bat, bludgeon, cudgel, truncheon ▶ *verb* 3 BEAT, bash, batter, bludgeon, hammer, pummel, strike

clue *noun* INDICATION, evidence, hint, lead, pointer, sign, suggestion, suspicion, trace

clueless *adjective* STUPID, dim, dull, half-witted, simple, slow, thick, unintelligent, witless

clump *noun* 1 CLUSTER, bunch, bundle, group, mass ▶ *verb* 2 STOMP, lumber, plod, thud, thump, tramp

clumsy *adjective* AWKWARD, bumbling, gauche, gawky, lumbering, maladroit, ponderous, uncoordinated, ungainly, unwieldy

cluster *noun* 1 GATHERING, assemblage, batch, bunch, clump, collection, group, knot ▶ *verb* 2 GATHER, assemble, bunch, collect, flock, group

clutch *verb* SEIZE, catch, clasp, cling to, embrace, grab, grasp, grip, snatch

clutches *plural noun* POWER, claws, control, custody, grasp, grip, hands, keeping, possession, sway

clutter *verb* 1 LITTER, scatter, strew ▶ *noun* 2 UNTIDINESS, confusion, disarray, disorder, jumble, litter, mess, muddle

coach *noun* 1 BUS, car, carriage, charabanc, vehicle 2 INSTRUCTOR, handler, teacher, trainer, tutor ▶ *verb* 3 INSTRUCT, drill, exercise, prepare, train, tutor

coalesce *verb* BLEND, amalgamate, combine, fuse, incorporate, integrate, merge, mix, unite

coalition *noun* ALLIANCE, amalgamation, association, bloc, combination, confederation, conjunction, fusion, merger, union

coarse *adjective* 1 ROUGH, crude, homespun, impure, unfinished, unpolished, unprocessed, unpurified, unrefined 2 VULGAR, earthy, improper, indecent, indelicate, ribald, rude, smutty

coarseness *noun* 1 ROUGHNESS, crudity, unevenness 2 VULGARITY, bawdiness, crudity, earthiness, indelicacy, ribaldry, smut, uncouthness

coast *noun* 1 SHORE, beach, border, coastline, seaboard, seaside ▶ *verb* 2 CRUISE, drift, freewheel, glide, sail, taxi

coat *noun* 1 FUR, fleece, hair, hide, pelt, skin, wool 2 LAYER, coating, covering, overlay ▶ *verb* 3 COVER, apply, plaster, smear, spread

coax *verb* PERSUADE, allure, cajole, entice, prevail upon, sweet-talk (*informal*), talk into, wheedle

cocktail *noun* MIXTURE, blend, combination, mix

cocky *adjective* OVERCONFIDENT, arrogant, brash, cocksure, conceited, egotistical, full of oneself, swaggering, vain

code *noun* 1 CIPHER, cryptograph 2 PRINCIPLES, canon, convention, custom, ethics, etiquette, manners, maxim, regulations, rules, system

cogent *adjective* CONVINCING, compelling, effective, forceful, influential, potent, powerful, strong, weighty

cogitate *verb* THINK, consider, contemplate, deliberate, meditate, mull over, muse, ponder, reflect, ruminate

coherent *adjective* 1 CONSISTENT, logical, lucid, meaningful, orderly, organized, rational, reasoned, systematic 2 INTELLIGIBLE, articulate, comprehensible

coil *verb* WIND, curl, loop, snake, spiral, twine, twist, wreathe, writhe

coin *noun* 1 MONEY, cash, change, copper, silver, specie ▸ *verb* 2 INVENT, create, fabricate, forge, make up, mint, mold, originate

coincide *verb* 1 OCCUR SIMULTANEOUSLY, be concurrent, coexist, synchronize 2 AGREE, accord, concur, correspond, harmonize, match, square, tally

coincidence *noun* 1 CHANCE, accident, fluke, happy accident, luck, stroke of luck 2 COINCIDING, concurrence, conjunction, correlation, correspondence

coincidental *adjective* CHANCE, accidental, casual, fluky (*informal*), fortuitous, unintentional, unplanned

cold *adjective* 1 CHILLY, arctic, bleak, cool, freezing, frigid, frosty, frozen, icy, wintry 2 UNFRIENDLY, aloof, distant, frigid, indifferent, reserved, standoffish ▸ *noun* 3 COLDNESS, chill, frigidity, frostiness, iciness

cold-blooded *adjective* CALLOUS, dispassionate, heartless, ruthless, steely, stony-hearted, unemotional, unfeeling

collaborate *verb* 1 WORK TOGETHER, cooperate, join forces, participate, play ball (*informal*), team up 2 CONSPIRE, collude, cooperate, fraternize

collaboration *noun* TEAMWORK, alliance, association, cooperation, partnership

collaborator *noun* 1 CO-WORKER, associate, colleague, confederate, partner, team-mate 2 TRAITOR, fraternizer, quisling, turncoat

collapse *verb* 1 FALL DOWN, cave in, crumple, fall, fall apart at the seams, give way, subside 2 FAIL, come to nothing, fold, founder, go belly-up (*informal*) ▸ *noun* 3 FALLING DOWN, cave-in, disintegration, falling apart, ruin, subsidence 4 FAILURE, downfall, flop, slump 5 FAINT, breakdown, exhaustion, prostration

collar *verb* Informal SEIZE, apprehend, arrest, capture, catch, grab, nail (*informal*)

colleague *noun* FELLOW WORKER, ally, assistant, associate, collaborator, comrade, helper, partner, team-mate, workmate

collect verb 1 ASSEMBLE, cluster, congregate, convene, converge, flock together, rally 2 GATHER, accumulate, amass, assemble, heap, hoard, save, stockpile

collected adjective CALM, composed, cool, poised, self-possessed, serene, unperturbed, unruffled

collection noun 1 ACCUMULATION, anthology, compilation, heap, hoard, mass, pile, set, stockpile, store 2 GROUP, assembly, assortment, cluster, company, crowd 3 CONTRIBUTION, alms, offering, offertory

collective adjective COMBINED, aggregate, composite, corporate, cumulative, joint, shared, unified, united

collide verb 1 CRASH, clash, come into collision, meet head-on 2 CONFLICT, clash

collision noun 1 CRASH, accident, bump, impact, pile-up (informal), smash 2 CONFLICT, clash, confrontation, encounter, opposition, skirmish

colloquial adjective INFORMAL, conversational, demotic, everyday, familiar, idiomatic, vernacular

colony noun SETTLEMENT, community, dependency, dominion, outpost, possession, province, satellite state, territory

color noun 1 HUE, colorant, dye, paint, pigment, shade, tint ▶verb 2 PAINT, dye, stain, tinge, tint 3 BLUSH, flush, redden

colorful adjective 1 BRIGHT, brilliant, multicolored, psychedelic, variegated 2 INTERESTING, distinctive, graphic, lively, picturesque, rich, vivid

colorless adjective 1 DRAB, achromatic, anemic, ashen, bleached, faded, wan, washed out 2 UNINTERESTING, characterless, dreary, dull, insipid, lackluster, vapid

colossal adjective HUGE, enormous, gigantic, immense, mammoth, massive, monumental, prodigious, vast

column noun 1 PILLAR, obelisk, post, shaft, support, upright 2 LINE, cavalcade, file, procession, rank, row

coma noun UNCONSCIOUSNESS, oblivion, stupor, trance

comb verb 1 UNTANGLE, arrange, dress, groom 2 SEARCH, forage, hunt, rake, ransack, rummage, scour, sift

combat noun 1 FIGHT, action, battle, conflict, contest, encounter, engagement, skirmish, struggle, war, warfare ▶verb 2 FIGHT, defy, do battle with, oppose, resist, withstand

combatant noun FIGHTER, adversary, antagonist, enemy, opponent, soldier, warrior

combination noun 1 MIXTURE, amalgamation, blend, coalescence, composite, connection, mix 2 ASSOCIATION, alliance, coalition, confederation, consortium, federation, syndicate, union

combine verb JOIN TOGETHER, amalgamate, blend, connect, integrate, link, merge, mix, pool, unite

come *verb* 1 MOVE TOWARDS, advance, approach, draw near, near 2 ARRIVE, appear, enter, materialize, reach, show up (*informal*), turn up (*informal*) 3 HAPPEN, fall, occur, take place 4 RESULT, arise, emanate, emerge, flow, issue, originate 5 REACH, extend 6 BE AVAILABLE, be made, be offered, be on offer, be produced

come about *verb* HAPPEN, arise, befall, come to pass, occur, result, take place, transpire (*informal*)

come across *verb* FIND, bump into (*informal*), chance upon, discover, encounter, meet, notice, stumble upon, unearth

comeback *noun* 1 *Informal* RETURN, rally, rebound, recovery, resurgence, revival, triumph 2 RESPONSE, rejoinder, reply, retaliation, retort, riposte

come back *verb* RETURN, reappear, recur, re-enter

comedian *noun* COMIC, card (*informal*), clown, funny man, humorist, jester, joker, wag, wit

comedown *noun* 1 DECLINE, deflation, demotion, reverse 2 *Informal* DISAPPOINTMENT, anticlimax, blow, humiliation, letdown

comedy *noun* HUMOR, farce, fun, hilarity, jesting, joking, light entertainment

comfort *noun* 1 LUXURY, cosiness, ease, opulence, snugness, wellbeing 2 RELIEF, compensation, consolation, help, succor, support ▸ *verb* 3 CONSOLE, commiserate with, hearten, reassure, soothe

comfortable *adjective* 1 RELAXING, agreeable, convenient, cozy, homely, homey, pleasant, restful, snug 2 HAPPY, at ease, at home, contented, gratified, relaxed, serene 3 *Informal* WELL-OFF, affluent, in clover (*informal*), prosperous, well-to-do

comforting *adjective* CONSOLING, cheering, consolatory, encouraging, heart-warming, reassuring, soothing

comic *adjective* 1 FUNNY, amusing, comical, droll, farcical, humorous, jocular, witty ▸ *noun* 2 COMEDIAN, buffoon, clown, funny man, humorist, jester, wag, wit

comical *adjective* FUNNY, amusing, comic, droll, farcical, hilarious, humorous, priceless, side-splitting

coming *adjective* 1 APPROACHING, at hand, forthcoming, imminent, impending, in store, near, nigh ▸ *noun* 2 ARRIVAL, advent, approach

command *verb* 1 ORDER, bid, charge, compel, demand, direct, require 2 HAVE AUTHORITY OVER, control, dominate, govern, handle, head, lead, manage, rule, supervise ▸ *noun* 3 ORDER, commandment, decree, demand, directive, instruction, requirement, ultimatum 4 AUTHORITY, charge, control, government, management, mastery, power, rule, supervision

commandeer *verb* SEIZE, appropriate, confiscate, requisition, sequester, sequestrate

commander noun OFFICER, boss (*informal*), captain, chief, commanding officer, head, leader, ruler

commanding adjective CONTROLLING, advantageous, decisive, dominant, dominating, superior

commemorate verb REMEMBER, celebrate, honor, immortalize, pay tribute to, salute

commemoration noun REMEMBRANCE, ceremony, honoring, memorial service, tribute

commence verb BEGIN, embark on, enter upon, initiate, open, originate, start

commend verb PRAISE, acclaim, applaud, approve, compliment, extol, recommend, speak highly of

commendable adjective PRAISEWORTHY, admirable, creditable, deserving, estimable, exemplary, laudable, meritorious, worthy

commendation noun PRAISE, acclaim, acclamation, approbation, approval, credit, encouragement, good opinion, kudos, panegyric, recommendation

comment noun 1 REMARK, observation, statement 2 NOTE, annotation, commentary, explanation, exposition, illustration ▶ verb 3 REMARK, mention, note, observe, point out, say, utter 4 ANNOTATE, elucidate, explain, interpret

commentary noun 1 NARRATION, description, voice-over 2 NOTES, analysis, critique, explanation, review, treatise

commentator noun 1 REPORTER, special correspondent, sportscaster 2 CRITIC, annotator, interpreter

commerce noun TRADE, business, dealing, exchange, traffic

commercial adjective 1 MERCANTILE, trading 2 MATERIALISTIC, mercenary, profit-making ▶ noun 3 ADVERTISEMENT, ad (*informal*), announcement, plug (*informal*)

commiserate verb SYMPATHIZE, console, feel for, pity

commission noun 1 DUTY, errand, mandate, mission, task 2 FEE, cut, percentage, rake-off (*slang*), royalties 3 COMMITTEE, board, commissioners, delegation, deputation, representatives ▶ verb 4 APPOINT, authorize, contract, delegate, depute, empower, engage, nominate, order, select

commit verb 1 DO, carry out, enact, execute, perform, perpetrate 2 PUT IN CUSTODY, confine, imprison

commitment noun 1 DEDICATION, devotion, involvement, loyalty 2 RESPONSIBILITY, duty, engagement, liability, obligation, tie

common adjective 1 AVERAGE, commonplace, conventional, customary, everyday, familiar, frequent, habitual, ordinary, regular, routine, standard, stock, usual 2 POPULAR, accepted, general, prevailing, prevalent, universal, widespread 3 COLLECTIVE, communal, popular, public, social 4 VULGAR, coarse, inferior, plebeian

commonplace *adjective*
1 EVERYDAY, banal, common, humdrum, mundane, obvious, ordinary, widespread ▶ *noun*
2 CLICHÉ, banality, platitude, truism

common sense *noun* GOOD SENSE, horse sense, level-headedness, native intelligence, prudence, sound judgment, wit

commotion *noun* DISTURBANCE, disorder, excitement, furor, fuss, hue and cry, rumpus, tumult, turmoil, upheaval, uproar

communal *adjective* PUBLIC, collective, general, joint, shared

commune *noun* COMMUNITY, collective, cooperative, kibbutz

commune with *verb* CONTEMPLATE, meditate on, muse on, ponder, reflect on

communicate *verb* MAKE KNOWN, convey, declare, disclose, impart, inform, pass on, proclaim, transmit

communication *noun* 1 PASSING ON, contact, conversation, correspondence, dissemination, link, transmission 2 MESSAGE, announcement, disclosure, dispatch, information, news, report, statement, word

communicative *adjective* TALKATIVE, chatty, expansive, forthcoming, frank, informative, loquacious, open, outgoing, voluble

Communism *noun* SOCIALISM, Bolshevism, collectivism, Marxism, state socialism

Communist *noun* SOCIALIST, Bolshevik, collectivist, Marxist, Red (*informal*)

community *noun* SOCIETY, brotherhood, commonwealth, company, general public, people, populace, public, residents, state

commuter *noun* DAILY TRAVELER, straphanger (*informal*), suburbanite

compact[1] *adjective* 1 CLOSELY PACKED, compressed, condensed, dense, pressed together, solid, thick 2 BRIEF, compendious, concise, succinct, terse, to the point ▶ *verb* 3 PACK CLOSELY, compress, condense, cram, stuff, tamp

compact[2] *noun* AGREEMENT, arrangement, bargain, bond, contract, covenant, deal, pact, treaty, understanding

companion *noun* 1 FRIEND, accomplice, ally, associate, colleague, comrade, consort, homeboy (*slang*), homegirl (*slang*), mate (*informal*), partner 2 ESCORT, aide, assistant, attendant, chaperon, squire

companionship *noun* FELLOWSHIP, camaraderie, company, comradeship, conviviality, esprit de corps, friendship, rapport, togetherness

company *noun* 1 BUSINESS, association, concern, corporation, establishment, firm, house, partnership, syndicate 2 GROUP, assembly, band, collection, community, crowd, gathering, party, set 3 GUESTS, callers, party, visitors

comparable *adjective* 1 ON A PAR, a match for, as good as, commensurate, equal, equivalent, in a class with, on a level playing field (*informal*), proportionate, tantamount **2** SIMILAR, akin, alike, analogous, cognate, corresponding, cut from the same cloth, of a piece, related

comparative *adjective* RELATIVE, by comparison, qualified

compare *verb* **1** WEIGH, balance, contrast, juxtapose, set against **2** (usually with *with*) BE ON A PAR WITH, approach, bear comparison, be in the same class as, be the equal of, compete with, equal, hold a candle to, match **3 compare to** LIKEN TO, correlate to, equate to, identify with, mention in the same breath as, parallel, resemble

comparison *noun* **1** CONTRAST, distinction, juxtaposition **2** SIMILARITY, analogy, comparability, correlation, likeness, resemblance

compartment *noun* SECTION, alcove, bay, berth, booth, carriage, cubbyhole, cubicle, locker, niche, pigeonhole

compass *noun* RANGE, area, boundary, circumference, extent, field, limit, reach, realm, scope

compassion *noun* SYMPATHY, condolence, fellow feeling, humanity, kindness, mercy, pity, sorrow, tender-heartedness, tenderness, understanding

compassionate *adjective* SYMPATHETIC, benevolent, charitable, humane, humanitarian, kind-hearted, merciful, pitying, tender-hearted, understanding

compatibility *noun* HARMONY, affinity, agreement, concord, empathy, like-mindedness, rapport, sympathy

compatible *adjective* HARMONIOUS, adaptable, congruous, consistent, in harmony, in keeping, suitable

compel *verb* FORCE, coerce, constrain, dragoon, impel, make, oblige, railroad (*informal*)

compelling *adjective* **1** FASCINATING, enchanting, enthralling, gripping, hypnotic, irresistible, mesmeric, spellbinding **2** PRESSING, binding, coercive, imperative, overriding, peremptory, unavoidable, urgent **3** CONVINCING, cogent, conclusive, forceful, irrefutable, powerful, telling, weighty

compensate *verb* **1** RECOMPENSE, atone, make amends, make good, refund, reimburse, remunerate, repay **2** CANCEL (OUT), balance, counteract, counterbalance, make up for, offset, redress

compensation *noun* RECOMPENSE, amends, atonement, damages, reimbursement, remuneration, reparation, restitution, satisfaction

compete *verb* CONTEND, be in the running, challenge, contest, fight, strive, struggle, vie

competence *noun* ABILITY, capability, capacity, expertise, fitness, proficiency, skill, suitability

competent *adjective* ABLE, adequate, capable, fit, proficient, qualified, suitable

competition *noun* 1 RIVALRY, opposition, strife, struggle 2 CONTEST, championship, event, head-to-head, puzzle, quiz, tournament 3 OPPOSITION, challengers, field, rivals

competitive *adjective* 1 CUT-THROAT, aggressive, antagonistic, at odds, dog-eat-dog, opposing, rival 2 AMBITIOUS, combative

competitor *noun* CONTESTANT, adversary, antagonist, challenger, opponent, rival

compilation *noun* COLLECTION, accumulation, anthology, assemblage, assortment, treasury

compile *verb* PUT TOGETHER, accumulate, amass, collect, cull, garner, gather, marshal, organize

complacency *noun* SELF-SATISFACTION, contentment, satisfaction, smugness

complacent *adjective* SELF-SATISFIED, contented, pleased with oneself, resting on one's laurels, satisfied, serene, smug, unconcerned

complain *verb* FIND FAULT, bemoan, bewail, carp, deplore, groan, grouse, grumble, lament, moan, whine

complaint *noun* 1 CRITICISM, charge, grievance, gripe (*informal*), grouse, grumble, lament, moan, protest 2 ILLNESS, affliction, ailment, disease, disorder, malady, sickness, upset

complement *noun* 1 COMPLETION, companion, consummation, counterpart, finishing touch, rounding-off,

supplement 2 TOTAL, aggregate, capacity, entirety, quota, totality, wholeness ▶*verb* 3 COMPLETE, cap (*informal*), crown, round off, set off

complementary *adjective* COMPLETING, companion, corresponding, interdependent, interrelating, matched, reciprocal

complete *adjective* 1 TOTAL, absolute, consummate, outright, perfect, thorough, thoroughgoing, utter 2 FINISHED, accomplished, achieved, concluded, ended 3 ENTIRE, all, faultless, full, intact, plenary, unbroken, whole ▶*verb* 4 FINISH, close, conclude, crown, end, finalize, round off, settle, wind up (*informal*), wrap up (*informal*)

completely *adverb* TOTALLY, absolutely, altogether, entirely, every inch, fully, hook, line and sinker, in full, lock, stock and barrel, one hundred per cent, perfectly, thoroughly, utterly, wholly

completion *noun* FINISHING, bitter end, close, conclusion, culmination, end, fruition, fulfillment

complex *adjective* 1 COMPOUND, composite, heterogeneous, manifold, multifarious, multiple 2 COMPLICATED, convoluted, elaborate, intricate, involved, labyrinthine, tangled, tortuous ▶*noun* 3 STRUCTURE, aggregate, composite, network, organization, scheme, system 4 OBSESSION, fixation, fixed idea, *idée fixe*, phobia, preoccupation

complexion *noun* 1 SKIN, color, coloring, hue, pigmentation, skin tone 2 NATURE, appearance, aspect, character, guise, light, look, make-up

complexity noun COMPLICATION, elaboration, entanglement, intricacy, involvement, ramification

complicate verb MAKE DIFFICULT, confuse, entangle, involve, muddle, ravel

complicated adjective
1 DIFFICULT, involved, perplexing, problematic, puzzling, troublesome
2 INVOLVED, complex, convoluted, elaborate, intricate, labyrinthine

complication noun
1 COMPLEXITY, confusion, entanglement, intricacy, web
2 PROBLEM, difficulty, drawback, embarrassment, obstacle, snag

compliment noun 1 PRAISE, bouquet, commendation, congratulations, eulogy, flattery, honor, tribute ▸ verb
2 PRAISE, brown-nose (slang), commend, congratulate, extol, flatter, pay tribute to, salute, speak highly of

complimentary adjective
1 FLATTERING, appreciative, approving, commendatory, congratulatory, laudatory
2 FREE, courtesy, donated, gratis, gratuitous, honorary, on the house

compliments plural noun GREETINGS, good wishes, regards, remembrances, respects, salutation

comply verb OBEY, abide by, acquiesce, adhere to, conform to, follow, observe, submit, toe the line

component noun 1 PART, constituent, element, ingredient, item, piece, unit
▸ adjective 2 CONSTITUENT, inherent, intrinsic

compose verb 1 PUT TOGETHER, build, comprise, constitute, construct, fashion, form, make, make up 2 CREATE, contrive, devise, invent, produce, write
3 CALM, collect, control, pacify, placate, quiet, soothe
4 ARRANGE, adjust

composed adjective CALM, at ease, collected, cool, level-headed, poised, relaxed, sedate, self-possessed, serene, unflappable

composition noun 1 CREATION, compilation, fashioning, formation, formulation, making, production, putting together 2 DESIGN, arrangement, configuration, formation, layout, make-up, organization, structure 3 ESSAY, exercise, literary work, opus, piece, treatise, work

composure noun CALMNESS, aplomb, equanimity, poise, sang-froid, self-assurance, self-possession, serenity

compound noun 1 COMBINATION, alloy, amalgam, blend, composite, fusion, medley, mixture, synthesis ▸ verb
2 COMBINE, amalgamate, blend, intermingle, mix, synthesize, unite 3 INTENSIFY, add to, aggravate, augment, complicate, exacerbate, heighten, magnify, worsen
▸ adjective 4 COMPLEX, composite, intricate, multiple

comprehend verb UNDERSTAND, apprehend, conceive, fathom, grasp, know, make out, perceive, see, take in

comprehensible *adjective* UNDERSTANDABLE, clear, coherent, conceivable, explicit, intelligible, plain

comprehension *noun* UNDERSTANDING, conception, discernment, grasp, intelligence, perception, realization

comprehensive *adjective* BROAD, all-embracing, all-inclusive, blanket, complete, encyclopedic, exhaustive, full, inclusive, thorough

compress *verb* SQUEEZE, abbreviate, concentrate, condense, contract, crush, press, shorten, squash

comprise *verb* 1 BE COMPOSED OF, consist of, contain, embrace, encompass, include, take in 2 MAKE UP, compose, constitute, form

compromise *noun* 1 GIVE-AND-TAKE, accommodation, adjustment, agreement, concession, settlement, trade-off ▸*verb* 2 MEET HALFWAY, adjust, agree, concede, give and take, go fifty-fifty (*informal*), settle, strike a balance 3 DISHONOR, discredit, embarrass, expose, jeopardize, prejudice, weaken

compulsion *noun* 1 URGE, drive, necessity, need, obsession, preoccupation 2 FORCE, coercion, constraint, demand, duress, obligation, pressure, urgency

compulsive *adjective* IRRESISTIBLE, compelling, driving, neurotic, obsessive, overwhelming, uncontrollable, urgent

compulsory *adjective* OBLIGATORY, binding, *de rigueur*, forced, imperative, mandatory, required, requisite

compute *verb* CALCULATE, add up, count, enumerate, figure out, reckon, tally, total

comrade *noun* COMPANION, ally, associate, colleague, co-worker, fellow, friend, homeboy (*slang*), homegirl (*slang*), partner

con *Informal* ▸*noun* 1 SWINDLE, deception, fraud, scam (*slang*), sting (*informal*), trick ▸*verb* 2 SWINDLE, cheat, deceive, defraud, double-cross (*informal*), dupe, hoodwink, rip off (*slang*), trick

concave *adjective* HOLLOW, indented

conceal *verb* HIDE, bury, camouflage, cover, disguise, mask, obscure, screen

concede *verb* 1 ADMIT, accept, acknowledge, allow, confess, grant, own 2 GIVE UP, cede, hand over, relinquish, surrender, yield

conceit *noun* SELF-IMPORTANCE, arrogance, egotism, narcissism, pride, swagger, vanity

conceited *adjective* SELF-IMPORTANT, arrogant, bigheaded (*informal*), cocky, egotistical, full of oneself, immodest, narcissistic, too big for one's boots *or* breeches, vain

conceivable *adjective* IMAGINABLE, believable, credible, possible, thinkable

conceive *verb* 1 IMAGINE, believe, comprehend, envisage, fancy, suppose, think, understand 2 THINK UP, contrive, create, design, devise, formulate 3 BECOME PREGNANT, become impregnated

concentrate verb 1 FOCUS ONE'S ATTENTION ON, be engrossed in, put one's mind to, rack one's brains 2 FOCUS, bring to bear, center, cluster, converge 3 GATHER, accumulate, cluster, collect, congregate, huddle

concentrated adjective 1 INTENSE, all-out (informal), deep, hard, intensive 2 CONDENSED, boiled down, evaporated, reduced, rich, thickened, undiluted

concentration noun 1 SINGLE-MINDEDNESS, absorption, application, heed 2 FOCUSING, bringing to bear, centralization, centring, consolidation, convergence, intensification 3 CONVERGENCE, accumulation, aggregation, cluster, collection, horde, mass

concept noun IDEA, abstraction, conception, conceptualization, hypothesis, image, notion, theory, view

conception noun 1 IDEA, concept, design, image, notion, plan 2 IMPREGNATION, fertilization, germination, insemination

concern noun 1 WORRY, anxiety, apprehension, burden, care, disquiet, distress 2 IMPORTANCE, bearing, interest, relevance 3 BUSINESS, affair, interest, job, responsibility, task 4 BUSINESS, company, corporation, enterprise, establishment, firm, organization ▶ verb 5 WORRY, bother, disquiet, distress, disturb, make anxious, perturb, trouble 6 BE RELEVANT TO, affect, apply to, bear on, interest, involve, pertain to, regard, touch

concerned adjective 1 INVOLVED, active, implicated, interested, mixed up, privy to 2 WORRIED, anxious, bothered, distressed, disturbed, troubled, uneasy, upset

concerning preposition REGARDING, about, apropos of, as regards, on the subject of, re, relating to, respecting, touching, with reference to

concession noun 1 GRANT, adjustment, allowance, boon, compromise, indulgence, permit, privilege, sop 2 CONCEDING, acknowledgment, admission, assent, confession, surrender, yielding

conciliate verb PACIFY, appease, clear the air, mediate, mollify, placate, reconcile, soothe, win over

conciliation noun PACIFICATION, appeasement, mollification, placation, reconciliation, soothing

conciliatory adjective PACIFYING, appeasing, mollifying, pacific, peaceable, placatory

concise adjective BRIEF, compendious, condensed, laconic, pithy, short, succinct, terse

conclude verb 1 DECIDE, assume, deduce, gather, infer, judge, surmise, work out 2 END, cease, close, complete, finish, round off, terminate, wind up 3 ACCOMPLISH, bring about, carry out, effect, pull off

conclusion noun 1 DECISION, conviction, deduction, inference, judgment, opinion, verdict 2 END, bitter end, close, completion, ending, finale, finish, result, termination 3 OUTCOME, consequence, culmination, end result, result, upshot

conclusive adjective DECISIVE, clinching, convincing, definite, final, irrefutable, ultimate, unanswerable

concoct verb MAKE UP, brew, contrive, devise, formulate, hatch, invent, prepare, think up

concoction noun MIXTURE, blend, brew, combination, compound, creation, preparation

concrete adjective 1 SPECIFIC, definite, explicit 2 REAL, actual, factual, material, sensible, substantial, tangible

concur verb AGREE, acquiesce, assent, consent

condemn verb 1 DISAPPROVE, blame, censure, damn, denounce, reproach, reprove, upbraid 2 SENTENCE, convict, damn, doom, pass sentence on

condemnation noun 1 DISAPPROVAL, blame, censure, denunciation, reproach, reproof, stricture 2 SENTENCE, conviction, damnation, doom, judgment

condensation noun 1 DISTILLATION, liquefaction, precipitate, precipitation 2 ABRIDGMENT, contraction, digest, précis, synopsis 3 CONCENTRATION, compression, consolidation, crystallization, curtailment, reduction

condense verb 1 ABRIDGE, abbreviate, compress, concentrate, epitomize, shorten, summarize 2 CONCENTRATE, boil down, reduce, thicken

condensed adjective 1 ABRIDGED, compressed, concentrated, shortened, shrunken, slimmed-down, summarized 2 CONCENTRATED, boiled down, reduced, thickened

condescend verb 1 PATRONIZE, talk down to 2 LOWER ONESELF, bend, deign, humble or demean oneself, see fit, stoop

condescending adjective PATRONIZING, disdainful, lofty, lordly, snobbish, snooty (informal), supercilious, superior

condition noun 1 STATE, circumstances, lie of the land, position, shape, situation, state of affairs 2 REQUIREMENT, limitation, prerequisite, proviso, qualification, restriction, rider, stipulation, terms 3 HEALTH, fettle, fitness, kilter, order, shape, state of health, trim 4 AILMENT, complaint, infirmity, malady, problem, weakness ▶verb 5 ACCUSTOM, adapt, equip, prepare, ready, tone up, train, work out

conditional adjective DEPENDENT, contingent, limited, provisional, qualified, subject to, with reservations

conditions plural noun CIRCUMSTANCES, environment, milieu, situation, surroundings, way of life

condone verb OVERLOOK, excuse, forgive, let pass, look the other way, make allowance for, pardon, turn a blind eye to

conduct noun 1 BEHAVIOR,
attitude, bearing, demeanor,
deportment, manners, ways
2 MANAGEMENT, administration,
control, direction, guidance,
handling, organization,
running, supervision ▶ verb
3 CARRY OUT, administer,
control, direct, handle,
manage, organize, preside
over, run, supervise 4 BEHAVE,
acquit, act, carry, comport,
deport 5 ACCOMPANY, convey,
escort, guide, lead, steer, usher

confederacy noun UNION,
alliance, coalition,
confederation, federation,
league

confer verb 1 DISCUSS, consult,
converse, deliberate, discourse,
talk 2 GRANT, accord, award,
bestow, give, hand out, present

conference noun MEETING,
colloquium, congress,
consultation, convention,
discussion, forum, seminar,
symposium

confess verb 1 ADMIT,
acknowledge, come clean
(informal), concede, confide,
disclose, divulge, fess up
(informal), own up 2 DECLARE,
affirm, assert, confirm, profess,
reveal

confession noun ADMISSION,
acknowledgment, disclosure,
exposure, revelation,
unbosoming

confidant, confidante noun
CLOSE FRIEND, alter ego, bosom
friend, crony, familiar, intimate

confide verb 1 TELL, admit,
confess, disclose, divulge,
impart, reveal, whisper

2 Formal ENTRUST, commend,
commit, consign

confidence noun 1 TRUST, belief,
credence, dependence, faith,
reliance 2 SELF-ASSURANCE,
aplomb, assurance, boldness,
courage, firmness, nerve,
self-possession 3 **in confidence**
IN SECRECY, between you and
me (and the gatepost),
confidentially, privately

confident adjective 1 CERTAIN,
convinced, counting on,
positive, satisfied, secure, sure
2 SELF-ASSURED, assured, bold,
dauntless, fearless, self-reliant

confidential adjective SECRET,
classified, hush-hush (informal),
intimate, off the record,
private, privy

confidentially adverb IN SECRET,
behind closed doors, between
ourselves, in camera, in
confidence, personally,
privately, sub rosa

confine verb RESTRICT, cage,
enclose, hem in, hold back,
imprison, incarcerate, intern,
keep, limit, shut up

confinement noun IMPRISONMENT,
custody, detention,
incarceration, internment

confines plural noun LIMITS,
boundaries, bounds,
circumference, edge, precincts

confirm verb 1 PROVE,
authenticate, bear out,
corroborate, endorse, ratify,
substantiate, validate, verify
2 STRENGTHEN, buttress,
establish, fix, fortify, reinforce

confirmation noun 1 PROOF,
authentication, corroboration,
evidence, substantiation,
testimony, validation,

verification **2** SANCTION, acceptance, agreement, approval, assent, endorsement, ratification

confirmed *adjective* LONG-ESTABLISHED, chronic, dyed-in-the-wool, habitual, hardened, ingrained, inveterate, seasoned

confiscate *verb* SEIZE, appropriate, commandeer, impound, sequester, sequestrate

confiscation *noun* SEIZURE, appropriation, forfeiture, impounding, sequestration, takeover

conflict *noun* **1** OPPOSITION, antagonism, difference, disagreement, discord, dissension, friction, hostility, strife **2** BATTLE, clash, combat, contest, encounter, fight, strife, war ▶ *verb* **3** BE INCOMPATIBLE, be at variance, clash, collide, differ, disagree, interfere

conflicting *adjective* INCOMPATIBLE, antagonistic, clashing, contradictory, contrary, discordant, inconsistent, opposing, paradoxical

conform *verb* **1** COMPLY, adapt, adjust, fall in with, follow, obey, toe the line **2** AGREE, accord, correspond, harmonize, match, suit, tally

conformist *noun* TRADITIONALIST, stick-in-the-mud (*informal*), yes man

conformity *noun* COMPLIANCE, conventionality, observance, orthodoxy, traditionalism

confound *verb* BEWILDER, astound, baffle, confuse, dumbfound, flummox, mystify, nonplus, perplex

confront *verb* FACE, accost, challenge, defy, encounter, oppose, stand up to, tackle

confrontation *noun* CONFLICT, contest, encounter, fight, head-to-head, showdown (*informal*)

confuse *verb* **1** MIX UP, disarrange, disorder, jumble, mingle, muddle, ravel **2** BEWILDER, baffle, bemuse, faze, flummox, mystify, nonplus, perplex, puzzle **3** DISCONCERT, discompose, disorient, fluster, rattle (*informal*), throw off balance, unnerve, upset

confused *adjective* **1** BEWILDERED, at sea, baffled, disorientated, flummoxed, muddled, nonplussed, perplexed, puzzled, taken aback **2** DISORDERED, chaotic, disorganized, in disarray, jumbled, mixed up, topsy-turvy, untidy

confusing *adjective* BEWILDERING, baffling, contradictory, disconcerting, misleading, perplexing, puzzling, unclear

confusion *noun* **1** BEWILDERMENT, disorientation, mystification, perplexity, puzzlement **2** DISORDER, chaos, commotion, jumble, mess, muddle, shambles, turmoil, untidiness, upheaval

congenial *adjective* **1** PLEASANT, affable, agreeable, companionable, favorable, friendly, genial, kindly **2** COMPATIBLE, kindred, like-minded, sympathetic, well-suited

congenital *adjective* INBORN,

immanent, inbred, inherent, innate, natural

congested *adjective*
1 OVERCROWDED, crowded, teeming **2** CLOGGED, blocked-up, crammed, jammed, overfilled, overflowing, packed, stuffed

congestion *noun*
1 OVERCROWDING, crowding **2** CLOGGING, bottleneck, jam, surfeit

congratulate *verb* COMPLIMENT, pat on the back, wish joy to

congratulations *plural noun, interjection* GOOD WISHES, best wishes, compliments, felicitations, greetings

congregate *verb* COME TOGETHER, assemble, collect, convene, converge, flock, gather, mass, meet

congregation *noun* ASSEMBLY, brethren, crowd, fellowship, flock, multitude, throng

congress *noun* MEETING, assembly, caucus, conclave, conference, convention, council, legislature, parliament

conjecture *noun* **1** GUESS, hypothesis, shot in the dark, speculation, supposition, surmise, theory ▶ *verb* **2** GUESS, hypothesize, imagine, speculate, suppose, surmise, theorize

conjugal *adjective* MARITAL, bridal, connubial, married, matrimonial, nuptial, wedded

conjure *verb* PERFORM TRICKS, juggle

conjurer, conjuror *noun* MAGICIAN, illusionist, sorcerer, wizard

conjure up *verb* BRING TO MIND,

contrive, create, evoke, produce as if by magic, recall, recollect

connect *verb* LINK, affix, attach, couple, fasten, join, unite

connected *adjective* LINKED, affiliated, akin, allied, associated, combined, coupled, joined, related, united

connection *noun* **1** ASSOCIATION, affinity, bond, liaison, link, relationship, relevance, tie-in **2** LINK, alliance, association, attachment, coupling, fastening, junction, tie, union **3** CONTACT, acquaintance, ally, associate, friend, homeboy (*slang*), homegirl (*slang*), sponsor

connivance *noun* COLLUSION, abetting, complicity, conspiring, tacit consent

connive *verb* **1** CONSPIRE, collude, cook up (*informal*), intrigue, plot, scheme **2 connive at** TURN A BLIND EYE TO, abet, disregard, let pass, look the other way, overlook, wink at

connoisseur *noun* EXPERT, aficionado, appreciator, authority, buff (*informal*), devotee, judge

conquer *verb* **1** DEFEAT, beat, crush, get the better of, master, overcome, overpower, overthrow, quell, subjugate, vanquish **2** SEIZE, acquire, annex, obtain, occupy, overrun, win

conqueror *noun* WINNER, conquistador, defeater, master, subjugator, vanquisher, victor

conquest *noun* **1** DEFEAT, mastery, overthrow, rout,

triumph, victory **2** TAKEOVER, annexation, coup, invasion, occupation, subjugation

conscience noun PRINCIPLES, moral sense, scruples, sense of right and wrong, still small voice

conscientious adjective THOROUGH, careful, diligent, exact, faithful, meticulous, painstaking, particular, punctilious

conscious adjective **1** AWARE, alert, alive to, awake, responsive, sensible, sentient **2** DELIBERATE, calculated, intentional, knowing, premeditated, self-conscious, studied, willful

consciousness noun AWARENESS, apprehension, knowledge, realization, recognition, sensibility

consecrate verb SANCTIFY, dedicate, devote, hallow, ordain, set apart, venerate

consecutive adjective SUCCESSIVE, in sequence, in turn, running, sequential, succeeding, uninterrupted

consensus noun AGREEMENT, assent, common consent, concord, general agreement, harmony, unanimity, unity

consent noun **1** AGREEMENT, acquiescence, approval, assent, compliance, go-ahead (informal), O.K. or okay (informal), permission, sanction ▶ verb **2** AGREE, acquiesce, allow, approve, assent, concur, permit

consequence noun **1** RESULT, effect, end result, issue, outcome, repercussion, sequel, upshot **2** IMPORTANCE, account,

concern, import, moment, significance, value, weight

consequent adjective FOLLOWING, ensuing, resultant, resulting, subsequent, successive

consequently adverb AS A RESULT, accordingly, ergo, hence, subsequently, therefore, thus

conservation noun PROTECTION, guardianship, husbandry, maintenance, preservation, safeguarding, safekeeping, saving, upkeep

conservative adjective **1** TRADITIONAL, cautious, conventional, die-hard, hidebound, reactionary, sober ▶ noun **2** TRADITIONALIST, reactionary, stick-in-the-mud (informal)

conserve verb PROTECT, hoard, husband, keep, nurse, preserve, save, store up, take care of, use sparingly

consider verb **1** THINK, believe, deem, hold to be, judge, rate, regard as **2** THINK ABOUT, cogitate, contemplate, deliberate, meditate, ponder, reflect, ruminate, turn over in one's mind, weigh **3** BEAR IN MIND, keep in view, make allowance for, reckon with, remember, respect, take into account

considerable adjective LARGE, appreciable, goodly, great, marked, noticeable, plentiful, sizable or sizeable, substantial

considerably adverb GREATLY, appreciably, markedly, noticeably, remarkably, significantly, substantially, very much

considerate *adjective*
THOUGHTFUL, attentive,
concerned, kindly, mindful,
obliging, patient, tactful,
unselfish

consideration *noun* 1 THOUGHT,
analysis, deliberation,
discussion, examination,
reflection, review, scrutiny
2 FACTOR, concern, issue, point
3 THOUGHTFULNESS, concern,
considerateness, kindness,
respect, tact 4 PAYMENT, fee,
recompense, remuneration,
reward, tip

considering *preposition* TAKING
INTO ACCOUNT, in the light of, in
view of

consignment *noun* SHIPMENT,
batch, delivery, goods

consist *verb* 1 **consist of** BE
MADE UP OF, amount to, be
composed of, comprise,
contain, embody, include,
incorporate, involve 2 **consist
in** LIE IN, be expressed by, be
found *or* contained in, inhere
in, reside in

consistency *noun* 1 TEXTURE,
compactness, density, firmness,
thickness, viscosity
2 CONSTANCY, evenness,
regularity, steadfastness,
steadiness, uniformity

consistent *adjective*
1 UNCHANGING, constant,
dependable, persistent, regular,
steady, true to type,
undeviating 2 AGREEING,
coherent, compatible,
congruous, consonant,
harmonious, logical

consolation *noun* COMFORT,
cheer, encouragement, help,
relief, solace, succor, support

console *verb* COMFORT, calm,
cheer, encourage, express
sympathy for, soothe

consolidate *verb* 1 STRENGTHEN,
fortify, reinforce, secure,
stabilize 2 COMBINE,
amalgamate, federate, fuse,
join, unite

consort *verb* 1 ASSOCIATE,
fraternize, go around with,
hang about, around *or* out
with, keep company, mix
▶ *noun* 2 SPOUSE, companion,
husband, partner, wife

conspicuous *adjective*
1 OBVIOUS, blatant, clear,
evident, noticeable, patent,
salient 2 NOTEWORTHY, illustrious,
notable, outstanding,
prominent, remarkable, salient,
signal, striking

conspiracy *noun* PLOT, collusion,
intrigue, machination, scheme,
treason

conspirator *noun* PLOTTER,
conspirer, intriguer, schemer,
traitor

conspire *verb* 1 PLOT, contrive,
intrigue, machinate, maneuver,
plan, scheme 2 WORK TOGETHER,
combine, concur, contribute,
cooperate, tend

constant *adjective* 1 CONTINUOUS,
ceaseless, incessant,
interminable, nonstop,
perpetual, sustained,
twenty-four-seven (*slang*),
unrelenting 2 UNCHANGING,
even, fixed, invariable,
permanent, stable, steady,
uniform, unvarying 3 FAITHFUL,
devoted, loyal, stalwart,
staunch, true, trustworthy,
trusty

constantly *adverb* CONTINUOUSLY,

all the time, always,
continually, endlessly,
incessantly, interminably,
invariably, nonstop,
perpetually, twenty-four-seven
(*slang*)

consternation *noun* DISMAY,
alarm, anxiety, distress, dread,
fear, trepidation

constituent *noun* 1 VOTER,
elector 2 COMPONENT, element,
factor, ingredient, part, unit
▶ *adjective* 3 COMPONENT, basic,
elemental, essential, integral

constitute *verb* MAKE UP,
compose, comprise, establish,
form, found, set up

constitution *noun* 1 HEALTH,
build, character, disposition,
physique 2 STRUCTURE,
composition, form, make-up,
nature

constitutional *adjective*
1 STATUTORY, chartered, vested
▶ *noun* 2 WALK, airing, stroll, turn

constrain *verb* 1 FORCE, bind,
coerce, compel, impel,
necessitate, oblige, pressurize
2 RESTRICT, check, confine,
constrict, curb, restrain, straiten

constraint *noun* 1 RESTRICTION,
check, curb, deterrent,
hindrance, limitation, rein
2 FORCE, coercion, compulsion,
necessity, pressure, restraint

construct *verb* BUILD, assemble,
compose, create, fashion,
form, make, manufacture, put
together, shape

construction *noun* 1 BUILDING,
composition, creation, edifice
2 INTERPRETATION, explanation,
inference, reading, rendering

constructive *adjective* HELPFUL,
positive, practical, productive,

useful, valuable

consult *verb* ASK, compare
notes, confer, pick (someone's)
brains, question, refer to, take
counsel, turn to

consultant *noun* SPECIALIST,
adviser, authority

consultation *noun* SEMINAR,
appointment, conference,
council, deliberation, dialogue,
discussion, examination,
hearing, interview, meeting,
session

consume *verb* 1 EAT, chow
down (*slang*), devour, eat up,
gobble (up), put away,
swallow 2 USE UP, absorb,
dissipate, exhaust, expend,
spend, squander, waste
3 DESTROY, annihilate, demolish,
devastate, lay waste, ravage 4
(*often passive*) OBSESS, absorb,
dominate, eat up, engross,
monopolize, preoccupy

consumer *noun* BUYER,
customer, purchaser, shopper,
user

consummate *verb* 1 COMPLETE,
accomplish, conclude, crown,
end, finish, fulfill ▶ *adjective*
2 SKILLED, accomplished,
matchless, perfect, polished,
practiced, superb, supreme
3 COMPLETE, absolute,
conspicuous, extreme,
supreme, total, utter

consumption *noun* 1 USING UP,
depletion, diminution,
dissipation, exhaustion,
expenditure, loss, waste
2 *Old-fashioned* TUBERCULOSIS, T.B.

contact *noun* 1 COMMUNICATION,
association, connection
2 TOUCH, contiguity
3 ACQUAINTANCE, connection

►*verb* 4 GET *or* BE IN TOUCH WITH, approach, call, communicate with, reach, speak to, write to

contagious *adjective* INFECTIOUS, catching, communicable, spreading, transmissible

contain *verb* 1 HOLD, accommodate, enclose, have capacity for, incorporate, seat 2 INCLUDE, comprehend, comprise, consist of, embody, embrace, involve 3 RESTRAIN, control, curb, hold back, hold in, keep a tight rein on, repress, stifle

container *noun* HOLDER, receptacle, repository, vessel

contaminate *verb* POLLUTE, adulterate, befoul, corrupt, defile, infect, stain, taint, tarnish

contamination *noun* POLLUTION, contagion, corruption, defilement, impurity, infection, poisoning, taint

contemplate *verb* 1 THINK ABOUT, consider, deliberate, meditate, muse over, ponder, reflect upon, ruminate (upon) 2 CONSIDER, envisage, expect, foresee, intend, plan, think of 3 LOOK AT, examine, eye up, gaze at, inspect, regard, stare at, study, survey, view

contemporary *adjective* 1 COEXISTING, concurrent, contemporaneous 2 MODERN, à la mode, current, newfangled, present, present-day, recent, up-to-date ►*noun* 3 PEER, fellow

contempt *noun* SCORN, derision, disdain, disregard, disrespect, mockery, neglect, slight

contemptible *adjective* DESPICABLE, detestable, ignominious, lousy (*slang*), measly, paltry, pitiful, scuzzy (*slang*), shameful, worthless

contemptuous *adjective* SCORNFUL, arrogant, condescending, derisive, disdainful, haughty, sneering, supercilious, withering

contend *verb* 1 COMPETE, clash, contest, fight, jostle, strive, struggle, vie 2 ARGUE, affirm, allege, assert, dispute, hold, maintain

content[1] *noun* 1 MEANING, essence, gist, significance, substance 2 AMOUNT, capacity, load, measure, size, volume

content[2] *adjective* 1 SATISFIED, agreeable, at ease, comfortable, contented, fulfilled, willing to accept ►*verb* 2 SATISFY, appease, humor, indulge, mollify, placate, please ►*noun* 3 SATISFACTION, comfort, contentment, ease, gratification, peace of mind, pleasure

contented *adjective* SATISFIED, comfortable, content, glad, gratified, happy, pleased, serene, thankful

contentious *adjective* ARGUMENTATIVE, bickering, captious, cavilling, disputatious, quarrelsome, querulous, wrangling

contentment *noun* SATISFACTION, comfort, content, ease, equanimity, fulfillment, happiness, peace, pleasure, serenity

contents *plural noun* CONSTITUENTS, elements, ingredients, load

contest *noun* 1 COMPETITION, game, match, tournament, trial

2 STRUGGLE, battle, combat, conflict, controversy, dispute, fight ▶ *verb* 3 DISPUTE, argue, call in *or* into question, challenge, debate, doubt, object to, oppose, question 4 COMPETE, contend, fight, strive, vie

contestant *noun* COMPETITOR, candidate, contender, entrant, participant, player

context *noun* 1 CIRCUMSTANCES, ambience, conditions, situation 2 FRAME OF REFERENCE, background, connection, framework, relation

contingency *noun* POSSIBILITY, accident, chance, emergency, event, eventuality, happening, incident

continual *adjective* CONSTANT, frequent, incessant, interminable, recurrent, regular, repeated, twenty-four-seven (*slang*), unremitting

continually *adverb* CONSTANTLY, all the time, always, forever, incessantly, interminably, nonstop, persistently, repeatedly, twenty-four-seven (*slang*)

continuation *noun* 1 CONTINUING, perpetuation, prolongation, resumption 2 ADDITION, extension, furtherance, postscript, sequel, supplement

continue *verb* 1 REMAIN, abide, carry on, endure, last, live on, persist, stay, survive 2 KEEP ON, carry on, go on, maintain, persevere, persist in, stick at, sustain 3 RESUME, carry on, pick up where one left off, proceed,

recommence, return to, take up

continuing *adjective* LASTING, enduring, in progress, ongoing, sustained

continuity *noun* SEQUENCE, cohesion, connection, flow, progression, succession

continuous *adjective* CONSTANT, extended, prolonged, twenty-four-seven (*slang*), unbroken, unceasing, undivided, uninterrupted

contraband *noun* 1 SMUGGLING, black-marketing, bootlegging, trafficking ▶ *adjective* 2 SMUGGLED, banned, bootleg, forbidden, hot (*informal*), illegal, illicit, prohibited, unlawful

contract *noun* 1 AGREEMENT, arrangement, bargain, commitment, covenant, pact, settlement ▶ *verb* 2 AGREE, bargain, come to terms, commit oneself, covenant, negotiate, pledge 3 SHORTEN, abbreviate, curtail, diminish, dwindle, lessen, narrow, reduce, shrink, shrivel 4 CATCH, acquire, be afflicted with, develop, get, go down with, incur

contraction *noun* SHORTENING, abbreviation, compression, narrowing, reduction, shrinkage, shriveling, tightening

contradict *verb* DENY, be at variance with, belie, challenge, controvert, fly in the face of, negate, rebut

contradiction *noun* DENIAL, conflict, contravention, incongruity, inconsistency, negation, opposite

contradictory *adjective*

INCONSISTENT, conflicting, contrary, incompatible, opposed, opposite, paradoxical

contraption noun Informal DEVICE, apparatus, contrivance, gadget, instrument, mechanism

contrary noun 1 OPPOSITE, antithesis, converse, reverse ▶ adjective 2 OPPOSED, adverse, clashing, contradictory, counter, discordant, hostile, inconsistent, opposite, paradoxical 3 PERVERSE, awkward, cantankerous, difficult, disobliging, intractable, obstinate, unaccommodating

contrast noun 1 DIFFERENCE, comparison, disparity, dissimilarity, distinction, divergence, foil, opposition ▶ verb 2 DIFFERENTIATE, compare, differ, distinguish, oppose, set in opposition, set off

contribute verb 1 GIVE, add, bestow, chip in (informal), donate, provide, subscribe, supply 2 **contribute to** BE PARTLY RESPONSIBLE FOR, be conducive to, be instrumental in, help, lead to, tend to

contribution noun GIFT, addition, donation, grant, input, offering, subscription

contributor noun GIVER, donor, patron, subscriber, supporter

contrite adjective SORRY, chastened, conscience-stricken, humble, penitent, regretful, remorseful, repentant, sorrowful

contrivance noun 1 DEVICE, apparatus, appliance, contraption, gadget, implement, instrument, invention, machine,

mechanism 2 PLAN, intrigue, machination, plot, ruse, scheme, stratagem, trick

contrive verb 1 BRING ABOUT, arrange, effect, manage, maneuver, plan, plot, scheme, succeed 2 DEVISE, concoct, construct, create, design, fabricate, improvise, invent, manufacture

contrived adjective FORCED, artificial, elaborate, labored, overdone, planned, strained, unnatural

control noun 1 POWER, authority, charge, command, guidance, management, oversight, supervision, supremacy 2 RESTRAINT, brake, check, curb, limitation, regulation ▶ verb 3 HAVE POWER OVER, administer, command, direct, govern, handle, have charge of, manage, manipulate, supervise 4 RESTRAIN, check, constrain, contain, curb, hold back, limit, repress, subdue

controls plural noun INSTRUMENTS, console, control panel, dash, dashboard, dials

controversial adjective DISPUTED, at issue, contentious, debatable, disputable, open to question, under discussion

controversy noun ARGUMENT, altercation, debate, dispute, quarrel, row, squabble, wrangling

convalescence noun RECOVERY, improvement, recuperation, rehabilitation, return to health

convalescent adjective RECOVERING, getting better, improving, mending, on the mend, recuperating

convene verb GATHER, assemble, bring together, call, come together, congregate, convoke, meet, summon

convenience noun 1 AVAILABILITY, accessibility, advantage, appropriateness, benefit, fitness, suitability, usefulness, utility 2 APPLIANCE, amenity, comfort, facility, help, labor-saving device

convenient adjective 1 USEFUL, appropriate, fit, handy, helpful, labor-saving, serviceable, suitable, timely 2 NEARBY, accessible, at hand, available, close at hand, handy, just round the corner, within reach

convention noun 1 CUSTOM, code, etiquette, practice, propriety, protocol, tradition, usage 2 AGREEMENT, bargain, contract, pact, protocol, treaty 3 ASSEMBLY, conference, congress, convocation, council, meeting

conventional adjective 1 ORDINARY, accepted, customary, normal, orthodox, regular, standard, traditional, usual 2 UNORIGINAL, banal, hackneyed, prosaic, routine, stereotyped

converge verb COME TOGETHER, coincide, combine, gather, join, meet, merge

conversation noun TALK, chat, conference, dialogue, discourse, discussion, gossip, tête-à-tête

converse[1] verb TALK, chat, chew the fat (slang), commune, confer, discourse, exchange views

converse[2] noun 1 OPPOSITE,

antithesis, contrary, obverse, other side of the coin, reverse
▶ adjective 2 OPPOSITE, contrary, counter, reverse, reversed, transposed

conversion noun 1 CHANGE, metamorphosis, transformation 2 ADAPTATION, alteration, modification, reconstruction, remodeling, reorganization

convert verb 1 CHANGE, alter, transform, transpose, turn 2 ADAPT, apply, customize, modify, remodel, reorganize, restyle, revise 3 REFORM, convince, proselytize ▶ noun 4 NEOPHYTE, disciple, proselyte

convex adjective ROUNDED, bulging, gibbous, protuberant

convey verb 1 COMMUNICATE, disclose, impart, make known, relate, reveal, tell 2 CARRY, bear, bring, conduct, fetch, guide, move, send, transport

convict verb 1 FIND GUILTY, condemn, imprison, pronounce guilty, sentence ▶ noun 2 PRISONER, criminal, culprit, felon, jailbird, lag (slang)

conviction noun 1 BELIEF, creed, faith, opinion, persuasion, principle, tenet, view 2 CONFIDENCE, assurance, certainty, certitude, firmness, reliance

convince verb PERSUADE, assure, bring round, prevail upon, satisfy, sway, win over

convincing adjective PERSUASIVE, cogent, conclusive, credible, impressive, plausible, powerful, telling

convulse verb SHAKE, agitate, churn up, derange, disorder, disturb, twist, work

convulsion *noun* SPASM, contraction, cramp, fit, paroxysm, seizure

cool *adjective* **1** COLD, chilled, chilly, nippy, refreshing **2** CALM, collected, composed, relaxed, sedate, self-controlled, self-possessed, unemotional, unruffled **3** UNFRIENDLY, aloof, distant, indifferent, lukewarm, offhand, standoffish, unenthusiastic, unwelcoming **4** *Informal* FASHIONABLE, hip, phat (*slang*), trendy (*informal*) ▶*verb* **5** CHILL, cool off, freeze, lose heat, refrigerate ▶*noun* **6** *Slang* CALMNESS, composure, control, poise, self-control, self-discipline, self-possession, temper

cooperate *verb* WORK TOGETHER, collaborate, combine, conspire, coordinate, join forces, pool resources, pull together

cooperation *noun* TEAMWORK, collaboration, combined effort, esprit de corps, give-and-take, unity

cooperative *adjective* **1** HELPFUL, accommodating, obliging, onside (*informal*), responsive, supportive **2** SHARED, collective, combined, joint

coordinate *verb* BRING TOGETHER, harmonize, integrate, match, organize, synchronize, systematize

cope *verb* **1** MANAGE, carry on, get by (*informal*), hold one's own, make the grade, struggle through, survive **2 cope with** DEAL WITH, contend with, grapple with, handle, struggle with, weather, wrestle with

copious *adjective* ABUNDANT, ample, bountiful, extensive, full, lavish, plentiful, profuse

copy *noun* **1** REPRODUCTION, counterfeit, duplicate, facsimile, forgery, imitation, likeness, model, replica ▶*verb* **2** REPRODUCE, counterfeit, duplicate, replicate, transcribe **3** IMITATE, ape, emulate, follow, mimic, mirror, repeat

cord *noun* ROPE, line, string, twine

cordial *adjective* WARM, affable, agreeable, cheerful, congenial, friendly, genial, hearty, sociable

cordon *noun* **1** CHAIN, barrier, line, ring ▶*verb* **2 cordon off** SURROUND, close off, encircle, enclose, fence off, isolate, picket, separate

core *noun* CENTER, crux, essence, gist, heart, kernel, nub, nucleus, pith

corner *noun* **1** ANGLE, bend, crook, joint **2** SPACE, hideaway, hideout, nook, retreat ▶*verb* **3** TRAP, run to earth **4** *As in* **corner the market** MONOPOLIZE, dominate, engross, hog (*slang*)

corny *adjective Slang* UNORIGINAL, banal, dull, hackneyed, old-fashioned, old hat, stale, stereotyped, trite

corporation *noun* **1** BUSINESS, association, corporate body, society **2** TOWN COUNCIL, civic authorities, council, municipal authorities

corps *noun* TEAM, band, company, detachment, division, regiment, squadron, troop, unit

corpse *noun* BODY, cadaver, carcass, remains, stiff (*slang*)

correct *adjective* **1** TRUE,

accurate, exact, faultless,
flawless, O.K. *or* okay
(*informal*), precise, right
2 PROPER, acceptable,
appropriate, fitting, kosher
(*informal*), O.K. *or* okay
(*informal*), seemly, standard
▶ *verb* **3** RECTIFY, adjust, amend,
cure, emend, redress, reform,
remedy, right **4** PUNISH,
admonish, chasten, chastise,
chide, discipline, rebuke,
reprimand, reprove

correction *noun* **1** RECTIFICATION,
adjustment, alteration,
amendment, emendation,
improvement, modification
2 PUNISHMENT, admonition,
castigation, chastisement,
discipline, reformation, reproof

correctly *adverb* RIGHTLY,
accurately, perfectly, precisely,
properly, right

correctness *noun* **1** TRUTH,
accuracy, exactitude,
exactness, faultlessness, fidelity,
preciseness, precision,
regularity **2** DECORUM, civility,
good breeding, propriety,
seemliness

correspond *verb* **1** BE
CONSISTENT, accord, agree,
conform, fit, harmonize,
match, square, tally
2 COMMUNICATE, exchange
letters, keep in touch, write

correspondence *noun*
1 LETTERS, communication, mail,
post, writing **2** RELATION,
agreement, coincidence,
comparison, conformity,
correlation, harmony, match,
similarity

correspondent *noun* **1** LETTER
WRITER, pen friend *or* pal
2 REPORTER, contributor,

journalist

corresponding *adjective* RELATED,
analogous, answering,
complementary, equivalent,
matching, reciprocal, similar

corridor *noun* PASSAGE, aisle,
alley, hallway, passageway

corroborate *verb* SUPPORT,
authenticate, back up, bear
out, confirm, endorse, ratify,
substantiate, validate

corrode *verb* EAT AWAY,
consume, corrupt, erode,
gnaw, oxidize, rust, wear away

corrosive *adjective* CORRODING,
caustic, consuming, erosive,
virulent, vitriolic, wasting,
wearing

corrupt *adjective* **1** DISHONEST,
bent (*slang*), bribable, crooked
(*informal*), fraudulent,
unprincipled, unscrupulous,
venal **2** DEPRAVED, debased,
degenerate, dissolute,
profligate, vicious **3** DISTORTED,
altered, doctored, falsified
▶ *verb* **4** BRIBE, buy off, entice,
fix (*informal*), grease
(someone's) palm (*slang*), lure,
suborn **5** DEPRAVE, debauch,
pervert, subvert **6** DISTORT,
doctor, tamper with

corruption *noun* **1** DISHONESTY,
bribery, extortion, fraud, shady
dealings (*informal*),
unscrupulousness, venality
2 DEPRAVITY, decadence, evil,
immorality, perversion, vice,
wickedness **3** DISTORTION,
doctoring, falsification

corset *noun* GIRDLE, belt, bodice

cosmetic *adjective* BEAUTIFYING,
nonessential, superficial, surface

cosmic *adjective* UNIVERSAL, stellar

cosmopolitan *adjective*

1 SOPHISTICATED, broad-minded, catholic, open-minded, universal, urbane, well-traveled, worldly-wise ▶ noun 2 MAN or WOMAN OF THE WORLD, jet-setter, sophisticate

cost noun 1 PRICE, amount, charge, damage (informal), expense, outlay, payment, worth 2 LOSS, damage, detriment, expense, harm, hurt, injury, penalty, sacrifice, suffering ▶ verb 3 SELL AT, come to, command a price of, set (someone) back (informal) 4 LOSE, do disservice to, harm, hurt, injure

costly adjective 1 EXPENSIVE, dear, exorbitant, extortionate, highly-priced, steep (informal), stiff 2 DAMAGING, catastrophic, deleterious, disastrous, harmful, loss-making, ruinous

costs plural noun EXPENSES, budget, outgoings, overheads

costume noun OUTFIT, apparel, attire, clothing, dress, ensemble, garb, livery, uniform

cottage noun CABIN, chalet, hut, lodge, shack

cough noun 1 FROG or TICKLE IN ONE'S THROAT, bark, hack ▶ verb 2 CLEAR ONE'S THROAT, bark, hack

council noun GOVERNING BODY, assembly, board, cabinet, committee, conference, congress, convention, panel, parliament

counsel noun 1 ADVICE, direction, guidance, information, recommendation, suggestion, warning 2 LEGAL ADVISER, advocate, attorney, barrister, lawyer ▶ verb 3 ADVISE, advocate, exhort, instruct,

recommend, urge, warn

count verb 1 ADD (UP), calculate, compute, enumerate, number, reckon, tally, tot up 2 MATTER, be important, carry weight, rate, signify, tell, weigh 3 CONSIDER, deem, judge, look upon, rate, regard, think 4 TAKE INTO ACCOUNT or CONSIDERATION, include, number among ▶ noun 5 CALCULATION, computation, enumeration, numbering, poll, reckoning, sum, tally

counter verb 1 RETALIATE, answer, hit back, meet, oppose, parry, resist, respond, ward off ▶ adverb 2 OPPOSITE TO, against, at variance with, contrariwise, conversely, in defiance of, versus

counteract verb ACT AGAINST, foil, frustrate, negate, neutralize, offset, resist, thwart

counterbalance verb OFFSET, balance, compensate, make up for, set off

counterfeit adjective 1 FAKE, bogus, false, forged, imitation, phoney or phony (informal), sham, simulated ▶ noun 2 FAKE, copy, forgery, fraud, imitation, phoney or phony (informal), reproduction, sham ▶ verb 3 FAKE, copy, fabricate, feign, forge, imitate, impersonate, pretend, sham, simulate

countermand verb CANCEL, annul, override, repeal, rescind, retract, reverse, revoke

counterpart noun OPPOSITE NUMBER, complement, equal, fellow, match, mate, supplement, tally, twin

countless adjective INNUMERABLE, endless, immeasurable,

incalculable, infinite, legion, limitless, myriad, numberless, uncountable, untold

count on or **upon** verb DEPEND ON, bank on, believe (in), lean on, pin one's faith on, reckon on, rely on, take for granted, take on trust, trust

country noun 1 NATION, commonwealth, kingdom, people, realm, state 2 TERRITORY, land, region, terrain 3 PEOPLE, citizens, community, inhabitants, nation, populace, public, society 4 COUNTRYSIDE, backwoods, farmland, green belt, outback (Austral. & N.Z.), provinces, sticks (informal)

countryside noun COUNTRY, farmland, green belt, outback (Austral. & N.Z.), outdoors, sticks (informal)

count up verb ADD, reckon up, sum, tally, total

county noun PROVINCE, shire

coup noun MASTERSTROKE, accomplishment, action, deed, exploit, feat, maneuver, stunt

couple noun 1 PAIR, brace, duo, two, twosome ▶ verb 2 LINK, connect, hitch, join, marry, pair, unite, wed, yoke

coupon noun SLIP, card, certificate, ticket, token, voucher

courage noun BRAVERY, daring, fearlessness, gallantry, heroism, mettle, nerve, pluck, resolution, valor

courageous adjective BRAVE, bold, daring, fearless, gallant, gritty, intrepid, lion-hearted, stouthearted, valiant

courier noun 1 GUIDE, representative 2 MESSENGER, bearer, carrier, envoy, runner

course noun 1 CLASSES, curriculum, lectures, program, schedule 2 PROGRESSION, development, flow, movement, order, progress, sequence, unfolding 3 ROUTE, direction, line, passage, path, road, track, trajectory, way 4 RACECOURSE, cinder track, circuit 5 PROCEDURE, behavior, conduct, manner, method, mode, plan, policy, program 6 PERIOD, duration, lapse, passage, passing, sweep, term, time 7 **of course** NATURALLY, certainly, definitely, indubitably, needless to say, obviously, undoubtedly, without a doubt ▶ verb 8 RUN, flow, gush, race, speed, stream, surge 9 HUNT, chase, follow, pursue, stalk

court noun 1 LAW COURT, bar, bench, tribunal 2 COURTYARD, cloister, piazza, plaza, quad (informal), quadrangle, square, yard 3 PALACE, hall, manor 4 ROYAL HOUSEHOLD, attendants, cortege, entourage, retinue, suite, train ▶ verb 5 WOO, date, go (out) with, run after, serenade, set one's cap at, take out, walk out with 6 CULTIVATE, brown-nose (slang), curry favor with, fawn upon, flatter, pander to, seek, solicit 7 INVITE, attract, bring about, incite, prompt, provoke, seek

courteous adjective POLITE, affable, attentive, civil, gallant, gracious, refined, respectful, urbane, well-mannered

courtesy noun 1 POLITENESS, affability, civility, courteousness, gallantry, good manners, graciousness, urbanity **2** FAVOR, benevolence, indulgence, kindness

courtier noun ATTENDANT, follower, squire

courtly adjective CEREMONIOUS, chivalrous, dignified, elegant, formal, gallant, polished, refined, stately, urbane

courtyard noun YARD, enclosure, quad, quadrangle

cove noun BAY, anchorage, inlet, sound

covenant noun **1** PROMISE, agreement, arrangement, commitment, contract, pact, pledge ▶ verb **2** PROMISE, agree, contract, pledge, stipulate, undertake

cover verb **1** CLOTHE, dress, envelop, put on, wrap **2** OVERLAY, coat, daub, encase, envelop **3** SUBMERGE, engulf, flood, overrun, wash over **4** CONCEAL, cloak, disguise, enshroud, hide, mask, obscure, shroud, veil **5** TRAVEL OVER, cross, pass through or over, traverse **6** PROTECT, defend, guard, shield **7** REPORT, describe, investigate, narrate, relate, tell of, write up ▶ noun **8** COVERING, canopy, case, coating, envelope, jacket, lid, top, wrapper **9** DISGUISE, façade, front, mask, pretext, screen, smoke screen, veil **10** PROTECTION, camouflage, concealment, defense, guard, shelter, shield **11** INSURANCE, compensation, indemnity, protection, reimbursement

covering adjective **1** EXPLANATORY, accompanying, descriptive, introductory ▶ noun

2 COVER, blanket, casing, coating, layer, wrapping

cover-up noun CONCEALMENT, complicity, conspiracy, front, smoke screen, whitewash (informal)

cover up verb CONCEAL, draw a veil over, hide, hush up, suppress, sweep under the carpet, whitewash (informal)

covet verb LONG FOR, aspire to, crave, desire, envy, lust after, set one's heart on, yearn for

covetous adjective ENVIOUS, acquisitive, avaricious, close-fisted, grasping, greedy, jealous, rapacious, yearning

coward noun WIMP (informal), chicken (slang), scaredy-cat (informal), yellow-belly (slang)

cowardice noun FAINT-HEARTEDNESS, fearfulness, spinelessness, weakness

cowardly adjective FAINT-HEARTED, chicken (slang), craven, fearful, scared, soft, spineless, timorous, weak, yellow (informal)

cowboy noun COWHAND, cattleman, drover, gaucho (S. American), herdsman, rancher, stockman

cower verb CRINGE, draw back, flinch, grovel, quail, shrink, tremble

coy adjective SHY, bashful, demure, modest, reserved, retiring, shrinking, timid

cozy adjective SNUG, comfortable, comfy (informal), homely, homey, intimate, sheltered, tucked up, warm

crack verb **1** BREAK, burst, cleave, fracture, snap, splinter, split **2** SNAP, burst, crash, detonate, explode, pop, ring **3** GIVE IN, break down, collapse, give way, go to pieces, lose control, succumb, yield **4** *Informal* HIT, clip (*informal*), clout (*informal*), cuff, slap, smack, whack **5** SOLVE, decipher, fathom, get the answer to, work out ▸*noun* **6** SNAP, burst, clap, crash, explosion, pop, report **7** BREAK, chink, cleft, cranny, crevice, fissure, fracture, gap, rift **8** *Informal* BLOW, clip (*informal*), clout (*informal*), cuff, slap, smack, whack **9** *Informal* JOKE, dig, funny remark, gag (*informal*), jibe, quip, wisecrack (*informal*), witticism

crackdown *noun* SUPPRESSION, clampdown, crushing, repression

cracked *adjective* BROKEN, chipped, damaged, defective, faulty, flawed, imperfect, split

cradle *noun* **1** CRIB, bassinet, cot **2** BIRTHPLACE, beginning, fount, fountainhead, origin, source, spring, wellspring ▸*verb* **3** HOLD, lull, nestle, nurse, rock, support

craft *noun* **1** OCCUPATION, business, employment, handicraft, pursuit, trade, vocation, work **2** SKILL, ability, aptitude, art, artistry, expertise, ingenuity, know-how (*informal*), technique, workmanship **3** VESSEL, aircraft, boat, plane, ship, spacecraft

craftsman *noun* SKILLED WORKER, artisan, maker, master, smith, technician, wright

craftsmanship *noun* WORKMANSHIP, artistry, expertise, mastery, technique

crafty *adjective* CUNNING, artful, calculating, devious, sharp, shrewd, sly, subtle, wily

crag *noun* ROCK, bluff, peak, pinnacle, tor

cram *verb* **1** STUFF, compress, force, jam, pack in, press, shove, squeeze **2** OVEREAT, glut, gorge, satiate, stuff **3** STUDY, bone up (*informal*), review

cramp[1] *noun* SPASM, ache, contraction, convulsion, pain, pang, stitch, twinge

cramp[2] *verb* RESTRICT, constrain, hamper, handicap, hinder, impede, inhibit, obstruct

cramped *adjective* CLOSED IN, confined, congested, crowded, hemmed in, overcrowded, packed, uncomfortable

cranny *noun* CREVICE, chink, cleft, crack, fissure, gap, hole, opening

crash *noun* **1** COLLISION, accident, bump, pile-up (*informal*), smash, wreck **2** SMASH, bang, boom, clang, clash, clatter, din, racket, thunder **3** COLLAPSE, debacle, depression, downfall, failure, ruin ▸*verb* **4** COLLIDE, bump (into), crash-land (*an aircraft*), drive into, have an accident, hit, plow into, wreck **5** COLLAPSE, be ruined, fail, fold, fold up, go belly up (*informal*), go bust (*informal*), go to the wall, go under **6** HURTLE, fall headlong, give way, lurch, overbalance, plunge, topple

crass *adjective* INSENSITIVE, boorish, gross, indelicate, oafish, stupid, unrefined, witless

crate *noun* CONTAINER, box, case, packing case, tea chest

crater noun HOLLOW, depression, dip

crave verb 1 LONG FOR, desire, hanker after, hope for, lust after, want, yearn for 2 BEG, ask, beseech, entreat, implore, petition, plead for, pray for, seek, solicit, supplicate

craving noun LONGING, appetite, desire, hankering, hope, hunger, thirst, yearning, yen (informal)

crawl verb 1 CREEP, advance slowly, inch, slither, worm one's way, wriggle, writhe 2 GROVEL, brown-nose (slang), creep, fawn, humble oneself, kiss ass (slang), toady 3 BE FULL OF, be alive, be overrun (slang), swarm, teem

craze noun FAD, enthusiasm, fashion, infatuation, mania, rage, trend, vogue

crazy adjective 1 RIDICULOUS, absurd, foolish, idiotic, ill-conceived, ludicrous, nonsensical, preposterous, senseless 2 FANATICAL, devoted, enthusiastic, infatuated, mad, passionate, wild (informal) 3 INSANE, crazed, demented, deranged, mad, nuts (slang), out of one's mind, unbalanced

creak verb SQUEAK, grate, grind, groan, scrape, scratch, screech

cream noun 1 LOTION, cosmetic, emulsion, essence, liniment, oil, ointment, paste, salve, unguent 2 BEST, crème de la crème, elite, flower, pick, prime ▶ adjective 3 OFF-WHITE, yellowish-white

creamy adjective SMOOTH, buttery, milky, rich, soft, velvety

crease noun 1 LINE, corrugation, fold, groove, ridge, wrinkle ▶ verb 2 WRINKLE, corrugate, crumple, double up, fold, rumple, screw up

create verb 1 MAKE, compose, devise, formulate, invent, originate, produce, spawn 2 CAUSE, bring about, lead to, occasion 3 APPOINT, constitute, establish, install, invest, make, set up

creation noun 1 MAKING, conception, formation, generation, genesis, procreation 2 SETTING UP, development, establishment, formation, foundation, inception, institution, production 3 INVENTION, achievement, brainchild (informal), concoction, handiwork, magnum opus, pièce de résistance, production 4 UNIVERSE, cosmos, nature, world

creative adjective IMAGINATIVE, artistic, clever, gifted, ingenious, inspired, inventive, original, visionary

creativity noun IMAGINATION, cleverness, ingenuity, inspiration, inventiveness, originality

creator noun MAKER, architect, author, designer, father, inventor, originator, prime mover

creature noun 1 LIVING THING, animal, beast, being, brute 2 PERSON, human being, individual, man, mortal, soul, woman

credentials plural noun CERTIFICATION, authorization, document, license, papers, passport, reference(s), testimonial

credibility noun BELIEVABILITY, integrity, plausibility, reliability, trustworthiness

credible adjective 1 BELIEVABLE, conceivable, imaginable, likely, plausible, possible, probable, reasonable, thinkable 2 RELIABLE, dependable, honest, sincere, trustworthy, trusty

credit noun 1 PRAISE, acclaim, acknowledgment, approval, commendation, honor, kudos, recognition, tribute 2 As in **be a credit to** SOURCE OF SATISFACTION or PRIDE, feather in one's cap, honor 3 PRESTIGE, esteem, good name, influence, position, regard, reputation, repute, standing, status 4 BELIEF, confidence, credence, faith, reliance, trust 5 **on credit** ON ACCOUNT, by deferred payment, by installments, on the card ▶ verb 6 BELIEVE, accept, have faith in, rely on, trust 7 **credit with** ATTRIBUTE TO, ascribe to, assign to, impute to

creditable adjective PRAISEWORTHY, admirable, commendable, honorable, laudable, reputable, respectable, worthy

credulity noun GULLIBILITY, blind faith, credulousness, naivety

creed noun BELIEF, articles of faith, catechism, credo, doctrine, dogma, principles

creek noun STREAM, bayou, brook, rivulet, runnel, tributary, watercourse

creep verb 1 SNEAK, approach unnoticed, skulk, slink, steal, tiptoe 2 CRAWL, glide, slither,

squirm, wriggle, writhe ▶ noun 3 Slang BROWN-NOSER (slang), crawler (slang), scuzzbucket (slang), sneak, sycophant, toady 4 Slang JERK, loser, lowlife, pervert, scumbag (slang), scuzzbucket (slang)

creeper noun CLIMBING PLANT, rambler, runner, trailing plant, vine

creeps plural noun **give one the creeps** Informal DISGUST, frighten, make one's hair stand on end, make one squirm, repel, repulse, scare

creepy adjective Informal DISTURBING, eerie, frightening, hair-raising, macabre, menacing, scary (informal), sinister

crescent noun MENISCUS, new moon, sickle

crest noun 1 TOP, apex, crown, highest point, peak, pinnacle, ridge, summit 2 TUFT, comb, crown, mane, plume 3 EMBLEM, badge, bearings, device, insignia, symbol

crestfallen adjective DISAPPOINTED, dejected, depressed, despondent, discouraged, disheartened, downcast, downhearted

crevice noun GAP, chink, cleft, crack, cranny, fissure, hole, opening, slit

crew noun 1 (SHIP'S) COMPANY, hands, (ship's) complement 2 TEAM, corps, gang, posse, squad 3 Informal CROWD, band, bunch (informal), gang, horde, mob, pack, set

crib noun 1 CRADLE, bassinet, bed, cot 2 MANGER, rack, stall ▶ verb 3 Informal COPY, cheat, pirate, plagiarize, purloin, steal

crime noun 1 OFFENSE, felony, misdeed, misdemeanor, transgression, trespass, unlawful act, violation 2 LAWBREAKING, corruption, illegality, misconduct, vice, wrongdoing

criminal noun 1 LAWBREAKER, convict, crook (informal), culprit, felon, offender, sinner, villain ▶ adjective 2 UNLAWFUL, corrupt, crooked (informal), illegal, illicit, immoral, lawless, wicked, wrong 3 DISGRACEFUL, deplorable, foolish, preposterous, ridiculous, scandalous, senseless

cringe verb SHRINK, cower, draw back, flinch, recoil, shy, wince

cripple verb 1 DISABLE, hamstring, incapacitate, lame, maim, paralyze, weaken 2 DAMAGE, destroy, impair, put out of action, put paid to, ruin, spoil

crippled adjective DISABLED, challenged, handicapped, incapacitated, laid up (informal), lame, paralyzed

crisis noun 1 CRITICAL POINT, climax, crunch (informal), crux, culmination, height, moment of truth, turning point 2 EMERGENCY, deep water, dire straits, meltdown (informal), panic stations (informal), plight, predicament, trouble

crisp adjective 1 CRUNCHY, brittle, crispy, crumbly, firm, fresh 2 CLEAN, neat, smart, spruce, tidy, trim, well-groomed, well-pressed 3 BRACING, brisk, fresh, invigorating, refreshing

criterion noun STANDARD, bench

mark, gauge, measure, principle, rule, test, touchstone, yardstick

critic noun 1 JUDGE, analyst, authority, commentator, connoisseur, expert, pundit, reviewer 2 FAULT-FINDER, attacker, detractor, knocker (informal)

critical adjective 1 CRUCIAL, all-important, decisive, pivotal, precarious, pressing, serious, urgent, vital 2 DISPARAGING, captious, censorious, derogatory, disapproving, fault-finding, nagging, nit-picking (informal), scathing 3 ANALYTICAL, discerning, discriminating, fastidious, judicious, penetrating, perceptive

criticism noun 1 FAULT-FINDING, bad press, censure, character assassination, disapproval, disparagement, flak (informal), stick (slang) 2 ANALYSIS, appraisal, appreciation, assessment, comment, commentary, critique, evaluation, judgment

criticize verb FIND FAULT WITH, carp, censure, condemn, disapprove of, disparage, knock (informal), put down

croak verb SQUAWK, caw, grunt, utter or speak huskily, wheeze

crook noun CRIMINAL, cheat, racketeer, robber, rogue, shark, swindler, thief, villain

crooked adjective 1 BENT, curved, deformed, distorted, hooked, irregular, misshapen, out of shape, twisted, warped, zigzag 2 AT AN ANGLE, askew, awry, lopsided, off-center, slanting, squint, uneven

3 DISHONEST, bent (*slang*), corrupt, criminal, fraudulent, illegal, shady (*informal*), underhand, unlawful

croon *verb* SING, hum, purr, warble

crop *noun* **1** PRODUCE, fruits, gathering, harvest, reaping, vintage, yield ▶ *verb* **2** CUT, clip, lop, pare, prune, shear, snip, trim GRAZE, browse, nibble

crop up *verb* HAPPEN, appear, arise, emerge, occur, spring up, turn up

cross *verb* **1** GO ACROSS, bridge, cut across, extend over, move across, pass over, span, traverse **2** INTERSECT, crisscross, intertwine **3** OPPOSE, block, impede, interfere, obstruct, resist **4** INTERBREED, blend, crossbreed, cross-fertilize, cross-pollinate, hybridize, intercross, mix, mongrelize ▶ *noun* **5** CRUCIFIX, rood **6** CROSSROADS, crossing, intersection, junction **7** MIXTURE, amalgam, blend, combination **8** TROUBLE, affliction, burden, grief, load, misfortune, trial, tribulation, woe, worry ▶ *adjective* **9** ANGRY, annoyed, grumpy, ill-tempered, in a bad mood, irascible, put out, short **10** TRANSVERSE, crosswise, diagonal, intersecting, oblique

cross-examine *verb* QUESTION, grill (*informal*), interrogate, pump, quiz

cross out *or* **off** *verb* STRIKE OFF *or* OUT, blue-pencil, cancel, delete, eliminate, score off *or* out

crouch *verb* BEND DOWN, bow, duck, hunch, kneel, squat, stoop

crow *verb* GLOAT, blow one's own trumpet, boast, brag, exult, strut, swagger, triumph

crowd *noun* **1** MULTITUDE, army, horde, host, mass, mob, pack, swarm, throng **2** GROUP, bunch (*informal*), circle, clique, lot, set **3** AUDIENCE, attendance, gate, house, spectators ▶ *verb* **4** FLOCK, congregate, gather, mass, stream, surge, swarm, throng **5** SQUEEZE, bundle, congest, cram, pack, pile

crowded *adjective* PACKED, busy, congested, cramped, full, jam-packed, swarming, teeming

crown *noun* **1** CORONET, circlet, diadem, tiara **2** LAUREL WREATH, garland, honor, laurels, prize, trophy, wreath **3** HIGH POINT, apex, crest, pinnacle, summit, tip, top ▶ *verb* **4** HONOR, adorn, dignify, festoon **5** CAP, be the climax *or* culmination of, complete, finish, perfect, put the finishing touch to, round off, top **6** *Slang* STRIKE, belt (*informal*), box, hit over the head, punch

Crown *noun* **1** MONARCHY, royalty, sovereignty **2** MONARCH, emperor *or* empress, king *or* queen, ruler, sovereign

crucial *adjective* **1** VITAL, essential, high-priority, important, momentous, pressing, urgent **2** CRITICAL, central, decisive, pivotal

crucify *verb* EXECUTE, persecute, torment, torture

crude *adjective* **1** PRIMITIVE, clumsy, makeshift, rough, rough-and-ready, rudimentary, unpolished **2** VULGAR, coarse, dirty, gross, indecent, obscene, off-color, scuzzy (*slang*), smutty, tasteless, uncouth **3** UNREFINED, natural, raw, unprocessed

crudely *adverb* VULGARLY, bluntly, coarsely, impolitely, roughly, rudely, tastelessly

crudity *noun* **1** ROUGHNESS, clumsiness, crudeness **2** VULGARITY, coarseness, impropriety, indecency, indelicacy, obscenity, smuttiness

cruel *adjective* **1** BRUTAL, barbarous, callous, hard-hearted, heartless, inhumane, malevolent, sadistic, spiteful, unkind, vicious **2** MERCILESS, pitiless, ruthless, unrelenting

cruelly *adverb* **1** BRUTALLY, barbarously, callously, heartlessly, in cold blood, mercilessly, pitilessly, sadistically, spitefully **2** BITTERLY, deeply, fearfully, grievously, monstrously, severely

cruelty *noun* BRUTALITY, barbarity, callousness, depravity, fiendishness, inhumanity, mercilessness, ruthlessness, spitefulness

cruise *noun* **1** SAIL, boat trip, sea trip, voyage ▶ *verb* **2** SAIL, coast, voyage **3** TRAVEL ALONG, coast, drift, keep a steady pace

crumb *noun* BIT, fragment, grain, morsel, scrap, shred, soupçon

crumble *verb* **1** DISINTEGRATE, collapse, decay, degenerate, deteriorate, fall apart, go to pieces, go to rack and ruin, tumble down **2** CRUSH, fragment, granulate, grind,

pound, powder, pulverize

crummy *adjective Informal* **1** DESPICABLE, contemptible, lousy (*slang*), mean, scuzzy (*slang*) **2** INFERIOR, deficient, inadequate, lousy (*slang*), of poor quality, poor, substandard **3** UNWELL, below par, off color, under the weather (*informal*)

crumple *verb* **1** CRUSH, crease, rumple, screw up, scrumple, wrinkle **2** COLLAPSE, break down, cave in, fall, give way, go to pieces

crunch *verb* **1** CHOMP, champ, chew noisily, grind, munch ▶ *noun* **2** *Informal* CRITICAL POINT, crisis, crux, emergency, moment of truth, test

crusade *noun* CAMPAIGN, cause, drive, movement, push

crush *verb* **1** SQUASH, break, compress, press, pulverize, squeeze **2** OVERCOME, conquer, overpower, overwhelm, put down, quell, stamp out, subdue **3** HUMILIATE, abash, mortify, put down (*slang*), quash, shame ▶ *noun* **4** CROWD, huddle, jam

crust *noun* LAYER, coating, covering, shell, skin, surface

crusty *adjective* **1** CRISPY, hard **2** IRRITABLE, cantankerous, cross, gruff, prickly, short-tempered, testy

cry *verb* **1** WEEP, blubber, shed tears, snivel, sob **2** SHOUT, bawl, bellow, call out, exclaim, howl, roar, scream, shriek, yell ▶ *noun* **3** WEEPING, blubbering, snivelling, sob, sobbing, weep **4** SHOUT, bellow, call, exclamation, howl, roar,

scream, screech, shriek, yell
5 APPEAL, plea

cub *noun* YOUNG, offspring, whelp

cuckoo *adjective Slang* INSANE, bonkers (*informal*), crazy, daft (*informal*), foolish, idiotic, nuts (*slang*), out of one's mind, stupid

cuddle *verb* HUG, bill and coo, cosset, embrace, fondle, pet, snuggle

cudgel *noun* CLUB, baton, bludgeon, stick, truncheon

cue *noun* SIGNAL, catchword, hint, key, prompting, reminder, sign, suggestion

cul-de-sac *noun* DEAD END, blind alley

culminate *verb* END UP, climax, close, come to a climax, come to a head, conclude, finish, wind up

culmination *noun* CLIMAX, acme, conclusion, consummation, finale, peak, pinnacle, zenith

culpable *adjective* BLAMEWORTHY, at fault, found wanting, guilty, in the wrong, to blame, wrong

culprit *noun* OFFENDER, criminal, evildoer, felon, guilty party, miscreant, transgressor, wrongdoer

cult *noun* **1** SECT, clique, faction, religion, school **2** DEVOTION, idolization, worship

cultivate *verb* **1** FARM, plant, plow, tend, till, work **2** DEVELOP, foster, improve, promote, refine **3** COURT, dance attendance upon, run after, seek out

cultivation *noun* **1** FARMING, gardening, husbandry, planting, plowing, tillage
2 DEVELOPMENT, encouragement, fostering, furtherance, nurture, patronage, promotion, support

cultural *adjective* ARTISTIC, civilizing, edifying, educational, enlightening, enriching, humane, liberal

culture *noun* **1** CIVILIZATION, customs, lifestyle, mores, society, way of life
2 REFINEMENT, education, enlightenment, good taste, sophistication, urbanity
3 FARMING, cultivation, husbandry

cultured *adjective* REFINED, educated, enlightened, highbrow, sophisticated, urbane, well-informed, well-read

culvert *noun* DRAIN, channel, conduit, gutter, watercourse

cumbersome *adjective* AWKWARD, bulky, burdensome, heavy, unmanageable, unwieldy, weighty

cunning *adjective* **1** CRAFTY, artful, devious, Machiavellian, sharp, shifty, sly, wily **2** SKILLFUL, imaginative, ingenious ▶ *noun* **3** CRAFTINESS, artfulness, deviousness, guile, slyness, trickery **4** SKILL, artifice, cleverness, ingenuity, subtlety

cup *noun* **1** MUG, beaker, bowl, chalice, goblet, teacup **2** TROPHY

cupboard *noun* CABINET, press

curb *noun* **1** RESTRAINT, brake, bridle, check, control, deterrent, limitation, rein ▶ *verb* **2** RESTRAIN, check, control, hinder, impede, inhibit, restrict, retard, suppress

cure *verb* **1** MAKE BETTER, correct, ease, heal, mend, relieve, remedy, restore 2 PRESERVE, dry, pickle, salt, smoke ▶*noun* 3 REMEDY, antidote, medicine, nostrum, panacea, treatment

curiosity *noun* 1 INQUISITIVENESS, interest, nosiness (*informal*), prying, snooping (*informal*) 2 ODDITY, freak, novelty, phenomenon, rarity, sight, spectacle, wonder

curious *adjective* 1 INQUIRING, inquisitive, interested, questioning, searching 2 INQUISITIVE, meddling, nosy (*informal*), prying 3 UNUSUAL, bizarre, extraordinary, mysterious, novel, odd, peculiar, rare, strange, unexpected

curl *verb* 1 TWIRL, bend, coil, curve, loop, spiral, turn, twist, wind ▶*noun* 2 TWIST, coil, kink, ringlet, spiral, whorl

curly *adjective* CURLING, crinkly, curled, frizzy, fuzzy, wavy, winding

currency *noun* 1 MONEY, coinage, coins, notes 2 ACCEPTANCE, circulation, exposure, popularity, prevalence, vogue

current *adjective* 1 PRESENT, contemporary, cool (*informal*), fashionable, in fashion, in vogue, phat (*slang*), present-day, trendy (*informal*), up-to-date 2 PREVALENT, accepted, common, customary, in circulation, popular, topical, widespread ▶*noun* 3 FLOW, course, draft, jet, progression, river, stream, tide, undertow 4 MOOD, atmosphere, feeling, tendency, trend, undercurrent

curse *verb* 1 SWEAR, blaspheme, cuss (*informal*), take the Lord's name in vain 2 DAMN, anathematize, excommunicate ▶*noun* 3 OATH, blasphemy, expletive, obscenity, swearing, swearword 4 DENUNCIATION, anathema, ban, excommunication, hoodoo (*informal*), jinx 5 AFFLICTION, bane, hardship, plague, scourge, torment, trouble

cursed *adjective* DAMNED, accursed, bedevilled, doomed, ill-fated

curt *adjective* SHORT, abrupt, blunt, brief, brusque, gruff, monosyllabic, succinct, terse

curtail *verb* CUT SHORT, cut back, decrease, diminish, dock, lessen, reduce, shorten, truncate

curtain *noun* HANGING, drape

curve *noun* 1 BEND, arc, curvature, loop, trajectory, turn ▶*verb* 2 BEND, arc, arch, coil, hook, spiral, swerve, turn, twist, wind

curved *adjective* BENT, arched, bowed, rounded, serpentine, sinuous, twisted

cushion *noun* 1 PILLOW, beanbag, bolster, hassock, headrest, pad ▶*verb* 2 SOFTEN, dampen, deaden, muffle, stifle, suppress

custody *noun* 1 SAFEKEEPING, care, charge, keeping, protection, supervision 2 IMPRISONMENT, confinement, detention, incarceration

custom *noun* 1 TRADITION, convention, policy, practice, ritual, rule, usage 2 HABIT, practice, procedure, routine,

way, wont **3** CUSTOMERS,
patronage, trade

customary *adjective* USUAL,
accepted, accustomed,
common, conventional,
established, normal, ordinary,
routine, traditional

customer *noun* CLIENT, buyer,
consumer, patron, purchaser,
regular (*informal*), shopper

customs *plural noun* DUTY,
import charges, tariff, tax, toll

cut *verb* **1** PENETRATE, chop,
pierce, score, sever, slash, slice,
slit, wound **2** DIVIDE, bisect,
dissect, slice, split **3** TRIM, clip,
hew, lop, mow, pare, prune,
shave, snip **4** ABRIDGE,
abbreviate, condense, curtail,
delete, shorten **5** REDUCE,
contract, cut back, decrease,
diminish, lower, slash, slim
(down) **6** SHAPE, carve, chisel,
engrave, fashion, form, sculpt,
whittle **7** HURT, insult, put
down, snub, sting, wound
▶ *noun* **8** INCISION, gash,
laceration, nick, slash, slit,
stroke, wound **9** REDUCTION,
cutback, decrease, fall,
lowering, saving **10** *Informal*
SHARE, percentage, piece,
portion, section, slice **11** STYLE,
fashion, look, shape

cutback *noun* REDUCTION, cut,
decrease, economy, lessening,
retrenchment

cut down *verb* **1** FELL, hew,
level, lop **2** REDUCE, decrease,
lessen, lower

cute *adjective* APPEALING,
attractive, charming, delightful,
engaging, lovable, sweet,
winning, winsome

cut in *verb* INTERRUPT, break in,

butt in, intervene, intrude

cut off *verb* **1** SEPARATE, isolate,
sever **2** INTERRUPT, disconnect,
intercept

cut out *verb* STOP, cease, give
up, refrain from

cutthroat *adjective*
1 COMPETITIVE, dog-eat-dog,
fierce, relentless, ruthless,
unprincipled ▶ *noun* **2** MURDERER,
assassin, butcher, executioner,
hit man (*slang*), killer

cutting *adjective* HURTFUL,
acrimonious, barbed, bitter,
caustic, malicious, sarcastic,
scathing, vitriolic, wounding

cycle *noun* ERA, circle, period,
phase, revolution, rotation

cynic *noun* SKEPTIC, doubter,
misanthrope, misanthropist,
pessimist, scoffer

cynical *adjective* SKEPTICAL,
contemptuous, derisive,
distrustful, misanthropic,
mocking, pessimistic, scoffing,
scornful, unbelieving

cynicism *noun* SKEPTICISM,
disbelief, doubt, misanthropy,
pessimism

— D d —

dab *verb* **1** PAT, daub, stipple,
tap, touch ▶ *noun* **2** SPOT, bit,
drop, pat, smudge, speck
3 PAT, flick, stroke, tap, touch

dabble *verb* **1** PLAY AT, dip into,
potter, tinker, trifle (with)
2 SPLASH, dip

daft *adjective* *Informal* **1** FOOLISH,
absurd, asinine, bonkers
(*informal*), crackpot (*informal*),

crazy, idiotic, silly, stupid, witless **2** CRAZY, bonkers (*slang*), demented, deranged, insane, nuts (*slang*), touched, unhinged

dagger *noun* KNIFE, bayonet, dirk, stiletto

daily *adjective* **1** EVERYDAY, diurnal, quotidian ▶*adverb* **2** EVERY DAY, day by day, once a day

dainty *adjective* DELICATE, charming, elegant, exquisite, fine, graceful, neat, petite, pretty

dam *noun* **1** BARRIER, barrage, embankment, obstruction, wall ▶*verb* **2** BLOCK UP, barricade, hold back, obstruct, restrict

damage *verb* **1** HARM, hurt, impair, injure, ruin, spoil, weaken, wreck ▶*noun* **2** HARM, destruction, detriment, devastation, hurt, injury, loss, suffering **3** *Informal* COST, bill, charge, expense

damages *plural noun* Law COMPENSATION, fine, reimbursement, reparation, satisfaction

damaging *adjective* HARMFUL, deleterious, detrimental, disadvantageous, hurtful, injurious, ruinous

dame *noun* NOBLEWOMAN, baroness, dowager, *grande dame*, lady, peeress

damn *verb* **1** CONDEMN, blast, censure, criticize, denounce, put down **2** SENTENCE, condemn, doom

damnation *noun* CONDEMNATION, anathema, damning, denunciation, doom

damned *adjective* **1** DOOMED, accursed, condemned, lost

2 *Slang* DETESTABLE, confounded, hateful, infernal, loathsome

damp *adjective* **1** MOIST, clammy, dank, dewy, drizzly, humid, soggy, sopping, wet ▶*noun* **2** MOISTURE, dampness, dankness, drizzle ▶*verb* **3** MOISTEN, dampen, wet **4** **damp down** REDUCE, allay, check, curb, diminish, inhibit, pour cold water on, stifle

dampen *verb* **1** REDUCE, check, dull, lessen, moderate, restrain, stifle **2** MOISTEN, make damp, spray, wet

damper *noun* As in **put a damper on** DISCOURAGEMENT, cold water (*informal*), hindrance, restraint, wet blanket (*informal*)

dance *verb* **1** PRANCE, hop, jig, skip, sway, trip, whirl ▶*noun* **2** BALL, disco, discotheque, hop (*informal, dated*), social

dancer *noun* BALLERINA, Terpsichorean

danger *noun* PERIL, hazard, jeopardy, menace, pitfall, risk, threat, vulnerability

dangerous *adjective* PERILOUS, breakneck, chancy (*informal*), hazardous, insecure, precarious, risky, unsafe, vulnerable

dangerously *adverb* PERILOUSLY, alarmingly, hazardously, precariously, recklessly, riskily, unsafely

dangle *verb* **1** HANG, flap, hang down, sway, swing, trail **2** WAVE, brandish, flaunt, flourish

dapper *adjective* NEAT, smart, soigné *or* soignée, spruce, spry, trim, well-groomed, well turned out

dare *verb* **1** RISK, hazard, make bold, presume, venture **2** CHALLENGE, defy, goad, provoke, taunt, throw down the gauntlet ▶ *noun* **3** CHALLENGE, provocation, taunt

daredevil *noun* **1** ADVENTURER, desperado, exhibitionist, show-off (*informal*), stunt man ▶ *adjective* **2** DARING, adventurous, audacious, bold, death-defying, reckless

daring *adjective* **1** BRAVE, adventurous, audacious, bold, daredevil, fearless, intrepid, reckless, venturesome ▶ *noun* **2** BRAVERY, audacity, boldness, courage, fearlessness, nerve (*informal*), pluck, temerity

dark *adjective* **1** DIM, dingy, murky, shadowy, shady, sunless, unlit **2** BLACK, dark-skinned, dusky, ebony, sable, swarthy **3** GLOOMY, bleak, dismal, grim, morose, mournful, sad, somber **4** EVIL, foul, infernal, sinister, vile, wicked **5** SECRET, concealed, hidden, mysterious ▶ *noun* **6** DARKNESS, dimness, dusk, gloom, murk, obscurity, semi-darkness **7** NIGHT, evening, nightfall, night-time, twilight

darken *verb* MAKE DARK, blacken, dim, obscure, overshadow

darkness *noun* DARK, blackness, duskiness, gloom, murk, nightfall, shade, shadows

darling *noun* **1** BELOVED, dear, dearest, love, sweetheart, truelove ▶ *adjective* **2** BELOVED, adored, cherished, dear, precious, treasured

darn *verb* **1** MEND, cobble up, patch, repair, sew up, stitch ▶ *noun* **2** MEND, invisible repair, patch, reinforcement

dart *verb* DASH, fly, race, run, rush, shoot, spring, sprint, tear

dash *verb* **1** RUSH, bolt, fly, hurry, race, run, speed, sprint, tear **2** THROW, cast, fling, hurl, slam, sling **3** CRASH, break, destroy, shatter, smash, splinter **4** FRUSTRATE, blight, foil, ruin, spoil, thwart, undo ▶ *noun* **5** RUSH, dart, race, run, sortie, sprint, spurt **6** LITTLE, bit, drop, hint, pinch, soupçon, sprinkling, tinge, touch **7** STYLE, brio, élan, flair, flourish, panache, spirit, verve

dashing *adjective* **1** BOLD, debonair, gallant, lively, spirited, swashbuckling **2** STYLISH, elegant, flamboyant, jaunty, showy, smart, sporty

data *noun* INFORMATION, details, facts, figures, statistics

date *noun* **1** TIME, age, epoch, era, period, stage **2** APPOINTMENT, assignation, engagement, meeting, rendezvous, tryst **3** PARTNER, escort, friend ▶ *verb* **4** PUT A DATE ON, assign a date to, fix the period of **5** BECOME OLD-FASHIONED, be dated, show one's age **6** **date from** or **date back to** COME FROM, bear a date of, belong to, exist from, originate in

dated *adjective* OLD-FASHIONED, obsolete, old hat, outdated, outmoded, out of date, passé, unfashionable

daub *verb* SMEAR, coat, cover, paint, plaster, slap on (*informal*)

daunting *adjective* INTIMIDATING, alarming, demoralizing, disconcerting, discouraging, disheartening, frightening, unnerving

dauntless *adjective* FEARLESS, bold, doughty, gallant, indomitable, intrepid, resolute, stouthearted, undaunted, unflinching

dawdle *verb* WASTE TIME, dally, delay, drag one's feet *or* heels, hang about, idle, loaf, loiter, trail

dawn *noun* 1 DAYBREAK, aurora (*poetic*), cockcrow, crack of dawn, daylight, morning, sunrise, sunup 2 BEGINNING, advent, birth, emergence, genesis, origin, rise, start ▶ *verb* 3 GROW LIGHT, break, brighten, lighten 4 BEGIN, appear, develop, emerge, originate, rise, unfold 5 **dawn on** *or* **upon** HIT, become apparent, come into one's head, come to mind, occur, register (*informal*), strike

day *noun* 1 TWENTY-FOUR HOURS, daylight, daytime 2 POINT IN TIME, date, time 3 TIME, age, epoch, era, heyday, period, zenith

daybreak *noun* DAWN, break of day, cockcrow, crack of dawn, first light, morning, sunrise, sunup

daydream *noun* 1 FANTASY, dream, fancy, imagining, pipe dream, reverie, wish ▶ *verb* 2 FANTASIZE, dream, envision, fancy, imagine, muse

daylight *noun* SUNLIGHT, light of day, sunshine

daze *verb* 1 STUN, benumb, numb, paralyze, shock, stupefy ▶ *noun* 2 SHOCK, bewilderment, confusion, distraction, stupor, trance, trancelike state

dazed *adjective* SHOCKED, bewildered, confused, disorientated, dizzy, muddled, punch-drunk, staggered, stunned

dazzle *verb* 1 IMPRESS, amaze, astonish, bowl over (*informal*), overpower, overwhelm, take one's breath away 2 BLIND, bedazzle, blur, confuse, daze ▶ *noun* 3 SPLENDOR, brilliance, glitter, magnificence, razzmatazz (*slang*), sparkle

dazzling *adjective* SPLENDID, brilliant, glittering, glorious, scintillating, sensational (*informal*), sparkling, stunning, virtuoso

dead *adjective* 1 DECEASED, defunct, departed, extinct, late, passed away, perished 2 NOT WORKING, inactive, inoperative, stagnant, unemployed, useless 3 NUMB, inert, paralyzed 4 TOTAL, absolute, complete, outright, thorough, unqualified, utter 5 *Informal* EXHAUSTED, spent, tired, worn out 6 BORING, dull, flat, uninteresting ▶ *noun* 7 MIDDLE, depth, midst

deaden *verb* REDUCE, alleviate, blunt, cushion, diminish, dull, lessen, muffle, smother, stifle, suppress, weaken

deadline *noun* TIME LIMIT, cutoff point, limit, target date

deadlock *noun* 1 DRAW, dead heat, tie 2 IMPASSE, gridlock, stalemate, standoff, standstill

deadlocked *adjective* 1 EVEN, equal, level, neck and neck, on a level playing field (*informal*)

2 GRIDLOCKED, at an impasse, at a standstill

deadly *adjective* LETHAL, dangerous, death-dealing, deathly, fatal, malignant, mortal

deadpan *adjective* EXPRESSIONLESS, blank, impassive, inexpressive, inscrutable, poker-faced, straight-faced

deaf *adjective* **1** HARD OF HEARING, stone deaf, without hearing **2** OBLIVIOUS, indifferent, unconcerned, unhearing, unmoved

deafen *verb* MAKE DEAF, din, drown out, split *or* burst the eardrums

deafening *adjective* EAR-PIERCING, booming, ear-splitting, overpowering, piercing, resounding, ringing, thunderous

deal *noun* **1** AGREEMENT, arrangement, bargain, contract, pact, transaction, understanding **2** AMOUNT, degree, extent, portion, quantity, share ▶ *verb* **3** SELL, bargain, buy and sell, do business, negotiate, stock, trade, traffic

dealer *noun* TRADER, merchant, purveyor, supplier, tradesman, wholesaler

deal out *verb* DISTRIBUTE, allot, apportion, assign, dispense, dole out, give, mete out, share

deal with *verb* **1** HANDLE, attend to, cope with, get to grips with, manage, see to, take care of, treat **2** BE CONCERNED WITH, consider

dear *noun* **1** BELOVED, angel, darling, loved one, precious, treasure ▶ *adjective* **2** BELOVED, cherished, close, favorite,

intimate, precious, prized, treasured **3** EXPENSIVE, at a premium, costly, high-priced, overpriced, pricey (*informal*)

dearly *adverb* **1** VERY MUCH, extremely, greatly, profoundly **2** AT GREAT COST, at a high price

dearth *noun* SCARCITY, deficiency, inadequacy, insufficiency, lack, paucity, poverty, shortage, want

death *noun* **1** DYING, demise, departure, end, exit, passing **2** DESTRUCTION, downfall, extinction, finish, ruin, undoing

deathly *adjective* DEATHLIKE, ghastly, grim, pale, pallid, wan

debacle *noun* DISASTER, catastrophe, collapse, defeat, fiasco, reversal, rout

debase *verb* DEGRADE, cheapen, devalue, lower, reduce

debatable *adjective* DOUBTFUL, arguable, controversial, dubious, moot, problematical, questionable, uncertain

debate *noun* **1** DISCUSSION, argument, contention, controversy, dispute ▶ *verb* **2** DISCUSS, argue, dispute, question **3** CONSIDER, deliberate, ponder, reflect, ruminate, weigh

debauchery *noun* DEPRAVITY, dissipation, dissoluteness, excess, indulgence, intemperance, lewdness, overindulgence

debonair *adjective* ELEGANT, charming, courteous, dashing, refined, smooth, suave, urbane, well-bred

debrief *verb* INTERROGATE, cross-examine, examine, probe, question, quiz

debris *noun* REMAINS, bits, detritus, fragments, rubble, ruins, waste, wreckage

debt *noun* **1** DEBIT, commitment, liability, obligation **2 in debt** OWING, in arrears, in the red (*informal*), liable

debtor *noun* BORROWER, mortgagor

debunk *verb* EXPOSE, cut down to size, deflate, disparage, mock, ridicule, show up

debut *noun* INTRODUCTION, beginning, bow, coming out, entrance, first appearance, initiation, presentation

decadence *noun* DEGENERATION, corruption, decay, decline, deterioration, dissipation, dissolution

decadent *adjective* DEGENERATE, corrupt, decaying, declining, dissolute, immoral, self-indulgent

decapitate *verb* BEHEAD, execute, guillotine

decay *verb* **1** DECLINE, crumble, deteriorate, disintegrate, dwindle, shrivel, wane, waste away, wither **2** ROT, corrode, decompose, perish, putrefy ▶ *noun* **3** DECLINE, collapse, degeneration, deterioration, fading, failing, wasting, withering **4** ROT, caries, decomposition, gangrene, putrefaction

decease *noun* Formal DEATH, demise, departure, dying, release

deceased *adjective* DEAD, defunct, departed, expired, former, late, lifeless

deceit *noun* DISHONESTY, cheating, chicanery, deception, fraud, lying, pretense, treachery, trickery

deceitful *adjective* DISHONEST, deceptive, down and dirty (*informal*), false, fraudulent, sneaky, treacherous, two-faced, untrustworthy

deceive *verb* DUPE (*informal*), cheat, con (*informal*), fool, hoodwink, mislead, swindle, trick

deceiver *noun* LIAR, cheat, con man (*informal*), double-dealer, fraud, impostor, swindler, trickster

decency *noun* RESPECTABILITY, civility, correctness, courtesy, decorum, etiquette, modesty, propriety

decent *adjective* **1** REASONABLE, adequate, ample, fair, passable, satisfactory, sufficient, tolerable **2** RESPECTABLE, chaste, decorous, modest, proper, pure **3** PROPER, appropriate, becoming, befitting, fitting, seemly, suitable **4** Informal KIND, accommodating, courteous, friendly, generous, gracious, helpful, obliging, thoughtful

deception *noun* **1** TRICKERY, cunning, deceit, fraud, guile, legerdemain, treachery **2** TRICK, bluff, decoy, hoax, illusion, lie, ruse, subterfuge

deceptive *adjective* MISLEADING, ambiguous, deceitful, dishonest, false, fraudulent, illusory, unreliable

decide *verb* REACH *or* COME TO A DECISION, adjudge, adjudicate, choose, conclude, determine, make up one's mind, resolve

decidedly *adverb* DEFINITELY,

clearly, distinctly, downright, positively, unequivocally, unmistakably

decimate verb DEVASTATE, ravage, wreak havoc on

decipher verb FIGURE OUT (informal), crack, decode, deduce, interpret, make out, read, solve

decision noun 1 JUDGMENT, arbitration, conclusion, finding, resolution, ruling, sentence, verdict 2 DECISIVENESS, determination, firmness, purpose, resolution, resolve, strength of mind or will

decisive adjective 1 INFLUENTIAL, conclusive, critical, crucial, fateful, momentous, significant 2 RESOLUTE, decided, determined, firm, forceful, incisive, strong-minded, trenchant

deck verb DECORATE, adorn, array, beautify, clothe, dress, embellish, festoon

declaim verb 1 ORATE, harangue, hold forth, lecture, proclaim, rant, recite, speak 2 **declaim against** PROTEST AGAINST, attack, decry, denounce, inveigh, rail

declaration noun 1 STATEMENT, acknowledgment, affirmation, assertion, avowal, disclosure, protestation, revelation, testimony 2 ANNOUNCEMENT, edict, notification, proclamation, profession, pronouncement

declare verb 1 STATE, affirm, announce, assert, claim, maintain, proclaim, profess, pronounce, swear, utter 2 MAKE KNOWN, confess, disclose, reveal, show

decline verb 1 LESSEN, decrease, diminish, dwindle, ebb, fade, fall off, shrink, sink, wane 2 DETERIORATE, decay, degenerate, droop, languish, pine, weaken, worsen 3 REFUSE, abstain, avoid, reject, say 'no', turn down ▶noun 4 LESSENING, downturn, drop, dwindling, falling off, recession, slump 5 DETERIORATION, decay, degeneration, failing, weakening, worsening

decode verb DECIPHER, crack, decrypt, interpret, solve, unscramble, work out

decompose verb ROT, break up, crumble, decay, fall apart, fester, putrefy

decor noun DECORATION, color scheme, furnishing style, ornamentation

decorate verb 1 ADORN, beautify, embellish, festoon, grace, ornament, trim 2 RENOVATE, do up (informal), color, furbish, paint, paper, wallpaper 3 PIN A MEDAL ON, cite, confer an honor on or upon

decoration noun 1 ADORNMENT, beautification, elaboration, embellishment, enrichment, ornamentation, trimming 2 ORNAMENT, bauble, frill, garnish, trimmings 3 MEDAL, award, badge, ribbon, star

decorative adjective ORNAMENTAL, beautifying, fancy, nonfunctional, pretty

decorous adjective PROPER, becoming, correct, decent, dignified, fitting, polite, seemly, well-behaved

decorum noun PROPRIETY,

decency, dignity, etiquette, good manners, politeness, protocol, respectability

decoy noun 1 LURE, bait, enticement, inducement, pretense, trap ▶ verb 2 LURE, deceive, ensnare, entice, entrap, seduce, tempt

decrease verb 1 LESSEN, cut down, decline, diminish, drop, dwindle, lower, reduce, shrink, subside ▶ noun 2 LESSENING, contraction, cutback, decline, dwindling, falling off, loss, reduction, subsidence

decree noun 1 LAW, act, command, edict, order, proclamation, ruling, statute ▶ verb 2 ORDER, command, demand, ordain, prescribe, proclaim, pronounce, rule

decrepit adjective 1 WEAK, aged, doddering, feeble, frail, infirm 2 WORN-OUT, battered, beat-up (informal), broken-down, dilapidated, ramshackle, rickety, run-down, tumbledown, weather-beaten

decry verb CONDEMN, belittle, criticize, denigrate, denounce, discredit, disparage, put down, run down

dedicate verb 1 DEVOTE, commit, give over to, pledge, surrender 2 INSCRIBE, address

dedicated adjective DEVOTED, committed, enthusiastic, purposeful, single-minded, wholehearted, zealous

dedication noun 1 DEVOTION, adherence, allegiance, commitment, faithfulness, loyalty, single-mindedness, wholeheartedness 2 INSCRIPTION, address, message

deduce verb CONCLUDE, draw, gather, glean, infer, reason, take to mean, understand

deduct verb SUBTRACT, decrease by, knock off (informal), reduce by, remove, take away, take off

deduction noun 1 SUBTRACTION, decrease, diminution, discount, reduction, withdrawal 2 CONCLUSION, assumption, finding, inference, reasoning, result

deed noun 1 ACTION, achievement, act, exploit, fact, feat, performance 2 Law DOCUMENT, contract, title

deep adjective 1 WIDE, bottomless, broad, far, profound, unfathomable, yawning 2 MYSTERIOUS, abstract, abstruse, arcane, esoteric, hidden, obscure, recondite, secret 3 INTENSE, extreme, grave, great, profound, serious (informal), unqualified 4 ABSORBED, engrossed, immersed, lost, preoccupied, rapt 5 DARK, intense, rich, strong, vivid 6 LOW, bass, booming, low-pitched, resonant, sonorous ▶ noun 7 **the deep** Poetic OCEAN, briny (informal), high seas, main, sea

deepen verb INTENSIFY, grow, increase, magnify, reinforce, strengthen

deeply adverb 1 THOROUGHLY, completely, gravely, profoundly, seriously, severely, to the core, to the heart, to the quick 2 INTENSELY, acutely, affectingly, distressingly, feelingly, mournfully, movingly, passionately, sadly

deface verb VANDALIZE, damage,

deform, disfigure, mar, mutilate, spoil, tarnish

de facto *adverb* **1** IN FACT, actually, in effect, in reality, really ▶ *adjective* **2** ACTUAL, existing, real

defame *verb* SLANDER, bad-mouth (*slang*), cast aspersions on, denigrate, discredit, disparage, knock (*informal*), libel, malign, smear

default *noun* **1** FAILURE, deficiency, dereliction, evasion, lapse, neglect, nonpayment, omission ▶ *verb* **2** FAIL, dodge, evade, neglect

defeat *verb* **1** BEAT, conquer, crush, master, overwhelm, rout, trounce, vanquish, wipe the floor with (*informal*) **2** FRUSTRATE, baffle, balk, confound, foil, get the better of, ruin, thwart ▶ *noun* **3** CONQUEST, beating, overthrow, rout **4** FRUSTRATION, failure, rebuff, reverse, setback, thwarting

defeatist *noun* **1** PESSIMIST, prophet of doom, quitter ▶ *adjective* **2** PESSIMISTIC

defect *noun* **1** IMPERFECTION, blemish, blotch, error, failing, fault, flaw, spot, taint ▶ *verb* **2** DESERT, abandon, change sides, go over, rebel, revolt, walk out on (*informal*)

defection *noun* DESERTION, apostasy, rebellion

defective *adjective* FAULTY, broken, deficient, flawed, imperfect, not working, on the blink (*slang*), out of order

defector *noun* DESERTER, apostate, renegade, turncoat

defend *verb* **1** PROTECT, cover, guard, keep safe, preserve, safeguard, screen, shelter, shield **2** SUPPORT, champion, endorse, justify, speak up for, stand up for, stick up for (*informal*), uphold, vindicate

defendant *noun* THE ACCUSED, defense, offender, prisoner at the bar, respondent

defender *noun* **1** PROTECTOR, bodyguard, escort, guard **2** SUPPORTER, advocate, champion, sponsor

defense *noun* **1** PROTECTION, cover, guard, immunity, resistance, safeguard, security, shelter **2** SHIELD, barricade, bulwark, buttress, fortification, rampart **3** ARGUMENT, excuse, explanation, justification, plea, vindication **4** *Law* PLEA, alibi, denial, rebuttal, testimony

defenseless *adjective* HELPLESS, exposed, naked, powerless, unarmed, unguarded, unprotected, vulnerable, wide open

defensive *adjective* ON GUARD, on the defensive, protective, uptight (*informal*), watchful

defer[1] *verb* POSTPONE, delay, hold over, procrastinate, put off, put on ice, shelve, suspend

defer[2] *verb* COMPLY, accede, bow, capitulate, give in, give way to, submit, yield

deference *noun* RESPECT, attention, civility, consideration, courtesy, honor, politeness, regard, reverence

deferential *adjective* RESPECTFUL, ingratiating, obedient, obeisant, obsequious, polite, reverential, submissive

defiance *noun* RESISTANCE,

confrontation, contempt,
disobedience, disregard,
insolence, insubordination,
opposition, rebelliousness

defiant *adjective* RESISTING,
audacious, bold, daring,
disobedient, insolent,
insubordinate, mutinous,
provocative, rebellious

deficiency *noun* 1 LACK,
absence, dearth, deficit,
scarcity, shortage 2 FAILING,
defect, demerit, fault, flaw,
frailty, imperfection,
shortcoming, weakness

deficient *adjective* 1 LACKING,
inadequate, insufficient,
meager, scant, scarce, short,
skimpy, wanting
2 UNSATISFACTORY, defective,
faulty, flawed, impaired,
imperfect, incomplete, inferior,
lousy (*slang*), weak

deficit *noun* SHORTFALL, arrears,
deficiency, loss, shortage

define *verb* 1 DESCRIBE,
characterize, designate,
explain, expound, interpret,
specify, spell out 2 MARK OUT,
bound, circumscribe, delineate,
demarcate, limit, outline

definite *adjective* 1 CLEAR,
black-and-white, cut-and-dried
(*informal*), exact, fixed, marked,
particular, precise, specific
2 CERTAIN, assured, decided,
guaranteed, positive, settled,
sure

definitely *adverb* CERTAINLY,
absolutely, categorically,
clearly, positively, surely,
undeniably, unmistakably,
unquestionably, without doubt

definition *noun* 1 EXPLANATION,
clarification, elucidation,

exposition, statement of
meaning 2 SHARPNESS, clarity,
contrast, distinctness, focus,
precision

definitive *adjective* 1 FINAL,
absolute, complete, conclusive,
decisive 2 AUTHORITATIVE,
exhaustive, perfect, reliable,
ultimate

deflate *verb* 1 COLLAPSE, empty,
exhaust, flatten, puncture,
shrink 2 HUMILIATE, chasten,
disconcert, dispirit, humble,
mortify, put down (*slang*),
squash 3 *Economics* REDUCE,
depress, devalue, diminish

deflect *verb* TURN ASIDE, bend,
deviate, diverge, glance off,
ricochet, swerve, veer

deflection *noun* DEVIATION,
bend, divergence, swerve

deform *verb* 1 DISTORT, buckle,
contort, gnarl, mangle,
misshape, twist, warp
2 DISFIGURE, deface, maim, mar,
mutilate, ruin, spoil

deformity *noun* ABNORMALITY,
defect, disfigurement,
malformation

defraud *verb* CHEAT, con
(*informal*), embezzle, fleece,
pilfer, rip off (*slang*), swindle,
trick

deft *adjective* SKILLFUL, adept,
adroit, agile, dexterous, expert,
neat, nimble, proficient

defunct *adjective* 1 DEAD,
deceased, departed, extinct,
gone 2 OBSOLETE, bygone,
expired, inoperative, invalid,
nonexistent, out of commission

defy *verb* RESIST, brave, confront,
disregard, flout, scorn, slight,
spurn

degenerate *adjective*

1 DEPRAVED, corrupt, debauched, decadent, dissolute, immoral, low, perverted ► verb **2** WORSEN, decay, decline, decrease, deteriorate, fall off, lapse, sink, slip

degradation noun **1** DISGRACE, discredit, dishonor, humiliation, ignominy, mortification, shame **2** DETERIORATION, decline, degeneration, demotion, downgrading

degrade verb **1** DISGRACE, debase, demean, discredit, dishonor, humble, humiliate, shame **2** DEMOTE, downgrade, lower

degrading adjective DEMEANING, dishonorable, humiliating, shameful, undignified, unworthy

degree noun STAGE, grade, notch, point, rung, step, unit

deity noun GOD, divinity, goddess, godhead, idol, immortal, supreme being

dejected adjective DOWNHEARTED, crestfallen, depressed, despondent, disconsolate, disheartened, downcast, glum, miserable, sad

dejection noun LOW SPIRITS, depression, despair, despondency, doldrums, downheartedness, gloom, melancholy, sadness, sorrow, unhappiness

de jure adverb LEGALLY, by right, rightfully

delay verb **1** PUT OFF, defer, hold over, postpone, procrastinate, shelve, suspend **2** HOLD UP, bog down, detain, hinder, hold

back, impede, obstruct, set back, slow up ► noun **3** PUTTING OFF, deferment, postponement, procrastination, suspension **4** HOLD-UP, hindrance, impediment, interruption, interval, setback, stoppage, wait

delegate noun **1** REPRESENTATIVE, agent, ambassador, commissioner, deputy, envoy, legate ► verb **2** ENTRUST, assign, consign, devolve, give, hand over, pass on, transfer **3** APPOINT, accredit, authorize, commission, depute, designate, empower, mandate

delegation noun **1** DEPUTATION, commission, contingent, embassy, envoys, legation, mission **2** DEVOLUTION, assignment, commissioning, committal

delete verb REMOVE, cancel, cross out, efface, erase, expunge, obliterate, rub out, strike out

deliberate adjective **1** INTENTIONAL, calculated, conscious, planned, prearranged, premeditated, purposeful, willful **2** UNHURRIED, careful, cautious, circumspect, measured, methodical, ponderous, slow, thoughtful ► verb **3** CONSIDER, cogitate, consult, debate, discuss, meditate, ponder, reflect, think, weigh

deliberately adverb INTENTIONALLY, by design, calculatingly, consciously, in cold blood, knowingly, on purpose, willfully, wittingly

deliberation noun **1** CONSIDERATION, calculation, circumspection, forethought,

meditation, reflection, thought
2 DISCUSSION, conference,
consultation, debate

delicacy noun **1** FINENESS,
accuracy, daintiness, elegance,
exquisiteness, lightness,
precision, subtlety **2** FRAGILITY,
flimsiness, frailty, slenderness,
tenderness, weakness **3** TREAT,
dainty, luxury, savory, tidbit
4 FASTIDIOUSNESS, discrimination,
finesse, purity, refinement,
sensibility, taste **5** SENSITIVITY,
sensitiveness, tact

delicate adjective **1** FINE, deft,
elegant, exquisite, graceful,
precise, skilled, subtle **2** SUBTLE,
choice, dainty, delicious, fine,
savory, tender, yummy
(informal) **3** FRAGILE, flimsy, frail,
slender, slight, tender, weak
4 CONSIDERATE, diplomatic,
discreet, sensitive, tactful

delicately adverb **1** FINELY,
daintily, deftly, elegantly,
exquisitely, gracefully,
precisely, skillfully, subtly
2 TACTFULLY, diplomatically,
sensitively

delicious adjective DELECTABLE,
appetizing, choice, dainty,
mouthwatering, savory, tasty,
toothsome, yummy (informal)

delight noun **1** PLEASURE, ecstasy,
enjoyment, gladness, glee,
happiness, joy, rapture ▶verb
2 PLEASE, amuse, charm, cheer,
enchant, gratify, thrill
3 delight in TAKE PLEASURE IN,
appreciate, enjoy, feast on,
like, love, relish, revel in, savor

delighted adjective PLEASED,
ecstatic, elated, enchanted,
happy, joyous, jubilant,
overjoyed, thrilled

delightful adjective PLEASANT,
agreeable, charming,
delectable, enchanting,
enjoyable, pleasurable,
rapturous, thrilling

delinquent noun CRIMINAL,
culprit, lawbreaker, miscreant,
offender, villain, wrongdoer

delirious adjective **1** MAD, crazy,
demented, deranged,
incoherent, insane, raving,
unhinged **2** ECSTATIC, beside
oneself, carried away, excited,
frantic, frenzied, hysterical,
wild, wired (slang)

delirium noun **1** MADNESS,
derangement, hallucination,
insanity, raving **2** FRENZY,
ecstasy, fever, hysteria, passion

deliver verb **1** CARRY, bear,
bring, cart, convey, distribute,
transport **2** HAND OVER, commit,
give up, grant, make over,
relinquish, surrender, transfer,
turn over, yield **3** GIVE,
announce, declare, present,
read, utter **4** RELEASE,
emancipate, free, liberate,
loose, ransom, rescue, save
5 STRIKE, administer, aim, deal,
direct, give, inflict, launch

deliverance noun RELEASE,
emancipation, escape,
liberation, ransom,
redemption, rescue, salvation

delivery noun **1** HANDING OVER,
consignment, conveyance,
dispatch, distribution,
surrender, transfer,
transmission **2** SPEECH,
articulation, elocution,
enunciation, intonation,
utterance **3** CHILDBIRTH,
confinement, labor, parturition

delude verb DECEIVE, beguile,

dupe, fool, hoodwink, kid
(*informal*), mislead, trick

deluge *noun* 1 FLOOD,
cataclysm, downpour,
inundation, overflowing, spate,
torrent 2 RUSH, avalanche,
barrage, flood, spate, torrent
▶ *verb* 3 FLOOD, douse, drench,
drown, inundate, soak,
submerge, swamp
4 OVERWHELM, engulf, inundate,
overload, overrun, swamp

delusion *noun* MISCONCEPTION,
error, fallacy, false impression,
fancy, hallucination, illusion,
misapprehension, mistake

deluxe *adjective* LUXURIOUS,
costly, exclusive, expensive,
grand, opulent, select, special,
splendid, superior

delve *verb* RESEARCH, burrow,
explore, ferret out, forage,
investigate, look into, probe,
rummage, search

demagogue *noun* AGITATOR,
firebrand, rabble-rouser

demand *verb* 1 REQUEST, ask,
challenge, inquire, interrogate,
question 2 REQUIRE, call for, cry
out for, entail, involve,
necessitate, need, want
3 CLAIM, exact, expect, insist
on, order ▶ *noun* 4 REQUEST,
inquiry, order, question,
requisition 5 NEED, call, claim,
market, requirement, want

demanding *adjective* DIFFICULT,
challenging, exacting, hard,
taxing, tough, trying, wearing

demarcation *noun* DELIMITATION,
differentiation, distinction,
division, separation

demean *verb* LOWER, abase,
debase, degrade, descend,
humble, stoop

demeanor *noun* BEHAVIOR, air,
bearing, carriage,
comportment, conduct,
deportment, manner

demented *adjective* MAD,
crazed, crazy, deranged,
frenzied, insane, maniacal,
unbalanced, unhinged

demise *noun* 1 FAILURE, collapse,
downfall, end, fall, ruin
2 *Euphemistic* DEATH, decease,
departure

democracy *noun*
SELF-GOVERNMENT,
commonwealth, republic

democratic *adjective*
SELF-GOVERNING, autonomous,
egalitarian, popular, populist,
representative

demolish *verb* 1 KNOCK DOWN,
bulldoze, destroy, dismantle,
flatten, level, raze, tear down
2 DEFEAT, annihilate, destroy,
overthrow, overturn, undo,
wreck

demolition *noun* KNOCKING
DOWN, bulldozing, destruction,
explosion, levelling, razing,
tearing down, wrecking

demon *noun* 1 EVIL SPIRIT, devil,
fiend, ghoul, goblin, malignant
spirit 2 WIZARD, ace (*informal*),
fiend, master

**demonic, demoniac,
demoniacal** *adjective*
1 DEVILISH, diabolic, diabolical,
fiendish, hellish, infernal,
satanic 2 FRENZIED, crazed,
frantic, frenetic, furious, hectic,
maniacal, manic

demonstrable *adjective*
PROVABLE, evident, irrefutable,
obvious, palpable, self-evident,
unmistakable, verifiable

demonstrate *verb* 1 PROVE,

display, exhibit, indicate, manifest, show, testify to
2 SHOW HOW, describe, explain, illustrate, make clear, teach
3 MARCH, parade, picket, protest, rally

demonstration noun **1** MARCH, mass lobby, parade, picket, protest, rally, sit-in
2 EXPLANATION, description, exposition, presentation, test, trial **3** PROOF, confirmation, display, evidence, exhibition, expression, illustration, testimony

demoralize verb DISHEARTEN, deject, depress, discourage, dispirit, undermine, unnerve, weaken

demote verb DOWNGRADE, degrade, kick downstairs (slang), lower in rank, relegate

demur verb **1** OBJECT, balk, dispute, hesitate, protest, refuse, take exception, waver
▶ noun **2** As in **without demur** OBJECTION, compunction, dissent, hesitation, misgiving, protest, qualm

demure adjective SHY, diffident, modest, reserved, reticent, retiring, sedate, unassuming

den noun **1** LAIR, cave, cavern, haunt, hideout, hole, shelter
2 Chiefly U.S. STUDY, cubbyhole, hideaway, living room, retreat, sanctuary, sanctum

denial noun **1** NEGATION, contradiction, dissent, renunciation, repudiation, retraction **2** REFUSAL, prohibition, rebuff, rejection, repulse, veto

denigrate verb DISPARAGE, bad-mouth (slang), belittle,

knock (informal), malign, run down, slander, vilify

denomination noun **1** RELIGIOUS GROUP, belief, creed, persuasion, school, sect **2** UNIT, grade, size, value

denote verb INDICATE, betoken, designate, express, imply, mark, mean, show, signify

denounce verb CONDEMN, accuse, attack, censure, denunciate, revile, stigmatize, vilify

dense adjective **1** THICK, close-knit, compact, condensed, heavy, impenetrable, opaque, solid
2 STUPID, dull, obtuse, slow-witted, stolid, thick

density noun TIGHTNESS, bulk, compactness, consistency, denseness, impenetrability, mass, solidity, thickness

dent noun **1** HOLLOW, chip, crater, depression, dimple, dip, impression, indentation, pit
▶ verb **2** MAKE A DENT IN, gouge, hollow, press in, push in

deny verb **1** CONTRADICT, disagree with, disprove, rebuff, rebut, refute **2** REFUSE, begrudge, disallow, forbid, reject, turn down, withhold
3 RENOUNCE, disclaim, disown, recant, repudiate, retract

depart verb **1** LEAVE, absent (oneself), disappear, exit, go, go away, quit, retire, retreat, withdraw **2** DEVIATE, differ, digress, diverge, stray, swerve, turn aside, vary, veer

department noun SECTION, branch, bureau, division, office, station, subdivision, unit

departure noun **1** LEAVING, exit,

exodus, going, going away, leave-taking, removal, retirement, withdrawal **2** DIVERGENCE, deviation, digression, variation **3** SHIFT, change, difference, innovation, novelty, whole new ball game (*informal*)

depend *verb* **1** TRUST IN, bank on, count on, lean on, reckon on, rely upon, turn to **2** BE DETERMINED BY, be based on, be contingent on, be subject to, be subordinate to, hang on, hinge on, rest on, revolve around

dependable *adjective* RELIABLE, faithful, reputable, responsible, staunch, steady, sure, trustworthy, trusty, unfailing

dependant *noun* RELATIVE, child, minor, protégé, subordinate

dependent *adjective* **1** RELYING ON, defenseless, helpless, reliant, vulnerable, weak **2 dependent on** *or* **upon** DETERMINED BY, conditional on, contingent on, depending on, influenced by, subject to

depict *verb* **1** DRAW, delineate, illustrate, outline, paint, picture, portray, sketch **2** DESCRIBE, characterize, narrate, outline, represent

depiction *noun* REPRESENTATION, delineation, description, picture, portrayal, sketch

deplete *verb* USE UP, consume, drain, empty, exhaust, expend, impoverish, lessen, reduce

deplorable *adjective*
1 REGRETTABLE, grievous, lamentable, pitiable, sad, unfortunate, wretched **2** DISGRACEFUL, dishonorable,

reprehensible, scandalous, shameful

deplore *verb* DISAPPROVE OF, abhor, censure, condemn, denounce, object to, take a dim view of

deploy *verb* POSITION, arrange, set out, station, use, utilize

deployment *noun* POSITION, arrangement, organization, spread, stationing, use, utilization

deport *verb* **1** EXPEL, banish, exile, expatriate, extradite, oust **2 deport oneself** BEHAVE, acquit oneself, act, bear oneself, carry oneself, comport oneself, conduct oneself, hold oneself

depose *verb* **1** REMOVE FROM OFFICE, demote, dethrone, dismiss, displace, oust **2** *Law* TESTIFY, avouch, declare, make a deposition

deposit *verb* **1** PUT, drop, lay, locate, place **2** STORE, bank, consign, entrust, lodge ▶ *noun* **3** DOWN PAYMENT, installment, part payment, pledge, retainer, security, stake **4** SEDIMENT, accumulation, dregs, lees, precipitate, silt

depot *noun* **1** STOREHOUSE, depository, repository, warehouse **2** BUS STATION, garage, terminus

depraved *adjective* CORRUPT, degenerate, dissolute, evil, immoral, sinful, vicious, vile, wicked

depravity *noun* CORRUPTION, debauchery, evil, immorality, sinfulness, vice, wickedness

depreciate *verb* **1** DEVALUE, decrease, deflate, lessen, lose value, lower, reduce

2 DISPARAGE, belittle, denigrate, deride, detract, run down, scorn, sneer at

depreciation *noun*
1 DEVALUATION, deflation, depression, drop, fall, slump
2 DISPARAGEMENT, belittlement, denigration, deprecation, detraction

depress *verb* 1 SADDEN, deject, discourage, dishearten, dispirit, make despondent, oppress, weigh down 2 LOWER, cheapen, depreciate, devalue, diminish, downgrade, lessen, reduce
3 PRESS DOWN, flatten, level, lower, push down

depressed *adjective*
1 LOW-SPIRITED, blue, dejected, despondent, discouraged, dispirited, downcast, downhearted, fed up, sad, unhappy 2 POVERTY-STRICKEN, deprived, disadvantaged, needy, poor, run-down
3 LOWERED, cheapened, depreciated, devalued, weakened 4 SUNKEN, concave, hollow, indented, recessed

depressing *adjective* BLEAK, discouraging, disheartening, dismal, dispiriting, gloomy, harrowing, sad, saddening

depression *noun* 1 LOW SPIRITS, dejection, despair, despondency, downheartedness, dumps (*informal*), gloominess, melancholy, sadness, the blues
2 RECESSION, economic decline, hard *or* bad times, inactivity, slump, stagnation 3 HOLLOW, bowl, cavity, dent, dimple, dip, indentation, pit, valley

deprivation *noun*
1 WITHHOLDING, denial, dispossession, expropriation, removal, withdrawal 2 WANT, destitution, distress, hardship, need, privation

deprive *verb* WITHHOLD, bereave, despoil, dispossess, rob, strip

deprived *adjective* POOR, bereft, destitute, disadvantaged, down at heel, in need, lacking, needy

depth *noun* 1 DEEPNESS, drop, extent, measure 2 INSIGHT, astuteness, discernment, penetration, profoundness, profundity, sagacity, wisdom

deputation *noun* DELEGATION, commission, embassy, envoys, legation

deputize *verb* STAND IN FOR, act for, take the place of, understudy

deputy *noun* SUBSTITUTE, delegate, legate, lieutenant, number two, proxy, representative, second-in-command, surrogate

deranged *adjective* MAD, crazed, crazy, demented, distracted, insane, irrational, unbalanced, unhinged

derelict *adjective* 1 ABANDONED, deserted, dilapidated, discarded, forsaken, neglected, ruined ▶ *noun* 2 TRAMP, bag lady, down-and-out, outcast, vagrant

deride *verb* MOCK, disdain, disparage, insult, jeer, ridicule, scoff, scorn, sneer, taunt

derisory *adjective* RIDICULOUS, contemptible, insulting, laughable, lousy (*slang*), ludicrous, outrageous, preposterous

derivation *noun* ORIGIN, beginning, foundation,

root, source

derive from *verb* COME FROM, arise from, emanate from, flow from, issue from, originate from, proceed from, spring from, stem from

derogatory *adjective* DISPARAGING, belittling, defamatory, offensive, slighting, uncomplimentary, unfavorable, unflattering

descend *verb* **1** MOVE DOWN, drop, fall, go down, plummet, plunge, sink, subside, tumble **2** SLOPE, dip, incline, slant **3** LOWER ONESELF, degenerate, deteriorate, stoop **4** **be descended** ORIGINATE, be handed down, be passed down, derive, issue, proceed, spring **5 descend on** ATTACK, arrive, invade, raid, swoop

descent *noun* **1** COMING DOWN, drop, fall, plunge, swoop **2** SLOPE, declivity, dip, drop, incline, slant **3** ANCESTRY, extraction, family tree, genealogy, lineage, origin, parentage **4** DECLINE, degeneration, deterioration

describe *verb* **1** RELATE, depict, explain, express, narrate, portray, recount, report, tell **2** TRACE, delineate, draw, mark out, outline

description *noun* **1** ACCOUNT, depiction, explanation, narrative, portrayal, report, representation, sketch **2** KIND, brand, category, class, order, sort, type, variety

descriptive *adjective* GRAPHIC, detailed, explanatory, expressive, illustrative, pictorial, picturesque, vivid

desert[1] *noun* WILDERNESS, solitude, waste, wasteland, wilds

desert[2] *verb* ABANDON, abscond, forsake, jilt, leave, leave stranded, maroon, quit, strand, walk out on (*informal*)

deserted *adjective* ABANDONED, derelict, desolate, empty, forsaken, neglected, unoccupied, vacant

deserter *noun* DEFECTOR, absconder, escapee, fugitive, renegade, runaway, traitor, truant

desertion *noun* ABANDONMENT, absconding, apostasy, betrayal, defection, dereliction, escape, evasion, flight, relinquishment

deserve *verb* MERIT, be entitled to, be worthy of, earn, justify, rate, warrant

deserved *adjective* WELL-EARNED, due, earned, fitting, justified, merited, proper, rightful, warranted

deserving *adjective* WORTHY, commendable, estimable, laudable, meritorious, praiseworthy, righteous

design *verb* **1** PLAN, draft, draw, outline, sketch, trace **2** CREATE, conceive, fabricate, fashion, invent, originate, think up **3** INTEND, aim, mean, plan, propose, purpose ▶ *noun* **4** PLAN, blueprint, draft, drawing, model, outline, scheme, sketch **5** ARRANGEMENT, construction, form, organization, pattern, shape, style **6** INTENTION, aim, end, goal, object, objective, purpose, target

designate *verb* **1** NAME, call,

dub, entitle, label, style, term
2 APPOINT, assign, choose,
delegate, depute, nominate,
select

designation *noun* NAME,
description, label, mark, title

designer *noun* CREATOR,
architect, deviser, inventor,
originator, planner

desirable *adjective*
1 WORTHWHILE, advantageous,
advisable, beneficial, good,
preferable, profitable, win-win
(*informal*) 2 ATTRACTIVE,
adorable, alluring, fetching,
glamorous, seductive, sexy
(*informal*)

desire *verb* 1 WANT, crave,
hanker after, hope for, long
for, set one's heart on, thirst
for, wish for, yearn for ▶*noun*
2 WISH, aspiration, craving,
hankering, hope, longing,
thirst, want 3 LUST, appetite,
libido, passion

desist *verb* STOP, break off,
cease, discontinue, end,
forbear, leave off, pause,
refrain from

desolate *adjective* 1 UNINHABITED,
bare, barren, bleak, dreary,
godforsaken, solitary, wild
2 MISERABLE, dejected,
despondent, disconsolate,
downcast, forlorn, gloomy,
wretched ▶*verb* 3 LAY WASTE,
depopulate, despoil, destroy,
devastate, lay low, pillage,
plunder, ravage, ruin 4 DEJECT,
depress, discourage,
dishearten, dismay, distress,
grieve

desolation *noun* 1 RUIN,
destruction, devastation, havoc
2 BLEAKNESS, barrenness,

isolation, solitude 3 MISERY,
anguish, dejection, despair,
distress, gloom, sadness, woe,
wretchedness

despair *noun* 1 DESPONDENCY,
anguish, dejection, depression,
desperation, gloom,
hopelessness, misery,
wretchedness ▶*verb* 2 LOSE
HOPE, give up, lose heart

despairing *adjective* HOPELESS,
dejected, desperate,
despondent, disconsolate,
frantic, grief-stricken,
inconsolable, miserable,
wretched

despatch see DISPATCH

desperado *noun* CRIMINAL,
bandit, lawbreaker, outlaw,
villain

desperate *adjective* 1 RECKLESS,
audacious, daring, frantic,
furious, risky 2 GRAVE, drastic,
extreme, urgent

desperately *adverb* 1 GRAVELY,
badly, dangerously, perilously,
seriously, severely 2 HOPELESSLY,
appallingly, fearfully, frightfully,
shockingly

desperation *noun*
1 RECKLESSNESS, foolhardiness,
frenzy, impetuosity, madness,
rashness 2 MISERY, agony,
anguish, despair, hopelessness,
trouble, unhappiness, worry

despicable *adjective*
CONTEMPTIBLE, detestable,
disgraceful, hateful, lousy
(*slang*), mean, scuzzy (*slang*),
shameful, sordid, vile,
worthless, wretched

despise *verb* LOOK DOWN ON,
abhor, detest, loathe, revile,
scorn

despite *preposition* IN SPITE OF,

against, even with, in the face of, in the teeth of, notwithstanding, regardless of, undeterred by

despondency noun DEJECTION, depression, despair, desperation, gloom, low spirits, melancholy, misery, sadness

despondent adjective DEJECTED, depressed, disconsolate, disheartened, dispirited, downhearted, glum, in despair, sad, sorrowful

despot noun TYRANT, autocrat, dictator, oppressor

despotic adjective TYRANNICAL, authoritarian, autocratic, dictatorial, domineering, imperious, oppressive

despotism noun TYRANNY, autocracy, dictatorship, oppression, totalitarianism

destination noun JOURNEY'S END, haven, resting-place, station, stop, terminus

destined adjective FATED, bound, certain, doomed, intended, meant, predestined

destiny noun FATE, doom, fortune, karma, kismet, lot, portion

destitute adjective PENNILESS, down and out, down on one's luck (*informal*), impoverished, indigent, insolvent, moneyless, penurious, poor, poverty-stricken

destroy verb RUIN, annihilate, crush, demolish, devastate, eradicate, shatter, wipe out, wreck

destruction noun RUIN, annihilation, demolition, devastation, eradication, extermination, havoc,

slaughter, wreckage

destructive adjective DAMAGING, calamitous, catastrophic, deadly, devastating, fatal, harmful, lethal, ruinous

detach verb SEPARATE, cut off, disconnect, disengage, divide, remove, sever, tear off, unfasten

detached adjective 1 SEPARATE, disconnected, discrete, unconnected 2 UNINVOLVED, disinterested, dispassionate, impartial, impersonal, neutral, objective, reserved, unbiased

detachment noun 1 INDIFFERENCE, aloofness, coolness, nonchalance, remoteness, unconcern 2 IMPARTIALITY, fairness, neutrality, objectivity 3 *Military* UNIT, body, force, party, patrol, squad, task force

detail noun 1 POINT, aspect, component, element, fact, factor, feature, particular, respect 2 FINE POINT, nicety, particular, triviality 3 *Military* PARTY, assignment, body, detachment, duty, fatigue, force, squad ▶ verb 4 LIST, catalog, enumerate, itemize, recite, recount, rehearse, relate, tabulate 5 APPOINT, allocate, assign, charge, commission, delegate, send

detailed adjective COMPREHENSIVE, blow-by-blow, exhaustive, full, intricate, minute, particular, thorough

detain verb 1 DELAY, check, hinder, hold up, impede, keep back, retard, slow up (*or* down) 2 HOLD, arrest, confine, intern, restrain

detect verb 1 NOTICE, ascertain,

identify, note, observe, perceive, recognize, spot
2 DISCOVER, find, track down, uncover, unmask

detective *noun* INVESTIGATOR, cop (*slang*), gumshoe (*slang*), private eye, private investigator, sleuth (*informal*)

detention *noun* IMPRISONMENT, confinement, custody, incarceration, quarantine

deter *verb* DISCOURAGE, dissuade, frighten, inhibit from, intimidate, prevent, put off, stop, talk out of

detergent *noun* CLEANER, cleanser

deteriorate *verb* DECLINE, degenerate, go downhill (*informal*), lower, slump, worsen

determination *noun* TENACITY, dedication, doggedness, fortitude, perseverance, persistence, resolve, single-mindedness, steadfastness, willpower

determine *verb* **1** SETTLE, conclude, decide, end, finish, ordain, regulate **2** FIND OUT, ascertain, detect, discover, learn, verify, work out **3** DECIDE, choose, elect, make up one's mind, resolve

determined *adjective* RESOLUTE, dogged, firm, intent, persevering, persistent, single-minded, steadfast, tenacious, unwavering

deterrent *noun* DISCOURAGEMENT, check, curb, disincentive, hindrance, impediment, obstacle, restraint

detest *verb* HATE, abhor, abominate, despise, dislike intensely, loathe, recoil from

detonate *verb* EXPLODE, blast, blow up, discharge, set off, trigger

detour *noun* DIVERSION, bypass, circuitous *or* indirect route, roundabout way

detract *verb* LESSEN, devaluate, diminish, lower, reduce, take away from

detriment *noun* DAMAGE, disadvantage, disservice, harm, hurt, impairment, injury, loss

detrimental *adjective* DAMAGING, adverse, deleterious, destructive, disadvantageous, harmful, prejudicial, unfavorable

devastate *verb* DESTROY, demolish, lay waste, level, ravage, raze, ruin, sack, wreck

devastating *adjective* OVERWHELMING, cutting, overpowering, savage, trenchant, vitriolic, withering

devastation *noun* DESTRUCTION, demolition, desolation, havoc, ruin

develop *verb* **1** ADVANCE, evolve, flourish, grow, mature, progress, prosper, ripen **2** FORM, breed, establish, generate, invent, originate **3** EXPAND, amplify, augment, broaden, elaborate, enlarge, unfold, work out

development *noun* **1** GROWTH, advance, evolution, expansion, improvement, increase, progress, spread **2** EVENT, happening, incident, occurrence, result, turn of events, upshot

deviant *adjective* **1** PERVERTED, kinky (*slang*), sick (*informal*), twisted, warped ▶ *noun* **2** PERVERT, freak, misfit

deviate *verb* DIFFER, depart,

diverge, stray, swerve, veer, wander

deviation noun DEPARTURE, digression, discrepancy, disparity, divergence, inconsistency, irregularity, shift, variation

device noun 1 GADGET, apparatus, appliance, contraption, implement, instrument, machine, tool 2 PLOY, gambit, maneuver, plan, scheme, stratagem, trick, wile

devil noun 1 **the Devil** SATAN, Beelzebub, Evil One, Lucifer, Mephistopheles, Prince of Darkness 2 BRUTE, beast, demon, fiend, monster, ogre, terror 3 SCAMP, rascal, rogue, scoundrel 4 PERSON, beggar, creature, thing, wretch

devilish adjective FIENDISH, atrocious, damnable, detestable, diabolical, hellish, infernal, satanic, wicked

devious adjective 1 SLY, calculating, deceitful, dishonest, double-dealing, insincere, scheming, surreptitious, underhand, wily 2 INDIRECT, circuitous, rambling, roundabout

devise verb WORK OUT, conceive, construct, contrive, design, dream up, formulate, invent, think up

devoid adjective LACKING, bereft, deficient, destitute, empty, free from, wanting, without

devote verb DEDICATE, allot, apply, assign, commit, give, pledge, reserve, set apart

devoted adjective DEDICATED, ardent, committed, constant, devout, faithful, loyal, staunch, steadfast, true

devotee noun ENTHUSIAST, adherent, admirer, aficionado, buff (*informal*), disciple, fan, fanatic, follower, supporter

devotion noun 1 DEDICATION, adherence, allegiance, commitment, constancy, faithfulness, fidelity, loyalty 2 LOVE, affection, attachment, fondness, passion 3 DEVOUTNESS, godliness, holiness, piety, reverence, spirituality 4 **devotions** PRAYERS, church service, divine office, religious observance

devour verb 1 EAT, chow down (*slang*), consume, gobble, gulp, guzzle, polish off (*informal*), swallow, wolf 2 DESTROY, annihilate, consume, ravage, waste, wipe out 3 ENJOY, read compulsively or voraciously, take in

devout adjective RELIGIOUS, godly, holy, orthodox, pious, prayerful, pure, reverent, saintly

dexterity noun 1 SKILL, adroitness, deftness, expertise, finesse, nimbleness, proficiency, touch 2 CLEVERNESS, ability, aptitude, ingenuity

diabolical adjective Informal DREADFUL, abysmal, appalling, atrocious, hellish, outrageous, shocking, terrible

diagnose verb IDENTIFY, analyze, determine, distinguish, interpret, pinpoint, pronounce, recognize

diagnosis noun 1 EXAMINATION, analysis, investigation, scrutiny 2 OPINION, conclusion, interpretation, pronouncement

diagonal *adjective* SLANTING, angled, cross, crossways, crosswise, oblique

diagonally *adverb* ASLANT, at an angle, cornerwise, crosswise, obliquely

diagram *noun* PLAN, chart, drawing, figure, graph, representation, sketch

dialect *noun* LANGUAGE, brogue, idiom, jargon, patois, provincialism, speech, vernacular

dialogue *noun* CONVERSATION, communication, conference, discourse, discussion

diary *noun* JOURNAL, appointment book, chronicle, daily record, engagement book, Filofax (*Trademark*)

dictate *verb* 1 SPEAK, read out, say, utter 2 ORDER, command, decree, demand, direct, impose, lay down the law, pronounce ▶*noun* 3 COMMAND, decree, demand, direction, edict, fiat, injunction, order 4 PRINCIPLE, code, law, rule

dictator *noun* ABSOLUTE RULER, autocrat, despot, oppressor, tyrant

dictatorial *adjective* 1 ABSOLUTE, arbitrary, autocratic, despotic, totalitarian, tyrannical, unlimited, unrestricted 2 DOMINEERING, authoritarian, bossy (*informal*), imperious, oppressive, overbearing

dictatorship *noun* ABSOLUTE RULE, absolutism, authoritarianism, autocracy, despotism, totalitarianism, tyranny

diction *noun* PRONUNCIATION, articulation, delivery, elocution, enunciation, fluency, inflection,

intonation, speech

dictionary *noun* WORDBOOK, glossary, lexicon, vocabulary

die *verb* 1 PASS AWAY, breathe one's last, croak (*slang*), expire, give up the ghost, kick the bucket (*slang*), perish, snuff it (*slang*) 2 DWINDLE, decay, decline, fade, sink, subside, wane, wilt, wither 3 STOP, break down, fade out *or* away, fail, fizzle out, halt, lose power, peter out, run down 4 **be dying** LONG, ache, be eager, desire, hunger, pine for, yearn

die-hard *noun* REACTIONARY, fanatic, old fogey, stick-in-the-mud (*informal*)

diet¹ *noun* 1 FOOD, fare, nourishment, nutriment, provisions, rations, sustenance, victuals 2 REGIME, abstinence, fast, regimen ▶*verb* 3 SLIM, abstain, eat sparingly, fast, lose weight

diet² *noun* COUNCIL, chamber, congress, convention, legislature, meeting, parliament

differ *verb* 1 BE DISSIMILAR, contradict, contrast, depart from, diverge, run counter to, stand apart, vary 2 DISAGREE, clash, contend, debate, demur, dispute, dissent, oppose, take exception, take issue

difference *noun* 1 DISSIMILARITY, alteration, change, contrast, discrepancy, disparity, diversity, variation, variety 2 DISAGREEMENT, argument, clash, conflict, contretemps, debate, dispute, quarrel 3 REMAINDER, balance, rest, result

different *adjective* 1 UNLIKE, altered, changed, contrasting,

disparate, dissimilar, divergent, inconsistent, opposed
2 VARIOUS, assorted, diverse, miscellaneous, sundry, varied
3 UNUSUAL, atypical, distinctive, extraordinary, peculiar, singular, special, strange, uncommon

differentiate *verb* **1** DISTINGUISH, contrast, discriminate, make a distinction, mark off, separate, set off *or* apart, tell apart
2 MAKE DIFFERENT, adapt, alter, change, convert, modify, transform

difficult *adjective* **1** HARD, arduous, demanding, formidable, laborious, onerous, strenuous, uphill
2 PROBLEMATICAL, abstruse, baffling, complex, complicated, intricate, involved, knotty, obscure **3** HARD TO PLEASE, demanding, fastidious, fussy, perverse, refractory, unaccommodating

difficulty *noun* **1** LABORIOUSNESS, arduousness, awkwardness, hardship, strain, strenuousness, tribulation **2** PREDICAMENT, dilemma, embarrassment, hot water (*informal*), jam (*informal*), mess, plight, quandary, trouble **3** PROBLEM, complication, hindrance, hurdle, impediment, obstacle, pitfall, snag, stumbling block

diffidence *noun* SHYNESS, bashfulness, hesitancy, insecurity, modesty, reserve, self-consciousness, timidity

diffident *adjective* SHY, bashful, doubtful, hesitant, insecure, modest, reserved, self-conscious, timid, unassertive, unassuming

dig *verb* **1** EXCAVATE, burrow, delve, hollow out, mine, quarry, scoop, tunnel
2 INVESTIGATE, delve, dig down, go into, probe, research, search **3** (with *out* or *up*) FIND, discover, expose, uncover, unearth, uproot **4** POKE, drive, jab, prod, punch, thrust ▸ *noun*
5 POKE, jab, prod, punch, thrust **6** CUTTING REMARK, barb, gibe, insult, jeer, sneer, taunt, wisecrack (*informal*)

digest *verb* **1** INGEST, absorb, assimilate, dissolve, incorporate
2 TAKE IN, absorb, consider, contemplate, grasp, study, understand ▸ *noun* **3** SUMMARY, abridgment, abstract, epitome, précis, résumé, synopsis

digestion *noun* INGESTION, absorption, assimilation, conversion, incorporation, transformation

dignified *adjective* DISTINGUISHED, formal, grave, imposing, noble, reserved, solemn, stately

dignitary *noun* PUBLIC FIGURE, high-up (*informal*), notable, personage, pillar of society, V.I.P., worthy

dignity *noun* **1** DECORUM, courtliness, grandeur, gravity, loftiness, majesty, nobility, solemnity, stateliness **2** HONOR, eminence, importance, rank, respectability, standing, status **3** SELF-IMPORTANCE, pride, self-esteem, self-respect

digress *verb* WANDER, depart, deviate, diverge, drift, get off the point *or* subject, go off at a tangent, ramble, stray

digression *noun* DEPARTURE, aside, detour, deviation,

divergence, diversion, straying, wandering

dilapidated *adjective* RUINED, broken-down, crumbling, decrepit, in ruins, ramshackle, rickety, run-down, tumbledown

dilate *verb* ENLARGE, broaden, expand, puff out, stretch, swell, widen

dilatory *adjective* TIME-WASTING, delaying, lingering, procrastinating, slow, sluggish, tardy, tarrying

dilemma *noun* PREDICAMENT, difficulty, mess, plight, problem, puzzle, quandary, spot (*informal*)

dilettante *noun* AMATEUR, aesthete, dabbler, trifler

diligence *noun* APPLICATION, attention, care, industry, laboriousness, perseverance

diligent *adjective* HARD-WORKING, assiduous, attentive, careful, conscientious, industrious, painstaking, persistent, studious, tireless

dilute *verb* 1 WATER DOWN, adulterate, cut, make thinner, thin (out), weaken 2 REDUCE, attenuate, decrease, diffuse, diminish, lessen, mitigate, temper, weaken

dim *adjective* 1 POORLY LIT, cloudy, dark, gray, overcast, shadowy, tenebrous 2 UNCLEAR, bleary, blurred, faint, fuzzy, ill-defined, indistinct, obscured, shadowy 3 **take a dim view** DISAPPROVE, be displeased, be skeptical, look askance, reject, suspect, take exception, view with disfavor ▶*verb* 4 DULL, blur, cloud, darken, fade, obscure

dimension *noun* (often plural) MEASUREMENT, amplitude, bulk, capacity, extent, proportions, size, volume

diminish *verb* 1 DECREASE, curtail, cut, lessen, lower, reduce, shrink 2 DWINDLE, decline, die out, recede, subside, wane

diminutive *adjective* SMALL, little, mini, miniature, minute, petite, tiny, undersized

din *noun* 1 NOISE, clamor, clatter, commotion, crash, pandemonium, racket, row, uproar ▶*verb* 2 **din (something) into (someone)** INSTILL, drum into, go on at, hammer into, inculcate, instruct, teach

dine *verb* EAT, banquet, chow down (*slang*), feast, lunch, sup

dingy *adjective* DULL, dark, dim, drab, dreary, gloomy, murky, obscure, somber

dinner *noun* MEAL, banquet, feast, main meal, repast, spread (*informal*)

dip *verb* 1 PLUNGE, bathe, douse, duck, dunk, immerse 2 SLOPE, decline, descend, drop (down), fall, lower, sink, subside ▶*noun* 3 PLUNGE, douche, drenching, ducking, immersion, soaking 4 BATHE, dive, plunge, swim 5 HOLLOW, basin, concavity, depression, hole, incline, slope 6 DROP, decline, fall, lowering, sag, slip, slump

dip into *verb* SAMPLE, browse, glance at, peruse, skim

diplomacy *noun* 1 STATESMANSHIP, international negotiation, statecraft 2 TACT, artfulness, craft, delicacy, discretion, finesse, savoir-faire, skill, subtlety

diplomat *noun* NEGOTIATOR, conciliator, go-between, mediator, moderator, politician, tactician

diplomatic *adjective* TACTFUL, adept, discreet, polite, politic, prudent, sensitive, subtle

dire *adjective* 1 DISASTROUS, awful, calamitous, catastrophic, horrible, ruinous, terrible, woeful 2 DESPERATE, critical, crucial, drastic, extreme, now or never, pressing, urgent 3 GRIM, dismal, dreadful, fearful, gloomy, ominous, portentous

direct *adjective* 1 STRAIGHT, nonstop, not crooked, shortest, through, unbroken, uninterrupted 2 IMMEDIATE, face-to-face, first-hand, head-on, personal 3 HONEST, candid, frank, open, plain-spoken, straight, straightforward, upfront (*informal*) 4 EXPLICIT, absolute, blunt, categorical, downright, express, plain, point-blank, unambiguous, unequivocal
▶ *verb* 5 CONTROL, conduct, guide, handle, lead, manage, oversee, run, supervise 6 ORDER, bid, charge, command, demand, dictate, instruct 7 GUIDE, indicate, lead, point in the direction of, point the way, show 8 ADDRESS, label, mail, route, send 9 AIM, focus, level, point, train

direction *noun* 1 WAY, aim, bearing, course, line, path, road, route, track 2 MANAGEMENT, administration, charge, command, control, guidance, leadership, order, supervision

directions *plural noun* INSTRUCTIONS, briefing, guidance, guidelines, plan, recommendation, regulations

directive *noun* ORDER, command, decree, edict, injunction, instruction, mandate, regulation, ruling

directly *adverb* 1 STRAIGHT, by the shortest route, exactly, in a beeline, precisely, unswervingly, without deviation 2 HONESTLY, openly, plainly, point-blank, straightforwardly, truthfully, unequivocally 3 AT ONCE, as soon as possible, forthwith, immediately, promptly, right away, straightaway

director *noun* CONTROLLER, administrator, chief, executive, governor, head, leader, manager, supervisor

dirge *noun* LAMENT, dead march, elegy, funeral song, requiem, threnody

dirt *noun* 1 FILTH, dust, grime, impurity, muck, mud 2 SOIL, clay, earth, loam 3 OBSCENITY, indecency, pornography, sleaze, smut

dirty *adjective* 1 FILTHY, foul, grimy, grubby, messy, mucky, muddy, polluted, scuzzy (*slang*), soiled, unclean 2 DISHONEST, crooked, fraudulent, illegal, lowdown (*slang*), scuzzy (*slang*), treacherous, unfair, unscrupulous, unsporting 3 OBSCENE, blue, indecent, pornographic, salacious, scuzzy (*slang*), sleazy, smutty, X-rated 4 As in **a dirty look** ANGRY,

annoyed, bitter, choked,
indignant, offended, resentful,
scorching ▶*verb* **5** SOIL,
blacken, defile, foul, muddy,
pollute, smirch, spoil, stain

disability *noun* **1** HANDICAP,
affliction, ailment, complaint,
defect, disorder, impairment,
infirmity, malady **2** INCAPACITY,
inability, unfitness

disable *verb* **1** HANDICAP, cripple,
damage, enfeeble, immobilize,
impair, incapacitate, paralyze
2 DISQUALIFY, invalidate, render
or declare incapable

disabled *adjective* HANDICAPPED,
challenged (*informal*), crippled,
incapacitated, infirm, lame,
paralyzed, weakened

disadvantage *noun* **1** HARM,
damage, detriment, disservice,
hurt, injury, loss, prejudice
2 DRAWBACK, downside,
handicap, inconvenience,
nuisance, snag, trouble

disagree *verb* **1** DIFFER (IN
OPINION), argue, clash, cross
swords, dispute, dissent,
object, quarrel, take issue with
2 CONFLICT, be dissimilar,
contradict, counter, differ,
diverge, run counter to, vary
3 MAKE ILL, bother, discomfort,
distress, hurt, nauseate, sicken,
trouble, upset

disagreeable *adjective* **1** NASTY,
disgusting, displeasing,
distasteful, objectionable,
obnoxious, offensive,
repugnant, repulsive, scuzzy
(*slang*), unpleasant **2** RUDE,
bad-tempered, churlish,
difficult, disobliging, irritable,
surly, unpleasant

disagreement *noun*

1 INCOMPATIBILITY, difference,
discrepancy, disparity,
dissimilarity, divergence,
incongruity, variance
2 ARGUMENT, altercation, clash,
conflict, dispute, dissent,
quarrel, row, squabble

disallow *verb* REJECT, disavow,
dismiss, disown, rebuff, refuse,
repudiate

disappear *verb* **1** VANISH,
evanesce, fade away, pass,
recede **2** CEASE, die out,
dissolve, evaporate, leave no
trace, melt away, pass away,
perish

disappearance *noun* VANISHING,
departure, eclipse,
evanescence, evaporation,
going, melting, passing

disappoint *verb* LET DOWN,
disenchant, disgruntle,
dishearten, disillusion, dismay,
dissatisfy, fail

disappointed *adjective* LET
DOWN, cast down, despondent,
discouraged, disenchanted,
disgruntled, dissatisfied,
downhearted, frustrated

disappointing *adjective*
UNSATISFACTORY, depressing,
disconcerting, discouraging,
inadequate, insufficient, lousy
(*slang*), sad, sorry

disappointment *noun*
1 FRUSTRATION, chagrin,
discontent, discouragement,
disenchantment,
disillusionment, dissatisfaction,
regret **2** LETDOWN, blow,
calamity, choker (*informal*),
misfortune, setback

disapproval *noun* DISPLEASURE,
censure, condemnation,
criticism, denunciation,

dissatisfaction, objection, reproach

disapprove verb CONDEMN, deplore, dislike, find unacceptable, frown on, look down one's nose at (informal), object to, reject, take a dim view of, take exception to

disarm verb 1 RENDER DEFENSELESS, disable 2 WIN OVER, persuade, set at ease 3 DEMILITARIZE, deactivate, demobilize, disband

disarmament noun ARMS REDUCTION, arms limitation, de-escalation, demilitarization, demobilization

disarming adjective CHARMING, irresistible, likable or likeable, persuasive, winning

disarrange verb DISORDER, confuse, disorganize, disturb, jumble (up), mess (up), scatter, shake (up), shuffle

disarray noun 1 CONFUSION, disorder, disorganization, disunity, indiscipline, unruliness 2 UNTIDINESS, chaos, clutter, jumble, mess, muddle, shambles

disaster noun CATASTROPHE, adversity, calamity, cataclysm, misfortune, ruin, tragedy, trouble

disastrous adjective TERRIBLE, calamitous, cataclysmic, catastrophic, devastating, fatal, ruinous, tragic

disbelief noun SKEPTICISM, distrust, doubt, dubiety, incredulity, mistrust, unbelief

discard verb GET RID OF, abandon, cast aside, dispense with, dispose of, drop, dump (informal), jettison, reject, throw away or out

discharge verb 1 RELEASE, allow to go, clear, free, liberate, pardon, set free 2 DISMISS, cashier, discard, expel, fire (informal), oust, remove, sack (informal) 3 FIRE, detonate, explode, let loose (informal), let off, set off, shoot 4 POUR FORTH, dispense, emit, exude, give off, leak, ooze, release 5 CARRY OUT, accomplish, do, execute, fulfill, observe, perform 6 PAY, clear, honor, meet, relieve, satisfy, settle, square up ▶ noun 7 RELEASE, acquittal, clearance, liberation, pardon 8 DISMISSAL, demobilization, ejection 9 FIRING, blast, burst, detonation, explosion, report, salvo, shot, volley 10 EMISSION, excretion, ooze, pus, secretion, seepage, suppuration

disciple noun FOLLOWER, adherent, apostle, devotee, pupil, student, supporter

disciplinarian noun AUTHORITARIAN, despot, martinet, stickler, taskmaster, tyrant

discipline noun 1 TRAINING, drill, exercise, method, practice, regimen, regulation 2 PUNISHMENT, castigation, chastisement, correction 3 SELF-CONTROL, conduct, control, orderliness, regulation, restraint, strictness 4 FIELD OF STUDY, area, branch of knowledge, course, curriculum, speciality, subject ▶ verb 5 TRAIN, bring up, drill, educate, exercise, prepare 6 PUNISH, bring to book, castigate, chasten, chastise, correct, penalize, reprimand, reprove

disclose verb 1 MAKE KNOWN,

broadcast, communicate, confess, divulge, let slip, publish, relate, reveal **2** SHOW, bring to light, expose, lay bare, reveal, uncover, unveil

disclosure noun REVELATION, acknowledgment, admission, announcement, confession, declaration, divulgence, leak, publication

discolor verb STAIN, fade, mark, soil, streak, tarnish, tinge

discomfort noun **1** PAIN, ache, hurt, irritation, malaise, soreness **2** UNEASINESS, annoyance, distress, hardship, irritation, nuisance, trouble

disconcert verb DISTURB, faze, fluster, perturb, rattle (informal), take aback, unsettle, upset, worry

disconcerting adjective DISTURBING, alarming, awkward, bewildering, confusing, distracting, embarrassing, perplexing, upsetting

disconnect verb CUT OFF, detach, disengage, divide, part, separate, sever, take apart, uncouple

disconnected adjective ILLOGICAL, confused, disjointed, incoherent, jumbled, mixed-up, rambling, unintelligible

disconsolate adjective INCONSOLABLE, crushed, dejected, desolate, forlorn, grief-stricken, heartbroken, miserable, wretched

discontent noun DISSATISFACTION, displeasure, envy, regret, restlessness, uneasiness, unhappiness

discontented adjective

DISSATISFIED, disaffected, disgruntled, displeased, exasperated, fed up, unhappy, vexed

discontinue verb STOP, abandon, break off, cease, drop, end, give up, quit, suspend, terminate

discord noun **1** DISAGREEMENT, conflict, dissension, disunity, division, friction, incompatibility, strife **2** DISHARMONY, cacophony, din, dissonance, harshness, jarring, racket, tumult

discordant adjective **1** DISAGREEING, at odds, clashing, conflicting, contradictory, contrary, different, incompatible **2** INHARMONIOUS, cacophonous, dissonant, grating, harsh, jarring, shrill, strident

discount verb **1** LEAVE OUT, brush off (slang), disbelieve, disregard, ignore, overlook, pass over **2** DEDUCT, lower, mark down, reduce, take off ▶noun **3** DEDUCTION, concession, cut, rebate, reduction

discourage verb **1** DISHEARTEN, dampen, deject, demoralize, depress, dispirit, intimidate, overawe, put a damper on **2** PUT OFF, deter, dissuade, inhibit, prevent, talk out of

discouraged adjective PUT OFF, crestfallen, deterred, disheartened, dismayed, dispirited, downcast, down in the mouth, glum

discouragement noun **1** LOSS OF CONFIDENCE, dejection, depression, despair, despondency, disappointment, dismay, downheartedness **2** DETERRENT, damper, disincentive, hindrance, impediment, obstacle, opposition, setback

discouraging *adjective* DISHEARTENING, dampening, daunting, depressing, disappointing, dispiriting, unfavorable

discourse *noun* **1** CONVERSATION, chat, communication, dialogue, discussion, seminar, speech, talk **2** SPEECH, dissertation, essay, homily, lecture, oration, sermon, treatise ▶*verb* **3** HOLD FORTH, expatiate, speak, talk

discourteous *adjective* RUDE, bad-mannered, boorish, disrespectful, ill-mannered, impolite, insolent, offhand, ungentlemanly, ungracious

discourtesy *noun* **1** RUDENESS, bad manners, disrespectfulness, impertinence, impoliteness, incivility, insolence **2** INSULT, affront, cold shoulder, kick in the teeth (*slang*), rebuff, slight, snub

discover *verb* **1** FIND, come across, come upon, dig up, locate, turn up, uncover, unearth **2** FIND OUT, ascertain, detect, learn, notice, perceive, realize, recognize, uncover

discovery *noun* **1** FINDING, detection, disclosure, exploration, location, revelation, uncovering **2** BREAKTHROUGH, find, innovation, invention, secret

discredit *verb* **1** DISGRACE, bring into disrepute, defame, dishonor, disparage, slander,

smear, vilify **2** DOUBT, challenge, deny, disbelieve, discount, dispute, distrust, mistrust, question ▶*noun* **3** DISGRACE, dishonor, disrepute, ignominy, ill-repute, scandal, shame, stigma

discreditable *adjective* DISGRACEFUL, dishonorable, ignominious, reprehensible, scandalous, shameful, unworthy

discreet *adjective* TACTFUL, careful, cautious, circumspect, considerate, diplomatic, guarded, judicious, prudent, wary

discrepancy *noun* DISAGREEMENT, conflict, contradiction, difference, disparity, divergence, incongruity, inconsistency, variation

discretion *noun* **1** TACT, carefulness, caution, consideration, diplomacy, judiciousness, prudence, wariness **2** CHOICE, inclination, pleasure, preference, volition, will

discriminate *verb* **1** SHOW PREJUDICE, favor, show bias, single out, treat as inferior, treat differently, victimize **2** DIFFERENTIATE, distinguish, draw a distinction, segregate, separate, tell the difference

discriminating *adjective* DISCERNING, cultivated, fastidious, particular, refined, selective, tasteful

discrimination *noun* **1** PREJUDICE, bias, bigotry, favoritism, intolerance, unfairness **2** DISCERNMENT, judgment, perception, refinement, subtlety, taste

discuss verb TALK ABOUT, argue, confer, consider, converse, debate, deliberate, examine

discussion noun TALK, analysis, argument, conference, consultation, conversation, debate, deliberation, dialogue, discourse, exchange

disdain noun 1 CONTEMPT, arrogance, derision, haughtiness, scorn, superciliousness ▶ verb 2 SCORN, deride, disregard, look down on, reject, slight, sneer at, spurn

disdainful adjective CONTEMPTUOUS, aloof, arrogant, derisive, haughty, proud, scornful, sneering, supercilious, superior

disease noun ILLNESS, affliction, ailment, complaint, condition, disorder, infection, infirmity, malady, sickness

diseased adjective SICK, ailing, infected, rotten, sickly, unhealthy, unsound, unwell, unwholesome

disembark verb LAND, alight, arrive, get off, go ashore, step out of

disenchanted adjective DISILLUSIONED, cynical, disappointed, indifferent, jaundiced, let down, sick of, soured

disenchantment noun DISILLUSIONMENT, disappointment, disillusion, rude awakening

disengage verb RELEASE, disentangle, extricate, free, loosen, set free, unloose, untie

disentangle verb UNTANGLE, disconnect, disengage, extricate, free, loose, unravel

disfavor noun DISAPPROVAL, disapprobation, dislike, displeasure

disfigure verb DAMAGE, blemish, deface, deform, distort, mar, mutilate, scar

disgorge verb VOMIT, discharge, eject, empty, expel

disgrace noun 1 SHAME, degradation, dishonor, disrepute, ignominy, infamy, odium, opprobrium 2 STAIN, blemish, blot, reproach, scandal, slur, stigma ▶ verb 3 BRING SHAME UPON, degrade, discredit, dishonor, humiliate, shame, sully, taint

disgraceful adjective SHAMEFUL, contemptible, detestable, dishonorable, disreputable, ignominious, lousy (slang), scandalous, shocking, unworthy

disgruntled adjective DISCONTENTED, annoyed, displeased, dissatisfied, grumpy, irritated, peeved, put out, vexed

disguise verb 1 HIDE, camouflage, cloak, conceal, cover, mask, screen, shroud, veil 2 MISREPRESENT, fake, falsify ▶ noun 3 COSTUME, camouflage, cover, mask, screen, veil 4 FAÇADE, deception, dissimulation, front, pretense, semblance, trickery, veneer

disguised adjective IN DISGUISE, camouflaged, covert, fake, false, feigned, incognito, masked, undercover

disgust noun 1 LOATHING, abhorrence, aversion, dislike, distaste, hatred, nausea, repugnance, repulsion, revulsion ▶ verb 2 SICKEN, displease, nauseate, offend, put off, repel, revolt

disgusted *adjective* SICKENED, appalled, nauseated, offended, repulsed, scandalized

disgusting *adjective* SICKENING, foul, gross, loathsome, nauseating, offensive, repellent, repugnant, revolting

dish *noun* **1** BOWL, plate, platter, salver **2** FOOD, fare, recipe

dishearten *verb* DISCOURAGE, cast down, deject, depress, deter, dismay, dispirit, put a damper on

disheveled *adjective* UNTIDY, bedraggled, disordered, messy, ruffled, rumpled, tousled, uncombed, unkempt

dishonest *adjective* DECEITFUL, bent (*slang*), cheating, corrupt, crooked (*informal*), disreputable, double-dealing, false, lying, treacherous

dishonesty *noun* DECEIT, cheating, chicanery, corruption, fraud, treachery, trickery, unscrupulousness

dishonor *verb* **1** SHAME, debase, debauch, defame, degrade, discredit, disgrace, sully ▶*noun* **2** SHAME, discredit, disgrace, disrepute, ignominy, infamy, obloquy, reproach, scandal **3** INSULT, abuse, affront, discourtesy, indignity, offense, outrage, sacrilege, slight

dishonorable *adjective* **1** SHAMEFUL, contemptible, despicable, discreditable, disgraceful, ignominious, infamous, lousy (*slang*), scandalous, scuzzy (*slang*) **2** UNTRUSTWORTHY, corrupt, disreputable, shameless,

treacherous, unprincipled, unscrupulous

disillusioned *adjective* DISENCHANTED, disabused, disappointed, enlightened, undeceived

disinclination *noun* RELUCTANCE, aversion, dislike, hesitance, objection, opposition, repugnance, resistance, unwillingness

disinclined *adjective* RELUCTANT, averse, hesitating, loath, not in the mood, opposed, resistant, unwilling

disinfect *verb* STERILIZE, clean, cleanse, decontaminate, deodorize, fumigate, purify, sanitize

disinfectant *noun* ANTISEPTIC, germicide, sterilizer

disinherit *verb Law* CUT OFF, disown, dispossess, oust, repudiate

disintegrate *verb* BREAK UP, break apart, crumble, fall apart, go to pieces, separate, shatter, splinter

disinterest *noun* IMPARTIALITY, detachment, fairness, neutrality

disinterested *adjective* IMPARTIAL, detached, dispassionate, even-handed, impersonal, neutral, objective, unbiased, unprejudiced

disjointed *adjective* INCOHERENT, confused, disconnected, disordered, rambling

dislike *verb* **1** BE AVERSE TO, despise, detest, disapprove, hate, loathe, not be able to bear *or* abide *or* stand, object to, take a dim view of ▶*noun* **2** AVERSION, animosity, antipathy, disapproval, disinclination, displeasure, distaste, enmity, hostility, repugnance

dislodge verb DISPLACE, disturb, extricate, force out, knock loose, oust, remove, uproot

disloyal adjective TREACHEROUS, faithless, false, subversive, traitorous, two-faced, unfaithful, untrustworthy

disloyalty noun TREACHERY, breach of trust, deceitfulness, double-dealing, falseness, inconstancy, infidelity, treason, unfaithfulness

dismal adjective GLOOMY, bleak, cheerless, dark, depressing, discouraging, dreary, forlorn, somber, wretched

dismantle verb TAKE APART, demolish, disassemble, strip, take to pieces

dismay verb 1 ALARM, appall, distress, frighten, horrify, paralyze, scare, terrify, unnerve 2 DISAPPOINT, daunt, discourage, dishearten, disillusion, dispirit, put off ▶ noun 3 ALARM, anxiety, apprehension, consternation, dread, fear, horror, trepidation 4 DISAPPOINTMENT, chagrin, discouragement, disillusionment

dismember verb CUT INTO PIECES, amputate, dissect, mutilate, sever

dismiss verb 1 SACK (informal), ax (informal), cashier, discharge, fire (informal), give notice to, give (someone) their marching orders, lay off, remove 2 LET GO, disperse, dissolve, free, release, send away 3 PUT OUT OF ONE'S MIND, banish, discard, dispel, disregard, lay aside, reject,
set aside

dismissal noun THE SACK (informal), expulsion, marching orders, notice, removal, the boot (slang)

disobedience noun DEFIANCE, indiscipline, insubordination, mutiny, noncompliance, nonobservance, recalcitrance, revolt, unruliness, waywardness

disobedient adjective DEFIANT, contrary, disorderly, insubordinate, intractable, naughty, refractory, undisciplined, unruly, wayward

disobey verb REFUSE TO OBEY, contravene, defy, disregard, flout, ignore, infringe, rebel, violate

disorder noun 1 UNTIDINESS, chaos, clutter, confusion, disarray, jumble, mess, muddle, shambles 2 DISTURBANCE, commotion, riot, turmoil, unrest, unruliness, uproar 3 ILLNESS, affliction, ailment, complaint, disease, malady, sickness

disorderly adjective 1 UNTIDY, chaotic, confused, disorganized, jumbled, messy 2 UNRULY, disruptive, indisciplined, lawless, riotous, rowdy, tumultuous, turbulent, ungovernable

disorganized adjective MUDDLED, chaotic, confused, disordered, haphazard, jumbled, unsystematic

disown verb DENY, cast off, disavow, disclaim, reject, renounce, repudiate

disparage verb RUN DOWN, belittle, denigrate, deprecate, deride, malign, put down, ridicule, slander, vilify

dispassionate *adjective*
1 UNEMOTIONAL, calm, collected, composed, cool, imperturbable, serene, unruffled 2 OBJECTIVE, detached, disinterested, fair, impartial, impersonal, neutral, unbiased, unprejudiced

dispatch, despatch *verb*
1 SEND, consign, dismiss, hasten 2 CARRY OUT, discharge, dispose of, finish, perform, settle 3 MURDER, assassinate, execute, kill, slaughter, slay ▸*noun* 4 MESSAGE, account, bulletin, communication, communiqué, news, report, story

dispel *verb* DRIVE AWAY, banish, chase away, dismiss, disperse, eliminate, expel

dispense *verb* 1 DISTRIBUTE, allocate, allot, apportion, assign, deal out, dole out, share 2 PREPARE, measure, mix, supply 3 ADMINISTER, apply, carry out, discharge, enforce, execute, implement, operate 4 **dispense with: a** DO AWAY WITH, abolish, brush aside, cancel, dispose of, get rid of **b** DO WITHOUT, abstain from, forgo, give up, relinquish

disperse *verb* 1 SCATTER, broadcast, diffuse, disseminate, distribute, spread, strew 2 BREAK UP, disband, dissolve, scatter, separate

dispirited *adjective* DISHEARTENED, crestfallen, dejected, depressed, despondent, discouraged, downcast, gloomy, glum, sad

displace *verb* 1 MOVE, disturb, misplace, shift, transpose 2 REPLACE, oust, succeed, supersede, supplant, take the place of

display *verb* 1 SHOW, demonstrate, disclose, exhibit, expose, manifest, present, reveal 2 SHOW OFF, flaunt, flourish, parade, vaunt ▸*noun* 3 EXHIBITION, array, demonstration, presentation, revelation, show 4 SHOW, flourish, ostentation, pageant, parade, pomp, spectacle

displease *verb* ANNOY, anger, irk, irritate, offend, pique, put out, upset, vex

displeasure *noun* ANNOYANCE, anger, disapproval, dissatisfaction, distaste, indignation, irritation, resentment

disposable *adjective*
1 THROWAWAY, biodegradable, nonreturnable 2 AVAILABLE, consumable, expendable

disposal *noun* 1 THROWING AWAY, discarding, dumping (*informal*), ejection, jettisoning, removal, riddance, scrapping 2 **at one's disposal** AVAILABLE, at one's service, consumable, expendable, free for use

dispose *verb* ARRANGE, array, distribute, group, marshal, order, place, put

dispose of *verb* 1 GET RID OF, destroy, discard, dump (*informal*), jettison, scrap, throw out *or* away, unload 2 DEAL WITH, decide, determine, end, finish with, settle

disposition *noun* 1 CHARACTER, constitution, make-up, nature, spirit, temper, temperament

2 TENDENCY, bent, bias, habit, inclination, leaning, proclivity, propensity **3** ARRANGEMENT, classification, distribution, grouping, ordering, organization, placement

disproportion noun INEQUALITY, asymmetry, discrepancy, disparity, imbalance, lopsidedness, unevenness

disproportionate adjective UNEQUAL, excessive, inordinate, out of proportion, unbalanced, uneven, unreasonable

disprove verb PROVE FALSE, contradict, discredit, expose, give the lie to, invalidate, negate, rebut, refute

dispute noun **1** DISAGREEMENT, altercation, argument, conflict, feud, quarrel **2** ARGUMENT, contention, controversy, debate, discussion, dissension ▸ verb **3** DOUBT, challenge, contest, contradict, deny, impugn, question, rebut **4** ARGUE, clash, cross swords, debate, quarrel, squabble

disqualification noun BAN, elimination, exclusion, ineligibility, rejection

disqualified adjective INELIGIBLE, debarred, eliminated, knocked out, out of the running

disqualify verb BAN, debar, declare ineligible, preclude, prohibit, rule out

disquiet noun **1** UNEASINESS, alarm, anxiety, concern, disturbance, foreboding, nervousness, trepidation, worry ▸ verb **2** MAKE UNEASY, bother, concern, disturb, perturb, trouble, unsettle, upset, worry

disregard verb **1** IGNORE, brush aside or away, discount, make light of, neglect, overlook, pass over, pay no heed to, turn a blind eye to ▸ noun **2** INATTENTION, contempt, disdain, disrespect, indifference, neglect, negligence, oversight

disrepair noun DILAPIDATION, collapse, decay, deterioration, ruination

disreputable adjective DISCREDITABLE, dishonorable, ignominious, infamous, louche, notorious, scandalous, shady (informal), shameful

disrepute noun DISCREDIT, disgrace, dishonor, ignominy, ill repute, infamy, obloquy, shame, unpopularity

disrespect noun CONTEMPT, cheek, impertinence, impoliteness, impudence, insolence, irreverence, lack of respect, rudeness, sauce

disrespectful adjective CONTEMPTUOUS, cheeky, discourteous, impertinent, impolite, impudent, insolent, insulting, irreverent, rude

disrupt verb **1** DISTURB, confuse, disorder, disorganize, spoil, upset **2** INTERRUPT, break up or into, interfere with, intrude, obstruct, unsettle, upset

disruption noun DISTURBANCE, interference, interruption, stoppage

disruptive adjective DISTURBING, disorderly, distracting, troublesome, unruly, unsettling, upsetting

dissatisfaction noun DISCONTENT, annoyance, chagrin, disappointment, displeasure,

frustration, irritation,
resentment, unhappiness

dissatisfied *adjective*
DISCONTENTED, disappointed,
disgruntled, displeased, fed up,
frustrated, unhappy, unsatisfied

dissect *verb* 1 CUT UP *or* APART,
anatomize, dismember, lay
open 2 ANALYZE, break down,
explore, inspect, investigate,
research, scrutinize, study

disseminate *verb* SPREAD,
broadcast, circulate, disperse,
distribute, publicize, scatter

dissension *noun* DISAGREEMENT,
conflict, discord, dispute,
dissent, friction, quarrel, row,
strife

dissent *verb* 1 DISAGREE, differ,
object, protest, refuse,
withhold assent *or* approval
▶ *noun* 2 DISAGREEMENT, discord,
dissension, objection,
opposition, refusal, resistance

dissenter *noun* OBJECTOR,
dissident, nonconformist

dissertation *noun* THESIS,
critique, discourse, disquisition,
essay, exposition, treatise

disservice *noun* BAD TURN, harm,
injury, injustice, unkindness,
wrong

dissident *adjective* 1 DISSENTING,
disagreeing, discordant,
heterodox, nonconformist
▶ *noun* 2 PROTESTER, agitator,
dissenter, rebel

dissimilar *adjective* DIFFERENT,
disparate, divergent, diverse,
heterogeneous, unlike,
unrelated, various

dissipate *verb* 1 SQUANDER,
consume, deplete, expend,
fritter away, run through,
spend, waste 2 DISPERSE,

disappear, dispel, dissolve,
drive away, evaporate, scatter,
vanish

dissipation *noun* 1 DISPERSAL,
disappearance, disintegration,
dissolution, scattering,
vanishing 2 DEBAUCHERY,
dissoluteness, excess,
extravagance, indulgence,
intemperance, prodigality,
profligacy, wantonness, waste

dissociate *verb* 1 BREAK AWAY,
break off, part company, quit
2 SEPARATE, detach, disconnect,
distance, divorce, isolate,
segregate, set apart

dissolute *adjective* IMMORAL,
debauched, degenerate,
depraved, dissipated,
profligate, rakish, wanton, wild

dissolution *noun* 1 BREAKING UP,
disintegration, division,
parting, separation
2 ADJOURNMENT, discontinuation,
end, finish, suspension,
termination

dissolve *verb* 1 MELT,
deliquesce, fuse, liquefy,
soften, thaw 2 END, break up,
discontinue, suspend,
terminate, wind up

dissuade *verb* DETER, advise
against, discourage, put off,
remonstrate, talk out of, warn

distance *noun* 1 SPACE, extent,
gap, interval, length, range,
span, stretch 2 RESERVE,
aloofness, coldness, coolness,
remoteness, restraint, stiffness
3 **in the distance** FAR OFF, afar,
far away, on the horizon,
yonder ▶ *verb* 4 **distance
oneself** SEPARATE ONESELF, be
distanced from, dissociate
oneself

distant adjective 1 FAR-OFF, abroad, far, faraway, far-flung, outlying, out-of-the-way, remote 2 APART, dispersed, distinct, scattered, separate 3 RESERVED, aloof, cool, reticent, standoffish, unapproachable, unfriendly, withdrawn

distaste noun DISLIKE, aversion, disgust, horror, loathing, odium, repugnance, revulsion

distasteful adjective UNPLEASANT, disagreeable, objectionable, offensive, repugnant, repulsive, scuzzy (slang), uninviting, unpalatable, unsavory

distill verb EXTRACT, condense, purify, refine

distinct adjective 1 DIFFERENT, detached, discrete, individual, separate, unconnected 2 DEFINITE, clear, decided, evident, marked, noticeable, obvious, palpable, unmistakable, well-defined

distinction noun 1 DIFFERENTIATION, discernment, discrimination, perception, separation 2 FEATURE, characteristic, distinctiveness, individuality, mark, particularity, peculiarity, quality 3 DIFFERENCE, contrast, differential, division, separation 4 EXCELLENCE, eminence, fame, greatness, honor, importance, merit, prominence, repute

distinctive adjective CHARACTERISTIC, idiosyncratic, individual, original, peculiar, singular, special, typical, unique

distinctly adverb DEFINITELY, clearly, decidedly, markedly, noticeably, obviously, patently, plainly, unmistakably

distinguish verb 1 DIFFERENTIATE, ascertain, decide, determine, discriminate, judge, tell apart, tell the difference 2 CHARACTERIZE, categorize, classify, mark, separate, set apart, single out 3 MAKE OUT, discern, know, perceive, pick out, recognize, see, tell

distinguished adjective EMINENT, acclaimed, celebrated, famed, famous, illustrious, noted, renowned, well-known

distort verb 1 MISREPRESENT, bias, color, falsify, pervert, slant, twist 2 DEFORM, bend, buckle, contort, disfigure, misshape, twist, warp

distortion noun 1 MISREPRESENTATION, bias, falsification, perversion, slant 2 DEFORMITY, bend, buckle, contortion, crookedness, malformation, twist, warp

distract verb 1 DIVERT, draw away, sidetrack, turn aside 2 AMUSE, beguile, engross, entertain, occupy

distracted adjective AGITATED, at sea, flustered, harassed, in a flap (informal), perplexed, puzzled, troubled

distraction noun 1 DIVERSION, disturbance, interference, interruption 2 ENTERTAINMENT, amusement, diversion, pastime, recreation 3 AGITATION, bewilderment, commotion, confusion, discord, disorder, disturbance

distraught adjective FRANTIC, agitated, beside oneself, desperate, distracted, distressed, out of one's mind, overwrought, worked-up

distress noun **1** WORRY, grief, heartache, misery, pain, sorrow, suffering, torment, wretchedness **2** NEED, adversity, difficulties, hardship, misfortune, poverty, privation, trouble ▶ verb **3** UPSET, disturb, grieve, harass, sadden, torment, trouble, worry

distressed adjective **1** UPSET, agitated, distracted, distraught, tormented, troubled, worried, wretched **2** POVERTY-STRICKEN, destitute, down at heel, indigent, needy, poor, straitened

distressing adjective UPSETTING, disturbing, harrowing, heart-breaking, painful, sad, worrying

distribute verb **1** HAND OUT, circulate, convey, deliver, pass round **2** SHARE, allocate, allot, apportion, deal, dispense, dole out

distribution noun **1** DELIVERY, dealing, handling, mailing, transportation **2** SHARING, allocation, allotment, apportionment, division **3** CLASSIFICATION, arrangement, grouping, organization, placement

district noun AREA, locale, locality, neighborhood, parish, quarter, region, sector, vicinity

distrust verb **1** SUSPECT, be suspicious of, be wary of, disbelieve, doubt, mistrust, question, smell a rat (informal) ▶ noun **2** SUSPICION, disbelief, doubt, misgiving, mistrust, question, skepticism, wariness

disturb verb **1** INTERRUPT, bother, butt in on, disrupt, interfere with, intrude on, pester **2** UPSET, alarm, distress, fluster, harass, perturb, trouble, unnerve, unsettle, worry **3** MUDDLE, disarrange, disorder

disturbance noun **1** INTERRUPTION, annoyance, bother, distraction, intrusion **2** DISORDER, brawl, commotion, fracas, fray, rumpus

disturbed adjective **1** Psychiatry UNBALANCED, disordered, maladjusted, neurotic, troubled, upset **2** WORRIED, anxious, apprehensive, bothered, concerned, nervous, troubled, uneasy, upset, wired (slang)

disturbing adjective WORRYING, alarming, disconcerting, distressing, frightening, harrowing, startling, unsettling, upsetting

disuse noun NEGLECT, abandonment, decay, idleness

ditch noun **1** CHANNEL, drain, dyke, furrow, gully, moat, trench, watercourse ▶ verb **2** Slang GET RID OF, abandon, discard, dispose of, drop, dump (informal), jettison, scrap, throw out or overboard

dither verb **1** VACILLATE, hesitate, hum and haw, shillyshally (informal), teeter, waver ▶ noun **2** FLUTTER, flap (informal), fluster, tizzy (informal)

dive verb **1** PLUNGE, descend, dip, drop, duck, nose-dive, plummet, swoop ▶ noun **2** PLUNGE, jump, leap, lunge, nose dive, spring

diverge verb **1** SEPARATE, branch, divide, fork, part, split, spread **2** DEVIATE, depart, digress, meander, stray, turn aside, wander

diverse *adjective* 1 VARIOUS, assorted, manifold, miscellaneous, of every description, several, sundry, varied 2 DIFFERENT, discrete, disparate, dissimilar, distinct, divergent, separate, unlike, varying

diversify *verb* VARY, branch out, change, expand, have a finger in every pie, spread out

diversion *noun* PASTIME, amusement, distraction, entertainment, game, recreation, relaxation, sport

diversity *noun* DIFFERENCE, distinctiveness, diverseness, heterogeneity, multiplicity, range, variety

divert *verb* 1 REDIRECT, avert, deflect, switch, turn aside 2 DISTRACT, draw *or* lead away from, lead astray, sidetrack 3 ENTERTAIN, amuse, beguile, delight, gratify, regale

diverting *adjective* ENTERTAINING, amusing, beguiling, enjoyable, fun, humorous, pleasant

divide *verb* 1 SEPARATE, bisect, cut (up), part, partition, segregate, split 2 SHARE, allocate, allot, deal out, dispense, distribute 3 CAUSE TO DISAGREE, break up, come between, estrange, split

dividend *noun* BONUS, cut (*informal*), divvy (*informal*), extra, gain, plus, portion, share, surplus

divine *adjective* 1 HEAVENLY, angelic, celestial, godlike, holy, spiritual, superhuman, supernatural 2 SACRED,

consecrated, holy, religious, sanctified, spiritual 3 *Informal* WONDERFUL, beautiful, excellent, glorious, marvelous, perfect, splendid, superlative ▶*verb* 4 INFER, apprehend, deduce, discern, guess, perceive, suppose, surmise

divinity *noun* 1 THEOLOGY, religion, religious studies 2 GOD *or* GODDESS, deity, guardian spirit, spirit 3 GODLINESS, deity, divine nature, holiness, sanctity

divisible *adjective* DIVIDABLE, separable, splittable

division *noun* 1 SEPARATION, cutting up, dividing, partition, splitting up 2 SHARING, allotment, apportionment, distribution 3 PART, branch, category, class, department, group, section 4 DISAGREEMENT, difference of opinion, discord, rupture, split, variance

divorce *noun* 1 SEPARATION, annulment, dissolution, split-up ▶*verb* 2 SEPARATE, disconnect, dissociate, dissolve (*marriage*), divide, part, sever, split up

divulge *verb* MAKE KNOWN, confess, declare, disclose, let slip, proclaim, reveal, tell

dizzy *adjective* 1 GIDDY, faint, light-headed, off balance, reeling, shaky, swimming, wobbly, woozy (*informal*) 2 CONFUSED, at sea, befuddled, bemused, bewildered, dazed, dazzled, muddled

do *verb* 1 PERFORM, accomplish, achieve, carry out, complete, execute 2 BE ADEQUATE, be sufficient, cut the mustard, pass muster, satisfy, suffice 3 GET READY, arrange, fix, look after, prepare, see to **4** SOLVE, decipher, decode, figure out, puzzle out, resolve, work out **5** CAUSE, bring about, create, effect, produce

do away with verb **1** KILL, exterminate, murder, slay **2** GET RID OF, abolish, discard, discontinue, eliminate, put an end to, put paid to, remove

docile adjective SUBMISSIVE, amenable, biddable, compliant, manageable, obedient, pliant

docility noun SUBMISSIVENESS, compliance, manageability, meekness, obedience

dock¹ noun **1** WHARF, harbor, pier, quay, waterfront ▸verb **2** MOOR, anchor, berth, drop anchor, land, put in, tie up **3** Of spacecraft LINK UP, couple, hook up, join, rendezvous, unite

dock² verb **1** DEDUCT, decrease, diminish, lessen, reduce, subtract, withhold **2** CUT OFF, clip, crop, curtail, cut short, shorten

doctor noun **1** G.P., general practitioner, medic (informal), medical practitioner, physician ▸verb **2** CHANGE, alter, disguise, falsify, misrepresent, pervert, tamper with **3** ADD TO, adulterate, cut, dilute, mix with, spike, water down

doctrinaire adjective DOGMATIC, biased, fanatical, inflexible, insistent, opinionated, rigid

doctrine noun TEACHING, article of faith, belief, conviction, creed, dogma, opinion, precept, principle, tenet

document noun **1** PAPER,

certificate, record, report ▸verb **2** SUPPORT, authenticate, certify, corroborate, detail, substantiate, validate, verify

dodge verb **1** DUCK, dart, sidestep, swerve, turn aside **2** EVADE, avoid, elude, get out of, shirk

dog noun **1** HOUND, canine, cur, man's best friend, pooch (slang) **2 go to the dogs** Informal GO TO RUIN, degenerate, deteriorate, go down the drain, go to pot ▸verb **3** TROUBLE, follow, haunt, hound, plague, pursue, stalk, track, trail

dogged adjective DETERMINED, indefatigable, obstinate, persistent, resolute, steadfast, stubborn, tenacious, unflagging, unshakable

dogma noun DOCTRINE, belief, credo, creed, opinion, teachings

dogmatic adjective OPINIONATED, arrogant, assertive, doctrinaire, emphatic, obdurate, overbearing

doldrums noun **the doldrums** INACTIVITY, depression, dumps (informal), gloom, listlessness, malaise

dole verb **dole out** GIVE OUT, allocate, allot, apportion, assign, dispense, distribute, hand out

dollop noun LUMP, helping, portion, scoop, serving

dolt noun IDIOT, ass, blockhead, chump (informal), dope (informal), dork (slang), dunce, fool, oaf, schmuck (slang)

domestic adjective **1** HOME, family, household, private **2** HOME-LOVING, domesticated, homely, housewifely, stay-at-home **3** DOMESTICATED, house-trained, pet, tame, trained **4** NATIVE, indigenous, internal ▶*noun* **5** SERVANT, charwoman, daily, help, maid

dominant *adjective* **1** CONTROLLING, assertive, authoritative, commanding, governing, ruling, superior, supreme **2** MAIN, chief, predominant, pre-eminent, primary, principal, prominent

dominate *verb* **1** CONTROL, direct, govern, have the whip hand over, monopolize, rule, tyrannize **2** TOWER ABOVE, loom over, overlook, stand head and shoulders above, stand over, survey

domination *noun* CONTROL, ascendancy, authority, command, influence, power, rule, superiority, supremacy

domineering *adjective* OVERBEARING, arrogant, authoritarian, bossy (*informal*), dictatorial, high-handed, imperious, oppressive, tyrannical

dominion *noun* **1** CONTROL, authority, command, jurisdiction, power, rule, sovereignty, supremacy **2** KINGDOM, country, domain, empire, realm, territory

don *verb* PUT ON, clothe oneself in, dress in, get into, pull on, slip on *or* into

donate *verb* GIVE, contribute, make a gift of, present, subscribe

donation *noun* CONTRIBUTION, gift, grant, hand-out, offering, present, subscription

donor *noun* GIVER, benefactor, contributor, donator, philanthropist

doom *noun* **1** DESTRUCTION, catastrophe, downfall, fate, fortune, lot, ruin ▶*verb* **2** CONDEMN, consign, damn, destine, sentence

doomed *adjective* CONDEMNED, bewitched, cursed, fated, hopeless, ill-fated, ill-omened, luckless, star-crossed

door *noun* OPENING, doorway, entrance, entry, exit

dope *noun* **1** *Slang* DRUG, narcotic, opiate **2** *Informal* IDIOT, dimwit (*informal*), doofus (*slang*), dork (*slang*), dunce, dweeb (*slang*), fool, nitwit (*informal*), schmuck (*slang*) ▶*verb* **3** DRUG, anesthetize, knock out, narcotize, sedate, stupefy

dork *noun* *Slang* IDIOT, doofus (*slang*), dope (*slang*), dunce, dweeb (*slang*), fool, geek (*slang*), nerd

dormant *adjective* INACTIVE, asleep, hibernating, inert, inoperative, latent, sleeping, slumbering, suspended

dose *noun* QUANTITY, dosage, draft, measure, portion, potion, prescription

dot *noun* **1** SPOT, fleck, jot, mark, point, speck, speckle **2 on the dot** ON TIME, exactly, on the button (*informal*), precisely, promptly, punctually, to the minute ▶*verb* **3** SPOT, dab, dabble, fleck, speckle, sprinkle, stipple, stud

dotage *noun* SENILITY, decrepitude, feebleness, imbecility, old age, second childhood, weakness

dote on *or* **upon** *verb* ADORE, admire, hold dear, idolize, lavish affection on, prize, treasure

doting *adjective* ADORING, devoted, fond, foolish, indulgent, lovesick

double *adjective* 1 TWICE, coupled, dual, duplicate, in pairs, paired, twin, twofold ▶ *verb* 2 MULTIPLY, duplicate, enlarge, grow, increase, magnify ▶ *noun* 3 TWIN, clone, dead ringer (*slang*), Doppelgänger, duplicate, lookalike, replica, spitting image (*informal*) 4 **at** *or* **on the double** QUICKLY, at full speed, briskly, immediately, posthaste, without delay

double-cross *verb* BETRAY, cheat, defraud, hoodwink, mislead, swindle, trick, two-time (*informal*)

doubt *noun* 1 UNCERTAINTY, hesitancy, hesitation, indecision, irresolution, lack of conviction, suspense 2 SUSPICION, apprehension, distrust, misgiving, mistrust, qualm, skepticism ▶ *verb* 3 BE UNCERTAIN, be dubious, demur, fluctuate, hesitate, scruple, vacillate, waver 4 SUSPECT, discredit, distrust, fear, lack confidence in, mistrust, query, question

doubtful *adjective* 1 UNLIKELY, debatable, dubious, equivocal, improbable, problematic(al), questionable, unclear 2 UNSURE, distrustful, hesitating, in two minds (*informal*), skeptical, suspicious, tentative, uncertain, unconvinced, wavering

doubtless *adverb* 1 CERTAINLY, assuredly, indisputably, of course, surely, undoubtedly, unquestionably, without doubt 2 PROBABLY, apparently, most likely, ostensibly, presumably, seemingly, supposedly

dour *adjective* GLOOMY, dismal, dreary, forbidding, grim, morose, sour, sullen, unfriendly

dowdy *adjective* FRUMPY, dingy, drab, dumpy (*informal*), frowzy, homely (*U.S.*), shabby, unfashionable

do without *verb* MANAGE WITHOUT, abstain from, dispense with, forgo, get along without, give up, kick (*informal*)

down *adjective* 1 DEPRESSED, dejected, disheartened, downcast, low, miserable, sad, unhappy ▶ *verb* 2 *Informal* SWALLOW, drain, drink (down), gulp, put away, toss off ▶ *noun* 3 **be down on** *Informal* BE ANTAGONISTIC *or* HOSTILE TO, bear a grudge towards, be prejudiced against, be set against, have it in for (*slang*)

down-and-out *noun* 1 TRAMP, bag lady, beggar, derelict, pauper, vagabond, vagrant ▶ *adjective* 2 DESTITUTE, derelict, down on one's luck (*informal*), impoverished, penniless, short, without two pennies to rub together (*informal*)

downcast *adjective* DEJECTED, crestfallen, depressed, despondent, disappointed, disconsolate, discouraged, disheartened, dismayed, dispirited

downer *noun Informal* MOANER, killjoy, pessimist, prophet of doom, sourpuss (*informal*), spoilsport, wet blanket (*informal*)

downfall *noun* RUIN, collapse, destruction, disgrace, fall, overthrow, undoing

downgrade *verb* DEMOTE, degrade, humble, lower *or* reduce in rank, take down a peg (*informal*)

downhearted *adjective* DEJECTED, crestfallen, depressed, despondent, discouraged, disheartened, dispirited, downcast, sad, unhappy

downpour *noun* RAINSTORM, cloudburst, deluge, flood, inundation, torrential rain

downright *adjective* COMPLETE, absolute, out-and-out, outright, plain, thoroughgoing, total, undisguised, unqualified, utter

down-to-earth *adjective* SENSIBLE, matter-of-fact, no-nonsense, plain-spoken, practical, realistic, sane, unsentimental

downtrodden *adjective* OPPRESSED, exploited, helpless, subjugated, subservient, tyrannized

downward *adjective* DESCENDING, declining, earthward, heading down, sliding, slipping

doze *verb* 1 NAP, nod off (*informal*), sleep, slumber, snooze (*informal*) ▶*noun* 2 NAP, catnap, forty winks (*informal*), shuteye (*slang*), siesta, snooze (*informal*)

drab *adjective* DULL, dingy, dismal, dreary, flat, gloomy, shabby, somber

draft[1] *noun* 1 OUTLINE, abstract,

plan, rough, sketch, version 2 ORDER, bill (*of exchange*), check, postal order ▶*verb* 3 OUTLINE, compose, design, draw, draw up, formulate, plan, sketch

draft[2] *noun* 1 BREEZE, current, flow, movement, puff 2 DRINK, cup, dose, potion, quantity

drag *verb* 1 PULL, draw, haul, lug, tow, trail, tug 2 **drag on** *or* **out** LAST, draw out, extend, keep going, lengthen, persist, prolong, protract, spin out, stretch out ▶*noun* 3 *Informal* NUISANCE, annoyance, bore, bother, downer (*informal*), pain (*informal*), pest

dragoon *verb* FORCE, browbeat, bully, coerce, compel, constrain, drive, impel, intimidate, railroad (*informal*)

drain *noun* 1 PIPE, channel, conduit, culvert, ditch, duct, sewer, sink, trench 2 REDUCTION, depletion, drag, exhaustion, sap, strain, withdrawal ▶*verb* 3 REMOVE, bleed, draw off, dry, empty, pump off *or* out, tap, withdraw 4 FLOW OUT, effuse, exude, leak, ooze, seep, trickle, well out 5 DRINK UP, finish, gulp down, quaff, swallow 6 EXHAUST, consume, deplete, dissipate, empty, sap, strain, use up

drama *noun* 1 PLAY, dramatization, show, stage show 2 THEATER, acting, dramaturgy, stagecraft 3 EXCITEMENT, crisis, histrionics, scene, spectacle, turmoil

dramatic *adjective* 1 THEATRICAL, dramaturgical, Thespian 2 POWERFUL, expressive, impressive, moving, striking, vivid **3** EXCITING, breathtaking, climactic, electrifying, melodramatic, sensational, suspenseful, tense, thrilling

dramatist *noun* PLAYWRIGHT, dramaturge, screenwriter, scriptwriter

dramatize *verb* EXAGGERATE, lay it on (thick) (*slang*), overdo, overstate, play to the gallery

drape *verb* COVER, cloak, fold, swathe, wrap

drastic *adjective* EXTREME, desperate, dire, forceful, harsh, radical, severe, strong

draw *verb* **1** SKETCH, depict, design, map out, mark out, outline, paint, portray, trace **2** PULL, drag, haul, tow, tug **3** TAKE OUT, extract, pull out **4** ATTRACT, allure, elicit, entice, evoke, induce, influence, invite, persuade **5** DEDUCE, derive, infer, make, take ▶ *noun* **6** *Informal* ATTRACTION, enticement, lure, pull (*informal*) **7** TIE, dead heat, deadlock, gridlock, impasse, stalemate

drawback *noun* DISADVANTAGE, deficiency, difficulty, downside, flaw, handicap, hitch, snag, stumbling block

drawing *noun* PICTURE, cartoon, depiction, illustration, outline, portrayal, representation, sketch, study

drawn *adjective* TENSE, haggard, pinched, stressed, tired, worn

draw on *verb* MAKE USE OF, employ, exploit, extract, fall back on, have recourse to, rely on, take from, use

draw out *verb* EXTEND, drag out, lengthen, make longer, prolong, protract, spin out,

stretch, string out

draw up *verb* **1** DRAFT, compose, formulate, frame, prepare, write out **2** HALT, bring to a stop, pull up, stop

dread *verb* **1** FEAR, cringe at, have cold feet (*informal*), quail, shrink from, shudder, tremble ▶ *noun* **2** FEAR, alarm, apprehension, dismay, fright, horror, terror, trepidation

dreadful *adjective* TERRIBLE, abysmal, appalling, atrocious, awful, fearful, frightful, hideous, horrible, shocking

dream *noun* **1** VISION, delusion, hallucination, illusion, imagination, trance **2** DAYDREAM, fantasy, pipe dream **3** AMBITION, aim, aspiration, desire, goal, hope, wish **4** DELIGHT, beauty, gem, joy, marvel, pleasure, treasure ▶ *verb* **5** HAVE DREAMS, conjure up, envisage, fancy, hallucinate, imagine, think, visualize **6** DAYDREAM, build castles in the air *or* in Spain, fantasize, stargaze

dreamer *noun* IDEALIST, daydreamer, escapist, fantasist, utopian, visionary, Walter Mitty

dreamy *adjective* **1** VAGUE, absent, abstracted, daydreaming, faraway, pensive, preoccupied, with one's head in the clouds **2** IMPRACTICAL, airy-fairy, fanciful, imaginary, quixotic, speculative

dreary *adjective* DULL, boring, drab, humdrum, monotonous, tedious, tiresome, uneventful, wearisome

dregs *plural noun* **1** SEDIMENT, deposit, dross, grounds, lees, residue, residuum, scum, waste

2 SCUM, good-for-nothings, rabble, riffraff

drench verb SOAK, drown, flood, inundate, saturate, souse, steep, swamp, wet

dress noun 1 FROCK, gown, outfit, robe 2 CLOTHING, apparel, attire, clothes, costume, garb, garments, togs ▶ verb 3 PUT ON, attire, change, clothe, don, garb, robe, slip on or into 4 BANDAGE, bind up, plaster, treat 5 ARRANGE, adjust, align, get ready, prepare, straighten

dressmaker noun SEAMSTRESS, couturier, tailor

dribble verb 1 RUN, drip, drop, fall in drops, leak, ooze, seep, trickle 2 DROOL, drivel, slaver, slobber

drift verb 1 FLOAT, be carried along, coast, go (aimlessly), meander, stray, waft, wander 2 PILE UP, accumulate, amass, bank up, drive, gather ▶ noun 3 PILE, accumulation, bank, heap, mass, mound 4 MEANING, direction, gist, import, intention, purport, significance, tendency, thrust

drifter noun WANDERER, beachcomber, bum (informal), hobo, itinerant, rolling stone, vagrant

drill noun 1 BORING TOOL, bit, borer, gimlet 2 TRAINING, discipline, exercise, instruction, practice, preparation, repetition ▶ verb 3 BORE, penetrate, perforate, pierce, puncture, sink in 4 TRAIN, coach, discipline, exercise, instruct, practice, rehearse, teach

drink verb 1 SWALLOW, gulp, guzzle, imbibe, quaff, sip, suck, sup 2 BOOZE (informal), hit the bottle (informal), tipple, tope ▶ noun 3 BEVERAGE, liquid, potion, refreshment 4 ALCOHOL, booze (informal), hooch or hootch, liquor, spirits, the bottle (informal) 5 GLASS, cup, draft

drip verb 1 DROP, dribble, exude, plop, splash, sprinkle, trickle ▶ noun 2 DROP, dribble, leak, trickle 3 Informal WEAKLING, mama's boy (informal)

drive verb 1 OPERATE, direct, guide, handle, manage, motor, ride, steer, travel 2 GOAD, coerce, constrain, force, press, prod, prompt, spur 3 PUSH, herd, hurl, impel, propel, send, urge 4 PUSH, hammer, ram, thrust ▶ noun 5 RUN, excursion, jaunt, journey, outing, ride, spin (informal), trip 6 CAMPAIGN, action, appeal, crusade, effort, push (informal) 7 INITIATIVE, ambition, energy, enterprise, get-up-and-go (informal), motivation, vigor, zip (informal)

drivel noun 1 NONSENSE, garbage (informal), gibberish, hogwash, hot air (informal), poppycock (informal), rubbish, trash ▶ verb 2 BABBLE, blether, gab (informal), prate, ramble

driving adjective FORCEFUL, compelling, dynamic, energetic, sweeping, vigorous, violent

drizzle noun 1 FINE RAIN, mist ▶ verb 2 RAIN, shower, spot or spit with rain, spray, sprinkle

droll adjective AMUSING, comical, entertaining, funny, humorous, jocular, waggish, whimsical

drone verb 1 HUM, buzz, purr, thrum, vibrate, whirr 2 **drone on** SPEAK MONOTONOUSLY, be boring, chant, intone, spout, talk interminably ▶ noun 3 HUM, buzz, murmuring, purr, thrum, vibration, whirring

drool verb 1 DRIBBLE, drivel, salivate, slaver, slobber, water at the mouth 2 **drool over** GLOAT OVER, dote on, gush, make much of, rave about (informal)

droop verb SAG, bend, dangle, drop, fall down, hang (down), sink

drop verb 1 FALL, decline, descend, diminish, plummet, plunge, sink, tumble 2 DRIP, dribble, fall in drops, trickle 3 DISCONTINUE, ax (informal), give up, kick (informal), quit, relinquish ▶ noun 4 DROPLET, bead, bubble, drip, globule, pearl, tear 5 DASH, mouthful, shot (informal), sip, spot, swig (informal), trace, trickle 6 DECREASE, cut, decline, deterioration, downturn, fall-off, lowering, reduction, slump 7 FALL, descent, plunge

drop off verb 1 SET DOWN, deliver, leave, let off 2 Informal FALL ASLEEP, doze (off), have forty winks (informal), nod (off), snooze (informal) 3 DECREASE, decline, diminish, dwindle, fall off, lessen, slacken

drop out verb LEAVE, abandon, fall by the wayside, give up, quit, stop, withdraw

drought noun DRY SPELL, aridity, dehydration, dryness

drove noun HERD, collection, company, crowd, flock, horde, mob, multitude, swarm, throng

drown verb 1 DRENCH, deluge, engulf, flood, go under, immerse, inundate, sink, submerge, swamp 2 OVERPOWER, deaden, muffle, obliterate, overcome, overwhelm, stifle, swallow up, wipe out

drowsy adjective SLEEPY, dopey (slang), dozy, half asleep, heavy, lethargic, somnolent, tired, torpid

drudge noun MENIAL, factotum, servant, slave, toiler, worker

drudgery noun MENIAL LABOR, donkey-work, grind (informal), hard work, labor, slog, toil

drug noun 1 MEDICATION, medicament, medicine, physic, poison, remedy 2 DOPE (slang), narcotic, opiate, stimulant ▶ verb 3 DOSE, administer a drug, dope (slang), medicate, treat 4 KNOCK OUT, anesthetize, deaden, numb, poison, stupefy

drum verb 1 BEAT, pulsate, rap, reverberate, tap, tattoo, throb 2 **drum into** DRIVE HOME, din into, hammer away, harp on, instill into, reiterate

drunk adjective 1 INTOXICATED, drunken, inebriated, plastered (slang), tipsy, under the influence (informal) ▶ noun 2 DRUNKARD, alcoholic, boozer (informal), inebriate, lush (slang), wino (informal)

drunkard noun DRINKER, alcoholic, dipsomaniac, drunk, lush (slang), tippler, wino (informal)

drunkenness noun INTOXICATION, alcoholism, bibulousness, dipsomania, inebriation, insobriety, intemperance

dry *adjective* 1 DEHYDRATED, arid, barren, desiccated, dried up, parched, thirsty 2 DULL, boring, dreary, monotonous, plain, tedious, tiresome, uninteresting 3 SARCASTIC, deadpan, droll, low-key, sly ▸ *verb* 4 DEHYDRATE, dehumidify, desiccate, drain, make dry, parch, sear

dry out *or* **up** *verb* BECOME DRY, harden, shrivel up, wilt, wither, wizen

dual *adjective* TWOFOLD, binary, double, duplex, duplicate, matched, paired, twin

dubious *adjective* 1 SUSPECT, fishy (*informal*), questionable, suspicious, unreliable, untrustworthy 2 UNSURE, doubtful, hesitant, skeptical, uncertain, unconvinced, undecided, wavering

duck *verb* 1 BOB, bend, bow, crouch, dodge, drop, lower, stoop 2 PLUNGE, dip, dive, douse, dunk, immerse, souse, submerge, wet 3 *Informal* DODGE, avoid, escape, evade, shirk, shun, sidestep

dud *Informal* ▸ *noun* 1 FAILURE, flop (*informal*), washout (*informal*) ▸ *adjective* 2 USELESS, broken, failed, inoperative, worthless

dudgeon *noun* **in high dudgeon** INDIGNANT, angry, choked, fuming, offended, resentful, ticked off (*informal*), vexed

due *adjective* 1 EXPECTED, scheduled 2 PAYABLE, in arrears, outstanding, owed, owing, unpaid 3 FITTING, appropriate, deserved, justified, merited, proper, rightful, suitable,

well-earned ▸ *noun* 4 RIGHT(S), deserts, merits, privilege ▸ *adverb* 5 DIRECTLY, exactly, straight, undeviatingly

duel *noun* 1 SINGLE COMBAT, affair of honor 2 CONTEST, clash, competition, encounter, engagement, fight, head-to-head, rivalry ▸ *verb* 3 FIGHT, clash, compete, contend, contest, lock horns, rival, struggle, vie with

dues *plural noun* MEMBERSHIP FEE, charge, charges, contribution, fee, levy

dull *adjective* 1 BORING, dreary, dumpy (*informal*), flat, frowzy, homely (*U.S.*), humdrum, monotonous, plain, tedious, uninteresting 2 STUPID, dense, dim-witted (*informal*), slow, thick, unintelligent 3 CLOUDY, dim, dismal, gloomy, leaden, overcast 4 LIFELESS, apathetic, blank, indifferent, listless, passionless, unresponsive 5 BLUNT, blunted, unsharpened ▸ *verb* 6 RELIEVE, allay, alleviate, blunt, lessen, moderate, soften, take the edge off

duly *adverb* 1 PROPERLY, accordingly, appropriately, befittingly, correctly, decorously, deservedly, fittingly, rightfully, suitably 2 ON TIME, at the proper time, punctually

dumb *adjective* 1 MUTE, mum, silent, soundless, speechless, tongue-tied, voiceless, wordless 2 *Informal* STUPID, asinine, dense, dim-witted (*informal*), dull, foolish, thick, unintelligent

dumbfounded *adjective* AMAZED, astonished, astounded, flabbergasted (*informal*), lost

for words, nonplussed,
overwhelmed, speechless,
staggered, stunned

dummy *noun* 1 MODEL, figure,
form, manikin, mannequin
2 COPY, counterfeit, duplicate,
imitation, sham, substitute
3 *Slang* FOOL, blockhead, dork
(*slang*), dunce, idiot, nitwit
(*informal*), oaf, schmuck
(*slang*), simpleton ▶ *adjective*
4 IMITATION, artificial, bogus,
fake, false, mock, phoney *or*
phony (*informal*), sham,
simulated

dump *verb* 1 DROP, deposit,
fling down, let fall, throw
down 2 GET RID OF, dispose of,
ditch (*slang*), empty out,
jettison, scrap, throw away *or*
out, tip, unload ▶ *noun*
3 RUBBISH TIP, junkyard, refuse
heap, rubbish heap, tip
4 *Informal* PIGSTY, hovel, mess,
slum

dumpy *adjective Informal* DOWDY,
frowzy, frumpy, homely (*U.S.*),
unfashionable

dunce *noun* SIMPLETON,
blockhead, dunderhead,
ignoramus, moron, thickhead

dungeon *noun* PRISON, cage,
cell, oubliette, vault

duplicate *adjective* 1 IDENTICAL,
corresponding, matched,
matching, twin, twofold ▶ *noun*
2 COPY, carbon copy, clone,
double, facsimile, photocopy,
replica, reproduction ▶ *verb*
3 COPY, clone, double, repeat,
replicate, reproduce

durability *noun* DURABLENESS,
constancy, endurance,
imperishability, permanence,
persistence

durable *adjective* LONG-LASTING,
dependable, enduring,
hard-wearing, persistent,
reliable, resistant, strong,
sturdy, tough

duration *noun* LENGTH, extent,
period, span, spell, stretch,
term, time

duress *noun* PRESSURE, coercion,
compulsion, constraint, threat

dusk *noun* TWILIGHT, dark,
evening, eventide, gloaming
(*Scot. or poetic*), nightfall,
sundown, sunset

dusky *adjective* 1 DARK,
dark-complexioned, sable,
swarthy 2 DIM, cloudy, gloomy,
murky, obscure, shadowy,
shady, tenebrous, twilit

dust *noun* 1 GRIME, grit,
particles, powder ▶ *verb*
2 SPRINKLE, cover, dredge,
powder, scatter, sift, spray,
spread

dusty *adjective* DIRTY, grubby,
scuzzy (*slang*), sooty, unclean,
unswept

dutiful *adjective* CONSCIENTIOUS,
devoted, obedient, respectful,
reverential, submissive

duty *noun* 1 RESPONSIBILITY,
assignment, function, job,
obligation, role, task, work
2 LOYALTY, allegiance, deference,
obedience, respect, reverence
3 TAX, excise, levy, tariff, toll
4 **on duty** AT WORK, busy,
engaged, on active service

dwarf *verb* 1 TOWER ABOVE *or*
OVER, diminish, dominate,
overshadow ▶ *adjective*
2 MINIATURE, baby, bonsai,
diminutive, small, tiny,
undersized ▶ *noun* 3 MIDGET,
Lilliputian, pygmy *or* pigmy,

Tom Thumb

dweeb *noun Slang* IDIOT, doofus (*slang*), dope (*slang*), dunce, fool, geek, slang, nerd

dwell *verb* LIVE, abide, inhabit, lodge, reside

dwelling *noun* HOME, abode, domicile, habitation, house, lodging, pad (*slang*), quarters, residence

dwindle *verb* LESSEN, decline, decrease, die away, diminish, fade, peter out, shrink, subside, taper off, wane

dye *noun* 1 COLORING, color, colorant, pigment, stain, tinge, tint ▸ *verb* 2 COLOR, pigment, stain, tinge, tint

dying *adjective* EXPIRING, at death's door, failing, *in extremis*, moribund, not long for this world

dynamic *adjective* ENERGETIC, forceful, go-ahead, go-getting (*informal*), high-powered, lively, powerful, vital

dynasty *noun* EMPIRE, government, house, regime, rule, sovereignty

E e

each *adjective* 1 EVERY ▸ *pronoun* 2 EVERY ONE, each and every one, each one, one and all ▸ *adverb* 3 APIECE, for each, individually, per capita, per head, per person, respectively, to each

eager *adjective* KEEN, agog, anxious, athirst, avid, enthusiastic, fervent, gung ho (*slang*), hungry, impatient, longing

eagerness *noun* KEENNESS, ardor, enthusiasm, fervor, hunger, impatience, thirst, yearning, zeal

ear *noun* SENSITIVITY, appreciation, discrimination, perception, taste

early *adjective* 1 PREMATURE, advanced, forward, untimely 2 PRIMITIVE, primeval, primordial, undeveloped, young ▸ *adverb* 3 TOO SOON, ahead of time, beforehand, in advance, in good time, prematurely

earmark *verb* SET ASIDE, allocate, designate, flag, label, mark out, reserve

earn *verb* 1 MAKE, bring in, collect, gain, get, gross, net, receive 2 DESERVE, acquire, attain, be entitled to, be worthy of, merit, rate, warrant, win

earnest *adjective* 1 SERIOUS, grave, intent, resolute, resolved, sincere, solemn, thoughtful ▸ *noun* 2 As in **in earnest** SERIOUSNESS, sincerity, truth

earnings *plural noun* INCOME, pay, proceeds, profits, receipts, remuneration, salary, takings, wages

earth *noun* 1 WORLD, globe, orb, planet, sphere 2 SOIL, clay, dirt, ground, land, turf

earthenware *noun* CROCKERY, ceramics, pots, pottery, terracotta

earthly *adjective* WORLDLY, human, material, mortal, secular, temporal

earthy adjective CRUDE, bawdy, coarse, raunchy (slang), ribald, robust, uninhibited, unsophisticated

ease noun 1 EASINESS, effortlessness, facility, readiness, simplicity 2 CONTENT, comfort, happiness, peace, peace of mind, quiet, serenity, tranquillity 3 REST, leisure, relaxation, repose, restfulness ▶verb 4 RELIEVE, alleviate, calm, comfort, lessen, lighten, relax, soothe 5 MOVE CAREFULLY, edge, inch, maneuver, slide, slip

easily adverb WITHOUT DIFFICULTY, comfortably, effortlessly, readily, smoothly, with ease, with one hand tied behind one's back

easy adjective 1 NOT DIFFICULT, a piece of cake (informal), child's play (informal), effortless, no trouble, painless, plain sailing, simple, straightforward, uncomplicated, undemanding 2 CAREFREE, comfortable, leisurely, peaceful, quiet, relaxed, serene, tranquil, untroubled 3 TOLERANT, easy-going, indulgent, lenient, mild, permissive, unoppressive

easy-going adjective RELAXED, carefree, casual, easy, even-tempered, happy-go-lucky, laid-back (informal), nonchalant, placid, tolerant, undemanding

eat verb 1 CONSUME, chew, devour, gobble, ingest, munch, scoff (slang), swallow 2 HAVE A MEAL, chow down (slang), dine, feed, take nourishment 3 DESTROY, corrode, decay, dissolve, erode, rot, waste away, wear away

eavesdrop verb LISTEN IN, monitor, overhear, snoop (informal), spy

ebb verb 1 FLOW BACK, go out, recede, retire, retreat, subside, wane, withdraw 2 DECLINE, decrease, diminish, dwindle, fade away, fall away, flag, lessen, peter out ▶noun 3 FLOWING BACK, going out, low tide, low water, retreat, subsidence, wane, withdrawal

eccentric adjective 1 ODD, freakish, idiosyncratic, irregular, outlandish, peculiar, quirky, strange, unconventional ▶noun 2 CRANK (informal), character (informal), nonconformist, oddball (informal), weirdo or weirdie (informal)

eccentricity noun ODDITY, abnormality, caprice, capriciousness, foible, idiosyncrasy, irregularity, peculiarity, quirk

ecclesiastic noun 1 CLERGYMAN, churchman, cleric, holy man, man of the cloth, minister, parson, pastor, priest ▶adjective 2 Also **ecclesiastical** CLERICAL, divine, holy, pastoral, priestly, religious, spiritual

echo noun 1 REPETITION, answer, reverberation 2 COPY, imitation, mirror image, parallel, reflection, reiteration, reproduction ▶verb 3 REPEAT, resound, reverberate 4 COPY, ape, imitate, mirror, parallel, recall, reflect, resemble

eclipse noun 1 OBSCURING, darkening, dimming, extinction, shading ▶verb 2 SURPASS, exceed, excel, outdo, outshine, put in the shade (informal), transcend

economic *adjective* **1** FINANCIAL, commercial, industrial **2** PROFITABLE, money-making, productive, profit-making, remunerative, viable

economical *adjective* **1** THRIFTY, careful, frugal, prudent, scrimping, sparing **2** COST-EFFECTIVE, efficient, money-saving, sparing, time-saving **3** INEXPENSIVE, cheap, low-priced, modest, reasonable

economize *verb* CUT BACK, be economical, be frugal, draw in one's horns, retrench, save, scrimp, tighten one's belt

economy *noun* THRIFT, frugality, husbandry, parsimony, prudence, restraint

ecstasy *noun* RAPTURE, bliss, delight, elation, euphoria, fervor, joy, seventh heaven

ecstatic *adjective* RAPTUROUS, blissful, elated, enraptured, entranced, euphoric, in seventh heaven, joyous, on cloud nine (*informal*), overjoyed

eddy *noun* **1** SWIRL, counter-current, counterflow, undertow, vortex, whirlpool ▶ *verb* **2** SWIRL, whirl

edge *noun* **1** BORDER, boundary, brink, fringe, limit, outline, perimeter, rim, side, verge **2** SHARPNESS, bite, effectiveness, force, incisiveness, keenness, point **3** As in **have the edge on** ADVANTAGE, ascendancy, dominance, lead, superiority, upper hand **4 on edge** NERVOUS, apprehensive, edgy, ill at ease, impatient, irritable, keyed up, on tenterhooks, tense, wired (*slang*) ▶ *verb*

5 BORDER, fringe, hem **6** INCH, creep, ease, sidle, steal

edgy *adjective* NERVOUS, anxious, ill at ease, irritable, keyed up, on edge, on tenterhooks, restive, tense, wired (*slang*)

edible *adjective* EATABLE, digestible, fit to eat, good, harmless, palatable, wholesome

edict *noun* DECREE, act, command, injunction, law, order, proclamation, ruling

edifice *noun* BUILDING, construction, erection, house, structure

edify *verb* INSTRUCT, educate, enlighten, guide, improve, inform, nurture, school, teach

edit *verb* REVISE, adapt, condense, correct, emend, polish, rewrite

edition *noun* VERSION, copy, impression, issue, number, printing, program (*TV, Radio*), volume

educate *verb* TEACH, civilize, develop, discipline, enlighten, improve, inform, instruct, school, train, tutor

educated *adjective* **1** TAUGHT, coached, informed, instructed, nurtured, schooled, tutored **2** CULTURED, civilized, cultivated, enlightened, knowledgeable, learned, refined, sophisticated

education *noun* TEACHING, development, discipline, enlightenment, instruction, nurture, schooling, training, tuition

educational *adjective* INSTRUCTIVE, cultural, edifying, educative, enlightening, improving, informative

eerie *adjective* FRIGHTENING,

creepy (*informal*), ghostly, mysterious, scary (*informal*), spooky (*informal*), strange, uncanny, unearthly, weird

efface *verb* OBLITERATE, blot out, cancel, delete, destroy, eradicate, erase, expunge, rub out, wipe out

effect *noun* 1 RESULT, conclusion, consequence, end result, event, outcome, upshot 2 OPERATION, action, enforcement, execution, force, implementation 3 IMPRESSION, essence, impact, sense, significance, tenor ▶ *verb* 4 BRING ABOUT, accomplish, achieve, complete, execute, fulfill, perform, produce

effective *adjective* 1 EFFICIENT, active, adequate, capable, competent, productive, serviceable, useful 2 IN OPERATION, active, current, in effect, in force, operative 3 POWERFUL, cogent, compelling, convincing, forceful, impressive, persuasive, telling

effects *plural noun* BELONGINGS, gear, goods, paraphernalia, possessions, property, things

effeminate *adjective* WOMANLY, camp (*informal*), feminine, sissy, soft, tender, unmanly, weak, womanish

effervescent *adjective* 1 BUBBLING, carbonated, fizzy, foaming, frothy, sparkling 2 LIVELY, animated, bubbly, ebullient, enthusiastic, exuberant, irrepressible, vivacious

effete *adjective* DECADENT, dissipated, enfeebled, feeble, ineffectual, spoiled, weak

efficacious *adjective* EFFECTIVE, adequate, efficient, operative, potent, powerful, productive, successful, useful

efficiency *noun* COMPETENCE, adeptness, capability, economy, effectiveness, power, productivity, proficiency

efficient *adjective* COMPETENT, businesslike, capable, economic, effective, organized, productive, proficient, well-organized, workmanlike

effigy *noun* LIKENESS, dummy, figure, guy, icon, idol, image, picture, portrait, representation, statue

effluent *noun* WASTE, effluvium, pollutant, sewage

effort *noun* 1 EXERTION, application, elbow grease (*facetious*), endeavor, energy, pains, struggle, toil, trouble, work 2 ATTEMPT, endeavor, essay, go (*informal*), shot (*informal*), stab (*informal*), try

effortless *adjective* EASY, painless, plain sailing, simple, smooth, uncomplicated, undemanding

effrontery *noun* INSOLENCE, arrogance, audacity, brazenness, cheek (*informal*), impertinence, impudence, nerve, presumption, temerity

effusive *adjective* DEMONSTRATIVE, ebullient, expansive, exuberant, gushing, lavish, unreserved, unrestrained

egg on *verb* ENCOURAGE, exhort, goad, incite, prod, prompt, push, spur, urge

egocentric *adjective* SELF-CENTERED, egoistic,

egoistical, egotistic, egotistical,
selfish

egotism, egoism *noun*
SELF-CENTEREDNESS, conceitedness,
narcissism, self-absorption,
self-esteem, self-importance,
self-interest, selfishness, vanity

egotist, egoist *noun*
EGOMANIAC, bighead (*informal*),
boaster, braggart, narcissist

egotistic, egotistical, egoistic
or **egoistical** *adjective*
SELF-CENTERED, boasting,
conceited, egocentric, full of
oneself, narcissistic,
self-absorbed, self-important,
vain

egress *noun Formal* EXIT,
departure, exodus, way out,
withdrawal

eject *verb* THROW OUT, banish,
drive out, evict, expel, oust,
remove, turn out

ejection *noun* EXPULSION,
banishment, deportation,
eviction, exile, removal

eke out *verb* BE SPARING WITH,
economize on, husband,
stretch out

elaborate *adjective* **1** DETAILED,
intricate, minute, painstaking,
precise, studied, thorough
2 COMPLICATED, complex, fancy,
fussy, involved, ornamented,
ornate ▶ *verb* **3** EXPAND (UPON),
add detail, amplify, develop,
embellish, enlarge, flesh out

elapse *verb* PASS, glide by, go
by, lapse, roll by, slip away

elastic *adjective* **1** STRETCHY,
plastic, pliable, pliant, resilient,
rubbery, springy, supple,
tensile **2** ADAPTABLE,
accommodating, adjustable,
compliant, flexible, supple,

tolerant, variable, yielding

elated *adjective* JOYFUL,
delighted, ecstatic, euphoric,
exhilarated, gleeful, jubilant,
overjoyed

elation *noun* JOY, bliss, delight,
ecstasy, euphoria, exhilaration,
glee, high spirits, jubilation,
rapture

elbow *noun* **1** JOINT, angle ▶ *verb*
2 PUSH, jostle, knock, nudge,
shove

elbow room *noun* SCOPE,
freedom, latitude, leeway, play,
room, space

elder *adjective* **1** OLDER,
first-born, senior ▶ *noun* **2** OLDER
PERSON, senior

elect *verb* CHOOSE, appoint,
determine, opt for, pick,
prefer, select, settle on, vote

election *noun* VOTING,
appointment, choice,
judgment, preference,
selection, vote

elector *noun* VOTER, constituent,
selector

electric *adjective* CHARGED,
dynamic, exciting, rousing,
stimulating, stirring, tense,
thrilling

electrify *verb* STARTLE, astound,
excite, galvanize, invigorate,
jolt, shock, stir, thrill

elegance *noun* STYLE, dignity,
exquisiteness, grace,
gracefulness, grandeur, luxury,
refinement, taste

elegant *adjective* STYLISH, chic,
delicate, exquisite, fine,
graceful, handsome, polished,
refined, tasteful

element *noun* **1** COMPONENT,
constituent, factor, ingredient,
part, section, subdivision, unit

2 *As in* **in one's element** ENVIRONMENT, domain, field, habitat, medium, milieu, sphere

elementary *adjective* SIMPLE, clear, easy, plain, rudimentary, straightforward, uncomplicated

elements *plural noun* **1** BASICS, essentials, foundations, fundamentals, nuts and bolts (*informal*), principles, rudiments **2** WEATHER CONDITIONS, atmospheric conditions, powers of nature

elevate *verb* **1** RAISE, heighten, hoist, lift, lift up, uplift **2** PROMOTE, advance, aggrandize, exalt, prefer, upgrade

elevated *adjective* HIGH-MINDED, dignified, exalted, grand, high-flown, inflated, lofty, noble, sublime

elevation *noun* **1** PROMOTION, advancement, aggrandizement, exaltation, preferment, upgrading **2** ALTITUDE, height

elicit *verb* **1** BRING ABOUT, bring forth, bring out, bring to light, call forth, cause, derive, evolve, give rise to **2** OBTAIN, draw out, evoke, exact, extort, extract, wrest

eligible *adjective* QUALIFIED, acceptable, appropriate, desirable, fit, preferable, proper, suitable, worthy

eliminate *verb* GET RID OF, cut out, dispose of, do away with, eradicate, exterminate, remove, stamp out, take out

elite *noun* BEST, aristocracy, cream, crème de la crème, flower, nobility, pick, upper class

elitist *adjective* SNOBBISH, exclusive, selective

elixir *noun* PANACEA, nostrum

elocution *noun* DICTION, articulation, declamation, delivery, enunciation, oratory, pronunciation, speech, speechmaking

elongate *verb* MAKE LONGER, draw out, extend, lengthen, prolong, protract, stretch

elope *verb* RUN AWAY, abscond, bolt, decamp, disappear, escape, leave, run off, slip away, steal away

eloquence *noun* EXPRESSIVENESS, expression, fluency, forcefulness, oratory, persuasiveness, rhetoric, way with words

eloquent *adjective* **1** SILVER-TONGUED, articulate, fluent, forceful, moving, persuasive, stirring, well-expressed **2** EXPRESSIVE, meaningful, suggestive, telling, vivid

elsewhere *adverb* IN *or* TO ANOTHER PLACE, abroad, away, hence (*archaic*), not here, somewhere else

elucidate *verb* CLARIFY, clear up, explain, explicate, expound, illuminate, illustrate, make plain, shed *or* throw light upon, spell out

elude *verb* **1** ESCAPE, avoid, dodge, duck (*informal*), evade, flee, get away from, outrun **2** BAFFLE, be beyond (someone), confound, escape, foil, frustrate, puzzle, stump, thwart

elusive *adjective* **1** DIFFICULT TO CATCH, shifty, slippery, tricky **2** INDEFINABLE, fleeting, intangible, subtle, transient, transitory

emaciated *adjective* SKELETAL, cadaverous, gaunt, haggard, lean, pinched, scrawny, thin, undernourished, wasted

emanate *verb* FLOW, arise, come forth, derive, emerge, issue, originate, proceed, spring, stem

emancipate *verb* FREE, deliver, liberate, release, set free, unchain, unfetter

emancipation *noun* FREEDOM, deliverance, liberation, liberty, release

embalm *verb* PRESERVE, mummify

embargo *noun* 1 BAN, bar, boycott, interdiction, prohibition, restraint, restriction, stoppage ▶*verb* 2 BAN, bar, block, boycott, prohibit, restrict, stop

embark *verb* 1 GO ABOARD, board ship, take ship
2 **embark on** *or* **upon** BEGIN, commence, enter, launch, plunge into, set about, set out, start, take up

embarrass *verb* SHAME, discomfit, disconcert, distress, fluster, humiliate, mortify, show up (*informal*)

embarrassed *adjective* ASHAMED, awkward, blushing, discomfited, disconcerted, humiliated, mortified, red-faced, self-conscious, sheepish

embarrassing *adjective* HUMILIATING, awkward, compromising, discomfiting, disconcerting, mortifying, sensitive, shameful, toe-curling (*informal*), uncomfortable

embarrassment *noun* 1 SHAME, awkwardness, bashfulness, distress, humiliation, mortification, self-consciousness, showing up (*informal*) 2 PREDICAMENT, bind (*informal*), difficulty, mess, pickle (*informal*), scrape (*informal*)

embellish *verb* DECORATE, adorn, beautify, elaborate, embroider, enhance, enrich, festoon, ornament

embellishment *noun* DECORATION, adornment, elaboration, embroidery, enhancement, enrichment, exaggeration, ornament, ornamentation

embezzle *verb* MISAPPROPRIATE, appropriate, filch, misuse, peculate, pilfer, purloin, rip off (*slang*), steal

embezzlement *noun* MISAPPROPRIATION, appropriation, filching, fraud, misuse, peculation, pilfering, stealing, theft

embittered *adjective* RESENTFUL, angry, bitter, disaffected, disillusioned, rancorous, soured, with a chip on one's shoulder (*informal*)

emblem *noun* SYMBOL, badge, crest, image, insignia, mark, sign, token

embodiment *noun* PERSONIFICATION, epitome, example, exemplar, expression, incarnation, representation, symbol

embody *verb* 1 PERSONIFY, exemplify, manifest, represent, stand for, symbolize, typify
2 INCORPORATE, collect, combine, comprise, contain, include

embolden *verb* ENCOURAGE, fire,

inflame, invigorate, rouse, stimulate, stir, strengthen

embrace verb 1 HUG, clasp, cuddle, envelop, hold, seize, squeeze, take or hold in one's arms 2 ACCEPT, adopt, espouse, seize, take on board, take up, welcome 3 INCLUDE, comprehend, comprise, contain, cover, encompass, involve, take in ▶noun 4 HUG, clasp, clinch (slang), cuddle, squeeze

embroil verb INVOLVE, enmesh, ensnare, entangle, implicate, incriminate, mire, mix up

embryo noun GERM, beginning, nucleus, root, rudiment

emend verb REVISE, amend, correct, edit, improve, rectify

emendation noun REVISION, amendment, correction, editing, improvement, rectification

emerge verb 1 COME INTO VIEW, appear, arise, come forth, emanate, issue, rise, spring up, surface 2 BECOME APPARENT, become known, come out, come out in the wash, come to light, crop up, transpire

emergence noun COMING, advent, appearance, arrival, development, materialization, rise

emergency noun CRISIS, danger, difficulty, extremity, necessity, plight, predicament, quandary, scrape (informal)

emigrate verb MOVE ABROAD, migrate, move

emigration noun DEPARTURE, exodus, migration

eminence noun PROMINENCE, distinction, esteem, fame, greatness, importance, note, prestige, renown, repute

eminent adjective PROMINENT, celebrated, distinguished, esteemed, famous, high-ranking, illustrious, noted, renowned, well-known

emission noun GIVING OFF or OUT, discharge, ejaculation, ejection, exhalation, radiation, shedding, transmission

emit verb GIVE OFF, cast out, discharge, eject, emanate, exude, radiate, send out, transmit

emotion noun FEELING, ardor, excitement, fervor, passion, sensation, sentiment, vehemence, warmth

emotional adjective 1 SENSITIVE, demonstrative, excitable, hot-blooded, passionate, sentimental, temperamental 2 MOVING, affecting, emotive, heart-warming, poignant, sentimental, stirring, touching

emotive adjective SENSITIVE, controversial, delicate, touchy

emphasis noun STRESS, accent, attention, force, importance, priority, prominence, significance, weight

emphasize verb STRESS, accentuate, dwell on, give priority to, highlight, lay stress on, play up, press home, underline

emphatic adjective FORCEFUL, categorical, definite, insistent, positive, pronounced, resounding, unequivocal, unmistakable, vigorous

empire noun KINGDOM, commonwealth, domain, realm

empirical adjective FIRST-HAND,

experiential, experimental, observed, practical, pragmatic

employ verb 1 HIRE, commission, engage, enlist, retain, take on 2 KEEP BUSY, engage, fill, make use of, occupy, take up, use up 3 USE, apply, bring to bear, exercise, exert, make use of, ply, put to use, utilize ▶ noun 4 As in **in the employ of** SERVICE, employment, engagement, hire

employed adjective WORKING, active, busy, engaged, in a job, in employment, in work, occupied

employee noun WORKER, hand, job-holder, staff member, wage-earner, workman

employer noun BOSS (informal), company, firm, owner, patron, proprietor

employment noun 1 TAKING ON, engagement, enlistment, hire, retaining 2 USE, application, exercise, exertion, utilization 3 JOB, line, occupation, profession, trade, vocation, work

emporium noun Old-fashioned SHOP, bazaar, market, mart, store, warehouse

empower verb ENABLE, allow, authorize, commission, delegate, entitle, license, permit, qualify, sanction, warrant

emptiness noun 1 BARENESS, blankness, desolation, vacancy, vacuum, void, waste 2 PURPOSELESSNESS, banality, futility, hollowness, inanity, meaninglessness, senselessness, vanity, worthlessness 3 INSINCERITY, cheapness,

hollowness, idleness

empty adjective 1 BARE, blank, clear, deserted, desolate, hollow, unfurnished, uninhabited, unoccupied, vacant, void 2 PURPOSELESS, banal, fruitless, futile, hollow, inane, meaningless, senseless, vain, worthless 3 INSINCERE, cheap, hollow, idle ▶ verb 4 EVACUATE, clear, drain, exhaust, pour out, unload, vacate, void

empty-headed adjective SCATTERBRAINED, brainless, dizzy (informal), featherbrained, harebrained, silly, vacuous

emulate verb IMITATE, compete with, copy, echo, follow, mimic, rival

enable verb ALLOW, authorize, empower, entitle, license, permit, qualify, sanction, warrant

enact verb 1 ESTABLISH, authorize, command, decree, legislate, ordain, order, proclaim, sanction 2 PERFORM, act out, depict, play, play the part of, portray, represent

enamored adjective IN LOVE, captivated, charmed, enraptured, fond, infatuated, smitten, taken

encampment noun CAMP, base, bivouac, camping ground, campsite, cantonment, quarters, tents

encapsulate verb SUM UP, abridge, compress, condense, digest, epitomize, précis, summarize

enchant verb FASCINATE, beguile, bewitch, captivate, charm, delight, enrapture, enthrall, ravish, spellbind

enchanter noun SORCERER, conjurer, magician, magus, necromancer, warlock, witch, wizard

enchanting adjective FASCINATING, alluring, attractive, bewitching, captivating, charming, delightful, entrancing, lovely, pleasant

enclose verb 1 SURROUND, bound, encase, encircle, fence, hem in, shut in, wall in 2 SEND WITH, include, insert, put in

encompass verb 1 SURROUND, circle, encircle, enclose, envelop, ring 2 INCLUDE, admit, comprise, contain, cover, embrace, hold, incorporate, take in

encounter verb 1 MEET, bump into (informal), chance upon, come upon, confront, experience, face, run across ▶ noun 2 MEETING, brush, confrontation, rendezvous 3 BATTLE, clash, conflict, contest, head-to-head, run-in (informal)

encourage verb 1 INSPIRE, buoy up, cheer, comfort, console, embolden, hearten, reassure 2 SPUR, advocate, egg on, foster, promote, prompt, support, urge

encouragement noun INSPIRATION, cheer, incitement, promotion, reassurance, stimulation, stimulus, support

encouraging adjective PROMISING, bright, cheerful, comforting, good, heartening, hopeful, reassuring, rosy

encroach verb INTRUDE, impinge, infringe, invade, make inroads,

overstep, trespass, usurp

encumber verb BURDEN, hamper, handicap, hinder, impede, inconvenience, obstruct, saddle, weigh down

end noun 1 EXTREMITY, boundary, edge, extent, extreme, limit, point, terminus, tip 2 FINISH, cessation, close, closure, ending, expiration, expiry, stop, termination 3 CONCLUSION, culmination, denouement, ending, finale, resolution 4 REMNANT, butt, fragment, leftover, oddment, remainder, scrap, stub 5 DESTRUCTION, death, demise, doom, extermination, extinction, ruin 6 PURPOSE, aim, goal, intention, object, objective, point, reason ▶ verb 7 FINISH, cease, close, conclude, culminate, stop, terminate, wind up

endanger verb PUT AT RISK, compromise, imperil, jeopardize, put in danger, risk, threaten

endearing adjective ATTRACTIVE, captivating, charming, cute, engaging, lovable, sweet, winning

endearment noun LOVING WORD, sweet nothing

endeavor verb 1 TRY, aim, aspire, attempt, labor, make an effort, strive, struggle, take pains ▶ noun 2 EFFORT, attempt, enterprise, trial, try, undertaking, venture

ending noun FINISH, cessation, close, completion, conclusion, culmination, denouement, end, finale

endless adjective ETERNAL, boundless, continual,

everlasting, incessant, infinite, interminable, unlimited

endorse *verb* 1 APPROVE, advocate, authorize, back, champion, promote, ratify, recommend, support 2 SIGN, countersign

endorsement *noun* 1 APPROVAL, advocacy, approbation, authorization, backing, bequest, ratification, recommendation, seal of approval, support 2 SIGNATURE, countersignature

endow *verb* PROVIDE, award, bequeath, bestow, confer, donate, finance, fund, give

endowment *noun* PROVISION, award, benefaction, bequest, donation, gift, grant, legacy

endurable *adjective* BEARABLE, acceptable, sufferable, sustainable, tolerable

endurance *noun* 1 STAYING POWER, fortitude, patience, perseverance, persistence, resolution, stamina, strength, tenacity, toleration 2 PERMANENCE, continuity, durability, duration, longevity, stability

endure *verb* 1 BEAR, cope with, experience, stand, suffer, sustain, undergo, withstand 2 LAST, continue, live on, persist, remain, stand, stay, survive

enduring *adjective* LONG-LASTING, abiding, continuing, lasting, perennial, persistent, steadfast, unfaltering, unwavering

enemy *noun* FOE, adversary, antagonist, competitor, opponent, rival, the other side, opposition

energetic *adjective* VIGOROUS, active, animated, dynamic, forceful, indefatigable, lively, strenuous, tireless

energy *noun* VIGOR, drive, forcefulness, get-up-and-go (*informal*), liveliness, pep, stamina, verve, vitality

enforce *verb* IMPOSE, administer, apply, carry out, execute, implement, insist on, prosecute, put into effect

engage *verb* 1 PARTICIPATE, embark on, enter into, join, set about, take part, undertake 2 OCCUPY, absorb, engross, grip, involve, preoccupy 3 CAPTIVATE, arrest, catch, fix, gain 4 EMPLOY, appoint, enlist, enroll, hire, retain, take on 5 *Military* BEGIN BATTLE WITH, assail, attack, encounter, fall on, join battle with, meet, take on 6 SET GOING, activate, apply, bring into operation, energize, switch on

engaged *adjective* 1 BETROTHED (*archaic*), affianced, pledged, promised, spoken for 2 OCCUPIED, busy, employed, in use, tied up, unavailable

engagement *noun* 1 APPOINTMENT, arrangement, commitment, date, meeting 2 BETROTHAL, troth (*archaic*) 3 BATTLE, action, combat, conflict, encounter, fight

engaging *adjective* CHARMING, agreeable, attractive, fetching (*informal*), likable *or* likeable, pleasing, winning, winsome

engender *verb* PRODUCE, breed, cause, create, generate, give rise to, induce, instigate, lead to

engine *noun* MACHINE, mechanism, motor

engineer *verb* BRING ABOUT, contrive, create, devise, effect, mastermind, plan, plot, scheme

engrave *verb* 1 CARVE, chisel, cut, etch, inscribe 2 FIX, embed, impress, imprint, ingrain, lodge

engraving *noun* CARVING, etching, inscription, plate, woodcut

engross *verb* ABSORB, engage, immerse, involve, occupy, preoccupy

engrossed *adjective* ABSORBED, caught up, enthralled, fascinated, gripped, immersed, lost, preoccupied, rapt, riveted

engulf *verb* IMMERSE, envelop, inundate, overrun, overwhelm, submerge, swallow up, swamp

enhance *verb* IMPROVE, add to, boost, heighten, increase, lift, reinforce, strengthen, swell

enigma *noun* MYSTERY, conundrum, problem, puzzle, riddle, teaser

enigmatic *adjective* MYSTERIOUS, ambiguous, cryptic, equivocal, inscrutable, obscure, puzzling, unfathomable

enjoy *verb* 1 TAKE PLEASURE IN *or* FROM, appreciate, be entertained by, be pleased with, delight in, like, relish 2 HAVE, be blessed *or* favored with, experience, have the benefit of, own, possess, reap the benefits of, use

enjoyable *adjective* PLEASURABLE, agreeable, delightful, entertaining, gratifying, pleasant, satisfying, to one's liking

enjoyment *noun* PLEASURE, amusement, delectation, delight, entertainment, fun, gratification, happiness, joy, relish

enlarge *verb* 1 INCREASE, add to, amplify, broaden, expand, extend, grow, magnify, swell, widen 2 **enlarge on** EXPAND ON, descant on, develop, elaborate on, expatiate on, give further details about

enlighten *verb* INFORM, advise, cause to understand, counsel, edify, educate, instruct, make aware, teach

enlightened *adjective* INFORMED, aware, civilized, cultivated, educated, knowledgeable, open-minded, reasonable, sophisticated

enlightenment *noun* UNDERSTANDING, awareness, comprehension, education, insight, instruction, knowledge, learning, wisdom

enlist *verb* 1 JOIN UP, enroll, enter (into), join, muster, register, sign up, volunteer 2 OBTAIN, engage, procure, recruit

enliven *verb* CHEER UP, animate, excite, inspire, invigorate, pep up, rouse, spark, stimulate, vitalize

enmity *noun* HOSTILITY, acrimony, animosity, bad blood, bitterness, hatred, ill will, malice

ennoble *verb* DIGNIFY, aggrandize, elevate, enhance, exalt, glorify, honor, magnify, raise

enormity *noun* 1 WICKEDNESS, atrocity, depravity, monstrousness, outrageousness, vileness, villainy 2 ATROCITY, abomination, crime, disgrace, evil, horror, monstrosity, outrage **3** *Informal* HUGENESS, greatness, immensity, magnitude, vastness

enormous *adjective* HUGE, colossal, gigantic, gross, immense, mammoth, massive, mountainous, tremendous, vast

enough *adjective* **1** SUFFICIENT, abundant, adequate, ample, plenty ▶*noun* **2** SUFFICIENCY, abundance, adequacy, ample supply, plenty, right amount ▶*adverb* **3** SUFFICIENTLY, abundantly, adequately, amply, reasonably, satisfactorily, tolerably

enquire see INQUIRE

enquiry see INQUIRY

enrage *verb* ANGER, exasperate, incense, inflame, infuriate, madden

enrich *verb* **1** ENHANCE, augment, develop, improve, refine, supplement **2** MAKE RICH, make wealthy

enroll *verb* ENLIST, accept, admit, join up, recruit, register, sign up *or* on, take on

enrollment *noun* ENLISTMENT, acceptance, admission, engagement, matriculation, recruitment, registration

en route *adverb* ON *or* ALONG THE WAY, in transit, on the road

ensemble *noun* **1** WHOLE, aggregate, collection, entirety, set, sum, total, totality **2** OUTFIT, costume, get-up (*informal*), suit **3** GROUP, band, cast, chorus, company, troupe

ensign *noun* FLAG, banner, colors, jack, pennant, pennon, standard, streamer

ensue *verb* FOLLOW, arise, come next, derive, flow, issue, proceed, result, stem

ensure *verb* **1** MAKE CERTAIN, certify, confirm, effect, guarantee, make sure, secure, warrant **2** PROTECT, guard, make safe, safeguard, secure

entail *verb* INVOLVE, bring about, call for, demand, give rise to, necessitate, occasion, require

entangle *verb* **1** TANGLE, catch, embroil, enmesh, ensnare, entrap, implicate, snag, snare, trap **2** MIX UP, complicate, confuse, jumble, muddle, perplex, puzzle

enter *verb* **1** COME *or* GO IN *or* INTO, arrive, make an entrance, pass into, penetrate, pierce **2** JOIN, commence, embark upon, enlist, enroll, set out on, start, take up **3** RECORD, inscribe, list, log, note, register, set down, take down

enterprise *noun* **1** FIRM, business, company, concern, establishment, operation **2** UNDERTAKING, adventure, effort, endeavor, operation, plan, program, project, venture **3** INITIATIVE, adventurousness, boldness, daring, drive, energy, enthusiasm, resourcefulness

enterprising *adjective* RESOURCEFUL, adventurous, bold, daring, energetic, enthusiastic, go-ahead, intrepid, spirited

entertain *verb* **1** AMUSE, charm, cheer, delight, please, regale **2** SHOW HOSPITALITY TO, accommodate, be host to, harbor, have company, lodge, put up, treat **3** CONSIDER, conceive, contemplate, imagine, keep in mind, think about

entertaining adjective ENJOYABLE, amusing, cheering, diverting, funny, humorous, interesting, pleasant, pleasurable

entertainment noun ENJOYMENT, amusement, fun, leisure activity, pastime, pleasure, recreation, sport, treat

enthrall verb FASCINATE, captivate, charm, enchant, enrapture, entrance, grip, mesmerize

enthusiasm noun KEENNESS, eagerness, fervor, interest, passion, relish, zeal, zest

enthusiast noun LOVER, aficionado, buff (informal), devotee, fan, fanatic, follower, supporter

enthusiastic adjective KEEN, avid, eager, fervent, gung ho (slang), passionate, vigorous, wholehearted, zealous

entice verb ATTRACT, allure, cajole, coax, lead on, lure, persuade, seduce, tempt

entire adjective WHOLE, complete, full, gross, total

entirely adverb COMPLETELY, absolutely, altogether, fully, in every respect, thoroughly, totally, utterly, wholly

entitle verb 1 GIVE THE RIGHT TO, allow, authorize, empower, enable, license, permit 2 CALL, christen, dub, label, name, term, title

entity noun THING, being, creature, individual, object, organism, substance

entourage noun RETINUE, associates, attendants, company, court, escort,

followers, staff, train

entrails plural noun INTESTINES, bowels, guts, innards (informal), insides (informal), offal, viscera

entrance[1] noun 1 WAY IN, access, door, doorway, entry, gate, opening, passage 2 APPEARANCE, arrival, coming in, entry, introduction 3 ADMISSION, access, admittance, entrée, entry, permission to enter

entrance[2] verb 1 ENCHANT, bewitch, captivate, charm, delight, enrapture, enthrall, fascinate 2 MESMERIZE, hypnotize, put in a trance

entrant noun COMPETITOR, candidate, contestant, entry, participant, player

entreaty noun PLEA, appeal, earnest request, exhortation, petition, prayer, request, supplication

entrenched adjective FIXED, deep-rooted, deep-seated, ineradicable, ingrained, rooted, set, unshakable, well-established

entrepreneur noun BUSINESSMAN or BUSINESSWOMAN, impresario, industrialist, magnate, tycoon

entrust verb GIVE CUSTODY OF, assign, commit, confide, delegate, deliver, hand over, turn over

entry noun 1 WAY IN, access, door, doorway, entrance, gate, opening, passage 2 COMING IN, appearance, entering, entrance, initiation, introduction 3 ADMISSION, access, entrance, entrée, permission to enter 4 RECORD, account, item, listing, note

entwine verb TWIST, interlace,

interweave, knit, plait, twine, weave, wind

enumerate *verb* LIST, cite, itemize, mention, name, quote, recite, recount, relate, spell out

enunciate *verb* 1 PRONOUNCE, articulate, enounce, say, sound, speak, utter, vocalize, voice 2 STATE, declare, proclaim, promulgate, pronounce, propound, publish

envelop *verb* ENCLOSE, cloak, cover, encase, encircle, engulf, shroud, surround, wrap

envelope *noun* WRAPPING, case, casing, cover, covering, jacket, wrapper

enviable *adjective* DESIRABLE, advantageous, favored, fortunate, lucky, privileged, to die for (*informal*), win-win (*informal*)

envious *adjective* COVETOUS, green with envy, grudging, jealous, resentful

environment *noun* SURROUNDINGS, atmosphere, background, conditions, habitat, medium, setting, situation

environmental *adjective* ECOLOGICAL, green

environmentalist *noun* CONSERVATIONIST, ecologist, green

environs *plural noun* SURROUNDING AREA, district, locality, neighborhood, outskirts, precincts, suburbs, vicinity

envisage *verb* 1 IMAGINE, conceive (of), conceptualize, contemplate, fancy, picture, think up, visualize 2 FORESEE, anticipate, envision, predict, see

envoy *noun* MESSENGER, agent, ambassador, courier, delegate, diplomat, emissary, intermediary, representative

envy *noun* 1 COVETOUSNESS, enviousness, jealousy, resentfulness, resentment ▶ *verb* 2 COVET, be envious (of), begrudge, be jealous (of), grudge, resent

ephemeral *adjective* BRIEF, fleeting, momentary, passing, short-lived, temporary, transient, transitory

epidemic *noun* SPREAD, contagion, growth, outbreak, plague, rash, upsurge, wave

epigram *noun* WITTICISM, aphorism, bon mot, quip

epilogue *noun* CONCLUSION, coda, concluding speech, postscript

episode *noun* 1 EVENT, adventure, affair, escapade, experience, happening, incident, matter, occurrence 2 PART, chapter, installment, passage, scene, section

epistle *noun* LETTER, communication, message, missive, note

epitaph *noun* MONUMENT, inscription

epithet *noun* NAME, appellation, description, designation, moniker *or* monicker (*slang*), nickname, sobriquet, tag, title

epitome *noun* PERSONIFICATION, archetype, embodiment, essence, quintessence, representation, type, typical example

epitomize *verb* TYPIFY, embody, exemplify, illustrate, personify, represent, symbolize

epoch noun ERA, age, date, period, time

equable adjective EVEN-TEMPERED, calm, composed, easy-going, imperturbable, level-headed, placid, serene, unflappable (informal)

equal adjective 1 IDENTICAL, alike, corresponding, equivalent, the same, uniform 2 REGULAR, symmetrical, uniform, unvarying 3 EVEN, balanced, evenly matched, fifty-fifty (informal) 4 FAIR, egalitarian, even-handed, impartial, just, on a level playing field (informal), unbiased 5 **equal to** CAPABLE OF, competent to, fit for, good enough for, ready for, strong enough, suitable for, up to ▶ noun 6 MATCH, counterpart, equivalent, rival, twin ▶ verb 7 MATCH, amount to, be tantamount to, correspond to, equate, level, parallel, tie with

equality noun 1 SAMENESS, balance, correspondence, equivalence, evenness, identity, likeness, similarity, uniformity 2 FAIRNESS, egalitarianism, equal opportunity, parity

equalize verb MAKE EQUAL, balance, equal, even up, level, match, regularize, smooth, square, standardize

equate verb MAKE or BE EQUAL, be commensurate, compare, correspond with or to, liken, mention in the same breath, parallel

equation noun EQUATING, comparison, correspondence, parallel

equilibrium noun STABILITY, balance, equipoise, evenness, rest, steadiness, symmetry

equip verb SUPPLY, arm, array, fit out, furnish, provide, stock

equipment noun TOOLS, accouterments, apparatus, gear, paraphernalia, stuff, supplies, tackle

equitable adjective FAIR, even-handed, honest, impartial, just, proper, reasonable, unbiased

equivalence noun EQUALITY, correspondence, evenness, likeness, parity, sameness, similarity

equivalent noun 1 EQUAL, counterpart, match, opposite number, parallel, twin ▶ adjective 2 EQUAL, alike, commensurate, comparable, corresponding, interchangeable, of a piece, on a level playing field (informal), same, similar, tantamount

equivocal adjective AMBIGUOUS, evasive, indefinite, indeterminate, misleading, oblique, obscure, uncertain, vague

era noun AGE, date, day or days, epoch, generation, period, time

eradicate verb WIPE OUT, annihilate, destroy, eliminate, erase, exterminate, extinguish, obliterate, remove, root out

erase verb WIPE OUT, blot, cancel, delete, expunge, obliterate, remove, rub out

erect verb 1 BUILD, construct, put up, raise, set up 2 FOUND, create, establish, form, initiate, institute, organize, set up ▶ adjective 3 UPRIGHT, elevated, perpendicular, pricked-up, stiff, straight, vertical

erode verb WEAR DOWN or AWAY, abrade, consume, corrode, destroy, deteriorate, disintegrate, eat away, grind down

erosion noun DETERIORATION, abrasion, attrition, destruction, disintegration, eating away, grinding down, wearing down or away

erotic adjective SEXUAL, amatory, carnal, lustful, seductive, sensual, sexy (informal), voluptuous

err verb MAKE A MISTAKE, blunder, go wrong, miscalculate, misjudge, mistake, slip up (informal)

errand noun JOB, charge, commission, message, mission, task

erratic adjective UNPREDICTABLE, changeable, inconsistent, irregular, uneven, unreliable, unstable, variable, wayward

erroneous adjective INCORRECT, fallacious, false, faulty, flawed, invalid, mistaken, unsound, wrong

error noun MISTAKE, bloomer (informal), blunder, miscalculation, oversight, slip, solecism

erstwhile adjective FORMER, bygone, late, old, once, one-time, past, previous, sometime

erudite adjective LEARNED, cultivated, cultured, educated, knowledgeable, scholarly, well-educated, well-read

erupt verb 1 EXPLODE, belch forth, blow up, burst out, gush, pour forth, spew forth or out, spout, throw off 2 Medical BREAK OUT, appear

eruption noun 1 EXPLOSION, discharge, ejection, flare-up, outbreak, outburst 2 Medical INFLAMMATION, outbreak, rash

escalate verb INCREASE, expand, extend, grow, heighten, intensify, mount, rise

escapade noun ADVENTURE, antic, caper, prank, scrape (informal), stunt

escape verb 1 GET AWAY, abscond, bolt, break free or out, flee, fly, make one's getaway, run away or off, slip away 2 AVOID, dodge, duck, elude, evade, pass, shun, slip 3 LEAK, emanate, exude, flow, gush, issue, pour forth, seep ▸ noun 4 GETAWAY, break, break-out, flight 5 AVOIDANCE, circumvention, evasion 6 RELAXATION, distraction, diversion, pastime, recreation 7 LEAK, emanation, emission, seepage

escort noun 1 GUARD, bodyguard, convoy, cortege, entourage, retinue, train 2 COMPANION, attendant, beau, chaperon, guide, partner ▸ verb 3 ACCOMPANY, chaperon, conduct, guide, lead, partner, shepherd, usher

especial adjective Formal EXCEPTIONAL, noteworthy, outstanding, principal, special, uncommon, unusual

especially adverb EXCEPTIONALLY, conspicuously, markedly, notably, outstandingly, remarkably, specially, strikingly, uncommonly, unusually

espionage noun SPYING,

counter-intelligence,
intelligence, surveillance,
undercover work

espousal noun SUPPORT,
adoption, advocacy, backing,
championing, championship,
defense, embracing,
promotion, taking up

espouse verb SUPPORT, adopt,
advocate, back, champion,
embrace, promote, stand up
for, take up, uphold

essay noun 1 COMPOSITION,
article, discourse, dissertation,
paper, piece, tract, treatise
▶ verb 2 Formal ATTEMPT, aim,
endeavor, try, undertake

essence noun 1 FUNDAMENTAL
NATURE, being, core, heart,
nature, quintessence, soul,
spirit, substance 2 CONCENTRATE,
distillate, extract, spirits,
tincture

essential adjective 1 VITAL,
crucial, important,
indispensable, necessary,
needed, requisite
2 FUNDAMENTAL, basic, cardinal,
elementary, innate, intrinsic,
main, principal ▶ noun
3 PREREQUISITE, basic,
fundamental, must, necessity,
rudiment, sine qua non

establish verb 1 CREATE,
constitute, form, found,
ground, inaugurate, institute,
settle, set up 2 PROVE,
authenticate, certify, confirm,
corroborate, demonstrate,
substantiate, verify

establishment noun 1 CREATION,
formation, foundation,
founding, inauguration,
installation, institution,
organization, setting up

2 ORGANIZATION, business,
company, concern,
corporation, enterprise, firm,
institution, outfit (informal)
3 **the Establishment** THE
AUTHORITIES, ruling class, the
powers that be, the system

estate noun 1 LANDS, area,
domain, holdings, manor,
property 2 Law PROPERTY, assets,
belongings, effects, fortune,
goods, possessions, wealth

esteem noun 1 RESPECT,
admiration, credit, estimation,
good opinion, honor, kudos,
regard, reverence, veneration
▶ verb 2 RESPECT, admire, love,
prize, regard highly, revere,
think highly of, treasure, value
3 CONSIDER, believe, deem,
estimate, judge, reckon,
regard, think, view

estimate verb 1 CALCULATE
ROUGHLY, assess, evaluate,
gauge, guess, judge, number,
reckon, value 2 FORM AN
OPINION, believe, conjecture,
consider, judge, rank, rate,
reckon, surmise ▶ noun
3 APPROXIMATE CALCULATION,
assessment, ballpark figure
(informal), guess, guesstimate
(informal), judgment, valuation
4 OPINION, appraisal,
assessment, belief, estimation,
judgment

estimation noun OPINION,
appraisal, appreciation,
assessment, belief,
consideration, considered
opinion, judgment, view

estuary noun INLET, creek, firth,
fjord, mouth

et cetera adverb 1 AND SO ON,
and so forth ▶ noun 2 AND THE
REST, and others, and the like,

et al.

etch verb CUT, carve, eat into, engrave, impress, imprint, inscribe, stamp

etching noun PRINT, carving, engraving, impression, imprint, inscription

eternal adjective 1 EVERLASTING, endless, immortal, infinite, never-ending, perpetual, timeless, unceasing, unending 2 PERMANENT, deathless, enduring, immutable, imperishable, indestructible, lasting, unchanging

eternity noun 1 INFINITY, ages, endlessness, immortality, perpetuity, timelessness 2 *Theology* THE AFTERLIFE, heaven, paradise, the hereafter, the next world

ethical adjective MORAL, conscientious, fair, good, honorable, just, principled, proper, right, upright, virtuous

ethics plural noun MORAL CODE, conscience, morality, moral philosophy, moral values, principles, rules of conduct, standards

ethnic adjective CULTURAL, folk, indigenous, national, native, racial, traditional

etiquette noun GOOD or PROPER BEHAVIOR, civility, courtesy, decorum, formalities, manners, politeness, propriety, protocol

euphoria noun ELATION, ecstasy, exaltation, exhilaration, intoxication, joy, jubilation, rapture

evacuate verb CLEAR, abandon, desert, forsake, leave, move out, pull out, quit, vacate, withdraw

evade verb 1 AVOID, dodge, duck, elude, escape, get away from, sidestep, steer clear of 2 AVOID ANSWERING, equivocate, fend off, fudge, hedge, parry

evaluate verb ASSESS, appraise, calculate, estimate, gauge, judge, rate, reckon, size up (*informal*), weigh

evaporate verb 1 DRY UP, dehydrate, desiccate, dry, vaporize 2 DISAPPEAR, dematerialize, dissolve, fade away, melt away, vanish

evasion noun 1 AVOIDANCE, dodging, escape 2 DECEPTION, equivocation, evasiveness, prevarication

evasive adjective DECEPTIVE, cagey (*informal*), equivocating, indirect, oblique, prevaricating, shifty, slippery

eve noun 1 NIGHT BEFORE, day before, vigil 2 BRINK, edge, point, threshold, verge

even adjective 1 LEVEL, flat, horizontal, parallel, smooth, steady, straight, true, uniform 2 REGULAR, constant, smooth, steady, unbroken, uniform, uninterrupted, unvarying, unwavering 3 EQUAL, comparable, fifty-fifty (*informal*), identical, level, like, matching, neck and neck, on a level playing field (*informal*), on a par, similar, tied 4 CALM, composed, cool, even-tempered, imperturbable, placid, unruffled, well-balanced 5 **get even (with)** PAY BACK, give tit for tat, reciprocate, repay, requite, retaliate

evening noun DUSK, gloaming (*Scot. or poetic*), twilight

event noun 1 INCIDENT, affair, business, circumstance, episode, experience, happening, occasion, occurrence 2 COMPETITION, bout, contest, game, tournament

even-tempered adjective CALM, composed, cool, imperturbable, level-headed, placid, tranquil, unexcitable, unruffled

eventful adjective EXCITING, active, busy, dramatic, full, lively, memorable, remarkable

eventual adjective FINAL, concluding, overall, ultimate

eventuality noun POSSIBILITY, case, chance, contingency, event, likelihood, probability

eventually adverb IN THE END, after all, at the end of the day, finally, one day, some time, ultimately, when all is said and done

ever adverb 1 AT ANY TIME, at all, at any period, at any point, by any chance, in any case, on any occasion 2 ALWAYS, at all times, constantly, continually, evermore, for ever, perpetually, twenty-four-seven (slang)

everlasting adjective ETERNAL, endless, immortal, indestructible, never-ending, perpetual, timeless, undying

evermore adverb FOR EVER, always, eternally, ever, to the end of time

every adjective EACH, all, each one

everybody pronoun EVERYONE, all and sundry, each one, each person, every person, one and all, the whole world

everyday adjective COMMON, customary, mundane, ordinary, routine, stock, usual, workaday

everyone pronoun EVERYBODY, all and sundry, each one, each person, every person, one and all, the whole world

everything pronoun ALL, each thing, the lot, the whole lot

everywhere adverb TO or IN EVERY PLACE, all around, all over, far and wide or near, high and low, in every nook and cranny, the world over, ubiquitously

evict verb EXPEL, boot out (informal), eject, kick out (informal), oust, remove, throw out, turn out

evidence noun 1 PROOF, confirmation, corroboration, demonstration, grounds, indication, sign, substantiation, testimony ▸verb 2 SHOW, demonstrate, display, exhibit, indicate, prove, reveal, signify, witness

evident adjective OBVIOUS, apparent, clear, manifest, noticeable, perceptible, plain, unmistakable, visible

evidently adverb 1 OBVIOUSLY, clearly, manifestly, plainly, undoubtedly, unmistakably, without question 2 APPARENTLY, ostensibly, outwardly, seemingly, to all appearances

evil noun 1 WICKEDNESS, badness, depravity, malignity, sin, vice, villainy, wrongdoing 2 HARM, affliction, disaster, hurt, ill, injury, mischief, misfortune, suffering, woe ▸adjective 3 WICKED, bad, depraved, immoral, malevolent, malicious, sinful, villainous 4 HARMFUL, calamitous, catastrophic, destructive, dire, disastrous, pernicious, ruinous **5** OFFENSIVE, foul, noxious, pestilential, unpleasant, vile

evoke verb RECALL, arouse, awaken, call, give rise to, induce, rekindle, stir up, summon up

evolution noun DEVELOPMENT, expansion, growth, increase, maturation, progress, unfolding, working out

evolve verb DEVELOP, expand, grow, increase, mature, progress, unfold, work out

exact adjective **1** ACCURATE, correct, definite, faultless, precise, right, specific, true, unerring ▶ verb **2** DEMAND, claim, command, compel, extort, extract, force

exacting adjective DEMANDING, difficult, hard, harsh, rigorous, severe, strict, stringent, taxing, tough

exactly adverb **1** PRECISELY, accurately, correctly, explicitly, faithfully, scrupulously, truthfully, unerringly **2** IN EVERY RESPECT, absolutely, indeed, precisely, quite, specifically, to the letter

exactness noun PRECISION, accuracy, correctness, exactitude, rigorousness, scrupulousness, strictness, veracity

exaggerate verb OVERSTATE, amplify, embellish, embroider, enlarge, overemphasize, overestimate

exaggeration noun OVERSTATEMENT, amplification, embellishment, enlargement, hyperbole, overemphasis,

overestimation

exalt verb **1** PRAISE, acclaim, extol, glorify, idolize, set on a pedestal, worship **2** RAISE, advance, elevate, ennoble, honor, promote, upgrade

exaltation noun **1** PRAISE, acclaim, glorification, idolization, reverence, tribute, worship **2** RISE, advancement, elevation, ennoblement, promotion, upgrading

exalted adjective HIGH-RANKING, dignified, eminent, grand, honored, lofty, prestigious

examination noun **1** INSPECTION, analysis, exploration, interrogation, investigation, research, scrutiny, study, test **2** QUESTIONING, inquiry, inquisition, probe, quiz, test

examine verb **1** INSPECT, analyze, explore, investigate, peruse, scrutinize, study, survey **2** QUESTION, cross-examine, grill (*informal*), inquire, interrogate, quiz, test

example noun **1** SPECIMEN, case, illustration, instance, sample **2** MODEL, archetype, ideal, paradigm, paragon, prototype, standard **3** WARNING, caution, lesson

exasperate verb IRRITATE, anger, annoy, enrage, incense, inflame, infuriate, madden, pique

exasperation noun IRRITATION, anger, annoyance, fury, pique, provocation, rage, wrath

excavate verb DIG OUT, burrow, delve, dig up, mine, quarry, tunnel, uncover, unearth

exceed verb **1** SURPASS, beat, better, cap (*informal*), eclipse, outdo, outstrip, overtake, pass, top **2** GO OVER THE LIMIT OF, go over the top, overstep

exceedingly adverb EXTREMELY, enormously, exceptionally, extraordinarily, hugely, superlatively, surpassingly, unusually, very

excel verb **1** BE SUPERIOR, beat, eclipse, outdo, outshine, surpass, transcend **2 excel in** or **at** BE GOOD AT, be proficient in, be skillful at, be talented at, shine at, show talent in

excellence noun HIGH QUALITY, distinction, eminence, goodness, greatness, merit, pre-eminence, superiority, supremacy

excellent adjective OUTSTANDING, brilliant, exquisite, fine, first-class, first-rate, good, great, superb, superlative, world-class

except preposition **1** Also **except for** APART FROM, barring, besides, but, excepting, excluding, omitting, other than, saving, with the exception of ▶ verb **2** EXCLUDE, leave out, omit, pass over

exception noun **1** SPECIAL CASE, anomaly, deviation, freak, inconsistency, irregularity, oddity, peculiarity **2** EXCLUSION, leaving out, omission, passing over

exceptional adjective **1** SPECIAL, abnormal, atypical, extraordinary, irregular, odd, peculiar, strange, unusual **2** REMARKABLE, excellent, extraordinary, marvelous, outstanding, phenomenal, prodigious, special, superior

excerpt noun EXTRACT, fragment, part, passage, piece, quotation, section, selection

excess noun **1** SURFEIT, glut, overload, superabundance, superfluity, surplus, too much **2** OVERINDULGENCE, debauchery, dissipation, dissoluteness, extravagance, intemperance, prodigality

excessive adjective IMMODERATE, disproportionate, exaggerated, extreme, inordinate, overmuch, superfluous, too much, undue, unfair, unreasonable

exchange verb **1** INTERCHANGE, barter, change, convert into, swap, switch, trade ▶ noun **2** INTERCHANGE, barter, quid pro quo, reciprocity, substitution, swap, switch, tit for tat, trade

excitable adjective NERVOUS, emotional, highly strung, hot-headed, mercurial, quick-tempered, temperamental, volatile, wired (slang)

excite verb AROUSE, animate, galvanize, inflame, inspire, provoke, rouse, stir up, thrill

excitement noun AGITATION, action, activity, animation, commotion, furor, passion, thrill

exciting adjective STIMULATING, dramatic, electrifying, exhilarating, rousing, sensational, stirring, thrilling

exclaim verb CRY OUT, call out, declare, proclaim, shout, utter, yell

exclamation noun CRY, call, interjection, outcry, shout, utterance, yell

exclude verb **1** KEEP OUT, ban, bar, boycott, disallow, forbid,

prohibit, refuse, shut out
2 LEAVE OUT, count out,
eliminate, ignore, omit, pass
over, reject, rule out, set aside

exclusion *noun* **1** BAN, bar,
boycott, disqualification,
embargo, prohibition, veto
2 ELIMINATION, omission, rejection

exclusive *adjective* **1** SOLE,
absolute, complete, entire, full,
total, undivided, whole
2 LIMITED, confined, peculiar,
restricted, unique **3** SELECT,
chic, cliquish, cool (*informal*),
fashionable, phat (*slang*),
restricted, snobbish, up-market

excommunicate *verb* EXPEL,
anathematize, ban, banish, cast
out, denounce, exclude,
repudiate

excruciating *adjective*
AGONIZING, harrowing,
insufferable, intense, piercing,
severe, unbearable, violent

exculpate *verb* ABSOLVE, acquit,
clear, discharge, excuse,
exonerate, pardon, vindicate

excursion *noun* TRIP, day trip,
expedition, jaunt, journey,
outing, pleasure trip, ramble,
tour

excusable *adjective* FORGIVABLE,
allowable, defensible,
justifiable, pardonable,
permissible, understandable,
warrantable

excuse *noun* **1** JUSTIFICATION,
apology, defense, explanation,
grounds, mitigation, plea,
reason, vindication ▸*verb*
2 JUSTIFY, apologize for, defend,
explain, mitigate, vindicate
3 FORGIVE, acquit, exculpate,
exonerate, make allowances
for, overlook, pardon, tolerate,

turn a blind eye to **4** FREE,
absolve, discharge, exempt, let
off, release, relieve, spare

execute *verb* **1** PUT TO DEATH,
behead, electrocute, guillotine,
hang, kill, shoot **2** CARRY OUT,
accomplish, administer,
discharge, effect, enact,
implement, perform, prosecute

execution *noun* **1** CARRYING OUT,
accomplishment,
administration, enactment,
enforcement, implementation,
operation, performance,
prosecution **2** KILLING, capital
punishment, hanging

executioner *noun* **1** HANGMAN,
headsman **2** KILLER, assassin,
exterminator, hit man (*slang*),
liquidator, murderer, slayer

executive *noun* **1** ADMINISTRATOR,
director, manager, official
2 ADMINISTRATION, directorate,
directors, government,
hierarchy, leadership,
management ▸*adjective*
3 ADMINISTRATIVE, controlling,
decision-making, directing,
governing, managerial

exemplary *adjective* **1** IDEAL,
admirable, commendable,
excellent, fine, good, model,
praiseworthy **2** WARNING,
cautionary

exemplify *verb* SHOW,
demonstrate, display, embody,
exhibit, illustrate, represent,
serve as an example of

exempt *adjective* **1** IMMUNE,
excepted, excused, free, not
liable, released, spared ▸*verb*
2 GRANT IMMUNITY, absolve,
discharge, excuse, free, let off,
release, relieve, spare

exemption *noun* IMMUNITY,

absolution, discharge, dispensation, exception, exoneration, freedom, release

exercise noun 1 EXERTION, activity, effort, labor, toil, training, work, work-out 2 TASK, drill, lesson, practice, problem 3 USE, application, discharge, fulfillment, implementation, practice, utilization ▶verb 4 PUT TO USE, apply, bring to bear, employ, exert, use, utilize 5 TRAIN, practice, work out

exert verb 1 USE, apply, bring to bear, employ, exercise, make use of, utilize, wield 2 **exert oneself** MAKE AN EFFORT, apply oneself, do one's best, endeavor, labor, strain, strive, struggle, toil, work

exertion noun EFFORT, elbow grease (facetious), endeavor, exercise, industry, strain, struggle, toil

exhaust verb 1 TIRE OUT, debilitate, drain, enervate, enfeeble, fatigue, sap, weaken, wear out 2 USE UP, consume, deplete, dissipate, expend, run through, spend, squander, waste

exhausted adjective 1 WORN OUT, debilitated, done in (informal), drained, fatigued, spent, tired out 2 USED UP, consumed, depleted, dissipated, expended, finished, spent, squandered, wasted

exhausting adjective TIRING, backbreaking, debilitating, grueling, laborious, punishing, sapping, strenuous, taxing

exhaustion noun 1 TIREDNESS, debilitation, fatigue, weariness 2 DEPLETION, consumption, emptying, using up

exhaustive adjective THOROUGH, all-embracing, complete, comprehensive, extensive, full-scale, in-depth, intensive

exhibit verb DISPLAY, demonstrate, express, indicate, manifest, parade, put on view, reveal, show

exhibition noun DISPLAY, demonstration, exposition, performance, presentation, representation, show, spectacle

exhilarating adjective EXCITING, breathtaking, enlivening, invigorating, stimulating, thrilling

exhort verb URGE, advise, beseech, call upon, entreat, persuade, press, spur

exhume verb DIG UP, disentomb, disinter, unearth

exigency noun NEED, constraint, demand, necessity, requirement

exile noun 1 BANISHMENT, deportation, expatriation, expulsion 2 EXPATRIATE, deportee, émigré, outcast, refugee ▶verb 3 BANISH, deport, drive out, eject, expatriate, expel

exist verb 1 BE, be present, endure, live, occur, survive 2 SURVIVE, eke out a living, get along or by, keep one's head above water, stay alive, subsist

existence noun BEING, actuality, life, subsistence

existent adjective IN EXISTENCE, alive, existing, extant, living, present, standing, surviving

exit noun 1 WAY OUT, door, gate, outlet 2 DEPARTURE, exodus, farewell, going, good-bye, leave-taking, retreat, withdrawal ▸ *verb* 3 DEPART, go away, go offstage (*Theatre*), go out, leave, make tracks, retire, retreat, take one's leave, withdraw

exodus *noun* DEPARTURE, evacuation, exit, flight, going out, leaving, migration, retreat, withdrawal

exonerate *verb* CLEAR, absolve, acquit, discharge, exculpate, excuse, justify, pardon, vindicate

exorbitant *adjective* EXCESSIVE, extortionate, extravagant, immoderate, inordinate, outrageous, preposterous, unreasonable

exorcise *verb* DRIVE OUT, cast out, deliver (from), expel, purify

exotic *adjective* 1 UNUSUAL, colorful, fascinating, glamorous, mysterious, strange, striking, unfamiliar 2 FOREIGN, alien, external, imported, naturalized

expand *verb* 1 INCREASE, amplify, broaden, develop, enlarge, extend, grow, magnify, swell, widen 2 SPREAD (OUT), diffuse, stretch (out), unfold, unfurl, unravel, unroll 3 **expand on** GO INTO DETAIL ABOUT, amplify, develop, elaborate on, embellish, enlarge on, expatiate on, expound on, flesh out

expanse *noun* AREA, breadth, extent, range, space, stretch, sweep, tract

expansion *noun* INCREASE, amplification, development, enlargement, growth, magnification, opening out, spread

expansive *adjective* 1 WIDE, broad, extensive, far-reaching, voluminous, wide-ranging, widespread 2 TALKATIVE, affable, communicative, effusive, friendly, loquacious, open, outgoing, sociable, unreserved

expatriate *adjective* 1 EXILED, banished, emigrant, émigré ▸ *noun* 2 EXILE, emigrant, émigré, refugee

expect *verb* 1 THINK, assume, believe, imagine, presume, reckon, suppose, surmise, trust 2 LOOK FORWARD TO, anticipate, await, contemplate, envisage, hope for, predict, watch for 3 REQUIRE, call for, demand, insist on, want

expectant *adjective* 1 EXPECTING, anticipating, apprehensive, eager, hopeful, in suspense, ready, watchful 2 PREGNANT, expecting (*informal*), gravid

expectation *noun* 1 PROBABILITY, assumption, belief, conjecture, forecast, likelihood, presumption, supposition 2 ANTICIPATION, apprehension, expectancy, hope, promise, suspense

expediency *noun* SUITABILITY, advisability, benefit, convenience, pragmatism, profitability, prudence, usefulness, utility

expedient *noun* 1 MEANS, contrivance, device, makeshift, measure, method, resort, scheme, stopgap ▸ *adjective* 2 ADVANTAGEOUS, appropriate, beneficial, convenient, effective, helpful, opportune, practical, suitable, useful, win-win (*informal*)

expedition noun JOURNEY, excursion, mission, quest, safari, tour, trek, voyage

expel verb 1 DRIVE OUT, belch, cast out, discharge, eject, remove, spew 2 DISMISS, ban, banish, chuck out (slang), drum out, evict, exclude, exile, throw out

expend verb SPEND, consume, dissipate, exhaust, go through, pay out, use (up)

expendable adjective DISPENSABLE, inessential, nonessential, replaceable, unimportant, unnecessary

expenditure noun SPENDING, consumption, cost, expense, outgoings, outlay, output, payment

expense noun COST, charge, expenditure, loss, outlay, payment, spending

expensive adjective DEAR, costly, exorbitant, extravagant, high-priced, lavish, overpriced, steep (informal), stiff

experience noun 1 KNOWLEDGE, contact, exposure, familiarity, involvement, participation, practice, training 2 EVENT, adventure, affair, encounter, episode, happening, incident, occurrence ▶verb 3 UNDERGO, encounter, endure, face, feel, go through, live through, sample, taste

experienced adjective KNOWLEDGEABLE, accomplished, expert, practiced, seasoned, tested, tried, veteran, well-versed

experiment noun 1 TEST, examination, experimentation, investigation, procedure, proof, research, trial, trial run ▶verb 2 TEST, examine, investigate, put to the test, research, sample, try, verify

experimental adjective TEST, exploratory, pilot, preliminary, probationary, provisional, speculative, tentative, trial, trial-and-error

expert noun 1 MASTER, authority, connoisseur, past master, professional, specialist, virtuoso ▶adjective 2 SKILLFUL, adept, adroit, experienced, masterly, practiced, professional, proficient, qualified, virtuoso

expertise noun SKILL, adroitness, command, facility, judgment, know-how (informal), knowledge, mastery, proficiency

expire verb 1 FINISH, cease, close, come to an end, conclude, end, lapse, run out, stop, terminate 2 BREATHE OUT, emit, exhale, expel 3 DIE, depart, kick the bucket (informal), pass away or on, perish

explain verb 1 MAKE CLEAR or PLAIN, clarify, clear up, define, describe, elucidate, expound, resolve, teach 2 ACCOUNT FOR, excuse, give a reason for, justify

explanation noun 1 REASON, account, answer, excuse, justification, motive, vindication 2 DESCRIPTION, clarification, definition, elucidation, illustration, interpretation

explanatory adjective DESCRIPTIVE, illustrative, interpretive

explicit adjective CLEAR,

categorical, definite, frank, precise, specific, straightforward, unambiguous

explode *verb* 1 BLOW UP, burst, detonate, discharge, erupt, go off, set off, shatter 2 DISPROVE, debunk, discredit, give the lie to, invalidate, refute, repudiate

exploit *verb* 1 TAKE ADVANTAGE OF, abuse, manipulate, milk, misuse, play on *or* upon 2 MAKE THE BEST USE OF, capitalize on, cash in on (*informal*), profit by *or* from, use, utilize ▶ *noun* 3 FEAT, accomplishment, achievement, adventure, attainment, deed, escapade, stunt

exploitation *noun* MISUSE, abuse, manipulation

exploration *noun* 1 INVESTIGATION, analysis, examination, inquiry, inspection, research, scrutiny, search 2 EXPEDITION, reconnaissance, survey, tour, travel, trip

exploratory *adjective* INVESTIGATIVE, experimental, fact-finding, probing, searching, trial

explore *verb* 1 INVESTIGATE, examine, inquire into, inspect, look into, probe, research, search 2 TRAVEL, reconnoiter, scout, survey, tour

explosion *noun* 1 BANG, blast, burst, clap, crack, detonation, discharge, report 2 OUTBURST, eruption, fit, outbreak

explosive *adjective* 1 UNSTABLE, volatile 2 VIOLENT, fiery, stormy, touchy, vehement

exponent *noun* 1 ADVOCATE, backer, champion, defender,

promoter, proponent, supporter, upholder 2 PERFORMER, player

expose *verb* 1 UNCOVER, display, exhibit, present, reveal, show, unveil 2 MAKE VULNERABLE, endanger, imperil, jeopardize, lay open, leave open, subject

exposed *adjective* 1 UNCONCEALED, bare, on display, on show, on view, revealed, uncovered 2 UNSHELTERED, open, unprotected 3 VULNERABLE, in peril, laid bare, susceptible, wide open

exposure *noun* PUBLICITY, display, exhibition, presentation, revelation, showing, uncovering, unveiling

expound *verb* EXPLAIN, describe, elucidate, interpret, set forth, spell out, unfold

express *verb* 1 STATE, articulate, communicate, declare, phrase, put into words, say, utter, voice, word 2 SHOW, convey, exhibit, indicate, intimate, make known, represent, reveal, signify, stand for, symbolize ▶ *adjective* 3 EXPLICIT, categorical, clear, definite, distinct, plain, unambiguous 4 SPECIFIC, clear-cut, especial, particular, singular, special 5 FAST, direct, high-speed, nonstop, rapid, speedy, swift

expression *noun* 1 STATEMENT, announcement, communication, declaration, utterance 2 INDICATION, demonstration, exhibition, manifestation, representation, show, sign, symbol, token 3 LOOK, air, appearance, aspect, countenance, face

4 PHRASE, idiom, locution, remark, term, turn of phrase, word

expressive *adjective* VIVID, eloquent, moving, poignant, striking, telling

expressly *adverb* 1 DEFINITELY, categorically, clearly, distinctly, explicitly, in no uncertain terms, plainly, unambiguously 2 SPECIFICALLY, especially, particularly, specially

expulsion *noun* EJECTION, banishment, dismissal, eviction, exclusion, removal

exquisite *adjective* 1 BEAUTIFUL, attractive, charming, comely, lovely, pleasing, striking 2 FINE, beautiful, dainty, delicate, elegant, lovely, precious 3 INTENSE, acute, keen, sharp

extempore *adverb, adjective* IMPROMPTU, ad lib, freely, improvised, offhand, off the cuff (*informal*), spontaneously, unpremeditated, unprepared

extend *verb* 1 MAKE LONGER, drag out, draw out, lengthen, prolong, spin out, spread out, stretch 2 LAST, carry on, continue, go on 3 WIDEN, add to, augment, broaden, enhance, enlarge, expand, increase, supplement 4 OFFER, confer, impart, present, proffer

extension *noun* 1 ANNEX, addition, appendage, appendix, supplement 2 LENGTHENING, broadening, development, enlargement, expansion, increase, spread, widening

extensive *adjective* WIDE, broad, far-flung, far-reaching, large-scale, pervasive, spacious, vast, voluminous, widespread

extent *noun* SIZE, amount, area, breadth, expanse, length, stretch, volume, width

extenuating *adjective* MITIGATING, justifying, moderating, qualifying

exterior *noun* 1 OUTSIDE, coating, covering, façade, face, shell, skin, surface ▶ *adjective* 2 OUTSIDE, external, outer, outermost, outward, surface

exterminate *verb* DESTROY, abolish, annihilate, eliminate, eradicate

external *adjective* 1 OUTER, exterior, outermost, outside, outward, surface 2 OUTSIDE, alien, extrinsic, foreign

extinct *adjective* DEAD, defunct, gone, lost, vanished

extinction *noun* DYING OUT, abolition, annihilation, destruction, eradication, extermination, obliteration, oblivion

extinguish *verb* 1 PUT OUT, blow out, douse, quench, smother, snuff out, stifle 2 DESTROY, annihilate, eliminate, end, eradicate, exterminate, remove, wipe out

extol *verb* PRAISE, acclaim, commend, eulogize, exalt, glorify, sing the praises of

extort *verb* FORCE, blackmail, bully, coerce, extract, squeeze

extortionate *adjective* EXORBITANT, excessive, extravagant, inflated, outrageous, preposterous, sky-high, unreasonable

extra *adjective* 1 ADDITIONAL, added, ancillary, auxiliary, further, more, supplementary

2 SURPLUS, excess, leftover, redundant, spare, superfluous, unused ▶*noun* **3** ADDITION, accessory, attachment, bonus, extension, supplement ▶*adverb* **4** EXCEPTIONALLY, especially, extraordinarily, extremely, particularly, remarkably, uncommonly, unusually

extract *verb* **1** PULL OUT, draw, pluck out, pull, remove, take out, uproot, withdraw **2** DERIVE, draw, elicit, glean, obtain ▶*noun* **3** PASSAGE, citation, clipping, cutting, excerpt, quotation, selection **4** ESSENCE, concentrate, distillation, juice

extraneous *adjective* IRRELEVANT, beside the point, immaterial, inappropriate, off the subject, unconnected, unrelated

extraordinary *adjective* UNUSUAL, amazing, exceptional, fantastic, outstanding, phenomenal, remarkable, strange, uncommon

extravagance *noun* **1** WASTE, lavishness, overspending, prodigality, profligacy, squandering, wastefulness **2** EXCESS, exaggeration, outrageousness, preposterousness, wildness

extravagant *adjective* **1** WASTEFUL, lavish, prodigal, profligate, spendthrift **2** EXCESSIVE, outrageous, over the top (*slang*), preposterous, reckless, unreasonable

extreme *adjective* **1** MAXIMUM, acute, great, highest, intense, severe, supreme, ultimate, utmost **2** SEVERE, drastic, harsh, radical, rigid, strict, uncompromising **3** EXCESSIVE, fanatical, immoderate, radical

4 FARTHEST, far-off, most distant, outermost, remotest ▶*noun* **5** LIMIT, boundary, edge, end, extremity, pole

extremely *adverb* VERY, awfully (*informal*), exceedingly, exceptionally, extraordinarily, severely, terribly, uncommonly, unusually

extremist *noun* FANATIC, die-hard, radical, zealot

extremity *noun* **1** LIMIT, border, boundary, edge, extreme, frontier, pinnacle, tip **2** CRISIS, adversity, dire straits, disaster, emergency, exigency, trouble **3 extremities** HANDS AND FEET, fingers and toes, limbs

extricate *verb* FREE, disengage, disentangle, get out, release, remove, rescue, wriggle out of

extrovert *adjective* OUTGOING, exuberant, gregarious, sociable

exuberance *noun* **1** HIGH SPIRITS, cheerfulness, ebullience, enthusiasm, liveliness, spirit, vitality, vivacity, zest **2** LUXURIANCE, abundance, copiousness, lavishness, profusion

exuberant *adjective* **1** HIGH-SPIRITED, animated, cheerful, ebullient, energetic, enthusiastic, lively, spirited, vivacious **2** LUXURIANT, abundant, copious, lavish, plentiful, profuse

exult *verb* BE JOYFUL, be overjoyed, celebrate, jump for joy, rejoice

eye *noun* **1** EYEBALL, optic (*informal*) **2** APPRECIATION, discernment, discrimination, judgment, perception, recognition, taste ▶*verb* **3** LOOK

AT, check out (*informal*), contemplate, inspect, study, survey, view, watch

eyesight *noun* VISION, perception, sight

eyesore *noun* MESS, blemish, blot, disfigurement, horror, monstrosity, sight (*informal*)

eyewitness *noun* OBSERVER, bystander, onlooker, passer-by, spectator, viewer, witness

F f

fable *noun* 1 STORY, allegory, legend, myth, parable, tale 2 FICTION, fabrication, fantasy, fish story (*informal*), invention, tall tale (*informal*), urban legend, yarn (*informal*)

fabric *noun* 1 CLOTH, material, stuff, textile, web 2 FRAMEWORK, constitution, construction, foundations, make-up, organization, structure

fabricate *verb* 1 MAKE UP, concoct, devise, fake, falsify, feign, forge, invent, trump up 2 BUILD, assemble, construct, erect, form, make, manufacture, shape

fabrication *noun* 1 FORGERY, concoction, fake, falsehood, fiction, invention, lie, myth 2 CONSTRUCTION, assembly, building, erection, manufacture, production

fabulous *adjective* 1 *Informal* WONDERFUL, brilliant, fantastic (*informal*), marvelous, out-of-this-world (*informal*), sensational (*informal*),

spectacular, superb 2 ASTOUNDING, amazing, breathtaking, inconceivable, incredible, phenomenal, unbelievable 3 LEGENDARY, apocryphal, fantastic, fictitious, imaginary, invented, made-up, mythical, unreal

façade *noun* APPEARANCE, exterior, face, front, guise, mask, pretense, semblance, show

face *noun* 1 COUNTENANCE, features, mug (*slang*), visage 2 EXPRESSION, appearance, aspect, look 3 SCOWL, frown, grimace, pout, smirk 4 FAÇADE, appearance, display, exterior, front, mask, show 5 SIDE, exterior, front, outside, surface 6 SELF-RESPECT, authority, dignity, honor, image, prestige, reputation, standing, status ▸*verb* 7 MEET, brave, come up against, confront, deal with, encounter, experience, oppose, tackle 8 LOOK ONTO, be opposite, front onto, overlook 9 COAT, clad, cover, dress, finish

faceless *adjective* IMPERSONAL, anonymous, remote

facet *noun* ASPECT, angle, face, part, phase, plane, side, slant, surface

facetious *adjective* FUNNY, amusing, comical, droll, flippant, frivolous, humorous, jocular, playful, tongue in cheek

face up to *verb* ACCEPT, acknowledge, come to terms with, confront, cope with, deal with, meet head-on, tackle

facile *adjective* SUPERFICIAL, cursory, glib, hasty, shallow, slick

facilitate verb PROMOTE, expedite, forward, further, help, make easy, pave the way for, speed up

facility noun 1 SKILL, ability, adroitness, dexterity, ease, efficiency, effortlessness, fluency, proficiency 2 (often plural) EQUIPMENT, advantage, aid, amenity, appliance, convenience, means, opportunity, resource

facsimile noun COPY, carbon copy, duplicate, fax, photocopy, print, replica, reproduction, transcript

fact noun 1 EVENT, act, deed, *fait accompli*, happening, incident, occurrence, performance 2 TRUTH, certainty, reality

faction noun 1 GROUP, bloc, cabal, clique, contingent, coterie, gang, party, set, splinter group 2 DISSENSION, conflict, disagreement, discord, disunity, division, infighting, rebellion

factor noun ELEMENT, aspect, cause, component, consideration, influence, item, part

factory noun WORKS, mill, plant

factual adjective TRUE, authentic, correct, exact, genuine, precise, real, true-to-life

faculties plural noun POWERS, capabilities, intelligence, reason, senses, wits

faculty noun 1 ABILITY, aptitude, capacity, facility, power, propensity, skill 2 DEPARTMENT, school

fad noun CRAZE, fashion, mania, rage, trend, vogue, whim

fade verb 1 PALE, bleach, discolor, lose color, wash out 2 DWINDLE, decline, die away, disappear, dissolve, melt away, vanish, wane

faded adjective DISCOLORED, bleached, dull, indistinct, pale, washed out

fading adjective DECLINING, decreasing, disappearing, dying, on the decline, vanishing

fail verb 1 BE UNSUCCESSFUL, bite the dust, break down, come to grief, come unstuck, fall, fizzle out (*informal*), flop (*informal*), founder, miscarry, misfire 2 DISAPPOINT, abandon, desert, forget, forsake, let down, neglect, omit 3 GIVE OUT, conk out (*informal*), cut out, die, peter out, stop working 4 GO BANKRUPT, become insolvent, close down, fold (*informal*), go broke (*informal*), go bust (*informal*), go into receivership, go out of business, go to the wall, go under ▶ noun 5 **without fail** REGULARLY, conscientiously, constantly, dependably, like clockwork, punctually, religiously, twenty-four-seven (*slang*), without exception

failing noun 1 WEAKNESS, blemish, defect, deficiency, drawback, fault, flaw, imperfection, shortcoming ▶ preposition 2 IN THE ABSENCE OF, in default of, lacking

failure noun 1 DEFEAT, breakdown, collapse, downfall, fiasco, lack of success, miscarriage, overthrow 2 LOSER, dead duck (*slang*), disappointment, dud (*informal*), flop (*informal*), nonstarter, washout (*informal*)

3 BANKRUPTCY, crash, downfall, insolvency, liquidation, ruin

faint *adjective* **1** DIM, distant, faded, indistinct, low, muted, soft, subdued, vague **2** SLIGHT, feeble, remote, unenthusiastic, weak **3** DIZZY, exhausted, giddy, light-headed, muzzy, weak, woozy (*informal*) ▶ *verb* **4** PASS OUT, black out, collapse, keel over (*informal*), lose consciousness, swoon (*literary*) ▶ *noun* **5** BLACKOUT, collapse, swoon (*literary*), unconsciousness

faintly *adverb* **1** SOFTLY, feebly, in a whisper, indistinctly, weakly **2** SLIGHTLY, a little, dimly, somewhat

fair[1] *adjective* **1** UNBIASED, above board, equitable, even-handed, honest, impartial, just, lawful, legitimate, proper, unprejudiced **2** LIGHT, blond, blonde, fair-haired, flaxen-haired, towheaded **3** RESPECTABLE, adequate, average, decent, moderate, O.K. *or* okay (*informal*), passable, reasonable, satisfactory, tolerable **4** BEAUTIFUL, bonny, comely, handsome, lovely, pretty **5** FINE, bright, clear, cloudless, dry, sunny, unclouded

fair[2] *noun* CARNIVAL, bazaar, festival, fête, gala, show

fairly *adverb* **1** MODERATELY, adequately, pretty well, quite, rather, reasonably, somewhat, tolerably **2** DESERVEDLY, equitably, honestly, impartially, justly, objectively, properly, without fear or favor **3** POSITIVELY, absolutely, really

fairness *noun* IMPARTIALITY, decency, disinterestedness, equitableness, equity, justice, legitimacy, rightfulness

fairy *noun* SPRITE, brownie, elf, imp, leprechaun, peri, pixie, Robin Goodfellow

fairy tale *or* **fairy story** *noun* **1** FOLK TALE, romance **2** LIE, cock-and-bull story (*informal*), fabrication, fiction, invention, tall tale (*informal*), untruth

faith *noun* **1** CONFIDENCE, assurance, conviction, credence, credit, dependence, reliance, trust **2** RELIGION, belief, church, communion, creed, denomination, dogma, persuasion **3** ALLEGIANCE, constancy, faithfulness, fidelity, loyalty

faithful *adjective* **1** LOYAL, constant, dependable, devoted, reliable, staunch, steadfast, true, trusty **2** ACCURATE, close, exact, precise, strict, true

faithless *adjective* DISLOYAL, false, fickle, inconstant, traitorous, treacherous, unfaithful, unreliable

fake *verb* **1** FORGE, copy, counterfeit, fabricate, feign, pretend, put on, sham, simulate ▶ *noun* **2** IMPOSTOR, charlatan, copy, forgery, fraud, hoax, imitation, reproduction, sham ▶ *adjective* **3** ARTIFICIAL, counterfeit, false, forged, imitation, mock, phoney *or* phony (*informal*), sham

fall *verb* **1** DESCEND, cascade, collapse, dive, drop, plummet, plunge, sink, subside, tumble **2** DECREASE, decline, diminish, drop, dwindle, go down, lessen, slump, subside **3** BE OVERTHROWN, capitulate, pass into enemy hands, succumb, surrender **4** DIE, be killed, meet one's end, perish **5** OCCUR, befall, chance, come about, come to pass, happen, take place **6** SLOPE, fall away, incline **7** LAPSE, err, go astray, offend, sin, transgress, trespass ▶*noun* **8** DESCENT, dive, drop, nose dive, plummet, plunge, slip, tumble **9** DECREASE, cut, decline, dip, drop, lessening, lowering, reduction, slump **10** COLLAPSE, capitulation, defeat, destruction, downfall, overthrow, ruin **11** LAPSE, sin, transgression

fallacy *noun* ERROR, delusion, falsehood, flaw, misapprehension, misconception, mistake, untruth

fallible *adjective* IMPERFECT, erring, frail, ignorant, uncertain, weak

fall out *verb* ARGUE, clash, come to blows, differ, disagree, fight, quarrel, squabble

fallow *adjective* UNCULTIVATED, dormant, idle, inactive, resting, unplanted, unused

false *adjective* **1** INCORRECT, erroneous, faulty, inaccurate, inexact, invalid, mistaken, wrong **2** UNTRUE, lying, unreliable, unsound, untruthful **3** ARTIFICIAL, bogus, counterfeit, fake, forged, imitation, sham, simulated **4** DECEPTIVE, deceitful, fallacious, fraudulent, hypocritical, misleading, trumped up

falsehood *noun* **1** UNTRUTHFULNESS, deceit, deception, dishonesty,

dissimulation, mendacity **2** LIE, fabrication, fib, fiction, story, untruth

falsify *verb* FORGE, alter, counterfeit, distort, doctor, fake, misrepresent, tamper with

falter *verb* HESITATE, stammer, stumble, stutter, totter, vacillate, waver

faltering *adjective* HESITANT, broken, irresolute, stammering, tentative, timid, uncertain, weak

fame *noun* PROMINENCE, celebrity, glory, honor, kudos, renown, reputation, repute, stardom

familiar *adjective* **1** WELL-KNOWN, accustomed, common, customary, frequent, ordinary, recognizable, routine **2** FRIENDLY, amicable, close, easy, intimate, relaxed **3** DISRESPECTFUL, bold, forward, impudent, intrusive, presumptuous

familiarity *noun* **1** ACQUAINTANCE, awareness, experience, grasp, understanding **2** FRIENDLINESS, ease, informality, intimacy, openness, sociability **3** DISRESPECT, boldness, forwardness, presumption

familiarize *verb* ACCUSTOM, habituate, instruct, inure, school, season, train

family *noun* **1** RELATIONS, folk (*informal*), household, kin, kith and kin, one's nearest and dearest, one's own flesh and blood, relatives **2** CLAN, dynasty, house, race, tribe **3** GROUP, class, genre, network, subdivision, system

famine *noun* HUNGER, dearth, scarcity, starvation

famished *adjective* STARVING,

ravenous, voracious

famous *adjective* WELL-KNOWN, acclaimed, celebrated, distinguished, eminent, illustrious, legendary, noted, prominent, renowned

fan[1] *noun* 1 BLOWER, air conditioner, ventilator ▸ *verb* 2 BLOW, air-condition, cool, refresh, ventilate

fan[2] *noun* SUPPORTER, admirer, aficionado, buff (*informal*), devotee, enthusiast, follower, lover

fanatic *noun* EXTREMIST, activist, bigot, militant, zealot

fanatical *adjective* PASSIONATE, bigoted, extreme, fervent, frenzied, immoderate, obsessive, overenthusiastic, wild, zealous

fanciful *adjective* UNREAL, imaginary, mythical, romantic, visionary, whimsical, wild

fancy *adjective* 1 ELABORATE, baroque, decorative, embellished, extravagant, intricate, ornamental, ornate ▸ *noun* 2 WHIM, caprice, desire, humor, idea, impulse, inclination, notion, thought, urge 3 DELUSION, chimera, daydream, dream, fantasy, vision ▸ *verb* 4 SUPPOSE, believe, conjecture, imagine, reckon, think, think likely 5 WISH FOR, crave, desire, hanker after, hope for, long for, thirst for, yearn for

fantasize *verb* DAYDREAM, dream, envision, imagine

fantastic *adjective* 1 *Informal* EXCELLENT, awesome (*slang*), first-rate, marvelous, sensational (*informal*), superb,

wonderful 2 STRANGE, fanciful, grotesque, outlandish 3 UNREALISTIC, extravagant, far-fetched, ludicrous, ridiculous, wild 4 IMPLAUSIBLE, absurd, cock-and-bull (*informal*), incredible, preposterous, unlikely

fantasy *noun* 1 IMAGINATION, creativity, fancy, invention, originality 2 DAYDREAM, dream, flight of fancy, illusion, mirage, pipe dream, reverie, vision

far *adverb* 1 A LONG WAY, afar, a good way, a great distance, deep, miles 2 MUCH, considerably, decidedly, extremely, greatly, incomparably, very much ▸ *adjective* 3 REMOTE, distant, faraway, far-flung, far-off, outlying, out-of-the-way

farce *noun* 1 COMEDY, buffoonery, burlesque, satire, slapstick 2 MOCKERY, joke, nonsense, parody, sham, travesty

farcical *adjective* LUDICROUS, absurd, comic, derisory, laughable, nonsensical, preposterous, ridiculous, risible

fare *noun* 1 CHARGE, price, ticket money 2 FOOD, provisions, rations, sustenance, victuals ▸ *verb* 3 GET ON, do, get along, make out, manage, prosper

farewell *noun* GOOD-BYE, adieu, departure, leave-taking, parting, sendoff (*informal*), valediction

far-fetched *adjective* UNCONVINCING, cock-and-bull (*informal*), fantastic, implausible, incredible, preposterous, unbelievable, unlikely, unrealistic

farm noun 1 SMALLHOLDING, farmstead, grange, homestead, plantation, ranch ▶verb 2 CULTIVATE, plant, work

fascinate verb INTRIGUE, absorb, beguile, captivate, engross, enthrall, entrance, hold spellbound, rivet, transfix

fascinating adjective GRIPPING, alluring, captivating, compelling, engaging, engrossing, enticing, intriguing, irresistible, riveting

fascination noun ATTRACTION, allure, charm, enchantment, lure, magic, magnetism, pull

fashion noun 1 STYLE, craze, custom, fad, look, mode, rage, trend, vogue 2 METHOD, manner, mode, style, way ▶verb 3 MAKE, construct, create, forge, form, manufacture, mold, shape

fashionable adjective POPULAR, à la mode, chic, cool (informal), in (informal), in vogue, modern, phat (slang), stylish, trendy (informal), up-to-date, with it (informal)

fast[1] adjective 1 QUICK, brisk, fleet, flying, hasty, rapid, speedy, swift 2 FIXED, close, fastened, firm, immovable, secure, sound, steadfast, tight 3 DISSIPATED, dissolute, extravagant, loose, profligate, reckless, self-indulgent, wanton, wild ▶adverb 4 QUICKLY, hastily, hurriedly, in haste, like lightning, rapidly, speedily, swiftly 5 SOUNDLY, deeply, firmly, fixedly, securely, tightly

fast[2] verb 1 GO HUNGRY, abstain,

deny oneself, go without food ▶noun 2 FASTING, abstinence

fasten verb FIX, affix, attach, bind, connect, join, link, secure, tie

fat adjective 1 OVERWEIGHT, corpulent, heavy, obese, plump, portly, rotund, stout, tubby 2 FATTY, adipose, greasy, oily, oleaginous ▶noun 3 FATNESS, blubber, bulk, corpulence, flab, flesh, lard (slang), obesity, paunch, spare tire (informal)

fatal adjective 1 LETHAL, deadly, final, incurable, killing, malignant, mortal, terminal 2 RUINOUS, baleful, baneful, calamitous, catastrophic, disastrous

fatality noun DEATH, casualty, loss, mortality

fate noun 1 DESTINY, chance, divine will, fortune, kismet, nemesis, predestination, providence 2 FORTUNE, cup, horoscope, lot, portion, stars

fated adjective DESTINED, doomed, foreordained, inescapable, inevitable, predestined, preordained, sure, written

fateful adjective 1 CRUCIAL, critical, decisive, important, portentous, significant 2 DISASTROUS, deadly, destructive, fatal, lethal, ominous, ruinous

father noun 1 PARENT, dad (informal), daddy (informal), old man (informal), pa (informal), papa (old-fashioned informal), pater (old-fashioned informal, chiefly Brit.), pop (informal), sire 2 FOREFATHER, ancestor, forebear,

predecessor, progenitor
3 FOUNDER, architect, author, creator, inventor, maker, originator, prime mover
4 PRIEST, padre (*informal*), pastor ▶*verb* **5** SIRE, beget, get, procreate

fatherland *noun* HOMELAND, motherland, native land

fatherly *adjective* PATERNAL, affectionate, benevolent, benign, kindly, patriarchal, protective, supportive

fathom *verb* UNDERSTAND, comprehend, get to the bottom of, grasp, interpret

fatigue *noun* **1** TIREDNESS, heaviness, languor, lethargy, listlessness ▶*verb* **2** TIRE, drain, exhaust, take it out of (*informal*), weaken, wear out, weary

fatten *verb* **1** GROW FAT, expand, gain weight, put on weight, spread, swell, thicken **2** (often with *up*) FEED UP, build up, feed, nourish, overfeed, stuff

fatty *adjective* GREASY, adipose, fat, oily, oleaginous, rich

fatuous *adjective* FOOLISH, brainless, idiotic, inane, ludicrous, mindless, moronic, silly, stupid, witless

fault *noun* **1** FLAW, blemish, defect, deficiency, failing, imperfection, shortcoming, weakness, weak point
2 MISTAKE, blunder, error, indiscretion, lapse, oversight, slip **3** RESPONSIBILITY, accountability, culpability, liability **4 at fault** GUILTY, answerable, blamable, culpable, in the wrong, responsible, to blame **5 find**

fault with CRITICIZE, carp at, complain, pick holes in, pull to pieces, quibble, take to task
6 to a fault EXCESSIVELY, immoderately, in the extreme, overmuch, unduly ▶*verb*
7 CRITICIZE, blame, censure, find fault with, hold (someone) responsible, impugn

faultless *adjective* FLAWLESS, correct, exemplary, foolproof, impeccable, model, perfect, unblemished

faulty *adjective* DEFECTIVE, broken, damaged, flawed, impaired, imperfect, incorrect, malfunctioning, out of order, unsound

favor *noun* **1** APPROVAL, approbation, backing, good opinion, goodwill, patronage, support **2** GOOD TURN, benefit, boon, courtesy, indulgence, kindness, service ▶*verb* **3** SIDE WITH, indulge, reward, smile upon **4** ADVOCATE, approve, champion, commend, encourage, incline towards, prefer, support

favorable *adjective*
1 ADVANTAGEOUS, auspicious, beneficial, encouraging, helpful, opportune, promising, propitious, suitable, win-win (*informal*) **2** POSITIVE, affirmative, agreeable, approving, encouraging, enthusiastic, reassuring, sympathetic

favorably *adverb*
1 ADVANTAGEOUSLY, auspiciously, conveniently, fortunately, opportunely, profitably, to one's advantage, well
2 POSITIVELY, approvingly, enthusiastically, helpfully, with approval

favorite adjective **1** PREFERRED, best-loved, choice, dearest, esteemed, favored ▶ noun **2** DARLING, beloved, blue-eyed boy (informal), idol, pet, teacher's pet, the apple of one's eye

fawn¹ verb (often with on or upon) CURRY FAVOR, brown-nose (slang), crawl, creep, cringe, dance attendance, flatter, grovel, ingratiate oneself, kiss ass (slang), kowtow, pander to

fawn² adjective BEIGE, buff, grayish-brown, neutral

fawning adjective OBSEQUIOUS, crawling, cringing, deferential, flattering, grovelling, servile, sycophantic

fear noun **1** ALARM, apprehensiveness, dread, fright, horror, panic, terror, trepidation **2** BUGBEAR, bête noire, bogey, horror, nightmare, specter ▶ verb **3** BE AFRAID, dread, shake in one's shoes, shudder at, take fright, tremble at **4 fear for** WORRY ABOUT, be anxious about, feel concern for

fearful adjective **1** SCARED, afraid, alarmed, frightened, jumpy, nervous, timid, timorous, uneasy, wired (slang) **2** FRIGHTFUL, awful, dire, dreadful, gruesome, hair-raising, horrendous, horrific, terrible

fearfully adverb **1** NERVOUSLY, apprehensively, diffidently, timidly, timorously, uneasily **2** VERY, awfully, exceedingly, excessively, frightfully, terribly, tremendously

fearless adjective BRAVE, bold, courageous, dauntless, indomitable, intrepid, plucky, unafraid, undaunted, valiant

fearsome adjective TERRIFYING, awe-inspiring, daunting, formidable, frightening, horrifying, menacing, unnerving

feasible adjective POSSIBLE, achievable, attainable, likely, practicable, reasonable, viable, workable

feast noun **1** BANQUET, dinner, repast, spread (informal), treat **2** FESTIVAL, celebration, fête, holiday, holy day, red-letter day, saint's day **3** TREAT, delight, enjoyment, gratification, pleasure ▶ verb **4** EAT ONE'S FILL, gorge, gormandize, indulge, overindulge, pig out (slang), wine and dine

feat noun ACCOMPLISHMENT, achievement, act, attainment, deed, exploit, performance

feathers plural noun PLUMAGE, down, plumes

feature noun **1** ASPECT, characteristic, facet, factor, hallmark, peculiarity, property, quality, trait **2** HIGHLIGHT, attraction, main item, speciality **3** ARTICLE, column, item, piece, report, story ▶ verb **4** SPOTLIGHT, emphasize, foreground, give prominence to, play up, present, star

features plural noun FACE, countenance, lineaments, physiognomy

feckless adjective IRRESPONSIBLE, good-for-nothing, hopeless, incompetent, ineffectual, shiftless, worthless

federation noun UNION, alliance,

amalgamation, association, coalition, combination, league, syndicate

fed up *adjective* DISSATISFIED, bored, depressed, discontented, down in the mouth, glum, sick and tired (*informal*), tired

fee *noun* CHARGE, bill, payment, remuneration, toll

feeble *adjective* **1** WEAK, debilitated, doddering, effete, frail, infirm, puny, sickly, weedy (*informal*) **2** UNCONVINCING, flimsy, inadequate, insufficient, lame, lousy (*slang*), paltry, pathetic, poor, tame, thin

feebleness *noun* WEAKNESS, effeteness, frailty, infirmity, languor, lassitude, sickliness

feed *verb* **1** CATER FOR, nourish, provide for, provision, supply, sustain, victual, wine and dine **2** (sometimes with *on*) EAT, chow down (*slang*), devour, exist on, live on, partake of ▶ *noun* **3** FOOD, fodder, pasturage, provender **4** *Informal* MEAL, feast, repast, spread (*informal*)

feel *verb* **1** TOUCH, caress, finger, fondle, handle, manipulate, paw, stroke **2** EXPERIENCE, be aware of, notice, observe, perceive **3** SENSE, be convinced, intuit **4** BELIEVE, consider, deem, hold, judge, think ▶ *noun* **5** TEXTURE, finish, surface, touch **6** IMPRESSION, air, ambience, atmosphere, feeling, quality, sense

feeler *noun* **1** ANTENNA, tentacle, whisker **2** APPROACH, advance, probe

feeling *noun* **1** EMOTION, ardor, fervor, intensity, passion, sentiment, warmth **2** IMPRESSION, hunch, idea, inkling, notion, presentiment, sense, suspicion **3** OPINION, inclination, instinct, point of view, view **4** SYMPATHY, compassion, concern, empathy, pity, sensibility, sensitivity, understanding **5** SENSE OF TOUCH, perception, sensation **6** ATMOSPHERE, air, ambience, aura, feel, mood, quality

fell *verb* CUT DOWN, cut, demolish, hew, knock down, level

fellow *noun* **1** MAN, chap (*informal*), character, guy (*informal*), individual, person **2** ASSOCIATE, colleague, companion, comrade, partner, peer

fellowship *noun* **1** CAMARADERIE, brotherhood, companionship, sociability **2** SOCIETY, association, brotherhood, club, fraternity, guild, league, order

feminine *adjective* WOMANLY, delicate, gentle, ladylike, soft, tender

femme fatale *noun* SEDUCTRESS, enchantress, siren, succubus, vamp (*informal*)

fen *noun* MARSH, bog, morass, quagmire, slough, swamp

fence *noun* **1** BARRIER, barricade, defense, hedge, palisade, railings, rampart, wall ▶ *verb* **2** (often with *in* or *off*) ENCLOSE, bound, confine, encircle, pen, protect, surround **3** EVADE, dodge, equivocate, parry

ferment *noun* COMMOTION,

disruption, excitement, frenzy, furor, stir, tumult, turmoil, unrest, uproar

ferocious *adjective* 1 FIERCE, predatory, rapacious, ravening, savage, violent, wild 2 CRUEL, barbaric, bloodthirsty, brutal, ruthless, vicious

ferocity *noun* SAVAGERY, bloodthirstiness, brutality, cruelty, fierceness, viciousness, wildness

ferret out *verb* TRACK DOWN, dig up, discover, elicit, root out, search out, trace, unearth

ferry *noun* 1 FERRY BOAT, packet, packet boat ▶ *verb* 2 CARRY, chauffeur, convey, run, ship, shuttle, transport

fertile *adjective* RICH, abundant, fecund, fruitful, luxuriant, plentiful, productive, prolific, teeming

fertility *noun* FRUITFULNESS, abundance, fecundity, luxuriance, productiveness, richness

fertilizer *noun* COMPOST, dressing, dung, manure

fervent, fervid *adjective* ARDENT, devout, earnest, enthusiastic, heartfelt, impassioned, intense, vehement

fervor *noun* INTENSITY, ardor, enthusiasm, excitement, passion, vehemence, warmth, zeal

fester *verb* 1 DECAY, putrefy, suppurate, ulcerate 2 INTENSIFY, aggravate, smolder

festival *noun* 1 CELEBRATION, carnival, entertainment, fête, gala, jubilee 2 HOLY DAY, anniversary, commemoration, feast, fête, fiesta, holiday,

red-letter day, saint's day

festive *adjective* CELEBRATORY, cheery, convivial, happy, jovial, joyful, joyous, jubilant, merry

festivity *noun* (often plural) CELEBRATION, entertainment, festival, party

festoon *verb* DECORATE, array, deck, drape, garland, hang, swathe, wreathe

fetch *verb* 1 BRING, carry, convey, deliver, get, go for, obtain, retrieve, transport 2 SELL FOR, bring in, earn, go for, make, realize, yield

fetching *adjective* ATTRACTIVE, alluring, captivating, charming, cute, enticing, winsome

fetish *noun* 1 FIXATION, mania, obsession, thing (*informal*) 2 TALISMAN, amulet

feud *noun* 1 HOSTILITY, argument, conflict, disagreement, enmity, quarrel, rivalry, row, vendetta ▶ *verb* 2 QUARREL, bicker, clash, contend, dispute, fall out, row, squabble, war

fever *noun* EXCITEMENT, agitation, delirium, ferment, fervor, frenzy, restlessness

feverish *adjective* 1 HOT, febrile, fevered, flushed, inflamed, pyretic (*Medical*) 2 EXCITED, agitated, frantic, frenetic, frenzied, overwrought, restless, wired (*slang*)

few *adjective* NOT MANY, meager, negligible, rare, scanty, scarcely any, sparse, sporadic

fiasco *noun* DEBACLE, catastrophe, disaster, failure, mess, washout (*informal*)

fib *noun* LIE, fiction, story, untruth, white lie

fiber noun 1 THREAD, filament, pile, strand, texture, wisp 2 ESSENCE, nature, quality, spirit, substance 3 As in **moral fiber** RESOLUTION, stamina, strength, toughness

fickle adjective CHANGEABLE, capricious, faithless, inconstant, irresolute, temperamental, unfaithful, variable, volatile

fiction noun 1 TALE, fantasy, legend, myth, novel, romance, story, yarn (informal) 2 LIE, cock and bull story (informal), fabrication, falsehood, invention, tall tale (informal), untruth, urban legend

fictional adjective IMAGINARY, invented, legendary, made-up, nonexistent, unreal

fictitious adjective FALSE, bogus, fabricated, imaginary, invented, made-up, make-believe, mythical, untrue

fiddle verb 1 FIDGET, finger, interfere with, mess about or around, play, tamper with, tinker ▶ noun 2 VIOLIN 3 **fit as a fiddle** HEALTHY, blooming, hale and hearty, in fine fettle, in good form, in good shape, in rude health, in the pink, sound, strong

fiddling adjective TRIVIAL, futile, insignificant, pettifogging, petty, trifling

fidelity noun 1 LOYALTY, allegiance, constancy, dependability, devotion, faithfulness, staunchness, trustworthiness 2 ACCURACY, closeness, correspondence, exactness, faithfulness, precision, scrupulousness

fidget verb 1 MOVE RESTLESSLY,

fiddle (informal), fret, squirm, twitch ▶ noun 2 **the fidgets** RESTLESSNESS, fidgetiness, jitters (informal), nervousness, unease, uneasiness

fidgety adjective RESTLESS, antsy (slang), impatient, jittery (informal), jumpy, nervous, on edge, restive, twitchy (informal), uneasy, wired (slang)

field noun 1 MEADOW, grassland, green, lea (poetic), pasture 2 COMPETITORS, applicants, candidates, competition, contestants, entrants, possibilities, runners 3 SPECIALITY, area, department, discipline, domain, line, province, territory ▶ verb 4 RETRIEVE, catch, pick up, return, stop 5 DEAL WITH, deflect, handle, turn aside

fiend noun 1 DEMON, devil, evil spirit 2 BRUTE, barbarian, beast, ghoul, monster, ogre, savage 3 Informal ENTHUSIAST, addict, fanatic, freak (informal), maniac

fiendish adjective WICKED, cruel, devilish, diabolical, hellish, infernal, malignant, monstrous, satanic, unspeakable

fierce adjective 1 WILD, brutal, cruel, dangerous, ferocious, fiery, menacing, savage, vicious 2 STRONG, furious, howling, inclement, powerful, raging, stormy, tempestuous, violent 3 INTENSE, cut-throat, keen, relentless, strong

fiercely adverb FEROCIOUSLY, furiously, passionately, savagely, tempestuously, tigerishly, tooth and nail, viciously, with no holds barred

fiery adjective 1 BURNING, ablaze,

afire, aflame, blazing, flaming, on fire 2 EXCITABLE, fierce, hot-headed, impetuous, irascible, irritable, passionate

fight verb 1 BATTLE, box, clash, combat, do battle, grapple, spar, struggle, tussle, wrestle 2 OPPOSE, contest, defy, dispute, make a stand against, resist, stand up to, withstand 3 ENGAGE IN, carry on, conduct, prosecute, wage ▶noun 4 CONFLICT, battle, clash, contest, dispute, duel, encounter, struggle, tussle 5 RESISTANCE, belligerence, militancy, pluck, spirit

fighter noun 1 SOLDIER, fighting man, man-at-arms, warrior 2 BOXER, prize fighter, pugilist

fight off verb REPEL, beat off, keep or hold at bay, repress, repulse, resist, stave off, ward off

figure noun 1 NUMBER, character, digit, numeral, symbol 2 AMOUNT, cost, price, sum, total, value 3 SHAPE, body, build, frame, physique, proportions 4 DIAGRAM, design, drawing, illustration, pattern, representation, sketch 5 CHARACTER, big name, celebrity, dignitary, personality ▶verb 6 CALCULATE, compute, count, reckon, tally, tot up, work out 7 (usually with in) FEATURE, act, appear, be featured, contribute to, play a part

figurehead noun FRONT MAN, mouthpiece, puppet, titular or nominal head

figure out verb 1 CALCULATE, compute, reckon, work out 2 UNDERSTAND, comprehend,

decipher, fathom, make out, see

filch verb STEAL, embezzle, misappropriate, pilfer, pinch (informal), take, thieve, walk off with

file[1] noun 1 FOLDER, case, data, documents, dossier, information, portfolio 2 LINE, column, queue, row ▶verb 3 REGISTER, document, enter, pigeonhole, put in place, record 4 MARCH, parade, troop

file[2] verb SMOOTH, abrade, polish, rasp, rub, scrape, shape

fill verb 1 STUFF, cram, crowd, glut, pack, stock, supply, swell 2 SATURATE, charge, imbue, impregnate, pervade, suffuse 3 PLUG, block, bung, close, cork, seal, stop 4 PERFORM, carry out, discharge, execute, fulfill, hold, occupy ▶noun 5 **one's fill** SUFFICIENT, all one wants, ample, enough, plenty

filler noun PADDING, makeweight, stopgap

fill in verb 1 INFORM, acquaint, apprise, bring up to date, give the facts or background 2 REPLACE, deputize, represent, stand in, sub, substitute, take the place of

filling noun 1 STUFFING, contents, filler, inside, insides, padding, wadding ▶adjective 2 SATISFYING, ample, heavy, square, substantial

fill out verb COMPLETE, answer, fill in, fill up

film noun 1 MOVIE, flick (slang), motion picture 2 LAYER, coating, covering, dusting, membrane, skin, tissue ▶verb 3 PHOTOGRAPH, shoot, take, video, videotape

filter *noun* 1 SIEVE, gauze, membrane, mesh, riddle, strainer ▶ *verb* 2 PURIFY, clarify, filtrate, refine, screen, sieve, sift, strain, winnow 3 TRICKLE, dribble, escape, exude, leak, ooze, penetrate, percolate, seep

filth *noun* 1 DIRT, excrement, grime, muck, refuse, sewage, slime, sludge, squalor 2 OBSCENITY, impurity, indecency, pornography, smut, vulgarity

filthy *adjective* 1 DIRTY, foul, polluted, putrid, slimy, squalid, unclean 2 MUDDY, begrimed, blackened, grimy, grubby, scuzzy (*slang*) 3 OBSCENE, corrupt, depraved, impure, indecent, lewd, licentious, pornographic, smutty, X-rated

final *adjective* 1 LAST, closing, concluding, latest, terminal, ultimate 2 DEFINITIVE, absolute, conclusive, decided, definite, incontrovertible, irrevocable, settled

finale *noun* ENDING, climax, close, conclusion, culmination, denouement, epilogue

finalize *verb* COMPLETE, clinch, conclude, decide, settle, tie up, wind up, work out, wrap up (*informal*)

finally *adverb* 1 EVENTUALLY, at last, at length, at long last, in the end, lastly, ultimately 2 IN CONCLUSION, in summary, to conclude

finance *noun* 1 ECONOMICS, accounts, banking, business, commerce, investment, money ▶ *verb* 2 FUND, back, bankroll, guarantee, pay for, subsidize,

support, underwrite

finances *plural noun* RESOURCES, affairs, assets, capital, cash, funds, money, wherewithal

financial *adjective* ECONOMIC, fiscal, monetary, pecuniary

find *verb* 1 DISCOVER, come across, encounter, hit upon, locate, meet, recognize, spot, uncover 2 PERCEIVE, detect, discover, learn, note, notice, observe, realize ▶ *noun* 3 DISCOVERY, acquisition, asset, bargain, catch, good buy

find out *verb* 1 LEARN, detect, discover, note, observe, perceive, realize 2 DETECT, catch, disclose, expose, reveal, uncover, unmask

fine[1] *adjective* 1 EXCELLENT, accomplished, exceptional, exquisite, first-rate, magnificent, masterly, outstanding, splendid, superior 2 SUNNY, balmy, bright, clear, clement, cloudless, dry, fair, pleasant 3 SATISFACTORY, acceptable, all right, convenient, good, O.K. *or* okay (*informal*), suitable 4 DELICATE, dainty, elegant, expensive, exquisite, fragile, quality 5 SUBTLE, abstruse, acute, hairsplitting, minute, nice, precise, sharp 6 SLENDER, diaphanous, flimsy, gauzy, gossamer, light, sheer, thin

fine[2] *noun* 1 PENALTY, damages, forfeit, punishment ▶ *verb* 2 PENALIZE, punish

finery *noun* SPLENDOR, frippery, gear (*informal*), glad rags (*informal*), ornaments, showiness, Sunday best, trappings, trinkets

finesse noun SKILL, adeptness, adroitness, craft, delicacy, diplomacy, discretion, savoir-faire, sophistication, subtlety, tact

finger verb TOUCH, feel, fiddle with (*informal*), handle, manipulate, maul, paw (*informal*), toy with

finish verb 1 STOP, cease, close, complete, conclude, end, round off, terminate, wind up, wrap up (*informal*) 2 CONSUME, devour, dispose of, eat, empty, exhaust, use up 3 DESTROY, bring down, defeat, dispose of, exterminate, overcome, put an end to, put paid to, rout, ruin 4 PERFECT, polish, refine 5 COAT, gild, lacquer, polish, stain, texture, veneer, wax ▶noun 6 END, cessation, close, completion, conclusion, culmination, denouement, finale, run-in 7 DEFEAT, annihilation, curtains (*informal*), death, end, end of the road, ruin 8 SURFACE, luster, patina, polish, shine, smoothness, texture

finished adjective 1 POLISHED, accomplished, perfected, professional, refined 2 OVER, closed, complete, done, ended, finalized, through 3 SPENT, done, drained, empty, exhausted, used up 4 RUINED, defeated, done for (*informal*), doomed, lost, through, undone, wiped out

finite adjective LIMITED, bounded, circumscribed, delimited, demarcated, restricted

fire noun 1 FLAMES, blaze, combustion, conflagration, inferno 2 BOMBARDMENT, barrage, cannonade, flak, fusillade, hail, salvo, shelling, sniping, volley 3 PASSION, ardor, eagerness, enthusiasm, excitement, fervor, intensity, sparkle, spirit, verve, vigor ▶verb 4 SHOOT, detonate, discharge, explode, let off, pull the trigger, set off, shell 5 INSPIRE, animate, enliven, excite, galvanize, impassion, inflame, rouse, stir 6 DISMISS, cashier, discharge, make redundant, sack (*informal*), show the door

firebrand noun RABBLE-ROUSER, agitator, demagogue, incendiary, instigator, tub-thumper

fireworks plural noun 1 PYROTECHNICS, illuminations 2 RAGE, hysterics, row, storm, trouble, uproar

firm[1] adjective 1 HARD, dense, inflexible, rigid, set, solid, solidified, stiff, unyielding 2 SECURE, embedded, fast, fixed, immovable, rooted, stable, steady, tight, unshakable 3 DEFINITE, adamant, inflexible, resolute, resolved, set on, unbending, unshakable, unyielding

firm[2] noun COMPANY, association, business, concern, conglomerate, corporation, enterprise, organization, partnership

firmly adverb 1 SECURELY, immovably, like a rock, steadily, tightly, unflinchingly, unshakably 2 RESOLUTELY, staunchly, steadfastly, unchangeably, unwaveringly

firmness noun 1 HARDNESS, inelasticity, inflexibility,

resistance, rigidity, solidity, stiffness 2 RESOLVE, constancy, inflexibility, resolution, staunchness, steadfastness

first *adjective* 1 FOREMOST, chief, head, highest, leading, pre-eminent, prime, principal, ruling 2 EARLIEST, initial, introductory, maiden, opening, original, premier, primordial 3 ELEMENTARY, basic, cardinal, fundamental, key, primary, rudimentary ▶ *noun* 4 *As in* **from the first** START, beginning, commencement, inception, introduction, outset, starting point ▶ *adverb* 5 BEFOREHAND, at the beginning, at the outset, firstly, initially, in the first place, to begin with, to start with

first-rate *adjective* EXCELLENT, crack (*slang*), elite, exceptional, first class, outstanding, superb, superlative, top-notch (*informal*), world-class

fishy *adjective* 1 *Informal* SUSPICIOUS, dubious, funny (*informal*), implausible, odd, questionable, suspect, unlikely 2 FISHLIKE, piscatorial, piscatory, piscine

fissure *noun* CRACK, breach, cleft, crevice, fault, fracture, opening, rift, rupture, split

fit¹ *verb* 1 MATCH, accord, belong, conform, correspond, meet, suit, tally 2 PREPARE, arm, equip, fit out, provide 3 ADAPT, adjust, alter, arrange, customize, modify, shape ▶ *adjective* 4 APPROPRIATE, apt, becoming, correct, fitting, proper, right, seemly, suitable 5 HEALTHY, able-bodied, hale, in good shape, robust, strapping,

trim, well

fit² *noun* 1 SEIZURE, attack, bout, convulsion, paroxysm, spasm 2 OUTBREAK, bout, burst, outburst, spell

fitful *adjective* IRREGULAR, broken, desultory, disturbed, inconstant, intermittent, spasmodic, sporadic, uneven

fitness *noun* 1 APPROPRIATENESS, aptness, competence, eligibility, propriety, readiness, suitability 2 HEALTH, good condition, good health, robustness, strength, vigor

fitting *adjective* 1 APPROPRIATE, apposite, becoming, correct, decent, proper, right, seemly, suitable ▶ *noun* 2 ACCESSORY, attachment, component, part, piece, unit

fix *verb* 1 PLACE, embed, establish, implant, install, locate, plant, position, set 2 FASTEN, attach, bind, connect, link, secure, stick, tie 3 DECIDE, agree on, arrange, arrive at, determine, establish, set, settle, specify 4 REPAIR, correct, mend, patch up, put to rights, see to 5 FOCUS, direct 6 *Informal* MANIPULATE, influence, rig ▶ *noun* 7 *Informal* PREDICAMENT, difficulty, dilemma, embarrassment, mess, pickle (*informal*), plight, quandary

fixation *noun* PREOCCUPATION, complex, hang-up (*informal*), *idée fixe*, infatuation, mania, obsession, thing (*informal*)

fixed *adjective* 1 PERMANENT, established, immovable, rigid, rooted, secure, set 2 INTENT, resolute, steady, unwavering 3 AGREED, arranged, decided, definite, established, planned, resolved, settled

fix up *verb* **1** ARRANGE, agree on, fix, organize, plan, settle, sort out **2** (often with *with*) PROVIDE, arrange for, bring about, lay on

fizz *verb* BUBBLE, effervesce, fizzle, froth, hiss, sparkle, sputter

fizzy *adjective* BUBBLY, bubbling, carbonated, effervescent, gassy, sparkling

flabbergasted *adjective* ASTONISHED, amazed, astounded, dumbfounded, lost for words, overwhelmed, speechless, staggered, stunned

flabby *adjective* LIMP, baggy, drooping, flaccid, floppy, loose, pendulous, sagging

flag[1] *noun* **1** BANNER, colors, ensign, pennant, pennon, standard, streamer ▶*verb* **2** MARK, indicate, label, note **3** (sometimes with *down*) HAIL, signal, warn, wave

flag[2] *verb* WEAKEN, abate, droop, fade, languish, peter out, sag, wane, weary, wilt

flagging *adjective* FADING, declining, deteriorating, faltering, waning, weakening, wilting

flagrant *adjective* OUTRAGEOUS, barefaced, blatant, brazen, glaring, heinous, scandalous, shameless

flagstone *noun* PAVING STONE, block, flag, slab

flail *verb* THRASH, beat, thresh, windmill

flair *noun* **1** ABILITY, aptitude, faculty, feel, genius, gift, knack, mastery, talent **2** STYLE, chic, dash, discernment, elegance, panache, stylishness, taste

flake *noun* **1** WAFER, layer, peeling, scale, shaving, sliver ▶*verb* **2** BLISTER, chip, peel (off)

flake out *verb* COLLAPSE, faint, keel over, pass out

flamboyant *adjective* **1** EXTRAVAGANT, dashing, elaborate, florid, ornate, ostentatious, showy, swashbuckling, theatrical **2** COLORFUL, brilliant, dazzling, glamorous, glitzy (*slang*)

flame *noun* **1** FIRE, blaze, brightness, light **2** *Informal* SWEETHEART, beau, boyfriend, girlfriend, heart-throb (*Brit.*), lover ▶*verb* **3** BURN, blaze, flare, flash, glare, glow, shine

flaming *adjective* BURNING, ablaze, blazing, fiery, glowing, raging, red-hot

flank *noun* **1** SIDE, hip, loin, thigh **2** WING, side

flap *verb* **1** FLUTTER, beat, flail, shake, thrash, vibrate, wag, wave ▶*noun* **2** FLUTTER, beating, shaking, swinging, swish, waving

flare *verb* **1** BLAZE, burn up, flicker, glare **2** WIDEN, broaden, spread out ▶*noun* **3** FLAME, blaze, burst, flash, flicker, glare

flare up *verb* LOSE ONE'S TEMPER, blow one's top (*informal*), boil over, explode, fly off the handle (*informal*), throw a tantrum

flash *noun* **1** BLAZE, burst, dazzle, flare, flicker, gleam, shimmer, spark, streak **2** MOMENT, instant, jiffy (*informal*), second, split second, trice, twinkling of an eye ▶*verb*

3 BLAZE, flare, flicker, glare, gleam, shimmer, sparkle, twinkle **4** SPEED, dart, dash, fly, race, shoot, streak, whistle, zoom **5** SHOW, display, exhibit, expose, flaunt, flourish

flashy adjective SHOWY, flamboyant, garish, gaudy, glitzy (slang), jazzy (informal), ostentatious, snazzy (informal)

flat¹ adjective **1** EVEN, horizontal, level, levelled, low, smooth **2** DULL, boring, dead, lackluster, lifeless, monotonous, tedious, tiresome, uninteresting **3** ABSOLUTE, categorical, downright, explicit, out-and-out, positive, unequivocal, unqualified **4** PUNCTURED, blown out, burst, collapsed, deflated, empty ▸adverb **5** COMPLETELY, absolutely, categorically, exactly, point blank, precisely, utterly **6 flat out** AT FULL SPEED, all out, at full tilt, for all one is worth

flat² noun APARTMENT, rooms

flatly adverb ABSOLUTELY, categorically, completely, positively, unhesitatingly

flatness noun **1** EVENNESS, smoothness, uniformity **2** DULLNESS, monotony, tedium

flatten verb LEVEL, compress, even out, iron out, raze, smooth off, squash, trample

flatter verb **1** PRAISE, brown-nose (slang), butter up, compliment, pander to, sweet-talk (informal), wheedle **2** SUIT, become, do something for, enhance, set off, show to advantage

flattering adjective **1** BECOMING, effective, enhancing, kind, well-chosen **2** INGRATIATING, adulatory, complimentary, fawning, fulsome, laudatory

flattery noun OBSEQUIOUSNESS, adulation, blandishment, fawning, servility, sweet-talk (informal), sycophancy

flaunt verb SHOW OFF, brandish, display, exhibit, flash about, flourish, parade, sport (informal)

flavor noun **1** TASTE, aroma, flavoring, piquancy, relish, savor, seasoning, smack, tang, zest **2** QUALITY, character, essence, feel, feeling, style, tinge, tone ▸verb **3** SEASON, ginger up, imbue, infuse, leaven, spice

flaw noun WEAKNESS, blemish, chink in one's armor, defect, failing, fault, imperfection, weak spot

flawed adjective DAMAGED, blemished, defective, erroneous, faulty, imperfect, unsound

flawless adjective PERFECT, faultless, impeccable, spotless, unblemished, unsullied

flee verb RUN AWAY, bolt, depart, escape, fly, make one's getaway, take flight, take off (informal), take to one's heels, turn tail

fleet noun NAVY, armada, flotilla, task force

fleeting adjective MOMENTARY, brief, ephemeral, passing, short-lived, temporary, transient, transitory

flesh noun **1** MEAT, brawn, fat, tissue, weight **2** HUMAN NATURE, carnality, flesh and blood **3 one's own flesh and blood**

FAMILY, blood, kin, kinsfolk, kith and kin, relations, relatives

flexibility noun ADAPTABILITY, adjustability, elasticity, give (*informal*), pliability, pliancy, resilience, springiness

flexible adjective 1 PLIABLE, elastic, lithe, plastic, pliant, springy, stretchy, supple 2 ADAPTABLE, adjustable, discretionary, open, variable

flick verb 1 STRIKE, dab, flip, hit, tap, touch 2 **flick through** BROWSE, flip through, glance at, skim, skip, thumb

flicker verb 1 TWINKLE, flare, flash, glimmer, gutter, shimmer, sparkle 2 FLUTTER, quiver, vibrate, waver ▶ noun 3 GLIMMER, flare, flash, gleam, spark 4 TRACE, breath, glimmer, iota, spark

flight[1] noun 1 *Of air travel* JOURNEY, trip, voyage 2 AVIATION, aeronautics, flying 3 FLOCK, cloud, formation, squadron, swarm, unit

flight[2] noun ESCAPE, departure, exit, exodus, fleeing, getaway, retreat, running away

flimsy adjective 1 FRAGILE, delicate, frail, insubstantial, makeshift, rickety, shaky 2 THIN, gauzy, gossamer, light, sheer, transparent 3 UNCONVINCING, feeble, implausible, inadequate, lousy (*slang*), pathetic, poor, unsatisfactory, weak

flinch verb RECOIL, cower, cringe, draw back, quail, shirk, shrink, shy away, wince

fling verb 1 THROW, cast, catapult, heave, hurl, propel, sling, toss ▶ noun 2 BINGE

(*informal*), bash, good time, party, spree

flip verb, noun TOSS, flick, snap, spin, throw

flippancy noun FRIVOLITY, impertinence, irreverence, levity, pertness, sauciness

flippant adjective FRIVOLOUS, cheeky, disrespectful, glib, impertinent, irreverent, offhand, superficial

flirt verb 1 LEAD ON, hit on (*slang*), make advances, make eyes at, philander 2 (usually with *with*) TOY WITH, consider, dabble in, entertain, expose oneself to, give a thought to, play with, trifle with ▶ noun 3 TEASE, coquette, heart-breaker, hussy, philanderer

flirtatious adjective TEASING, amorous, come-hither, coquettish, coy, enticing, flirty, provocative, sportive

float verb 1 BE BUOYANT, hang, hover 2 GLIDE, bob, drift, move gently, sail, slide, slip along 3 LAUNCH, get going, promote, set up

floating adjective 1 BUOYANT, afloat, buoyed up, sailing, swimming 2 FLUCTUATING, free, movable, unattached, variable, wandering

flock noun 1 HERD, colony, drove, flight, gaggle, skein 2 CROWD, collection, company, congregation, gathering, group, herd, host, mass ▶ verb 3 GATHER, collect, congregate, converge, crowd, herd, huddle, mass, throng

flog verb BEAT, flagellate, flay, lash, scourge, thrash, trounce, whack, whip

flood noun 1 DELUGE, downpour, inundation, overflow, spate, tide, torrent 2 ABUNDANCE, flow, glut, profusion, rush, stream, torrent ▶verb 3 IMMERSE, drown, inundate, overflow, pour over, submerge, swamp 4 ENGULF, overwhelm, surge, swarm, sweep 5 OVERSUPPLY, choke, fill, glut, saturate

floor noun 1 TIER, level, stage, story ▶verb 2 KNOCK DOWN, deck (slang), prostrate 3 Informal BEWILDER, baffle, confound, defeat, disconcert, dumbfound, perplex, puzzle, stump, throw (informal)

flop verb 1 FALL, collapse, dangle, droop, drop, sag, slump 2 Informal FAIL, come unstuck, fall flat, fold (informal), founder, go belly-up (slang), misfire ▶noun 3 Informal FAILURE, debacle, disaster, fiasco, nonstarter, washout (informal)

floppy adjective DROOPY, baggy, flaccid, limp, loose, pendulous, sagging, soft

floral adjective FLOWERY, flower-patterned

florid adjective 1 FLUSHED, blowsy, high-colored, rubicund, ruddy 2 FLOWERY, baroque, flamboyant, fussy, high-flown, ornate, overelaborate

flotsam noun DEBRIS, detritus, jetsam, junk, odds and ends, wreckage

flounder verb FUMBLE, grope, struggle, stumble, thrash, toss

flourish verb 1 PROSPER, bloom, blossom, boom, flower, grow, increase, succeed, thrive 2 WAVE, brandish, display, flaunt, shake, wield ▶noun 3 WAVE, display, fanfare, parade, show 4 ORNAMENTATION, curlicue, decoration, embellishment, plume, sweep

flourishing adjective SUCCESSFUL, blooming, going places, in the pink, luxuriant, prospering, rampant, thriving

flout verb DEFY, laugh in the face of, mock, scoff at, scorn, sneer at, spurn

flow verb 1 RUN, circulate, course, move, roll 2 POUR, cascade, flood, gush, rush, stream, surge, sweep 3 RESULT, arise, emanate, emerge, issue, proceed, spring ▶noun 4 TIDE, course, current, drift, flood, flux, outpouring, spate, stream

flower noun 1 BLOOM, blossom, efflorescence 2 ELITE, best, cream, crème de la crème, pick ▶verb 3 BLOSSOM, bloom, flourish, mature, open, unfold

flowery adjective ORNATE, baroque, embellished, fancy, florid, high-flown

flowing adjective 1 STREAMING, falling, gushing, rolling, rushing, smooth, sweeping 2 FLUENT, continuous, easy, smooth, unbroken, uninterrupted

fluctuate verb CHANGE, alternate, oscillate, seesaw, shift, swing, vary, veer, waver

fluency noun EASE, articulateness, assurance, command, control, facility, glibness, readiness, slickness, smoothness

fluent adjective SMOOTH,

articulate, easy, effortless,
flowing, natural, voluble,
well-versed

fluff noun FUZZ, down, nap, pile

fluffy adjective SOFT, downy,
feathery, fleecy, fuzzy

fluid noun 1 LIQUID, liquor,
solution ▶ adjective 2 LIQUID,
flowing, liquefied, melted,
molten, runny, watery

fluke noun LUCKY BREAK, accident,
chance, coincidence, quirk of
fate, serendipity, stroke of luck

flurry noun 1 COMMOTION, ado,
bustle, disturbance,
excitement, flutter, fuss, stir
2 GUST, squall

flush[1] verb 1 BLUSH, color, glow,
go red, redden 2 RINSE OUT,
cleanse, flood, hose down,
wash out ▶ noun 3 BLUSH, color,
glow, redness, rosiness

flush[2] adjective 1 LEVEL, even,
flat, square, true 2 Informal
WEALTHY, in the money
(informal), moneyed, rich,
well-heeled (informal), well-off

flushed adjective BLUSHING,
crimson, embarrassed,
glowing, hot, red, rosy, ruddy

fluster verb 1 UPSET, agitate,
bother, confuse, disturb,
perturb, rattle (informal), ruffle,
unnerve ▶ noun 2 TURMOIL,
disturbance, dither, flap
(informal), flurry, flutter, furor

flutter verb 1 BEAT, flap,
palpitate, quiver, ripple,
tremble, vibrate, waver ▶ noun
2 VIBRATION, palpitation, quiver,
shiver, shudder, tremble,
tremor, twitching 3 AGITATION,
commotion, confusion, dither,
excitement, fluster

fly verb 1 TAKE WING, flit, flutter,

hover, sail, soar, wing 2 PILOT,
control, maneuver, operate
3 DISPLAY, flap, float, flutter,
show, wave 4 PASS, elapse, flit,
glide, pass swiftly, roll on, run
its course, slip away 5 RUSH,
career, dart, dash, hurry, race,
shoot, speed, sprint, tear
6 FLEE, escape, get away, run
for it, skedaddle (informal), take
to one's heels

flying adjective HURRIED, brief,
fleeting, hasty, rushed,
short-lived, transitory

foam noun 1 FROTH, bubbles,
head, lather, spray, spume,
suds ▶ verb 2 BUBBLE, boil,
effervesce, fizz, froth, lather

focus noun 1 CENTER, focal
point, heart, hub, target ▶ verb
2 CONCENTRATE, aim, center,
direct, fix, pinpoint, spotlight,
zoom in

foe noun ENEMY, adversary,
antagonist, opponent, rival

fog noun MIST, gloom, miasma,
murk, smog

foggy adjective MISTY, cloudy,
dim, hazy, indistinct, murky,
smoggy, vaporous

foil[1] verb THWART, balk, counter,
defeat, disappoint, frustrate,
nullify, stop

foil[2] noun CONTRAST, antithesis,
complement

foist verb IMPOSE, fob off, palm
off, pass off, sneak in, unload

fold verb 1 BEND, crease, double
over 2 Informal GO BANKRUPT,
collapse, crash, fail, go bust
(informal), go to the wall, go
under, shut down ▶ noun
3 CREASE, bend, furrow, overlap,
pleat, wrinkle

folder noun FILE, binder,

envelope, portfolio

folk noun PEOPLE, clan, family, kin, kindred, race, tribe

follow verb 1 COME AFTER, come next, succeed, supersede, supplant, take the place of 2 PURSUE, chase, dog, hound, hunt, shadow, stalk, track, trail 3 ACCOMPANY, attend, escort, tag along 4 OBEY, be guided by, conform, heed, observe 5 UNDERSTAND, appreciate, catch on (*informal*), comprehend, fathom, grasp, realize, take in 6 RESULT, arise, develop, ensue, flow, issue, proceed, spring 7 BE INTERESTED IN, cultivate, keep abreast of, support

follower noun SUPPORTER, adherent, apostle, devotee, disciple, fan, pupil

following adjective 1 NEXT, consequent, ensuing, later, subsequent, succeeding, successive ▶noun 2 SUPPORTERS, clientele, coterie, entourage, fans, retinue, suite, train

folly noun FOOLISHNESS, imprudence, indiscretion, lunacy, madness, nonsense, rashness, stupidity

fond adjective 1 LOVING, adoring, affectionate, amorous, caring, devoted, doting, indulgent, tender, warm 2 FOOLISH, deluded, delusive, empty, naive, overoptimistic, vain 3 **fond of** KEEN ON, addicted to, attached to, enamored of, having a soft spot for, hooked on, into (*informal*), partial to

fondle verb CARESS, cuddle, dandle, pat, pet, stroke

fondly adverb 1 LOVINGLY, affectionately, dearly,

indulgently, possessively, tenderly, with affection 2 FOOLISHLY, credulously, naively, stupidly, vainly

fondness noun 1 LIKING, attachment, fancy, love, partiality, penchant, soft spot, taste, weakness 2 DEVOTION, affection, attachment, kindness, love, tenderness

food noun NOURISHMENT, cuisine, diet, fare, grub (*slang*), nutrition, rations, refreshment

fool noun 1 SIMPLETON, blockhead, dork (*slang*), dunce, halfwit, idiot, ignoramus, imbecile (*informal*), schmuck (*slang*) 2 DUPE, fall guy (*informal*), laughing stock, mug (*Brit. slang*), stooge (*slang*), sucker (*slang*) 3 CLOWN, buffoon, harlequin, jester ▶verb 4 DECEIVE, beguile, con (*informal*), delude, dupe, hoodwink, mislead, take in, trick

foolhardy adjective RASH, hot-headed, impetuous, imprudent, irresponsible, reckless

foolish adjective UNWISE, absurd, ill-judged, imprudent, injudicious, senseless, silly

foolishly adverb UNWISELY, idiotically, ill-advisedly, imprudently, injudiciously, mistakenly, stupidly

foolishness noun STUPIDITY, absurdity, folly, imprudence, indiscretion, irresponsibility, silliness, weakness

foolproof adjective INFALLIBLE, certain, guaranteed, safe, sure-fire (*informal*), unassailable, unbreakable

footing noun 1 BASIS, foundation, groundwork 2 RELATIONSHIP, grade, position, rank, standing, status

footstep noun STEP, footfall, tread

forage verb 1 SEARCH, cast about, explore, hunt, rummage, scour, seek ▶ noun 2 *Cattle, etc.* FODDER, feed, food, provender

foray noun RAID, incursion, inroad, invasion, sally, sortie, swoop

forbear verb REFRAIN, abstain, cease, desist, hold back, keep from, restrain oneself, stop

forbearance noun PATIENCE, long-suffering, moderation, resignation, restraint, self-control, temperance, tolerance

forbearing adjective PATIENT, forgiving, indulgent, lenient, long-suffering, merciful, moderate, tolerant

forbid verb PROHIBIT, ban, disallow, exclude, outlaw, preclude, rule out, veto

forbidden adjective PROHIBITED, banned, outlawed, out of bounds, proscribed, taboo, vetoed

forbidding adjective THREATENING, daunting, frightening, hostile, menacing, ominous, sinister, unfriendly

force noun 1 POWER, energy, impulse, might, momentum, pressure, strength, vigor 2 COMPULSION, arm-twisting (*informal*), coercion, constraint, duress, pressure, violence 3 INTENSITY, emphasis, fierceness, vehemence, vigor

4 ARMY, host, legion, patrol, regiment, squad, troop, unit 5 **in force: a** VALID, binding, current, effective, in operation, operative, working **b** IN GREAT NUMBERS, all together, in full strength ▶ verb 6 COMPEL, coerce, constrain, dragoon, drive, impel, make, oblige, press, pressurize 7 BREAK OPEN, blast, prise, wrench, wrest 8 PUSH, propel, thrust

forced adjective 1 COMPULSORY, conscripted, enforced, involuntary, mandatory, obligatory 2 FALSE, affected, artificial, contrived, insincere, labored, stiff, strained, unnatural, wooden

forceful adjective POWERFUL, cogent, compelling, convincing, dynamic, effective, persuasive

forcible adjective 1 VIOLENT, aggressive, armed, coercive, compulsory 2 STRONG, compelling, energetic, forceful, potent, powerful, weighty

forebear noun ANCESTOR, father, forefather, forerunner, predecessor

foreboding noun DREAD, anxiety, apprehension, apprehensiveness, chill, fear, misgiving, premonition, presentiment

forecast verb 1 PREDICT, anticipate, augur, divine, foresee, foretell, prophesy ▶ noun 2 PREDICTION, conjecture, guess, prognosis, prophecy

forefather noun ANCESTOR, father, forebear, forerunner, predecessor

forefront noun LEAD, center,

fore, foreground, front, prominence, spearhead, vanguard

foregoing *adjective* PRECEDING, above, antecedent, anterior, former, previous, prior

foreign *adjective* ALIEN, exotic, external, imported, remote, strange, unfamiliar, unknown

foreigner *noun* ALIEN, immigrant, incomer, stranger

foremost *adjective* LEADING, chief, highest, paramount, pre-eminent, primary, prime, principal, supreme

forerunner *noun* PRECURSOR, envoy, harbinger, herald, prototype

foresee *verb* ANTICIPATE, envisage, forecast, foretell, predict, prophesy

foreshadow *verb* PREDICT, augur, forebode, indicate, portend, prefigure, presage, promise, signal

foresight *noun* ANTICIPATION, far-sightedness, forethought, precaution, preparedness, prescience, prudence

foretell *verb* PREDICT, forecast, forewarn, presage, prognosticate, prophesy

forethought *noun* ANTICIPATION, far-sightedness, foresight, precaution, providence, provision, prudence

forever *adverb* **1** EVERMORE, always, for all time, for keeps, in perpetuity, till Doomsday, till the cows come home (*informal*) **2** CONSTANTLY, all the time, continually, endlessly, eternally, incessantly, interminably, perpetually, twenty-four-seven (*slang*), unremittingly

forewarn *verb* CAUTION, advise, alert, apprise, give fair warning, put on guard, tip off

forfeit *noun* **1** PENALTY, damages, fine, forfeiture, loss ▶ *verb* **2** LOSE, be deprived of, be stripped of, give up, relinquish, renounce, say good-bye to, surrender

forge *verb* **1** CREATE, construct, devise, fashion, form, frame, make, mold, shape, work **2** FALSIFY, copy, counterfeit, fake, feign, imitate

forgery *noun* **1** FRAUDULENCE, coining, counterfeiting, falsification, fraudulent imitation **2** FAKE, counterfeit, falsification, imitation, phoney or phony (*informal*), sham

forget *verb* NEGLECT, leave behind, lose sight of, omit, overlook

forgetful *adjective* ABSENT-MINDED, careless, inattentive, neglectful, oblivious, unmindful, vague

forgive *verb* EXCUSE, absolve, acquit, condone, exonerate, let bygones be bygones, let off (*informal*), pardon

forgiveness *noun* PARDON, absolution, acquittal, amnesty, exoneration, mercy, remission

forgiving *adjective* MERCIFUL, clement, compassionate, forbearing, lenient, magnanimous, soft-hearted, tolerant

forgo *verb* GIVE UP, abandon, do without, relinquish, renounce, resign, surrender, waive, yield

forgotten *adjective* LEFT BEHIND, bygone, lost, omitted, past, past recall, unremembered

fork *verb* BRANCH, bifurcate, diverge, divide, part, split

forked *adjective* BRANCHING, angled, bifurcate(d), branched, divided, pronged, split, zigzag

forlorn *adjective* MISERABLE, disconsolate, down in the dumps (*informal*), helpless, hopeless, pathetic, pitiful, unhappy, woebegone, wretched

form *noun* 1 SHAPE, appearance, configuration, formation, pattern, structure 2 TYPE, kind, sort, style, variety 3 CONDITION, fettle, fitness, health, shape, trim 4 PROCEDURE, convention, custom, etiquette, protocol 5 DOCUMENT, application, paper, sheet 6 CLASS, grade, rank ▶ *verb* 7 MAKE, build, construct, create, fashion, forge, mold, produce, shape 8 ARRANGE, combine, draw up, organize 9 TAKE SHAPE, appear, become visible, come into being, crystallize, grow, materialize, rise 10 DEVELOP, acquire, contract, cultivate, pick up 11 CONSTITUTE, compose, comprise, make up

formal *adjective* 1 OFFICIAL, ceremonial, ritualistic, solemn 2 CONVENTIONAL, affected, correct, precise, stiff, unbending

formality *noun* 1 CONVENTION, custom, procedure, red tape, rite, ritual 2 CORRECTNESS, decorum, etiquette, protocol

format *noun* STYLE, appearance, arrangement, construction, form, layout, look, make-up, plan, type

formation *noun* 1 ESTABLISHMENT, constitution, development, forming, generation, genesis, manufacture, production 2 PATTERN, arrangement, configuration, design, grouping, structure

formative *adjective* DEVELOPMENTAL, influential

former *adjective* PREVIOUS, earlier, erstwhile, one-time, prior

formerly *adverb* PREVIOUSLY, at one time, before, lately, once

formidable *adjective* 1 INTIMIDATING, daunting, dismaying, fearful, frightful, menacing, terrifying 2 IMPRESSIVE, awesome, cool (*informal*), great, mighty, phat (*slang*), powerful, redoubtable, terrific (*informal*), tremendous

formula *noun* METHOD, blueprint, precept, principle, procedure, recipe, rule

formulate *verb* 1 DEFINE, detail, express, frame, give form to, set down, specify, systematize 2 DEVISE, develop, forge, invent, map out, originate, plan, work out

forsake *verb* 1 DESERT, abandon, disown, leave in the lurch, strand 2 GIVE UP, forgo, relinquish, renounce, set aside, surrender, yield

forsaken *adjective* DESERTED, abandoned, disowned, forlorn, left in the lurch, marooned, outcast, stranded

fort *noun* 1 FORTRESS, blockhouse, camp, castle, citadel, fortification, garrison, stronghold 2 **hold the fort** STAND IN, carry on, keep things on an even keel, take over the reins

forte noun SPECIALITY, gift,
métier, strength, strong point,
talent

forth adverb FORWARD, ahead,
away, onward, out, outward

forthcoming adjective
1 APPROACHING, coming,
expected, future, imminent,
impending, prospective,
upcoming **2** ACCESSIBLE, at hand,
available, in evidence,
obtainable, on tap (*informal*),
ready **3** COMMUNICATIVE, chatty,
expansive, free, informative,
open, sociable, talkative,
unreserved

forthright adjective OUTSPOKEN,
blunt, candid, direct, frank,
open, plain-spoken,
straightforward, upfront
(*informal*)

forthwith adverb AT ONCE,
directly, immediately, instantly,
quickly, right away,
straightaway, without delay

fortification noun **1** DEFENSE,
bastion, fastness, fort, fortress,
protection, stronghold
2 STRENGTHENING, reinforcement

fortify verb STRENGTHEN,
augment, buttress, protect,
reinforce, shore up, support

fortitude noun COURAGE,
backbone, bravery,
fearlessness, grit, perseverance,
resolution, strength, valor

fortress noun CASTLE, citadel,
fastness, fort, redoubt,
stronghold

fortunate adjective **1** LUCKY,
favored, in luck, successful,
well-off **2** FAVORABLE,
advantageous, convenient,
expedient, felicitous, fortuitous,
helpful, opportune,

providential, timely, win-win
(*informal*)

fortunately adverb LUCKILY, by a
happy chance, by good luck,
happily, providentially

fortune noun **1** WEALTH,
affluence, opulence,
possessions, property,
prosperity, riches, treasure
2 LUCK, chance, destiny, fate,
kismet, providence **3 fortunes**
DESTINY, adventures,
experiences, history, lot, success

forward adjective **1** LEADING,
advance, first, foremost, front,
head **2** PRESUMPTUOUS, bold,
brash, brazen, cheeky, familiar,
impertinent, impudent, pushy
(*informal*) **3** WELL-DEVELOPED,
advanced, precocious,
premature ▶ adverb **4** AHEAD,
forth, on, onward ▶ verb
5 PROMOTE, advance, assist,
expedite, further, hasten, hurry
6 SEND, dispatch, post, send on

foster verb **1** PROMOTE, cultivate,
encourage, feed, nurture,
stimulate, support, uphold
2 BRING UP, mother, nurse,
raise, rear, take care of

foul adjective **1** DIRTY, fetid,
filthy, funky (*slang*),
malodorous, nauseating,
putrid, repulsive, scuzzy
(*slang*), squalid, stinking,
unclean **2** OBSCENE, abusive,
blue, coarse, indecent, lewd,
profane, scurrilous, vulgar
3 OFFENSIVE, abhorrent,
despicable, detestable,
disgraceful, lousy (*slang*),
scandalous, scuzzy (*slang*),
shameful, wicked **4** UNFAIR,
crooked, dishonest, fraudulent,
shady (*informal*), underhand,
unscrupulous ▶ verb **5** POLLUTE,

besmirch, contaminate, defile, dirty, stain, sully, taint

found *verb* ESTABLISH, constitute, create, inaugurate, institute, organize, originate, set up, start

foundation *noun*
1 GROUNDWORK, base, basis, bedrock, bottom, footing, substructure, underpinning
2 SETTING UP, endowment, establishment, inauguration, institution, organization, settlement

founder[1] *noun* INITIATOR, architect, author, beginner, father, inventor, originator

founder[2] *verb* 1 SINK, be lost, go down, go to the bottom, submerge 2 FAIL, break down, collapse, come to grief, come unstuck, fall through, miscarry, misfire 3 STUMBLE, lurch, sprawl, stagger, trip

foundling *noun* STRAY, orphan, outcast, waif

fountain *noun* 1 JET, font, fount, reservoir, spout, spray, spring, well 2 SOURCE, cause, derivation, fount, fountainhead, origin, wellspring

foyer *noun* ENTRANCE HALL, antechamber, anteroom, lobby, reception area, vestibule

fracas *noun* BRAWL, affray (*Law*), disturbance, melee *or* mêlée, riot, rumpus, scuffle, skirmish

fraction *noun* PIECE, part, percentage, portion, section, segment, share, slice

fractious *adjective* IRRITABLE, captious, cross, petulant, querulous, refractory, testy, tetchy, touchy

fracture *noun* 1 BREAK, cleft, crack, fissure, opening, rift,

rupture, split ▶ *verb* 2 BREAK, crack, rupture, splinter, split

fragile *adjective* DELICATE, breakable, brittle, dainty, fine, flimsy, frail, frangible, weak

fragment *noun* 1 PIECE, bit, chip, particle, portion, scrap, shred, sliver ▶ *verb* 2 BREAK, break up, come apart, come to pieces, crumble, disintegrate, shatter, splinter, split up

fragmentary *adjective* INCOMPLETE, bitty, broken, disconnected, incoherent, partial, piecemeal, scattered, scrappy, sketchy

fragrance *noun* SCENT, aroma, balm, bouquet, fragrancy, perfume, redolence, smell, sweet odor

fragrant *adjective* PERFUMED, aromatic, balmy, odorous, redolent, sweet-scented, sweet-smelling

frail *adjective* WEAK, delicate, feeble, flimsy, fragile, infirm, insubstantial, puny, vulnerable

frailty *noun* FEEBLENESS, fallibility, frailness, infirmity, susceptibility, weakness

frame *noun* 1 CASING, construction, framework, shell, structure 2 PHYSIQUE, anatomy, body, build, carcass 3 **frame of mind** MOOD, attitude, disposition, humor, outlook, state, temper ▶ *verb* 4 CONSTRUCT, assemble, build, make, manufacture, put together 5 DRAFT, compose, devise, draw up, formulate, map out, sketch 6 MOUNT, case, enclose, surround

framework *noun* STRUCTURE, foundation, frame,

groundwork, plan, shell, skeleton, the bare bones

frank *adjective* HONEST, blunt, candid, direct, forthright, open, outspoken, plain-spoken, sincere, straightforward, truthful

frankly *adverb* 1 HONESTLY, candidly, in truth, to be honest 2 OPENLY, bluntly, directly, freely, plainly, without reserve

frankness *noun* OUTSPOKENNESS, bluntness, candor, forthrightness, openness, plain speaking, truthfulness

frantic *adjective* 1 FURIOUS, at the end of one's tether, berserk, beside oneself, distracted, distraught, wild 2 HECTIC, desperate, fraught (*informal*), frenetic, frenzied

fraternity *noun* 1 CLUB, association, brotherhood, circle, company, guild, league, union 2 COMPANIONSHIP, brotherhood, camaraderie, fellowship, kinship

fraternize *verb* ASSOCIATE, consort, cooperate, hobnob, keep company, mingle, mix, socialize

fraud *noun* 1 DECEPTION, chicanery, deceit, double-dealing, duplicity, sharp practice, swindling, treachery, trickery 2 IMPOSTOR, charlatan, fake, fraudster, hoaxer, phoney *or* phony (*informal*), pretender, swindler

fraudulent *adjective* DECEITFUL, crooked (*informal*), dishonest, double-dealing, duplicitous, sham, swindling, treacherous

fray *verb* WEAR THIN, chafe, rub, wear

freak *noun* 1 ODDITY, aberration, anomaly, malformation, monstrosity, weirdo *or* weirdie (*informal*) 2 ENTHUSIAST, addict, aficionado, buff (*informal*), devotee, fan, fanatic, fiend (*informal*), nut (*slang*) ▶ *adjective* 3 ABNORMAL, exceptional, unparalleled, unusual

free *adjective* 1 FOR NOTHING, complimentary, for free (*informal*), free of charge, gratis, gratuitous, on the house, unpaid, without charge 2 AT LIBERTY, at large, footloose, independent, liberated, loose, on the loose, unfettered 3 ALLOWED, able, clear, permitted, unimpeded, unrestricted 4 AVAILABLE, empty, idle, spare, unemployed, unoccupied, unused, vacant 5 GENEROUS, lavish, liberal, unsparing, unstinting ▶ *verb* 6 RELEASE, deliver, let out, liberate, loose, set free, turn loose, unchain, untie 7 EXTRICATE, cut loose, disengage, disentangle, rescue

freedom *noun* 1 LIBERTY, deliverance, emancipation, independence, release 2 OPPORTUNITY, a blank check, carte blanche, discretion, free rein, latitude, license

free-for-all *noun* FIGHT, brawl, fracas, melee *or* mêlée, riot, row, scrimmage

freely *adverb* 1 WILLINGLY, of one's own accord, of one's own free will, spontaneously, voluntarily, without prompting 2 OPENLY, candidly, frankly, plainly, unreservedly, without reserve 3 ABUNDANTLY, amply, copiously, extravagantly, lavishly, liberally, unstintingly

freeze verb 1 CHILL, harden, ice over or up, stiffen 2 SUSPEND, fix, hold up, inhibit, peg, stop

freezing adjective ICY, arctic, biting, bitter, chill, frosty, glacial, raw, wintry

freight noun 1 TRANSPORTATION, carriage, conveyance, shipment 2 CARGO, burden, consignment, goods, load, merchandise, payload

French adjective GALLIC

frenzied adjective FURIOUS, distracted, feverish, frantic, frenetic, rabid, uncontrolled, wild

frenzy noun FURY, derangement, hysteria, paroxysm, passion, rage, seizure

frequent adjective 1 COMMON, customary, everyday, familiar, habitual, persistent, recurrent, repeated, usual ▶verb 2 VISIT, attend, be found at, hang out at (informal), haunt, patronize

frequently adverb OFTEN, commonly, habitually, many times, much, not infrequently, repeatedly

fresh adjective 1 NEW, different, modern, novel, original, recent, up-to-date 2 ADDITIONAL, added, auxiliary, extra, further, more, other, supplementary 3 INVIGORATING, bracing, brisk, clean, cool, crisp, pure, refreshing, unpolluted 4 LIVELY, alert, energetic, keen, refreshed, sprightly, spry, vigorous 5 NATURAL, unprocessed 6 Informal CHEEKY, disrespectful, familiar, forward, impudent, insolent, presumptuous

freshen verb REFRESH, enliven,

freshen up, liven up, restore, revitalize

freshness noun 1 NOVELTY, inventiveness, newness, originality 2 CLEANNESS, brightness, clearness, glow, shine, sparkle, vigor, wholesomeness

fret verb WORRY, agonize, brood, grieve, lose sleep over, upset or distress oneself

fretful adjective IRRITABLE, crotchety, edgy, fractious, querulous, short-tempered, testy, touchy, uneasy

friction noun 1 RUBBING, abrasion, chafing, grating, rasping, resistance, scraping 2 HOSTILITY, animosity, bad blood, conflict, disagreement, discord, dissension, resentment

friend noun 1 COMPANION, buddy (informal), chum (informal), comrade, homeboy (slang), homegirl (slang), pal (informal), playmate 2 SUPPORTER, ally, associate, patron, well-wisher

friendliness noun KINDLINESS, affability, amiability, congeniality, conviviality, geniality, neighborliness, sociability, warmth

friendly adjective SOCIABLE, affectionate, amicable, buddy-buddy (informal), close, familiar, helpful, intimate, neighborly, on good terms, pally (informal), sympathetic, welcoming

friendship noun GOODWILL, affection, amity, attachment, concord, familiarity, friendliness, harmony, intimacy

fright noun FEAR, alarm,

consternation, dread, horror, panic, scare, shock, trepidation

frighten verb SCARE, alarm, intimidate, petrify, shock, startle, terrify, terrorize, unnerve

frightened adjective AFRAID, alarmed, petrified, scared, scared stiff, startled, terrified, terrorized, terror-stricken

frightening adjective TERRIFYING, alarming, fearful, fearsome, horrifying, menacing, scary (informal), shocking, unnerving

frightful adjective TERRIFYING, alarming, awful, dreadful, fearful, ghastly, horrendous, horrible, terrible, traumatic

frigid adjective 1 COLD, arctic, frosty, frozen, glacial, icy, wintry 2 FORBIDDING, aloof, austere, formal, unapproachable, unfeeling, unresponsive

frills plural noun TRIMMINGS, additions, bells and whistles, embellishments, extras, frippery, fuss, ornamentation, ostentation

fringe noun 1 BORDER, edging, hem, trimming 2 EDGE, borderline, limits, margin, outskirts, perimeter, periphery ▶ adjective 3 UNOFFICIAL, unconventional, unorthodox

frisk verb 1 FROLIC, caper, cavort, gambol, jump, play, prance, skip, trip 2 SEARCH, check, inspect, run over, shake down (U.S. slang)

frisky adjective LIVELY, coltish, frolicsome, high-spirited, kittenish, playful, sportive

fritter away verb WASTE, dissipate, idle away, misspend, run through, spend like

water, squander

frivolity noun FUN, flippancy, frivolousness, gaiety, levity, light-heartedness, silliness, superficiality, triviality

frivolous adjective 1 FLIPPANT, childish, foolish, idle, juvenile, puerile, silly, superficial 2 TRIVIAL, minor, petty, shallow, trifling, unimportant

frolic verb 1 PLAY, caper, cavort, frisk, gambol, lark, make merry, romp, sport ▶ noun 2 REVEL, antic, game, lark, romp, spree

frolicsome adjective PLAYFUL, coltish, frisky, kittenish, lively, merry, sportive

front noun 1 EXTERIOR, façade, face, foreground, frontage 2 FOREFRONT, front line, head, lead, vanguard 3 DISGUISE, blind, cover, cover-up, façade, mask, pretext, show ▶ adjective 4 FIRST, foremost, head, lead, leading, topmost ▶ verb 5 FACE ONTO, look over or onto, overlook

frontier noun BOUNDARY, borderline, edge, limit, perimeter, verge

frost noun HOARFROST, freeze, rime

frosty adjective 1 COLD, chilly, frozen, icy, wintry 2 UNFRIENDLY, discouraging, frigid, standoffish, unenthusiastic, unwelcoming

froth noun 1 FOAM, bubbles, effervescence, head, lather, scum, spume, suds ▶ verb 2 FIZZ, bubble over, come to a head, effervesce, foam, lather

frothy adjective FOAMY, foaming, sudsy

frown verb 1 SCOWL, glare, glower, knit one's brows, look daggers, lour or lower 2 **frown on** DISAPPROVE OF, discourage, dislike, look askance at, take a dim view of

frozen adjective ICY, arctic, chilled, frigid, frosted, icebound, ice-cold, ice-covered, numb

frugal adjective THRIFTY, abstemious, careful, economical, niggardly, parsimonious, prudent, sparing

fruit noun 1 PRODUCE, crop, harvest, product, yield 2 RESULT, advantage, benefit, consequence, effect, end result, outcome, profit, return, reward

fruitful adjective USEFUL, advantageous, beneficial, effective, productive, profitable, rewarding, successful, win-win (informal), worthwhile

fruition noun MATURITY, attainment, completion, fulfillment, materialization, perfection, realization, ripeness

fruitless adjective USELESS, futile, ineffectual, pointless, profitless, unavailing, unproductive, unprofitable, unsuccessful, vain

frustrate verb THWART, balk, block, check, counter, defeat, disappoint, foil, forestall, nullify, stymie

frustrated adjective DISAPPOINTED, discouraged, disheartened, embittered, resentful

frustration noun 1 OBSTRUCTION, blocking, circumvention, foiling, thwarting 2 ANNOYANCE, disappointment, dissatisfaction, grievance, irritation, resentment, vexation

fuel noun INCITEMENT, ammunition, provocation

fugitive noun 1 RUNAWAY, deserter, escapee, refugee ▶adjective 2 MOMENTARY, brief, ephemeral, fleeting, passing, short-lived, temporary, transient, transitory

fulfill verb 1 ACHIEVE, accomplish, carry out, complete, perform, realize, satisfy 2 COMPLY WITH, answer, conform to, fill, meet, obey, observe

fulfillment noun ACHIEVEMENT, accomplishment, attainment, completion, consummation, implementation, realization

full adjective 1 SATURATED, brimming, complete, filled, loaded, replete, satiated, stocked 2 PLENTIFUL, abundant, adequate, ample, comprehensive, exhaustive, extensive, generous 3 RICH, clear, deep, distinct, loud, resonant, rounded 4 PLUMP, buxom, curvaceous, rounded, voluptuous 5 LOOSE, baggy, capacious, large, puffy, voluminous ▶noun 6 **in full** COMPLETELY, in its entirety, in total, without exception

full-blooded adjective VIGOROUS, hearty, lusty, red-blooded, virile

fullness noun 1 PLENTY, abundance, copiousness, fill, profusion, satiety, saturation, sufficiency 2 RICHNESS, clearness, loudness, resonance, strength

full-scale adjective MAJOR, all-out, comprehensive, exhaustive, in-depth, sweeping, thorough, thoroughgoing, wide-ranging

fully adverb TOTALLY, altogether, completely, entirely, in all respects, one hundred per cent, perfectly, thoroughly, utterly, wholly

fulsome adjective INSINCERE, excessive, extravagant, immoderate, inordinate, sycophantic, unctuous

fumble verb GROPE, feel around, flounder, scrabble

fume verb RAGE, get hot under the collar (informal), rant, see red (informal), seethe, smolder, storm

fumes plural noun SMOKE, exhaust, gas, pollution, smog, vapor

fumigate verb DISINFECT, clean out or up, cleanse, purify, sanitize, sterilize

fuming adjective ANGRY, enraged, in a rage, incensed, on the warpath (informal), raging, seething, up in arms

fun noun 1 ENJOYMENT, amusement, entertainment, jollity, merriment, mirth, pleasure, recreation, sport 2 **make fun of** MOCK, lampoon, laugh at, parody, poke fun at, ridicule, satirize ▶ adjective 3 ENJOYABLE, amusing, convivial, diverting, entertaining, lively, witty

function noun 1 PURPOSE, business, duty, job, mission, raison d'être, responsibility, role, task 2 RECEPTION, affair, gathering, social occasion ▶ verb 3 WORK, act, behave, do duty, go, operate, perform, run

functional adjective 1 PRACTICAL, hard-wearing, serviceable, useful, utilitarian 2 WORKING, operative

fund noun 1 RESERVE, kitty, pool, stock, store, supply ▶ verb 2 FINANCE, pay for, subsidize, support

fundamental adjective 1 ESSENTIAL, basic, cardinal, central, elementary, key, primary, principal, rudimentary, underlying ▶ noun 2 PRINCIPLE, axiom, cornerstone, law, rudiment, rule

fundamentally adverb ESSENTIALLY, at bottom, at heart, basically, intrinsically, primarily, radically

funds plural noun MONEY, capital, cash, finance, ready money, resources, savings, the wherewithal

funeral noun BURIAL, cremation, inhumation, interment, obsequies

funnel verb CHANNEL, conduct, convey, direct, filter, move, pass, pour

funny adjective 1 HUMOROUS, amusing, comic, comical, droll, entertaining, hilarious, riotous, side-splitting, witty 2 PECULIAR, curious, mysterious, odd, queer, strange, suspicious, unusual, weird

furious adjective 1 ANGRY, beside oneself, enraged, fuming, incensed, infuriated, livid (informal), raging, up in arms 2 VIOLENT, fierce, intense, savage, turbulent, unrestrained, vehement

furnish verb 1 DECORATE, equip, fit out, stock 2 SUPPLY, give, grant, hand out, offer, present, provide

furniture noun HOUSEHOLD

GOODS, appliances, fittings, furnishings, goods, possessions, things (*informal*)

furor *noun* DISTURBANCE, commotion, hullabaloo, outcry, stir, to-do, uproar

furrow *noun* 1 GROOVE, channel, crease, hollow, line, rut, seam, trench, wrinkle ▶*verb* 2 WRINKLE, corrugate, crease, draw together, knit

further *adverb* 1 IN ADDITION, additionally, also, besides, furthermore, into the bargain, moreover, to boot ▶*adjective* 2 ADDITIONAL, extra, fresh, more, new, other, supplementary ▶*verb* 3 PROMOTE, advance, assist, encourage, forward, help, lend support to, work for

furthermore *adverb* BESIDES, additionally, as well, further, in addition, into the bargain, moreover, to boot, too

furthest *adjective* MOST DISTANT, extreme, farthest, furthermost, outmost, remotest, ultimate

furtive *adjective* SLY, clandestine, conspiratorial, secretive, sneaky, stealthy, surreptitious, underhand, under-the-table

fury *noun* 1 ANGER, frenzy, impetuosity, madness, passion, rage, wrath 2 VIOLENCE, ferocity, fierceness, force, intensity, savagery, severity, vehemence

fuss *noun* 1 BOTHER, ado, commotion, excitement, palaver, stir, to-do 2 ARGUMENT, complaint, furor, objection, row, squabble, trouble ▶*verb* 3 WORRY, fidget, fret, get worked up, take pains

fussy *adjective* 1 HARD TO PLEASE, choosy (*informal*), difficult,

fastidious, finicky, nit-picking (*informal*), particular, picky (*informal*) 2 OVERELABORATE, busy, cluttered, overworked, rococo

fusty *adjective* STALE, airless, damp, mildewed, moldering, musty, stuffy

futile *adjective* USELESS, fruitless, ineffectual, unavailing, unprofitable, unsuccessful, vain, worthless

futility *noun* USELESSNESS, emptiness, hollowness, ineffectiveness

future *noun* 1 HEREAFTER, time to come 2 OUTLOOK, expectation, prospect ▶*adjective* 3 FORTHCOMING, approaching, coming, fated, impending, later, subsequent, to come

fuzzy *adjective* 1 FLUFFY, downy, frizzy, woolly 2 INDISTINCT, bleary, blurred, distorted, ill-defined, obscure, out of focus, unclear, vague

G g

gabble *verb* 1 PRATTLE, babble, blabber, gibber, gush, jabber, spout ▶*noun* 2 GIBBERISH, babble, blabber, chatter, drivel, prattle, twaddle

gadabout *noun* PLEASURE-SEEKER, gallivanter, rambler, rover, wanderer

gadget *noun* DEVICE, appliance, contraption (*informal*), contrivance, gizmo (*slang*), instrument, invention, thing, tool

gaffe *noun* BLUNDER, bloomer

(*informal*), faux pas, indiscretion, lapse, mistake, slip, solecism

gag[1] *verb* 1 SUPPRESS, curb, muffle, muzzle, quiet, silence, stifle, stop up 2 RETCH, barf (*slang*), heave, puke (*slang*), spew, throw up (*informal*), toss one's cookies (*slang*), vomit

gag[2] *noun* JOKE, crack (*slang*), funny (*informal*), hoax, jest, wisecrack (*informal*), witticism

gaiety *noun* 1 CHEERFULNESS, blitheness, exhilaration, glee, high spirits, jollity, light-heartedness, merriment, mirth 2 MERRYMAKING, conviviality, festivity, fun, jollification, revelry

gaily *adverb* 1 CHEERFULLY, blithely, gleefully, happily, joyfully, light-heartedly, merrily 2 COLORFULLY, brightly, brilliantly, flamboyantly, flashily, gaudily, showily

gain *verb* 1 OBTAIN, acquire, attain, capture, collect, gather, get, land, pick up, secure, win 2 REACH, arrive at, attain, come to, get to 3 **gain on** GET NEARER, approach, catch up with, close, narrow the gap, overtake ▶*noun* 4 PROFIT, advantage, benefit, dividend, return, yield 5 INCREASE, advance, growth, improvement, progress, rise

gainful *adjective* PROFITABLE, advantageous, beneficial, fruitful, lucrative, productive, remunerative, rewarding, useful, win-win (*informal*), worthwhile

gains *plural noun* PROFITS, earnings, prize, proceeds, revenue, takings, winnings

gainsay *verb* CONTRADICT, contravene, controvert, deny, disagree with, dispute, rebut, retract

gait *noun* WALK, bearing, carriage, pace, step, stride, tread

gala *noun* FESTIVAL, carnival, celebration, festivity, fête, jamboree, pageant

gale *noun* 1 STORM, blast, cyclone, hurricane, squall, tempest, tornado, typhoon 2 OUTBURST, burst, eruption, explosion, fit, howl, outbreak, peal, shout, shriek

gall[1] *noun* 1 *Informal* IMPUDENCE, brazenness, cheek (*informal*), chutzpah (*informal*), effrontery, impertinence, insolence, nerve (*informal*) 2 BITTERNESS, acrimony, animosity, bile, hostility, rancor

gall[2] *verb* 1 SCRAPE, abrade, chafe, irritate 2 ANNOY, exasperate, irk, irritate, provoke, rankle, vex

gallant *adjective* 1 BRAVE, bold, courageous, heroic, honorable, intrepid, manly, noble, valiant 2 CHIVALROUS, attentive, courteous, gentlemanly, gracious, noble, polite

gallantry *noun* 1 BRAVERY, boldness, courage, heroism, intrepidity, manliness, spirit, valor 2 ATTENTIVENESS, chivalry, courteousness, courtesy, gentlemanliness, graciousness, nobility, politeness

galling *adjective* ANNOYING, bitter, exasperating, irksome, irritating, provoking, vexatious

gallivant *verb* WANDER, gad about, ramble, roam, rove

gallop verb RUN, bolt, career, dash, hurry, race, rush, speed, sprint

galore adverb IN ABUNDANCE, all over the place, aplenty, everywhere, in great quantity, in great numbers, in profusion, to spare

galvanize verb STIMULATE, electrify, excite, inspire, invigorate, jolt, provoke, spur, stir

gamble verb 1 BET, game, play, wager 2 RISK, chance, hazard, speculate, stick one's neck out (informal), take a chance ▶ noun 3 RISK, chance, leap in the dark, lottery, speculation, uncertainty, venture 4 BET, wager

gambol verb 1 FROLIC, caper, cavort, frisk, hop, jump, prance, skip ▶ noun 2 FROLIC, caper, hop, jump, prance, skip

game noun 1 PASTIME, amusement, distraction, diversion, entertainment, lark, recreation, sport 2 MATCH, competition, contest, event, head-to-head, meeting, tournament 3 WILD ANIMALS, prey, quarry 4 SCHEME, design, plan, plot, ploy, stratagem, tactic, trick ▶ adjective 5 BRAVE, courageous, gallant, gritty, intrepid, persistent, plucky, spirited 6 WILLING, desirous, eager, interested, keen, prepared, ready

gamut noun RANGE, area, catalog, compass, field, scale, scope, series, sweep

gang noun GROUP, band, clique, club, company, coterie, crowd, mob, pack, squad, team

gangling adjective TALL, angular, awkward, lanky, rangy, rawboned, spindly

gangster noun RACKETEER, crook (informal), hood (slang), hoodlum, mobster (slang)

gap noun 1 OPENING, break, chink, cleft, crack, hole, space 2 INTERVAL, breathing space, hiatus, interlude, intermission, interruption, lacuna, lull, pause, respite 3 DIFFERENCE, disagreement, disparity, divergence, inconsistency

gape verb 1 STARE, gawk, goggle, wonder 2 OPEN, crack, split, yawn

gaping adjective WIDE, broad, cavernous, great, open, vast, wide open, yawning

garbage noun RUBBISH, litter, refuse, trash, waste

garbled adjective JUMBLED, confused, distorted, double-Dutch, incomprehensible, mixed up, unintelligible

garish adjective GAUDY, brash, brassy, flashy, loud, showy, tacky (informal), tasteless, vulgar

garland noun 1 WREATH, bays, chaplet, crown, festoon, honors, laurels ▶ verb 2 ADORN, crown, deck, festoon, wreathe

garments plural noun CLOTHES, apparel, attire, clothing, costume, dress, garb, gear (slang), outfit, uniform

garner verb COLLECT, accumulate, amass, gather, hoard, save, stockpile, store, stow away

garnish verb 1 DECORATE, adorn, embellish, enhance, ornament, set off, trim ▶ noun

2 DECORATION, adornment, embellishment, enhancement, ornamentation, trimming

garrison noun 1 TROOPS, armed force, command, detachment, unit 2 FORT, base, camp, encampment, fortification, fortress, post, station, stronghold ▶verb 3 STATION, assign, position, post, put on duty

garrulous adjective TALKATIVE, chatty, gossiping, loquacious, prattling, verbose, voluble

gash verb 1 CUT, gouge, lacerate, slash, slit, split, tear, wound ▶noun 2 CUT, gouge, incision, laceration, slash, slit, split, tear, wound

gasp verb 1 GULP, blow, catch one's breath, choke, pant, puff ▶noun 2 GULP, exclamation, pant, puff, sharp intake of breath

gate noun BARRIER, door, entrance, exit, gateway, opening, passage, portal

gather verb 1 ASSEMBLE, accumulate, amass, collect, garner, mass, muster, stockpile 2 LEARN, assume, conclude, deduce, hear, infer, surmise, understand 3 PICK, cull, garner, glean, harvest, pluck, reap, select 4 INTENSIFY, deepen, expand, grow, heighten, increase, rise, swell, thicken 5 FOLD, pleat, tuck

gathering noun ASSEMBLY, company, conclave, congress, convention, crowd, group, meeting

gauche adjective AWKWARD, clumsy, ill-mannered, inelegant, tactless, unsophisticated

gaudy adjective GARISH, bright, flashy, loud, showy, tacky (informal), tasteless, vulgar

gauge verb 1 MEASURE, ascertain, calculate, check, compute, count, determine, weigh 2 JUDGE, adjudge, appraise, assess, estimate, evaluate, guess, rate, reckon, value ▶noun 3 INDICATOR, criterion, guide, guideline, measure, meter, standard, test, touchstone, yardstick

gaunt adjective EMACIATED, angular, anorexic, bony, cadaverous, lean, pinched, scrawny, skeletal, skinny, spare

gawky adjective AWKWARD, clumsy, gauche, loutish, lumbering, maladroit, ungainly

gay adjective 1 HOMOSEXUAL, bent (informal, derogatory), lesbian, queer (informal, derogatory) 2 CAREFREE, blithe, cheerful, jovial, light-hearted, lively, merry, sparkling 3 COLORFUL, bright, brilliant, flamboyant, flashy, rich, showy, vivid ▶noun 4 HOMOSEXUAL, lesbian

gaze verb 1 STARE, gape, look, regard, view, watch, wonder ▶noun 2 STARE, fixed look, look

gazette noun NEWSPAPER, journal, news-sheet, paper, periodical

gear noun 1 COG, cogwheel, gearwheel 2 MECHANISM, cogs, machinery, works 3 EQUIPMENT, accouterments, apparatus, instruments, paraphernalia, supplies, tackle, tools 4 CLOTHING, clothes, costume, dress, garments, outfit, togs, wear ▶verb 5 EQUIP, adapt, adjust, fit

geek *noun Slang* BORE, anorak (*informal*), dork (*slang*), drip (*informal*), obsessive, trainspotter (*informal*), wonk (*informal*)

gelatinous *adjective* JELLY-LIKE, gluey, glutinous, gummy, sticky, viscous

gelid *adjective* COLD, arctic, chilly, freezing, frigid, frosty, frozen, glacial, ice-cold, icy

gem *noun* 1 PRECIOUS STONE, jewel, stone 2 PRIZE, jewel, masterpiece, pearl, treasure

general *adjective* 1 COMMON, accepted, broad, extensive, popular, prevalent, public, universal, widespread
2 IMPRECISE, approximate, ill-defined, indefinite, inexact, loose, unspecific, vague
3 UNIVERSAL, across-the-board, blanket, collective, comprehensive, indiscriminate, miscellaneous, sweeping, total

generally *adverb* 1 USUALLY, as a rule, by and large, customarily, normally, on the whole, ordinarily, typically
2 COMMONLY, extensively, popularly, publicly, universally, widely

generate *verb* PRODUCE, breed, cause, create, engender, give rise to, make, propagate

generation *noun* 1 PRODUCTION, creation, formation, genesis, propagation, reproduction
2 AGE GROUP, breed, crop 3 AGE, epoch, era, period, time

generic *adjective* COLLECTIVE, blanket, common, comprehensive, general, inclusive, universal, wide

generosity *noun* 1 CHARITY, beneficence, bounty, kindness, largesse *or* largess, liberality, munificence, open-handedness
2 UNSELFISHNESS, goodness, high-mindedness, magnanimity, nobleness

generous *adjective* 1 CHARITABLE, beneficent, bountiful, hospitable, kind, lavish, liberal, open-handed, unstinting
2 UNSELFISH, big-hearted, good, high-minded, lofty, magnanimous, noble
3 PLENTIFUL, abundant, ample, copious, full, lavish, liberal, rich, unstinting

genesis *noun* BEGINNING, birth, creation, formation, inception, origin, start

genial *adjective* CHEERFUL, affable, agreeable, amiable, congenial, friendly, good-natured, jovial, pleasant, warm

geniality *noun* CHEERFULNESS, affability, agreeableness, amiability, conviviality, cordiality, friendliness, good cheer, joviality, warmth

genius *noun* 1 MASTER, brainbox, expert, hotshot (*informal*), maestro, mastermind, savant, virtuoso, whiz (*informal*)
2 BRILLIANCE, ability, aptitude, bent, capacity, flair, gift, knack, talent

genre *noun* TYPE, category, class, group, kind, sort, species, style

genteel *adjective* REFINED, courteous, cultured, elegant, gentlemanly, ladylike, polite, respectable, urbane, well-mannered

gentle *adjective* 1 SWEET-TEMPERED, compassionate, humane, kindly, meek, mild, placid, tender **2** MODERATE, light, mild, muted, slight, soft, soothing **3** GRADUAL, easy, imperceptible, light, mild, moderate, slight, slow **4** TAME, biddable, broken, docile, manageable, placid, tractable

gentlemanly *adjective* POLITE, civil, courteous, gallant, genteel, honorable, refined, urbane, well-mannered

gentleness *noun* TENDERNESS, compassion, kindness, mildness, softness, sweetness

gentry *noun* NOBILITY, aristocracy, elite, upper class, upper crust (*informal*)

genuine *adjective* **1** AUTHENTIC, actual, bona fide, legitimate, real, the real McCoy, true, veritable **2** SINCERE, candid, earnest, frank, heartfelt, honest, unaffected, unfeigned

germ *noun* **1** MICROBE, bacterium, bug (*informal*), microorganism, virus **2** BEGINNING, embryo, origin, root, rudiment, seed, source, spark

germane *adjective* RELEVANT, apposite, appropriate, apropos, connected, fitting, material, pertinent, related, to the point or purpose

germinate *verb* SPROUT, bud, develop, generate, grow, originate, shoot, swell, vegetate

gesticulate *verb* SIGNAL, gesture, indicate, make a sign, motion, sign, wave

gesture *noun* **1** SIGNAL, action, gesticulation, indication, motion, sign ▶*verb* **2** SIGNAL, sign, wave, gesticulate, indicate, motion,

get *verb* **1** OBTAIN, acquire, attain, fetch, gain, land, net, pick up, procure, receive, secure, win **2** CONTRACT, catch, come down with, fall victim to, take **3** CAPTURE, grab, lay hold of, seize, take **4** BECOME, come to be, grow, turn **5** UNDERSTAND, catch, comprehend, fathom, follow, perceive, see, take in, work out **6** PERSUADE, convince, induce, influence, prevail upon **7** *Informal* ANNOY, bug (*informal*), gall, irritate, upset, vex

get across *verb* **1** CROSS, ford, negotiate, pass over, traverse **2** COMMUNICATE, bring home to, convey, impart, make clear or understood, put over, transmit

get along *verb* BE FRIENDLY, agree, be compatible, click (*slang*), concur, hit it off (*informal*)

get at *verb* **1** GAIN ACCESS TO, acquire, attain, come to grips with, get hold of, reach **2** IMPLY, hint, intend, lead up to, mean, suggest **3** CRITICIZE, attack, blame, find fault with, nag, pick on

getaway *noun* ESCAPE, break, break-out, flight

get by *verb* MANAGE, cope, exist, fare, get along, keep one's head above water, make both ends meet, survive

get off *verb* LEAVE, alight, depart, descend, disembark, dismount, escape, exit

get on *verb* BOARD, ascend, climb, embark, mount

get over *verb* RECOVER FROM, come round, get better, mend, pull through, rally, revive, survive

ghastly *adjective* HORRIBLE, dreadful, frightful, gruesome, hideous, horrendous, loathsome, shocking, terrible, terrifying

ghost *noun* 1 SPIRIT, apparition, phantom, poltergeist, soul, specter, spook (*informal*), wraith 2 TRACE, glimmer, hint, possibility, semblance, shadow, suggestion

ghostly *adjective* SUPERNATURAL, eerie, ghostlike, phantom, spectral, spooky (*informal*), unearthly, wraithlike

ghoulish *adjective* MACABRE, disgusting, grisly, gruesome, morbid, sick (*informal*), unwholesome

giant *noun* 1 OGRE, colossus, monster, titan ▶ *adjective* 2 HUGE, colossal, enormous, gargantuan, gigantic, immense, mammoth, titanic, vast

gibberish *noun* NONSENSE, babble, drivel, gobbledygook (*informal*), mumbo jumbo, twaddle

gibe, jibe *verb* 1 TAUNT, jeer, make fun of, mock, poke fun at, ridicule, scoff, scorn, sneer ▶ *noun* 2 TAUNT, barb, crack (*slang*), dig, jeer, sarcasm, scoffing, sneer

giddiness *noun* DIZZINESS, faintness, light-headedness, vertigo

giddy *adjective* DIZZY, dizzying, faint, light-headed, reeling, unsteady, vertiginous

gift *noun* 1 DONATION, bequest, bonus, contribution, grant, hand-out, legacy, offering,

present 2 TALENT, ability, capability, capacity, flair, genius, knack, power

gifted *adjective* TALENTED, able, accomplished, brilliant, capable, clever, expert, ingenious, masterly, skilled

gigantic *adjective* ENORMOUS, colossal, giant, huge, immense, mammoth, stupendous, titanic, tremendous

giggle *verb, noun* LAUGH, cackle, chortle, chuckle, snigger, titter, twitter

gild *verb* EMBELLISH, adorn, beautify, brighten, coat, dress up, embroider, enhance, ornament

gimmick *noun* STUNT, contrivance, device, dodge, ploy, scheme

gingerly *adverb* CAUTIOUSLY, carefully, charily, circumspectly, hesitantly, reluctantly, suspiciously, timidly, warily

gird *verb* SURROUND, encircle, enclose, encompass, enfold, hem in, ring

girdle *noun* 1 BELT, band, cummerbund, sash, waistband ▶ *verb* 2 SURROUND, bound, encircle, enclose, encompass, gird, ring

girl *noun* FEMALE CHILD, damsel (*archaic*), daughter, lass, maid (*archaic*), maiden (*archaic*), miss

girth *noun* CIRCUMFERENCE, bulk, measure, size

gist *noun* POINT, core, essence, force, idea, meaning, sense, significance, substance

give *verb* 1 PRESENT, award, contribute, deliver, donate, grant, hand over *or* out, provide, supply 2 ANNOUNCE, communicate, issue, notify, pronounce, transmit, utter **3** CONCEDE, grant, hand over, relinquish, surrender, yield **4** PRODUCE, cause, engender, make, occasion

give away verb REVEAL, betray, disclose, divulge, expose, leak, let out, let slip, uncover

give in verb ADMIT DEFEAT, capitulate, collapse, concede, quit, submit, succumb, surrender, yield

give off verb EMIT, discharge, exude, produce, release, send out, throw out

give out verb EMIT, discharge, exude, produce, release, send out, throw out

give up verb ABANDON, call it a day or night, cease, desist, leave off, quit, relinquish, renounce, stop, surrender

glad adjective **1** HAPPY, contented, delighted, gratified, joyful, overjoyed, pleased **2** PLEASING, cheerful, cheering, gratifying, pleasant

gladden verb PLEASE, cheer, delight, gratify, hearten

gladly adverb HAPPILY, cheerfully, freely, gleefully, readily, willingly, with pleasure

gladness noun HAPPINESS, cheerfulness, delight, gaiety, glee, high spirits, joy, mirth, pleasure

glamorous adjective ELEGANT, attractive, dazzling, exciting, fascinating, glittering, glossy, prestigious, smart

glamour noun CHARM, allure, appeal, attraction, beauty, enchantment, fascination, prestige

glance verb **1** LOOK, glimpse, peek, peep, scan, view **2** GLEAM, flash, glimmer, glint, glisten, glitter, reflect, shimmer, shine, twinkle ▸ noun **3** LOOK, glimpse, peek, peep, view

glare verb **1** SCOWL, frown, glower, look daggers, lour or lower **2** DAZZLE, blaze, flame, flare ▸ noun **3** SCOWL, black look, dirty look, frown, glower, lour or lower **4** DAZZLE, blaze, brilliance, flame, glow

glaring adjective **1** CONSPICUOUS, blatant, flagrant, gross, manifest, obvious, outrageous, unconcealed **2** DAZZLING, blazing, bright, garish, glowing

glassy adjective **1** TRANSPARENT, clear, glossy, shiny, slippery, smooth **2** EXPRESSIONLESS, blank, cold, dull, empty, fixed, glazed, lifeless, vacant

glaze verb **1** COAT, enamel, gloss, lacquer, polish, varnish ▸ noun **2** COAT, enamel, finish, gloss, lacquer, luster, patina, polish, shine, varnish

gleam noun **1** GLOW, beam, flash, glimmer, ray, sparkle **2** TRACE, flicker, glimmer, hint, inkling, suggestion ▸ verb **3** SHINE, flash, glimmer, glint, glisten, glitter, glow, shimmer, sparkle

glee noun DELIGHT, elation, exhilaration, exuberance, exultation, joy, merriment, triumph

gleeful adjective DELIGHTED, elated, exuberant, exultant, joyful, jubilant, overjoyed, triumphant

glib adjective SMOOTH, easy,

fluent, insincere, plausible, quick, ready, slick, suave, voluble

glide *verb* SLIDE, coast, drift, float, flow, roll, run, sail, skate, slip

glimmer *verb* 1 FLICKER, blink, gleam, glisten, glitter, glow, shimmer, shine, sparkle, twinkle ▶ *noun* 2 GLEAM, blink, flicker, glow, ray, shimmer, sparkle, twinkle 3 TRACE, flicker, gleam, hint, inkling, suggestion

glimpse *noun* 1 LOOK, glance, peek, peep, sight, sighting ▶ *verb* 2 CATCH SIGHT OF, espy, sight, spot, spy, view

glint *verb* 1 GLEAM, flash, glimmer, glitter, shine, sparkle, twinkle ▶ *noun* 2 GLEAM, flash, glimmer, glitter, shine, sparkle, twinkle, twinkling

glisten *verb* GLEAM, flash, glance, glare, glimmer, glint, glitter, shimmer, shine, sparkle, twinkle

glitch *noun* PROBLEM, blip, difficulty, gremlin, hitch, interruption, malfunction, snag

glitter *verb* 1 SHINE, flash, glare, gleam, glimmer, glint, glisten, shimmer, sparkle, twinkle ▶ *noun* 2 SHINE, brightness, flash, glare, gleam, radiance, sheen, shimmer, sparkle 3 GLAMOUR, display, gaudiness, pageantry, show, showiness, splendor, tinsel

gloat *verb* RELISH, brag, crow, drool, exult, glory, revel in, rub it in (*informal*), triumph

global *adjective* 1 WORLDWIDE, international, planetary, universal, world 2 COMPREHENSIVE, all-inclusive, exhaustive, general, total,

unlimited

globe *noun* SPHERE, ball, earth, orb, planet, world

globule *noun* DROPLET, bead, bubble, drop, particle, pearl, pellet

gloom *noun* 1 DARKNESS, blackness, dark, dusk, murk, obscurity, shade, shadow, twilight 2 DEPRESSION, dejection, despondency, low spirits, melancholy, sorrow, unhappiness, woe

gloomy *adjective* 1 DARK, black, dim, dismal, dreary, dull, gray, murky, somber 2 DEPRESSING, bad, cheerless, disheartening, dispiriting, dreary, sad, somber 3 MISERABLE, crestfallen, dejected, dispirited, downcast, downhearted, glum, melancholy, morose, pessimistic, sad

glorify *verb* 1 ENHANCE, aggrandize, dignify, elevate, ennoble, magnify 2 WORSHIP, adore, bless, exalt, honor, idolize, pay homage to, revere, venerate 3 PRAISE, celebrate, eulogize, extol, sing *or* sound the praises of

glorious *adjective* 1 FAMOUS, celebrated, distinguished, eminent, honored, illustrious, magnificent, majestic, renowned 2 SPLENDID, beautiful, brilliant, dazzling, gorgeous, shining, superb 3 DELIGHTFUL, excellent, fine, gorgeous, marvelous, wonderful

glory *noun* 1 HONOR, dignity, distinction, eminence, fame, kudos, praise, prestige, renown 2 SPLENDOR, grandeur, greatness, magnificence, majesty, nobility, pageantry, pomp ▸ *verb* 3 TRIUMPH, boast, exult, pride oneself, relish, revel, take delight

gloss[1] *noun* SHINE, brightness, gleam, luster, patina, polish, sheen, veneer

gloss[2] *noun* 1 COMMENT, annotation, commentary, elucidation, explanation, footnote, interpretation, note, translation ▸ *verb* 2 INTERPRET, annotate, comment, elucidate, explain, translate

glossy *adjective* SHINY, bright, glassy, glazed, lustrous, polished, shining, silky

glow *verb* 1 SHINE, brighten, burn, gleam, glimmer, redden, smolder ▸ *noun* 2 LIGHT, burning, gleam, glimmer, luminosity, phosphorescence 3 RADIANCE, brightness, brilliance, effulgence, splendor, vividness

glower *verb* 1 SCOWL, frown, give a dirty look, glare, look daggers, lour *or* lower ▸ *noun* 2 SCOWL, black look, dirty look, frown, glare, lour *or* lower

glowing *adjective* 1 BRIGHT, aglow, flaming, luminous, radiant 2 COMPLIMENTARY, adulatory, ecstatic, enthusiastic, laudatory, rave (*informal*), rhapsodic

glue *noun* 1 ADHESIVE, cement, gum, paste ▸ *verb* 2 STICK, affix, cement, fix, gum, paste, seal

glum *adjective* GLOOMY, crestfallen, dejected, doleful, low, morose, pessimistic, sullen

glut *noun* 1 SURFEIT, excess, oversupply, plethora, saturation, superfluity, surplus ▸ *verb* 2 SATURATE, choke, clog, deluge, flood, inundate, overload, oversupply

glutton *noun* GOURMAND, pig (*informal*)

gluttonous *adjective* GREEDY, gormandizing, insatiable, piggish, ravenous, voracious

gluttony *noun* GREED, gormandizing, greediness, voracity

gnarled *adjective* TWISTED, contorted, knotted, knotty, rough, rugged, weather-beaten, wrinkled

gnaw *verb* BITE, chew, munch, nibble

go *verb* 1 MOVE, advance, journey, make for, pass, proceed, set off, travel 2 LEAVE, depart, make tracks, move out, slope off, withdraw 3 FUNCTION, move, operate, perform, run, work 4 CONTRIBUTE, lead to, serve, tend, work towards 5 HARMONIZE, agree, blend, chime, complement, correspond, fit, match, suit 6 ELAPSE, expire, flow, lapse, pass, slip away ▸ *noun* 7 ATTEMPT, bid, crack (*informal*), effort, shot (*informal*), try, turn 8 *Informal* ENERGY, drive, force, life, spirit, verve, vigor, vitality, vivacity

goad *verb* 1 PROVOKE, drive, egg on, exhort, incite, prod, prompt, spur ▸ *noun* 2 PROVOCATION, impetus, incentive, incitement, irritation, spur, stimulus, urge

goal *noun* AIM, ambition, end, intention, object, objective, purpose, target

gobble *verb* DEVOUR, bolt, cram,

gorge, gulp, guzzle, stuff, swallow, wolf

go-between noun INTERMEDIARY, agent, broker, dealer, mediator, medium, middleman

godforsaken adjective DESOLATE, abandoned, bleak, deserted, dismal, dreary, forlorn, gloomy, lonely, remote, wretched

godlike adjective DIVINE, celestial, heavenly, superhuman, transcendent

godly adjective DEVOUT, god-fearing, good, holy, pious, religious, righteous, saintly

godsend noun BLESSING, boon, manna, stroke of luck, windfall

go for verb 1 FAVOR, admire, be attracted to, be fond of, choose, like, prefer 2 ATTACK, assail, assault, launch oneself at, rush upon, set about or upon, spring upon

golden adjective 1 YELLOW, blond or blonde, flaxen 2 SUCCESSFUL, flourishing, glorious, halcyon, happy, prosperous, rich 3 PROMISING, excellent, favorable, opportune

gone adjective 1 FINISHED, elapsed, ended, over, past 2 MISSING, absent, astray, away, lacking, lost, vanished

good adjective 1 PLEASING, acceptable, admirable, excellent, fine, first-class, first-rate, great, satisfactory, splendid, superior 2 PRAISEWORTHY, admirable, ethical, honest, honorable, moral, righteous, trustworthy, upright, virtuous, worthy 3 EXPERT, able, accomplished, adept, adroit, clever,

competent, proficient, skilled, talented 4 BENEFICIAL, advantageous, convenient, favorable, fitting, helpful, profitable, suitable, useful, wholesome, win-win (informal) 5 KIND, altruistic, benevolent, charitable, friendly, humane, kind-hearted, kindly, merciful, obliging 6 VALID, authentic, bona fide, genuine, legitimate, proper, real, true 7 WELL-BEHAVED, dutiful, obedient, orderly, polite, well-mannered 8 FULL, adequate, ample, complete, considerable, extensive, large, substantial, sufficient ▶ noun 9 BENEFIT, advantage, gain, interest, profit, use, usefulness, welfare, wellbeing 10 VIRTUE, excellence, goodness, merit, morality, rectitude, right, righteousness, worth 11 **for good** PERMANENTLY, finally, for ever, irrevocably, once and for all

good-bye noun FAREWELL, adieu, leave-taking, parting

good-for-nothing noun 1 IDLER, couch potato (slang), slacker (informal), waster, wastrel ▶ adjective 2 WORTHLESS, feckless, idle, irresponsible, useless

goodly adjective CONSIDERABLE, ample, large, significant, sizable or sizeable, substantial, tidy (informal)

goodness noun 1 EXCELLENCE, merit, quality, superiority, value, worth 2 KINDNESS, benevolence, friendliness, generosity, goodwill, humaneness, kind-heartedness, kindliness, mercy 3 VIRTUE, honesty, honor, integrity, merit, morality, probity, rectitude, righteousness, uprightness **4** BENEFIT, advantage, salubriousness, wholesomeness

goods *plural noun* **1** PROPERTY, belongings, chattels, effects, gear, paraphernalia, possessions, things, trappings **2** MERCHANDISE, commodities, stock, stuff, wares

goodwill *noun* FRIENDLINESS, amity, benevolence, friendship, heartiness, kindliness

go off *verb* **1** EXPLODE, blow up, detonate, fire **2** LEAVE, decamp, depart, go away, move out, part, quit, slope off

go out *verb* **1** LEAVE, depart, exit **2** BE EXTINGUISHED, die out, expire, fade out

go over *verb* EXAMINE, inspect, rehearse, reiterate, review, revise, study, work over

gore¹ *noun* BLOOD, bloodshed, butchery, carnage, slaughter

gore² *verb* PIERCE, impale, transfix, wound

gorge *noun* **1** RAVINE, canyon, chasm, cleft, defile, fissure, pass ▶ *verb* **2** OVEREAT, cram, devour, feed, glut, gobble, gulp, guzzle, stuff, wolf

gorgeous *adjective* **1** BEAUTIFUL, dazzling, elegant, magnificent, ravishing, splendid, stunning (*informal*), sumptuous, superb **2** *Informal* PLEASING, delightful, enjoyable, exquisite, fine, glorious, good, lovely

gory *adjective* BLOODTHIRSTY, blood-soaked, bloodstained, bloody, murderous, sanguinary

gospel *noun* **1** TRUTH, certainty, fact, the last word **2** DOCTRINE,

credo, creed, message, news, revelation, tidings

gossip *noun* **1** IDLE TALK, blether, chitchat, hearsay, scandal, small talk, tittle-tattle **2** BUSYBODY, chatterbox (*informal*), chatterer, gossipmonger, scandalmonger, tattler, telltale ▶ *verb* **3** CHAT, blether, chew the fat (*slang*), gabble, jaw (*slang*), prate, prattle, tattle

go through *verb* **1** SUFFER, bear, brave, endure, experience, tolerate, undergo, withstand **2** EXAMINE, check, explore, forage, hunt, look, search

gouge *verb* **1** SCOOP, chisel, claw, cut, dig (out), hollow (out) ▶ *noun* **2** GASH, cut, furrow, groove, hollow, scoop, scratch, trench

gourmet *noun* CONNOISSEUR, *bon vivant*, epicure, foodie (*informal*), gastronome

govern *verb* **1** RULE, administer, command, control, direct, guide, handle, lead, manage, order **2** RESTRAIN, check, control, curb, discipline, hold in check, master, regulate, subdue, tame

government *noun* **1** RULE, administration, authority, governance, sovereignty, statecraft **2** EXECUTIVE, administration, ministry, powers-that-be, regime

governor *noun* LEADER, administrator, chief, commander, controller, director, executive, head, manager, ruler

gown *noun* DRESS, costume, frock, garb, garment, habit, robe

grab verb SNATCH, capture, catch, catch or take hold of, clutch, grasp, grip, pluck, seize, snap up

grace noun 1 ELEGANCE, attractiveness, beauty, charm, comeliness, ease, gracefulness, poise, polish, refinement, tastefulness 2 GOODWILL, benefaction, benevolence, favor, generosity, goodness, kindliness, kindness 3 MANNERS, consideration, decency, decorum, etiquette, propriety, tact 4 INDULGENCE, mercy, pardon, reprieve 5 PRAYER, benediction, blessing, thanks, thanksgiving ▶verb 6 HONOR, adorn, decorate, dignify, embellish, enhance, enrich, favor, ornament, set off

graceful adjective ELEGANT, beautiful, charming, comely, easy, pleasing, tasteful

gracious adjective KIND, charitable, civil, considerate, cordial, courteous, friendly, polite, well-mannered

grade noun 1 LEVEL, category, class, degree, echelon, group, rank, stage ▶verb 2 CLASSIFY, arrange, class, group, order, range, rank, rate, sort

gradient noun SLOPE, bank, declivity, grade, hill, incline, rise

gradual adjective STEADY, gentle, graduated, piecemeal, progressive, regular, slow, unhurried

gradually adverb STEADILY, by degrees, gently, little by little, progressively, slowly, step by step, unhurriedly

graduate verb 1 MARK OFF, calibrate, grade, measure out, proportion, regulate 2 CLASSIFY, arrange, grade, group, order, rank, sort

graft noun 1 SHOOT, bud, implant, scion, splice, sprout ▶verb 2 TRANSPLANT, affix, implant, ingraft, insert, join, splice

grain noun 1 CEREALS, corn 2 SEED, grist, kernel 3 BIT, fragment, granule, modicum, morsel, particle, piece, scrap, speck, trace 4 TEXTURE, fiber, nap, pattern, surface, weave 5 As in **go against the grain** INCLINATION, character, disposition, humor, make-up, temper

grand adjective 1 IMPRESSIVE, dignified, grandiose, great, imposing, large, magnificent, regal, splendid, stately, sublime 2 EXCELLENT, cool (informal), fine, first-class, great (informal), outstanding, phat (slang), splendid, wonderful

grandeur noun SPLENDOR, dignity, magnificence, majesty, nobility, pomp, stateliness, sublimity

grandiose adjective 1 PRETENTIOUS, affected, bombastic, extravagant, flamboyant, high-flown, ostentatious, pompous, showy 2 IMPOSING, grand, impressive, lofty, magnificent, majestic, monumental, stately

grant verb 1 CONSENT TO, accede to, agree to, allow, permit 2 GIVE, allocate, allot, assign, award, donate, hand out, present 3 ADMIT, acknowledge, concede ▶noun 4 AWARD, allowance, donation, endowment, gift, hand-out, present, subsidy

granule noun GRAIN, atom, crumb, fragment, molecule, particle, scrap, speck

graphic adjective 1 VIVID, clear, detailed, explicit, expressive, lively, lucid, striking 2 PICTORIAL, diagrammatic, visual

grapple verb 1 GRIP, clutch, grab, grasp, seize, wrestle 2 DEAL WITH, address oneself to, confront, get to grips with, struggle, tackle, take on

grasp verb 1 GRIP, catch, clasp, clinch, clutch, grab, grapple, hold, lay or take hold of, seize, snatch 2 UNDERSTAND, catch on, catch or get the drift of, comprehend, get, realize, see, take in ▶ noun 3 GRIP, clasp, clutches, embrace, hold, possession, tenure 4 CONTROL, power, reach, scope 5 UNDERSTANDING, awareness, comprehension, grip, knowledge, mastery

grasping adjective GREEDY, acquisitive, avaricious, covetous, rapacious

grate verb 1 SHRED, mince, pulverize, triturate 2 SCRAPE, creak, grind, rasp, rub, scratch 3 ANNOY, exasperate, get on one's nerves (informal), irritate, jar, rankle, set one's teeth on edge

grateful adjective THANKFUL, appreciative, beholden, indebted, obliged

gratification noun SATISFACTION, delight, enjoyment, fulfillment, indulgence, pleasure, relish, reward, thrill

gratify verb PLEASE, delight, give pleasure, gladden, humor,

requite, satisfy

grating[1] adjective IRRITATING, annoying, discordant, displeasing, harsh, jarring, offensive, raucous, strident, unpleasant

grating[2] noun GRILLE, grate, grid, gridiron, lattice, trellis

gratitude noun THANKFULNESS, appreciation, gratefulness, indebtedness, obligation, recognition, thanks

gratuitous adjective 1 FREE, complimentary, gratis, spontaneous, unasked-for, unpaid, unrewarded, voluntary 2 UNJUSTIFIED, baseless, causeless, groundless, needless, superfluous, uncalled-for, unmerited, unnecessary, unwarranted, wanton

gratuity noun TIP, bonus, donation, gift, largesse or largess, reward

grave[1] noun BURYING PLACE, crypt, mausoleum, pit, sepulcher, tomb, vault

grave[2] adjective 1 SOLEMN, dignified, dour, earnest, serious, sober, somber, unsmiling 2 IMPORTANT, acute, critical, dangerous, pressing, serious, severe, threatening, urgent

graveyard noun CEMETERY, burial ground, charnel house, churchyard, necropolis

gravity noun 1 IMPORTANCE, acuteness, momentousness, perilousness, seriousness, severity, significance, urgency, weightiness 2 SOLEMNITY, dignity, earnestness, gravitas, seriousness, sobriety

gray adjective 1 PALE, ashen,

pallid, wan **2** DISMAL, dark, depressing, dim, drab, dreary, dull, gloomy **3** CHARACTERLESS, anonymous, colorless, dull

graze[1] *verb* FEED, browse, crop, pasture

graze[2] *verb* **1** TOUCH, brush, glance off, rub, scrape, shave, skim **2** SCRATCH, abrade, chafe, scrape, skin ▶*noun* **3** SCRATCH, abrasion, scrape

greasy *adjective* FATTY, oily, oleaginous, slimy, slippery

great *adjective* **1** LARGE, big, enormous, gigantic, huge, immense, prodigious, vast, voluminous **2** IMPORTANT, critical, crucial, momentous, serious, significant **3** FAMOUS, eminent, illustrious, noteworthy, outstanding, prominent, remarkable, renowned **4** *Informal* EXCELLENT, fantastic (*informal*), fine, marvelous, superb, terrific (*informal*), tremendous (*informal*), wonderful

greatly *adverb* VERY MUCH, considerably, enormously, exceedingly, hugely, immensely, remarkably, tremendously, vastly

greatness *noun* **1** IMMENSITY, enormity, hugeness, magnitude, prodigiousness, size, vastness **2** IMPORTANCE, gravity, momentousness, seriousness, significance, urgency, weight **3** FAME, celebrity, distinction, eminence, glory, grandeur, illustriousness, kudos, note, renown

greed, greediness *noun* **1** GLUTTONY, edacity, esurience, gormandizing, hunger, voracity **2** AVARICE, acquisitiveness, avidity, covetousness, craving, desire, longing, selfishness

greedy *adjective* **1** GLUTTONOUS, gormandizing, hungry, insatiable, piggish, ravenous, voracious **2** GRASPING, acquisitive, avaricious, avid, covetous, craving, desirous, rapacious, selfish

green *adjective* **1** LEAFY, grassy, verdant **2** ECOLOGICAL, conservationist, environment-friendly, non-polluting, ozone-friendly **3** IMMATURE, gullible, inexperienced, naive, new, raw, untrained, wet behind the ears (*informal*) **4** JEALOUS, covetous, envious, grudging, resentful ▶*noun* **5** LAWN, common, sward, turf

greet *verb* WELCOME, accost, address, compliment, hail, meet, receive, salute

greeting *noun* WELCOME, address, reception, salutation, salute

gregarious *adjective* OUTGOING, affable, companionable, convivial, cordial, friendly, sociable, social

gridlock *noun* STANDSTILL, deadlock, impasse, stalemate

grief *noun* SADNESS, anguish, distress, heartache, misery, regret, remorse, sorrow, suffering, woe

grievance *noun* COMPLAINT, ax to grind, gripe (*informal*), injury, injustice

grieve *verb* **1** MOURN, complain, deplore, lament, regret, rue, suffer, weep **2** SADDEN, afflict, distress, hurt, injure, pain, wound

grievous *adjective* 1 PAINFUL, dreadful, grave, harmful, severe 2 DEPLORABLE, atrocious, dreadful, monstrous, offensive, outrageous, shameful, shocking

grim *adjective* FORBIDDING, formidable, harsh, merciless, ruthless, severe, sinister, stern, terrible

grimace *noun* 1 SCOWL, face, frown, sneer ▶ *verb* 2 SCOWL, frown, lour *or* lower, make a face *or* faces, sneer

grime *noun* DIRT, filth, grease, smut, soot

grimy *adjective* DIRTY, filthy, foul, grubby, scuzzy (*slang*), soiled, sooty, unclean

grind *verb* 1 CRUSH, abrade, granulate, grate, mill, pound, powder, pulverize, triturate 2 SMOOTH, polish, sand, sharpen, whet 3 SCRAPE, gnash, grate ▶ *noun* 4 *Informal* HARD WORK, chore, drudgery, labor, sweat (*informal*), toil

grip *noun* 1 CLASP, hold 2 CONTROL, clutches, domination, influence, possession, power 3 UNDERSTANDING, command, comprehension, grasp, mastery ▶ *verb* 4 GRASP, clasp, clutch, hold, seize, take hold of 5 ENGROSS, absorb, enthrall, entrance, fascinate, hold, mesmerize, rivet

gripping *adjective* FASCINATING, compelling, engrossing, enthralling, entrancing, exciting, riveting, spellbinding, thrilling

grisly *adjective* GRUESOME,

appalling, awful, dreadful, ghastly, horrible, macabre, shocking, terrifying

grit *noun* 1 GRAVEL, dust, pebbles, sand 2 COURAGE, backbone, determination, fortitude, guts (*informal*), perseverance, resolution, spirit, tenacity ▶ *verb* 3 GRIND, clench, gnash, grate

gritty *adjective* 1 ROUGH, dusty, granular, gravelly, rasping, sandy 2 COURAGEOUS, brave, determined, dogged, plucky, resolute, spirited, steadfast, tenacious

groan *noun* 1 MOAN, cry, sigh, whine ▶ *verb* 2 MOAN, cry, sigh, whine

groggy *adjective* DIZZY, confused, dazed, faint, shaky, unsteady, weak, wobbly

groom *noun* 1 STABLEMAN, stableboy ▶ *verb* 2 SMARTEN UP, clean, preen, primp, spruce up, tidy 3 RUB DOWN, brush, clean, curry, tend 4 TRAIN, coach, drill, educate, make ready, nurture, prepare, prime, ready

groove *noun* INDENTATION, channel, cut, flute, furrow, hollow, rut, trench, trough

grope *verb* FEEL, cast about, fish, flounder, forage, fumble, scrabble, search

gross *adjective* 1 FAT, corpulent, hulking, obese, overweight 2 TOTAL, aggregate, before deductions, before tax, entire, whole 3 VULGAR, coarse, crude, indelicate, obscene, offensive 4 BLATANT, flagrant, grievous, heinous, rank, sheer, unmitigated, utter ▶ *verb* 5 EARN, bring in, make, rake in (*informal*), take

grotesque *adjective* UNNATURAL, bizarre, deformed, distorted, fantastic, freakish, outlandish, preposterous, strange

ground *noun* **1** EARTH, dry land, land, soil, terra firma, terrain, turf **2** STADIUM, arena, field, park, pitch **3** (often plural) LAND, estate, fields, gardens, terrain, territory **4** (usually plural) DREGS, deposit, lees, sediment **5 grounds** REASON, basis, cause, excuse, foundation, justification, motive, occasion, pretext, rationale ▶ *verb* **6** BASE, establish, fix, found, set, settle **7** INSTRUCT, acquaint with, familiarize with, initiate, teach, train, tutor

groundless *adjective* UNJUSTIFIED, baseless, empty, idle, uncalled-for, unfounded, unwarranted

groundwork *noun* PRELIMINARIES, foundation, fundamentals, preparation, spadework, underpinnings

group *noun* **1** SET, band, bunch, cluster, collection, crowd, gang, pack, party ▶ *verb* **2** ARRANGE, bracket, class, classify, marshal, order, sort

grouse *verb* **1** COMPLAIN, bellyache (*slang*), carp, gripe (*informal*), grumble, moan, whine ▶ *noun* **2** COMPLAINT, grievance, gripe (*informal*), grouch (*informal*), grumble, moan, objection, protest

grove *noun* WOOD, coppice, copse, covert, plantation, spinney, thicket

grovel *verb* HUMBLE ONESELF,

abase oneself, bow and scrape, brown-nose (*slang*), crawl, creep, cringe, demean oneself, fawn, kiss ass (*slang*), kowtow, toady

grow *verb* **1** INCREASE, develop, enlarge, expand, get bigger, multiply, spread, stretch, swell **2** ORIGINATE, arise, issue, spring, stem **3** IMPROVE, advance, flourish, progress, prosper, succeed, thrive **4** BECOME, come to be, get, turn **5** CULTIVATE, breed, farm, nurture, produce, propagate, raise

grown-up *adjective* **1** MATURE, adult, fully-grown, of age ▶ *noun* **2** ADULT, man, woman

growth *noun* **1** INCREASE, development, enlargement, expansion, multiplication, proliferation, stretching **2** IMPROVEMENT, advance, expansion, progress, prosperity, rise, success **3** *Medical* TUMOR, lump

grub *noun* **1** LARVA, caterpillar, maggot **2** *Slang* FOOD, rations, sustenance, victuals ▶ *verb* **3** DIG UP, burrow, pull up, root (*informal*) **4** SEARCH, ferret, forage, hunt, rummage, scour, uncover, unearth

grubby *adjective* DIRTY, filthy, grimy, messy, mucky, scuzzy (*slang*), seedy, shabby, sordid, squalid, unwashed

grudge *verb* **1** RESENT, begrudge, complain, covet, envy, mind ▶ *noun* **2** RESENTMENT, animosity, antipathy, bitterness, dislike, enmity, grievance, rancor

grueling *adjective* EXHAUSTING, arduous, backbreaking,

demanding, laborious,
punishing, severe, strenuous,
taxing, tiring

gruesome *adjective* HORRIFIC,
ghastly, grim, grisly, horrible,
macabre, shocking, terrible

gruff *adjective* **1** SURLY,
bad-tempered, brusque,
churlish, grumpy, rough, rude,
sullen, ungracious **2** HOARSE,
croaking, guttural, harsh,
husky, low, rasping, rough,
throaty

grumble *verb* **1** COMPLAIN, bleat,
carp, gripe (*informal*), grouch
(*informal*), grouse, moan,
whine **2** RUMBLE, growl, gurgle,
murmur, mutter, roar ▶*noun*
3 COMPLAINT, grievance, gripe
(*informal*), grouch (*informal*),
grouse, moan, objection,
protest **4** RUMBLE, growl, gurgle,
murmur, muttering, roar

grumpy *adjective* IRRITABLE,
cantankerous, crotchety,
ill-tempered, peevish, sulky,
sullen, surly, testy

guarantee *noun* **1** ASSURANCE,
bond, certainty, pledge,
promise, security, surety,
warranty, word of honor ▶*verb*
2 MAKE CERTAIN, assure, certify,
ensure, pledge, promise,
secure, vouch for, warrant

guard *verb* **1** WATCH OVER,
defend, mind, preserve,
protect, safeguard, secure,
shield ▶*noun* **2** PROTECTOR,
custodian, defender, lookout,
picket, sentinel, sentry,
warden, watch, watchman
3 PROTECTION, buffer, defense,
safeguard, screen, security,
shield **4 off guard** UNPREPARED,
napping, unready, unwary
5 on guard PREPARED, alert,

cautious, circumspect, on the
alert, on the lookout, ready,
vigilant, wary, watchful

guarded *adjective* CAUTIOUS,
cagey (*informal*), careful,
circumspect, noncommittal,
prudent, reserved, reticent,
suspicious, wary

guardian *noun* KEEPER,
champion, curator, custodian,
defender, guard, protector,
warden

guerrilla *noun* FREEDOM FIGHTER,
partisan, underground fighter

guess *verb* **1** ESTIMATE,
conjecture, hypothesize,
predict, speculate, work out
2 SUPPOSE, believe, conjecture,
fancy, imagine, judge, reckon,
suspect, think ▶*noun*
3 PREDICTION, conjecture,
hypothesis, shot in the dark,
speculation, supposition, theory

guesswork *noun* SPECULATION,
conjecture, estimation,
supposition, surmise, theory

guest *noun* VISITOR, boarder,
caller, company, lodger, visitant

guidance *noun* ADVICE,
counseling, direction, help,
instruction, leadership,
management, teaching

guide *noun* **1** ESCORT, adviser,
conductor, counselor, leader,
mentor, teacher, usher
2 MODEL, example, ideal,
inspiration, paradigm, standard
3 POINTER, beacon, guiding
light, landmark, lodestar,
marker, sign, signpost
4 GUIDEBOOK, Baedeker, catalog,
directory, handbook,
instructions, key, manual ▶*verb*
5 LEAD, accompany, conduct,
direct, escort, shepherd, show

the way, usher **6** STEER, command, control, direct, handle, manage, maneuver **7** SUPERVISE, advise, counsel, influence, instruct, oversee, superintend, teach, train

guild noun SOCIETY, association, brotherhood, club, company, corporation, fellowship, fraternity, league, lodge, order, organization, union

guile noun CUNNING, artifice, cleverness, craft, deceit, slyness, trickery, wiliness

guilt noun **1** CULPABILITY, blame, guiltiness, misconduct, responsibility, sinfulness, wickedness, wrongdoing **2** REMORSE, contrition, guilty conscience, regret, self-reproach, shame, stigma

guiltless adjective INNOCENT, blameless, clean (slang), irreproachable, pure, sinless, spotless, squeaky-clean, untainted

guilty adjective **1** RESPONSIBLE, at fault, blameworthy, culpable, reprehensible, sinful, to blame, wrong **2** REMORSEFUL, ashamed, conscience-stricken, contrite, regretful, rueful, shamefaced, sheepish, sorry

guise noun FORM, appearance, aspect, demeanor, disguise, mode, pretense, semblance, shape

gulf noun **1** BAY, bight, sea inlet **2** CHASM, abyss, gap, opening, rift, separation, split, void

gullibility noun CREDULITY, innocence, naivety, simplicity

gullible adjective NAIVE, born yesterday, credulous, innocent, simple, trusting, unsuspecting,

wet behind the ears (informal)

gully noun CHANNEL, ditch, gutter, watercourse

gulp verb **1** SWALLOW, devour, gobble, guzzle, quaff, swig (informal), swill, wolf **2** GASP, choke, swallow ▶ noun **3** SWALLOW, draft, mouthful, swig (informal)

gum noun **1** GLUE, adhesive, cement, paste, resin ▶ verb **2** STICK, affix, cement, glue, paste

gun noun FIREARM, handgun, piece (slang), pistol, revolver, rifle, saturday night special (slang)

gunman noun TERRORIST, bandit, gunslinger (slang), killer

gurgle verb **1** MURMUR, babble, bubble, lap, plash, purl, ripple, splash ▶ noun **2** MURMUR, babble, purl, ripple

guru noun TEACHER, authority, leader, master, mentor, sage, Svengali, tutor

gush verb **1** FLOW, cascade, flood, pour, run, rush, spout, spurt, stream **2** ENTHUSE, babble, chatter, effervesce, effuse, overstate, spout ▶ noun **3** STREAM, cascade, flood, flow, jet, rush, spout, spurt, torrent

gust noun **1** BLAST, blow, breeze, puff, rush, squall ▶ verb **2** BLOW, blast, squall

gusto noun RELISH, delight, enjoyment, enthusiasm, fervor, pleasure, verve, zeal

gut noun **1** Informal PAUNCH, belly, potbelly, spare tire (slang) **2 guts: a** INTESTINES, belly, bowels, entrails, innards (informal), insides (informal), stomach, viscera **b** Informal

COURAGE, audacity, backbone, daring, mettle, nerve, pluck, spirit ▶ verb **3** DISEMBOWEL, clean **4** RAVAGE, clean out, despoil, empty ▶ adjective **5** As in **gut reaction** INSTINCTIVE, basic, heartfelt, intuitive, involuntary, natural, spontaneous, unthinking, visceral

gutsy adjective BRAVE, bold, courageous, determined, gritty, indomitable, plucky, resolute, spirited

gutter noun DRAIN, channel, conduit, ditch, sluice, trench, trough

guttural adjective THROATY, deep, gravelly, gruff, hoarse, husky, rasping, rough, thick

guy noun Informal MAN, chap, dude (slang), fellow, lad, person

guzzle verb DEVOUR, bolt, cram, drink, gobble, stuff (oneself), swill, wolf

Gypsy noun TRAVELER, Bohemian, nomad, rambler, roamer, Romany, rover, wanderer

H h

habit noun **1** MANNERISM, custom, practice, proclivity, propensity, quirk, tendency, way **2** ADDICTION, dependence

habitation noun **1** DWELLING, abode, domicile, home, house, living quarters, lodging, quarters, residence **2** OCCUPANCY, inhabitance, occupation, tenancy

habitual adjective CUSTOMARY, accustomed, familiar, normal,

regular, routine, standard, traditional, usual

hack[1] verb CUT, chop, hew, lacerate, mangle, mutilate, slash

hack[2] noun **1** SCRIBBLER, literary hack, penny-a-liner **2** HORSE, crock, nag

hackneyed adjective UNORIGINAL, clichéd, commonplace, overworked, stale, stereotyped, stock, threadbare, tired, trite

hag noun WITCH, crone, harridan

haggard adjective GAUNT, careworn, drawn, emaciated, pinched, thin, wan

haggle verb BARGAIN, barter, beat down

hail[1] noun **1** BOMBARDMENT, barrage, downpour, rain, shower, storm, volley ▶ verb **2** RAIN DOWN ON, batter, beat down upon, bombard, pelt, rain, shower

hail[2] verb **1** GREET, acclaim, acknowledge, applaud, cheer, honor, salute, welcome **2** FLAG DOWN, signal to, wave down **3 hail from** COME FROM, be a native of, be born in, originate in

hair noun LOCKS, head of hair, mane, mop, shock, tresses

hairdresser noun STYLIST, barber, coiffeur or coiffeuse

hair-raising adjective FRIGHTENING, alarming, bloodcurdling, horrifying, scary, shocking, spine-chilling, terrifying

hairstyle noun HAIRCUT, coiffure, cut, hairdo, style

hairy adjective SHAGGY, bushy, furry, hirsute, stubbly, unshaven, woolly

halcyon adjective **1** PEACEFUL,

calm, gentle, quiet, serene, tranquil, undisturbed **2** As in **halcyon days** HAPPY, carefree, flourishing, golden, palmy, prosperous

hale adjective HEALTHY, able-bodied, fit, flourishing, in the pink, robust, sound, strong, vigorous, well

half noun **1** EQUAL PART, fifty per cent, hemisphere, portion, section ▶ adjective **2** PARTIAL, halved, limited, moderate ▶ adverb **3** PARTIALLY, in part, partly

half-baked adjective ILL-JUDGED, ill-conceived, impractical, poorly planned, short-sighted, unformed, unthought out or through

half-hearted adjective UNENTHUSIASTIC, apathetic, indifferent, lackluster, listless, lukewarm, perfunctory, tame

halfway adverb **1** MIDWAY, to or in the middle ▶ adjective **2** MIDWAY, central, equidistant, intermediate, mid, middle

halfwit noun FOOL, airhead (slang), dork (slang), dunderhead, idiot, imbecile (informal), moron, schmuck (slang), simpleton

hall noun **1** ENTRANCE HALL, corridor, entry, foyer, hallway, lobby, passage, passageway, vestibule **2** MEETING PLACE, assembly room, auditorium, chamber, concert hall

hallmark noun **1** SEAL, device, endorsement, mark, sign, stamp, symbol **2** INDICATION, sure sign, telltale sign

hallucination noun ILLUSION, apparition, delusion, dream, fantasy, figment of the imagination, mirage, vision

halo noun RING OF LIGHT, aura, corona, nimbus, radiance

halt verb **1** STOP, break off, cease, come to an end, desist, rest, stand still, wait **2** END, block, bring to an end, check, curb, cut short, nip in the bud, terminate ▶ noun **3** STOP, close, end, pause, standstill, stoppage

halting adjective FALTERING, awkward, hesitant, labored, stammering, stumbling, stuttering

halve verb BISECT, cut in half, divide equally, share equally, split in two

hammer verb **1** HIT, bang, beat, drive, knock, strike, tap **2** Informal DEFEAT, beat, drub, run rings around (informal), thrash, trounce, wipe the floor with (informal)

hamper verb HINDER, frustrate, hamstring, handicap, impede, interfere with, obstruct, prevent, restrict

hand noun **1** PALM, fist, mitt (slang), paw (informal) **2** HIRED MAN, artisan, craftsman, employee, laborer, operative, worker, workman **3** PENMANSHIP, calligraphy, handwriting, script **4** OVATION, clap, round of applause **5 at** or **on hand** NEARBY, at one's fingertips, available, close, handy, near, ready, within reach ▶ verb **6** PASS, deliver, hand over

handbook noun GUIDEBOOK, Baedeker, guide, instruction book, manual

handcuff verb SHACKLE, fetter, manacle

handcuffs plural noun SHACKLES, cuffs (informal), fetters, manacles

handful noun FEW, small number, smattering, sprinkling

handicap noun 1 DISADVANTAGE, barrier, drawback, hindrance, impediment, limitation, obstacle, restriction, stumbling block 2 ADVANTAGE, head start 3 DISABILITY, defect, impairment ▶verb 4 RESTRICT, burden, encumber, hamper, hamstring, hinder, hold back, impede, limit

handicraft noun CRAFTSMANSHIP, art, craft, handiwork, skill, workmanship

handiwork noun CREATION, achievement, design, invention, product, production

handle noun 1 GRIP, haft, hilt, stock ▶verb 2 HOLD, feel, finger, grasp, pick up, touch 3 CONTROL, direct, guide, manage, maneuver, manipulate 4 DEAL WITH, cope with, manage

hand-out noun 1 CHARITY, alms 2 LEAFLET, bulletin, circular, literature (informal), mailshot, press release

handsome adjective 1 GOOD-LOOKING, attractive, comely, elegant, gorgeous, personable, well-proportioned 2 LARGE, abundant, ample, considerable, generous, liberal, plentiful, sizable or sizeable

handwriting noun PENMANSHIP, calligraphy, hand, scrawl, script

handy adjective 1 AVAILABLE, accessible, at hand, at one's fingertips, close, convenient, nearby, on hand, within reach 2 USEFUL, convenient, easy to use, helpful, manageable, neat, practical, serviceable, user-friendly 3 SKILLFUL, adept, adroit, deft, dexterous, expert, proficient, skilled

hang verb 1 SUSPEND, dangle, droop 2 EXECUTE, lynch, string up (informal) ▶noun 3 **get the hang of** GRASP, comprehend, understand

hang back verb HESITATE, be reluctant, demur, hold back, recoil

hangdog adjective GUILTY, cowed, cringing, defeated, downcast, furtive, shamefaced, wretched

hangover noun AFTEREFFECTS, crapulence, morning after (informal)

hang-up noun PREOCCUPATION, block, difficulty, inhibition, obsession, problem, thing (informal)

hank noun COIL, length, loop, piece, roll, skein

hanker verb (with for or after) DESIRE, crave, hunger, itch, long, lust, pine, thirst, yearn

haphazard adjective DISORGANIZED, aimless, casual, hit or miss (informal), indiscriminate, random, slapdash

happen verb 1 OCCUR, come about, come to pass, develop, result, take place, transpire (informal) 2 CHANCE, turn out

happening noun EVENT, affair, episode, experience, incident, occurrence, proceeding

happily adverb 1 WILLINGLY, freely, gladly, with pleasure 2 JOYFULLY, blithely, cheerfully, gaily, gleefully, joyously, merrily **3** LUCKILY, fortunately, opportunely, providentially

happiness *noun* JOY, bliss, cheerfulness, contentment, delight, ecstasy, elation, jubilation, pleasure, satisfaction

happy *adjective* **1** JOYFUL, blissful, cheerful, content, delighted, ecstatic, elated, glad, jubilant, merry, overjoyed, pleased, thrilled **2** FORTUNATE, advantageous, auspicious, favorable, lucky, timely, win-win (*informal*)

happy-go-lucky *adjective* CAREFREE, blithe, easy-going, light-hearted, nonchalant, unconcerned, untroubled

harangue *verb* **1** RANT, address, declaim, exhort, hold forth, lecture, spout (*informal*) ▶ *noun* **2** SPEECH, address, declamation, diatribe, exhortation, tirade

harass *verb* ANNOY, bother, harry, hassle (*informal*), hound, persecute, pester, plague, trouble, vex

harassed *adjective* WORRIED, careworn, distraught, hassled (*informal*), strained, tormented, troubled, under pressure, vexed

harassment *noun* TROUBLE, annoyance, bother, hassle (*informal*), irritation, nuisance, persecution, pestering

harbor *noun* **1** PORT, anchorage, haven ▶ *verb* **2** SHELTER, hide, protect, provide refuge, shield **3** MAINTAIN, cling to, entertain, foster, hold, nurse, nurture, retain

hard *adjective* **1** SOLID, firm, inflexible, rigid, rocklike, stiff, strong, tough, unyielding **2** STRENUOUS, arduous, backbreaking, exacting, exhausting, laborious, rigorous, tough **3** DIFFICULT, complicated, intricate, involved, knotty, perplexing, puzzling, thorny **4** UNFEELING, callous, cold, cruel, hardhearted, pitiless, stern, unkind, unsympathetic **5** PAINFUL, disagreeable, distressing, grievous, intolerable, unpleasant ▶ *adverb* **6** ENERGETICALLY, fiercely, forcefully, forcibly, heavily, intensely, powerfully, severely, sharply, strongly, vigorously, violently, with all one's might, with might and main **7** DILIGENTLY, doggedly, industriously, persistently, steadily, untiringly

hard-boiled *adjective* TOUGH, cynical, hard-nosed (*informal*), matter-of-fact, practical, realistic, unsentimental

harden *verb* **1** SOLIDIFY, anneal, bake, cake, freeze, set, stiffen **2** ACCUSTOM, habituate, inure, season, train

hardened *adjective* **1** HABITUAL, chronic, incorrigible, inveterate, shameless **2** ACCUSTOMED, habituated, inured, seasoned, toughened

hard-headed *adjective* SENSIBLE, level-headed, practical, pragmatic, realistic, shrewd, tough, unsentimental

hardhearted *adjective* UNSYMPATHETIC, callous, cold, hard, heartless, insensitive, uncaring, unfeeling

hardiness *noun* RESILIENCE, resolution, robustness, ruggedness, sturdiness, toughness

hardly *adverb* BARELY, just, only just, scarcely, with difficulty

hardship *noun* SUFFERING, adversity, difficulty, misfortune, need, privation, tribulation

hard up *adjective* POOR, broke (*informal*), impecunious, impoverished, on the breadline, out of pocket, penniless, short, strapped for cash (*informal*)

hardy *adjective* STRONG, robust, rugged, sound, stout, sturdy, tough

harm *verb* 1 INJURE, abuse, damage, hurt, ill-treat, maltreat, ruin, spoil, wound ▶ *noun* 2 INJURY, abuse, damage, hurt, ill, loss, mischief, misfortune

harmful *adjective* DESTRUCTIVE, damaging, deleterious, detrimental, hurtful, injurious, noxious, pernicious

harmless *adjective* INNOCUOUS, gentle, innocent, inoffensive, nontoxic, safe, unobjectionable

harmonious *adjective*
1 MELODIOUS, agreeable, concordant, consonant, dulcet, mellifluous, musical, sweet-sounding, tuneful
2 FRIENDLY, agreeable, amicable, compatible, congenial, cordial, sympathetic

harmonize *verb* BLEND, chime with, cohere, coordinate, correspond, match, tally, tone in with

harmony *noun* 1 AGREEMENT, accord, amicability, compatibility, concord, cooperation, friendship, peace, rapport, sympathy
2 TUNEFULNESS, euphony, melody, tune, unison

harness *noun* 1 EQUIPMENT, gear, tack, tackle ▶ *verb* 2 EXPLOIT, channel, control, employ, mobilize, utilize

harrowing *adjective* DISTRESSING, agonizing, disturbing, heart-rending, nerve-racking, painful, terrifying, tormenting, traumatic

harry *verb* PESTER, badger, bother, chivvy, harass, hassle (*informal*), molest, plague

harsh *adjective* 1 RAUCOUS, discordant, dissonant, grating, guttural, rasping, rough, strident 2 SEVERE, austere, cruel, draconian, drastic, pitiless, punitive, ruthless, stern

harshly *adverb* SEVERELY, brutally, cruelly, roughly, sternly, strictly

harshness *noun* SEVERITY, asperity, austerity, brutality, rigor, roughness, sternness

harvest *noun* 1 CROP, produce, yield ▶ *verb* 2 GATHER, mow, pick, pluck, reap

hassle *noun* 1 ARGUMENT, bickering, disagreement, dispute, fight, quarrel, row, squabble 2 TROUBLE, bother, difficulty, grief (*informal*), inconvenience, problem ▶ *verb* 3 BOTHER, annoy, badger, bug (*informal*), harass, hound, pester

haste *noun* 1 SPEED, alacrity, quickness, rapidity, swiftness, urgency, velocity 2 RUSH, hurry, hustle, impetuosity

hasten *verb* RUSH, dash, fly, hurry (up), make haste, race, scurry, speed

hastily *adverb* 1 SPEEDILY, promptly, quickly, rapidly
2 HURRIEDLY, impetuously,

precipitately, rashly

hasty *adjective* 1 SPEEDY, brisk, hurried, prompt, rapid, swift, urgent 2 IMPETUOUS, impulsive, precipitate, rash, thoughtless

hatch *verb* 1 INCUBATE, breed, bring forth, brood 2 DEVISE, conceive, concoct, contrive, cook up (*informal*), design, dream up (*informal*), think up

hate *verb* 1 DETEST, abhor, despise, dislike, loathe, recoil from 2 BE UNWILLING, be loath, be reluctant, be sorry, dislike, feel disinclined, shrink from ▶ *noun* 3 DISLIKE, animosity, antipathy, aversion, detestation, enmity, hatred, hostility, loathing

hateful *adjective* DESPICABLE, abhorrent, detestable, horrible, loathsome, lousy (*slang*), obnoxious, odious, offensive, repellent, repugnant, repulsive, scuzzy (*slang*)

hatred *noun* DISLIKE, animosity, antipathy, aversion, detestation, enmity, hate, repugnance, revulsion

haughty *adjective* PROUD, arrogant, conceited, contemptuous, disdainful, imperious, scornful, snooty (*informal*), stuck-up (*informal*), supercilious

haul *verb* 1 DRAG, draw, heave, lug, pull, tug ▶ *noun* 2 GAIN, booty, catch, harvest, loot, spoils, takings, yield

haunt *verb* 1 PLAGUE, obsess, possess, prey on, recur, stay with, torment, trouble, weigh on ▶ *noun* 2 MEETING PLACE, hangout (*informal*), rendezvous, stamping ground

haunted *adjective* 1 POSSESSED, cursed, eerie, ghostly, jinxed, spooky (*informal*) 2 PREOCCUPIED, obsessed, plagued, tormented, troubled, worried

haunting *adjective* POIGNANT, evocative, nostalgic, persistent, unforgettable

have *verb* 1 POSSESS, hold, keep, obtain, own, retain 2 RECEIVE, accept, acquire, gain, get, obtain, procure, secure, take 3 EXPERIENCE, endure, enjoy, feel, meet with, suffer, sustain, undergo 4 GIVE BIRTH TO, bear, beget, bring forth, deliver 5 **have to** BE OBLIGED, be bound, be compelled, be forced, have got to, must, ought, should

haven *noun* SANCTUARY, asylum, refuge, retreat, sanctum, shelter

havoc *noun* DISORDER, chaos, confusion, disruption, mayhem, shambles

haywire *adjective* As in **go haywire** TOPSY-TURVY, chaotic, confused, disordered, disorganized, mixed up, out of order, shambolic (*informal*)

hazard *noun* 1 DANGER, jeopardy, peril, pitfall, risk, threat ▶ *verb* 2 JEOPARDIZE, endanger, expose, imperil, risk, threaten 3 As in **hazard a guess** CONJECTURE, advance, offer, presume, throw out, venture, volunteer

hazardous *adjective* DANGEROUS, difficult, insecure, perilous, precarious, risky, unsafe

haze *noun* MIST, cloud, fog, obscurity, vapor

hazy *adjective* 1 MISTY, cloudy, dim, dull, foggy, overcast

2 VAGUE, fuzzy, ill-defined, indefinite, indistinct, muddled, nebulous, uncertain, unclear

head noun **1** SKULL, crown, noodle (slang), nut (slang), pate **2** LEADER, boss (informal), captain, chief, commander, director, manager, master, principal, supervisor **3** TOP, crest, crown, peak, pinnacle, summit, tip **4** BRAIN, brains (informal), intellect, intelligence, mind, thought, understanding **5 go to one's head** EXCITE, intoxicate, make conceited, puff up **6 head over heels** UNCONTROLLABLY, completely, intensely, thoroughly, utterly, wholeheartedly ▶ adjective **7** CHIEF, arch, first, leading, main, pre-eminent, premier, prime, principal, supreme ▶ verb **8** LEAD, be or go first, cap, crown, lead the way, precede, top **9** CONTROL, be in charge of, command, direct, govern, guide, lead, manage, run **10** MAKE FOR, aim, go to, make a beeline for, point, set off for, set out, start towards, steer, turn

headache noun **1** MIGRAINE, neuralgia **2** PROBLEM, bane, bother, inconvenience, nuisance, trouble, vexation, worry

heading noun TITLE, caption, headline, name, rubric

headlong adverb, adjective **1** HEADFIRST, head-on ▶ adverb **2** HASTILY, heedlessly, helter-skelter, hurriedly, pell-mell, precipitately, rashly, thoughtlessly ▶ adjective **3** HASTY, breakneck, dangerous, impetuous, impulsive, inconsiderate, precipitate, reckless, thoughtless

headstrong adjective OBSTINATE, foolhardy, heedless, impulsive, perverse, pig-headed, self-willed, stubborn, unruly, willful

headway noun PROGRESS, advance, improvement, progression, way

heady adjective **1** INEBRIATING, intoxicating, potent, strong **2** EXCITING, exhilarating, intoxicating, stimulating, thrilling

heal verb CURE, make well, mend, regenerate, remedy, restore, treat

health noun **1** WELLBEING, fitness, good condition, healthiness, robustness, soundness, strength, vigor **2** CONDITION, constitution, fettle, shape, state

healthy adjective **1** WELL, active, fit, hale and hearty, in fine fettle, in good shape (informal), in the pink, robust, strong **2** WHOLESOME, beneficial, hygienic, invigorating, nourishing, nutritious, salubrious, salutary

heap noun **1** PILE, accumulation, collection, hoard, lot, mass, mound, stack **2** (often plural) A LOT, great deal, lots (informal), mass, plenty, pot(s) (informal), stack(s), tons ▶ verb **3** PILE, accumulate, amass, collect, gather, hoard, stack **4** CONFER, assign, bestow, load, shower upon

hear verb **1** LISTEN TO, catch, overhear **2** LEARN, ascertain, discover, find out, gather, get

wind of (*informal*), pick up
3 *Law* TRY, examine,
investigate, judge

hearing *noun* INQUIRY, industrial
tribunal, investigation, review,
trial

hearsay *noun* RUMOR, gossip,
idle talk, report, talk,
tittle-tattle, word of mouth

heart *noun* **1** NATURE, character,
disposition, soul, temperament
2 BRAVERY, courage, fortitude,
pluck, purpose, resolution,
spirit, will **3** CENTER, core, hub,
middle, nucleus, quintessence
4 by heart BY MEMORY, by rote,
off pat, parrot-fashion
(*informal*), pat, word for word

heartache *noun* SORROW, agony,
anguish, despair, distress, grief,
heartbreak, pain, remorse,
suffering, torment, torture

heartbreak *noun* GRIEF, anguish,
desolation, despair, misery,
pain, sorrow, suffering

heartbreaking *adjective* TRAGIC,
agonizing, distressing,
harrowing, heart-rending,
pitiful, poignant, sad

heartbroken *adjective* MISERABLE,
brokenhearted, crushed,
desolate, despondent,
disconsolate, dispirited,
heartsick

heartfelt *adjective* SINCERE, deep,
devout, earnest, genuine,
honest, profound, unfeigned,
wholehearted

heartily *adverb* ENTHUSIASTICALLY,
eagerly, earnestly, resolutely,
vigorously, zealously

heartless *adjective* CRUEL,
callous, cold, hard,
hardhearted, merciless, pitiless,
uncaring, unfeeling

heart-rending *adjective* MOVING,
affecting, distressing,
harrowing, heartbreaking,
poignant, sad, tragic

hearty *adjective* **1** FRIENDLY,
back-slapping, ebullient,
effusive, enthusiastic, genial,
jovial, warm **2** SUBSTANTIAL,
ample, filling, nourishing,
sizable *or* sizeable, solid, square

heat *verb* **1** WARM UP, make hot,
reheat ▶ *noun* **2** HOTNESS, high
temperature, warmth
3 INTENSITY, excitement, fervor,
fury, passion, vehemence

heated *adjective* ANGRY, excited,
fierce, frenzied, furious,
impassioned, intense,
passionate, stormy, vehement

heathen *noun* **1** UNBELIEVER,
infidel, pagan ▶ *adjective*
2 PAGAN, godless, idolatrous,
irreligious

heave *verb* **1** LIFT, drag (up),
haul (up), hoist, pull (up),
raise, tug **2** THROW, cast, fling,
hurl, pitch, send, sling, toss
3 SIGH, groan, puff **4** VOMIT,
barf (*slang*), gag, retch, spew,
throw up (*informal*)

heaven *noun* **1** PARADISE, bliss,
Elysium *or* Elysian fields (*Greek
myth*), hereafter, life
everlasting, next world, nirvana
(*Buddhism, Hinduism*), Zion
(*Christianity*) **2** HAPPINESS, bliss,
ecstasy, paradise, rapture,
seventh heaven, utopia **3 the
heavens** SKY, ether, firmament

heavenly *adjective* **1** BEAUTIFUL,
blissful, delightful, divine
(*informal*), exquisite, lovely,
ravishing, sublime, wonderful
2 CELESTIAL, angelic, blessed,
divine, holy, immortal

heavily adverb 1 PONDEROUSLY, awkwardly, clumsily, weightily 2 DENSELY, closely, compactly, thickly 3 CONSIDERABLY, a great deal, copiously, excessively, to excess, very much

heaviness noun WEIGHT, gravity, heftiness, ponderousness

heavy adjective 1 WEIGHTY, bulky, hefty, massive, ponderous 2 CONSIDERABLE, abundant, copious, excessive, large, profuse

heckle verb JEER, boo, disrupt, interrupt, shout down, taunt

hectic adjective FRANTIC, animated, chaotic, feverish, frenetic, heated, turbulent

hedge noun 1 BARRIER, boundary, screen, windbreak ▶ verb 2 DODGE, duck, equivocate, evade, prevaricate, sidestep, temporize 3 INSURE, cover, guard, protect, safeguard, shield

heed noun 1 CARE, attention, caution, mind, notice, regard, respect, thought ▶ verb 2 PAY ATTENTION TO, bear in mind, consider, follow, listen to, note, obey, observe, take notice of

heedless adjective CARELESS, foolhardy, inattentive, oblivious, thoughtless, unmindful

heel noun Slang SWINE, louse, rat, scumbag, scuzzbucket (slang), skunk

heel over verb LEAN OVER, keel over, list, tilt

hefty adjective STRONG, big, burly, hulking, massive, muscular, robust, strapping

height noun 1 ALTITUDE, elevation, highness, loftiness, stature, tallness 2 PEAK, apex, crest, crown, pinnacle, summit, top, zenith 3 CULMINATION, climax, limit, maximum, ultimate

heighten verb INTENSIFY, add to, amplify, enhance, improve, increase, magnify, sharpen, strengthen

heir noun SUCCESSOR, beneficiary, heiress (fem.), inheritor, next in line

hell noun 1 UNDERWORLD, abyss, fire and brimstone, Hades (Greek myth), hellfire, inferno, nether world 2 TORMENT, agony, anguish, misery, nightmare, ordeal, suffering, wretchedness

hellish adjective DEVILISH, damnable, diabolical, fiendish, infernal

hello interjection WELCOME, good afternoon, good evening, good morning, greetings

helm noun 1 TILLER, rudder, wheel 2 **at the helm** IN CHARGE, at the wheel, in command, in control, in the driving seat, in the saddle

help verb 1 AID, abet, assist, cooperate, lend a hand, succor, support 2 IMPROVE, alleviate, ameliorate, ease, facilitate, mitigate, relieve 3 REFRAIN FROM, avoid, keep from, prevent, resist ▶ noun 4 ASSISTANCE, advice, aid, cooperation, guidance, helping hand, support

helper noun ASSISTANT, adjutant, aide, ally, attendant, collaborator, helpmate, mate, partner, right-hand man, second, supporter

helpful *adjective* 1 USEFUL, advantageous, beneficial, constructive, practical, profitable, timely, win-win (*informal*) 2 COOPERATIVE, accommodating, considerate, friendly, kind, neighborly, supportive, sympathetic

helping *noun* PORTION, dollop (*informal*), piece, plateful, ration, serving

helpless *adjective* WEAK, challenged, disabled, impotent, incapable, infirm, paralyzed, powerless

helter-skelter *adjective* 1 HAPHAZARD, confused, disordered, hit-or-miss, jumbled, muddled, random, topsy-turvy ▶*adverb* 2 CARELESSLY, anyhow, hastily, headlong, hurriedly, pell-mell, rashly, recklessly, wildly

hem *noun* 1 EDGE, border, fringe, margin, trimming ▶*verb* 2 **hem in** SURROUND, beset, circumscribe, confine, enclose, restrict, shut in

hence *conjunction* THEREFORE, ergo, for this reason, on that account, thus

henchman *noun* ATTENDANT, associate, bodyguard, follower, minder (*slang*), right-hand man, sidekick (*slang*), subordinate, supporter

henpecked *adjective* BULLIED, browbeaten, dominated, meek, subjugated, timid

herald *noun* 1 MESSENGER, crier 2 FORERUNNER, harbinger, indication, omen, precursor, sign, signal, token ▶*verb* 3 INDICATE, foretoken, portend,

presage, promise, show, usher in

herd *noun* 1 MULTITUDE, collection, crowd, drove, flock, horde, mass, mob, swarm, throng ▶*verb* 2 CONGREGATE, assemble, collect, flock, gather, huddle, muster, rally

hereafter *adverb* 1 IN FUTURE, from now on, hence, henceforth, henceforward ▶*noun* 2 AFTERLIFE, life after death, next world

hereditary *adjective* 1 GENETIC, inborn, inbred, inheritable, transmissible 2 INHERITED, ancestral, traditional

heredity *noun* GENETICS, constitution, genetic make-up, inheritance

heresy *noun* DISSIDENCE, apostasy, heterodoxy, iconoclasm, unorthodoxy

heretic *noun* DISSIDENT, apostate, dissenter, nonconformist, renegade, revisionist

heretical *adjective* UNORTHODOX, heterodox, iconoclastic, idolatrous, impious, revisionist

heritage *noun* INHERITANCE, bequest, birthright, endowment, legacy, tradition

hermit *noun* RECLUSE, anchorite, eremite, loner (*informal*), monk

hero *noun* 1 IDOL, champion, conqueror, star, superstar, victor 2 LEADING MAN, protagonist

heroic *adjective* COURAGEOUS, brave, daring, fearless, gallant, intrepid, lion-hearted, valiant

heroine *noun* LEADING LADY, diva, prima donna, protagonist

heroism *noun* BRAVERY, courage, courageousness, fearlessness, gallantry, intrepidity, spirit, valor

hesitant *adjective* UNCERTAIN, diffident, doubtful, half-hearted, halting, irresolute, reluctant, unsure, vacillating, wavering

hesitate *verb* 1 WAVER, delay, dither, doubt, hum and haw, pause, vacillate, wait 2 BE RELUCTANT, balk, be unwilling, demur, hang back, scruple, shrink from, think twice

hesitation *noun* 1 INDECISION, delay, doubt, hesitancy, irresolution, uncertainty, vacillation 2 RELUCTANCE, misgiving(s), qualm(s), scruple(s), unwillingness

hew *verb* 1 CUT, ax, chop, hack, lop, split 2 CARVE, fashion, form, make, model, sculpt, sculpture, shape, smooth

heyday *noun* PRIME, bloom, pink, prime of life, salad days

hiatus *noun* PAUSE, break, discontinuity, gap, interruption, interval, respite, space

hidden *adjective* CONCEALED, clandestine, covert, latent, secret, under wraps, unseen, veiled

hide[1] *verb* 1 CONCEAL, secrete, stash (*informal*) 2 GO INTO HIDING, go to ground, go underground, hole up, lie low, take cover 3 DISGUISE, camouflage, cloak, conceal, cover, mask, obscure, shroud, veil 4 SUPPRESS, draw a veil over, hush up, keep dark, keep secret, keep under one's hat, withhold

hide[2] *noun* SKIN, pelt

hidebound *adjective* CONVENTIONAL, narrow-minded, rigid, set in one's ways, strait-laced, ultraconservative

hideous *adjective* UGLY, ghastly, grim, grisly, grotesque, gruesome, monstrous, repulsive, revolting, scuzzy (*slang*), unsightly

hideout *noun* HIDEAWAY, den, hiding place, lair, shelter

hierarchy *noun* GRADING, pecking order, ranking

high *adjective* 1 TALL, elevated, lofty, soaring, steep, towering 2 EXTREME, excessive, extraordinary, great, intensified, sharp, strong 3 IMPORTANT, arch, chief, eminent, exalted, powerful, superior 4 *Informal* INTOXICATED, stoned (*slang*), tripping (*informal*) 5 HIGH-PITCHED, acute, penetrating, piercing, piping, sharp, shrill, strident ▶ *adverb* 6 ALOFT, at great height, far up, way up

highbrow *noun* 1 INTELLECTUAL, aesthete, egghead (*informal*), scholar ▶ *adjective* 2 INTELLECTUAL, bookish, cultivated, cultured, sophisticated

high-flown *adjective* EXTRAVAGANT, elaborate, exaggerated, florid, grandiose, inflated, lofty, overblown, pretentious

high-handed *adjective* DICTATORIAL, despotic, domineering, imperious, oppressive, overbearing, tyrannical, willful

highlight *noun* 1 FEATURE, climax, focal point, focus, high point, high spot, peak ▶ *verb*

2 EMPHASIZE, accent, accentuate, bring to the fore, show up, spotlight, stress, underline

highly adverb EXTREMELY, exceptionally, greatly, immensely, tremendously, vastly, very, very much

highly strung adjective NERVOUS, edgy, excitable, neurotic, sensitive, stressed, temperamental, tense, twitchy (informal), wired (slang)

hijack verb SEIZE, commandeer, expropriate, take over

hike noun **1** WALK, march, ramble, tramp, trek ▸verb **2** WALK, back-pack, ramble, tramp **3 hike up** RAISE, hitch up, jack up, lift, pull up

hilarious adjective FUNNY, amusing, comical, entertaining, humorous, rollicking, side-splitting, uproarious

hilarity noun LAUGHTER, amusement, exhilaration, glee, high spirits, jollity, merriment, mirth

hill noun MOUNT, fell, height, hillock, hilltop, knoll, mound, tor

hillock noun MOUND, hummock, knoll

hilly adjective MOUNTAINOUS, rolling, undulating

hilt noun HANDLE, grip, haft, handgrip

hinder verb OBSTRUCT, block, check, delay, encumber, frustrate, hamper, handicap, hold up or back, impede, interrupt, stop

hindmost adjective LAST, final, furthest, furthest behind, rearmost, trailing

hindrance noun OBSTACLE, barrier, deterrent, difficulty, drawback, handicap, hitch, impediment, obstruction, restriction, snag, stumbling block

hinge verb DEPEND, be contingent, hang, pivot, rest, revolve around, turn

hint noun **1** INDICATION, allusion, clue, implication, innuendo, insinuation, intimation, suggestion **2** ADVICE, help, pointer, suggestion, tip **3** TRACE, dash, suggestion, suspicion, tinge, touch, undertone ▸verb **4** SUGGEST, imply, indicate, insinuate, intimate

hippie noun BOHEMIAN, beatnik, dropout

hire verb **1** EMPLOY, appoint, commission, engage, sign up, take on **2** RENT, charter, engage, lease, let ▸noun **3** RENTAL, charge, cost, fee, price, rent

hiss noun **1** SIBILATION, buzz, hissing **2** CATCALL, boo, jeer ▸verb **3** WHISTLE, sibilate, wheeze, whirr, whiz **4** JEER, boo, deride, hoot, mock

historic adjective SIGNIFICANT, epoch-making, extraordinary, famous, ground-breaking, momentous, notable, outstanding, remarkable

historical adjective FACTUAL, actual, attested, authentic, documented, real

history noun **1** CHRONICLE, account, annals, narrative, recital, record, story **2** THE PAST, antiquity, olden days, yesterday, yesteryear

hit verb **1** STRIKE, bang, beat,

clout (*informal*), knock, slap, smack, thump, wallop (*informal*), whack **2** COLLIDE WITH, bang into, bump, clash with, crash against, run into, smash into **3** REACH, accomplish, achieve, arrive at, attain, gain **4** AFFECT, damage, devastate, impact on, influence, leave a mark on, overwhelm, touch **5 hit it off** *Informal* GET ON (WELL), be on good terms, click (*slang*), get on like a house on fire (*informal*) ▶ *noun* **6** STROKE, belt (*informal*), blow, clout (*informal*), knock, rap, slap, smack, wallop (*informal*) **7** SUCCESS, sensation, smash (*informal*), triumph, winner

hit-and-miss *adjective* HAPHAZARD, aimless, casual, disorganized, indiscriminate, random, undirected, uneven

hitch *noun* **1** PROBLEM, catch, difficulty, drawback, hindrance, hold-up, impediment, obstacle, snag ▶ *verb* **2** FASTEN, attach, connect, couple, harness, join, tether, tie **3** *Informal* HITCHHIKE, thumb a lift **4 hitch up** PULL UP, jerk, tug, yank

hitherto *adverb* PREVIOUSLY, heretofore, so far, thus far, until now

hit on *verb* THINK UP, arrive at, discover, invent, light upon, strike upon, stumble on

hoard *noun* **1** STORE, accumulation, cache, fund, pile, reserve, stockpile, supply, treasure-trove ▶ *verb* **2** SAVE, accumulate, amass, collect, gather, lay up, put by, stash away (*informal*), stockpile, store

hoarse *adjective* RAUCOUS, croaky, grating, gravelly, gruff, guttural, husky, rasping, rough, throaty

hoax *noun* **1** TRICK, con (*informal*), deception, fraud, practical joke, prank, spoof (*informal*), swindle ▶ *verb* **2** DECEIVE, con (*slang*), dupe, fool, hoodwink, swindle, trick

hobby *noun* PASTIME, diversion, (leisure) activity, leisure pursuit, relaxation

hobnob *verb* SOCIALIZE, associate, consort, fraternize, hang about, hang out (*informal*), keep company, mingle, mix

hoist *verb* **1** RAISE, elevate, erect, heave, lift ▶ *noun* **2** LIFT, crane, elevator, winch

hold *verb* **1** OWN, have, keep, maintain, occupy, possess, retain **2** GRASP, clasp, cling, clutch, cradle, embrace, enfold, grip **3** RESTRAIN, confine, detain, impound, imprison **4** CONSIDER, assume, believe, deem, judge, presume, reckon, regard, think **5** CONVENE, call, conduct, preside over, run **6** ACCOMMODATE, contain, have a capacity for, seat, take ▶ *noun* **7** GRIP, clasp, grasp **8** FOOTHOLD, footing, support **9** CONTROL, influence, mastery

holder *noun* **1** OWNER, bearer, keeper, possessor, proprietor **2** CASE, container, cover

hold forth *verb* SPEAK, declaim, discourse, go on, lecture, preach, spiel (*informal*), spout (*informal*)

hold-up *noun* **1** DELAY, bottleneck, hitch, setback, snag, stoppage, traffic jam, wait **2** ROBBERY, mugging (*informal*), stick-up (*slang*), theft

hold up *verb* 1 DELAY, detain, hinder, retard, set back, slow down, stop 2 SUPPORT, prop, shore up, sustain 3 ROB, mug (*informal*), waylay

hold with *verb* APPROVE OF, agree to *or* with, be in favor of, countenance, subscribe to, support

hole *noun* 1 OPENING, aperture, breach, crack, fissure, gap, orifice, perforation, puncture, tear, vent 2 CAVITY, cave, cavern, chamber, hollow, pit 3 BURROW, den, earth, lair, shelter 4 *Informal* HOVEL, dive (*slang*), dump (*informal*), slum

holiday *noun* 1 VACATION, break, leave, recess, time off 2 FESTIVAL, celebration, feast, fête, gala

holiness *noun* DIVINITY, godliness, piety, purity, righteousness, sacredness, saintliness, sanctity, spirituality

hollow *adjective* 1 EMPTY, unfilled, vacant, void 2 DEEP, dull, low, muted, reverberant 3 WORTHLESS, fruitless, futile, meaningless, pointless, useless, vain ▶ *noun* 4 CAVITY, basin, bowl, crater, depression, hole, pit, trough 5 VALLEY, dale, dell, dingle, glen ▶ *verb* 6 SCOOP, dig, excavate, gouge

holocaust *noun* GENOCIDE, annihilation, conflagration, destruction, devastation, massacre

holy *adjective* 1 DEVOUT, god-fearing, godly, pious, pure, religious, righteous, saintly, virtuous 2 SACRED, blessed, consecrated, hallowed, sacrosanct, sanctified, venerable

homage *noun* RESPECT, adoration, adulation, deference, devotion, honor, reverence, worship

home *noun* 1 HOUSE, abode, domicile, dwelling, habitation, pad (*slang, dated*), residence 2 BIRTHPLACE, home town 3 **at home: a** IN, available, present **b** AT EASE, comfortable, familiar, relaxed 4 **bring home to** MAKE CLEAR, drive home, emphasize, impress upon, press home ▶ *adjective* 5 DOMESTIC, familiar, internal, local, native

homeboy *or* **home girl** *noun Slang* FRIEND, buddy (*informal*), chum (*informal*), comrade, crony, pal (*informal*)

homeland *noun* NATIVE LAND, country of origin, fatherland, mother country, motherland

homeless *adjective* 1 DESTITUTE, displaced, dispossessed, down-and-out, down on one's luck (*informal*) ▶ *noun* 2 **the homeless** VAGRANTS, squatters

homely *adjective U.S.* DOWDY, dumpy (*informal*), frowzy, frumpy, ugly, unattractive, unfashionable

homespun *adjective* UNSOPHISTICATED, coarse, dumpy (*informal*), homely (*U.S.*), home-made, plain, rough

homey *adjective* COMFORTABLE, cozy, friendly, homespun, modest, ordinary, plain, simple, welcoming

homicidal *adjective* MURDEROUS, deadly, lethal, maniacal, mortal

homicide *noun* 1 MURDER, bloodshed, killing, manslaughter, slaying

2 MURDERER, killer, slayer

homily *noun* SERMON, address, discourse, lecture, preaching

homogeneity *noun* UNIFORMITY, consistency, correspondence, sameness, similarity

homogeneous *adjective* UNIFORM, akin, alike, analogous, comparable, consistent, identical, similar, unvarying

hone *verb* SHARPEN, edge, file, grind, point, polish, whet

honest *adjective* **1** TRUSTWORTHY, ethical, honorable, law-abiding, reputable, scrupulous, truthful, upright, virtuous **2** OPEN, candid, direct, forthright, frank, plain, sincere, upfront (*informal*)

honestly *adverb* **1** ETHICALLY, by fair means, cleanly, honorably, lawfully, legally **2** FRANKLY, candidly, in all sincerity, plainly, straight (out), to one's face, truthfully

honesty *noun* **1** INTEGRITY, honor, incorruptibility, morality, probity, rectitude, scrupulousness, trustworthiness, truthfulness, uprightness, virtue **2** FRANKNESS, bluntness, candor, openness, outspokenness, sincerity, straightforwardness

honor *noun* **1** GLORY, credit, dignity, distinction, fame, kudos, prestige, renown, reputation **2** TRIBUTE, accolade, commendation, homage, praise, recognition **3** FAIRNESS, decency, goodness, honesty, integrity, morality, probity, rectitude **4** PRIVILEGE, compliment, credit, pleasure ▶ *verb* **5** RESPECT, adore,

appreciate, esteem, prize, value **6** FULFILL, be true to, carry out, discharge, keep, live up to, observe **7** ACCLAIM, commemorate, commend, decorate, praise **8** ACCEPT, acknowledge, pass, pay, take

honorable *adjective* RESPECTED, creditable, estimable, reputable, respectable, virtuous

honorary *adjective* NOMINAL, complimentary, in name *or* title only, titular, unofficial, unpaid

hoodwink *verb* DECEIVE, con (*informal*), delude, dupe, fool, mislead, swindle, trick

hook *noun* **1** FASTENER, catch, clasp, link, peg ▶ *verb* **2** FASTEN, clasp, fix, secure **3** CATCH, ensnare, entrap, snare, trap

hooked *adjective* **1** BENT, aquiline, curved, hook-shaped **2** ADDICTED, devoted, enamored, obsessed, taken, turned on (*slang*)

hooligan *noun* DELINQUENT, lager lout, ruffian, vandal

hooliganism *noun* DELINQUENCY, disorder, loutishness, rowdiness, vandalism, violence

hoop *noun* RING, band, circlet, girdle, loop, wheel

hoot *noun* **1** CRY, call, toot **2** CATCALL, boo, hiss, jeer ▶ *verb* **3** JEER, boo, hiss, howl down

hop *verb* **1** JUMP, bound, caper, leap, skip, spring, trip, vault ▶ *noun* **2** JUMP, bounce, bound, leap, skip, spring, step, vault

hope *verb* **1** DESIRE, aspire, cross one's fingers, long, look forward to, set one's heart on ▶ *noun* **2** DESIRE, ambition, assumption, dream, expectation, longing

hopeful *adjective* **1** OPTIMISTIC, buoyant, confident, expectant, looking forward to, sanguine **2** PROMISING, auspicious, bright, encouraging, heartening, reassuring, rosy

hopefully *adverb* OPTIMISTICALLY, confidently, expectantly

hopeless *adjective* POINTLESS, futile, impossible, no-win, unattainable, useless, vain

horde *noun* CROWD, band, drove, gang, host, mob, multitude, pack, swarm, throng

horizon *noun* SKYLINE, vista

horizontal *adjective* LEVEL, flat, parallel

horrible *adjective* **1** TERRIFYING, appalling, dreadful, frightful, ghastly, grim, grisly, gruesome, hideous, repulsive, revolting, shocking **2** UNPLEASANT, awful, cruel, disagreeable, dreadful, horrid, lousy (*slang*), mean, nasty, scuzzy (*slang*), terrible

horrid *adjective* **1** UNPLEASANT, awful, disagreeable, dreadful, horrible, terrible **2** UNKIND, beastly (*informal*), cruel, mean, nasty

horrific *adjective* TERRIFYING, appalling, awful, dreadful, frightful, ghastly, grisly, horrendous, horrifying, shocking

horrify *verb* **1** TERRIFY, alarm, frighten, intimidate, make one's hair stand on end, petrify, scare **2** SHOCK, appall, dismay, outrage, sicken

horror *noun* **1** TERROR, alarm, consternation, dread, fear, fright, panic **2** HATRED, aversion, detestation, disgust, loathing,

odium, repugnance, revulsion

horse *noun* NAG, colt, filly, mare, mount, stallion, steed (*archaic or literary*)

horseman *noun* RIDER, cavalier, cavalryman, dragoon, equestrian

horseplay *noun* BUFFOONERY, clowning, fooling around, high jinks, pranks, romping, rough-and-tumble, skylarking (*informal*)

hospitable *adjective* WELCOMING, cordial, friendly, generous, gracious, kind, liberal, sociable

hospitality *noun* WELCOME, conviviality, cordiality, friendliness, neighborliness, sociability, warmth

host¹ *noun* **1** MASTER OF CEREMONIES, entertainer, innkeeper, landlord *or* landlady, proprietor **2** PRESENTER, anchorman *or* anchorwoman ▶ *verb* **3** PRESENT, front (*informal*), introduce

host² *noun* MULTITUDE, army, array, drove, horde, legion, myriad, swarm, throng

hostage *noun* PRISONER, captive, pawn

hostile *adjective* **1** OPPOSED, antagonistic, belligerent, contrary, ill-disposed, rancorous **2** UNFRIENDLY, adverse, inhospitable, unsympathetic, unwelcoming

hostilities *plural noun* WARFARE, conflict, fighting, war

hostility *noun* OPPOSITION, animosity, antipathy, enmity, hatred, ill will, malice, resentment, unfriendliness

hot *adjective* **1** HEATED, boiling, roasting, scalding, scorching, searing, steaming, sultry, sweltering, torrid, warm **2** SPICY, biting, peppery, piquant, pungent, sharp **3** FIERCE, fiery, intense, passionate, raging, stormy, violent **4** RECENT, fresh, just out, latest, new, up to the minute **5** POPULAR, approved, favored, in demand, in vogue, sought-after

hot air *noun* EMPTY TALK, bombast, claptrap (*informal*), guff (*slang*), verbiage, wind

hot-blooded *adjective* PASSIONATE, ardent, excitable, fiery, impulsive, spirited, temperamental, wild

hot-headed *adjective* RASH, fiery, foolhardy, hasty, hot-tempered, impetuous, quick-tempered, reckless, volatile

hot water *noun* (usually preceded by *in*) *Informal* PREDICAMENT, dilemma, fix (*informal*), jam (*informal*), mess, scrape (*informal*), spot (*informal*), tight spot

hound *verb* HARASS, badger, goad, harry, impel, persecute, pester, provoke

house *noun* **1** HOME, abode, domicile, dwelling, habitation, homestead, pad (*slang, dated*), residence **2** FAMILY, household **3** DYNASTY, clan, tribe **4** FIRM, business, company, organization, outfit (*informal*) **5** ASSEMBLY, Commons, legislative body, parliament **6 on the house** FREE, for nothing, gratis ▶*verb* **7** ACCOMMODATE, billet, harbor, lodge, put up, quarter, take in **8** CONTAIN, cover, keep, protect,

sheathe, shelter, store

household *noun* FAMILY, home, house

householder *noun* OCCUPANT, homeowner, resident, tenant

housing *noun* **1** ACCOMMODATION, dwellings, homes, houses **2** CASE, casing, container, cover, covering, enclosure, sheath

hovel *noun* HUT, cabin, den, hole, shack, shanty, shed

hover *verb* **1** FLOAT, drift, flutter, fly, hang **2** LINGER, hang about **3** WAVER, dither, fluctuate, oscillate, vacillate

however *adverb* NEVERTHELESS, after all, anyhow, but, nonetheless, notwithstanding, still, though, yet

howl *noun* **1** CRY, bawl, bay, clamor, groan, roar, scream, shriek, wail ▶*verb* **2** CRY, bawl, bellow, roar, scream, shriek, wail, weep, yell

hub *noun* CENTER, core, focal point, focus, heart, middle, nerve center

huddle *verb* **1** CROWD, cluster, converge, flock, gather, press, throng **2** CURL UP, crouch, hunch up ▶*noun* **3** *Informal* CONFERENCE, discussion, meeting, powwow

hue *noun* COLOR, dye, shade, tinge, tint, tone

hug *verb* **1** CLASP, cuddle, embrace, enfold, hold close, squeeze, take in one's arms ▶*noun* **2** EMBRACE, bear hug, clasp, clinch (*slang*), squeeze

huge *adjective* LARGE, colossal, enormous, gigantic, immense, mammoth, massive, monumental, tremendous, vast

hulk noun 1 WRECK, frame, hull, shell, shipwreck 2 OAF, lout, lubber, lump (*informal*)

hull noun FRAME, body, casing, covering, framework

hum verb 1 MURMUR, buzz, drone, purr, throb, thrum, vibrate, whir 2 BE BUSY, bustle, buzz, pulsate, pulse, stir

human adjective 1 MORTAL, manlike ▶ noun 2 HUMAN BEING, creature, individual, man *or* woman, mortal, person, soul

humane adjective KIND, benign, compassionate, forgiving, good-natured, merciful, sympathetic, tender, understanding

humanitarian adjective 1 COMPASSIONATE, altruistic, benevolent, charitable, humane, philanthropic, public-spirited ▶ noun 2 PHILANTHROPIST, altruist, benefactor, Good Samaritan

humanity noun 1 HUMAN RACE, Homo sapiens, humankind, man, mankind, people 2 HUMAN NATURE, mortality 3 SYMPATHY, charity, compassion, fellow feeling, kind-heartedness, kindness, mercy, philanthropy

humanize verb CIVILIZE, educate, enlighten, improve, soften, tame

humble adjective 1 MODEST, meek, self-effacing, unassuming, unostentatious, unpretentious 2 LOWLY, mean, modest, obscure, ordinary, plebeian, poor, simple, undistinguished ▶ verb 3 HUMILIATE, chasten, crush, disgrace, put (someone) in

their place, subdue, take down a peg (*informal*)

humbug noun 1 FRAUD, charlatan, con man (*informal*), faker, impostor, phoney *or* phony (*informal*), swindler, trickster 2 NONSENSE, baloney (*informal*), cant, claptrap (*informal*), hypocrisy, quackery, rubbish 3 KILLJOY, scrooge (*informal*), spoilsport, wet blanket (*informal*)

humdrum adjective DULL, banal, boring, dreary, monotonous, mundane, ordinary, tedious, tiresome, uneventful

humid adjective DAMP, clammy, dank, moist, muggy, steamy, sticky, sultry, wet

humidity noun DAMP, clamminess, dampness, dankness, moistness, moisture, mugginess, wetness

humiliate verb EMBARRASS, bring low, chasten, crush, degrade, humble, mortify, put down, put (someone) in their place, shame

humiliating adjective EMBARRASSING, crushing, degrading, humbling, ignominious, mortifying, shaming

humiliation noun EMBARRASSMENT, degradation, disgrace, dishonor, humbling, ignominy, indignity, loss of face, mortification, put-down, shame

humility noun MODESTY, humbleness, lowliness, meekness, submissiveness, unpretentiousness

humor noun 1 FUNNINESS, amusement, comedy, drollery, facetiousness, fun, jocularity, ludicrousness 2 JOKING, comedy, farce, jesting, pleasantry, wisecracks (*informal*), wit, witticisms 3 MOOD, disposition, frame of mind, spirits, temper ▸*verb* 4 INDULGE, accommodate, flatter, go along with, gratify, mollify, pander to

humorist *noun* COMEDIAN, card (*informal*), comic, funny man, jester, joker, wag, wit

humorous *adjective* FUNNY, amusing, comic, comical, droll, entertaining, jocular, playful, waggish, witty

hump *noun* LUMP, bulge, bump, mound, projection, protrusion, protuberance, swelling

hunch *noun* 1 FEELING, idea, impression, inkling, intuition, premonition, presentiment, suspicion ▸*verb* 2 DRAW IN, arch, bend, curve

hunger *noun* 1 FAMINE, starvation 2 APPETITE, emptiness, hungriness, ravenousness 3 DESIRE, ache, appetite, craving, itch, lust, thirst, yearning ▸*verb* 4 WANT, ache, crave, desire, hanker, itch, long, thirst, wish, yearn

hungry *adjective* 1 EMPTY, famished, ravenous, starved, starving, voracious 2 EAGER, athirst, avid, covetous, craving, desirous, greedy, keen, yearning

hunk *noun* LUMP, block, chunk, mass, nugget, piece, slab, wedge

hunt *verb* 1 STALK, chase, hound, pursue, track, trail 2 SEARCH, ferret about, forage, look, scour, seek ▸*noun* 3 SEARCH, chase, hunting, investigation, pursuit, quest

hurdle *noun* 1 FENCE, barricade, barrier 2 OBSTACLE, barrier, difficulty, handicap, hazard, hindrance, impediment, obstruction, stumbling block

hurl *verb* THROW, cast, fling, heave, launch, let fly, pitch, propel, sling, toss

hurricane *noun* STORM, cyclone, gale, tempest, tornado, twister (*informal*), typhoon

hurried *adjective* HASTY, brief, cursory, perfunctory, quick, rushed, short, speedy, swift

hurry *verb* 1 RUSH, dash, fly, get a move on (*informal*), make haste, scoot, scurry, step on it (*informal*) ▸*noun* 2 URGENCY, flurry, haste, quickness, rush, speed

hurt *verb* 1 HARM, bruise, damage, disable, impair, injure, mar, spoil, wound 2 ACHE, be sore, be tender, burn, smart, sting, throb 3 SADDEN, annoy, distress, grieve, pain, upset, wound ▸*noun* 4 DISTRESS, discomfort, pain, pang, soreness, suffering ▸*adjective* 5 INJURED, bruised, cut, damaged, harmed, scarred, wounded 6 OFFENDED, aggrieved, crushed, wounded

hurtful *adjective* UNKIND, cruel, cutting, damaging, destructive, malicious, nasty, spiteful, upsetting, wounding

hurtle *verb* RUSH, charge, crash, fly, plunge, race, shoot, speed, stampede, tear

husband *noun* 1 PARTNER, better half (*humorous*), mate, spouse ▸*verb* 2 ECONOMIZE, budget, conserve, hoard, save, store

husbandry noun 1 FARMING, agriculture, cultivation, tillage 2 THRIFT, economy, frugality

hush verb 1 QUIETEN, mute, muzzle, shush, silence ▸ noun 2 QUIET, calm, peace, silence, stillness, tranquillity

hush-hush adjective SECRET, classified, confidential, restricted, top-secret, under wraps

husky adjective 1 HOARSE, croaky, gruff, guttural, harsh, raucous, rough, throaty 2 MUSCULAR, burly, hefty, powerful, rugged, stocky, strapping, thickset

hustle verb JOSTLE, elbow, force, jog, push, shove

hut noun SHED, cabin, den, hovel, lean-to, shanty, shelter

hybrid noun CROSSBREED, amalgam, composite, compound, cross, half-breed, mixture, mongrel

hygiene noun CLEANLINESS, sanitation

hygienic adjective CLEAN, aseptic, disinfected, germ-free, healthy, pure, sanitary, sterile

hymn noun ANTHEM, carol, chant, paean, psalm

hype noun PUBLICITY, ballyhoo (informal), brouhaha, plugging (informal), promotion, razzmatazz (slang)

hypnotic adjective MESMERIC, mesmerizing, sleep-inducing, soothing, soporific, spellbinding

hypnotize verb MESMERIZE, put in a trance, put to sleep

hypocrisy noun INSINCERITY, cant, deceitfulness, deception, duplicity, pretense

hypocrite noun FRAUD, charlatan, deceiver, impostor, phoney or phony (informal), pretender

hypocritical adjective INSINCERE, canting, deceitful, duplicitous, false, fraudulent, phoney or phony (informal), sanctimonious, two-faced

hypothesis noun ASSUMPTION, postulate, premise, proposition, supposition, theory, thesis

hypothetical adjective THEORETICAL, academic, assumed, conjectural, imaginary, putative, speculative, supposed

hysteria noun FRENZY, agitation, delirium, hysterics, madness, panic

hysterical adjective 1 FRENZIED, crazed, distracted, distraught, frantic, overwrought, raving 2 Informal HILARIOUS, comical, side-splitting, uproarious

——— **I i** ———

icy adjective 1 COLD, biting, bitter, chill, chilly, freezing, frosty, ice-cold, raw 2 SLIPPERY, glassy, slippy (informal or dialect) 3 UNFRIENDLY, aloof, cold, distant, frigid, frosty, unwelcoming

idea noun 1 THOUGHT, concept, impression, perception 2 BELIEF, conviction, notion, opinion, teaching, view 3 PLAN, aim, intention, object, objective, purpose

ideal adjective 1 PERFECT, archetypal, classic, complete, consummate, model,

quintessential, supreme ▶ noun
2 MODEL, last word, paradigm,
paragon, pattern, perfection,
prototype, standard

idealist noun ROMANTIC,
dreamer, Utopian, visionary

idealistic adjective PERFECTIONIST,
impracticable, optimistic,
romantic, starry-eyed, Utopian,
visionary

idealize verb ROMANTICIZE,
apotheosize, ennoble, exalt,
glorify, magnify, put on a
pedestal, worship

ideally adverb IN A PERFECT WORLD,
all things being equal, if one
had one's way

identical adjective ALIKE,
duplicate, indistinguishable,
interchangeable, matching,
twin

identification noun
1 RECOGNITION, naming,
pinpointing 2 EMPATHY,
association, connection, fellow
feeling, involvement, rapport,
relationship, sympathy

identify verb 1 RECOGNIZE,
diagnose, make out, name,
pick out, pinpoint, place, point
out, put one's finger on
(informal), spot 2 **identify with**
RELATE TO, associate with,
empathize with, feel for,
respond to

identity noun 1 EXISTENCE,
individuality, personality, self
2 SAMENESS, correspondence,
unity

idiocy noun FOOLISHNESS,
asininity, fatuousness,
imbecility, inanity, insanity,
lunacy, senselessness

idiom noun 1 PHRASE, expression,
turn of phrase 2 LANGUAGE,

jargon, parlance, style,
vernacular

idiosyncrasy noun PECULIARITY,
characteristic, eccentricity,
mannerism, oddity, quirk, trick

idiot noun FOOL, chump, cretin
(offensive), dork (slang),
dunderhead, halfwit, imbecile,
moron, schmuck (slang),
simpleton

idiotic adjective FOOLISH, asinine,
bonkers (informal), crazy, daft
(informal), foolhardy,
harebrained, insane, moronic,
senseless, stupid

idle adjective 1 INACTIVE,
redundant, unemployed,
unoccupied, unused, vacant
2 LAZY, good-for-nothing,
indolent, lackadaisical, shiftless,
slothful, sluggish 3 USELESS,
fruitless, futile, groundless,
ineffective, pointless,
unavailing, unsuccessful, vain,
worthless ▶ verb 4 (often with
away) LAZE, dally, dawdle, kill
time, loaf, loiter, lounge, potter

idleness noun 1 INACTIVITY,
inaction, leisure, time on one's
hands, unemployment
2 LAZINESS, inertia, shiftlessness,
sloth, sluggishness, torpor

idol noun 1 GRAVEN IMAGE, deity,
god 2 HERO, beloved, darling,
favorite, pet, pin-up (slang)

idolatry noun ADORATION,
adulation, exaltation,
glorification

idolize verb WORSHIP, adore, dote
upon, exalt, glorify,
hero-worship, look up to, love,
revere, venerate

idyllic adjective IDEALIZED,
charming, halcyon, heavenly,
ideal, picturesque, unspoiled

if *conjunction* PROVIDED, assuming, on condition that, providing, supposing

ignite *verb* 1 CATCH FIRE, burn, burst into flames, flare up, inflame, take fire 2 SET FIRE TO, kindle, light, set alight, torch

ignominious *adjective* HUMILIATING, discreditable, disgraceful, dishonorable, indecorous, inglorious, shameful, sorry, undignified

ignominy *noun* DISGRACE, discredit, dishonor, disrepute, humiliation, infamy, obloquy, shame, stigma

ignorance *noun* UNAWARENESS, inexperience, innocence, unconsciousness, unfamiliarity

ignorant *adjective* 1 UNINFORMED, benighted, inexperienced, innocent, oblivious, unaware, unconscious, unenlightened, uninitiated, unwitting 2 UNEDUCATED, illiterate 3 INSENSITIVE, crass, half-baked (*informal*), rude

ignore *verb* OVERLOOK, blow off (*slang*), discount, disregard, neglect, pass over, reject, take no notice of, turn a blind eye to

ill *adjective* 1 UNWELL, ailing, diseased, indisposed, infirm, off-color, sick, under the weather (*informal*), unhealthy 2 HARMFUL, bad, damaging, deleterious, detrimental, evil, foul, injurious, unfortunate ▶ *noun* 3 HARM, affliction, hardship, hurt, injury, misery, misfortune, trouble, unpleasantness, woe ▶ *adverb* 4 BADLY, inauspiciously, poorly, unfavorably, unfortunately,

unluckily 5 HARDLY, barely, by no means, scantily

ill-advised *adjective* MISGUIDED, foolhardy, ill-considered, ill-judged, imprudent, incautious, injudicious, rash, reckless, thoughtless, unwise

ill-disposed *adjective* UNFRIENDLY, antagonistic, disobliging, hostile, inimical, uncooperative, unwelcoming

illegal *adjective* UNLAWFUL, banned, criminal, felonious, forbidden, illicit, outlawed, prohibited, unauthorized, unlicensed

illegality *noun* CRIME, felony, illegitimacy, lawlessness, wrong

illegible *adjective* INDECIPHERABLE, obscure, scrawled, unreadable

illegitimate *adjective* 1 UNLAWFUL, illegal, illicit, improper, unauthorized 2 BORN OUT OF WEDLOCK, bastard

ill-fated *adjective* DOOMED, hapless, ill-omened, ill-starred, luckless, star-crossed, unfortunate, unhappy, unlucky

illicit *adjective* 1 ILLEGAL, criminal, felonious, illegitimate, prohibited, unauthorized, unlawful, unlicensed 2 FORBIDDEN, clandestine, furtive, guilty, immoral, improper

illiterate *adjective* UNEDUCATED, ignorant, uncultured, untaught, untutored

ill-mannered *adjective* RUDE, badly behaved, boorish, churlish, discourteous, impolite, insolent, loutish, uncouth

illness *noun* DISEASE, affliction, ailment, disorder, infirmity, malady, sickness

illogical *adjective* IRRATIONAL, absurd, inconsistent, invalid, meaningless, senseless, unreasonable, unscientific, unsound

ill-treat *verb* ABUSE, damage, harm, injure, maltreat, mishandle, misuse, oppress

illuminate *verb* **1** LIGHT UP, brighten **2** EXPLAIN, clarify, clear up, elucidate, enlighten, interpret, make clear, shed light on

illuminating *adjective* INFORMATIVE, enlightening, explanatory, helpful, instructive, revealing

illumination *noun* **1** LIGHT, brightness, lighting, radiance **2** ENLIGHTENMENT, clarification, insight, revelation

illusion *noun* **1** FANTASY, chimera, daydream, figment of the imagination, hallucination, mirage, will-o'-the-wisp **2** MISCONCEPTION, deception, delusion, error, fallacy, misapprehension

illusory *adjective* UNREAL, chimerical, deceptive, delusive, fallacious, false, hallucinatory, mistaken, sham

illustrate *verb* DEMONSTRATE, bring home, elucidate, emphasize, explain, point up, show

illustrated *adjective* PICTORIAL, decorated, graphic

illustration *noun* **1** EXAMPLE, case, instance, specimen **2** PICTURE, decoration, figure, plate, sketch

illustrious *adjective* FAMOUS, celebrated, distinguished, eminent, glorious, great, notable, prominent, renowned

ill will *noun* HOSTILITY, animosity, bad blood, dislike, enmity, hatred, malice, rancor, resentment, venom

image *noun* **1** REPRESENTATION, effigy, figure, icon, idol, likeness, picture, portrait, statue **2** REPLICA, counterpart, (dead) ringer (*slang*), Doppelgänger, double, facsimile, spitting image (*informal*) **3** CONCEPT, idea, impression, mental picture, perception

imaginable *adjective* POSSIBLE, believable, comprehensible, conceivable, credible, likely, plausible

imaginary *adjective* FICTIONAL, fictitious, hypothetical, illusory, imagined, invented, made-up, nonexistent, unreal

imagination *noun* **1** CREATIVITY, enterprise, ingenuity, invention, inventiveness, originality, resourcefulness, vision **2** UNREALITY, illusion, supposition

imaginative *adjective* CREATIVE, clever, enterprising, ingenious, inspired, inventive, original

imagine *verb* **1** ENVISAGE, conceive, conceptualize, conjure up, picture, plan, think of, think up, visualize **2** BELIEVE, assume, conjecture, fancy, guess (*informal*), infer, suppose, surmise, suspect, take it, think

imbecile *noun* **1** IDIOT, chump, cretin (*offensive*), dork (*slang*), fool, halfwit, moron, schmuck (*slang*), thickhead ▶ *adjective* **2** STUPID, asinine, fatuous, feeble-minded, foolish, idiotic, moronic, thick, witless

imbibe verb **1** DRINK, consume, knock back (informal), quaff, sink (informal), swallow, swig (informal) **2** Literary ABSORB, acquire, assimilate, gain, gather, ingest, receive, take in

imbroglio noun COMPLICATION, embarrassment, entanglement, involvement, misunderstanding, quandary

imitate verb COPY, ape, echo, emulate, follow, mimic, mirror, repeat, simulate

imitation noun **1** MIMICRY, counterfeiting, duplication, likeness, resemblance, simulation **2** REPLICA, fake, forgery, impersonation, impression, reproduction, sham, substitution ▶ adjective **3** ARTIFICIAL, dummy, ersatz, man-made, mock, phoney or phony (informal), reproduction, sham, simulated, synthetic

imitative adjective DERIVATIVE, copycat (informal), mimetic, parrot-like, second-hand, simulated, unoriginal

imitator noun IMPERSONATOR, copier, copycat (informal), impressionist, mimic, parrot

immaculate adjective **1** CLEAN, neat, spick-and-span, spotless, spruce, squeaky-clean **2** FLAWLESS, above reproach, faultless, impeccable, perfect, unblemished, unexceptionable, untarnished

immaterial adjective IRRELEVANT, extraneous, inconsequential, inessential, insignificant, of no importance, trivial, unimportant

immature adjective **1** YOUNG, adolescent, undeveloped, unformed, unripe **2** CHILDISH, callow, inexperienced, infantile, juvenile, puerile

immaturity noun **1** UNRIPENESS, greenness, imperfection, rawness, unpreparedness **2** CHILDISHNESS, callowness, inexperience, puerility

immediate adjective **1** INSTANT, instantaneous **2** NEAREST, close, direct, near, next

immediately adverb AT ONCE, directly, forthwith, instantly, now, promptly, right away, straight away, this instant, without delay

immense adjective HUGE, colossal, enormous, extensive, gigantic, great, massive, monumental, stupendous, tremendous, vast

immensity noun SIZE, bulk, enormity, expanse, extent, greatness, hugeness, magnitude, vastness

immerse verb **1** PLUNGE, bathe, dip, douse, duck, dunk, sink, submerge **2** ENGROSS, absorb, busy, engage, involve, occupy, take up

immersion noun **1** DIPPING, dousing, ducking, dunking, plunging, submerging **2** INVOLVEMENT, absorption, concentration, preoccupation

immigrant noun SETTLER, incomer, newcomer

imminent adjective NEAR, at hand, close, coming, forthcoming, gathering, impending, in the pipeline, looming

immobile adjective STATIONARY, at a standstill, at rest, fixed, immovable, motionless, rigid, rooted, static, still, stock-still, unmoving

immobility *noun* STILLNESS, fixity, inertness, motionlessness, stability, steadiness

immobilize *verb* PARALYZE, bring to a standstill, cripple, disable, freeze, halt, stop, transfix

immoderate *adjective* EXCESSIVE, exaggerated, exorbitant, extravagant, extreme, inordinate, over the top (*slang*), undue, unjustified, unreasonable

immoral *adjective* WICKED, bad, corrupt, debauched, depraved, dissolute, indecent, sinful, unethical, unprincipled, wrong

immorality *noun* WICKEDNESS, corruption, debauchery, depravity, dissoluteness, sin, vice, wrong

immortal *adjective* 1 ETERNAL, deathless, enduring, everlasting, imperishable, lasting, perennial, undying ▶ *noun* 2 GOD, goddess 3 GREAT, genius, hero

immortality *noun* 1 ETERNITY, everlasting life, perpetuity 2 FAME, celebrity, glory, greatness, renown

immortalize *verb* COMMEMORATE, celebrate, exalt, glorify

immovable *adjective* 1 FIXED, firm, immutable, jammed, secure, set, stable, stationary, stuck 2 INFLEXIBLE, adamant, obdurate, resolute, steadfast, unshakable, unwavering, unyielding

immune *adjective* EXEMPT, clear, free, invulnerable, proof (against), protected, resistant, safe, unaffected

immunity *noun* 1 EXEMPTION, amnesty, freedom, indemnity, invulnerability, license, release 2 RESISTANCE, immunization, protection

immunize *verb* VACCINATE, inoculate, protect, safeguard

imp *noun* 1 DEMON, devil, sprite 2 RASCAL, brat, minx, rogue, scamp

impact *noun* 1 COLLISION, blow, bump, contact, crash, jolt, knock, smash, stroke, thump 2 EFFECT, consequences, impression, influence, repercussions, significance ▶ *verb* 3 HIT, clash, collide, crash, crush, strike

impair *verb* WORSEN, blunt, damage, decrease, diminish, harm, hinder, injure, lessen, reduce, undermine, weaken

impaired *adjective* DAMAGED, defective, faulty, flawed, imperfect, unsound

impart *verb* 1 COMMUNICATE, convey, disclose, divulge, make known, pass on, relate, reveal, tell 2 GIVE, accord, afford, bestow, confer, grant, lend, yield

impartial *adjective* NEUTRAL, detached, disinterested, equitable, even-handed, fair, just, objective, open-minded, unbiased, unprejudiced

impartiality *noun* NEUTRALITY, detachment, disinterestedness, dispassion, equity, even-handedness, fairness, objectivity, open-mindedness

impassable *adjective* BLOCKED, closed, impenetrable, obstructed

impasse *noun* DEADLOCK, dead end, gridlock, stalemate, standoff, standstill

impassioned *adjective* INTENSE, animated, fervent, fiery, heated, inspired, passionate, rousing, stirring

impatience *noun* 1 HASTE, impetuosity, intolerance, rashness 2 RESTLESSNESS, agitation, anxiety, eagerness, edginess, fretfulness, nervousness, uneasiness

impatient *adjective* 1 HASTY, demanding, hot-tempered, impetuous, intolerant 2 RESTLESS, eager, edgy, fretful, straining at the leash

impeach *verb* CHARGE, accuse, arraign, indict

impeccable *adjective* FAULTLESS, blameless, flawless, immaculate, irreproachable, perfect, unblemished, unimpeachable

impecunious *adjective* POOR, broke (*informal*), destitute, down and out, down on one's luck (*informal*), indigent, insolvent, penniless, poverty-stricken

impede *verb* HINDER, block, check, disrupt, hamper, hold up, obstruct, slow (down), thwart

impediment *noun* OBSTACLE, barrier, difficulty, encumbrance, hindrance, obstruction, snag, stumbling block

impel *verb* FORCE, compel, constrain, drive, induce, oblige, push, require

impending *adjective* LOOMING, approaching, coming, forthcoming, gathering, imminent, in the pipeline, near, upcoming

impenetrable *adjective* 1 SOLID, dense, impassable, impermeable, impervious, inviolable, thick 2 INCOMPREHENSIBLE, arcane, enigmatic, inscrutable, mysterious, obscure, unfathomable, unintelligible

imperative *adjective* URGENT, crucial, essential, pressing, vital

imperceptible *adjective* UNDETECTABLE, faint, indiscernible, microscopic, minute, slight, small, subtle, tiny

imperfect *adjective* FLAWED, damaged, defective, faulty, impaired, incomplete, limited, unfinished

imperfection *noun* FAULT, blemish, defect, deficiency, failing, flaw, frailty, shortcoming, taint, weakness

imperial *adjective* ROYAL, kingly, majestic, princely, queenly, regal, sovereign

imperil *verb* ENDANGER, expose, jeopardize, risk

impersonal *adjective* REMOTE, aloof, cold, detached, dispassionate, formal, inhuman, neutral

impersonate *verb* IMITATE, ape, do (*informal*), masquerade as, mimic, pass oneself off as, pose as (*informal*)

impersonation *noun* IMITATION, caricature, impression, mimicry, parody

impertinence *noun* RUDENESS, brazenness, cheek (*informal*), disrespect, effrontery, front, impudence, insolence, nerve (*informal*), presumption

impertinent *adjective* RUDE, brazen, cheeky (*informal*), disrespectful, impolite, impudent, insolent, presumptuous

imperturbable *adjective* CALM, collected, composed, cool, nerveless, self-possessed, serene, unexcitable, unflappable (*informal*), unruffled

impervious *adjective* 1 SEALED, impassable, impenetrable, impermeable, resistant 2 UNAFFECTED, immune, invulnerable, proof against, unmoved, untouched

impetuosity *noun* HASTE, impulsiveness, precipitateness, rashness

impetuous *adjective* RASH, hasty, impulsive, precipitate, unthinking

impetus *noun* 1 INCENTIVE, catalyst, goad, impulse, motivation, push, spur, stimulus 2 FORCE, energy, momentum, power

impinge *verb* 1 ENCROACH, infringe, invade, obtrude, trespass, violate 2 AFFECT, bear upon, have a bearing on, impact, influence, relate to, touch

impious *adjective* SACRILEGIOUS, blasphemous, godless, irreligious, irreverent, profane, sinful, ungodly, unholy, wicked

impish *adjective* MISCHIEVOUS, devilish, puckish, rascally, roguish, sportive, waggish

implacable *adjective* UNYIELDING, inflexible, intractable, merciless, pitiless, unbending,

uncompromising, unforgiving

implant *verb* 1 INSTILL, inculcate, infuse 2 INSERT, fix, graft

implement *verb* 1 CARRY OUT, bring about, complete, effect, enforce, execute, fulfill, perform, realize ▶ *noun* 2 TOOL, apparatus, appliance, device, gadget, instrument, utensil

implicate *verb* INCRIMINATE, associate, embroil, entangle, include, inculpate, involve

implication *noun* SUGGESTION, inference, innuendo, meaning, overtone, presumption, significance

implicit *adjective* 1 IMPLIED, inferred, latent, tacit, taken for granted, undeclared, understood, unspoken 2 ABSOLUTE, constant, firm, fixed, full, steadfast, unqualified, unreserved, wholehearted

implied *adjective* UNSPOKEN, hinted at, implicit, indirect, suggested, tacit, undeclared, unexpressed, unstated

implore *verb* BEG, beseech, entreat, importune, plead with, pray

imply *verb* 1 HINT, insinuate, intimate, signify, suggest 2 ENTAIL, indicate, involve, mean, point to, presuppose

impolite *adjective* BAD-MANNERED, discourteous, disrespectful, ill-mannered, insolent, loutish, rude, uncouth

impoliteness *noun* BAD MANNERS, boorishness, churlishness, discourtesy, disrespect, insolence, rudeness

import *verb* 1 BRING IN, introduce ▶ *noun* 2 MEANING,

drift, gist, implication, intention, sense, significance, thrust 3 IMPORTANCE, consequence, magnitude, moment, significance, substance, weight

importance noun 1 SIGNIFICANCE, concern, consequence, import, interest, moment, substance, usefulness, value, weight 2 PRESTIGE, distinction, eminence, esteem, influence, prominence, standing, status

important adjective 1 SIGNIFICANT, far-reaching, momentous, seminal, serious, substantial, urgent, weighty 2 POWERFUL, eminent, high-ranking, influential, noteworthy, pre-eminent, prominent

importunate adjective PERSISTENT, demanding, dogged, insistent, pressing, urgent

impose verb 1 ESTABLISH, decree, fix, institute, introduce, levy, ordain 2 INFLICT, appoint, enforce, saddle (someone) with

imposing adjective IMPRESSIVE, commanding, dignified, grand, majestic, stately, striking

imposition noun 1 APPLICATION, introduction, levying 2 INTRUSION, liberty, presumption

impossibility noun HOPELESSNESS, impracticability, inability

impossible adjective 1 UNATTAINABLE, impracticable, inconceivable, out of the question, unachievable, unobtainable, unthinkable 2 ABSURD, ludicrous, outrageous, preposterous, unreasonable

impostor noun IMPERSONATOR,

charlatan, deceiver, fake, fraud, phoney or phony (informal), pretender, sham, trickster

impotence noun POWERLESSNESS, feebleness, frailty, helplessness, inability, incapacity, incompetence, ineffectiveness, paralysis, uselessness, weakness

impotent adjective POWERLESS, feeble, frail, helpless, incapable, incapacitated, incompetent, ineffective, paralyzed, weak

impoverish verb 1 BANKRUPT, beggar, break, ruin 2 DIMINISH, deplete, drain, exhaust, reduce, sap, use up, wear out

impoverished adjective POOR, bankrupt, destitute, impecunious, needy, penurious, poverty-stricken

impracticable adjective UNFEASIBLE, impossible, out of the question, unachievable, unattainable, unworkable

impractical adjective 1 UNWORKABLE, impossible, impracticable, inoperable, nonviable, unrealistic, wild 2 IDEALISTIC, romantic, starry-eyed, unrealistic

imprecise adjective INDEFINITE, equivocal, hazy, ill-defined, indeterminate, inexact, inexplicit, loose, rough, vague, woolly

impregnable adjective INVULNERABLE, impenetrable, indestructible, invincible, secure, unassailable, unbeatable, unconquerable

impregnate verb 1 SATURATE, infuse, permeate, soak, steep, suffuse 2 FERTILIZE, inseminate, make pregnant

impress verb 1 EXCITE, affect,

inspire, make an impression, move, stir, strike, touch **2** STRESS, bring home to, emphasize, fix, inculcate, instill into **3** IMPRINT, emboss, engrave, indent, mark, print, stamp

impression *noun* **1** EFFECT, feeling, impact, influence, reaction **2** IDEA, belief, conviction, feeling, hunch, notion, sense, suspicion **3** MARK, dent, hollow, imprint, indentation, outline, stamp **4** IMITATION, impersonation, parody

impressionable *adjective* SUGGESTIBLE, gullible, ingenuous, open, receptive, responsive, sensitive, susceptible, vulnerable

impressive *adjective* GRAND, awesome, cool (*informal*), dramatic, exciting, moving, phat (*slang*), powerful, stirring, striking

imprint *noun* **1** MARK, impression, indentation, sign, stamp ▶ *verb* **2** FIX, engrave, etch, impress, print, stamp

imprison *verb* JAIL, confine, detain, incarcerate, intern, lock up, put away, send down (*informal*)

imprisoned *adjective* JAILED, behind bars, captive, confined, incarcerated, in jail, inside (*slang*), locked up, under lock and key

imprisonment *noun* CUSTODY, confinement, detention, incarceration

improbability *noun* DOUBT, dubiety, uncertainty, unlikelihood

improbable *adjective* DOUBTFUL,

dubious, fanciful, far-fetched, implausible, questionable, unconvincing, unlikely, weak

impromptu *adjective* UNPREPARED, ad-lib, extemporaneous, improvised, offhand, off the cuff (*informal*), spontaneous, unrehearsed, unscripted

improper *adjective* **1** INDECENT, risqué, smutty, suggestive, unbecoming, unseemly, untoward, vulgar **2** UNWARRANTED, inappropriate, out of place, uncalled-for, unfit, unsuitable

impropriety *noun* INDECENCY, bad taste, incongruity, vulgarity

improve *verb* **1** ENHANCE, advance, better, correct, help, rectify, touch up, upgrade **2** PROGRESS, develop, make strides, pick up, rally, rise

improvement *noun* **1** ENHANCEMENT, advancement, betterment **2** PROGRESS, development, rally, recovery, upswing

improvident *adjective* IMPRUDENT, careless, negligent, prodigal, profligate, reckless, short-sighted, spendthrift, thoughtless, wasteful

improvisation *noun* **1** SPONTANEITY, ad-libbing, extemporizing, invention **2** MAKESHIFT, ad-lib, expedient

improvise *verb* **1** EXTEMPORIZE, ad-lib, busk, invent, play it by ear (*informal*), speak off the cuff (*informal*), wing it (*informal*) **2** CONCOCT, contrive, devise, throw together

imprudent *adjective* UNWISE, careless, foolhardy, ill-advised, ill-considered, ill-judged, injudicious, irresponsible, rash, reckless

impudence noun BOLDNESS, audacity, brazenness, cheek (*informal*), effrontery, impertinence, insolence, nerve (*informal*), presumption, shamelessness

impudent adjective BOLD, audacious, brazen, cheeky (*informal*), impertinent, insolent, pert, presumptuous, rude, shameless

impulse noun URGE, caprice, feeling, inclination, notion, whim, wish

impulsive adjective INSTINCTIVE, devil-may-care, hasty, impetuous, intuitive, passionate, precipitate, rash, spontaneous

impunity noun SECURITY, dispensation, exemption, freedom, immunity, liberty, license, permission

impure adjective 1 UNREFINED, adulterated, debased, mixed 2 CONTAMINATED, defiled, dirty, infected, polluted, tainted 3 IMMORAL, corrupt, indecent, lascivious, lewd, licentious, obscene, unchaste

impurity noun CONTAMINATION, defilement, dirtiness, infection, pollution, taint

imputation noun BLAME, accusation, aspersion, censure, insinuation, reproach, slander, slur

inability noun INCAPABILITY, disability, disqualification, impotence, inadequacy, incapacity, incompetence, ineptitude, powerlessness

inaccessible adjective OUT OF REACH, impassable, out of the way, remote, unapproachable, unattainable, unreachable

inaccuracy noun ERROR, defect, erratum, fault, lapse, mistake

inaccurate adjective INCORRECT, defective, erroneous, faulty, imprecise, mistaken, out, unreliable, unsound, wrong

inactive adjective UNUSED, dormant, idle, inoperative, unemployed, unoccupied

inactivity noun IMMOBILITY, dormancy, hibernation, inaction, passivity, unemployment

inadequacy noun 1 SHORTAGE, dearth, insufficiency, meagerness, paucity, poverty, scantiness 2 INCOMPETENCE, deficiency, inability, incapacity, ineffectiveness 3 SHORTCOMING, defect, failing, imperfection, weakness

inadequate adjective 1 INSUFFICIENT, meager, scant, sketchy, sparse 2 INCOMPETENT, deficient, faulty, found wanting, incapable, lousy (*slang*), not up to scratch (*informal*), unqualified

inadmissible adjective UNACCEPTABLE, inappropriate, irrelevant, unallowable

inadvertently adverb UNINTENTIONALLY, accidentally, by accident, by mistake, involuntarily, mistakenly, unwittingly

inadvisable adjective UNWISE, ill-advised, impolitic, imprudent, inexpedient, injudicious

inane adjective SENSELESS, empty, fatuous, frivolous, futile, idiotic,

mindless, silly, stupid, vacuous
inanimate *adjective* LIFELESS, cold, dead, defunct, extinct, inert
inapplicable *adjective* IRRELEVANT, inappropriate, unsuitable
inappropriate *adjective* UNSUITABLE, improper, incongruous, out of place, unbecoming, unbefitting, unfitting, unseemly, untimely
inarticulate *adjective* FALTERING, halting, hesitant, poorly spoken
inattention *noun* NEGLECT, absent-mindedness, carelessness, daydreaming, inattentiveness, preoccupation, thoughtlessness
inattentive *adjective* PREOCCUPIED, careless, distracted, dreamy, negligent, unobservant, vague
inaudible *adjective* INDISTINCT, low, mumbling, out of earshot, stifled, unheard
inaugural *adjective* FIRST, initial, introductory, maiden, opening
inaugurate *verb* 1 LAUNCH, begin, commence, get under way, initiate, institute, introduce, set in motion
2 INVEST, induct, install
inauguration *noun* 1 LAUNCH, initiation, institution, opening, setting up 2 INVESTITURE, induction, installation
inauspicious *adjective* UNPROMISING, bad, discouraging, ill-omened, ominous, unfavorable, unfortunate, unlucky, unpropitious
inborn *adjective* NATURAL, congenital, hereditary, inbred, ingrained, inherent, innate, instinctive, intuitive, native
inbred *adjective* INNATE,

constitutional, deep-seated, ingrained, inherent, native, natural
incalculable *adjective* COUNTLESS, boundless, infinite, innumerable, limitless, numberless, untold, vast
incantation *noun* CHANT, charm, formula, invocation, spell
incapable *adjective*
1 INCOMPETENT, feeble, inadequate, ineffective, inept, inexpert, insufficient, lousy (*slang*), unfit, unqualified, weak
2 UNABLE, helpless, impotent, powerless
incapacitate *verb* DISABLE, cripple, immobilize, lay up (*informal*), paralyze, put out of action (*informal*)
incapacitated *adjective* INDISPOSED, *hors de combat*, immobilized, laid up (*informal*), out of action (*informal*), unfit
incapacity *noun* INABILITY, impotence, inadequacy, incapability, incompetency, ineffectiveness, powerlessness, unfitness, weakness
incarcerate *verb* IMPRISON, confine, detain, impound, intern, jail, lock up, throw in jail
incarceration *noun* IMPRISONMENT, captivity, confinement, detention, internment
incarnate *adjective* PERSONIFIED, embodied, typified
incarnation *noun* EMBODIMENT, epitome, manifestation, personification, type
incense *verb* ANGER, enrage, inflame, infuriate, irritate, madden, make one's hackles rise, rile (*informal*)

incensed *adjective* ANGRY, enraged, fuming, furious, indignant, infuriated, irate, maddened, steamed up (*slang*), up in arms

incentive *noun* ENCOURAGEMENT, bait, carrot (*informal*), enticement, inducement, lure, motivation, spur, stimulus

inception *noun* BEGINNING, birth, commencement, dawn, initiation, origin, outset, start

incessant *adjective* ENDLESS, ceaseless, constant, continual, eternal, interminable, never-ending, nonstop, perpetual, twenty-four-seven (*slang*), unceasing, unending

incessantly *adverb* ENDLESSLY, ceaselessly, constantly, continually, eternally, interminably, nonstop, perpetually, persistently, twenty-four-seven (*slang*)

incident *noun* **1** HAPPENING, adventure, episode, event, fact, matter, occasion, occurrence **2** DISTURBANCE, clash, commotion, confrontation, contretemps, scene

incidental *adjective* SECONDARY, ancillary, minor, nonessential, occasional, subordinate, subsidiary

incidentally *adverb* PARENTHETICALLY, by the bye, by the way, in passing

incinerate *verb* BURN UP, carbonize, char, cremate, reduce to ashes

incipient *adjective* BEGINNING, commencing, developing, embryonic, inchoate, nascent, starting

incision *noun* CUT, gash, notch, opening, slash, slit

incisive *adjective* PENETRATING, acute, keen, perspicacious, piercing, trenchant

incite *verb* PROVOKE, encourage, foment, inflame, instigate, spur, stimulate, stir up, urge, whip up

incitement *noun* PROVOCATION, agitation, encouragement, impetus, instigation, prompting, spur, stimulus

incivility *noun* RUDENESS, bad manners, boorishness, discourteousness, discourtesy, disrespect, ill-breeding, impoliteness

inclement *adjective* STORMY, foul, harsh, intemperate, rough, severe, tempestuous

inclination *noun* **1** TENDENCY, disposition, liking, partiality, penchant, predilection, predisposition, proclivity, proneness, propensity **2** SLOPE, angle, gradient, incline, pitch, slant, tilt

incline *verb* **1** PREDISPOSE, influence, persuade, prejudice, sway **2** SLOPE, lean, slant, tilt, tip, veer ▶ *noun* **3** SLOPE, ascent, descent, dip, grade, gradient, rise

inclined *adjective* DISPOSED, apt, given, liable, likely, minded, predisposed, prone, willing

include *verb* **1** CONTAIN, comprise, cover, embrace, encompass, incorporate, involve, subsume, take in **2** INTRODUCE, add, enter, insert

inclusion *noun* ADDITION, incorporation, insertion

inclusive *adjective* COMPREHENSIVE, across-the-board,

all-embracing, blanket, general, global, sweeping, umbrella

incognito *adjective* IN DISGUISE, disguised, under an assumed name, unknown, unrecognized

incoherence *noun* UNINTELLIGIBILITY, disjointedness, inarticulateness

incoherent *adjective* UNINTELLIGIBLE, confused, disjointed, disordered, inarticulate, inconsistent, jumbled, muddled, rambling, stammering, stuttering

income *noun* REVENUE, earnings, pay, proceeds, profits, receipts, salary, takings, wages

incoming *adjective* ARRIVING, approaching, entering, homeward, landing, new, returning

incomparable *adjective* UNEQUALED, beyond compare, inimitable, matchless, peerless, superlative, supreme, transcendent, unmatched, unparalleled, unrivaled

incompatible *adjective* INCONSISTENT, conflicting, contradictory, incongruous, mismatched, unsuited

incompetence *noun* INEPTITUDE, inability, inadequacy, incapability, incapacity, ineffectiveness, unfitness, uselessness

incompetent *adjective* INEPT, bungling, floundering, incapable, ineffectual, inexpert, unfit, useless

incomplete *adjective* UNFINISHED, deficient, fragmentary, imperfect, partial, wanting

incomprehensible *adjective* UNINTELLIGIBLE, baffling, beyond

one's grasp, impenetrable, obscure, opaque, perplexing, puzzling, unfathomable

inconceivable *adjective* UNIMAGINABLE, beyond belief, incomprehensible, incredible, mind-boggling (*informal*), out of the question, unbelievable, unheard-of, unthinkable

inconclusive *adjective* INDECISIVE, ambiguous, indeterminate, open, unconvincing, undecided, up in the air (*informal*), vague

incongruity *noun* INAPPROPRIATENESS, conflict, discrepancy, disparity, incompatibility, inconsistency, unsuitability

incongruous *adjective* INAPPROPRIATE, discordant, improper, incompatible, out of keeping, out of place, unbecoming, unsuitable

inconsiderable *adjective* INSIGNIFICANT, inconsequential, minor, negligible, slight, small, trifling, trivial, unimportant

inconsiderate *adjective* SELFISH, indelicate, insensitive, rude, tactless, thoughtless, unkind, unthinking

inconsistency *noun*
1 INCOMPATIBILITY, disagreement, discrepancy, disparity, divergence, incongruity, variance 2 UNRELIABILITY, fickleness, instability, unpredictability, unsteadiness

inconsistent *adjective*
1 INCOMPATIBLE, at odds, conflicting, contradictory, discordant, incongruous, irreconcilable, out of step
2 CHANGEABLE, capricious,

erratic, fickle, unpredictable, unstable, unsteady, variable

inconsolable *adjective*
HEARTBROKEN, brokenhearted, desolate, despairing

inconspicuous *adjective*
UNOBTRUSIVE, camouflaged, hidden, insignificant, ordinary, plain, unassuming, unnoticeable, unostentatious

incontrovertible *adjective*
INDISPUTABLE, certain, established, incontestable, indubitable, irrefutable, positive, sure, undeniable, unquestionable

inconvenience *noun* 1 TROUBLE, awkwardness, bother, difficulty, disadvantage, disruption, disturbance, fuss, hindrance, nuisance ▶ *verb* 2 TROUBLE, bother, discommode, disrupt, disturb, put out, upset

inconvenient *adjective*
TROUBLESOME, awkward, bothersome, disadvantageous, disturbing, inopportune, unsuitable, untimely

incorporate *verb* INCLUDE, absorb, assimilate, blend, combine, integrate, merge, subsume

incorrect *adjective* FALSE, erroneous, faulty, flawed, inaccurate, mistaken, untrue, wrong

incorrigible *adjective* INCURABLE, hardened, hopeless, intractable, inveterate, irredeemable, unreformed

incorruptible *adjective*
1 HONEST, above suspicion, straight, trustworthy, upright
2 IMPERISHABLE, everlasting, undecaying

increase *verb* 1 GROW, advance,

boost, develop, enlarge, escalate, expand, extend, multiply, raise, spread, swell ▶ *noun* 2 GROWTH, development, enlargement, escalation, expansion, extension, gain, increment, rise, upturn

increasingly *adverb*
PROGRESSIVELY, more and more

incredible *adjective*
1 IMPLAUSIBLE, beyond belief, far-fetched, improbable, inconceivable, preposterous, unbelievable, unimaginable, unthinkable 2 *Informal* AMAZING, astonishing, astounding, extraordinary, prodigious, sensational (*informal*), wonderful

incredulity *noun* DISBELIEF, distrust, doubt, skepticism

incredulous *adjective*
DISBELIEVING, distrustful, doubtful, dubious, skeptical, suspicious, unbelieving, unconvinced

increment *noun* INCREASE, accrual, addition, advancement, augmentation, enlargement, gain, step up, supplement

incriminate *verb* IMPLICATE, accuse, blame, charge, impeach, inculpate, involve

incumbent *adjective* OBLIGATORY, binding, compulsory, mandatory, necessary

incur *verb* EARN, arouse, bring (upon oneself), draw, expose oneself to, gain, meet with, provoke

incurable *adjective* FATAL, inoperable, irremediable, terminal

indebted *adjective* GRATEFUL, beholden, in debt, obligated, obliged, under an obligation

indecency noun OBSCENITY, immodesty, impropriety, impurity, indelicacy, lewdness, licentiousness, pornography, vulgarity

indecent adjective 1 LEWD, crude, dirty, filthy, immodest, improper, impure, licentious, pornographic, salacious, scuzzy (*slang*), X-rated 2 UNBECOMING, in bad taste, indecorous, unseemly, vulgar

indecipherable adjective ILLEGIBLE, indistinguishable, unintelligible, unreadable

indecision noun HESITATION, dithering, doubt, indecisiveness, uncertainty, vacillation, wavering

indecisive adjective HESITATING, dithering, faltering, in two minds (*informal*), tentative, uncertain, undecided, vacillating, wavering

indeed adverb REALLY, actually, certainly, in truth, truly, undoubtedly

indefensible adjective UNFORGIVABLE, inexcusable, unjustifiable, unpardonable, untenable, unwarrantable, wrong

indefinable adjective INEXPRESSIBLE, impalpable, indescribable

indefinite adjective UNCLEAR, doubtful, equivocal, ill-defined, imprecise, indeterminate, inexact, uncertain, unfixed, vague

indefinitely adverb ENDLESSLY, ad infinitum, continually, for ever

indelible adjective PERMANENT, enduring, indestructible,

ineradicable, ingrained, lasting

indelicate adjective OFFENSIVE, coarse, crude, embarrassing, immodest, off-color, risqué, rude, suggestive, tasteless, vulgar

indemnify verb 1 INSURE, guarantee, protect, secure, underwrite 2 COMPENSATE, reimburse, remunerate, repair, repay

indemnity noun 1 INSURANCE, guarantee, protection, security 2 COMPENSATION, redress, reimbursement, remuneration, reparation, restitution

independence noun FREEDOM, autonomy, liberty, self-reliance, self-rule, self-sufficiency, sovereignty

independent adjective 1 FREE, liberated, separate, unconstrained, uncontrolled 2 SELF-GOVERNING, autonomous, nonaligned, self-determining, sovereign 3 SELF-SUFFICIENT, liberated, self-contained, self-reliant, self-supporting

independently adverb SEPARATELY, alone, autonomously, by oneself, individually, on one's own, solo, unaided

indescribable adjective UNUTTERABLE, beyond description, beyond words, indefinable, inexpressible

indestructible adjective PERMANENT, enduring, everlasting, immortal, imperishable, incorruptible, indelible, indissoluble, lasting, unbreakable

indeterminate adjective UNCERTAIN, imprecise, indefinite, inexact, undefined, unfixed, unspecified, unstipulated, vague

indicate verb 1 SIGNIFY, betoken, denote, imply, manifest, point to, reveal, suggest 2 POINT OUT, designate, specify 3 SHOW, display, express, read, record, register

indication noun SIGN, clue, evidence, hint, inkling, intimation, manifestation, mark, suggestion, symptom

indicative adjective SUGGESTIVE, pointing to, significant, symptomatic

indicator noun SIGN, gauge, guide, mark, meter, pointer, signal, symbol

indict verb CHARGE, accuse, arraign, impeach, prosecute, summon

indictment noun CHARGE, accusation, allegation, impeachment, prosecution, summons

indifference noun DISREGARD, aloofness, apathy, coldness, coolness, detachment, inattention, negligence, nonchalance, unconcern

indifferent adjective 1 UNCONCERNED, aloof, callous, cold, cool, detached, impervious, inattentive, uninterested, unmoved, unsympathetic 2 MEDIOCRE, moderate, ordinary, passable, so-so (informal), undistinguished

indigestion noun HEARTBURN, dyspepsia, upset stomach

indignant adjective RESENTFUL, angry, disgruntled, exasperated, incensed, irate, peeved (informal), riled, scornful, ticked off (informal), up in arms (informal)

indignation noun RESENTMENT, anger, exasperation, pique, rage, scorn, umbrage

indignity noun HUMILIATION, affront, dishonor, disrespect, injury, insult, opprobrium, slight, snub

indirect adjective 1 CIRCUITOUS, long-drawn-out, meandering, oblique, rambling, roundabout, tortuous, wandering 2 INCIDENTAL, secondary, subsidiary, unintended

indiscreet adjective TACTLESS, impolitic, imprudent, incautious, injudicious, naive, rash, reckless, unwise

indiscretion noun MISTAKE, error, faux pas, folly, foolishness, gaffe, lapse, slip

indiscriminate adjective RANDOM, careless, desultory, general, uncritical, undiscriminating, unsystematic, wholesale

indispensable adjective ESSENTIAL, crucial, imperative, key, necessary, needed, requisite, vital

indisposed adjective ILL, ailing, sick, under the weather, unwell

indisposition noun ILLNESS, ailment, ill health, sickness

indisputable adjective UNDENIABLE, beyond doubt, certain, incontestable, incontrovertible, indubitable, irrefutable, unquestionable

indistinct adjective UNCLEAR, blurred, faint, fuzzy, hazy, ill-defined, indeterminate, shadowy, undefined, vague

individual adjective 1 PERSONAL, characteristic, distinctive, exclusive, idiosyncratic, own, particular, peculiar, singular, special, specific, unique ▸ *noun* **2** PERSON, being, character, creature, soul, unit

individualist *noun* MAVERICK, freethinker, independent, loner, lone wolf, nonconformist, original

individuality *noun* DISTINCTIVENESS, character, originality, personality, separateness, singularity, uniqueness

individually *adverb* SEPARATELY, apart, independently, one at a time, one by one, singly

indoctrinate *verb* TRAIN, brainwash, drill, ground, imbue, initiate, instruct, school, teach

indoctrination *noun* TRAINING, brainwashing, drilling, grounding, inculcation, instruction, schooling

indolent *adjective* LAZY, idle, inactive, inert, languid, lethargic, listless, slothful, sluggish, workshy

indomitable *adjective* INVINCIBLE, bold, resolute, staunch, steadfast, unbeatable, unconquerable, unflinching, unyielding

indubitable *adjective* CERTAIN, incontestable, incontrovertible, indisputable, irrefutable, obvious, sure, undeniable, unquestionable

induce *verb* **1** PERSUADE, convince, encourage, incite, influence, instigate, prevail upon, prompt, talk into **2** CAUSE, bring about, effect, engender, generate, give rise to, lead to, occasion, produce

inducement *noun* INCENTIVE, attraction, bait, carrot (*informal*), encouragement, incitement, lure, reward

indulge *verb* **1** GRATIFY, feed, give way to, pander to, satisfy, yield to **2** SPOIL, cosset, give in to, go along with, humor, pamper

indulgence *noun* **1** GRATIFICATION, appeasement, fulfillment, satiation, satisfaction **2** LUXURY, extravagance, favor, privilege, treat **3** TOLERANCE, forbearance, patience, understanding

indulgent *adjective* LENIENT, compliant, easy-going, forbearing, kindly, liberal, permissive, tolerant, understanding

industrialist *noun* CAPITALIST, big businessman, captain of industry, magnate, manufacturer, tycoon

industrious *adjective* HARD-WORKING, busy, conscientious, diligent, energetic, persistent, purposeful, tireless, zealous

industry *noun* **1** BUSINESS, commerce, manufacturing, production, trade **2** EFFORT, activity, application, diligence, labor, tirelessness, toil, zeal

inebriated *adjective* DRUNK, crocked (*slang*), intoxicated, paralytic (*informal*), plastered (*slang*), three sheets to the wind (*slang*), tipsy, under the influence (*informal*)

ineffective *adjective* USELESS, fruitless, futile, idle, impotent, inefficient, unavailing, unproductive, vain, worthless

ineffectual *adjective* WEAK,

feeble, impotent, inadequate, incompetent, ineffective, inept, lousy (*slang*)

inefficiency *noun* INCOMPETENCE, carelessness, disorganization, muddle, slackness, sloppiness

inefficient *adjective* INCOMPETENT, disorganized, ineffectual, inept, wasteful, weak

ineligible *adjective* UNQUALIFIED, disqualified, ruled out, unacceptable, unfit, unsuitable

inept *adjective* INCOMPETENT, bumbling, bungling, clumsy, inexpert, maladroit

ineptitude *noun* INCOMPETENCE, clumsiness, inexpertness, unfitness

inequality *noun* DISPARITY, bias, difference, disproportion, diversity, irregularity, prejudice, unevenness

inequitable *adjective* UNFAIR, biased, discriminatory, one-sided, partial, partisan, preferential, prejudiced, unjust

inert *adjective* INACTIVE, dead, dormant, immobile, lifeless, motionless, static, still, unreactive, unresponsive

inertia *noun* INACTIVITY, apathy, immobility, lethargy, listlessness, passivity, sloth, unresponsiveness

inescapable *adjective* UNAVOIDABLE, certain, destined, fated, ineluctable, inevitable, inexorable, sure

inestimable *adjective* INCALCULABLE, immeasurable, invaluable, precious, priceless, prodigious

inevitable *adjective* UNAVOIDABLE, assured, certain, destined, fixed, ineluctable, inescapable,

inexorable, sure

inevitably *adverb* UNAVOIDABLY, as a result, automatically, certainly, necessarily, of necessity, perforce, surely, willy-nilly

inexcusable *adjective* UNFORGIVABLE, indefensible, outrageous, unjustifiable, unpardonable, unwarrantable

inexorable *adjective* UNRELENTING, inescapable, relentless, remorseless, unbending, unyielding

inexpensive *adjective* CHEAP, bargain, budget, economical, modest, reasonable

inexperience *noun* UNFAMILIARITY, callowness, greenness, ignorance, newness, rawness

inexperienced *adjective* IMMATURE, callow, green, new, raw, unpracticed, untried, unversed

inexpert *adjective* AMATEURISH, bungling, clumsy, inept, maladroit, unpracticed, unprofessional, unskilled

inexplicable *adjective* UNACCOUNTABLE, baffling, enigmatic, incomprehensible, insoluble, mysterious, mystifying, strange, unfathomable, unintelligible

inextricably *adverb* INSEPARABLY, indissolubly, indistinguishably, intricately, irretrievably, totally

infallibility *noun* PERFECTION, impeccability, omniscience, supremacy, unerringness

infallible *adjective* FOOLPROOF, certain, dependable, reliable, sure, sure-fire (*informal*), trustworthy, unbeatable, unfailing

infamous *adjective* NOTORIOUS, disreputable, ignominious, ill-famed

infancy *noun* BEGINNINGS, cradle, dawn, inception, origins, outset, start

infant *noun* BABY, babe, child, minor, toddler, tot

infantile *adjective* CHILDISH, babyish, immature, puerile

infatuate *verb* OBSESS, besot, bewitch, captivate, enchant, enrapture, fascinate

infatuated *adjective* OBSESSED, besotted, bewitched, captivated, carried away, enamored, enraptured, fascinated, possessed, smitten (*informal*), spellbound

infatuation *noun* OBSESSION, crush (*informal*), fixation, madness, passion, thing (*informal*)

infect *verb* CONTAMINATE, affect, blight, corrupt, defile, poison, pollute, taint

infection *noun* CONTAMINATION, contagion, corruption, defilement, poison, pollution, virus

infectious *adjective* CATCHING, communicable, contagious, spreading, transmittable, virulent

infer *verb* DEDUCE, conclude, derive, gather, presume, surmise, understand

inference *noun* DEDUCTION, assumption, conclusion, presumption, reading, surmise

inferior *adjective* **1** LOWER, lesser, menial, minor, secondary, subordinate, subsidiary ▶ *noun* **2** UNDERLING, junior, menial, subordinate

inferiority *noun* **1** INADEQUACY, deficiency, imperfection, insignificance, mediocrity, shoddiness, worthlessness **2** SUBSERVIENCE, abasement, lowliness, subordination

infernal *adjective* DEVILISH, accursed, damnable, damned, diabolical, fiendish, hellish, satanic

infertile *adjective* BARREN, sterile, unfruitful, unproductive

infertility *noun* STERILITY, barrenness, infecundity, unproductiveness

infest *verb* OVERRUN, beset, invade, penetrate, permeate, ravage, swarm, throng

infested *adjective* OVERRUN, alive, crawling, ravaged, ridden, swarming, teeming

infiltrate *verb* PENETRATE, filter through, insinuate oneself, make inroads (into), percolate, permeate, pervade, sneak in (*informal*)

infinite *adjective* NEVER-ENDING, boundless, eternal, everlasting, illimitable, immeasurable, inexhaustible, limitless, measureless, unbounded

infinitesimal *adjective* MICROSCOPIC, insignificant, minuscule, minute, negligible, teeny, tiny, unnoticeable

infinity *noun* ETERNITY, boundlessness, endlessness, immensity, vastness

infirm *adjective* FRAIL, ailing, debilitated, decrepit, doddering, enfeebled, failing, feeble, weak

infirmity *noun* FRAILTY, decrepitude, ill health, sickliness, vulnerability

inflame *verb* ENRAGE, anger, arouse, excite, incense, infuriate, madden, provoke, rouse, stimulate

inflamed *adjective* SORE, fevered, hot, infected, red, swollen

inflammable *adjective* FLAMMABLE, combustible, incendiary

inflammation *noun* SORENESS, painfulness, rash, redness, tenderness

inflammatory *adjective* PROVOCATIVE, explosive, fiery, intemperate, like a red rag to a bull, rabble-rousing

inflate *verb* EXPAND, bloat, blow up, dilate, distend, enlarge, increase, puff up *or* out, pump up, swell

inflated *adjective* EXAGGERATED, ostentatious, overblown, swollen

inflation *noun* EXPANSION, enlargement, escalation, extension, increase, rise, spread, swelling

inflexibility *noun* OBSTINACY, intransigence, obduracy

inflexible *adjective* 1 OBSTINATE, implacable, intractable, obdurate, resolute, set in one's ways, steadfast, stubborn, unbending, uncompromising 2 INELASTIC, hard, rigid, stiff, taut

inflict *verb* IMPOSE, administer, apply, deliver, levy, mete *or* deal out, visit, wreak

infliction *noun* IMPOSITION, administration, perpetration, wreaking

influence *noun* 1 EFFECT, authority, control, domination, magnetism, pressure, weight 2 POWER, clout (*informal*), hold, importance, leverage, prestige, pull (*informal*) ▶ *verb* 3 AFFECT, control, direct, guide, manipulate, sway

influential *adjective* IMPORTANT, authoritative, instrumental, leading, potent, powerful, significant, telling, weighty

influx *noun* ARRIVAL, incursion, inrush, inundation, invasion, rush

inform *verb* 1 TELL, advise, communicate, enlighten, instruct, notify, teach, tip off 2 INCRIMINATE, betray, blow the whistle on (*informal*), denounce, inculpate, squeal (*slang*)

informal *adjective* RELAXED, casual, colloquial, cozy, easy, familiar, homey, natural, simple, unofficial

informality *noun* FAMILIARITY, casualness, ease, naturalness, relaxation, simplicity

information *noun* FACTS, data, intelligence, knowledge, message, news, notice, report

informative *adjective* INSTRUCTIVE, chatty, communicative, edifying, educational, enlightening, forthcoming, illuminating, revealing

informed *adjective* KNOWLEDGEABLE, enlightened, erudite, expert, familiar, in the picture, learned, up to date, versed, well-read

informer *noun* BETRAYER, accuser, Judas, sneak, stool pigeon

infrequent *adjective* OCCASIONAL, few and far between, once in a blue moon, rare, sporadic, uncommon, unusual

infringe *verb* BREAK, contravene,

disobey, transgress, violate

infringement *noun* CONTRAVENTION, breach, infraction, transgression, trespass, violation

infuriate *verb* ENRAGE, anger, exasperate, incense, irritate, madden, provoke, rile

infuriating *adjective* ANNOYING, exasperating, galling, irritating, maddening, mortifying, provoking, vexatious

ingenious *adjective* CREATIVE, bright, brilliant, clever, crafty, inventive, original, resourceful, shrewd

ingenuity *noun* ORIGINALITY, cleverness, flair, genius, gift, inventiveness, resourcefulness, sharpness, shrewdness

ingenuous *adjective* NAIVE, artless, guileless, honest, innocent, open, plain, simple, sincere, trusting, unsophisticated

inglorious *adjective* DISHONORABLE, discreditable, disgraceful, disreputable, ignoble, ignominious, infamous, shameful, unheroic

ingratiate *verb* PANDER TO, brown-nose (*slang*), crawl, curry favor, fawn, flatter, grovel, insinuate oneself, kiss ass (*slang*), toady

ingratiating *adjective* SYCOPHANTIC, crawling, fawning, flattering, humble, obsequious, servile, toadying, unctuous

ingratitude *noun* UNGRATEFULNESS, thanklessness

ingredient *noun* COMPONENT, constituent, element, part

inhabit *verb* LIVE, abide, dwell, occupy, populate, reside

inhabitant *noun* DWELLER, citizen, denizen, inmate, native, occupant, occupier, resident, tenant

inhabited *adjective* POPULATED, colonized, developed, occupied, peopled, settled, tenanted

inhale *verb* BREATHE IN, draw in, gasp, respire, suck in

inherent *adjective* INNATE, essential, hereditary, inborn, inbred, inbuilt, ingrained, inherited, intrinsic, native, natural

inherit *verb* BE LEFT, come into, fall heir to, succeed to

inheritance *noun* LEGACY, bequest, birthright, heritage, patrimony

inhibit *verb* RESTRAIN, check, constrain, curb, discourage, frustrate, hinder, hold back *or* in, impede, obstruct

inhibited *adjective* SHY, constrained, guarded, repressed, reserved, reticent, self-conscious, subdued

inhibition *noun* SHYNESS, block, hang-up (*informal*), reserve, restraint, reticence, self-consciousness

inhospitable *adjective* 1 UNWELCOMING, cool, uncongenial, unfriendly, unreceptive, unsociable, xenophobic 2 BLEAK, barren, desolate, forbidding, godforsaken, hostile

inhuman *adjective* CRUEL, barbaric, brutal, cold-blooded, heartless, merciless, pitiless, ruthless, savage, unfeeling

inhumane *adjective* CRUEL, brutal, heartless, pitiless, unfeeling, unkind, unsympathetic

inhumanity noun CRUELTY, atrocity, barbarism, brutality, heartlessness, pitilessness, ruthlessness, unkindness

inimical adjective HOSTILE, adverse, antagonistic, ill-disposed, opposed, unfavorable, unfriendly, unwelcoming

inimitable adjective UNIQUE, consummate, incomparable, matchless, peerless, unparalleled, unrivaled

iniquitous adjective WICKED, criminal, evil, immoral, reprehensible, sinful, unjust

iniquity noun WICKEDNESS, abomination, evil, injustice, sin, wrong

initial adjective FIRST, beginning, incipient, introductory, opening, primary

initially adverb AT FIRST, at or in the beginning, first, firstly, originally, primarily

initiate verb 1 BEGIN, commence, get under way, kick off (informal), launch, open, originate, set in motion, start 2 INDUCT, indoctrinate, introduce, invest 3 INSTRUCT, acquaint with, coach, familiarize with, teach, train ▶noun 4 NOVICE, beginner, convert, entrant, learner, member, probationer

initiation noun INTRODUCTION, debut, enrollment, entrance, inauguration, induction, installation, investiture

initiative noun 1 FIRST STEP, advantage, first move, lead 2 RESOURCEFULNESS, ambition,

drive, dynamism, enterprise, get-up-and-go (informal), leadership

inject verb 1 VACCINATE, inoculate 2 INTRODUCE, bring in, infuse, insert, instill

injection noun 1 VACCINATION, inoculation, shot (informal) 2 INTRODUCTION, dose, infusion, insertion

injudicious adjective UNWISE, foolish, ill-advised, ill-judged, impolitic, imprudent, incautious, inexpedient, rash, unthinking

injunction noun ORDER, command, exhortation, instruction, mandate, precept, ruling

injure verb HURT, damage, harm, impair, ruin, spoil, undermine, wound

injured adjective HURT, broken, challenged, damaged, disabled, undermined, weakened, wounded

injury noun HARM, damage, detriment, disservice, hurt, ill, trauma (Pathology), wound, wrong

injustice noun UNFAIRNESS, bias, discrimination, inequality, inequity, iniquity, oppression, partisanship, prejudice, wrong

inkling noun SUSPICION, clue, conception, hint, idea, indication, intimation, notion, suggestion, whisper

inland adjective INTERIOR, domestic, internal, upcountry

inlet noun BAY, bight, creek, firth or frith (Scot.), fjord, passage

inmost or **innermost** adjective DEEPEST, basic, central, essential, intimate, personal, private, secret

innate *adjective* INBORN, congenital, constitutional, essential, inbred, ingrained, inherent, instinctive, intuitive, native, natural

inner *adjective* **1** INSIDE, central, interior, internal, inward, middle **2** PRIVATE, hidden, intimate, personal, repressed, secret, unrevealed

innkeeper *noun* PUBLICAN, host *or* hostess, hotelier, landlord *or* landlady, mine host

innocence *noun* **1** GUILTLESSNESS, blamelessness, clean hands, incorruptibility, probity, purity, uprightness, virtue **2** HARMLESSNESS, innocuousness, inoffensiveness **3** INEXPERIENCE, artlessness, credulousness, gullibility, ingenuousness, naivety, simplicity, unworldliness

innocent *adjective* **1** NOT GUILTY, blameless, guiltless, honest, in the clear, uninvolved **2** HARMLESS, innocuous, inoffensive, unobjectionable, well-intentioned, well-meant **3** NAIVE, artless, childlike, credulous, gullible, ingenuous, open, simple, unworldly

innovation *noun* MODERNIZATION, alteration, change, departure, introduction, newness, novelty, variation

innuendo *noun* INSINUATION, aspersion, hint, implication, imputation, intimation, overtone, suggestion, whisper

innumerable *adjective* COUNTLESS, beyond number, incalculable, infinite, multitudinous, myriad, numberless, numerous, unnumbered, untold

inoffensive *adjective* HARMLESS, innocent, innocuous, mild, quiet, retiring, unobjectionable, unobtrusive

inoperative *adjective* OUT OF ACTION, broken, defective, ineffective, invalid, null and void, out of order, out of service, useless

inopportune *adjective* INCONVENIENT, ill-chosen, ill-timed, inappropriate, unfavorable, unfortunate, unpropitious, unseasonable, unsuitable, untimely

inordinate *adjective* EXCESSIVE, disproportionate, extravagant, immoderate, intemperate, preposterous, unconscionable, undue, unreasonable, unwarranted

inorganic *adjective* ARTIFICIAL, chemical, man-made

inquest *noun* INQUIRY, inquisition, investigation, probe

inquire *verb* **1** INVESTIGATE, examine, explore, look into, make inquiries, probe, research **2** *Also* **enquire** ASK, query, question

inquiry *noun* **1** INVESTIGATION, examination, exploration, inquest, interrogation, probe, research, study, survey **2** *Also* **enquiry** QUESTION, query

inquisition *noun* INVESTIGATION, cross-examination, examination, grilling (*informal*), inquest, inquiry, questioning, third degree (*informal*)

inquisitive *adjective* CURIOUS, inquiring, nosy (*informal*), probing, prying, questioning

insane adjective **1** MAD, crazed, crazy, demented, deranged, mentally ill, out of one's mind, unhinged **2** STUPID, bonkers (informal), daft (informal), foolish, idiotic, impractical, irrational, irresponsible, preposterous, senseless

insanitary adjective UNHEALTHY, dirty, disease-ridden, filthy, infested, insalubrious, polluted, scuzzy (slang), unclean, unhygienic

insanity noun **1** MADNESS, delirium, dementia, mental disorder, mental illness **2** STUPIDITY, folly, irresponsibility, lunacy, senselessness

insatiable adjective UNQUENCHABLE, greedy, intemperate, rapacious, ravenous, voracious

inscribe verb CARVE, cut, engrave, etch, impress, imprint

inscription noun ENGRAVING, dedication, legend, words

inscrutable adjective **1** ENIGMATIC, blank, deadpan, impenetrable, poker-faced (informal) **2** MYSTERIOUS, hidden, incomprehensible, inexplicable, unexplainable, unfathomable, unintelligible

insecure adjective **1** ANXIOUS, afraid, uncertain, unsure **2** UNSAFE, defenseless, exposed, unguarded, unprotected, vulnerable, wide-open

insecurity noun ANXIETY, fear, uncertainty, worry

insensible adjective UNAWARE, impervious, oblivious, unaffected, unconscious, unmindful

insensitive adjective UNFEELING,

callous, hardened, indifferent, thick-skinned, tough, uncaring, unconcerned

inseparable adjective **1** INDIVISIBLE, indissoluble **2** DEVOTED, bosom, close, intimate

insert verb ENTER, embed, implant, introduce, place, put, stick in

insertion noun INCLUSION, addition, implant, interpolation, introduction, supplement

inside adjective **1** INNER, interior, internal, inward **2** CONFIDENTIAL, classified, exclusive, internal, private, restricted, secret ▶ adverb **3** INDOORS, under cover, within ▶ noun **4** INTERIOR, contents **5 insides** Informal STOMACH, belly, bowels, entrails, guts, innards (informal), viscera, vitals

insidious adjective STEALTHY, deceptive, sly, smooth, sneaking, subtle, surreptitious

insight noun UNDERSTANDING, awareness, comprehension, discernment, judgment, observation, penetration, perception, perspicacity, vision

insignia noun BADGE, crest, emblem, symbol

insignificance noun UNIMPORTANCE, inconsequence, irrelevance, meaninglessness, pettiness, triviality, worthlessness

insignificant adjective UNIMPORTANT, inconsequential, irrelevant, meaningless, minor, nondescript, paltry, petty, trifling, trivial

insincere adjective DECEITFUL,

dishonest, disingenuous,
duplicitous, false, hollow,
hypocritical, lying, two-faced,
untruthful

insincerity noun DECEITFULNESS,
dishonesty, dissimulation,
duplicity, hypocrisy, pretense,
untruthfulness

insinuate verb 1 IMPLY, allude,
hint, indicate, intimate,
suggest 2 INGRATIATE, curry
favor, get in with, worm or
work one's way in

insinuation noun IMPLICATION,
allusion, aspersion, hint,
innuendo, slur, suggestion

insipid adjective 1 BLAND,
anemic, characterless, colorless,
prosaic, uninteresting, vapid,
wishy-washy (informal)
2 TASTELESS, bland, flavorless,
unappetizing, watery

insist verb 1 DEMAND, lay down
the law, put one's foot down
(informal), require 2 ASSERT,
aver, claim, maintain, reiterate,
repeat, swear, vow

insistence noun PERSISTENCE,
emphasis, importunity, stress

insistent adjective PERSISTENT,
dogged, emphatic,
importunate, incessant,
persevering, unrelenting, urgent

insolence noun RUDENESS,
boldness, cheek (informal),
disrespect, effrontery,
impertinence, impudence

insolent adjective RUDE, bold,
contemptuous, impertinent,
impudent, insubordinate,
insulting

insoluble adjective INEXPLICABLE,
baffling, impenetrable,
indecipherable, mysterious,
unaccountable, unfathomable,

unsolvable

insolvency noun BANKRUPTCY,
failure, liquidation, ruin

insolvent adjective BANKRUPT,
broke (informal), failed, gone
bust (informal), gone to the
wall, in receivership, ruined

insomnia noun SLEEPLESSNESS,
wakefulness

inspect verb EXAMINE, check, go
over or through, investigate,
look over, scrutinize, survey, vet

inspection noun EXAMINATION,
check, checkup, investigation,
once-over (informal), review,
scrutiny, search, survey

inspector noun EXAMINER,
censor, investigator, overseer,
scrutinizer, superintendent,
supervisor

inspiration noun 1 INFLUENCE,
muse, spur, stimulus
2 REVELATION, creativity,
illumination, insight

inspire verb 1 STIMULATE,
animate, encourage, enliven,
galvanize, influence, spur
2 AROUSE, enkindle, excite, give
rise to, produce

inspired adjective 1 BRILLIANT,
cool (informal), dazzling,
impressive, memorable,
outstanding, phat (slang),
superlative, thrilling, wonderful
2 UPLIFTED, elated, enthused,
exhilarated, stimulated

inspiring adjective UPLIFTING,
exciting, exhilarating,
heartening, moving, rousing,
stimulating, stirring

instability noun UNPREDICTABILITY,
changeableness, fickleness,
fluctuation, impermanence,
inconstancy, insecurity,
unsteadiness, variability,

volatility, wavering

install *verb* **1** SET UP, fix, lay, lodge, place, position, put in, station **2** INDUCT, establish, inaugurate, institute, introduce, invest **3** SETTLE, ensconce, position

installation *noun* **1** SETTING UP, establishment, fitting, installment, placing, positioning **2** INDUCTION, inauguration, investiture **3** EQUIPMENT, machinery, plant, system

installment *noun* PORTION, chapter, division, episode, part, repayment, section

instance *noun* **1** EXAMPLE, case, illustration, occasion, occurrence, situation ▸*verb* **2** QUOTE, adduce, cite, mention, name, specify

instant *noun* **1** SECOND, flash, jiffy (*informal*), moment, split second, trice, twinkling of an eye (*informal*) **2** JUNCTURE, moment, occasion, point, time ▸*adjective* **3** IMMEDIATE, direct, instantaneous, on-the-spot, prompt, quick, split-second **4** PRECOOKED, convenience, fast, ready-mixed

instantaneous *adjective* IMMEDIATE, direct, instant, on-the-spot, prompt

instantaneously *adverb* IMMEDIATELY, at once, instantly, in the twinkling of an eye (*informal*), on the spot, promptly, straight away

instantly *adverb* IMMEDIATELY, at once, directly, instantaneously, now, right away, straight away, this minute

instead *adverb* **1** RATHER,

alternatively, in lieu, in preference, on second thoughts, preferably **2 instead of** IN PLACE OF, in lieu of, rather than

instigate *verb* PROVOKE, bring about, incite, influence, initiate, prompt, set off, start, stimulate, trigger

instigation *noun* PROMPTING, behest, bidding, encouragement, incentive, incitement, urging

instigator *noun* RINGLEADER, agitator, leader, motivator, prime mover, troublemaker

instill *verb* INTRODUCE, engender, imbue, implant, inculcate, infuse, insinuate

instinct *noun* INTUITION, faculty, gift, impulse, knack, predisposition, proclivity, talent, tendency

instinctive *adjective* INBORN, automatic, inherent, innate, intuitive, involuntary, natural, reflex, spontaneous, unpremeditated, visceral

instinctively *adverb* INTUITIVELY, automatically, by instinct, involuntarily, naturally, without thinking

institute *noun* **1** SOCIETY, academy, association, college, foundation, guild, institution, school ▸*verb* **2** ESTABLISH, fix, found, initiate, introduce, launch, organize, originate, pioneer, set up, start

institution *noun* **1** ESTABLISHMENT, academy, college, foundation, institute, school, society **2** CUSTOM, convention, law, practice, ritual, rule, tradition

institutional *adjective*

CONVENTIONAL, accepted, established, formal, orthodox

instruct *verb* **1** ORDER, bid, charge, command, direct, enjoin, tell **2** TEACH, coach, drill, educate, ground, school, train, tutor

instruction *noun* **1** TEACHING, coaching, education, grounding, guidance, lesson(s), schooling, training, tuition **2** ORDER, command, demand, directive, injunction, mandate, ruling

instructions *plural noun* ORDERS, advice, directions, guidance, information, key, recommendations, rules

instructive *adjective* INFORMATIVE, edifying, educational, enlightening, helpful, illuminating, revealing, useful

instructor *noun* TEACHER, adviser, coach, demonstrator, guide, mentor, trainer, tutor

instrument *noun* **1** TOOL, apparatus, appliance, contraption (*informal*), device, gadget, implement, mechanism **2** MEANS, agency, agent, mechanism, medium, organ, vehicle

instrumental *adjective* ACTIVE, contributory, helpful, influential, involved, useful

insubordinate *adjective* DISOBEDIENT, defiant, disorderly, mutinous, rebellious, recalcitrant, refractory, undisciplined, ungovernable, unruly

insubordination *noun* DISOBEDIENCE, defiance, indiscipline, insurrection, mutiny, rebellion, recalcitrance, revolt

insubstantial *adjective* FLIMSY, feeble, frail, poor, slight, tenuous, thin, weak

insufferable *adjective* UNBEARABLE, detestable, dreadful, impossible, insupportable, intolerable, unendurable

insufficient *adjective* INADEQUATE, deficient, incapable, lacking, scant, short

insular *adjective* NARROW-MINDED, blinkered, circumscribed, inward-looking, limited, narrow, parochial, petty, provincial

insulate *verb* ISOLATE, close off, cocoon, cushion, cut off, protect, sequester, shield

insult *verb* **1** OFFEND, abuse, affront, call names, put down, slander, slight, snub ▶ *noun* **2** ABUSE, affront, aspersion, insolence, offense, put-down, slap in the face (*informal*), slight, snub

insulting *adjective* OFFENSIVE, abusive, contemptuous, degrading, disparaging, insolent, rude, scurrilous

insuperable *adjective* INSURMOUNTABLE, impassable, invincible, unconquerable

insupportable *adjective* **1** INTOLERABLE, insufferable, unbearable, unendurable **2** UNJUSTIFIABLE, indefensible, untenable

insurance *noun* PROTECTION, assurance, cover, guarantee, indemnity, safeguard, security, warranty

insure *verb* PROTECT, assure, cover, guarantee, indemnify, underwrite, warrant

insurgent *noun* 1 REBEL, insurrectionist, mutineer, revolutionary, rioter ▶ *adjective* 2 REBELLIOUS, disobedient, insubordinate, mutinous, revolting, revolutionary, riotous, seditious

insurmountable *adjective* INSUPERABLE, hopeless, impassable, impossible, invincible, overwhelming, unconquerable

insurrection *noun* REBELLION, coup, insurgency, mutiny, revolt, revolution, riot, uprising

intact *adjective* UNDAMAGED, complete, entire, perfect, sound, unbroken, unharmed, unimpaired, unscathed, whole

integral *adjective* ESSENTIAL, basic, component, constituent, fundamental, indispensable, intrinsic, necessary

integrate *verb* COMBINE, amalgamate, assimilate, blend, fuse, incorporate, join, merge, unite

integration *noun* ASSIMILATION, amalgamation, blending, combining, fusing, incorporation, mixing, unification

integrity *noun* 1 HONESTY, goodness, honor, incorruptibility, principle, probity, purity, rectitude, uprightness, virtue 2 UNITY, coherence, cohesion, completeness, soundness, wholeness

intellect *noun* INTELLIGENCE, brains (*informal*), judgment, mind, reason, sense, understanding

intellectual *adjective*

1 SCHOLARLY, bookish, cerebral, highbrow, intelligent, studious, thoughtful ▶ *noun* 2 THINKER, academic, egghead (*informal*), highbrow

intelligence *noun* 1 UNDERSTANDING, acumen, brain power, brains (*informal*), cleverness, comprehension, intellect, perception, sense 2 INFORMATION, data, facts, findings, knowledge, news, notification, report

intelligent *adjective* CLEVER, brainy (*informal*), bright, enlightened, perspicacious, quick-witted, sharp, smart, well-informed

intelligentsia *noun* INTELLECTUALS, highbrows, literati

intelligible *adjective* UNDERSTANDABLE, clear, comprehensible, distinct, lucid, open, plain

intemperate *adjective* EXCESSIVE, extreme, immoderate, profligate, self-indulgent, unbridled, unrestrained, wild

intend *verb* PLAN, aim, have in mind *or* view, mean, propose, purpose

intense *adjective* 1 EXTREME, acute, deep, excessive, fierce, great, powerful, profound, severe 2 PASSIONATE, ardent, fanatical, fervent, fierce, heightened, impassioned, vehement

intensify *verb* INCREASE, add to, aggravate, deepen, escalate, heighten, magnify, redouble, reinforce, sharpen, strengthen

intensity *noun* FORCE, ardor, emotion, fanaticism, fervor, fierceness, passion, strength, vehemence, vigor

intensive *adjective* CONCENTRATED, comprehensive, demanding, exhaustive, in-depth, thorough, thoroughgoing

intent *noun* 1 INTENTION, aim, design, end, goal, meaning, object, objective, plan, purpose ▶ *adjective* 2 ATTENTIVE, absorbed, determined, eager, engrossed, preoccupied, rapt, resolved, steadfast, watchful

intention *noun* PURPOSE, aim, design, end, goal, idea, object, objective, point, target

intentional *adjective* DELIBERATE, calculated, intended, meant, planned, premeditated, willful

intentionally *adverb* DELIBERATELY, designedly, on purpose, willfully

inter *verb* BURY, entomb, lay to rest

intercede *verb* MEDIATE, arbitrate, intervene, plead

intercept *verb* SEIZE, block, catch, cut off, head off, interrupt, obstruct, stop

interchange *verb* 1 SWITCH, alternate, exchange, reciprocate, swap ▶ *noun* 2 JUNCTION, intersection

interchangeable *adjective* IDENTICAL, equivalent, exchangeable, reciprocal, synonymous

intercourse *noun* 1 COMMUNICATION, commerce, contact, dealings 2 SEXUAL INTERCOURSE, carnal knowledge, coitus, copulation, sex

interest *noun* 1 CURIOSITY, attention, concern, notice, regard 2 HOBBY, activity, diversion, pastime, preoccupation, pursuit

3 ADVANTAGE, benefit, good, profit 4 STAKE, claim, investment, right, share ▶ *verb* 5 INTRIGUE, attract, catch one's eye, divert, engross, fascinate

interested *adjective* 1 CURIOUS, attracted, drawn, excited, fascinated, keen 2 INVOLVED, concerned, implicated

interesting *adjective* INTRIGUING, absorbing, appealing, attractive, compelling, engaging, engrossing, gripping, stimulating, thought-provoking

interface *noun* CONNECTION, border, boundary, frontier, link

interfere *verb* 1 INTRUDE, butt in, intervene, meddle, stick one's oar in (*informal*), tamper 2 (often with *with*) CONFLICT, clash, hamper, handicap, hinder, impede, inhibit, obstruct

interference *noun* 1 INTRUSION, intervention, meddling, prying 2 CONFLICT, clashing, collision, obstruction, opposition

interim *adjective* TEMPORARY, acting, caretaker, improvised, makeshift, provisional, stopgap

interior *noun* 1 INSIDE, center, core, heart ▶ *adjective* 2 INSIDE, inner, internal, inward 3 MENTAL, hidden, inner, intimate, personal, private, secret, spiritual

interloper *noun* TRESPASSER, gate-crasher (*informal*), intruder, meddler

interlude *noun* INTERVAL, break, breathing space, delay, hiatus, intermission, pause, respite, rest, spell, stoppage

intermediary *noun* MEDIATOR,

agent, broker, go-between, middleman

intermediate *adjective* MIDDLE, halfway, in-between (*informal*), intervening, mid, midway, transitional

interment *noun* BURIAL, funeral

interminable *adjective* ENDLESS, ceaseless, everlasting, infinite, long-drawn-out, long-winded, never-ending, perpetual, protracted

intermingle *verb* MIX, blend, combine, fuse, interlace, intermix, interweave, merge

intermission *noun* INTERVAL, break, interlude, pause, recess, respite, rest, stoppage

intermittent *adjective* PERIODIC, broken, fitful, irregular, occasional, spasmodic, sporadic

intern *verb* IMPRISON, confine, detain, hold, hold in custody

internal *adjective* 1 INNER, inside, interior 2 DOMESTIC, civic, home, in-house, intramural

international *adjective* UNIVERSAL, cosmopolitan, global, intercontinental, worldwide

Internet *noun* INFORMATION SUPERHIGHWAY, cyberspace, the net (*informal*), the web (*informal*), World Wide Web

interpose *verb* INTERRUPT, insert, interject, put one's oar in

interpret *verb* EXPLAIN, construe, decipher, decode, elucidate, make sense of, render, translate

interpretation *noun* EXPLANATION, analysis, clarification, elucidation, exposition, portrayal, rendition, translation, version

interpreter *noun* TRANSLATOR, commentator

interrogate *verb* QUESTION, cross-examine, examine, grill (*informal*), investigate, pump, quiz

interrogation *noun* QUESTIONING, cross-examination, examination, grilling (*informal*), inquiry, inquisition, third degree (*informal*)

interrupt *verb* 1 INTRUDE, barge in (*informal*), break in, butt in, disturb, heckle, interfere (with) 2 SUSPEND, break off, cut short, delay, discontinue, hold up, lay aside, stop

interruption *noun* STOPPAGE, break, disruption, disturbance, hitch, intrusion, pause, suspension

intersection *noun* JUNCTION, crossing, crossroads, interchange

interval *noun* BREAK, delay, gap, interlude, intermission, pause, respite, rest, space, spell

intervene *verb* 1 INVOLVE ONESELF, arbitrate, intercede, interfere, intrude, lend a hand, mediate, step in (*informal*) 2 HAPPEN, befall, come to pass, ensue, occur, take place

intervention *noun* MEDIATION, agency, interference, intrusion

interview *noun* 1 MEETING, audience, conference, consultation, dialogue, press conference, talk ▶ *verb* 2 QUESTION, examine, interrogate, talk to

interviewer *noun* QUESTIONER, examiner, interrogator, investigator, reporter

intestines *plural noun* GUTS,

bowels, entrails, innards (*informal*), insides (*informal*), viscera

intimacy noun FAMILIARITY, closeness, confidentiality

intimate[1] *adjective* 1 CLOSE, bosom, buddy-buddy (*informal*), confidential, dear, near, thick (*informal*) 2 PERSONAL, confidential, private, secret 3 DETAILED, deep, exhaustive, first-hand, immediate, in-depth, profound, thorough 4 SNUG, comfy (*informal*), cozy, friendly, homey, warm ▸*noun* 5 FRIEND, close friend, confidant *or (fem.)* confidante, (constant) companion, crony, homeboy (*slang*), homegirl (*slang*), soul mate

intimate[2] *verb* 1 SUGGEST, hint, imply, indicate, insinuate 2 ANNOUNCE, communicate, declare, make known, state

intimately *adverb* 1 CONFIDINGLY, affectionately, confidentially, familiarly, personally, tenderly, warmly 2 IN DETAIL, fully, inside out, thoroughly, very well

intimation *noun* 1 HINT, allusion, indication, inkling, insinuation, reminder, suggestion, warning 2 ANNOUNCEMENT, communication, declaration, notice

intimidate *verb* FRIGHTEN, browbeat, bully, coerce, daunt, overawe, scare, subdue, terrorize, threaten

intimidation *noun* BULLYING, arm-twisting (*informal*), browbeating, coercion, menaces, pressure,

terrorization, threat(s)

intolerable *adjective* UNBEARABLE, excruciating, impossible, insufferable, insupportable, painful, unendurable

intolerance *noun* NARROW-MINDEDNESS, bigotry, chauvinism, discrimination, dogmatism, fanaticism, illiberality, prejudice

intolerant *adjective* NARROW-MINDED, bigoted, chauvinistic, dictatorial, dogmatic, fanatical, illiberal, prejudiced, small-minded

intone *verb* RECITE, chant

intoxicated *adjective* 1 DRUNK, drunken, inebriated, paralytic (*informal*), plastered (*slang*), tipsy, under the influence (*informal*) 2 EUPHORIC, dizzy, elated, enraptured, excited, exhilarated, high (*informal*), wired (*slang*)

intoxicating *adjective* 1 ALCOHOLIC, strong 2 EXCITING, exhilarating, heady, thrilling

intoxication *noun* 1 DRUNKENNESS, inebriation, insobriety, tipsiness 2 EXCITEMENT, delirium, elation, euphoria, exhilaration

intransigent *adjective* UNCOMPROMISING, hardline, intractable, obdurate, obstinate, stiff-necked, stubborn, unbending, unyielding

intrepid *adjective* FEARLESS, audacious, bold, brave, courageous, daring, gallant, plucky, stouthearted, valiant

intricacy *noun* COMPLEXITY, complication, convolutions, elaborateness

intricate adjective COMPLICATED, complex, convoluted, elaborate, fancy, involved, labyrinthine, tangled, tortuous

intrigue verb 1 INTEREST, attract, fascinate, rivet, titillate 2 PLOT, connive, conspire, machinate, maneuver, scheme ▶noun 3 PLOT, chicanery, collusion, conspiracy, machination, maneuver, scheme, stratagem, wile 4 AFFAIR, amour, intimacy, liaison, romance

intriguing adjective INTERESTING, beguiling, compelling, diverting, exciting, fascinating, tantalizing, titillating

intrinsic adjective INBORN, basic, built-in, congenital, constitutional, essential, fundamental, inbred, inherent, native, natural

introduce verb 1 PRESENT, acquaint, familiarize, make known 2 BRING IN, establish, found, initiate, institute, launch, pioneer, set up, start 3 BRING UP, advance, air, broach, moot, put forward, submit 4 INSERT, add, inject, put in, throw in (informal)

introduction noun 1 LAUNCH, establishment, inauguration, institution, pioneering 2 OPENING, foreword, intro (informal), lead-in, preamble, preface, prelude, prologue

introductory adjective PRELIMINARY, first, inaugural, initial, opening, preparatory

introspective adjective INWARD-LOOKING, brooding, contemplative, introverted, meditative, pensive

introverted adjective INTROSPECTIVE, inner-directed, inward-looking, self-contained, withdrawn

intrude verb INTERFERE, butt in, encroach, infringe, interrupt, meddle, push in, trespass

intruder noun TRESPASSER, gate-crasher (informal), infiltrator, interloper, invader, prowler

intrusion noun INVASION, encroachment, infringement, interference, interruption, trespass, violation

intrusive adjective INTERFERING, impertinent, importunate, meddlesome, nosy (informal), presumptuous, pushy (informal), uncalled-for, unwanted

intuition noun INSTINCT, hunch, insight, perception, presentiment, sixth sense

intuitive adjective INSTINCTIVE, innate, spontaneous, untaught

inundate verb FLOOD, drown, engulf, immerse, overflow, overrun, overwhelm, submerge, swamp

invade verb 1 ATTACK, assault, burst in, descend upon, encroach, infringe, make inroads, occupy, raid, violate 2 INFEST, overrun, permeate, pervade, swarm over

invader noun ATTACKER, aggressor, plunderer, raider, trespasser

invalid[1] adjective 1 DISABLED, ailing, bedridden, challenged, frail, ill, infirm, sick ▶noun 2 PATIENT, convalescent, valetudinarian

invalid[2] adjective NULL AND VOID, fallacious, false, illogical,

inoperative, irrational,
unfounded, unsound, void,
worthless

invalidate *verb* NULLIFY, annul,
cancel, overthrow, undermine,
undo

invaluable *adjective* PRECIOUS,
inestimable, priceless, valuable,
worth one's *or* its weight in
gold

invariably *adverb* CONSISTENTLY,
always, customarily, day in,
day out, habitually,
perpetually, regularly,
unfailingly, without exception

invasion *noun* **1** ATTACK, assault,
campaign, foray, incursion,
inroad, offensive, onslaught,
raid **2** INTRUSION, breach,
encroachment, infraction,
infringement, usurpation,
violation

invective *noun* ABUSE, censure,
denunciation, diatribe, tirade,
tongue-lashing, vilification,
vituperation

invent *verb* **1** CREATE, coin,
conceive, design, devise,
discover, formulate, improvise,
originate, think up **2** MAKE UP,
concoct, cook up (*informal*),
fabricate, feign, forge,
manufacture, trump up

invention *noun* **1** CREATION,
brainchild (*informal*),
contraption, contrivance,
design, device, discovery,
gadget, instrument **2** CREATIVITY,
genius, imagination, ingenuity,
inventiveness, originality,
resourcefulness **3** FICTION,
fabrication, falsehood, fantasy,
forgery, lie, untruth, yarn

inventive *adjective* CREATIVE,
fertile, imaginative, ingenious,

innovative, inspired, original,
resourceful

inventor *noun* CREATOR,
architect, author, coiner,
designer, maker, originator

inventory *noun* LIST, account,
catalog, file, record, register,
roll, roster

inverse *adjective* OPPOSITE,
contrary, converse, reverse,
reversed, transposed

invert *verb* OVERTURN, reverse,
transpose, upset, upturn

invest *verb* **1** SPEND, advance,
devote, lay out, put in, sink
2 EMPOWER, authorize, charge,
license, sanction, vest

investigate *verb* EXAMINE,
explore, go into, inquire into,
inspect, look into, probe,
research, study

investigation *noun* EXAMINATION,
exploration, inquest, inquiry,
inspection, probe, review,
search, study, survey

investigator *noun* EXAMINER,
gumshoe (*slang*), inquirer,
(private) detective, private eye
(*informal*), researcher, sleuth

investiture *noun* INSTALLATION,
enthronement, inauguration,
induction, ordination

investment *noun* **1** TRANSACTION,
speculation, venture **2** STAKE,
ante (*informal*), contribution

inveterate *adjective*
LONG-STANDING, chronic,
confirmed, deep-seated,
dyed-in-the-wool, entrenched,
habitual, hardened,
incorrigible, incurable

invidious *adjective* UNDESIRABLE,
hateful

invigorate *verb* REFRESH,
energize, enliven, exhilarate,

fortify, galvanize, liven up, revitalize, stimulate

invincible *adjective* UNBEATABLE, impregnable, indestructible, indomitable, insuperable, invulnerable, unassailable, unconquerable

inviolable *adjective* SACROSANCT, hallowed, holy, inalienable, sacred, unalterable

inviolate *adjective* INTACT, entire, pure, unbroken, undefiled, unhurt, unpolluted, unsullied, untouched, whole

invisible *adjective* UNSEEN, imperceptible, indiscernible

invitation *noun* REQUEST, call, invite (*informal*), summons

invite *verb* 1 REQUEST, ask, beg, bid, summon 2 ENCOURAGE, ask for (*informal*), attract, court, entice, provoke, tempt, welcome

inviting *adjective* TEMPTING, alluring, appealing, attractive, enticing, mouthwatering, seductive, welcoming

invocation *noun* APPEAL, entreaty, petition, prayer, supplication

invoke *verb* 1 CALL UPON, appeal to, beg, beseech, entreat, implore, petition, pray, supplicate 2 APPLY, implement, initiate, put into effect, resort to, use

involuntary *adjective* UNINTENTIONAL, automatic, instinctive, reflex, spontaneous, unconscious, uncontrolled, unthinking

involve *verb* 1 ENTAIL, imply, mean, necessitate, presuppose, require 2 CONCERN, affect, draw in, implicate, touch

involved *adjective* 1 COMPLICATED, complex, confusing, convoluted, elaborate, intricate, labyrinthine, tangled, tortuous 2 CONCERNED, caught (up), implicated, mixed up in *or* with, participating, taking part

involvement *noun* CONNECTION, association, commitment, interest, participation

invulnerable *adjective* SAFE, impenetrable, indestructible, insusceptible, invincible, proof against, secure, unassailable

inward *adjective* 1 INCOMING, entering, inbound, ingoing 2 INTERNAL, inner, inside, interior 3 PRIVATE, confidential, hidden, inmost, innermost, personal, secret

inwardly *adverb* PRIVATELY, at heart, deep down, inside, secretly

irate *adjective* ANGRY, annoyed, cross, enraged, furious, incensed, indignant, infuriated, livid

irksome *adjective* IRRITATING, annoying, bothersome, disagreeable, exasperating, tiresome, troublesome, trying, vexing, wearisome

iron *adjective* 1 FERROUS, chalybeate, ferric 2 INFLEXIBLE, adamant, hard, implacable, indomitable, rigid, steely, strong, tough, unbending, unyielding

ironic *adjective* 1 SARCASTIC, double-edged, mocking, sardonic, satirical, with tongue in cheek, wry 2 PARADOXICAL, incongruous

iron out *verb* SETTLE, clear up,

get rid of, put right, reconcile, resolve, smooth over, sort out, straighten out

irony noun **1** SARCASM, mockery, satire **2** PARADOX, incongruity

irrational adjective ILLOGICAL, absurd, crazy, nonsensical, preposterous, unreasonable

irrefutable adjective UNDENIABLE, certain, incontestable, incontrovertible, indisputable, sure, unquestionable

irregular adjective **1** VARIABLE, erratic, fitful, haphazard, occasional, random, spasmodic, sporadic, unsystematic **2** UNCONVENTIONAL, abnormal, exceptional, extraordinary, peculiar, unofficial, unorthodox, unusual **3** UNEVEN, asymmetrical, bumpy, crooked, jagged, lopsided, ragged, rough

irregularity noun **1** UNCERTAINTY, desultoriness, disorganization, haphazardness **2** ABNORMALITY, anomaly, oddity, peculiarity, unorthodoxy **3** UNEVENNESS, asymmetry, bumpiness, jaggedness, lopsidedness, raggedness, roughness

irrelevant adjective UNCONNECTED, beside the point, extraneous, immaterial, impertinent, inapplicable, inappropriate, neither here nor there, unrelated

irreparable adjective BEYOND REPAIR, incurable, irremediable, irretrievable, irreversible

irrepressible adjective EBULLIENT, boisterous, buoyant, effervescent, unstoppable

irreproachable adjective BLAMELESS, beyond reproach, faultless, impeccable, innocent, perfect, pure, unimpeachable

irresistible adjective OVERWHELMING, compelling, compulsive, overpowering, urgent

irresponsible adjective IMMATURE, careless, reckless, scatterbrained, shiftless, thoughtless, unreliable, untrustworthy

irreverent adjective DISRESPECTFUL, cheeky (informal), flippant, iconoclastic, impertinent, impudent, mocking, tongue-in-cheek

irreversible adjective IRREVOCABLE, final, incurable, irreparable, unalterable

irrevocable adjective FIXED, fated, immutable, irreversible, predestined, predetermined, settled, unalterable

irrigate verb WATER, flood, inundate, moisten, wet

irritability noun BAD TEMPER, ill humor, impatience, irascibility, prickliness, testiness, tetchiness, touchiness

irritable adjective BAD-TEMPERED, cantankerous, crotchety, ill-tempered, irascible, oversensitive, prickly, testy, tetchy, touchy

irritate verb **1** ANNOY, anger, bother, exasperate, get on one's nerves (informal), infuriate, needle (informal), nettle, rankle with, try one's patience **2** RUB, chafe, inflame, pain

irritated adjective ANNOYED, angry, bothered, cross, exasperated, nettled, piqued, put out, vexed

irritating *adjective* ANNOYING, disturbing, infuriating, irksome, maddening, nagging, troublesome, trying

irritation *noun* 1 ANNOYANCE, anger, displeasure, exasperation, indignation, resentment, testiness, vexation 2 NUISANCE, drag (*informal*), irritant, pain in the neck (*informal*), thorn in one's flesh

island *noun* ISLE, atoll, cay *or* key, islet

isolate *verb* SEPARATE, cut off, detach, disconnect, insulate, segregate, set apart

isolated *adjective* REMOTE, hidden, lonely, off the beaten track, outlying, out-of-the-way, secluded

isolation *noun* SEPARATION, detachment, remoteness, seclusion, segregation, solitude

issue *noun* 1 TOPIC, bone of contention, matter, point, problem, question, subject 2 OUTCOME, consequence, effect, end result, result, upshot 3 EDITION, copy, number, printing 4 CHILDREN, descendants, heirs, offspring, progeny 5 **take issue** DISAGREE, challenge, dispute, object, oppose, raise an objection, take exception 6 PUBLISH, announce, broadcast, circulate, deliver, distribute, give out, put out, release

isthmus *noun* STRIP, spit

itch *noun* 1 IRRITATION, itchiness, prickling, tingling 2 DESIRE, craving, hankering, hunger, longing, lust, passion, yearning, yen (*informal*) ▶ *verb*

3 PRICKLE, irritate, tickle, tingle 4 LONG, ache, crave, hanker, hunger, lust, pine, yearn

itchy *adjective* IMPATIENT, eager, edgy, fidgety, restive, restless, unsettled

item *noun* 1 DETAIL, article, component, entry, matter, particular, point, thing 2 REPORT, account, article, bulletin, dispatch, feature, note, notice, paragraph, piece

itinerant *adjective* WANDERING, migratory, nomadic, peripatetic, roaming, roving, traveling, vagrant

itinerary *noun* SCHEDULE, program, route, timetable

—— **J j** ——

jab *verb, noun* POKE, dig, lunge, nudge, prod, punch, stab, tap, thrust

jabber *verb* CHATTER, babble, blether, gabble, mumble, ramble, yap (*informal*)

jacket *noun* COVERING, case, casing, coat, sheath, skin, wrapper, wrapping

jackpot *noun* PRIZE, award, bonanza, reward, winnings

jack up *verb* RAISE, elevate, hoist, lift, lift up

jaded *adjective* TIRED, exhausted, fatigued, spent, weary

jagged *adjective* UNEVEN, barbed, craggy, indented, ragged, serrated, spiked, toothed

jail *noun* 1 PRISON, penitentiary, reformatory, slammer (*slang*) ▶ *verb* 2 IMPRISON, confine, detain, incarcerate, lock up, send down

jailer noun GUARD, keeper, warden

jam verb 1 PACK, cram, force, press, ram, squeeze, stuff, wedge 2 CROWD, crush, throng 3 CONGEST, block, clog, obstruct, stall, stick ▶ noun 4 PREDICAMENT, deep water, fix (*informal*), hot water, pickle (*informal*), tight spot, trouble

jamboree noun FESTIVAL, carnival, celebration, festivity, fête, revelry, spree

jangle verb RATTLE, chime, clank, clash, clatter, jingle, vibrate

janitor noun CARETAKER, concierge, custodian, doorkeeper, porter

jar[1] noun POT, container, crock, jug, pitcher, urn, vase

jar[2] verb 1 JOLT, bump, convulse, rattle, rock, shake, vibrate 2 IRRITATE, annoy, get on one's nerves (*informal*), grate, irk, nettle, offend ▶ noun 3 JOLT, bump, convulsion, shock, vibration

jargon noun PARLANCE, argot, idiom, usage

jaundiced adjective 1 CYNICAL, skeptical 2 BITTER, envious, hostile, jealous, resentful, spiteful, suspicious

jaunt noun OUTING, airing, excursion, expedition, ramble, stroll, tour, trip

jaunty adjective SPRIGHTLY, buoyant, carefree, high-spirited, lively, perky, self-confident, sparky

jaw verb TALK, chat, chatter, chew the fat (*slang*), gossip, spout

jaws plural noun OPENING, entrance, mouth

jazz up verb ENLIVEN, animate, enhance, improve

jazzy adjective FLASHY, fancy, gaudy, snazzy (*informal*)

jealous adjective 1 ENVIOUS, covetous, desirous, green, grudging, resentful 2 WARY, mistrustful, protective, suspicious, vigilant, watchful

jealousy noun ENVY, covetousness, mistrust, possessiveness, resentment, spite, suspicion

jeans plural noun DENIMS, Levis (*Trademark*)

jeer verb 1 SCOFF, barrack, deride, gibe, heckle, mock, ridicule, taunt ▶ noun 2 TAUNT, abuse, boo, catcall, derision, gibe, ridicule

jell verb 1 SOLIDIFY, congeal, harden, set, thicken 2 TAKE SHAPE, come together, crystallize, materialize

jeopardize verb ENDANGER, chance, expose, gamble, imperil, risk, stake, venture

jeopardy noun DANGER, insecurity, peril, risk, vulnerability

jerk verb, noun TUG, jolt, lurch, pull, thrust, twitch, wrench, yank

jerky adjective BUMPY, convulsive, jolting, jumpy, shaky, spasmodic, twitchy

jest noun 1 JOKE, bon mot, crack (*slang*), jape, pleasantry, prank, quip, wisecrack (*informal*), witticism ▶ verb 2 JOKE, kid (*informal*), mock, quip, tease

jester noun CLOWN, buffoon, fool, harlequin

jet[1] *adjective* BLACK, coal-black, ebony, inky, pitch-black, raven, sable

jet[2] *noun* 1 STREAM, flow, fountain, gush, spout, spray, spring 2 NOZZLE, atomizer, sprayer, sprinkler ▶ *verb* 3 FLY, soar, zoom

jettison *verb* ABANDON, discard, dump, eject, expel, scrap, throw overboard, unload

jetty *noun* PIER, breakwater, dock, groyne, mole, quay, wharf

jewel *noun* 1 GEMSTONE, ornament, rock (*slang*), sparkler (*informal*) 2 RARITY, collector's item, find, gem, pearl, treasure, wonder

jewelry *noun* JEWELS, finery, gems, ornaments, regalia, treasure, trinkets

jib *verb* REFUSE, balk, recoil, retreat, shrink, stop short

jibe see GIBE

jiffy *noun Slang* INSTANT, blink of an eye (*informal*), flash, heartbeat (*informal*), second, two shakes of a lamb's tail (*slang*)

jig *verb* SKIP, bob, bounce, caper, prance, wiggle

jingle *noun* 1 RATTLE, clang, clink, reverberation, ringing, tinkle 2 SONG, chorus, ditty, melody, tune ▶ *verb* 3 RING, chime, clatter, clink, jangle, rattle, tinkle

jinx *noun* 1 CURSE, evil eye (*informal*), hex (*informal*), hoodoo (*informal*), nemesis ▶ *verb* 2 CURSE, bewitch, hex (*informal*)

jitters *plural noun* NERVES, anxiety, butterflies (in one's stomach) (*informal*), cold feet (*informal*), fidgets, nervousness, the shakes (*informal*)

jittery *adjective* NERVOUS, agitated, anxious, fidgety, jumpy, shaky, trembling, twitchy, wired (*slang*)

job *noun* 1 TASK, assignment, chore, duty, enterprise, errand, undertaking, venture 2 OCCUPATION, business, calling, career, employment, livelihood, profession, vocation

jobless *adjective* UNEMPLOYED, idle, inactive, out of work, unoccupied

jocular *adjective* HUMOROUS, amusing, droll, facetious, funny, joking, jovial, playful, sportive, teasing, waggish

jog *verb* 1 NUDGE, prod, push, shake, stir 2 RUN, canter, lope, trot

John Doe *noun Informal* MAN IN THE STREET, average guy, average person, know-nothing (*slang*)

joie de vivre *noun* ENTHUSIASM, ebullience, enjoyment, gusto, relish, zest

join *verb* 1 CONNECT, add, append, attach, combine, couple, fasten, link, unite 2 ENROLL, enlist, enter, sign up

joint *adjective* 1 SHARED, collective, combined, communal, cooperative, joined, mutual, united ▶ *noun* 2 JUNCTION, connection, hinge, intersection, nexus, node ▶ *verb* 3 DIVIDE, carve, cut up, dissect, segment, sever

jointly *adverb* COLLECTIVELY, as one, in common, in conjunction, in league, in partnership, mutually, together

joke noun **1** JEST, gag (informal), jape, prank, pun, quip, wisecrack (informal), witticism **2** CLOWN, buffoon, laughing stock ▶verb **3** JEST, banter, kid (informal), mock, play the fool, quip, taunt, tease

joker noun COMEDIAN, buffoon, clown, comic, humorist, jester, prankster, trickster, wag, wit

jolly adjective HAPPY, cheerful, chirpy (informal), genial, jovial, merry, playful, sprightly, upbeat (informal)

jolt noun **1** JERK, bump, jar, jog, jump, lurch, shake, start **2** SURPRISE, blow, bolt from the blue, bombshell, setback, shock ▶verb **3** JERK, jar, jog, jostle, knock, push, shake, shove **4** SURPRISE, discompose, disturb, perturb, stagger, startle, stun

jostle verb PUSH, bump, elbow, hustle, jog, jolt, shake, shove

jot verb **1** NOTE DOWN, list, record, scribble ▶noun **2** BIT, fraction, grain, morsel, scrap, speck

journal noun **1** NEWSPAPER, daily, gazette, magazine, monthly, periodical, weekly **2** DIARY, chronicle, log, record

journalist noun REPORTER, broadcaster, columnist, commentator, correspondent, hack, newsman or newswoman, pressman

journey noun **1** TRIP, excursion, expedition, odyssey, pilgrimage, tour, trek, voyage ▶verb **2** TRAVEL, go, proceed, roam, rove, tour, traverse, trek, voyage, wander

jovial adjective CHEERFUL, animated, cheery, convivial, happy, jolly, merry, mirthful

joy noun DELIGHT, bliss, ecstasy, elation, gaiety, glee, pleasure, rapture, satisfaction

joyful adjective DELIGHTED, elated, enraptured, glad, gratified, happy, jubilant, merry, pleased

joyless adjective UNHAPPY, cheerless, depressed, dismal, dreary, gloomy, miserable, sad

joyous adjective JOYFUL, festive, merry, rapturous

jubilant adjective OVERJOYED, elated, enraptured, euphoric, exuberant, exultant, thrilled, triumphant

jubilation noun JOY, celebration, ecstasy, elation, excitement, exultation, festivity, triumph

jubilee noun CELEBRATION, festival, festivity, holiday

judge noun **1** REFEREE, adjudicator, arbiter, arbitrator, moderator, umpire **2** CRITIC, arbiter, assessor, authority, connoisseur, expert **3** MAGISTRATE, justice ▶verb **4** ARBITRATE, adjudicate, decide, mediate, referee, umpire **5** CONSIDER, appraise, assess, esteem, estimate, evaluate, rate, value

judgment noun **1** SENSE, acumen, discernment, discrimination, prudence, shrewdness, understanding, wisdom **2** VERDICT, arbitration, decision, decree, finding, ruling, sentence **3** OPINION, appraisal, assessment, belief, diagnosis, estimate, finding, valuation, view

judicial adjective LEGAL, official

judicious adjective SENSIBLE,

astute, careful, discriminating, enlightened, prudent, shrewd, thoughtful, well-judged, wise

jug noun CONTAINER, carafe, crock, ewer, jar, pitcher, urn, vessel

juggle verb MANIPULATE, alter, change, maneuver, modify

juice noun LIQUID, extract, fluid, liquor, nectar, sap

juicy adjective 1 MOIST, lush, succulent 2 INTERESTING, colorful, provocative, racy, risqué, sensational, spicy (informal), suggestive, vivid

jumble noun 1 MUDDLE, clutter, confusion, disarray, disorder, mess, mishmash, mixture ▶ verb 2 MIX, confuse, disorder, disorganize, mistake, muddle, shuffle

jumbo adjective GIANT, gigantic, huge, immense, large, oversized

jump verb 1 LEAP, bounce, bound, hop, hurdle, skip, spring, vault 2 RECOIL, flinch, jerk, start, wince 3 MISS, avoid, evade, omit, skip 4 INCREASE, advance, ascend, escalate, rise, surge ▶ noun 5 LEAP, bound, hop, skip, spring, vault 6 INTERRUPTION, break, gap, hiatus, lacuna, space 7 RISE, advance, increase, increment, upsurge, upturn

jumped-up adjective CONCEITED, arrogant, insolent, overbearing, pompous, presumptuous

jumpy adjective NERVOUS, agitated, anxious, apprehensive, fidgety, jittery (informal), on edge, restless, tense, wired (slang)

junction noun CONNECTION, coupling, linking, union

juncture noun MOMENT, occasion, point, time

junior adjective MINOR, inferior, lesser, lower, secondary, subordinate, younger

junk noun RUBBISH, clutter, debris, litter, odds and ends, refuse, scrap, trash, waste

jurisdiction noun 1 AUTHORITY, command, control, influence, power, rule 2 RANGE, area, bounds, compass, field, province, scope, sphere

just adverb 1 EXACTLY, absolutely, completely, entirely, perfectly, precisely 2 RECENTLY, hardly, lately, only now, scarcely 3 MERELY, by the skin of one's teeth, only, simply, solely ▶ adjective 4 FAIR, conscientious, equitable, fair-minded, good, honest, upright, virtuous 5 PROPER, appropriate, apt, deserved, due, fitting, justified, merited, rightful

justice noun 1 FAIRNESS, equity, honesty, integrity, law, legality, legitimacy, right 2 JUDGE, magistrate

justifiable adjective REASONABLE, acceptable, defensible, excusable, legitimate, sensible, understandable, valid, warrantable

justification noun 1 EXPLANATION, defense, excuse, rationalization, vindication 2 REASON, basis, grounds, warrant

justify verb EXPLAIN, defend, exculpate, excuse, exonerate, support, uphold, vindicate, warrant

justly adverb PROPERLY, correctly, equitably, fairly, lawfully

jut *verb* STICK OUT, bulge, extend, overhang, poke, project, protrude

juvenile *adjective* **1** YOUNG, babyish, callow, childish, immature, inexperienced, infantile, puerile, youthful ▸*noun* **2** CHILD, adolescent, boy, girl, infant, minor, youth

juxtaposition *noun* PROXIMITY, adjacency, closeness, contact, nearness, propinquity, vicinity

K k

kamikaze *adjective* SELF-DESTRUCTIVE, foolhardy, suicidal

keel over *verb* COLLAPSE, black out (*informal*), faint, pass out

keen *adjective* **1** EAGER, ardent, avid, enthusiastic, impassioned, intense, zealous **2** SHARP, cutting, incisive, razor-like **3** ASTUTE, canny, clever, perceptive, quick, shrewd, wise

keenness *noun* EAGERNESS, ardor, enthusiasm, fervor, intensity, passion, zeal, zest

keep *verb* **1** RETAIN, conserve, control, hold, maintain, possess, preserve **2** STORE, carry, deposit, hold, place, stack, stock **3** LOOK AFTER, care for, guard, maintain, manage, mind, protect, tend, watch over **4** SUPPORT, feed, maintain, provide for, subsidize, sustain **5** DETAIN, delay, hinder, hold back, keep back, obstruct, prevent, restrain ▸*noun* **6** BOARD, food, living,

maintenance **7** TOWER, castle

keeper *noun* GUARDIAN, attendant, caretaker, curator, custodian, guard, preserver, steward, warden

keeping *noun* **1** CARE, charge, custody, guardianship, possession, protection, safekeeping **2** As in **in keeping with** AGREEMENT, accord, balance, compliance, conformity, correspondence, harmony, observance, proportion

keepsake *noun* SOUVENIR, memento, relic, reminder, symbol, token

keep up *verb* MAINTAIN, continue, keep pace, preserve, sustain

keg *noun* BARREL, cask, drum, vat

kernel *noun* ESSENCE, core, germ, gist, nub, pith, substance

key *noun* **1** OPENER, latchkey **2** ANSWER, explanation, solution ▸*adjective* **3** ESSENTIAL, crucial, decisive, fundamental, important, leading, main, major, pivotal, principal

key in *verb* TYPE, enter, input, keyboard

keynote *noun* HEART, center, core, essence, gist, substance, theme

kick *verb* **1** BOOT, punt **2** *Informal* GIVE UP, abandon, desist from, leave off, quit, stop ▸*noun* **3** *Informal* THRILL, buzz (*slang*), pleasure, stimulation

kick off *verb* BEGIN, commence, get the show on the road, initiate, open, start

kick out *verb* DISMISS, eject, evict, expel, get rid of, remove, sack (*informal*)

kid[1] *noun Informal* CHILD, baby, infant, minor, teenager, tot, youngster, youth

kid[2] *verb* TEASE, delude, fool, hoax, jest, joke, pretend, trick

kidnap *verb* ABDUCT, capture, hijack, hold to ransom, seize

kill *verb* 1 SLAY, assassinate, butcher, destroy, execute, exterminate, liquidate, massacre, murder, slaughter 2 SUPPRESS, extinguish, halt, quash, quell, scotch, smother, stifle, stop

killer *noun* ASSASSIN, butcher, cut-throat, executioner, exterminator, gunman, hit man (*slang*), murderer, slayer

killing *noun* 1 SLAUGHTER, bloodshed, carnage, extermination, homicide, manslaughter, massacre, murder, slaying 2 *Informal* BONANZA, cleanup (*informal*), coup, gain, profit, success, windfall

killjoy *noun* SPOILSPORT, dampener, wet blanket (*informal*)

kin *noun* FAMILY, kindred, kinsfolk, relations, relatives

kind[1] *adjective* CONSIDERATE, benign, charitable, compassionate, courteous, friendly, generous, humane, kindly, obliging, philanthropic, tender-hearted

kind[2] *noun* CLASS, brand, breed, family, set, sort, species, variety

kind-hearted *adjective* SYMPATHETIC, altruistic, compassionate, considerate, generous, good-natured, helpful, humane, kind, tender-hearted

kindle *verb* 1 SET FIRE TO, ignite, inflame, light 2 AROUSE, awaken, induce, inspire, provoke, rouse, stimulate, stir

kindliness *noun* KINDNESS, amiability, benevolence, charity, compassion, friendliness, gentleness, humanity, kind-heartedness

kindly *adjective* 1 GOOD-NATURED, benevolent, benign, compassionate, helpful, kind, pleasant, sympathetic, warm ▶ *adverb* 2 POLITELY, agreeably, cordially, graciously, tenderly, thoughtfully

kindness *noun* GOODWILL, benevolence, charity, compassion, generosity, humanity, kindliness, philanthropy, understanding

kindred *adjective* 1 SIMILAR, akin, corresponding, like, matching, related ▶ *noun* 2 FAMILY, kin, kinsfolk, relations, relatives

king *noun* RULER, emperor, monarch, sovereign

kingdom *noun* COUNTRY, nation, realm, state, territory

kink *noun* 1 TWIST, bend, coil, wrinkle 2 QUIRK, eccentricity, fetish, foible, idiosyncrasy, vagary, whim

kinky *adjective* 1 *Slang* WEIRD, eccentric, odd, outlandish, peculiar, queer, quirky, strange 2 TWISTED, coiled, curled, tangled

kinship *noun* 1 RELATION, consanguinity, kin, ties of blood 2 SIMILARITY, affinity, association, connection, correspondence, relationship

kiosk *noun* BOOTH, bookstall,

counter, newsstand, stall, stand

kiss verb 1 OSCULATE, neck (*informal*), peck (*informal*) 2 BRUSH, glance, graze, scrape, touch ▸ noun 3 OSCULATION, peck (*informal*), smacker (*slang*), smooch (*slang*)

kit noun EQUIPMENT, apparatus, gear, paraphernalia, tackle, tools

knack noun SKILL, ability, aptitude, capacity, expertise, facility, gift, propensity, talent, trick

knave noun ROGUE, rascal, scoundrel, villain

knead verb SQUEEZE, form, manipulate, massage, mold, press, rub, shape, work

kneel verb GENUFLECT, get (down) on one's knees, stoop

knell noun RINGING, chime, peal, sound, toll

knick-knack noun TRINKET, bagatelle, bauble, bric-a-brac, plaything, trifle

knife noun 1 BLADE, cutter ▸ verb 2 CUT, lacerate, pierce, slash, stab, wound

knit verb 1 JOIN, bind, fasten, intertwine, link, tie, unite, weave 2 WRINKLE, crease, furrow, knot, pucker

knob noun LUMP, bump, hump, knot, projection, protrusion, stud

knock verb 1 HIT, belt (*informal*), cuff, punch, rap, smack, strike, thump 2 *Informal* CRITICIZE, abuse, belittle, censure, condemn, denigrate, deprecate, disparage, find fault, run down ▸ noun 3 BLOW, clip, clout (*informal*), cuff, rap, slap, smack, thump 4 SETBACK,

defeat, failure, rebuff, rejection, reversal

knock down verb DEMOLISH, destroy, fell, level, raze

knock off verb 1 STOP WORK, clock off, clock out, finish 2 STEAL, pinch, rob, thieve

knockout noun 1 KILLER BLOW, *coup de grâce*, KO or K.O. (*slang*) 2 SUCCESS, hit, sensation, smash, smash hit, triumph, winner

knot noun 1 CONNECTION, bond, joint, ligature, loop, tie 2 CLUSTER, bunch, clump, collection ▸ verb 3 TIE, bind, loop, secure, tether

know verb 1 REALIZE, comprehend, feel certain, notice, perceive, recognize, see, understand 2 BE ACQUAINTED WITH, be familiar with, have dealings with, have knowledge of, recognize

know-how noun CAPABILITY, ability, aptitude, expertise, ingenuity, knack, knowledge, savoir-faire, skill, talent

knowing adjective MEANINGFUL, expressive, significant

knowingly adverb DELIBERATELY, consciously, intentionally, on purpose, purposely, willfully, wittingly

knowledge noun 1 LEARNING, education, enlightenment, erudition, instruction, intelligence, scholarship, wisdom 2 ACQUAINTANCE, cognizance, familiarity, intimacy

knowledgeable adjective 1 WELL-INFORMED, *au fait*, aware, clued-up (*informal*), cognizant, conversant, experienced, familiar, in the know (*informal*)

2 INTELLIGENT, educated, erudite, learned, scholarly

known *adjective* FAMOUS, acknowledged, avowed, celebrated, noted, recognized, well-known

knuckle under *verb* GIVE WAY, accede, acquiesce, capitulate, cave in (*informal*), give in, submit, succumb, surrender, yield

kudos *noun* PRAISE, acclaim, applause, credit, laudation, plaudits, recognition

L l

label *noun* **1** TAG, marker, sticker, ticket ▸ *verb* **2** MARK, stamp, tag

labor *noun* **1** WORK, industry, toil **2** WORKERS, employees, hands, laborers, workforce **3** CHILDBIRTH, delivery, parturition ▸ *verb* **4** WORK, endeavor, slave, strive, struggle, sweat (*informal*), toil **5** (usually with *under*) BE DISADVANTAGED, be a victim of, be burdened by, suffer **6** OVEREMPHASIZE, dwell on, elaborate, overdo, strain

labored *adjective* FORCED, awkward, difficult, heavy, stiff, strained

laborer *noun* WORKER, blue-collar worker, drudge, hand, manual worker

laborious *adjective* HARD, arduous, backbreaking, exhausting, onerous, strenuous, tiring, tough, wearisome

labyrinth *noun* MAZE, intricacy, jungle, tangle

lace *noun* **1** NETTING, filigree, openwork **2** CORD, bootlace, shoelace, string, tie ▸ *verb* **3** FASTEN, bind, do up, thread, tie **4** MIX IN, add to, fortify, spike

lacerate *verb* TEAR, claw, cut, gash, mangle, rip, slash, wound

laceration *noun* CUT, gash, rent, rip, slash, tear, wound

lack *noun* **1** SHORTAGE, absence, dearth, deficiency, need, scarcity, want ▸ *verb* **2** NEED, be deficient in, be short of, be without, miss, require, want

lackadaisical *adjective* **1** LETHARGIC, apathetic, dull, half-hearted, indifferent, languid, listless **2** LAZY, abstracted, dreamy, idle, indolent, inert

lackey *noun* **1** HANGER-ON, brown-noser (*slang*), flatterer, minion, sycophant, toady, yes man **2** MANSERVANT, attendant, flunky, footman, valet

lackluster *adjective* FLAT, drab, dull, leaden, lifeless, muted, prosaic, uninspired, vapid

laconic *adjective* TERSE, brief, concise, curt, monosyllabic, pithy, short, succinct

lad *noun* BOY, fellow, guy (*informal*), juvenile, kid (*informal*), youngster, youth

laden *adjective* LOADED, burdened, charged, encumbered, full, weighed down

lady *noun* **1** GENTLEWOMAN, dame **2** WOMAN, female

ladylike *adjective* REFINED,

elegant, genteel, modest, polite, proper, respectable, sophisticated, well-bred

lag *verb* HANG BACK, dawdle, delay, linger, loiter, straggle, tarry, trail

laggard *noun* STRAGGLER, dawdler, idler, loiterer, slowpoke (*informal*), sluggard, snail

laid-back *adjective* RELAXED, casual, easy-going, free and easy, unflappable (*informal*), unhurried

lair *noun* NEST, burrow, den, earth, hole

laissez faire *noun* NONINTERVENTION, free enterprise, free trade

lake *noun* POND, basin, lagoon, mere, pool, reservoir, tarn

lame *adjective* 1 DISABLED, challenged, crippled, game, handicapped, hobbling, limping 2 UNCONVINCING, feeble, flimsy, inadequate, lousy (*slang*), pathetic, poor, thin, unsatisfactory, weak

lament *verb* 1 COMPLAIN, bemoan, bewail, deplore, grieve, mourn, regret, sorrow, wail, weep ▶ *noun* 2 COMPLAINT, lamentation, moan, wailing 3 DIRGE, elegy, requiem, threnody

lamentable *adjective* REGRETTABLE, deplorable, distressing, grievous, mournful, tragic, unfortunate, woeful

lampoon *noun* 1 SATIRE, burlesque, caricature, parody, spoof (*informal*) ▶ *verb* 2 RIDICULE, caricature, make fun of, mock, parody, satirize

land *noun* 1 GROUND, dry land, earth, terra firma 2 SOIL, dirt, ground, loam 3 COUNTRYSIDE, farmland 4 PROPERTY, estate, grounds, realty 5 COUNTRY, district, nation, province, region, territory, tract ▶ *verb* 6 ARRIVE, alight, come to rest, disembark, dock, touch down 7 END UP, turn up, wind up 8 *Informal* OBTAIN, acquire, gain, get, secure, win

landlord *noun* 1 INNKEEPER, host, hotelier 2 OWNER, freeholder, lessor, proprietor

landmark *noun* 1 FEATURE, monument 2 MILESTONE, turning point, watershed

landscape *noun* SCENERY, countryside, outlook, panorama, prospect, scene, view, vista

landslide *noun* 1 ROCKFALL, avalanche, landslip ▶ *adjective* 2 OVERWHELMING, conclusive, decisive, runaway

lane *noun* ROAD, alley, footpath, passageway, path, pathway, street, way

language *noun* 1 SPEECH, communication, discourse, expression, parlance, talk 2 TONGUE, dialect, patois, vernacular

languid *adjective* 1 LAZY, indifferent, lackadaisical, languorous, listless, unenthusiastic 2 LETHARGIC, dull, heavy, sluggish, torpid

languish *verb* 1 WEAKEN, decline, droop, fade, fail, faint, flag, wilt, wither 2 (often with *for*) PINE, desire, hanker, hunger, long, yearn 3 BE NEGLECTED, be abandoned, rot, suffer, waste away

lank *adjective* **1** LIMP, lifeless, straggling **2** THIN, emaciated, gaunt, lean, scrawny, skinny, slender, slim, spare

lanky *adjective* GANGLING, angular, bony, gaunt, rangy, spare, tall

lap[1] *noun* CIRCUIT, circle, loop, orbit, tour

lap[2] *verb* **1** RIPPLE, gurgle, plash, purl, splash, swish, wash **2** DRINK, lick, sip, sup

lapse *noun* **1** MISTAKE, error, failing, fault, indiscretion, negligence, omission, oversight, slip **2** INTERVAL, break, breathing space, gap, intermission, interruption, lull, pause **3** DROP, decline, deterioration, fall ▶*verb* **4** DROP, decline, degenerate, deteriorate, fall, sink, slide, slip **5** END, expire, run out, stop, terminate

lapsed *adjective* OUT OF DATE, discontinued, ended, expired, finished, invalid, run out

large *adjective* **1** BIG, considerable, enormous, gigantic, great, huge, immense, massive, monumental, sizable *or* sizeable, substantial, vast **2 at large: a** FREE, at liberty, on the loose, on the run, unconfined **b** IN GENERAL, as a whole, chiefly, generally, in the main, mainly **c** AT LENGTH, exhaustively, greatly, in full detail

largely *adverb* MAINLY, as a rule, by and large, chiefly, generally, mostly, predominantly, primarily, principally, to a great extent

large-scale *adjective* WIDE-RANGING, broad, extensive, far-reaching, global, sweeping, vast, wholesale, wide

lark *noun* **1** PRANK, caper, escapade, fun, game, jape, mischief ▶*verb* **2 lark about** PLAY, caper, cavort, have fun, make mischief

lash[1] *noun* **1** BLOW, hit, stripe, stroke, swipe (*informal*) ▶*verb* **2** WHIP, beat, birch, flog, scourge, thrash **3** POUND, beat, buffet, dash, drum, hammer, smack, strike **4** SCOLD, attack, blast, censure, criticize, put down, upbraid

lash[2] *verb* FASTEN, bind, make fast, secure, strap, tie

lass *noun* GIRL, damsel, maid, maiden, young woman

last[1] *adjective* **1** HINDMOST, at the end, rearmost **2** MOST RECENT, latest **3** FINAL, closing, concluding, terminal, ultimate ▶*adverb* **4** IN THE REAR, after, behind, bringing up the rear, in or at the end

last[2] *verb* CONTINUE, abide, carry on, endure, keep on, persist, remain, stand up, survive

lasting *adjective* CONTINUING, abiding, durable, enduring, long-standing, long-term, perennial, permanent

latch *noun* **1** FASTENING, bar, bolt, catch, hasp, hook, lock ▶*verb* **2** FASTEN, bar, bolt, make fast, secure

late *adjective* **1** OVERDUE, behind, behindhand, belated, delayed, last-minute, tardy **2** RECENT, advanced, fresh, modern, new **3** DEAD, deceased, defunct, departed, former, past ▶*adverb*

4 BELATEDLY, at the last minute, behindhand, behind time, dilatorily, tardily

lately *adverb* RECENTLY, in recent times, just now, latterly, not long ago, of late

lateness *noun* DELAY, belatedness, tardiness

latent *adjective* HIDDEN, concealed, dormant, invisible, potential, undeveloped, unrealized

later *adverb* AFTERWARDS, after, by and by, in a while, in time, later on, subsequently, thereafter

lateral *adjective* SIDEWAYS, edgeways, flanking

latest *adjective* UP-TO-DATE, cool (*informal*), current, fashionable, modern, most recent, newest, phat (*slang*), up-to-the-minute

lather *noun* **1** FROTH, bubbles, foam, soapsuds, suds ▶ *verb* **2** FROTH, foam, soap

latitude *noun* SCOPE, elbowroom, freedom, laxity, leeway, liberty, license, play

latter *adjective* LAST-MENTIONED, closing, concluding, last, second

latterly *adverb* RECENTLY, lately, of late

lattice *noun* GRID, grating, grille, trellis

laudable *adjective* PRAISEWORTHY, admirable, commendable, creditable, excellent, meritorious, of note, worthy

laugh *verb* **1** CHUCKLE, be in stitches, chortle, giggle, guffaw, snigger, split one's sides, titter ▶ *noun* **2** CHUCKLE, chortle, giggle, guffaw, snigger, titter **3** *Informal* JOKE, hoot (*informal*), lark, scream (*informal*)

laughable *adjective* RIDICULOUS, absurd, derisory, farcical, ludicrous, nonsensical, preposterous, risible

laughing stock *noun* FIGURE OF FUN, butt, target, victim

laugh off *verb* DISREGARD, brush aside, dismiss, ignore, minimize, pooh-pooh, shrug off

laughter *noun* AMUSEMENT, glee, hilarity, merriment, mirth

launch *verb* **1** PROPEL, discharge, dispatch, fire, project, send off, set in motion **2** BEGIN, commence, embark upon, inaugurate, initiate, instigate, introduce, open, start

laurels *plural noun* GLORY, credit, distinction, fame, honor, kudos, praise, prestige, recognition, renown

lavatory *noun* TOILET, bathroom, latrine, powder room, (public) convenience, washroom, water closet, W.C.

lavish *adjective* **1** PLENTIFUL, abundant, copious, profuse, prolific **2** GENEROUS, bountiful, free, liberal, munificent, open-handed, unstinting **3** EXTRAVAGANT, exaggerated, excessive, immoderate, prodigal, unrestrained, wasteful, wild ▶ *verb* **4** SPEND, deluge, dissipate, expend, heap, pour, shower, squander, waste

law *noun* **1** CONSTITUTION, charter, code **2** RULE, act, command, commandment, decree, edict, order, ordinance, regulation, statute **3** PRINCIPLE, axiom, canon, precept

law-abiding *adjective* OBEDIENT, compliant, dutiful, good, honest, honorable, lawful, orderly, peaceable

law-breaker *noun* CRIMINAL, convict, crook (*informal*), culprit, delinquent, felon, miscreant, offender, villain, wrongdoer

lawful *adjective* LEGAL, authorized, constitutional, legalized, legitimate, licit, permissible, rightful, valid, warranted

lawless *adjective* DISORDERLY, anarchic, chaotic, rebellious, riotous, unruly, wild

lawlessness *noun* ANARCHY, chaos, disorder, mob rule

lawsuit *noun* CASE, action, dispute, industrial tribunal, litigation, proceedings, prosecution, suit, trial

lawyer *noun* LEGAL ADVISER, advocate, attorney, barrister (*chiefly Brit.*), counsel, counselor

lax *adjective* SLACK, careless, casual, lenient, negligent, overindulgent, remiss, slapdash, slipshod

lay[1] *verb* 1 PLACE, deposit, leave, plant, put, set, set down, spread 2 ARRANGE, organize, position, set out 3 PRODUCE, bear, deposit 4 PUT FORWARD, advance, bring forward, lodge, offer, present, submit 5 ATTRIBUTE, allocate, allot, ascribe, assign, impute 6 DEVISE, concoct, contrive, design, hatch, plan, plot, prepare, work out 7 BET, gamble, give odds, hazard, risk, stake, wager

lay[2] *adjective* 1 NONCLERICAL, secular 2 NONSPECIALIST,

amateur, inexpert, nonprofessional

layer *noun* TIER, row, seam, stratum, thickness

layman *noun* AMATEUR, lay person, nonprofessional, outsider

layoff *noun* DISMISSAL, discharge, unemployment

lay off *verb* DISMISS, discharge, let go, pay off

lay on *verb* PROVIDE, cater (for), furnish, give, purvey, supply

layout *noun* ARRANGEMENT, design, formation, outline, plan

lay out *verb* 1 ARRANGE, design, display, exhibit, plan, spread out 2 *Informal* SPEND, disburse, expend, fork out (*slang*), invest, pay, shell out (*informal*) 3 *Informal* KNOCK OUT, knock for six (*informal*), knock unconscious, KO *or* K.O. (*slang*)

laziness *noun* IDLENESS, inactivity, indolence, slackness, sloth, sluggishness

lazy *adjective* 1 IDLE, inactive, indolent, inert, slack, slothful, slow, workshy 2 LETHARGIC, drowsy, languid, languorous, sleepy, slow-moving, sluggish, somnolent, torpid

lead *verb* 1 GUIDE, conduct, escort, pilot, precede, show the way, steer, usher 2 PERSUADE, cause, dispose, draw, incline, induce, influence, prevail, prompt 3 COMMAND, direct, govern, head, manage, preside over, supervise 4 BE AHEAD (OF), blaze a trail, come first, exceed, excel, outdo, outstrip, surpass, transcend 5 LIVE, experience, have, pass, spend, undergo

6 RESULT IN, bring on, cause, contribute, produce ▸ *noun* **7** FIRST PLACE, precedence, primacy, priority, supremacy, vanguard **8** ADVANTAGE, edge, margin, start **9** EXAMPLE, direction, guidance, leadership, model **10** CLUE, hint, indication, suggestion **11** LEADING ROLE, principal, protagonist, title role ▸ *adjective* **12** MAIN, chief, first, foremost, head, leading, premier, primary, prime, principal

leader *noun* PRINCIPAL, boss (*informal*), captain, chief, chieftain, commander, director, guide, head, ringleader, ruler

leadership *noun* **1** GUIDANCE, direction, domination, management, running, superintendency **2** AUTHORITY, command, control, influence, initiative, pre-eminence, supremacy

leading *adjective* MAIN, chief, dominant, first, foremost, greatest, highest, primary, principal

lead on *verb* ENTICE, beguile, deceive, draw on, lure, seduce, string along (*informal*), tempt

lead up to *verb* INTRODUCE, pave the way, prepare for

leaf *noun* **1** FROND, blade **2** PAGE, folio, sheet ▸ *verb* **3 leaf through** BROWSE, flip, glance, riffle, skim, thumb (through)

leaflet *noun* BOOKLET, brochure, circular, pamphlet

leafy *adjective* GREEN, bosky (*literary*), shaded, shady, verdant

league *noun* **1** ASSOCIATION, alliance, coalition,

confederation, consortium, federation, fraternity, group, guild, partnership, union **2** CLASS, category, level

leak *noun* **1** HOLE, aperture, chink, crack, crevice, fissure, opening, puncture **2** DRIP, leakage, percolation, seepage **3** DISCLOSURE, divulgence ▸ *verb* **4** DRIP, escape, exude, ooze, pass, percolate, seep, spill, trickle **5** DISCLOSE, divulge, give away, let slip, make known, make public, pass on, reveal, tell

leaky *adjective* PUNCTURED, cracked, holey, leaking, perforated, porous, split

lean[1] *verb* **1** REST, be supported, prop, recline, repose **2** BEND, heel, incline, slant, slope, tilt, tip **3** TEND, be disposed to, be prone to, favor, prefer **4 lean on** DEPEND ON, count on, have faith in, rely on, trust

lean[2] *adjective* **1** SLIM, angular, bony, gaunt, rangy, skinny, slender, spare, thin, wiry **2** UNPRODUCTIVE, barren, meager, poor, scanty, unfruitful

leaning *noun* TENDENCY, bent, bias, disposition, inclination, partiality, penchant, predilection, proclivity, propensity

leap *verb* **1** JUMP, bounce, bound, hop, skip, spring ▸ *noun* **2** JUMP, bound, spring, vault **3** INCREASE, escalation, rise, surge, upsurge, upswing

learn *verb* **1** MASTER, grasp, pick up **2** MEMORIZE, commit to memory, get off pat, learn by heart **3** DISCOVER, ascertain, detect, discern, find out, gather, hear, understand

learned *adjective* SCHOLARLY, academic, erudite, highbrow, intellectual, versed, well-informed, well-read

learner *noun* BEGINNER, apprentice, neophyte, novice, tyro

learning *noun* KNOWLEDGE, culture, education, erudition, information, lore, scholarship, study, wisdom

lease *verb* HIRE, charter, let, loan, rent

leash *noun* LEAD, rein, tether

least *adjective* SMALLEST, fewest, lowest, meanest, minimum, poorest, slightest, tiniest

leathery *adjective* TOUGH, hard, rough

leave¹ *verb* 1 DEPART, decamp, disappear, exit, go away, make tracks, move, pull out, quit, retire, slope off, withdraw 2 FORGET, leave behind, mislay 3 CAUSE, deposit, generate, produce, result in 4 GIVE UP, abandon, drop, relinquish, renounce, surrender 5 ENTRUST, allot, assign, cede, commit, consign, give over, refer 6 BEQUEATH, hand down, will

leave² *noun* 1 PERMISSION, allowance, authorization, concession, consent, dispensation, freedom, liberty, sanction 2 HOLIDAY, furlough, leave of absence, sabbatical, time off, vacation 3 PARTING, adieu, departure, farewell, good-bye, leave-taking, retirement, withdrawal

leave out *verb* OMIT, blow off (*slang*), cast aside, disregard, exclude, ignore, neglect,

overlook, reject

lecherous *adjective* LUSTFUL, lascivious, lewd, libidinous, licentious, prurient, salacious

lecture *noun* 1 TALK, address, discourse, instruction, lesson, speech 2 REBUKE, reprimand, reproof, scolding, talking-to (*informal*), telling off (*informal*) ▶*verb* 3 TALK, address, discourse, expound, hold forth, speak, spout, teach 4 SCOLD, admonish, berate, castigate, censure, reprimand, reprove, tell off (*informal*)

ledge *noun* SHELF, mantle, projection, ridge, sill, step

leer *noun, verb* GRIN, gloat, goggle, ogle, smirk, squint, stare

lees *plural noun* SEDIMENT, deposit, dregs, grounds

leeway *noun* ROOM, elbowroom, latitude, margin, play, scope, space

left *adjective* 1 LEFT-HAND, larboard (*Nautical*), port, sinistral 2 *Of politics* SOCIALIST, leftist, left-wing, radical

leftover *noun* REMNANT, oddment, scrap

left-wing *adjective* SOCIALIST, communist, radical, red (*informal*)

leg *noun* 1 LIMB, lower limb, member, pin (*informal*), stump (*informal*) 2 SUPPORT, brace, prop, upright 3 STAGE, lap, part, portion, section, segment, stretch 4 **pull someone's leg** *Informal* TEASE, fool, kid (*informal*), make fun of, trick

legacy *noun* BEQUEST, estate, gift, heirloom, inheritance

legal *adjective* **1** LEGITIMATE, allowed, authorized, constitutional, lawful, licit, permissible, sanctioned, valid **2** JUDICIAL, forensic, juridical

legality *noun* LEGITIMACY, lawfulness, rightfulness, validity

legalize *verb* ALLOW, approve, authorize, decriminalize, legitimate, legitimize, license, permit, sanction, validate

legation *noun* DELEGATION, consulate, embassy, representation

legend *noun* **1** MYTH, fable, fiction, folk tale, saga, story, tale **2** CELEBRITY, luminary, megastar (*informal*), phenomenon, prodigy **3** INSCRIPTION, caption, motto

legendary *adjective* **1** MYTHICAL, apocryphal, fabled, fabulous, fictitious, romantic, traditional **2** FAMOUS, celebrated, famed, illustrious, immortal, renowned, well-known

legibility *noun* CLARITY, neatness, readability

legible *adjective* CLEAR, decipherable, distinct, easy to read, neat, readable

legion *noun* **1** ARMY, brigade, company, division, force, troop **2** MULTITUDE, drove, horde, host, mass, myriad, number, throng

legislation *noun* **1** LAWMAKING, enactment, prescription, regulation **2** LAW, act, bill, charter, measure, regulation, ruling, statute

legislative *adjective* LAW-MAKING, judicial, law-giving

legislator *noun* LAWMAKER, lawgiver

legislature *noun* PARLIAMENT, assembly, chamber, congress, senate

legitimate *adjective* **1** LEGAL, authentic, authorized, genuine, kosher (*informal*), lawful, licit, rightful **2** REASONABLE, admissible, correct, justifiable, logical, sensible, valid, warranted, well-founded ▶*verb* **3** AUTHORIZE, legalize, legitimize, permit, pronounce lawful, sanction

legitimize *verb* LEGALIZE, authorize, permit, sanction

leisure *noun* SPARE TIME, ease, freedom, free time, liberty, recreation, relaxation, rest

leisurely *adjective* UNHURRIED, comfortable, easy, gentle, lazy, relaxed, slow

lend *verb* **1** LOAN, advance **2** ADD, bestow, confer, give, grant, impart, provide, supply **3 lend itself to** SUIT, be appropriate, be serviceable

length *noun* **1** *Of linear extent* DISTANCE, extent, longitude, measure, reach, span **2** *Of time* DURATION, period, space, span, stretch, term **3** PIECE, measure, portion, section, segment **4 at length: a** IN DETAIL, completely, fully, in depth, thoroughly, to the full **b** FOR A LONG TIME, for ages, for hours, interminably **c** AT LAST, at long last, eventually, finally, in the end

lengthen *verb* EXTEND, continue, draw out, elongate, expand, increase, prolong, protract, spin out, stretch

lengthy *adjective* LONG, drawn-out, extended, interminable, long-drawn-out, long-winded, prolonged, protracted, tedious

leniency noun TOLERANCE, clemency, compassion, forbearance, indulgence, mercy, moderation, pity, quarter

lenient adjective TOLERANT, compassionate, forbearing, forgiving, indulgent, kind, merciful, sparing

lesbian adjective HOMOSEXUAL, gay, sapphic

less adjective 1 SMALLER, shorter ▶preposition 2 MINUS, excepting, lacking, subtracting, without

lessen verb REDUCE, contract, decrease, diminish, ease, lower, minimize, narrow, shrink

lesser adjective MINOR, inferior, less important, lower, secondary

lesson noun 1 CLASS, coaching, instruction, period, schooling, teaching, tutoring 2 EXAMPLE, deterrent, message, moral

let[1] verb 1 ALLOW, authorize, entitle, give permission, give the go-ahead, permit, sanction, tolerate 2 LEASE, hire, rent

let[2] noun HINDRANCE, constraint, impediment, interference, obstacle, obstruction, prohibition, restriction

letdown noun DISAPPOINTMENT, anticlimax, blow, comedown (informal), setback, washout (informal)

let down verb DISAPPOINT, disenchant, disillusion, dissatisfy, fail, fall short, leave in the lurch, leave stranded

lethal adjective DEADLY, dangerous, destructive, devastating, fatal, mortal, murderous, virulent

lethargic adjective SLUGGISH, apathetic, drowsy, dull, languid, listless, sleepy, slothful

lethargy noun SLUGGISHNESS, apathy, drowsiness, inertia, languor, lassitude, listlessness, sleepiness, sloth

let off verb 1 FIRE, detonate, discharge, explode 2 EMIT, exude, give off, leak, release 3 EXCUSE, absolve, discharge, exempt, exonerate, forgive, pardon, release, spare

let on verb REVEAL, admit, disclose, divulge, give away, let the cat out of the bag (informal), make known, say

let out verb 1 EMIT, give vent to, produce 2 RELEASE, discharge, free, let go, liberate

letter noun 1 CHARACTER, sign, symbol 2 MESSAGE, communication, dispatch, epistle, line, missive, note

let-up noun LESSENING, break, breathing space, interval, lull, pause, remission, respite, slackening

let up verb STOP, abate, decrease, diminish, ease (up), moderate, relax, slacken, subside

level adjective 1 HORIZONTAL, flat 2 EVEN, consistent, plain, smooth, uniform 3 EQUAL, balanced, commensurate, comparable, equivalent, even, neck and neck, on a level playing field (informal), on a par, proportionate ▶verb 4 FLATTEN, even off or out, plane, smooth 5 EQUALIZE, balance, even up 6 RAZE, bulldoze, demolish, destroy, devastate, flatten, knock down, pull down, tear down 7 DIRECT,

aim, focus, point, train ▶ *noun*
8 POSITION, achievement,
degree, grade, rank, stage,
standard, standing, status **9 on
the level** *Informal* HONEST,
above board, fair, genuine,
square, straight

level-headed *adjective* STEADY,
balanced, calm, collected,
composed, cool, sensible,
unflappable (*informal*)

lever *noun* **1** HANDLE, bar ▶ *verb*
2 PRISE, force

leverage *noun* INFLUENCE,
authority, clout (*informal*), pull
(*informal*), weight

levity *noun* LIGHT-HEARTEDNESS,
facetiousness, flippancy,
frivolity, silliness, skittishness,
triviality

levy *verb* **1** IMPOSE, charge,
collect, demand, exact
2 CONSCRIPT, call up, mobilize,
muster, raise ▶ *noun*
3 IMPOSITION, assessment,
collection, exaction, gathering
4 TAX, duty, excise, fee, tariff,
toll

lewd *adjective* INDECENT, bawdy,
lascivious, libidinous, licentious,
lustful, obscene, pornographic,
smutty, wanton, X-rated

lewdness *noun* INDECENCY,
bawdiness, carnality,
debauchery, depravity,
lasciviousness, lechery,
licentiousness, obscenity,
pornography, wantonness

liability *noun* **1** RESPONSIBILITY,
accountability, answerability,
culpability **2** DEBT, debit,
obligation **3** DISADVANTAGE,
burden, drawback,
encumbrance, handicap,
hindrance, inconvenience,

millstone, nuisance

liable *adjective* **1** RESPONSIBLE,
accountable, answerable,
obligated **2** VULNERABLE,
exposed, open, subject,
susceptible **3** LIKELY, apt,
disposed, inclined, prone,
tending

liaise *verb* LINK, communicate,
keep contact, mediate

liaison *noun* **1** COMMUNICATION,
connection, contact, hook-up,
interchange **2** AFFAIR, amour,
entanglement, intrigue, love
affair, romance

liar *noun* FALSIFIER, fabricator,
fibber, perjurer

libel *noun* **1** DEFAMATION,
aspersion, calumny,
denigration, smear ▶ *verb*
2 DEFAME, blacken, malign,
revile, slur, smear, vilify

libelous *adjective* DEFAMATORY,
derogatory, false, injurious,
malicious, scurrilous, untrue

liberal *adjective* **1** PROGRESSIVE,
libertarian, radical, reformist
2 GENEROUS, beneficent,
bountiful, charitable, kind,
open-handed, open-hearted,
unstinting **3** TOLERANT,
broad-minded, indulgent,
permissive **4** ABUNDANT, ample,
bountiful, copious, handsome,
lavish, munificent, plentiful,
profuse, rich

liberality *noun* **1** GENEROSITY,
beneficence, benevolence,
bounty, charity, kindness,
largesse *or* largess,
munificence, philanthropy
2 TOLERATION,
broad-mindedness, latitude,
liberalism, libertarianism,
permissiveness

liberalize verb RELAX, ease, loosen, moderate, modify, slacken, soften

liberate verb FREE, deliver, emancipate, let loose, let out, release, rescue, set free

liberation noun DELIVERANCE, emancipation, freedom, freeing, liberty, release

liberator noun DELIVERER, emancipator, freer, redeemer, rescuer, savior

libertine noun REPROBATE, debauchee, lecher, profligate, rake, roué, sensualist, voluptuary, womanizer

liberty noun 1 FREEDOM, autonomy, emancipation, immunity, independence, liberation, release, self-determination, sovereignty 2 IMPERTINENCE, impropriety, impudence, insolence, presumption 3 **at liberty** FREE, on the loose, unrestricted

libidinous adjective LUSTFUL, carnal, debauched, lascivious, lecherous, sensual, wanton

license noun 1 CERTIFICATE, charter, permit, warrant 2 PERMISSION, authority, authorization, blank check, carte blanche, dispensation, entitlement, exemption, immunity, leave, liberty, right 3 LATITUDE, freedom, independence, leeway, liberty 4 LAXITY, excess, immoderation, indulgence, irresponsibility

license verb PERMIT, accredit, allow, authorize, certify, empower, sanction, warrant

licentious adjective PROMISCUOUS, abandoned, debauched, dissolute, immoral, lascivious, lustful, sensual, wanton

lick verb 1 TASTE, lap, tongue 2 Of flames FLICKER, dart, flick, play over, ripple, touch 3 Slang BEAT, defeat, master, outdo, outstrip, overcome, rout, trounce, vanquish ▶ noun 4 DAB, bit, stroke, touch 5 Informal PACE, clip (informal), rate, speed

lie¹ verb 1 FALSIFY, dissimulate, equivocate, fabricate, fib, prevaricate, tell untruths ▶ noun 2 FALSEHOOD, deceit, fabrication, fib, fiction, invention, prevarication, untruth

lie² verb 1 RECLINE, loll, lounge, repose, rest, sprawl, stretch out 2 BE SITUATED, be, be placed, exist, remain

life noun 1 BEING, sentience, vitality 2 EXISTENCE, being, lifetime, span, time 3 BIOGRAPHY, autobiography, confessions, history, life story, memoirs, story 4 BEHAVIOR, conduct, life style, way of life 5 LIVELINESS, animation, energy, high spirits, spirit, verve, vigor, vitality, vivacity, zest

lifeless adjective 1 DEAD, deceased, defunct, extinct, inanimate 2 DULL, colorless, flat, lackluster, lethargic, listless, sluggish, wooden 3 UNCONSCIOUS, comatose, dead to the world (informal), insensible

lifelike adjective REALISTIC, authentic, exact, faithful, natural, true-to-life, vivid

lifelong adjective LONG-STANDING, enduring, lasting, long-lasting, perennial, persistent

lifetime noun EXISTENCE, career, day(s), span, time

lift *verb* 1 RAISE, draw up, elevate, hoist, pick up, uplift, upraise 2 REVOKE, annul, cancel, countermand, end, remove, rescind, stop, terminate 3 DISAPPEAR, be dispelled, disperse, dissipate, vanish ▶*noun* 4 RIDE, drive, run 5 BOOST, encouragement, pick-me-up, shot in the arm (*informal*)

light¹ *noun* 1 BRIGHTNESS, brilliance, glare, gleam, glint, glow, illumination, luminosity, radiance, shine 2 LAMP, beacon, candle, flare, lantern, taper, torch 3 ASPECT, angle, context, interpretation, point of view, slant, vantage point, viewpoint 4 MATCH, flame, lighter ▶*adjective* 5 BRIGHT, brilliant, illuminated, luminous, lustrous, shining, well-lit 6 PALE, bleached, blond, faded, fair, pastel ▶*verb* 7 IGNITE, inflame, kindle 8 ILLUMINATE, brighten, light up

light² *adjective* 1 INSUBSTANTIAL, airy, buoyant, flimsy, portable, slight, underweight 2 WEAK, faint, gentle, indistinct, mild, moderate, slight, soft 3 INSIGNIFICANT, inconsequential, inconsiderable, scanty, slight, small, trifling, trivial 4 NIMBLE, agile, graceful, lithe, sprightly, sylphlike 5 LIGHT-HEARTED, amusing, entertaining, frivolous, funny, humorous, witty 6 DIGESTIBLE, frugal, modest ▶*verb* 7 SETTLE, alight, land, perch 8 **light on** or **upon** COME ACROSS, chance upon, discover, encounter, find, happen upon, hit upon, stumble on

lighten¹ *verb* BRIGHTEN, become light, illuminate, irradiate, light up

lighten² *verb* 1 EASE, allay, alleviate, ameliorate, assuage, lessen, mitigate, reduce, relieve 2 CHEER, brighten, buoy up, lift, perk up, revive

light-headed *adjective* FAINT, dizzy, giddy, hazy, vertiginous, woozy (*informal*)

light-hearted *adjective* CAREFREE, blithe, cheerful, happy-go-lucky, jolly, jovial, playful, upbeat (*informal*)

lightly *adverb* 1 GENTLY, delicately, faintly, slightly, softly 2 MODERATELY, sparingly, sparsely, thinly 3 EASILY, effortlessly, readily, simply 4 CARELESSLY, breezily, flippantly, frivolously, heedlessly, thoughtlessly

lightweight *adjective* UNIMPORTANT, inconsequential, insignificant, paltry, petty, slight, trifling, trivial, worthless

likable, likeable *adjective* ATTRACTIVE, agreeable, amiable, appealing, charming, engaging, nice, pleasant, sympathetic

like¹ *adjective* SIMILAR, akin, alike, analogous, corresponding, equivalent, identical, parallel, same

like² *verb* 1 ENJOY, be fond of, be keen on, be partial to, delight in, go for, love, relish, revel in 2 ADMIRE, appreciate, approve, cherish, esteem, hold dear, prize, take to 3 WISH, care to, choose, desire, fancy, feel inclined, prefer, want 4 *Informal* BE ATTRACTED TO, be captivated by, be turned on by (*informal*), lust after, take a liking to, take to

likelihood *noun* PROBABILITY, chance, possibility, prospect

likely *adjective* 1 INCLINED, apt, disposed, liable, prone, tending 2 PROBABLE, anticipated, expected, odds-on, on the cards, to be expected 3 PLAUSIBLE, believable, credible, feasible, possible, reasonable 4 PROMISING, hopeful, up-and-coming

liken *verb* COMPARE, equate, match, parallel, relate, set beside

likeness *noun* 1 RESEMBLANCE, affinity, correspondence, similarity 2 PORTRAIT, depiction, effigy, image, picture, representation

likewise *adverb* SIMILARLY, in like manner, in the same way

liking *noun* FONDNESS, affection, inclination, love, partiality, penchant, preference, soft spot, taste, weakness

limb *noun* 1 PART, appendage, arm, extremity, leg, member, wing 2 BRANCH, bough, offshoot, projection, spur

limelight *noun* PUBLICITY, attention, celebrity, fame, prominence, public eye, recognition, stardom, the spotlight

limit *noun* 1 BREAKING POINT, deadline, end, ultimate 2 BOUNDARY, border, edge, frontier, perimeter ▶ *verb* 3 RESTRICT, bound, check, circumscribe, confine, curb, ration, restrain

limitation *noun* RESTRICTION,

check, condition, constraint, control, curb, qualification, reservation, restraint

limited *adjective* RESTRICTED, bounded, checked, circumscribed, confined, constrained, controlled, curbed, finite

limitless *adjective* INFINITE, boundless, countless, endless, inexhaustible, unbounded, unlimited, untold, vast

limp[1] *verb* 1 HOBBLE, falter, hop, shamble, shuffle ▶ *noun* 2 LAMENESS, hobble

limp[2] *adjective* FLOPPY, drooping, flabby, flaccid, pliable, slack, soft

line *noun* 1 STROKE, band, groove, mark, score, scratch, streak, stripe 2 WRINKLE, crease, crow's foot, furrow, mark 3 BOUNDARY, border, borderline, edge, frontier, limit 4 STRING, cable, cord, rope, thread, wire 5 TRAJECTORY, course, direction, path, route, track 6 JOB, area, business, calling, employment, field, occupation, profession, specialization, trade 7 ROW, column, file, procession, queue, rank 8 **in line for** DUE FOR, in the running for ▶ *verb* 9 MARK, crease, furrow, rule, score 10 BORDER, bound, edge, fringe

lineaments *plural noun* FEATURES, countenance, face, physiognomy

lined *adjective* 1 RULED, feint 2 WRINKLED, furrowed, wizened, worn

lines *plural noun* WORDS, part, script

line-up *noun* ARRANGEMENT, array,

row, selection, team

linger verb 1 STAY, hang around, loiter, remain, stop, tarry, wait 2 DELAY, dally, dawdle, drag one's feet or heels, idle, take one's time

link noun 1 COMPONENT, constituent, element, member, part, piece 2 CONNECTION, affinity, association, attachment, bond, relationship, tie-up ▶ verb 3 FASTEN, attach, bind, connect, couple, join, tie, unite 4 ASSOCIATE, bracket, connect, identify, relate

lip noun 1 EDGE, brim, brink, margin, rim 2 Slang IMPUDENCE, backchat (informal), cheek (informal), effrontery, impertinence, insolence

liquid noun 1 FLUID, juice, solution ▶ adjective 2 FLUID, aqueous, flowing, melted, molten, running, runny 3 Of assets CONVERTIBLE, negotiable

liquidate verb 1 PAY, clear, discharge, honor, pay off, settle, square 2 DISSOLVE, abolish, annul, cancel, terminate 3 KILL, destroy, dispatch, eliminate, exterminate, get rid of, murder, wipe out (informal)

liquor noun 1 ALCOHOL, booze (informal), drink, hard stuff (informal), spirits, strong drink 2 JUICE, broth, extract, liquid, stock

list[1] noun 1 REGISTER, catalog, directory, index, inventory, record, roll, series, tally ▶ verb 2 TABULATE, catalog, enter, enumerate, itemize, record, register

list[2] verb 1 LEAN, careen, heel over, incline, tilt, tip ▶ noun 2 TILT, cant, leaning, slant

listen verb 1 HEAR, attend, lend an ear, prick up one's ears 2 PAY ATTENTION, heed, mind, obey, observe, take notice

listless adjective LANGUID, apathetic, indifferent, indolent, lethargic, sluggish

literacy noun EDUCATION, knowledge, learning

literal adjective 1 EXACT, accurate, close, faithful, strict, verbatim, word for word 2 ACTUAL, bona fide, genuine, plain, real, simple, true, unvarnished

literally adverb STRICTLY, actually, exactly, faithfully, precisely, really, to the letter, truly, verbatim, word for word

literary adjective WELL-READ, bookish, erudite, formal, learned, scholarly

literate adjective EDUCATED, informed, knowledgeable

literature noun WRITINGS, letters, lore

lithe adjective SUPPLE, flexible, limber, lissom(e), loose-limbed, pliable

litigant noun CLAIMANT, party, plaintiff

litigate verb SUE, go to court, press charges, prosecute

litigation noun LAWSUIT, action, case, prosecution

litter noun 1 RUBBISH, debris, detritus, garbage, muck, refuse, trash 2 BROOD, offspring, progeny, young ▶ verb 3 CLUTTER, derange, disarrange, disorder, mess up 4 SCATTER, strew

little *adjective* **1** SMALL, diminutive, miniature, minute, petite, short, tiny, wee **2** YOUNG, babyish, immature, infant, junior, undeveloped ▶ *adverb* **3** HARDLY, barely **4** RARELY, hardly ever, not often, scarcely, seldom ▶ *noun* **5** BIT, fragment, hint, particle, speck, spot, touch, trace

live¹ *verb* **1** EXIST, be, be alive, breathe **2** PERSIST, last, prevail **3** DWELL, abide, inhabit, lodge, occupy, reside, settle **4** SURVIVE, endure, get along, make ends meet, subsist, support oneself **5** THRIVE, flourish, prosper

live² *adjective* **1** LIVING, alive, animate, breathing **2** TOPICAL, burning, controversial, current, hot, pertinent, pressing, prevalent **3** BURNING, active, alight, blazing, glowing, hot, ignited, smoldering

livelihood *noun* OCCUPATION, bread and butter (*informal*), employment, job, living, work

liveliness *noun* ENERGY, animation, boisterousness, dynamism, spirit, sprightliness, vitality, vivacity

lively *adjective* **1** VIGOROUS, active, agile, alert, brisk, energetic, keen, perky, quick, sprightly **2** ANIMATED, cheerful, chirpy (*informal*), sparky, spirited, upbeat (*informal*), vivacious **3** VIVID, bright, colorful, exciting, forceful, invigorating, refreshing, stimulating

liven up *verb* STIR, animate, brighten, buck up (*informal*), enliven, perk up, rouse

liverish *adjective* **1** SICK, bilious,

queasy **2** IRRITABLE, crotchety, crusty, disagreeable, grumpy, ill-humored, irascible, splenetic, tetchy

livery *noun* COSTUME, attire, clothing, dress, garb, regalia, suit, uniform

livid *adjective* **1** *Informal* ANGRY, beside oneself, enraged, fuming, furious, incensed, indignant, infuriated, outraged **2** DISCOLORED, black-and-blue, bruised, contused, purple

living *adjective* **1** ALIVE, active, breathing, existing **2** CURRENT, active, contemporary, extant, in use ▶ *noun* **3** EXISTENCE, being, existing, life, subsistence **4** LIFE STYLE, way of life

load *noun* **1** CARGO, consignment, freight, shipment **2** BURDEN, albatross, encumbrance, millstone, onus, trouble, weight, worry ▶ *verb* **3** FILL, cram, freight, heap, pack, pile, stack, stuff **4** BURDEN, encumber, oppress, saddle with, weigh down, worry **5** *Of firearms* MAKE READY, charge, prime

loaded *adjective* **1** WEIGHTED, biased, distorted **2** TRICKY, artful, insidious, manipulative, prejudicial **3** *Slang* RICH, affluent, flush (*informal*), moneyed, wealthy, well-heeled (*informal*), well off, well-to-do

loaf¹ *noun* LUMP, block, cake, cube, slab

loaf² *verb* IDLE, laze, lie around, loiter, lounge around, take it easy

loan *noun* **1** ADVANCE, credit ▶ *verb* **2** LEND, advance, let out

loath, loth *adjective* UNWILLING,

averse, disinclined, opposed, reluctant

loathe *verb* HATE, abhor, abominate, despise, detest, dislike

loathing *noun* HATRED, abhorrence, antipathy, aversion, detestation, disgust, repugnance, repulsion, revulsion

loathsome *adjective* HATEFUL, abhorrent, detestable, disgusting, nauseating, obnoxious, odious, offensive, repugnant, repulsive, revolting, scuzzy (*slang*), vile

lobby *noun* **1** CORRIDOR, entrance hall, foyer, hallway, passage, porch, vestibule **2** PRESSURE GROUP ▶ *verb* **3** CAMPAIGN, influence, persuade, press, pressure, promote, push, urge

local *adjective* **1** REGIONAL, provincial **2** RESTRICTED, confined, limited ▶ *noun* **3** RESIDENT, inhabitant, native

locality *noun* **1** NEIGHBORHOOD, area, district, neck of the woods (*informal*), region, vicinity **2** SITE, locale, location, place, position, scene, setting, spot

localize *verb* RESTRICT, circumscribe, confine, contain, delimit, limit

locate *verb* **1** FIND, come across, detect, discover, pin down, pinpoint, track down, unearth **2** PLACE, establish, fix, put, seat, set, settle, situate

location *noun* POSITION, locale, place, point, site, situation, spot, venue

lock[1] *noun* **1** FASTENING, bolt,

clasp, padlock ▶ *verb* **2** FASTEN, bolt, close, seal, secure, shut **3** UNITE, clench, engage, entangle, entwine, join, link **4** EMBRACE, clasp, clutch, encircle, enclose, grasp, hug, press

lock[2] *noun* STRAND, curl, ringlet, tress, tuft

lockup *noun* PRISON, cell, jail

lock up *verb* IMPRISON, cage, confine, detain, incarcerate, jail, put behind bars, shut up

lodge *noun* **1** CABIN, chalet, cottage, gatehouse, hut, shelter **2** SOCIETY, branch, chapter, club, group ▶ *verb* **3** STAY, board, room **4** STICK, come to rest, imbed, implant **5** REGISTER, file, put on record, submit

lodger *noun* TENANT, boarder, paying guest, resident

lodging *noun* (*often plural*) ACCOMMODATION, abode, apartments, quarters, residence, rooms, shelter

lofty *adjective* **1** HIGH, elevated, raised, soaring, towering **2** NOBLE, dignified, distinguished, elevated, exalted, grand, illustrious, renowned **3** HAUGHTY, arrogant, condescending, disdainful, patronizing, proud, supercilious

log *noun* **1** STUMP, block, chunk, trunk **2** RECORD, account, journal, logbook ▶ *verb* **3** CHOP, cut, fell, hew **4** RECORD, chart, note, register, set down

loggerheads *plural noun* **at loggerheads** QUARRELING, at daggers drawn, at each other's throats, at odds, feuding, in dispute, opposed

logic noun REASON, good sense, sense

logical adjective 1 RATIONAL, clear, cogent, coherent, consistent, sound, valid, well-organized 2 REASONABLE, plausible, sensible, wise

loiter verb LINGER, dally, dawdle, dilly-dally (informal), hang about or around, idle, loaf, skulk

loll verb 1 LOUNGE, loaf, recline, relax, slouch, slump, sprawl 2 DROOP, dangle, drop, flap, flop, hang, sag

lone adjective SOLITARY, one, only, single, sole, unaccompanied

loneliness noun SOLITUDE, desolation, isolation, seclusion

lonely adjective 1 ABANDONED, destitute, forlorn, forsaken, friendless, lonesome 2 SOLITARY, alone, apart, companionless, isolated, lone, single, withdrawn 3 REMOTE, deserted, desolate, godforsaken, isolated, out-of-the-way, secluded, unfrequented, uninhabited

loner noun INDIVIDUALIST, lone wolf, maverick, outsider, recluse

lonesome adjective LONELY, companionless, desolate, dreary, forlorn, friendless, gloomy

long[1] adjective 1 ELONGATED, expanded, extended, extensive, far-reaching, lengthy, spread out, stretched 2 PROLONGED, interminable, lengthy, lingering, long-drawn-out, protracted, sustained

long[2] verb DESIRE, crave, hanker, itch, lust, pine, want, wish, yearn

longing noun DESIRE, ambition, aspiration, craving, hope, itch, thirst, urge, wish, yearning, yen (informal)

long-lived adjective LONG-LASTING, enduring

long shot noun OUTSIDER, dark horse

long-standing adjective ESTABLISHED, abiding, enduring, fixed, long-established, long-lasting, time-honored

long-suffering adjective UNCOMPLAINING, easy-going, forbearing, forgiving, patient, resigned, stoical, tolerant

long-winded adjective RAMBLING, lengthy, long-drawn-out, prolix, prolonged, repetitious, tedious, tiresome, verbose, wordy

look verb 1 SEE, contemplate, examine, eye, gaze, glance, observe, scan, study, survey, view, watch 2 SEEM, appear, look like, strike one as 3 FACE, front, overlook 4 HOPE, anticipate, await, expect, reckon on 5 SEARCH, forage, hunt, seek ▶noun 6 VIEW, examination, gaze, glance, glimpse, inspection, observation, peek, sight 7 APPEARANCE, air, aspect, bearing, countenance, demeanor, expression, manner, semblance

look after verb TAKE CARE OF, attend to, care for, guard, keep an eye on, mind, nurse, protect, supervise, take charge of, tend

look down on verb DISDAIN, contemn, despise, scorn, sneer, spurn

look forward to *verb* ANTICIPATE, await, expect, hope for, long for, look for, wait for

lookout *noun* 1 VIGIL, guard, readiness, watch 2 WATCHMAN, guard, sentinel, sentry 3 WATCHTOWER, observation post, observatory, post

look out *verb* BE CAREFUL, beware, keep an eye out, pay attention, watch out

look up *verb* 1 RESEARCH, find, hunt for, search for, seek out, track down 2 IMPROVE, get better, perk up, pick up, progress, shape up (*informal*) 3 VISIT, call on, drop in on (*informal*), look in on 4 **look up to** RESPECT, admire, defer to, esteem, honor, revere

loom *verb* APPEAR, bulk, emerge, hover, impend, menace, take shape, threaten

loop *noun* 1 CURVE, circle, coil, curl, ring, spiral, twirl, twist, whorl ▶ *verb* 2 TWIST, coil, curl, knot, roll, spiral, turn, wind round

loophole *noun* LET-OUT, escape, excuse

loose *adjective* 1 UNTIED, free, insecure, unattached, unbound, unfastened, unfettered, unrestricted 2 SLACK, easy, relaxed, sloppy 3 VAGUE, ill-defined, imprecise, inaccurate, indistinct, inexact, rambling, random 4 PROMISCUOUS, abandoned, debauched, dissipated, dissolute, fast, immoral, profligate ▶ *verb* 5 FREE, detach, disconnect, liberate, release, set free, unfasten, unleash, untie

loosen *verb* 1 UNTIE, detach, separate, undo, unloose 2 FREE, liberate, release, set free 3 **loosen up** RELAX, ease up *or* off, go easy (*informal*), let up, soften

loot *noun* 1 PLUNDER, booty, goods, haul, prize, spoils, swag (*slang*) ▶ *verb* 2 PLUNDER, despoil, pillage, raid, ransack, ravage, rifle, rob, sack

lopsided *adjective* CROOKED, askew, asymmetrical, awry, cockeyed, disproportionate, squint, unbalanced, uneven, warped

lord *noun* 1 MASTER, commander, governor, leader, liege, overlord, ruler, superior 2 NOBLEMAN, earl, noble, peer, viscount 3 **Our Lord** *or* **the Lord** JESUS CHRIST, Christ, God, Jehovah, the Almighty ▶ *verb* 4 **lord it over** ORDER AROUND, boss around (*informal*), domineer, pull rank, put on airs, swagger

lordly *adjective* PROUD, arrogant, condescending, disdainful, domineering, haughty, high-handed, imperious, lofty, overbearing

lore *noun* TRADITIONS, beliefs, doctrine, sayings, teaching, wisdom

lose *verb* 1 MISLAY, be deprived of, drop, forget, misplace 2 FORFEIT, miss, pass up (*informal*), yield 3 BE DEFEATED, come to grief, lose out

loser *noun* 1 FAILURE, also-ran, dud (*informal*), flop (*informal*) 2 NERD, dork (*slang*), drip (*informal*), dweeb (*slang*), geek (*slang*)

loss noun 1 DEFEAT, failure, forfeiture, mislaying, squandering, waste 2 DAMAGE, cost, destruction, harm, hurt, injury, ruin 3 (sometimes plural) DEFICIT, debit, debt, deficiency, depletion 4 **at a loss** CONFUSED, at one's wits' end, baffled, bewildered, helpless, nonplussed, perplexed, puzzled, stumped

lost adjective 1 MISSING, disappeared, mislaid, misplaced, vanished, wayward 2 OFF-COURSE, adrift, astray, at sea, disoriented, off-track

lot noun 1 COLLECTION, assortment, batch, bunch (informal), consignment, crowd, group, quantity, set 2 DESTINY, accident, chance, doom, fate, fortune 3 **a lot** or **lots** PLENTY, abundance, a great deal, heap(s), masses (informal), piles (informal), scores, stack(s)

loth see LOATH

lotion noun CREAM, balm, embrocation, liniment, salve, solution

lottery noun 1 RAFFLE, drawing, sweepstakes 2 GAMBLE, chance, hazard, risk, toss-up (informal)

loud adjective 1 NOISY, blaring, booming, clamorous, deafening, ear-splitting, forte (Music), resounding, thundering, tumultuous, vociferous 2 GARISH, brash, flamboyant, flashy, gaudy, glaring, lurid, showy

loudly adverb NOISILY, deafeningly, fortissimo (Music), lustily, shrilly, uproariously, vehemently, vigorously, vociferously

lounge verb RELAX, laze, lie about, loaf, loiter, loll, sprawl, take it easy

lousy adjective Informal CRUMMY, awful, crappy (slang), inadequate, inferior, shabby, shoddy, terrible

lout noun OAF, boor, dolt, lummox (informal)

lovable, loveable adjective ENDEARING, adorable, amiable, charming, cute, delightful, enchanting, likable or likeable, lovely, sweet

love verb 1 ADORE, cherish, dote on, hold dear, idolize, prize, treasure, worship 2 ENJOY, appreciate, delight in, like, relish, savor, take pleasure in ▶noun 3 PASSION, adoration, affection, ardor, attachment, devotion, infatuation, tenderness, warmth 4 LIKING, devotion, enjoyment, fondness, inclination, partiality, relish, soft spot, taste, weakness 5 BELOVED, darling, dear, dearest, lover, sweetheart, truelove 6 **in love** ENAMORED, besotted, charmed, enraptured, infatuated, smitten

love affair noun ROMANCE, affair, amour, intrigue, liaison, relationship

lovely adjective 1 ATTRACTIVE, adorable, beautiful, charming, comely, exquisite, graceful, handsome, pretty 2 ENJOYABLE, agreeable, delightful, engaging, nice, pleasant, pleasing

lover noun SWEETHEART, admirer, beloved, boyfriend or girlfriend, flame (informal), mistress, suitor

loving *adjective* AFFECTIONATE, amorous, dear, devoted, doting, fond, tender, warm-hearted

low *adjective* **1** SMALL, little, short, squat, stunted **2** INFERIOR, deficient, inadequate, lousy (*slang*), poor, second-rate, shoddy **3** COARSE, common, crude, disreputable, rough, rude, undignified, vulgar **4** DEJECTED, depressed, despondent, disheartened, downcast, down in the dumps (*informal*), fed up, gloomy, glum, miserable **5** ILL, debilitated, frail, stricken, weak **6** QUIET, gentle, hushed, muffled, muted, soft, subdued, whispered

lowdown *noun Informal* INFORMATION, info (*informal*), inside story, intelligence

lower *adjective* **1** MINOR, inferior, junior, lesser, secondary, second-class, smaller, subordinate **2** REDUCED, curtailed, decreased, diminished, lessened ▶ *verb* **3** DROP, depress, fall, let down, sink, submerge, take down **4** LESSEN, cut, decrease, diminish, minimize, prune, reduce, slash

low-key *adjective* SUBDUED, muted, quiet, restrained, toned down, understated

lowly *adjective* HUMBLE, meek, mild, modest, unassuming

low-spirited *adjective* DEPRESSED, dejected, despondent, dismal, down, down-hearted, fed up, low, miserable, sad

loyal *adjective* FAITHFUL, constant, dependable, devoted, dutiful, staunch, steadfast, true, trustworthy, trusty, unwavering

loyalty *noun* FAITHFULNESS, allegiance, constancy, dependability, devotion, fidelity, staunchness, steadfastness, trustworthiness

lubricate *verb* OIL, grease, smear

lucid *adjective* **1** CLEAR, comprehensible, explicit, intelligible, transparent **2** TRANSLUCENT, clear, crystalline, diaphanous, glassy, limpid, pellucid, transparent **3** CLEAR-HEADED, all there, *compos mentis*, in one's right mind, rational, sane

luck *noun* **1** FORTUNE, accident, chance, destiny, fate **2** GOOD FORTUNE, advantage, blessing, godsend, prosperity, serendipity, success, windfall

luckily *adverb* FORTUNATELY, favorably, happily, opportunely, propitiously, providentially

luckless *adjective* ILL-FATED, cursed, doomed, hapless, hopeless, jinxed, unfortunate, unlucky

lucky *adjective* FORTUNATE, advantageous, blessed, charmed, favored, serendipitous, successful, win-win (*informal*)

lucrative *adjective* PROFITABLE, advantageous, fruitful, productive, remunerative, well-paid

lucre *noun* MONEY, gain, mammon, pelf, profit, riches, spoils, wealth

ludicrous *adjective* RIDICULOUS, absurd, crazy, farcical, laughable, nonsensical, outlandish, preposterous, silly

luggage *noun* BAGGAGE, bags, cases, gear, impedimenta, paraphernalia, suitcases, things

lugubrious *adjective* GLOOMY, doleful, melancholy, mournful, sad, serious, somber, sorrowful, woebegone

lukewarm *adjective* **1** TEPID, warm **2** HALF-HEARTED, apathetic, cool, indifferent, unenthusiastic, unresponsive

lull *verb* **1** CALM, allay, pacify, quell, soothe, subdue, tranquilize ▶ *noun* **2** RESPITE, calm, hush, let-up (*informal*), pause, quiet, silence

lumber *verb* PLOD, clump, shamble, shuffle, stump, trudge, trundle, waddle

lumbering *adjective* AWKWARD, clumsy, heavy, hulking, ponderous, ungainly

luminous *adjective* BRIGHT, glowing, illuminated, luminescent, lustrous, radiant, shining

lump *noun* **1** PIECE, ball, chunk, hunk, mass, nugget **2** SWELLING, bulge, bump, growth, hump, protrusion, tumor ▶ *verb* **3** GROUP, collect, combine, conglomerate, consolidate, mass, pool

lumpy *adjective* BUMPY, knobbly, uneven

lunacy *noun* **1** INSANITY, dementia, derangement, madness, mania, psychosis **2** FOOLISHNESS, absurdity, craziness, folly, foolhardiness, madness, stupidity

lunatic *adjective* **1** IRRATIONAL, bonkers (*informal*),

crackbrained (*informal*), crackpot (*informal*), crazy, daft, deranged, insane, mad ▶ *noun* **2** MADMAN, maniac, nutcase (*slang*), psychopath

lunge *noun* **1** THRUST, charge, jab, pounce, spring, swing ▶ *verb* **2** POUNCE, charge, dive, leap, plunge, thrust

lurch *verb* **1** TILT, heave, heel, lean, list, pitch, rock, roll **2** STAGGER, reel, stumble, sway, totter, weave

lure *verb* **1** TEMPT, allure, attract, draw, ensnare, entice, invite, seduce ▶ *noun* **2** TEMPTATION, allurement, attraction, bait, carrot (*informal*), enticement, incentive, inducement

lurid *adjective* **1** SENSATIONAL, graphic, melodramatic, shocking, vivid **2** GLARING, intense

lurk *verb* HIDE, conceal oneself, lie in wait, prowl, skulk, slink, sneak

luscious *adjective* DELICIOUS, appetizing, juicy, mouth-watering, palatable, succulent, sweet, toothsome, yummy (*informal*)

lush *adjective* **1** ABUNDANT, dense, flourishing, green, rank, verdant **2** LUXURIOUS, elaborate, extravagant, grand, lavish, opulent, ornate, palatial, plush (*informal*), sumptuous

lust *noun* **1** LECHERY, lasciviousness, lewdness, sensuality **2** APPETITE, craving, desire, greed, longing, passion, thirst ▶ *verb* **3** DESIRE, covet, crave, hunger for *or* after, want, yearn

luster *noun* **1** SPARKLE, gleam,

glint, glitter, gloss, glow, sheen, shimmer, shine 2 GLORY, distinction, fame, honor, kudos, prestige, renown

lusty *adjective* VIGOROUS, energetic, healthy, hearty, powerful, robust, strong, sturdy, virile

luxurious *adjective* SUMPTUOUS, comfortable, expensive, lavish, magnificent, opulent, plush (*informal*), rich, splendid

luxury *noun* 1 OPULENCE, affluence, hedonism, richness, splendor, sumptuousness 2 EXTRAVAGANCE, extra, frill, indulgence, treat

lying *noun* 1 DISHONESTY, deceit, mendacity, perjury, untruthfulness ▸ *adjective* 2 DECEITFUL, dishonest, false, mendacious, perfidious, treacherous, two-faced, untruthful

lyrical *adjective* ENTHUSIASTIC, effusive, impassioned, inspired, poetic, rhapsodic

M m

macabre *adjective* GRUESOME, dreadful, eerie, frightening, ghastly, ghostly, ghoulish, grim, grisly, morbid

machiavellian *adjective* SCHEMING, astute, crafty, cunning, cynical, double-dealing, opportunist, sly, underhand, unscrupulous

machine *noun* 1 APPLIANCE, apparatus, contraption, contrivance, device, engine,

instrument, mechanism, tool 2 SYSTEM, machinery, organization, setup (*informal*), structure

machinery *noun* EQUIPMENT, apparatus, gear, instruments, tackle, tools

macho *adjective* MANLY, chauvinist, masculine, virile

mad *adjective* 1 INSANE, crazy (*informal*), demented, deranged, *non compos mentis*, nuts (*slang*), of unsound mind, out of one's mind, psychotic, raving, unhinged, unstable 2 FOOLISH, absurd, asinine, bonkers (*informal*), daft (*informal*), foolhardy, irrational, nonsensical, preposterous, senseless, wild 3 ANGRY, berserk, enraged, furious, incensed, livid (*informal*), wild 4 ENTHUSIASTIC, ardent, avid, crazy (*informal*), fanatical, impassioned, infatuated, wild 5 FRENZIED, excited, frenetic, uncontrolled, unrestrained, wild, wired (*slang*) 6 **like mad** *Informal* ENERGETICALLY, enthusiastically, excitedly, furiously, rapidly, speedily, violently, wildly

madden *verb* INFURIATE, annoy, derange, drive one crazy, enrage, incense, inflame, irritate, upset

madly *adverb* 1 INSANELY, crazily, deliriously, distractedly, frantically, frenziedly, hysterically 2 FOOLISHLY, absurdly, irrationally, ludicrously, senselessly, wildly 3 ENERGETICALLY, excitedly, furiously, like mad (*informal*), recklessly, speedily, wildly 4 *Informal* PASSIONATELY,

desperately, devotedly,
intensely, to distraction

madman or **madwoman** noun
LUNATIC, maniac, nutcase
(slang), psycho (slang),
psychopath

madness noun 1 INSANITY,
aberration, craziness, delusion,
dementia, derangement,
distraction, lunacy, mania,
mental illness, psychopathy,
psychosis 2 FOOLISHNESS,
absurdity, daftness (informal),
folly, foolhardiness, idiocy,
nonsense, preposterousness,
wildness

maelstrom noun 1 WHIRLPOOL,
vortex 2 TURMOIL, chaos,
confusion, disorder, tumult,
upheaval

maestro noun MASTER, expert,
genius, virtuoso

magazine noun 1 JOURNAL,
pamphlet, periodical
2 STOREHOUSE, arsenal, depot,
store, warehouse

magic noun 1 SORCERY, black art,
enchantment, necromancy,
witchcraft, wizardry
2 CONJURING, illusion,
legerdemain, prestidigitation,
sleight of hand, trickery
3 CHARM, allurement,
enchantment, fascination,
glamour, magnetism, power
▶adjective 4 Also **magical**
MIRACULOUS, bewitching,
charming, enchanting,
entrancing, fascinating,
marvelous, spellbinding

magician noun SORCERER,
conjurer, enchanter or
enchantress, illusionist,
necromancer, warlock, witch,
wizard

magisterial adjective
AUTHORITATIVE, commanding,
lordly, masterful

magistrate noun JUDGE, J.P.,
justice, justice of the peace

magnanimity noun GENEROSITY,
benevolence, big-heartedness,
largesse or largess, nobility,
selflessness, unselfishness

magnanimous adjective
GENEROUS, big-hearted,
bountiful, charitable, kind,
noble, selfless, unselfish

magnate noun TYCOON, baron,
captain of industry, mogul,
plutocrat

magnetic adjective ATTRACTIVE,
captivating, charismatic,
charming, fascinating,
hypnotic, irresistible,
mesmerizing, seductive

magnetism noun CHARM, allure,
appeal, attraction, charisma,
drawing power, magic, pull,
seductiveness

magnification noun INCREASE,
amplification, enhancement,
enlargement, expansion,
heightening, intensification

magnificence noun SPLENDOR,
brilliance, glory, grandeur,
majesty, nobility, opulence,
stateliness, sumptuousness

magnificent adjective
1 SPLENDID, cool (informal),
glorious, gorgeous, imposing,
impressive, majestic, regal,
sublime, sumptuous
2 EXCELLENT, brilliant, fine,
outstanding, phat (slang),
splendid, superb

magnify verb 1 ENLARGE, amplify,
blow up (informal), boost,
dilate, expand, heighten,
increase, intensify 2 OVERSTATE,

exaggerate, inflate, overemphasize, overplay

magnitude noun 1 IMPORTANCE, consequence, greatness, moment, note, significance, weight 2 SIZE, amount, amplitude, extent, mass, quantity, volume

maid noun 1 GIRL, damsel, lass, maiden, wench 2 SERVANT, housemaid, maidservant, serving-maid

maiden noun 1 GIRL, damsel, lass, maid, virgin, wench ▶adjective 2 UNMARRIED, unwed 3 FIRST, inaugural, initial, introductory

maidenly adjective MODEST, chaste, decent, decorous, demure, pure, virginal

mail noun 1 LETTERS, correspondence, junk mail, post (chiefly Brit.) 2 POSTAL SERVICE, collection, delivery, post office ▶verb 3 POST, dispatch, forward, send, transmit

maim verb CRIPPLE, disable, hurt, injure, mutilate, wound

main adjective 1 CHIEF, central, essential, foremost, head, leading, pre-eminent, primary, principal ▶noun 2 CONDUIT, cable, channel, duct, line, pipe 3 in the main ON THE WHOLE, for the most part, generally, in general, mainly, mostly

mainly adverb CHIEFLY, for the most part, in the main, largely, mostly, on the whole, predominantly, primarily, principally

mainstay noun PILLAR, anchor, backbone, bulwark, buttress, lynchpin, prop

mainstream adjective

CONVENTIONAL, accepted, current, established, general, orthodox, prevailing, received

maintain verb 1 KEEP UP, carry on, continue, perpetuate, preserve, prolong, retain, sustain 2 SUPPORT, care for, look after, provide for, supply, take care of 3 ASSERT, avow, claim, contend, declare, insist, profess, state

maintenance noun 1 CONTINUATION, carrying-on, perpetuation, prolongation 2 UPKEEP, care, conservation, keeping, nurture, preservation, repairs 3 ALLOWANCE, alimony, keep, support

majestic adjective GRAND, grandiose, impressive, magnificent, monumental, regal, splendid, stately, sublime, superb

majesty noun GRANDEUR, glory, magnificence, nobility, pomp, splendor, stateliness

major adjective 1 MAIN, bigger, chief, greater, higher, leading, senior, supreme 2 IMPORTANT, critical, crucial, great, notable, outstanding, serious, significant

majority noun 1 PREPONDERANCE, best part, bulk, greater number, mass, most 2 ADULTHOOD, manhood or womanhood, maturity, seniority

make verb 1 CREATE, assemble, build, construct, fashion, form, manufacture, produce, put together, synthesize 2 PRODUCE, accomplish, bring about, cause, create, effect, generate, give rise to, lead to 3 FORCE, cause, compel, constrain, drive, impel, induce, oblige, prevail upon, require **4** AMOUNT TO, add up to, compose, constitute, form **5** PERFORM, carry out, do, effect, execute **6** EARN, clear, gain, get, net, obtain, win **7 make it** *Informal* SUCCEED, arrive (*informal*), get on, prosper ▸ *noun* **8** BRAND, kind, model, sort, style, type, variety

make-believe *noun* FANTASY, imagination, play-acting, pretense, unreality

make for *verb* HEAD FOR, aim for, be bound for, head towards

make off *verb* **1** FLEE, bolt, clear out (*informal*), run away *or* off, take to one's heels **2 make off with** STEAL, abduct, carry off, filch, kidnap, pinch (*informal*), run away *or* off with

make out *verb* **1** SEE, detect, discern, discover, distinguish, perceive, recognize **2** UNDERSTAND, comprehend, decipher, fathom, follow, grasp, work out **3** WRITE OUT, complete, draw up, fill in *or* out **4** PRETEND, assert, claim, let on, make as if *or* though **5** FARE, get on, manage

maker *noun* MANUFACTURER, builder, constructor, producer

makeshift *adjective* TEMPORARY, expedient, provisional, stopgap, substitute

make-up *noun* **1** COSMETICS, face (*informal*), greasepaint (*Theatre*), paint (*informal*), powder **2** STRUCTURE, arrangement, assembly, composition, configuration, constitution, construction, format, organization **3** NATURE, character, constitution,

disposition, temperament

make up *verb* **1** FORM, compose, comprise, constitute **2** INVENT, coin, compose, concoct, construct, create, devise, dream up, formulate, frame, originate **3** COMPLETE, fill, supply **4** SETTLE, bury the hatchet, call it quits, reconcile **5 make up for** COMPENSATE FOR, atone for, balance, make amends for, offset, recompense

making *noun* CREATION, assembly, building, composition, construction, fabrication, manufacture, production

makings *plural noun* BEGINNINGS, capacity, ingredients, potential

maladjusted *adjective* DISTURBED, alienated, neurotic, unstable

maladministration *noun* MISMANAGEMENT, corruption, dishonesty, incompetence, inefficiency, malpractice, misrule

maladroit *adjective* CLUMSY, awkward, inept, inexpert, unskillful

malady *noun* DISEASE, affliction, ailment, complaint, disorder, illness, infirmity, sickness

malaise *noun* UNEASE, anxiety, depression, disquiet, melancholy

malcontent *noun* TROUBLEMAKER, agitator, mischief-maker, rebel, stirrer (*informal*)

male *adjective* MASCULINE, manly, virile

malefactor *noun* WRONGDOER, criminal, delinquent, evildoer, miscreant, offender, villain

malevolence *noun* MALICE, hate, hatred, ill will, rancor, spite, vindictiveness

malevolent *adjective* SPITEFUL, hostile, ill-natured, malicious, malign, vengeful, vindictive

malformation *noun* DEFORMITY, distortion, misshapenness

malformed *adjective* MISSHAPEN, abnormal, crooked, deformed, distorted, irregular, twisted

malfunction *verb* 1 BREAK DOWN, fail, go wrong ▸*noun* 2 FAULT, breakdown, defect, failure, flaw, glitch

malice *noun* ILL WILL, animosity, enmity, evil intent, hate, hatred, malevolence, spite, vindictiveness

malicious *adjective* SPITEFUL, ill-disposed, ill-natured, malevolent, rancorous, resentful, vengeful

malign *verb* 1 DISPARAGE, abuse, defame, denigrate, libel, run down, slander, smear, vilify ▸*adjective* 2 EVIL, bad, destructive, harmful, hostile, injurious, malevolent, malignant, pernicious, wicked

malignant *adjective* 1 HARMFUL, destructive, hostile, hurtful, malevolent, malign, pernicious, spiteful 2 *Medical* UNCONTROLLABLE, cancerous, dangerous, deadly, fatal, irremediable

malleable *adjective* 1 WORKABLE, ductile, plastic, soft, tensile 2 MANAGEABLE, adaptable, biddable, compliant, impressionable, pliable, tractable

malodorous *adjective* SMELLY, fetid, funky (*slang*), mephitic, nauseating, noisome, offensive, putrid, reeking, stinking

malpractice *noun* MISCONDUCT, abuse, dereliction, mismanagement, negligence

maltreat *verb* ABUSE, bully, harm, hurt, ill-treat, injure, mistreat

mammoth *adjective* COLOSSAL, enormous, giant, gigantic, huge, immense, massive, monumental, mountainous, prodigious

man *noun* 1 MALE, chap (*informal*), dude (*informal*), gentleman, guy (*informal*) 2 HUMAN, human being, individual, person, soul 3 MANKIND, Homo sapiens, humanity, humankind, human race, people 4 MANSERVANT, attendant, retainer, servant, valet ▸*verb* 5 STAFF, crew, garrison, occupy, people

manacle *noun* 1 HANDCUFF, bond, chain, fetter, iron, shackle ▸*verb* 2 HANDCUFF, bind, chain, fetter, put in chains, shackle

manage *verb* 1 ADMINISTER, be in charge (of), command, conduct, direct, handle, run, supervise 2 SUCCEED, accomplish, arrange, contrive, effect, engineer 3 HANDLE, control, manipulate, operate, use 4 COPE, carry on, get by (*informal*), make do, muddle through, survive

manageable *adjective* DOCILE, amenable, compliant, easy, submissive

management *noun* 1 DIRECTORS, administration, board, employers, executive(s) 2 ADMINISTRATION, command, control, direction, handling, operation, running, supervision

manager noun SUPERVISOR, administrator, boss (*informal*), director, executive, governor, head, organizer

mandate noun COMMAND, commission, decree, directive, edict, instruction, order

mandatory adjective COMPULSORY, binding, obligatory, required, requisite

maneuver noun 1 STRATAGEM, dodge, intrigue, machination, ploy, ruse, scheme, subterfuge, tactic, trick 2 MOVEMENT, exercise, operation ▶ verb 3 MANIPULATE, contrive, engineer, machinate, pull strings, scheme, wangle (*informal*) 4 MOVE, deploy, exercise

manfully adverb BRAVELY, boldly, courageously, determinedly, gallantly, hard, resolutely, stoutly, valiantly

mangle verb CRUSH, deform, destroy, disfigure, distort, mutilate, ruin, spoil, tear, wreck

mangy adjective DIRTY, moth-eaten, scuzzy (*slang*), seedy, shabby, shoddy, squalid

manhandle verb ROUGH UP, knock about or around, maul, paw (*informal*)

manhood noun MANLINESS, masculinity, virility

mania noun 1 MADNESS, delirium, dementia, derangement, insanity, lunacy 2 OBSESSION, craze, fad (*informal*), fetish, fixation, passion, preoccupation, thing (*informal*)

maniac noun 1 MADMAN or MADWOMAN, lunatic, psycho (*slang*), psychopath 2 FANATIC,

enthusiast, fan, fiend (*informal*), freak (*informal*)

manifest adjective 1 OBVIOUS, apparent, blatant, clear, conspicuous, evident, glaring, noticeable, palpable, patent ▶ verb 2 DISPLAY, demonstrate, exhibit, expose, express, reveal, show

manifestation noun DISPLAY, demonstration, exhibition, expression, indication, mark, show, sign, symptom

manifold adjective NUMEROUS, assorted, copious, diverse, many, multifarious, multiple, varied, various

manipulate verb 1 WORK, handle, operate, use 2 INFLUENCE, control, direct, engineer, maneuver

mankind noun PEOPLE, Homo sapiens, humanity, humankind, human race, man

manliness noun VIRILITY, boldness, bravery, courage, fearlessness, masculinity, valor, vigor

manly adjective VIRILE, bold, brave, courageous, fearless, manful, masculine, strapping, strong, vigorous

man-made adjective ARTIFICIAL, ersatz, manufactured, mock, synthetic

manner noun 1 BEHAVIOR, air, aspect, bearing, conduct, demeanor 2 STYLE, custom, fashion, method, mode, way 3 TYPE, brand, category, form, kind, sort, variety

mannered adjective AFFECTED, artificial, pretentious, stilted

mannerism noun HABIT, characteristic, foible,

idiosyncrasy, peculiarity, quirk, trait, trick

manners *plural noun* 1 BEHAVIOR, conduct, demeanor 2 POLITENESS, courtesy, decorum, etiquette, p's and q's, refinement

mansion *noun* RESIDENCE, hall, manor, seat, villa

mantle *noun* 1 CLOAK, cape, hood, shawl, wrap 2 COVERING, blanket, canopy, curtain, pall, screen, shroud, veil

manual *adjective* 1 HAND-OPERATED, human, physical ▶*noun* 2 HANDBOOK, bible, instructions

manufacture *verb* 1 MAKE, assemble, build, construct, create, mass-produce, produce, put together, turn out 2 CONCOCT, cook up (*informal*), devise, fabricate, invent, make up, think up, trump up ▶*noun* 3 MAKING, assembly, construction, creation, production

manufacturer *noun* MAKER, builder, constructor, creator, industrialist, producer

manure *noun* COMPOST, droppings, dung, excrement, fertilizer, muck, ordure

many *adjective* 1 NUMEROUS, abundant, countless, innumerable, manifold, myriad, umpteen (*informal*), various ▶*noun* 2 A LOT, heaps (*informal*), lots (*informal*), plenty, scores

mar *verb* SPOIL, blemish, damage, detract from, disfigure, hurt, impair, ruin, scar, stain, taint, tarnish

maraud *verb* RAID, forage, loot,

pillage, plunder, ransack, ravage

marauder *noun* RAIDER, bandit, buccaneer, outlaw, plunderer

march *verb* 1 WALK, file, pace, parade, stride, strut ▶*noun* 2 WALK, routemarch, trek 3 PROGRESS, advance, development, evolution, progression

margin *noun* EDGE, border, boundary, brink, perimeter, periphery, rim, side, verge

marginal *adjective* 1 BORDERLINE, bordering, on the edge, peripheral 2 INSIGNIFICANT, minimal, minor, negligible, slight, small

marijuana *noun* CANNABIS, dope (*slang*), grass (*slang*), hemp, pot (*slang*)

marine *adjective* NAUTICAL, maritime, naval, seafaring, seagoing

mariner *noun* SAILOR, salt, sea dog, seafarer, seaman

marital *adjective* MATRIMONIAL, conjugal, connubial, nuptial

maritime *adjective* 1 NAUTICAL, marine, naval, oceanic, seafaring 2 COASTAL, littoral, seaside

mark *noun* 1 SPOT, blemish, blot, line, scar, scratch, smudge, stain, streak 2 SIGN, badge, device, emblem, flag, hallmark, label, symbol, token 3 CRITERION, measure, norm, standard, yardstick 4 TARGET, aim, goal, object, objective, purpose ▶*verb* 5 SCAR, blemish, blot, scratch, smudge, stain, streak 6 CHARACTERIZE, brand, flag, identify, label, stamp 7 DISTINGUISH, denote, exemplify, illustrate, show

8 OBSERVE, attend, mind, note, notice, pay attention, pay heed, watch **9** GRADE, appraise, assess, correct, evaluate

marked *adjective* NOTICEABLE, blatant, clear, conspicuous, decided, distinct, obvious, patent, prominent, pronounced, striking

markedly *adverb* NOTICEABLY, clearly, considerably, conspicuously, decidedly, distinctly, obviously, strikingly

market *noun* **1** FAIR, bazaar, mart ▶ *verb* **2** SELL, retail, vend

marketable *adjective* SOUGHT AFTER, in demand, salable, wanted

marksman, markswoman *noun* SHARPSHOOTER, crack shot (*informal*), good shot

maroon *verb* ABANDON, desert, leave, leave high and dry (*informal*), strand

marriage *noun* WEDDING, match, matrimony, nuptials, wedlock

marry *verb* **1** WED, get hitched (*slang*), tie the knot (*informal*) **2** UNITE, ally, bond, join, knit, link, merge, unify, yoke

marsh *noun* SWAMP, bog, fen, morass, quagmire, slough

marshal *verb* **1** ARRANGE, align, array, deploy, draw up, group, line up, order, organize **2** CONDUCT, escort, guide, lead, shepherd, usher

marshy *adjective* SWAMPY, boggy, quaggy, waterlogged, wet

martial *adjective* MILITARY, bellicose, belligerent, warlike

martinet *noun* DISCIPLINARIAN, stickler

martyrdom *noun* PERSECUTION, ordeal, suffering

marvel *verb* **1** WONDER, be amazed, be awed, gape ▶ *noun* **2** WONDER, miracle, phenomenon, portent, prodigy

marvelous *adjective* **1** AMAZING, astonishing, astounding, breathtaking, brilliant, extraordinary, miraculous, phenomenal, prodigious, spectacular, stupendous **2** EXCELLENT, fabulous (*informal*), fantastic (*informal*), great (*informal*), splendid, superb, terrific (*informal*), wonderful

masculine *adjective* MALE, manlike, manly, mannish, virile

mask *noun* **1** DISGUISE, camouflage, cover, façade, front, guise, screen, veil ▶ *verb* **2** DISGUISE, camouflage, cloak, conceal, cover, hide, obscure, screen, veil

masquerade *noun* **1** MASKED BALL, fancy dress party, revel **2** PRETENSE, cloak, cover-up, deception, disguise, mask, pose, screen, subterfuge ▶ *verb* **3** POSE, disguise, dissemble, dissimulate, impersonate, pass oneself off, pretend (to be)

mass *noun* **1** PIECE, block, chunk, hunk, lump **2** LOT, bunch, collection, heap, load, pile, quantity, stack **3** SIZE, bulk, greatness, magnitude ▶ *adjective* **4** LARGE-SCALE, extensive, general, indiscriminate, wholesale, widespread ▶ *verb* **5** GATHER, accumulate, assemble, collect, congregate, rally, swarm, throng

massacre *noun* **1** SLAUGHTER, annihilation, blood bath, butchery, carnage, extermination, holocaust, murder ▶verb 2 SLAUGHTER, butcher, cut to pieces, exterminate, kill, mow down, murder, wipe out

massage noun 1 RUB-DOWN, manipulation ▶verb 2 RUB DOWN, knead, manipulate

massive adjective HUGE, big, colossal, enormous, gigantic, hefty, immense, mammoth, monumental, whopping (informal)

master noun 1 RULER, boss (informal), chief, commander, controller, director, governor, lord, manager 2 EXPERT, ace (informal), doyen, genius, maestro, past master, virtuoso, wizard 3 TEACHER, guide, guru, instructor, tutor ▶adjective 4 MAIN, chief, foremost, leading, predominant, prime, principal ▶verb 5 LEARN, get the hang of (informal), grasp 6 OVERCOME, conquer, defeat, tame, triumph over, vanquish

masterful adjective 1 SKILLFUL, adroit, consummate, expert, fine, first-rate, masterly, superlative, supreme, world-class 2 DOMINEERING, arrogant, bossy (informal), high-handed, imperious, overbearing, overweening

masterly adjective SKILLFUL, adroit, consummate, crack (slang), expert, first-rate, masterful, supreme, world-class

mastermind verb 1 PLAN, conceive, devise, direct, manage, organize ▶noun 2 ORGANIZER, architect, brain(s) (informal), director, engineer, manager, planner

masterpiece noun CLASSIC, jewel, magnum opus, pièce de résistance, tour de force

mastery noun 1 EXPERTISE, finesse, know-how (informal), proficiency, prowess, skill, virtuosity 2 CONTROL, ascendancy, command, domination, superiority, supremacy, upper hand, whip hand

match noun 1 GAME, bout, competition, contest, head-to-head, test, trial 2 EQUAL, counterpart, peer, rival 3 MARRIAGE, alliance, pairing, partnership ▶verb 4 CORRESPOND, accord, agree, fit, go with, harmonize, tally 5 RIVAL, compare, compete, emulate, equal, measure up to

matching adjective IDENTICAL, coordinating, corresponding, equivalent, like, twin

matchless adjective UNEQUALED, incomparable, inimitable, superlative, supreme, unmatched, unparalleled, unrivaled, unsurpassed

mate noun 1 PARTNER, husband or wife, spouse 2 COLLEAGUE, associate, companion 3 ASSISTANT, helper, subordinate ▶verb 4 PAIR, breed, couple

material noun 1 SUBSTANCE, matter, stuff 2 INFORMATION, data, evidence, facts, notes 3 CLOTH, fabric ▶adjective 4 PHYSICAL, bodily, concrete, corporeal, palpable, substantial, tangible 5 IMPORTANT, essential, meaningful, momentous, serious, significant, vital, weighty 6 RELEVANT, applicable, apposite, apropos, germane, pertinent

materialize *verb* OCCUR, appear, come about, come to pass, happen, take shape, turn up

materially *adverb* SIGNIFICANTLY, essentially, gravely, greatly, much, seriously, substantially

maternal *adjective* MOTHERLY

maternity *noun* MOTHERHOOD, motherliness

matrimonial *adjective* MARITAL, conjugal, connubial, nuptial

matrimony *noun* MARRIAGE, nuptials, wedding ceremony, wedlock

matted *adjective* TANGLED, knotted, tousled, uncombed

matter *noun* 1 SUBSTANCE, body, material, stuff 2 SITUATION, affair, business, concern, event, incident, proceeding, question, subject, topic 3 *As in* **what's the matter?** PROBLEM, complication, difficulty, distress, trouble, worry ▶ *verb* 4 BE IMPORTANT, carry weight, count, make a difference, signify

matter-of-fact *adjective* UNSENTIMENTAL, deadpan, down-to-earth, emotionless, mundane, plain, prosaic, sober, unimaginative

mature *adjective* 1 GROWN-UP, adult, full-grown, fully fledged, mellow, of age, ready, ripe, seasoned ▶ *verb* 2 DEVELOP, age, bloom, blossom, come of age, grow up, mellow, ripen

maturity *noun* ADULTHOOD, experience, manhood *or* womanhood, ripeness, wisdom

maudlin *adjective* SENTIMENTAL, mawkish, overemotional, slushy (*informal*), tearful,

weepy (*informal*)

maul *verb* 1 ILL-TREAT, abuse, manhandle, molest, paw 2 TEAR, batter, claw, lacerate, mangle

maverick *noun* 1 REBEL, dissenter, eccentric, heretic, iconoclast, individualist, nonconformist, protester, radical ▶ *adjective* 2 REBEL, dissenting, eccentric, heretical, iconoclastic, individualistic, nonconformist, radical

mawkish *adjective* SENTIMENTAL, emotional, maudlin, schmaltzy (*slang*), slushy (*informal*)

maxim *noun* SAYING, adage, aphorism, axiom, dictum, motto, proverb, rule

maximum *noun* 1 TOP, ceiling, height, peak, pinnacle, summit, upper limit, utmost, zenith ▶ *adjective* 2 GREATEST, highest, most, paramount, supreme, topmost, utmost

maybe *adverb* PERHAPS, perchance (*archaic*), possibly

mayhem *noun* CHAOS, commotion, confusion, destruction, disorder, fracas, havoc, trouble, violence

maze *noun* 1 LABYRINTH 2 WEB, confusion, imbroglio, tangle

meadow *noun* FIELD, grassland, lea (*poetic*), pasture

meager *adjective* INSUBSTANTIAL, inadequate, lousy (*slang*), measly, paltry, poor, puny, scanty, slight, small

meal *noun* Informal FEAST, feed, repast, spread (*informal*)

mean[1] *verb* 1 SIGNIFY, convey, denote, express, imply, indicate, represent, spell, stand for, symbolize 2 INTEND, aim, aspire, design, desire, plan, set out, want, wish

mean[2] *adjective* **1** MISERLY, mercenary, niggardly, parsimonious, penny-pinching, stingy, tight-fisted, ungenerous **2** DESPICABLE, callous, contemptible, hard-hearted, lousy (*slang*), petty, scuzzy (*slang*), shabby, shameful, sordid, vile

mean[3] *noun* **1** AVERAGE, balance, compromise, happy medium, middle, midpoint, norm ▶ *adjective* **2** AVERAGE, middle, standard

meander *verb* **1** WIND, snake, turn, zigzag **2** WANDER, ramble, stroll ▶ *noun* **3** CURVE, bend, coil, loop, turn, twist, zigzag

meaning *noun* SENSE, connotation, drift, gist, message, significance, substance

meaningful *adjective* SIGNIFICANT, important, material, purposeful, relevant, useful, valid, worthwhile

meaningless *adjective* POINTLESS, empty, futile, inane, inconsequential, insignificant, senseless, useless, vain, worthless

meanness *noun* **1** MISERLINESS, niggardliness, parsimony, selfishness, stinginess **2** PETTINESS, disgracefulness, ignobility, narrow-mindedness, shabbiness, shamefulness

means *plural noun* **1** METHOD, agency, instrument, medium, mode, process, way **2** MONEY, affluence, capital, fortune, funds, income, resources, wealth, wherewithal **3 by all**

means CERTAINLY, definitely, doubtlessly, of course, surely **4 by no means** IN NO WAY, definitely not, not in the least, on no account

meantime, meanwhile *adverb* AT THE SAME TIME, concurrently, in the interim, simultaneously

measly *adjective* MEAGER, miserable, paltry, pathetic, pitiful, poor, puny, scanty, skimpy

measurable *adjective* QUANTIFIABLE, assessable, perceptible, significant

measure *noun* **1** QUANTITY, allotment, allowance, amount, portion, quota, ration, share **2** GAUGE, meter, rule, scale, yardstick **3** ACTION, act, deed, expedient, maneuver, means, procedure, step **4** LAW, act, bill, resolution, statute **5** RHYTHM, beat, cadence, meter, verse ▶ *verb* **6** QUANTIFY, assess, calculate, calibrate, compute, determine, evaluate, gauge, weigh

measured *adjective* **1** STEADY, dignified, even, leisurely, regular, sedate, slow, solemn, stately, unhurried **2** CONSIDERED, calculated, deliberate, reasoned, sober, studied, well-thought-out

measurement *noun* CALCULATION, assessment, calibration, computation, evaluation, mensuration, valuation

measure up to *verb* FULFILL THE EXPECTATIONS, be equal to, be suitable, come up to scratch (*informal*), fit *or* fill the bill, make the grade (*informal*)

meat *noun* FLESH

meaty adjective 1 BRAWNY, beefy (*informal*), burly, heavily built, heavy, muscular, solid, strapping, sturdy 2 INTERESTING, meaningful, profound, rich, significant, substantial

mechanical adjective 1 AUTOMATIC, automated 2 UNTHINKING, automatic, cursory, impersonal, instinctive, involuntary, perfunctory, routine, unfeeling

mechanism noun 1 MACHINE, apparatus, appliance, contrivance, device, instrument, tool 2 PROCESS, agency, means, method, operation, procedure, system, technique

meddle verb INTERFERE, butt in, intervene, intrude, pry, tamper

meddlesome adjective INTERFERING, intrusive, meddling, mischievous, officious, prying

mediate verb INTERVENE, arbitrate, conciliate, intercede, reconcile, referee, step in (*informal*), umpire

mediation noun ARBITRATION, conciliation, intercession, intervention, reconciliation

mediator noun NEGOTIATOR, arbiter, arbitrator, go-between, honest broker, intermediary, middleman, peacemaker, referee, umpire

medicinal adjective THERAPEUTIC, curative, healing, medical, remedial, restorative

medicine noun REMEDY, cure, drug, medicament, medication, nostrum

mediocre adjective SECOND-RATE, average, indifferent, inferior, middling, ordinary, passable, pedestrian, so-so (*informal*), undistinguished

mediocrity noun INSIGNIFICANCE, indifference, inferiority, ordinariness, unimportance

meditate verb 1 REFLECT, cogitate, consider, contemplate, deliberate, muse, ponder, ruminate, think 2 PLAN, have in mind, intend, purpose, scheme

meditation noun REFLECTION, cogitation, contemplation, musing, pondering, rumination, study, thought

medium adjective 1 MIDDLE, average, fair, intermediate, mean, median, mediocre, middling, midway ▶noun 2 MIDDLE, average, center, compromise, mean, midpoint 3 MEANS, agency, channel, instrument, mode, organ, vehicle, way 4 ENVIRONMENT, atmosphere, conditions, milieu, setting, surroundings 5 SPIRITUALIST

medley noun MIXTURE, assortment, farrago, jumble, *mélange*, miscellany, mishmash, mixed bag (*informal*), potpourri

meek adjective SUBMISSIVE, acquiescent, compliant, deferential, docile, gentle, humble, mild, modest, timid, unassuming, unpretentious

meekness noun SUBMISSIVENESS, acquiescence, compliance, deference, docility, gentleness, humility, mildness, modesty, timidity

meet verb 1 ENCOUNTER, bump into, chance on, come across, confront, contact, find, happen on, run across, run into

2 CONVERGE, come together, connect, cross, intersect, join, link up, touch **3** SATISFY, answer, come up to, comply with, discharge, fulfill, match, measure up to **4** GATHER, assemble, collect, come together, congregate, convene, muster **5** EXPERIENCE, bear, encounter, endure, face, go through, suffer, undergo

meeting *noun* **1** ENCOUNTER, assignation, confrontation, engagement, introduction, rendezvous, tryst **2** CONFERENCE, assembly, conclave, congress, convention, gathering, get-together (*informal*), reunion, session

melancholy *noun* **1** SADNESS, dejection, depression, despondency, gloom, low spirits, misery, sorrow, unhappiness ▶ *adjective* **2** SAD, depressed, despondent, dispirited, downhearted, gloomy, glum, miserable, mournful, sorrowful

melee, mêlée *noun* FIGHT, brawl, fracas, free-for-all (*informal*), rumpus, scrimmage, scuffle, skirmish, tussle

mellifluous *adjective* SWEET, dulcet, euphonious, honeyed, silvery, smooth, soft, soothing, sweet-sounding

mellow *adjective* **1** SOFT, delicate, full-flavored, mature, rich, ripe, sweet ▶ *verb* **2** MATURE, develop, improve, ripen, season, soften, sweeten

melodious *adjective* TUNEFUL, dulcet, euphonious, harmonious, melodic, musical, sweet-sounding

melodramatic *adjective* SENSATIONAL, blood-and-thunder, extravagant, histrionic, overdramatic, overemotional, theatrical

melody *noun* **1** TUNE, air, music, song, strain, theme **2** TUNEFULNESS, euphony, harmony, melodiousness, musicality

melt *verb* **1** DISSOLVE, fuse, liquefy, soften, thaw **2** (often with *away*) DISAPPEAR, disperse, dissolve, evanesce, evaporate, fade, vanish **3** SOFTEN, disarm, mollify, relax

member *noun* **1** REPRESENTATIVE, associate, fellow **2** LIMB, appendage, arm, extremity, leg, part

membership *noun* **1** MEMBERS, associates, body, fellows **2** PARTICIPATION, belonging, enrollment, fellowship

memento *noun* SOUVENIR, keepsake, memorial, relic, remembrance, reminder, token, trophy

memoir *noun* ACCOUNT, biography, essay, journal, life, monograph, narrative, record

memoirs *plural noun* AUTOBIOGRAPHY, diary, experiences, journals, life story, memories, recollections, reminiscences

memorable *adjective* NOTEWORTHY, celebrated, famous, historic, momentous, notable, remarkable, significant, striking, unforgettable

memorandum *noun* NOTE, communication, jotting, memo, message, minute, reminder

memorial noun 1 MONUMENT, memento, plaque, record, remembrance, souvenir ▶adjective 2 COMMEMORATIVE, monumental

memorize verb REMEMBER, commit to memory, learn, learn by heart, learn by rote

memory noun 1 RECALL, recollection, remembrance, reminiscence, retention 2 COMMEMORATION, honor, remembrance

menace noun 1 THREAT, intimidation, warning 2 Informal NUISANCE, annoyance, pest, plague, troublemaker ▶verb 3 THREATEN, bully, frighten, intimidate, loom, lour or lower, terrorize

menacing adjective THREATENING, forbidding, frightening, intimidating, looming, louring or lowering, ominous

mend verb 1 REPAIR, darn, fix, patch, refit, renew, renovate, restore, retouch 2 IMPROVE, ameliorate, amend, correct, emend, rectify, reform, revise 3 HEAL, convalesce, get better, recover, recuperate ▶noun 4 REPAIR, darn, patch, stitch 5 **on the mend** CONVALESCENT, getting better, improving, recovering, recuperating

mendacious adjective LYING, deceitful, deceptive, dishonest, duplicitous, fallacious, false, fraudulent, insincere, untruthful

menial adjective 1 UNSKILLED, boring, dull, humdrum, low-status, routine ▶noun 2 SERVANT, attendant, drudge, flunky, lackey, underling

mental adjective 1 INTELLECTUAL, cerebral 2 Informal INSANE, deranged, disturbed, mad, mentally ill, psychotic, unbalanced, unstable

mentality noun ATTITUDE, cast of mind, character, disposition, make-up, outlook, personality, psychology

mentally adverb IN THE MIND, in one's head, intellectually, inwardly, psychologically

mention verb 1 REFER TO, bring up, declare, disclose, divulge, intimate, point out, reveal, state, touch upon ▶noun 2 ACKNOWLEDGMENT, citation, recognition, tribute 3 REFERENCE, allusion, indication, observation, remark

mentor noun GUIDE, adviser, coach, counselor, guru, instructor, teacher, tutor

menu noun BILL OF FARE, carte du jour

mercantile adjective COMMERCIAL, trading

mercenary adjective 1 GREEDY, acquisitive, avaricious, grasping, money-grubbing (informal), sordid, venal ▶noun 2 HIRELING, soldier of fortune

merchandise noun GOODS, commodities, produce, products, stock, wares

merchant noun TRADESMAN, broker, dealer, purveyor, retailer, salesman, seller, shopkeeper, supplier, trader, trafficker, vendor, wholesaler

merciful adjective COMPASSIONATE, clement, forgiving, generous, gracious, humane, kind, lenient, sparing, sympathetic, tender-hearted

merciless *adjective* CRUEL, barbarous, callous, hard-hearted, harsh, heartless, pitiless, ruthless, unforgiving

mercurial *adjective* LIVELY, active, capricious, changeable, impulsive, irrepressible, mobile, quicksilver, spirited, sprightly, unpredictable, volatile

mercy *noun* 1 COMPASSION, clemency, forbearance, forgiveness, grace, kindness, leniency, pity 2 BLESSING, boon, godsend

mere *adjective* SIMPLE, bare, common, nothing more than, plain, pure, sheer

meretricious *adjective* TRASHY, flashy, garish, gaudy, gimcrack, showy, tawdry, tinsel

merge *verb* COMBINE, amalgamate, blend, coalesce, converge, fuse, join, meet, mingle, mix, unite

merger *noun* UNION, amalgamation, coalition, combination, consolidation, fusion, incorporation

merit *noun* 1 WORTH, advantage, asset, excellence, goodness, integrity, quality, strong point, talent, value, virtue ▶ *verb* 2 DESERVE, be entitled to, be worthy of, earn, have a right to, rate, warrant

meritorious *adjective* PRAISEWORTHY, admirable, commendable, creditable, deserving, excellent, good, laudable, virtuous, worthy

merriment *noun* FUN, amusement, festivity, glee, hilarity, jollity, joviality, laughter, mirth, revelry

merry *adjective* CHEERFUL, blithe,

carefree, convivial, festive, happy, jolly, joyous

mesh *noun* 1 NET, netting, network, tracery, web ▶ *verb* 2 ENGAGE, combine, connect, coordinate, dovetail, harmonize, interlock, knit

mesmerize *verb* ENTRANCE, captivate, enthrall, fascinate, grip, hold spellbound, hypnotize

mess *noun* 1 DISORDER, chaos, clutter, confusion, disarray, disorganization, jumble, litter, shambles, untidiness 2 DIFFICULTY, dilemma, fix (*informal*), hot water, jam (*informal*), muddle, pickle (*informal*), plight, predicament, tight spot ▶ *verb* 3 (often with *up*) DIRTY, clutter, disarrange, dishevel, muddle, pollute, scramble 4 (often with *with*) INTERFERE, meddle, play, tamper, tinker

message *noun* 1 COMMUNICATION, bulletin, communiqué, dispatch, letter, memorandum, note, tidings, word 2 POINT, idea, import, meaning, moral, purport, theme

messenger *noun* COURIER, carrier, delivery boy, emissary, envoy, errand-boy, go-between, herald, runner

messy *adjective* UNTIDY, chaotic, cluttered, confused, dirty, disheveled, disordered, disorganized, muddled, scuzzy (*slang*), shambolic, sloppy (*informal*)

metamorphosis *noun* TRANSFORMATION, alteration, change, conversion, mutation, transmutation

metaphor *noun* FIGURE OF SPEECH, allegory, analogy, image, symbol, trope

metaphorical *adjective* FIGURATIVE, allegorical, emblematic, symbolic

mete *verb* DISTRIBUTE, administer, apportion, assign, deal, dispense, portion

meteoric *adjective* SPECTACULAR, brilliant, dazzling, fast, overnight, rapid, speedy, sudden, swift

method *noun* 1 MANNER, approach, mode, modus operandi, procedure, process, routine, style, system, technique, way 2 ORDERLINESS, order, organization, pattern, planning, purpose, regularity, system

methodical *adjective* ORDERLY, businesslike, deliberate, disciplined, meticulous, organized, precise, regular, structured, systematic

meticulous *adjective* THOROUGH, exact, fastidious, fussy, painstaking, particular, precise, punctilious, scrupulous, strict

mettle *noun* COURAGE, bravery, fortitude, gallantry, life, nerve, pluck, resolution, spirit, valor, vigor

microbe *noun* MICROORGANISM, bacillus, bacterium, bug (*informal*), germ, virus

microscopic *adjective* TINY, imperceptible, infinitesimal, invisible, minuscule, minute, negligible

midday *noun* NOON, noonday, twelve o'clock

middle *adjective* 1 CENTRAL,

halfway, intermediate, intervening, mean, median, medium, mid ▶*noun* 2 CENTER, focus, halfway point, heart, midpoint, midsection, midst

middle-class *adjective* BOURGEOIS, conventional, traditional

middling *adjective* 1 MEDIOCRE, indifferent, so-so (*informal*), tolerable, unexceptional, unremarkable 2 MODERATE, adequate, all right, average, fair, medium, modest, O.K. *or* okay (*informal*), ordinary, passable, serviceable

midget *noun* DWARF, pygmy *or* pigmy, shrimp (*informal*), Tom Thumb

midnight *noun* TWELVE O'CLOCK, dead of night, middle of the night, the witching hour

midst *noun* **in the midst of** AMONG, amidst, during, in the middle of, in the thick of, surrounded by

midway *adjective, adverb* HALFWAY, betwixt and between, in the middle

might *noun* 1 POWER, energy, force, strength, vigor 2 **with might and main** FORCEFULLY, lustily, manfully, mightily, vigorously

mightily *adverb* 1 VERY, decidedly, exceedingly, extremely, greatly, highly, hugely, intensely, much 2 POWERFULLY, energetically, forcefully, lustily, manfully, strongly, vigorously

mighty *adjective* POWERFUL, forceful, lusty, robust, strapping, strong, sturdy, vigorous

migrant *noun* 1 WANDERER,

drifter, emigrant, immigrant, itinerant, nomad, rover, traveler ▸ *adjective* **2** TRAVELING, drifting, immigrant, itinerant, migratory, nomadic, roving, shifting, transient, vagrant, wandering

migrate *verb* MOVE, emigrate, journey, roam, rove, travel, trek, voyage, wander

migration *noun* WANDERING, emigration, journey, movement, roving, travel, trek, voyage

migratory *adjective* NOMADIC, itinerant, migrant, peripatetic, roving, transient

mild *adjective* **1** GENTLE, calm, docile, easy-going, equable, meek, peaceable, placid **2** BLAND, smooth **3** CALM, balmy, moderate, temperate, tranquil, warm

mildness *noun* GENTLENESS, calmness, clemency, docility, moderation, placidity, tranquillity, warmth

milieu *noun* SURROUNDINGS, background, element, environment, locale, location, scene, setting

militant *adjective* AGGRESSIVE, active, assertive, combative, vigorous

military *adjective* **1** WARLIKE, armed, martial, soldierly ▸ *noun* **2** ARMED FORCES, army, forces, services

militate *verb* **militate against** COUNTERACT, be detrimental to, conflict with, counter, oppose, resist, tell against, weigh against

milk *verb* EXPLOIT, extract, pump, take advantage of

mill *noun* **1** FACTORY, foundry, plant, works **2** GRINDER, crusher ▸ *verb* **3** GRIND, crush, grate, pound, powder **4** SWARM, crowd, throng

millstone *noun* **1** GRINDSTONE, quernstone **2** BURDEN, affliction, albatross, encumbrance, load, weight

mime *verb* ACT OUT, gesture, represent, simulate

mimic *verb* **1** IMITATE, ape, caricature, do (*informal*), impersonate, parody ▸ *noun* **2** IMITATOR, caricaturist, copycat (*informal*), impersonator, impressionist

mimicry *noun* IMITATION, burlesque, caricature, impersonation, mimicking, mockery, parody

mince *verb* **1** CUT, chop, crumble, grind, hash **2** *As in* **mince one's words** TONE DOWN, moderate, soften, spare, weaken

mincing *adjective* AFFECTED, camp (*informal*), dainty, effeminate, foppish, precious, pretentious, sissy

mind *noun* **1** INTELLIGENCE, brain(s) (*informal*), gray matter (*informal*), intellect, reason, sense, understanding, wits **2** MEMORY, recollection, remembrance **3** INTENTION, desire, disposition, fancy, inclination, leaning, notion, urge, wish **4** SANITY, judgment, marbles (*informal*), mental balance, rationality, reason, senses, wits **5** **make up one's mind** DECIDE, choose, determine, resolve ▸ *verb* **6** TAKE OFFENSE, be affronted, be bothered, care, disapprove, dislike, object, resent **7** PAY ATTENTION, heed, listen to, mark, note, obey, observe, pay heed to, take heed **8** GUARD, attend to, keep an eye on, look after, take care of, tend, watch **9** BE CAREFUL, be cautious, be on (one's) guard, be wary, take care, watch

mindful *adjective* AWARE, alert, alive to, careful, conscious, heedful, wary, watchful

mindless *adjective* STUPID, foolish, idiotic, inane, moronic, thoughtless, unthinking, witless

mine *noun* **1** PIT, colliery, deposit, excavation, shaft **2** SOURCE, abundance, fund, hoard, reserve, stock, store, supply, treasury, wealth ▶*verb* **3** DIG UP, dig for, excavate, extract, hew, quarry, unearth

mingle *verb* **1** MIX, blend, combine, intermingle, interweave, join, merge, unite **2** ASSOCIATE, consort, fraternize, hang about *or* around, hobnob, rub shoulders (*informal*), socialize

miniature *adjective* SMALL, diminutive, little, minuscule, minute, scaled-down, tiny, toy

minimal *adjective* MINIMUM, least, least possible, nominal, slightest, smallest, token

minimize *verb* **1** REDUCE, curtail, decrease, diminish, miniaturize, prune, shrink **2** PLAY DOWN, belittle, decry, deprecate, discount, disparage, make light *or* little of, underrate

minimum *adjective* **1** LEAST, least possible, lowest, minimal, slightest, smallest ▶*noun*

2 LEAST, lowest, nadir

minion *noun* FOLLOWER, flunky, hanger-on, henchman, hireling, lackey, underling, yes man

minister *noun* **1** CLERGYMAN, cleric, parson, pastor, preacher, priest, rector, vicar ▶*verb* **2** ATTEND, administer, cater to, pander to, serve, take care of, tend

ministry *noun* **1** DEPARTMENT, bureau, council, office, quango **2** THE PRIESTHOOD, holy orders, the church

minor *adjective* SMALL, inconsequential, insignificant, lesser, petty, slight, trivial, unimportant ▶*noun* UNDERAGE PERSON, adolescent, child, juvenile, teenager, youngster (*informal*), youth

minstrel *noun* MUSICIAN, bard, singer, songstress, troubadour

mint *verb* MAKE, cast, coin, produce, punch, stamp, strike

minuscule *adjective* TINY, diminutive, infinitesimal, little, microscopic, miniature, minute

minute¹ *noun* MOMENT, flash, instant, jiffy (*informal*), second, trice

minute² *adjective* **1** SMALL, diminutive, infinitesimal, little, microscopic, miniature, minuscule, tiny **2** PRECISE, close, critical, detailed, exact, exhaustive, meticulous, painstaking, punctilious

minutes *plural noun* RECORD, memorandum, notes, proceedings, transactions, transcript

minutiae *plural noun* DETAILS, finer points, ins and outs, niceties, particulars, subtleties, trifles, trivia

minx noun FLIRT, coquette, hussy

miracle noun WONDER, marvel, phenomenon, prodigy

miraculous adjective WONDERFUL, amazing, astonishing, astounding, extraordinary, incredible, phenomenal, prodigious, unaccountable, unbelievable

mirage noun ILLUSION, hallucination, optical illusion

mire noun 1 SWAMP, bog, marsh, morass, quagmire 2 MUD, dirt, muck, ooze, slime

mirror noun 1 LOOKING-GLASS, glass, reflector ▸verb 2 REFLECT, copy, echo, emulate, follow

mirth noun MERRIMENT, amusement, cheerfulness, fun, gaiety, glee, hilarity, jollity, joviality, laughter, revelry

mirthful adjective MERRY, blithe, cheerful, cheery, festive, happy, jolly, jovial, light-hearted, playful, sportive

misadventure noun MISFORTUNE, accident, bad luck, calamity, catastrophe, debacle, disaster, mishap, reverse, setback

misanthropic adjective ANTISOCIAL, cynical, malevolent, unfriendly

misapprehend verb MISUNDERSTAND, misconstrue, misinterpret, misread, mistake

misapprehension noun MISUNDERSTANDING, delusion, error, fallacy, misconception, misinterpretation, mistake

misappropriate verb STEAL, embezzle, misspend, misuse, peculate, pocket

misbehave verb ACT UP, be disobedient, make a fuss, make trouble, make waves

miscalculate verb MISJUDGE, blunder, err, overestimate, overrate, slip up, underestimate, underrate

miscarriage noun FAILURE, breakdown, error, mishap, perversion

miscarry verb FAIL, come to grief, fall through, go awry, go wrong, misfire

miscellaneous adjective MIXED, assorted, diverse, jumbled, motley, sundry, varied, various

miscellany noun ASSORTMENT, anthology, collection, jumble, medley, *mélange*, mixed bag, mixture, potpourri, variety

mischance noun MISFORTUNE, accident, calamity, disaster, misadventure, mishap

mischief noun 1 TROUBLE, impishness, misbehavior, monkey business (*informal*), naughtiness, shenanigans (*informal*), waywardness 2 HARM, damage, evil, hurt, injury, misfortune, trouble

mischievous adjective 1 NAUGHTY, impish, playful, puckish, rascally, roguish, sportive, troublesome, wayward 2 MALICIOUS, damaging, destructive, evil, harmful, hurtful, spiteful, vicious, wicked

misconception noun DELUSION, error, fallacy, misapprehension, misunderstanding

misconduct noun IMMORALITY, impropriety, malpractice, mismanagement, wrongdoing

miscreant noun WRONGDOER,

criminal, rascal, reprobate, rogue, scoundrel, sinner, vagabond, villain

misdeed noun OFFENSE, crime, fault, misconduct, misdemeanor, sin, transgression, wrong

misdemeanor noun OFFENSE, fault, infringement, misdeed, peccadillo, transgression

miser noun SKINFLINT, cheapskate (informal), niggard, penny-pincher (informal), Scrooge

miserable adjective 1 UNHAPPY, dejected, depressed, despondent, disconsolate, forlorn, gloomy, sorrowful, woebegone, wretched 2 SQUALID, deplorable, lamentable, shameful, sordid, sorry, wretched

miserly adjective MEAN, avaricious, grasping, niggardly, parsimonious, penny-pinching (informal), stingy, tightfisted, ungenerous

misery noun UNHAPPINESS, anguish, depression, desolation, despair, distress, gloom, grief, sorrow, suffering, torment, woe

misfire verb FAIL, fall through, go wrong, miscarry

misfit noun NONCONFORMIST, eccentric, fish out of water (informal), oddball (informal), square peg (in a round hole) (informal)

misfortune noun 1 BAD LUCK, adversity, hard luck, ill luck, infelicity 2 MISHAP, affliction, calamity, disaster, reverse, setback, tragedy, tribulation, trouble

misgiving noun UNEASE, anxiety, apprehension, distrust, doubt, qualm, reservation, suspicion, trepidation, uncertainty, worry

misguided adjective UNWISE, deluded, erroneous, ill-advised, imprudent, injudicious, misplaced, mistaken, unwarranted

mishandle verb MISMANAGE, botch, bungle, make a mess of, mess up (informal), muff

mishap noun ACCIDENT, calamity, misadventure, mischance, misfortune

misinform verb MISLEAD, deceive, misdirect, misguide

misinterpret verb MISUNDERSTAND, distort, misapprehend, misconceive, misconstrue, misjudge, misread, misrepresent, mistake

misjudge verb MISCALCULATE, overestimate, overrate, underestimate, underrate

mislay verb LOSE, lose track of, misplace

mislead verb DECEIVE, delude, fool, hoodwink, misdirect, misguide, misinform

misleading adjective CONFUSING, ambiguous, deceptive, disingenuous, evasive, false

mismanage verb MISHANDLE, botch, bungle, make a mess of, mess up, misconduct, misdirect, misgovern

misplace verb LOSE, lose track of, mislay

misprint noun MISTAKE, corrigendum, erratum, literal, typo (informal)

misquote verb MISREPRESENT, falsify, twist

misrepresent verb DISTORT, disguise, falsify, misinterpret

misrule noun DISORDER, anarchy, chaos, confusion, lawlessness, turmoil

miss verb **1** OMIT, leave out, let go, overlook, pass over, skip **2** AVOID, escape, evade **3** LONG FOR, pine for, yearn for ▶noun **4** MISTAKE, blunder, error, failure, omission, oversight

misshapen adjective DEFORMED, contorted, crooked, distorted, grotesque, malformed, twisted, warped

missile noun ROCKET, projectile, weapon

missing adjective ABSENT, astray, lacking, left out, lost, mislaid, misplaced, unaccounted-for

mission noun TASK, assignment, commission, duty, errand, job, quest, undertaking, vocation

missionary noun EVANGELIST, apostle, preacher

missive noun LETTER, communication, dispatch, epistle, memorandum, message, note, report

misspent adjective WASTED, dissipated, imprudent, profitless, squandered

mist noun FOG, cloud, film, haze, smog, spray, steam, vapor

mistake noun **1** ERROR, blunder, erratum, fault, faux pas, miscalculation, oversight, slip ▶verb **2** MISUNDERSTAND, misapprehend, misconstrue, misinterpret, misjudge, misread **3** CONFUSE WITH, mix up with, take for

mistaken adjective WRONG, erroneous, false, faulty, inaccurate, incorrect,

misguided, unsound, wide of the mark

mistakenly adverb INCORRECTLY, by mistake, erroneously, fallaciously, falsely, inaccurately, misguidedly, wrongly

mistimed adjective INOPPORTUNE, badly timed, ill-timed, untimely

mistreat verb ABUSE, harm, ill-treat, injure, knock about or around, maltreat, manhandle, misuse, molest

mistress noun LOVER, concubine, girlfriend, kept woman, paramour

mistrust verb **1** DOUBT, be wary of, distrust, fear, suspect ▶noun **2** SUSPICION, distrust, doubt, misgiving, skepticism, uncertainty, wariness

mistrustful adjective SUSPICIOUS, chary, cynical, distrustful, doubtful, fearful, hesitant, skeptical, uncertain, wary

misty adjective FOGGY, blurred, cloudy, dim, hazy, indistinct, murky, obscure, opaque, overcast

misunderstand verb MISINTERPRET, be at cross-purposes, get the wrong end of the stick, misapprehend, misconstrue, misjudge, misread, mistake

misunderstanding noun MISTAKE, error, misconception, misinterpretation, misjudgment, mix-up

misuse noun **1** WASTE, abuse, desecration, misapplication, squandering ▶verb **2** WASTE, abuse, desecrate, misapply, prostitute, squander

mitigate verb EASE, extenuate,

lessen, lighten, moderate, soften, subdue, temper

mitigation *noun* RELIEF, alleviation, diminution, extenuation, moderation, remission

mix *verb* 1 COMBINE, blend, cross, fuse, intermingle, interweave, join, jumble, merge, mingle 2 SOCIALIZE, associate, consort, fraternize, hang out (*informal*), hobnob, mingle ▸ *noun* 3 MIXTURE, alloy, amalgam, assortment, blend, combination, compound, fusion, medley

mixed *adjective* 1 COMBINED, amalgamated, blended, composite, compound, joint, mingled, united 2 VARIED, assorted, cosmopolitan, diverse, heterogeneous, miscellaneous, motley

mixed-up *adjective* CONFUSED, at sea, bewildered, distraught, disturbed, maladjusted, muddled, perplexed, puzzled, upset

mixture *noun* BLEND, amalgam, assortment, brew, compound, fusion, jumble, medley, mix, potpourri, variety

mix-up *noun* CONFUSION, mess, mistake, misunderstanding, muddle, tangle

mix up *verb* 1 COMBINE, blend, mix 2 CONFUSE, confound, muddle

moan *noun* 1 GROAN, lament, sigh, sob, wail, whine 2 *Informal* GRUMBLE, complaint, gripe (*informal*), grouch (*informal*), grouse, protest, whine ▸ *verb* 3 GROAN, lament, sigh, sob, whine 4 *Informal* GRUMBLE, bleat, carp, complain, groan, grouse, whine

mob *noun* 1 CROWD, drove, flock, horde, host, mass, multitude, pack, swarm, throng 2 *Slang* GANG, crew (*informal*), group, lot, set ▸ *verb* 3 SURROUND, crowd around, jostle, set upon, swarm around

mobile *adjective* MOVABLE, itinerant, moving, peripatetic, portable, traveling, wandering

mobilize *verb* PREPARE, activate, call to arms, call up, get *or* make ready, marshal, organize, rally, ready

mock *verb* 1 LAUGH AT, deride, jeer, make fun of, poke fun at, ridicule, scoff, scorn, sneer, taunt, tease 2 MIMIC, ape, caricature, imitate, lampoon, parody, satirize ▸ *adjective* 3 IMITATION, artificial, dummy, fake, false, feigned, phoney *or* phony (*informal*), pretended, sham, spurious

mockery *noun* 1 DERISION, contempt, disdain, disrespect, insults, jeering, ridicule, scoffing, scorn 2 FARCE, disappointment, joke, letdown

mocking *adjective* SCORNFUL, contemptuous, derisive, disdainful, disrespectful, sarcastic, sardonic, satirical, scoffing

mode *noun* 1 METHOD, form, manner, procedure, process, style, system, technique, way 2 FASHION, craze, look, rage, style, trend, vogue

model *noun* 1 REPRESENTATION, copy, dummy, facsimile, image, imitation, miniature, mock-up, replica 2 PATTERN, archetype, example, ideal, original, paradigm, paragon, prototype, standard **3** SITTER, poser, subject ▶*verb* **4** SHAPE, carve, design, fashion, form, mold, sculpt **5** SHOW OFF, display, sport (*informal*), wear

moderate *adjective* **1** MILD, controlled, gentle, limited, middle-of-the-road, modest, reasonable, restrained, steady **2** AVERAGE, fair, indifferent, mediocre, middling, ordinary, passable, so-so (*informal*), unexceptional ▶*verb* **3** REGULATE, control, curb, ease, modulate, restrain, soften, subdue, temper, tone down

moderately *adverb* REASONABLY, fairly, passably, quite, rather, slightly, somewhat, tolerably

moderation *noun* RESTRAINT, fairness, reasonableness, temperance

modern *adjective* CURRENT, contemporary, fresh, new, newfangled, novel, present-day, recent, up-to-date

modernity *noun* NOVELTY, currency, freshness, innovation, newness

modernize *verb* UPDATE, make over, rejuvenate, remake, remodel, renew, renovate, revamp

modest *adjective* **1** UNPRETENTIOUS, bashful, coy, demure, diffident, reserved, reticent, retiring, self-effacing, shy **2** MODERATE, fair, limited, middling, ordinary, small, unexceptional

modesty *noun* RESERVE, bashfulness, coyness, demureness, diffidence,

humility, reticence, shyness, timidity

modicum *noun* LITTLE, bit, crumb, drop, fragment, scrap, shred, touch

modification *noun* CHANGE, adjustment, alteration, qualification, refinement, revision, variation

modify *verb* **1** CHANGE, adapt, adjust, alter, convert, reform, remodel, revise, rework **2** TONE DOWN, ease, lessen, lower, moderate, qualify, restrain, soften, temper

modish *adjective* FASHIONABLE, chic, contemporary, cool (*informal*), current, in, phat (*slang*), smart, stylish, trendy (*informal*), up-to-the-minute, voguish

modulate *verb* ADJUST, attune, balance, regulate, tune, vary

mogul *noun* TYCOON, baron, big cheese (*informal*), big shot (*informal*), magnate, V.I.P.

moist *adjective* DAMP, clammy, dewy, humid, soggy, wet

moisten *verb* DAMPEN, damp, moisturize, soak, water, wet

moisture *noun* DAMPNESS, dew, liquid, water, wetness

mold[1] *noun* **1** CAST, pattern, shape **2** DESIGN, build, construction, fashion, form, format, kind, pattern, shape, style **3** NATURE, caliber, character, kind, quality, sort, stamp, type ▶*verb* **4** SHAPE, construct, create, fashion, forge, form, make, model, sculpt, work **5** INFLUENCE, affect, control, direct, form, make, shape

mold[2] *noun* FUNGUS, blight,

mildew, mustiness

moldy *adjective* STALE, bad, blighted, decaying, fusty, mildewed, musty, rotten

molecule *noun* PARTICLE, jot, speck

molest *verb* 1 ANNOY, badger, beset, bother, disturb, harass, persecute, pester, plague, torment, worry 2 ABUSE, attack, harm, hurt, ill-treat, interfere with, maltreat

mollify *verb* PACIFY, appease, calm, conciliate, placate, quiet, soothe, sweeten

moment *noun* 1 INSTANT, flash, jiffy (*informal*), second, split second, trice, twinkling 2 TIME, juncture, point, stage

momentarily *adverb* BRIEFLY, for a moment, temporarily

momentary *adjective* SHORT-LIVED, brief, fleeting, passing, short, temporary, transitory

momentous *adjective* SIGNIFICANT, critical, crucial, fateful, historic, important, pivotal, vital, weighty

momentum *noun* IMPETUS, drive, energy, force, power, propulsion, push, strength, thrust

monarch *noun* RULER, emperor *or* empress, king, potentate, prince *or* princess, queen, sovereign

monarchy *noun* 1 SOVEREIGNTY, autocracy, kingship, monocracy, royalism 2 KINGDOM, empire, principality, realm

monastery *noun* ABBEY, cloister, convent, friary, nunnery, priory

monastic *adjective* MONKISH, ascetic, cloistered,

contemplative, hermit-like, reclusive, secluded, sequestered, withdrawn

monetary *adjective* FINANCIAL, budgetary, capital, cash, fiscal, pecuniary

money *noun* CASH, capital, coin, currency, hard cash, legal tender, riches, silver, wealth

mongrel *noun* 1 HYBRID, cross, crossbreed, half-breed ▶ *adjective* 2 HYBRID, crossbred

monitor *noun* 1 WATCHDOG, guide, invigilator, supervisor ▶ *verb* 2 CHECK, follow, keep an eye on, keep tabs on, keep track of, observe, stalk, survey, watch

monk *noun* FRIAR, brother

monkey *noun* 1 SIMIAN, primate 2 RASCAL, devil, imp, rogue, scamp ▶ *verb* 3 FOOL, meddle, mess, play, tinker

monolithic *adjective* HUGE, colossal, impenetrable, intractable, massive, monumental, solid

monologue *noun* SPEECH, harangue, lecture, sermon, soliloquy

monopolize *verb* CONTROL, corner the market in, dominate, hog (*slang*), keep to oneself, take over

monotonous *adjective* TEDIOUS, boring, dull, humdrum, mind-numbing, repetitive, tiresome, unchanging, wearisome

monotony *noun* TEDIUM, boredom, monotonousness, repetitiveness, routine, sameness, tediousness

monster *noun* 1 BRUTE, beast, demon, devil, fiend, villain

2 FREAK, monstrosity, mutant **3** GIANT, colossus, mammoth, titan ▶ *adjective* **4** HUGE, colossal, enormous, gigantic, immense, mammoth, massive, stupendous, tremendous

monstrosity *noun* EYESORE, freak, horror, monster

monstrous *adjective*
1 UNNATURAL, fiendish, freakish, frightful, grotesque, gruesome, hideous, horrible **2** OUTRAGEOUS, diabolical, disgraceful, foul, inhuman, intolerable, scandalous, shocking **3** HUGE, colossal, enormous, immense, mammoth, massive, prodigious, stupendous, tremendous

monument *noun* MEMORIAL, cairn, cenotaph, commemoration, gravestone, headstone, marker, mausoleum, shrine, tombstone

monumental *adjective*
1 IMPORTANT, awesome, enormous, epoch-making, historic, majestic, memorable, significant, unforgettable **2** *Informal* IMMENSE, colossal, great, massive, staggering

mood *noun* STATE OF MIND, disposition, frame of mind, humor, spirit, temper

moody *adjective* **1** SULLEN, gloomy, glum, ill-tempered, irritable, morose, sad, sulky, temperamental, touchy **2** CHANGEABLE, capricious, erratic, fickle, flighty, impulsive, mercurial, temperamental, unpredictable, volatile

moon *noun* **1** SATELLITE ▶ *verb* **2** IDLE, daydream, languish, mope, waste time

moor¹ *noun* MOORLAND, heath

moor² *verb* TIE UP, anchor, berth, dock, lash, make fast, secure

moot *adjective* **1** DEBATABLE, arguable, contestable, controversial, disputable, doubtful, undecided, unresolved, unsettled ▶ *verb* **2** BRING UP, broach, propose, put forward, suggest

mop *noun* **1** SQUEEGEE, sponge, swab **2** MANE, shock, tangle, thatch

mope *verb* BROOD, fret, languish, moon, pine, pout, sulk

mop up *verb* CLEAN UP, soak up, sponge, swab, wash, wipe

moral *adjective* **1** GOOD, decent, ethical, high-minded, honorable, just, noble, principled, right, virtuous ▶ *noun* **2** LESSON, meaning, message, point, significance

morale *noun* CONFIDENCE, esprit de corps, heart, self-esteem, spirit

morality *noun* **1** INTEGRITY, decency, goodness, honesty, justice, righteousness, virtue **2** STANDARDS, conduct, ethics, manners, morals, mores, philosophy, principles

morals *plural noun* MORALITY, behavior, conduct, ethics, habits, integrity, manners, mores, principles, scruples, standards

morass *noun* **1** MARSH, bog, fen, quagmire, slough, swamp **2** MESS, confusion, mix-up, muddle, tangle

moratorium *noun* POSTPONEMENT, freeze, halt, standstill, suspension

morbid *adjective*
1 UNWHOLESOME, ghoulish, gloomy, melancholy, sick, somber, unhealthy 2 GRUESOME, dreadful, ghastly, grisly, hideous, horrid, macabre

mordant *adjective* SARCASTIC, biting, caustic, cutting, incisive, pungent, scathing, stinging, trenchant

more *adjective* 1 EXTRA, added, additional, further, new, other, supplementary ▶ *adverb* 2 TO A GREATER EXTENT, better, further, longer

moreover *adverb* FURTHERMORE, additionally, also, as well, besides, further, in addition, too

morgue *noun* MORTUARY

moribund *adjective* DECLINING, on its last legs, stagnant, waning, weak

morning *noun* DAWN, a.m., break of day, daybreak, forenoon, morn (*poetic*), sunrise

moron *noun* FOOL, blockhead, cretin (*offensive*), dork (*slang*), dunce, dunderhead, halfwit, idiot, imbecile, oaf, schmuck (*slang*)

moronic *adjective* IDIOTIC, cretinous (*offensive*), foolish, halfwitted, imbecilic, mindless, stupid, unintelligent

morose *adjective* SULLEN, depressed, dour, gloomy, glum, ill-tempered, moody, sour, sulky, surly, taciturn

morsel *noun* PIECE, bit, bite, crumb, mouthful, part, scrap, soupçon, taste, tidbit

mortal *adjective* 1 HUMAN, ephemeral, impermanent, passing, temporal, transient, worldly 2 FATAL, deadly,

death-dealing, destructive, killing, lethal, murderous, terminal ▶ *noun* 3 HUMAN BEING, being, earthling, human, individual, man, person, woman

mortality *noun* 1 HUMANITY, impermanence, transience 2 KILLING, bloodshed, carnage, death, destruction, fatality

mortification *noun*
1 HUMILIATION, annoyance, chagrin, discomfiture, embarrassment, shame, vexation 2 DISCIPLINE, abasement, chastening, control, denial, subjugation 3 *Medical* GANGRENE, corruption, festering

mortified *adjective* HUMILIATED, ashamed, chagrined, chastened, crushed, deflated, embarrassed, humbled, shamed

mortify *verb* 1 HUMILIATE, chagrin, chasten, crush, deflate, embarrass, humble, shame 2 DISCIPLINE, abase, chasten, control, deny, subdue 3 *Of flesh* PUTREFY, deaden, die, fester

mortuary *noun* MORGUE, funeral parlour

mostly *adverb* GENERALLY, as a rule, chiefly, largely, mainly, on the whole, predominantly, primarily, principally, usually

moth-eaten *adjective* DECAYED, decrepit, dilapidated, ragged, shabby, tattered, threadbare, worn-out

mother *noun* 1 PARENT, dam, ma (*informal*), mama *or* mamma (*old-fashioned informal*), mater (*old-fashioned informal, chiefly Brit.*), mom (*informal*), mommy (*informal*), old lady (*informal*)

▶ *adjective* **2** NATIVE, inborn, innate, natural ▶ *verb* **3** NURTURE, care for, cherish, nurse, protect, raise, rear, tend

motherly *adjective* MATERNAL, affectionate, caring, comforting, loving, protective, sheltering

motif *noun* **1** THEME, concept, idea, leitmotif, subject **2** DESIGN, decoration, ornament, shape

motion *noun* **1** MOVEMENT, flow, locomotion, mobility, move, progress, travel **2** PROPOSAL, proposition, recommendation, submission, suggestion ▶ *verb* **3** GESTURE, beckon, direct, gesticulate, nod, signal, wave

motionless *adjective* STILL, fixed, frozen, immobile, paralyzed, standing, static, stationary, stock-still, transfixed, unmoving

motivate *verb* INSPIRE, arouse, cause, drive, induce, move, persuade, prompt, stimulate, stir

motivation *noun* INCENTIVE, incitement, inducement, inspiration, motive, reason, spur, stimulus

motive *noun* REASON, ground(s), incentive, inducement, inspiration, object, purpose, rationale, stimulus

motley *adjective*
1 MISCELLANEOUS, assorted, disparate, heterogeneous, mixed, varied **2** MULTICOLORED, checkered, variegated

mottled *adjective* BLOTCHY, dappled, flecked, piebald, speckled, spotted, stippled, streaked

motto *noun* SAYING, adage, dictum, maxim, precept, proverb, rule, slogan, watchword

mound *noun* **1** HEAP, drift, pile, rick, stack **2** HILL, bank, dune, embankment, hillock, knoll, rise

mount *verb* **1** CLIMB, ascend, clamber up, go up, scale **2** BESTRIDE, climb onto, jump on **3** INCREASE, accumulate, build, escalate, grow, intensify, multiply, pile up, swell ▶ *noun* **4** BACKING, base, frame, setting, stand, support **5** HORSE, steed (*archaic or literary*)

mountain *noun* **1** PEAK, alp, fell (*Brit.*), mount **2** HEAP, abundance, mass, mound, pile, stack, ton

mountainous *adjective* **1** HIGH, alpine, highland, rocky, soaring, steep, towering, upland **2** HUGE, daunting, enormous, gigantic, great, immense, mammoth, mighty, monumental

mourn *verb* GRIEVE, bemoan, bewail, deplore, lament, rue, wail, weep

mournful *adjective* **1** SAD, melancholy, piteous, plaintive, sorrowful, tragic, unhappy, woeful **2** DISMAL, disconsolate, downcast, gloomy, grieving, heavy-hearted, lugubrious, miserable, rueful, somber

mourning *noun* **1** GRIEVING, bereavement, grief, lamentation, weeping, woe **2** BLACK, sackcloth and ashes, widow's weeds

mouth *noun* **1** LIPS, jaws, maw **2** OPENING, aperture, door, entrance, gateway, inlet, orifice

mouthful *noun* TASTE, bit, bite, little, morsel, sample, spoonful, swallow

mouthpiece *noun* SPOKESPERSON, agent, delegate, representative, spokesman *or* spokeswoman

movable *adjective* PORTABLE, detachable, mobile, transferable, transportable

move *verb* 1 GO, advance, budge, proceed, progress, shift, stir 2 CHANGE, shift, switch, transfer, transpose 3 LEAVE, migrate, pack one's bags (*informal*), quit, relocate, remove 4 DRIVE, activate, operate, propel, shift, start, turn 5 TOUCH, affect, excite, impress 6 INCITE, cause, induce, influence, inspire, motivate, persuade, prompt, rouse 7 PROPOSE, advocate, put forward, recommend, suggest, urge ▶*noun* 8 ACTION, maneuver, measure, ploy, step, stratagem, stroke, turn 9 TRANSFER, relocation, removal, shift

movement *noun* 1 MOTION, action, activity, change, development, flow, maneuver, progress, stirring 2 GROUP, campaign, crusade, drive, faction, front, grouping, organization, party 3 WORKINGS, action, machinery, mechanism, works 4 *Music* SECTION, division, part, passage

movie *noun* FILM, feature, flick (*slang*), picture

moving *adjective* 1 EMOTIONAL, affecting, inspiring, pathetic, persuasive, poignant, stirring, touching 2 MOBILE, movable, portable, running, unfixed

mow *verb* CUT, crop, scythe, shear, trim

mow down *verb* MASSACRE, butcher, cut down, cut to pieces, shoot down, slaughter

much *adjective* 1 GREAT, abundant, a lot of, ample, considerable, copious, plenty of, sizable *or* sizeable, substantial ▶*noun* 2 A LOT, a good deal, a great deal, heaps (*informal*), lots (*informal*), plenty ▶*adverb* 3 GREATLY, a great deal, a lot, considerably, decidedly, exceedingly

muck *noun* 1 MANURE, dung, ordure 2 DIRT, filth, mire, mud, ooze, slime, sludge

mucky *adjective* DIRTY, begrimed, filthy, grimy, messy, muddy, scuzzy (*slang*)

mud *noun* DIRT, clay, mire, ooze, silt, slime, sludge

muddle *verb* 1 JUMBLE, disarrange, disorder, disorganize, mess, scramble, spoil, tangle 2 CONFUSE, befuddle, bewilder, confound, daze, disorient, perplex, stupefy ▶*noun* 3 CONFUSION, chaos, disarray, disorder, disorganization, jumble, mess, mix-up, predicament, tangle

muddy *adjective* 1 DIRTY, bespattered, grimy, mucky, mud-caked, scuzzy (*slang*), soiled 2 BOGGY, marshy, quaggy, swampy

muffle *verb* 1 WRAP UP, cloak, cover, envelop, shroud, swaddle, swathe 2 DEADEN, muzzle, quieten, silence, soften, stifle, suppress

muffled *adjective* INDISTINCT, faint, muted, stifled, strangled, subdued, suppressed

mug[1] *noun* CUP, beaker, flagon,

pot, tankard

mug² noun FACE, countenance, features, visage **1** FOOL, dork (slang), schmuck (slang), sucker (slang) ▸ verb **2** ATTACK, assault, beat up, rob, set about or upon

muggy adjective HUMID, clammy, close, moist, oppressive, sticky, stuffy, sultry

mull verb PONDER, consider, contemplate, deliberate, meditate, reflect on, ruminate, think over, weigh

multifarious adjective DIVERSE, different, legion, manifold, many, miscellaneous, multiple, numerous, sundry, varied

multiple adjective MANY, manifold, multitudinous, numerous, several, sundry, various

multiply verb **1** INCREASE, build up, expand, extend, proliferate, spread **2** REPRODUCE, breed, propagate

multitude noun MASS, army, crowd, horde, host, mob, myriad, swarm, throng

munch verb CHEW, champ, chomp, crunch

mundane adjective **1** ORDINARY, banal, commonplace, day-to-day, everyday, humdrum, prosaic, routine, workaday **2** EARTHLY, mortal, secular, temporal, terrestrial, worldly

municipal adjective CIVIC, public, urban

municipality noun TOWN, borough, city, district, township

munificence noun GENEROSITY, beneficence, benevolence, bounty, largesse or largess, liberality, magnanimousness, philanthropy

munificent adjective GENEROUS, beneficent, benevolent, bountiful, lavish, liberal, magnanimous, open-handed, philanthropic, unstinting

murder noun **1** KILLING, assassination, bloodshed, butchery, carnage, homicide, manslaughter, massacre, slaying ▸ verb **2** KILL, assassinate, bump off (slang), butcher, eliminate (slang), massacre, slaughter, slay

murderer noun KILLER, assassin, butcher, cut-throat, hit man (slang), homicide, slaughterer, slayer

murderous adjective DEADLY, bloodthirsty, brutal, cruel, cut-throat, ferocious, lethal, savage

murky adjective DARK, cloudy, dim, dull, gloomy, gray, misty, overcast

murmur verb **1** MUMBLE, mutter, whisper **2** GRUMBLE, complain, moan (informal) ▸ noun **3** DRONE, buzzing, humming, purr, rumble, whisper

muscle noun **1** TENDON, sinew **2** STRENGTH, brawn, clout (informal), forcefulness, might, power, stamina, weight

muscular adjective STRONG, athletic, powerful, robust, sinewy, strapping, sturdy, vigorous

muse verb PONDER, brood, cogitate, consider, contemplate, deliberate, meditate, mull over, reflect, ruminate

mushy adjective **1** SOFT, pulpy, semi-solid, slushy, squashy, squelchy **2** *Informal* SENTIMENTAL, maudlin, mawkish, saccharine, schmaltzy (*slang*), sloppy (*informal*), slushy (*informal*)

musical *adjective* MELODIOUS, dulcet, euphonious, harmonious, lyrical, melodic, sweet-sounding, tuneful

must *noun* NECESSITY, essential, fundamental, imperative, prerequisite, requirement, requisite, *sine qua non*

muster *verb* **1** ASSEMBLE, call together, convene, gather, marshal, mobilize, rally, summon ▶*noun* **2** ASSEMBLY, collection, congregation, convention, gathering, meeting, rally, roundup

musty *adjective* STALE, airless, dank, funky (*slang*), fusty, mildewed, moldy, old, smelly, stuffy

mutability *noun* CHANGE, alteration, evolution, metamorphosis, transition, variation, vicissitude

mutable *adjective* CHANGEABLE, adaptable, alterable, fickle, inconsistent, inconstant, unsettled, unstable, variable, volatile

mutation *noun* CHANGE, alteration, evolution, metamorphosis, modification, transfiguration, transformation, variation

mute *adjective* SILENT, dumb, mum, speechless, unspoken, voiceless, wordless

mutilate *verb* **1** MAIM, amputate, cut up, damage, disfigure, dismember, injure, lacerate, mangle **2** DISTORT, adulterate, bowdlerize, censor, cut, damage, expurgate

mutinous *adjective* REBELLIOUS, disobedient, insubordinate, insurgent, refractory, riotous, subversive, unmanageable, unruly

mutiny *noun* **1** REBELLION, disobedience, insubordination, insurrection, revolt, revolution, riot, uprising ▶*verb* **2** REBEL, disobey, resist, revolt, rise up

mutter *verb* GRUMBLE, complain, grouse, mumble, murmur, rumble

mutual *adjective* SHARED, common, interchangeable, joint, reciprocal, requited, returned

muzzle *noun* **1** JAWS, mouth, nose, snout **2** GAG, guard ▶*verb* **3** SUPPRESS, censor, curb, gag, restrain, silence, stifle

myopic *adjective* SHORT-SIGHTED, near-sighted

myriad *adjective* **1** INNUMERABLE, countless, immeasurable, incalculable, multitudinous, untold ▶*noun* **2** MULTITUDE, army, horde, host, swarm

mysterious *adjective* STRANGE, arcane, enigmatic, inexplicable, inscrutable, mystifying, perplexing, puzzling, secret, uncanny, unfathomable, weird

mystery *noun* PUZZLE, conundrum, enigma, problem, question, riddle, secret, teaser

mystic, mystical *adjective* SUPERNATURAL, inscrutable, metaphysical, mysterious, occult, otherworldly, paranormal, preternatural, transcendental

mystify *verb* PUZZLE, baffle, bewilder, confound, confuse, flummox, nonplus, perplex, stump

mystique *noun* FASCINATION, awe, charisma, charm, glamour, magic, spell

myth *noun* 1 LEGEND, allegory, fable, fairy story, fiction, folk tale, saga, story, urban legend *or* myth 2 ILLUSION, delusion, fancy, fantasy, figment, imagination, superstition, tall tale (*informal*)

mythical *adjective* 1 LEGENDARY, fabled, fabulous, fairy-tale, mythological 2 IMAGINARY, fabricated, fantasy, fictitious, invented, made-up, make-believe, nonexistent, pretended, unreal, untrue

mythological *adjective* LEGENDARY, fabulous, mythic, mythical, traditional

mythology *noun* LEGEND, folklore, lore, tradition

—— N n ——

nadir *noun* BOTTOM, depths, lowest point, minimum, rock bottom

nag[1] *verb* 1 SCOLD, annoy, badger, harass, hassle (*informal*), henpeck, irritate, pester, plague, upbraid, worry ▶ *noun* 2 SCOLD, harpy, shrew, tartar, virago

nag[2] *noun* HORSE, hack

nagging *adjective* IRRITATING, persistent, scolding, shrewish, worrying

nail *verb* FASTEN, attach, fix, hammer, join, pin, secure, tack

naive *adjective* 1 GULLIBLE, callow, credulous, green, unsuspicious, wet behind the ears (*informal*) 2 INNOCENT, artless, guileless, ingenuous, open, simple, trusting, unsophisticated, unworldly

naivety, naïveté *noun* 1 GULLIBILITY, callowness, credulity 2 INNOCENCE, artlessness, guilelessness, inexperience, ingenuousness, naturalness, openness, simplicity

naked *adjective* NUDE, bare, exposed, in one's birthday suit (*informal*), stripped, unclothed, undressed, without a stitch on (*informal*)

nakedness *noun* NUDITY, bareness, undress

name *noun* 1 TITLE, designation, epithet, handle (*slang*), moniker *or* monicker (*slang*), nickname, sobriquet, term 2 FAME, distinction, eminence, esteem, honor, note, praise, renown, repute ▶ *verb* 3 CALL, baptize, christen, dub, entitle, label, style, term 4 NOMINATE, appoint, choose, designate, select, specify

named *adjective* 1 CALLED, baptized, christened, dubbed, entitled, known as, labeled, styled, termed 2 NOMINATED, appointed, chosen, designated, mentioned, picked, selected, singled out, specified

nameless *adjective* 1 ANONYMOUS, unnamed, untitled 2 UNKNOWN, incognito, obscure, undistinguished, unheard-of, unsung 3 HORRIBLE, abominable, indescribable, unmentionable, unspeakable, unutterable

namely adverb SPECIFICALLY, to wit, viz.

nap[1] noun 1 SLEEP, catnap, forty winks (informal), rest, siesta ▶verb 2 SLEEP, catnap, doze, drop off (informal), nod off (informal), rest, snooze (informal)

nap[2] noun WEAVE, down, fiber, grain, pile

napkin noun CLOTH, linen, wipe

narcissism noun EGOTISM, self-love, vanity

narcotic noun 1 DRUG, analgesic, anesthetic, anodyne, opiate, painkiller, sedative, tranquilizer ▶adjective 2 SEDATIVE, analgesic, calming, hypnotic, painkilling, soporific

narrate verb TELL, chronicle, describe, detail, recite, recount, relate, report

narration noun TELLING, description, explanation, reading, recital, relation

narrative noun STORY, account, chronicle, history, report, statement, tale

narrator noun STORYTELLER, author, chronicler, commentator, reporter, writer

narrow adjective 1 THIN, attenuated, fine, slender, slim, spare, tapering 2 LIMITED, close, confined, constricted, contracted, meager, restricted, tight 3 INSULAR, dogmatic, illiberal, intolerant, narrow-minded, partial, prejudiced, small-minded ▶verb 4 TIGHTEN, constrict, limit, reduce

narrowly adverb JUST, barely, by the skin of one's teeth, only just, scarcely

narrow-minded adjective INTOLERANT, bigoted, hidebound, illiberal, opinionated, parochial, prejudiced, provincial, small-minded

nastiness noun UNPLEASANTNESS, malice, meanness, spitefulness

nasty adjective 1 OBJECTIONABLE, disagreeable, loathsome, obnoxious, offensive, unpleasant, vile 2 SPITEFUL, despicable, disagreeable, distasteful, lousy (slang), malicious, mean, scuzzy (slang), unpleasant, vicious, vile 3 PAINFUL, bad, critical, dangerous, serious, severe

nation noun COUNTRY, people, race, realm, society, state, tribe

national adjective 1 NATIONWIDE, countrywide, public, widespread ▶noun 2 CITIZEN, inhabitant, native, resident, subject

nationalism noun PATRIOTISM, allegiance, chauvinism, jingoism, loyalty

nationality noun RACE, birth, nation

nationwide adjective NATIONAL, countrywide, general, widespread

native adjective 1 LOCAL, domestic, home, indigenous 2 INBORN, congenital, hereditary, inbred, ingrained, innate, instinctive, intrinsic, natural ▶noun 3 INHABITANT, aborigine, citizen, countryman, dweller, national, resident

natty adjective SMART, dapper, elegant, fashionable, neat, phat (slang), snazzy (informal), spruce, stylish, trim

natural adjective 1 NORMAL,

common, everyday, legitimate, logical, ordinary, regular, typical, usual 2 UNAFFECTED, genuine, ingenuous, open, real, simple, spontaneous, unpretentious, unsophisticated 3 INNATE, characteristic, essential, inborn, inherent, instinctive, intuitive, native 4 PURE, organic, plain, unrefined, whole

naturalist noun BIOLOGIST, botanist, ecologist, zoologist

naturalistic adjective REALISTIC, lifelike, true-to-life

naturally adverb 1 OF COURSE, certainly 2 GENUINELY, normally, simply, spontaneously, typically, unaffectedly, unpretentiously

nature noun 1 CREATION, cosmos, earth, environment, universe, world 2 MAKE-UP, character, complexion, constitution, essence 3 KIND, category, description, sort, species, style, type, variety 4 TEMPERAMENT, disposition, humor, mood, outlook, temper

naughty adjective 1 DISOBEDIENT, bad, impish, misbehaved, mischievous, refractory, wayward, wicked, worthless 2 OBSCENE, improper, lewd, ribald, risqué, smutty, vulgar

nausea noun SICKNESS, biliousness, queasiness, retching, squeamishness, vomiting

nauseate verb SICKEN, disgust, offend, repel, repulse, revolt, turn one's stomach

nauseous adjective SICKENING, abhorrent, disgusting, distasteful, nauseating,

offensive, repugnant, repulsive, revolting, scuzzy (slang)

nautical adjective MARITIME, marine, naval

naval adjective NAUTICAL, marine, maritime

navigable adjective 1 PASSABLE, clear, negotiable, unobstructed 2 SAILABLE, controllable, dirigible

navigate verb SAIL, drive, guide, handle, maneuver, pilot, steer, voyage

navigation noun SAILING, helmsmanship, seamanship, voyaging

navigator noun PILOT, mariner, seaman

navy noun FLEET, armada, flotilla

near adjective 1 CLOSE, adjacent, adjoining, nearby, neighboring 2 FORTHCOMING, approaching, imminent, impending, in the offing, looming, nigh, upcoming

nearby adjective NEIGHBORING, adjacent, adjoining, convenient, handy

nearly adverb ALMOST, approximately, as good as, just about, practically, roughly, virtually, well-nigh

nearness noun CLOSENESS, accessibility, availability, handiness, proximity, vicinity

near-sighted adjective SHORT-SIGHTED, myopic

neat adjective 1 TIDY, orderly, shipshape, smart, spick-and-span, spruce, systematic, trim 2 ELEGANT, adept, adroit, deft, dexterous, efficient, graceful, nimble, skillful, stylish 3 Of alcoholic drinks STRAIGHT, pure, undiluted, unmixed

neatly adverb 1 TIDILY, daintily, fastidiously, methodically, smartly, sprucely, systematically 2 ELEGANTLY, adeptly, adroitly, deftly, dexterously, efficiently, expertly, gracefully, nimbly, skillfully

neatness noun 1 TIDINESS, daintiness, orderliness, smartness, spruceness, trimness 2 ELEGANCE, adroitness, deftness, dexterity, efficiency, grace, nimbleness, skill, style

nebulous adjective VAGUE, confused, dim, hazy, imprecise, indefinite, indistinct, shadowy, uncertain, unclear

necessarily adverb CERTAINLY, automatically, compulsorily, incontrovertibly, inevitably, inexorably, naturally, of necessity, undoubtedly

necessary adjective 1 NEEDED, compulsory, essential, imperative, indispensable, mandatory, obligatory, required, requisite, vital 2 CERTAIN, fated, inescapable, inevitable, inexorable, unavoidable

necessitate verb COMPEL, call for, coerce, constrain, demand, force, impel, oblige, require

necessities plural noun ESSENTIALS, exigencies, fundamentals, needs, requirements

necessity noun 1 INEVITABILITY, compulsion, inexorableness, obligation 2 NEED, desideratum, essential, fundamental, prerequisite, requirement, requisite, sine qua non

necromancy noun MAGIC, black magic, divination,

enchantment, sorcery, witchcraft, wizardry

necropolis noun CEMETERY, burial ground, churchyard, graveyard

need verb 1 REQUIRE, call for, demand, entail, lack, miss, necessitate, want ▶noun 2 POVERTY, deprivation, destitution, inadequacy, insufficiency, lack, paucity, penury, shortage 3 REQUIREMENT, demand, desideratum, essential, requisite 4 EMERGENCY, exigency, necessity, obligation, urgency, want

needed adjective NECESSARY, called for, desired, lacked, required, wanted

needful adjective NECESSARY, essential, indispensable, needed, required, requisite, stipulated, vital

needle verb IRRITATE, annoy, get on one's nerves (informal), goad, harass, nag, pester, provoke, rile, taunt

needless adjective UNNECESSARY, gratuitous, groundless, pointless, redundant, superfluous, uncalled-for, unwanted, useless

needlework noun EMBROIDERY, needlecraft, sewing, stitching, tailoring

needy adjective POOR, deprived, destitute, disadvantaged, impoverished, penniless, poverty-stricken, underprivileged

nefarious adjective WICKED, criminal, depraved, evil, foul, heinous, infernal, villainous

negate verb 1 INVALIDATE, annul, cancel, countermand, neutralize, nullify, obviate, reverse, wipe out **2** DENY, contradict, disallow, disprove, gainsay (*archaic or literary*), oppose, rebut, refute

negation *noun* **1** CANCELLATION, neutralization, nullification **2** DENIAL, contradiction, converse, disavowal, inverse, opposite, rejection, renunciation, reverse

negative *adjective* **1** CONTRADICTORY, contrary, denying, dissenting, opposing, refusing, rejecting, resisting **2** PESSIMISTIC, cynical, gloomy, jaundiced, uncooperative, unenthusiastic, unwilling ▶*noun* **3** CONTRADICTION, denial, refusal

neglect *verb* **1** DISREGARD, blow off (*slang*), disdain, ignore, overlook, rebuff, scorn, slight, spurn **2** FORGET, be remiss, evade, omit, pass over, shirk, skimp ▶*noun* **3** DISREGARD, disdain, inattention, indifference **4** NEGLIGENCE, carelessness, dereliction, failure, laxity, oversight, slackness

neglected *adjective* **1** ABANDONED, derelict, overgrown **2** DISREGARDED, unappreciated, underestimated, undervalued

neglectful *adjective* CARELESS, heedless, inattentive, indifferent, lax, negligent, remiss, thoughtless, uncaring

negligence *noun* CARELESSNESS, dereliction, disregard, inattention, indifference, laxity, neglect, slackness, thoughtlessness

negligent *adjective* CARELESS, forgetful, heedless, inattentive, neglectful, remiss, slack,

slapdash, thoughtless, unthinking

negligible *adjective* INSIGNIFICANT, imperceptible, inconsequential, minor, minute, small, trifling, trivial, unimportant

negotiable *adjective* DEBATABLE, variable

negotiate *verb* **1** DEAL, arrange, bargain, conciliate, debate, discuss, haggle, mediate, transact, work out **2** GET ROUND, clear, cross, get over, get past, pass, surmount

negotiation *noun* BARGAINING, arbitration, debate, diplomacy, discussion, haggling, mediation, transaction, wheeling and dealing (*informal*)

negotiator *noun* MEDIATOR, ambassador, delegate, diplomat, honest broker, intermediary, moderator

neighborhood *noun* DISTRICT, community, environs, locale, locality, quarter, region, vicinity

neighboring *adjective* NEARBY, adjacent, adjoining, bordering, connecting, near, next, surrounding

neighborly *adjective* HELPFUL, considerate, friendly, harmonious, hospitable, kind, obliging, sociable

nemesis *noun* RETRIBUTION, destiny, destruction, fate, vengeance

nepotism *noun* FAVORITISM, bias, partiality, patronage, preferential treatment

nerd *noun* BORE, doofus (*slang*), dork (*slang*), drip (*informal*), dweeb (*slang*), egghead (*informal*), geek (*slang*), goober (*informal*)

nerve *noun* 1 BRAVERY, courage, daring, fearlessness, grit, guts (*informal*), pluck, resolution, will 2 IMPUDENCE, audacity, boldness, brazenness, cheek (*informal*), impertinence, insolence, temerity ▸ *verb* 3 **nerve oneself** BRACE ONESELF, fortify oneself, steel oneself

nerveless *adjective* CALM, composed, controlled, cool, impassive, imperturbable, self-possessed, unemotional

nerve-racking *adjective* TENSE, difficult, distressing, frightening, harrowing, stressful, trying, worrying

nerves *plural noun* TENSION, anxiety, butterflies (in one's stomach) (*informal*), cold feet (*informal*), fretfulness, nervousness, strain, stress, worry

nervous *adjective* APPREHENSIVE, anxious, edgy, fearful, jumpy, on edge, tense, uneasy, uptight (*informal*), wired (*slang*), worried

nervousness *noun* ANXIETY, agitation, disquiet, excitability, fluster, tension, touchiness, worry

nervy *adjective* ANXIOUS, agitated, fidgety, jittery (*informal*), jumpy, nervous, on edge, tense, twitchy (*informal*), wired (*slang*)

nest *noun* REFUGE, den, haunt, hideaway, retreat

nest egg *noun* RESERVE, cache, deposit, fall-back, fund(s), savings, store

nestle *verb* SNUGGLE, cuddle, curl up, huddle, nuzzle

nestling *noun* CHICK, fledgling

net[1] *noun* 1 MESH, lattice, netting, network, openwork, tracery, web ▸ *verb* 2 CATCH, bag, capture, enmesh, ensnare, entangle, trap

net[2] *adjective* 1 FINAL, after taxes, clear, take-home ▸ *verb* 2 EARN, accumulate, bring in, clear, gain, make, realize, reap

nether *adjective* LOWER, below, beneath, bottom, inferior, under, underground

nettled *adjective* IRRITATED, annoyed, exasperated, galled, harassed, incensed, peeved, put out, riled, vexed

network *noun* SYSTEM, arrangement, complex, grid, labyrinth, lattice, maze, organization, structure, web

neurosis *noun* OBSESSION, abnormality, affliction, derangement, instability, maladjustment, mental illness, phobia

neurotic *adjective* UNSTABLE, abnormal, compulsive, disturbed, maladjusted, manic, nervous, obsessive, unhealthy

neuter *verb* CASTRATE, doctor (*informal*), emasculate, fix (*informal*), geld, spay

neutral *adjective* 1 UNBIASED, disinterested, even-handed, impartial, nonaligned, nonpartisan, uncommitted, uninvolved, unprejudiced 2 INDETERMINATE, dull, indistinct, intermediate, undefined

neutrality *noun* IMPARTIALITY, detachment, nonalignment, noninterference, noninvolvement, nonpartisanship

neutralize *verb* COUNTERACT,

cancel, compensate for, counterbalance, frustrate, negate, nullify, offset, undo

never adverb AT NO TIME, not at all, on no account, under no circumstances

nevertheless adverb NONETHELESS, but, even so, (even) though, however, notwithstanding, regardless, still, yet

new adjective 1 MODERN, contemporary, current, fresh, ground-breaking, latest, novel, original, recent, state-of-the-art, unfamiliar, up-to-date 2 CHANGED, altered, improved, modernized, redesigned, renewed, restored 3 EXTRA, added, more, supplementary

newcomer noun NOVICE, arrival, beginner, Johnny-come-lately (*informal*), new kid in town (*informal*), parvenu

newfangled adjective NEW, contemporary, cool (*informal*), fashionable, gimmicky, modern, novel, phat (*slang*), recent, state-of-the-art

newly adverb RECENTLY, anew, freshly, just, lately, latterly

newness noun NOVELTY, freshness, innovation, oddity, originality, strangeness, unfamiliarity, uniqueness

news noun INFORMATION, bulletin, communiqué, exposé, gossip, hearsay, intelligence, latest (*informal*), report, revelation, rumor, story

newsworthy adjective INTERESTING, important, notable, noteworthy, remarkable, significant, stimulating

next adjective 1 FOLLOWING, consequent, ensuing, later, subsequent, succeeding 2 NEAREST, adjacent, adjoining, closest, neighboring ▶ adverb 3 AFTERWARDS, following, later, subsequently, thereafter

nibble verb 1 BITE, eat, gnaw, munch, nip, peck, pick at ▶ noun 2 SNACK, bite, crumb, morsel, peck, soupçon, taste, tidbit

nice adjective 1 PLEASANT, agreeable, attractive, charming, delightful, good, pleasurable 2 KIND, courteous, friendly, likable *or* likeable, polite, well-mannered 3 NEAT, dainty, fine, tidy, trim 4 SUBTLE, careful, delicate, fastidious, fine, meticulous, precise, strict

nicely adverb 1 PLEASANTLY, acceptably, agreeably, attractively, charmingly, delightfully, pleasurably, well 2 KINDLY, amiably, commendably, courteously, politely 3 NEATLY, daintily, finely, tidily, trimly

nicety noun SUBTLETY, daintiness, delicacy, discrimination, distinction, nuance, refinement

niche noun 1 ALCOVE, corner, hollow, nook, opening, recess 2 POSITION, calling, pigeonhole (*informal*), place, slot (*informal*), vocation

nick verb 1 CUT, chip, dent, mark, notch, scar, score, scratch, snick ▶ noun 2 CUT, chip, dent, mark, notch, scar, scratch

nickname noun PET NAME, diminutive, epithet, label, moniker *or* monicker (*slang*), sobriquet

nifty *adjective* NEAT, attractive, chic, deft, pleasing, smart, stylish

niggard *noun* MISER, cheapskate (*informal*), Scrooge, skinflint

niggardly *adjective* STINGY, avaricious, frugal, grudging, mean, miserly, parsimonious, tightfisted, ungenerous

niggle *verb* 1 WORRY, annoy, irritate, rankle 2 CRITICIZE, carp, cavil, find fault, fuss

niggling *adjective* 1 PERSISTENT, gnawing, irritating, troubling, worrying 2 PETTY, finicky, fussy, nit-picking (*informal*), pettifogging, picky (*informal*), quibbling

night *noun* DARKNESS, dark, night-time

nightfall *noun* EVENING, dusk, sundown, sunset, twilight

nightly *adjective* 1 NOCTURNAL, night-time ▶ *adverb* 2 EVERY NIGHT, each night, night after night, nights (*informal*)

nightmare *noun* 1 BAD DREAM, hallucination 2 ORDEAL, horror, torment, trial, tribulation

nil *noun* NOTHING, love, naught, none, zero

nimble *adjective* AGILE, brisk, deft, dexterous, lively, quick, sprightly, spry, swift

nimbly *adverb* QUICKLY, briskly, deftly, dexterously, easily, readily, smartly, spryly, swiftly

nip¹ *verb* PINCH, bite, squeeze, tweak

nip² *noun* DRAM, draft, drop, mouthful, shot (*informal*), sip, snifter (*informal*)

nippy *adjective* CHILLY, biting,

sharp, stinging

nirvana *noun* PARADISE, bliss, joy, peace, serenity, tranquillity

nit-picking *adjective* FUSSY, captious, carping, finicky, hairsplitting, pedantic, pettifogging, quibbling

nitty-gritty *noun* BASICS, brass tacks (*informal*), core, crux, essentials, fundamentals, gist, substance

nitwit *noun* *Informal* FOOL, dimwit (*informal*), doofus (*slang*), dork (*slang*), dummy (*slang*), halfwit, oaf, schmuck (*slang*), simpleton

no *interjection* 1 NEVER, nay, not at all, no way ▶ *noun* 2 REFUSAL, denial, negation

nobility *noun* 1 INTEGRITY, honor, incorruptibility, uprightness, virtue 2 ARISTOCRACY, elite, lords, nobles, patricians, peerage, upper class

noble *adjective* 1 WORTHY, generous, honorable, magnanimous, upright, virtuous 2 ARISTOCRATIC, blue-blooded, highborn, lordly, patrician, titled 3 GREAT, dignified, distinguished, grand, imposing, impressive, lofty, splendid, stately ▶ *noun* 4 LORD, aristocrat, nobleman, peer

nobody *pronoun* 1 NO-ONE ▶ *noun* 2 NONENTITY, cipher, lightweight (*informal*), menial

nocturnal *adjective* NIGHTLY, night-time

nod *verb* 1 ACKNOWLEDGE, bow, gesture, indicate, signal 2 SLEEP, doze, drowse, nap ▶ *noun* 3 GESTURE, acknowledgment, greeting, indication, sign, signal

noggin *noun* 1 CUP, dram, mug,

nip, tot **2** *Informal* HEAD, block (*informal*), noodle (*slang*), nut (*slang*)

no go *adjective* IMPOSSIBLE, futile, hopeless, vain

noise *noun* SOUND, clamor, commotion, din, hubbub, racket, row, uproar

noiseless *adjective* SILENT, hushed, inaudible, mute, quiet, soundless, still

noisome *adjective* **1** POISONOUS, bad, harmful, pernicious, pestilential, unhealthy, unwholesome **2** OFFENSIVE, disgusting, fetid, foul, funky (*slang*), malodorous, noxious, putrid, smelly, stinking

noisy *adjective* LOUD, boisterous, cacophonous, clamorous, deafening, ear-splitting, strident, tumultuous, uproarious, vociferous

nomad *noun* WANDERER, drifter, itinerant, migrant, rambler, rover, vagabond

nomadic *adjective* WANDERING, itinerant, migrant, peripatetic, roaming, roving, traveling, vagrant

nom de plume *noun* PSEUDONYM, alias, assumed name, nom de guerre, pen name

nomenclature *noun* TERMINOLOGY, classification, codification, phraseology, taxonomy, vocabulary

nominal *adjective* **1** SO-CALLED, formal, ostensible, professed, puppet, purported, supposed, theoretical, titular **2** SMALL, inconsiderable, insignificant, minimal, symbolic, token, trifling, trivial

nominate *verb* NAME, appoint, assign, choose, designate, elect, propose, recommend, select, suggest

nomination *noun* CHOICE, appointment, designation, election, proposal, recommendation, selection, suggestion

nominee *noun* CANDIDATE, aspirant, contestant, entrant, protégé, runner

nonaligned *adjective* NEUTRAL, impartial, uncommitted, undecided

nonchalance *noun* INDIFFERENCE, calm, composure, equanimity, imperturbability, sang-froid, self-possession, unconcern

nonchalant *adjective* CASUAL, blasé, calm, careless, indifferent, insouciant, laid-back (*informal*), offhand, unconcerned, unperturbed

noncombatant *noun* CIVILIAN, neutral, nonbelligerent

noncommittal *adjective* EVASIVE, cautious, circumspect, equivocal, guarded, neutral, politic, temporizing, tentative, vague, wary

non compos mentis *adjective* INSANE, crazy, deranged, mentally ill, unbalanced, unhinged

nonconformist *noun* MAVERICK, dissenter, eccentric, heretic, iconoclast, individualist, protester, radical, rebel

nonconformity *noun* DISSENT, eccentricity, heresy, heterodoxy

nondescript *adjective* ORDINARY, commonplace, dull, featureless, undistinguished, unexceptional, unremarkable

none *pronoun* NOT ANY, nil, nobody, no-one, nothing, not one, zero

nonentity *noun* NOBODY, cipher, lightweight (*informal*), mediocrity, small fry

nonessential *adjective* UNNECESSARY, dispensable, expendable, extraneous, inessential, peripheral, superfluous, unimportant

nonetheless *adverb* NEVERTHELESS, despite that, even so, however, in spite of that, yet

nonevent *noun* FLOP (*informal*), disappointment, dud (*informal*), failure, fiasco, washout

nonexistent *adjective* IMAGINARY, chimerical, fictional, hypothetical, illusory, legendary, mythical, unreal

nonsense *noun* RUBBISH, balderdash, claptrap (*informal*), drivel, gibberish, hot air (*informal*), stupidity, tripe (*informal*), twaddle

nonsensical *adjective* SENSELESS, absurd, crazy, foolish, inane, incomprehensible, irrational, meaningless, ridiculous, silly

nonstarter *noun* DEAD LOSS, dud (*informal*), lemon (*informal*), loser, no-hoper (*informal*), turkey (*informal*), washout (*informal*)

nonstop *adjective* 1 CONTINUOUS, constant, endless, incessant, interminable, relentless, twenty-four-seven (*slang*), unbroken, uninterrupted ▶ *adverb* 2 CONTINUOUSLY, ceaselessly, constantly, endlessly, incessantly, interminably, perpetually, relentlessly, twenty-four-seven

(*slang*), unremittingly

noodle *noun Slang* HEAD, common sense, gut feeling (*informal*), intuition, sense

nook *noun* NICHE, alcove, corner, cubbyhole, hideout, opening, recess, retreat

noon *noun* MIDDAY, high noon, noonday, noontide, twelve noon

norm *noun* STANDARD, average, benchmark, criterion, par, pattern, rule, yardstick

normal *adjective* 1 USUAL, average, common, conventional, natural, ordinary, regular, routine, standard, typical 2 SANE, rational, reasonable, well-adjusted

normality *noun* 1 REGULARITY, conventionality, naturalness 2 SANITY, balance, rationality, reason

normally *adverb* USUALLY, as a rule, commonly, generally, habitually, ordinarily, regularly, typically

north *adjective* 1 NORTHERN, Arctic, boreal, northerly, polar ▶ *adverb* 2 NORTHWARD(S), northerly

nose *noun* 1 SNOUT, beak, bill, honker (*slang*), proboscis ▶ *verb* 2 EASE FORWARD, nudge, nuzzle, push, shove 3 PRY, meddle, snoop (*informal*)

nosegay *noun* POSY, bouquet

nostalgia *noun* REMINISCENCE, homesickness, longing, pining, regretfulness, remembrance, wistfulness, yearning

nostalgic *adjective* SENTIMENTAL, emotional, homesick, longing, maudlin, regretful, wistful

nostrum *noun* MEDICINE, cure,

drug, elixir, panacea, potion, remedy, treatment

nosy adjective INQUISITIVE, curious, eavesdropping, interfering, intrusive, meddlesome, prying, snooping (informal)

notability noun FAME, celebrity, distinction, eminence, esteem, renown

notable adjective 1 REMARKABLE, conspicuous, extraordinary, memorable, noteworthy, outstanding, rare, striking, uncommon, unusual ▸noun 2 CELEBRITY, big name, dignitary, personage, V.I.P.

notably adverb PARTICULARLY, especially, outstandingly, strikingly

notation noun SIGNS, characters, code, script, symbols, system

notch noun 1 CUT, cleft, incision, indentation, mark, nick, score 2 Informal LEVEL, degree, grade, step ▸verb 3 CUT, indent, mark, nick, score, scratch

notch up verb REGISTER, achieve, gain, make, score

note noun 1 MESSAGE, comment, communication, epistle, jotting, letter, memo, memorandum, minute, remark, reminder 2 SYMBOL, indication, mark, sign, token ▸verb 3 SEE, notice, observe, perceive 4 MARK, denote, designate, indicate, record, register 5 MENTION, remark

notebook noun JOTTER, diary, exercise book, journal, notepad

noted adjective FAMOUS, acclaimed, celebrated, distinguished, eminent,

illustrious, notable, prominent, renowned, well-known

noteworthy adjective REMARKABLE, exceptional, extraordinary, important, notable, outstanding, significant, unusual

nothing noun NOUGHT, emptiness, nada (informal), nil, nothingness, nullity, void, zero

nothingness noun 1 OBLIVION, nonbeing, nonexistence, nullity 2 INSIGNIFICANCE, unimportance, worthlessness

notice noun 1 OBSERVATION, cognizance, consideration, heed, interest, note, regard 2 ATTENTION, civility, respect 3 ANNOUNCEMENT, advice, communication, instruction, intimation, news, notification, order, warning ▸verb 4 OBSERVE, detect, discern, distinguish, mark, note, perceive, see, spot

noticeable adjective OBVIOUS, appreciable, clear, conspicuous, evident, manifest, perceptible, plain, striking

notification noun ANNOUNCEMENT, advice, declaration, information, intelligence, message, notice, statement, warning

notify verb INFORM, advise, alert, announce, declare, make known, publish, tell, warn

notion noun 1 IDEA, belief, concept, impression, inkling, opinion, sentiment, view 2 WHIM, caprice, desire, fancy, impulse, inclination, wish

notional adjective SPECULATIVE, abstract, conceptual, hypothetical, imaginary, theoretical, unreal

notoriety noun SCANDAL, dishonor, disrepute, infamy, obloquy, opprobrium

notorious adjective INFAMOUS, dishonorable, disreputable, opprobrious, scandalous

notoriously adverb INFAMOUSLY, dishonorably, disreputably, opprobriously, scandalously

notwithstanding preposition DESPITE, in spite of

nought noun ZERO, nil, nothing

nourish verb 1 FEED, nurse, nurture, supply, sustain, tend 2 ENCOURAGE, comfort, cultivate, foster, maintain, promote, support

nourishing adjective NUTRITIOUS, beneficial, nutritive, wholesome

nourishment noun FOOD, nutriment, nutrition, sustenance

novel[1] noun STORY, fiction, narrative, romance, tale

novel[2] adjective NEW, different, fresh, innovative, original, strange, uncommon, unfamiliar, unusual

novelty noun 1 NEWNESS, freshness, innovation, oddity, originality, strangeness, surprise, unfamiliarity, uniqueness 2 GIMMICK, curiosity, gadget 3 KNICK-KNACK, bauble, memento, souvenir, trifle, trinket

novice noun BEGINNER, amateur, apprentice, learner, newcomer, probationer, pupil, trainee

now adverb 1 NOWADAYS, anymore, at the moment 2 IMMEDIATELY, at once, instantly, promptly, straightaway 3 **now and then** or **again** OCCASIONALLY, from time to time, infrequently, intermittently, on

and off, sometimes, sporadically

nowadays adverb NOW, anymore, at the moment, in this day and age, today

noxious adjective HARMFUL, deadly, destructive, foul, hurtful, injurious, poisonous, unhealthy, unwholesome

nuance noun SUBTLETY, degree, distinction, gradation, nicety, refinement, shade, tinge

nubile adjective MARRIAGEABLE, ripe (informal)

nucleus noun CENTER, basis, core, focus, heart, kernel, nub, pivot

nude adjective NAKED, bare, disrobed, in one's birthday suit, stark-naked, stripped, unclad, unclothed, undressed, without a stitch on (informal)

nudge verb PUSH, bump, dig, elbow, jog, poke, prod, shove, touch

nudity noun NAKEDNESS, bareness, deshabille, nudism, undress

nugget noun LUMP, chunk, clump, hunk, mass, piece

nuisance noun PROBLEM, annoyance, bother, drag (informal), hassle (informal), inconvenience, irritation, pain in the neck, pest, trouble

null adjective **null and void** INVALID, inoperative, useless, valueless, void, worthless

nullify verb CANCEL, counteract, invalidate, negate, neutralize, obviate, render null and void, veto

nullity noun NONEXISTENCE, invalidity, powerlessness, uselessness, worthlessness

numb *adjective* **1** UNFEELING, benumbed, dead, deadened, frozen, immobilized, insensitive, paralyzed, torpid ▶ *verb* **2** DEADEN, benumb, dull, freeze, immobilize, paralyze

number *noun* **1** NUMERAL, character, digit, figure, integer **2** QUANTITY, aggregate, amount, collection, crowd, horde, multitude, throng **3** ISSUE, copy, edition, imprint, printing ▶ *verb* **4** COUNT, account, add, calculate, compute, enumerate, include, reckon, total

numberless *adjective* INFINITE, countless, endless, innumerable, multitudinous, myriad, unnumbered, untold

numbness *noun* DEADNESS, dullness, insensitivity, paralysis, torpor

numeral *noun* NUMBER, digit, figure, integer

numerous *adjective* MANY, abundant, copious, plentiful, profuse, several, thick on the ground

nunnery *noun* CONVENT, abbey, cloister, house

nuptial *adjective* MARITAL, bridal, conjugal, connubial, matrimonial

nuptials *plural noun* WEDDING, marriage, matrimony

nurse *verb* **1** LOOK AFTER, care for, minister to, tend, treat **2** BREAST-FEED, feed, nourish, nurture, suckle, wet-nurse **3** FOSTER, cherish, cultivate, encourage, harbor, preserve, promote, succor, support

nursery *noun* CRECHE, kindergarten, playgroup

nurture *noun* **1** DEVELOPMENT, discipline, education, instruction, rearing, training, upbringing ▶ *verb* **2** DEVELOP, bring up, discipline, educate, instruct, rear, school, train

nut *noun* **1** *Slang* MADMAN, crank (*informal*), lunatic, maniac, nutcase (*slang*), psycho (*slang*) **2** *Slang* HEAD, brain, mind, reason, senses

nutrition *noun* FOOD, nourishment, nutriment, sustenance

nutritious *adjective* NOURISHING, beneficial, health-giving, invigorating, nutritive, strengthening, wholesome

nuts *adjective* *Informal* INSANE, deranged, disturbed, mad, mentally ill, psychotic, unbalanced, unstable

nuzzle *verb* SNUGGLE, burrow, cuddle, fondle, nestle, pet

nymph *noun* SYLPH, dryad, girl, maiden, naiad

oaf *noun* IDIOT, blockhead, clod, dolt, dork (*slang*), dunce, fool, goon, lout, moron, schmuck (*slang*)

oafish *adjective* MORONIC, dense, dim-witted (*informal*), doltish, dumb (*informal*), loutish, stupid, thick

oath *noun* **1** PROMISE, affirmation, avowal, bond, pledge, vow, word **2** SWEARWORD, blasphemy, curse, expletive, profanity

obdurate *adjective* STUBBORN,

dogged, hard-hearted,
immovable, implacable,
inflexible, obstinate,
pig-headed, unyielding

obedience noun RESPECT,
acquiescence, compliance,
docility, observance, reverence,
submissiveness, subservience

obedient adjective RESPECTFUL,
acquiescent, biddable,
compliant, deferential, docile,
dutiful, submissive, subservient,
well-trained

obelisk noun COLUMN, monolith,
monument, needle, pillar, shaft

obese adjective FAT, corpulent,
gross, heavy, overweight,
paunchy, plump, portly,
rotund, stout, tubby

obesity noun FATNESS, bulk,
corpulence, grossness,
portliness, stoutness, tubbiness

obey verb CARRY OUT, abide by,
act upon, adhere to, comply,
conform, follow, heed, keep,
observe

obfuscate verb CONFUSE, befog,
cloud, darken, muddy the
waters, obscure, perplex

object[1] noun 1 THING, article,
body, entity, item,
phenomenon 2 TARGET, focus,
recipient, victim 3 PURPOSE, aim,
design, end, goal, idea,
intention, objective, point

object[2] verb PROTEST, argue
against, demur, draw the line
(at something), expostulate,
oppose, take exception

objection noun PROTEST,
counter-argument, demur,
doubt, opposition,
remonstrance, scruple

objectionable adjective
UNPLEASANT, deplorable,

disagreeable, intolerable,
obnoxious, offensive,
regrettable, repugnant,
unseemly

objective noun 1 PURPOSE, aim,
ambition, end, goal, intention,
mark, object, target ▶adjective
2 UNBIASED, detached,
disinterested, dispassionate,
even-handed, fair, impartial,
open-minded, unprejudiced

objectively adverb IMPARTIALLY,
disinterestedly, dispassionately,
even-handedly, with an open
mind

objectivity noun IMPARTIALITY,
detachment, disinterestedness,
dispassion

obligation noun DUTY,
accountability, burden, charge,
compulsion, liability,
requirement, responsibility

obligatory adjective COMPULSORY,
binding, de rigueur, essential,
imperative, mandatory,
necessary, required, requisite,
unavoidable

oblige verb 1 COMPEL, bind,
constrain, force, impel, make,
necessitate, require 2 INDULGE,
accommodate, benefit, gratify,
please

obliged adjective 1 GRATEFUL,
appreciative, beholden,
indebted, in (someone's) debt,
thankful 2 BOUND, compelled,
forced, required

obliging adjective COOPERATIVE,
accommodating, agreeable,
considerate, good-natured,
helpful, kind, polite, willing

oblique adjective 1 SLANTING,
angled, aslant, sloping, tilted
2 INDIRECT, backhanded,
circuitous, implied,

roundabout, sidelong

obliterate verb DESTROY,
annihilate, blot out, efface,
eradicate, erase, expunge,
extirpate, root out, wipe out

obliteration noun ANNIHILATION,
elimination, eradication,
extirpation, wiping out

oblivion noun 1 NEGLECT,
abeyance, disregard,
forgetfulness
2 UNCONSCIOUSNESS, insensibility,
obliviousness, unawareness

oblivious adjective UNAWARE,
forgetful, heedless, ignorant,
insensible, neglectful,
negligent, regardless,
unconcerned, unconscious,
unmindful

obloquy noun 1 ABUSE,
aspersion, attack, blame,
censure, criticism, invective,
reproach, slander, vilification
2 DISCREDIT, disgrace, dishonor,
humiliation, ignominy, infamy,
shame, stigma

obnoxious adjective OFFENSIVE,
disagreeable, insufferable,
loathsome, nasty, nauseating,
objectionable, odious,
repulsive, revolting, scuzzy
(slang), unpleasant

obscene adjective 1 INDECENT,
dirty, filthy, immoral,
improper, lewd, offensive,
pornographic, salacious, scuzzy
(slang), X-rated 2 SICKENING,
atrocious, disgusting, evil,
heinous, loathsome,
outrageous, shocking, vile,
wicked

obscenity noun 1 INDECENCY,
coarseness, dirtiness,
impropriety, lewdness,
licentiousness, pornography,

smut 2 SWEARWORD, four-letter
word, profanity, vulgarism
3 OUTRAGE, abomination,
affront, atrocity, blight, evil,
offense, wrong

obscure adjective 1 VAGUE,
ambiguous, arcane, confusing,
cryptic, enigmatic, esoteric,
mysterious, opaque, recondite
2 INDISTINCT, blurred, cloudy,
dim, faint, gloomy, murky,
shadowy 3 LITTLE-KNOWN,
humble, lowly, out-of-the-way,
remote, undistinguished,
unheard-of, unknown ▶ verb
4 CONCEAL, cover, disguise,
hide, obfuscate, screen, veil

obscurity noun 1 DARKNESS,
dimness, dusk, gloom, haze,
shadows 2 INSIGNIFICANCE,
lowliness, unimportance

obsequious adjective
SYCOPHANTIC, cringing,
deferential, fawning, flattering,
grovelling, ingratiating, servile,
submissive, unctuous

observable adjective NOTICEABLE,
apparent, detectable,
discernible, evident, obvious,
perceptible, recognizable, visible

observance noun HONORING,
carrying out, compliance,
fulfillment, performance

observant adjective ATTENTIVE,
alert, eagle-eyed, perceptive,
quick, sharp-eyed, vigilant,
watchful, wide-awake

observation noun 1 STUDY,
examination, inspection,
monitoring, review, scrutiny,
surveillance, watching
2 REMARK, comment, note,
opinion, pronouncement,
reflection, thought, utterance

observe verb 1 SEE, detect,

discern, discover, note, notice, perceive, spot, witness **2** WATCH, check, keep an eye on (*informal*), keep track of, look at, monitor, scrutinize, study, survey, view **3** REMARK, comment, mention, note, opine, say, state **4** HONOR, abide by, adhere to, comply, conform to, follow, heed, keep, obey, respect

observer noun SPECTATOR, beholder, bystander, eyewitness, fly on the wall, looker-on, onlooker, viewer, watcher, witness

obsessed adjective PREOCCUPIED, dominated, gripped, haunted, hung up on (*slang*), infatuated, troubled

obsession noun PREOCCUPATION, complex, fetish, fixation, hang-up (*informal*), infatuation, mania, phobia, thing (*informal*)

obsessive adjective COMPULSIVE, besetting, consuming, gripping, haunting

obsolescent adjective WANING, ageing, declining, dying out, on the wane, on the way out, past its prime

obsolete adjective EXTINCT, antiquated, archaic, discarded, disused, old, old-fashioned, outmoded, out of date, passé

obstacle noun DIFFICULTY, bar, barrier, block, hindrance, hitch, hurdle, impediment, obstruction, snag, stumbling block

obstinacy noun STUBBORNNESS, doggedness, inflexibility, intransigence, obduracy, persistence, pig-headedness, tenacity, willfulness

obstinate adjective STUBBORN, determined, dogged, inflexible, intractable, intransigent, pig-headed, refractory, self-willed, strong-minded, willful

obstreperous adjective UNRULY, disorderly, loud, noisy, riotous, rowdy, turbulent, unmanageable, wild

obstruct verb BLOCK, bar, barricade, check, hamper, hinder, impede, restrict, stop, thwart

obstruction noun OBSTACLE, bar, barricade, barrier, blockage, difficulty, hindrance, impediment

obstructive adjective UNCOOPERATIVE, awkward, blocking, delaying, hindering, restrictive, stalling, unhelpful

obtain verb **1** GET, achieve, acquire, attain, earn, gain, land, procure, secure **2** EXIST, be in force, be prevalent, be the case, hold, prevail

obtainable adjective AVAILABLE, achievable, attainable, on tap (*informal*), to be had

obtrusive adjective NOTICEABLE, blatant, obvious, prominent, protruding, protuberant, sticking out

obtuse adjective SLOW, dense, dull, stolid, stupid, thick, uncomprehending

obviate verb PRECLUDE, avert, prevent, remove

obvious adjective EVIDENT, apparent, clear, conspicuous, distinct, indisputable, manifest, noticeable, plain, self-evident, undeniable, unmistakable

obviously adverb CLEARLY,

manifestly, of course, palpably,
patently, plainly, undeniably,
unmistakably, unquestionably,
without doubt

occasion noun 1 TIME, chance,
moment, opening,
opportunity, window 2 EVENT,
affair, celebration, experience,
happening, occurrence
3 REASON, call, cause, excuse,
ground(s), justification, motive,
prompting, provocation ▶ verb
4 CAUSE, bring about,
engender, generate, give rise
to, induce, inspire, lead to,
produce, prompt, provoke

occasional adjective INFREQUENT,
incidental, intermittent,
irregular, odd, rare, sporadic,
uncommon

occasionally adverb SOMETIMES,
at times, from time to time,
irregularly, now and again,
once in a while, periodically

occult adjective SUPERNATURAL,
arcane, esoteric, magical,
mysterious, mystical

occupancy noun TENURE,
possession, residence, tenancy,
use

occupant noun INHABITANT,
incumbent, indweller, inmate,
lessee, occupier, resident,
tenant

occupation noun 1 PROFESSION,
business, calling, employment,
job, line (of work), pursuit,
trade, vocation, walk of life
2 POSSESSION, control, holding,
occupancy, residence, tenancy,
tenure 3 INVASION, conquest,
seizure, subjugation

occupied adjective 1 BUSY,
employed, engaged, working
2 IN USE, engaged, full, taken,

unavailable 3 INHABITED, lived-in,
peopled, settled, tenanted

occupy verb 1 (often passive)
TAKE UP, divert, employ,
engage, engross, involve,
monopolize, preoccupy, tie up
2 LIVE IN, dwell in, inhabit,
own, possess, reside in 3 FILL,
cover, permeate, pervade, take
up 4 INVADE, capture, overrun,
seize, take over

occur verb 1 HAPPEN, befall,
come about, crop up
(informal), take place, turn up
(informal) 2 EXIST, appear, be
found, be present, develop,
manifest itself, show itself
3 **occur to** COME TO MIND, cross
one's mind, dawn on, enter
one's head, spring to mind,
strike one, suggest itself

occurrence noun 1 INCIDENT,
adventure, affair, circumstance,
episode, event, happening,
instance 2 EXISTENCE,
appearance, development,
manifestation, materialization

odd adjective 1 UNUSUAL, bizarre,
extraordinary, freakish,
irregular, peculiar, rare,
remarkable, singular, strange
2 OCCASIONAL, casual, incidental,
irregular, periodic, random,
sundry, various 3 SPARE,
leftover, remaining, solitary,
surplus, unmatched, unpaired

oddity noun 1 IRREGULARITY,
abnormality, anomaly,
eccentricity, freak, idiosyncrasy,
peculiarity, quirk 2 MISFIT, crank
(informal), maverick, oddball
(informal)

oddment noun LEFTOVER, bit, fag
end, fragment, off cut,
remnant, scrap, snippet

odds *plural noun* 1 PROBABILITY, chances, likelihood 2 **at odds** IN CONFLICT, at daggers drawn, at loggerheads, at sixes and sevens, at variance, out of line

odds and ends *plural noun* SCRAPS, bits, bits and pieces, debris, oddments, remnants

odious *adjective* OFFENSIVE, detestable, horrid, loathsome, obnoxious, repulsive, revolting, scuzzy (*slang*), unpleasant

odor *noun* SMELL, aroma, bouquet, essence, fragrance, perfume, redolence, scent, stench, stink

odyssey *noun* JOURNEY, crusade, pilgrimage, quest, trek, voyage

off *adverb* 1 AWAY, apart, aside, elsewhere, out ▶*adjective* 2 UNAVAILABLE, canceled, finished, gone, postponed

offbeat *adjective* UNUSUAL, eccentric, left-field (*informal*), novel, outré, strange, unconventional, unorthodox, way-out (*informal*)

off color *adjective* ILL, out of sorts, peaky, poorly (*informal*), queasy, run down, sick, under the weather (*informal*), unwell

offend *verb* INSULT, affront, annoy, displease, hurt (someone's) feelings, outrage, slight, snub, upset, wound

offended *adjective* RESENTFUL, affronted, disgruntled, displeased, outraged, piqued, put out (*informal*), smarting, stung, upset

offender *noun* CRIMINAL, crook, culprit, delinquent, lawbreaker, miscreant, sinner, transgressor, villain, wrongdoer

offense *noun* 1 CRIME, fault,

misdeed, misdemeanor, sin, transgression, trespass, wrongdoing 2 SNUB, affront, hurt, indignity, injustice, insult, outrage, slight 3 ANNOYANCE, anger, displeasure, indignation, pique, resentment, umbrage, wrath

offensive *adjective* 1 INSULTING, abusive, discourteous, disrespectful, impertinent, insolent, objectionable, rude 2 DISAGREEABLE, disgusting, nauseating, obnoxious, odious, repellent, revolting, unpleasant, vile 3 AGGRESSIVE, attacking, invading ▶*noun* 4 ATTACK, campaign, drive, onslaught, push (*informal*)

offer *verb* 1 BID, proffer, tender 2 PROVIDE, afford, furnish, present 3 PROPOSE, advance, submit, suggest 4 VOLUNTEER, come forward, offer one's services ▶*noun* 5 BID, proposal, proposition, submission, suggestion, tender

offering *noun* DONATION, contribution, gift, hand-out, present, sacrifice, subscription

offhand *adjective* 1 CASUAL, aloof, brusque, careless, curt, glib ▶*adverb* 2 IMPROMPTU, ad lib, extempore, off the cuff (*informal*)

office *noun* POST, function, occupation, place, responsibility, role, situation

officer *noun* OFFICIAL, agent, appointee, executive, functionary, office-holder, representative

official *adjective* 1 AUTHORIZED, accredited, authentic, certified, formal, legitimate, licensed,

proper, sanctioned ▶ noun
2 OFFICER, agent, bureaucrat, executive, functionary, office bearer, representative

officiate verb PRESIDE, chair, conduct, manage, oversee, serve, superintend

officious adjective INTERFERING, dictatorial, intrusive, meddlesome, obtrusive, overzealous, pushy (informal), self-important

offing noun **in the offing** IN PROSPECT, imminent, on the horizon, upcoming

offset verb CANCEL OUT, balance out, compensate for, counteract, counterbalance, make up for, neutralize

offshoot noun BY-PRODUCT, adjunct, appendage, development, spin-off

offspring noun 1 CHILD, descendant, heir, scion, successor 2 CHILDREN, brood, descendants, family, heirs, issue, progeny, young

often adverb FREQUENTLY, generally, repeatedly, time and again

ogle verb LEER, eye up (informal)

ogre noun MONSTER, bogeyman, bugbear, demon, devil, giant, specter

oil verb LUBRICATE, grease

oily adjective GREASY, fatty, oleaginous

ointment noun LOTION, balm, cream, embrocation, emollient, liniment, salve, unguent

O.K., okay interjection 1 ALL RIGHT, agreed, right, roger, very good, very well, yes ▶ adjective 2 ALL RIGHT, acceptable, adequate, fine, good, in order,

permitted, satisfactory, up to scratch (informal) ▶ verb 3 APPROVE, agree to, authorize, endorse, give the green light, rubber-stamp (informal), sanction ▶ noun 4 APPROVAL, agreement, assent, authorization, consent, go-ahead (informal), green light, permission, sanction, say-so (informal), seal of approval

old adjective 1 SENILE, aged, ancient, decrepit, elderly, mature, venerable 2 ANTIQUE, antediluvian, antiquated, dated, obsolete, timeworn 3 FORMER, earlier, erstwhile, one-time, previous

old-fashioned adjective OUT OF DATE, behind the times, dated, obsolescent, obsolete, old hat, outdated, outmoded, passé, unfashionable

omen noun SIGN, foreboding, indication, portent, premonition, presage, warning

ominous adjective SINISTER, fateful, foreboding, inauspicious, portentous, threatening, unpromising, unpropitious

omission noun EXCLUSION, failure, lack, neglect, oversight

omit verb LEAVE OUT, drop, eliminate, exclude, forget, neglect, overlook, pass over, skip

omnipotence noun SUPREMACY, invincibility, mastery

omnipotent adjective ALMIGHTY, all-powerful, supreme

omniscient adjective ALL-KNOWING, all-wise

once adverb 1 FORMERLY, at one

time, long ago, once upon a
time, previously **2 at once:**
a IMMEDIATELY, directly,
forthwith, instantly, now, right
away, straight away, this (very)
minute **b** SIMULTANEOUSLY, at the
same time, together

oncoming *adjective* APPROACHING,
advancing, forthcoming,
looming, onrushing

onerous *adjective* DIFFICULT,
burdensome, demanding,
exacting, hard, heavy,
laborious, oppressive, taxing

one-sided *adjective* BIASED,
lopsided, partial, partisan,
prejudiced, unfair, unjust

ongoing *adjective* EVOLVING,
continuous, developing,
progressing, unfinished,
unfolding

onlooker *noun* OBSERVER,
bystander, eyewitness,
looker-on, spectator, viewer,
watcher, witness

only *adjective* **1** SOLE, exclusive,
individual, lone, single, solitary,
unique ▶*adverb* **2** MERELY,
barely, just, purely, simply

onset *noun* BEGINNING, inception,
outbreak, start

onslaught *noun* ATTACK, assault,
blitz, charge, offensive, onrush,
onset

onus *noun* BURDEN, liability, load,
obligation, responsibility, task

onward, onwards *adverb*
AHEAD, beyond, forth, forward,
in front, on

ooze[1] *verb* SEEP, drain, dribble,
drip, escape, filter, leak

ooze[2] *noun* MUD, alluvium, mire,
silt, slime, sludge

opaque *adjective* CLOUDY, dim,
dull, filmy, hazy, impenetrable,

muddy, murky

open *adjective* **1** UNFASTENED,
agape, ajar, gaping,
uncovered, unfolded, unfurled,
unlocked, yawning **2** ACCESSIBLE,
available, free, public,
unoccupied, unrestricted,
vacant **3** UNRESOLVED, arguable,
debatable, moot, undecided,
unsettled **4** FRANK, candid,
guileless, honest, sincere,
transparent ▶*verb* **5** START,
begin, commence, inaugurate,
initiate, kick off (*informal*),
launch, set in motion
6 UNFASTEN, unblock, uncork,
uncover, undo, unlock, untie,
unwrap **7** UNFOLD, expand,
spread (out), unfurl, unroll

open-air *adjective* OUTDOOR,
alfresco

open-handed *adjective*
GENEROUS, bountiful, free, lavish,
liberal, munificent, unstinting

opening *noun* **1** HOLE, aperture,
chink, cleft, crack, fissure, gap,
orifice, perforation, slot, space
2 OPPORTUNITY, chance,
occasion, vacancy **3** BEGINNING,
commencement, dawn,
inception, initiation, launch,
outset, start ▶*adjective* **4** FIRST,
beginning, inaugural, initial,
introductory, maiden, primary

openly *adverb* CANDIDLY,
forthrightly, frankly, overtly,
plainly, unhesitatingly,
unreservedly

open-minded *adjective* TOLERANT,
broad-minded, impartial,
liberal, reasonable, receptive,
unbiased, undogmatic,
unprejudiced

operate *verb* **1** WORK, act,
function, go, perform, run

2 HANDLE, be in charge of, manage, maneuver, use, work

operation noun PROCEDURE, action, course, exercise, motion, movement, performance, process

operational adjective WORKING, functional, going, operative, prepared, ready, up and running, usable, viable, workable

operative adjective **1** IN FORCE, active, effective, functioning, in operation, operational ▶noun **2** WORKER, artisan, employee, laborer

operator noun WORKER, conductor, driver, handler, mechanic, operative, practitioner, technician

opinion noun BELIEF, assessment, feeling, idea, impression, judgment, point of view, sentiment, theory, view

opinionated adjective DOGMATIC, bigoted, cocksure, doctrinaire, overbearing, pig-headed, prejudiced, single-minded

opponent noun COMPETITOR, adversary, antagonist, challenger, contestant, enemy, foe, rival

opportune adjective TIMELY, advantageous, appropriate, apt, auspicious, convenient, favorable, fitting, suitable, well-timed

opportunism noun EXPEDIENCY, exploitation, pragmatism, unscrupulousness

opportunity noun CHANCE, moment, occasion, opening, scope, time

oppose verb FIGHT, block, combat, counter, defy, resist,

take issue with, take on, thwart, withstand

opposed adjective AVERSE, antagonistic, clashing, conflicting, contrary, dissentient, hostile

opposing adjective HOSTILE, conflicting, contrary, enemy, incompatible, opposite, rival

opposite adjective **1** FACING, fronting **2** DIFFERENT, antithetical, conflicting, contrary, contrasted, reverse, unlike ▶noun **3** REVERSE, antithesis, contradiction, contrary, converse, inverse

opposition noun **1** HOSTILITY, antagonism, competition, disapproval, obstruction, prevention, resistance, unfriendliness **2** OPPONENT, antagonist, competition, foe, other side, rival

oppress verb **1** DEPRESS, afflict, burden, dispirit, harass, sadden, torment, vex **2** PERSECUTE, abuse, maltreat, subdue, subjugate, suppress, wrong

oppressed adjective DOWNTRODDEN, abused, browbeaten, disadvantaged, harassed, maltreated, tyrannized, underprivileged

oppression noun PERSECUTION, abuse, brutality, cruelty, injury, injustice, maltreatment, subjection, tyranny

oppressive adjective **1** TYRANNICAL, brutal, cruel, despotic, harsh, inhuman, repressive, severe, unjust **2** SULTRY, airless, close, muggy, stifling, stuffy

oppressor noun PERSECUTOR,

autocrat, bully, despot, scourge, slave-driver, tormentor, tyrant

opt *verb* (often with *for*) CHOOSE, decide (on), elect, go for, plump for, prefer

optimistic *adjective* HOPEFUL, buoyant, cheerful, confident, encouraged, expectant, positive, rosy, sanguine

optimum *adjective* IDEAL, best, highest, optimal, peak, perfect, superlative

option *noun* CHOICE, alternative, preference, selection

optional *adjective* VOLUNTARY, discretionary, elective, extra, open, possible

opulence *noun* 1 WEALTH, affluence, luxuriance, luxury, plenty, prosperity, riches 2 ABUNDANCE, copiousness, cornucopia, fullness, profusion, richness, superabundance

opulent *adjective* 1 RICH, affluent, lavish, luxurious, moneyed, prosperous, sumptuous, wealthy, well-off, well-to-do 2 ABUNDANT, copious, lavish, luxuriant, plentiful, profuse, prolific

opus *noun* WORK, brainchild, composition, creation, *oeuvre*, piece, production

oracle *noun* 1 PROPHECY, divination, prediction, prognostication, revelation 2 PUNDIT, adviser, authority, guru, mastermind, mentor, wizard

oral *adjective* SPOKEN, verbal, vocal

oration *noun* SPEECH, address, discourse, harangue, homily, lecture

orator *noun* PUBLIC SPEAKER, declaimer, lecturer, rhetorician, speaker

oratorical *adjective* RHETORICAL, bombastic, declamatory, eloquent, grandiloquent, high-flown, magniloquent, sonorous

oratory *noun* ELOQUENCE, declamation, elocution, grandiloquence, public speaking, rhetoric, speech-making

orb *noun* SPHERE, ball, circle, globe, ring

orbit *noun* 1 PATH, circle, course, cycle, revolution, rotation, trajectory 2 SPHERE OF INFLUENCE, ambit, compass, domain, influence, range, reach, scope, sweep ▶ *verb* 3 CIRCLE, circumnavigate, encircle, revolve around

orchestrate *verb* 1 SCORE, arrange 2 ORGANIZE, arrange, coordinate, put together, set up, stage-manage

ordain *verb* APPOINT, anoint, consecrate, invest, nominate 2 ORDER, decree, demand, dictate, fix, lay down, legislate, prescribe, rule, will

ordeal *noun* HARDSHIP, agony, anguish, baptism of fire, nightmare, suffering, test, torture, trial, tribulation(s)

order *noun* 1 INSTRUCTION, command, decree, dictate, direction, directive, injunction, law, mandate, regulation, rule 2 SEQUENCE, arrangement, array, grouping, layout, line-up, progression, series, structure 3 TIDINESS, method, neatness, orderliness, organization,

pattern, regularity, symmetry, system **4** DISCIPLINE, calm, control, law, law and order, peace, quiet, tranquillity
5 REQUEST, application, booking, commission, requisition, reservation **6** CLASS, caste, grade, position, rank, status **7** KIND, class, family, genre, ilk, sort, type **8** SOCIETY, association, brotherhood, community, company, fraternity, guild, organization ►*verb* **9** INSTRUCT, bid, charge, command, decree, demand, direct, require
10 REQUEST, apply for, book, reserve, send away for
11 ARRANGE, catalog, classify, group, marshal, organize, sort out, systematize

orderly *adjective*
1 WELL-ORGANIZED, businesslike, in order, methodical, neat, regular, scientific, shipshape, systematic, tidy **2** WELL-BEHAVED, controlled, disciplined, law-abiding, peaceable, quiet, restrained

ordinarily *adverb* USUALLY, as a rule, commonly, customarily, generally, habitually, in general, normally

ordinary *adjective* **1** USUAL, common, conventional, everyday, normal, regular, routine, standard, stock, typical **2** COMMONPLACE, banal, humble, humdrum, modest, mundane, plain, unremarkable, workaday

organ *noun* **1** PART, element, structure, unit **2** MOUTHPIECE, forum, medium, vehicle, voice

organic *adjective* **1** NATURAL, animate, biological, live, living **2** SYSTEMATIC, integrated, methodical, ordered,

organized, structured

organism *noun* CREATURE, animal, being, body, entity, structure

organization *noun* **1** GROUP, association, body, company, confederation, corporation, institution, outfit (*informal*), syndicate **2** MANAGEMENT, construction, coordination, direction, organizing, planning, running, structuring
3 ARRANGEMENT, chemistry, composition, format, make-up, pattern, structure, unity

organize *verb* ARRANGE, classify, coordinate, group, marshal, put together, run, set up, systematize, take care of

orgy *noun* **1** REVEL, bacchanalia, carousal, debauch, revelry, Saturnalia **2** SPREE, binge (*informal*), bout, excess, indulgence, overindulgence, splurge, surfeit

orient *verb* FAMILIARIZE, acclimatize, adapt, adjust, align, get one's bearings, orientate

orientation *noun* **1** POSITION, bearings, direction, location
2 FAMILIARIZATION, acclimatization, adaptation, adjustment, assimilation, introduction, settling in

orifice *noun* OPENING, aperture, cleft, hole, mouth, pore, rent, vent

origin *noun* **1** ROOT, base, basis, derivation, fount, fountainhead, source, wellspring **2** BEGINNING, birth, creation, emergence, foundation, genesis, inception, launch, start

original *adjective* **1** FIRST,

earliest, initial, introductory, opening, primary, starting **2** NEW, fresh, ground-breaking, innovative, novel, seminal, unprecedented, unusual **3** CREATIVE, fertile, imaginative, ingenious, inventive, resourceful ▶ noun **4** PROTOTYPE, archetype, master, model, paradigm, pattern, precedent, standard

originality noun NOVELTY, creativity, freshness, imagination, ingenuity, innovation, inventiveness, newness, unorthodoxy

originally adverb INITIALLY, at first, first, in the beginning, to begin with

originate verb **1** BEGIN, arise, come, derive, emerge, result, rise, spring, start, stem **2** INTRODUCE, bring about, create, formulate, generate, institute, launch, pioneer

originator noun CREATOR, architect, author, father or mother, founder, inventor, maker, pioneer

ornament noun **1** DECORATION, accessory, adornment, bauble, embellishment, festoon, knick-knack, trimming, trinket ▶ verb **2** DECORATE, adorn, beautify, embellish, festoon, grace, prettify

ornamental adjective DECORATIVE, attractive, beautifying, embellishing, for show, showy

ornamentation noun DECORATION, adornment, elaboration, embellishment, embroidery, frills, ornateness

ornate adjective ELABORATE, baroque, busy, decorated,

fancy, florid, fussy, ornamented, overelaborate, rococo

orthodox adjective ESTABLISHED, accepted, approved, conventional, customary, official, received, traditional, well-established

orthodoxy noun CONFORMITY, authority, conventionality, received wisdom, traditionalism

oscillate verb FLUCTUATE, seesaw, sway, swing, vacillate, vary, vibrate, waver

oscillation noun SWING, fluctuation, instability, vacillation, variation, wavering

ossify verb HARDEN, fossilize, solidify, stiffen

ostensible adjective APPARENT, outward, pretended, professed, purported, seeming, so-called, superficial, supposed

ostensibly adverb APPARENTLY, on the face of it, professedly, seemingly, supposedly

ostentation noun DISPLAY, affectation, exhibitionism, flamboyance, flashiness, flaunting, parade, pomp, pretentiousness, show, showing off (informal)

ostentatious adjective PRETENTIOUS, brash, conspicuous, flamboyant, flashy, gaudy, loud, obtrusive, showy

ostracism noun EXCLUSION, banishment, exile, isolation, rejection

ostracize verb EXCLUDE, banish, cast out, cold-shoulder, exile, give (someone) the cold shoulder, reject, shun

other adjective **1** ADDITIONAL, added, alternative, auxiliary, extra, further, more, spare, supplementary **2** DIFFERENT, contrasting, dissimilar, distinct, diverse, separate, unrelated, variant

otherwise conjunction **1** OR ELSE, if not, or then ▶adverb **2** DIFFERENTLY, any other way, contrarily

ounce noun SHRED, atom, crumb, drop, grain, scrap, speck, trace

oust verb EXPEL, depose, dislodge, displace, dispossess, eject, throw out, topple, turn out, unseat

out adjective **1** AWAY, abroad, absent, elsewhere, gone, not at home, outside **2** EXTINGUISHED, at an end, dead, ended, exhausted, expired, finished, used up

outbreak noun ERUPTION, burst, epidemic, explosion, flare-up, outburst, rash, upsurge

outburst noun OUTPOURING, eruption, explosion, flare-up, outbreak, paroxysm, spasm, surge

outcast noun PARIAH, castaway, exile, leper, persona non grata, refugee, vagabond, wretch

outclass verb SURPASS, eclipse, excel, leave standing (informal), outdo, outshine, outstrip, overshadow, run rings around (informal)

outcome noun RESULT, conclusion, consequence, end, issue, payoff (informal), upshot

outcry noun PROTEST, clamor, commotion, complaint, hue and cry, hullaballoo, outburst, uproar

outdated adjective OLD-FASHIONED, antiquated, archaic, obsolete, outmoded, out of date, passé, unfashionable

outdo verb SURPASS, beat, best, eclipse, exceed, get the better of, outclass, outmaneuver, overcome, top, transcend

outdoor adjective OPEN-AIR, alfresco, out-of-door(s), outside

outer adjective EXTERNAL, exposed, exterior, outlying, outside, outward, peripheral, surface

outfit noun **1** COSTUME, clothes, ensemble, garb, get-up (informal), kit, suit **2** GROUP, company, crew, organization, setup (informal), squad, team, unit

outgoing adjective **1** LEAVING, departing, former, retiring, withdrawing **2** SOCIABLE, approachable, communicative, expansive, extrovert, friendly, gregarious, open, warm

outgoings plural noun EXPENSES, costs, expenditure, outlay, overheads

outing noun TRIP, excursion, expedition, jaunt, spin (informal)

outlandish adjective STRANGE, bizarre, exotic, fantastic, far-out (slang), freakish, outré, preposterous, unheard-of, weird

outlaw noun **1** BANDIT, desperado, fugitive, highwayman, marauder, outcast, robber ▶verb **2** FORBID, ban, bar, disallow, exclude, prohibit, proscribe

outlay noun EXPENDITURE, cost, expenses, investment, outgoings, spending

outlet noun **1** RELEASE, avenue,

channel, duct, exit, opening, vent 2 SHOP, market, store

outline *noun* 1 SUMMARY, recapitulation, résumé, rundown, synopsis, thumbnail sketch 2 SHAPE, configuration, contour, delineation, figure, form, profile, silhouette ▶ *verb* 3 SUMMARIZE, adumbrate, delineate, draft, plan, rough out, sketch (in), trace

outlive *verb* SURVIVE, outlast

outlook *noun* 1 ATTITUDE, angle, frame of mind, perspective, point of view, slant, standpoint, viewpoint 2 PROSPECT, expectations, forecast, future

outlying *adjective* REMOTE, distant, far-flung, out-of-the-way, peripheral, provincial

outmoded *adjective* OLD-FASHIONED, anachronistic, antiquated, archaic, obsolete, out-of-date, outworn, passé, unfashionable

out-of-date *adjective* OLD-FASHIONED, antiquated, dated, expired, invalid, lapsed, obsolete, outmoded, outworn, passé

outpouring *noun* STREAM, cascade, effusion, flow, spate, spurt, torrent

output *noun* PRODUCTION, achievement, manufacture, productivity, yield

outrage *noun* 1 VIOLATION, abuse, affront, desecration, indignity, insult, offense, sacrilege, violence 2 INDIGNATION, anger, fury, hurt, resentment, shock, wrath ▶ *verb* 3 OFFEND, affront, incense,

infuriate, madden, scandalize, shock

outrageous *adjective* 1 OFFENSIVE, atrocious, disgraceful, flagrant, heinous, iniquitous, nefarious, unspeakable, villainous, wicked 2 SHOCKING, exorbitant, extravagant, immoderate, preposterous, scandalous, steep (*informal*), unreasonable

outré *adjective* ECCENTRIC, bizarre, fantastic, freakish, odd, off-the-wall (*slang*), outlandish, unconventional, weird

outright *adjective* 1 ABSOLUTE, complete, out-and-out, perfect, thorough, thoroughgoing, total, unconditional, unmitigated, unqualified 2 DIRECT, definite, flat, straightforward, unequivocal, unqualified ▶ *adverb* 3 ABSOLUTELY, completely, openly, overtly, straightforwardly, thoroughly, to the full

outset *noun* BEGINNING, commencement, inauguration, inception, kickoff (*informal*), onset, opening, start

outshine *verb* OVERSHADOW, eclipse, leave *or* put in the shade, outclass, outdo, outstrip, surpass, transcend, upstage

outside *adjective* 1 EXTERNAL, exterior, extraneous, outer, outward 2 *As in* **an outside chance** UNLIKELY, distant, faint, marginal, remote, slight, slim, small ▶ *noun* 3 SURFACE, exterior, façade, face, front, skin, topside

outsider *noun* INTERLOPER, incomer, intruder, newcomer, odd man out, stranger

outsize *adjective* EXTRA-LARGE, giant, gigantic, huge, jumbo (*informal*), mammoth, monster, oversized

outskirts *plural noun* EDGE, boundary, environs, periphery, suburbia, suburbs

outspoken *adjective* FORTHRIGHT, abrupt, blunt, explicit, frank, open, plain-spoken, unceremonious, unequivocal

outstanding *adjective*
1 EXCELLENT, cool (*informal*), exceptional, great, important, impressive, phat (*slang*), special, superior, superlative
2 UNPAID, due, payable, pending, remaining, uncollected, unsettled

outstrip *verb* SURPASS, better, eclipse, exceed, excel, outdistance, outdo, overtake, transcend

outward *adjective* APPARENT, noticeable, observable, obvious, ostensible, perceptible, surface, visible

outwardly *adverb* OSTENSIBLY, apparently, externally, on the face of it, on the surface, seemingly, superficially, to all intents and purposes

outweigh *verb* OVERRIDE, cancel (out), compensate for, eclipse, prevail over, take precedence over, tip the scales

outwit *verb* OUTTHINK, cheat, dupe, fool, get the better of, outfox, outmaneuver, outsmart (*informal*), swindle

outworn *adjective* OUTDATED, antiquated, discredited, disused, hackneyed, obsolete, outmoded, out-of-date, threadbare, worn-out

oval *adjective* ELLIPTICAL, egg-shaped, ovoid

ovation *noun* APPLAUSE, acclaim, acclamation, big hand, cheers, clapping, plaudits, tribute

over *preposition* 1 ON, above, on top of, upon 2 EXCEEDING, above, in excess of, more than ▸*adverb* 3 ABOVE, aloft, on high, overhead 4 EXTRA, beyond, in addition, in excess, left over ▸*adjective* 5 FINISHED, bygone, closed, completed, concluded, done (with), ended, gone, past

overact *verb* EXAGGERATE, ham *or* ham up (*informal*), overdo, overplay

overall *adjective* 1 TOTAL, all-embracing, blanket, complete, comprehensive, general, global, inclusive ▸*adverb* 2 IN GENERAL, on the whole

overawe *verb* INTIMIDATE, abash, alarm, daunt, frighten, scare, terrify

overbalance *verb* OVERTURN, capsize, keel over, slip, tip over, topple over, tumble, turn turtle

overbearing *adjective* ARROGANT, bossy (*informal*), dictatorial, domineering, haughty, high-handed, imperious, supercilious, superior

overblown *adjective* EXCESSIVE, disproportionate, immoderate, inflated, overdone, over the top, undue

overcast *adjective* CLOUDY, dismal, dreary, dull, gray, leaden, louring *or* lowering, murky

overcharge *verb* CHEAT, fleece,

rip off (*slang*), short-change, sting (*informal*), surcharge

overcome *verb* **1** CONQUER, beat, defeat, master, overpower, overwhelm, prevail, subdue, subjugate, surmount, triumph over, vanquish ▶ *adjective* **2** AFFECTED, at a loss for words, bowled over (*informal*), overwhelmed, speechless, swept off one's feet

overconfident *adjective* BRASH, cocksure, foolhardy, overweening, presumptuous

overcrowded *adjective* CONGESTED, bursting at the seams, choked, jam-packed, overloaded, overpopulated, packed (out), swarming

overdo *verb* **1** EXAGGERATE, belabor, gild the lily, go overboard (*informal*), overindulge, overreach, overstate **2 overdo it** OVERWORK, bite off more than one can chew, burn the candle at both ends (*informal*), overload, strain or overstrain oneself, wear oneself out

overdone *adjective* **1** EXCESSIVE, exaggerated, fulsome, immoderate, inordinate, overelaborate, too much, undue, unnecessary **2** OVERCOOKED, burnt, charred, dried up, spoiled

overdue *adjective* LATE, behindhand, behind schedule, belated, owing, tardy, unpunctual

overeat *verb* OVERINDULGE, binge (*informal*), gorge, gormandize, guzzle, pig out (*slang*), stuff oneself

overemphasize *verb* OVERSTRESS,

belabor, blow up out of all proportion, make a mountain out of a molehill (*informal*), overdramatize

overflow *verb* **1** SPILL, brim over, bubble over, pour over, run over, well over ▶ *noun* **2** SURPLUS, overabundance, spilling over

overhang *verb* PROJECT, extend, jut, loom, protrude, stick out

overhaul *verb* **1** REPAIR, check, do up (*informal*), examine, inspect, recondition, refurbish, restore, service **2** OVERTAKE, catch up with, get ahead of, pass ▶ *noun* **3** CHECKUP, check, examination, inspection, reconditioning, service

overhead *adverb* **1** ABOVE, aloft, in the sky, on high, skyward, up above, upward ▶ *adjective* **2** AERIAL, overhanging, upper

overheads *plural noun* RUNNING COSTS, operating costs

overindulgence *noun* EXCESS, immoderation, intemperance, overeating, surfeit

overjoyed *adjective* DELIGHTED, elated, euphoric, jubilant, on cloud nine (*informal*), over the moon (*informal*), thrilled

overload *verb* OVERBURDEN, burden, encumber, oppress, overtax, saddle (with), strain, weigh down

overlook *verb* **1** FORGET, disregard, miss, neglect, omit, pass **2** IGNORE, condone, disregard, excuse, forgive, make allowances for, pardon, turn a blind eye to, wink at **3** HAVE A VIEW OF, look over or out on

overpower *verb* OVERWHELM,

conquer, crush, defeat, master, overcome, overthrow, quell, subdue, subjugate, vanquish

overpowering *adjective* IRRESISTIBLE, forceful, invincible, irrefutable, overwhelming, powerful, strong

overrate *verb* OVERESTIMATE, exaggerate, overvalue

override *verb* OVERRULE, annul, cancel, countermand, nullify, outweigh, supersede

overriding *adjective* ULTIMATE, dominant, paramount, predominant, primary, supreme

overrule *verb* REVERSE, alter, annul, cancel, countermand, override, overturn, repeal, rescind, veto

overrun *verb* 1 INVADE, occupy, overwhelm, rout 2 INFEST, choke, inundate, permeate, ravage, spread over, swarm over 3 EXCEED, go beyond, overshoot, run over *or* on

overseer *noun* SUPERVISOR, boss (*informal*), chief, foreman, master, superintendent

overshadow *verb* 1 OUTSHINE, dominate, dwarf, eclipse, leave *or* put in the shade, surpass, tower above 2 SPOIL, blight, mar, put a damper on, ruin, temper

oversight *noun* MISTAKE, blunder, carelessness, error, fault, lapse, neglect, omission, slip

overt *adjective* OPEN, blatant, manifest, observable, obvious, plain, public, unconcealed, undisguised

overtake *verb* 1 PASS, catch up with, get past, leave behind, outdistance, outdo, outstrip,

overhaul 2 BEFALL, engulf, happen, hit, overwhelm, strike

overthrow *verb* 1 DEFEAT, bring down, conquer, depose, dethrone, oust, overcome, overpower, topple, unseat, vanquish ▶ *noun* 2 DOWNFALL, defeat, destruction, dethronement, fall, ousting, undoing, unseating

overtone *noun* CONNOTATION, hint, implication, innuendo, intimation, nuance, sense, suggestion, undercurrent

overture *noun* 1 *Music* INTRODUCTION, opening, prelude 2 **overtures** APPROACH, advance, invitation, offer, proposal, proposition

overturn *verb* 1 TIP OVER, capsize, keel over, overbalance, topple, upend, upturn 2 OVERTHROW, bring down, depose, destroy, unseat

overweight *adjective* FAT, bulky, chubby, chunky, corpulent, heavy, hefty, obese, plump, portly, stout, tubby (*informal*)

overwhelm *verb* 1 DEVASTATE, bowl over (*informal*), knock (someone) for six (*informal*), overcome, stagger, sweep (someone) off his *or* her feet, take (someone's) breath away 2 DESTROY, crush, cut to pieces, massacre, overpower, overrun, rout

overwhelming *adjective* DEVASTATING, breathtaking, crushing, irresistible, overpowering, shattering, stunning, towering

overwork *verb* 1 STRAIN, burn the midnight oil, sweat (*informal*), work one's fingers to the bone 2 OVERUSE, exhaust, exploit, fatigue, oppress, wear out, weary

overwrought *adjective* AGITATED, distracted, excited, frantic, keyed up, on edge, overexcited, tense, uptight (*informal*), wired (*slang*)

owe *verb* BE IN DEBT, be in arrears, be obligated *or* indebted

owing *adjective* UNPAID, due, outstanding, overdue, owed, payable, unsettled

owing to *preposition* BECAUSE OF, as a result of, on account of

own *adjective* 1 PERSONAL, individual, particular, private ▶*pronoun* 2 **hold one's own** COMPETE, keep going, keep one's end up, keep one's head above water 3 **on one's own** ALONE, by oneself, independently, singly, unaided, unassisted, under one's own steam ▶*verb* 4 POSSESS, be in possession of, enjoy, have, hold, keep, retain 5 ACKNOWLEDGE, admit, allow, concede, confess, grant, recognize 6 **own up** CONFESS, admit, come clean, make a clean breast, tell the truth

owner *noun* POSSESSOR, holder, landlord *or* landlady, proprietor

ownership *noun* POSSESSION, dominion, title

P p

pace *noun* 1 STEP, gait, stride, tread, walk 2 SPEED, rate, tempo, velocity ▶*verb* 3 STRIDE, march, patrol, pound 4 **pace out** MEASURE, count, mark out, step

pacifist *noun* PEACE LOVER, conscientious objector, dove

pacify *verb* CALM, allay, appease, assuage, mollify, placate, propitiate, soothe

pack *verb* 1 PACKAGE, bundle, load, store, stow 2 CRAM, compress, crowd, fill, jam, press, ram, stuff 3 **pack off** SEND AWAY, dismiss, send packing (*informal*) ▶*noun* 4 BUNDLE, back pack, burden, kitbag, knapsack, load, parcel, rucksack 5 PACKET, package 6 GROUP, band, bunch, company, crowd, flock, gang, herd, mob, troop

package *noun* 1 PARCEL, box, carton, container, packet 2 UNIT, combination, whole ▶*verb* 3 PACK, box, parcel (up), wrap

packed *adjective* FULL, chock-a-block, chock-full, crammed, crowded, filled, jammed, jam-packed

packet *noun* PACKAGE, bag, carton, container, parcel

pack up *verb* 1 PUT AWAY, store 2 *Informal* STOP, finish, give up, pack it in (*informal*) 3 BREAK DOWN, conk out (*informal*), fail

pact *noun* AGREEMENT, alliance, bargain, covenant, deal, treaty, understanding

pad[1] *noun* 1 CUSHION, buffer, protection, stuffing, wad 2 NOTEPAD, block, jotter, writing pad 3 PAW, foot, sole 4 *Slang, dated* HOME, apartment, flat, place ▶*verb* 5 PACK, cushion, fill,

protect, stuff **6 pad out**
LENGTHEN, elaborate, fill out,
flesh out, protract, spin out,
stretch

pad[2] *verb* SNEAK, creep, go
barefoot, steal

padding *noun* **1** FILLING,
packing, stuffing, wadding
2 WORDINESS, hot air (*informal*),
verbiage, verbosity

paddle[1] *noun* **1** OAR, scull ▶ *verb*
2 ROW, propel, pull, scull

paddle[2] *verb* **1** WADE, slop,
splash (about) **2** DABBLE, stir

pagan *adjective* **1** HEATHEN,
idolatrous, infidel, polytheistic
▶ *noun* **2** HEATHEN, idolater,
infidel, polytheist

page[1] *noun* FOLIO, leaf, sheet,
side

page[2] *noun* **1** ATTENDANT,
pageboy, servant, squire ▶ *verb*
2 CALL, send for, summon

pageant *noun* SHOW, display,
parade, procession, spectacle,
tableau

pageantry *noun* SPECTACLE,
display, grandeur, parade,
pomp, show, splendor,
theatricality

pain *noun* **1** HURT, ache,
discomfort, irritation, pang,
soreness, tenderness, throb,
twinge **2** SUFFERING, agony,
anguish, distress, heartache,
misery, torment, torture ▶ *verb*
3 HURT, smart, sting, throb
4 DISTRESS, agonize, cut to the
quick, grieve, hurt, sadden,
torment, torture

pained *adjective* DISTRESSED,
aggrieved, hurt, injured,
offended, upset, wounded

painful *adjective* **1** DISTRESSING,
disagreeable, distasteful,

grievous, unpleasant **2** SORE,
aching, agonizing, smarting,
tender **3** DIFFICULT, arduous,
hard, laborious, troublesome,
trying

painfully *adverb* DISTRESSINGLY,
clearly, dreadfully, sadly,
unfortunately

painkiller *noun* ANALGESIC,
anesthetic, anodyne, drug

painless *adjective* SIMPLE, easy,
effortless, fast, quick

pains *plural noun* TROUBLE,
bother, care, diligence, effort

painstaking *adjective* THOROUGH,
assiduous, careful,
conscientious, diligent,
meticulous, scrupulous

paint *noun* **1** COLORING, color,
dye, pigment, stain, tint ▶ *verb*
2 DEPICT, draw, picture, portray,
represent, sketch **3** COAT, apply,
color, cover, daub

pair *noun* **1** COUPLE, brace, duo,
twins ▶ *verb* **2** COUPLE, bracket,
join, match (up), team, twin

pal *noun* *Informal* FRIEND, buddy
(*informal*), chum (*informal*),
companion, comrade, crony,
homeboy (*slang*), homegirl
(*slang*)

palatable *adjective* DELICIOUS,
appetizing, luscious,
mouthwatering, tasty, yummy
(*informal*)

palate *noun* TASTE, appetite,
stomach

palatial *adjective* MAGNIFICENT,
grand, imposing, majestic,
opulent, regal, splendid, stately

palaver *noun* FUSS, big deal
(*informal*), performance
(*informal*), rigmarole, song and
dance (*informal*), to-do

pale *adjective* **1** WHITE, ashen,

bleached, colorless, faded, light, pallid, pasty, wan ▶*verb* **2** BECOME PALE, blanch, go white, lose color, whiten

pall[1] *noun* **1** CLOUD, mantle, shadow, veil **2** GLOOM, check, damp, damper

pall[2] *verb* BECOME BORING, become dull, become tedious, cloy, jade, sicken, tire, weary

pallid *adjective* PALE, anemic, ashen, colorless, pasty, wan

pallor *noun* PALENESS, lack of color, pallidness, wanness, whiteness

palm off *verb* FOB OFF, foist off, pass off

palpable *adjective* OBVIOUS, clear, conspicuous, evident, manifest, plain, unmistakable, visible

palpitate *verb* BEAT, flutter, pound, pulsate, throb, tremble

paltry *adjective* INSIGNIFICANT, contemptible, despicable, inconsiderable, lousy (*slang*), meager, mean, measly, minor, miserable, petty, poor, puny, scuzzy (*slang*), slight, small, trifling, trivial, unimportant, worthless

pamper *verb* SPOIL, cater to, coddle, cosset, indulge, overindulge, pet

pamphlet *noun* BOOKLET, brochure, circular, leaflet, tract

pan[1] *noun* **1** POT, container, saucepan ▶*verb* **2** SIFT OUT, look for, search for **3** *Informal* CRITICIZE, censure, knock (*informal*), slam (*slang*)

pan[2] *verb* MOVE, follow, sweep, track

panacea *noun* CURE-ALL, nostrum, universal cure

panache *noun* STYLE, dash, élan, flamboyance

pandemonium *noun* UPROAR, bedlam, chaos, confusion, din, hullabaloo, racket, rumpus, turmoil

pander *verb* **pander to** INDULGE, cater to, gratify, play up to (*informal*), please, satisfy

pang *noun* TWINGE, ache, pain, prick, spasm, stab, sting

panic *noun* **1** FEAR, alarm, fright, hysteria, scare, terror ▶*verb* **2** GO TO PIECES, become hysterical, lose one's nerve **3** ALARM, scare, unnerve

panic-stricken *adjective* FRIGHTENED, frightened out of one's wits, hysterical, in a cold sweat (*informal*), panicky, scared, scared stiff, terrified

panoply *noun* ARRAY, attire, dress, garb, regalia, trappings

panorama *noun* VIEW, prospect, vista

panoramic *adjective* WIDE, comprehensive, extensive, overall, sweeping

pant *verb* PUFF, blow, breathe, gasp, heave, wheeze

pants *plural noun* TROUSERS, slacks

paper *noun* **1** NEWSPAPER, daily, gazette, journal **2** ESSAY, article, dissertation, report, treatise **3 papers: a** DOCUMENTS, certificates, deeds, records **b** LETTERS, archive, diaries, documents, dossier, file, records ▶*verb* **4** WALLPAPER, hang

par *noun* AVERAGE, level, mean, norm, standard, usual

parable *noun* LESSON, allegory, fable, moral tale, story

parade *noun* **1** PROCESSION,

array, cavalcade, march, pageant 2 SHOW, display, spectacle ▶ *verb* 3 FLAUNT, display, exhibit, show off (*informal*) 4 MARCH, process

paradigm *noun* MODEL, example, ideal, pattern

paradise *noun* 1 HEAVEN, Elysian fields, Happy Valley, Promised Land 2 BLISS, delight, felicity, heaven, utopia

paradox *noun* CONTRADICTION, anomaly, enigma, oddity, puzzle

paradoxical *adjective* CONTRADICTORY, baffling, confounding, enigmatic, puzzling

paragon *noun* MODEL, epitome, exemplar, ideal, nonpareil, pattern, quintessence

paragraph *noun* SECTION, clause, item, part, passage, subdivision

parallel *adjective* 1 EQUIDISTANT, alongside, side by side 2 MATCHING, analogous, corresponding, like, resembling, similar ▶ *noun* 3 EQUIVALENT, analogue, counterpart, equal, match, twin 4 SIMILARITY, analogy, comparison, likeness, resemblance

paralysis *noun* 1 IMMOBILITY, palsy 2 STANDSTILL, breakdown, halt, stoppage

paralytic *adjective* PARALYZED, challenged, crippled, disabled, incapacitated, lame, palsied

paralyze *verb* 1 DISABLE, cripple, incapacitate, lame 2 IMMOBILIZE, freeze, halt, numb, petrify, stun

parameter *noun* LIMIT, framework, limitation, restriction, specification

paramount *adjective* PRINCIPAL, cardinal, chief, first, foremost, main, primary, prime, supreme

paranoid *adjective* 1 MENTALLY ILL, deluded, disturbed, manic, neurotic, paranoiac, psychotic 2 *Informal* SUSPICIOUS, fearful, nervous, wired (*slang*), worried

paraphernalia *noun* EQUIPMENT, apparatus, baggage, belongings, effects, gear, stuff, tackle, things, trappings

paraphrase *noun* 1 REWORDING, rephrasing, restatement ▶ *verb* 2 REWORD, express in other words *or* one's own words, rephrase, restate

parasite *noun* SPONGER (*informal*), bloodsucker (*informal*), hanger-on, leech, scrounger (*informal*)

parasitic, parasitical *adjective* SCROUNGING (*informal*), bloodsucking (*informal*), sponging (*informal*)

parcel *noun* 1 PACKAGE, bundle, pack ▶ *verb* 2 (often with *up*) WRAP, do up, pack, package, tie up

parch *verb* DRY UP, dehydrate, desiccate, evaporate, shrivel, wither

parched *adjective* DRIED OUT *or* UP, arid, dehydrated, dry, thirsty

pardon *verb* 1 FORGIVE, absolve, acquit, excuse, exonerate, let off (*informal*), overlook ▶ *noun* 2 FORGIVENESS, absolution, acquittal, amnesty, exoneration

pardonable *adjective* FORGIVABLE, excusable, minor, understandable, venial

pare *verb* 1 PEEL, clip, cut, shave, skin, trim 2 CUT BACK, crop, cut, decrease, dock, reduce

parent *noun* FATHER *or* MOTHER, procreator, progenitor, sire

parentage *noun* FAMILY, ancestry, birth, descent, lineage, pedigree, stock

pariah *noun* OUTCAST, exile, undesirable, untouchable

parish *noun* COMMUNITY, church, congregation, flock

parity *noun* EQUALITY, consistency, equivalence, uniformity, unity

park *noun* PARKLAND, estate, garden, grounds, woodland

parlance *noun* LANGUAGE, idiom, jargon, phraseology, speech, talk, tongue

parliament *noun* ASSEMBLY, congress, convention, council, legislature, senate

parliamentary *adjective* GOVERNMENTAL, law-making, legislative

parlor *noun* Old-fashioned SITTING ROOM, drawing room, front room, living room, lounge

parochial *adjective* PROVINCIAL, insular, limited, narrow, narrow-minded, petty, small-minded

parody *noun* 1 SATIRE (*informal*), burlesque, caricature, skit, spoof (*informal*) ▶*verb* 2 SATIRIZE (*informal*), burlesque, caricature

paroxysm *noun* OUTBURST, attack, convulsion, fit, seizure, spasm

parrot *verb* REPEAT, copy, echo, imitate, mimic

parry *verb* 1 WARD OFF, block, deflect, rebuff, repel, repulse 2 EVADE, avoid, dodge, sidestep

parsimonious *adjective* MEAN,

close, frugal, miserly, niggardly, penny-pinching (*informal*), stingy, tightfisted

parson *noun* CLERGYMAN, churchman, cleric, minister, pastor, preacher, priest, vicar

part *noun* 1 PIECE, bit, fraction, fragment, portion, scrap, section, share 2 COMPONENT, branch, constituent, division, member, unit 3 *Theatre* ROLE, character, lines 4 SIDE, behalf, cause, concern, interest 5 (often plural) REGION, area, district, neighborhood, quarter, vicinity **6 in good part** GOOD-NATUREDLY, cheerfully, well, without offense **7 in part** PARTLY, a little, in some measure, partially, somewhat ▶*verb* 8 DIVIDE, break, come apart, detach, rend, separate, sever, split, tear 9 SEPARATE, depart, go, go away, leave, split up, withdraw

partake *verb* 1 **partake of** CONSUME, chow down (*slang*), eat, take 2 **partake in** PARTICIPATE IN, engage in, share in, take part in

partial *adjective* 1 INCOMPLETE, imperfect, uncompleted, unfinished 2 BIASED, discriminatory, one-sided, partisan, prejudiced, unfair, unjust

partiality *noun* 1 BIAS, favoritism, preference, prejudice 2 LIKING, fondness, inclination, love, penchant, predilection, taste, weakness

partially *adverb* PARTLY, fractionally, incompletely, in part, not wholly, somewhat

participant *noun* PARTICIPATOR,

contributor, member, player, stakeholder

participate *verb* TAKE PART, be involved in, join in, partake, perform, share

participation *noun* TAKING PART, contribution, involvement, joining in, partaking, sharing in

particle *noun* BIT, grain, iota, jot, mite, piece, scrap, shred, speck

particular *adjective* **1** SPECIFIC, distinct, exact, peculiar, precise, special **2** SPECIAL, especial, exceptional, marked, notable, noteworthy, remarkable, singular, uncommon, unusual **3** FUSSY, choosy (*informal*), demanding, fastidious, finicky, picky (*informal*) ▶ *noun* **4** (usually plural) DETAIL, circumstance, fact, feature, item, specification **5 in particular** ESPECIALLY, distinctly, exactly, particularly, specifically

particularly *adverb* **1** ESPECIALLY, exceptionally, notably, singularly, uncommonly, unusually **2** SPECIFICALLY, distinctly, especially, explicitly, expressly, in particular

parting *noun* **1** GOING, farewell, good-bye **2** DIVISION, breaking, rift, rupture, separation, split

partisan *noun* **1** SUPPORTER, adherent, devotee, upholder **2** UNDERGROUND FIGHTER, guerrilla, resistance fighter ▶ *adjective* **3** PREJUDICED, biased, interested, one-sided, partial, sectarian

partition *noun* **1** SCREEN, barrier, wall **2** DIVISION, segregation, separation **3** ALLOTMENT, apportionment, distribution

▶ *verb* **4** SEPARATE, divide, screen

partly *adverb* PARTIALLY, slightly, somewhat

partner *noun* **1** SPOUSE, consort, husband *or* wife, mate, significant other (*informal*) **2** COMPANION, ally, associate, colleague, comrade, helper, mate

partnership *noun* COMPANY, alliance, cooperative, firm, house, society, union

party *noun* **1** GET-TOGETHER (*informal*), celebration, festivity, function, gathering, reception, social gathering **2** GROUP, band, company, crew, gang, squad, team, unit **3** FACTION, camp, clique, coterie, league, set, side **4** PERSON, individual, someone

pass *verb* **1** GO BY *or* PAST, elapse, go, lapse, move, proceed, run **2** QUALIFY, do, get through, graduate, succeed **3** SPEND, fill, occupy, while away **4** GIVE, convey, deliver, hand, send, transfer **5** APPROVE, accept, decree, enact, legislate, ordain, ratify **6** EXCEED, beat, go beyond, outdo, outstrip, surpass **7** END, blow over, cease, go ▶ *noun* **8** GAP, canyon, gorge, ravine, route **9** LICENSE, authorization, passport, permit, ticket, warrant

passable *adjective* ADEQUATE, acceptable, all right, average, fair, mediocre, so-so (*informal*), tolerable

passage *noun* **1** WAY, alley, avenue, channel, course, path, road, route **2** CORRIDOR, hall, lobby, vestibule **3** EXTRACT, excerpt, piece, quotation, reading, section, text **4** JOURNEY,

crossing, trek, trip, voyage
5 SAFE-CONDUCT, freedom,
permission, right

passageway noun CORRIDOR,
aisle, alley, hall, hallway, lane,
passage

pass away verb Euphemistic DIE,
expire, kick the bucket (slang),
pass on, pass over, shuffle off
this mortal coil, snuff it
(informal)

passé adjective OUT-OF-DATE,
dated, obsolete, old-fashioned,
old hat, outdated, outmoded,
unfashionable

passenger noun TRAVELER, fare,
rider

passer-by noun BYSTANDER,
onlooker, witness

passing adjective 1 MOMENTARY,
brief, ephemeral, fleeting,
short-lived, temporary,
transient, transitory
2 SUPERFICIAL, casual, cursory,
glancing, quick, short

passion noun 1 LOVE, ardor,
desire, infatuation, lust
2 EMOTION, ardor, excitement,
feeling, fervor, fire, heat,
intensity, warmth, zeal 3 RAGE,
anger, fit, frenzy, fury,
outburst, paroxysm, storm
4 MANIA, bug (informal),
craving, craze, enthusiasm,
fascination, obsession

passionate adjective 1 LOVING,
amorous, ardent, erotic, hot,
lustful 2 EMOTIONAL, ardent,
eager, fervent, fierce, heartfelt,
impassioned, intense, strong

passive adjective SUBMISSIVE,
compliant, docile, inactive,
quiescent, receptive

pass off verb FAKE, counterfeit,
make a pretense of, palm off

pass out verb FAINT, become
unconscious, black out
(informal), lose consciousness

pass over verb DISREGARD,
ignore, overlook, take no
notice of

pass up verb MISS, abstain,
decline, forgo, let slip, neglect

password noun SIGNAL, key
word, watchword

past adjective 1 FORMER, ancient,
bygone, early, olden, previous
2 OVER, done, ended, finished,
gone ▶noun 3 BACKGROUND,
history, life, past life 4 **the
past** FORMER TIMES, days gone
by, long ago, olden days
▶preposition 5 AFTER, beyond,
later than 6 BEYOND, across, by,
over

paste noun 1 ADHESIVE, cement,
glue, gum ▶verb 2 STICK,
cement, glue, gum

pastel adjective PALE, delicate,
light, muted, soft

pastiche noun MEDLEY, blend,
mélange, miscellany, mixture

pastime noun ACTIVITY,
amusement, diversion,
entertainment, game, hobby,
recreation

pastor noun CLERGYMAN,
churchman, ecclesiastic,
minister, parson, priest, rector,
vicar

pastoral adjective 1 RUSTIC,
bucolic, country, rural
2 ECCLESIASTICAL, clerical,
ministerial, priestly

pasture noun GRASSLAND, grass,
grazing, meadow

pasty adjective PALE, anemic,
pallid, sickly, wan

pat verb 1 STROKE, caress, fondle,
pet, tap, touch ▶noun 2 STROKE,

clap, tap

patch noun **1** REINFORCEMENT **2** SPOT, bit, scrap, shred, small piece **3** PLOT, area, ground, land, tract ▸verb **4** MEND, cover, reinforce, repair, sew up

patchwork noun MIXTURE, jumble, medley, pastiche

patchy adjective UNEVEN, erratic, fitful, irregular, sketchy, spotty, variable

patent noun **1** COPYRIGHT, license ▸adjective **2** OBVIOUS, apparent, clear, evident, glaring, manifest

paternal adjective FATHERLY, concerned, protective, solicitous

paternity noun **1** FATHERHOOD **2** PARENTAGE, descent, extraction, family, lineage

path noun **1** WAY, footpath, road, track, trail **2** COURSE, direction, road, route, way

pathetic adjective SAD, affecting, distressing, heart-rending, moving, pitiable, plaintive, poignant, tender, touching

pathos noun SADNESS, pitifulness, plaintiveness, poignancy

patience noun **1** FORBEARANCE, calmness, restraint, serenity, sufferance, tolerance **2** ENDURANCE, constancy, fortitude, long-suffering, perseverance, resignation, stoicism, submission

patient adjective **1** LONG-SUFFERING, calm, enduring, persevering, philosophical, resigned, stoical, submissive, uncomplaining **2** FORBEARING, even-tempered, forgiving, indulgent, lenient, mild, tolerant, understanding ▸noun **3** SICK PERSON, case, invalid, sufferer

patriot noun NATIONALIST, chauvinist, loyalist

patriotic adjective NATIONALISTIC, chauvinistic, jingoistic, loyal

patriotism noun NATIONALISM, jingoism

patrol noun **1** POLICING, guarding, protecting, vigilance, watching **2** GUARD, patrolman, sentinel, watch, watchman ▸verb **3** POLICE, guard, inspect, keep guard, keep watch, safeguard

patron noun **1** SUPPORTER, backer, benefactor, champion, friend, helper, philanthropist, sponsor **2** CUSTOMER, buyer, client, frequenter, habitué, shopper

patronage noun **1** SUPPORT, aid, assistance, backing, help, promotion, sponsorship **2** CUSTOM, business, clientele, commerce, trade, trading, traffic

patronize verb **1** TALK DOWN TO, look down on **2** BE A CUSTOMER or CLIENT OF, do business with, frequent, shop at **3** SUPPORT, back, fund, help, maintain, promote, sponsor

patronizing adjective CONDESCENDING, disdainful, gracious, haughty, snobbish, supercilious, superior

patter[1] verb **1** TAP, beat, pat, pitter-patter **2** WALK LIGHTLY, scurry, scuttle, skip, trip ▸noun **3** TAPPING, pattering, pitter-patter

patter[2] noun **1** SPIEL (informal), line, pitch **2** CHATTER, gabble, jabber, nattering, prattle **3** JARGON, argot, cant, lingo (informal), patois, slang, vernacular ▶ verb 4 CHATTER, jabber, prate, rattle on, spout (informal)

pattern noun 1 DESIGN, arrangement, decoration, device, figure, motif 2 ORDER, method, plan, sequence, system 3 PLAN, design, diagram, guide, original, stencil, template ▶ verb 4 MODEL, copy, follow, form, imitate, mold, style

paucity noun Formal SCARCITY, dearth, deficiency, lack, rarity, scantiness, shortage, sparseness

paunch noun BELLY, pot, potbelly, spare tire (slang)

pauper noun DOWN-AND-OUT, bankrupt, beggar, mendicant, poor person

pause verb 1 STOP BRIEFLY, break, cease, delay, halt, have a breather (informal), interrupt, rest, take a break, wait ▶ noun 2 STOP, break, breather (informal), cessation, gap, halt, interlude, intermission, interval, lull, respite, rest, stoppage

pave verb COVER, concrete, floor, surface, tile

paw verb MANHANDLE, grab, handle roughly, maul, molest

pawn[1] verb HOCK (informal), deposit, mortgage, pledge

pawn[2] noun TOOL, cat's-paw, instrument, plaything, puppet, stooge (slang)

pay verb 1 REIMBURSE, compensate, give, recompense, remit, remunerate, requite, reward, settle 2 GIVE, bestow, extend, grant, hand out, present 3 BENEFIT, be worthwhile, repay 4 BE PROFITABLE, make a return, make money 5 YIELD, bring in, produce, return ▶ noun 6 WAGES, allowance, earnings, fee, income, payment, recompense, reimbursement, remuneration, reward, salary, stipend

payable adjective DUE, outstanding, owed, owing

pay back verb 1 REPAY, refund, reimburse, settle up, square 2 GET EVEN WITH (informal), hit back, retaliate

payment noun 1 PAYING, discharge, remittance, settlement 2 REMITTANCE, advance, deposit, installment, premium 3 WAGE, fee, hire, remuneration, reward

pay off verb 1 SETTLE, clear, discharge, pay in full, square 2 SUCCEED, be effective, work

pay out verb SPEND, disburse, expend, fork out or over or up (slang), shell out (informal)

peace noun 1 STILLNESS, calm, calmness, hush, quiet, repose, rest, silence, tranquillity 2 SERENITY, calm, composure, contentment, repose 3 HARMONY, accord, agreement, concord 4 TRUCE, armistice, treaty

peaceable adjective PEACE-LOVING, conciliatory, friendly, gentle, mild, peaceful, unwarlike

peaceful adjective 1 AT PEACE, amicable, friendly, harmonious, nonviolent 2 CALM, placid, quiet, restful, serene, still, tranquil, undisturbed 3 PEACE-LOVING, conciliatory, peaceable, unwarlike

peacemaker noun MEDIATOR, arbitrator, conciliator, pacifier

peak noun 1 POINT, apex, brow,

crest, pinnacle, summit, tip,
top 2 HIGH POINT, acme, climax,
crown, culmination, zenith
▶ verb 3 CULMINATE, climax,
come to a head

peal noun 1 RING, blast, chime,
clang, clap, crash,
reverberation, roar, rumble
▶ verb 2 RING, chime, crash,
resound, roar, rumble

peasant noun RUSTIC,
countryman

peccadillo noun MISDEED, error,
indiscretion, lapse,
misdemeanor, slip

peck verb, noun PICK, dig, hit,
jab, poke, prick, strike, tap

peculiar adjective 1 ODD,
abnormal, bizarre, curious,
eccentric, extraordinary,
freakish, funny, offbeat,
outlandish, outré, quaint,
queer, singular, strange,
uncommon, unconventional,
unusual, weird 2 SPECIFIC,
characteristic, distinctive,
particular, special, unique

peculiarity noun 1 ECCENTRICITY,
abnormality, foible,
idiosyncrasy, mannerism,
oddity, quirk 2 CHARACTERISTIC,
attribute, feature, mark,
particularity, property, quality,
trait

pedagogue noun TEACHER,
instructor, master or mistress,
schoolmaster or schoolmistress

pedant noun HAIRSPLITTER,
nit-picker (informal), quibbler

pedantic adjective HAIRSPLITTING,
academic, bookish, donnish,
formal, fussy, nit-picking
(informal), particular, precise,
punctilious

pedantry noun HAIRSPLITTING,

punctiliousness, quibbling

peddle verb SELL, hawk, market,
push (informal), trade

peddler noun SELLER,
door-to-door salesman,
hawker, huckster, vendor

pedestal noun SUPPORT, base,
foot, mounting, plinth, stand

pedestrian noun 1 WALKER,
foot-traveler ▶ adjective 2 DULL,
banal, boring, commonplace,
humdrum, mediocre,
mundane, ordinary, prosaic,
uninspired

pedigree noun 1 LINEAGE,
ancestry, blood, breed,
descent, extraction, family,
family tree, genealogy, line,
race, stock ▶ adjective
2 PUREBRED, full-blooded,
thoroughbred

peek verb 1 GLANCE, look, peep
▶ noun 2 GLANCE, glimpse, look,
look-see (slang), peep

peel verb 1 SKIN, flake off, pare,
scale, strip off ▶ noun 2 SKIN,
peeling, rind

peep[1] verb 1 PEEK, look, sneak a
look, steal a look ▶ noun
2 LOOK, glimpse, look-see
(slang), peek

peep[2] verb, noun TWEET, cheep,
chirp, squeak

peephole noun SPYHOLE,
aperture, chink, crack, hole,
opening

peer[1] noun 1 NOBLE, aristocrat,
lord, nobleman 2 EQUAL,
compeer, fellow, like

peer[2] verb SQUINT, gaze, inspect,
peep, scan, snoop, spy

peerage noun ARISTOCRACY, lords
and ladies, nobility, peers

peerless adjective UNEQUALED,

beyond compare, excellent,
incomparable, matchless,
outstanding, unmatched,
unparalleled, unrivaled

peevish *adjective* IRRITABLE,
cantankerous, childish,
churlish, cross, crotchety,
fractious, fretful, grumpy,
petulant, querulous, snappy,
sulky, sullen, surly

peg *verb* FASTEN, attach, fix, join,
secure

pejorative *adjective* DEROGATORY,
deprecatory, depreciatory,
disparaging, negative,
uncomplimentary, unpleasant

pelt[1] *verb* 1 THROW, batter,
bombard, cast, hurl, pepper,
shower, sling, strike 2 RUSH,
belt (*slang*), charge, dash,
hurry, run fast, shoot, speed,
tear 3 POUR, bucket down
(*informal*), rain cats and dogs
(*informal*), rain hard, teem

pelt[2] *noun* COAT, fell, hide, skin

pen[1] *verb* WRITE, compose, draft,
draw up, jot down

pen[2] *noun* 1 ENCLOSURE, cage,
coop, fold, hutch, pound, sty
▶ *verb* 2 ENCLOSE, cage, confine,
coop up, fence in, hedge, shut
up *or* in

penal *adjective* DISCIPLINARY,
corrective, punitive

penalize *verb* PUNISH, discipline,
handicap, impose a penalty on

penalty *noun* PUNISHMENT, fine,
forfeit, handicap, price

penance *noun* ATONEMENT,
penalty, reparation, sackcloth
and ashes

penchant *noun* LIKING, bent,
bias, fondness, inclination,
leaning, partiality, predilection,
proclivity, propensity, taste,
tendency

pending *adjective* UNDECIDED,
awaiting, imminent,
impending, in the balance,
undetermined, unsettled

penetrate *verb* 1 PIERCE, bore,
enter, go through, prick, stab
2 GRASP, comprehend,
decipher, fathom, figure out
(*informal*), get to the bottom
of, work out

penetrating *adjective* 1 SHARP,
carrying, harsh, piercing, shrill
2 PERCEPTIVE, acute, astute,
incisive, intelligent, keen,
perspicacious, quick, sharp,
sharp-witted, shrewd

penetration *noun* 1 PIERCING,
entrance, entry, incision,
puncturing 2 PERCEPTION,
acuteness, astuteness, insight,
keenness, sharpness,
shrewdness

penitence *noun* REPENTANCE,
compunction, contrition,
regret, remorse, shame, sorrow

penitent *adjective* REPENTANT,
abject, apologetic,
conscience-stricken, contrite,
regretful, remorseful, sorry

pen name *noun* PSEUDONYM,
nom de plume

pennant *noun* FLAG, banner,
ensign, pennon, streamer

penniless *adjective* POOR, broke
(*informal*), destitute, dirt-poor
(*informal*), down and out,
down on one's luck (*informal*),
flat broke (*informal*),
impecunious, impoverished,
indigent, penurious,
poverty-stricken

pension *noun* ALLOWANCE,
annuity, benefit,
superannuation

pensive *adjective* THOUGHTFUL, contemplative, dreamy, meditative, musing, preoccupied, reflective, sad, serious, solemn, wistful

pent-up *adjective* SUPPRESSED, bottled up, curbed, held back, inhibited, repressed, smothered, stifled

penury *noun* POVERTY, beggary, destitution, indigence, need, privation, want

people *plural noun* 1 PERSONS, humanity, mankind, men and women, mortals 2 NATION, citizens, community, folk, inhabitants, population, public 3 FAMILY, clan, race, tribe ▶ *verb* 4 INHABIT, colonize, occupy, populate, settle

pepper *noun* 1 SEASONING, flavor, spice ▶ *verb* 2 SPRINKLE, dot, fleck, spatter, speck 3 PELT, bombard, shower

perceive *verb* 1 SEE, behold, discern, discover, espy, make out, note, notice, observe, recognize, spot 2 UNDERSTAND, comprehend, gather, grasp, learn, realize, see

perceptible *adjective* VISIBLE, apparent, appreciable, clear, detectable, discernible, evident, noticeable, observable, obvious, recognizable, tangible

perception *noun* UNDERSTANDING, awareness, conception, consciousness, feeling, grasp, idea, impression, notion, sensation, sense

perceptive *adjective* OBSERVANT, acute, alert, astute, aware, percipient, perspicacious, quick, sharp

perch *noun* 1 RESTING PLACE, branch, pole, post ▶ *verb* 2 SIT, alight, balance, land, rest, roost, settle

percussion *noun* IMPACT, blow, bump, clash, collision, crash, knock, smash, thump

peremptory *adjective* 1 IMPERATIVE, absolute, binding, compelling, decisive, final, obligatory 2 IMPERIOUS, authoritative, bossy (*informal*), dictatorial, dogmatic, domineering, overbearing

perennial *adjective* LASTING, abiding, constant, continual, enduring, incessant, persistent, recurrent, twenty-four-seven (*slang*)

perfect *adjective* 1 COMPLETE, absolute, consummate, entire, finished, full, sheer, unmitigated, utter, whole 2 FAULTLESS, flawless, immaculate, impeccable, pure, spotless, unblemished 3 EXCELLENT, ideal, splendid, sublime, superb, superlative, supreme 4 EXACT, accurate, correct, faithful, precise, true, unerring ▶ *verb* 5 IMPROVE, develop, polish, refine 6 ACCOMPLISH, achieve, carry out, complete, finish, fulfill, perform

perfection *noun* 1 COMPLETENESS, maturity 2 PURITY, integrity, perfectness, wholeness 3 EXCELLENCE, exquisiteness, sublimity, superiority 4 EXACTNESS, faultlessness, precision

perfectionist *noun* STICKLER, precisionist, purist

perfectly *adverb* 1 COMPLETELY, absolutely, altogether, fully,

quite, thoroughly, totally,
utterly, wholly **2** FLAWLESSLY,
faultlessly, ideally, impeccably,
superbly, supremely,
wonderfully

perfidious *adjective Literary*
TREACHEROUS, disloyal,
double-dealing, traitorous,
two-faced, unfaithful

perforate *verb* PIERCE, bore, drill,
penetrate, punch, puncture

perform *verb* **1** CARRY OUT,
accomplish, achieve, complete,
discharge, do, execute, fulfill,
pull off, work **2** PRESENT, act,
enact, play, produce, put on,
represent, stage

performance *noun* **1** CARRYING
OUT, accomplishment,
achievement, act, completion,
execution, fulfillment, work
2 PRESENTATION, acting,
appearance, exhibition, gig
(*informal*), play, portrayal,
production, show

performer *noun* ARTISTE, actor *or*
actress, player, Thespian,
trouper

perfume *noun* FRAGRANCE,
aroma, bouquet, odor, scent,
smell

perfunctory *adjective* OFFHAND,
cursory, heedless, indifferent,
mechanical, routine, sketchy,
superficial

perhaps *adverb* MAYBE,
conceivably, feasibly, it may
be, perchance (*archaic*), possibly

peril *noun* DANGER, hazard,
jeopardy, menace, risk,
uncertainty

perilous *adjective* DANGEROUS,
hazardous, precarious, risky,
threatening, unsafe

perimeter *noun* BOUNDARY,

ambit, border, bounds,
circumference, confines, edge,
limit, margin, periphery

period *noun* TIME, interval,
season, space, span, spell,
stretch, term, while

periodic *adjective* RECURRENT,
cyclical, intermittent,
occasional, regular, repeated,
sporadic

periodical *noun* PUBLICATION,
journal, magazine, monthly,
paper, quarterly, weekly

peripheral *adjective*
1 INCIDENTAL, inessential,
irrelevant, marginal, minor,
secondary, unimportant
2 OUTERMOST, exterior, external,
outer, outside

perish *verb* **1** DIE, be killed,
expire, lose one's life, pass
away **2** BE DESTROYED, collapse,
decline, disappear, fall, vanish
3 ROT, decay, decompose,
disintegrate, molder, waste

perishable *adjective* SHORT-LIVED,
decaying, decomposable

perjure *verb* **perjure oneself**
Criminal law COMMIT PERJURY,
bear false witness, forswear,
give false testimony, lie under
oath, swear falsely

perjury *noun* LYING UNDER OATH,
bearing false witness, false
statement, forswearing, giving
false testimony

perk *noun Informal* BONUS,
benefit, extra, fringe benefit,
perquisite, plus

permanence *noun* CONTINUITY,
constancy, continuance,
durability, endurance, finality,
indestructibility, perpetuity,
stability

permanent *adjective* LASTING,

abiding, constant, enduring, eternal, everlasting, immutable, perpetual, persistent, stable, steadfast, twenty-four-seven (*slang*), unchanging

permeate *verb* PERVADE, charge, fill, imbue, impregnate, infiltrate, penetrate, saturate, spread through

permissible *adjective* PERMITTED, acceptable, allowable, all right, authorized, lawful, legal, legitimate, O.K. *or* okay (*informal*)

permission *noun* AUTHORIZATION, allowance, approval, assent, consent, dispensation, go-ahead (*informal*), green light, leave, liberty, license, sanction

permissive *adjective* TOLERANT, easy-going, forbearing, free, indulgent, lax, lenient, liberal

permit *verb* 1 ALLOW, authorize, consent, enable, entitle, give leave *or* permission, give the green light to, grant, let, license, sanction ▶ *noun* 2 LICENSE, authorization, pass, passport, permission, warrant

permutation *noun* TRANSFORMATION, alteration, change, transposition

pernicious *adjective* WICKED, bad, damaging, dangerous, deadly, destructive, detrimental, evil, fatal, harmful, hurtful, malign, poisonous

perpendicular *adjective* UPRIGHT, at right angles to, on end, plumb, straight, vertical

perpetrate *verb* COMMIT, carry out, do, enact, execute, perform, wreak

perpetual *adjective*

1 EVERLASTING, endless, eternal, infinite, lasting, never-ending, perennial, permanent, unchanging, unending
2 CONTINUAL, constant, continuous, endless, incessant, interminable, never-ending, persistent, recurrent, repeated, twenty-four-seven (*slang*)

perpetuate *verb* MAINTAIN, immortalize, keep going, preserve

perplex *verb* PUZZLE, baffle, bewilder, confound, confuse, mystify, stump

perplexing *adjective* PUZZLING, baffling, bewildering, complex, complicated, confusing, difficult, enigmatic, hard, inexplicable, mystifying

perplexity *noun* 1 PUZZLEMENT, bafflement, bewilderment, confusion, incomprehension, mystification 2 PUZZLE, difficulty, fix (*informal*), mystery, paradox

perquisite *noun Formal* BONUS, benefit, dividend, extra, perk (*informal*), plus

persecute *verb* 1 VICTIMIZE, afflict, ill-treat, maltreat, oppress, torment, torture
2 HARASS, annoy, badger, bother, hassle (*informal*), pester, tease

perseverance *noun* PERSISTENCE, determination, diligence, doggedness, endurance, pertinacity, resolution, tenacity

persevere *verb* KEEP GOING, carry on, continue, go on, hang on, persist, remain, stick at *or* to

persist *verb* 1 CONTINUE, carry on, keep up, last, linger, remain 2 PERSEVERE, continue, insist, stand firm

persistence noun DETERMINATION, doggedness, endurance, grit, perseverance, pertinacity, resolution, tenacity, tirelessness

persistent adjective
1 CONTINUOUS, constant, continual, endless, incessant, never-ending, perpetual, repeated, twenty-four-seven (slang) 2 DETERMINED, dogged, obdurate, obstinate, persevering, pertinacious, steadfast, steady, stubborn, tenacious, tireless, unflagging

person noun 1 INDIVIDUAL, being, body, human, soul 2 in person PERSONALLY, bodily, in the flesh, oneself

personable adjective PLEASANT, agreeable, amiable, attractive, charming, good-looking, handsome, likable or likeable, nice

personage noun PERSONALITY, big shot (informal), celebrity, dignitary, luminary, megastar (informal), notable, public figure, somebody, V.I.P.

personal adjective 1 PRIVATE, exclusive, individual, intimate, own, particular, peculiar, special 2 OFFENSIVE, derogatory, disparaging, insulting, nasty

personality noun 1 NATURE, character, disposition, identity, individuality, make-up, temperament 2 CELEBRITY, famous name, household name, megastar (informal), notable, personage, star

personally adverb 1 BY ONESELF, alone, independently, on one's own, solely 2 IN ONE'S OPINION, for one's part, from one's own

viewpoint, in one's books, in one's own view 3 INDIVIDUALLY, individualistically, privately, specially, subjectively

personification noun EMBODIMENT, epitome, image, incarnation, portrayal, representation

personify verb EMBODY, epitomize, exemplify, represent, symbolize, typify

personnel noun EMPLOYEES, helpers, human resources, people, staff, workers, workforce

perspective noun 1 OUTLOOK, angle, attitude, context, frame of reference 2 OBJECTIVITY, proportion, relation, relative importance, relativity

perspicacious adjective PERCEPTIVE, acute, alert, astute, discerning, keen, percipient, sharp, shrewd

perspiration noun SWEAT, moisture, wetness

perspire verb SWEAT, exude, glow, pour with sweat, secrete, swelter

persuade verb 1 TALK INTO, coax, entice, impel, incite, induce, influence, sway, urge, win over 2 CONVINCE, cause to believe, satisfy

persuasion noun 1 URGING, cajolery, enticement, inducement, wheedling 2 PERSUASIVENESS, cogency, force, potency, power 3 CREED, belief, conviction, credo, faith, opinion, tenet, views 4 FACTION, camp, denomination, party, school, school of thought, side

persuasive adjective CONVINCING, cogent, compelling, credible, effective, eloquent, forceful, influential, plausible, sound, telling, valid, weighty

pert *adjective* IMPUDENT, bold, cheeky, forward, impertinent, insolent, sassy (*informal*), saucy

pertain *verb* RELATE, apply, befit, belong, be relevant, concern, refer, regard

pertinent *adjective* RELEVANT, applicable, apposite, appropriate, apt, fit, fitting, germane, material, proper, to the point

pertness *noun* IMPUDENCE, audacity, cheek (*informal*), cheekiness, effrontery, forwardness, front, impertinence, insolence, sauciness

perturb *verb* DISTURB, agitate, bother, disconcert, faze, fluster, ruffle, trouble, unsettle, vex, worry

perturbed *adjective* DISTURBED, agitated, anxious, disconcerted, flustered, shaken, troubled, uncomfortable, uneasy, worried

peruse *verb* READ, browse, check, examine, inspect, scan, scrutinize, study

pervade *verb* SPREAD THROUGH, charge, fill, imbue, infuse, penetrate, permeate, suffuse

pervasive *adjective* WIDESPREAD, common, extensive, general, omnipresent, prevalent, rife, ubiquitous, universal

perverse *adjective* **1** ABNORMAL, contrary, deviant, disobedient, improper, rebellious, refractory, troublesome, unhealthy **2** WILLFUL, contrary, dogged, headstrong, intractable,

intransigent, obdurate, wrong-headed **3** STUBBORN, contrary, mulish, obstinate, pig-headed, stiff-necked, wayward **4** ILL-NATURED, churlish, cross, fractious, ill-tempered, peevish, surly

perversion *noun* **1** DEVIATION, aberration, abnormality, debauchery, depravity, immorality, kink (*informal*), kinkiness (*slang*), unnaturalness, vice **2** DISTORTION, corruption, falsification, misinterpretation, misrepresentation, twisting

perversity *noun* CONTRARINESS, contradictoriness, intransigence, obduracy, refractoriness, waywardness, wrong-headedness

pervert *verb* **1** DISTORT, abuse, falsify, garble, misrepresent, misuse, twist, warp **2** CORRUPT, debase, debauch, degrade, deprave, lead astray ▶ *noun* **3** DEVIANT, degenerate, sicko (*informal*), weirdo or weirdie (*informal*)

perverted *adjective* UNNATURAL, abnormal, corrupt, debased, debauched, depraved, deviant, kinky (*slang*), sick, twisted, unhealthy, warped

pessimism *noun* GLOOMINESS, dejection, depression, despair, despondency, distrust, gloom, hopelessness, melancholy

pessimist *noun* WET BLANKET (*informal*), cynic, defeatist, killjoy, prophet of doom, worrier

pessimistic *adjective* GLOOMY, bleak, cynical, dark, dejected, depressed, despairing, despondent, glum, hopeless, morose

pest noun 1 NUISANCE, annoyance, bane, bother, drag (*informal*), irritation, pain (*informal*), thorn in one's flesh, trial, vexation 2 INFECTION, blight, bug, epidemic, pestilence, plague, scourge

pester verb ANNOY, badger, bedevil, bother, bug (*informal*), harass, harry, hassle (*informal*), nag, plague, torment

pestilence noun PLAGUE, epidemic, visitation

pestilent adjective 1 ANNOYING, bothersome, irksome, irritating, tiresome, vexing 2 HARMFUL, detrimental, evil, injurious, pernicious 3 CONTAMINATED, catching, contagious, diseased, disease-ridden, infected, infectious

pestilential adjective DEADLY, dangerous, destructive, detrimental, harmful, hazardous, injurious, pernicious

pet noun 1 FAVORITE, darling, idol, jewel, treasure ▶adjective 2 FAVORITE, cherished, dearest, dear to one's heart ▶verb 3 PAMPER, baby, coddle, cosset, spoil 4 FONDLE, caress, pat, stroke 5 CUDDLE, kiss, make out, neck (*informal*), smooch (*informal*)

peter out verb DIE OUT, dwindle, ebb, fade, fail, run out, stop, taper off, wane

petite adjective SMALL, dainty, delicate, elfin, little, slight

petition noun 1 APPEAL, entreaty, plea, prayer, request, solicitation ▶verb 2 APPEAL, adjure, ask,

beg, beseech, entreat, plead, pray, solicit, supplicate

petrify verb 1 TERRIFY, horrify, immobilize, paralyze, stun, stupefy, transfix 2 FOSSILIZE, calcify, harden, turn to stone

petty adjective 1 TRIVIAL, contemptible, inconsiderable, insignificant, little, lousy (*slang*), measly (*informal*), negligible, paltry, slight, small, trifling, unimportant 2 SMALL-MINDED, mean, mean-minded, shabby, spiteful, ungenerous

petulance noun SULKINESS, bad temper, ill humor, irritability, peevishness, pique, sullenness

petulant adjective SULKY, bad-tempered, huffy, ill-humored, moody, peevish, sullen

phantom noun 1 SPECTER, apparition, ghost, phantasm, shade (*literary*), spirit, spook (*informal*), wraith 2 ILLUSION, figment of the imagination, hallucination, vision

phase noun STAGE, chapter, development, juncture, period, point, position, step, time

phase out verb WIND DOWN, close, ease off, eliminate, pull out, remove, run down, terminate, wind up, withdraw

phenomenal adjective EXTRAORDINARY, exceptional, fantastic, marvelous, miraculous, outstanding, prodigious, remarkable, unusual

phenomenon noun 1 OCCURRENCE, circumstance, episode, event, fact, happening, incident 2 WONDER, exception, marvel, miracle, prodigy, rarity, sensation

philanderer noun WOMANIZER (*informal*), Casanova, Don Juan, flirt, gigolo, ladies' man, playboy, stud (*slang*), wolf (*informal*)

philanthropic adjective HUMANITARIAN, beneficent, benevolent, charitable, humane, kind, kind-hearted, munificent, public-spirited

philanthropist noun HUMANITARIAN, benefactor, contributor, donor, giver, patron

philanthropy noun HUMANITARIANISM, almsgiving, beneficence, benevolence, brotherly love, charitableness, charity, generosity, kind-heartedness

philistine noun 1 BOOR, barbarian, ignoramus, lout, lowbrow, vulgarian, yahoo ▶ adjective 2 UNCULTURED, boorish, ignorant, lowbrow, tasteless, uncultivated, uneducated, unrefined

philosopher noun THINKER, logician, metaphysician, sage, theorist, wise man

philosophical adjective 1 WISE, abstract, logical, rational, sagacious, theoretical, thoughtful 2 STOICAL, calm, collected, composed, cool, serene, tranquil, unruffled

philosophy noun 1 THOUGHT, knowledge, logic, metaphysics, rationalism, reasoning, thinking, wisdom 2 OUTLOOK, beliefs, convictions, doctrine, ideology, principles, tenets, thinking, values, viewpoint, world view 3 STOICISM,

calmness, composure, equanimity, self-possession, serenity

phlegmatic adjective UNEMOTIONAL, apathetic, impassive, indifferent, placid, stoical, stolid, undemonstrative, unfeeling

phobia noun TERROR, aversion, detestation, dread, fear, hatred, horror, loathing, repulsion, revulsion, thing (*informal*)

phone noun 1 TELEPHONE, blower (*informal*), horn (*informal*) 2 CALL ▶ verb 3 CALL, get on the blower (*informal*), get on the horn (*informal*), give someone a call, make a call, telephone

phony Informal ▶ adjective 1 FAKE, bogus, counterfeit, ersatz, false, imitation, pseudo (*informal*), sham ▶ noun 2 FAKE, counterfeit, forgery, fraud, impostor, pseud (*informal*), sham

photograph noun 1 PICTURE, photo (*informal*), print, shot, snap (*informal*), snapshot, transparency ▶ verb 2 TAKE A PICTURE OF, film, record, shoot, snap (*informal*), take (someone's) picture

photographic adjective 1 LIFELIKE, graphic, natural, pictorial, realistic, visual, vivid 2 Of a person's memory ACCURATE, exact, faithful, precise, retentive

phrase noun 1 EXPRESSION, group of words, idiom, remark, saying ▶ verb 2 EXPRESS, put, put into words, say, voice, word

phraseology noun WORDING, choice of words, expression,

idiom, language, parlance, phrase, phrasing, speech, style, syntax

physical adjective 1 BODILY, corporal, corporeal, earthly, fleshly, incarnate, mortal 2 MATERIAL, natural, palpable, real, solid, substantial, tangible

physician noun DOCTOR, doc (informal), doctor of medicine, general practitioner, G.P., M.D., medic (informal), medical practitioner

physique noun BUILD, body, constitution, figure, form, frame, shape, structure

pick verb 1 SELECT, choose, decide upon, elect, fix upon, hand-pick, opt for, settle upon, single out 2 GATHER, collect, harvest, pluck, pull 3 NIBBLE, have no appetite, peck at, play or toy with, push the food round the plate 4 PROVOKE, incite, instigate, start 5 OPEN, break into, break open, crack, force ▶noun 6 CHOICE, decision, option, preference, selection 7 THE BEST, crème de la crème, elect, elite, the cream

picket noun 1 PROTESTER, demonstrator, picketer 2 LOOKOUT, guard, patrol, sentinel, sentry, watch 3 STAKE, pale, paling, post, stanchion, upright ▶verb 4 BLOCKADE, boycott, demonstrate

pickle noun 1 Informal PREDICAMENT, bind (informal), difficulty, dilemma, fix (informal), hot water (informal), jam (informal), quandary, scrape (informal), tight spot ▶verb 2 PRESERVE, marinade, steep

pick-me-up noun Informal TONIC, bracer (informal), refreshment, restorative, shot in the arm (informal), stimulant

pick on verb TORMENT, badger, bait, bully, goad, hector, tease

pick out verb IDENTIFY, discriminate, distinguish, make out, perceive, recognize, tell apart

pick up verb 1 LIFT, gather, grasp, raise, take up, uplift 2 OBTAIN, buy, come across, find, purchase 3 RECOVER, be on the mend, get better, improve, mend, rally, take a turn for the better, turn the corner 4 LEARN, acquire, get the hang of (informal), master 5 COLLECT, call for, get

pick-up noun IMPROVEMENT, change for the better, rally, recovery, revival, rise, strengthening, upswing, upturn

picnic noun EXCURSION, outdoor meal, outing

pictorial adjective GRAPHIC, illustrated, picturesque, representational, scenic

picture noun 1 REPRESENTATION, drawing, engraving, illustration, image, likeness, painting, photograph, portrait, print, sketch 2 DESCRIPTION, account, depiction, image, impression, report 3 DOUBLE, carbon copy, copy, dead ringer (slang), duplicate, image, likeness, lookalike, replica, spitting image (informal), twin 4 PERSONIFICATION, embodiment, epitome, essence 5 FILM, flick (slang), motion picture, movie (informal) ▶verb 6 IMAGINE, conceive of, envision, see, visualize **7** REPRESENT, depict, draw, illustrate, paint, photograph, show, sketch

picturesque *adjective* **1** PRETTY, attractive, beautiful, charming, quaint, scenic, striking **2** VIVID, colorful, graphic

piebald *adjective* PIED, black and white, brindled, dappled, flecked, mottled, speckled, spotted

piece *noun* **1** BIT, chunk, fragment, morsel, part, portion, quantity, segment, slice **2** WORK, article, composition, creation, item, study, work of art

piecemeal *adverb* BIT BY BIT, by degrees, gradually, little by little

pier *noun* **1** JETTY, landing place, promenade, quay, wharf **2** PILLAR, buttress, column, pile, post, support, upright

pierce *verb* PENETRATE, bore, drill, enter, perforate, prick, puncture, spike, stab, stick into

piercing *adjective* **1** *Usually of sound* PENETRATING, ear-splitting, high-pitched, loud, sharp, shrill **2** KEEN, alert, penetrating, perceptive, perspicacious, quick-witted, sharp, shrewd **3** *Usually of weather* COLD, arctic, biting, bitter, freezing, nippy, wintry **4** SHARP, acute, agonizing, excruciating, intense, painful, severe, stabbing

piety *noun* HOLINESS, faith, godliness, piousness, religion, reverence

pig *noun* **1** HOG, boar, porker, sow, swine **2** *Informal* SLOB (*slang*), boor, brute, glutton,

hog (*informal*), swine

pigeonhole *noun* **1** COMPARTMENT, cubbyhole, locker, niche, place, section ▶ *verb* **2** CLASSIFY, categorize, characterize, compartmentalize, ghettoize, label, slot (*informal*) **3** PUT OFF, defer, postpone, shelve

pig-headed *adjective* STUBBORN, contrary, inflexible, mulish, obstinate, self-willed, stiff-necked, unyielding

pigment *noun* COLOR, coloring, dye, paint, stain, tincture, tint

pile¹ *noun* **1** HEAP, accumulation, collection, hoard, mass, mound, mountain, stack **2** BUILDING, edifice, erection, structure ▶ *verb* **3** COLLECT, accumulate, amass, assemble, gather, heap, hoard, stack **4** CROWD, crush, flock, flood, jam, pack, rush, stream

pile² *noun* FOUNDATION, beam, column, pillar, post, support, upright

pile³ *noun* NAP, down, fiber, fur, hair, plush

pile-up *noun Informal* COLLISION, accident, crash, multiple collision, smash, smash-up (*informal*)

pilfer *verb* STEAL, appropriate, embezzle, filch, lift (*informal*), pinch (*informal*), purloin, swipe (*slang*), take

pilgrim *noun* TRAVELER, wanderer, wayfarer

pilgrimage *noun* JOURNEY, excursion, expedition, mission, tour, trip

pill *noun* **1** TABLET, capsule, pellet **2 the pill** ORAL CONTRACEPTIVE

pillage *verb* **1** PLUNDER, despoil,

loot, maraud, raid, ransack, ravage, sack ▸ *noun* 2 PLUNDER, marauding, robbery, sack, spoliation

pillar *noun* 1 SUPPORT, column, pier, post, prop, shaft, stanchion, upright 2 SUPPORTER, follower, mainstay, upholder

pillory *verb* RIDICULE, brand, denounce, stigmatize

pilot *noun* 1 AIRMAN, aviator, flyer 2 HELMSMAN, navigator, steersman ▸ *adjective* 3 TRIAL, experimental, model, test ▸ *verb* 4 FLY, conduct, direct, drive, guide, handle, navigate, operate, steer

pimple *noun* SPOT, boil, pustule, zit (*slang*)

pin *verb* 1 FASTEN, affix, attach, fix, join, secure 2 HOLD FAST, fix, hold down, immobilize, pinion

pinch *verb* 1 SQUEEZE, compress, grasp, nip, press 2 HURT, cramp, crush, pain 3 *Informal* STEAL, filch, lift (*informal*), pilfer, purloin, swipe (*slang*) ▸ *noun* 4 SQUEEZE, nip 5 DASH, bit, jot, mite, *soupçon*, speck 6 HARDSHIP, crisis, difficulty, emergency, necessity, plight, predicament, strait

pinched *adjective* THIN, drawn, gaunt, haggard, peaky, worn

pin down *verb* 1 FORCE, compel, constrain, make, press, pressurize 2 DETERMINE, identify, locate, name, pinpoint, specify

pine *verb* 1 (often with *for*) LONG, ache, crave, desire, eat one's heart out over, hanker, hunger for, thirst for, wish for, yearn for 2 WASTE, decline, fade, languish, sicken

pinion *verb* IMMOBILIZE, bind,

chain, fasten, fetter, manacle, shackle, tie

pink *adjective* ROSY, flushed, reddish, rose, roseate, salmon

pinnacle *noun* PEAK, apex, crest, crown, height, summit, top, vertex, zenith

pinpoint *verb* IDENTIFY, define, distinguish, locate

pioneer *noun* 1 SETTLER, colonist, explorer 2 FOUNDER, developer, innovator, leader, trailblazer ▸ *verb* 3 DEVELOP, create, discover, establish, initiate, instigate, institute, invent, originate, show the way, start

pious *adjective* RELIGIOUS, devout, God-fearing, godly, holy, reverent, righteous, saintly

pipe *noun* 1 TUBE, conduit, duct, hose, line, main, passage, pipeline ▸ *verb* 2 WHISTLE, cheep, peep, play, sing, sound, warble 3 CONVEY, channel, conduct

pipe down *verb Informal* BE QUIET, hold one's tongue, hush, quieten down, shush, shut one's mouth, shut up (*informal*)

pipeline *noun* TUBE, conduit, duct, passage, pipe

piquant *adjective* 1 SPICY, biting, pungent, savory, sharp, tangy, tart, zesty 2 INTERESTING, lively, provocative, scintillating, sparkling, stimulating

pique *noun* 1 RESENTMENT, annoyance, displeasure, huff, hurt feelings, irritation, offense, umbrage, wounded pride ▸ *verb* 2 DISPLEASE, affront, annoy, get (*informal*), irk, irritate, nettle, offend, rile, sting 3 AROUSE, excite, rouse, spur, stimulate, stir, whet

piracy *noun* ROBBERY,

buccaneering, freebooting,
stealing, theft

pirate *noun* 1 BUCCANEER, corsair,
freebooter, marauder, raider
2 PLAGIARIST, infringer,
plagiarizer ▶ *verb* 3 COPY,
appropriate, plagiarize, poach,
reproduce, steal

pit *noun* 1 HOLE, abyss, cavity,
chasm, crater, dent,
depression, hollow ▶ *verb*
2 SCAR, dent, indent, mark,
pockmark

pitch *verb* 1 THROW, cast, chuck
(*informal*), fling, heave, hurl,
lob (*informal*), sling, toss 2 SET
UP, erect, put up, raise, settle
3 FALL, dive, drop, topple,
tumble 4 TOSS, lurch, plunge,
roll ▶ *noun* 5 SPORTS FIELD, field
of play, ground, park 6 LEVEL,
degree, height, highest point,
point, summit 7 SLOPE, angle,
dip, gradient, incline, tilt
8 TONE, modulation, sound,
timbre 9 SALES TALK, patter, spiel
(*informal*)

pitch-black *adjective* JET-BLACK,
dark, inky, pitch-dark, unlit

pitch in *verb* HELP, chip in
(*informal*), contribute,
cooperate, do one's bit, join
in, lend a hand, participate

piteous *adjective* PATHETIC,
affecting, distressing,
harrowing, heartbreaking,
heart-rending, moving,
pitiable, pitiful, plaintive,
poignant, sad

pitfall *noun* DANGER, catch,
difficulty, drawback, hazard,
peril, snag, trap

pith *noun* ESSENCE, core, crux,
gist, heart, kernel, nub, point,
quintessence, salient point

pithy *adjective* SUCCINCT, brief,
cogent, concise, epigrammatic,
laconic, pointed, short, terse,
to the point, trenchant

pitiful *adjective* 1 PATHETIC,
distressing, grievous,
harrowing, heartbreaking,
heart-rending, piteous, pitiable,
sad, wretched 2 CONTEMPTIBLE,
abject, base, lousy (*slang*), low,
mean, miserable, paltry,
shabby, sorry

pitiless *adjective* MERCILESS,
callous, cold-blooded,
cold-hearted, cruel,
hardhearted, heartless,
implacable, relentless, ruthless,
unmerciful

pittance *noun* PEANUTS (*slang*),
chicken feed (*slang*), drop,
mite, slave wages, trifle

pity *noun* 1 COMPASSION, charity,
clemency, fellow feeling,
forbearance, kindness, mercy,
sympathy 2 SHAME, bummer
(*slang*), crying shame,
misfortune, sin ▶ *verb* 3 FEEL
SORRY FOR, bleed for, feel for,
grieve for, have compassion
for, sympathize with, weep for

pivot *noun* 1 AXIS, axle, fulcrum,
spindle, swivel 2 HUB, center,
heart, hinge, kingpin ▶ *verb*
3 TURN, revolve, rotate, spin,
swivel, twirl 4 RELY, be
contingent, depend, hang,
hinge

pivotal *adjective* CRUCIAL, central,
critical, decisive, vital

pixie *noun* ELF, brownie, fairy,
sprite

placard *noun* NOTICE,
advertisement, bill, poster

placate *verb* CALM, appease,
assuage, conciliate, humor,

mollify, pacify, propitiate, soothe

place noun 1 SPOT, area, location, point, position, site, venue, whereabouts 2 REGION, district, locale, locality, neighborhood, quarter, vicinity 3 POSITION, grade, rank, station, status 4 SPACE, accommodation, room 5 HOME, abode, domicile, dwelling, house, pad (slang, dated), property, residence 6 DUTY, affair, charge, concern, function, prerogative, responsibility, right, role 7 JOB, appointment, employment, position, post 8 **take place** HAPPEN, come about, go on, occur, transpire (informal) ▶verb 9 PUT, deposit, install, lay, locate, position, rest, set, situate, stand, station, stick (informal) 10 CLASSIFY, arrange, class, grade, group, order, rank, sort 11 IDENTIFY, know, put one's finger on, recognize, remember 12 ASSIGN, allocate, appoint, charge, entrust, give

placid adjective CALM, collected, composed, equable, even-tempered, imperturbable, serene, tranquil, unexcitable, unruffled, untroubled

plagiarism noun COPYING, borrowing, infringement, piracy, theft

plagiarize verb COPY, borrow, lift (informal), pirate, steal

plague noun 1 DISEASE, epidemic, infection, pestilence 2 AFFLICTION, bane, blight, curse, evil, scourge, torment ▶verb 3 PESTER, annoy, badger, bother, harass, harry, hassle (informal), tease, torment, torture, trouble, vex

plain adjective 1 CLEAR, comprehensible, distinct, evident, manifest, obvious, overt, patent, unambiguous, understandable, unmistakable, visible 2 HONEST, blunt, candid, direct, downright, forthright, frank, open, outspoken, straightforward, upfront (informal) 3 UNADORNED, austere, bare, basic, severe, simple, Spartan, stark, unembellished, unfussy, unornamented 4 UGLY, dumpy (informal), frowzy, homely (U.S.), ill-favored, no oil painting (informal), not beautiful, unattractive, unlovely, unprepossessing 5 ORDINARY, common, commonplace, everyday, simple, unaffected, unpretentious ▶noun 6 FLATLAND, grassland, plateau, prairie, steppe, veld

plain-spoken adjective BLUNT, candid, direct, downright, forthright, frank, outspoken

plaintive adjective SORROWFUL, heart-rending, mournful, pathetic, piteous, pitiful, sad

plan noun 1 SCHEME, design, method, plot, program, proposal, strategy, suggestion, system 2 DIAGRAM, blueprint, chart, drawing, layout, map, representation, sketch ▶verb 3 DEVISE, arrange, contrive, design, draft, formulate, organize, outline, plot, scheme, think out 4 INTEND, aim, mean, propose, purpose

plane noun 1 AIRPLANE, aircraft, jet 2 FLAT SURFACE, level surface 3 LEVEL, condition, degree, position ▶adjective 4 LEVEL, even, flat, horizontal, regular, smooth ▸*verb* **5** SKIM, glide, sail, skate

plant *noun* **1** VEGETABLE, bush, flower, herb, shrub, weed **2** FACTORY, foundry, mill, shop, works, yard **3** MACHINERY, apparatus, equipment, gear ▸*verb* **4** SOW, put in the ground, scatter, seed, transplant **5** PLACE, establish, fix, found, insert, put, set

plaster *noun* **1** MORTAR, gypsum, plaster of Paris, stucco **2** BANDAGE, adhesive plaster, dressing, Elastoplast (*Trademark*), sticking plaster ▸*verb* **3** COVER, coat, daub, overlay, smear, spread

plastic *adjective* **1** MANAGEABLE, docile, malleable, pliable, receptive, responsive, tractable **2** PLIANT, ductile, flexible, moldable, pliable, soft, supple

plate *noun* **1** PLATTER, dish, trencher (*archaic*) **2** HELPING, course, dish, portion, serving **3** LAYER, panel, sheet, slab **4** ILLUSTRATION, lithograph, print ▸*verb* **5** COAT, cover, gild, laminate, overlay

plateau *noun* **1** UPLAND, highland, table, tableland **2** LEVELLING OFF, level, stability, stage

platform *noun* **1** STAGE, dais, podium, rostrum, stand **2** POLICY, manifesto, objective(s), party line, principle, program

platitude *noun* CLICHÉ, banality, commonplace, truism

platoon *noun* SQUAD, company, group, outfit (*informal*), patrol, squadron, team

platter *noun* PLATE, dish, salver, tray, trencher (*archaic*)

plaudits *plural noun* APPROVAL, acclaim, acclamation, applause, approbation, praise

plausible *adjective* **1** REASONABLE, believable, conceivable, credible, likely, persuasive, possible, probable, tenable **2** GLIB, smooth, smooth-talking, smooth-tongued, specious

play *verb* **1** AMUSE ONESELF, entertain oneself, fool, have fun, revel, romp, sport, trifle **2** COMPETE, challenge, contend against, participate, take on, take part **3** ACT, act the part of, perform, portray, represent ▸*noun* **4** DRAMA, comedy, dramatic piece, farce, pantomime, piece, show, stage show, tragedy **5** AMUSEMENT, diversion, entertainment, fun, game, pastime, recreation, sport **6** FUN, humor, jest, joking, lark (*informal*), prank, sport **7** SPACE, elbowroom, latitude, leeway, margin, room, scope

playboy *noun* WOMANIZER, ladies' man, philanderer, rake, roué

play down *verb* MINIMIZE, gloss over, make light of, make little of, underplay, underrate

player *noun* **1** SPORTSMAN *or* SPORTSWOMAN, competitor, contestant, participant **2** MUSICIAN, artist, instrumentalist, performer, virtuoso **3** PERFORMER, actor *or* actress, entertainer, Thespian, trouper

playful *adjective* LIVELY, frisky, impish, merry, mischievous, spirited, sportive, sprightly, vivacious

playmate noun FRIEND, chum (*informal*), companion, comrade, pal (*informal*), playfellow

play on or **upon** verb TAKE ADVANTAGE OF, abuse, capitalize on, exploit, impose on, trade on

plaything noun TOY, amusement, game, pastime, trifle

play up verb EMPHASIZE, accentuate, highlight, stress, underline

plea noun 1 APPEAL, entreaty, intercession, petition, prayer, request, suit, supplication 2 EXCUSE, defense, explanation, justification

plead verb APPEAL, ask, beg, beseech, entreat, implore, petition, request

pleasant adjective 1 PLEASING, agreeable, amusing, delightful, enjoyable, fine, lovely, nice, pleasurable 2 NICE, affable, agreeable, amiable, charming, congenial, engaging, friendly, genial, likable or likeable

pleasantry noun JOKE, badinage, banter, jest, quip, witticism

please verb DELIGHT, amuse, entertain, gladden, gratify, humor, indulge, satisfy, suit

pleased adjective HAPPY, contented, delighted, euphoric, glad, gratified, over the moon (*informal*), satisfied, thrilled

pleasing adjective ENJOYABLE, agreeable, charming, delightful, engaging, gratifying, likable or likeable, pleasurable, satisfying

pleasurable adjective ENJOYABLE, agreeable, delightful, fun, good, lovely, nice, pleasant

pleasure noun HAPPINESS, amusement, bliss, delectation, delight, enjoyment, gladness, gratification, joy, satisfaction

plebeian adjective 1 COMMON, base, coarse, low, lower-class, proletarian, uncultivated, unrefined, vulgar, working-class ▶ noun 2 COMMONER, common man, man in the street, pleb, proletarian

pledge noun 1 PROMISE, assurance, covenant, oath, undertaking, vow, warrant, word 2 GUARANTEE, bail, collateral, deposit, pawn, security, surety ▶ verb 3 PROMISE, contract, engage, give one's oath, give one's word, swear, vow

plentiful adjective ABUNDANT, ample, bountiful, copious, generous, lavish, liberal, overflowing, plenteous, profuse

plenty noun 1 LOTS (*informal*), abundance, enough, great deal, heap(s) (*informal*), masses, pile(s) (*informal*), plethora, quantity, stack(s) 2 ABUNDANCE, affluence, copiousness, fertility, fruitfulness, plenitude, profusion, prosperity, wealth

plethora noun EXCESS, glut, overabundance, profusion, superabundance, surfeit, surplus

pliable adjective 1 FLEXIBLE, bendable, bendy, malleable, plastic, pliant, supple 2 IMPRESSIONABLE, adaptable, compliant, docile, easily led, pliant, receptive, responsive, susceptible, tractable

pliant *adjective* 1 FLEXIBLE, bendable, bendy, plastic, pliable, supple 2 IMPRESSIONABLE, biddable, compliant, easily led, pliable, susceptible, tractable

plight *noun* DIFFICULTY, condition, jam (*informal*), predicament, scrape (*informal*), situation, spot (*informal*), state, trouble

plod *verb* 1 TRUDGE, clump, drag, lumber, tramp, tread 2 SLOG, grind (*informal*), labor, persevere, plow through, soldier on, toil

plot[1] *noun* 1 PLAN, cabal, conspiracy, intrigue, machination, scheme, stratagem 2 STORY, action, narrative, outline, scenario, story line, subject, theme ▶ *verb* 3 PLAN, collude, conspire, contrive, intrigue, machinate, maneuver, scheme 4 DEVISE, conceive, concoct, contrive, cook up (*informal*), design, hatch, lay 5 CHART, calculate, locate, map, mark, outline

plot[2] *noun* PATCH, allotment, area, ground, lot, parcel, tract

plow *verb* 1 TURN OVER, cultivate, dig, till 2 (usually with *through*) FORGE, cut, drive, plunge, press, push, wade

ploy *noun* TACTIC, device, dodge, maneuver, move, ruse, scheme, stratagem, trick, wile

pluck *verb* 1 PULL OUT *or* OFF, collect, draw, gather, harvest, pick 2 TUG, catch, clutch, jerk, pull at, snatch, tweak, yank 3 STRUM, finger, pick, twang ▶ *noun* 4 COURAGE, backbone, boldness, bravery, grit, guts (*informal*), nerve

plucky *adjective* COURAGEOUS, bold, brave, daring, game, gutsy (*slang*), intrepid

plug *noun* 1 STOPPER, bung, cork, spigot 2 *Informal* MENTION, advertisement, hype, publicity, push ▶ *verb* 3 SEAL, block, bung, close, cork, fill, pack, stop, stopper, stop up, stuff 4 *Informal* MENTION, advertise, build up, hype, promote, publicize, push

plum *adjective* CHOICE, best, first-class, prize

plumb *verb* 1 DELVE, explore, fathom, gauge, go into, penetrate, probe, unravel ▶ *noun* 2 WEIGHT, lead, plumb bob, plummet ▶ *adverb* 3 EXACTLY, bang, precisely, slap

plume *noun* FEATHER, crest, pinion, quill

plummet *verb* PLUNGE, crash, descend, dive, drop down, fall, nose-dive, tumble

plump *adjective* CHUBBY, corpulent, dumpy, fat, roly-poly, rotund, round, stout, tubby

plunder *verb* 1 LOOT, pillage, raid, ransack, rifle, rob, sack, strip ▶ *noun* 2 LOOT, booty, ill-gotten gains, pillage, prize, spoils, swag (*slang*)

plunge *verb* 1 THROW, cast, pitch 2 HURTLE, career, charge, dash, jump, rush, tear 3 DESCEND, dip, dive, drop, fall, nose-dive, plummet, sink, tumble ▶ *noun* 4 DIVE, descent, drop, fall, jump

plus *preposition* 1 AND, added to, coupled with, with ▶ *adjective* 2 ADDITIONAL, added, add-on, extra, supplementary ▶ *noun* 3 ADVANTAGE, asset, benefit, bonus, extra, gain, good point

plush *adjective* LUXURIOUS, deluxe, lavish, luxury, opulent, rich, sumptuous

ply *verb* 1 WORK AT, carry on, exercise, follow, practice, pursue 2 USE, employ, handle, manipulate, wield

poach *verb* ENCROACH, appropriate, infringe, intrude, trespass

pocket *noun* 1 POUCH, bag, compartment, receptacle, sack ▶ *verb* 2 STEAL, appropriate, filch, lift (*informal*), pilfer, purloin, take ▶ *adjective* 3 SMALL, abridged, compact, concise, little, miniature, portable

pod *noun, verb* SHELL, hull, husk, shuck

podium *noun* PLATFORM, dais, rostrum, stage

poem *noun* VERSE, lyric, ode, rhyme, song, sonnet

poet *noun* BARD, lyricist, rhymer, versifier

poetic *adjective* LYRICAL, elegiac, lyric, metrical

poetry *noun* VERSE, poems, rhyme, rhyming

poignancy *noun* 1 SADNESS, emotion, feeling, pathos, sentiment, tenderness 2 SHARPNESS, bitterness, intensity, keenness

poignant *adjective* MOVING, bitter, distressing, heart-rending, intense, painful, pathetic, sad, touching

point *noun* 1 ESSENCE, crux, drift, gist, heart, import, meaning, nub, pith, question, subject, thrust 2 AIM, end, goal, intent, intention, motive, object,

objective, purpose, reason 3 ITEM, aspect, detail, feature, particular 4 CHARACTERISTIC, aspect, attribute, quality, respect, trait 5 PLACE, location, position, site, spot, stage 6 FULL STOP, dot, mark, period, stop 7 END, apex, prong, sharp end, spike, spur, summit, tip, top 8 HEADLAND, cape, head, promontory 9 STAGE, circumstance, condition, degree, extent, position 10 MOMENT, instant, juncture, time, very minute 11 UNIT, score, tally ▶ *verb* 12 INDICATE, call attention to, denote, designate, direct, show, signify 13 AIM, direct, level, train

point-blank *adjective* 1 DIRECT, blunt, downright, explicit, express, plain ▶ *adverb* 2 DIRECTLY, bluntly, candidly, explicitly, forthrightly, frankly, openly, plainly, straight

pointed *adjective* 1 SHARP, acute, barbed, edged 2 CUTTING, acute, biting, incisive, keen, penetrating, pertinent, sharp, telling

pointer *noun* 1 HINT, advice, caution, information, recommendation, suggestion, tip 2 INDICATOR, guide, hand, needle

pointless *adjective* SENSELESS, absurd, aimless, fruitless, futile, inane, irrelevant, meaningless, silly, stupid, useless

point out *verb* MENTION, allude to, bring up, identify, indicate, show, specify

poise *noun* COMPOSURE, aplomb, assurance, calmness, cool (*slang*), dignity, presence, sang-froid, self-possession

poised *adjective* **1** READY, all set, prepared, standing by, waiting **2** COMPOSED, calm, collected, dignified, self-confident, self-possessed, together (*informal*)

poison *noun* **1** TOXIN, bane, venom ▸*verb* **2** MURDER, give (someone) poison, kill **3** CONTAMINATE, infect, pollute **4** CORRUPT, defile, deprave, pervert, subvert, taint, undermine, warp

poisonous *adjective* **1** TOXIC, deadly, fatal, lethal, mortal, noxious, venomous, virulent **2** EVIL, baleful, corrupting, malicious, noxious, pernicious

poke *verb* **1** JAB, dig, nudge, prod, push, shove, stab, stick, thrust ▸*noun* **2** JAB, dig, nudge, prod, thrust

poky *adjective* SMALL, confined, cramped, narrow, tiny

pole *noun* ROD, bar, mast, post, shaft, spar, staff, stick

police *noun* **1** THE LAW (*informal*), boys in blue (*informal*), constabulary, fuzz (*slang*), police force ▸*verb* **2** CONTROL, guard, patrol, protect, regulate, watch

policeman *noun* COP (*slang*), constable, copper (*slang*), fuzz (*slang*), officer

policy *noun* PROCEDURE, action, approach, code, course, custom, plan, practice, rule, scheme

polish *verb* **1** SHINE, brighten, buff, burnish, rub, smooth, wax **2** PERFECT, brush up, enhance, finish, improve, refine, touch up ▸*noun* **3** VARNISH, wax **4** SHEEN, brightness, finish, glaze, gloss, luster **5** STYLE, breeding, class (*informal*), elegance, finesse, finish, grace, refinement

polished *adjective* **1** ACCOMPLISHED, adept, expert, fine, masterly, professional, skillful, superlative **2** SHINING, bright, burnished, gleaming, glossy, smooth **3** ELEGANT, cultivated, polite, refined, sophisticated, well-bred

polite *adjective* **1** MANNERLY, civil, complaisant, courteous, gracious, respectful, well-behaved, well-mannered **2** REFINED, civilized, cultured, elegant, genteel, polished, sophisticated, well-bred

politeness *noun* COURTESY, civility, courteousness, decency, etiquette, mannerliness

politic *adjective* WISE, advisable, diplomatic, expedient, judicious, prudent, sensible

political *adjective* GOVERNMENTAL, parliamentary, policy-making

politician *noun* STATESMAN, bureaucrat, congressman, legislator, office bearer, public servant, representative

politics *noun* STATESMANSHIP, affairs of state, civics, government, political science

poll *noun* **1** CANVASS, ballot, census, count, sampling, survey **2** VOTE, figures, returns, tally, voting ▸*verb* **3** TALLY, register **4** QUESTION, ballot, canvass, interview, sample, survey

pollute *verb* **1** CONTAMINATE, dirty, foul, infect, poison, soil, spoil, stain, taint **2** DEFILE, corrupt, debase, debauch, deprave, desecrate, dishonor, profane, sully

pollution noun CONTAMINATION, corruption, defilement, dirtying, foulness, impurity, taint, uncleanness

pomp noun 1 CEREMONY, flourish, grandeur, magnificence, pageant, pageantry, splendor, state 2 SHOW, display, grandiosity, ostentation

pomposity noun SELF-IMPORTANCE, affectation, airs, grandiosity, pompousness, portentousness, pretension, pretentiousness

pompous adjective 1 SELF-IMPORTANT, arrogant, grandiose, ostentatious, pretentious, puffed up, showy 2 GRANDILOQUENT, boastful, bombastic, high-flown, inflated

pond noun POOL, duck pond, fish pond, millpond, small lake, tarn

ponder verb THINK, brood, cogitate, consider, contemplate, deliberate, meditate, mull over, muse, reflect, ruminate

ponderous adjective 1 DULL, heavy, long-winded, pedantic, tedious 2 UNWIELDY, bulky, cumbersome, heavy, huge, massive, weighty 3 CLUMSY, awkward, heavy-footed, lumbering

pontificate verb EXPOUND, hold forth, lay down the law, preach, pronounce, sound off

pool[1] noun 1 POND, lake, mere, puddle, tarn 2 SWIMMING POOL, swimming bath

pool[2] noun 1 SYNDICATE,

collective, consortium, group, team, trust 2 KITTY, bank, funds, jackpot, pot ▶ verb 3 COMBINE, amalgamate, join forces, league, merge, put together, share

poor adjective 1 IMPOVERISHED, broke (informal), destitute, down and out, down on one's luck (informal), hard up (informal), impecunious, indigent, needy, on the breadline, penniless, penurious, poverty-stricken, short 2 INADEQUATE, deficient, incomplete, insufficient, lacking, lousy (slang), meager, measly, scant, scanty, skimpy 3 INFERIOR, below par, lousy (slang), low-grade, mediocre, rotten (informal), rubbishy, second-rate, substandard, unsatisfactory 4 UNFORTUNATE, hapless, ill-fated, luckless, pitiable, unhappy, unlucky, wretched

poorly adverb BADLY, inadequately, incompetently, inexpertly, insufficiently, unsatisfactorily, unsuccessfully

pop verb 1 BURST, bang, crack, explode, go off, snap 2 PUT, insert, push, shove, slip, stick, thrust, tuck ▶ noun 3 BANG, burst, crack, explosion, noise, report

pope noun HOLY FATHER, Bishop of Rome, pontiff, Vicar of Christ

populace noun PEOPLE, general public, hoi polloi, masses, mob, multitude

popular adjective 1 WELL-LIKED, accepted, approved, cool (informal), fashionable, favorite, in (informal), in demand, in favor, liked, phat (slang), sought-after 2 COMMON, conventional, current, general, prevailing, prevalent, universal

popularity noun FAVOR, acceptance, acclaim, approval, currency, esteem, regard, vogue

popularize verb MAKE POPULAR, disseminate, give currency to, give mass appeal, make available to all, spread, universalize

popularly adverb GENERALLY, commonly, conventionally, customarily, ordinarily, traditionally, universally, usually, widely

populate verb INHABIT, colonize, live in, occupy, settle

population noun INHABITANTS, community, denizens, folk, natives, people, residents, society

populous adjective POPULATED, crowded, heavily populated, overpopulated, packed, swarming, teeming

pore[1] verb **pore over** STUDY, examine, peruse, ponder, read, scrutinize

pore[2] noun OPENING, hole, orifice, outlet

pornographic adjective OBSCENE, blue, dirty, filthy, indecent, lewd, salacious, scuzzy (slang), smutty, X-rated

pornography noun OBSCENITY, dirt, filth, indecency, porn (informal), smut

porous adjective PERMEABLE, absorbent, absorptive, penetrable, spongy

port noun HARBOR, anchorage, haven, seaport

portable adjective LIGHT, compact, convenient, easily carried, handy, manageable, movable

portend verb FORETELL, augur, betoken, bode, foreshadow, herald, indicate, predict, prognosticate, promise, warn of

portent noun OMEN, augury, forewarning, indication, prognostication, sign, warning

portentous adjective 1 SIGNIFICANT, crucial, fateful, important, menacing, momentous, ominous 2 POMPOUS, ponderous, self-important, solemn

porter[1] noun BAGGAGE ATTENDANT, bearer, carrier

porter[2] noun DOORMAN, caretaker, concierge, gatekeeper, janitor

portion noun 1 PART, bit, fragment, morsel, piece, scrap, section, segment 2 SHARE, allocation, allotment, allowance, lot, measure, quantity, quota, ration 3 HELPING, piece, serving 4 DESTINY, fate, fortune, lot, luck ▶ verb 5 **portion out** DIVIDE, allocate, allot, apportion, deal, distribute, dole out, share out

portly adjective STOUT, burly, corpulent, fat, fleshy, heavy, large, plump

portrait noun 1 PICTURE, image, likeness, painting, photograph, representation 2 DESCRIPTION, characterization, depiction, portrayal, profile, thumbnail sketch

portray verb 1 REPRESENT, depict, draw, figure, illustrate, paint, picture, sketch 2 DESCRIBE, characterize, depict, put in words 3 PLAY, act the part of, represent

portrayal noun REPRESENTATION, characterization, depiction, interpretation, performance, picture

pose verb 1 POSITION, model, sit 2 PUT ON AIRS, posture, show off (informal) 3 **pose as** IMPERSONATE, masquerade as, pass oneself off as, pretend to be, profess to be ▶ noun 4 POSTURE, attitude, bearing, position, stance 5 ACT, affectation, air, façade, front, mannerism, posturing, pretense

poser noun PUZZLE, enigma, problem, question, riddle

posit verb PUT FORWARD, advance, assume, postulate, presume, propound, state

position noun 1 PLACE, area, bearings, locale, location, point, post, situation, spot, station, whereabouts 2 POSTURE, arrangement, attitude, pose, stance 3 ATTITUDE, belief, opinion, outlook, point of view, slant, stance, view, viewpoint 4 STATUS, importance, place, prestige, rank, reputation, standing, station, stature 5 JOB, duty, employment, occupation, office, place, post, role, situation ▶ verb 6 PLACE, arrange, lay out, locate, put, set, stand

positive adjective 1 CERTAIN, assured, confident, convinced, sure 2 DEFINITE, absolute, categorical, certain, clear, conclusive, decisive, explicit, express, firm, real 3 HELPFUL, beneficial, constructive, practical, productive, progressive, useful

positively adverb DEFINITELY, absolutely, assuredly, categorically, certainly, emphatically, firmly, surely, unequivocally, unquestionably

possess verb 1 HAVE, enjoy, hold, own 2 CONTROL, acquire, dominate, hold, occupy, seize, take over

possessed adjective CRAZED, berserk, demented, frenzied, obsessed, raving

possession noun 1 OWNERSHIP, control, custody, hold, occupation, tenure, title 2 **possessions** PROPERTY, assets, belongings, chattels, effects, estate, things

possessive adjective JEALOUS, controlling, covetous, dominating, domineering, overprotective, selfish

possibility noun 1 FEASIBILITY, likelihood, potentiality, practicability, workableness 2 LIKELIHOOD, chance, hope, liability, odds, probability, prospect, risk 3 (often plural) POTENTIAL, capabilities, potentiality, promise, prospects, talent

possible adjective 1 CONCEIVABLE, credible, hypothetical, imaginable, likely, potential 2 LIKELY, hopeful, potential, probable, promising 3 FEASIBLE, attainable, doable, practicable, realizable, viable, workable

possibly adverb PERHAPS, maybe, perchance (archaic)

post[1] noun **keep someone posted** NOTIFY, advise, brief, fill in on (informal), inform, report to

post[2] noun 1 SUPPORT, column,

picket, pillar, pole, shaft, stake, upright ▶ *verb* **2** PUT UP, affix, display, pin up

post³ *noun* **1** JOB, appointment, assignment, employment, office, place, position, situation **2** STATION, beat, place, position ▶ *verb* **3** STATION, assign, place, position, put, situate

poster *noun* NOTICE, advertisement, announcement, bill, placard, public notice, sticker

posterity *noun* **1** FUTURE, succeeding generations **2** DESCENDANTS, children, family, heirs, issue, offspring, progeny

postpone *verb* PUT OFF, adjourn, defer, delay, put back, put on the back burner (*informal*), shelve, suspend

postponement *noun* DELAY, adjournment, deferment, deferral, stay, suspension

postscript *noun* P.S., addition, afterthought, supplement

postulate *verb* PRESUPPOSE, assume, hypothesize, posit, propose, suppose, take for granted, theorize

posture *noun* **1** BEARING, attitude, carriage, disposition, set, stance ▶ *verb* **2** SHOW OFF (*informal*), affect, pose, put on airs

pot *noun* CONTAINER, bowl, pan, vessel

potency *noun* POWER, effectiveness, force, influence, might, strength

potent *adjective* **1** POWERFUL, authoritative, commanding, dominant, dynamic, influential **2** STRONG, forceful, mighty, powerful, vigorous

potential *adjective* **1** POSSIBLE, dormant, future, hidden, inherent, latent, likely, promising ▶ *noun* **2** ABILITY, aptitude, capability, capacity, possibility, potentiality, power, wherewithal

potion *noun* CONCOCTION, brew, dose, draft, elixir, mixture, philtre

pottery *noun* CERAMICS, earthenware, stoneware, terracotta

pouch *noun* BAG, container, pocket, purse, sack

pounce *verb* **1** SPRING, attack, fall upon, jump, leap at, strike, swoop ▶ *noun* **2** SPRING, assault, attack, bound, jump, leap, swoop

pound¹ *verb* **1** BEAT, batter, belabor, clobber (*slang*), hammer, pummel, strike, thrash, thump **2** CRUSH, powder, pulverize **3** PULSATE, beat, palpitate, pulse, throb **4** STOMP (*informal*), march, thunder, tramp

pound² *noun* ENCLOSURE, compound, pen, yard

pour *verb* **1** FLOW, course, emit, gush, run, rush, spew, spout, stream **2** LET FLOW, decant, spill, splash **3** RAIN, bucket down (*informal*), pelt (down), teem **4** STREAM, crowd, swarm, teem, throng

pout *verb* **1** SULK, glower, look petulant, pull a long face ▶ *noun* **2** SULLEN LOOK, glower, long face

poverty *noun* **1** PENNILESSNESS, beggary, destitution, hardship, indigence, insolvency, need, penury, privation, want

2 SCARCITY, dearth, deficiency, insufficiency, lack, paucity, shortage

poverty-stricken *adjective* PENNILESS, broke (*informal*), destitute, down and out, down on one's luck (*informal*), flat broke (*informal*), impecunious, impoverished, indigent, poor

powder *noun* **1** DUST, fine grains, loose particles, talc ▶*verb* **2** DUST, cover, dredge, scatter, sprinkle, strew

powdery *adjective* FINE, crumbly, dry, dusty, grainy, granular

power *noun* **1** ABILITY, capability, capacity, competence, competency, faculty, potential **2** CONTROL, ascendancy, authority, command, dominance, domination, dominion, influence, mastery, rule **3** AUTHORITY, authorization, license, prerogative, privilege, right, warrant **4** STRENGTH, brawn, energy, force, forcefulness, intensity, might, muscle, potency, vigor

powerful *adjective* **1** CONTROLLING, authoritative, commanding, dominant, influential, prevailing **2** STRONG, energetic, mighty, potent, strapping, sturdy, vigorous **3** PERSUASIVE, cogent, compelling, convincing, effectual, forceful, impressive, striking, telling, weighty

powerless *adjective* **1** DEFENSELESS, dependent, ineffective, subject, tied, unarmed, vulnerable **2** HELPLESS, challenged, debilitated, disabled, feeble, frail, impotent, incapable,

incapacitated, ineffectual, weak

practicability *noun* FEASIBILITY, advantage, possibility, practicality, use, usefulness, viability

practicable *adjective* FEASIBLE, achievable, attainable, doable, possible, viable

practical *adjective* **1** FUNCTIONAL, applied, empirical, experimental, factual, pragmatic, realistic, utilitarian **2** SENSIBLE, businesslike, down-to-earth, hard-headed, matter-of-fact, ordinary, realistic **3** FEASIBLE, doable, practicable, serviceable, useful, workable **4** SKILLED, accomplished, efficient, experienced, proficient

practically *adverb* **1** ALMOST, all but, basically, essentially, fundamentally, in effect, just about, nearly, very nearly, virtually, well-nigh **2** SENSIBLY, clearly, matter-of-factly, rationally, realistically, reasonably

practice *noun* **1** CUSTOM, habit, method, mode, routine, rule, system, tradition, usage, way, wont **2** REHEARSAL, drill, exercise, preparation, repetition, study, training **3** PROFESSION, business, career, vocation, work **4** USE, action, application, exercise, experience, operation ▶*verb* **5** REHEARSE, drill, exercise, go over, go through, prepare, repeat, study, train **6** DO, apply, carry out, follow, observe, perform **7** WORK AT, carry on, engage in, pursue

practiced *adjective* SKILLED, able, accomplished, experienced, expert, proficient, seasoned, trained, versed

pragmatic *adjective* PRACTICAL, businesslike, down-to-earth, hard-headed, realistic, sensible, utilitarian

praise *verb* 1 APPROVE, acclaim, admire, applaud, cheer, compliment, congratulate, eulogize, extol, honor, laud 2 GIVE THANKS TO, adore, bless, exalt, glorify, worship ▶*noun* 3 APPROVAL, acclaim, acclamation, approbation, commendation, compliment, congratulation, eulogy, kudos, plaudit, tribute 4 THANKS, adoration, glory, homage, kudos, worship

praiseworthy *adjective* CREDITABLE, admirable, commendable, laudable, meritorious, worthy

prance *verb* 1 DANCE, caper, cavort, frisk, gambol, romp, skip 2 STRUT, parade, show off (*informal*), stalk, swagger

prank *noun* TRICK, antic, escapade, jape, lark (*informal*), practical joke

pray *verb* 1 SAY ONE'S PRAYERS, offer a prayer, recite the rosary 2 BEG, adjure, ask, beseech, entreat, implore, petition, plead, request, solicit

prayer *noun* 1 ORISON, devotion, invocation, litany, supplication 2 PLEA, appeal, entreaty, petition, request, supplication

preach *verb* 1 DELIVER A SERMON, address, evangelize 2 LECTURE, advocate, exhort, moralize, sermonize

preacher *noun* CLERGYMAN, evangelist, minister, missionary, parson

preamble *noun* INTRODUCTION, foreword, opening statement or remarks, preface, prelude

precarious *adjective* DANGEROUS, hazardous, insecure, perilous, risky, shaky, tricky, unreliable, unsafe, unsure

precaution *noun* 1 SAFEGUARD, insurance, protection, provision, safety measure 2 FORETHOUGHT, care, caution, providence, prudence, wariness

precede *verb* GO BEFORE, antedate, come first, head, introduce, lead, preface

precedence *noun* PRIORITY, antecedence, pre-eminence, primacy, rank, seniority, superiority, supremacy

precedent *noun* INSTANCE, antecedent, example, model, paradigm, pattern, prototype, standard

preceding *adjective* PREVIOUS, above, aforementioned, aforesaid, earlier, foregoing, former, past, prior

precept *noun* RULE, canon, command, commandment, decree, instruction, law, order, principle, regulation, statute

precinct *noun* 1 ENCLOSURE, confine, limit 2 AREA, district, quarter, section, sector, zone

precious *adjective* 1 VALUABLE, costly, dear, expensive, fine, invaluable, priceless, prized 2 LOVED, adored, beloved, cherished, darling, dear, prized, treasured 3 AFFECTED, artificial, overnice, overrefined

precipice *noun* CLIFF, bluff, crag, height, rock face

precipitate *verb* 1 QUICKEN, accelerate, advance, bring on, expedite, hasten, hurry, speed up, trigger **2** THROW, cast, fling, hurl, launch, let fly ▶ *adjective* **3** HASTY, heedless, impetuous, impulsive, precipitous, rash, reckless **4** SWIFT, breakneck, headlong, rapid, rushing **5** SUDDEN, abrupt, brief, quick, unexpected, without warning

precipitous *adjective* **1** SHEER, abrupt, dizzy, high, perpendicular, steep **2** HASTY, heedless, hurried, precipitate, rash, reckless

précis *noun* **1** SUMMARY, abridgment, outline, résumé, synopsis ▶ *verb* **2** SUMMARIZE, abridge, outline, shorten, sum up

precise *adjective* **1** EXACT, absolute, accurate, correct, definite, explicit, express, particular, specific, strict **2** STRICT, careful, exact, fastidious, finicky, formal, meticulous, particular, punctilious, rigid, scrupulous, stiff

precisely *adverb* EXACTLY, absolutely, accurately, correctly, just so, plumb (*informal*), smack (*informal*), square, squarely, strictly

precision *noun* EXACTNESS, accuracy, care, meticulousness, particularity, preciseness

preclude *verb* PREVENT, check, debar, exclude, forestall, inhibit, obviate, prohibit, rule out, stop

precocious *adjective* ADVANCED, ahead, bright, developed, forward, quick, smart

preconceived *adjective* PRESUMED, forejudged, prejudged, presupposed

preconception *noun* PRECONCEIVED IDEA *or* NOTION, bias, notion, predisposition, prejudice, presupposition

precursor *noun* **1** HERALD, forerunner, harbinger, vanguard **2** FORERUNNER, antecedent, forebear, predecessor

predatory *adjective* HUNTING, carnivorous, predacious, raptorial

predecessor *noun* **1** PREVIOUS JOB HOLDER, antecedent, forerunner, precursor **2** ANCESTOR, antecedent, forebear, forefather

predestination *noun* FATE, destiny, foreordainment, foreordination, predetermination

predestined *adjective* FATED, doomed, meant, preordained

predetermined *adjective* PREARRANGED, agreed, fixed, preplanned, set

predicament *noun* FIX (*informal*), dilemma, jam (*informal*), mess, pinch, plight, quandary, scrape (*informal*), situation, spot (*informal*)

predict *verb* FORETELL, augur, divine, forecast, portend, prophesy

predictable *adjective* LIKELY, anticipated, certain, expected, foreseeable, reliable, sure

prediction *noun* PROPHECY, augury, divination, forecast, prognosis, prognostication

predilection *noun* LIKING, bias, fondness, inclination, leaning, love, partiality, penchant, preference, propensity, taste, weakness

predispose *verb* INCLINE, affect, bias, dispose, influence, lead, prejudice, prompt

predisposed *adjective* INCLINED, given, liable, minded, ready, subject, susceptible, willing

predominant *adjective* MAIN, ascendant, chief, dominant, leading, paramount, prevailing, prevalent, prime, principal

predominantly *adverb* MAINLY, chiefly, for the most part, generally, largely, mostly, primarily, principally

predominate *verb* PREVAIL, be most noticeable, carry weight, hold sway, outweigh, overrule, overshadow

pre-eminence *noun* SUPERIORITY, distinction, excellence, predominance, prestige, prominence, renown, supremacy

pre-eminent *adjective* OUTSTANDING, chief, distinguished, excellent, foremost, incomparable, matchless, predominant, renowned, superior, supreme

pre-empt *verb* ANTICIPATE, appropriate, assume, usurp

preen *verb* 1 *Of birds* CLEAN, plume 2 SMARTEN, dress up, spruce up, titivate 3 **preen oneself (on)** PRIDE ONESELF, congratulate oneself

preface *noun* 1 INTRODUCTION, foreword, preamble, preliminary, prelude, prologue ▶ *verb* 2 INTRODUCE, begin, open, prefix

prefer *verb* LIKE BETTER, be partial to, choose, desire, fancy, favor, go for, incline towards,

opt for, pick

preferable *adjective* BETTER, best, chosen, favored, more desirable, superior

preferably *adverb* RATHER, by choice, first, in *or* for preference, sooner

preference *noun* 1 FIRST CHOICE, choice, desire, favorite, option, partiality, pick, predilection, selection 2 PRIORITY, favored treatment, favoritism, first place, precedence

preferential *adjective* PRIVILEGED, advantageous, better, favored, special

preferment *noun* PROMOTION, advancement, elevation, exaltation, rise, upgrading

pregnant *adjective* 1 EXPECTANT, big *or* heavy with child, expecting (*informal*), with child 2 MEANINGFUL, charged, eloquent, expressive, loaded, pointed, significant, telling, weighty

prehistoric *adjective* EARLIEST, early, primeval, primitive, primordial

prejudge *verb* JUMP TO CONCLUSIONS, anticipate, presume, presuppose

prejudice *noun* 1 BIAS, partiality, preconceived notion, preconception, prejudgment 2 DISCRIMINATION, bigotry, chauvinism, injustice, intolerance, narrow-mindedness, unfairness ▶ *verb* 3 BIAS, color, distort, influence, poison, predispose, slant 4 HARM, damage, hinder, hurt, impair, injure, mar, spoil, undermine

prejudiced *adjective* BIASED,

bigoted, influenced, intolerant, narrow-minded, one-sided, opinionated, unfair

prejudicial *adjective* HARMFUL, damaging, deleterious, detrimental, disadvantageous, hurtful, injurious, unfavorable

preliminary *adjective* 1 FIRST, initial, introductory, opening, pilot, prefatory, preparatory, prior, test, trial ▶ *noun* 2 INTRODUCTION, beginning, opening, overture, preamble, preface, prelude, start

prelude *noun* INTRODUCTION, beginning, foreword, overture, preamble, preface, prologue, start

premature *adjective* 1 EARLY, forward, unseasonable, untimely 2 HASTY, ill-timed, overhasty, rash, too soon, untimely

premeditated *adjective* PLANNED, calculated, conscious, considered, deliberate, intentional, willful

premeditation *noun* PLANNING, design, forethought, intention, plotting, prearrangement, predetermination, purpose

premier *noun* 1 HEAD OF GOVERNMENT, chancellor, chief minister, chief officer, prime minister ▶ *adjective* 2 CHIEF, first, foremost, head, highest, leading, main, primary, prime, principal

premiere *noun* FIRST NIGHT, debut, opening

premise *noun* ASSUMPTION, argument, assertion, hypothesis, postulation, presupposition, proposition, supposition

premises *plural noun* BUILDING, establishment, place, property, site

premium *noun* 1 BONUS, bounty, fee, perk (*informal*), perquisite, prize, reward 2 **at a premium** IN GREAT DEMAND, hard to come by, in short supply, rare, scarce

premonition *noun* FEELING, foreboding, hunch, idea, intuition, presentiment, suspicion

preoccupation *noun* 1 OBSESSION, bee in one's bonnet, fixation 2 ABSORPTION, absent-mindedness, abstraction, daydreaming, engrossment, immersion, reverie, woolgathering

preoccupied *adjective* ABSORBED, absent-minded, distracted, engrossed, immersed, lost in, oblivious, rapt, wrapped up

preparation *noun* 1 GROUNDWORK, getting ready, preparing 2 (often plural) ARRANGEMENT, measure, plan, provision 3 MIXTURE, compound, concoction, medicine

preparatory *adjective* INTRODUCTORY, opening, prefatory, preliminary, primary

prepare *verb* MAKE or GET READY, adapt, adjust, arrange, practice, prime, train, warm up

prepared *adjective* 1 READY, arranged, in order, in readiness, primed, set 2 WILLING, disposed, inclined

preponderance *noun* PREDOMINANCE, dominance, domination, extensiveness, greater numbers, greater part, lion's share, mass, prevalence, supremacy

prepossessing *adjective*
ATTRACTIVE, appealing, charming, engaging, fetching, good-looking, handsome, likable *or* likeable, pleasing

preposterous *adjective*
RIDICULOUS, absurd, crazy, incredible, insane, laughable, ludicrous, nonsensical, out of the question, outrageous, unthinkable

prerequisite *noun*
1 REQUIREMENT, condition, essential, must, necessity, precondition, qualification, requisite, *sine qua non*
▶ *adjective* 2 REQUIRED, essential, indispensable, mandatory, necessary, obligatory, requisite, vital

prerogative *noun* RIGHT, advantage, due, exemption, immunity, liberty, privilege

presage *verb* PORTEND, augur, betoken, bode, foreshadow, foretoken, signify

prescience *noun* FORESIGHT, clairvoyance, foreknowledge, precognition, second sight

prescribe *verb* ORDER, decree, dictate, direct, lay down, ordain, recommend, rule, set, specify, stipulate

prescription *noun*
1 INSTRUCTION, direction, formula, recipe 2 MEDICINE, drug, mixture, preparation, remedy

presence *noun* 1 BEING, attendance, existence, inhabitance, occupancy, residence 2 PERSONALITY, air, appearance, aspect, aura,

bearing, carriage, demeanor, poise, self-assurance

presence of mind *noun*
LEVEL-HEADEDNESS, calmness, composure, cool (*slang*), coolness, self-possession, wits

present[1] *adjective* 1 HERE, at hand, near, nearby, ready, there 2 CURRENT, contemporary, existent, existing, immediate, present-day ▶ *noun* 3 **the present** NOW, here and now, the present moment, the time being, today 4 **at present** JUST NOW, at the moment, now, right now 5 **for the present** FOR NOW, for the moment, for the time being, in the meantime, temporarily

present[2] *noun* 1 GIFT, boon, donation, endowment, grant, gratuity, hand-out, offering ▶ *verb* 2 INTRODUCE, acquaint with, make known 3 PUT ON, display, exhibit, give, show, stage 4 GIVE, award, bestow, confer, grant, hand out, hand over

presentable *adjective* DECENT, acceptable, becoming, fit to be seen, O.K. *or* okay (*informal*), passable, respectable, satisfactory, suitable

presentation *noun* 1 GIVING, award, bestowal, conferral, donation, offering 2 PRODUCTION, demonstration, display, exhibition, performance, show

presently *adverb* SOON, anon (*archaic*), before long, by and by, shortly

preservation *noun* PROTECTION, conservation, maintenance, safeguarding, safekeeping, safety, salvation, support

preserve verb **1** SAVE, care for, conserve, defend, keep, protect, safeguard, shelter, shield **2** MAINTAIN, continue, keep, keep up, perpetuate, sustain, uphold ▶noun **3** AREA, domain, field, realm, sphere

preside verb RUN, administer, chair, conduct, control, direct, govern, head, lead, manage, officiate

press verb **1** FORCE DOWN, compress, crush, depress, jam, mash, push, squeeze **2** HUG, clasp, crush, embrace, fold in one's arms, hold close, squeeze **3** SMOOTH, flatten, iron **4** URGE, beg, entreat, exhort, implore, petition, plead, pressurize **5** CROWD, flock, gather, herd, push, seethe, surge, swarm, throng ▶noun **6 the press:** a NEWSPAPERS, Fleet Street, fourth estate, news media, the papers b JOURNALISTS, columnists, correspondents, newsmen, pressmen, reporters

pressing adjective URGENT, crucial, high-priority, imperative, important, importunate, serious, vital

pressure noun **1** FORCE, compressing, compression, crushing, squeezing, weight **2** POWER, coercion, compulsion, constraint, force, influence, sway **3** STRESS, burden, demands, hassle (informal), heat, load, strain, urgency

prestige noun STATUS, credit, distinction, eminence, fame, honor, importance, kudos, renown, reputation, standing

prestigious adjective CELEBRATED,

eminent, esteemed, great, illustrious, important, notable, prominent, renowned, respected

presumably adverb IT WOULD SEEM, apparently, in all likelihood, in all probability, on the face of it, probably, seemingly

presume verb **1** BELIEVE, assume, conjecture, guess (informal), infer, postulate, suppose, surmise, take for granted, think **2** DARE, go so far, make so bold, take the liberty, venture

presumption noun **1** CHEEK (informal), audacity, boldness, effrontery, gall (informal), impudence, insolence, nerve (informal) **2** PROBABILITY, basis, chance, likelihood

presumptuous adjective PUSHY (informal), audacious, bold, forward, insolent, overconfident, too big for one's boots

presuppose verb PRESUME, assume, imply, posit, postulate, take as read, take for granted

presupposition noun ASSUMPTION, belief, preconception, premise, presumption, supposition

pretend verb **1** FEIGN, affect, allege, assume, fake, falsify, impersonate, profess, sham, simulate **2** MAKE BELIEVE, act, imagine, make up, suppose

pretended adjective FEIGNED, bogus, counterfeit, fake, false, phoney or phony (informal), pretend (informal), pseudo (informal), sham, so-called

pretender noun CLAIMANT, aspirant

pretense noun **1** DECEPTION, acting, charade, deceit, falsehood, feigning, sham, simulation, trickery **2** SHOW, affectation, artifice, display, façade, veneer

pretension noun **1** CLAIM, aspiration, assumption, demand, pretense, profession **2** AFFECTATION, airs, conceit, ostentation, pretentiousness, self-importance, show, snobbery, vanity

pretentious adjective AFFECTED, conceited, grandiloquent, grandiose, high-flown, inflated, mannered, ostentatious, pompous, puffed up, showy, snobbish

pretext noun GUISE, cloak, cover, excuse, ploy, pretense, ruse, show

pretty adjective **1** ATTRACTIVE, beautiful, bonny, charming, comely, fair, good-looking, lovely ▶adverb **2** FAIRLY, kind of (informal), moderately, quite, rather, reasonably, somewhat

prevail verb **1** WIN, be victorious, overcome, overrule, succeed, triumph **2** BE WIDESPREAD, abound, be current, be prevalent, exist generally, predominate

prevailing adjective **1** WIDESPREAD, common, cool (informal), current, customary, established, fashionable, general, in vogue, ordinary, phat (slang), popular, prevalent, usual **2** PREDOMINATING, dominant, main, principal, ruling

prevalence noun COMMONNESS, currency, frequency, popularity, universality

prevalent adjective COMMON, current, customary, established, frequent, general, popular, universal, usual, widespread

prevaricate verb EVADE, beat about the bush, cavil, deceive, dodge, equivocate, hedge

prevent verb STOP, avert, avoid, foil, forestall, frustrate, hamper, hinder, impede, inhibit, obstruct, obviate, preclude, thwart

prevention noun ELIMINATION, avoidance, deterrence, precaution, safeguard, thwarting

preventive adjective **1** HINDERING, hampering, impeding, obstructive **2** PROTECTIVE, counteractive, deterrent, precautionary ▶noun **3** HINDRANCE, block, impediment, obstacle, obstruction **4** PROTECTION, deterrent, prevention, remedy, safeguard, shield

preview noun ADVANCE SHOWING, foretaste, sneak preview, taster, trailer

previous adjective EARLIER, erstwhile, foregoing, former, past, preceding, prior

previously adverb BEFORE, beforehand, earlier, formerly, hitherto, in the past, once

prey noun **1** QUARRY, game, kill **2** VICTIM, dupe, fall guy (informal), mug (Brit. slang), target

price noun **1** COST, amount, charge, damage (informal), estimate, expense, fee, figure, rate, value, worth

2 CONSEQUENCES, cost, penalty, toll ▶ *verb* **3** EVALUATE, assess, cost, estimate, rate, value

priceless *adjective* **1** VALUABLE, costly, dear, expensive, invaluable, precious **2** *Informal* HILARIOUS, amusing, comic, droll, funny, rib-tickling, side-splitting

pricey *adjective* EXPENSIVE, costly, dear, high-priced, steep (*informal*)

prick *verb* **1** PIERCE, jab, lance, perforate, punch, puncture, stab **2** STING, bite, itch, prickle, smart, tingle ▶ *noun* **3** PUNCTURE, hole, perforation, pinhole, wound

prickle *noun* **1** SPIKE, barb, needle, point, spine, spur, thorn ▶ *verb* **2** TINGLE, itch, smart, sting **3** PRICK, jab, stick

prickly *adjective* **1** SPINY, barbed, bristly, thorny **2** ITCHY, crawling, scratchy, sharp, smarting, stinging, tingling

pride *noun* **1** SATISFACTION, delight, gratification, joy, pleasure **2** SELF-RESPECT, dignity, honor, self-esteem, self-worth **3** CONCEIT, arrogance, egotism, hubris, pretension, pretentiousness, self-importance, self-love, superciliousness, vanity **4** GEM, jewel, pride and joy, treasure

priest *noun* CLERGYMAN, cleric, curate, divine, ecclesiastic, father, minister, pastor, vicar

prig *noun* GOODY-GOODY (*informal*), prude, puritan, stuffed shirt (*informal*)

priggish *adjective* SELF-RIGHTEOUS, goody-goody (*informal*), holier-than-thou, prim,

prudish, puritanical

prim *adjective* PRUDISH, demure, fastidious, fussy, priggish, prissy (*informal*), proper, puritanical, strait-laced

prima donna *noun* DIVA, leading lady, star

primarily *adverb* **1** CHIEFLY, above all, essentially, fundamentally, generally, largely, mainly, mostly, principally **2** AT FIRST, at or from the start, first and foremost, initially, in the beginning, in the first place, originally

primary *adjective* **1** CHIEF, cardinal, first, greatest, highest, main, paramount, prime, principal **2** ELEMENTARY, introductory, rudimentary, simple

prime *adjective* **1** MAIN, chief, leading, predominant, pre-eminent, primary, principal **2** BEST, choice, excellent, first-class, first-rate, highest, quality, select, top ▶ *noun* **3** PEAK, bloom, flower, height, heyday, zenith ▶ *verb* **4** INFORM, brief, clue in (*informal*), fill in (*informal*), notify, tell **5** PREPARE, coach, get ready, make ready, train

primeval *adjective* EARLIEST, ancient, early, first, old, prehistoric, primal, primitive, primordial

primitive *adjective* **1** EARLY, earliest, elementary, first, original, primary, primeval, primordial **2** CRUDE, rough, rudimentary, simple, unrefined

prince *noun* RULER, lord, monarch, sovereign

princely *adjective* **1** REGAL,

imperial, majestic, noble, royal, sovereign **2** GENEROUS, bounteous, gracious, lavish, liberal, munificent, open-handed, rich

principal *adjective* **1** MAIN, cardinal, chief, essential, first, foremost, key, leading, paramount, pre-eminent, primary, prime ▶ *noun* **2** HEAD (*informal*), dean, headmaster *or* headmistress, superintendent **3** STAR, lead, leader **4** CAPITAL, assets, money

principally *adverb* MAINLY, above all, chiefly, especially, largely, mostly, predominantly, primarily

principle *noun* **1** RULE, canon, criterion, doctrine, dogma, fundamental, law, maxim, precept, standard, truth **2** MORALS, conscience, integrity, probity, scruples, sense of honor **3 in principle** IN THEORY, ideally, theoretically

print *verb* **1** PUBLISH, engrave, impress, imprint, issue, mark, stamp ▶ *noun* **2** PUBLICATION, book, magazine, newspaper, newsprint, periodical, printed matter **3** REPRODUCTION, copy, engraving, photo (*informal*), photograph, picture

prior *adjective* **1** EARLIER, foregoing, former, preceding, pre-existent, pre-existing, previous **2 prior to** BEFORE, earlier than, preceding, previous

priority *noun* PRECEDENCE, pre-eminence, preference, rank, right of way, seniority

priory *noun* MONASTERY, abbey, convent, nunnery,

religious house

prison *noun* JAIL, clink (*slang*), confinement, cooler (*slang*), dungeon, lockup, penitentiary, slammer (*slang*)

prisoner *noun* **1** CONVICT, con (*slang*), jailbird, lag (*slang*) **2** CAPTIVE, detainee, hostage, internee

prissy *adjective* PRIM, old-maidish (*informal*), prim and proper, prudish, strait-laced

pristine *adjective* NEW, immaculate, pure, uncorrupted, undefiled, unspoiled, unsullied, untouched, virginal

privacy *noun* SECLUSION, isolation, retirement, retreat, solitude

private *adjective* **1** EXCLUSIVE, individual, intimate, own, personal, reserved, special **2** SECRET, clandestine, confidential, covert, hush-hush (*informal*), off the record, unofficial **3** SECLUDED, concealed, isolated, secret, separate, sequestered, solitary

privilege *noun* RIGHT, advantage, claim, concession, due, entitlement, freedom, liberty, prerogative

privileged *adjective* SPECIAL, advantaged, elite, entitled, favored, honored

privy *adjective* **1 privy to** INFORMED OF, apprised of, aware of, cognizant of, in on, in the know about (*informal*), wise to (*slang*) ▶ *noun* **2** LAVATORY, latrine, outside toilet

prize[1] *noun* **1** REWARD, accolade, award, honor, trophy **2** WINNINGS, haul, jackpot,

purse, stakes ▶ *adjective*
3 CHAMPION, award-winning, best, first-rate, outstanding, top, winning

prize[2] *verb* VALUE, cherish, esteem, hold dear, treasure

probability *noun* LIKELIHOOD, chance(s), expectation, liability, likeliness, odds, prospect

probable *adjective* LIKELY, apparent, credible, feasible, plausible, possible, presumable, reasonable

probably *adverb* LIKELY, doubtless, maybe, most likely, perchance (*archaic*), perhaps, possibly, presumably

probation *noun* TRIAL PERIOD, apprenticeship, trial

probe *verb* **1** EXAMINE, explore, go into, investigate, look into, scrutinize, search **2** EXPLORE, feel around, poke, prod ▶ *noun* **3** EXAMINATION, detection, exploration, inquiry, investigation, scrutiny, study

problem *noun* **1** DIFFICULTY, complication, dilemma, dispute, predicament, quandary, trouble **2** PUZZLE, conundrum, enigma, poser, question, riddle

problematic *adjective* TRICKY, debatable, doubtful, dubious, problematical, puzzling

procedure *noun* METHOD, action, conduct, course, custom, modus operandi, policy, practice, process, routine, strategy, system

proceed *verb* **1** GO ON, carry on, continue, go ahead, move on, press on, progress **2** ARISE, come, derive, emanate, flow, issue, originate, result,

spring, stem

proceeding *noun* **1** ACTION, act, deed, measure, move, procedure, process, step **2 proceedings** BUSINESS, account, affairs, archives, doings, minutes, records, report, transactions

proceeds *plural noun* INCOME, earnings, gain, products, profit, returns, revenue, takings, yield

process *noun* **1** PROCEDURE, action, course, manner, means, measure, method, operation, performance, practice, system **2** DEVELOPMENT, advance, evolution, growth, movement, progress, progression ▶ *verb* **3** HANDLE, deal with, fulfill

procession *noun* PARADE, cavalcade, cortege, file, march, train

proclaim *verb* DECLARE, advertise, announce, circulate, herald, indicate, make known, profess, publish

proclamation *noun* DECLARATION, announcement, decree, edict, notice, notification, pronouncement, publication

procrastinate *verb* DELAY, dally, drag one's feet (*informal*), gain time, play for time, postpone, put off, stall, temporize

procure *verb* OBTAIN, acquire, buy, come by, find, gain, get, pick up, purchase, score (*slang*), secure, win

prod *verb* **1** POKE, dig, drive, jab, nudge, push, shove **2** PROMPT, egg on, goad, impel, incite, motivate, move, rouse, spur, stimulate, urge ▶ *noun* **3** POKE, dig, jab, nudge, push, shove **4** PROMPT, cue, reminder, signal, stimulus

prodigal *adjective* 1 EXTRAVAGANT, excessive, immoderate, improvident, profligate, reckless, spendthrift, wasteful

prodigious *adjective* 1 HUGE, colossal, enormous, giant, gigantic, immense, massive, monstrous, vast 2 WONDERFUL, amazing, exceptional, extraordinary, fabulous, fantastic (*informal*), marvelous, phenomenal, remarkable, staggering

prodigy *noun* 1 GENIUS, mastermind, talent, whizz (*informal*), wizard 2 WONDER, marvel, miracle, phenomenon, sensation

produce *verb* 1 CAUSE, bring about, effect, generate, give rise to 2 BRING FORTH, bear, beget, breed, deliver 3 SHOW, advance, demonstrate, exhibit, offer, present 4 MAKE, compose, construct, create, develop, fabricate, invent, manufacture 5 PRESENT, direct, do, exhibit, mount, put on, show, stage
▶*noun* 6 FRUIT AND VEGETABLES, crop, greengrocery, harvest, product, yield

producer *noun* 1 DIRECTOR, impresario 2 MAKER, farmer, grower, manufacturer

product *noun* 1 GOODS, artefact, commodity, creation, invention, merchandise, produce, work 2 RESULT, consequence, effect, outcome, upshot

production *noun* 1 PRODUCING, construction, creation, fabrication, formation, making, manufacture, manufacturing 2 PRESENTATION, direction, management, staging

productive *adjective* 1 FERTILE, creative, fecund, fruitful, inventive, plentiful, prolific, rich 2 USEFUL, advantageous, beneficial, constructive, effective, profitable, rewarding, valuable, win-win (*informal*), worthwhile

productivity *noun* OUTPUT, production, work rate, yield

profane *adjective* 1 SACRILEGIOUS, disrespectful, godless, impious, impure, irreligious, irreverent, sinful, ungodly, wicked 2 CRUDE, blasphemous, coarse, filthy, foul, obscene, vulgar
▶*verb* 3 DESECRATE, commit sacrilege, debase, defile, violate

profanity *noun* 1 SACRILEGE, blasphemy, impiety, profaneness 2 SWEARING, curse, cursing, irreverence, obscenity

profess *verb* 1 CLAIM, allege, fake, feign, make out, pretend, purport 2 STATE, admit, affirm, announce, assert, avow, confess, declare, proclaim, vouch

professed *adjective* 1 SUPPOSED, alleged, ostensible, pretended, purported, self-styled, so-called, would-be 2 DECLARED, avowed, confessed, confirmed, proclaimed, self-acknowledged, self-confessed

profession *noun* 1 OCCUPATION, business, calling, career, employment, office, position, sphere, vocation 2 DECLARATION, affirmation, assertion, avowal, claim, confession, statement

professional *adjective* 1 EXPERT, adept, competent, efficient, experienced, masterly, proficient, qualified, skilled ▶ noun 2 EXPERT, adept, maestro, master, past master, pro (slang), specialist, virtuoso

professor noun TEACHER, don (Brit.), fellow (Brit.), prof (informal)

proficiency noun SKILL, ability, aptitude, competence, dexterity, expertise, knack, know-how (informal), mastery

proficient adjective SKILLED, able, accomplished, adept, capable, competent, efficient, expert, gifted, masterly, skillful

profile noun 1 OUTLINE, contour, drawing, figure, form, side view, silhouette, sketch 2 BIOGRAPHY, characterization, sketch, thumbnail sketch, vignette

profit noun 1 (often plural) EARNINGS, gain, proceeds, receipts, return, revenue, takings, yield 2 BENEFIT, advancement, advantage, gain, good, use, value ▶ verb 3 BENEFIT, be of advantage to, gain, help, improve, promote, serve 4 MAKE MONEY, earn, gain

profitable adjective 1 MONEY-MAKING, commercial, cost-effective, fruitful, lucrative, paying, remunerative, worthwhile 2 BENEFICIAL, advantageous, fruitful, productive, rewarding, useful, valuable, win-win (informal), worthwhile

profiteer noun 1 RACKETEER, exploiter ▶ verb 2 RACKETEER, exploit, make a quick buck (slang)

profligate adjective

1 EXTRAVAGANT, immoderate, improvident, prodigal, reckless, spendthrift, wasteful 2 DEPRAVED, debauched, degenerate, dissolute, immoral, licentious, shameless, wanton, wicked, wild ▶ noun 3 SPENDTHRIFT, squanderer, waster, wastrel 4 DEGENERATE, debauchee, libertine, rake, reprobate, roué

profound adjective 1 WISE, abstruse, deep, learned, penetrating, philosophical, sagacious, sage 2 INTENSE, acute, deeply felt, extreme, great, heartfelt, keen

profuse adjective PLENTIFUL, abundant, ample, bountiful, copious, luxuriant, overflowing, prolific

profusion noun ABUNDANCE, bounty, excess, extravagance, glut, plethora, quantity, surplus, wealth

progeny noun CHILDREN, descendants, family, issue, lineage, offspring, posterity, race, stock, young

prognosis noun FORECAST, diagnosis, prediction, prognostication, projection

program noun 1 SCHEDULE, agenda, curriculum, line-up, list, listing, order of events, plan, syllabus, timetable 2 SHOW, broadcast, performance, presentation, production

progress noun 1 DEVELOPMENT, advance, breakthrough, gain, growth, headway, improvement 2 MOVEMENT, advance, course, passage, way 3 in progress GOING ON, being done, happening, occurring, proceeding, taking place, under way ▶ *verb* **4** DEVELOP, advance, gain, grow, improve **5** MOVE ON, advance, continue, go forward, make headway, proceed, travel

progression *noun* **1** PROGRESS, advance, advancement, furtherance, gain, headway, movement forward **2** SEQUENCE, chain, course, cycle, series, string, succession

progressive *adjective* **1** ENLIGHTENED, advanced, avant-garde, forward-looking, liberal, modern, radical, reformist, revolutionary **2** GROWING, advancing, continuing, developing, increasing, ongoing

prohibit *verb* **1** FORBID, ban, debar, disallow, outlaw, proscribe, veto **2** PREVENT, hamper, hinder, impede, restrict, stop

prohibition *noun* **1** PREVENTION, constraint, exclusion, obstruction, restriction **2** BAN, bar, boycott, embargo, injunction, interdict, proscription, veto

prohibitive *adjective* EXORBITANT, excessive, extortionate, steep (*informal*)

project *noun* **1** SCHEME, activity, assignment, enterprise, job, occupation, plan, task, undertaking, venture, work ▶ *verb* **2** FORECAST, calculate, estimate, extrapolate, gauge, predict, reckon **3** STICK OUT, bulge, extend, jut, overhang, protrude, stand out

projectile *noun* MISSILE, bullet,

rocket, shell

projection *noun* **1** PROTRUSION, bulge, ledge, overhang, protuberance, ridge, shelf **2** FORECAST, calculation, computation, estimate, estimation, extrapolation, reckoning

proletarian *adjective* **1** WORKING-CLASS, common, plebeian ▶ *noun* **2** WORKER, commoner, man of the people, pleb, plebeian

proletariat *noun* WORKING CLASS, commoners, hoi polloi, laboring classes, lower classes, plebs, the common people, the masses

proliferate *verb* INCREASE, breed, expand, grow rapidly, multiply

proliferation *noun* MULTIPLICATION, expansion, increase, spread

prolific *adjective* PRODUCTIVE, abundant, copious, fecund, fertile, fruitful, luxuriant, profuse

prologue *noun* INTRODUCTION, foreword, preamble, preface, preliminary, prelude

prolong *verb* LENGTHEN, continue, delay, drag out, draw out, extend, perpetuate, protract, spin out, stretch

promenade *noun* **1** WALKWAY, esplanade, parade, prom **2** STROLL, constitutional, saunter, turn, walk ▶ *verb* **3** STROLL, perambulate, saunter, take a walk, walk

prominence *noun* **1** CONSPICUOUSNESS, markedness **2** FAME, celebrity, distinction, eminence, importance, name, prestige, reputation

prominent *adjective*

1 NOTICEABLE, conspicuous, eye-catching, obtrusive, obvious, outstanding, pronounced **2** FAMOUS, distinguished, eminent, foremost, important, leading, main, notable, renowned, top, well-known

promiscuity noun LICENTIOUSNESS, debauchery, immorality, looseness, permissiveness, promiscuousness, wantonness

promiscuous adjective LICENTIOUS, abandoned, debauched, fast, immoral, libertine, loose, wanton, wild

promise verb **1** GUARANTEE, assure, contract, give an undertaking, give one's word, pledge, swear, take an oath, undertake, vow, warrant **2** SEEM LIKELY, augur, betoken, indicate, look like, show signs of, suggest ▶ noun **3** GUARANTEE, assurance, bond, commitment, oath, pledge, undertaking, vow, word **4** POTENTIAL, ability, aptitude, capability, capacity, flair, talent

promising adjective **1** ENCOURAGING, auspicious, bright, favorable, hopeful, likely, propitious, reassuring, rosy **2** TALENTED, able, gifted, rising

promontory noun POINT, cape, foreland, head, headland

promote verb **1** HELP, advance, aid, assist, back, boost, encourage, forward, foster, support **2** RAISE, elevate, exalt, upgrade **3** ADVERTISE, hype, plug (informal), publicize, push, sell

promotion noun **1** RISE, advancement, elevation,

exaltation, honor, move up, preferment, upgrading **2** PUBLICITY, advertising, plugging (informal) **3** ENCOURAGEMENT, advancement, boosting, furtherance, support

prompt verb **1** CAUSE, elicit, give rise to, occasion, provoke **2** REMIND, assist, cue, help out ▶ adjective **3** IMMEDIATE, early, instant, quick, rapid, speedy, swift, timely ▶ adverb **4** Informal EXACTLY, on the dot, promptly, punctually, sharp

promptly adverb IMMEDIATELY, at once, directly, on the dot, on time, punctually, quickly, speedily, swiftly

promptness noun SWIFTNESS, briskness, eagerness, haste, punctuality, quickness, speed, willingness

promulgate verb MAKE KNOWN, broadcast, circulate, communicate, disseminate, make public, proclaim, promote, publish, spread

prone adjective **1** LIABLE, apt, bent, disposed, given, inclined, likely, predisposed, subject, susceptible, tending **2** FACE DOWN, flat, horizontal, prostrate, recumbent

prong noun POINT, spike, tine

pronounce verb **1** SAY, accent, articulate, enunciate, sound, speak **2** DECLARE, affirm, announce, decree, deliver, proclaim

pronounced adjective NOTICEABLE, conspicuous, decided, definite, distinct, evident, marked, obvious, striking

pronouncement noun
ANNOUNCEMENT, declaration,
decree, dictum, edict,
judgment, proclamation,
statement

pronunciation noun INTONATION,
accent, articulation, diction,
enunciation, inflection, speech,
stress

proof noun 1 EVIDENCE,
authentication, confirmation,
corroboration, demonstration,
substantiation, testimony,
verification ▶ adjective
2 IMPERVIOUS, impenetrable,
repellent, resistant, strong

prop verb 1 SUPPORT, bolster,
brace, buttress, hold up, stay,
sustain, uphold ▶ noun
2 SUPPORT, brace, buttress,
mainstay, stanchion, stay

propaganda noun INFORMATION,
advertising, disinformation,
hype, promotion, publicity

propagate verb 1 SPREAD,
broadcast, circulate,
disseminate, promote,
promulgate, publish, transmit
2 REPRODUCE, beget, breed,
engender, generate, increase,
multiply, procreate, produce

propel verb DRIVE, force, impel,
launch, push, send, shoot,
shove, thrust

propensity noun TENDENCY,
bent, disposition, inclination,
liability, penchant,
predisposition, proclivity

proper adjective 1 SUITABLE,
appropriate, apt, becoming,
befitting, fit, fitting, right
2 CORRECT, accepted,
conventional, established,
formal, orthodox, precise, right
3 POLITE, decent, decorous,

genteel, gentlemanly, ladylike,
mannerly, respectable, seemly

properly adverb 1 SUITABLY,
appropriately, aptly, fittingly,
rightly 2 CORRECTLY, accurately
3 POLITELY, decently, respectably

property noun 1 POSSESSIONS,
assets, belongings, capital,
effects, estate, goods, holdings,
riches, wealth 2 LAND, estate,
freehold, holding, real estate
3 QUALITY, attribute,
characteristic, feature,
hallmark, trait

prophecy noun PREDICTION,
augury, divination, forecast,
prognostication, second sight,
soothsaying

prophesy verb PREDICT, augur,
divine, forecast, foresee,
foretell, prognosticate

prophet noun SOOTHSAYER,
diviner, forecaster, oracle,
prophesier, seer, sibyl

prophetic adjective PREDICTIVE,
oracular, prescient, prognostic,
sibylline

propitious adjective FAVORABLE,
auspicious, bright,
encouraging, fortunate, happy,
lucky, promising

proportion noun 1 RELATIVE
AMOUNT, ratio, relationship
2 BALANCE, congruity,
correspondence, harmony,
symmetry 3 PART, amount,
division, fraction, percentage,
quota, segment, share
4 **proportions** DIMENSIONS,
capacity, expanse, extent, size,
volume

proportional, proportionate
adjective BALANCED,
commensurate, compatible,
consistent, corresponding,

equitable, even, in proportion

proposal *noun* SUGGESTION, bid, offer, plan, presentation, program, project, recommendation, scheme

propose *verb* 1 PUT FORWARD, advance, present, submit, suggest 2 NOMINATE, name, present, recommend 3 INTEND, aim, design, have in mind, mean, plan, scheme 4 OFFER MARRIAGE, ask for someone's hand (in marriage), pop the question (*informal*)

proposition *noun* 1 PROPOSAL, plan, recommendation, scheme, suggestion ▶*verb* 2 MAKE A PASS AT, accost, make an improper suggestion, solicit

propound *verb* PUT FORWARD, advance, postulate, present, propose, submit, suggest

proprietor, proprietress *noun* OWNER, landlord *or* landlady, titleholder

propriety *noun* 1 CORRECTNESS, aptness, fitness, rightness, seemliness 2 DECORUM, courtesy, decency, etiquette, manners, politeness, respectability, seemliness

propulsion *noun* DRIVE, impetus, impulse, propelling force, push, thrust

prosaic *adjective* DULL, boring, everyday, humdrum, matter-of-fact, mundane, ordinary, pedestrian, routine, trite, unimaginative

proscribe *verb* 1 PROHIBIT, ban, embargo, forbid, interdict 2 OUTLAW, banish, deport, exclude, exile, expatriate, expel, ostracize

prosecute *verb* Law PUT ON TRIAL, arraign, bring to trial, indict, litigate, sue, take to court, try

prospect *noun* 1 EXPECTATION, anticipation, future, hope, odds, outlook, probability, promise 2 (sometimes plural) LIKELIHOOD, chance, possibility 3 VIEW, landscape, outlook, scene, sight, spectacle, vista ▶*verb* 4 LOOK FOR, search for, seek

prospective *adjective* FUTURE, anticipated, coming, destined, expected, forthcoming, imminent, intended, likely, possible, potential

prospectus *noun* CATALOG, list, outline, program, syllabus, synopsis

prosper *verb* SUCCEED, advance, do well, flourish, get on, progress, thrive

prosperity *noun* SUCCESS, affluence, fortune, good fortune, luxury, plenty, prosperousness, riches, wealth

prosperous *adjective* 1 WEALTHY, affluent, moneyed, rich, well-heeled (*informal*), well-off, well-to-do 2 SUCCESSFUL, booming, doing well, flourishing, fortunate, lucky, thriving

prostitute *noun* 1 WHORE, call girl, fallen woman, harlot, ho (*slang*), hooker (*slang*), loose woman, streetwalker, strumpet, tart (*informal*), trollop ▶*verb* 2 CHEAPEN, debase, degrade, demean, devalue, misapply, pervert, profane

prostrate *adjective* 1 PRONE, flat, horizontal 2 EXHAUSTED, dejected, depressed, desolate,

drained, inconsolable,
overcome, spent, worn out
▶ *verb* **3** EXHAUST, drain, fatigue,
sap, tire, wear out, weary
4 prostrate oneself BOW DOWN
TO, abase oneself, fall at
(someone's) feet, grovel, kiss
ass (*slang*), kneel, kowtow

protagonist *noun* **1** SUPPORTER,
advocate, champion, exponent
2 LEADING CHARACTER, central
character, hero *or* heroine,
principal

protect *verb* KEEP SAFE, defend,
guard, look after, preserve,
safeguard, save, screen, shelter,
shield, stick up for (*informal*),
support, watch over

protection *noun* **1** SAFETY, aegis,
care, custody, defense,
protecting, safeguard,
safekeeping, security
2 SAFEGUARD, barrier, buffer,
cover, guard, screen, shelter,
shield

protective *adjective* PROTECTING,
defensive, fatherly, maternal,
motherly, paternal, vigilant,
watchful

protector *noun* DEFENDER,
bodyguard, champion, guard,
guardian, patron

protest *noun* **1** OBJECTION,
complaint, dissent, outcry,
protestation, remonstrance
▶ *verb* **2** OBJECT, complain, cry
out, demonstrate, demur,
disagree, disapprove, express
disapproval, oppose,
remonstrate **3** ASSERT, affirm,
attest, avow, declare, insist,
maintain, profess

protestation *noun* DECLARATION,
affirmation, avowal, profession,
vow

protester *noun* DEMONSTRATOR,
agitator, rebel

protocol *noun* CODE OF BEHAVIOR,
conventions, customs,
decorum, etiquette, manners,
propriety

prototype *noun* ORIGINAL,
example, first, model, pattern,
standard, type

protracted *adjective* EXTENDED,
dragged out, drawn-out,
long-drawn-out, prolonged,
spun out

protrude *verb* STICK OUT, bulge,
come through, extend, jut,
obtrude, project, stand out

protrusion *noun* PROJECTION,
bulge, bump, lump,
outgrowth, protuberance

protuberance *noun* BULGE,
bump, excrescence, hump,
knob, lump, outgrowth,
process, prominence,
protrusion, swelling

proud *adjective* **1** SATISFIED,
content, glad, gratified,
pleased, well-pleased
2 CONCEITED, arrogant, boastful,
disdainful, haughty, imperious,
lordly, overbearing,
self-satisfied, snobbish,
supercilious

prove *verb* **1** VERIFY,
authenticate, confirm,
demonstrate, determine,
establish, justify, show,
substantiate **2** TEST, analyze,
assay, check, examine, try
3 TURN OUT, come out, end up,
result

proven *adjective* ESTABLISHED,
attested, confirmed, definite,
proved, reliable, tested, verified

proverb *noun* SAYING, adage,
dictum, maxim, saw

proverbial *adjective*
CONVENTIONAL, acknowledged, axiomatic, current, famed, famous, legendary, notorious, traditional, typical, well-known

provide *verb* 1 SUPPLY, cater, equip, furnish, outfit, purvey, stock up 2 GIVE, add, afford, bring, impart, lend, present, produce, render, serve, yield 3 **provide for** or **against** TAKE PRECAUTIONS, anticipate, forearm, plan ahead, plan for, prepare for 4 **provide for** SUPPORT, care for, keep, maintain, sustain, take care of

providence *noun* FATE, destiny, fortune

provident *adjective* 1 THRIFTY, economical, frugal, prudent 2 FORESIGHTED, careful, cautious, discreet, far-seeing, forearmed, shrewd, vigilant, well-prepared, wise

providential *adjective* LUCKY, fortuitous, fortunate, happy, heaven-sent, opportune, timely

provider *noun* 1 SUPPLIER, donor, giver, source 2 BREADWINNER, earner, supporter, wage earner

providing, provided *conjunction* ON CONDITION THAT, as long as, given

province *noun* 1 REGION, colony, department, district, division, domain, patch, section, zone 2 AREA, business, capacity, concern, duty, field, function, line, responsibility, role, sphere

provincial *adjective* 1 RURAL, country, hick (*informal*), homespun, local, rustic 2 NARROW-MINDED, insular, inward-looking, limited, narrow, parochial,

small-minded, small-town, unsophisticated ▶*noun* 3 YOKEL, country cousin, hayseed (*informal*), hick (*informal*), rustic

provision *noun* 1 SUPPLYING, catering, equipping, furnishing, providing 2 CONDITION, clause, demand, proviso, requirement, rider, stipulation, term

provisional *adjective* 1 TEMPORARY, interim 2 CONDITIONAL, contingent, limited, qualified, tentative

provisions *plural noun* FOOD, comestibles, eatables, edibles, fare, foodstuff, rations, stores, supplies, victuals

proviso *noun* CONDITION, clause, qualification, requirement, rider, stipulation

provocation *noun* 1 CAUSE, grounds, incitement, motivation, reason, stimulus 2 OFFENSE, affront, annoyance, challenge, dare, grievance, indignity, injury, insult, taunt

provocative *adjective* OFFENSIVE, annoying, galling, goading, insulting, provoking, stimulating

provoke *verb* 1 ANGER, aggravate (*informal*), annoy, enrage, hassle (*informal*), incense, infuriate, irk, irritate, madden, rile 2 CAUSE, bring about, elicit, evoke, incite, induce, occasion, produce, promote, prompt, rouse, stir

prowess *noun* 1 SKILL, accomplishment, adeptness, aptitude, excellence, expertise, genius, mastery, talent 2 BRAVERY, courage, daring, fearlessness, heroism, mettle, valiance, valor

prowl *verb* MOVE STEALTHILY, skulk,

slink, sneak, stalk, steal

proximity *noun* NEARNESS, closeness

proxy *noun* REPRESENTATIVE, agent, delegate, deputy, factor, substitute

prudence *noun* COMMON SENSE, care, caution, discretion, good sense, judgment, vigilance, wariness, wisdom

prudent *adjective* 1 SENSIBLE, careful, cautious, discerning, discreet, judicious, politic, shrewd, vigilant, wary, wise 2 THRIFTY, canny, careful, economical, far-sighted, frugal, provident, sparing

prudish *adjective* PRIM, old-maidish (*informal*), overmodest, priggish, prissy (*informal*), proper, puritanical, starchy (*informal*), strait-laced, stuffy, Victorian

prune *verb* CUT, clip, dock, reduce, shape, shorten, snip, trim

pry *verb* BE INQUISITIVE, be nosy (*informal*), interfere, intrude, meddle, poke, snoop (*informal*)

prying *adjective* INQUISITIVE, curious, interfering, meddlesome, meddling, nosy (*informal*), snooping (*informal*), spying

psalm *noun* HYMN, chant

pseudo- *adjective* FALSE, artificial, fake, imitation, mock, phoney or phony (*informal*), pretended, sham, spurious

pseudonym *noun* FALSE NAME, alias, assumed name, incognito, nom de plume, pen name

psyche *noun* SOUL, anima, individuality, mind, personality, self, spirit

psychiatrist *noun* PSYCHOTHERAPIST, analyst, headshrinker (*slang*), psychoanalyst, psychologist, shrink (*slang*), therapist

psychic *adjective* 1 SUPERNATURAL, mystic, occult 2 MENTAL, psychological, spiritual

psychological *adjective* 1 MENTAL, cerebral, intellectual 2 IMAGINARY, all in the mind, irrational, psychosomatic, unreal

psychology *noun* 1 BEHAVIORISM, science of mind, study of personality 2 WAY OF THINKING, attitude, mental make-up, mental processes, thought processes, what makes one tick

psychopath *noun* MADMAN, headcase (*informal*), lunatic, maniac, nutcase (*slang*), psychotic, sociopath

psychotic *adjective* MAD, certifiable, demented, deranged, insane, loony (*informal*), lunatic, non compos mentis, unbalanced

puberty *noun* ADOLESCENCE, pubescence, teens

public *adjective* 1 GENERAL, civic, common, national, popular, social, state, universal, widespread 2 COMMUNAL, accessible, open, unrestricted 3 WELL-KNOWN, important, prominent, respected 4 PLAIN, acknowledged, known, obvious, open, overt, patent ▶ *noun* 5 PEOPLE, citizens, community, electorate, everyone, nation, populace, society

publication *noun* 1 PAMPHLET, brochure, issue, leaflet,

magazine, newspaper, periodical, title
2 ANNOUNCEMENT, broadcasting, declaration, disclosure, notification, proclamation, publishing, reporting

publicity noun ADVERTISING, attention, boost, hype, plug (*informal*), press, promotion

publicize verb ADVERTISE, hype, make known, play up, plug (*informal*), promote, push

public-spirited adjective ALTRUISTIC, charitable, humanitarian, philanthropic, unselfish

publish verb 1 PUT OUT, issue, print, produce 2 ANNOUNCE, advertise, broadcast, circulate, disclose, divulge, proclaim, publicize, reveal, spread

pucker verb 1 WRINKLE, contract, crease, draw together, gather, knit, purse, screw up, tighten ▶ noun 2 WRINKLE, crease, fold

puerile adjective CHILDISH, babyish, foolish, immature, juvenile, silly, trivial

puff noun 1 BLAST, breath, draft, gust, whiff 2 SMOKE, drag (*slang*), pull ▶ verb 3 BLOW, breathe, exhale, gasp, gulp, pant, wheeze 4 SMOKE, drag (*slang*), draw, inhale, pull at or on, suck 5 (usually with *up*) SWELL, bloat, dilate, distend, expand, inflate

puffy adjective SWOLLEN, bloated, distended, enlarged, puffed up

pugilist noun BOXER, fighter, prizefighter

pugnacious adjective AGGRESSIVE, belligerent, combative, hot-tempered, quarrelsome

pull verb 1 DRAW, drag, haul,

jerk, tow, trail, tug, yank
2 STRAIN, dislocate, rip, sprain, stretch, tear, wrench 3 EXTRACT, draw out, gather, pick, pluck, remove, take out, uproot ▶ noun 4 TUG, jerk, twitch, yank
5 PUFF, drag (*slang*), inhalation
6 Informal INFLUENCE, clout (*informal*), muscle, power, weight

pull down verb DEMOLISH, bulldoze, destroy, raze, remove

pull off verb SUCCEED, accomplish, carry out, do the trick, manage

pull out verb WITHDRAW, depart, evacuate, leave, quit, retreat

pull through verb SURVIVE, get better, rally, recover

pulp noun 1 PASTE, mash, mush
2 FLESH, soft part ▶ verb 3 CRUSH, mash, pulverize, squash ▶ adjective 4 CHEAP, lurid, rubbishy, trashy

pulsate verb THROB, beat, palpitate, pound, pulse, quiver, thump

pulse noun 1 BEAT, beating, pulsation, rhythm, throb, throbbing, vibration ▶ verb
2 BEAT, pulsate, throb, vibrate

pulverize verb 1 CRUSH, granulate, grind, mill, pound
2 DEFEAT, annihilate, crush, demolish, destroy, flatten, smash, wreck

pummel verb BEAT, batter, hammer, pound, punch, strike, thump

pump verb 1 (often with *into*) DRIVE, force, inject, pour, push, send, supply 2 INTERROGATE, cross-examine, probe, quiz

pun noun PLAY ON WORDS, double entendre, quip, witticism

punch[1] *verb* **1** HIT, belt (*informal*), bop (*informal*), box, pummel, smash, sock (*slang*), strike ▶ *noun* **2** BLOW, bop (*informal*), hit, jab, sock (*slang*), wallop (*informal*) **3** *Informal* EFFECTIVENESS, bite, drive, forcefulness, impact, verve, vigor

punch[2] *verb* PIERCE, bore, cut, drill, perforate, prick, puncture, stamp

punctilious *adjective* PARTICULAR, exact, finicky, formal, fussy, meticulous, nice, precise, proper, strict

punctual *adjective* ON TIME, exact, on the dot, precise, prompt, timely

punctuality *noun* PROMPTNESS, promptitude, readiness

punctuate *verb* **1** INTERRUPT, break, intersperse, pepper, sprinkle **2** EMPHASIZE, accentuate, stress, underline

puncture *noun* **1** HOLE, break, cut, damage, leak, nick, opening, slit **2** FLAT TIRE, flat ▶ *verb* **3** PIERCE, bore, cut, nick, penetrate, perforate, prick, rupture

pungent *adjective* STRONG, acrid, bitter, hot, peppery, piquant, sharp, sour, spicy, tart

punish *verb* DISCIPLINE, castigate, chasten, chastise, correct, penalize, sentence

punishable *adjective* CULPABLE, blameworthy, criminal, indictable

punishing *adjective* HARD, arduous, backbreaking, exhausting, grueling, strenuous, taxing, tiring, wearing

punishment *noun* PENALTY, chastening, chastisement, correction, discipline, penance, retribution

punitive *adjective* RETALIATORY, in reprisal, retaliative

punt *verb* **1** BET, back, gamble, lay, stake, wager ▶ *noun* **2** BET, gamble, stake, wager

puny *adjective* FEEBLE, frail, little, sickly, stunted, tiny, weak

pupil *noun* LEARNER, beginner, disciple, novice, schoolboy *or* schoolgirl, student

puppet *noun* **1** MARIONETTE, doll, ventriloquist's dummy **2** PAWN, cat's-paw, instrument, mouthpiece, stooge, tool

purchase *verb* **1** BUY, acquire, come by, gain, get, obtain, pay for, pick up, score (*slang*) ▶ *noun* **2** BUY, acquisition, asset, gain, investment, possession, property **3** GRIP, foothold, hold, leverage, support

pure *adjective* **1** UNMIXED, authentic, flawless, genuine, natural, neat, real, simple, straight, unalloyed **2** CLEAN, germ-free, sanitary, spotless, squeaky-clean, sterilized, uncontaminated, unpolluted, untainted, wholesome **3** INNOCENT, blameless, chaste, impeccable, modest, uncorrupted, unsullied, virginal, virtuous **4** COMPLETE, absolute, outright, sheer, thorough, unmitigated, unqualified, utter

purely *adverb* ABSOLUTELY, completely, entirely, exclusively, just, merely, only, simply, solely, wholly

purge *verb* **1** GET RID OF, do

away with, eradicate, expel, exterminate, remove, wipe out ▶*noun* **2** REMOVAL, ejection, elimination, eradication, expulsion

purify *verb* **1** CLEAN, clarify, cleanse, decontaminate, disinfect, refine, sanitize, wash **2** ABSOLVE, cleanse, redeem, sanctify

purist *noun* STICKLER, formalist, pedant

puritan *noun* **1** MORALIST, fanatic, prude, rigorist, zealot ▶*adjective* **2** STRICT, ascetic, austere, moralistic, narrow-minded, prudish, severe, strait-laced

puritanical *adjective* STRICT, ascetic, austere, narrow-minded, proper, prudish, puritan, severe, strait-laced

purity *noun* **1** CLEANNESS, cleanliness, faultlessness, immaculateness, pureness, wholesomeness **2** INNOCENCE, chasteness, chastity, decency, honesty, integrity, virginity, virtue, virtuousness

purloin *verb* STEAL, appropriate, filch, pilfer, pinch (*informal*), swipe (*slang*), thieve

purport *verb* **1** CLAIM, allege, assert, profess ▶*noun* **2** SIGNIFICANCE, drift, gist, idea, implication, import, meaning

purpose *noun* **1** REASON, aim, idea, intention, object, point **2** AIM, ambition, desire, end, goal, hope, intention, object, plan, wish **3** DETERMINATION, firmness, persistence, resolution, resolve, single-mindedness, tenacity,

will **4 on purpose** DELIBERATELY, designedly, intentionally, knowingly, purposely

purposeless *adjective* POINTLESS, aimless, empty, motiveless, needless, senseless, uncalled-for, unnecessary

purposely *adverb* DELIBERATELY, consciously, expressly, intentionally, knowingly, on purpose, with intent

purse *noun* **1** POUCH, money-bag, wallet **2** MONEY, exchequer, funds, means, resources, treasury, wealth ▶*verb* **3** PUCKER, contract, pout, press together, tighten

pursue *verb* **1** FOLLOW, chase, dog, hound, hunt, hunt down, run after, shadow, stalk, tail (*informal*), track **2** TRY FOR, aim for, desire, seek, strive for, work towards **3** ENGAGE IN, carry on, conduct, perform, practice **4** CONTINUE, carry on, keep on, maintain, persevere in, persist, proceed

pursuit *noun* **1** PURSUING, chase, hunt, quest, search, seeking, trailing **2** OCCUPATION, activity, hobby, interest, line, pastime, pleasure

purvey *verb* SUPPLY, cater, deal in, furnish, provide, sell, trade in

push *verb* **1** SHOVE, depress, drive, press, propel, ram, thrust **2** MAKE or FORCE ONE'S WAY, elbow, jostle, move, shoulder, shove, squeeze, thrust **3** URGE, encourage, hurry, impel, incite, persuade, press, spur ▶*noun* **4** SHOVE, butt, nudge, thrust **5** DRIVE, ambition, dynamism, energy, enterprise, go (*informal*), initiative, vigor, vitality

pushed *adjective* (often with *for*) SHORT OF, hurried, pressed, rushed, under pressure

pushover *noun* 1 PIECE OF CAKE (*informal*), breeze (*informal*), child's play (*informal*), cinch (*slang*), picnic (*informal*), plain sailing, walkover (*informal*) 2 SUCKER (*slang*), easy game (*informal*), easy *or* soft mark (*informal*), mug (*Brit. slang*), walkover (*informal*)

pushy *adjective* FORCEFUL, ambitious, assertive, bold, brash, bumptious, obtrusive, presumptuous, self-assertive

pussyfoot *verb* HEDGE, beat about the bush, be noncommittal, equivocate, hum and haw, prevaricate, sit on the fence

put *verb* 1 PLACE, deposit, lay, position, rest, set, settle, situate 2 EXPRESS, phrase, state, utter, word 3 THROW, cast, fling, heave, hurl, lob, pitch, toss

put across *or* **over** *verb* COMMUNICATE, convey, explain, get across, make clear, make oneself understood

put aside *or* **by** *verb* SAVE, deposit, lay by, stockpile, store

put away *verb* 1 SAVE, deposit, keep, put by 2 COMMIT, certify, institutionalize, lock up 3 CONSUME, devour, eat up, gobble, wolf down 4 PUT BACK, replace, tidy away

put down *verb* 1 RECORD, enter, set down, take down, write down 2 STAMP OUT, crush, quash, quell, repress, suppress 3 (usually with *to*) ATTRIBUTE,

ascribe, impute, set down 4 PUT TO SLEEP, destroy, do away with, put out of its misery 5 *Slang* HUMILIATE, disparage, mortify, shame, slight, snub

put forward *verb* RECOMMEND, advance, nominate, propose, submit, suggest, tender

put off *verb* 1 POSTPONE, defer, delay, hold over, put on the back burner (*informal*), take a rain check on (*informal*) 2 DISCONCERT, confuse, discomfit, dismay, faze, nonplus, perturb, throw (*informal*), unsettle 3 DISCOURAGE, dishearten, dissuade

put on *verb* 1 DON, change into, dress, get dressed in, slip into 2 FAKE, affect, assume, feign, pretend, sham, simulate 3 PRESENT, do, mount, produce, show, stage 4 ADD, gain, increase by

put out *verb* 1 ANNOY, anger, exasperate, irk, irritate, nettle, vex 2 EXTINGUISH, blow out, douse, quench 3 INCONVENIENCE, bother, discomfit, discommode, impose upon, incommode, trouble

putrid *adjective* ROTTEN, bad, decayed, decomposed, putrefied, rancid, rotting, spoiled

putter *verb* MESS AROUND, dabble, dawdle, monkey around (*informal*), tinker

put up *verb* 1 ERECT, build, construct, fabricate, raise 2 ACCOMMODATE, board, house, lodge, take in 3 RECOMMEND, nominate, offer, present,

propose, put forward, submit
4 put up with STAND, abide,
bear, endure, stand for,
swallow, take, tolerate

puzzle *verb* **1** PERPLEX, baffle,
bewilder, confound, confuse,
mystify, stump ▶ *noun*
2 PROBLEM, conundrum,
enigma, mystery, paradox,
poser, question, riddle

puzzled *adjective* PERPLEXED, at a
loss, at sea, baffled,
bewildered, confused, lost,
mystified

puzzlement *noun* PERPLEXITY,
bafflement, bewilderment,
confusion, doubt, mystification

puzzling *adjective* PERPLEXING,
abstruse, baffling, bewildering,
enigmatic, incomprehensible,
involved, mystifying

Q q

quack *noun* CHARLATAN, fake,
fraud, humbug, impostor,
mountebank, phoney *or* phony
(*informal*), pretender

quaff *verb* DRINK, down, gulp,
imbibe, swallow, swig (*informal*)

quagmire *noun* BOG, fen,
marsh, mire, morass,
quicksand, slough, swamp

quail *verb* SHRINK, blanch,
blench, cower, cringe, falter,
flinch, have cold feet
(*informal*), recoil, shudder

quaint *adjective* **1** UNUSUAL,
bizarre, curious, droll,
eccentric, fanciful, odd,
old-fashioned, peculiar, queer,
singular, strange

2 OLD-FASHIONED, antiquated,
old-world, picturesque

quake *verb* SHAKE, move, quiver,
rock, shiver, shudder, tremble,
vibrate

qualification *noun* **1** ATTRIBUTE,
ability, aptitude, capability,
eligibility, fitness, quality, skill,
suitability **2** CONDITION, caveat,
limitation, modification,
proviso, requirement,
reservation, rider, stipulation

qualified *adjective* **1** CAPABLE,
able, adept, competent,
efficient, experienced, expert,
fit, practiced, proficient, skillful,
trained **2** RESTRICTED, bounded,
conditional, confined,
contingent, limited, modified,
provisional, reserved

qualify *verb* **1** CERTIFY, empower,
equip, fit, permit, prepare,
ready, train **2** MODERATE,
diminish, ease, lessen, limit,
reduce, regulate, restrain,
restrict, soften, temper

quality *noun* **1** EXCELLENCE,
caliber, distinction, grade,
merit, position, rank, standing,
status **2** CHARACTERISTIC, aspect,
attribute, condition, feature,
mark, property, trait **3** NATURE,
character, kind, make, sort

qualm *noun* MISGIVING, anxiety,
apprehension, compunction,
disquiet, doubt, hesitation,
scruple, twinge *or* pang of
conscience, uneasiness

quandary *noun* DIFFICULTY,
Catch-22, dilemma, impasse,
plight, predicament, puzzle,
strait

quantity *noun* **1** AMOUNT, lot,
number, part, sum, total **2** SIZE,
bulk, capacity, extent, length,

magnitude, mass, measure, volume

quarrel noun 1 DISAGREEMENT, argument, brawl, breach, contention, controversy, dispute, dissension, feud, fight, row, squabble, tiff ▶ verb 2 DISAGREE, argue, bicker, brawl, clash, differ, dispute, fall out (informal), fight, row, squabble

quarrelsome adjective ARGUMENTATIVE, belligerent, combative, contentious, disputatious, pugnacious

quarry noun PREY, aim, game, goal, objective, prize, victim

quarter noun 1 DISTRICT, area, locality, neighborhood, part, place, province, region, side, zone 2 MERCY, clemency, compassion, forgiveness, leniency, pity ▶ verb 3 ACCOMMODATE, billet, board, house, lodge, place, post, station

quarters plural noun LODGINGS, abode, barracks, billet, chambers, dwelling, habitation, residence, rooms

quash verb 1 ANNUL, cancel, invalidate, overrule, overthrow, rescind, reverse, revoke 2 SUPPRESS, beat, crush, overthrow, put down, quell, repress, squash, subdue

quasi- adjective PSEUDO-, apparent, seeming, semi-, so-called, would-be

quaver verb 1 TREMBLE, flicker, flutter, quake, quiver, shake, vibrate, waver ▶ noun 2 TREMBLING, quiver, shake, tremble, tremor, vibration

queasy adjective 1 SICK, bilious, green around the gills

(informal), ill, nauseated, off color, squeamish, upset 2 UNEASY, anxious, fidgety, ill at ease, restless, troubled, uncertain, worried

queen noun 1 SOVEREIGN, consort, monarch, ruler 2 IDEAL, mistress, model, star

queer adjective 1 STRANGE, abnormal, curious, droll, extraordinary, funny, odd, peculiar, uncommon, unusual, weird 2 FAINT, dizzy, giddy, light-headed, queasy

quell verb 1 SUPPRESS, conquer, crush, defeat, overcome, overpower, put down, quash, subdue, vanquish 2 ASSUAGE, allay, appease, calm, mollify, pacify, quiet, soothe

quench verb 1 SATISFY, allay, appease, sate, satiate, slake 2 PUT OUT, crush, douse, extinguish, smother, stifle, suppress

querulous adjective COMPLAINING, captious, carping, critical, discontented, dissatisfied, fault-finding, grumbling, peevish, whining

query noun 1 QUESTION, doubt, inquiry, objection, problem, suspicion ▶ verb 2 DOUBT, challenge, disbelieve, dispute, distrust, mistrust, suspect 3 ASK, inquire or enquire, question

quest noun SEARCH, adventure, crusade, enterprise, expedition, hunt, journey, mission

question noun 1 ISSUE, motion, point, point at issue, proposal, proposition, subject, theme, topic 2 DIFFICULTY, argument, contention, controversy,

dispute, doubt, problem, query
3 in question UNDER DISCUSSION,
at issue, in doubt, open to
debate **4 out of the question**
IMPOSSIBLE, inconceivable,
unthinkable ▶ verb **5** ASK,
cross-examine, examine,
inquire, interrogate, interview,
probe, quiz **6** DISPUTE,
challenge, disbelieve, doubt,
mistrust, oppose, query, suspect

questionable adjective DUBIOUS,
controversial, debatable,
doubtful, iffy (informal), moot,
suspect, suspicious

queue noun LINE, chain, file,
sequence, series, string, train

quibble verb **1** SPLIT HAIRS, carp,
cavil ▶ noun **2** OBJECTION, cavil,
complaint, criticism, nicety,
niggle

quick adjective **1** FAST, brisk,
express, fleet, hasty, rapid,
speedy, swift **2** BRIEF, cursory,
hasty, hurried, perfunctory
3 SUDDEN, prompt **4** INTELLIGENT,
acute, alert, astute, bright
(informal), clever, perceptive,
quick-witted, sharp, shrewd,
smart **5** DEFT, adept, adroit,
dexterous, skillful **6** EXCITABLE,
irascible, irritable, passionate,
testy, touchy

quicken verb **1** SPEED, accelerate,
expedite, hasten, hurry, impel,
precipitate **2** INVIGORATE, arouse,
energize, excite, incite, inspire,
revive, stimulate, vitalize

quickly adverb SWIFTLY, abruptly,
apace, briskly, fast, hastily,
hurriedly, promptly, pronto
(informal), rapidly, soon,
speedily

quick-tempered adjective
HOT-TEMPERED, choleric, fiery,

irascible, irritable, quarrelsome,
testy

quick-witted adjective CLEVER,
alert, astute, bright (informal),
keen, perceptive, sharp,
shrewd, smart

quiet adjective **1** SILENT, hushed,
inaudible, low, noiseless,
peaceful, soft, soundless
2 CALM, mild, peaceful, placid,
restful, serene, smooth,
tranquil **3** UNDISTURBED, isolated,
private, secluded, sequestered,
unfrequented **4** RESERVED,
gentle, meek, mild, retiring,
sedate, shy ▶ noun **5** PEACE,
calmness, ease, quietness,
repose, rest, serenity, silence,
stillness, tranquillity

quieten verb **1** SILENCE,
compose, hush, muffle, mute,
quell, quiet, stifle, still, stop,
subdue **2** SOOTHE, allay,
appease, blunt, calm, deaden,
dull

quietly adverb **1** SILENTLY, in an
undertone, inaudibly, in
silence, mutely, noiselessly,
softly **2** CALMLY, mildly,
patiently, placidly, serenely

quietness noun PEACE, calm,
hush, quiet, silence, stillness,
tranquillity

quilt noun BEDSPREAD, continental
quilt, counterpane, coverlet,
duvet, eiderdown

quintessence noun ESSENCE,
distillation, soul, spirit

quintessential adjective
ULTIMATE, archetypal, definitive,
prototypical, typical

quip noun JOKE, gibe, jest,
pleasantry, retort, riposte, sally,
wisecrack (informal), witticism

quirk noun PECULIARITY,

aberration, characteristic, eccentricity, foible, habit, idiosyncrasy, kink, mannerism, oddity, trait

quirky *adjective* ODD, eccentric, idiosyncratic, offbeat, peculiar, unusual

quit *verb* 1 STOP, abandon, cease, discontinue, drop, end, give up, halt 2 RESIGN, abdicate, go, leave, pull out, retire, step down (*informal*) 3 DEPART, go, leave, pull out

quite *adverb* 1 SOMEWHAT, fairly, moderately, rather, reasonably, relatively 2 ABSOLUTELY, completely, entirely, fully, perfectly, totally, wholly 3 TRULY, in fact, in reality, in truth, really

quiver *verb* 1 SHAKE, oscillate, quake, quaver, shiver, shudder, tremble, vibrate ▶*noun* 2 SHAKE, oscillation, shiver, shudder, tremble, tremor, vibration

quixotic *adjective* UNREALISTIC, dreamy, fanciful, idealistic, impractical, romantic

quiz *noun* 1 EXAMINATION, investigation, questioning, test ▶*verb* 2 QUESTION, ask, examine, interrogate, investigate

quizzical *adjective* MOCKING, arch, questioning, sardonic, teasing

quota *noun* SHARE, allowance, assignment, part, portion, ration, slice

quotation *noun* 1 PASSAGE, citation, excerpt, extract, quote (*informal*), reference 2 *Commerce* ESTIMATE, charge, cost, figure, price, quote (*informal*), rate, tender

quote *verb* REPEAT, cite, detail, instance, name, recall, recite, recollect, refer to

—— **R r** ——

rabble *noun* MOB, canaille, crowd, herd, horde, swarm, throng

rabid *adjective* 1 FANATICAL, extreme, fervent, irrational, narrow-minded, zealous 2 MAD, hydrophobic

race[1] *noun* 1 CONTEST, chase, competition, dash, pursuit, rivalry ▶*verb* 2 RUN, career, compete, contest, dart, dash, fly, gallop, hurry, speed, tear, zoom

race[2] *noun* PEOPLE, blood, folk, nation, stock, tribe, type

racial *adjective* ETHNIC, ethnological, folk, genealogical, genetic, national, tribal

rack *noun* 1 FRAME, framework, stand, structure ▶*verb* 2 TORTURE, afflict, agonize, crucify, harrow, oppress, pain, torment

racket *noun* 1 NOISE, clamor, din, disturbance, fuss, outcry, pandemonium, row 2 FRAUD, scheme

racy *adjective* 1 RISQUÉ, bawdy, blue, naughty, smutty, suggestive 2 LIVELY, animated, energetic, entertaining, exciting, sparkling, spirited

radiance *noun* 1 HAPPINESS, delight, gaiety, joy, pleasure, rapture, warmth 2 BRIGHTNESS, brilliance, glare, gleam, glow, light, luster, shine

radiant *adjective* 1 HAPPY, blissful, delighted, ecstatic, glowing, joyful, joyous, on cloud nine (*informal*), rapturous 2 BRIGHT, brilliant, gleaming, glittering, glowing, luminous, lustrous, shining

radiate *verb* 1 SPREAD OUT, branch out, diverge, issue 2 EMIT, diffuse, give off *or* out, pour, scatter, send out, shed, spread

radical *adjective* 1 FUNDAMENTAL, basic, deep-seated, innate, natural, profound 2 EXTREME, complete, drastic, entire, extremist, fanatical, severe, sweeping, thorough ▸ *noun* 3 EXTREMIST, fanatic, militant, revolutionary

raffle *noun* DRAW, lottery, sweep, sweepstake

ragamuffin *noun* URCHIN, guttersnipe

rage *noun* 1 FURY, anger, frenzy, ire, madness, passion, rampage, wrath 2 *As in* **all the rage** CRAZE, enthusiasm, fad (*informal*), fashion, latest thing, trend, vogue ▸ *verb* 3 BE FURIOUS, blow one's top, blow up (*informal*), fly off the handle (*informal*), fume, go ballistic (*slang*), go up the wall (*slang*), see red, seethe, storm, wig out (*slang*)

ragged *adjective* 1 TATTERED, in rags, in tatters, shabby, tatty, threadbare, torn, unkempt 2 ROUGH, jagged, rugged, serrated, uneven, unfinished

raging *adjective* FURIOUS, beside oneself, enraged, fuming, incensed, infuriated, mad, raving, seething

rags *plural noun* TATTERS, castoffs, old clothes, tattered clothing

raid *noun* 1 ATTACK, foray, incursion, inroad, invasion, sally, sortie ▸ *verb* 2 ATTACK, assault, foray, invade, pillage, plunder, sack

raider *noun* ATTACKER, invader, marauder, plunderer, robber, thief

railing *noun* FENCE, balustrade, barrier, paling, rails

rain *noun* 1 RAINFALL, cloudburst, deluge, downpour, drizzle, fall, raindrops, showers, torrent ▸ *verb* 2 POUR, bucket down (*informal*), come down in buckets (*informal*), drizzle, pelt (down), rain cats and dogs, teem 3 FALL, deposit, drop, shower, sprinkle

rainy *adjective* WET, damp, drizzly, showery

raise *verb* 1 LIFT, build, elevate, erect, heave, hoist, rear, uplift 2 INCREASE, advance, amplify, boost, enhance, enlarge, heighten, inflate, intensify, magnify, strengthen 3 COLLECT, assemble, form, gather, mass, obtain, rally, recruit 4 CAUSE, create, engender, occasion, originate, produce, provoke, start 5 BRING UP, develop, nurture, rear 6 SUGGEST, advance, broach, introduce, moot, put forward

rake[1] *verb* 1 GATHER, collect, remove 2 SEARCH, comb, scour, scrutinize

rake[2] *noun* LIBERTINE, debauchee, lecher, playboy, roué

rakish *adjective* DASHING, dapper, debonair, devil-may-care, jaunty, raffish

rally noun 1 GATHERING, assembly, congress, convention, meeting 2 RECOVERY, improvement, recuperation, revival ▸ verb 3 REASSEMBLE, regroup, reorganize, unite 4 GATHER, assemble, collect, convene, marshal, muster, round up, unite 5 RECOVER, get better, improve, recuperate, revive

ram verb 1 HIT, butt, crash, dash, drive, force, impact, smash 2 CRAM, crowd, force, jam, stuff, thrust

ramble verb 1 WALK, range, roam, rove, saunter, stray, stroll, wander 2 BABBLE ▸ noun 3 WALK, hike, roaming, roving, saunter, stroll, tour

rambler noun WALKER, hiker, rover, wanderer, wayfarer

rambling adjective LONG-WINDED, circuitous, digressive, disconnected, discursive, disjointed, incoherent, wordy

ramification noun **ramifications** CONSEQUENCES, developments, results, sequel, upshot

ramp noun SLOPE, gradient, incline, rise

rampage verb 1 GO BERSERK, rage, run amok, run riot, storm ▸ noun 2 **on the rampage** BERSERK, amok, out of control, raging, riotous, violent, wild

rampant adjective 1 WIDESPREAD, prevalent, profuse, rife, spreading like wildfire, unchecked, uncontrolled, unrestrained 2 *Heraldry* UPRIGHT, erect, rearing, standing

rampart noun DEFENSE, bastion, bulwark, fence, fortification, wall

ramshackle adjective RICKETY, crumbling, decrepit, derelict, flimsy, shaky, tumbledown, unsafe, unsteady

rancid adjective ROTTEN, bad, fetid, foul, putrid, rank, sour, stale, strong-smelling, tainted

rancor noun HATRED, animosity, bad blood, bitterness, hate, ill feeling, ill will

random adjective 1 CHANCE, accidental, adventitious, casual, fortuitous, haphazard, hit or miss, incidental ▸ noun 2 **at random** HAPHAZARDLY, arbitrarily, by chance, randomly, unsystematically, willy-nilly

range noun 1 LIMITS, area, bounds, orbit, province, radius, reach, scope, sphere 2 SERIES, assortment, collection, gamut, lot, selection, variety ▸ verb 3 VARY, extend, reach, run, stretch 4 ROAM, ramble, rove, traverse, wander

rangy adjective LONG-LIMBED, gangling, lanky, leggy, long-legged

rank[1] noun 1 STATUS, caste, class, degree, division, grade, level, order, position, sort, type 2 ROW, column, file, group, line, range, series, tier ▸ verb 3 ARRANGE, align, array, dispose, line up, order, sort

rank[2] adjective 1 ABSOLUTE, arrant, blatant, complete, downright, flagrant, gross, sheer, thorough, total, utter 2 FOUL, bad, disgusting, funky (*slang*), noisome, noxious, offensive, rancid, revolting, smelly, stinking 3 ABUNDANT, dense, lush, luxuriant, profuse

rank and file noun GENERAL

PUBLIC, majority, mass, masses

rankle verb ANNOY, anger, gall, get on one's nerves (informal), irk, irritate, rile

ransack verb 1 SEARCH, comb, explore, go through, rummage, scour, turn inside out 2 PLUNDER, loot, pillage, raid, strip

ransom noun PAYMENT, money, payoff, price

rant verb SHOUT, cry, declaim, rave, roar, yell

rap verb 1 HIT, crack, knock, strike, tap ▶ noun 2 BLOW, clout (informal), crack, knock, tap 3 Slang PUNISHMENT, blame, responsibility

rapacious adjective GREEDY, avaricious, grasping, insatiable, predatory, preying, voracious

rape verb 1 SEXUALLY ASSAULT, abuse, force, outrage, ravish, violate ▶ noun 2 SEXUAL ASSAULT, outrage, ravishment, violation 3 DESECRATION, abuse, defilement, violation

rapid adjective QUICK, brisk, express, fast, hasty, hurried, prompt, speedy, swift

rapidity noun SPEED, alacrity, briskness, fleetness, haste, hurry, promptness, quickness, rush, swiftness, velocity

rapidly adverb QUICKLY, briskly, fast, hastily, hurriedly, in haste, promptly, pronto (informal), speedily, swiftly

rapport noun BOND, affinity, empathy, harmony, link, relationship, sympathy, tie, understanding

rapprochement noun RECONCILIATION, detente, reunion

rapt adjective SPELLBOUND,

absorbed, engrossed, enthralled, entranced, fascinated, gripped

rapture noun ECSTASY, bliss, delight, euphoria, joy, rhapsody, seventh heaven, transport

rapturous adjective ECSTATIC, blissful, euphoric, in seventh heaven, joyful, overjoyed, over the moon (informal), transported

rare adjective 1 UNCOMMON, few, infrequent, scarce, singular, sparse, strange, unusual 2 SUPERB, choice, excellent, fine, great, peerless, superlative

rarefied adjective EXALTED, elevated, high, lofty, noble, spiritual, sublime

rarely adverb SELDOM, hardly, hardly ever, infrequently

raring adjective As in **raring to** EAGER, desperate, enthusiastic, impatient, keen, longing, ready

rarity noun 1 CURIO, collector's item, find, gem, treasure 2 UNCOMMONNESS, infrequency, scarcity, shortage, sparseness, strangeness, unusualness

rascal noun ROGUE, devil, good-for-nothing, imp, scamp, scoundrel, villain

rash[1] adjective RECKLESS, careless, foolhardy, hasty, heedless, ill-advised, impetuous, imprudent, impulsive, incautious

rash[2] noun 1 OUTBREAK, eruption 2 SPATE, flood, outbreak, plague, series, wave

rashness noun RECKLESSNESS, carelessness, foolhardiness, hastiness, heedlessness, indiscretion, thoughtlessness

rate noun **1** SPEED, pace, tempo, velocity **2** DEGREE, proportion, ratio, scale, standard **3** CHARGE, cost, fee, figure, price **4 at any rate** IN ANY CASE, anyhow, anyway, at all events ▸ verb **5** EVALUATE, consider, count, estimate, grade, measure, rank, reckon, value **6** DESERVE, be entitled to, be worthy of, merit

rather adverb **1** TO SOME EXTENT, a little, fairly, moderately, quite, relatively, somewhat, to some degree **2** PREFERABLY, more readily, more willingly, sooner

ratify verb APPROVE, affirm, authorize, confirm, endorse, establish, sanction, uphold

rating noun POSITION, class, degree, grade, order, placing, rank, rate, status

ratio noun PROPORTION, fraction, percentage, rate, relation

ration noun **1** ALLOWANCE, allotment, helping, measure, part, portion, quota, share ▸ verb **2** LIMIT, budget, control, restrict

rational adjective SANE, intelligent, logical, lucid, realistic, reasonable, sensible, sound, wise

rationale noun REASON, grounds, logic, motivation, philosophy, principle, raison d'être, theory

rationalize verb JUSTIFY, account for, excuse, vindicate

rattle verb **1** CLATTER, bang, jangle **2** SHAKE, bounce, jar, jolt, vibrate **3** Informal FLUSTER, disconcert, disturb, faze, perturb, shake, upset

raucous adjective HARSH, grating, hoarse, loud, noisy, rough, strident

raunchy adjective Slang SEXY, coarse, earthy, lusty, sexual, steamy (informal)

ravage verb **1** DESTROY, demolish, despoil, devastate, lay waste, ransack, ruin, spoil ▸ noun **2 ravages** DAMAGE, destruction, devastation, havoc, ruin, ruination, spoliation

rave verb **1** RANT, babble, be delirious, go mad (informal), rage, roar **2** ENTHUSE, be excited about (informal), be wild about (informal), gush, praise

ravenous adjective STARVING, famished, starved

ravine noun CANYON, defile, gorge, gulch, gully, pass

raving adjective MAD, crazed, crazy, delirious, hysterical, insane, irrational, wild

ravish verb **1** ENCHANT, captivate, charm, delight, enrapture, entrance, fascinate, spellbind **2** RAPE, abuse, force, sexually assault, violate

ravishing adjective ENCHANTING, beautiful, bewitching, charming, entrancing, gorgeous, lovely

raw adjective **1** UNCOOKED, fresh, natural **2** UNREFINED, basic, coarse, crude, natural, rough, unfinished, unprocessed **3** INEXPERIENCED, callow, green, immature, new **4** CHILLY, biting, bitter, cold, freezing, piercing

ray noun BEAM, bar, flash, gleam, shaft

raze verb DESTROY, demolish, flatten, knock down, level, pull down, ruin

re preposition CONCERNING, about, apropos, regarding, with reference to, with regard to

reach verb 1 ARRIVE AT, attain, get to, make 2 TOUCH, contact, extend to, grasp, stretch to 3 CONTACT, communicate with, get hold of, get in touch with, get through to ▸noun 4 RANGE, capacity, distance, extension, extent, grasp, influence, power, scope, stretch

react verb 1 RESPOND, answer, reply 2 ACT, behave, function, operate, proceed, work

reaction noun 1 RESPONSE, answer, reply 2 RECOIL, counteraction 3 CONSERVATISM, the right

reactionary adjective 1 CONSERVATIVE, right-wing ▸noun 2 CONSERVATIVE, die-hard, right-winger

read verb 1 LOOK AT, peruse, pore over, scan, study 2 INTERPRET, comprehend, construe, decipher, discover, see, understand 3 REGISTER, display, indicate, record, show

readable adjective 1 ENJOYABLE, entertaining, enthralling, gripping, interesting 2 LEGIBLE, clear, comprehensible, decipherable

readily adverb 1 WILLINGLY, eagerly, freely, gladly, promptly, quickly 2 EASILY, effortlessly, quickly, smoothly, speedily, unhesitatingly

readiness noun 1 WILLINGNESS, eagerness, keenness 2 EASE, adroitness, dexterity, facility, promptness

reading noun 1 PERUSAL, examination, inspection, scrutiny, study 2 RECITAL, lesson, performance, sermon

3 INTERPRETATION, grasp, impression, version 4 LEARNING, education, erudition, knowledge, scholarship

ready adjective 1 PREPARED, arranged, fit, organized, primed, ripe, set 2 WILLING, agreeable, disposed, eager, glad, happy, inclined, keen, prone 3 PROMPT, alert, bright, clever, intelligent, keen, perceptive, quick, sharp, smart 4 AVAILABLE, accessible, convenient, handy, near, present

real adjective GENUINE, actual, authentic, factual, rightful, sincere, true, unfeigned, valid

realistic adjective 1 PRACTICAL, common-sense, down-to-earth, level-headed, matter-of-fact, real, sensible 2 LIFELIKE, authentic, faithful, genuine, natural, true, true to life

reality noun TRUTH, actuality, fact, realism, validity, verity

realization noun 1 AWARENESS, cognizance, comprehension, conception, grasp, perception, recognition, understanding 2 ACHIEVEMENT, accomplishment, fulfillment

realize verb 1 BECOME AWARE OF, comprehend, get the message, grasp, take in, understand 2 ACHIEVE, accomplish, carry out or through, complete, do, effect, fulfill, perform

really adverb TRULY, actually, certainly, genuinely, in actuality, indeed, in fact, positively, surely

realm noun 1 KINGDOM, country, domain, dominion, empire, land 2 SPHERE, area, branch, department, field, province, territory, world

reap verb 1 COLLECT, bring in, cut, garner, gather, harvest 2 OBTAIN, acquire, derive, gain, get

rear[1] noun 1 BACK, end, rearguard, stern, tail, tail end ▶ adjective 2 BACK, following, hind, last

rear[2] verb 1 BRING UP, breed, educate, foster, nurture, raise, train 2 RISE, loom, soar, tower

reason noun 1 CAUSE, aim, goal, grounds, incentive, intention, motive, object, purpose 2 SENSE(S), intellect, judgment, logic, mind, rationality, sanity, soundness, understanding ▶ verb 3 DEDUCE, conclude, infer, make out, think, work out 4 **reason with** PERSUADE, bring round (informal), prevail upon, talk into or out of, urge, win over

reasonable adjective 1 SENSIBLE, logical, plausible, practical, sane, sober, sound, tenable, wise 2 MODERATE, equitable, fair, fit, just, modest, O.K. or okay (informal), proper, right

reasoned adjective SENSIBLE, clear, logical, well-thought-out

reasoning noun THINKING, analysis, logic, thought

reassure verb ENCOURAGE, comfort, hearten, put or set one's mind at rest, restore confidence to

rebate noun REFUND, allowance, bonus, deduction, discount, reduction

rebel verb 1 REVOLT, mutiny, resist, rise up 2 DEFY, disobey, dissent ▶ noun 3 REVOLUTIONARY, insurgent, revolutionist, secessionist 4 NONCONFORMIST, apostate, dissenter, heretic, schismatic ▶ adjective 5 REBELLIOUS, insurgent, insurrectionary, revolutionary

rebellion noun 1 RESISTANCE, mutiny, revolt, revolution, rising, uprising 2 NONCONFORMITY, defiance, heresy, schism

rebellious adjective 1 REVOLUTIONARY, disloyal, disobedient, disorderly, insurgent, mutinous, rebel, seditious, unruly 2 DEFIANT, difficult, refractory, resistant, unmanageable

rebound verb 1 BOUNCE, recoil, ricochet 2 MISFIRE, backfire, boomerang, recoil

rebuff verb 1 REJECT, cold-shoulder, cut, knock back (slang), refuse, repulse, slight, snub, spurn, turn down ▶ noun 2 REJECTION, cold shoulder, kick in the teeth (slang), knock-back (slang), refusal, repulse, slap in the face (informal), slight, snub

rebuke verb 1 SCOLD, admonish, castigate, censure, chide, reprimand, reprove, tell off (informal) ▶ noun 2 SCOLDING, admonition, censure, reprimand, row, telling-off (informal)

rebut verb DISPROVE, confute, invalidate, negate, overturn, prove wrong, refute

rebuttal noun DISPROOF, confutation, invalidation, negation, refutation

recalcitrant adjective DISOBEDIENT, defiant, insubordinate, refractory, unmanageable, unruly, wayward, willful

recall verb 1 RECOLLECT, bring or call to mind, evoke, remember 2 ANNUL, cancel, countermand, repeal, retract, revoke, withdraw ▶noun 3 RECOLLECTION, memory, remembrance 4 ANNULMENT, cancellation, repeal, rescindment, retraction, withdrawal

recant verb WITHDRAW, disclaim, forswear, renege, repudiate, retract, revoke, take back

recapitulate verb REPEAT, outline, recap (informal), recount, restate, summarize

recede verb FALL BACK, abate, ebb, regress, retire, retreat, return, subside, withdraw

receipt noun 1 SALES SLIP, counterfoil, proof of purchase 2 RECEIVING, acceptance, delivery, reception

receive verb 1 GET, accept, acquire, be given, collect, obtain, pick up, take 2 EXPERIENCE, bear, encounter, suffer, sustain, undergo 3 GREET, accommodate, admit, entertain, meet, welcome

recent adjective NEW, current, fresh, late, modern, novel, present-day, up-to-date

recently adverb NEWLY, currently, freshly, lately, latterly, not long ago, of late

receptacle noun CONTAINER, holder, repository

reception noun 1 PARTY, function, levee, soirée 2 WELCOME, acknowledgment, greeting, reaction, response, treatment

receptive adjective OPEN,

amenable, interested, open-minded, open to suggestions, susceptible, sympathetic

recess noun 1 ALCOVE, bay, corner, hollow, niche, nook 2 BREAK, holiday, intermission, interval, respite, rest, vacation

recession noun DEPRESSION, decline, drop, slump

recipe noun 1 DIRECTIONS, ingredients, instructions 2 METHOD, formula, prescription, procedure, process, technique

reciprocal adjective MUTUAL, alternate, complementary, correlative, corresponding, equivalent, exchanged, interchangeable

reciprocate verb RETURN, exchange, reply, requite, respond, swap, trade

recital noun 1 PERFORMANCE, rehearsal, rendering 2 RECITATION, account, narrative, reading, relation, statement, telling

recitation noun RECITAL, lecture, passage, performance, piece, reading

recite verb REPEAT, declaim, deliver, narrate, perform, speak

reckless adjective CARELESS, hasty, headlong, heedless, imprudent, mindless, precipitate, rash, thoughtless, wild

reckon verb 1 THINK, assume, believe, guess (informal), imagine, suppose 2 CONSIDER, account, count, deem, esteem, judge, rate, regard 3 COUNT, add up, calculate, compute, figure, number, tally, total

reckoning noun 1 COUNT, addition, calculation, estimate 2 BILL, account, charge, due, score

reclaim verb REGAIN, recapture, recover, redeem, reform, retrieve, salvage

recline verb LEAN, lie (down), loll, lounge, repose, rest, sprawl

recluse noun HERMIT, anchoress, anchorite, monk, solitary

reclusive adjective SOLITARY, hermit-like, isolated, retiring, withdrawn

recognition noun 1 IDENTIFICATION, discovery, recollection, remembrance 2 ACCEPTANCE, admission, allowance, confession 3 APPRECIATION, notice, respect

recognize verb 1 IDENTIFY, know, notice, place, recall, recollect, remember, spot 2 ACCEPT, acknowledge, admit, allow, concede, grant 3 APPRECIATE, notice, respect

recoil verb 1 JERK BACK, kick, react, rebound, spring back 2 DRAW BACK, falter, quail, shrink 3 BACKFIRE, boomerang, misfire, rebound ▶ noun 4 REACTION, backlash, kick, rebound, repercussion

recollect verb REMEMBER, place, recall, summon up

recollection noun MEMORY, impression, recall, remembrance, reminiscence

recommend verb 1 ADVISE, advance, advocate, counsel, prescribe, propose, put forward, suggest 2 PRAISE, approve, commend, endorse

recommendation noun 1 ADVICE, counsel, proposal, suggestion 2 PRAISE, advocacy, approval, commendation, endorsement, reference, sanction, testimonial

recompense verb 1 REWARD, pay, remunerate 2 COMPENSATE, make up for, pay for, redress, reimburse, repay, requite ▶ noun 3 COMPENSATION, amends, damages, payment, remuneration, reparation, repayment, requital, restitution 4 REWARD, payment, return, wages

reconcile verb 1 RESOLVE, adjust, compose, put to rights, rectify, settle, square 2 REUNITE, appease, conciliate, make peace between, propitiate 3 ACCEPT, put up with (informal), resign oneself, submit, yield

reconciliation noun REUNION, conciliation, pacification, reconcilement

recondite adjective OBSCURE, arcane, concealed, dark, deep, difficult, hidden, mysterious, occult, profound, secret

recondition verb RESTORE, do up (informal), overhaul, remodel, renew, renovate, repair, revamp

reconnaissance noun INSPECTION, exploration, investigation, observation, scan, survey

reconnoiter verb INSPECT, case (slang), explore, investigate, observe, scan, spy out, survey

reconsider verb RETHINK, reassess, review, revise, think again

reconstruct verb 1 REBUILD, recreate, regenerate, remake, remodel, renovate, restore

2 DEDUCE, build up, piece
together

record noun 1 DOCUMENT,
account, chronicle, diary,
entry, file, journal, log, register,
report 2 EVIDENCE,
documentation, testimony,
trace, witness 3 DISC, album,
LP, single, vinyl 4 BACKGROUND,
career, history, performance
5 **off the record** CONFIDENTIAL,
not for publication, private,
unofficial ▶ verb 6 WRITE DOWN,
chronicle, document, enter,
log, minute, note, register, set
down, take down 7 TAPE, make
a recording of, tape-record,
video, video-tape 8 REGISTER,
give evidence of, indicate, say,
show

recorder noun CHRONICLER,
archivist, clerk, diarist,
historian, scribe

recording noun RECORD, disc,
tape, video

recount verb TELL, depict,
describe, narrate, recite, relate,
repeat, report

recoup verb 1 REGAIN, recover,
retrieve, win back
2 COMPENSATE, make up for,
refund, reimburse, remunerate,
repay, requite

recourse noun OPTION,
alternative, choice, expedient,
remedy, resort, resource, way
out

recover verb 1 GET BETTER,
convalesce, get well, heal,
improve, mend, rally,
recuperate, revive 2 REGAIN, get
back, recapture, reclaim,
redeem, repossess, restore,
retrieve

recovery noun 1 IMPROVEMENT,

convalescence, healing,
mending, recuperation, revival
2 RETRIEVAL, reclamation,
repossession, restoration

recreation noun PASTIME,
amusement, diversion,
enjoyment, entertainment, fun,
hobby, leisure activity, play,
relaxation, sport

recrimination noun BICKERING,
counterattack, mutual
accusation, quarrel, squabbling

recruit verb 1 ENLIST, draft,
enroll, levy, mobilize, muster,
raise 2 WIN (OVER), engage,
obtain, procure ▶ noun
3 BEGINNER, apprentice, convert,
helper, initiate, learner, novice,
trainee

rectify verb CORRECT, adjust,
emend, fix, improve, redress,
remedy, repair, right

rectitude noun MORALITY,
decency, goodness, honesty,
honor, integrity, principle,
probity, virtue

recuperate verb RECOVER,
convalesce, get better,
improve, mend

recur verb HAPPEN AGAIN, come
again, persist, reappear, repeat,
return, revert

recurrent adjective PERIODIC,
continued, frequent, habitual,
recurring

recycle verb REPROCESS, reclaim,
reuse, salvage, save

red adjective 1 CRIMSON,
carmine, cherry, coral, ruby,
scarlet, vermilion 2 Of hair
CHESTNUT, carroty,
flame-colored, reddish, sandy,
titian 3 FLUSHED, blushing,
embarrassed, florid,
shamefaced ▶ noun 4 **in the**

red *Informal* IN DEBT, in arrears, insolvent, overdrawn **5 see**

red *Informal* LOSE ONE'S TEMPER, blow one's top, crack up (*informal*), fly off the handle (*informal*), go ballistic (*slang*), go mad (*informal*)

red-blooded *adjective Informal* VIGOROUS, lusty, robust, strong, virile

redden *verb* FLUSH, blush, color (up), crimson, go red

redeem *verb* **1** MAKE UP FOR, atone for, compensate for, make amends for **2** REINSTATE, absolve, restore to favor **3** SAVE, deliver, emancipate, free, liberate, ransom **4** BUY BACK, reclaim, recover, regain, repurchase, retrieve

redemption *noun* **1** COMPENSATION, amends, atonement, reparation **2** SALVATION, deliverance, emancipation, liberation, release, rescue **3** REPURCHASE, reclamation, recovery, repossession, retrieval

red-handed *adjective* IN THE ACT, (in) flagrante delicto

redolent *adjective* **1** REMINISCENT, evocative, suggestive **2** SCENTED, aromatic, fragrant, odorous, perfumed, sweet-smelling

redoubtable *adjective* FORMIDABLE, fearful, fearsome, mighty, powerful, strong

redress *verb* **1** MAKE AMENDS FOR, compensate for, make up for **2** PUT RIGHT, adjust, balance, correct, even up, rectify, regulate ▶ *noun* **3** AMENDS, atonement, compensation, payment, recompense, reparation

reduce *verb* **1** LESSEN, abate, curtail, cut down, decrease, diminish, lower, moderate, shorten, weaken **2** DEGRADE, break, bring low, downgrade, humble

redundant *adjective* SUPERFLUOUS, extra, inessential, supernumerary, surplus, unnecessary, unwanted

reek *verb* **1** STINK, smell ▶ *noun* **2** STINK, fetor, odor, smell, stench

reel *verb* **1** STAGGER, lurch, pitch, rock, roll, sway **2** WHIRL, revolve, spin, swirl

refer *verb* **1** ALLUDE, bring up, cite, mention, speak of **2** RELATE, apply, belong, be relevant to, concern, pertain **3** CONSULT, apply, go, look up, turn to **4** DIRECT, guide, point, send

referee *noun* **1** UMPIRE, adjudicator, arbiter, arbitrator, judge, ref (*informal*) ▶ *verb* **2** UMPIRE, adjudicate, arbitrate, judge, mediate

reference *noun* **1** CITATION, allusion, mention, note, quotation **2** TESTIMONIAL, character, credentials, endorsement, recommendation **3** RELEVANCE, applicability, bearing, connection, relation

referendum *noun* PUBLIC VOTE, plebiscite, popular vote

refine *verb* **1** PURIFY, clarify, cleanse, distill, filter, process **2** IMPROVE, hone, perfect, polish

refined *adjective* **1** CULTURED, civilized, cultivated, elegant, polished, polite, well-bred **2** PURE, clarified, clean, distilled, filtered, processed, purified

3 DISCERNING, delicate, discriminating, fastidious, fine, precise, sensitive

refinement noun
1 SOPHISTICATION, breeding, civility, courtesy, cultivation, culture, discrimination, gentility, good breeding, polish, taste 2 SUBTLETY, fine point, nicety, nuance
3 PURIFICATION, clarification, cleansing, distillation, filtering, processing

reflect verb 1 THROW BACK, echo, mirror, reproduce, return
2 SHOW, demonstrate, display, indicate, manifest, reveal
3 THINK, cogitate, consider, meditate, muse, ponder, ruminate, wonder

reflection noun 1 IMAGE, echo, mirror image 2 THOUGHT, cogitation, consideration, contemplation, idea, meditation, musing, observation, opinion, thinking

reflective adjective THOUGHTFUL, contemplative, meditative, pensive

reform noun 1 IMPROVEMENT, amendment, betterment, rehabilitation ▶ verb 2 IMPROVE, amend, correct, mend, rectify, restore 3 MEND ONE'S WAYS, clean up one's act (informal), go straight (informal), shape up (informal), turn over a new leaf

refractory adjective UNMANAGEABLE, difficult, disobedient, headstrong, intractable, uncontrollable, unruly, willful

refrain[1] verb STOP, abstain, avoid, cease, desist, forbear, leave off, renounce

refrain[2] noun CHORUS, melody, tune

refresh verb 1 REVIVE, brace, enliven, freshen, reinvigorate, revitalize, stimulate 2 STIMULATE, jog, prompt, renew

refreshing adjective
1 STIMULATING, bracing, fresh, invigorating 2 NEW, novel, original

refreshment noun
refreshments FOOD AND DRINK, drinks, snacks, tidbits

refrigerate verb COOL, chill, freeze, keep cold

refuge noun SHELTER, asylum, haven, hideout, protection, retreat, sanctuary

refugee noun EXILE, displaced person, émigré, escapee

refund verb 1 REPAY, pay back, reimburse, restore, return
▶ noun 2 REPAYMENT, reimbursement, return

refurbish verb RENOVATE, clean up, do up (informal), mend, overhaul, repair, restore, revamp

refusal noun DENIAL, knock-back (slang), rebuff, rejection

refuse[1] verb REJECT, decline, deny, say no, spurn, turn down, withhold

refuse[2] noun RUBBISH, garbage, junk (informal), litter, trash, waste

refute verb DISPROVE, discredit, negate, overthrow, prove false, rebut

regain verb 1 RECOVER, get back, recapture, recoup, retrieve, take back, win back 2 GET BACK TO, reach again, return to

regal adjective ROYAL, kingly or

queenly, magnificent, majestic, noble, princely

regale *verb* ENTERTAIN, amuse, delight, divert

regalia *plural noun* EMBLEMS, accouterments, decorations, finery, paraphernalia, trappings

regard *verb* 1 CONSIDER, believe, deem, esteem, judge, rate, see, suppose, think, view 2 LOOK AT, behold, check out (*informal*), eye, gaze at, observe, scrutinize, view, watch 3 HEED, attend, listen to, mind, pay attention to, take notice of 4 **as regards** CONCERNING, pertaining to, regarding, relating to ▶ *noun* 5 HEED, attention, interest, mind, notice 6 RESPECT, care, concern, consideration, esteem, thought 7 LOOK, gaze, glance, scrutiny, stare

regarding *preposition* CONCERNING, about, as regards, in or with regard to, on the subject of, re, respecting, with reference to

regardless *adjective* 1 HEEDLESS, inconsiderate, indifferent, neglectful, negligent, rash, reckless, unmindful ▶ *adverb* 2 ANYWAY, in any case, in spite of everything, nevertheless

regards *plural noun* GOOD WISHES, best wishes, compliments, greetings, respects

regenerate *verb* RENEW, breathe new life into, invigorate, reawaken, reinvigorate, rejuvenate, restore, revive

regime *noun* GOVERNMENT, leadership, management, reign, rule, system

regimented *adjective* CONTROLLED, disciplined, ordered, organized, regulated, systematized

region *noun* AREA, district, locality, part, place, quarter, section, sector, territory, tract, zone

regional *adjective* LOCAL, district, parochial, provincial, zonal

register *noun* 1 LIST, archives, catalog, chronicle, diary, file, log, record, roll, roster ▶ *verb* 2 RECORD, catalog, chronicle, enlist, enroll, enter, list, note 3 SHOW, display, exhibit, express, indicate, manifest, mark, reveal

regress *verb* REVERT, backslide, degenerate, deteriorate, fall away *or* off, go back, lapse, relapse, return

regret *verb* 1 FEEL SORRY ABOUT, bemoan, bewail, deplore, grieve, lament, miss, mourn, repent, rue 2 SORROW, bitterness, compunction, contrition, penitence, remorse, repentance, ruefulness

regretful *adjective* SORRY, apologetic, contrite, penitent, remorseful, repentant, rueful, sad, sorrowful

regrettable *adjective* UNFORTUNATE, disappointing, distressing, lamentable, sad, shameful

regular *adjective* 1 NORMAL, common, customary, habitual, ordinary, routine, typical, usual 2 EVEN, balanced, flat, level, smooth, straight, symmetrical, uniform 3 SYSTEMATIC, consistent, constant, even, fixed, ordered, set, stated, steady, uniform

regulate _verb_ 1 CONTROL, direct, govern, guide, handle, manage, rule, run, supervise 2 ADJUST, balance, fit, moderate, modulate, tune

regulation _noun_ 1 RULE, decree, dictate, edict, law, order, precept, statute 2 CONTROL, direction, government, management, supervision 3 ADJUSTMENT, modulation, tuning

regurgitate _verb_ VOMIT, barf (_slang_), disgorge, puke (_slang_), spew (out _or_ up), throw up (_informal_)

rehabilitate _verb_ 1 REINTEGRATE, adjust 2 REDEEM, clear, reform, restore, save

rehash _verb_ 1 REWORK, refashion, rejig (_informal_), reuse, rewrite ▶ _noun_ 2 REWORKING, new version, rearrangement, rewrite

rehearsal _noun_ PRACTICE, drill, preparation, rehearsing, run-through

rehearse _verb_ PRACTICE, drill, go over, prepare, recite, repeat, run through, train

reign _noun_ 1 RULE, command, control, dominion, monarchy, power ▶ _verb_ 2 RULE, be in power, command, govern, influence 3 BE SUPREME, hold sway, predominate, prevail

reimburse _verb_ PAY BACK, compensate, recompense, refund, remunerate, repay, return

rein _verb_ 1 CONTROL, check, curb, halt, hold back, limit, restrain, restrict ▶ _noun_ 2 CONTROL, brake, bridle, check, curb, harness, hold, restraint

reincarnation _noun_ REBIRTH, transmigration of souls

reinforce _verb_ SUPPORT, bolster, emphasize, fortify, prop, strengthen, stress, supplement, toughen

reinforcement _noun_ 1 STRENGTHENING, augmentation, fortification, increase 2 SUPPORT, brace, buttress, prop, stay 3 **reinforcements** RESERVES, additional _or_ fresh troops, auxiliaries, support

reinstate _verb_ RESTORE, recall, re-establish, replace, return

reiterate _verb_ REPEAT, do again, restate, say again

reject _verb_ 1 DENY, decline, disallow, exclude, renounce, repudiate, veto 2 REBUFF, jilt, refuse, repulse, say no to, spurn, turn down 3 DISCARD, eliminate, jettison, scrap, throw away _or_ out ▶ _noun_ 4 CASTOFF, discard, failure, second

rejection _noun_ 1 DENIAL, dismissal, exclusion, renunciation, repudiation, thumbs down, veto 2 REBUFF, brushoff (_slang_), kick in the teeth (_slang_), knock-back (_slang_), refusal

rejig _verb_ REARRANGE, alter, juggle, manipulate, reorganize, tweak

rejoice _verb_ BE GLAD, be happy, be overjoyed, celebrate, exult, glory

rejoicing _noun_ HAPPINESS, celebration, elation, exultation, gladness, joy, jubilation, merrymaking

rejoin _verb_ REPLY, answer, respond, retort, riposte

rejoinder _noun_ REPLY, answer,

comeback (*informal*), response, retort, riposte

rejuvenate *verb* REVITALIZE, breathe new life into, refresh, regenerate, reinvigorate, renew, restore

relapse *verb* 1 LAPSE, backslide, degenerate, fail, regress, revert, slip back 2 WORSEN, deteriorate, fade, fail, sicken, sink, weaken ▶ *noun* 3 LAPSE, backsliding, regression, retrogression 4 WORSENING, deterioration, turn for the worse, weakening

relate *verb* 1 CONNECT, associate, correlate, couple, join, link 2 CONCERN, apply, be relevant to, have to do with, pertain, refer 3 TELL, describe, detail, narrate, recite, recount, report

related *adjective* 1 AKIN, kindred 2 ASSOCIATED, affiliated, akin, connected, interconnected, joint, linked

relation *noun* 1 CONNECTION, bearing, bond, comparison, correlation, link 2 RELATIVE, kin, kinsman *or* kinswoman 3 KINSHIP, affinity, kindred

relations *plural noun* 1 DEALINGS, affairs, connections, contact, interaction, intercourse, relationship 2 FAMILY, clan, kin, kindred, kinsfolk, kinsmen, relatives, tribe

relationship *noun* 1 ASSOCIATION, affinity, bond, connection, kinship, rapport 2 AFFAIR, liaison 3 CONNECTION, correlation, link, parallel, similarity, tie-up

relative *adjective* 1 DEPENDENT, allied, associated, comparative, contingent, corresponding, proportionate, related 2 RELEVANT, applicable, apposite,

appropriate, apropos, germane, pertinent ▶ *noun* 3 RELATION, kinsman *or* kinswoman, member of one's *or* the family

relatively *adverb* COMPARATIVELY, rather, somewhat

relax *verb* 1 BE *or* FEEL AT EASE, calm, chill out (*slang*), lighten up (*slang*), rest, take it easy, unwind 2 LESSEN, abate, ease, ebb, let up, loosen, lower, moderate, reduce, relieve, slacken, weaken

relaxation *noun* LEISURE, enjoyment, fun, pleasure, recreation, rest

relaxed *adjective* EASY-GOING, casual, comfortable, easy, free and easy, homey, informal, laid-back (*informal*), leisurely

relay *noun* 1 SHIFT, relief, turn 2 MESSAGE, dispatch, transmission ▶ *verb* 3 PASS ON, broadcast, carry, communicate, send, spread, transmit

release *verb* 1 SET FREE, discharge, drop, extricate, free, liberate, loose, unbridle, undo, unfasten 2 ACQUIT, absolve, exonerate, let go, let off 3 ISSUE, circulate, distribute, launch, make known, make public, publish, put out ▶ *noun* 4 LIBERATION, deliverance, discharge, emancipation, freedom, liberty 5 ACQUITTAL, absolution, exemption, exoneration 6 ISSUE, proclamation, publication

relegate *verb* DEMOTE, downgrade

relent *verb* BE MERCIFUL, capitulate, change one's mind, come round, have pity, show mercy, soften, yield

relentless adjective
1 UNREMITTING, incessant, nonstop, persistent, unrelenting, unrelieved
2 MERCILESS, cruel, fierce, implacable, pitiless, remorseless, ruthless, unrelenting

relevant adjective SIGNIFICANT, apposite, appropriate, apt, fitting, germane, pertinent, related, to the point

reliable adjective DEPENDABLE, faithful, safe, sound, staunch, sure, true, trustworthy

reliance noun TRUST, belief, confidence, dependence, faith

relic noun REMNANT, fragment, keepsake, memento, souvenir, trace, vestige

relief noun 1 EASE, comfort, cure, deliverance, mitigation, release, remedy, solace 2 REST, break, breather (informal), relaxation, respite 3 AID, assistance, help, succor, support

relieve verb 1 EASE, alleviate, assuage, calm, comfort, console, cure, mitigate, relax, soften, soothe 2 HELP, aid, assist, succor, support, sustain

religious adjective 1 DEVOUT, devotional, faithful, godly, holy, pious, sacred, spiritual 2 CONSCIENTIOUS, faithful, meticulous, punctilious, rigid, scrupulous

relinquish verb GIVE UP, abandon, abdicate, cede, drop, forsake, leave, let go, renounce, surrender

relish verb 1 ENJOY, delight in, fancy, like, revel in, savor ▶ noun 2 ENJOYMENT, fancy,

fondness, gusto, liking, love, partiality, penchant, predilection, taste 3 CONDIMENT, sauce, seasoning 4 FLAVOR, piquancy, smack, spice, tang, taste, trace

reluctance noun UNWILLINGNESS, aversion, disinclination, dislike, distaste, loathing, repugnance

reluctant adjective UNWILLING, disinclined, hesitant, loath, unenthusiastic

rely verb DEPEND, bank, bet, count, trust

remain verb 1 CONTINUE, abide, dwell, endure, go on, last, persist, stand, stay, survive 2 STAY BEHIND, be left, delay, linger, wait

remainder noun REST, balance, excess, leavings, remains, remnant, residue, surplus

remaining adjective LEFT-OVER, lingering, outstanding, persisting, surviving, unfinished

remains plural noun 1 REMNANTS, debris, dregs, leavings, leftovers, relics, residue, rest 2 BODY, cadaver, carcass, corpse

remark verb 1 COMMENT, declare, mention, observe, pass comment, reflect, say, state 2 NOTICE, espy, make out, mark, note, observe, perceive, see ▶ noun 3 COMMENT, observation, reflection, statement, utterance

remarkable adjective EXTRAORDINARY, notable, outstanding, rare, singular, striking, surprising, uncommon, unusual, wonderful

remedy noun 1 CURE, medicine, nostrum, treatment ▶ verb 2 PUT RIGHT, correct, fix, rectify, set to rights

remember verb 1 RECALL, call to mind, commemorate, look back (on), recollect, reminisce, think back 2 BEAR IN MIND, keep in mind

remembrance noun 1 MEMORY, recall, recollection, reminiscence, thought 2 SOUVENIR, commemoration, keepsake, memento, memorial, monument, reminder, token

remind verb CALL TO MIND, jog one's memory, make (someone) remember, prompt

reminisce verb RECALL, hark back, look back, recollect, remember, think back

reminiscence noun RECOLLECTION, anecdote, memoir, memory, recall, remembrance

reminiscent adjective SUGGESTIVE, evocative, similar

remiss adjective CARELESS, forgetful, heedless, lax, neglectful, negligent, thoughtless

remission noun 1 PARDON, absolution, amnesty, discharge, exemption, release, reprieve 2 LESSENING, abatement, alleviation, ebb, lull, relaxation, respite

remit verb 1 SEND, dispatch, forward, mail, post, transmit 2 CANCEL, halt, repeal, rescind, stop 3 POSTPONE, defer, delay, put off, shelve, suspend ▶ noun 4 INSTRUCTIONS, brief, guidelines, orders

remittance noun PAYMENT, allowance, fee

remnant noun REMAINDER, end, fragment, leftovers, remains, residue, rest, trace, vestige

remonstrate verb ARGUE, dispute, dissent, object, protest, take issue

remorse noun REGRET, anguish, compunction, contrition, grief, guilt, penitence, repentance, shame, sorrow

remorseful adjective REGRETFUL, apologetic, ashamed, conscience-stricken, contrite, guilty, penitent, repentant, sorry

remorseless adjective 1 PITILESS, callous, cruel, inhumane, merciless, ruthless 2 RELENTLESS, inexorable

remote adjective 1 DISTANT, far, inaccessible, in the middle of nowhere, isolated, out-of-the-way, secluded 2 ALOOF, abstracted, cold, detached, distant, reserved, standoffish, uncommunicative, withdrawn 3 SLIGHT, doubtful, dubious, faint, outside, slender, slim, small, unlikely

removal noun 1 TAKING AWAY or OFF or OUT, dislodgment, ejection, elimination, eradication, extraction, uprooting, withdrawal 2 DISMISSAL, expulsion 3 MOVE, departure, relocation, transfer

remove verb 1 TAKE AWAY or OFF or OUT, abolish, delete, detach, displace, eject, eliminate, erase, excise, extract, get rid of, wipe from the face of the earth, withdraw 2 DISMISS, depose, dethrone, discharge, expel, oust, throw out 3 MOVE, depart, flit (Scot. & Northern English dialect), relocate

remunerate verb PAY, compensate, recompense,

reimburse, repay, requite, reward

remuneration *noun* PAYMENT, earnings, fee, income, pay, return, reward, salary, stipend, wages

remunerative *adjective* PROFITABLE, economic, lucrative, moneymaking, paying, rewarding, worthwhile

renaissance, renascence *noun* REBIRTH, reappearance, reawakening, renewal, restoration, resurgence, revival

rend *verb* TEAR, rip, rupture, separate, wrench

render *verb* 1 MAKE, cause to become, leave 2 PROVIDE, furnish, give, hand out, pay, present, submit, supply, tender 3 PORTRAY, act, depict, do, give, perform, play, represent

rendezvous *noun* 1 APPOINTMENT, assignation, date, engagement, meeting, tryst 2 MEETING PLACE, gathering point, venue ▶ *verb* 3 MEET, assemble, come together, gather, join up

rendition *noun* 1 PERFORMANCE, arrangement, interpretation, portrayal, presentation, reading, rendering, version 2 TRANSLATION, interpretation, reading, transcription, version

renegade *noun* 1 DESERTER, apostate, defector, traitor, turncoat ▶ *adjective* 2 REBELLIOUS, apostate, disloyal, traitorous, unfaithful

renege *verb* BREAK ONE'S WORD, back out, break a promise, default, go back

renew *verb* 1 RECOMMENCE, continue, extend, reaffirm,

recreate, reopen, repeat, resume 2 RESTORE, mend, modernize, overhaul, refit, refurbish, renovate, repair 3 REPLACE, refresh, replenish, restock

renounce *verb* GIVE UP, abjure, deny, disown, forsake, forswear, quit, recant, relinquish, waive

renovate *verb* RESTORE, do up (*informal*), modernize, overhaul, recondition, refit, refurbish, renew, repair

renown *noun* FAME, distinction, eminence, note, reputation, repute

renowned *adjective* FAMOUS, celebrated, distinguished, eminent, esteemed, notable, noted, well-known

rent[1] *verb* 1 HIRE, charter, lease, let ▶ *noun* 2 HIRE, fee, lease, payment, rental

rent[2] *noun* TEAR, gash, hole, opening, rip, slash, slit, split

renunciation *noun* GIVING UP, abandonment, abdication, abjuration, denial, disavowal, forswearing, rejection, relinquishment, repudiation

reorganize *verb* REARRANGE, reshuffle, restructure

repair *verb* 1 MEND, fix, heal, patch, patch up, renovate, restore ▶ *noun* 2 MEND, darn, overhaul, patch, restoration

reparation *noun* COMPENSATION, atonement, damages, recompense, restitution, satisfaction

repartee *noun* WIT, badinage, banter, riposte, wittiness, wordplay

repast *noun* MEAL, food

repay verb 1 PAY BACK, compensate, recompense, refund, reimburse, requite, return, square 2 GET EVEN WITH (informal), avenge, hit back, reciprocate, retaliate, revenge

repeal verb 1 ABOLISH, annul, cancel, invalidate, nullify, recall, reverse, revoke ▶noun 2 ABOLITION, annulment, cancellation, invalidation, rescindment

repeat verb 1 REITERATE, echo, replay, reproduce, rerun, reshow, restate, retell ▶noun 2 REPETITION, echo, reiteration, replay, rerun, reshowing

repeatedly adverb OVER AND OVER, frequently, many times, often

repel verb 1 DISGUST, gross out (slang), nauseate, offend, revolt, sicken 2 DRIVE OFF, fight, hold off, parry, rebuff, repulse, resist, ward off

repellent adjective 1 DISGUSTING, abhorrent, hateful, horrid, loathsome, nauseating, noxious, offensive, repugnant, repulsive, revolting, scuzzy (slang), sickening 2 PROOF, impermeable, repelling, resistant

repent verb REGRET, be sorry, feel remorse, rue

repentance noun REGRET, compunction, contrition, grief, guilt, penitence, remorse

repentant adjective REGRETFUL, contrite, penitent, remorseful, rueful, sorry

repercussion noun

repercussions CONSEQUENCES, backlash, result, sequel, side effects

repertoire noun RANGE, collection, list, repertory, stock, store, supply

repetition noun REPEATING, echo, recurrence, reiteration, renewal, replication, restatement, tautology

repetitious adjective LONG-WINDED, prolix, tautological, tedious, verbose, wordy

repetitive adjective MONOTONOUS, boring, dull, mechanical, recurrent, tedious, unchanging, unvaried

rephrase verb REWORD, paraphrase, put differently

repine verb COMPLAIN, fret, grumble, moan

replace verb TAKE THE PLACE OF, follow, oust, substitute, succeed, supersede, supplant, take over from

replacement noun SUCCESSOR, double, proxy, stand-in, substitute, surrogate, understudy

replenish verb REFILL, fill, provide, reload, replace, restore, top up

replete adjective FULL, crammed, filled, full up, glutted, gorged, stuffed

replica noun DUPLICATE, carbon copy (informal), copy, facsimile, imitation, model, reproduction

replicate verb COPY, duplicate, mimic, recreate, reduplicate, reproduce

reply verb 1 ANSWER, counter, reciprocate, rejoin, respond, retaliate, retort ▶noun 2 ANSWER, counter, counterattack, reaction, rejoinder, response, retaliation, retort, riposte

report verb 1 COMMUNICATE, broadcast, cover, describe, detail, inform of, narrate, pass on, recount, relate, state, tell 2 PRESENT ONESELF, appear, arrive, come, turn up ▶ noun 3 ACCOUNT, communication, description, narrative, news, record, statement, word 4 ARTICLE, piece, story, write-up 5 RUMOR, buzz, gossip, hearsay, talk 6 BANG, blast, boom, crack, detonation, discharge, explosion, noise, sound

reporter noun JOURNALIST, correspondent, hack (derogatory), pressman, writer

repose noun 1 PEACE, ease, quietness, relaxation, respite, rest, stillness, tranquillity 2 COMPOSURE, calmness, poise, self-possession 3 SLEEP, slumber ▶ verb 4 REST, lie, lie down, recline, rest upon

repository noun STORE, depository, storehouse, treasury, vault

reprehensible adjective BLAMEWORTHY, bad, culpable, disgraceful, shameful, unworthy

represent verb 1 STAND FOR, act for, betoken, mean, serve as, speak for, symbolize 2 SYMBOLIZE, embody, epitomize, exemplify, personify, typify 3 PORTRAY, denote, depict, describe, illustrate, outline, picture, show

representation noun PORTRAYAL, account, depiction, description, illustration, image, likeness, model, picture, portrait

representative noun 1 DELEGATE, agent, deputy, member, proxy, spokesman or spokeswoman 2 SALESMAN, agent, commercial traveler, rep ▶ adjective 3 TYPICAL, archetypal, characteristic, exemplary, symbolic

repress verb 1 INHIBIT, bottle up, check, control, curb, hold back, restrain, stifle, suppress 2 SUBDUE, quell, subjugate

repression noun SUBJUGATION, constraint, control, despotism, domination, restraint, suppression, tyranny

repressive adjective OPPRESSIVE, absolute, authoritarian, despotic, dictatorial, tyrannical

reprieve verb 1 GRANT A STAY OF EXECUTION TO, let off the hook (slang), pardon 2 RELIEVE, abate, allay, alleviate, mitigate, palliate ▶ noun 3 STAY OF EXECUTION, amnesty, deferment, pardon, postponement, remission 4 RELIEF, alleviation, mitigation, palliation, respite

reprimand verb 1 BLAME, censure, rap over the knuckles, rebuke, scold ▶ noun 2 BLAME, censure, rebuke, reproach, reproof, talking-to (informal)

reprisal noun RETALIATION, retribution, revenge, vengeance

reproach noun 1 BLAME, censure, condemnation, disapproval, opprobrium, rebuke ▶ verb 2 BLAME, censure, condemn, criticize, lambast(e), rebuke, reprimand, scold, upbraid

reproachful adjective CRITICAL, censorious, condemnatory, disapproving, fault-finding, reproving

reprobate noun 1 SCOUNDREL,

bad egg (*old-fashioned informal*), degenerate, evildoer, miscreant, profligate, rake, rascal, villain ▶ *adjective* **2** DEPRAVED, abandoned, bad, base, corrupt, degenerate, dissolute, immoral, sinful, wicked

reproduce *verb* **1** COPY, duplicate, echo, imitate, match, mirror, recreate, repeat, replicate **2** BREED, multiply, procreate, propagate, spawn

reproduction *noun* **1** BREEDING, generation, increase, multiplication **2** COPY, duplicate, facsimile, imitation, picture, print, replica

reproof *noun* REBUKE, blame, censure, condemnation, criticism, reprimand, scolding

reprove *verb* REBUKE, berate, blame, censure, condemn, reprimand, scold, tell off (*informal*)

repudiate *verb* REJECT, deny, disavow, disclaim, disown, renounce

repugnance *noun* DISTASTE, abhorrence, aversion, disgust, dislike, hatred, loathing

repugnant *adjective* DISTASTEFUL, abhorrent, disgusting, loathsome, nauseating, offensive, repellent, revolting, sickening, vile

repulse *verb* **1** DRIVE BACK, beat off, fight off, rebuff, repel, ward off **2** REBUFF, refuse, reject, snub, spurn, turn down

repulsion *noun* DISTASTE, abhorrence, aversion, detestation, disgust, hatred, loathing, repugnance, revulsion

repulsive *adjective* DISGUSTING,

abhorrent, foul, loathsome, nauseating, repellent, revolting, scuzzy (*slang*), sickening, vile

reputable *adjective* RESPECTABLE, creditable, excellent, good, honorable, reliable, trustworthy, well-thought-of, worthy

reputation *noun* ESTIMATION, character, esteem, name, renown, repute, standing, stature

repute *noun* REPUTATION, celebrity, distinction, eminence, fame, name, renown, standing, stature

reputed *adjective* SUPPOSED, alleged, believed, considered, deemed, estimated, held, reckoned, regarded

reputedly *adverb* SUPPOSEDLY, allegedly, apparently, seemingly

request *verb* **1** ASK (FOR), appeal for, demand, desire, entreat, invite, seek, solicit ▶ *noun* **2** ASKING, appeal, call, demand, desire, entreaty, suit

require *verb* **1** NEED, crave, desire, lack, miss, want, wish **2** DEMAND, ask, bid, call upon, command, compel, exact, insist upon, oblige, order

required *adjective* NEEDED, called for, essential, necessary, obligatory, requisite

requirement *noun* NECESSITY, demand, essential, lack, must, need, prerequisite, stipulation, want

requisite *adjective* **1** NECESSARY, called for, essential, indispensable, needed, needful, obligatory, required ▶ *noun* **2** NECESSITY, condition, essential, must, need, prerequisite, requirement

requisition verb 1 DEMAND, call for, request ▶noun 2 DEMAND, call, request, summons

requital noun RETURN, repayment

requite verb RETURN, get even, give in return, pay (someone) back in his or her own coin, reciprocate, repay, respond, retaliate

rescind verb ANNUL, cancel, countermand, declare null and void, invalidate, repeal, set aside

rescue verb 1 SAVE, deliver, get out, liberate, recover, redeem, release, salvage ▶noun 2 LIBERATION, deliverance, recovery, redemption, release, salvage, salvation, saving

research noun 1 INVESTIGATION, analysis, examination, exploration, probe, study ▶verb 2 INVESTIGATE, analyze, examine, explore, probe, study

resemblance noun SIMILARITY, correspondence, kinship, likeness, parallel, sameness, similitude

resemble verb BE LIKE, bear a resemblance to, be similar to, look like, mirror, parallel

resent verb BE BITTER ABOUT, begrudge, grudge, object to, take exception to, take offense at

resentful adjective BITTER, angry, embittered, grudging, indignant, miffed (informal), offended, piqued, ticked off (informal)

resentment noun BITTERNESS, animosity, bad blood, grudge, ill feeling, ill will, indignation, pique, rancor, umbrage

reservation noun 1 DOUBT, hesitancy, scruple 2 CONDITION, proviso, qualification, rider, stipulation 3 RESERVE, preserve, sanctuary, territory

reserve verb 1 KEEP, hoard, hold, put by, retain, save, set aside, stockpile, store 2 BOOK, engage, prearrange, secure ▶noun 3 STORE, cache, fund, hoard, reservoir, savings, stock, supply 4 RESERVATION, park, preserve, sanctuary, tract 5 SHYNESS, constraint, reservation, restraint, reticence, secretiveness, silence, taciturnity ▶adjective 6 SUBSTITUTE, auxiliary, extra, fall-back, secondary, spare

reserved adjective 1 UNCOMMUNICATIVE, restrained, reticent, retiring, secretive, shy, silent, standoffish, taciturn, undemonstrative 2 SET ASIDE, booked, engaged, held, kept, restricted, retained, spoken for, taken

reservoir noun 1 LAKE, basin, pond, tank 2 STORE, pool, reserves, source, stock, supply

reshuffle noun 1 REORGANIZATION, change, rearrangement, redistribution, regrouping, restructuring, revision ▶verb 2 REORGANIZE, change around, rearrange, redistribute, regroup, restructure, revise

reside verb LIVE, abide, dwell, inhabit, lodge, stay

residence noun HOME, abode, domicile, dwelling, flat, habitation, house, lodging, place

resident noun INHABITANT, citizen, local, lodger, occupant, occupier, tenant

residual *adjective* REMAINING, leftover, unconsumed, unused, vestigial

residue *noun* REMAINDER, dregs, excess, extra, leftovers, remains, remnant, rest, surplus

resign *verb* 1 QUIT, abdicate, give in one's notice, leave, step down (*informal*), vacate 2 GIVE UP, abandon, forgo, forsake, relinquish, renounce, surrender, yield 3 **resign oneself** ACCEPT, acquiesce, give in, submit, succumb, yield

resignation *noun* 1 LEAVING, abandonment, abdication, departure 2 ENDURANCE, acceptance, acquiescence, compliance, nonresistance, passivity, patience, submission, sufferance

resigned *adjective* STOICAL, compliant, long-suffering, patient, subdued, unresisting

resilient *adjective* 1 TOUGH, buoyant, hardy, irrepressible, strong 2 FLEXIBLE, elastic, plastic, pliable, rubbery, springy, supple

resist *verb* 1 OPPOSE, battle, combat, defy, hinder, stand up to 2 REFRAIN FROM, abstain from, avoid, forbear, forgo, keep from 3 WITHSTAND, be proof against

resistance *noun* FIGHTING, battle, defiance, fight, hindrance, impediment, obstruction, opposition, struggle

resistant *adjective* 1 IMPERVIOUS, hard, proof against, strong, tough, unaffected by 2 OPPOSED, antagonistic, hostile, intractable, intransigent, unwilling

resolute *adjective* DETERMINED, dogged, firm, fixed, immovable, inflexible, set, steadfast, strong-willed, tenacious, unshakable, unwavering

resolution *noun* 1 DETERMINATION, doggedness, firmness, perseverance, purpose, resoluteness, resolve, steadfastness, tenacity, willpower 2 DECISION, aim, declaration, determination, intent, intention, purpose, resolve

resolve *verb* 1 DECIDE, agree, conclude, determine, fix, intend, purpose 2 BREAK DOWN, analyze, reduce, separate 3 WORK OUT, answer, clear up, crack, fathom ▶*noun* 4 DETERMINATION, firmness, resoluteness, resolution, steadfastness, willpower 5 DECISION, intention, objective, purpose, resolution

resonant *adjective* ECHOING, booming, resounding, reverberating, ringing, sonorous

resort *verb* 1 **resort to** USE, employ, fall back on, have recourse to, turn to, utilize ▶*noun* 2 HOLIDAY CENTER, haunt, retreat, spot, tourist center 3 RECOURSE, reference

resound *verb* ECHO, re-echo, resonate, reverberate, ring

resounding *adjective* ECHOING, booming, full, powerful, resonant, reverberating, ringing, sonorous

resource *noun* 1 INGENUITY, ability, capability, cleverness, initiative, inventiveness 2 MEANS, course, device, expedient, resort

resourceful *adjective* INGENIOUS, able, bright, capable, clever, creative, inventive

resources *plural noun* RESERVES, assets, capital, funds, holdings, money, riches, supplies, wealth

respect *noun* 1 REGARD, admiration, consideration, deference, esteem, estimation, honor, recognition 2 POINT, aspect, characteristic, detail, feature, matter, particular, sense, way 3 RELATION, bearing, connection, reference, regard ▶ *verb* 4 THINK HIGHLY OF, admire, defer to, esteem, have a good *or* high opinion of, honor, look up to, value 5 SHOW CONSIDERATION FOR, abide by, adhere to, comply with, follow, heed, honor, obey, observe

respectable *adjective* 1 HONORABLE, decent, estimable, good, honest, reputable, upright, worthy 2 REASONABLE, ample, appreciable, considerable, decent, fair, sizable *or* sizeable, substantial

respectful *adjective* POLITE, civil, courteous, deferential, mannerly, reverent, well-mannered

respective *adjective* SPECIFIC, individual, own, particular, relevant

respite *noun* PAUSE, break, cessation, halt, interval, lull, recess, relief, rest

resplendent *adjective* BRILLIANT, bright, dazzling, glorious, radiant, shining, splendid

respond *verb* ANSWER, counter, react, reciprocate, rejoin, reply, retort, return

response *noun* ANSWER, counterattack, feedback, reaction, rejoinder, reply, retort, return

responsibility *noun* 1 AUTHORITY, importance, power 2 FAULT, blame, culpability, guilt 3 DUTY, care, charge, liability, obligation, onus 4 LEVEL-HEADEDNESS, conscientiousness, dependability, rationality, sensibleness, trustworthiness

responsible *adjective* 1 IN CHARGE, in authority, in control 2 TO BLAME, at fault, culpable, guilty 3 ACCOUNTABLE, answerable, liable 4 SENSIBLE, dependable, level-headed, rational, reliable, trustworthy

responsive *adjective* SENSITIVE, alive, impressionable, open, reactive, receptive, susceptible

rest[1] *noun* 1 REPOSE, calm, inactivity, leisure, relaxation, relief, stillness, tranquillity 2 PAUSE, break, cessation, halt, interlude, intermission, interval, lull, respite, stop 3 SUPPORT, base, holder, prop, stand ▶ *verb* 4 RELAX, be at ease, put one's feet up, sit down, take it easy 5 BE SUPPORTED, lean, lie, prop, recline, repose, sit

rest[2] *noun* REMAINDER, balance, excess, others, remains, remnants, residue, surplus

restaurant *noun* BISTRO, café, cafeteria, diner, eatery, tearoom

restful *adjective* RELAXING, calm, calming, peaceful, quiet, relaxed, serene, soothing, tranquil

restitution *noun* COMPENSATION, amends, recompense,

reparation, requital

restive *adjective* RESTLESS, edgy, fidgety, impatient, jumpy, nervous, on edge, wired (*slang*)

restless *adjective* 1 MOVING, nomadic, roving, transient, unsettled, unstable, wandering 2 UNSETTLED, antsy (*slang*), edgy, fidgeting, fidgety, jumpy, nervous, on edge, restive, wired (*slang*)

restlessness *noun* 1 MOVEMENT, activity, bustle, unrest, unsettledness 2 RESTIVENESS, edginess, jitters (*informal*), jumpiness, nervousness

restoration *noun* 1 REPAIR, reconstruction, renewal, renovation, revitalization, revival 2 REINSTATEMENT, re-establishment, replacement, restitution, return

restore *verb* 1 REPAIR, fix, mend, rebuild, recondition, reconstruct, refurbish, renew, renovate 2 REVIVE, build up, refresh, revitalize, strengthen 3 RETURN, bring back, give back, hand back, recover, reinstate, replace, send back 4 REINSTATE, reintroduce

restrain *verb* HOLD BACK, check, constrain, contain, control, curb, curtail, hamper, hinder, inhibit, restrict

restrained *adjective* CONTROLLED, calm, mild, moderate, self-controlled, undemonstrative

restraint *noun* 1 SELF-CONTROL, control, inhibition, moderation, self-discipline, self-possession, self-restraint 2 LIMITATION, ban, check, curb, embargo, interdict, limit, rein

restrict *verb* LIMIT, bound,

confine, contain, hamper, handicap, inhibit, regulate, restrain

restriction *noun* LIMITATION, confinement, control, curb, handicap, inhibition, regulation, restraint, rule

result *noun* 1 CONSEQUENCE, effect, end, end result, outcome, product, sequel, upshot ▶ *verb* 2 HAPPEN, appear, arise, derive, develop, ensue, follow, issue, spring 3 **result in** END IN, culminate in, finish with

resume *verb* BEGIN AGAIN, carry on, continue, go on, proceed, reopen, restart

résumé *noun* SUMMARY, précis, recapitulation, rundown, synopsis

resumption *noun* CONTINUATION, carrying on, re-establishment, renewal, reopening, restart, resurgence

resurgence *noun* REVIVAL, rebirth, re-emergence, renaissance, resumption, resurrection, return

resurrect *verb* REVIVE, bring back, reintroduce, renew

resurrection *noun* REVIVAL, reappearance, rebirth, renaissance, renewal, restoration, resurgence, return

resuscitate *verb* REVIVE, bring round, resurrect, revitalize, save

retain *verb* 1 KEEP, hold, hold back, maintain, preserve, reserve, save 2 HIRE, commission, employ, engage, pay, reserve

retainer *noun* 1 FEE, advance, deposit 2 SERVANT, attendant, domestic

retaliate *verb* PAY (SOMEONE) BACK,

get even with (*informal*), hit back, reciprocate, strike back, take revenge

retaliation *noun* REVENGE, an eye for an eye, counterblow, reciprocation, repayment, reprisal, requital, vengeance

retard *verb* SLOW DOWN, arrest, check, delay, handicap, hinder, hold back *or* up, impede, set back

retch *verb* GAG, barf (*slang*), heave, puke (*slang*), regurgitate, spew, throw up (*informal*), vomit

reticence *noun* SILENCE, quietness, reserve, taciturnity

reticent *adjective* UNCOMMUNICATIVE, close-lipped, quiet, reserved, silent, taciturn, tight-lipped, unforthcoming

retinue *noun* ATTENDANTS, aides, entourage, escort, followers, servants

retire *verb* 1 STOP WORKING, give up work 2 WITHDRAW, depart, exit, go away, leave 3 GO TO BED, hit the hay (*slang*), hit the sack (*slang*), turn in (*informal*)

retirement *noun* WITHDRAWAL, privacy, retreat, seclusion, solitude

retiring *adjective* SHY, bashful, quiet, reserved, self-effacing, timid, unassertive, unassuming

retort *verb* 1 REPLY, answer, come back with, counter, respond, return, riposte ▶ *noun* 2 REPLY, answer, comeback (*informal*), rejoinder, response, riposte

retract *verb* 1 WITHDRAW, deny, disavow, disclaim, eat one's words, recant, renege, renounce, revoke, take back

2 DRAW IN, pull back, pull in, sheathe

retreat *verb* 1 WITHDRAW, back away, back off, depart, draw back, fall back, go back, leave, pull back ▶ *noun* 2 WITHDRAWAL, departure, evacuation, flight, retirement 3 REFUGE, haven, hideaway, sanctuary, seclusion, shelter

retrench *verb* CUT BACK, economize, make economies, save, tighten one's belt

retrenchment *noun* CUTBACK, cost-cutting, cut, economy, tightening one's belt

retribution *noun* PUNISHMENT, justice, Nemesis, reckoning, reprisal, retaliation, revenge, vengeance

retrieve *verb* GET BACK, recapture, recoup, recover, redeem, regain, restore, save, win back

retrograde *adjective* DECLINING, backward, degenerative, deteriorating, downward, regressive, retrogressive, worsening

retrogress *verb* DECLINE, backslide, deteriorate, go back, go downhill (*informal*), regress, relapse, worsen

retrospect *noun* HINDSIGHT, re-examination, review

return *verb* 1 COME BACK, go back, reappear, rebound, recur, retreat, revert, turn back 2 PUT BACK, re-establish, reinstate, replace, restore 3 GIVE BACK, pay back, recompense, refund, reimburse, repay 4 REPLY, answer, respond, retort 5 ELECT, choose, vote in ▶ *noun* 6 RESTORATION, re-establishment, reinstatement **7** REAPPEARANCE, recurrence **8** RETREAT, rebound, recoil **9** PROFIT, gain, income, interest, proceeds, revenue, takings, yield **10** REPORT, account, form, list, statement, summary **11** REPLY, answer, comeback (*informal*), rejoinder, response, retort

revamp *verb* RENOVATE, do up (*informal*), overhaul, recondition, refurbish, restore

reveal *verb* **1** MAKE KNOWN, announce, disclose, divulge, give away, impart, let out, let slip, make public, proclaim, tell **2** SHOW, display, exhibit, manifest, uncover, unearth, unmask, unveil

revel *verb* **1** CELEBRATE, carouse, live it up (*informal*), make merry **2** **revel in** ENJOY, delight in, indulge in, lap up, luxuriate in, relish, take pleasure in, thrive on ▶ *noun* **3** (often plural) MERRYMAKING, carousal, celebration, festivity, party, spree

revelation *noun* DISCLOSURE, exhibition, exposé, exposure, news, proclamation, publication, uncovering, unearthing, unveiling

reveller *noun* CAROUSER, merrymaker, partygoer

revelry *noun* FESTIVITY, carousal, celebration, fun, jollity, merrymaking, party, spree

revenge *noun* **1** RETALIATION, an eye for an eye, reprisal, retribution, vengeance ▶ *verb* **2** AVENGE, get even, hit back, repay, retaliate, take revenge for

revenue *noun* INCOME, gain,

proceeds, profits, receipts, returns, takings, yield

reverberate *verb* ECHO, re-echo, resound, ring, vibrate

revere *verb* BE IN AWE OF, exalt, honor, look up to, respect, reverence, venerate, worship

reverence *noun* AWE, admiration, high esteem, honor, respect, veneration, worship

reverent *adjective* RESPECTFUL, awed, deferential, humble, reverential

reverie *noun* DAYDREAM, abstraction, brown study, woolgathering

reverse *verb* **1** TURN ROUND, invert, transpose, turn back, turn over, turn upside down, upend **2** CHANGE, annul, cancel, countermand, invalidate, overrule, overthrow, overturn, quash, repeal, rescind, revoke, undo **3** GO BACKWARDS, back, back up, move backwards, retreat ▶ *noun* **4** OPPOSITE, contrary, converse, inverse **5** BACK, other side, rear, underside, wrong side **6** MISFORTUNE, adversity, affliction, blow, disappointment, failure, hardship, misadventure, mishap, reversal, setback ▶ *adjective* **7** OPPOSITE, contrary, converse

revert *verb* RETURN, come back, go back, resume

review *noun* **1** CRITIQUE, commentary, criticism, evaluation, judgment, notice **2** MAGAZINE, journal, periodical **3** SURVEY, analysis, examination, scrutiny, study **4** *Military*

INSPECTION, march past, parade ▶ *verb* 5 ASSESS, criticize, evaluate, judge, study 6 RECONSIDER, reassess, re-evaluate, re-examine, rethink, revise, think over 7 LOOK BACK ON, recall, recollect, reflect on, remember 8 INSPECT, examine 9 STUDY, cram (*informal*), revise (*chiefly Brit.*)

reviewer *noun* CRITIC, commentator, judge

revile *verb* MALIGN, abuse, bad-mouth (*slang*), denigrate, knock (*informal*), reproach, run down, vilify

revise *verb* CHANGE, alter, amend, correct, edit, emend, redo, review, rework, update

revision *noun* CHANGE, amendment, correction, emendation, updating

revival *noun* RENEWAL, reawakening, rebirth, renaissance, resurgence, resurrection, revitalization

revive *verb* REVITALIZE, awaken, bring round, come round, invigorate, reanimate, recover, refresh, rekindle, renew, restore

revoke *verb* CANCEL, annul, countermand, disclaim, invalidate, negate, nullify, obviate, quash, repeal, rescind, retract, reverse, set aside, withdraw

revolt *noun* 1 UPRISING, insurgency, insurrection, mutiny, rebellion, revolution, rising ▶ *verb* 2 REBEL, mutiny, resist, rise 3 DISGUST, gross out (*slang*), make one's flesh creep, nauseate, repel, repulse, sicken, turn one's stomach

revolting *adjective* DISGUSTING, foul, horrible, horrid, nauseating, repellent, repugnant, repulsive, scuzzy (*slang*), sickening, yucky *or* yukky (*slang*)

revolution *noun* 1 REVOLT, coup, insurgency, mutiny, rebellion, rising, uprising 2 TRANSFORMATION, innovation, reformation, sea change, shift, upheaval 3 ROTATION, circle, circuit, cycle, lap, orbit, spin, turn

revolutionary *adjective* 1 REBEL, extremist, insurgent, radical, subversive 2 NEW, different, drastic, ground-breaking, innovative, novel, progressive, radical ▶ *noun* 3 REBEL, insurgent, revolutionist

revolutionize *verb* TRANSFORM, modernize, reform

revolve *verb* ROTATE, circle, go round, orbit, spin, turn, twist, wheel, whirl

revulsion *noun* DISGUST, abhorrence, detestation, loathing, repugnance, repulsion

reward *noun* 1 PAYMENT, bonus, bounty, premium, prize, recompense, repayment, return, wages 2 PUNISHMENT, just deserts, retribution ▶ *verb* 3 PAY, compensate, recompense, remunerate, repay

rewarding *adjective* WORTHWHILE, beneficial, enriching, fruitful, fulfilling, productive, profitable, satisfying, valuable

rhapsodize *verb* ENTHUSE, go into ecstasies, gush, rave (*informal*)

rhetoric *noun* 1 ORATORY, eloquence 2 HYPERBOLE,

bombast, grandiloquence, magniloquence, verbosity, wordiness

rhetorical *adjective* ORATORICAL, bombastic, declamatory, grandiloquent, high-flown, magniloquent, verbose

rhyme *noun* 1 POETRY, ode, poem, song, verse ▶*verb* 2 SOUND LIKE, harmonize

rhythm *noun* BEAT, accent, cadence, lilt, meter, pulse, swing, tempo, time

rhythmic, rhythmical *adjective* CADENCED, lilting, metrical, musical, periodic, pulsating, throbbing

ribald *adjective* RUDE, bawdy, blue, broad, coarse, earthy, naughty, obscene, racy, smutty, vulgar

rich *adjective* 1 WEALTHY, affluent, loaded (*slang*), moneyed, prosperous, well-heeled (*informal*), well-off, well-to-do 2 WELL-STOCKED, full, productive, well-supplied 3 ABUNDANT, abounding, ample, copious, fertile, fruitful, lush, luxurious, plentiful, productive, prolific 4 FULL-BODIED, creamy, fatty, luscious, succulent, sweet, tasty

riches *plural noun* WEALTH, affluence, assets, fortune, plenty, resources, substance, treasure

richly *adverb* 1 ELABORATELY, elegantly, expensively, exquisitely, gorgeously, lavishly, luxuriously, opulently, splendidly, sumptuously 2 FULLY, amply, appropriately, properly, suitably, thoroughly, well

rickety *adjective* SHAKY, insecure, precarious, ramshackle, tottering, unsound, unsteady, wobbly

rid *verb* 1 FREE, clear, deliver, disburden, disencumber, make free, purge, relieve, unburden 2 **get rid of** DISPOSE OF, dump, eject, eliminate, expel, remove, throw away *or* out

riddle *noun* PUZZLE, conundrum, enigma, mystery, poser, problem

riddled *adjective* FILLED, damaged, infested, permeated, pervaded, spoilt

ride *verb* 1 CONTROL, handle, manage 2 TRAVEL, be carried, go, move ▶*noun* 3 TRIP, drive, jaunt, journey, lift, outing

ridicule *noun* 1 MOCKERY, chaff, derision, gibe, jeer, laughter, raillery, scorn ▶*verb* 2 LAUGH AT, chaff, deride, jeer, make fun of, mock, poke fun at, sneer

ridiculous *adjective* LAUGHABLE, absurd, comical, farcical, funny, ludicrous, risible, silly, stupid

rife *adjective* WIDESPREAD, common, frequent, general, prevalent, rampant, ubiquitous, universal

riffraff *plural noun* RABBLE, dregs of society (*slang*), hoi polloi, scum of the earth (*slang*)

rifle *verb* RANSACK, burgle, go through, loot, pillage, plunder, rob, sack, strip

rift *noun* 1 BREACH, disagreement, division, falling out (*informal*), quarrel, separation, split 2 SPLIT, break, cleft, crack, crevice, fault, fissure, flaw, gap, opening

rig *verb* 1 FIX (*informal*), arrange,

engineer, gerrymander,
manipulate, tamper with
2 EQUIP, fit out, furnish, outfit,
supply ▶ *noun* **3** APPARATUS,
equipment, fittings, fixtures,
gear, tackle

right *adjective* **1** JUST, equitable,
ethical, fair, good, honest,
lawful, moral, proper
2 CORRECT, accurate, exact,
factual, genuine, precise, true,
valid **3** PROPER, appropriate,
becoming, desirable, done, fit,
fitting, seemly, suitable ▶ *adverb*
4 CORRECTLY, accurately, exactly,
genuinely, precisely, truly
5 PROPERLY, appropriately, aptly,
fittingly, suitably **6** STRAIGHT,
directly, promptly, quickly,
straightaway **7** EXACTLY,
precisely, squarely ▶ *noun*
8 CLAIM, authority, business,
due, freedom, liberty, license,
permission, power, prerogative,
privilege ▶ *verb* **9** RECTIFY,
correct, fix, put right, redress,
settle, sort out, straighten

right away *adverb* IMMEDIATELY,
at once, directly, forthwith,
instantly, now, pronto
(*informal*), straightaway

righteous *adjective* VIRTUOUS,
ethical, fair, good, honest,
honorable, just, moral, pure,
upright

righteousness *noun* VIRTUE,
goodness, honesty, honor,
integrity, justice, morality,
probity, purity, rectitude,
uprightness

rightful *adjective* LAWFUL, due,
just, legal, legitimate, proper,
real, true, valid

rigid *adjective* **1** STRICT, exact,
fixed, inflexible, rigorous, set,
stringent, unbending,

uncompromising **2** STIFF,
inflexible, unyielding

rigmarole *noun* PROCEDURE,
bother, fuss, hassle (*informal*),
nonsense, palaver

rigor *noun* **1** STRICTNESS,
harshness, inflexibility, rigidity,
sternness, stringency
2 HARDSHIP, ordeal, privation,
suffering, trial

rigorous *adjective* STRICT,
demanding, exacting, hard,
harsh, inflexible, severe, stern,
stringent, tough

rig-out *noun* OUTFIT, costume,
dress, garb, gear (*informal*),
get-up (*informal*), togs

rig out *verb* **1** DRESS, array,
attire, clothe, costume **2** EQUIP,
fit, furnish, outfit

rig up *verb* SET UP, arrange,
assemble, build, construct,
erect, fix up, improvise, put
together, put up

rile *verb* ANGER, aggravate
(*informal*), annoy, get *or* put
one's back up, irk, irritate

rim *noun* EDGE, border, brim,
brink, lip, margin, verge

rind *noun* SKIN, crust, husk,
outer layer, peel

ring[1] *verb* **1** CHIME, clang, peal,
reverberate, sound, toll
2 PHONE, buzz (*informal*), call,
telephone ▶ *noun* **3** CHIME, knell,
peal **4** CALL, buzz (*informal*),
phone call

ring[2] *noun* **1** CIRCLE, band,
circuit, halo, hoop, loop, round
2 ARENA, circus, enclosure, rink
3 GANG, association, band,
cartel, circle, group, mob,
syndicate ▶ *verb* **4** ENCIRCLE,
enclose, gird, girdle, surround

rinse *verb* **1** WASH, bathe, clean,

cleanse, dip, splash ▸ *noun*
2 WASH, bath, dip, splash

riot *noun* 1 DISTURBANCE,
anarchy, confusion, disorder,
lawlessness, strife, tumult,
turbulence, turmoil, upheaval
2 REVELRY, carousal, festivity,
frolic, high jinks, merrymaking
3 PROFUSION, display,
extravaganza, show, splash
4 **run riot: a** RAMPAGE, be out of
control, go wild **b** GROW
PROFUSELY, spread like wildfire
▸ *verb* 5 RAMPAGE, go on the
rampage, run riot

riotous *adjective* 1 UNRESTRAINED,
boisterous, loud, noisy,
uproarious, wild 2 UNRULY,
anarchic, disorderly, lawless,
rebellious, rowdy,
ungovernable, violent

rip *verb* 1 TEAR, burst, claw, cut,
gash, lacerate, rend, slash, slit,
split ▸ *noun* 2 TEAR, cut, gash,
hole, laceration, rent, slash, slit,
split

ripe *adjective* 1 MATURE, mellow,
ready, ripened, seasoned
2 SUITABLE, auspicious,
favorable, ideal, opportune,
right, timely

ripen *verb* MATURE, burgeon,
develop, grow ripe, season

rip-off *noun* SWINDLE, cheat, con
(*informal*), con trick (*informal*),
fraud, scam (*slang*), theft

rip off *verb* Slang SWINDLE, cheat,
con (*informal*), defraud, fleece,
rob

riposte *noun* 1 RETORT, answer,
comeback (*informal*), rejoinder,
reply, response, sally ▸ *verb*
2 RETORT, answer, come back,
reply, respond

rise *verb* 1 GET UP, arise, get to

one's feet, stand up 2 GO UP,
ascend, climb 3 ADVANCE, get
on, progress, prosper 4 GET
STEEPER, ascend, go uphill, slope
upwards 5 INCREASE, go up,
grow, intensify, mount 6 REBEL,
mutiny, revolt 7 ORIGINATE,
happen, issue, occur, spring
▸ *noun* 8 INCREASE, upsurge,
upswing, upturn
9 ADVANCEMENT, climb, progress,
promotion 10 UPWARD SLOPE,
ascent, elevation, incline
11 **give rise to** CAUSE, bring
about, effect, produce, result in

risk *noun* 1 DANGER, chance,
gamble, hazard, jeopardy,
peril, pitfall, possibility ▸ *verb*
2 DARE, chance, endanger,
gamble, hazard, imperil,
jeopardize, venture

risky *adjective* DANGEROUS,
chancy (*informal*), hazardous,
perilous, uncertain, unsafe

risqué *adjective* SUGGESTIVE,
bawdy, blue, improper,
indelicate, naughty, racy, ribald

rite *noun* CEREMONY, custom,
observance, practice,
procedure, ritual

ritual *noun* 1 CEREMONY,
observance, rite 2 CUSTOM,
convention, habit, practice,
procedure, protocol, routine,
tradition ▸ *adjective*
3 CEREMONIAL, conventional,
customary, habitual, routine

rival *noun* 1 OPPONENT,
adversary, competitor,
contender, contestant
▸ *adjective* 2 COMPETING,
conflicting, opposing ▸ *verb*
3 EQUAL, be a match for, come
up to, compare with, compete,
match

rivalry *noun* COMPETITION, conflict, contention, contest, opposition

river *noun* 1 STREAM, brook, creek, tributary, waterway 2 FLOW, flood, rush, spate, torrent

riveting *adjective* ENTHRALLING, absorbing, captivating, engrossing, fascinating, gripping, hypnotic, spellbinding

road *noun* WAY, course, highway, lane, motorway, path, pathway, roadway, route, track

roam *verb* WANDER, prowl, ramble, range, rove, stray, travel, walk

roar *verb* 1 CRY, bawl, bay, bellow, howl, shout, yell 2 GUFFAW, hoot, laugh heartily, split one's sides (*informal*) ▸ *noun* 3 CRY, bellow, howl, outcry, shout, yell 4 GUFFAW, hoot

rob *verb* STEAL FROM, burgle, cheat, con (*informal*), defraud, deprive, dispossess, hold up, loot, mug (*informal*), pillage, plunder, raid

robber *noun* THIEF, bandit, burglar, cheat, con man (*informal*), fraud, looter, mugger (*informal*), plunderer, raider, stealer

robbery *noun* THEFT, burglary, hold-up, larceny, mugging (*informal*), pillage, plunder, raid, rip-off (*slang*), stealing, stick-up (*slang*), swindle

robe *noun* 1 GOWN, costume, habit ▸ *verb* 2 CLOTHE, dress, garb

robot *noun* MACHINE, android, automaton, mechanical man

robust *adjective* STRONG, fit, hale, hardy, healthy, muscular, powerful, stout, strapping, sturdy, tough, vigorous

rock[1] *noun* STONE, boulder

rock[2] *verb* 1 SWAY, lurch, pitch, reel, roll, swing, toss 2 SHOCK, astonish, astound, shake, stagger, stun, surprise

rocky[1] *adjective* ROUGH, craggy, rugged, stony

rocky[2] *adjective* UNSTABLE, rickety, shaky, unsteady, wobbly

rod *noun* STICK, bar, baton, cane, pole, shaft, staff, wand

rogue *noun* SCOUNDREL, crook (*informal*), fraud, rascal, scamp, villain

role *noun* 1 JOB, capacity, duty, function, part, position, post, task 2 PART, character, portrayal, representation

roll *verb* 1 TURN, go round, revolve, rotate, spin, swivel, trundle, twirl, wheel, whirl 2 WIND, bind, enfold, envelop, furl, swathe, wrap 3 FLOW, run, undulate 4 LEVEL, even, flatten, press, smooth 5 TUMBLE, lurch, reel, rock, sway, toss ▸ *noun* 6 TURN, cycle, reel, revolution, rotation, spin, twirl, wheel, whirl 7 REGISTER, census, index, list, record 8 RUMBLE, boom, reverberation, roar, thunder

rollicking *adjective* BOISTEROUS, carefree, devil-may-care, exuberant, hearty, jaunty, lively, playful

roly-poly *adjective* PLUMP, buxom, chubby, fat, rounded, tubby

romance *noun* 1 LOVE AFFAIR, affair, amour, attachment, liaison, relationship

2 EXCITEMENT, charm, color, fascination, glamour, mystery
3 STORY, fairy tale, fantasy, legend, love story, melodrama, tale

romantic *adjective* **1** LOVING, amorous, fond, passionate, sentimental, tender **2** IDEALISTIC, dreamy, impractical, starry-eyed, unrealistic **3** EXCITING, colorful, fascinating, glamorous, mysterious ▶ *noun* **4** IDEALIST, dreamer, sentimentalist

romp *verb* **1** FROLIC, caper, cavort, frisk, gambol, have fun, sport **2** WIN EASILY, walk it (*informal*), win by a mile (*informal*), win hands down ▶ *noun* **3** FROLIC, caper, lark (*informal*)

room *noun* **1** CHAMBER, apartment, office **2** SPACE, area, capacity, expanse, extent, leeway, margin, range, scope **3** OPPORTUNITY, chance, occasion, scope

roomy *adjective* SPACIOUS, ample, broad, capacious, commodious, extensive, generous, large, sizable *or* sizeable, wide

root[1] *noun* **1** STEM, rhizome, tuber **2** SOURCE, base, bottom, cause, core, foundation, heart, nucleus, origin, seat, seed **3** **roots** SENSE OF BELONGING, birthplace, cradle, family, heritage, home, origins ▶ *verb* **4** ESTABLISH, anchor, fasten, fix, ground, implant, moor, set, stick

root[2] *verb* DIG, burrow, ferret

rooted *adjective* DEEP-SEATED, confirmed, deep, deeply felt,

entrenched, established, firm, fixed, ingrained

root out *verb* GET RID OF, abolish, do away with, eliminate, eradicate, exterminate, extirpate, remove, weed out

rope *noun* **1** CORD, cable, hawser, line, strand **2** **know the ropes** BE EXPERIENCED, be an old hand, be knowledgeable

rope in *verb* PERSUADE, engage, enlist, inveigle, involve, talk into

roster *noun* ROTA, agenda, catalog, list, register, roll, schedule, table

rostrum *noun* STAGE, dais, platform, podium, stand

rosy *adjective* **1** PINK, red **2** GLOWING, blooming, healthy-looking, radiant, ruddy **3** PROMISING, auspicious, bright, cheerful, encouraging, favorable, hopeful, optimistic

rot *verb* **1** DECAY, crumble, decompose, deteriorate, go bad, molder, perish, putrefy, spoil **2** DETERIORATE, decline, waste away ▶ *noun* **3** DECAY, blight, canker, corruption, decomposition, mold, putrefaction

rotary *adjective* REVOLVING, rotating, spinning, turning

rotate *verb* **1** REVOLVE, go round, gyrate, pivot, reel, spin, swivel, turn, wheel **2** TAKE TURNS, alternate, switch

rotation *noun* **1** REVOLUTION, orbit, reel, spin, spinning, turn, turning, wheel **2** SEQUENCE, alternation, cycle, succession, switching

rotten *adjective* **1** DECAYING, bad, corrupt, crumbling, decomposing, festering, funky (*slang*), moldy, perished, putrescent, rank, smelly, sour, stinking 2 CORRUPT, crooked (*informal*), dishonest, dishonorable, immoral, perfidious 3 *Informal* DESPICABLE, base, contemptible, dirty, lousy (*slang*), mean, nasty, scuzzy (*slang*)

rotund *adjective* 1 ROUND, globular, rounded, spherical 2 PLUMP, chubby, corpulent, fat, fleshy, portly, stout, tubby

rough *adjective* 1 UNEVEN, broken, bumpy, craggy, irregular, jagged, rocky, stony 2 UNGRACIOUS, blunt, brusque, coarse, impolite, rude, unceremonious, uncivil, uncouth, unmannerly 3 APPROXIMATE, estimated, general, imprecise, inexact, sketchy, vague 4 STORMY, choppy, squally, turbulent, wild 5 NASTY, cruel, hard, harsh, tough, unfeeling, unpleasant, violent 6 BASIC, crude, imperfect, incomplete, rudimentary, sketchy, unfinished, unpolished, unrefined 7 UNPLEASANT, arduous, hard, tough, uncomfortable ▶*verb* 8 **rough out** OUTLINE, draft, plan, sketch ▶*noun* 9 OUTLINE, draft, mock-up, preliminary sketch

rough-and-ready *adjective* MAKESHIFT, crude, improvised, provisional, sketchy, stopgap, unpolished, unrefined

round *adjective* 1 SPHERICAL, circular, curved, cylindrical, globular, rotund, rounded 2 PLUMP, ample, fleshy, full, full-fleshed, rotund ▶*verb* 3 GO

ROUND, bypass, circle, encircle, flank, skirt, turn ▶*noun* 4 SPHERE, ball, band, circle, disc, globe, orb, ring 5 STAGE, division, lap, level, period, session, turn 6 SERIES, cycle, sequence, session, succession 7 COURSE, beat, circuit, routine, schedule, series, tour

roundabout *adjective* INDIRECT, circuitous, devious, discursive, evasive, oblique, tortuous

round off *verb* COMPLETE, close, conclude, finish off

roundup *noun* GATHERING, assembly, collection, herding, marshalling, muster, rally

round up *verb* GATHER, collect, drive, group, herd, marshal, muster, rally

rouse *verb* 1 WAKE UP, awaken, call, rise, wake 2 EXCITE, agitate, anger, animate, incite, inflame, move, provoke, stimulate, stir

rousing *adjective* LIVELY, exciting, inspiring, moving, spirited, stimulating, stirring

rout *noun* 1 DEFEAT, beating, debacle, drubbing, overthrow, thrashing ▶*verb* 2 DEFEAT, beat, conquer, crush, destroy, drub, overthrow, thrash, trounce, wipe the floor with (*informal*)

route *noun* WAY, beat, circuit, course, direction, itinerary, journey, path, road

routine *noun* 1 PROCEDURE, custom, method, order, pattern, practice, program ▶*adjective* 2 USUAL, customary, everyday, habitual, normal, ordinary, standard, typical 3 BORING, dull, humdrum, predictable, tedious, tiresome

rove *verb* WANDER, drift, ramble,

range, roam, stray, traipse (*informal*)

row¹ *noun* LINE, bank, column, file, range, series, string

row² *noun* **1** DISPUTE, brawl, quarrel, squabble, tiff, trouble **2** DISTURBANCE, commotion, noise, racket, rumpus, tumult, uproar ▶*verb* **3** QUARREL, argue, dispute, fight, squabble, wrangle

rowdy *adjective* **1** DISORDERLY, loud, noisy, rough, unruly, wild ▶*noun* **2** HOOLIGAN, lout, ruffian

royal *adjective* **1** REGAL, imperial, kingly, princely, queenly, sovereign **2** SPLENDID, grand, impressive, magnificent, majestic, stately

rub *verb* **1** POLISH, clean, scour, shine, wipe **2** CHAFE, abrade, fray, grate, scrape ▶*noun* **3** POLISH, shine, stroke, wipe **4** MASSAGE, caress, kneading

rubbish *noun* **1** WASTE, garbage, junk (*informal*), litter, lumber, refuse, scrap, trash **2** NONSENSE, claptrap (*informal*), garbage, hogwash, hot air (*informal*), trash, tripe (*informal*)

rub out *verb* ERASE, cancel, delete, efface, obliterate, remove, wipe out

ruckus *noun* Informal UPROAR, commotion, disturbance, fracas, fuss, hoopla, trouble

ruddy *adjective* ROSY, blooming, fresh, glowing, healthy, radiant, red, reddish, rosy-cheeked

rude *adjective* **1** IMPOLITE, abusive, cheeky, discourteous, disrespectful, ill-mannered, impertinent, impudent, insolent, insulting, uncivil,

unmannerly **2** VULGAR, boorish, brutish, coarse, graceless, loutish, oafish, rough, uncivilized, uncouth, uncultured **3** UNPLEASANT, abrupt, harsh, sharp, startling, sudden **4** ROUGHLY-MADE, artless, crude, inartistic, inelegant, makeshift, primitive, raw, rough, simple

rudimentary *adjective* BASIC, early, elementary, fundamental, initial, primitive, undeveloped

rudiments *plural noun* BASICS, beginnings, elements, essentials, foundation, fundamentals

rue *verb* REGRET, be sorry for, kick oneself for, lament, mourn, repent

rueful *adjective* REGRETFUL, contrite, mournful, penitent, remorseful, repentant, sorrowful, sorry

ruffian *noun* THUG, brute, bully, hoodlum, hooligan, tough

ruffle *verb* **1** DISARRANGE, dishevel, disorder, mess up, rumple, tousle **2** ANNOY, agitate, fluster, irritate, nettle, peeve (*informal*), tick off, upset

rugged *adjective* **1** ROUGH, broken, bumpy, craggy, difficult, irregular, jagged, ragged, rocky, uneven **2** STRONG-FEATURED, rough-hewn, weather-beaten **3** TOUGH, brawny, burly, husky (*informal*), muscular, robust, strong, sturdy, well-built

ruin *verb* **1** DESTROY, crush, defeat, demolish, devastate, lay waste, smash, wreck **2** BANKRUPT, impoverish, pauperize 3 SPOIL, blow (*slang*), botch, damage, make a mess of, mess up, screw up (*informal*) ▶ *noun* 4 DESTRUCTION, breakdown, collapse, defeat, devastation, downfall, fall, undoing, wreck 5 DISREPAIR, decay, disintegration, ruination, wreckage 6 BANKRUPTCY, destitution, insolvency

ruinous *adjective* 1 DEVASTATING, calamitous, catastrophic, destructive, dire, disastrous, shattering 2 EXTRAVAGANT, crippling, immoderate, wasteful

rule *noun* 1 REGULATION, axiom, canon, decree, direction, guideline, law, maxim, precept, principle, tenet 2 CUSTOM, convention, habit, practice, procedure, routine, tradition 3 GOVERNMENT, authority, command, control, dominion, jurisdiction, mastery, power, regime, reign 4 **as a rule** USUALLY, generally, mainly, normally, on the whole, ordinarily ▶ *verb* 5 GOVERN, be in authority, be in power, command, control, direct, reign 6 BE PREVALENT, be customary, predominate, preponderate, prevail 7 DECREE, decide, judge, pronounce, settle

rule out *verb* EXCLUDE, ban, debar, dismiss, disqualify, eliminate, leave out, preclude, prohibit, reject

ruler *noun* 1 GOVERNOR, commander, controller, head of state, king *or* queen, leader, lord, monarch, potentate, sovereign 2 MEASURE, rule, yardstick

ruling *noun* 1 DECISION, adjudication, decree, judgment, pronouncement, verdict ▶ *adjective* 2 GOVERNING, commanding, controlling, reigning 3 PREDOMINANT, chief, dominant, main, pre-eminent, preponderant, prevailing, principal

ruminate *verb* PONDER, cogitate, consider, contemplate, deliberate, mull over, muse, reflect, think, turn over in one's mind

rummage *verb* SEARCH, delve, forage, hunt, ransack, root

rumor *noun* STORY, buzz, dirt (*slang*), gossip, hearsay, news, report, talk, whisper, word

rump *noun* BUTTOCKS, backside (*informal*), bottom, buns (*slang*), butt (*informal*), derrière (*euphemistic*), hindquarters, posterior, rear, rear end, seat

rumpus *noun* COMMOTION, disturbance, furor, fuss, hue and cry, noise, row, uproar

run *verb* 1 RACE, bolt, dash, gallop, hurry, jog, lope, rush, scurry, sprint 2 FLEE, beat a retreat, beat it (*slang*), bolt, escape, make a run for it, take flight, take off (*informal*), take to one's heels 3 MOVE, course, glide, go, pass, roll, skim 4 WORK, function, go, operate, perform 5 MANAGE, administer, be in charge of, control, direct, handle, head, lead, operate 6 CONTINUE, extend, go, proceed, reach, stretch 7 FLOW, discharge, go, gush, leak, pour, spill, spout, stream 8 MELT, dissolve, go soft, liquefy 9 PUBLISH, display, feature, print 10 COMPETE, be a candidate, contend, put oneself up for, stand, take part **11** SMUGGLE, bootleg, traffic in ▶ noun **12** RACE, dash, gallop, jog, rush, sprint, spurt **13** RIDE, drive, excursion, jaunt, outing, spin (informal), trip **14** SEQUENCE, course, period, season, series, spell, stretch, string **15** ENCLOSURE, coop, pen **16 in the long run** EVENTUALLY, in the end, ultimately

run across verb MEET, bump into, come across, encounter, run into

runaway noun **1** FUGITIVE, deserter, escapee, refugee, truant ▶ adjective **2** ESCAPED, fleeing, fugitive, loose, wild

run away verb FLEE, abscond, bolt, escape, fly the coop (informal), make a run for it, scram (informal), take to one's heels

run-down adjective **1** EXHAUSTED, below par, debilitated, drained, enervated, unhealthy, weak, weary, worn-out **2** DILAPIDATED, broken-down, decrepit, ramshackle, seedy, shabby, worn-out

run down verb **1** CRITICIZE, bad-mouth (slang), belittle, decry, denigrate, disparage, knock (informal) **2** REDUCE, curtail, cut, cut back, decrease, downsize, trim **3** KNOCK DOWN, hit, knock over, run into, run over **4** WEAKEN, debilitate, exhaust

run into verb **1** MEET, bump into, come across or upon, encounter, run across **2** HIT, collide with, strike

runner noun **1** ATHLETE, jogger, sprinter **2** MESSENGER, courier,

dispatch bearer, errand boy

running adjective **1** CONTINUOUS, constant, incessant, perpetual, twenty-four-seven (slang), unbroken, uninterrupted **2** FLOWING, moving, streaming ▶ noun **3** MANAGEMENT, administration, control, direction, leadership, organization, supervision **4** WORKING, functioning, maintenance, operation, performance

runny adjective FLOWING, fluid, liquefied, liquid, melted, watery

run off verb FLEE, bolt, escape, fly the coop (informal), make off, run away, take flight, take to one's heels

run out verb BE USED UP, be exhausted, dry up, end, fail, finish, give out

run over verb **1** KNOCK DOWN, hit, knock over, run down **2** GO THROUGH, check, go over, rehearse, run through

run through verb REHEARSE, go over, practise, read, run over

rupture noun **1** BREAK, breach, burst, crack, fissure, rent, split, tear ▶ verb **2** BREAK, burst, crack, separate, sever, split, tear

rural adjective RUSTIC, agricultural, country, pastoral, sylvan

ruse noun TRICK, device, dodge, hoax, maneuver, ploy, stratagem, subterfuge

rush verb **1** HURRY, bolt, career, dash, fly, hasten, race, run, shoot, speed, tear **2** PUSH, hurry, hustle, press **3** ATTACK, charge, storm ▶ noun **4** HURRY, charge, dash, haste, race, scramble, stampede, surge

5 ATTACK, assault, charge, onslaught ▶*adjective* **6** HASTY, fast, hurried, quick, rapid, swift, urgent

rust *noun* **1** CORROSION, oxidation **2** MILDEW, blight, mold, must, rot ▶*verb* **3** CORRODE, oxidize

rustic *adjective* **1** RURAL, country, pastoral, sylvan **2** UNCOUTH, awkward, coarse, crude, rough ▶*noun* **3** YOKEL, boor, bumpkin, clod, clodhopper (*informal*), hick (*informal*), hillbilly, peasant, redneck (*slang*)

rustle *verb* **1** CRACKLE, crinkle, whisper ▶*noun* **2** CRACKLE, crinkling, rustling, whisper

rusty *adjective* **1** CORRODED, oxidized, rust-covered, rusted **2** REDDISH, chestnut, coppery, reddish-brown, russet, rust-colored **3** OUT OF PRACTICE, stale, unpracticed, weak

rut *noun* **1** GROOVE, furrow, indentation, track, trough, wheel mark **2** HABIT, dead end, pattern, routine, system

ruthless *adjective* MERCILESS, brutal, callous, cruel, harsh, heartless, pitiless, relentless, remorseless

rutted *adjective* GROOVED, cut, furrowed, gouged, holed, indented, marked, scored

—— **S s** ——

sabotage *noun* **1** DAMAGE, destruction, disruption, subversion, wrecking ▶*verb* **2** DAMAGE, destroy, disable, disrupt, incapacitate, subvert, vandalize, wreck

saccharine *adjective* OVERSWEET, cloying, honeyed, nauseating, sickly, sugary, syrupy

sack¹ *noun* **1 the sack** DISMISSAL, discharge, the ax (*informal*), the boot (*slang*) ▶*verb* **2** DISMISS, ax (*informal*), discharge, fire (*informal*)

sack² *noun* **1** PLUNDERING, looting, pillage ▶*verb* **2** PLUNDER, loot, pillage, raid, rob, ruin, strip

sacred *adjective* **1** HOLY, blessed, divine, hallowed, revered, sanctified **2** RELIGIOUS, ecclesiastical, holy **3** INVIOLABLE, protected, sacrosanct

sacrifice *noun* **1** SURRENDER, loss, renunciation **2** OFFERING, oblation ▶*verb* **3** GIVE UP, forego, forfeit, let go, lose, say good-bye to, surrender **4** OFFER, immolate, offer up

sacrilege *noun* DESECRATION, blasphemy, heresy, impiety, irreverence, profanation, violation

sacrilegious *adjective* PROFANE, blasphemous, desecrating, impious, irreligious, irreverent

sacrosanct *adjective* INVIOLABLE, hallowed, inviolate, sacred, sanctified, set apart, untouchable

sad *adjective* **1** UNHAPPY, blue, dejected, depressed, doleful, down, low, low-spirited, melancholy, mournful, woebegone **2** TRAGIC, depressing, dismal, grievous, harrowing, heart-rending, moving, pathetic, pitiful, poignant, upsetting

3 DEPLORABLE, bad, lamentable, sorry, wretched

sadden verb UPSET, deject, depress, distress, grieve, make sad

saddle verb BURDEN, encumber, load

sadistic adjective CRUEL, barbarous, brutal, ruthless, vicious

sadness noun UNHAPPINESS, dejection, depression, despondency, grief, melancholy, misery, poignancy, sorrow, the blues

safe adjective **1** SECURE, impregnable, in safe hands, out of danger, out of harm's way, protected, safe and sound **2** UNHARMED, all right, intact, O.K. or okay (informal), undamaged, unhurt, unscathed **3** RISK-FREE, certain, impregnable, secure, sound ▶noun **4** STRONGBOX, coffer, deposit box, repository, safe-deposit box, vault

safeguard verb **1** PROTECT, defend, guard, look after, preserve ▶noun **2** PROTECTION, defense, guard, security

safely adverb IN SAFETY, in one piece, safe and sound, with impunity, without risk

safety noun **1** SECURITY, impregnability, protection **2** SHELTER, cover, refuge, sanctuary

sag verb **1** SINK, bag, dip, droop, fall, give way, hang loosely, slump **2** TIRE, droop, flag, wane, weaken, wilt

saga noun TALE, epic, legend, narrative, story, yarn

sage noun **1** WISE MAN, elder,

guru, master, philosopher ▶adjective **2** WISE, judicious, sagacious, sapient, sensible

sail verb **1** EMBARK, set sail **2** GLIDE, drift, float, fly, skim, soar, sweep, wing **3** PILOT, steer

sailor noun MARINER, marine, sea dog, seafarer, seaman

saintly adjective VIRTUOUS, godly, holy, pious, religious, righteous, saintlike

sake noun **1** BENEFIT, account, behalf, good, interest, welfare **2** PURPOSE, aim, end, motive, objective, reason

salacious adjective LASCIVIOUS, carnal, erotic, lecherous, lewd, libidinous, lustful

salary noun PAY, earnings, income, wage, wages

sale noun **1** SELLING, deal, disposal, marketing, transaction **2 for sale** AVAILABLE, obtainable, on the market

salient adjective PROMINENT, conspicuous, important, noticeable, outstanding, pronounced, striking

sallow adjective WAN, anemic, pale, pallid, pasty, sickly, unhealthy, yellowish

salt noun **1** SEASONING, flavor, relish, savor, taste **2 with a grain** or **pinch of salt** SKEPTICALLY, cynically, disbelievingly, suspiciously, with reservations ▶adjective **3** SALTY, brackish, briny, saline

salty adjective SALT, brackish, briny, saline

salubrious adjective HEALTHY, beneficial, good for one, health-giving, wholesome

salutary adjective BENEFICIAL, advantageous, good for one, profitable, useful, valuable

salute *noun* 1 GREETING, address, recognition, salutation ▶ *verb* 2 GREET, acknowledge, address, hail, welcome 3 HONOR, acknowledge, pay tribute *or* homage to, recognize

salvage *verb* SAVE, recover, redeem, rescue, retrieve

salvation *noun* SAVING, deliverance, escape, preservation, redemption, rescue

salve *noun* OINTMENT, balm, cream, emollient, lotion

same *adjective* 1 AFOREMENTIONED, aforesaid 2 IDENTICAL, alike, corresponding, duplicate, equal, twin 3 UNCHANGED, changeless, consistent, constant, invariable, unaltered, unvarying

sample *noun* 1 SPECIMEN, example, instance, model, pattern ▶ *verb* 2 TEST, experience, inspect, taste, try ▶ *adjective* 3 TEST, representative, specimen, trial

sanctify *verb* CONSECRATE, cleanse, hallow

sanctimonious *adjective* HOLIER-THAN-THOU, hypocritical, pious, self-righteous, smug

sanction *noun* 1 PERMISSION, approval, authority, authorization, backing, O.K. *or* okay (*informal*), stamp *or* seal of approval 2 (often plural) BAN, boycott, coercive measures, embargo, penalty ▶ *verb* 3 PERMIT, allow, approve, authorize, endorse

sanctity *noun* 1 SACREDNESS, inviolability 2 HOLINESS, godliness, goodness, grace,

piety, righteousness

sanctuary *noun* 1 SHRINE, altar, church, temple 2 PROTECTION, asylum, haven, refuge, retreat, shelter 3 RESERVE, conservation area, national park, nature reserve

sane *adjective* 1 RATIONAL, all there (*informal*), compos mentis, in one's right mind, mentally sound, of sound mind 2 SENSIBLE, balanced, judicious, level-headed, reasonable, sound

sanguine *adjective* CHEERFUL, buoyant, confident, hopeful, optimistic

sanitary *adjective* HYGIENIC, clean, germ-free, healthy, wholesome

sanity *noun* 1 MENTAL HEALTH, normality, rationality, reason, saneness 2 GOOD SENSE, common sense, level-headedness, rationality, sense

sap^1 *noun* 1 VITAL FLUID, essence, lifeblood 2 *Informal Slang* FOOL, dork (*slang*), idiot, jerk (*slang*), ninny, schmuck (*slang*), simpleton

sap^2 *verb* WEAKEN, deplete, drain, exhaust, undermine

sarcasm *noun* IRONY, bitterness, cynicism, derision, mockery, satire

sarcastic *adjective* IRONIC, acid, biting, caustic, cutting, cynical, mocking, sardonic, satirical

sardonic *adjective* MOCKING, cynical, derisive, dry, ironic, sarcastic, sneering, wry

Satan *noun* THE DEVIL, Beelzebub, Lord of the Flies, Lucifer, Mephistopheles, Prince of Darkness, The Evil One

satanic *adjective* EVIL, black, demonic, devilish, diabolic, fiendish, hellish, infernal, wicked

satiate *verb* 1 GLUT, cloy, gorge, jade, nauseate, overfill, stuff, surfeit 2 SATISFY, sate, slake

satire *noun* MOCKERY, burlesque, caricature, irony, lampoon, parody, ridicule, spoof (*informal*)

satirical *adjective* MOCKING, biting, caustic, cutting, incisive, ironic

satirize *verb* RIDICULE, burlesque, deride, lampoon, parody, pillory

satisfaction *noun* 1 CONTENTMENT, comfort, content, enjoyment, happiness, pleasure, pride, repletion, satiety 2 FULFILLMENT, achievement, assuaging, gratification

satisfactory *adjective* ADEQUATE, acceptable, all right, average, fair, good enough, passable, sufficient

satisfy *verb* 1 CONTENT, assuage, gratify, indulge, pacify, pander to, please, quench, sate, slake 2 FULFILL, answer, do, meet, serve, suffice 3 PERSUADE, assure, convince, reassure

saturate *verb* SOAK, drench, imbue, souse, steep, suffuse, waterlog, wet through

saturated *adjective* SOAKED, drenched, dripping, soaking (wet), sodden, sopping (wet), waterlogged, wet through

saturnine *adjective* GLOOMY, dour, glum, grave, morose, somber

saucy *adjective* 1 IMPUDENT, cheeky (*informal*), forward, impertinent, insolent, pert, presumptuous, rude 2 JAUNTY,

dashing, gay, perky

saunter *verb* 1 STROLL, amble, meander, mosey (*informal*), ramble, roam, wander ▶ *noun* 2 STROLL, airing, amble, ramble, turn, walk

savage *adjective* 1 WILD, feral, undomesticated, untamed 2 UNCULTIVATED, rough, rugged, uncivilized 3 CRUEL, barbarous, bestial, bloodthirsty, brutal, ferocious, fierce, harsh, ruthless, sadistic, vicious 4 PRIMITIVE, rude, unspoilt ▶ *noun* 5 LOUT, boor, yahoo ▶ *verb* 6 ATTACK, lacerate, mangle, maul

savagery *noun* CRUELTY, barbarity, brutality, ferocity, ruthlessness, viciousness

save *verb* 1 RESCUE, deliver, free, liberate, recover, redeem, salvage 2 PROTECT, conserve, guard, keep safe, look after, preserve, safeguard 3 KEEP, collect, gather, hoard, hold, husband, lay by, put by, reserve, set aside, store

saving *noun* 1 ECONOMY, bargain, discount, reduction ▶ *adjective* 2 REDEEMING, compensatory, extenuating

savings *plural noun* NEST EGG, fund, reserves, resources, store

savior *noun* RESCUER, defender, deliverer, liberator, preserver, protector, redeemer

Savior *noun* CHRIST, Jesus, Messiah, Redeemer

savoir-faire *noun* SOCIAL KNOW-HOW (*informal*), diplomacy, discretion, finesse, poise, social graces, tact, urbanity, worldliness

savor *verb* 1 ENJOY, appreciate,

delight in, luxuriate in, relish, revel in **2** (often with *of*) SUGGEST, be suggestive, show signs, smack ▶ *noun* **3** FLAVOR, piquancy, relish, smack, smell, tang, taste

savory *adjective* SPICY, appetizing, full-flavored, luscious, mouthwatering, palatable, piquant, rich, tasty

say *verb* **1** SPEAK, affirm, announce, assert, declare, maintain, mention, pronounce, remark, state, utter, voice **2** SUPPOSE, assume, conjecture, estimate, guess, imagine, presume, surmise **3** EXPRESS, communicate, convey, imply ▶ *noun* **4** CHANCE TO SPEAK, voice, vote **5** INFLUENCE, authority, clout (*informal*), power, weight

saying *noun* PROVERB, adage, aphorism, axiom, dictum, maxim

scale¹ *noun* FLAKE, lamina, layer, plate

scale² *noun* **1** GRADUATION, gradation, hierarchy, ladder, progression, ranking, sequence, series, steps **2** RATIO, proportion **3** DEGREE, extent, range, reach, scope ▶ *verb* **4** CLIMB, ascend, clamber, escalade, mount, surmount **5** ADJUST, proportion, regulate

scam *verb Slang* **1** CHEAT, cook the books (*informal*), diddle (*informal*), fix, swindle, wangle (*informal*) ▶ *noun* **2** *Slang* FRAUD, fix, racket (*slang*), swindle

scamp *noun* RASCAL, devil, imp, monkey, rogue, scallywag (*informal*)

scamper *verb* RUN, dart, dash, hasten, hurry, romp, scoot,

scurry, scuttle

scan *verb* **1** GLANCE OVER, check, check out (*informal*), examine, eye, look through, run one's eye over, run over, skim **2** SCRUTINIZE, investigate, scour, search, survey, sweep

scandal *noun* **1** CRIME, disgrace, embarrassment, offense, sin, wrongdoing **2** SHAME, defamation, discredit, disgrace, dishonor, ignominy, infamy, opprobrium, stigma **3** GOSSIP, aspersion, dirt, rumors, slander, talk, tattle

scandalize *verb* SHOCK, affront, appall, horrify, offend, outrage

scandalous *adjective* **1** SHOCKING, disgraceful, disreputable, infamous, outrageous, shameful, unseemly **2** SLANDEROUS, defamatory, libelous, scurrilous, untrue

scant *adjective* MEAGER, barely sufficient, little, minimal, sparse

scanty *adjective* MEAGER, bare, deficient, inadequate, insufficient, lousy (*slang*), poor, scant, short, skimpy, sparse, thin

scapegoat *noun* WHIPPING BOY, fall guy (*informal*)

scar *noun* **1** MARK, blemish, injury, wound ▶ *verb* **2** MARK, damage, disfigure

scarce *adjective* RARE, few, few and far between, infrequent, in short supply, insufficient, uncommon

scarcely *adverb* **1** HARDLY, barely **2** DEFINITELY NOT, hardly

scarcity *noun* SHORTAGE, dearth, deficiency, insufficiency, lack, paucity, rareness, want

scare *verb* 1 FRIGHTEN, alarm, dismay, intimidate, panic, shock, startle, terrify ▶ *noun* 2 FRIGHT, panic, shock, start, terror

scared *adjective* FRIGHTENED, fearful, panicky, panic-stricken, petrified, shaken, startled, terrified

scary *adjective* FRIGHTENING, alarming, chilling, creepy (*informal*), horrifying, spine-chilling, spooky (*informal*), terrifying

scathing *adjective* CRITICAL, biting, caustic, cutting, harsh, sarcastic, scornful, trenchant, withering

scatter *verb* 1 THROW ABOUT, diffuse, disseminate, fling, shower, spread, sprinkle, strew 2 DISPERSE, disband, dispel, dissipate

scatterbrain *noun* FEATHERBRAIN, butterfly, flibbertigibbet

scenario *noun* STORY LINE, outline, résumé, summary, synopsis

scene *noun* 1 SITE, area, locality, place, position, setting, spot 2 SETTING, backdrop, background, location, set 3 SHOW, display, drama, exhibition, pageant, picture, sight, spectacle 4 ACT, division, episode, part 5 VIEW, landscape, panorama, prospect, vista 6 FUSS, commotion, exhibition, performance, row, tantrum, to-do 7 *Informal* WORLD, arena, business, environment

scenery *noun* 1 LANDSCAPE, surroundings, terrain, view, vista 2 *Theatre* SET, backdrop, flats, setting, stage set

scenic *adjective* PICTURESQUE, beautiful, panoramic, spectacular, striking

scent *noun* 1 FRAGRANCE, aroma, bouquet, odor, perfume, smell 2 TRAIL, spoor, track ▶ *verb* 3 DETECT, discern, nose out, sense, smell, sniff

scented *adjective* FRAGRANT, aromatic, odoriferous, perfumed, sweet-smelling

schedule *noun* 1 PLAN, agenda, calendar, catalog, inventory, list, program, timetable ▶ *verb* 2 PLAN, appoint, arrange, book, organize, program

scheme *noun* 1 PLAN, program, project, proposal, strategy, system, tactics 2 DIAGRAM, blueprint, chart, draft, layout, outline, pattern 3 PLOT, conspiracy, intrigue, maneuver, ploy, ruse, stratagem, subterfuge ▶ *verb* 4 PLAN, lay plans, project, work out 5 PLOT, collude, conspire, intrigue, machinate, maneuver

scheming *adjective* CALCULATING, artful, conniving, cunning, sly, tricky, underhand, wily

schism *noun* DIVISION, breach, break, rift, rupture, separation, split

scholar *noun* 1 INTELLECTUAL, academic, savant 2 STUDENT, disciple, learner, pupil, schoolboy *or* schoolgirl

scholarly *adjective* LEARNED, academic, bookish, erudite, intellectual, lettered, scholastic

scholarship *noun* 1 LEARNING, book-learning, education, erudition, knowledge 2 BURSARY, fellowship

scholastic *adjective* LEARNED, academic, lettered, scholarly

school *noun* 1 ACADEMY, college, faculty, institute, institution, seminary 2 GROUP, adherents, circle, denomination, devotees, disciples, faction, followers, set ▸ *verb* 3 TRAIN, coach, discipline, drill, educate, instruct, tutor

schooling *noun* 1 TEACHING, education, tuition 2 TRAINING, coaching, drill, instruction

science *noun* 1 DISCIPLINE, body of knowledge, branch of knowledge 2 SKILL, art, technique

scientific *adjective* SYSTEMATIC, accurate, controlled, exact, mathematical, precise

scientist *noun* INVENTOR, technophile

scintillating *adjective* BRILLIANT, animated, bright, dazzling, exciting, glittering, lively, sparkling, stimulating

scoff[1] *verb* SCORN, belittle, deride, despise, jeer, knock (*informal*), laugh at, mock, pooh-pooh, ridicule, sneer

scoff[2] *verb* GOBBLE (UP), bolt, devour, gorge oneself on, gulp down, guzzle, wolf

scold *verb* REPRIMAND, berate, castigate, censure, chew out (*slang*), find fault with, lecture, rebuke, reproach, reprove, tell off (*informal*), upbraid

scolding *noun* REBUKE, lecture, row, telling-off (*informal*)

scoop *noun* 1 LADLE, dipper, spoon 2 EXCLUSIVE, exposé, revelation, sensation ▸ *verb* 3 (often with *up*) LIFT, gather up, pick up, take up 4 (often with *out*) HOLLOW, bail, dig, empty,

excavate, gouge, shovel

scope *noun* 1 OPPORTUNITY, freedom, latitude, liberty, room, space 2 RANGE, area, capacity, orbit, outlook, reach, span, sphere

scorch *verb* BURN, parch, roast, sear, shrivel, singe, wither

scorching *adjective* BURNING, baking, boiling, fiery, flaming, red-hot, roasting, searing

score *noun* 1 POINTS, grade, mark, outcome, record, result, total 2 GROUNDS, basis, cause, ground, reason 3 GRIEVANCE, grudge, injury, injustice, wrong 4 **scores** LOTS, hundreds, masses, millions, multitudes, myriads, swarms ▸ *verb* 5 GAIN, achieve, chalk up (*informal*), make, notch up (*informal*), win 6 KEEP COUNT, count, record, register, tally 7 CUT, deface, gouge, graze, mark, scrape, scratch, slash 8 (with *out* or *through*) CROSS OUT, cancel, delete, obliterate, strike out 9 *Music* ARRANGE, adapt, orchestrate, set

scorn *noun* 1 CONTEMPT, derision, disdain, disparagement, mockery, sarcasm ▸ *verb* 2 DESPISE, be above, deride, disdain, flout, reject, scoff at, slight, spurn

scornful *adjective* CONTEMPTUOUS, derisive, disdainful, haughty, jeering, mocking, sarcastic, sardonic, scathing, scoffing, sneering

scoundrel *noun* ROGUE, bastard (*offensive*), good-for-nothing, heel (*slang*), miscreant, rascal, reprobate, scamp, swine, villain

scour[1] *verb* RUB, abrade, buff,

clean, polish, scrub, wash

scour[2] verb SEARCH, beat, comb, hunt, ransack

scourge noun 1 AFFLICTION, bane, curse, infliction, misfortune, pest, plague, terror, torment 2 WHIP, cat, lash, strap, switch, thong ▶ verb 3 AFFLICT, curse, plague, terrorize, torment 4 WHIP, beat, cane, flog, horsewhip, lash, thrash

scout noun 1 VANGUARD, advance guard, lookout, outrider, precursor, reconnoiterer ▶ verb 2 RECONNOITER, investigate, observe, probe, spy, survey, watch

scowl verb 1 GLOWER, frown, lour or lower ▶ noun 2 GLOWER, black look, dirty look, frown

scrabble verb SCRAPE, claw, scramble, scratch

scraggy adjective SCRAWNY, angular, bony, lean, skinny

scram verb GO AWAY, abscond, beat it (slang), clear off (informal), get lost (informal), leave, make oneself scarce (informal), make tracks, vamoose (slang)

scramble verb 1 STRUGGLE, climb, crawl, scrabble, swarm 2 STRIVE, contend, jostle, push, run, rush, vie ▶ noun 3 CLIMB, trek 4 STRUGGLE, commotion, competition, confusion, melee or mêlée, race, rush, tussle

scrap[1] noun 1 PIECE, bit, crumb, fragment, grain, morsel, part, particle, portion, sliver, snippet 2 WASTE, junk, off cuts 3 **scraps** LEFTOVERS, bits, leavings, remains ▶ verb 4 DISCARD, abandon, ditch (slang), drop, jettison,

throw away or out, write off

scrap[2] Informal ▶ noun 1 FIGHT, argument, battle, disagreement, dispute, quarrel, row, squabble, wrangle ▶ verb 2 FIGHT, argue, row, squabble, wrangle

scrape verb 1 GRAZE, bark, rub, scratch, scuff, skin 2 RUB, clean, erase, remove, scour 3 GRATE, grind, rasp, scratch, squeak 4 SCRIMP, pinch, save, skimp, stint 5 **scrape through** GET BY (informal), just make it, struggle ▶ noun 6 Informal PREDICAMENT, awkward situation, difficulty, dilemma, fix (informal), mess, plight, tight spot

scrapheap noun **on the scrapheap** DISCARDED, ditched (slang), jettisoned, put out to pasture (informal), redundant

scrappy adjective FRAGMENTARY, bitty, disjointed, incomplete, piecemeal, sketchy, thrown together

scratch verb 1 MARK, claw, cut, damage, etch, grate, graze, lacerate, score, scrape 2 WITHDRAW, abolish, call off, cancel, delete, eliminate, erase, pull out ▶ noun 3 MARK, blemish, claw mark, gash, graze, laceration, scrape 4 **up to scratch** ADEQUATE, acceptable, satisfactory, sufficient, up to standard ▶ adjective 5 IMPROVISED, impromptu, rough-and-ready

scrawl verb SCRIBBLE, doodle, squiggle, writing

scrawny adjective THIN, bony, gaunt, lean, scraggy, skin-and-bones (informal), skinny, undernourished

scream verb **1** CRY, bawl, screech, shriek, yell ▶noun **2** CRY, howl, screech, shriek, yell, yelp

screech noun, verb CRY, scream, shriek

screen noun **1** COVER, awning, canopy, cloak, guard, partition, room divider, shade, shelter, shield **2** MESH, net ▶verb **3** COVER, cloak, conceal, hide, mask, shade, veil **4** PROTECT, defend, guard, shelter, shield **5** VET, evaluate, examine, filter, gauge, scan, sift, sort **6** BROADCAST, present, put on, show

screw verb **1** TURN, tighten, twist **2** Informal, (often with out of) EXTORT, extract, wrest, wring

screw up verb **1** Informal BUNGLE, botch, make a mess of (slang), mess up, mishandle, spoil **2** DISTORT, contort, pucker, wrinkle

screwy adjective CRAZY, crackpot (informal), eccentric, loopy (informal), nutty (slang), odd, off-the-wall (slang), out to lunch (informal), weird

scribble verb SCRAWL, dash off, jot, write

scribe noun COPYIST, amanuensis, writer

scrimp verb ECONOMIZE, be frugal, save, scrape, skimp, stint, tighten one's belt

script noun **1** TEXT, book, copy, dialogue, libretto, lines, words **2** HANDWRITING, calligraphy, penmanship, writing

Scripture noun THE BIBLE, Holy Bible, Holy Scripture, Holy Writ, The Good Book, The Gospels, The Scriptures

scrounge verb Informal CADGE, beg, bum (informal), freeload (slang), sponge (informal)

scrounger adjective CADGER, freeloader (slang), parasite, sponger (informal)

scrub verb SCOUR, clean, cleanse, rub

scruple noun **1** MISGIVING, compunction, doubt, hesitation, qualm, reluctance, second thoughts, uneasiness ▶verb **2** HAVE MISGIVINGS ABOUT, demur, doubt, have qualms about, hesitate, think twice about

scrupulous adjective **1** MORAL, conscientious, honorable, principled, upright **2** CAREFUL, exact, fastidious, meticulous, precise, punctilious, rigorous, strict

scrutinize verb EXAMINE, explore, inspect, investigate, peruse, pore over, probe, scan, search, study

scrutiny noun EXAMINATION, analysis, exploration, inspection, investigation, perusal, search, study

scuffle verb **1** FIGHT, clash, grapple, jostle, struggle, tussle ▶noun **2** FIGHT, brawl, commotion, disturbance, fray, scrimmage, skirmish, tussle

sculpture verb SCULPT, carve, chisel, fashion, form, hew, model, mold, shape

scum noun **1** IMPURITIES, dross, film, froth **2** RABBLE, dregs of society, riffraff, trash

scurrilous adjective SLANDEROUS, abusive, defamatory, insulting, scandalous, vituperative

scurry verb 1 HURRY, dart, dash, race, scamper, scoot, scuttle, sprint ▶ noun 2 FLURRY, scampering, whirl

scuttle verb RUN, bustle, hasten, hurry, rush, scamper, scoot, scurry

sea noun 1 OCEAN, main, the deep, the waves 2 EXPANSE, abundance, mass, multitude, plethora, profusion 3 **at sea** BEWILDERED, baffled, confused, lost, mystified, puzzled

seafaring adjective NAUTICAL, marine, maritime, naval

seal noun 1 AUTHENTICATION, confirmation, imprimatur, insignia, ratification, stamp ▶ verb 2 CLOSE, bung, enclose, fasten, plug, shut, stop, stopper, stop up 3 AUTHENTICATE, confirm, ratify, stamp, validate 4 SETTLE, clinch, conclude, consummate, finalize 5 **seal off** ISOLATE, put out of bounds, quarantine, segregate

seam noun 1 JOINT, closure 2 LAYER, lode, stratum, vein 3 RIDGE, furrow, line, wrinkle

sear verb SCORCH, burn, sizzle

search verb 1 LOOK, comb, examine, explore, hunt, inspect, investigate, ransack, scour, scrutinize ▶ noun 2 LOOK, examination, exploration, hunt, inspection, investigation, pursuit, quest

searching adjective KEEN, close, intent, penetrating, piercing, probing, quizzical, sharp

season noun 1 PERIOD, spell, term, time ▶ verb 2 FLAVOR, enliven, pep up, salt, spice

seasonable adjective APPROPRIATE, convenient, fit, opportune, providential, suitable, timely, well-timed

seasoned adjective EXPERIENCED, hardened, practiced, time-served, veteran

seasoning noun FLAVORING, condiment, dressing, relish, salt and pepper, sauce, spice

seat noun 1 CHAIR, bench, pew, settle, stall, stool 2 CENTER, capital, heart, hub, place, site, situation, source 3 RESIDENCE, abode, ancestral hall, house, mansion 4 MEMBERSHIP, chair, constituency, incumbency, place ▶ verb 5 SIT, fix, install, locate, place, set, settle 6 HOLD, accommodate, cater for, contain, sit, take

seating noun ACCOMMODATION, chairs, places, room, seats

secede verb WITHDRAW, break with, leave, pull out, quit, resign, split from

secluded adjective PRIVATE, cloistered, cut off, isolated, lonely, out-of-the-way, sheltered, solitary

seclusion noun PRIVACY, isolation, shelter, solitude

second[1] adjective 1 NEXT, following, subsequent, succeeding 2 ADDITIONAL, alternative, extra, further, other 3 INFERIOR, lesser, lower, secondary, subordinate ▶ noun 4 SUPPORTER, assistant, backer, helper ▶ verb 5 SUPPORT, approve, assist, back, endorse, go along with

second[2] noun MOMENT, flash, instant, jiffy (informal), minute, sec (informal), trice

secondary adjective

1 SUBORDINATE, inferior, lesser, lower, minor, unimportant **2** RESULTANT, contingent, derived, indirect **3** BACKUP, auxiliary, fall-back, reserve, subsidiary, supporting

second-class *adjective* INFERIOR, indifferent, mediocre, second-best, second-rate, undistinguished, uninspiring

second-hand *adjective* **1** USED, hand-me-down (*informal*), nearly new ▸ *adverb* **2** INDIRECTLY

second in command *noun* DEPUTY, number two, right-hand man

secondly *adverb* NEXT, in the second place, second

second-rate *adjective* INFERIOR, low-grade, low-quality, mediocre, poor, rubbishy, shoddy, substandard, tacky (*informal*), tawdry, two-bit (*slang*)

secrecy *noun* **1** MYSTERY, concealment, confidentiality, privacy, silence **2** SECRETIVENESS, clandestineness, covertness, furtiveness, stealth

secret *adjective* **1** CONCEALED, close, disguised, furtive, hidden, undercover, underground, undisclosed, unknown, unrevealed **2** STEALTHY, secretive, sly, underhand **3** MYSTERIOUS, abstruse, arcane, clandestine, cryptic, occult ▸ *noun* **4** MYSTERY, code, enigma, key **5 in secret** SECRETLY, slyly, surreptitiously

secrete[1] *verb* GIVE OFF, emanate, emit, exude

secrete[2] *verb* HIDE, cache, conceal, harbor, stash (*informal*), stow

secretive *adjective* RETICENT, close, deep, reserved, tight-lipped, uncommunicative

secretly *adverb* IN SECRET, clandestinely, covertly, furtively, privately, quietly, stealthily, surreptitiously

sect *noun* GROUP, camp, denomination, division, faction, party, schism

sectarian *adjective* **1** NARROW-MINDED, bigoted, doctrinaire, dogmatic, factional, fanatical, limited, parochial, partisan ▸ *noun* **2** BIGOT, dogmatist, extremist, fanatic, partisan, zealot

section *noun* **1** PART, division, fraction, installment, passage, piece, portion, segment, slice **2** DISTRICT, area, region, sector, zone

sector *noun* PART, area, district, division, quarter, region, zone

secular *adjective* WORLDLY, civil, earthly, lay, nonspiritual, temporal

secure *adjective* **1** SAFE, immune, protected, unassailable **2** SURE, assured, certain, confident, easy, reassured **3** FIXED, fast, fastened, firm, immovable, stable, steady ▸ *verb* **4** OBTAIN, acquire, gain, get, procure, score (*slang*) **5** FASTEN, attach, bolt, chain, fix, lock, make fast, tie up

security *noun* **1** PRECAUTIONS, defense, protection, safeguards, safety measures **2** SAFETY, care, custody, refuge, safekeeping, sanctuary **3** SURENESS, assurance, certainty, confidence, conviction, positiveness, reliance **4** PLEDGE, collateral, gage, guarantee, hostage, insurance, pawn, surety

sedate *adjective* CALM, collected, composed, cool, dignified, serene, tranquil

sedative *adjective* **1** CALMING, anodyne, relaxing, soothing, tranquilizing ▸ *noun* **2** TRANQUILIZER, anodyne, downer *or* down (*slang*)

sedentary *adjective* INACTIVE, desk, desk-bound, seated, sitting

sediment *noun* DREGS, deposit, grounds, lees, residue

sedition *noun* RABBLE-ROUSING, agitation, incitement to riot, subversion

seditious *adjective* REVOLUTIONARY, dissident, mutinous, rebellious, refractory, subversive

seduce *verb* **1** CORRUPT, debauch, deflower, deprave, dishonor **2** TEMPT, beguile, deceive, entice, inveigle, lead astray, lure, mislead

seduction *noun* **1** CORRUPTION **2** TEMPTATION, enticement, lure, snare

seductive *adjective* ALLURING, attractive, bewitching, enticing, inviting, provocative, tempting

seductress *noun* TEMPTRESS, enchantress, *femme fatale*, siren, succubus, vamp (*informal*)

see *verb* **1** PERCEIVE, behold, catch sight of, discern, distinguish, espy, glimpse, look, make out, notice, observe, sight, spot, witness **2** UNDERSTAND, appreciate, comprehend, fathom, feel, follow, get, grasp, realize **3** FIND OUT, ascertain, determine, discover, learn **4** MAKE SURE, ensure, guarantee, make certain, see to it **5** CONSIDER, decide, deliberate, reflect, think over **6** VISIT, confer with, consult, interview, receive, speak to **7** GO OUT WITH, court, date (*informal*), go steady with (*informal*) **8** ACCOMPANY, escort, lead, show, usher, walk

seed *noun* **1** GRAIN, egg, embryo, germ, kernel, ovum, pip, spore **2** ORIGIN, beginning, germ, nucleus, source, start **3** OFFSPRING, children, descendants, issue, progeny **4 go** *or* **run to seed** DECLINE, decay, degenerate, deteriorate, go downhill (*informal*), go to pot, let oneself go

seedy *Informal* ▸ *adjective* SHABBY, dilapidated, dirty, grubby, mangy, run-down, scuzzy (*slang*), sleazy, squalid, tatty

seeing *conjunction* SINCE, as, inasmuch as, in view of the fact that

seek *verb* **1** LOOK FOR, be after, follow, hunt, pursue, search for, stalk **2** TRY, aim, aspire to, attempt, endeavor, essay, strive

seem *verb* APPEAR, assume, give the impression, look

seemly *adjective* FITTING, appropriate, becoming, correct, decent, decorous, fit, proper, suitable

seep *verb* OOZE, exude, leak, permeate, soak, trickle, well

seer *noun* PROPHET, sibyl, soothsayer

seesaw *verb* ALTERNATE, fluctuate,

oscillate, swing

seethe verb 1 BE FURIOUS, be livid, fume, go ballistic (slang), rage, see red (informal), simmer 2 BOIL, bubble, fizz, foam, froth

see through verb 1 BE UNDECEIVED BY, be wise to (informal), fathom, not fall for, penetrate 2 **see (something) through** PERSEVERE (WITH), keep at, persist, stick out (informal) 3 **see (someone) through** HELP OUT, stick by, support

segment noun SECTION, bit, division, part, piece, portion, slice, wedge

segregate verb SET APART, discriminate against, dissociate, isolate, separate

segregation noun SEPARATION, apartheid, discrimination, isolation

seize verb 1 GRAB, catch up, clutch, grasp, grip, lay hands on, snatch, take 2 CONFISCATE, appropriate, commandeer, impound, take possession of 3 CAPTURE, apprehend, arrest, catch, take captive

seizure noun 1 ATTACK, convulsion, fit, paroxysm, spasm 2 CAPTURE, apprehension, arrest 3 TAKING, annexation, commandeering, confiscation, grabbing

seldom adverb RARELY, hardly ever, infrequently, not often

select verb 1 CHOOSE, opt for, pick, single out ▶adjective 2 CHOICE, excellent, first-class, hand-picked, special, superior, top-notch (informal) 3 EXCLUSIVE, cliquish, elite, privileged

selection noun 1 CHOICE,

choosing, option, pick, preference 2 RANGE, assortment, choice, collection, medley, variety

selective adjective PARTICULAR, careful, discerning, discriminating

self-assurance noun CONFIDENCE, assertiveness, positiveness, self-confidence, self-possession

self-centered adjective SELFISH, egotistic, narcissistic, self-seeking

self-confidence noun SELF-ASSURANCE, aplomb, confidence, nerve, poise

self-confident adjective SELF-ASSURED, assured, confident, poised, sure of oneself

self-conscious adjective EMBARRASSED, awkward, bashful, diffident, ill at ease, insecure, nervous, uncomfortable, wired (slang)

self-control noun WILLPOWER, restraint, self-discipline, self-restraint

self-esteem noun SELF-RESPECT, confidence, faith in oneself, pride, self-assurance, self-regard

self-evident adjective OBVIOUS, clear, incontrovertible, inescapable, undeniable

self-important adjective CONCEITED, bigheaded, cocky, full of oneself, pompous, swollen-headed

self-indulgence noun INTEMPERANCE, excess, extravagance

selfish adjective SELF-CENTERED, egoistic, egoistical, egotistic, egotistical, greedy, self-interested, ungenerous

selfless adjective UNSELFISH,

altruistic, generous,
self-denying, self-sacrificing

self-possessed *adjective*
SELF-ASSURED, collected,
confident, cool, poised,
unruffled

self-reliant *adjective* INDEPENDENT,
self-sufficient, self-supporting

self-respect *noun* PRIDE, dignity,
morale, self-esteem

self-restraint *noun* SELF-CONTROL,
self-command, self-discipline,
willpower

self-righteous *adjective*
SANCTIMONIOUS, complacent,
holier-than-thou, priggish,
self-satisfied, smug, superior

self-sacrifice *noun* SELFLESSNESS,
altruism, generosity, self-denial

self-satisfied *adjective* SMUG,
complacent, pleased with
oneself, self-congratulatory

self-seeking *adjective* SELFISH,
careerist, looking out for
number one (*informal*), out for
what one can get,
self-interested, self-serving

sell *verb* **1** TRADE, barter,
exchange **2** DEAL IN, handle,
market, peddle, retail, stock,
trade in, traffic in

seller *noun* DEALER, agent,
merchant, purveyor, retailer,
salesman *or* saleswoman,
supplier, vendor

selling *noun* DEALING, business,
trading, traffic

sell out *verb* **1** DISPOSE OF, be
out of stock, get rid of, run
out of **2** *Informal* BETRAY,
double-cross (*informal*), sell
down the river (*informal*), stab
in the back

semblance *noun* APPEARANCE,
aspect, façade, mask, pretense,
resemblance, show, veneer

seminal *adjective* INFLUENTIAL,
formative, ground-breaking,
important, innovative, original

send *verb* **1** CONVEY, direct,
dispatch, forward, remit,
transmit **2** PROPEL, cast, fire,
fling, hurl, let fly, shoot

send for *verb* SUMMON, call for,
order, request

sendoff *noun* FAREWELL,
departure, leave-taking, start,
valediction

senile *adjective* DODDERING,
decrepit, doting, in one's
dotage

senility *noun* DOTAGE,
decrepitude, infirmity, loss of
one's faculties, senile dementia

senior *adjective* **1** HIGHER RANKING,
superior **2** OLDER, elder

senior citizen *noun* PENSIONER,
old fogey (*slang*), old *or* elderly
person, retired person

seniority *noun* SUPERIORITY,
precedence, priority, rank

sensation *noun* **1** FEELING,
awareness, consciousness,
impression, perception, sense
2 EXCITEMENT, commotion, furor,
stir, thrill

sensational *adjective*
1 DRAMATIC, amazing,
astounding, awesome,
exciting, melodramatic,
shock-horror (*facetious*),
shocking, thrilling **2** EXCELLENT,
awesome (*informal*), cool
(*informal*), fabulous (*informal*),
impressive, marvelous,
mind-blowing (*informal*), out of
this world (*informal*), phat
(*slang*), superb

sense *noun* **1** FACULTY, feeling,
sensation **2** FEELING,

atmosphere, aura, awareness, consciousness, impression, perception **3** (sometimes plural) INTELLIGENCE, brains (*informal*), cleverness, common sense, judgment, reason, sagacity, sanity, sharpness, understanding, wisdom, wit(s) **4** MEANING, drift, gist, implication, import, significance ▸*verb* **5** PERCEIVE, be aware of, discern, feel, get the impression, pick up, realize, understand

senseless *adjective* **1** STUPID, asinine, bonkers (*informal*), crazy, daft (*informal*), foolish, idiotic, illogical, inane, irrational, mad, mindless, nonsensical, pointless, ridiculous, silly **2** UNCONSCIOUS, insensible, out, out cold, stunned

sensibility *noun* **1** (often plural) FEELINGS, emotions, moral sense, sentiments, susceptibilities **2** SENSITIVITY, responsiveness, sensitiveness, susceptibility

sensible *adjective* **1** WISE, canny, down-to-earth, intelligent, judicious, practical, prudent, rational, realistic, sage, sane, shrewd, sound **2** (usually with *of*) AWARE, conscious, mindful, sensitive to

sensitive *adjective* **1** EASILY HURT, delicate, tender **2** SUSCEPTIBLE, easily affected, impressionable, responsive, touchy-feely (*informal*) **3** TOUCHY, easily offended, easily upset, thin-skinned **4** RESPONSIVE, acute, fine, keen, precise

sensitivity *noun* SENSITIVENESS, delicacy, receptiveness, responsiveness, susceptibility

sensual *adjective* **1** PHYSICAL, animal, bodily, carnal, fleshly, luxurious, voluptuous **2** EROTIC, lascivious, lecherous, lewd, lustful, raunchy (*slang*), sexual

sensuality *noun* EROTICISM, carnality, lasciviousness, lecherousness, lewdness, sexiness (*informal*), voluptuousness

sensuous *adjective* PLEASURABLE, gratifying, hedonistic, sybaritic

sentence *noun* **1** PUNISHMENT, condemnation, decision, decree, judgment, order, ruling, verdict ▸*verb* **2** CONDEMN, doom, penalize

sententious *adjective* POMPOUS, canting, judgmental, moralistic, preachifying (*informal*), sanctimonious

sentient *adjective* FEELING, conscious, living, sensitive

sentiment *noun* **1** EMOTION, sensibility, tenderness **2** (often plural) FEELING, attitude, belief, idea, judgment, opinion, view **3** SENTIMENTALITY, emotionalism, mawkishness, romanticism

sentimental *adjective* ROMANTIC, emotional, maudlin, nostalgic, overemotional, schmaltzy (*slang*), slushy (*informal*), soft-hearted, touching, weepy (*informal*)

sentimentality *noun* ROMANTICISM, corniness (*slang*), emotionalism, mawkishness, nostalgia, schmaltz (*slang*)

sentinel *noun* GUARD, lookout, sentry, watch, watchman

separable *adjective* DISTINGUISHABLE, detachable, divisible

separate *verb* **1** DIVIDE, come

apart, come away, detach, disconnect, disjoin, remove, sever, split, sunder **2** PART, break up, disunite, diverge, divorce, estrange, part company, split up **3** ISOLATE, segregate, single out ▶*adjective* **4** UNCONNECTED, detached, disconnected, divided, divorced, isolated, unattached **5** INDIVIDUAL, alone, apart, distinct, particular, single, solitary

separated *adjective* DISCONNECTED, apart, disassociated, disunited, divided, parted, separate, sundered

separately *adverb* INDIVIDUALLY, alone, apart, severally, singly

separation *noun* **1** DIVISION, break, disconnection, dissociation, disunion, gap **2** SPLIT-UP, break-up, divorce, parting, rift, split

septic *adjective* INFECTED, festering, poisoned, putrefying, putrid, suppurating

sepulcher *noun* TOMB, burial place, grave, mausoleum, vault

sequel *noun* **1** FOLLOW-UP, continuation, development **2** CONSEQUENCE, conclusion, end, outcome, result, upshot

sequence *noun* SUCCESSION, arrangement, chain, course, cycle, order, progression, series

serene *adjective* CALM, composed, peaceful, tranquil, unruffled, untroubled

serenity *noun* CALMNESS, calm, composure, peace, peacefulness, quietness, stillness, tranquillity

series *noun* SEQUENCE, chain,

course, order, progression, run, set, string, succession, train

serious *adjective* **1** SEVERE, acute, critical, dangerous **2** IMPORTANT, crucial, fateful, grim, momentous, no laughing matter, pressing, significant, urgent, worrying **3** SOLEMN, grave, humorless, sober, unsmiling **4** SINCERE, earnest, genuine, honest, in earnest

seriously *adverb* **1** GRAVELY, acutely, badly, critically, dangerously, severely **2** SINCERELY, gravely, in earnest

seriousness *noun* **1** IMPORTANCE, gravity, significance, urgency **2** SOLEMNITY, earnestness, gravitas, gravity

sermon *noun* **1** HOMILY, address **2** LECTURE, harangue, talking-to (*informal*)

servant *noun* ATTENDANT, domestic, help, maid, retainer, slave

serve *verb* **1** WORK FOR, aid, assist, attend to, help, minister to, wait on **2** PERFORM, act, complete, discharge, do, fulfill **3** PROVIDE, deliver, dish up, present, set out, supply **4** BE ADEQUATE, answer the purpose, be acceptable, do, function as, satisfy, suffice, suit

service *noun* **1** HELP, assistance, avail, benefit, use, usefulness **2** WORK, business, duty, employment, labor, office **3** OVERHAUL, check, maintenance **4** CEREMONY, observance, rite, worship ▶*verb* **5** OVERHAUL, check, fine tune, go over, maintain, tune (up)

serviceable *adjective* USEFUL, beneficial, functional, helpful, operative, practical, profitable, usable, utilitarian

servile *adjective* SUBSERVIENT, abject, fawning, grovelling, obsequious, sycophantic, toadying

serving *noun* PORTION, helping

session *noun* MEETING, assembly, conference, congress, discussion, hearing, period, sitting

set¹ *verb* **1** PUT, deposit, lay, locate, place, plant, position, rest, seat, situate, station, stick **2** PREPARE, arrange, lay, make ready, spread **3** HARDEN, cake, congeal, crystallize, solidify, stiffen, thicken **4** ARRANGE, appoint, decide (upon), determine, establish, fix, fix up, resolve, schedule, settle, specify **5** ASSIGN, allot, decree, impose, ordain, prescribe, specify **6** GO DOWN, decline, dip, disappear, sink, subside, vanish ▸ *noun* **7** POSITION, attitude, bearing, carriage, posture **8** SCENERY, scene, setting, stage set ▸ *adjective* **9** FIXED, agreed, appointed, arranged, decided, definite, established, prearranged, predetermined, scheduled, settled **10** INFLEXIBLE, hard and fast, immovable, rigid, stubborn **11** CONVENTIONAL, stereotyped, stock, traditional, unspontaneous **12 set on** or **upon** DETERMINED, bent, intent, resolute

set² *noun* **1** SERIES, assortment, batch, collection, compendium **2** GROUP, band, circle, clique, company, coterie, crowd, faction, gang

setback *noun* HOLD-UP, blow,

check, defeat, disappointment, hitch, misfortune, reverse

set back *verb* HOLD UP, delay, hinder, impede, retard, slow

set off *verb* **1** LEAVE, depart, embark, start out **2** DETONATE, explode, ignite

setting *noun* BACKGROUND, backdrop, context, location, scene, scenery, set, site, surroundings

settle *verb* **1** PUT IN ORDER, adjust, order, regulate, straighten out, work out **2** LAND, alight, come to rest, descend, light **3** MOVE TO, dwell, inhabit, live, make one's home, put down roots, reside, set up home, take up residence **4** COLONIZE, people, pioneer, populate **5** CALM, lull, pacify, quell, quiet, quieten, reassure, relax, relieve, soothe **6** PAY, clear, discharge, square (up) **7** (often with *on* or *upon*) DECIDE, agree, confirm, determine, establish, fix **8** RESOLVE, clear up, decide, put an end to, reconcile

settlement *noun* **1** AGREEMENT, arrangement, conclusion, confirmation, establishment, working out **2** PAYMENT, clearing, discharge **3** COLONY, community, encampment, outpost

settler *noun* COLONIST, colonizer, frontiersman, immigrant, pioneer

setup *noun* ARRANGEMENT, conditions, organization, regime, structure, system

set up *verb* **1** BUILD, assemble, construct, erect, put together, put up, raise **2** ESTABLISH, arrange, begin, found, initiate, institute, organize, prearrange, prepare

sever *verb* **1** CUT, cut in two, detach, disconnect, disjoin, divide, part, separate, split **2** BREAK OFF, dissociate, put an end to, terminate

several *adjective* SOME, different, diverse, manifold, many, sundry, various

severe *adjective* **1** STRICT, austere, cruel, drastic, hard, harsh, oppressive, rigid, unbending **2** GRIM, forbidding, grave, serious, stern, tight-lipped, unsmiling **3** INTENSE, acute, extreme, fierce **4** PLAIN, austere, classic, homely, restrained, simple, Spartan, unadorned, unembellished, unfussy

severely *adverb* **1** STRICTLY, harshly, sharply, sternly **2** SERIOUSLY, acutely, badly, extremely, gravely

severity *noun* STRICTNESS, hardness, harshness, severeness, sternness, toughness

sex *noun* **1** GENDER **2** (SEXUAL) INTERCOURSE, coition, coitus, copulation, fornication, lovemaking, sexual relations

sexual *adjective* **1** CARNAL, erotic, intimate, sensual, sexy **2** REPRODUCTIVE, genital, procreative, sex

sexual intercourse *noun* COPULATION, carnal knowledge, coition, coitus, sex, union

sexuality *noun* DESIRE, carnality, eroticism, lust, sensuality, sexiness (*informal*)

sexy *adjective* EROTIC, arousing, naughty, provocative, seductive, sensual, sensuous, suggestive, titillating

shabby *adjective* **1** TATTY, dilapidated, mean, ragged, run-down, seedy, tattered, threadbare, worn **2** MEAN, cheap, contemptible, despicable, dirty, dishonorable, lousy (*slang*), low, rotten (*informal*), scurvy, scuzzy (*slang*)

shack *noun* HUT, cabin, shanty

shackle *noun* **1** (often plural) FETTER, bond, chain, iron, leg-iron, manacle ▸*verb* **2** FETTER, bind, chain, manacle, put in irons

shade *noun* **1** DIMNESS, dusk, gloom, gloominess, semidarkness, shadow **2** SCREEN, blind, canopy, cover, covering, curtain, shield, veil **3** COLOR, hue, tinge, tint, tone **4** DASH, hint, suggestion, trace **5** *Literary* GHOST, apparition, phantom, specter, spirit **6 put into the shade** OUTSHINE, eclipse, outclass, overshadow ▸*verb* **7** COVER, conceal, hide, obscure, protect, screen, shield, veil **8** DARKEN, cloud, dim, shadow

shadow *noun* **1** DIMNESS, cover, darkness, dusk, gloom, shade **2** TRACE, hint, suggestion, suspicion **3** CLOUD, blight, gloom, sadness ▸*verb* **4** SHADE, darken, overhang, screen, shield **5** FOLLOW, stalk, tail (*informal*), trail

shadowy *adjective* **1** DARK, dim, dusky, gloomy, murky, shaded, shady **2** VAGUE, dim, dreamlike, faint, ghostly, nebulous, phantom, spectral, unsubstantial

shady *adjective* **1** SHADED, cool, dim **2** *Informal* CROOKED, disreputable, dubious, questionable, shifty, suspect, suspicious, unethical

shaft *noun* **1** HANDLE, pole, rod, shank, stem **2** RAY, beam, gleam

shaggy *adjective* UNKEMPT, hairy, hirsute, long-haired, rough, tousled, unshorn

shake *verb* **1** VIBRATE, bump, jar, jolt, quake, rock, shiver, totter, tremble **2** WAVE, brandish, flourish **3** UPSET, distress, disturb, frighten, rattle (*informal*), shock, unnerve ▶ *noun* **4** VIBRATION, agitation, convulsion, jerk, jolt, quaking, shiver, shudder, trembling, tremor

shake up *verb* **1** STIR (UP), agitate, churn (up), mix **2** UPSET, disturb, shock, unsettle

shaky *adjective* **1** UNSTEADY, faltering, precarious, quivery, rickety, trembling, unstable, weak **2** UNCERTAIN, dubious, iffy (*informal*), questionable, suspect

shallow *adjective* **1** SUPERFICIAL, empty, slight, surface, trivial **2** UNINTELLIGENT, foolish, frivolous, ignorant, puerile, simple

sham *noun* **1** PHONEY *or* PHONY (*informal*), counterfeit, forgery, fraud, hoax, humbug, imitation, impostor, pretense ▶ *adjective* **2** FALSE, artificial, bogus, counterfeit, feigned, imitation, mock, phoney *or* phony (*informal*), pretended, simulated ▶ *verb* **3** FAKE, affect, assume, feign, pretend, put on, simulate

shambles *noun* CHAOS,

confusion, disarray, disorder, havoc, madhouse, mess, muddle

shame *noun* **1** EMBARRASSMENT, abashment, humiliation, ignominy, mortification **2** DISGRACE, blot, discredit, dishonor, disrepute, infamy, reproach, scandal, smear ▶ *verb* **3** EMBARRASS, abash, disgrace, humble, humiliate, mortify **4** DISHONOR, blot, debase, defile, degrade, smear, stain

shamefaced *adjective* EMBARRASSED, abashed, ashamed, humiliated, mortified, red-faced, sheepish

shameful *adjective* **1** EMBARRASSING, humiliating, mortifying **2** DISGRACEFUL, base, dishonorable, low, mean, outrageous, scandalous, wicked

shameless *adjective* BRAZEN, audacious, barefaced, flagrant, hardened, insolent, unabashed, unashamed

shanty *noun* SHACK, cabin, hut, shed

shape *noun* **1** FORM, build, configuration, contours, figure, lines, outline, profile, silhouette **2** PATTERN, frame, model, mold **3** CONDITION, fettle, health, state, trim ▶ *verb* **4** FORM, create, fashion, make, model, mold, produce **5** DEVELOP, adapt, devise, frame, modify, plan

shapeless *adjective* FORMLESS, amorphous, irregular, misshapen, unstructured

shapely *adjective* WELL-FORMED, curvaceous, elegant, graceful, neat, trim, well-proportioned

share *noun* **1** PART, allotment,

allowance, contribution, due, lot, portion, quota, ration, whack (*informal*) ▶ *verb* 2 DIVIDE, assign, distribute, partake, participate, receive, split

sharp *adjective* 1 KEEN, acute, jagged, pointed, serrated, spiky 2 SUDDEN, abrupt, distinct, extreme, marked 3 CLEAR, crisp, distinct, well-defined 4 QUICK-WITTED, alert, astute, bright, clever, discerning, knowing, penetrating, perceptive, quick 5 DISHONEST, artful, crafty, cunning, sly, unscrupulous, wily 6 CUTTING, barbed, biting, bitter, caustic, harsh, hurtful 7 SOUR, acid, acrid, hot, piquant, pungent, tart 8 ACUTE, intense, painful, piercing, severe, shooting, stabbing ▶ *adverb* 9 PROMPTLY, exactly, on the dot, on time, precisely, punctually

sharpen *verb* WHET, edge, grind, hone

shatter *verb* 1 SMASH, break, burst, crack, crush, pulverize 2 DESTROY, demolish, ruin, torpedo, wreck

shattered *adjective* Informal DEVASTATED, blown away, crushed

shave *verb* TRIM, crop, pare, shear

shed[1] *noun* HUT, outhouse, shack

shed[2] *verb* 1 GIVE OUT, cast, drop, emit, give, radiate, scatter, shower, spill 2 CAST OFF, discard, moult, slough

sheen *noun* SHINE, brightness, gleam, gloss, luster, polish

sheepish *adjective* EMBARRASSED, abashed, ashamed, mortified, self-conscious, shamefaced

sheer *adjective* 1 TOTAL, absolute, complete, downright, out-and-out, pure, unmitigated, utter 2 STEEP, abrupt, precipitous 3 FINE, diaphanous, gauzy, gossamer, see-through, thin, transparent

sheet *noun* 1 COAT, film, lamina, layer, overlay, stratum, surface, veneer 2 PIECE, panel, plate, slab 3 EXPANSE, area, blanket, covering, stretch, sweep

shell *noun* 1 CASE, husk, pod 2 FRAME, framework, hull, structure ▶ *verb* 3 BOMB, attack, blitz, bombard, strafe

shell out *verb* PAY OUT, fork out (*slang*), give, hand over

shelter *noun* 1 PROTECTION, cover, defense, guard, screen 2 SAFETY, asylum, haven, refuge, retreat, sanctuary, security ▶ *verb* 3 PROTECT, cover, defend, guard, harbor, hide, safeguard, shield 4 TAKE SHELTER, hide, seek refuge

sheltered *adjective* PROTECTED, cloistered, isolated, quiet, screened, secluded, shaded, shielded

shelve *verb* POSTPONE, defer, freeze, put aside, put on ice, put on the back burner (*informal*), suspend, take a rain check on (*informal*)

shepherd *verb* GUIDE, conduct, herd, steer, usher

shield *noun* 1 PROTECTION, cover, defense, guard, safeguard, screen, shelter ▶ *verb* 2 PROTECT, cover, defend, guard, safeguard, screen, shelter

shift *verb* 1 MOVE, budge, displace, move around, rearrange, relocate, reposition ▶ *noun* 2 MOVE, displacement, rearrangement, shifting

shiftless *adjective* LAZY, aimless, good-for-nothing, idle, lackadaisical, slothful, unambitious, unenterprising

shifty *adjective* UNTRUSTWORTHY, deceitful, devious, evasive, furtive, slippery, sly, tricky, underhand

shimmer *verb* 1 GLEAM, glisten, scintillate, twinkle ▶ *noun* 2 GLEAM, iridescence

shine *verb* 1 GLEAM, beam, flash, glare, glisten, glitter, glow, radiate, sparkle, twinkle 2 POLISH, brush, buff, burnish 3 STAND OUT, be conspicuous, excel ▶ *noun* 4 BRIGHTNESS, glare, gleam, light, radiance, shimmer, sparkle 5 POLISH, gloss, luster, sheen

shining *adjective* BRIGHT, beaming, brilliant, gleaming, glistening, luminous, radiant, shimmering, sparkling

shiny *adjective* BRIGHT, gleaming, glistening, glossy, lustrous, polished

ship *noun* VESSEL, boat, craft

shipshape *adjective* TIDY, neat, orderly, spick-and-span, trim, well-ordered, well-organized

shirk *verb* DODGE, avoid, evade, get out of, slack

shirker *noun* SLACKER, clock-watcher, dodger, idler

shiver¹ *verb* 1 TREMBLE, quake, quiver, shake, shudder ▶ *noun* 2 TREMBLING, flutter, quiver, shudder, tremor

shiver² *verb* SPLINTER, break, crack, fragment, shatter, smash, smash to smithereens

shivery *adjective* SHAKING, chilled, chilly, cold, quaking, quivery, shaky

shock *verb* 1 HORRIFY, appall, disgust, nauseate, revolt, scandalize, sicken 2 ASTOUND, jolt, shake, stagger, stun, stupefy ▶ *noun* 3 IMPACT, blow, clash, collision 4 UPSET, blow, bombshell, distress, disturbance, stupefaction, stupor, trauma

shocking *adjective* DREADFUL, appalling, atrocious, disgraceful, disgusting, ghastly, horrifying, nauseating, outrageous, revolting, scandalous, sickening

shoddy *adjective* INFERIOR, poor, rubbishy, second-rate, slipshod, tawdry, trashy

shoot *verb* 1 HIT, blast (*slang*), bring down, kill, open fire, plug (*slang*) 2 FIRE, discharge, emit, fling, hurl, launch, project, propel 3 SPEED, bolt, charge, dart, dash, fly, hurtle, race, rush, streak, tear ▶ *noun* 4 BRANCH, bud, offshoot, sprig, sprout

shop *noun* STORE, boutique, emporium, hypermarket, supermarket

shore *noun* BEACH, coast, sands, seashore, strand (*poetic*)

shore up *verb* SUPPORT, brace, buttress, hold, prop, reinforce, strengthen, underpin

short *adjective* 1 CONCISE, brief, compressed, laconic, pithy, succinct, summary, terse 2 SMALL, diminutive, dumpy, little, petite, squat 3 BRIEF, fleeting, momentary 4 (often with *of*) LACKING, deficient, limited, low (on), scant, scarce, wanting 5 ABRUPT, brusque, curt, discourteous, impolite, sharp, terse, uncivil ▶ *adverb* **6** ABRUPTLY, suddenly, without warning

shortage *noun* DEFICIENCY, dearth, insufficiency, lack, paucity, scarcity, want

shortcoming *noun* FAILING, defect, fault, flaw, imperfection, weakness

shorten *verb* CUT, abbreviate, abridge, curtail, decrease, diminish, lessen, reduce

shortly *adverb* SOON, before long, in a little while, presently

short-sighted *adjective*
1 NEAR-SIGHTED, myopic
2 UNTHINKING, ill-advised, ill-considered, impolitic, impractical, improvident, imprudent, injudicious

short-tempered *adjective* QUICK-TEMPERED, hot-tempered, impatient, irascible, testy

shot *noun* **1** THROW, discharge, lob, pot shot **2** PELLET, ball, bullet, lead, projectile, slug
3 MARKSMAN, shooter **4** *Slang* ATTEMPT, effort, endeavor, go (*informal*), stab (*informal*), try, turn

shoulder *verb* **1** BEAR, accept, assume, be responsible for, carry, take on **2** PUSH, elbow, jostle, press, shove

shout *noun* **1** CRY, bellow, call, roar, scream, yell ▶ *verb* **2** CRY (OUT), bawl, bellow, call (out), holler (*informal*), roar, scream, yell

shout down *verb* SILENCE, drown, drown out, overwhelm

shove *verb* PUSH, drive, elbow, impel, jostle, press, propel, thrust

shovel *verb* MOVE, dredge, heap, ladle, load, scoop, toss

shove off *verb* GO AWAY, clear off (*informal*), depart, leave, push off (*informal*), scram (*informal*)

show *verb* **1** BE VISIBLE, appear **2** DISPLAY, exhibit, present **3** PROVE, clarify, demonstrate, elucidate, point out **4** INSTRUCT, demonstrate, explain, teach **5** DISPLAY, indicate, manifest, register, reveal **6** GUIDE, accompany, attend, conduct, escort, lead ▶ *noun*
7 ENTERTAINMENT, presentation, production **8** EXHIBITION, array, display, fair, pageant, parade, sight, spectacle **9** PRETENSE, affectation, air, appearance, display, illusion, parade, pose

showdown *noun* CONFRONTATION, clash, face-off (*slang*)

shower *noun* **1** DELUGE, barrage, stream, torrent, volley ▶ *verb* **2** INUNDATE, deluge, heap, lavish, pour, rain

showman *noun* PERFORMER, entertainer

show-off *noun* EXHIBITIONIST, boaster, braggart, poseur

show off *verb* **1** EXHIBIT, demonstrate, display, flaunt, parade **2** BOAST, blow one's own trumpet, brag, swagger

show up *verb* **1** STAND OUT, appear, be conspicuous, be visible **2** REVEAL, expose, highlight, lay bare **3** *Informal* EMBARRASS, let down, mortify, put to shame **4** ARRIVE, appear, come, turn up

showy *adjective* **1** OSTENTATIOUS, brash, flamboyant, flash (*informal*), flashy, over the top (*informal*) **2** GAUDY, garish, loud

shred *noun* **1** STRIP, bit, fragment, piece, scrap, sliver, tatter **2** PARTICLE, atom, grain, iota, jot, scrap, trace

shrew *noun* NAG, harpy, harridan, scold, spitfire, vixen

shrewd *adjective* CLEVER, astute, calculating, canny, crafty, cunning, intelligent, keen, perceptive, perspicacious, sharp, smart

shrewdness *noun* ASTUTENESS, canniness, discernment, judgment, perspicacity, quick wits, sharpness, smartness

shriek *verb, noun* CRY, scream, screech, squeal, yell

shrill *adjective* PIERCING, high, penetrating, sharp

shrink *verb* **1** DECREASE, contract, diminish, dwindle, grow smaller, lessen, narrow, shorten **2** RECOIL, cower, cringe, draw back, flinch, quail

shrivel *verb* WITHER, dehydrate, desiccate, shrink, wilt, wizen

shroud *noun* **1** WINDING SHEET, grave clothes **2** COVERING, mantle, pall, screen, veil ► *verb* **3** CONCEAL, blanket, cloak, cover, envelop, hide, screen, veil

shudder *verb* **1** SHIVER, convulse, quake, quiver, shake, tremble ► *noun* **2** SHIVER, quiver, spasm, tremor

shuffle *verb* **1** SCUFFLE, drag, scrape, shamble **2** REARRANGE, disarrange, disorder, jumble, mix

shun *verb* AVOID, keep away from, steer clear of

shut *verb* CLOSE, fasten, seal, secure, slam

shut down *verb* **1** STOP, halt, switch off **2** CLOSE, shut up

shut out *verb* EXCLUDE, bar, debar, keep out, lock out

shuttle *verb* GO BACK AND FORTH, alternate, commute, go to and fro

shut up *verb* **1** *Informal* BE QUIET, fall silent, gag, hold one's tongue, hush, silence **2** CONFINE, cage, coop up, immure, imprison, incarcerate

shy^1 *adjective* **1** TIMID, bashful, coy, diffident, retiring, self-conscious, self-effacing, shrinking **2** CAUTIOUS, chary, distrustful, hesitant, suspicious, wary ► *verb* **3** (sometimes with *off* or *away*) RECOIL, balk, draw back, flinch, start

shy^2 *verb* THROW, cast, fling, hurl, pitch, sling, toss

shyness *noun* TIMIDNESS, bashfulness, diffidence, lack of confidence, self-consciousness, timidity, timorousness

sick *adjective* **1** NAUSEOUS, ill, nauseated, queasy **2** UNWELL, ailing, diseased, indisposed, poorly (*informal*), under the weather (*informal*) **3** *Informal* MORBID, black, ghoulish, macabre, sadistic **4 sick of** TIRED, bored, fed up, jaded, weary

sicken *verb* **1** DISGUST, gross out (*slang*), nauseate, repel, revolt, turn one's stomach **2** FALL ILL, ail, take sick

sickening *adjective* DISGUSTING, distasteful, foul, gross (*slang*), loathsome, nauseating, noisome, offensive, repulsive, revolting, scuzzy (*slang*), stomach-turning (*informal*), vile, yucky *or* yukky (*slang*)

sickly *adjective* 1 UNHEALTHY, ailing, delicate, faint, feeble, infirm, pallid, peaky, wan, weak 2 NAUSEATING, cloying, mawkish

sickness *noun* 1 ILLNESS, affliction, ailment, bug (*informal*), complaint, disease, disorder, malady 2 NAUSEA, queasiness, vomiting

side *noun* 1 BORDER, boundary, division, edge, limit, margin, perimeter, rim, sector, verge 2 PART, aspect, face, facet, flank, hand, surface, view 3 PARTY, camp, cause, faction, sect, team 4 POINT OF VIEW, angle, opinion, position, slant, stand, standpoint, viewpoint ▶ *adjective* 5 SUBORDINATE, ancillary, incidental, lesser, marginal, minor, secondary, subsidiary ▶ *verb* 6 (usually with *with*) SUPPORT, ally with, favor, go along with, take the part of

sidelong *adjective* SIDEWAYS, covert, indirect, oblique

sidestep *verb* AVOID, circumvent, dodge, duck (*informal*), evade, skirt

sidetrack *verb* DIVERT, deflect, distract

sideways *adverb* 1 OBLIQUELY, edgeways, laterally, sidelong, to the side ▶ *adjective* 2 OBLIQUE, sidelong

sidle *verb* EDGE, creep, inch, slink, sneak, steal

siesta *noun* NAP, catnap, doze, forty winks (*informal*), sleep, snooze (*informal*)

sieve *noun* 1 STRAINER, colander ▶ *verb* 2 SIFT, separate, strain

sift *verb* 1 SIEVE, filter, separate

2 EXAMINE, analyze, go through, investigate, research, scrutinize, work over

sight *noun* 1 VISION, eye, eyes, eyesight, seeing 2 VIEW, appearance, perception, range of vision, visibility 3 SPECTACLE, display, exhibition, pageant, scene, show, vista 4 EYESORE, mess, monstrosity 5 **catch sight of** SPOT, espy, glimpse ▶ *verb* 6 SPOT, behold, discern, distinguish, make out, observe, perceive, see

sign *noun* 1 INDICATION, clue, evidence, hint, mark, proof, signal, symptom, token 2 NOTICE, board, placard, warning 3 SYMBOL, badge, device, emblem, logo, mark 4 OMEN, augury, auspice, foreboding, portent, warning ▶ *verb* 5 AUTOGRAPH, endorse, initial, inscribe 6 GESTURE, beckon, gesticulate, indicate, signal

signal *noun* 1 SIGN, beacon, cue, gesture, indication, mark, token ▶ *verb* 2 GESTURE, beckon, gesticulate, indicate, motion, sign, wave

significance *noun* 1 IMPORTANCE, consequence, moment, relevance, weight 2 MEANING, force, implication(s), import, message, point, purport, sense

significant *adjective* 1 IMPORTANT, critical, material, momentous, noteworthy, serious, vital, weighty 2 MEANINGFUL, eloquent, expressive, indicative, suggestive

signify *verb* 1 INDICATE, be a sign of, betoken, connote, denote, imply, intimate, mean,

portend, suggest **2** MATTER, be
important, carry weight, count
silence *noun* **1** QUIET, calm,
hush, lull, peace, stillness
2 MUTENESS, dumbness,
reticence, taciturnity ▶*verb*
3 QUIETEN, cut off, cut short,
deaden, gag, muffle, quiet,
stifle, still, suppress
silent *adjective* **1** QUIET, hushed,
muted, noiseless, soundless,
still **2** MUTE, dumb, speechless,
taciturn, voiceless, wordless
silently *adjective* QUIETLY,
inaudibly, in silence, mutely,
noiselessly, soundlessly,
without a sound, wordlessly
silhouette *noun* **1** OUTLINE,
form, profile, shape ▶*verb*
2 OUTLINE, etch, stand out
silky *adjective* SMOOTH, silken,
sleek, velvety
silly *adjective* FOOLISH, absurd,
asinine, fatuous, idiotic, inane,
ridiculous, senseless, stupid,
unwise
silt *noun* **1** SEDIMENT, alluvium,
deposit, ooze, sludge ▶*verb*
2 silt up CLOG, choke, congest
similar *adjective* ALIKE,
analogous, close, comparable,
like, resembling
similarity *noun* RESEMBLANCE,
affinity, agreement, analogy,
closeness, comparability,
correspondence, likeness,
sameness
simmer *verb* FUME, be angry,
rage, seethe, smolder
simmer down *verb* CALM DOWN,
control oneself, cool off *or*
down
simper *verb* SMILE COYLY, smile
affectedly, smirk
simple *adjective* **1** EASY, clear,

intelligible, lucid, plain,
straightforward,
uncomplicated,
understandable, uninvolved
2 PLAIN, classic, natural,
unembellished, unfussy **3** PURE,
elementary, unalloyed,
uncombined, unmixed
4 ARTLESS, childlike, guileless,
ingenuous, innocent, naive,
natural, sincere, unaffected,
unsophisticated **5** HONEST, bald,
basic, direct, frank, naked,
plain, sincere, stark **6** HUMBLE,
dumpy (*informal*), homely,
modest, unpretentious
7 FEEBLE-MINDED, foolish,
half-witted, moronic, slow,
stupid
simple-minded *adjective*
FEEBLE-MINDED, backward,
dim-witted, foolish, idiot,
idiotic, moronic, retarded,
simple, stupid
simpleton *noun* HALFWIT, doofus
(*slang*), dork (*slang*), dullard,
fool, idiot, imbecile (*informal*),
moron, schmuck (*slang*)
simplicity *noun* **1** EASE, clarity,
clearness, straightforwardness
2 PLAINNESS, lack of adornment,
purity, restraint **3** ARTLESSNESS,
candor, directness, innocence,
naivety, openness
simplify *verb* MAKE SIMPLER,
abridge, disentangle, dumb
down, reduce to essentials,
streamline
simply *adverb* **1** PLAINLY, clearly,
directly, easily, intelligibly,
naturally, straightforwardly,
unpretentiously **2** JUST, merely,
only, purely, solely **3** TOTALLY,
absolutely, completely, really,
utterly, wholly
simulate *verb* PRETEND, act,

affect, feign, put on, sham

simultaneous *adjective*
COINCIDING, at the same time,
coincident, concurrent,
contemporaneous, synchronous

simultaneously *adverb* AT THE
SAME TIME, concurrently, together

sin *noun* 1 WRONGDOING, crime,
error, evil, guilt, iniquity,
misdeed, offense, transgression
▶ *verb* 2 TRANSGRESS, err, fall, go
astray, lapse, offend

sincere *adjective* HONEST, candid,
earnest, frank, genuine,
guileless, heartfelt, real, serious,
true, unaffected

sincerely *adverb* HONESTLY,
earnestly, genuinely, in earnest,
seriously, truly, wholeheartedly

sincerity *noun* HONESTY, candor,
frankness, genuineness,
seriousness, truth

sinecure *noun* SOFT JOB
(*informal*), gravy train (*slang*),
money for jam *or* old rope
(*informal*), soft option

sinful *adjective* GUILTY, bad,
corrupt, criminal, erring,
immoral, iniquitous, wicked

sing *verb* 1 WARBLE, carol, chant,
chirp, croon, pipe, trill, yodel
2 HUM, buzz, purr, whine

singe *verb* BURN, char, scorch,
sear

singer *noun* VOCALIST, balladeer,
cantor, chorister, crooner,
minstrel, soloist

single *adjective* 1 ONE, distinct,
individual, lone, only, separate,
sole, solitary 2 INDIVIDUAL,
exclusive, separate, undivided,
unshared 3 SIMPLE, unblended,
unmixed 4 UNMARRIED, free,
unattached, unwed ▶ *verb* 5
(usually with *out*) PICK, choose,

distinguish, fix on, pick on *or*
out, select, separate, set apart

single-handed *adverb* UNAIDED,
alone, by oneself,
independently, on one's own,
solo, unassisted, without help

single-minded *adjective*
DETERMINED, dedicated, dogged,
fixed, unswerving

singly *adverb* ONE BY ONE,
individually, one at a time,
separately

singular *adjective* 1 SINGLE,
individual, separate, sole
2 REMARKABLE, eminent,
exceptional, notable,
noteworthy, outstanding
3 UNUSUAL, curious, eccentric,
extraordinary, odd, peculiar,
queer, strange

singularly *adverb* REMARKABLY,
especially, exceptionally,
notably, outstandingly,
particularly, uncommonly,
unusually

sinister *adjective* THREATENING,
dire, disquieting, evil, malign,
menacing, ominous

sink *verb* 1 DESCEND, dip, drop,
fall, founder, go down, go
under, lower, plunge,
submerge, subside 2 FALL,
abate, collapse, drop, lapse,
slip, subside 3 DECLINE, decay,
deteriorate, diminish, dwindle,
fade, fail, flag, lessen, weaken,
worsen 4 DIG, bore, drill, drive,
excavate 5 STOOP, be reduced
to, lower oneself

sink in *verb* BE UNDERSTOOD, get
through to, penetrate, register
(*informal*)

sinner *noun* WRONGDOER,
evildoer, malefactor, miscreant,
offender, transgressor

sip verb 1 DRINK, sample, sup, taste ▶ noun 2 SWALLOW, drop, taste, thimbleful

sissy noun 1 WIMP (informal), coward, mama's boy, softie (informal), weakling ▶ adjective 2 WIMPISH or WIMPY (informal), cowardly, effeminate, feeble, soft (informal), unmanly, weak

sit verb 1 REST, perch, settle 2 CONVENE, assemble, deliberate, meet, officiate, preside

site noun 1 LOCATION, place, plot, position, setting, spot ▶ verb 2 LOCATE, install, place, position, set, situate

situation noun 1 STATE OF AFFAIRS, case, circumstances, condition, plight, state 2 LOCATION, place, position, setting, site, spot 3 STATUS, rank, station 4 JOB, employment, office, place, position, post

sizable, sizeable adjective LARGE, considerable, decent, goodly, largish, respectable, substantial

size noun DIMENSIONS, amount, bulk, extent, immensity, magnitude, mass, proportions, range, volume

size up verb ASSESS, appraise, evaluate, take stock of

sizzle verb HISS, crackle, frizzle, fry, spit

skedaddle verb Slang RUN AWAY, abscond, beat it (slang), clear off (informal), disappear, flee, run for it, scram (informal), take to one's heels

skeleton noun FRAMEWORK, bare bones, draft, frame, outline, sketch, structure

skeptic noun DOUBTER, cynic,

disbeliever, doubting Thomas

skeptical adjective DOUBTFUL, cynical, disbelieving, dubious, incredulous, mistrustful, unconvinced

skepticism noun DOUBT, cynicism, disbelief, incredulity, unbelief

sketch noun 1 DRAWING, delineation, design, draft, outline, plan ▶ verb 2 DRAW, delineate, depict, draft, outline, represent, rough out

sketchy adjective INCOMPLETE, cursory, inadequate, perfunctory, rough, scrappy, skimpy, superficial

skill noun EXPERTISE, ability, art, cleverness, competence, craft, dexterity, facility, knack, proficiency, skillfulness, talent, technique

skilled adjective EXPERT, able, masterly, professional, proficient, skillful

skillful adjective EXPERT, able, adept, adroit, clever, competent, dexterous, masterly, practiced, professional, proficient, skilled

skim verb 1 SEPARATE, cream 2 GLIDE, coast, float, fly, sail, soar 3 (usually with through) SCAN, glance, run one's eye over

skimp verb STINT, be mean with, be sparing with, cut corners, scamp, scrimp

skin noun 1 HIDE, fell, pelt 2 COATING, casing, crust, film, husk, outside, peel, rind ▶ verb 3 PEEL, flay, scrape

skin alive verb Informal ATTACK, assail, assault, let have it (informal), let loose on (informal)

skinflint noun MISER, niggard,

penny-pincher (*informal*), Scrooge

skinny *adjective* THIN, emaciated, lean, scrawny, undernourished

skip *verb* 1 HOP, bob, bounce, caper, dance, flit, frisk, gambol, prance, trip 2 PASS OVER, eschew, give (something) a miss, leave out, miss out, omit

skirmish *noun* 1 FIGHT, battle, brush, clash, conflict, encounter, fracas, scrap (*informal*) ▶ *verb* 2 FIGHT, clash, collide

skirt *verb* 1 BORDER, edge, flank 2 (often with *around* or *round*) AVOID, circumvent, evade, steer clear of

skit *noun* 1 PARODY, burlesque, sketch, spoof (*informal*) 2 PLAY, comedy, drama, performance

skittish *adjective* LIVELY, excitable, fidgety, highly strung, jumpy, nervous, restive, wired (*slang*)

skulk *verb* LURK, creep, prowl, slink, sneak

sky *noun* HEAVENS, firmament

slab *noun* PIECE, chunk, lump, portion, slice, wedge

slack *adjective* 1 LOOSE, baggy, lax, limp, relaxed 2 NEGLIGENT, idle, inactive, lax, lazy, neglectful, remiss, slapdash, slipshod 3 SLOW, dull, inactive, quiet, slow-moving, sluggish ▶ *noun* 4 ROOM, excess, give (*informal*), leeway ▶ *verb* 5 SHIRK, dodge, idle

slacken *verb* (often with *off*) LESSEN, abate, decrease, diminish, drop off, moderate, reduce, relax

slacker *noun* IDLER, couch

potato (*slang*), dodger, loafer, shirker

slake *verb* SATISFY, assuage, quench, sate

slam *verb* BANG, crash, dash, fling, hurl, smash, throw

slander *noun* 1 DEFAMATION, calumny, libel, scandal, smear ▶ *verb* 2 DEFAME, blacken (someone's) name, libel, malign, smear

slanderous *adjective* DEFAMATORY, damaging, libelous, malicious

slant *verb* 1 SLOPE, bend, bevel, cant, heel, incline, lean, list, tilt 2 BIAS, angle, color, distort, twist ▶ *noun* 3 SLOPE, camber, gradient, incline, tilt 4 BIAS, angle, emphasis, one-sidedness, point of view, prejudice

slanting *adjective* SLOPING, angled, at an angle, bent, diagonal, inclined, oblique, tilted, tilting

slap *noun* 1 SMACK, blow, cuff, spank ▶ *verb* 2 SMACK, clap, cuff, paddle (*U.S. & Canad.*), spank

slapdash *adjective* CARELESS, clumsy, hasty, hurried, messy, slipshod, sloppy (*informal*)

slash *verb* 1 CUT, gash, hack, lacerate, rend, rip, score, slit 2 REDUCE, cut, drop, lower ▶ *noun* 3 CUT, gash, incision, laceration, rent, rip, slit

slaughter *verb* 1 MURDER, butcher, kill, massacre, slay ▶ *noun* 2 MURDER, bloodshed, butchery, carnage, killing, massacre, slaying

slaughterhouse *noun* ABATTOIR

slave *noun* 1 SERVANT, drudge, serf, vassal ▶ *verb* 2 TOIL, drudge, slog

slavery noun ENSLAVEMENT, bondage, captivity, servitude, subjugation

slavish adjective 1 SERVILE, abject, base, cringing, fawning, grovelling, obsequious, submissive, sycophantic 2 IMITATIVE, second-hand, unimaginative, unoriginal

slay verb KILL, butcher, massacre, mow down, murder, slaughter

sleaze noun CORRUPTION, bribery, dishonesty, extortion, fraud, unscrupulousness, venality

sleazy adjective SORDID, disreputable, low, run-down, scuzzy (slang), seedy, squalid

sleek adjective GLOSSY, lustrous, shiny, smooth

sleep noun 1 SLUMBER(S), doze, forty winks (informal), hibernation, nap, siesta, snooze (informal) ▸ verb 2 SLUMBER, catnap, doze, drowse, hibernate, snooze (informal), take a nap

sleepless adjective WAKEFUL, insomniac, restless

sleepy adjective DROWSY, dull, heavy, inactive, lethargic, sluggish

slender adjective 1 SLIM, lean, narrow, slight, willowy 2 FAINT, poor, remote, slight, slim, tenuous, thin 3 MEAGER, little, scant, scanty, small

sleuth noun DETECTIVE, gumshoe (slang), private eye (informal), (private) investigator

slice noun 1 SHARE, cut, helping, portion, segment, sliver, wedge ▸ verb 2 CUT, carve, divide, sever

slick adjective 1 GLIB, plausible, polished, smooth, specious 2 SKILLFUL, adroit, deft, dexterous, polished, professional ▸ verb 3 SMOOTH, plaster down, sleek

slide verb SLIP, coast, glide, skim, slither

slight adjective 1 SMALL, feeble, insignificant, meager, measly, minor, paltry, scanty, trifling, trivial, unimportant 2 SLIM, delicate, feeble, fragile, lightly-built, small, spare ▸ verb 3 SNUB, affront, blow off (slang), disdain, ignore, insult, scorn ▸ noun 4 SNUB, affront, insult, neglect, rebuff, slap in the face (informal), (the) cold shoulder

slightly adverb A LITTLE, somewhat

slim adjective 1 SLENDER, lean, narrow, slight, svelte, thin, trim 2 SLIGHT, faint, poor, remote, slender ▸ verb 3 LOSE WEIGHT, diet, reduce

slimy adjective 1 VISCOUS, clammy, glutinous, oozy 2 OBSEQUIOUS, creeping, grovelling, oily, servile, smarmy (Brit. informal), unctuous

sling verb 1 THROW, cast, chuck (informal), fling, heave, hurl, lob (informal), shy, toss 2 HANG, dangle, suspend

slink verb CREEP, prowl, skulk, slip, sneak, steal

slinky adjective FIGURE-HUGGING, clinging, close-fitting, skintight

slip verb 1 FALL, skid 2 SLIDE, glide, skate, slither 3 SNEAK, conceal, creep, hide, steal 4 (sometimes with up) MAKE A MISTAKE, blunder, err, miscalculate 5 **let slip** GIVE

AWAY, disclose, divulge, leak, reveal ► noun 6 MISTAKE, blunder, error, failure, fault, lapse, omission, oversight
7 give (someone) the slip ESCAPE FROM, dodge, elude, evade, get away from, lose (someone)

slippery adjective 1 SMOOTH, glassy, greasy, icy, slippy (informal or dialect), unsafe 2 DEVIOUS, crafty, cunning, dishonest, evasive, shifty, tricky, untrustworthy

slipshod adjective CARELESS, casual, slapdash, sloppy (informal), slovenly, untidy

slit noun 1 CUT, gash, incision, opening, rent, split, tear ► verb 2 CUT (OPEN), gash, knife, lance, pierce, rip, slash

slither verb SLIDE, glide, slink, slip, snake, undulate

sliver noun SHRED, fragment, paring, shaving, splinter

slobber verb DROOL, dribble, drivel, salivate, slaver

slobbish adjective MESSY, slovenly, unclean, unkempt, untidy

slog verb 1 WORK, labor, plod, plow through, slave, toil 2 TRUDGE, tramp, trek 3 HIT, punch, slug, sock (slang), strike, thump, wallop (informal) ► noun 4 LABOR, effort, exertion, struggle 5 TRUDGE, hike, tramp, trek

slogan noun CATCH PHRASE, catchword, motto

slop verb 1 SPILL, overflow, slosh (informal), splash ► noun 2 Informal FOOD, grub (slang), mess (slang)

slope noun 1 INCLINATION,

gradient, incline, ramp, rise, slant, tilt ► verb 2 SLANT, drop away, fall, incline, lean, rise, tilt
3 slope off SLINK AWAY, creep away, slip away

sloping adjective SLANTING, inclined, leaning, oblique

sloppy adjective 1 CARELESS, messy, slipshod, slovenly, untidy 2 SENTIMENTAL, gushing, mawkish, slushy (informal)

slot noun 1 OPENING, aperture, groove, hole, slit, vent 2 Informal PLACE, opening, position, space, time, vacancy ► verb 3 FIT IN, fit, insert

sloth noun LAZINESS, idleness, inactivity, inertia, slackness, sluggishness, torpor

slothful adjective LAZY, idle, inactive, indolent, workshy

slouch verb SLUMP, droop, loll, stoop

slovenly adjective CARELESS, disorderly, negligent, slack, slapdash, slipshod, sloppy (informal), untidy

slow adjective 1 PROLONGED, gradual, lingering, long-drawn-out, protracted 2 UNHURRIED, dawdling, lackadaisical, laggard, lazy, leisurely, ponderous, sluggish 3 LATE, backward, behind, delayed, tardy 4 STUPID, braindead (informal), dense, dim, dull-witted, obtuse, retarded, thick ► verb 5 (often with up or down) REDUCE SPEED, brake, decelerate, handicap, hold up, retard, slacken (off)

slowly adverb GRADUALLY, leisurely, unhurriedly

sludge noun SEDIMENT, mire, muck, mud, ooze, residue,

silt, slime

sluggish *adjective* INACTIVE, dull, heavy, indolent, inert, lethargic, slothful, slow, torpid

slum *noun* HOVEL, ghetto

slumber *verb* SLEEP, doze, drowse, nap, snooze (*informal*)

slump *verb* 1 FALL, collapse, crash, plunge, sink, slip 2 SAG, droop, hunch, loll, slouch ▶*noun* 3 FALL, collapse, crash, decline, downturn, drop, reverse, trough 4 RECESSION, depression

slur *noun* INSULT, affront, aspersion, calumny, innuendo, insinuation, smear, stain

slut *noun Offensive* TART, ho (*slang*), trollop, whore

sly *adjective* 1 CUNNING, artful, clever, crafty, devious, scheming, secret, shifty, stealthy, subtle, underhand, wily 2 ROGUISH, arch, impish, knowing, mischievous ▶*noun* 3 **on the sly** SECRETLY, covertly, on the quiet, privately, surreptitiously

smack *verb* 1 SLAP, clap, cuff, hit, paddle (*U.S. & Canad.*), spank, strike ▶*noun* 2 SLAP, blow ▶*adverb* 3 *Informal* DIRECTLY, exactly, precisely, right, slap (*informal*), squarely, straight

small *adjective* 1 LITTLE, diminutive, mini, miniature, minute, petite, pygmy *or* pigmy, teeny, teeny-weeny, tiny, undersized, wee 2 UNIMPORTANT, insignificant, minor, negligible, paltry, petty, trifling, trivial 3 PETTY, base, mean, narrow 4 MODEST, humble, unpretentious

small-minded *adjective* PETTY, bigoted, intolerant, mean, narrow-minded, ungenerous

small-time *adjective* MINOR, insignificant, of no account, petty, unimportant

smarmy *adjective Brit. informal* OBSEQUIOUS, crawling, ingratiating, servile, smooth, suave, sycophantic, toadying, unctuous

smart *adjective* 1 CLEVER, acute, astute, bright, canny, ingenious, intelligent, keen, quick, sharp, shrewd 2 BRISK, lively, quick, vigorous ▶*verb* 3 STING, burn, hurt ▶*noun* 4 STING, pain, soreness

smart aleck *noun Informal* KNOW-ALL (*informal*), smarty pants (*informal*), wise guy (*informal*)

smarten *verb* TIDY, groom, put in order, put to rights, spruce up

smash *verb* 1 BREAK, crush, demolish, pulverize, shatter 2 COLLIDE, crash 3 DESTROY, lay waste, ruin, trash (*slang*), wreck ▶*noun* 4 DESTRUCTION, collapse, downfall, failure, ruin 5 COLLISION, accident, crash

smattering *noun* MODICUM, bit, rudiments

smear *verb* 1 SPREAD OVER, bedaub, coat, cover, daub, rub on 2 DIRTY, smudge, soil, stain, sully 3 SLANDER, besmirch, blacken, malign ▶*noun* 4 SMUDGE, blot, blotch, daub, splotch, streak 5 SLANDER, calumny, defamation, libel

smell *verb* 1 SNIFF, scent 2 STINK, reek ▶*noun* 3 ODOR, aroma, bouquet, fragrance, perfume, scent 4 STINK, fetor, stench

smelly *adjective* STINKING, fetid, foul, foul-smelling, funky (*slang*), malodorous, noisome, reeking

smirk *noun* SMUG LOOK, simper

smitten *adjective* 1 AFFLICTED, laid low, plagued, struck 2 INFATUATED, beguiled, bewitched, captivated, charmed, enamored

smolder *verb* SEETHE, boil, fume, rage, simmer

smooth *adjective* 1 EVEN, flat, flush, horizontal, level, plane 2 SLEEK, glossy, polished, shiny, silky, soft, velvety 3 EASY, effortless, well-ordered 4 FLOWING, regular, rhythmic, steady, uniform 5 SUAVE, facile, glib, persuasive, slick, smarmy (*Brit. informal*), unctuous, urbane 6 MELLOW, agreeable, mild, pleasant ▶*verb* 7 FLATTEN, iron, level, plane, press 8 CALM, appease, assuage, ease, mitigate, mollify, soften

smother *verb* 1 SUFFOCATE, choke, stifle, strangle 2 SUPPRESS, conceal, hide, muffle, repress, stifle

smudge *verb* 1 SMEAR, daub, dirty, mark, smirch ▶*noun* 2 SMEAR, blemish, blot

smug *adjective* SELF-SATISFIED, complacent, conceited, superior

smuggler *noun* TRAFFICKER, bootlegger, runner

smutty *adjective* OBSCENE, bawdy, blue, coarse, crude, dirty, indecent, indelicate, suggestive, vulgar

snack *noun* LIGHT MEAL, bite, refreshment(s)

snag *noun* 1 DIFFICULTY, catch, complication, disadvantage, downside, drawback, hitch, obstacle, problem ▶*verb* 2 CATCH, rip, tear

snap *verb* 1 BREAK, crack, separate 2 CRACKLE, click, pop 3 BITE AT, bite, nip, snatch 4 SPEAK SHARPLY, bark, jump down (someone's) throat (*informal*), lash out at ▶*noun* 5 CRACKLE, pop 6 BITE, grab, nip ▶*adjective* 7 INSTANT, immediate, spur-of-the-moment, sudden

snappy *adjective* 1 IRRITABLE, cross, edgy, testy, touchy 2 SMART, chic, cool (*informal*), dapper, fashionable, phat (*slang*), stylish

snap up *verb* SEIZE, grab, pounce upon, take advantage of

snare *noun* 1 TRAP, gin, net, noose, wire ▶*verb* 2 TRAP, catch, entrap, net, seize, wire

snarl *verb* (often with *up*) TANGLE, entangle, entwine, muddle, ravel

snarl-up *noun* TANGLE, confusion, entanglement, muddle

snatch *verb* 1 SEIZE, clutch, grab, grasp, grip ▶*noun* 2 BIT, fragment, part, piece, snippet

sneak *verb* 1 SLINK, lurk, pad, skulk, slip, steal 2 SLIP, smuggle, spirit ▶*noun* 3 INFORMER, telltale

sneaking *adjective* 1 NAGGING, persistent, uncomfortable, worrying 2 SECRET, hidden, private, undivulged, unexpressed, unvoiced

sneaky *adjective* SLY, deceitful, devious, dishonest, double-dealing, down and dirty (*informal*), furtive, low, mean, shifty, untrustworthy

sneer *noun* 1 SCORN, derision, gibe, jeer, mockery, ridicule ▶ *verb* 2 SCORN, deride, disdain, jeer, laugh, mock, ridicule

snide *adjective* NASTY, cynical, disparaging, hurtful, ill-natured, malicious, sarcastic, scornful, sneering, spiteful

sniff *verb* INHALE, breathe, smell

snigger *noun, verb* LAUGH, giggle, snicker, titter

snip *verb* 1 CUT, clip, crop, dock, shave, trim ▶ *noun* 2 BIT, clipping, fragment, piece, scrap, shred

snipe *verb* CRITICIZE, carp, denigrate, disparage, jeer, knock (*informal*), put down

snippet *noun* PIECE, fragment, part, scrap, shred

snitch *verb* 1 *Informal* INFORM ON, grass on (*Brit. slang*), tattle on, tell on (*informal*), tell tales ▶ *noun* 2 INFORMER, tattletale, telltale

snivel *verb* WHINE, cry, moan, sniffle, whimper

snob *noun* ELITIST, highbrow, prig

snobbery *noun* ARROGANCE, airs, pretension, pride, snobbishness

snobbish *adjective* SUPERIOR, arrogant, patronizing, pretentious, snooty (*informal*), stuck-up (*informal*)

snoop *verb* PRY, interfere, poke one's nose in (*informal*), spy

snooper *noun* NOSY ROSY (*U.S. informal*), busybody, meddler, snoop (*informal*)

snooze *verb* 1 DOZE, catnap, nap, take forty winks (*informal*) ▶ *noun* 2 DOZE, catnap, forty winks (*informal*), nap, siesta

snub *verb* 1 PUT DOWN, avoid, blow off (*slang*), cold-shoulder, cut (*informal*), humiliate, ignore, rebuff, slight ▶ *noun* 2 INSULT, affront, put-down, slap in the face

snug *adjective* COZY, comfortable, comfy (*informal*), homey, warm

snuggle *verb* NESTLE, cuddle, nuzzle

soak *verb* 1 WET, bathe, damp, drench, immerse, moisten, saturate, steep 2 PENETRATE, permeate, seep 3 **soak up** ABSORB, assimilate

soaking *adjective* SOAKED, drenched, dripping, saturated, sodden, sopping, streaming, wet through, wringing wet

soar *verb* 1 ASCEND, fly, mount, rise, wing 2 RISE, climb, escalate, rocket, shoot up

sob *verb* CRY, howl, shed tears, weep

sober *adjective* 1 ABSTINENT, abstemious, moderate, temperate 2 SERIOUS, composed, cool, grave, level-headed, rational, reasonable, sedate, solemn, staid, steady 3 PLAIN, dark, drab, dumpy (*informal*), frowzy, homely (*U.S.*), quiet, somber, subdued

sobriety *noun* 1 ABSTINENCE, abstemiousness, moderation, nonindulgence, soberness, temperance 2 SERIOUSNESS, gravity, level-headedness, solemnity, staidness, steadiness

so-called *adjective* ALLEGED, pretended, professed, self-styled, supposed

sociable *adjective* FRIENDLY, affable, companionable, convivial, cordial, genial, gregarious, outgoing, social, warm

social *adjective* 1 COMMUNAL, collective, common, community, general, group, public ▸ *noun* 2 GET-TOGETHER (*informal*), gathering, party

socialize *verb* MIX, fraternize, get about *or* around, go out

society *noun* 1 MANKIND, civilization, humanity, people, the community, the public 2 ORGANIZATION, association, circle, club, fellowship, group, guild, institute, league, order, union 3 UPPER CLASSES, beau monde, elite, gentry, high society 4 COMPANIONSHIP, company, fellowship, friendship

sodden *adjective* SOAKED, drenched, saturated, soggy, sopping, waterlogged

sofa *noun* COUCH, chaise longue, divan, settee

soft *adjective* 1 PLIABLE, bendable, elastic, flexible, malleable, moldable, plastic, supple 2 YIELDING, elastic, gelatinous, pulpy, spongy, squashy 3 VELVETY, downy, feathery, fleecy, silky, smooth 4 QUIET, dulcet, gentle, murmured, muted, soft-toned 5 PALE, bland, light, mellow, pastel, subdued 6 DIM, dimmed, faint, restful 7 MILD, balmy, temperate 8 LENIENT, easy-going, indulgent, lax, overindulgent, permissive, spineless 9 OUT OF CONDITION, effeminate, flabby, flaccid, limp, weak 10 *Informal* EASY, comfortable, undemanding

11 KIND, compassionate, gentle, sensitive, sentimental, tenderhearted, touchy-feely (*informal*)

soften *verb* LESSEN, allay, appease, cushion, ease, mitigate, moderate, mollify, still, subdue, temper

softhearted *adjective* KIND, charitable, compassionate, sentimental, sympathetic, tender, tenderhearted, warm-hearted

soggy *adjective* SODDEN, dripping, moist, saturated, soaked, sopping, waterlogged

soil[1] *noun* 1 EARTH, clay, dirt, dust, ground 2 LAND, country

soil[2] *verb* DIRTY, befoul, besmirch, defile, foul, pollute, spot, stain, sully, tarnish

solace *noun* 1 COMFORT, consolation, relief ▸ *verb* 2 COMFORT, console

soldier *noun* FIGHTER, man-at-arms, serviceman, trooper, warrior

sole *adjective* ONLY, alone, exclusive, individual, one, single, solitary

solely *adverb* ONLY, alone, completely, entirely, exclusively, merely

solemn *adjective* 1 FORMAL, ceremonial, dignified, grand, grave, momentous, stately 2 SERIOUS, earnest, grave, sedate, sober, staid

solemnity *noun* 1 SERIOUSNESS, earnestness, gravity 2 FORMALITY, grandeur, impressiveness, momentousness

solicitous *adjective* CONCERNED, anxious, attentive, careful

solicitude *noun* CONCERN,

anxiety, attentiveness, care, consideration, regard

solid *adjective* **1** FIRM, compact, concrete, dense, hard **2** STRONG, stable, sturdy, substantial, unshakable **3** SOUND, genuine, good, pure, real, reliable **4** RELIABLE, dependable, trusty, upright, upstanding, worthy

solidarity *noun* UNITY, accord, cohesion, concordance, like-mindedness, team spirit, unanimity, unification

solidify *verb* HARDEN, cake, coagulate, cohere, congeal, jell, set

solitary *adjective* **1** UNSOCIABLE, cloistered, isolated, reclusive, unsocial **2** SINGLE, alone, lone, sole **3** LONELY, companionless, friendless, lonesome **4** ISOLATED, hidden, out-of-the-way, remote, unfrequented

solitude *noun* ISOLATION, loneliness, privacy, retirement, seclusion

solution *noun* **1** ANSWER, explanation, key, result **2** *Chemistry* MIXTURE, blend, compound, mix, solvent

solve *verb* ANSWER, clear up, crack, decipher, disentangle, get to the bottom of, resolve, unravel, work out

somber *adjective* **1** DARK, dim, drab, dull, gloomy, sober **2** GLOOMY, dismal, doleful, grave, joyless, lugubrious, mournful, sad, sober

somebody *noun* CELEBRITY, dignitary, household name, luminary, megastar (*informal*), name, notable, personage, star

someday *adverb* EVENTUALLY, one

day, one of these (fine) days, sooner or later

somehow *adverb* ONE WAY OR ANOTHER, by fair means or foul, by hook or (by) crook, by some means or other, come hell or high water (*informal*), come what may

sometimes *adverb* OCCASIONALLY, at times, now and then

song *noun* BALLAD, air, anthem, carol, chant, chorus, ditty, hymn, number, psalm, tune

soon *adverb* BEFORE LONG, in the near future, shortly

soothe *verb* **1** CALM, allay, appease, hush, lull, mollify, pacify, quiet, still **2** RELIEVE, alleviate, assuage, ease

soothing *adjective* CALMING, emollient, palliative, relaxing, restful

soothsayer *noun* PROPHET, diviner, fortune-teller, seer, sibyl

sophisticated *adjective* **1** CULTURED, cosmopolitan, cultivated, refined, urbane, worldly **2** COMPLEX, advanced, complicated, delicate, elaborate, intricate, refined, subtle

sophistication *noun* SAVOIR-FAIRE, finesse, poise, urbanity, worldliness, worldly wisdom

soporific *adjective* **1** SLEEP-INDUCING, sedative, somnolent, tranquilizing ▸ *noun* **2** SEDATIVE, narcotic, opiate, tranquilizer

sorcerer *noun* MAGICIAN, enchanter, necromancer, warlock, witch, wizard

sorcery *noun* BLACK MAGIC, black art, enchantment, magic, necromancy, witchcraft, wizardry

sordid *adjective* 1 DIRTY, filthy, foul, mean, scuzzy (*slang*), seedy, sleazy, squalid, unclean 2 BASE, debauched, degenerate, low, shabby, shameful, vicious, vile 3 MERCENARY, avaricious, covetous, grasping, selfish

sore *adjective* 1 PAINFUL, angry, burning, inflamed, irritated, raw, sensitive, smarting, tender 2 ANNOYING, severe, sharp, troublesome 3 ANNOYED, aggrieved, angry, cross, hurt, irked, irritated, pained, resentful, stung, upset 4 URGENT, acute, critical, desperate, dire, extreme, pressing

sorrow *noun* 1 GRIEF, anguish, distress, heartache, heartbreak, misery, mourning, regret, sadness, unhappiness, woe 2 AFFLICTION, hardship, misfortune, trial, tribulation, trouble, woe ▸ *verb* 3 GRIEVE, agonize, bemoan, be sad, bewail, lament, mourn

sorrowful *adjective* SAD, dejected, dismal, doleful, grieving, miserable, mournful, sorry, unhappy, woebegone, woeful, wretched

sorry *adjective* 1 REGRETFUL, apologetic, conscience-stricken, contrite, penitent, remorseful, repentant, shamefaced 2 SYMPATHETIC, commiserative, compassionate, full of pity, moved 3 WRETCHED, deplorable, mean, miserable, pathetic, pitiful, poor, sad

sort *noun* 1 KIND, brand, category, class, ilk, make, nature, order, quality, style, type, variety ▸ *verb* 2 ARRANGE,

categorize, classify, divide, grade, group, order, put in order, rank

sort out *verb* 1 RESOLVE, clarify, clear up 2 ORGANIZE, tidy up

soul *noun* 1 SPIRIT, essence, life, vital force 2 PERSONIFICATION, embodiment, epitome, essence, quintessence, type 3 PERSON, being, body, creature, individual, man *or* woman

sound[1] *noun* 1 NOISE, din, report, reverberation, tone 2 IMPRESSION, drift, idea, look ▸ *verb* 3 RESOUND, echo, reverberate 4 SEEM, appear, look 5 PRONOUNCE, announce, articulate, declare, express, utter

sound[2] *adjective* 1 PERFECT, fit, healthy, intact, solid, unhurt, unimpaired, uninjured, whole 2 SENSIBLE, correct, logical, proper, prudent, rational, reasonable, right, trustworthy, valid, well-founded, wise 3 DEEP, unbroken, undisturbed, untroubled

sound[3] *verb* FATHOM, plumb, probe

sound out *verb* PROBE, canvass, pump, question, see how the land lies

sour *adjective* 1 SHARP, acetic, acid, bitter, pungent, tart 2 GONE OFF, curdled, gone bad, turned 3 ILL-NATURED, acrimonious, disagreeable, embittered, ill-tempered, peevish, tart, ungenerous, waspish

source *noun* 1 ORIGIN, author, beginning, cause, derivation, fount, originator 2 INFORMANT, authority

souvenir noun KEEPSAKE, memento, reminder

sovereign noun 1 MONARCH, chief, emperor or empress, king or queen, potentate, prince, ruler ▶ adjective 2 SUPREME, absolute, imperial, kingly or queenly, principal, royal, ruling 3 EXCELLENT, effectual, efficacious, efficient

sovereignty noun SUPREME POWER, domination, kingship, primacy, supremacy

sow verb SCATTER, implant, plant, seed

space noun 1 ROOM, capacity, elbowroom, expanse, extent, leeway, margin, play, scope 2 GAP, blank, distance, interval, omission 3 TIME, duration, interval, period, span, while

spacious adjective ROOMY, ample, broad, capacious, commodious, expansive, extensive, huge, large, sizable or sizeable

spadework noun PREPARATION, donkey-work, groundwork, labor

span noun 1 EXTENT, amount, distance, length, reach, spread, stretch 2 PERIOD, duration, spell, term ▶ verb 3 EXTEND ACROSS, bridge, cover, cross, link, traverse

spank verb SMACK, cuff, paddle (U.S. & Canad.), slap

spar verb ARGUE, bicker, row, scrap (informal), squabble, wrangle

spare adjective 1 EXTRA, additional, free, leftover, odd, over, superfluous, surplus, unoccupied, unused, unwanted

2 THIN, gaunt, lean, meager, wiry ▶ verb 3 HAVE MERCY ON, be merciful to, go easy on (informal), leave, let off (informal), pardon, save from 4 AFFORD, do without, give, grant, let (someone) have, manage without, part with

spare time noun LEISURE, free time, odd moments

sparing adjective ECONOMICAL, careful, frugal, prudent, saving, thrifty

spark noun 1 FLICKER, flare, flash, gleam, glint 2 TRACE, atom, hint, jot, scrap, vestige ▶ verb 3 (often with off) START, inspire, precipitate, provoke, set off, stimulate, trigger (off)

sparkle verb 1 GLITTER, dance, flash, gleam, glint, glisten, scintillate, shimmer, shine, twinkle ▶ noun 2 GLITTER, brilliance, flash, flicker, gleam, glint, twinkle 3 VIVACITY, dash, élan, life, spirit, vitality

sparse adjective SCATTERED, few and far between, meager, scanty, scarce

spartan adjective AUSTERE, ascetic, disciplined, frugal, plain, rigorous, self-denying, severe, strict

spasm noun 1 CONVULSION, contraction, paroxysm, twitch 2 BURST, eruption, fit, frenzy, outburst, seizure

spasmodic adjective SPORADIC, convulsive, erratic, fitful, intermittent, irregular, jerky

spate noun FLOOD, deluge, flow, outpouring, rush, torrent

speak verb 1 TALK, articulate, converse, express, pronounce, say, state, tell, utter 2 LECTURE, address, declaim, discourse, hold forth

speaker noun LECTURER, orator, public speaker, spokesman or spokeswoman, spokesperson

speak out or **up** verb SPEAK ONE'S MIND, have one's say, make one's position plain, voice one's opinions

spearhead verb LEAD, head, initiate, launch, pioneer, set in motion, set off

special adjective 1 EXCEPTIONAL, extraordinary, important, memorable, significant, uncommon, unique, unusual 2 PARTICULAR, appropriate, distinctive, individual, precise, specific

specialist noun EXPERT, authority, buff (informal), connoisseur, consultant, master, professional

speciality noun FORTE, bag (slang, dated), métier, pièce de résistance, specialty

species noun KIND, breed, category, class, group, sort, type, variety

specific adjective 1 PARTICULAR, characteristic, distinguishing, special 2 DEFINITE, clear-cut, exact, explicit, express, precise, unequivocal

specification noun REQUIREMENT, condition, detail, particular, qualification, stipulation

specify verb STATE, define, designate, detail, indicate, mention, name, stipulate

specimen noun SAMPLE, example, exemplification, instance, model, pattern, representative, type

speck noun 1 MARK, blemish,

dot, fleck, mote, speckle, spot, stain 2 PARTICLE, atom, bit, grain, iota, jot, mite, shred

speckled adjective FLECKED, dappled, dotted, mottled, spotted, sprinkled

spectacle noun 1 SIGHT, curiosity, marvel, phenomenon, scene, wonder 2 SHOW, display, event, exhibition, extravaganza, pageant, performance

spectacular adjective 1 IMPRESSIVE, cool (informal), dazzling, dramatic, grand, magnificent, phat (slang), sensational, splendid, striking, stunning (informal) ▶ noun 2 SHOW, display, spectacle

spectator noun ONLOOKER, bystander, looker-on, observer, viewer, watcher

specter noun GHOST, apparition, phantom, spirit, vision, wraith

speculate verb 1 CONJECTURE, consider, guess, hypothesize, suppose, surmise, theorize, wonder 2 GAMBLE, hazard, risk, venture

speculation noun 1 GUESSWORK, conjecture, hypothesis, opinion, supposition, surmise, theory 2 GAMBLE, hazard, risk

speculative adjective HYPOTHETICAL, academic, conjectural, notional, suppositional, theoretical

speech noun 1 COMMUNICATION, conversation, dialogue, discussion, talk 2 TALK, address, discourse, homily, lecture, oration, spiel (informal) 3 LANGUAGE, articulation, dialect, diction, enunciation, idiom, jargon, parlance, tongue

speechless *adjective* 1 MUTE, dumb, inarticulate, silent, wordless 2 ASTOUNDED, aghast, amazed, dazed, shocked

speed *noun* 1 SWIFTNESS, haste, hurry, pace, quickness, rapidity, rush, velocity ▶ *verb* 2 RACE, career, gallop, hasten, hurry, make haste, rush, tear, zoom 3 HELP, advance, aid, assist, boost, expedite, facilitate

speed up *verb* ACCELERATE, gather momentum, increase the tempo

speedy *adjective* QUICK, express, fast, hasty, headlong, hurried, immediate, precipitate, prompt, rapid, swift

spell[1] *verb* INDICATE, augur, imply, mean, point to, portend, signify

spell[2] *noun* 1 INCANTATION, charm 2 FASCINATION, allure, bewitchment, enchantment, glamour, magic

spell[3] *noun* PERIOD, bout, course, interval, season, stretch, term, time

spellbound *adjective* ENTRANCED, bewitched, captivated, charmed, enthralled, fascinated, gripped, mesmerized, rapt

spend *verb* 1 PAY OUT, disburse, expend, fork out (*slang*) 2 PASS, fill, occupy, while away 3 USE UP, consume, dissipate, drain, empty, exhaust, run through, squander, waste

spendthrift *noun* 1 SQUANDERER, big spender, profligate, spender, waster ▶ *adjective* 2 WASTEFUL, extravagant, improvident, prodigal, profligate

spew *verb* VOMIT, barf (*slang*), disgorge, puke (*slang*), regurgitate, throw up (*informal*)

sphere *noun* 1 BALL, circle, globe, globule, orb 2 FIELD, capacity, department, domain, function, patch, province, realm, scope, territory, turf (*slang*)

spherical *adjective* ROUND, globe-shaped, globular, rotund

spice *noun* 1 SEASONING, relish, savor 2 EXCITEMENT, color, pep, piquancy, zest, zing (*informal*)

spicy *adjective* 1 HOT, aromatic, piquant, savory, seasoned 2 *Informal* SCANDALOUS, hot (*informal*), indelicate, racy, ribald, risqué, suggestive, titillating

spike *noun* 1 POINT, barb, prong, spine ▶ *verb* 2 IMPALE, spear, spit, stick

spill *verb* 1 POUR, discharge, disgorge, overflow, slop over ▶ *noun* 2 FALL, tumble

spin *verb* 1 REVOLVE, gyrate, pirouette, reel, rotate, turn, twirl, whirl 2 REEL, swim, whirl ▶ *noun* 3 REVOLUTION, gyration, roll, whirl 4 *Informal* DRIVE, joy ride (*informal*), ride

spine *noun* 1 BACKBONE, spinal column, vertebrae, vertebral column 2 BARB, needle, quill, ray, spike, spur

spine-chilling *adjective* FRIGHTENING, bloodcurdling, eerie, horrifying, scary (*informal*), spooky (*informal*), terrifying

spineless *adjective* WEAK, cowardly, faint-hearted, feeble, gutless (*informal*), lily-livered, soft, weak-kneed (*informal*)

spin out verb PROLONG, amplify, delay, drag out, draw out, extend, lengthen

spiral noun 1 COIL, corkscrew, helix, whorl ▶adjective 2 COILED, helical, whorled, winding

spirit noun 1 LIFE FORCE, life, soul, vital spark 2 FEELING, atmosphere, gist, tenor, tone 3 TEMPERAMENT, attitude, character, disposition, outlook, temper 4 LIVELINESS, animation, brio, energy, enthusiasm, fire, force, life, mettle, vigor, zest 5 COURAGE, backbone, gameness, grit, guts (informal), spunk (informal) 6 ESSENCE, intention, meaning, purport, purpose, sense, substance 7 GHOST, apparition, phantom, specter 8 **spirits** MOOD, feelings, frame of mind, morale ▶verb 9 (with away or off) REMOVE, abduct, abstract, carry, purloin, seize, steal, whisk

spirited adjective LIVELY, active, animated, energetic, feisty (informal), mettlesome, vivacious

spiritual adjective SACRED, devotional, divine, holy, religious

spit verb 1 EJECT, expectorate, splutter, throw out ▶noun 2 SALIVA, dribble, drool, slaver, spittle

spite noun 1 MALICE, animosity, hatred, ill will, malevolence, spitefulness, spleen, venom 2 **in spite of** DESPITE, (even) though, notwithstanding, regardless of ▶verb 3 HURT, annoy, harm, injure, vex

spiteful adjective MALICIOUS, bitchy (informal), ill-natured, malevolent, nasty, vindictive

splash verb 1 SCATTER, shower, slop, spatter, spray, sprinkle, wet 2 PUBLICIZE, broadcast, tout, trumpet ▶noun 3 DASH, burst, patch, spattering, touch 4 Informal DISPLAY, effect, impact, sensation, stir

splash out verb Informal SPEND, be extravagant, spare no expense, splurge

splendid adjective 1 MARVELOUS, fantastic (informal), first-class, glorious, great (informal), wonderful 2 MAGNIFICENT, cool (informal), costly, gorgeous, impressive, lavish, luxurious, ornate, phat (slang), resplendent, rich, sumptuous, superb

splendor noun MAGNIFICENCE, brightness, brilliance, display, glory, grandeur, pomp, richness, show, spectacle, sumptuousness

splinter noun 1 SLIVER, chip, flake, fragment ▶verb 2 SHATTER, disintegrate, fracture, split

split verb 1 BREAK, burst, come apart, come undone, crack, give way, open, rend, rip 2 SEPARATE, branch, cleave, disband, disunite, diverge, fork, part 3 SHARE OUT, allocate, allot, apportion, distribute, divide, halve, partition ▶noun 4 CRACK, breach, division, fissure, gap, rent, rip, separation, slit, tear 5 DIVISION, breach, break-up, discord, dissension, estrangement, rift, rupture, schism ▶adjective 6 DIVIDED, broken, cleft, cracked, fractured, ruptured

split up verb SEPARATE, break up,

divorce, part

spoil *verb* 1 RUIN, damage, destroy, disfigure, harm, impair, injure, mar, mess up, trash (*slang*), wreck 2 OVERINDULGE, coddle, cosset, indulge, pamper 3 GO BAD, addle, curdle, decay, decompose, rot, turn

spoils *plural noun* BOOTY, loot, plunder, prey, swag (*slang*), treasure

spoilsport *noun* KILLJOY, damper, misery (*informal*), sourpuss, wet blanket (*informal*)

spoken *adjective* SAID, expressed, oral, told, unwritten, uttered, verbal, viva voce, voiced

spokesperson *noun* SPEAKER, mouthpiece, official, spin doctor (*informal*), spokesman *or* spokeswoman, voice

spongy *adjective* POROUS, absorbent

sponsor *noun* 1 BACKER, patron, promoter ▶ *verb* 2 BACK, finance, fund, patronize, promote, subsidize

spontaneous *adjective* UNPLANNED, impromptu, impulsive, instinctive, natural, unprompted, voluntary, willing

spoof *noun* *Informal* PARODY, burlesque, caricature, mockery, satire

spooky *adjective* EERIE, chilling, creepy (*informal*), frightening, scary (*informal*), spine-chilling, uncanny, unearthly, weird

sporadic *adjective* INTERMITTENT, irregular, occasional, scattered, spasmodic

sport *noun* 1 GAME, amusement, diversion, exercise, pastime,

play, recreation 2 FUN, badinage, banter, jest, joking, teasing ▶ *verb* 3 *Old-fashioned, Informal* WEAR, display, exhibit, show off

sporting *adjective* FAIR, game (*informal*), sportsmanlike

sporty *adjective* ATHLETIC, energetic, outdoor

spot *noun* 1 MARK, blemish, blot, blotch, scar, smudge, speck, speckle, stain 2 PLACE, location, point, position, scene, site 3 *Informal* PREDICAMENT, difficulty, hot water (*informal*), mess, plight, quandary, tight spot, trouble ▶ *verb* 4 SEE, catch a glimpse of, catch sight of, detect, discern, espy, make out, observe, recognize, sight 5 MARK, dirty, fleck, mottle, smirch, soil, spatter, speckle, splodge, splotch, stain

spotless *adjective* CLEAN, flawless, gleaming, immaculate, impeccable, pure, shining, unblemished, unstained, unsullied, untarnished

spotlight *noun* 1 ATTENTION, fame, limelight, public eye ▶ *verb* 2 HIGHLIGHT, accentuate, draw attention to

spotted *adjective* SPECKLED, dappled, dotted, flecked, mottled

spouse *noun* PARTNER, consort, husband *or* wife, mate, significant other (*informal*)

spout *verb* STREAM, discharge, gush, shoot, spray, spurt, surge

sprawl *verb* LOLL, flop, lounge, slouch, slump

spray[1] *noun* 1 DROPLETS, drizzle, fine mist 2 AEROSOL, atomizer, sprinkler ▶ *verb* **3** SCATTER, diffuse, shower, sprinkle

spray² *noun* SPRIG, branch, corsage, floral arrangement

spread *verb* **1** OPEN (OUT), broaden, dilate, expand, extend, sprawl, stretch, unfold, unroll, widen **2** PROLIFERATE, escalate, multiply **3** CIRCULATE, broadcast, disseminate, make known, propagate ▶ *noun* **4** INCREASE, advance, development, dispersal, dissemination, expansion, proliferation **5** EXTENT, span, stretch, sweep

spree *noun* BINGE (*informal*), bacchanalia, carousal, fling, orgy, revel

sprightly *adjective* LIVELY, active, agile, brisk, energetic, nimble, spirited, spry, vivacious

spring *verb* **1** JUMP, bounce, bound, leap, vault **2** (often with *from*) ORIGINATE, arise, come, derive, descend, issue, proceed, start, stem **3** (often with *up*) APPEAR, develop, mushroom, shoot up ▶ *noun* **4** JUMP, bound, leap, vault **5** ELASTICITY, bounce, buoyancy, flexibility, resilience

springy *adjective* ELASTIC, bouncy, buoyant, flexible, resilient, rubbery

sprinkle *verb* SCATTER, dredge, dust, pepper, powder, shower, spray, strew

sprinkling *noun* SCATTERING, dash, dusting, few, handful, sprinkle

sprint *verb* RACE, dart, dash, shoot, tear

sprite *noun* SPIRIT, brownie, elf, fairy, goblin, imp, pixie

sprout *verb* GROW, bud, develop, shoot, spring

spruce *adjective* SMART, dapper, neat, trim, well-groomed, well turned out

spruce up *verb* SMARTEN UP, tidy, titivate

spry *adjective* ACTIVE, agile, nimble, sprightly, supple

spur *noun* **1** STIMULUS, impetus, impulse, incentive, incitement, inducement, motive **2** GOAD, prick **3** **on the spur of the moment** ON IMPULSE, impromptu, impulsively, on the spot, without planning ▶ *verb* **4** INCITE, animate, drive, goad, impel, prick, prod, prompt, stimulate, urge

spurious *adjective* FALSE, artificial, bogus, fake, phoney or phony (*informal*), pretended, sham, specious, unauthentic

spurn *verb* REJECT, despise, disdain, rebuff, repulse, scorn, slight, snub

spurt *verb* **1** GUSH, burst, erupt, shoot, squirt, surge ▶ *noun* **2** BURST, fit, rush, spate, surge

spy *noun* **1** UNDERCOVER AGENT, mole ▶ *verb* **2** CATCH SIGHT OF, espy, glimpse, notice, observe, spot

squabble *verb* **1** QUARREL, argue, bicker, dispute, fight, row, wrangle ▶ *noun* **2** QUARREL, argument, disagreement, dispute, fight, row, tiff

squad *noun* TEAM, band, company, crew, force, gang, group, troop

squalid *adjective* DIRTY, filthy, scuzzy (*slang*), seedy, sleazy, slummy, sordid, unclean

squalor *noun* FILTH, foulness,

sleaziness, squalidness

squander verb WASTE, blow (slang), expend, fritter away, misspend, misuse, spend

square adjective 1 HONEST, above board, ethical, fair, genuine, kosher (informal), straight 2 Informal UNCOOL, dorky (slang), nerdy, unhip ▶verb 3 EVEN UP, adjust, align, level 4 (sometimes with up) PAY OFF, settle 5 (often with with) AGREE, correspond, fit, match, reconcile, tally

squash verb 1 CRUSH, compress, distort, flatten, mash, press, pulp, smash 2 SUPPRESS, annihilate, crush, humiliate, quell, silence

squashy adjective SOFT, mushy, pulpy, spongy, yielding

squawk verb CRY, hoot, screech

squeak verb PEEP, pipe, squeal

squeal noun, verb SCREAM, screech, shriek, wail, yell

squeamish adjective 1 DELICATE, fastidious, prudish, strait-laced 2 SICK, nauseous, queasy

squeeze verb 1 PRESS, clutch, compress, crush, grip, pinch, squash, wring 2 CRAM, crowd, force, jam, pack, press, ram, stuff 3 HUG, clasp, cuddle, embrace, enfold 4 EXTORT, milk, pressurize, wrest ▶noun 5 HUG, clasp, embrace 6 CRUSH, congestion, crowd, jam, press, squash

squirm verb WRIGGLE, twist, writhe

squirt noun Informal CHILD, baby, boy, girl, infant, kid (informal), minor, toddler, tot, whippersnapper (old-fashioned), youngster

stab verb 1 PIERCE, impale, jab, knife, spear, stick, thrust, transfix, wound ▶noun 2 WOUND, gash, incision, jab, puncture, thrust 3 TWINGE, ache, pang, prick 4 **make** or **have a stab at** Informal ATTEMPT, endeavor, have a go, try

stability noun FIRMNESS, solidity, soundness, steadiness, strength

stable adjective 1 FIRM, constant, established, fast, fixed, immovable, lasting, permanent, secure, sound, strong 2 STEADY, reliable, staunch, steadfast, sure

stack noun 1 PILE, heap, load, mass, mound, mountain ▶verb 2 PILE, accumulate, amass, assemble, heap up, load

staff noun 1 WORKERS, employees, personnel, team, workforce 2 STICK, cane, crook, pole, rod, scepter, stave, wand

stage noun POINT, division, juncture, lap, leg, level, period, phase, step

stagger verb 1 TOTTER, lurch, reel, sway, wobble 2 ASTOUND, amaze, astonish, confound, overwhelm, shake, shock, stun, stupefy 3 OVERLAP, alternate, step

stagnant adjective STALE, quiet, sluggish, still

stagnate verb VEGETATE, decay, decline, idle, languish, rot, rust

staid adjective SEDATE, calm, composed, grave, serious, sober, solemn, steady

stain verb 1 MARK, blemish, blot, dirty, discolor, smirch, soil, spot, tinge ▶noun 2 MARK, blemish, blot, discoloration, smirch, spot 3 STIGMA, disgrace, dishonor, shame, slur

stake¹ noun POLE, pale, paling, palisade, picket, post, stick

stake² noun 1 BET, ante, pledge, wager 2 INTEREST, concern, investment, involvement, share ▶ verb 3 BET, chance, gamble, hazard, risk, venture, wager

stale adjective 1 OLD, decayed, dry, flat, fusty, hard, musty, sour 2 UNORIGINAL, banal, hackneyed, overused, stereotyped, threadbare, trite, worn-out

stalk verb PURSUE, follow, haunt, hunt, shadow, track

stall verb PLAY FOR TIME, hedge, temporize

stalwart adjective STRONG, staunch, stout, strapping, sturdy

stamina noun STAYING POWER, endurance, energy, force, power, resilience, strength

stammer verb STUTTER, falter, hesitate, pause, stumble

stamp noun 1 IMPRINT, brand, earmark, hallmark, mark, signature ▶ verb 2 TRAMPLE, crush 3 IDENTIFY, brand, categorize, label, mark, reveal, show to be 4 IMPRINT, impress, mark, print

stampede noun RUSH, charge, flight, rout

stamp out verb ELIMINATE, crush, destroy, eradicate, put down, quell, scotch, suppress

stance noun 1 ATTITUDE, position, stand, standpoint, viewpoint 2 POSTURE, bearing, carriage, deportment

stand verb 1 BE UPRIGHT, be erect, be vertical, rise 2 PUT, mount, place, position, set

3 EXIST, be valid, continue, hold, obtain, prevail, remain 4 TOLERATE, abide, allow, bear, brook, countenance, deal with (slang), endure, handle, put up with (informal), stomach, take ▶ noun 5 STALL, booth, table 6 POSITION, attitude, determination, opinion, stance 7 SUPPORT, base, bracket, dais, platform, rack, stage, tripod

standard noun 1 BENCHMARK, average, criterion, gauge, grade, guideline, measure, model, norm, yardstick 2 (often plural) PRINCIPLES, ethics, ideals, morals 3 FLAG, banner, ensign ▶ adjective 4 USUAL, average, basic, customary, normal, orthodox, regular, typical 5 ACCEPTED, approved, authoritative, definitive, established, official, recognized

standardize verb BRING INTO LINE, institutionalize, regiment

stand by verb 1 BE PREPARED, wait 2 SUPPORT, back, be loyal to, champion, take (someone's) part

stand for verb 1 REPRESENT, betoken, denote, indicate, mean, signify, symbolize 2 Informal TOLERATE, bear, brook, endure, put up with

stand-in noun SUBSTITUTE, deputy, locum, replacement, reserve, stopgap, surrogate, understudy

stand in for verb BE A SUBSTITUTE FOR, cover for, deputize for, represent, take the place of

standing adjective 1 PERMANENT, fixed, lasting, regular 2 UPRIGHT, erect, vertical ▶ noun 3 STATUS, eminence, footing, position,

rank, reputation, repute
4 DURATION, continuance,
existence

standoffish *adjective* RESERVED,
aloof, cold, distant, haughty,
remote, unapproachable,
unsociable

stand out *verb* BE CONSPICUOUS,
be distinct, be obvious, be
prominent

standpoint *noun* POINT OF VIEW,
angle, position, stance,
viewpoint

stand up for *verb* SUPPORT,
champion, defend, stick up for
(*informal*), uphold

staple *adjective* PRINCIPAL, basic,
chief, fundamental, key, main,
predominant

star *noun* 1 HEAVENLY BODY
2 CELEBRITY, big name, luminary,
main attraction, megastar
(*informal*), name, superstar
(*informal*) ▶ *adjective* 3 LEADING,
brilliant, celebrated, major,
prominent, well-known

stare *verb* GAZE, eyeball (*slang*),
gape, gawk, goggle, look,
watch

stark *adjective* 1 HARSH, austere,
bare, barren, bleak, grim, hard,
homely, plain, severe
2 ABSOLUTE, blunt, downright,
out-and-out, pure, sheer,
unmitigated, utter ▶ *adverb*
3 ABSOLUTELY, altogether,
completely, entirely, quite,
utterly, wholly

start *verb* 1 BEGIN, appear, arise,
commence, issue, originate
2 SET ABOUT, embark upon,
make a beginning, take the
first step 3 SET IN MOTION,
activate, get going, initiate,
instigate, kick-start, open,

originate, trigger 4 JUMP, flinch,
jerk, recoil, shy 5 ESTABLISH,
begin, create, found,
inaugurate, initiate, institute,
launch, pioneer, set up ▶ *noun*
6 BEGINNING, birth, dawn,
foundation, inception,
initiation, onset, opening,
outset 7 ADVANTAGE, edge, head
start, lead 8 JUMP, convulsion,
spasm

startle *verb* SURPRISE, frighten,
make (someone) jump, scare,
shock

starving *adjective* HUNGRY,
famished, ravenous, starved

state *noun* 1 CONDITION,
circumstances, position,
predicament, shape, situation
2 FRAME OF MIND, attitude,
humor, mood, spirits
3 COUNTRY, commonwealth,
federation, government,
kingdom, land, nation,
republic, territory 4 CEREMONY,
display, glory, grandeur,
majesty, pomp, splendor, style
▶ *verb* 5 EXPRESS, affirm,
articulate, assert, declare,
expound, present, say, specify,
utter, voice

stately *adjective* GRAND, august,
dignified, lofty, majestic, noble,
regal, royal

statement *noun* ACCOUNT,
announcement,
communication, communiqué,
declaration, proclamation,
report

state-of-the-art *adjective* LATEST,
newest, up-to-date,
up-to-the-minute

static *adjective* STATIONARY, fixed,
immobile, motionless, still,
unmoving

station noun 1 HEADQUARTERS, base, depot 2 PLACE, location, position, post, seat, situation 3 POSITION, post, rank, situation, standing, status ▶verb 4 ASSIGN, establish, install, locate, post, set

stationary adjective MOTIONLESS, fixed, parked, standing, static, stock-still, unmoving

statuesque adjective WELL-PROPORTIONED, imposing, Junoesque

stature noun IMPORTANCE, eminence, prestige, prominence, rank, standing

status noun POSITION, condition, consequence, eminence, grade, prestige, rank, standing

staunch[1] adjective LOYAL, faithful, firm, sound, stalwart, steadfast, true, trusty

staunch[2] verb STOP, check, dam, halt, stay, stem

stay verb 1 REMAIN, abide, continue, halt, linger, loiter, pause, stop, tarry, wait ▶noun 2 VISIT, holiday, sojourn, stop, stopover 3 POSTPONEMENT, deferment, delay, halt, stopping, suspension

steadfast adjective FIRM, faithful, fast, fixed, intent, loyal, resolute, stalwart, staunch, steady, unswerving, unwavering

steady adjective 1 FIRM, fixed, safe, stable 2 SENSIBLE, balanced, calm, dependable, equable, level-headed, reliable, sober 3 CONTINUOUS, ceaseless, consistent, constant, incessant, nonstop, persistent, regular, twenty-four-seven (slang), unbroken, uninterrupted ▶verb 4 STABILIZE, balance, brace, secure, support

steal verb 1 TAKE, appropriate, embezzle, filch, lift (informal), misappropriate, pilfer, pinch (informal), purloin, thieve 2 SNEAK, creep, slink, slip, tiptoe

stealth noun SECRECY, furtiveness, slyness, sneakiness, stealthiness, surreptitiousness, unobtrusiveness

stealthy adjective SECRET, furtive, secretive, sneaking, surreptitious

steep[1] adjective 1 SHEER, abrupt, precipitous 2 HIGH, exorbitant, extortionate, extreme, overpriced, unreasonable

steep[2] verb 1 SOAK, drench, immerse, macerate, marinate (Cookery), moisten, souse, submerge 2 SATURATE, fill, imbue, infuse, permeate, pervade, suffuse

steer verb DIRECT, conduct, control, guide, handle, pilot

stem[1] noun 1 STALK, axis, branch, shoot, trunk ▶verb 2 **stem from** ORIGINATE IN, arise from, be caused by, derive from

stem[2] verb STOP, check, curb, dam, hold back, staunch

stench noun STINK, foul smell, reek, whiff

step noun 1 FOOTSTEP, footfall, footprint, pace, print, stride, track 2 STAGE, move, phase, point 3 ACTION, act, deed, expedient, means, measure, move 4 DEGREE, level, rank ▶verb 5 WALK, move, pace, tread

step in verb INTERVENE, become involved, take action

step up verb INCREASE, intensify, raise

stereotype noun 1 FORMULA, pattern ▶verb 2 CATEGORIZE,

pigeonhole, standardize, typecast

sterile *adjective* **1** GERM-FREE, aseptic, disinfected, sterilized **2** BARREN, bare, dry, empty, fruitless, unfruitful, unproductive

sterilize *verb* DISINFECT, fumigate, purify

sterling *adjective* EXCELLENT, fine, genuine, sound, superlative, true

stern *adjective* SEVERE, austere, forbidding, grim, hard, harsh, inflexible, rigid, serious, strict

stick[1] *noun* **1** CANE, baton, crook, pole, rod, staff, twig **2** *Brit. slang* ABUSE, criticism, flak (*informal*)

stick[2] *verb* **1** POKE, dig, jab, penetrate, pierce, prod, puncture, spear, stab, thrust, transfix **2** FASTEN, adhere, affix, attach, bind, bond, cling, fix, glue, hold, join, paste, weld **3** (with *out, up,* etc.) PROTRUDE, bulge, extend, jut, obtrude, poke, project, show **4** PUT, deposit, lay, place, set **5** STAY, linger, persist, remain **6** *Slang* TOLERATE, abide, stand, stomach, take **7 stick up for** DEFEND, champion, stand up for, support

stickler *noun* PERFECTIONIST, fanatic, fusspot (*informal*), purist

sticky *adjective* **1** TACKY, adhesive, clinging, gluey, glutinous, gooey (*informal*), gummy, viscid, viscous **2** *Informal* DIFFICULT, awkward, delicate, embarrassing, nasty, tricky, unpleasant **3** HUMID, clammy, close, muggy, oppressive, sultry, sweltering

stiff *adjective* **1** INFLEXIBLE, firm, hard, inelastic, rigid, solid, taut, tense, tight, unbending, unyielding **2** AWKWARD, clumsy, graceless, inelegant, jerky (*informal*), ungainly, ungraceful **3** DIFFICULT, arduous, exacting, hard, tough **4** SEVERE, drastic, extreme, hard, harsh, heavy, strict **5** UNRELAXED, artifical, constrained, forced, formal, stilted, unnatural

stiffen *verb* **1** BRACE, reinforce, tauten, tense **2** SET, congeal, crystallize, harden, jell, solidify, thicken

stifle *verb* **1** SUPPRESS, check, hush, repress, restrain, silence, smother, stop **2** SUFFOCATE, asphyxiate, choke, smother, strangle

stigma *noun* DISGRACE, dishonor, shame, slur, smirch, stain

still *adjective* **1** MOTIONLESS, calm, peaceful, restful, serene, stationary, tranquil, undisturbed **2** SILENT, hushed, quiet ▶ *verb* **3** QUIETEN, allay, calm, hush, lull, pacify, quiet, settle, silence, soothe ▶ *conjunction* **4** HOWEVER, but, nevertheless, notwithstanding, yet

stilted *adjective* STIFF, constrained, forced, unnatural, wooden

stimulant *noun* PICK-ME-UP (*informal*), restorative, tonic, upper (*slang*)

stimulate *verb* AROUSE, encourage, fire, impel, incite, prompt, provoke, rouse, spur

stimulating *adjective* EXCITING, exhilarating, inspiring, provocative, rousing, stirring

stimulus *noun* INCENTIVE, encouragement, goad, impetus, incitement, inducement, spur

sting *verb* **1** HURT, burn, pain, smart, tingle, wound **2** *Informal* CHEAT, defraud, fleece, overcharge, rip off (*slang*), swindle

stingy *adjective* MEAN, miserly, niggardly, parsimonious, penny-pinching (*informal*), tightfisted, ungenerous

stink *noun* **1** STENCH, fetor, foul smell ▶ *verb* **2** REEK

stint *verb* **1** BE MEAN, be frugal, be sparing, hold back, skimp on ▶ *noun* **2** SHARE, period, quota, shift, spell, stretch, term, time, turn

stipulate *verb* SPECIFY, agree, contract, covenant, insist upon, require, settle

stipulation *noun* SPECIFICATION, agreement, clause, condition, precondition, proviso, qualification, requirement

stir *verb* **1** MIX, agitate, beat, shake **2** STIMULATE, arouse, awaken, excite, incite, provoke, rouse, spur ▶ *noun* **3** COMMOTION, activity, bustle, disorder, disturbance, excitement, flurry, fuss

stock *noun* **1** GOODS, array, choice, commodities, merchandise, range, selection, variety, wares **2** SUPPLY, fund, hoard, reserve, stockpile, store **3** PROPERTY, assets, capital, funds, investment **4** LIVESTOCK, beasts, cattle, domestic animals ▶ *adjective* **5** STANDARD, conventional, customary, ordinary, regular, routine, usual

6 HACKNEYED, banal, overused, trite ▶ *verb* **7** SELL, deal in, handle, keep, supply, trade in **8** PROVIDE WITH, equip, fit out, furnish, supply **9 stock up** STORE (UP), accumulate, amass, gather, hoard, lay in, put away, save

stocky *adjective* THICKSET, chunky, dumpy, solid, stubby, sturdy

stodgy *adjective* **1** HEAVY, filling, leaden, starchy **2** DULL, boring, heavy going, staid, stuffy, tedious, unexciting

stoical *adjective* RESIGNED, dispassionate, impassive, long-suffering, philosophical, phlegmatic, stoic, stolid

stoicism *noun* RESIGNATION, acceptance, forbearance, fortitude, impassivity, long-suffering, patience, stolidity

stolid *adjective* APATHETIC, dull, lumpish, unemotional, wooden

stomach *noun* **1** BELLY, abdomen, gut (*informal*), pot, tummy (*informal*) **2** INCLINATION, appetite, desire, relish, taste ▶ *verb* **3** BEAR, abide, endure, swallow, take, tolerate

stony *adjective* COLD, blank, chilly, expressionless, hard, hostile, icy, unresponsive

stoop *verb* **1** BEND, bow, crouch, duck, hunch, lean **2 stoop to** SINK TO, descend to, lower oneself by, resort to ▶ *noun* **3** SLOUCH, bad posture, round-shoulderedness

stop *verb* **1** HALT, cease, conclude, cut short, desist, discontinue, end, finish, pause, put an end to, quit, refrain,

shut down, terminate
2 PREVENT, arrest, forestall, hinder, hold back, impede, repress, restrain **3** PLUG, block, obstruct, seal, staunch, stem **4** STAY, lodge, rest ▶*noun* **5** END, cessation, finish, halt, standstill **6** STAY, break, rest **7** STATION, depot, terminus

stopgap *noun* MAKESHIFT, improvisation, resort, substitute

stoppage *noun* STOPPING, arrest, close, closure, cutoff, halt, hindrance, shutdown, standstill

. **store** *verb* **1** PUT BY, deposit, garner, hoard, keep, put aside, reserve, save, stockpile ▶*noun* **2** SHOP, market, mart, outlet **3** SUPPLY, accumulation, cache, fund, hoard, quantity, reserve, stock, stockpile **4** REPOSITORY, depository, storeroom, warehouse

storm *noun* **1** TEMPEST, blizzard, gale, hurricane, squall **2** OUTBURST, agitation, commotion, disturbance, furor, outbreak, outcry, row, rumpus, strife, tumult, turmoil ▶*verb* **3** ATTACK, assail, assault, charge, rush **4** RAGE, bluster, rant, rave, thunder **5** RUSH, flounce, fly, stamp

stormy *adjective* WILD, blustery, inclement, raging, rough, squally, turbulent, windy

story *noun* **1** TALE, account, anecdote, history, legend, narrative, romance, yarn **2** REPORT, article, feature, news, news item, scoop

stout *adjective* **1** FAT, big, bulky, burly, corpulent, fleshy, heavy, overweight, plump, portly, rotund, tubby **2** STRONG,

able-bodied, brawny, muscular, robust, stalwart, strapping, sturdy **3** BRAVE, bold, courageous, fearless, gallant, intrepid, plucky, resolute, valiant

stow *verb* PACK, bundle, load, put away, stash (*informal*), store

straight *adjective* **1** DIRECT, near, short **2** LEVEL, aligned, even, horizontal, right, smooth, square, true **3** UPRIGHT, erect, plumb, vertical **4** HONEST, above board, accurate, fair, honorable, just, law-abiding, trustworthy, upright **5** FRANK, blunt, bold, candid, forthright, honest, outright, plain, straightforward **6** SUCCESSIVE, consecutive, continuous, nonstop, running, solid **7** UNDILUTED, neat, pure, unadulterated, unmixed **8** ORDERLY, arranged, in order, neat, organized, shipshape, tidy **9** *Slang* CONVENTIONAL, bourgeois, conservative ▶*adverb* **10** DIRECTLY, at once, immediately, instantly

straight away *adverb* IMMEDIATELY, at once, directly, instantly, now, right away

straighten *verb* NEATEN, arrange, order, put in order, tidy (up)

straightforward *adjective* **1** HONEST, candid, direct, forthright, genuine, open, sincere, truthful, upfront (*informal*) **2** EASY, elementary, routine, simple, uncomplicated

strain[1] *verb* **1** STRETCH, distend, draw tight, tauten, tighten **2** OVEREXERT, injure, overtax, overwork, pull, sprain, tax, tear, twist, wrench **3** STRIVE, bend over backwards (*informal*), endeavor, give it one's best shot (*informal*), go for it (*informal*), knock oneself out (*informal*), labor, struggle **4** SIEVE, filter, purify, sift ▶*noun* **5** STRESS, anxiety, burden, pressure, tension **6** EXERTION, effort, force, struggle **7** INJURY, pull, sprain, wrench

strain² *noun* **1** BREED, ancestry, blood, descent, extraction, family, lineage, race **2** TRACE, streak, suggestion, tendency

strained *adjective* **1** FORCED, artificial, false, put on, unnatural **2** TENSE, awkward, difficult, embarrassed, stiff, uneasy

strait *noun* **1** (often plural) CHANNEL, narrows, sound **2 straits** DIFFICULTY, dilemma, extremity, hardship, plight, predicament

strait-laced *adjective* STRICT, moralistic, narrow-minded, prim, proper, prudish, puritanical

strand *noun* FILAMENT, fiber, string, thread

stranded *adjective* **1** BEACHED, aground, ashore, grounded, marooned, shipwrecked **2** HELPLESS, abandoned, high and dry

strange *adjective* **1** ODD, abnormal, bizarre, curious, extraordinary, peculiar, queer, uncommon, weird, wonderful **2** UNFAMILIAR, alien, exotic, foreign, new, novel, unknown, untried

stranger *noun* NEWCOMER, alien, foreigner, guest, incomer, outlander, visitor

strangle *verb* **1** THROTTLE,

asphyxiate, choke, strangulate **2** SUPPRESS, inhibit, repress, stifle

strap *noun* **1** BELT, thong, tie ▶*verb* **2** FASTEN, bind, buckle, lash, secure, tie

strapping *adjective* WELL-BUILT, big, brawny, husky (*informal*), powerful, robust, sturdy

stratagem *noun* TRICK, device, dodge, maneuver, plan, ploy, ruse, scheme, subterfuge

strategic *adjective* **1** TACTICAL, calculated, deliberate, diplomatic, planned, politic **2** CRUCIAL, cardinal, critical, decisive, important, key, vital

strategy *noun* PLAN, approach, policy, procedure, scheme

stray *verb* **1** WANDER, drift, err, go astray **2** DIGRESS, deviate, diverge, get off the point ▶*adjective* **3** LOST, abandoned, homeless, roaming, vagrant **4** RANDOM, accidental, chance

streak *noun* **1** BAND, layer, line, slash, strip, stripe, stroke, vein **2** TRACE, dash, element, strain, touch, vein ▶*verb* **3** SPEED, dart, flash, fly, hurtle, sprint, tear, whizz (*informal*), zoom

stream *noun* **1** RIVER, bayou, beck, brook, rivulet, tributary **2** FLOW, course, current, drift, run, rush, surge, tide, torrent ▶*verb* **3** FLOW, cascade, course, flood, gush, issue, pour, run, spill, spout

streamlined *adjective* EFFICIENT, organized, rationalized, slick, smooth-running

street *noun* ROAD, avenue, boulevard, lane, parkway, roadway, row, terrace

strength *noun* **1** MIGHT, brawn, courage, fortitude, muscle, robustness, stamina, sturdiness, toughness **2** INTENSITY, effectiveness, efficacy, force, potency, power, vigor **3** ADVANTAGE, asset, strong point

strengthen *verb* **1** FORTIFY, brace up, consolidate, harden, invigorate, restore, stiffen, toughen **2** REINFORCE, augment, bolster, brace, build up, buttress, harden, intensify, support

strenuous *adjective* DEMANDING, arduous, hard, laborious, taxing, tough, uphill

stress *noun* **1** STRAIN, anxiety, burden, pressure, tension, trauma, worry **2** EMPHASIS, force, significance, weight **3** ACCENT, accentuation, beat, emphasis ▶ *verb* **4** EMPHASIZE, accentuate, dwell on, underline

stretch *verb* **1** EXTEND, cover, put forth, reach, spread, unroll **2** PULL, distend, draw out, elongate, expand, strain, tighten ▶ *noun* **3** EXPANSE, area, distance, extent, spread, tract **4** PERIOD, space, spell, stint, term, time

strict *adjective* **1** SEVERE, authoritarian, firm, harsh, stern, stringent **2** EXACT, accurate, close, faithful, meticulous, precise, scrupulous, true **3** ABSOLUTE, total, utter

strident *adjective* HARSH, discordant, grating, jarring, raucous, screeching, shrill

strife *noun* CONFLICT, battle, clash, discord, dissension, friction, quarrel

strike *verb* **1** WALK OUT, down tools, mutiny, revolt **2** HIT, beat, clobber (*slang*), clout

(*informal*), cuff, hammer, knock, punch, slap, smack, thump, wallop (*informal*) **3** COLLIDE WITH, bump into, hit, run into **4** ATTACK, assail, assault, hit **5** OCCUR TO, come to, dawn on *or* upon, hit, register (*informal*)

striking *adjective* IMPRESSIVE, conspicuous, cool (*informal*), dramatic, noticeable, outstanding, phat (*slang*)

string *noun* **1** CORD, fiber, twine **2** SERIES, chain, file, line, procession, row, sequence, succession

stringent *adjective* STRICT, inflexible, rigid, rigorous, severe, tight, tough

stringy *adjective* FIBROUS, gristly, sinewy, tough

strip[1] *verb* **1** UNDRESS, disrobe, unclothe **2** PLUNDER, despoil, divest, empty, loot, pillage, ransack, rob, sack

strip[2] *noun* PIECE, band, belt, shred

strive *verb* TRY, attempt, bend over backwards (*informal*), break one's neck (*informal*), do one's best, give it one's best shot (*informal*), go all out (*informal*), knock oneself out (*informal*), labor, make an all-out effort (*informal*), struggle, toil

stroke *verb* **1** CARESS, fondle, pet, rub ▶ *noun* **2** APOPLEXY, attack, collapse, fit, seizure **3** BLOW, hit, knock, pat, rap, thump

stroll *verb* **1** WALK, amble, promenade, ramble, saunter ▶ *noun* **2** WALK, breath of air, constitutional, promenade, ramble, turn

strong *adjective* 1 POWERFUL, athletic, brawny, burly, hardy, lusty, muscular, robust, strapping, sturdy, tough 2 DURABLE, hard-wearing, heavy-duty, sturdy, substantial, well-built 3 PERSUASIVE, compelling, convincing, effective, potent, sound, telling, weighty, well-founded 4 INTENSE, acute, deep, fervent, fervid, fierce, firm, keen, vehement, violent, zealous 5 EXTREME, drastic, forceful, severe 6 BRIGHT, bold, brilliant, dazzling

stronghold *noun* FORTRESS, bastion, bulwark, castle, citadel, fort

structure *noun* 1 BUILDING, construction, edifice, erection 2 ARRANGEMENT, configuration, construction, design, form, formation, make-up, organization ▶*verb* 3 ARRANGE, assemble, build up, design, organize, shape

struggle *verb* 1 STRIVE, exert oneself, give it one's best shot (*informal*), go all out (*informal*), knock oneself out (*informal*), labor, make an all-out effort (*informal*), strain, toil, work 2 FIGHT, battle, compete, contend, grapple, wrestle ▶*noun* 3 EFFORT, exertion, labor, pains, scramble, toil, work 4 FIGHT, battle, brush, clash, combat, conflict, contest, tussle

strut *verb* SWAGGER, parade, peacock, prance

stub *noun* 1 BUTT, end, remainder, remnant, stump, tail, tail end 2 COUNTERFOIL

stubborn *adjective* OBSTINATE, dogged, headstrong, inflexible, intractable, obdurate, persistent, pig-headed, recalcitrant, tenacious, unyielding

stubby *adjective* STOCKY, chunky, dumpy, short, squat, thickset

stuck *adjective* 1 FASTENED, cemented, fast, fixed, glued, joined 2 *Informal* BAFFLED, beaten, stumped

stuck-up *adjective* SNOBBISH, arrogant, bigheaded (*informal*), conceited, haughty, proud, snooty (*informal*)

stud *verb* ORNAMENT, bejewel, dot, spangle, spot

student *noun* LEARNER, apprentice, disciple, pupil, scholar, trainee, undergraduate

studied *adjective* PLANNED, conscious, deliberate, intentional, premeditated

studio *noun* WORKSHOP, atelier

studious *adjective* SCHOLARLY, academic, assiduous, bookish, diligent, hard-working, intellectual

study *verb* 1 CONTEMPLATE, consider, examine, go into, ponder, pore over, read 2 LEARN, cram (*informal*), read up, review 3 EXAMINE, analyze, investigate, look into, research, scrutinize, survey ▶*noun* 4 LEARNING, application, lessons, reading, research, school work 5 EXAMINATION, analysis, consideration, contemplation, inquiry, inspection, investigation, review, scrutiny, survey

stuff *noun* 1 THINGS, belongings, effects, equipment, gear, kit, objects, paraphernalia, possessions, tackle **2** SUBSTANCE, essence, matter **3** MATERIAL, cloth, fabric, textile ▶ *verb* **4** CRAM, crowd, fill, force, jam, pack, push, ram, shove, squeeze

stuffing *noun* FILLING, packing, wadding

stuffy *adjective* **1** AIRLESS, close, frowsty, heavy, muggy, oppressive, stale, stifling, sultry, unventilated **2** *Informal* STAID, dreary, dull, pompous, priggish, prim, stodgy

stumble *verb* **1** TRIP, fall, falter, lurch, reel, slip, stagger **2** (with *across, on* or *upon*) DISCOVER, chance upon, come across, find

stump *verb* BAFFLE, bewilder, confuse, flummox, mystify, nonplus, perplex, puzzle

stumpy *adjective* STOCKY, dumpy, short, squat, stubby, thickset

stun *verb* OVERCOME, astonish, astound, bewilder, confound, confuse, overpower, shock, stagger, stupefy

stunning *adjective* WONDERFUL, beautiful, cool (*informal*), dazzling, gorgeous, impressive, lovely, marvelous, phat (*slang*), sensational (*informal*), spectacular, striking

stunt *noun* FEAT, act, deed, exploit, trick

stunted *adjective* UNDERSIZED, diminutive, little, small, tiny

stupefy *verb* ASTOUND, amaze, daze, dumbfound, shock, stagger, stun

stupendous *adjective*
1 WONDERFUL, amazing, astounding, breathtaking, marvelous, overwhelming, sensational (*informal*), staggering, superb **2** HUGE, colossal, enormous, gigantic, mega (*slang*), vast

stupid *adjective* **1** UNINTELLIGENT, brainless, dense, dim, dumb (*informal*), half-witted, moronic, obtuse, simple, simple-minded, slow, slow-witted, thick **2** FOOLISH, asinine, bonkers (*informal*), daft (*informal*), idiotic, imbecilic, inane, nonsensical, pointless, rash, senseless, unintelligent **3** DAZED, groggy, insensate, semiconscious, stunned, stupefied

stupidity *noun* **1** LACK OF INTELLIGENCE, brainlessness, denseness, dimness, dullness, imbecility, obtuseness, slowness, thickness **2** FOOLISHNESS, absurdity, fatuousness, folly, idiocy, inanity, lunacy, madness, silliness

stupor *noun* DAZE, coma, insensibility, stupefaction, unconsciousness

sturdy *adjective* **1** ROBUST, athletic, brawny, hardy, lusty, muscular, powerful **2** WELL-BUILT, durable, solid, substantial, well-made

stutter *verb* STAMMER, falter, hesitate, stumble

style *noun* **1** DESIGN, cut, form, manner **2** MANNER, approach, method, mode, technique, way **3** ELEGANCE, chic, élan, flair, panache, polish, smartness, sophistication, taste **4** TYPE, category, genre, kind, sort, variety **5** FASHION, mode, rage, trend, vogue **6** LUXURY, affluence, comfort, ease, elegance, grandeur ▶ *verb* **7** DESIGN, adapt, arrange, cut, fashion, shape, tailor **8** CALL, designate, dub, entitle, label, name, term

stylish *adjective* SMART, chic, cool (*informal*), dressy (*informal*), fashionable, modish, phat (*slang*), trendy (*informal*), voguish

suave *adjective* SMOOTH, charming, courteous, debonair, polite, sophisticated, urbane

subconscious *adjective* HIDDEN, inner, intuitive, latent, repressed, subliminal

subdue *verb* **1** OVERCOME, break, conquer, control, crush, defeat, master, overpower, quell, tame, vanquish **2** MODERATE, mellow, quieten down, soften, suppress, tone down

subdued *adjective* **1** QUIET, chastened, crestfallen, dejected, downcast, down in the mouth, sad, serious **2** SOFT, dim, hushed, muted, quiet, subtle, toned down, unobtrusive

subject *noun* **1** TOPIC, affair, business, issue, matter, object, point, question, substance, theme **2** CITIZEN, national, subordinate ▶ *adjective* **3** SUBORDINATE, dependent, inferior, obedient, satellite **4 subject to: a** LIABLE TO, exposed to, in danger of, open to, prone to, susceptible to, vulnerable to **b** CONDITIONAL ON, contingent on, dependent on ▶ *verb* **5** PUT THROUGH, expose, lay open, submit, treat

subjective *adjective* PERSONAL,

biased, nonobjective, prejudiced

subjugate *verb* CONQUER, enslave, master, overcome, overpower, quell, subdue, suppress, vanquish

sublime *adjective* NOBLE, elevated, exalted, glorious, grand, great, high, lofty

submerge *verb* IMMERSE, deluge, dip, duck, engulf, flood, inundate, overflow, overwhelm, plunge, sink, swamp

submission *noun* **1** SURRENDER, assent, capitulation, giving in, yielding **2** PRESENTATION, entry, handing in, tendering **3** MEEKNESS, compliance, deference, docility, obedience, passivity, resignation

submissive *adjective* MEEK, accommodating, acquiescent, amenable, compliant, docile, obedient, passive, pliant, tractable, unresisting, yielding

submit *verb* **1** SURRENDER, accede, agree, capitulate, comply, endure, give in, succumb, tolerate, yield **2** PUT FORWARD, hand in, present, proffer, table, tender

subordinate *adjective* **1** LESSER, dependent, inferior, junior, lower, minor, secondary, subject ▶ *noun* **2** INFERIOR, aide, assistant, attendant, junior, second

subordination *noun* INFERIORITY, inferior *or* secondary status, servitude, subjection

subscribe *verb* **1** DONATE, contribute, give **2** SUPPORT, advocate, endorse

subscription *noun* **1** MEMBERSHIP FEE, annual payment, dues

2 DONATION, contribution, gift

subsequent *adjective* FOLLOWING, after, ensuing, later, succeeding, successive

subsequently *adverb* LATER, afterwards

subservient *adjective* SERVILE, abject, deferential, obsequious, slavish, submissive, sycophantic

subside *verb* **1** DECREASE, abate, diminish, ease, ebb, lessen, quieten, slacken, wane **2** SINK, cave in, collapse, drop, lower, settle

subsidence *noun* **1** SINKING, settling **2** DECREASE, abatement, easing off, lessening, slackening

subsidiary *adjective* LESSER, ancillary, auxiliary, minor, secondary, subordinate, supplementary

subsidize *verb* FUND, finance, promote, sponsor, support

subsidy *noun* AID, allowance, assistance, grant, help, support

substance *noun* **1** MATERIAL, body, fabric, stuff **2** MEANING, essence, gist, import, main point, significance **3** REALITY, actuality, concreteness **4** WEALTH, assets, estate, means, property, resources

substantial *adjective* BIG, ample, considerable, important, large, significant, sizable *or* sizeable

substantiate *verb* SUPPORT, authenticate, confirm, establish, prove, verify

substitute *verb* **1** REPLACE, change, exchange, interchange, swap, switch ▶ *noun* **2** REPLACEMENT, agent, deputy, locum, proxy, reserve, sub, surrogate ▶ *adjective* **3** REPLACEMENT, alternative,

fall-back, proxy, reserve, second, surrogate

substitution *noun* REPLACEMENT, change, exchange, swap, switch

subterfuge *noun* TRICK, deception, dodge, maneuver, ploy, ruse, stratagem

subtle *adjective* **1** SOPHISTICATED, delicate, refined **2** FAINT, delicate, implied, slight, understated **3** CRAFTY, artful, cunning, devious, ingenious, shrewd, sly, wily

subtlety *noun* **1** SOPHISTICATION, delicacy, refinement **2** CUNNING, artfulness, cleverness, craftiness, deviousness, ingenuity, slyness, wiliness

subtract *verb* TAKE AWAY, deduct, diminish, remove, take from, take off

subversive *adjective* **1** SEDITIOUS, riotous, treasonous ▶ *noun* **2** DISSIDENT, fifth columnist, saboteur, terrorist, traitor

subvert *verb* OVERTURN, sabotage, undermine

succeed *verb* **1** MAKE IT (*informal*), be successful, flourish, make good, make the grade (*informal*), prosper, thrive, triumph, work **2** FOLLOW, come next, ensue, result

success *noun* **1** LUCK, fame, fortune, happiness, prosperity, triumph **2** HIT (*informal*), celebrity, megastar (*informal*), sensation, smash (*informal*), star, superstar, winner

successful *adjective* THRIVING, booming, flourishing, fortunate, fruitful, lucky, profitable, prosperous, rewarding, top, victorious

successfully *adverb* WELL, favorably, victoriously, with flying colors

succession *noun* 1 SERIES, chain, course, cycle, order, progression, run, sequence, train 2 TAKING OVER, accession, assumption, inheritance

successive *adjective* CONSECUTIVE, following, in succession

succinct *adjective* BRIEF, compact, concise, laconic, pithy, terse

succor *noun* 1 HELP, aid, assistance ▸*verb* 2 HELP, aid, assist

succulent *adjective* JUICY, luscious, lush, moist

succumb *verb* 1 SURRENDER, capitulate, give in, submit, yield 2 DIE, fall

sucker *noun Slang* FOOL, dork (*slang*), dupe, mug (*Brit. slang*), pushover (*slang*), schmuck (*slang*), victim

sudden *adjective* QUICK, abrupt, hasty, hurried, rapid, rash, swift, unexpected

suddenly *adverb* ABRUPTLY, all of a sudden, unexpectedly

sue *verb Law* TAKE (SOMEONE) TO COURT, charge, indict, prosecute, summon

suffer *verb* 1 UNDERGO, bear, endure, experience, go through, sustain 2 TOLERATE, put up with (*informal*)

suffering *noun* PAIN, agony, anguish, discomfort, distress, hardship, misery, ordeal, torment

suffice *verb* BE ENOUGH, be adequate, be sufficient, do, meet requirements, serve

sufficient *adjective* ADEQUATE, enough, satisfactory

suffocate *verb* CHOKE, asphyxiate, smother, stifle

suggest *verb* 1 RECOMMEND, advise, advocate, prescribe, propose 2 BRING TO MIND, evoke 3 HINT, imply, indicate, intimate

suggestion *noun* 1 RECOMMENDATION, motion, plan, proposal, proposition 2 HINT, breath, indication, intimation, trace, whisper

suggestive *adjective* SMUTTY, bawdy, blue, indelicate, provocative, racy, ribald, risqué, rude

suit *noun* 1 OUTFIT, clothing, costume, dress, ensemble, habit 2 LAWSUIT, action, case, cause, proceeding, prosecution, trial ▸*verb* 3 BE ACCEPTABLE TO, do, gratify, please, satisfy 4 BEFIT, become, go with, harmonize, match, tally

suitability *noun* APPROPRIATENESS, aptness, fitness, rightness

suitable *adjective* APPROPRIATE, apt, becoming, befitting, fit, fitting, proper, right, satisfactory

suite *noun* ROOMS, apartment

suitor *noun Old-fashioned* ADMIRER, beau (*old-fashioned*), young man

sulk *verb* BE SULLEN, be in a huff, pout

sulky *adjective* HUFFY, cross, disgruntled, in the sulks, moody, petulant, querulous, resentful, sullen

sullen *adjective* MOROSE, cross, dour, glowering, moody, sour, surly, unsociable

sully *verb* DEFILE, besmirch, disgrace, dishonor, smirch, stain, tarnish

sultry *adjective* 1 HUMID, close, hot, muggy, oppressive, sticky, stifling 2 SEDUCTIVE, provocative, sensual, sexy (*informal*)

sum *noun* TOTAL, aggregate, amount, tally, whole

summarize *verb* SUM UP, abridge, condense, encapsulate, epitomize, précis

summary *noun* SYNOPSIS, abridgment, outline, précis, résumé, review, rundown

summit *noun* PEAK, acme, apex, head, height, pinnacle, top, zenith

summon *verb* 1 SEND FOR, bid, call, invite 2 (often with *up*) GATHER, draw on, muster

sumptuous *adjective* LUXURIOUS, gorgeous, grand, lavish, opulent, splendid, superb

sum up *verb* SUMMARIZE, put in a nutshell, recapitulate, review

sunburned *adjective* TANNED, bronzed, brown, burnt, peeling, red

sundry *adjective* VARIOUS, assorted, different, miscellaneous, several, some

sunken *adjective* 1 HOLLOW, drawn, haggard 2 LOWER, buried, recessed, submerged

sunny *adjective* 1 BRIGHT, clear, fine, radiant, summery, sunlit, unclouded 2 CHEERFUL, buoyant, cheery, happy, joyful, light-hearted

sunrise *noun* DAWN, break of day, cockcrow, daybreak

sunset *noun* NIGHTFALL, close of (the) day, dusk, eventide

super *adjective* Informal EXCELLENT, glorious, magnificent, marvelous, outstanding, sensational (*informal*), superb, terrific (*informal*), wonderful

superb *adjective* SPLENDID, excellent, exquisite, fine, first-rate, grand, magnificent, marvelous, superior, superlative, world-class

supercilious *adjective* SCORNFUL, arrogant, contemptuous, disdainful, haughty, lofty, snooty (*informal*), stuck-up (*informal*)

superficial *adjective* 1 HASTY, casual, cursory, desultory, hurried, perfunctory, sketchy, slapdash 2 SHALLOW, empty-headed, frivolous, silly, trivial 3 SURFACE, exterior, external, on the surface, slight

superfluous *adjective* EXCESS, extra, left over, redundant, remaining, spare, supernumerary, surplus

superhuman *adjective* 1 HEROIC, phenomenal, prodigious 2 SUPERNATURAL, paranormal

superintendence *noun* SUPERVISION, charge, control, direction, government, management

superintendent *noun* SUPERVISOR, chief, controller, director, governor, inspector, manager, overseer

superior *adjective* 1 BETTER, grander, greater, higher, surpassing, unrivaled 2 SUPERCILIOUS, condescending, disdainful, haughty, lofty, lordly, patronizing, pretentious, snobbish 3 FIRST-CLASS, choice, deluxe, excellent, exceptional,

exclusive, first-rate ▶ *noun*
4 BOSS (*informal*), chief,
director, manager, principal,
senior, supervisor

superiority *noun* SUPREMACY,
advantage, ascendancy,
excellence, lead, predominance

superlative *adjective*
OUTSTANDING, excellent,
supreme, unparalleled,
unrivaled, unsurpassed

supernatural *adjective*
PARANORMAL, ghostly, hidden,
miraculous, mystic, occult,
psychic, spectral, uncanny,
unearthly

supersede *verb* REPLACE,
displace, oust, supplant, take
the place of, usurp

supervise *verb* OVERSEE, control,
direct, handle, look after,
manage, run, superintend

supervision *noun*
SUPERINTENDENCE, care, charge,
control, direction, guidance,
management

supervisor *noun* BOSS (*informal*),
administrator, chief, foreman,
inspector, manager, overseer

supplant *verb* REPLACE, displace,
oust, supersede, take the place
of

supple *adjective* FLEXIBLE, limber,
lissom(e), lithe, pliable, pliant

supplement *noun* 1 ADDITION,
add-on, appendix, extra, insert,
postscript, pull-out ▶ *verb*
2 ADD, augment, complement,
extend, reinforce

supplementary *adjective*
ADDITIONAL, add-on, ancillary,
auxiliary, extra, secondary

supplication *noun* PLEA, appeal,
entreaty, petition, prayer,
request

supply *verb* 1 PROVIDE,
contribute, endow, equip,
furnish, give, grant, produce,
stock, yield ▶ *noun* 2 STORE,
cache, fund, hoard, quantity,
reserve, source, stock 3 (usually
plural) PROVISIONS, equipment,
food, materials, necessities,
rations, stores

support *verb* 1 BEAR, brace,
buttress, carry, hold, prop,
reinforce, sustain 2 PROVIDE FOR,
finance, fund, keep, look after,
maintain, sustain 3 HELP, aid,
assist, back, champion, defend,
second, side with 4 BEAR OUT,
confirm, corroborate,
substantiate, verify ▶ *noun*
5 HELP, aid, assistance, backing,
encouragement, loyalty 6 PROP,
brace, foundation, pillar, post
7 SUPPORTER, backer, mainstay,
prop, second, tower of
strength 8 UPKEEP, keep,
maintenance, subsistence,
sustenance

supporter *noun* FOLLOWER,
adherent, advocate, champion,
fan, friend, helper, patron,
sponsor, well-wisher

supportive *adjective* HELPFUL,
encouraging, sympathetic,
understanding

suppose *verb* 1 PRESUME,
assume, conjecture, expect,
guess (*informal*), imagine, think
2 IMAGINE, conjecture, consider,
hypothesize, postulate, pretend

supposed *adjective* 1 PRESUMED,
accepted, alleged, assumed,
professed 2 (usually with *to*)
MEANT, expected, obliged,
required

supposedly *adverb* ALLEGEDLY,
hypothetically, ostensibly,
presumably, theoretically

supposition noun GUESS, conjecture, hypothesis, presumption, speculation, surmise, theory

suppress verb 1 STOP, check, conquer, crush, overpower, put an end to, quash, quell, subdue 2 RESTRAIN, conceal, contain, curb, hold in or back, repress, silence, smother, stifle

suppression noun ELIMINATION, check, crushing, quashing, smothering

supremacy noun DOMINATION, mastery, predominance, primacy, sovereignty, supreme power, sway

supreme adjective HIGHEST, chief, foremost, greatest, head, leading, paramount, pre-eminent, prime, principal, top, ultimate

sure adjective 1 CERTAIN, assured, confident, convinced, decided, definite, positive 2 RELIABLE, accurate, dependable, foolproof, infallible, undeniable, undoubted, unerring, unfailing 3 INEVITABLE, assured, bound, guaranteed, inescapable

surely adverb UNDOUBTEDLY, certainly, definitely, doubtlessly, indubitably, unquestionably, without doubt

surface noun 1 OUTSIDE, covering, exterior, face, side, top, veneer ▶ verb 2 APPEAR, arise, come to light, come up, crop up (informal), emerge, materialize, transpire

surfeit noun EXCESS, glut, plethora, superfluity

surge noun 1 RUSH, flood, flow, gush, outpouring 2 WAVE,

billow, roller, swell ▶ verb 3 RUSH, gush, heave, rise, roll

surly adjective ILL-TEMPERED, churlish, cross, grouchy (informal), morose, sulky, sullen, uncivil, ungracious

surmise verb 1 GUESS, conjecture, imagine, presume, speculate, suppose ▶ noun 2 GUESS, assumption, conjecture, presumption, speculation, supposition

surpass verb OUTDO, beat, eclipse, exceed, excel, outshine, outstrip, transcend

surpassing adjective SUPREME, exceptional, extraordinary, incomparable, matchless, outstanding, unrivaled

surplus noun 1 EXCESS, balance, remainder, residue, surfeit ▶ adjective 2 EXCESS, extra, odd, remaining, spare, superfluous

surprise noun 1 SHOCK, bombshell, eye-opener (informal), jolt, revelation 2 AMAZEMENT, astonishment, incredulity, wonder ▶ verb 3 AMAZE, astonish, stagger, stun, take aback 4 CATCH UNAWARES or OFF-GUARD, discover, spring upon, startle

surprised adjective AMAZED, astonished, speechless, taken by surprise, thunderstruck

surprising adjective AMAZING, astonishing, extraordinary, incredible, remarkable, staggering, unexpected, unusual

surrender verb 1 GIVE IN, capitulate, give way, submit, succumb, yield 2 GIVE UP, abandon, cede, concede, part with, relinquish, renounce,

waive, yield ▶ *noun*
3 SUBMISSION, capitulation, relinquishment, renunciation, resignation

surreptitious *adjective* SECRET, covert, furtive, sly, stealthy, underhand

surrogate *noun* SUBSTITUTE, proxy, representative, stand-in

surround *verb* ENCLOSE, encircle, encompass, envelop, hem in, ring

surroundings *plural noun* ENVIRONMENT, background, location, milieu, setting

surveillance *noun* OBSERVATION, inspection, scrutiny, supervision, watch

survey *verb* **1** LOOK OVER, contemplate, examine, inspect, observe, scan, scrutinize, view **2** ESTIMATE, appraise, assess, measure, plan, plot, size up ▶ *noun* **3** EXAMINATION, inspection, scrutiny **4** STUDY, inquiry, review

survive *verb* REMAIN ALIVE, endure, last, live on, outlast, outlive

susceptible *adjective* **1** (usually with *to*) LIABLE, disposed, given, inclined, prone, subject, vulnerable **2** IMPRESSIONABLE, receptive, responsive, sensitive, suggestible

suspect *verb* **1** BELIEVE, consider, feel, guess, speculate, suppose **2** DISTRUST, doubt, mistrust ▶ *adjective* **3** DUBIOUS, doubtful, iffy (*informal*), questionable

suspend *verb* **1** HANG, attach, dangle **2** POSTPONE, cease, cut short, defer, discontinue, interrupt, put off, shelve

suspense *noun* UNCERTAINTY,

anxiety, apprehension, doubt, expectation, insecurity, irresolution, tension

suspension *noun* POSTPONEMENT, abeyance, break, breaking off, deferment, discontinuation, interruption

suspicion *noun* **1** DISTRUST, doubt, dubiety, misgiving, mistrust, qualm, skepticism, wariness **2** IDEA, guess, hunch, impression, notion **3** TRACE, hint, shade, soupçon, streak, suggestion, tinge, touch

suspicious *adjective* **1** DISTRUSTFUL, doubtful, skeptical, unbelieving, wary **2** SUSPECT, doubtful, dubious, fishy (*informal*), questionable

sustain *verb* **1** MAINTAIN, continue, keep up, prolong, protract **2** KEEP ALIVE, aid, assist, help, nourish **3** WITHSTAND, bear, endure, experience, feel, suffer, undergo **4** SUPPORT, bear, uphold

sustained *adjective* CONTINUOUS, constant, nonstop, perpetual, prolonged, steady, twenty-four-seven (*slang*), unremitting

swagger *verb* SHOW OFF (*informal*), boast, brag, parade

swallow *verb* GULP, chow down (*slang*), consume, devour, drink, eat, swig (*informal*)

swamp *noun* **1** BOG, fen, marsh, mire, morass, quagmire, slough ▶ *verb* **2** FLOOD, capsize, engulf, inundate, sink, submerge **3** OVERWHELM, flood, inundate, overload

swarm *noun* **1** MULTITUDE, army, crowd, flock, herd, horde, host, mass, throng ▶ *verb*

2 CROWD, flock, mass, stream, throng 3 TEEM, abound, bristle, crawl

swarthy *adjective* DARK-SKINNED, black, brown, dark, dark-complexioned, dusky

swashbuckling *adjective* DASHING, bold, daredevil, flamboyant

swathe *verb* WRAP, bundle up, cloak, drape, envelop, shroud

sway *verb* 1 LEAN, bend, rock, roll, swing 2 INFLUENCE, affect, guide, induce, persuade ▶ *noun* 3 POWER, authority, clout (*informal*), control, influence

swear *verb* 1 CURSE, be foul-mouthed, blaspheme 2 DECLARE, affirm, assert, attest, promise, testify, vow

swearing *noun* BAD LANGUAGE, blasphemy, cursing, foul language, profanity

swearword *noun* OATH, curse, expletive, four-letter word, obscenity, profanity

sweat *noun* 1 PERSPIRATION 2 *Informal* LABOR, chore, drudgery, toil 3 *Informal* WORRY, agitation, anxiety, distress, panic, strain ▶ *verb* 4 PERSPIRE, glow 5 *Informal* WORRY, agonize, fret, suffer, torture oneself

sweaty *adjective* PERSPIRING, clammy, sticky

sweep *verb* 1 CLEAR, brush, clean, remove 2 SAIL, fly, glide, pass, skim, tear, zoom ▶ *noun* 3 ARC, bend, curve, move, stroke, swing 4 EXTENT, range, scope, stretch

sweeping *adjective* 1 WIDE-RANGING, all-embracing, all-inclusive, broad,

comprehensive, extensive, global, wide 2 INDISCRIMINATE, blanket, exaggerated, overstated, unqualified, wholesale

sweet *adjective* 1 SUGARY, cloying, saccharine 2 CHARMING, agreeable, appealing, cute, delightful, engaging, kind, likable *or* likeable, lovable, winning 3 MELODIOUS, dulcet, harmonious, mellow, musical 4 FRAGRANT, aromatic, clean, fresh, pure ▶ *noun* 5 (usually plural) CONFECTIONERY, bonbon

sweeten *verb* 1 SUGAR 2 MOLLIFY, appease, pacify, soothe

sweetheart *noun* LOVER, beloved, boyfriend *or* girlfriend, darling, dear, love

swell *verb* 1 EXPAND, balloon, bloat, bulge, dilate, distend, enlarge, grow, increase, rise ▶ *noun* 2 WAVE, billow, surge

swelling *noun* ENLARGEMENT, bulge, bump, distension, inflammation, lump, protuberance

sweltering *adjective* HOT, boiling, burning, oppressive, scorching, stifling

swerve *verb* VEER, bend, deflect, deviate, diverge, stray, swing, turn, turn aside

swift *adjective* QUICK, fast, hurried, prompt, rapid, speedy

swiftly *adverb* QUICKLY, fast, hurriedly, promptly, rapidly, speedily

swiftness *noun* SPEED, promptness, quickness, rapidity, speediness, velocity

swindle *verb* 1 CHEAT, con, defraud, fleece, rip (someone) off (*slang*), sting (*informal*), trick ▶noun 2 FRAUD, con trick (informal), deception, racket, rip-off (slang), scam (slang)

swindler noun CHEAT, con man (informal), fraud, rogue, shark, trickster

swing verb 1 SWAY, oscillate, rock, veer, wave 2 (usually with round) TURN, curve, pivot, rotate, swivel 3 HANG, dangle, suspend ▶noun 4 SWAYING, oscillation

swipe verb 1 HIT, lash out at, slap, strike, wallop (informal) 2 Slang STEAL, appropriate, filch, lift (informal), pinch (informal), purloin ▶noun 3 BLOW, clout (informal), cuff, slap, smack, wallop (informal)

swirl verb WHIRL, churn, eddy, spin, twist

switch noun 1 CHANGE, reversal, shift 2 EXCHANGE, substitution, swap ▶verb 3 CHANGE, deflect, deviate, divert, shift 4 EXCHANGE, substitute, swap

swivel verb TURN, pivot, revolve, rotate, spin

swollen adjective ENLARGED, bloated, distended, inflamed, puffed up

swoop verb 1 POUNCE, descend, dive, rush, stoop, sweep ▶noun 2 POUNCE, descent, drop, lunge, plunge, rush, stoop, sweep

swop verb EXCHANGE, barter, interchange, switch, trade

sycophant noun CRAWLER, brown-noser (slang), fawner, flatterer, toady, yes man

sycophantic adjective OBSEQUIOUS, crawling, fawning, flattering, grovelling, ingratiating, servile, slimy, smarmy (Brit. informal),

toadying, unctuous

syllabus noun COURSE OF STUDY, curriculum

symbol noun SIGN, badge, emblem, figure, icon, image, logo, mark, representation, token

symbolic adjective REPRESENTATIVE, allegorical, emblematic, figurative

symbolize verb REPRESENT, denote, mean, personify, signify, stand for, typify

symmetrical adjective BALANCED, in proportion, regular

symmetry noun BALANCE, evenness, order, proportion, regularity

sympathetic adjective 1 CARING, compassionate, concerned, interested, kind, pitying, supportive, understanding, warm 2 LIKE-MINDED, agreeable, companionable, compatible, congenial, friendly

sympathize verb 1 FEEL FOR, commiserate, condole, pity 2 AGREE, side with, understand

sympathizer noun SUPPORTER, partisan, well-wisher

sympathy noun 1 COMPASSION, commiseration, pity, understanding 2 AGREEMENT, affinity, fellow feeling, rapport

symptom noun SIGN, expression, indication, mark, token, warning

symptomatic adjective INDICATIVE, characteristic, suggestive

synthetic adjective ARTIFICIAL, fake, man-made

system noun 1 METHOD, practice, procedure, routine,

technique 2 ARRANGEMENT, classification, organization, scheme, structure

systematic *adjective* METHODICAL, efficient, orderly, organized

T t

table *noun* 1 COUNTER, bench, board, stand 2 LIST, catalog, chart, diagram, record, register, roll, schedule, tabulation ▶ *verb* 3 SUBMIT, enter, move, propose, put forward, suggest

tableau *noun* PICTURE, representation, scene, spectacle

taboo *noun* 1 PROHIBITION, anathema, ban, interdict, proscription, restriction ▶ *adjective* 2 FORBIDDEN, anathema, banned, outlawed, prohibited, proscribed, unacceptable, unmentionable

tacit *adjective* IMPLIED, implicit, inferred, undeclared, understood, unexpressed, unspoken, unstated

taciturn *adjective* UNCOMMUNICATIVE, quiet, reserved, reticent, silent, tight-lipped, unforthcoming, withdrawn

tack¹ *noun* 1 NAIL, drawing pin, pin ▶ *verb* 2 FASTEN, affix, attach, fix, nail, pin 3 STITCH, baste 4 **tack on** APPEND, add, attach, tag

tack² *noun* COURSE, approach, direction, heading, line, method, path, plan, procedure, way

tackle *verb* 1 DEAL WITH, attempt, come *or* get to grips with, embark upon, get stuck into (*informal*), set about, undertake 2 CONFRONT, challenge, grab, grasp, halt, intercept, seize, stop ▶ *noun* 3 CHALLENGE, block 4 EQUIPMENT, accoutrements, apparatus, gear, paraphernalia, tools, trappings

tacky¹ *adjective* STICKY, adhesive, gluey, gummy, wet

tacky² *adjective* Informal VULGAR, cheap, off-color, scuzzy (*slang*), seedy, shabby, shoddy, sleazy, tasteless, tatty

tact *noun* DIPLOMACY, consideration, delicacy, discretion, sensitivity, thoughtfulness, understanding

tactful *adjective* DIPLOMATIC, considerate, delicate, discreet, polite, politic, sensitive, thoughtful, understanding

tactic *noun* 1 POLICY, approach, maneuver, method, move, ploy, scheme, stratagem 2 **tactics** STRATEGY, campaigning, generalship, maneuvers, plans

tactical *adjective* STRATEGIC, cunning, diplomatic, shrewd, smart

tactician *noun* STRATEGIST, general, mastermind, planner

tactless *adjective* INSENSITIVE, impolite, impolitic, inconsiderate, indelicate, indiscreet, thoughtless, undiplomatic, unsubtle

tag *noun* 1 LABEL, flap, identification, mark, marker, note, slip, tab, ticket ▶ *verb* 2 LABEL, mark 3 (with *along* or on) ACCOMPANY, attend, follow, shadow, stalk, tail (*informal*), trail

tail noun 1 EXTREMITY, appendage, end, rear end, tailpiece 2 **turn tail** RUN AWAY, cut and run, flee, retreat, run off, take to one's heels ▸ verb 3 *Informal* FOLLOW, shadow, stalk, track, trail

tailor noun 1 OUTFITTER, clothier, costumier, couturier, dressmaker, seamstress ▸ verb 2 ADAPT, adjust, alter, customize, fashion, modify, mold, shape, style

taint verb 1 SPOIL, blemish, contaminate, corrupt, damage, defile, pollute, ruin, stain, sully, tarnish ▸ noun 2 STAIN, black mark, blemish, blot, defect, demerit, fault, flaw, spot

take verb 1 CAPTURE, acquire, catch, get, grasp, grip, obtain, secure, seize 2 ACCOMPANY, bring, conduct, convoy, escort, guide, lead, usher 3 CARRY, bear, bring, convey, ferry, fetch, haul, transport 4 STEAL, appropriate, misappropriate, pinch (*informal*), pocket, purloin 5 REQUIRE, call for, demand, necessitate, need 6 TOLERATE, abide, bear, endure, put up with (*informal*), stand, stomach, withstand 7 HAVE ROOM FOR, accommodate, contain, hold 8 SUBTRACT, deduct, eliminate, remove 9 ASSUME, believe, consider, perceive, presume, regard, understand

take in verb 1 UNDERSTAND, absorb, assimilate, comprehend, digest, get the hang of (*informal*), grasp

2 DECEIVE, cheat, con (*informal*), dupe, fool, hoodwink, mislead, swindle, trick

takeoff noun DEPARTURE, launch, liftoff

take off verb 1 REMOVE, discard, peel off, strip off 2 LIFT OFF, take to the air 3 *Informal* DEPART, abscond, decamp, disappear, go, leave, slope off

takeover noun MERGER, coup, incorporation

take up verb 1 OCCUPY, absorb, consume, cover, extend over, fill, use up 2 START, adopt, become involved in, engage in

taking adjective 1 CHARMING, attractive, beguiling, captivating, enchanting, engaging, fetching (*informal*), likable *or* likeable, prepossessing ▸ noun 2 **takings** REVENUE, earnings, income, proceeds, profits, receipts, returns, take

tale noun STORY, account, anecdote, fable, legend, narrative, saga, yarn (*informal*)

talent noun ABILITY, aptitude, capacity, flair, genius, gift, knack

talented adjective GIFTED, able, brilliant

talisman noun CHARM, amulet, fetish, lucky charm, mascot

talk verb 1 SPEAK, chat, chatter, chew the fat (*slang*), communicate, converse, gossip, natter, utter 2 NEGOTIATE, confabulate, confer, parley 3 INFORM, blab, give the game away, let the cat out of the bag, tell all ▸ noun 4 SPEECH, address, discourse, disquisition, lecture, oration, sermon

talkative *adjective* LOQUACIOUS, chatty, effusive, garrulous, gossipy, long-winded, mouthy, verbose, voluble, wordy

talker *noun* SPEAKER, chatterbox, conversationalist, lecturer, orator

talking-to *noun* REPRIMAND, criticism, lecture, rebuke, reproach, reproof, scolding, telling-off (*informal*)

tall *adjective* **1** HIGH, big, elevated, giant, lanky, lofty, soaring, towering **2** *As in* **tall tale** *Informal* IMPLAUSIBLE, absurd, cock-and-bull (*informal*), exaggerated, far-fetched, incredible, preposterous, unbelievable **3** *As in* **tall order** DIFFICULT, demanding, hard, unreasonable, well-nigh impossible

tally *verb* **1** CORRESPOND, accord, agree, coincide, concur, conform, fit, harmonize, match, square ▶*noun* **2** RECORD, count, mark, reckoning, running total, score, total

tame *adjective* **1** DOMESTICATED, amenable, broken, disciplined, docile, gentle, obedient, tractable **2** SUBMISSIVE, compliant, docile, manageable, meek, obedient, subdued, unresisting **3** UNINTERESTING, bland, boring, dull, humdrum, insipid, unexciting, uninspiring, vapid ▶*verb* **4** DOMESTICATE, break in, house-train, train **5** DISCIPLINE, bring to heel, conquer, humble, master, subdue, subjugate, suppress

tamper *verb* INTERFERE, alter, fiddle (*informal*), fool about

(*informal*), meddle, mess about, tinker

tangible *adjective* DEFINITE, actual, concrete, material, palpable, perceptible, positive, real

tangle *noun* **1** KNOT, coil, entanglement, jungle, twist, web **2** CONFUSION, complication, entanglement, fix (*informal*), imbroglio, jam, mess, mix-up ▶*verb* **3** TWIST, coil, entangle, interweave, knot, mat, mesh, ravel **4** (*often with* with) COME INTO CONFLICT, come up against, contend, contest, cross swords, dispute, lock horns

tangled *adjective* **1** TWISTED, entangled, jumbled, knotted, matted, messy, snarled, tousled **2** COMPLICATED, complex, confused, convoluted, involved, knotty, messy, mixed-up

tangy *adjective* SHARP, piquant, pungent, spicy, tart

tantalize *verb* TORMENT, frustrate, lead on, taunt, tease, torture

tantamount *adjective* EQUIVALENT, commensurate, equal, synonymous

tantrum *noun* OUTBURST, fit, flare-up, hysterics, temper

tap[1] *verb* **1** KNOCK, beat, drum, pat, rap, strike, touch ▶*noun* **2** KNOCK, pat, rap, touch

tap[2] *noun* **1** VALVE, stopcock **2 on tap:** a *Informal* AVAILABLE, at hand, in reserve, on hand, ready **b** ON DRAFT ▶*verb* **3** LISTEN IN ON, bug (*informal*), eavesdrop on **4** DRAW OFF, bleed, drain, siphon off

tape *noun* **1** STRIP, band, ribbon

▶ *verb* **2** RECORD, tape-record, video **3** BIND, seal, secure, stick, wrap

taper *verb* **1** NARROW, come to a point, thin **2 taper off** LESSEN, decrease, die away, dwindle, fade, reduce, subside, wane, wind down

target *noun* **1** GOAL, aim, ambition, end, intention, mark, object, objective **2** VICTIM, butt, scapegoat

tariff *noun* TAX, duty, excise, levy, toll

tarnish *verb* **1** STAIN, blacken, blemish, blot, darken, discolor, sully, taint ▶ *noun* **2** STAIN, blemish, blot, discoloration, spot, taint

tart[1] *noun* PIE, pastry, tartlet

tart[2] *adjective* SHARP, acid, bitter, piquant, pungent, sour, tangy, vinegary

tart[3] *noun* SLUT, call girl, floozy (*slang*), ho (*slang*), prostitute, trollop, whore

task *noun* **1** JOB, assignment, chore, duty, enterprise, exercise, mission, undertaking **2 take to task** CRITICIZE, blame, censure, reprimand, reproach, reprove, scold, tell off (*informal*), upbraid

taste *noun* **1** FLAVOR, relish, savor, smack, tang **2** BIT, bite, dash, morsel, mouthful, sample, *soupçon*, spoonful, tidbit **3** LIKING, appetite, fancy, fondness, inclination, partiality, penchant, predilection, preference **4** REFINEMENT, appreciation, discernment, discrimination, elegance, judgment, sophistication, style ▶ *verb* **5** DISTINGUISH,

differentiate, discern, perceive **6** SAMPLE, savor, sip, test, try **7** HAVE A FLAVOR OF, savor of, smack of **8** EXPERIENCE, encounter, know, meet with, partake of, undergo

tasteful *adjective* REFINED, artistic, cultivated, cultured, discriminating, elegant, exquisite, in good taste, polished, stylish

tasteless *adjective* **1** INSIPID, bland, boring, dull, flat, flavorless, mild, thin, weak **2** VULGAR, crass, crude, gaudy, gross, inelegant, off-color, tacky (*informal*), tawdry

tasty *adjective* DELICIOUS, appetizing, delectable, full-flavored, luscious, palatable, savory, toothsome, yummy (*informal*)

tatters *noun* **in tatters** RAGGED, down at heel, in rags, in shreds, ripped, tattered, threadbare, torn

tatty *adjective* RAGGED, bedraggled, dilapidated, down at heel, neglected, run-down, shabby, threadbare, worn

taunt *verb* **1** TEASE, deride, insult, jeer, mock, provoke, ridicule, torment ▶ *noun* **2** JEER, derision, dig, gibe, insult, provocation, ridicule, sarcasm, teasing

taut *adjective* TIGHT, flexed, rigid, strained, stressed, stretched, tense

tavern *noun* INN, alehouse (*archaic*), bar, hostelry, public house

tawdry *adjective* VULGAR, cheap, flashy, gaudy, gimcrack, tacky (*informal*), tasteless, tatty, tinselly

tax noun 1 CHARGE, duty, excise, levy, tariff, tithe, toll ► verb 2 CHARGE, assess, rate 3 STRAIN, burden, exhaust, load, stretch, test, try, weaken, weary

taxing adjective DEMANDING, exacting, exhausting, onerous, punishing, sapping, stressful, tiring, tough, trying

teach verb INSTRUCT, coach, drill, educate, enlighten, guide, inform, show, train, tutor

teacher noun INSTRUCTOR, coach, educator, guide, lecturer, master or mistress, mentor, schoolteacher, trainer, tutor

team noun 1 GROUP, band, body, bunch, company, gang, line-up, set, side, squad ► verb 2 (often with up) JOIN, band together, cooperate, couple, get together, link, unite, work together

teamwork noun COOPERATION, collaboration, coordination, esprit de corps, fellowship, harmony, unity

tear verb 1 RIP, claw, lacerate, mangle, mutilate, pull apart, rend, rupture, scratch, shred, split 2 RUSH, bolt, charge, dash, fly, hurry, race, run, speed, sprint, zoom ► noun 3 HOLE, laceration, rent, rip, rupture, scratch, split

tearful adjective WEEPING, blubbering, crying, in tears, lachrymose, sobbing, weepy (informal), whimpering

tears plural noun 1 CRYING, blubbering, sobbing, wailing, weeping 2 **in tears** CRYING, blubbering, distressed, sobbing, weeping

tease verb MOCK, goad, lead on, provoke, pull someone's leg (informal), tantalize, taunt, torment

technical adjective SCIENTIFIC, hi-tech or high-tech, skilled, specialist, specialized, technological

technique noun 1 METHOD, approach, manner, means, mode, procedure, style, system, way 2 SKILL, artistry, craft, craftsmanship, execution, performance, proficiency, touch

tedious adjective BORING, drab, dreary, dull, humdrum, irksome, laborious, mind-numbing, monotonous, tiresome, wearisome

tedium noun BOREDOM, drabness, dreariness, dullness, monotony, routine, sameness, tediousness

teeming¹ adjective FULL, abundant, alive, brimming, bristling, bursting, crawling, overflowing, swarming, thick

teeming² adjective POURING, pelting, raining cats and dogs (informal)

teenager noun YOUTH, adolescent, boy, girl, juvenile, minor

teeter verb WOBBLE, rock, seesaw, stagger, sway, totter, waver

teetotaler noun ABSTAINER, nondrinker

telepathy noun MIND-READING, E.S.P., sixth sense

telephone noun 1 PHONE, handset, line ► verb 2 CALL, dial, phone

telescope noun 1 GLASS, spyglass ► verb 2 SHORTEN,

abbreviate, abridge, compress, condense, contract, shrink

television *noun* TV, small screen (*informal*), the tube (*slang*)

tell *verb* 1 INFORM, announce, communicate, disclose, divulge, express, make known, notify, proclaim, reveal, state 2 INSTRUCT, bid, call upon, command, direct, order, require, summon 3 DESCRIBE, chronicle, depict, narrate, portray, recount, relate, report 4 DISTINGUISH, differentiate, discern, discriminate, identify 5 CARRY WEIGHT, count, have *or* take effect, make its presence felt, register, take its toll, weigh

telling *adjective* EFFECTIVE, considerable, decisive, forceful, impressive, influential, marked, powerful, significant, striking

telling-off *noun* REPRIMAND, criticism, lecture, rebuke, reproach, reproof, scolding, talking-to

tell off *verb* REPRIMAND, berate, censure, chide, lecture, rebuke, reproach, scold

temerity *noun* BOLDNESS, audacity, chutzpah (*informal*), effrontery, front, impudence, nerve (*informal*), rashness, recklessness

temper *noun* 1 RAGE, bad mood, fury, passion, tantrum 2 IRRITABILITY, hot-headedness, irascibility, passion, petulance, resentment, surliness 3 SELF-CONTROL, calmness, composure, cool (*slang*), equanimity 4 FRAME OF MIND, constitution, disposition, humor, mind, mood, nature, temperament ▸*verb* 5 MODERATE,

assuage, lessen, mitigate, mollify, restrain, soften, soothe, tone down 6 STRENGTHEN, anneal, harden, toughen

temperament *noun* 1 NATURE, bent, character, constitution, disposition, humor, make-up, outlook, personality, temper 2 EXCITABILITY, anger, hot-headedness, moodiness, petulance, volatility

temperamental *adjective* 1 MOODY, capricious, emotional, excitable, highly strung, hypersensitive, irritable, sensitive, touchy, volatile 2 UNRELIABLE, erratic, inconsistent, inconstant, unpredictable

temperance *noun* 1 MODERATION, continence, discretion, forbearance, restraint, self-control, self-discipline, self-restraint 2 TEETOTALISM, abstemiousness, abstinence, sobriety

temperate *adjective* 1 MILD, calm, cool, fair, gentle, moderate, pleasant 2 SELF-RESTRAINED, calm, composed, dispassionate, even-tempered, mild, moderate, reasonable, self-controlled, sensible

tempest *noun* GALE, cyclone, hurricane, squall, storm, tornado, typhoon

tempestuous *adjective* 1 STORMY, blustery, gusty, inclement, raging, squally, turbulent, windy 2 VIOLENT, boisterous, emotional, furious, heated, intense, passionate, stormy, turbulent, wild

temple *noun* SHRINE, church,

place of worship, sanctuary

temporarily adverb BRIEFLY, fleetingly, for the time being, momentarily, pro tem

temporary adjective IMPERMANENT, brief, ephemeral, fleeting, interim, momentary, provisional, short-lived, transitory

tempt verb ENTICE, allure, attract, coax, invite, lead on, lure, seduce, tantalize

temptation noun ENTICEMENT, allurement, inducement, lure, pull, seduction, tantalization

tempting adjective ENTICING, alluring, appetizing, attractive, inviting, mouthwatering, seductive, tantalizing

tenable adjective SOUND, arguable, believable, defensible, justifiable, plausible, rational, reasonable, viable

tenacious adjective 1 FIRM, clinging, forceful, immovable, iron, strong, tight, unshakable 2 STUBBORN, adamant, determined, dogged, obdurate, obstinate, persistent, resolute, steadfast, unswerving, unyielding

tenacity noun PERSEVERANCE, application, determination, doggedness, obduracy, persistence, resolve, steadfastness, stubbornness

tenancy noun LEASE, occupancy, possession, renting, residence

tenant noun LEASEHOLDER, inhabitant, lessee, occupant, occupier, renter, resident

tend¹ verb 1 BE INCLINED, be apt, be liable, gravitate, have a tendency, incline, lean 2 GO, aim, bear, head, lead,

make for, point

tend² verb TAKE CARE OF, attend, cultivate, keep, look after, maintain, manage, nurture, watch over

tendency noun INCLINATION, disposition, leaning, liability, proclivity, proneness, propensity, susceptibility

tender¹ adjective 1 GENTLE, affectionate, caring, compassionate, considerate, kind, loving, sympathetic, tenderhearted, warm-hearted 2 VULNERABLE, immature, impressionable, inexperienced, raw, sensitive, young, youthful 3 SENSITIVE, bruised, inflamed, painful, raw, sore

tender² verb 1 OFFER, give, hand in, present, proffer, propose, put forward, submit, volunteer ▶ noun 2 OFFER, bid, estimate, proposal, submission 3 As in **legal tender** CURRENCY, money, payment

tenderness noun 1 GENTLENESS, affection, care, compassion, consideration, kindness, love, sentimentality, sympathy, warmth 2 SORENESS, inflammation, pain, sensitivity

tense adjective 1 NERVOUS, anxious, apprehensive, edgy, jumpy, keyed up, on edge, on tenterhooks, strained, uptight (informal), wired (slang) 2 STRESSFUL, exciting, nerve-racking, worrying 3 TIGHT, rigid, strained, stretched, taut ▶ verb 4 TIGHTEN, brace, flex, strain, stretch

tension noun 1 SUSPENSE, anxiety, apprehension, hostility, nervousness, pressure,

strain, stress, unease
2 TIGHTNESS, pressure, rigidity, stiffness, stress, stretching, tautness

tentative *adjective*
1 EXPERIMENTAL, conjectural, indefinite, provisional, speculative, unconfirmed, unsettled **2** HESITANT, cautious, diffident, doubtful, faltering, timid, uncertain, undecided, unsure

tenuous *adjective* SLIGHT, doubtful, dubious, flimsy, insubstantial, nebulous, shaky, sketchy, weak

tepid *adjective* **1** LUKEWARM, warmish **2** HALF-HEARTED, apathetic, cool, indifferent, lukewarm, unenthusiastic

term *noun* **1** WORD, expression, name, phrase, title **2** PERIOD, duration, interval, season, span, spell, time, while ▶ *verb* **3** CALL, designate, dub, entitle, label, name, style

terminal *adjective* **1** DEADLY, fatal, incurable, killing, lethal, mortal **2** FINAL, concluding, extreme, last, ultimate, utmost ▶ *noun* **3** TERMINUS, depot, end of the line, station

terminate *verb* END, abort, cease, close, complete, conclude, discontinue, finish, stop

termination *noun* ENDING, abortion, cessation, completion, conclusion, discontinuation, end, finish

terminology *noun* LANGUAGE, jargon, nomenclature, phraseology, terms, vocabulary

terminus *noun* END OF THE LINE, depot, garage, last stop, station

terms *plural noun* **1** CONDITIONS, particulars, provisions, provisos, qualifications, specifications, stipulations **2** RELATIONSHIP, footing, relations, standing, status

terrain *noun* GROUND, country, going, land, landscape, topography

terrestrial *adjective* EARTHLY, global, worldly

terrible *adjective* **1** SERIOUS, dangerous, desperate, extreme, severe **2** BAD, abysmal, awful, dire, dreadful, poor, rotten (*informal*) **3** FEARFUL, dreadful, frightful, horrendous, horrible, horrifying, monstrous, shocking, terrifying

terribly *adverb* EXTREMELY, awfully (*informal*), decidedly, desperately, exceedingly, seriously, thoroughly, very

terrific *adjective* **1** GREAT, enormous, fearful, gigantic, huge, intense, tremendous **2** *Informal* EXCELLENT, amazing, brilliant, fantastic (*informal*), magnificent, marvelous, outstanding, sensational (*informal*), stupendous, superb, wonderful

terrified *adjective* FRIGHTENED, alarmed, appalled, horrified, horror-struck, panic-stricken, petrified, scared

terrify *verb* FRIGHTEN, alarm, appall, horrify, make one's hair stand on end, scare, shock, terrorize

territory *noun* DISTRICT, area, country, domain, land, patch, province, region, zone

terror *noun* **1** FEAR, alarm, anxiety, dread, fright, horror, panic, shock **2** SCOURGE, bogeyman, bugbear, devil, fiend, monster

terrorize verb OPPRESS, browbeat, bully, coerce, intimidate, menace, threaten

terse adjective **1** CONCISE, brief, condensed, laconic, monosyllabic, pithy, short, succinct **2** CURT, abrupt, brusque, short, snappy

test verb **1** CHECK, analyze, assess, examine, experiment, investigate, put to the test, research, try out ▶noun **2** EXAMINATION, acid test, analysis, assessment, check, evaluation, investigation, research, trial

testament noun **1** PROOF, demonstration, evidence, testimony, tribute, witness **2** WILL, last wishes

testify verb BEAR WITNESS, affirm, assert, attest, certify, corroborate, state, swear, vouch

testimonial noun TRIBUTE, commendation, endorsement, recommendation, reference

testimony noun **1** EVIDENCE, affidavit, deposition, statement, submission **2** PROOF, corroboration, demonstration, evidence, indication, manifestation, support, verification

testing adjective DIFFICULT, arduous, challenging, demanding, exacting, rigorous, searching, strenuous, taxing, tough

tether noun **1** ROPE, chain, fetter, halter, lead, leash **2 at the end of one's tether** EXASPERATED, at one's wits' end,

exhausted ▶verb **3** TIE, bind, chain, fasten, fetter, secure

text noun **1** CONTENTS, body **2** WORDS, wording

texture noun FEEL, consistency, grain, structure, surface, tissue

thank verb SAY THANK YOU, show one's appreciation

thankful adjective GRATEFUL, appreciative, beholden, indebted, obliged, pleased, relieved

thankless adjective UNREWARDING, fruitless, unappreciated, unprofitable, unrequited

thanks plural noun **1** GRATITUDE, acknowledgment, appreciation, credit, gratefulness, kudos, recognition **2 thanks to** BECAUSE OF, as a result of, due to, owing to, through

thaw verb MELT, defrost, dissolve, liquefy, soften, unfreeze, warm

theatrical adjective **1** DRAMATIC, Thespian **2** EXAGGERATED, affected, dramatic, histrionic, mannered, melodramatic, ostentatious, showy, stagy

theft noun STEALING, embezzlement, fraud, larceny, pilfering, purloining, robbery, thieving

theme noun **1** SUBJECT, idea, keynote, subject matter, topic **2** MOTIF, leitmotif

theological adjective RELIGIOUS, doctrinal, ecclesiastical

theoretical adjective ABSTRACT, academic, conjectural, hypothetical, notional, speculative

theorize verb SPECULATE, conjecture, formulate, guess, hypothesize, project, propound, suppose

theory *noun* SUPPOSITION, assumption, conjecture, hypothesis, presumption, speculation, surmise, thesis

therapeutic *adjective* BENEFICIAL, corrective, curative, good, healing, remedial, restorative, salutary

therapist *noun* HEALER, physician

therapy *noun* REMEDY, cure, healing, treatment

therefore *adverb* CONSEQUENTLY, accordingly, as a result, ergo, hence, so, then, thence, thus

thesis *noun* 1 DISSERTATION, essay, monograph, paper, treatise 2 PROPOSITION, contention, hypothesis, idea, opinion, proposal, theory, view

thick *adjective* 1 WIDE, broad, bulky, fat, solid, substantial 2 DENSE, close, compact, concentrated, condensed, heavy, impenetrable, opaque 3 *Informal* FRIENDLY, close, devoted, familiar, inseparable, intimate, pally (*informal*) 4 FULL, brimming, bristling, bursting, covered, crawling, packed, swarming, teeming 5 **a bit thick** UNFAIR, unjust, unreasonable

thicken *verb* SET, clot, coagulate, condense, congeal, jell

thicket *noun* WOOD, brake, coppice, copse, covert, grove

thickset *adjective* WELL-BUILT, bulky, burly, heavy, muscular, stocky, strong, sturdy

thief *noun* ROBBER, burglar, embezzler, housebreaker, pickpocket, pilferer, plunderer, shoplifter, stealer

thieve *verb* STEAL, filch, pilfer, pinch (*informal*), purloin, rob, swipe (*slang*)

thin *adjective* 1 NARROW, attenuated, fine 2 SLIM, bony, emaciated, lean, scrawny, skeletal, skinny, slender, slight, spare, spindly 3 MEAGER, deficient, scanty, scarce, scattered, skimpy, sparse, wispy 4 DELICATE, diaphanous, filmy, fine, flimsy, gossamer, sheer, unsubstantial 5 UNCONVINCING, feeble, flimsy, inadequate, lame, lousy (*slang*), poor, superficial, weak

thing *noun* 1 OBJECT, article, being, body, entity, something, substance 2 *Informal* OBSESSION, bee in one's bonnet, fetish, fixation, hang-up (*informal*), mania, phobia, preoccupation 3 **things** POSSESSIONS, belongings, effects, equipment, gear, luggage, stuff

think *verb* 1 BELIEVE, consider, deem, estimate, imagine, judge, reckon, regard, suppose 2 PONDER, cerebrate, cogitate, contemplate, deliberate, meditate, muse, reason, reflect, ruminate

thinker *noun* PHILOSOPHER, brain (*informal*), intellect (*informal*), mastermind, sage, theorist, wise man

thinking *noun* 1 REASONING, conjecture, idea, judgment, opinion, position, theory, view ▶*adjective* 2 THOUGHTFUL, contemplative, intelligent, meditative, philosophical, rational, reasoning, reflective

think up *verb* DEVISE, come up with, concoct, contrive, create, dream up, invent, visualize

thirst noun 1 THIRSTINESS, drought, dryness 2 CRAVING, appetite, desire, hankering, keenness, longing, passion, yearning

thirsty adjective 1 PARCHED, arid, dehydrated, dry 2 EAGER, avid, craving, desirous, greedy, hungry, longing, yearning

thorn noun PRICKLE, barb, spike, spine

thorny adjective PRICKLY, barbed, bristly, pointed, sharp, spiky, spiny

thorough adjective 1 CAREFUL, assiduous, conscientious, efficient, exhaustive, full, in-depth, intensive, meticulous, painstaking, sweeping 2 COMPLETE, absolute, out-and-out, outright, perfect, total, unmitigated, unqualified, utter

thoroughbred adjective PUREBRED, pedigree

thoroughfare noun ROAD, avenue, highway, passage, passageway, street, way

thoroughly adverb 1 CAREFULLY, assiduously, conscientiously, efficiently, exhaustively, from top to bottom, fully, intensively, meticulously, painstakingly, scrupulously 2 COMPLETELY, absolutely, downright, perfectly, quite, totally, to the hilt, utterly

though conjunction 1 ALTHOUGH, even if, even though, notwithstanding, while ▶ adverb 2 NEVERTHELESS, for all that, however, nonetheless, notwithstanding, still, yet

thought noun 1 THINKING, brainwork, cogitation, consideration, deliberation, meditation, musing, reflection, rumination 2 IDEA, concept, judgment, notion, opinion, view 3 CONSIDERATION, attention, heed, regard, scrutiny, study 4 INTENTION, aim, design, idea, notion, object, plan, purpose 5 EXPECTATION, anticipation, aspiration, hope, prospect

thoughtful adjective 1 CONSIDERATE, attentive, caring, helpful, kind, kindly, solicitous, unselfish 2 WELL-THOUGHT-OUT, astute, canny, prudent 3 REFLECTIVE, contemplative, deliberative, meditative, pensive, ruminative, serious, studious

thoughtless adjective INCONSIDERATE, impolite, insensitive, rude, selfish, tactless, uncaring, undiplomatic, unkind

thrash verb 1 BEAT, belt (informal), cane, flog, paddle (U.S. & Canad.), scourge, spank, whip 2 DEFEAT, beat, crush, run rings around (informal), slaughter (informal), trounce, wipe the floor with (informal) 3 THRESH, flail, jerk, toss and turn, writhe

thrashing noun 1 BEATING, belting (informal), flogging, punishment, whipping 2 DEFEAT, beating, hammering (informal), trouncing

thrash out verb SETTLE, argue out, debate, discuss, have out, resolve, solve, talk over

thread noun 1 STRAND, fiber, filament, line, string, yarn 2 THEME, direction, drift, plot, story line, train of thought

▶*verb* 3 PASS, ease, pick (one's way), squeeze through

threadbare *adjective* 1 SHABBY, down at heel, frayed, old, ragged, tattered, tatty, worn 2 HACKNEYED, commonplace, conventional, familiar, overused, stale, stereotyped, tired, trite, well-worn

threat *noun* 1 WARNING, foreboding, foreshadowing, omen, portent, presage, writing on the wall 2 DANGER, hazard, menace, peril, risk

threaten *verb* 1 INTIMIDATE, browbeat, bully, lean on (*slang*), menace, pressurize, terrorize 2 ENDANGER, imperil, jeopardize, put at risk, put in jeopardy, put on the line 3 FORESHADOW, forebode, impend, portend, presage

threatening *adjective* 1 MENACING, bullying, intimidatory 2 OMINOUS, forbidding, grim, inauspicious, sinister

threshold *noun* 1 ENTRANCE, door, doorstep, doorway 2 START, beginning, brink, dawn, inception, opening, outset, verge 3 MINIMUM, lower limit

thrift *noun* FRUGALITY, carefulness, economy, parsimony, prudence, saving, thriftiness

thrifty *adjective* ECONOMICAL, careful, frugal, parsimonious, provident, prudent, saving, sparing

thrill *noun* 1 PLEASURE, buzz (*slang*), kick (*informal*), stimulation, tingle, titillation ▶*verb* 2 EXCITE, arouse, electrify, move, stimulate, stir, titillate

thrilling *adjective* EXCITING, electrifying, gripping, riveting, rousing, sensational, stimulating, stirring

thrive *verb* PROSPER, boom, develop, do well, flourish, get on, grow, increase, succeed

thriving *adjective* PROSPEROUS, blooming, booming, burgeoning, flourishing, healthy, successful, well

throb *verb* 1 PULSATE, beat, palpitate, pound, pulse, thump, vibrate ▶*noun* 2 PULSE, beat, palpitation, pounding, pulsating, thump, thumping, vibration

throng *noun* 1 CROWD, crush, horde, host, mass, mob, multitude, pack, swarm ▶*verb* 2 CROWD, congregate, converge, flock, mill around, pack, swarm around

throttle *verb* STRANGLE, choke, garrotte, strangulate

through *preposition* 1 BETWEEN, by, past 2 BECAUSE OF, by means of, by way of, using, via 3 DURING, in, throughout ▶*adjective* 4 FINISHED, completed, done, ended ▶*adverb* 5 **through and through** COMPLETELY, altogether, entirely, fully, thoroughly, totally, utterly, wholly

throughout *adverb* EVERYWHERE, all over, from start to finish, right through

throw *verb* 1 HURL, cast, chuck (*informal*), fling, launch, lob (*informal*), pitch, send, sling, toss 2 *Informal* CONFUSE, astonish, baffle, confound, disconcert, dumbfound, faze ▶*noun* 3 TOSS, fling, heave, lob (*informal*), pitch, sling

throwaway *adjective* CASUAL, careless, offhand, passing, understated

throw away *verb* DISCARD, dispense with, dispose of, ditch (*slang*), dump (*informal*), get rid of, jettison, reject, scrap, throw out

thrust *verb* 1 PUSH, drive, force, jam, plunge, propel, ram, shove ▶ *noun* 2 PUSH, drive, lunge, poke, prod, shove, stab 3 MOMENTUM, impetus

thud *noun, verb* THUMP, clunk, crash, knock, smack

thug *noun* RUFFIAN, bruiser (*informal*), bully boy, gangster, hooligan, tough

thump *noun* 1 CRASH, bang, clunk, thud, thwack 2 BLOW, clout (*informal*), knock, punch, rap, smack, wallop (*informal*), whack ▶ *verb* 3 STRIKE, beat, clobber (*slang*), clout (*informal*), hit, knock, pound, punch, smack, wallop (*informal*), whack

thunder *noun* 1 RUMBLE, boom, crash, explosion ▶ *verb* 2 RUMBLE, boom, crash, peal, resound, reverberate, roar 3 SHOUT, bark, bellow, roar, yell

thunderous *adjective* LOUD, booming, deafening, ear-splitting, noisy, resounding, roaring, tumultuous

thunderstruck *adjective* AMAZED, astonished, astounded, dumbfounded, flabbergasted (*informal*), open-mouthed, shocked, staggered, stunned, taken aback

thus *adverb* 1 THEREFORE, accordingly, consequently, ergo, for this reason, hence, on that account, so, then 2 IN THIS WAY, as follows, like this, so

thwart *verb* FRUSTRATE, foil, hinder, obstruct, outwit, prevent, snooker, stymie

tick[1] *noun* 1 MITE, bug, insect 2 TAPPING, clicking, ticktock

tick[2] *noun* CREDIT, account

ticket *noun* 1 VOUCHER, card, certificate, coupon, pass, slip, token 2 LABEL, card, docket, marker, slip, sticker, tab, tag

tidbit *noun* DELICACY, dainty, morsel, snack, treat

tide *noun* 1 CURRENT, ebb, flow, stream, tideway, undertow 2 TENDENCY, direction, drift, movement, trend

tidy *adjective* 1 NEAT, clean, methodical, orderly, shipshape, spruce, well-kept, well-ordered 2 *Informal* CONSIDERABLE, ample, generous, goodly, handsome, healthy, large, sizable *or* sizeable, substantial ▶ *verb* 3 NEATEN, clean, groom, order, spruce up, straighten

tie *verb* 1 FASTEN, attach, bind, connect, join, knot, link, secure, tether 2 RESTRICT, bind, confine, hamper, hinder, limit, restrain 3 DRAW, equal, match ▶ *noun* 4 BOND, affiliation, allegiance, commitment, connection, liaison, relationship 5 FASTENING, bond, cord, fetter, knot, ligature, link 6 DRAW, dead heat, deadlock, gridlock, stalemate

tier *noun* ROW, bank, layer, level, line, rank, story, stratum

tight *adjective* 1 STRETCHED, close, constricted, cramped, narrow, rigid, snug, taut

2 *Informal* MISERLY, grasping, mean, niggardly, parsimonious, stingy, tightfisted **3** CLOSE, even, evenly-balanced, well-matched

tighten *verb* SQUEEZE, close, constrict, narrow

till[1] *verb* CULTIVATE, dig, plow, work

till[2] *noun* CASH REGISTER, cash box

tilt *verb* **1** SLANT, heel, incline, lean, list, slope, tip ▶*noun* **2** SLOPE, angle, inclination, incline, list, pitch, slant **3** *Medieval history* JOUST, combat, duel, fight, lists, tournament **4 (at) full tilt** FULL SPEED, for dear life, headlong

timber *noun* WOOD, beams, boards, logs, planks, trees

timbre *noun* TONE, color, resonance, ring

time *noun* **1** PERIOD, duration, interval, season, space, span, spell, stretch, term **2** OCCASION, instance, juncture, point, stage **3** *Music* TEMPO, beat, measure, rhythm ▶*verb* **4** SCHEDULE, set

timeless *adjective* ETERNAL, ageless, changeless, enduring, everlasting, immortal, lasting, permanent

timely *adjective* OPPORTUNE, appropriate, convenient, judicious, propitious, seasonable, suitable, well-timed

timetable *noun* SCHEDULE, agenda, calendar, curriculum, diary, list, program

timid *adjective* FEARFUL, apprehensive, bashful, coy, diffident, faint-hearted, shrinking, shy, timorous

timorous *adjective* TIMID, apprehensive, bashful, coy,

diffident, faint-hearted, fearful, shrinking, shy

tinge *noun* **1** TINT, color, shade **2** BIT, dash, drop, smattering, sprinkling, suggestion, touch, trace ▶*verb* **3** TINT, color, imbue, suffuse

tingle *verb* **1** PRICKLE, have goose pimples, itch, sting, tickle ▶*noun* **2** QUIVER, goose pimples, itch, pins and needles (*informal*), prickling, shiver, thrill

tinker *verb* MEDDLE, dabble, fiddle (*informal*), mess about, play, potter

tint *noun* **1** SHADE, color, hue, tone **2** DYE, rinse, tincture, tinge, wash ▶*verb* **3** DYE, color

tiny *adjective* SMALL, diminutive, infinitesimal, little, microscopic, miniature, minute, negligible, petite, slight

tip[1] *noun* **1** END, extremity, head, peak, pinnacle, point, summit, top ▶*verb* **2** CAP, crown, finish, surmount, top

tip[2] *noun* **1** GRATUITY, gift **2** HINT, clue, pointer, suggestion, warning ▶*verb* **3** REWARD, remunerate **4** ADVISE, caution, forewarn, suggest, warn

tip[3] *verb* **1** TILT, incline, lean, list, slant **2** DUMP, empty, pour out, unload ▶*noun* **3** DUMP, refuse heap, rubbish heap

tipple *verb* **1** DRINK, imbibe, indulge (*informal*), quaff, swig, tope ▶*noun* **2** ALCOHOL, booze (*informal*), drink, liquor

tipsy *adjective* DRUNK, fuzzy, happy, mellow, three sheets to the wind

tirade *noun* OUTBURST, diatribe, fulmination, harangue, invective, lecture

tire verb 1 FATIGUE, drain, exhaust, wear out, weary 2 BORE, exasperate, irk, irritate, weary

tired adjective 1 EXHAUSTED, drained, drowsy, fatigued, flagging, jaded, sleepy, weary, worn out 2 BORED, fed up, sick, weary 3 HACKNEYED, clichéd, corny (slang), old, outworn, stale, threadbare, trite, well-worn

tireless adjective ENERGETIC, indefatigable, industrious, resolute, unflagging, untiring, vigorous

tiresome adjective BORING, dull, irksome, irritating, tedious, trying, vexatious, wearing, wearisome

tiring adjective EXHAUSTING, arduous, demanding, exacting, laborious, strenuous, tough, wearing

titillate verb EXCITE, arouse, interest, stimulate, tantalize, tease, thrill

titillating adjective EXCITING, arousing, interesting, lurid, provocative, stimulating, suggestive, teasing

title noun 1 NAME, designation, handle (slang), moniker or monicker (slang), term 2 CHAMPIONSHIP, crown 3 OWNERSHIP, claim, entitlement, prerogative, privilege, right

titter verb LAUGH, chortle (informal), chuckle, giggle, snigger

tizzy noun Informal PANIC, agitation, commotion, fluster, state (informal), sweat (informal)

toady noun 1 SYCOPHANT, brown-noser (slang), creep (slang), flatterer, flunkey, hanger-on, lackey, minion, scuzzbucket (slang), yes man ▶ verb 2 FLATTER, brown-nose (slang), fawn on, grovel, kiss ass (slang), kowtow to, pander to, suck up to (informal)

toast[1] verb WARM, brown, grill, heat, roast

toast[2] noun 1 TRIBUTE, compliment, health, pledge, salutation, salute 2 FAVORITE, darling, hero or heroine ▶ verb 3 DRINK TO, drink (to) the health of, salute

together adverb 1 COLLECTIVELY, as one, hand in glove, in concert, in unison, jointly, mutually, shoulder to shoulder, side by side 2 AT THE SAME TIME, at one fell swoop, concurrently, contemporaneously, simultaneously ▶ adjective 3 Informal WELL-ORGANIZED, composed, well-adjusted, well-balanced

toil noun 1 HARD WORK, application, drudgery, effort, elbow grease (informal), exertion, slog, sweat ▶ verb 2 WORK, drudge, labor, slave, slog, strive, struggle, sweat (informal), work one's fingers to the bone

toilet noun LAVATORY, bathroom, convenience, gents (Brit. informal), ladies' room, latrine, privy, urinal, water closet, W.C.

token noun 1 SYMBOL, badge, expression, indication, mark, note, representation, sign ▶ adjective 2 NOMINAL, hollow, minimal, perfunctory, superficial, symbolic

tolerable *adjective* 1 BEARABLE, acceptable, allowable, endurable, sufferable, supportable 2 FAIR, acceptable, adequate, all right, average, O.K. *or* okay (*informal*), passable

tolerance *noun* 1 BROAD-MINDEDNESS, forbearance, indulgence, open-mindedness, permissiveness 2 ENDURANCE, fortitude, hardiness, resilience, resistance, stamina, staying power, toughness

tolerant *adjective* BROAD-MINDED, catholic, forbearing, liberal, long-suffering, open-minded, understanding, unprejudiced

tolerate *verb* ALLOW, accept, brook, condone, endure, permit, put up with (*informal*), stand, stomach, take

toleration *noun* ACCEPTANCE, allowance, endurance, indulgence, permissiveness, sanction

toll¹ *verb* 1 RING, chime, clang, knell, peal, sound, strike ▶*noun* 2 RINGING, chime, clang, knell, peal

toll² *noun* 1 CHARGE, duty, fee, levy, payment, tariff, tax 2 DAMAGE, cost, loss, penalty

tomb *noun* GRAVE, catacomb, crypt, mausoleum, sarcophagus, sepulcher, vault

tombstone *noun* GRAVESTONE, headstone, marker, memorial, monument

tomfoolery *noun* FOOLISHNESS, buffoonery, clowning, fooling around (*informal*), horseplay, shenanigans (*informal*), silliness, skylarking (*informal*), stupidity

ton *noun* (*often plural*) *Informal* A LOT, great deal, ocean, quantity, stacks

tone *noun* 1 PITCH, inflection, intonation, modulation, timbre 2 CHARACTER, air, attitude, feel, manner, mood, spirit, style, temper 3 COLOR, hue, shade, tinge, tint ▶*verb* 4 HARMONIZE, blend, go well with, match, suit

tone down *verb* MODERATE, play down, reduce, restrain, soften, subdue, temper

tongue *noun* LANGUAGE, dialect, parlance, speech

tonic *noun* STIMULANT, boost, pick-me-up (*informal*), restorative, shot in the arm (*informal*)

too *adverb* 1 ALSO, as well, besides, further, in addition, likewise, moreover, to boot 2 EXCESSIVELY, extremely, immoderately, inordinately, overly, unduly, unreasonably, very

tool *noun* 1 IMPLEMENT, appliance, contraption, contrivance, device, gadget, instrument, machine, utensil 2 PUPPET, cat's-paw, creature, flunkey, hireling, lackey, minion, pawn, stooge (*slang*)

top *noun* 1 PEAK, apex, crest, crown, culmination, head, height, pinnacle, summit, zenith 2 FIRST PLACE, head, lead 3 LID, cap, cover, stopper ▶*adjective* 4 LEADING, best, chief, elite, finest, first, foremost, head, highest, pre-eminent, principal, uppermost ▶*verb* 5 COVER, cap, crown, finish, garnish 6 LEAD, be first, head 7 SURPASS, beat, best, better, eclipse, exceed, excel, outstrip, transcend

topic *noun* SUBJECT, issue, matter, point, question, subject matter, theme

topical *adjective* CURRENT, contemporary, newsworthy, popular, up-to-date, up-to-the-minute

topmost *adjective* HIGHEST, dominant, foremost, leading, paramount, principal, supreme, top, uppermost

topple *verb* 1 FALL OVER, collapse, fall, keel over, overbalance, overturn, totter, tumble 2 OVERTHROW, bring down, bring low, oust, overturn, unseat

topsy-turvy *adjective* CONFUSED, chaotic, disorderly, disorganized, inside-out, jumbled, messy, mixed-up, upside-down

torment *verb* 1 TORTURE, crucify, distress, rack 2 TEASE, annoy, bother, harass, hassle (*informal*), irritate, nag, pester, vex ▸ *noun* 3 SUFFERING, agony, anguish, distress, hell, misery, pain, torture

torn *adjective* 1 CUT, lacerated, ragged, rent, ripped, slit, split 2 UNDECIDED, in two minds (*informal*), irresolute, uncertain, unsure, vacillating, wavering

tornado *noun* WHIRLWIND, cyclone, gale, hurricane, squall, storm, tempest, typhoon

torpor *noun* INACTIVITY, apathy, drowsiness, indolence, laziness, lethargy, listlessness, sloth, sluggishness

torrent *noun* STREAM, cascade, deluge, downpour, flood, flow, rush, spate, tide

torrid *adjective* 1 ARID, dried, parched, scorched 2 PASSIONATE, ardent, fervent, intense, steamy (*informal*)

tortuous *adjective* 1 WINDING, circuitous, convoluted, indirect, mazy, meandering, serpentine, sinuous, twisting, twisty 2 COMPLICATED, ambiguous, convoluted, devious, indirect, involved, roundabout, tricky

torture *verb* 1 TORMENT, afflict, crucify, distress, persecute, put on the rack, rack ▸ *noun* 2 AGONY, anguish, distress, pain, persecution, suffering, torment

toss *verb* 1 THROW, cast, fling, flip, hurl, launch, lob (*informal*), pitch, sling 2 THRASH, rock, roll, shake, wriggle, writhe ▸ *noun* 3 THROW, lob (*informal*), pitch

tot *noun* INFANT, baby, child, mite, toddler

total *noun* 1 WHOLE, aggregate, entirety, full amount, sum, totality ▸ *adjective* 2 COMPLETE, absolute, comprehensive, entire, full, gross, thoroughgoing, undivided, utter, whole ▸ *verb* 3 AMOUNT TO, come to, mount up to, reach 4 ADD UP, reckon, tot up

totalitarian *adjective* DICTATORIAL, authoritarian, despotic, oppressive, tyrannous, undemocratic

totality *noun* WHOLE, aggregate, entirety, sum, total

totally *adverb* COMPLETELY, absolutely, comprehensively, entirely, fully, one hundred per cent, thoroughly, utterly, wholly

totter *verb* STAGGER, falter, lurch,

reel, stumble, sway

touch verb 1 HANDLE, brush, caress, contact, feel, finger, fondle, stroke, tap 2 MEET, abut, adjoin, be in contact, border, contact, graze, impinge upon 3 AFFECT, disturb, impress, influence, inspire, move, stir 4 EAT, chow down (*slang*), consume, drink, partake of 5 MATCH, compare with, equal, hold a candle to (*informal*), parallel, rival 6 **touch on** REFER TO, allude to, bring in, cover, deal with, mention, speak of ▶ *noun* 7 FEELING, handling, physical contact 8 TAP, brush, contact, pat, stroke 9 BIT, dash, drop, jot, small amount, smattering, soupçon, spot, trace 10 STYLE, manner, method, technique, trademark, way

touch and go adjective RISKY, close, critical, near, nerve-racking, precarious

touching adjective MOVING, affecting, emotive, pathetic, pitiable, poignant, sad, stirring

touchstone noun STANDARD, criterion, gauge, measure, norm, par, yardstick

touchy adjective OVERSENSITIVE, irascible, irritable, querulous, quick-tempered, testy, tetchy, thin-skinned

tough adjective 1 RESILIENT, durable, hard, inflexible, leathery, resistant, rugged, solid, strong, sturdy 2 STRONG, hardy, seasoned, stout, strapping, sturdy, vigorous 3 ROUGH, hard-boiled, pugnacious, ruthless, violent 4 STRICT, firm, hard, merciless, resolute, severe, stern,

unbending 5 DIFFICULT, arduous, exacting, hard, laborious, strenuous, troublesome, uphill 6 *Informal* UNLUCKY, lamentable, regrettable, unfortunate ▶ *noun*

tour noun 1 JOURNEY, excursion, expedition, jaunt, outing, trip ▶ *verb* 2 VISIT, explore, go round, journey, sightsee, travel through

tourist noun TRAVELER, excursionist, globetrotter, holiday-maker, sightseer, tripper, voyager

tournament noun COMPETITION, contest, event, meeting, series

tow verb DRAG, draw, haul, lug, pull, tug

towards preposition 1 IN THE DIRECTION OF, en route for, for, on the way to, to 2 REGARDING, about, concerning, for, with regard to, with respect to

tower noun COLUMN, belfry, obelisk, pillar, skyscraper, steeple, turret

towering adjective HIGH, colossal, elevated, imposing, impressive, lofty, magnificent, soaring, tall

toxic adjective POISONOUS, deadly, harmful, lethal, noxious, pernicious, pestilential, septic

toy noun 1 PLAYTHING, doll, game ▶ *verb* 2 PLAY, amuse oneself, dally, fiddle (*informal*), fool (about or around), trifle

trace verb 1 FIND, detect, discover, ferret out, hunt down, track, unearth 2 COPY, draw, outline, sketch ▶ *noun* 3 TRACK, footmark, footprint, footstep, path, spoor, trail 4 BIT, drop, hint, shadow, suggestion, suspicion, tinge, touch, whiff **5** INDICATION, evidence, mark, record, remnant, sign, survival, vestige

track noun **1** PATH, course, line, orbit, pathway, road, trajectory, way **2** TRAIL, footmark, footprint, footstep, mark, path, spoor, trace, wake **3** LINE, permanent way, rails ▶verb **4** FOLLOW, chase, hunt down, pursue, shadow, stalk, tail (informal), trace, trail

track down verb FIND, dig up, discover, hunt down, run to earth or ground, sniff out, trace, unearth

tract[1] noun AREA, district, expanse, extent, plot, region, stretch, territory

tract[2] noun TREATISE, booklet, dissertation, essay, homily, monograph, pamphlet

tractable adjective MANAGEABLE, amenable, biddable, compliant, docile, obedient, submissive, tame, willing, yielding

traction noun GRIP, friction, pull, purchase, resistance

trade noun **1** COMMERCE, barter, business, dealing, exchange, traffic, transactions, truck **2** JOB, business, craft, employment, line of work, métier, occupation, profession ▶verb **3** DEAL, bargain, do business, have dealings, peddle, traffic, transact, truck **4** EXCHANGE, barter, swap, switch

trader noun DEALER, merchant, purveyor, seller, supplier

tradesman noun **1** CRAFTSMAN, artisan, journeyman, workman **2** SHOPKEEPER, dealer, merchant,

purveyor, retailer, seller, supplier

tradition noun CUSTOM, convention, folklore, habit, institution, lore, ritual

traditional adjective CUSTOMARY, accustomed, conventional, established, old, time-honored, usual

traffic noun **1** TRANSPORT, freight, transportation, vehicles **2** TRADE, business, commerce, dealings, exchange, peddling, truck ▶verb **3** TRADE, bargain, deal, do business, exchange, have dealings, peddle

tragedy noun DISASTER, adversity, calamity, catastrophe, misfortune

tragic adjective DISASTROUS, appalling, calamitous, catastrophic, deadly, dire, dreadful, miserable, pathetic, sad, unfortunate

trail noun **1** PATH, footpath, road, route, track, way **2** TRACKS, footprints, marks, path, scent, spoor, trace, wake ▶verb **3** DRAG, dangle, draw, haul, pull, tow **4** LAG, dawdle, follow, hang back, linger, loiter, straggle, traipse (informal) **5** FOLLOW, chase, hunt, pursue, shadow, stalk, tail (informal), trace, track

train verb **1** INSTRUCT, coach, drill, educate, guide, prepare, school, teach, tutor **2** EXERCISE, prepare, work out **3** AIM, direct, focus, level, point ▶noun **4** SEQUENCE, chain, progression, series, set, string, succession

trainer noun COACH, handler

training noun **1** INSTRUCTION, coaching, discipline, education, grounding, schooling, teaching, tuition 2 EXERCISE, practice, preparation, working out

traipse verb TRUDGE, drag oneself, footslog, slouch, trail, tramp

trait noun CHARACTERISTIC, attribute, feature, idiosyncrasy, mannerism, peculiarity, quality, quirk

traitor noun BETRAYER, apostate, back-stabber, defector, deserter, Judas, quisling, rebel, renegade, turncoat

trajectory noun PATH, course, flight path, line, route, track

tramp verb 1 HIKE, footslog, march, ramble, roam, rove, slog, trek, walk 2 TRUDGE, plod, stump, toil, traipse (informal) ▶ noun 3 VAGRANT, derelict, down-and-out, drifter 4 HIKE, march, ramble, slog, trek 5 TREAD, footfall, footstep, stamp

trample verb CRUSH, flatten, run over, squash, stamp, tread, walk over

trance noun DAZE, abstraction, dream, rapture, reverie, stupor, unconsciousness

tranquil adjective CALM, peaceful, placid, quiet, restful, sedate, serene, still, undisturbed

tranquilize verb CALM, lull, pacify, quell, quiet, relax, sedate, settle one's nerves, soothe

tranquilizer noun SEDATIVE, barbiturate, bromide, downer (slang), opiate

tranquillity noun CALM, hush, peace, placidity, quiet, repose, rest, serenity, stillness

transaction noun DEAL, bargain, business, enterprise, negotiation, undertaking

transcend verb SURPASS, eclipse, exceed, excel, go beyond, outdo, outstrip, rise above

transcendent adjective UNPARALLELED, consummate, incomparable, matchless, pre-eminent, sublime, unequaled, unrivaled

transcribe verb WRITE OUT, copy out, reproduce, take down, transfer

transcript noun COPY, duplicate, manuscript, record, reproduction, transcription

transfer verb 1 MOVE, change, convey, hand over, pass on, relocate, shift, transplant, transport, transpose ▶ noun 2 MOVE, change, handover, relocation, shift, transference, translation, transmission, transposition

transfix verb 1 STUN, engross, fascinate, hold, hypnotize, mesmerize, paralyze 2 PIERCE, impale, puncture, run through, skewer, spear

transform verb CHANGE, alter, convert, remodel, revolutionize, transmute

transformation noun CHANGE, alteration, conversion, metamorphosis, revolution, sea change, transmutation

transgress verb OFFEND, break the law, contravene, disobey, encroach, infringe, sin, trespass, violate

transgression noun OFFENSE, contravention, crime, encroachment, infraction, infringement, misdeed, misdemeanor, sin, trespass, violation, wrongdoing

transgressor noun OFFENDER, criminal, culprit, lawbreaker, miscreant, sinner, trespasser, villain, wrongdoer

transient adjective TEMPORARY, brief, ephemeral, fleeting, impermanent, momentary, passing, short-lived, transitory

transit noun MOVEMENT, carriage, conveyance, crossing, passage, transfer, transport, transportation

transition noun CHANGE, alteration, conversion, development, metamorphosis, passing, progression, shift, transmutation

transitional adjective CHANGING, developmental, fluid, intermediate, passing, provisional, temporary, unsettled

transitory adjective SHORT-LIVED, brief, ephemeral, fleeting, impermanent, momentary, passing, short, temporary, transient

translate verb INTERPRET, construe, convert, decipher, decode, paraphrase, render

translation noun INTERPRETATION, decoding, paraphrase, rendering, rendition, version

transmission noun 1 TRANSFER, conveyance, dissemination, sending, shipment, spread, transference 2 BROADCASTING, dissemination, putting out, relaying, sending, showing 3 PROGRAM, broadcast, show

transmit verb 1 PASS ON, bear, carry, convey, disseminate, hand on, impart, send, spread, transfer 2 BROADCAST,

disseminate, radio, relay, send out

transparency noun 1 CLARITY, clearness, limpidity, pellucidness, translucence 2 PHOTOGRAPH, slide

transparent adjective 1 CLEAR, crystalline, diaphanous, limpid, lucid, see-through, sheer, translucent 2 PLAIN, evident, explicit, manifest, obvious, patent, recognizable, unambiguous, undisguised

transpire verb 1 EMERGE, become known, come out, come to light 2 Informal HAPPEN, arise, befall, chance, come about, occur, take place

transplant verb TRANSFER, displace, relocate, remove, resettle, shift, uproot

transport verb 1 CONVEY, bear, bring, carry, haul, move, take, transfer 2 EXILE, banish, deport 3 ENRAPTURE, captivate, delight, enchant, entrance, move, ravish ▶noun 4 VEHICLE, conveyance, transportation 5 TRANSFERENCE, conveyance, shipment, transportation 6 ECSTASY, bliss, delight, enchantment, euphoria, heaven, rapture, ravishment

transpose verb INTERCHANGE, alter, change, exchange, move, reorder, shift, substitute, swap, switch, transfer

trap noun 1 SNARE, ambush, gin, net, noose, pitfall 2 TRICK, ambush, deception, ruse, stratagem, subterfuge, wile ▶verb 3 CATCH, corner, enmesh, ensnare, entrap, snare, take 4 TRICK, ambush, beguile, deceive, dupe, ensnare, inveigle

trappings *plural noun*
ACCESSORIES, accouterments, equipment, finery, furnishings, gear, panoply, paraphernalia, things, trimmings

trash *noun* 1 NONSENSE, drivel, hogwash, moonshine, rot, rubbish, tripe (*informal*), twaddle 2 LITTER, dross, garbage, junk (*informal*), refuse, rubbish, waste ▶ *verb* 3 DESTROY, defeat, demolish, put paid to, ruin, torpedo, trounce, wreck

trashy *adjective* WORTHLESS, cheap, inferior, rubbishy, shabby, shoddy, tawdry

trauma *noun* SUFFERING, agony, anguish, hurt, ordeal, pain, shock, torture

traumatic *adjective* SHOCKING, agonizing, damaging, disturbing, hurtful, injurious, painful, scarring, upsetting, wounding

travel *verb* 1 GO, journey, move, progress, roam, tour, trek, voyage, wander ▶ *noun* 2 (usually *plural*) WANDERING, excursion, expedition, globetrotting, journey, tour, trip, voyage

traveler *noun* WANDERER, explorer, globetrotter, gypsy, holiday-maker, tourist, voyager, wayfarer

traveling *adjective* MOBILE, itinerant, migrant, nomadic, peripatetic, roaming, roving, touring, wandering, wayfaring

traverse *verb* CROSS, go over, span, travel over

travesty *noun* 1 MOCKERY, burlesque, caricature, distortion, lampoon, parody, perversion ▶ *verb* 2 MOCK, burlesque, caricature, distort, lampoon, make a mockery of, parody, ridicule

treacherous *adjective* 1 DISLOYAL, deceitful, double-dealing, duplicitous, faithless, false, perfidious, traitorous, unfaithful, untrustworthy 2 DANGEROUS, deceptive, hazardous, icy, perilous, precarious, risky, slippery, unreliable, unsafe, unstable

treachery *noun* BETRAYAL, disloyalty, double-dealing, duplicity, faithlessness, infidelity, perfidy, treason

tread *verb* 1 STEP, hike, march, pace, stamp, stride, walk 2 TRAMPLE, crush underfoot, squash ▶ *noun* 3 STEP, footfall, footstep, gait, pace, stride, walk

treason *noun* DISLOYALTY, duplicity, lese-majesty, mutiny, perfidy, sedition, traitorousness, treachery

treasonable *adjective* DISLOYAL, mutinous, perfidious, seditious, subversive, traitorous, treacherous

treasure *noun* 1 RICHES, cash, fortune, gold, jewels, money, valuables, wealth 2 DARLING, apple of one's eye, gem, jewel, nonpareil, paragon, pride and joy ▶ *verb* 3 PRIZE, adore, cherish, esteem, hold dear, idolize, love, revere, value

treasury *noun* STOREHOUSE, bank, cache, hoard, repository, store, vault

treat *verb* 1 HANDLE, act towards, behave towards, consider, deal with, look upon, manage, regard, use 2 ATTEND

TO, care for, nurse **3** ENTERTAIN, lay on, provide, regale, stand (*informal*) ▶*noun* **4** ENTERTAINMENT, banquet, celebration, feast, gift, party, refreshment **5** PLEASURE, delight, enjoyment, fun, joy, satisfaction, surprise, thrill

treatise *noun* ESSAY, dissertation, monograph, pamphlet, paper, study, thesis, tract, work

treatment *noun* **1** CARE, cure, healing, medication, medicine, remedy, surgery, therapy **2** HANDLING, action, behavior, conduct, dealing, management, manipulation

treaty *noun* PACT, agreement, alliance, compact, concordat, contract, convention, covenant, entente

trek *noun* **1** JOURNEY, expedition, hike, march, odyssey, safari, slog, tramp ▶*verb* **2** JOURNEY, footslog, hike, march, rove, slog, traipse (*informal*), tramp, trudge

tremble *verb* **1** SHAKE, quake, quiver, shiver, shudder, totter, vibrate, wobble ▶*noun* **2** SHAKE, quake, quiver, shiver, shudder, tremor, vibration, wobble

tremendous *adjective* **1** HUGE, colossal, enormous, formidable, gigantic, great, immense, stupendous, terrific **2** *Informal* EXCELLENT, amazing, brilliant, exceptional, extraordinary, fantastic (*informal*), great, marvelous, sensational (*informal*), wonderful

tremor *noun* **1** SHAKE, quaking, quaver, quiver, shiver, trembling, wobble **2** EARTHQUAKE, quake (*informal*),

shock

trench *noun* DITCH, channel, drain, excavation, furrow, gutter, trough

trenchant *adjective* **1** INCISIVE, acerbic, caustic, cutting, penetrating, pointed, pungent, scathing **2** EFFECTIVE, energetic, forceful, potent, powerful, strong, vigorous

trend *noun* **1** TENDENCY, bias, current, direction, drift, flow, inclination, leaning **2** FASHION, craze, fad (*informal*), mode, rage, style, thing, vogue

trendy *adjective* Informal FASHIONABLE, cool (*informal*), in fashion, in vogue, modish, phat (*slang*), stylish, voguish, with it (*informal*)

trepidation *noun* ANXIETY, alarm, apprehension, consternation, disquiet, dread, fear, nervousness, uneasiness, worry

trespass *verb* **1** INTRUDE, encroach, infringe, invade, obtrude ▶*noun* **2** INTRUSION, encroachment, infringement, invasion, unlawful entry

trespasser *noun* INTRUDER, interloper, invader, poacher

trial *noun* **1** HEARING, litigation, tribunal **2** TEST, audition, dry run (*informal*), experiment, probation, test-run **3** HARDSHIP, adversity, affliction, distress, ordeal, suffering, tribulation, trouble

tribe *noun* RACE, clan, family, people

tribunal *noun* HEARING, court, trial

tribute *noun* **1** ACCOLADE, commendation, compliment, eulogy, panegyric, recognition, testimonial **2** TAX, charge, homage, payment, ransom

trick noun 1 DECEPTION, fraud, hoax, maneuver, ploy, ruse, stratagem, subterfuge, swindle, trap, wile 2 JOKE, antic, jape, practical joke, prank, stunt 3 SECRET, hang (informal), knack, know-how (informal), skill, technique 4 MANNERISM, characteristic, foible, habit, idiosyncrasy, peculiarity, practice, quirk, trait ▶verb 5 DECEIVE, cheat, con (informal), dupe, fool, hoodwink, kid (informal), mislead, swindle, take in (informal), trap

trickery noun DECEPTION, cheating, chicanery, deceit, dishonesty, guile, monkey business (informal)

trickle verb 1 DRIBBLE, drip, drop, exude, ooze, run, seep, stream ▶noun 2 DRIBBLE, drip, seepage

tricky adjective 1 DIFFICULT, complicated, delicate, knotty, problematic, risky, thorny, ticklish 2 CRAFTY, artful, cunning, deceitful, devious, scheming, slippery, sly, wily

trifle noun 1 KNICK-KNACK, bagatelle, bauble, plaything, toy ▶verb 2 TOY, dally, mess about, play

trifling adjective INSIGNIFICANT, measly, negligible, paltry, trivial, unimportant, worthless

trigger verb SET OFF, activate, cause, generate, produce, prompt, provoke, set in motion, spark off, start

trim adjective 1 NEAT, dapper, shipshape, smart, spruce, tidy, well-groomed 2 SLENDER, fit, shapely, sleek, slim,

streamlined, svelte, willowy ▶verb 3 CUT, clip, crop, even up, pare, prune, shave, tidy 4 DECORATE, adorn, array, beautify, deck out, dress, embellish, ornament ▶noun 5 DECORATION, adornment, border, edging, embellishment, frill, ornamentation, piping, trimming 6 CONDITION, fettle, fitness, health, shape (informal), state 7 CUT, clipping, crop, pruning, shave, shearing, tidying up

trimming noun 1 DECORATION, adornment, border, edging, embellishment, frill, ornamentation, piping 2 **trimmings** EXTRAS, accessories, accompaniments, frills, ornaments, paraphernalia, trappings

trinity noun THREESOME, triad, trio, triumvirate

trinket noun ORNAMENT, bagatelle, bauble, knick-knack, toy, trifle

trio noun THREESOME, triad, trilogy, trinity, triumvirate

trip noun 1 JOURNEY, errand, excursion, expedition, foray, jaunt, outing, run, tour, voyage 2 STUMBLE, fall, misstep, slip ▶verb 3 STUMBLE, fall, lose one's footing, misstep, slip, tumble 4 CATCH OUT, trap 5 SKIP, dance, gambol, hop

triple adjective 1 THREEFOLD, three-way, tripartite ▶verb 2 TREBLE, increase threefold

trite adjective UNORIGINAL, banal, clichéd, commonplace, hackneyed, stale, stereotyped, threadbare, tired

triumph noun 1 JOY, elation,

exultation, happiness,
jubilation, pride, rejoicing
2 SUCCESS, accomplishment,
achievement, attainment,
conquest, coup, feat, victory
▶ *verb* **3** (often with *over*) WIN,
overcome, prevail, prosper,
succeed, vanquish **4** REJOICE,
celebrate, crow, exult, gloat,
glory, revel

triumphant *adjective* VICTORIOUS,
celebratory, conquering,
elated, exultant, jubilant,
proud, successful, winning

trivia *plural noun* MINUTIAE,
details, trifles, trivialities

trivial *adjective* UNIMPORTANT,
incidental, inconsequential,
insignificant, meaningless,
minor, petty, small, trifling,
worthless

triviality *noun* INSIGNIFICANCE,
meaninglessness, pettiness,
unimportance, worthlessness

trivialize *verb* UNDERVALUE,
belittle, laugh off, make light
of, minimize, play down, scoff
at, underestimate, underplay

troop *noun* **1** GROUP, band,
body, company, crowd, horde,
multitude, squad, team, unit
2 troops SOLDIERS, armed
forces, army, men, servicemen,
soldiery ▶ *verb* **3** FLOCK, march,
stream, swarm, throng, traipse
(*informal*)

trophy *noun* PRIZE, award,
booty, cup, laurels, memento,
souvenir, spoils

tropical *adjective* HOT, steamy,
stifling, sultry, sweltering, torrid

trot *verb* **1** RUN, canter, jog,
lope, scamper ▶ *noun* **2** RUN,
canter, jog, lope

trouble *noun* **1** DISTRESS, anxiety,

disquiet, grief, misfortune,
pain, sorrow, torment, woe,
worry **2** DISEASE, ailment,
complaint, defect, disorder,
failure, illness, malfunction
3 DISORDER, agitation, bother
(*informal*), commotion, discord,
disturbance, strife, tumult,
unrest **4** EFFORT, care, exertion,
inconvenience, labor, pains,
thought, work ▶ *verb* **5** WORRY,
bother, disconcert, distress,
disturb, pain, perturb, plague,
sadden, upset **6** TAKE PAINS,
exert oneself, make an effort,
take the time **7** INCONVENIENCE,
bother, burden, disturb,
impose upon, incommode, put
out

troublesome *adjective*
1 WORRYING, annoying,
demanding, difficult,
inconvenient, irksome, taxing,
tricky, trying, vexatious
2 DISORDERLY, rebellious, rowdy,
turbulent, uncooperative,
undisciplined, unruly, violent

trough *noun* **1** MANGER, water
trough **2** CHANNEL, canal,
depression, ditch, duct, furrow,
gully, gutter, trench

trounce *verb* THRASH, beat,
crush, drub, hammer
(*informal*), rout, slaughter
(*informal*), wipe the floor with
(*informal*)

troupe *noun* COMPANY, band, cast

truancy *noun* ABSENCE, absence
without leave, malingering,
shirking

truant *noun* ABSENTEE,
malingerer, runaway, shirker

truce *noun* CEASEFIRE, armistice,
cessation, let-up (*informal*), lull,
moratorium, peace, respite

truculent *adjective* HOSTILE, aggressive, bellicose, belligerent, defiant, ill-tempered, obstreperous, pugnacious

trudge *verb* 1 PLOD, footslog, lumber, slog, stump, traipse (*informal*), tramp, trek ▸*noun* 2 HIKE, footslog, march, slog, traipse (*informal*), tramp, trek

true *adjective* 1 CORRECT, accurate, authentic, factual, genuine, precise, real, right, truthful, veracious 2 FAITHFUL, dedicated, devoted, dutiful, loyal, reliable, staunch, steady, trustworthy 3 EXACT, accurate, on target, perfect, precise, unerring

truism *noun* CLICHÉ, axiom, bromide, commonplace, platitude

truly *adverb* 1 CORRECTLY, authentically, exactly, factually, genuinely, legitimately, precisely, rightly, truthfully 2 FAITHFULLY, devotedly, dutifully, loyally, sincerely, staunchly, steadily 3 REALLY, extremely, greatly, indeed, of course, very

trumpet *noun* 1 HORN, bugle, clarion ▸*verb* 2 PROCLAIM, advertise, announce, broadcast, shout from the rooftops, tout (*informal*)

trump up *verb* FABRICATE, concoct, contrive, cook up (*informal*), create, fake, invent, make up

truncate *verb* SHORTEN, abbreviate, curtail, cut short, dock, lop, pare, prune, trim

truncheon *noun* CLUB, baton, cudgel, staff

trunk *noun* 1 STEM, bole, stalk 2 CHEST, box, case, casket, coffer, crate 3 BODY, torso 4 SNOUT, proboscis

truss *verb* 1 TIE, bind, fasten, make fast, secure, strap, tether ▸*noun* 2 *Medical* SUPPORT, bandage 3 JOIST, beam, brace, buttress, prop, stanchion, stay, strut, support

trust *verb* 1 BELIEVE IN, bank on, count on, depend on, have faith in, rely upon 2 CONSIGN, assign, commit, confide, delegate, entrust, give 3 EXPECT, assume, hope, presume, suppose, surmise ▸*noun* 4 CONFIDENCE, assurance, belief, certainty, conviction, credence, credit, expectation, faith, reliance

trustful, trusting *adjective* UNWARY, credulous, gullible, naive, unsuspecting, unsuspicious

trustworthy *adjective* HONEST, dependable, honorable, principled, reliable, reputable, responsible, staunch, steadfast, trusty

trusty *adjective* FAITHFUL, dependable, reliable, solid, staunch, steady, strong, trustworthy

truth *noun* TRUTHFULNESS, accuracy, exactness, fact, genuineness, legitimacy, precision, reality, validity, veracity

truthful *adjective* HONEST, candid, frank, precise, sincere, straight, true, trustworthy

try *verb* 1 ATTEMPT, aim, endeavor, have a go, make an effort, seek, strive, struggle

2 TEST, appraise, check out, evaluate, examine, investigate, put to the test, sample, taste ▶ *noun* **3** ATTEMPT, crack (*informal*), effort, go (*informal*), shot (*informal*), stab (*informal*), whack (*informal*)

trying *adjective* ANNOYING, bothersome, difficult, exasperating, hard, stressful, taxing, tiresome, tough, wearisome

tubby *adjective* FAT, chubby, corpulent, obese, overweight, plump, portly, stout

tuck *verb* **1** PUSH, fold, gather, insert ▶ *noun* **2** FOLD, gather, pinch, pleat

tuft *noun* CLUMP, bunch, cluster, collection, knot, tussock

tug *verb* **1** PULL, jerk, wrench, yank ▶ *noun* **2** PULL, jerk, yank

tuition *noun* TRAINING, education, instruction, lessons, schooling, teaching, tutelage, tutoring

tumble *verb* **1** FALL, drop, flop, plummet, stumble, topple ▶ *noun* **2** FALL, drop, plunge, spill, stumble, trip

tumbledown *adjective* DILAPIDATED, crumbling, decrepit, ramshackle, rickety, ruined

tumor *noun* GROWTH, cancer, carcinoma (*Pathology*), lump, sarcoma (*Medical*), swelling

tumult *noun* COMMOTION, clamor, din, hubbub, pandemonium, riot, row, turmoil, upheaval, uproar

tumultuous *adjective* WILD, boisterous, excited, noisy, riotous, rowdy, turbulent, unruly, uproarious, wired (*slang*)

tune *noun* **1** MELODY, air, song,

strain, theme **2** PITCH, concord, consonance, euphony, harmony ▶ *verb* **3** ADJUST, adapt, attune, harmonize, pitch, regulate

tuneful *adjective* MELODIOUS, catchy, euphonious, harmonious, mellifluous, melodic, musical, pleasant

tuneless *adjective* DISCORDANT, atonal, cacophonous, dissonant, harsh, unmusical

tunnel *noun* **1** PASSAGE, burrow, channel, hole, passageway, shaft, subway, underpass ▶ *verb* **2** DIG, burrow, excavate, mine, scoop out

turbulence *noun* CONFUSION, agitation, commotion, disorder, instability, tumult, turmoil, unrest, upheaval

turbulent *adjective* AGITATED, blustery, choppy, foaming, furious, raging, rough, tempestuous, tumultuous

turf *noun* **1** GRASS, sod, sward **2 the turf** HORSE-RACING, racing, the flat

turmoil *noun* CONFUSION, agitation, chaos, commotion, disarray, disorder, tumult, upheaval, uproar

turn *verb* **1** CHANGE COURSE, move, shift, swerve, switch, veer, wheel **2** ROTATE, circle, go round, gyrate, pivot, revolve, roll, spin, twist, whirl **3** CHANGE, alter, convert, mold, mutate, remodel, shape, transform **4** SHAPE, fashion, frame, make, mold **5** GO BAD, curdle, sour, spoil, taint ▶ *noun* **6** ROTATION, circle, cycle, gyration, revolution, spin, twist, whirl **7** SHIFT, departure, deviation

8 OPPORTUNITY, chance, crack (*informal*), go, stint, time, try **9** DIRECTION, drift, heading, tendency, trend **10** *As in* **good turn** ACT, action, deed, favor, gesture, service

turncoat *noun* TRAITOR, apostate, backslider, defector, deserter, renegade

turn down *verb* **1** LOWER, lessen, muffle, mute, quieten, soften **2** REFUSE, decline, rebuff, reject, repudiate, spurn

turn in *verb* **1** GO TO BED, go to sleep, hit the sack (*slang*) **2** HAND IN, deliver, give up, hand over, return, submit, surrender, tender

turning *noun* JUNCTION, bend, crossroads, curve, side road, turn, turn-off

turning point *noun* CROSSROADS, change, crisis, crux, moment of truth

turn off *verb* STOP, cut out, put out, shut down, switch off, turn out, unplug

turn on *verb* **1** START, activate, ignite, kick-start, start up, switch on **2** ATTACK, assail, assault, fall on, round on **3** *Informal* EXCITE, arouse, attract, please, stimulate, thrill, titillate

turnout *noun* ATTENDANCE, assembly, audience, congregation, crowd, gate, number, throng

turnover *noun* **1** OUTPUT, business, productivity **2** MOVEMENT, change, coming and going

turn up *verb* **1** ARRIVE, appear, attend, come, put in an appearance, show one's face,

show up (*informal*) **2** FIND, dig up, disclose, discover, expose, reveal, unearth **3** COME TO LIGHT, crop up (*informal*), pop up **4** INCREASE, amplify, boost, enhance, intensify, raise

tussle *noun* **1** FIGHT, battle, brawl, conflict, contest, scrap (*informal*), scuffle, struggle ▶*verb* **2** FIGHT, battle, grapple, scrap (*informal*), scuffle, struggle, vie, wrestle

tutor *noun* **1** TEACHER, coach, educator, guardian, guide, guru, instructor, lecturer, mentor ▶*verb* **2** TEACH, coach, drill, educate, guide, instruct, school, train

twaddle *noun* NONSENSE, claptrap (*informal*), drivel, garbage (*informal*), gobbledegook (*informal*), poppycock (*informal*), rubbish

tweak *verb, noun* TWIST, jerk, pinch, pull, squeeze

twig *noun* BRANCH, shoot, spray, sprig, stick

twilight *noun* DUSK, dimness, evening, gloaming (*Scot. or poetic*), gloom, half-light, sundown, sunset

twin *noun* **1** DOUBLE, clone, counterpart, duplicate, fellow, likeness, lookalike, match, mate ▶*verb* **2** PAIR, couple, join, link, match, yoke

twine *noun* **1** STRING, cord, yarn ▶*verb* **2** COIL, bend, curl, encircle, loop, spiral, twist, wind

twinge *noun* PAIN, pang, prick, spasm, stab, stitch

twinkle *verb* **1** SPARKLE, blink, flash, flicker, gleam, glint, glisten, glitter, shimmer, shine ▶*noun* **2** FLICKER, flash, gleam, glimmer, shimmer, spark, sparkle

twirl verb 1 TURN, pirouette, pivot, revolve, rotate, spin, twist, wheel, whirl, wind ▶ noun 2 TURN, pirouette, revolution, rotation, spin, twist, wheel, whirl

twist verb 1 WIND, coil, curl, screw, spin, swivel, wrap, wring 2 DISTORT, contort, screw up ▶ noun 3 WIND, coil, curl, spin, swivel 4 DEVELOPMENT, change, revelation, slant, surprise, turn, variation 5 CURVE, arc, bend, meander, turn, undulation, zigzag 6 DISTORTION, defect, deformation, flaw, imperfection, kink, warp

twitch verb 1 JERK, flutter, jump, squirm ▶ noun 2 SPASM, flutter, jerk, jump, tic

two-faced adjective HYPOCRITICAL, deceitful, dissembling, duplicitous, false, insincere, treacherous, untrustworthy

tycoon noun MAGNATE, baron, capitalist, fat cat (slang), financier, industrialist, mogul, plutocrat

type noun CATEGORY, class, genre, group, kind, order, sort, species, style, variety

typhoon noun STORM, cyclone, squall, tempest, tornado

typical adjective CHARACTERISTIC, archetypal, average, classic, model, normal, orthodox, representative, standard, stock, usual

typify verb SYMBOLIZE, characterize, embody, epitomize, exemplify, illustrate, personify, represent, sum up

tyrannical adjective OPPRESSIVE, authoritarian, autocratic, cruel, despotic, dictatorial, domineering, high-handed, imperious, overbearing, tyrannous

tyranny noun OPPRESSION, absolutism, authoritarianism, autocracy, cruelty, despotism, dictatorship, high-handedness, imperiousness

tyrant noun DICTATOR, absolutist, authoritarian, autocrat, bully, despot, martinet, oppressor, slave-driver

U u

ubiquitous adjective EVERYWHERE, ever-present, omnipresent, pervasive, universal

ugly adjective 1 UNATTRACTIVE, dumpy (informal), frowzy, hideous, homely (U.S.), ill-favored, plain, unlovely, unprepossessing, unsightly 2 UNPLEASANT, disagreeable, distasteful, horrid, objectionable, shocking, terrible 3 OMINOUS, baleful, dangerous, menacing, sinister

ulcer noun SORE, abscess, boil, gumboil, peptic ulcer, pustule

ulterior adjective HIDDEN, concealed, covert, secret, undisclosed

ultimate adjective 1 FINAL, end, last 2 SUPREME, extreme, greatest, highest, paramount, superlative, utmost

ultimately adverb FINALLY, after all, at last, eventually, in due time, in the end, sooner or later

umpire *noun* 1 REFEREE, arbiter, arbitrator, judge ▶*verb* 2 REFEREE, adjudicate, arbitrate, judge

unabashed *adjective* UNEMBARRASSED, blatant, bold, brazen

unable *adjective* INCAPABLE, impotent, ineffectual, powerless, unfit, unqualified

unabridged *adjective* UNCUT, complete, full-length, unexpurgated, whole

unacceptable *adjective* UNSATISFACTORY, displeasing, objectionable

unaccompanied *adjective* 1 ALONE, by oneself, lone, on one's own, solo, unescorted 2 *Music* A CAPPELLA

unaccountable *adjective* 1 INEXPLICABLE, baffling, mysterious, odd, puzzling, unexplainable, unfathomable 2 NOT ANSWERABLE, exempt, not responsible

unaccustomed *adjective* 1 UNFAMILIAR, new, strange, unwonted 2 **unaccustomed to** NOT USED TO, inexperienced at, unfamiliar with, unused to

unaffected[1] *adjective* NATURAL, artless, genuine, plain, simple, sincere, unpretentious

unaffected[2] *adjective* IMPERVIOUS, proof, unmoved, unresponsive, untouched

unafraid *adjective* FEARLESS, daring, dauntless, intrepid

unalterable *adjective* UNCHANGEABLE, fixed, immutable, permanent

unanimity *noun* AGREEMENT, accord, assent, concord,

concurrence, consensus, harmony, like-mindedness, unison

unanimous *adjective* AGREED, common, concerted, harmonious, in agreement, like-minded, united

unanimously *adverb* WITHOUT EXCEPTION, as one, in concert, of one mind, with one accord

unanswerable *adjective* CONCLUSIVE, absolute, incontestable, incontrovertible, indisputable

unanswered *adjective* UNRESOLVED, disputed, open, undecided

unappetizing *adjective* UNPLEASANT, distasteful, repulsive, scuzzy (*slang*), unappealing, unattractive, unpalatable

unapproachable *adjective* 1 UNFRIENDLY, aloof, chilly, cool, distant, remote, reserved, standoffish 2 INACCESSIBLE, out of reach, remote

unarmed *adjective* DEFENSELESS, exposed, helpless, open, unprotected, weak

unassailable *adjective* IMPREGNABLE, invincible, invulnerable, secure

unassuming *adjective* MODEST, humble, quiet, reserved, retiring, self-effacing, unassertive, unobtrusive, unpretentious

unattached *adjective* 1 FREE, independent 2 SINGLE, available, not spoken for, unengaged, unmarried

unattended *adjective* 1 ABANDONED, unguarded, unwatched 2 ALONE, on one's own, unaccompanied

unauthorized *adjective* ILLEGAL, unlawful, unofficial, unsanctioned

unavoidable *adjective* INEVITABLE, certain, fated, inescapable

unaware *adjective* IGNORANT, oblivious, unconscious, uninformed, unknowing

unawares *adverb* **1** BY SURPRISE, off guard, suddenly, unexpectedly **2** UNKNOWINGLY, accidentally, by accident, inadvertently, unwittingly

unbalanced *adjective* **1** BIASED, one-sided, partial, partisan, prejudiced, unfair **2** SHAKY, lopsided, uneven, unstable, wobbly **3** DERANGED, crazy, demented, disturbed, eccentric, insane, irrational, mad, *non compos mentis*, not all there, unhinged, unstable

unbearable *adjective* INTOLERABLE, insufferable, too much (*informal*), unacceptable

unbeatable *adjective* INVINCIBLE, indomitable

unbeaten *adjective* UNDEFEATED, triumphant, victorious

unbecoming *adjective* **1** UNSIGHTLY, unattractive, unbefitting, unflattering, unsuitable **2** UNSEEMLY, discreditable, improper, offensive

unbelievable *adjective* INCREDIBLE, astonishing, far-fetched, implausible, impossible, improbable, inconceivable, preposterous, unconvincing, unimaginable

unbending *adjective* INFLEXIBLE, firm, intractable, resolute, rigid, severe, strict, stubborn, tough,

uncompromising

unbiased *adjective* FAIR, disinterested, equitable, impartial, just, neutral, objective, unprejudiced

unblemished *adjective* SPOTLESS, flawless, immaculate, impeccable, perfect, pure, untarnished

unborn *adjective* EXPECTED, awaited, embryonic, fetal

unbreakable *adjective* INDESTRUCTIBLE, durable, lasting, rugged, strong

unbridled *adjective* UNRESTRAINED, excessive, intemperate, licentious, riotous, unchecked, unruly, wanton

unbroken *adjective* **1** INTACT, complete, entire, whole **2** CONTINUOUS, constant, incessant, twenty-four-seven (*slang*), uninterrupted

unburden *verb* CONFESS, confide, disclose, get (something) off one's chest (*informal*), reveal

uncalled-for *adjective* UNJUSTIFIED, gratuitous, needless, undeserved, unnecessary, unwarranted

uncanny *adjective* **1** WEIRD, mysterious, strange, supernatural, unearthly, unnatural **2** EXTRAORDINARY, astounding, exceptional, incredible, miraculous, unusual, remarkable, unusual

unceasing *adjective* CONTINUAL, constant, continuous, endless, incessant, nonstop, perpetual, twenty-four-seven (*slang*)

uncertain *adjective* **1** UNPREDICTABLE, doubtful, indefinite, questionable, risky, speculative **2** UNSURE, dubious, hazy, irresolute, unclear, unconfirmed, undecided, vague

uncertainty noun DOUBT, ambiguity, confusion, dubiety, hesitancy, indecision, unpredictability

unchangeable adjective UNALTERABLE, constant, fixed, immutable, invariable, irreversible, permanent, stable

unchanging adjective CONSTANT, continuing, enduring, eternal, immutable, lasting, permanent, perpetual, twenty-four-seven (slang), unvarying

uncharitable adjective UNKIND, cruel, hardhearted, unfeeling, ungenerous

uncharted adjective UNEXPLORED, strange, undiscovered, unfamiliar, unknown

uncivil adjective IMPOLITE, bad-mannered, discourteous, ill-mannered, rude, unmannerly

uncivilized adjective 1 PRIMITIVE, barbarian, savage, wild 2 UNCOUTH, boorish, coarse, philistine, uncultivated, uneducated

unclean adjective DIRTY, corrupt, defiled, evil, filthy, foul, impure, polluted, scuzzy (slang), soiled, stained

unclear adjective 1 INDISTINCT, blurred, dim, faint, fuzzy, hazy, obscure, shadowy, undefined, vague 2 DOUBTFUL, ambiguous, indefinite, indeterminate, vague

uncomfortable adjective 1 AWKWARD, cramped, painful, rough 2 UNEASY, awkward, discomfited, disturbed, embarrassed, troubled

uncommitted adjective UNINVOLVED, floating, free, neutral, nonaligned, not involved, unattached

uncommon adjective 1 RARE, infrequent, novel, odd, peculiar, queer, scarce, strange, unusual 2 EXTRAORDINARY, distinctive, exceptional, notable, outstanding, remarkable, special

uncommonly adverb 1 RARELY, hardly ever, infrequently, occasionally, seldom 2 EXCEPTIONALLY, particularly, very

uncommunicative adjective RETICENT, close, reserved, secretive, silent, taciturn, tight-lipped, unforthcoming

uncompromising adjective INFLEXIBLE, firm, inexorable, intransigent, rigid, strict, tough, unbending

unconcern noun INDIFFERENCE, aloofness, apathy, detachment, lack of interest, nonchalance

unconcerned adjective INDIFFERENT, aloof, apathetic, cool, detached, dispassionate, distant, uninterested, unmoved

unconditional adjective ABSOLUTE, complete, entire, full, outright, positive, total, unlimited, unqualified, unreserved

unconnected adjective 1 SEPARATE, detached, divided 2 MEANINGLESS, disjointed, illogical, incoherent, irrelevant

unconscious adjective 1 SENSELESS, insensible, knocked out, out, out cold, stunned 2 UNAWARE, ignorant, oblivious, unknowing 3 UNINTENTIONAL, accidental, inadvertent, unwitting

uncontrollable adjective WILD,

frantic, furious, mad, strong, unruly, violent

uncontrolled *adjective*
UNRESTRAINED, rampant, riotous, unbridled, unchecked, undisciplined

unconventional *adjective*
UNUSUAL, eccentric, individual, irregular, nonconformist, odd, offbeat, original, outré, unorthodox

unconvincing *adjective*
IMPLAUSIBLE, dubious, feeble, flimsy, improbable, lame, questionable, suspect, thin, unlikely, weak

uncooperative *adjective*
UNHELPFUL, awkward, difficult, disobliging, obstructive

uncoordinated *adjective* CLUMSY, awkward, bungling, graceless, lumbering, maladroit, ungainly, ungraceful

uncouth *adjective* COARSE, boorish, crude, graceless, ill-mannered, loutish, oafish, rough, rude, vulgar

uncover *verb* 1 REVEAL, disclose, divulge, expose, make known 2 OPEN, bare, show, strip, unwrap

uncritical *adjective*
UNDISCRIMINATING, indiscriminate, undiscerning

undecided *adjective* 1 UNSURE, dithering, hesitant, in two minds, irresolute, torn, uncertain 2 UNSETTLED, debatable, iffy (*informal*), indefinite, moot, open, unconcluded, undetermined

undefined *adjective*
1 UNSPECIFIED, imprecise, inexact, unclear 2 INDISTINCT, formless, indefinite, vague

undeniable *adjective* CERTAIN, clear, incontrovertible, indisputable, obvious, sure, unquestionable

under *preposition* 1 BELOW, beneath, underneath 2 SUBJECT TO, governed by, secondary to, subordinate to ▸ *adverb* 3 BELOW, beneath, down, lower

underclothes *plural noun*
UNDERWEAR, lingerie, undergarments, undies (*informal*)

undercover *adjective* SECRET, concealed, covert, hidden, private

undercurrent *noun* 1 UNDERTOW, riptide 2 UNDERTONE, atmosphere, feeling, hint, overtone, sense, suggestion, tendency, tinge, vibes (*slang*)

underdog *noun* OUTSIDER, little fellow (*informal*)

underestimate *verb* UNDERRATE, belittle, minimize, miscalculate, undervalue

undergo *verb* EXPERIENCE, bear, endure, go through, stand, suffer, sustain

underground *adjective*
1 SUBTERRANEAN, buried, covered 2 SECRET, clandestine, covert, hidden ▸ *noun* 3 **the underground** THE RESISTANCE, partisans

undergrowth *noun* SCRUB, bracken, briars, brush, underbrush

underhand, underhanded *adjective* SLY, crafty, deceitful, devious, dishonest, down and dirty (*informal*), furtive, secret, sneaky, stealthy

underline *verb* 1 UNDERSCORE, mark 2 EMPHASIZE, accentuate, highlight, stress

underlying *adjective*
FUNDAMENTAL, basic, elementary,
intrinsic, primary, prime

undermine *verb* WEAKEN, disable,
sabotage, sap, subvert

underprivileged *adjective*
DISADVANTAGED, deprived,
destitute, impoverished, needy,
poor

underrate *verb* UNDERESTIMATE,
belittle, discount, undervalue

undersized *adjective* STUNTED,
dwarfish, miniature, pygmy *or*
pigmy, small

understand *verb* 1 COMPREHEND,
conceive, fathom, follow, get,
grasp, perceive, realize, see,
take in 2 BELIEVE, assume,
gather, presume, suppose, think

understandable *adjective*
REASONABLE, justifiable,
legitimate, natural, to be
expected

understanding *noun*
1 PERCEPTION, appreciation,
awareness, comprehension,
discernment, grasp, insight,
judgment, knowledge, sense
2 INTERPRETATION, belief, idea,
judgment, notion, opinion,
perception, view 3 AGREEMENT,
accord, pact ▶ *adjective*
4 SYMPATHETIC, compassionate,
considerate, kind, patient,
sensitive, tolerant

understood *adjective* 1 IMPLIED,
implicit, inferred, tacit,
unspoken, unstated 2 ASSUMED,
accepted, taken for granted

understudy *noun* STAND-IN,
replacement, reserve, substitute

undertake *verb* AGREE, bargain,
contract, engage, guarantee,
pledge, promise

undertaking *noun* 1 TASK, affair,
attempt, business, effort,
endeavor, enterprise,
operation, project, venture
2 PROMISE, assurance,
commitment, pledge, vow,
word

undertone *noun* 1 MURMUR,
whisper 2 UNDERCURRENT, hint,
suggestion, tinge, touch, trace

undervalue *verb* UNDERRATE,
depreciate, hold cheap,
minimize, misjudge,
underestimate

underwater *adjective* SUBMERGED,
submarine, sunken

under way *adjective* BEGUN,
going on, in progress, started

underwear *noun* UNDERCLOTHES,
lingerie, undergarments,
underthings, undies (*informal*)

underweight *adjective* SKINNY,
emaciated, half-starved, puny,
skin and bone (*informal*),
undernourished, undersized

underworld *noun* 1 CRIMINALS,
gangland (*informal*), gangsters,
organized crime 2 NETHER
WORLD, Hades, nether regions

underwrite *verb* 1 FINANCE,
back, fund, guarantee, insure,
sponsor, subsidize 2 SIGN,
endorse, initial

undesirable *adjective*
OBJECTIONABLE, disagreeable,
distasteful, unacceptable,
unattractive, unsuitable,
unwanted, unwelcome

undeveloped *adjective*
POTENTIAL, immature, latent

undignified *adjective* UNSEEMLY,
improper, indecorous,
inelegant, unbecoming,
unsuitable

undisciplined *adjective*

UNCONTROLLED, obstreperous, unrestrained, unruly, wayward, wild, willful

undisguised *adjective* OBVIOUS, blatant, evident, explicit, open, overt, patent, unconcealed

undisputed *adjective* ACKNOWLEDGED, accepted, certain, indisputable, recognized, unchallenged, undeniable, undoubted

undistinguished *adjective* ORDINARY, everyday, mediocre, unexceptional, unimpressive, unremarkable

undisturbed *adjective* 1 QUIET, tranquil 2 CALM, collected, composed, placid, sedate, serene, tranquil, unfazed (*informal*), unperturbed, untroubled

undivided *adjective* COMPLETE, entire, exclusive, full, solid, thorough, undistracted, united, whole

undo *verb* 1 OPEN, disentangle, loose, unbutton, unfasten, untie 2 REVERSE, annul, cancel, invalidate, neutralize, offset 3 RUIN, defeat, destroy, overturn, quash, shatter, subvert, undermine, upset, wreck

undoing *noun* DOWNFALL, collapse, defeat, disgrace, overthrow, reversal, ruin, shame

undone *adjective* UNFINISHED, left, neglected, omitted, unfulfilled, unperformed

undoubted *adjective* CERTAIN, acknowledged, definite, indisputable, indubitable, sure, undisputed, unquestioned

undoubtedly *adverb* CERTAINLY, assuredly, definitely, doubtless,

surely, without doubt

undress *verb* 1 STRIP, disrobe, shed, take off one's clothes ▶*noun* 2 NAKEDNESS, nudity

undue *adjective* EXCESSIVE, extreme, improper, needless, uncalled-for, unnecessary, unwarranted

unduly *adverb* EXCESSIVELY, overly, unnecessarily, unreasonably

undying *adjective* ETERNAL, constant, deathless, everlasting, infinite, permanent, perpetual, twenty-four-seven (*slang*), unending

unearth *verb* 1 DISCOVER, expose, find, reveal, uncover 2 DIG UP, dredge up, excavate, exhume

unearthly *adjective* EERIE, ghostly, phantom, spectral, spooky (*informal*), strange, supernatural, uncanny, weird

uneasiness *noun* ANXIETY, disquiet, doubt, misgiving, qualms, trepidation, worry

uneasy *adjective* 1 ANXIOUS, disturbed, edgy, nervous, on edge, perturbed, troubled, twitchy (*informal*), uncomfortable, wired (*slang*), worried 2 AWKWARD, insecure, precarious, shaky, strained, tense, uncomfortable

uneconomic *adjective* UNPROFITABLE, loss-making, nonpaying

uneducated *adjective* 1 IGNORANT, illiterate, unlettered, unschooled, untaught 2 LOWBROW, uncultivated, uncultured

unemotional *adjective* IMPASSIVE, apathetic, cold, cool, phlegmatic, reserved, undemonstrative, unexcitable

unemployed *adjective* OUT OF WORK, idle, jobless, laid off, redundant

unending *adjective* PERPETUAL, continual, endless, eternal, everlasting, interminable, unceasing

unendurable *adjective* UNBEARABLE, insufferable, insupportable, intolerable

unenthusiastic *adjective* INDIFFERENT, apathetic, half-hearted, nonchalant

unenviable *adjective* UNPLEASANT, disagreeable, uncomfortable, undesirable

unequal *adjective* 1 DIFFERENT, differing, disparate, dissimilar, unlike, unmatched, varying 2 DISPROPORTIONATE, asymmetrical, ill-matched, irregular, unbalanced, uneven

unequaled *adjective* INCOMPARABLE, matchless, paramount, peerless, supreme, unparalleled, unrivaled

unequivocal *adjective* CLEAR, absolute, certain, definite, explicit, incontrovertible, indubitable, manifest, plain, unambiguous

unerring *adjective* ACCURATE, exact, infallible, perfect, sure, unfailing

unethical *adjective* DISHONEST, disreputable, illegal, immoral, improper, shady (*informal*), unprincipled, unscrupulous, wrong

uneven *adjective* 1 ROUGH, bumpy 2 VARIABLE, broken, fitful, irregular, jerky, patchy, spasmodic 3 UNBALANCED, lopsided, odd 4 UNEQUAL,

ill-matched, unfair

uneventful *adjective* HUMDRUM, boring, dull, ho-hum (*informal*), monotonous, routine, tedious, unexciting

unexceptional *adjective* ORDINARY, commonplace, conventional, mediocre, normal, pedestrian, undistinguished, unremarkable

unexpected *adjective* UNFORESEEN, abrupt, chance, fortuitous, sudden, surprising, unanticipated, unlooked-for, unpredictable

unfailing *adjective* 1 CONTINUOUS, boundless, endless, persistent, unflagging 2 RELIABLE, certain, dependable, faithful, loyal, staunch, sure, true

unfair *adjective* 1 BIASED, bigoted, one-sided, partial, partisan, prejudiced, unjust 2 UNSCRUPULOUS, dishonest, unethical, unsporting, wrongful

unfaithful *adjective* 1 FAITHLESS, adulterous, two-timing (*informal*), untrue 2 DISLOYAL, deceitful, faithless, false, traitorous, treacherous, untrustworthy

unfamiliar *adjective* STRANGE, alien, different, new, novel, unknown, unusual

unfashionable *adjective* PASSÉ, antiquated, dated, dumpy (*informal*), frowzy, homely (*U.S.*), obsolete, old-fashioned, old hat

unfasten *verb* UNDO, detach, let go, loosen, open, separate, unlace, untie

unfathomable *adjective* 1 BAFFLING, deep, impenetrable, incomprehensible, indecipherable, inexplicable, profound **2** IMMEASURABLE, bottomless, unmeasured

unfavorable *adjective* **1** ADVERSE, contrary, inauspicious, unfortunate, unlucky, unpropitious **2** HOSTILE, inimical, negative, unfriendly

unfeeling *adjective* **1** HARDHEARTED, apathetic, callous, cold, cruel, heartless, insensitive, pitiless, uncaring **2** NUMB, insensate, insensible

unfinished *adjective* **1** INCOMPLETE, half-done, uncompleted, undone **2** ROUGH, bare, crude, natural, raw, unrefined

unfit *adjective* **1** INCAPABLE, inadequate, incompetent, lousy (*slang*), no good, unqualified, useless **2** UNSUITABLE, inadequate, ineffective, unsuited, useless **3** OUT OF SHAPE, feeble, flabby, in poor condition, unhealthy

unflappable *adjective* IMPERTURBABLE, calm, collected, composed, cool, impassive, level-headed, self-possessed

unflattering *adjective* **1** BLUNT, candid, critical, honest **2** UNATTRACTIVE, dumpy (*informal*), frowzy, homely (*U.S.*), plain, unbecoming

unflinching *adjective* DETERMINED, firm, immovable, resolute, staunch, steadfast, steady, unfaltering

unfold *verb* **1** OPEN, expand, spread out, undo, unfurl, unravel, unroll, unwrap **2** REVEAL, disclose, divulge, make known, present, show, uncover

unforeseen *adjective* UNEXPECTED, accidental, sudden, surprising, unanticipated, unpredicted

unforgettable *adjective* MEMORABLE, exceptional, impressive, notable

unforgivable *adjective* INEXCUSABLE, deplorable, disgraceful, shameful, unpardonable

unfortunate *adjective* **1** DISASTROUS, adverse, calamitous, ill-fated **2** UNLUCKY, cursed, doomed, hapless, unhappy, unsuccessful, wretched **3** REGRETTABLE, deplorable, lamentable, unsuitable

unfounded *adjective* GROUNDLESS, baseless, false, idle, spurious, unjustified

unfriendly *adjective* **1** HOSTILE, aloof, chilly, cold, distant, uncongenial, unsociable **2** UNFAVORABLE, alien, hostile, inhospitable

ungainly *adjective* AWKWARD, clumsy, inelegant, lumbering, ungraceful

ungodly *adjective* **1** UNREASONABLE, dreadful, intolerable, outrageous, unearthly **2** WICKED, corrupt, depraved, godless, immoral, impious, irreligious, profane, sinful

ungracious *adjective* BAD-MANNERED, churlish, discourteous, impolite, rude, uncivil, unmannerly

ungrateful *adjective* UNAPPRECIATIVE, unmindful, unthankful

unguarded *adjective* **1** UNPROTECTED, defenseless,

undefended, vulnerable
2 CARELESS, heedless,
ill-considered, imprudent,
incautious, rash, thoughtless,
unthinking, unwary

unhappiness noun SADNESS,
blues, dejection, depression,
despondency, gloom,
heartache, low spirits,
melancholy, misery, sorrow,
wretchedness

unhappy adjective 1 SAD, blue,
dejected, depressed,
despondent, downcast,
melancholy, miserable,
mournful, sorrowful 2 UNLUCKY,
cursed, hapless, ill-fated,
unfortunate, wretched

unharmed adjective UNHURT,
intact, safe, sound,
undamaged, unscathed, whole

unhealthy adjective 1 HARMFUL,
detrimental, insalubrious,
insanitary, unwholesome
2 SICK, ailing, delicate, feeble,
frail, infirm, invalid, sickly,
unwell

unheard-of adjective
1 UNPRECEDENTED, inconceivable,
new, novel, singular, unique
2 SHOCKING, disgraceful,
outrageous, preposterous
3 OBSCURE, unfamiliar, unknown

unhesitating adjective 1 INSTANT,
immediate, prompt, ready
2 WHOLEHEARTED, resolute,
unfaltering, unquestioning,
unreserved

unholy adjective EVIL, corrupt,
profane, sinful, ungodly, wicked

unhurried adjective LEISURELY,
easy, sedate, slow

unidentified adjective UNNAMED,
anonymous, nameless,
unfamiliar, unrecognized

unification noun UNION, alliance,
amalgamation, coalescence,
coalition, confederation,
federation, uniting

uniform noun 1 OUTFIT,
costume, dress, garb, habit,
livery, regalia, suit ▶ adjective
2 UNVARYING, consistent,
constant, even, regular,
smooth, unchanging 3 ALIKE,
equal, like, on a level playing
field (informal), same, similar

uniformity noun 1 REGULARITY,
constancy, evenness,
invariability, sameness,
similarity 2 MONOTONY, dullness,
flatness, sameness, tedium

unify verb UNITE, amalgamate,
combine, confederate,
consolidate, join, merge

unimaginable adjective
INCONCEIVABLE, fantastic,
impossible, incredible,
unbelievable

unimaginative adjective
UNORIGINAL, banal, derivative,
dull, hackneyed, ordinary,
pedestrian, predictable,
prosaic, uncreative, uninspired

unimportant adjective
INSIGNIFICANT, inconsequential,
irrelevant, minor, paltry, petty,
trifling, trivial, worthless

uninhabited adjective DESERTED,
barren, desolate, empty,
unpopulated, vacant

uninhibited adjective
1 UNSELFCONSCIOUS, free,
liberated, natural, open,
relaxed, spontaneous,
unrepressed, unreserved
2 UNRESTRAINED, free, unbridled,
unchecked, unconstrained,
uncontrolled, unrestricted

uninspired adjective

UNIMAGINATIVE, banal, dull, humdrum, ordinary, prosaic, unexciting, unoriginal

unintelligent *adjective* STUPID, braindead (*informal*), brainless, dense, dull, foolish, obtuse, slow, thick

unintelligible *adjective* INCOMPREHENSIBLE, inarticulate, incoherent, indistinct, jumbled, meaningless, muddled

unintentional *adjective* ACCIDENTAL, casual, inadvertent, involuntary, unconscious, unintended

uninterested *adjective* INDIFFERENT, apathetic, blasé, bored, listless, unconcerned

uninteresting *adjective* BORING, drab, dreary, dry, dull, flat, humdrum, monotonous, tedious, unexciting

uninterrupted *adjective* CONTINUOUS, constant, nonstop, steady, sustained, unbroken

union *noun* **1** JOINING, amalgamation, blend, combination, conjunction, fusion, mixture, uniting **2** ALLIANCE, association, coalition, confederacy, federation, league **3** AGREEMENT, accord, concord, harmony, unanimity, unison, unity

unique *adjective* **1** SINGLE, lone, only, solitary **2** UNPARALLELED, incomparable, inimitable, matchless, unequaled, unmatched, unrivaled

unison *noun* AGREEMENT, accord, accordance, concert, concord, harmony, unity

unit *noun* **1** ITEM, entity, whole **2** PART, component, constituent, element, member,

section, segment **3** SECTION, detachment, group **4** MEASURE, measurement, quantity

unite *verb* **1** JOIN, amalgamate, blend, combine, couple, fuse, link, merge, unify **2** COOPERATE, ally, band, join forces, pool

united *adjective* **1** COMBINED, affiliated, allied, banded together, collective, concerted, pooled, unified **2** IN AGREEMENT, agreed, of one mind, of the same opinion, unanimous

unity *noun* **1** WHOLENESS, entity, integrity, oneness, singleness, union **2** AGREEMENT, accord, assent, concord, consensus, harmony, solidarity

universal *adjective* WIDESPREAD, common, general, total, unlimited, whole, worldwide

universally *adverb* EVERYWHERE, always, invariably, without exception

universe *noun* COSMOS, creation, macrocosm, nature

unjust *adjective* UNFAIR, biased, one-sided, partial, partisan, prejudiced, wrong, wrongful

unjustifiable *adjective* INEXCUSABLE, indefensible, outrageous, unacceptable, unforgivable, unpardonable, wrong

unkempt *adjective* **1** UNCOMBED, shaggy, tousled **2** UNTIDY, disheveled, disordered, messy, slovenly, ungroomed

unkind *adjective* CRUEL, harsh, malicious, mean, nasty, spiteful, uncharitable, unfeeling, unfriendly, unsympathetic

unknown *adjective* **1** HIDDEN, concealed, dark, mysterious, secret, unrevealed **2** STRANGE, alien, new **3** UNIDENTIFIED, anonymous, nameless, uncharted, undiscovered, unexplored, unnamed **4** OBSCURE, humble, unfamiliar

unlawful *adjective* ILLEGAL, banned, criminal, forbidden, illicit, outlawed, prohibited

unleash *verb* RELEASE, free, let go, let loose

unlike *adjective* DIFFERENT, dissimilar, distinct, diverse, not alike, opposite, unequal

unlikely *adjective* **1** IMPROBABLE, doubtful, faint, remote, slight **2** UNBELIEVABLE, implausible, incredible, questionable

unlimited *adjective* **1** INFINITE, boundless, countless, endless, extensive, great, immense, limitless, unbounded, vast **2** COMPLETE, absolute, full, total, unqualified, unrestricted

unload *verb* EMPTY, discharge, dump, lighten, relieve, unpack

unlock *verb* OPEN, release, undo, unfasten, unlatch

unlooked-for *adjective* UNEXPECTED, chance, fortuitous, surprising, unanticipated, unforeseen, unpredicted

unloved *adjective* NEGLECTED, forsaken, loveless, rejected, spurned, unpopular, unwanted

unlucky *adjective* **1** UNFORTUNATE, cursed, hapless, luckless, miserable, unhappy, wretched **2** ILL-FATED, doomed, inauspicious, ominous, unfavorable

unmarried *adjective* SINGLE, bachelor, maiden, unattached, unwed

unmask *verb* REVEAL, disclose,

discover, expose, lay bare, uncover

unmentionable *adjective* TABOO, forbidden, indecent, obscene, scandalous, shameful, shocking, unspeakable

unmerciful *adjective* MERCILESS, brutal, cruel, hard, implacable, pitiless, remorseless, ruthless

unmistakable *adjective* CLEAR, certain, distinct, evident, manifest, obvious, plain, sure, unambiguous

unmitigated *adjective* **1** UNRELIEVED, intense, persistent, unalleviated, unbroken, undiminished **2** COMPLETE, absolute, arrant, downright, outright, sheer, thorough, utter

unmoved *adjective* UNAFFECTED, cold, impassive, indifferent, unimpressed, unresponsive, untouched

unnatural *adjective* **1** STRANGE, extraordinary, freakish, outlandish, queer **2** ABNORMAL, anomalous, irregular, odd, perverse, perverted, unusual **3** FALSE, affected, artificial, feigned, forced, insincere, phoney *or* phony (*informal*), stiff, stilted

unnecessary *adjective* NEEDLESS, expendable, inessential, redundant, superfluous, unneeded, unrequired

unnerve *verb* INTIMIDATE, demoralize, discourage, dishearten, dismay, faze, fluster, frighten, psych out (*informal*), rattle, shake, upset

unnoticed *adjective* UNOBSERVED, disregarded, ignored, neglected, overlooked,

unheeded, unperceived,
unrecognized, unseen

unobtrusive *adjective*
INCONSPICUOUS, low-key, modest,
quiet, restrained, retiring,
self-effacing, unassuming

unoccupied *adjective* EMPTY,
uninhabited, vacant

unofficial *adjective* UNAUTHORIZED,
informal, private, unconfirmed

unorthodox *adjective*
UNCONVENTIONAL, abnormal,
irregular, off-the-wall (*slang*),
unusual

unpaid *adjective* 1 VOLUNTARY,
honorary, unsalaried 2 OWING,
due, outstanding, overdue,
payable, unsettled

unpalatable *adjective*
UNPLEASANT, disagreeable,
distasteful, horrid, offensive,
repugnant, unappetizing,
unsavory

unparalleled *adjective*
UNEQUALED, incomparable,
matchless, superlative, unique,
unmatched, unprecedented,
unsurpassed

unpardonable *adjective*
UNFORGIVABLE, deplorable,
disgraceful, indefensible,
inexcusable

unperturbed *adjective* CALM, as
cool as a cucumber,
composed, cool, placid,
unfazed (*informal*), unruffled,
untroubled, unworried

unpleasant *adjective* NASTY, bad,
disagreeable, displeasing,
distasteful, horrid, objectionable

unpopular *adjective* DISLIKED,
rejected, shunned, unwanted,
unwelcome

unprecedented *adjective*
EXTRAORDINARY, abnormal, new,

novel, original, remarkable,
singular, unheard-of

unpredictable *adjective*
INCONSTANT, chance,
changeable, doubtful, erratic,
random, unforeseeable,
unreliable, variable

unprejudiced *adjective* IMPARTIAL,
balanced, fair, just, objective,
open-minded, unbiased

unprepared *adjective* 1 TAKEN
OFF GUARD, surprised, unaware,
unready 2 IMPROVISED, ad-lib, off
the cuff (*informal*), spontaneous

unpretentious *adjective* MODEST,
dumpy (*informal*), homely,
humble, plain, simple,
straightforward, unaffected,
unassuming, unostentatious

unprincipled *adjective* DISHONEST,
amoral, crooked, devious,
immoral, underhand, unethical,
unscrupulous

unproductive *adjective*
1 USELESS, fruitless, futile, idle,
ineffective, unprofitable,
unrewarding, vain 2 BARREN,
fruitless, sterile

unprofessional *adjective*
1 UNETHICAL, improper, lax,
negligent, unprincipled
2 AMATEURISH, incompetent,
inefficient, inexpert

unprotected *adjective*
VULNERABLE, defenseless, helpless,
open, undefended

unqualified *adjective* 1 UNFIT,
ill-equipped, incapable,
incompetent, ineligible,
unprepared 2 TOTAL, absolute,
complete, downright, outright,
thorough, utter

unquestionable *adjective*
CERTAIN, absolute, clear,
conclusive, definite,

incontrovertible, indisputable, sure, undeniable, unequivocal, unmistakable

unravel verb 1 UNDO, disentangle, free, separate, untangle, unwind 2 SOLVE, explain, figure out (informal), resolve, work out

unreal adjective 1 IMAGINARY, dreamlike, fabulous, fanciful, illusory, make-believe, visionary 2 INSUBSTANTIAL, immaterial, intangible, nebulous 3 FAKE, artificial, false, insincere, mock, pretended, sham

unrealistic adjective IMPRACTICAL, impracticable, improbable, romantic, unworkable

unreasonable adjective 1 EXCESSIVE, extortionate, immoderate, undue, unfair, unjust, unwarranted 2 BIASED, blinkered, opinionated

unrelated adjective 1 DIFFERENT, unconnected, unlike 2 IRRELEVANT, extraneous, inapplicable, inappropriate, unconnected

unreliable adjective 1 UNDEPENDABLE, irresponsible, treacherous, untrustworthy 2 UNCERTAIN, deceptive, fallible, false, implausible, inaccurate, unsound

unrepentant adjective IMPENITENT, abandoned, callous, hardened, incorrigible, shameless, unremorseful

unreserved adjective 1 TOTAL, absolute, complete, entire, full, unlimited, wholehearted 2 OPEN, demonstrative, extrovert, free, outgoing, uninhibited, unrestrained

unresolved adjective UNDECIDED, doubtful, moot, unanswered, undetermined, unsettled, unsolved, vague

unrest noun DISCONTENT, agitation, discord, dissension, protest, rebellion, sedition, strife

unrestrained adjective UNCONTROLLED, abandoned, free, immoderate, intemperate, unbounded, unbridled, unchecked, uninhibited

unrestricted adjective 1 UNLIMITED, absolute, free, open, unbounded, unregulated 2 OPEN, public

unrivaled adjective UNPARALLELED, beyond compare, incomparable, matchless, supreme, unequaled, unmatched, unsurpassed

unruly adjective UNCONTROLLABLE, disobedient, mutinous, rebellious, wayward, wild, willful

unsafe adjective DANGEROUS, hazardous, insecure, perilous, risky, unreliable

unsatisfactory adjective UNACCEPTABLE, deficient, disappointing, inadequate, insufficient, lousy (slang), not good enough, not up to scratch (informal), poor

unsavory adjective 1 UNPLEASANT, distasteful, nasty, obnoxious, offensive, repellent, repulsive, revolting, scuzzy (slang) 2 UNAPPETIZING, nauseating, sickening, unpalatable

unscathed adjective UNHARMED, safe, unhurt, uninjured, unmarked, whole

unscrupulous adjective UNPRINCIPLED, corrupt, dishonest, dishonorable, immoral, improper, unethical

unseat *verb* 1 THROW, unhorse, unsaddle 2 DEPOSE, dethrone, displace, oust, overthrow, remove

unseemly *adjective* IMPROPER, inappropriate, indecorous, unbecoming, undignified, unsuitable

unseen *adjective* UNOBSERVED, concealed, hidden, invisible, obscure, undetected, unnoticed

unselfish *adjective* GENEROUS, altruistic, kind, magnanimous, noble, selfless, self-sacrificing

unsettle *verb* DISTURB, agitate, bother, confuse, disconcert, faze, fluster, perturb, ruffle, trouble, upset

unsettled *adjective* 1 UNSTABLE, disorderly, insecure, shaky, unsteady 2 RESTLESS, agitated, anxious, confused, disturbed, flustered, restive, shaken, tense, wired (*slang*) 3 CHANGING, inconstant, uncertain, variable

unshakable *adjective* FIRM, absolute, fixed, immovable, staunch, steadfast, sure, unswerving, unwavering

unsightly *adjective* UGLY, disagreeable, dumpy (*informal*), hideous, homely (*U.S.*), horrid, repulsive, scuzzy (*slang*), unattractive

unskilled *adjective* UNPROFESSIONAL, amateurish, inexperienced, unqualified, untrained

unsociable *adjective* UNFRIENDLY, chilly, cold, distant, hostile, retiring, unforthcoming, withdrawn

unsolicited *adjective*

UNREQUESTED, gratuitous, unasked for, uncalled-for, uninvited, unsought

unsophisticated *adjective* 1 NATURAL, artless, childlike, guileless, ingenuous, unaffected 2 SIMPLE, dumpy (*informal*), frowzy, homely (*U.S.*), plain, uncomplicated, unrefined, unspecialized

unsound *adjective* 1 UNHEALTHY, ailing, defective, diseased, ill, unbalanced, unstable, unwell, weak 2 UNRELIABLE, defective, fallacious, false, flawed, illogical, shaky, specious, weak

unspeakable *adjective* 1 INDESCRIBABLE, inconceivable, unbelievable, unimaginable 2 DREADFUL, abominable, appalling, awful, heinous, horrible, monstrous, shocking

unspoiled, unspoilt *adjective* 1 PERFECT, intact, preserved, unchanged, undamaged, untouched 2 NATURAL, artless, innocent, unaffected

unspoken *adjective* TACIT, implicit, implied, understood, unexpressed, unstated

unstable *adjective* 1 INSECURE, precarious, shaky, tottering, unsettled, unsteady, wobbly 2 CHANGEABLE, fitful, fluctuating, inconstant, unpredictable, variable, volatile 3 UNPREDICTABLE, capricious, changeable, erratic, inconsistent, irrational, temperamental

unsteady *adjective* 1 UNSTABLE, infirm, insecure, precarious, shaky, unsafe, wobbly 2 CHANGEABLE, erratic, inconstant, temperamental, unsettled, volatile

unsuccessful *adjective* **1** USELESS, failed, fruitless, futile, unavailing, unproductive, vain **2** UNLUCKY, hapless, luckless, unfortunate

unsuitable *adjective* INAPPROPRIATE, improper, inapposite, inapt, ineligible, unacceptable, unbecoming, unfit, unfitting, unseemly

unsure *adjective* **1** UNCONFIDENT, insecure, unassured **2** DOUBTFUL, distrustful, dubious, hesitant, mistrustful, skeptical, suspicious, unconvinced

unsuspecting *adjective* TRUSTING, credulous, gullible, trustful, unwary

unswerving *adjective* CONSTANT, firm, resolute, single-minded, staunch, steadfast, steady, true, unwavering

unsympathetic *adjective* HARD, callous, cold, cruel, harsh, heartless, insensitive, unfeeling, unkind, unmoved

untangle *verb* DISENTANGLE, extricate, unravel, unsnarl

untenable *adjective* UNSUSTAINABLE, groundless, illogical, indefensible, insupportable, shaky, unsound, weak

unthinkable *adjective* **1** IMPOSSIBLE, absurd, out of the question, unreasonable **2** INCONCEIVABLE, implausible, incredible, unimaginable

untidy *adjective* MESSY, chaotic, cluttered, disarrayed, disordered, jumbled, littered, muddled, shambolic, unkempt

untie *verb* UNDO, free, loosen, release, unbind, unfasten, unknot, unlace

untimely *adjective* **1** EARLY, premature **2** ILL-TIMED, awkward, inappropriate, inconvenient, inopportune, mistimed

untiring *adjective* TIRELESS, constant, determined, dogged, persevering, steady, unflagging, unremitting

untold *adjective* **1** INDESCRIBABLE, inexpressible, undreamed of, unimaginable, unthinkable, unutterable **2** COUNTLESS, incalculable, innumerable, myriad, numberless, uncountable

untouched *adjective* UNHARMED, intact, undamaged, unhurt, uninjured, unscathed

untoward *adjective* **1** ANNOYING, awkward, inconvenient, irritating, troublesome, unfortunate **2** UNLUCKY, adverse, inauspicious, inopportune, unfavorable

untrained *adjective* AMATEUR, green, inexperienced, raw, uneducated, unqualified, unschooled, unskilled, untaught

untroubled *adjective* UNDISTURBED, calm, cool, peaceful, placid, tranquil, unfazed (*informal*), unperturbed, unworried

untrue *adjective* **1** FALSE, deceptive, dishonest, erroneous, inaccurate, incorrect, lying, mistaken, wrong **2** UNFAITHFUL, deceitful, disloyal, faithless, false, inconstant, treacherous, untrustworthy

untrustworthy *adjective* UNRELIABLE, deceitful, devious, dishonest, disloyal, false, slippery, treacherous, tricky

untruth noun LIE, deceit, falsehood, fib, story, white lie

untruthful adjective DISHONEST, deceitful, deceptive, false, lying, mendacious

unusual adjective EXTRAORDINARY, curious, different, exceptional, odd, queer, rare, remarkable, singular, strange, uncommon, unconventional

unveil verb REVEAL, disclose, divulge, expose, make known, uncover

unwanted adjective UNDESIRED, outcast, rejected, uninvited, unneeded, unsolicited, unwelcome

unwarranted adjective UNNECESSARY, gratuitous, groundless, indefensible, inexcusable, uncalled-for, unjustified, unprovoked

unwavering adjective STEADY, consistent, determined, immovable, resolute, staunch, steadfast, unshakable, unswerving

unwelcome adjective
1 UNWANTED, excluded, rejected, unacceptable, undesirable
2 DISAGREEABLE, displeasing, distasteful, undesirable, unpleasant

unwell adjective ILL, ailing, sick, sickly, under the weather (informal), unhealthy

unwholesome adjective
1 HARMFUL, deleterious, noxious, poisonous, unhealthy 2 WICKED, bad, corrupting, degrading, demoralizing, evil, immoral

unwieldy adjective 1 AWKWARD, cumbersome, inconvenient,

unmanageable 2 BULKY, clumsy, hefty, massive, ponderous

unwilling adjective RELUCTANT, averse, disinclined, grudging, indisposed, loath, resistant, unenthusiastic

unwind verb 1 UNRAVEL, slacken, uncoil, undo, unroll, untwine, untwist 2 RELAX, loosen up, take it easy, wind down

unwise adjective FOOLISH, foolhardy, improvident, imprudent, inadvisable, injudicious, rash, reckless, senseless, silly, stupid

unwitting adjective
1 UNINTENTIONAL, accidental, chance, inadvertent, involuntary, unplanned
2 UNKNOWING, ignorant, innocent, unaware, unconscious, unsuspecting

unworldly adjective 1 SPIRITUAL, metaphysical, nonmaterialistic
2 NAIVE, idealistic, innocent, unsophisticated

unworthy adjective
1 UNDESERVING, not fit for, not good enough 2 DISHONORABLE, base, contemptible, degrading, discreditable, disgraceful, disreputable, ignoble, lousy (slang), shameful 3 **unworthy of** UNBEFITTING, beneath, inappropriate, unbecoming, unfitting, unseemly, unsuitable

unwritten adjective 1 ORAL, vocal 2 CUSTOMARY, accepted, tacit, understood

unyielding adjective FIRM, adamant, immovable, inflexible, obdurate, obstinate, resolute, rigid, stiff-necked, stubborn, tough, uncompromising

upbeat *adjective* CHEERFUL, cheery, encouraging, hopeful, optimistic, positive

upbraid *verb* SCOLD, admonish, berate, rebuke, reprimand, reproach, reprove

upbringing *noun* EDUCATION, breeding, raising, rearing, training

update *verb* REVISE, amend, bring up to date, modernize, renew

upgrade *verb* PROMOTE, advance, better, elevate, enhance, improve, raise

upheaval *noun* DISTURBANCE, disorder, disruption, revolution, turmoil

uphill *adjective* 1 ASCENDING, climbing, mounting, rising 2 ARDUOUS, difficult, exhausting, grueling, hard, laborious, strenuous, taxing, tough

uphold *verb* SUPPORT, advocate, aid, back, champion, defend, endorse, maintain, promote, sustain

upkeep *noun* 1 MAINTENANCE, keep, repair, running, subsistence 2 OVERHEADS, expenditure, expenses, running costs

uplift *verb* 1 RAISE, elevate, hoist, lift up 2 IMPROVE, advance, better, edify, inspire, raise, refine ▶ *noun* 3 IMPROVEMENT, advancement, edification, enhancement, enlightenment, enrichment, refinement

upmarket *adjective Informal* UPPER-CLASS, classy (*informal*), grand, high-class, luxurious, smart, stylish, swanky (*informal*)

upper *adjective* 1 HIGHER, high, loftier, top, topmost 2 SUPERIOR, eminent, greater, important

upper-class *adjective* ARISTOCRATIC, blue-blooded, highborn, high-class, noble, patrician

upper hand *noun* CONTROL, advantage, ascendancy, edge, mastery, supremacy

uppermost *adjective* 1 TOP, highest, loftiest, topmost 2 SUPREME, chief, dominant, foremost, greatest, leading, main, principal

uppity *adjective Informal* CONCEITED, bumptious, cocky, full of oneself, impertinent, self-important

upright *adjective* 1 VERTICAL, erect, perpendicular, straight 2 HONEST, conscientious, ethical, good, honorable, just, principled, righteous, virtuous

uprising *noun* REBELLION, disturbance, insurgence, insurrection, mutiny, revolt, revolution, rising

uproar *noun* COMMOTION, din, furor, mayhem, noise, outcry, pandemonium, racket, riot, turmoil

uproarious *adjective* 1 HILARIOUS, hysterical, rib-tickling, rip-roaring (*informal*), side-splitting, very funny 2 LOUD, boisterous, rollicking, unrestrained

uproot *verb* 1 PULL UP, dig up, rip up, root out, weed out 2 DISPLACE, exile

upset *adjective* 1 SICK, ill, queasy 2 DISTRESSED, agitated, bothered, dismayed, disturbed, grieved, hurt, put out, troubled, worried 3 DISORDERED, chaotic, confused, disarrayed,

in disarray, muddled
4 OVERTURNED, capsized, spilled, upside down ▶ *verb* **5** TIP OVER, capsize, knock over, overturn, spill **6** MESS UP, change, disorder, disorganize, disturb, spoil **7** DISTRESS, agitate, bother, disconcert, disturb, faze, fluster, grieve, perturb, ruffle, trouble ▶ *noun* **8** REVERSAL, defeat, shake-up (*informal*) **9** ILLNESS, bug (*informal*), complaint, disorder, malady, sickness **10** DISTRESS, agitation, bother, disturbance, shock, trouble, worry

upshot *noun* RESULT, culmination, end, end result, finale, outcome, sequel

upside down *adjective*
1 INVERTED, backward, overturned, upturned **2** CONFUSED, chaotic, disordered, muddled, topsy-turvy

upstanding *adjective* HONEST, ethical, good, honorable, incorruptible, moral, principled, upright

upstart *noun* SOCIAL CLIMBER, arriviste, *nouveau riche*, parvenu

uptight *adjective Informal* TENSE, anxious, edgy, on edge, uneasy, wired (*slang*)

up-to-date *adjective* MODERN, cool (*informal*), current, fashionable, in vogue, phat (*slang*), stylish, trendy (*informal*), up-to-the-minute

upturn *noun* RISE, advancement, improvement, increase, recovery, revival, upsurge, upswing

urban *adjective* CIVIC, city, metropolitan, municipal, town

urbane *adjective* SOPHISTICATED, courteous, cultivated, cultured, debonair, polished, refined, smooth, suave, well-bred

urchin *noun* RAGAMUFFIN, brat, gamin, waif

urge *noun* **1** IMPULSE, compulsion, desire, drive, itch, longing, thirst, wish, yearning ▶ *verb* **2** BEG, beseech, entreat, exhort, implore, plead **3** ADVOCATE, advise, counsel, recommend, support **4** DRIVE, compel, force, goad, impel, incite, induce, press, push, spur

urgency *noun* IMPORTANCE, extremity, gravity, hurry, necessity, need, pressure, seriousness

urgent *adjective* CRUCIAL, compelling, critical, immediate, imperative, important, pressing

usable *adjective* SERVICEABLE, available, current, functional, practical, utilizable, valid, working

usage *noun* **1** USE, control, employment, handling, management, operation, running **2** PRACTICE, convention, custom, habit, method, mode, procedure, regime, routine

use *verb* **1** EMPLOY, apply, exercise, exert, operate, practice, utilize, work **2** TAKE ADVANTAGE OF, exploit, manipulate **3** CONSUME, exhaust, expend, run through, spend ▶ *noun* **4** USAGE, application, employment, exercise, handling, operation, practice, service **5** GOOD, advantage, avail, benefit, help, point, profit, service, usefulness, value **6** PURPOSE,

end, object, reason

used *adjective* SECOND-HAND, cast-off, nearly new, shopsoiled

used to *adjective* ACCUSTOMED TO, familiar with

useful *adjective* HELPFUL, advantageous, beneficial, effective, fruitful, practical, profitable, serviceable, valuable, win-win (*informal*), worthwhile

usefulness *noun* HELPFULNESS, benefit, convenience, effectiveness, efficacy, practicality, use, utility, value, worth

useless *adjective* 1 WORTHLESS, fruitless, futile, impractical, ineffectual, pointless, unproductive, vain, valueless 2 *Informal* INEPT, hopeless, incompetent, ineffectual, no good

use up *verb* CONSUME, absorb, drain, exhaust, finish, run through

usher *noun* 1 ATTENDANT, doorkeeper, doorman, escort, guide ▸ *verb* 2 ESCORT, conduct, direct, guide, lead

usual *adjective* NORMAL, common, customary, everyday, general, habitual, ordinary, regular, routine, standard, typical

usually *adverb* NORMALLY, as a rule, commonly, generally, habitually, mainly, mostly, on the whole

usurp *verb* SEIZE, appropriate, assume, commandeer, take, take over, wrest

utility *noun* USEFULNESS, benefit, convenience, efficacy, practicality, serviceableness

utilize *verb* USE, avail oneself of, employ, make use of, put to use, take advantage of, turn to account

utmost *adjective* 1 GREATEST, chief, highest, maximum, paramount, pre-eminent, supreme 2 FARTHEST, extreme, final, last ▸ *noun* 3 GREATEST, best, hardest, highest

Utopia *noun* PARADISE, bliss, Eden, Garden of Eden, heaven, Shangri-la

Utopian *adjective* PERFECT, dream, fantasy, ideal, idealistic, imaginary, romantic, visionary

utter[1] *verb* EXPRESS, articulate, pronounce, say, speak, voice

utter[2] *adjective* ABSOLUTE, complete, downright, outright, sheer, thorough, total, unmitigated

utterance *noun* SPEECH, announcement, declaration, expression, remark, statement, words

utterly *adverb* TOTALLY, absolutely, completely, entirely, extremely, fully, perfectly, thoroughly

vacancy *noun* JOB, opening, opportunity, position, post, situation

vacant *adjective* 1 UNOCCUPIED, available, empty, free, idle, unfilled, untenanted, void 2 VAGUE, absent-minded, abstracted, blank, dreamy, idle, inane, vacuous

vacate verb LEAVE, evacuate, quit

vacuous adjective UNINTELLIGENT, blank, inane, stupid, uncomprehending, vacant

vacuum noun EMPTINESS, gap, nothingness, space, vacuity, void

vagabond noun BEGGAR, down-and-out, itinerant, rover, tramp, vagrant

vagrant noun 1 TRAMP, drifter, hobo, itinerant, rolling stone, wanderer ▶ adjective 2 ITINERANT, nomadic, roaming, rootless, roving, unsettled, vagabond

vague adjective UNCLEAR, equivocal, hazy, ill-defined, imprecise, indefinite, indeterminate, indistinct, loose, nebulous, uncertain, unspecified

vain adjective 1 PROUD, arrogant, conceited, egotistical, narcissistic, self-important, swaggering 2 FUTILE, abortive, fruitless, idle, pointless, senseless, unavailing, unprofitable, useless, worthless ▶ noun 3 **in vain** TO NO AVAIL, fruitless(ly), ineffectual(ly), unsuccessful(ly), useless(ly), vain(ly)

valiant adjective BRAVE, bold, courageous, fearless, gallant, heroic, intrepid, lion-hearted

valid adjective 1 LOGICAL, cogent, convincing, good, sound, telling, well-founded, well-grounded 2 LEGAL, authentic, bona fide, genuine, lawful, legitimate, official

validate verb CONFIRM, authenticate, authorize, certify, corroborate, endorse, ratify, substantiate

validity noun 1 SOUNDNESS, cogency, force, power, strength, weight 2 LEGALITY, authority, lawfulness, legitimacy, right

valley noun HOLLOW, dale, dell, depression, glen, vale

valor noun BRAVERY, boldness, courage, fearlessness, gallantry, heroism, intrepidity, spirit

valuable adjective 1 PRECIOUS, costly, dear, expensive, high-priced 2 USEFUL, beneficial, helpful, important, prized, profitable, worthwhile ▶ noun 3 **valuables** TREASURES, heirlooms

value noun 1 IMPORTANCE, advantage, benefit, desirability, merit, profit, usefulness, utility, worth 2 COST, market price, rate 3 **values** PRINCIPLES, ethics, (moral) standards ▶ verb 4 EVALUATE, appraise, assess, estimate, price, rate, set at 5 RESPECT, appreciate, cherish, esteem, hold dear, prize, regard highly, treasure

vandal noun HOOLIGAN, delinquent, rowdy

vanguard noun FORERUNNERS, cutting edge, forefront, front line, leaders, spearhead, trailblazers, trendsetters, van

vanish verb DISAPPEAR, dissolve, evanesce, evaporate, fade (away), melt (away)

vanity noun PRIDE, arrogance, conceit, conceitedness, egotism, narcissism

vanquish verb Literary DEFEAT, beat, conquer, crush, master, overcome, overpower, overwhelm, triumph over

vapid adjective DULL, bland, boring, flat, insipid, tame, uninspiring, uninteresting, weak, wishy-washy (*informal*)

vapor *noun* MIST, exhalation, fog, haze, steam

variable *adjective* CHANGEABLE, flexible, fluctuating, inconstant, mutable, shifting, temperamental, uneven, unstable, unsteady

variance *noun* **at variance** IN DISAGREEMENT, at loggerheads, at odds, conflicting, out of line

variant *adjective* 1 DIFFERENT, alternative, divergent, modified ▶*noun* 2 VARIATION, alternative, development, modification

variation *noun* DIFFERENCE, change, departure, deviation, diversity, innovation, modification, novelty, variety

varied *adjective* DIFFERENT, assorted, diverse, heterogeneous, miscellaneous, mixed, motley, sundry, various

variety *noun* 1 DIVERSITY, change, difference, discrepancy, diversification, multifariousness, variation 2 RANGE, array, assortment, collection, cross section, medley, miscellany, mixture 3 TYPE, brand, breed, category, class, kind, sort, species, strain

various *adjective* DIFFERENT, assorted, disparate, distinct, diverse, miscellaneous, several, sundry, varied

varnish *noun, verb* POLISH, glaze, gloss, lacquer

vary *verb* CHANGE, alter, differ, disagree, diverge, fluctuate

vast *adjective* HUGE, boundless, colossal, enormous, gigantic, great, immense, massive, monumental, wide

vault[1] *noun* 1 STRONGROOM,

depository, repository 2 CRYPT, catacomb, cellar, charnel house, mausoleum, tomb, undercroft

vault[2] *verb* JUMP, bound, clear, hurdle, leap, spring

vaulted *adjective* ARCHED, cavernous, domed

veer *verb* SWERVE, change course, change direction, sheer, shift, turn

vegetate *verb* STAGNATE, deteriorate, go to seed, idle, languish, loaf

vehemence *noun* FORCEFULNESS, ardor, emphasis, energy, fervor, force, intensity, passion, vigor

vehement *adjective* STRONG, ardent, emphatic, fervent, fierce, forceful, impassioned, intense, passionate, powerful

vehicle *noun* 1 TRANSPORT, conveyance, transportation 2 MEDIUM, apparatus, channel, means, mechanism, organ

veil *noun* 1 COVER, blind, cloak, curtain, disguise, film, mask, screen, shroud ▶*verb* 2 COVER, cloak, conceal, disguise, hide, mask, obscure, screen, shield

veiled *adjective* DISGUISED, concealed, covert, hinted at, implied, masked, suppressed

vein *noun* 1 BLOOD VESSEL 2 SEAM, course, current, lode, stratum, streak, stripe 3 MOOD, mode, note, style, temper, tenor, tone

velocity *noun* SPEED, pace, quickness, rapidity, swiftness

velvety *adjective* SMOOTH, delicate, downy, soft

vendetta *noun* FEUD, bad blood, quarrel

veneer *noun* MASK, appearance, façade, front, guise, pretense, semblance, show

venerable *adjective* RESPECTED, august, esteemed, honored, revered, sage, wise, worshipped

venerate *verb* RESPECT, adore, esteem, honor, look up to, revere, reverence, worship

vengeance *noun* REVENGE, reprisal, retaliation, retribution

venom *noun* 1 MALICE, acrimony, bitterness, hate, rancor, spite, spleen, virulence 2 POISON, bane, toxin

venomous *adjective* 1 MALICIOUS, hostile, malignant, rancorous, savage, spiteful, vicious, vindictive 2 POISONOUS, mephitic, noxious, toxic, virulent

vent *noun* 1 OUTLET, aperture, duct, opening, orifice ▸ *verb* 2 EXPRESS, air, discharge, emit, give vent to, pour out, release, utter, voice

venture *noun* 1 UNDERTAKING, adventure, endeavor, enterprise, gamble, hazard, project, risk ▸ *verb* 2 RISK, chance, hazard, speculate, stake, wager 3 DARE, hazard, make bold, presume, take the liberty, volunteer 4 GO, embark on, plunge into, set out

verbal *adjective* SPOKEN, oral, unwritten, word-of-mouth

verbatim *adverb* EXACTLY, precisely, to the letter, word for word

verbose *adjective* LONG-WINDED, circumlocutory, diffuse, periphrastic, prolix, tautological, windy, wordy

verbosity *noun* LONG-WINDEDNESS, loquaciousness, prolixity, verboseness, wordiness

verdant *adjective* GREEN, flourishing, fresh, grassy, leafy, lush

verdict *noun* DECISION, adjudication, conclusion, finding, judgment, opinion, sentence

verge *noun* 1 BORDER, boundary, brim, brink, edge, limit, margin, threshold ▸ *verb* 2 **verge on** BORDER, approach, come near

verification *noun* PROOF, authentication, confirmation, corroboration, substantiation, validation

verify *verb* CHECK, authenticate, bear out, confirm, corroborate, prove, substantiate, support, validate

vernacular *noun* DIALECT, idiom, parlance, patois, speech

versatile *adjective* ADAPTABLE, adjustable, all-purpose, all-round, flexible, multifaceted, resourceful, variable

versed *adjective* KNOWLEDGEABLE, acquainted, conversant, experienced, familiar, practiced, proficient, seasoned, well informed

version *noun* 1 FORM, design, model, style, variant 2 ACCOUNT, adaptation, interpretation, portrayal, rendering

vertical *adjective* UPRIGHT, erect, on end, perpendicular

vertigo *noun* DIZZINESS, giddiness, light-headedness

verve *noun* ENTHUSIASM, animation, energy, gusto,

liveliness, sparkle, spirit, vitality

very *adverb* 1 EXTREMELY, acutely, decidedly, deeply, exceedingly, greatly, highly, profoundly, uncommonly, unusually ▶ *adjective* 2 EXACT, precise, selfsame

vessel *noun* 1 SHIP, boat, craft 2 CONTAINER, pot, receptacle, utensil

vest *verb* (with *in* or *with*) PLACE, bestow, confer, consign, endow, entrust, invest, settle

vestibule *noun* HALL, anteroom, foyer, lobby, porch, portico

vestige *noun* TRACE, glimmer, indication, remnant, scrap, suspicion

vet *verb* CHECK, appraise, examine, investigate, review, scrutinize

veteran *noun* 1 OLD HAND, old stager, past master, warhorse (*informal*) ▶ *adjective* 2 LONG-SERVING, battle-scarred, old, seasoned

veto *noun* 1 BAN, boycott, embargo, interdict, prohibition ▶ *verb* 2 BAN, boycott, disallow, forbid, prohibit, reject, rule out, turn down

vex *verb* ANNOY, bother, distress, exasperate, irritate, plague, trouble, upset, worry

vexation *noun* 1 ANNOYANCE, chagrin, displeasure, dissatisfaction, exasperation, frustration, irritation, pique 2 PROBLEM, bother, difficulty, hassle (*informal*), headache (*informal*), nuisance, trouble, worry

viable *adjective* WORKABLE, applicable, feasible, operable, practicable, usable

vibrant *adjective* ENERGETIC, alive, animated, dynamic, sparkling, spirited, vigorous, vivacious, vivid

vibrate *verb* SHAKE, fluctuate, oscillate, pulsate, quiver, reverberate, shudder, sway, throb, tremble

vibration *noun* TREMOR, oscillation, pulsation, quiver, reverberation, shake, shudder, throbbing, trembling

vicarious *adjective* INDIRECT, delegated, substituted, surrogate

vice *noun* 1 WICKEDNESS, corruption, depravity, evil, immorality, iniquity, sin, turpitude 2 FAULT, blemish, defect, failing, imperfection, shortcoming, weakness

vice versa *adverb* CONVERSELY, contrariwise, in reverse, the other way round

vicinity *noun* NEIGHBORHOOD, area, district, environs, locality, neck of the woods (*informal*), proximity

vicious *adjective* 1 VIOLENT, barbarous, cruel, ferocious, savage, wicked 2 MALICIOUS, cruel, mean, spiteful, venomous, vindictive

victim *noun* CASUALTY, fatality, martyr, sacrifice, scapegoat, sufferer

victimize *verb* PERSECUTE, discriminate against, pick on

victor *noun* WINNER, champion, conqueror, prizewinner, vanquisher

victorious *adjective* WINNING, champion, conquering, first, prizewinning, successful, triumphant, vanquishing

victory noun WIN, conquest, success, triumph

vie verb COMPETE, contend, strive, struggle

view noun 1 (sometimes plural) OPINION, attitude, belief, conviction, feeling, impression, point of view, sentiment 2 SCENE, landscape, outlook, panorama, perspective, picture, prospect, spectacle, vista 3 VISION, sight ▸ verb 4 REGARD, consider, deem, look on

viewer noun WATCHER, observer, onlooker, spectator

vigilance noun WATCHFULNESS, alertness, attentiveness, carefulness, caution, circumspection, observance

vigilant adjective WATCHFUL, alert, attentive, careful, cautious, circumspect, on one's guard, on the lookout, wakeful

vigor noun ENERGY, animation, dynamism, forcefulness, gusto, liveliness, power, spirit, strength, verve, vitality

vigorous adjective ENERGETIC, active, dynamic, forceful, lively, lusty, powerful, spirited, strenuous, strong

vigorously adverb ENERGETICALLY, forcefully, hard, lustily, strenuously, strongly

vile adjective 1 WICKED, corrupt, degenerate, depraved, evil, nefarious, perverted 2 DISGUSTING, foul, horrid, nasty, nauseating, offensive, repugnant, repulsive, revolting, scuzzy (slang), sickening

vilify verb MALIGN, abuse, berate, denigrate, disparage, revile, slander, smear

villain noun 1 EVILDOER, criminal,

miscreant, reprobate, rogue, scoundrel, wretch 2 ANTIHERO, baddy (informal)

villainous adjective WICKED, bad, cruel, degenerate, depraved, evil, fiendish, nefarious, vicious, vile

villainy noun WICKEDNESS, delinquency, depravity, devilry, iniquity, turpitude, vice

vindicate verb 1 CLEAR, absolve, acquit, exculpate, exonerate, rehabilitate 2 JUSTIFY, defend, excuse

vindication noun 1 EXONERATION, exculpation, rehabilitation 2 JUSTIFICATION, defense, excuse

vindictive adjective VENGEFUL, implacable, malicious, resentful, revengeful, spiteful, unforgiving, unrelenting

vintage adjective BEST, choice, classic, prime, select, superior

violate verb 1 BREAK, contravene, disobey, disregard, encroach upon, infringe, transgress 2 DESECRATE, abuse, befoul, defile, dishonor, pollute, profane 3 RAPE, abuse, assault, debauch, ravish

violation noun 1 INFRINGEMENT, abuse, breach, contravention, encroachment, infraction, transgression, trespass 2 DESECRATION, defilement, profanation, sacrilege, spoliation

violence noun 1 FORCE, bloodshed, brutality, cruelty, ferocity, fighting, savagery, terrorism 2 INTENSITY, abandon, fervor, force, severity, vehemence

violent adjective DESTRUCTIVE, brutal, cruel, hot-headed, murderous, riotous, savage, uncontrollable, unrestrained, vicious

V.I.P. *noun* CELEBRITY, big name, luminary, somebody, star

virgin *noun* 1 MAIDEN, girl ▶ *adjective* 2 PURE, chaste, immaculate, uncorrupted, undefiled, vestal, virginal

virginity *noun* CHASTITY, maidenhood

virile *adjective* MANLY, lusty, macho, manlike, masculine, red-blooded, strong, vigorous

virility *noun* MASCULINITY, machismo, manhood, vigor

virtual *adjective* PRACTICAL, essential, in all but name

virtually *adverb* PRACTICALLY, almost, as good as, in all but name, in effect, in essence, nearly

virtue *noun* 1 GOODNESS, incorruptibility, integrity, morality, probity, rectitude, righteousness, uprightness, worth 2 MERIT, advantage, asset, attribute, credit, good point, plus (*informal*), strength

virtuosity *noun* MASTERY, brilliance, craft, expertise, flair, panache, polish, skill

virtuoso *noun* MASTER, artist, genius, maestro, magician

virtuous *adjective* GOOD, ethical, honorable, incorruptible, moral, praiseworthy, righteous, upright, worthy

virulent *adjective* POISONOUS, deadly, lethal, pernicious, toxic, venomous

viscous *adjective* THICK, gelatinous, sticky, syrupy

visible *adjective* APPARENT, clear, discernible, evident, in view,

manifest, observable, perceptible, unconcealed

vision *noun* 1 SIGHT, eyesight, perception, seeing, view 2 IMAGE, concept, conception, daydream, dream, fantasy, idea, ideal 3 HALLUCINATION, apparition, chimera, delusion, illusion, mirage, revelation 4 FORESIGHT, discernment, farsightedness, imagination, insight, intuition, penetration, prescience

visionary *adjective* 1 PROPHETIC, mystical 2 IMPRACTICAL, idealistic, quixotic, romantic, speculative, starry-eyed, unrealistic, unworkable, utopian ▶ *noun* 3 PROPHET, mystic, seer

visit *verb* 1 CALL ON, drop in on (*informal*), look (someone) up, stay with, stop by ▶ *noun* 2 CALL, sojourn, stay, stop

visitation *noun* 1 INSPECTION, examination, visit 2 CATASTROPHE, blight, calamity, cataclysm, disaster, ordeal, punishment, scourge

visitor *noun* GUEST, caller, company

vista *noun* VIEW, panorama, perspective, prospect

visual *adjective* 1 OPTICAL, ocular, optic 2 OBSERVABLE, discernible, perceptible, visible

visualize *verb* PICTURE, conceive of, envisage, imagine

vital *adjective* 1 ESSENTIAL, basic, fundamental, imperative, indispensable, necessary, requisite 2 IMPORTANT, critical, crucial, decisive, key, life-or-death, significant, urgent 3 LIVELY, animated, dynamic, energetic, spirited, vibrant, vigorous, vivacious, zestful

vitality *noun* ENERGY, animation, exuberance, life, liveliness, strength, vigor, vivacity

vitriolic *adjective* BITTER, acerbic, caustic, envenomed, sardonic, scathing, venomous, virulent, withering

vivacious *adjective* LIVELY, bubbling, ebullient, high-spirited, sparkling, spirited, sprightly, upbeat (*informal*), vital

vivacity *noun* LIVELINESS, animation, ebullience, energy, gaiety, high spirits, sparkle, spirit, sprightliness

vivid *adjective* 1 BRIGHT, brilliant, clear, colorful, glowing, intense, rich 2 LIFELIKE, dramatic, graphic, memorable, powerful, realistic, stirring, telling, true to life

vocabulary *noun* WORDS, dictionary, glossary, language, lexicon

vocal *adjective* 1 SPOKEN, oral, said, uttered, voiced 2 OUTSPOKEN, articulate, eloquent, expressive, forthright, frank, plain-spoken, strident, vociferous

vocation *noun* PROFESSION, calling, career, job, mission, pursuit, trade

vociferous *adjective* NOISY, clamorous, loud, outspoken, strident, uproarious, vehement, vocal

vogue *noun* 1 FASHION, craze, custom, mode, style, trend, way 2 As in **in vogue** POPULARITY, acceptance, currency, favor, prevalence, usage, use

voice *noun* 1 SOUND, articulation, tone, utterance 2 SAY, view, vote, will, wish ▶ *verb* 3 EXPRESS, air, articulate, declare, enunciate, utter

void *noun* 1 EMPTINESS, blankness, gap, lack, space, vacuity, vacuum ▶ *adjective* 2 INVALID, ineffective, inoperative, null and void, useless, vain, worthless 3 EMPTY, bare, free, tenantless, unfilled, unoccupied, vacant ▶ *verb* 4 INVALIDATE, cancel, nullify, rescind 5 EMPTY, drain, evacuate

volatile *adjective* 1 CHANGEABLE, explosive, inconstant, unsettled, unstable, unsteady, variable 2 TEMPERAMENTAL, erratic, fickle, mercurial, up and down (*informal*)

volition *noun* FREE WILL, choice, choosing, discretion, preference, will

volley *noun* BARRAGE, blast, bombardment, burst, cannonade, fusillade, hail, salvo, shower

voluble *adjective* TALKATIVE, articulate, fluent, forthcoming, glib, loquacious

volume *noun* 1 CAPACITY, compass, dimensions 2 AMOUNT, aggregate, body, bulk, mass, quantity, total 3 BOOK, publication, title, tome, treatise

voluminous *adjective* LARGE, ample, capacious, cavernous, roomy, vast

voluntarily *adverb* WILLINGLY, by choice, freely, off one's own bat, of one's own accord

voluntary *adjective* UNFORCED, discretionary, free, optional,

spontaneous, willing

volunteer *verb* OFFER, step forward

voluptuous *adjective* **1** BUXOM, ample, curvaceous (*informal*), enticing, seductive, shapely **2** SENSUAL, epicurean, hedonistic, licentious, luxurious, self-indulgent, sybaritic

vomit *verb* RETCH, barf (*slang*), disgorge, emit, heave, regurgitate, spew out *or* up, throw up (*informal*)

voracious *adjective* **1** GLUTTONOUS, greedy, hungry, insatiable, omnivorous, ravenous **2** AVID, hungry, insatiable, rapacious, uncontrolled, unquenchable

vortex *noun* WHIRLPOOL, eddy, maelstrom

vote *noun* **1** POLL, ballot, franchise, plebiscite, referendum, show of hands ▶ *verb* **2** ELECT, cast one's vote, opt

voucher *noun* TICKET, coupon, token

vouch for *verb* **1** GUARANTEE, answer for, certify, give assurance of, stand witness, swear to **2** CONFIRM, affirm, assert, attest to, support, uphold

vow *noun* **1** PROMISE, oath, pledge ▶ *verb* **2** PROMISE, affirm, pledge, swear

voyage *noun* JOURNEY, crossing, cruise, passage, trip

vulgar *adjective* CRUDE, coarse, common, impolite, indecent, off-color, ribald, risqué, rude, tasteless, uncouth, unrefined

vulgarity *noun* CRUDENESS, bad taste, coarseness, indelicacy, ribaldry, rudeness, tastelessness

vulnerable *adjective* **1** WEAK, sensitive, susceptible, tender, thin-skinned **2** EXPOSED, accessible, assailable, defenseless, unprotected, wide open

wacky *adjective Informal* FOOLISH, absurd, asinine, crackpot (*informal*), crazy, idiotic, silly, stupid, witless

wad *noun* MASS, bundle, hunk, roll

waddle *verb* SHUFFLE, sway, toddle, totter, wobble

wade *verb* **1** WALK THROUGH, ford, paddle, splash **2 wade through** PLOW THROUGH, drudge at, labor at, peg away at, toil at, work one's way through

waft *verb* CARRY, bear, convey, drift, float, transport

wag *verb* **1** WAVE, bob, nod, quiver, shake, stir, vibrate, wiggle ▶ *noun* **2** WAVE, bob, nod, quiver, shake, vibration, wiggle

wage *noun* **1** *Also* **wages** PAYMENT, allowance, emolument, fee, pay, recompense, remuneration, reward, stipend ▶ *verb* **2** ENGAGE IN, carry on, conduct, practice, proceed with, prosecute, pursue, undertake

wager *noun* **1** BET, gamble ▶ *verb* **2** BET, chance, gamble, lay, pledge, risk, speculate, stake, venture

waif *noun* STRAY, foundling, orphan

wail *verb* 1 CRY, bawl, grieve, howl, lament, weep, yowl ▸ *noun* 2 CRY, complaint, howl, lament, moan, weeping, yowl

wait *verb* 1 REMAIN, hang fire, hold back, linger, pause, rest, stay, tarry ▸ *noun* 2 DELAY, halt, hold-up, interval, pause, rest, stay

waiter, waitress *noun* ATTENDANT, server, steward *or* stewardess

wait on *or* **upon** *verb* SERVE, attend, minister to, tend

waive *verb* SET ASIDE, abandon, dispense with, forgo, give up, relinquish, remit, renounce

wake¹ *verb* 1 AWAKEN, arise, awake, bestir, come to, get up, rouse, stir 2 ACTIVATE, animate, arouse, excite, fire, galvanize, kindle, provoke, stimulate, stir up 3 *noun* VIGIL, deathwatch, funeral, watch

wake² *noun* SLIPSTREAM, aftermath, backwash, path, track, trail, train, wash, waves

wakeful *adjective* 1 SLEEPLESS, insomniac, restless 2 WATCHFUL, alert, alive, attentive, observant, on guard, vigilant, wary

waken *verb* AWAKEN, activate, arouse, awake, rouse, stir

walk *verb* 1 GO, amble, hike, march, move, pace, step, stride, stroll 2 ESCORT, accompany, convoy, take ▸ *noun* 3 STROLL, hike, march, promenade, ramble, saunter, trek, trudge 4 GAIT, carriage, step 5 PATH, alley, avenue,

esplanade, footpath, lane, promenade, trail 6 **walk of life** PROFESSION, calling, career, field, line, trade, vocation

walker *noun* PEDESTRIAN, hiker, rambler, wayfarer

walkout *noun* STRIKE, industrial action, protest, stoppage

walkover *noun* PUSHOVER (*slang*), breeze (*informal*), cakewalk (*informal*), child's play (*informal*), picnic (*informal*), piece of cake (*informal*)

wall *noun* 1 PARTITION, enclosure, screen 2 BARRIER, fence, hedge, impediment, obstacle, obstruction

wallet *noun* HOLDER, case, pocketbook, pouch, purse

wallop *verb* 1 HIT, batter, beat, clobber (*slang*), pound, pummel, strike, thrash, thump, whack ▸ *noun* 2 BLOW, bash, punch, slug, smack, thump, thwack, whack

wallow *verb* 1 REVEL, bask, delight, glory, luxuriate, relish, take pleasure 2 ROLL ABOUT, splash around

wan *adjective* PALE, anemic, ashen, pallid, pasty, sickly, washed out, white

wand *noun* STICK, baton, rod

wander *verb* 1 ROAM, drift, meander, ramble, range, rove, stray, stroll 2 DEVIATE, depart, digress, diverge, err, go astray, swerve, veer ▸ *noun* 3 EXCURSION, cruise, meander, ramble

wanderer *noun* TRAVELER, drifter, gypsy, nomad, rambler, rover, vagabond, voyager

wandering *adjective* NOMADIC, itinerant, migratory,

peripatetic, rootless, roving, traveling, vagrant, wayfaring

wane verb 1 DECLINE, decrease, diminish, dwindle, ebb, fade, fail, lessen, subside, taper off, weaken ▶ noun 2 **on the wane** DECLINING, dwindling, ebbing, fading, obsolescent, on the decline, tapering off, weakening

wangle verb CONTRIVE, arrange, engineer, fix (informal), maneuver, manipulate, pull off

want verb 1 DESIRE, covet, crave, hanker after, hope for, hunger for, long for, thirst for, wish, yearn for 2 NEED, call for, demand, lack, miss, require ▶ noun 3 WISH, appetite, craving, desire, longing, need, requirement, yearning 4 LACK, absence, dearth, deficiency, famine, insufficiency, paucity, scarcity, shortage 5 POVERTY, destitution, neediness, penury, privation

wanting adjective 1 LACKING, absent, incomplete, missing, short, shy 2 INADEQUATE, defective, deficient, faulty, imperfect, lousy (slang), poor, substandard, unsound

wanton adjective 1 UNPROVOKED, arbitrary, gratuitous, groundless, motiveless, needless, senseless, uncalled-for, unjustifiable, willful 2 PROMISCUOUS, dissipated, dissolute, immoral, lecherous, libidinous, loose, lustful, shameless, unchaste

war noun 1 FIGHTING, battle, combat, conflict, enmity, hostilities, struggle, warfare ▶ verb 2 FIGHT, battle, campaign against, clash, combat, take up arms, wage war

warble verb SING, chirp, trill, twitter

ward noun 1 ROOM, apartment, cubicle 2 DISTRICT, area, division, precinct, quarter, zone 3 DEPENDANT, charge, minor, protégé, pupil

warden noun KEEPER, administrator, caretaker, curator, custodian, guardian, ranger, superintendent

ward off verb REPEL, avert, avoid, deflect, fend off, parry, stave off

wardrobe noun 1 CLOTHES CUPBOARD, closet 2 CLOTHES, apparel, attire

warehouse noun STORE, depository, depot, stockroom, storehouse

wares plural noun GOODS, commodities, merchandise, produce, products, stock, stuff

warfare noun WAR, arms, battle, combat, conflict, fighting, hostilities

warily adverb CAUTIOUSLY, carefully, charily, circumspectly, distrustfully, gingerly, suspiciously, vigilantly, watchfully, with care

warlike adjective BELLIGERENT, aggressive, bellicose, bloodthirsty, hawkish, hostile, martial, warmongering

warlock noun MAGICIAN, conjurer, enchanter, sorcerer, wizard

warm adjective 1 HEATED, balmy, lukewarm, pleasant, sunny, tepid, thermal 2 AFFECTIONATE, amorous, cordial, friendly, hospitable, kindly, loving, tender ▶ verb 3 HEAT, heat up, melt, thaw, warm up

warmonger noun HAWK, belligerent, militarist, saber-rattler

warmth noun 1 HEAT, hotness, warmness 2 AFFECTION, amorousness, cordiality, heartiness, kindliness, love, tenderness

warn verb NOTIFY, advise, alert, apprise, caution, forewarn, give notice, inform, make (someone) aware, tip off

warning noun CAUTION, advice, alarm, alert, notification, omen, sign, tip-off

warp verb 1 TWIST, bend, contort, deform, distort ▶noun 2 TWIST, bend, contortion, distortion, kink

warrant noun 1 AUTHORIZATION, authority, license, permission, permit, sanction ▶verb 2 CALL FOR, demand, deserve, excuse, justify, license, necessitate, permit, require, sanction 3 GUARANTEE, affirm, attest, certify, declare, pledge, vouch for

warranty noun GUARANTEE, assurance, bond, certificate, contract, covenant, pledge

warrior noun SOLDIER, combatant, fighter, gladiator, man-at-arms

wary adjective CAUTIOUS, alert, careful, chary, circumspect, distrustful, guarded, suspicious, vigilant, watchful

wash verb 1 CLEAN, bathe, cleanse, launder, rinse, scrub 2 SWEEP AWAY, bear away, carry off, move 3 Informal BE PLAUSIBLE, bear scrutiny, be convincing, carry weight, hold up, hold water, stand up, stick ▶noun 4 CLEANING, cleansing, laundering, rinse, scrub 5 COAT, coating, film, layer, overlay 6 SWELL, surge, wave

washout noun FAILURE, disappointment, disaster, dud (informal), fiasco, flop (informal)

waste verb 1 MISUSE, blow (slang), dissipate, fritter away, lavish, squander, throw away 2 **waste away** DECLINE, atrophy, crumble, decay, dwindle, fade, wane, wear out, wither ▶noun 3 MISUSE, dissipation, extravagance, frittering away, prodigality, squandering, wastefulness 4 RUBBISH, debris, dross, garbage, leftovers, litter, refuse, scrap, trash 5 **wastes** DESERT, wasteland, wilderness ▶adjective 6 UNWANTED, leftover, superfluous, supernumerary, unused, useless, worthless 7 UNCULTIVATED, bare, barren, desolate, empty, uninhabited, unproductive, wild

wasteful adjective EXTRAVAGANT, lavish, prodigal, profligate, spendthrift, thriftless, uneconomical

waster noun IDLER, couch potato (slang), good-for-nothing, loafer, shirker, wastrel

watch verb 1 LOOK AT, contemplate, eye, observe, regard, see, view 2 GUARD, keep, look after, mind, protect, superintend, take care of, tend ▶noun 3 WRISTWATCH, chronometer, timepiece 4 LOOKOUT, observation, surveillance, vigil

watchdog noun 1 GUARD DOG 2 GUARDIAN, custodian, monitor, protector, scrutineer

watchful *adjective* ALERT, attentive, observant, on the lookout, suspicious, vigilant, wary, wide awake

watchman *noun* GUARD, caretaker, custodian, security guard

watchword *noun* MOTTO, battle cry, byword, catch phrase, catchword, maxim, rallying cry, slogan

water *noun* 1 LIQUID, H_2O ▶ *verb* 2 MOISTEN, dampen, douse, drench, hose, irrigate, soak, spray

water down *verb* DILUTE, thin, water, weaken

waterfall *noun* CASCADE, cataract, fall

watertight *adjective* 1 WATERPROOF 2 FOOLPROOF, airtight, flawless, impregnable, sound, unassailable

watery *adjective* 1 WET, aqueous, damp, fluid, liquid, moist, soggy 2 DILUTED, runny, thin, washy, watered-down, weak

wave *verb* 1 SIGNAL, beckon, direct, gesticulate, gesture, indicate, sign 2 FLAP, brandish, flourish, flutter, oscillate, shake, stir, swing, wag ▶ *noun* 3 RIPPLE, billow, breaker, ridge, roller, swell, undulation 4 OUTBREAK, flood, rash, rush, stream, surge, upsurge

waver *verb* 1 HESITATE, dither, falter, fluctuate, hum and haw, seesaw, vacillate 2 TREMBLE, flicker, quiver, shake, totter, wobble

wax *verb* INCREASE, develop, enlarge, expand, grow, magnify, swell

way *noun* 1 METHOD, fashion, manner, means, mode, procedure, process, system, technique 2 STYLE, custom, habit, manner, nature, personality, practice, wont 3 ROUTE, channel, course, direction, path, pathway, road, track, trail 4 JOURNEY, approach, march, passage 5 DISTANCE, length, stretch

wayfarer *noun* TRAVELER, gypsy, itinerant, nomad, rover, voyager, wanderer

wayward *adjective* ERRATIC, capricious, inconstant, ungovernable, unmanageable, unpredictable, unruly

weak *adjective* 1 FEEBLE, debilitated, effete, fragile, frail, infirm, puny, sickly, unsteady 2 UNSAFE, defenseless, exposed, helpless, unguarded, unprotected, vulnerable 3 UNCONVINCING, feeble, flimsy, hollow, lame, pathetic, unsatisfactory 4 TASTELESS, diluted, insipid, runny, thin, watery

weaken *verb* 1 LESSEN, diminish, dwindle, fade, flag, lower, moderate, reduce, sap, undermine, wane 2 DILUTE, thin out, water down

weakling *noun* SISSY, baby (*informal*), drip (*informal*), wimp (*informal*)

weakness *noun* 1 FRAILTY, decrepitude, feebleness, fragility, infirmity, powerlessness, vulnerability 2 FAILING, blemish, defect, deficiency, fault, flaw, imperfection, lack, shortcoming 3 LIKING, fondness, inclination, partiality, passion, penchant, soft spot

wealth noun 1 RICHES, affluence, capital, fortune, money, opulence, prosperity 2 PLENTY, abundance, copiousness, cornucopia, fullness, profusion, richness

wealthy adjective RICH, affluent, flush (informal), moneyed, opulent, prosperous, well-heeled (informal), well-off, well-to-do

wear verb 1 BE DRESSED IN, don, have on, put on, sport (informal) 2 SHOW, display, exhibit 3 DETERIORATE, abrade, corrode, erode, fray, grind, rub ▶ noun 4 CLOTHES, apparel, attire, costume, dress, garb, garments, gear (informal), things 5 DAMAGE, abrasion, attrition, corrosion, deterioration, erosion, wear and tear

weariness noun TIREDNESS, drowsiness, exhaustion, fatigue, languor, lassitude, lethargy, listlessness

wearing adjective TIRESOME, exasperating, fatiguing, irksome, oppressive, trying, wearisome

wearisome adjective TEDIOUS, annoying, boring, exhausting, fatiguing, irksome, oppressive, tiresome, troublesome, trying, wearing

wear off verb SUBSIDE, decrease, diminish, disappear, dwindle, fade, peter out, wane

weary adjective 1 TIRED, done in (informal), drained, drowsy, exhausted, fatigued, flagging, jaded, sleepy, worn out 2 TIRING, arduous, laborious, tiresome, wearisome ▶ verb 3 TIRE, drain, enervate, fatigue, sap, take it out of (informal), tax, tire out, wear out

weather noun 1 CLIMATE, conditions ▶ verb 2 WITHSTAND, brave, come through, endure, overcome, resist, ride out, stand, survive

weave verb 1 KNIT, braid, entwine, interlace, intertwine, plait 2 CREATE, build, construct, contrive, fabricate, make up, put together, spin 3 ZIGZAG, crisscross, wind

web noun 1 SPIDER'S WEB, cobweb 2 NETWORK, lattice, tangle

wed verb 1 MARRY, get married, take the plunge (informal), tie the knot (informal) 2 UNITE, ally, blend, combine, interweave, join, link, merge

wedding noun MARRIAGE, nuptials, wedlock

wedge noun 1 BLOCK, chunk, lump ▶ verb 2 SQUEEZE, cram, crowd, force, jam, lodge, pack, ram, stuff, thrust

wedlock noun MARRIAGE, matrimony

weed out verb ELIMINATE, dispense with, eradicate, get rid of, remove, root out, uproot

weedy adjective WEAK, feeble, frail, ineffectual, puny, skinny, thin

weep verb CRY, blubber, lament, mourn, shed tears, snivel, sob, whimper

weepy adjective Informal SENTIMENTAL, overemotional, schmaltzy (slang), slushy (informal)

weigh verb 1 HAVE A WEIGHT OF,

tip the scales at (*informal*)
2 CONSIDER, contemplate, deliberate upon, evaluate, examine, meditate upon, ponder, reflect upon, think over **3** MATTER, carry weight, count

weight *noun* **1** HEAVINESS, load, mass, poundage, tonnage **2** IMPORTANCE, authority, consequence, impact, import, influence, power, value ▶ *verb* **3** LOAD, freight **4** BIAS, load, slant, unbalance

weighty *adjective* **1** IMPORTANT, consequential, crucial, grave, momentous, portentous, serious, significant, solemn **2** HEAVY, burdensome, cumbersome, hefty (*informal*), massive, ponderous

weird *adjective* STRANGE, bizarre, creepy (*informal*), eerie, freakish, mysterious, odd, queer, spooky (*informal*), unnatural

welcome *verb* **1** GREET, embrace, hail, meet, receive ▶ *noun* **2** GREETING, acceptance, hospitality, reception, salutation ▶ *adjective* **3** ACCEPTABLE, agreeable, appreciated, delightful, desirable, gratifying, pleasant, refreshing **4** FREE, under no obligation

weld *verb* JOIN, bind, bond, connect, fuse, link, solder, unite

welfare *noun* **1** WELLBEING, advantage, benefit, good, happiness, health, interest, prosperity **2** BENEFIT, allowance, gift, grant, handout

well[1] *adverb* **1** SATISFACTORILY, agreeably, nicely, pleasantly,

smoothly, splendidly, successfully **2** SKILLFULLY, ably, adeptly, adequately, admirably, correctly, efficiently, expertly, proficiently, properly **3** PROSPEROUSLY, comfortably **4** SUITABLY, fairly, fittingly, justly, properly, rightly **5** INTIMATELY, deeply, fully, profoundly, thoroughly **6** FAVORABLY, approvingly, glowingly, highly, kindly, warmly **7** CONSIDERABLY, abundantly, amply, fully, greatly, heartily, highly, substantially, thoroughly, very much ▶ *adjective* **8** HEALTHY, fit, in fine fettle, sound **9** SATISFACTORY, agreeable, fine, pleasing, proper, right, thriving

well[2] *noun* **1** HOLE, bore, pit, shaft ▶ *verb* **2** FLOW, gush, jet, pour, spout, spring, spurt, surge

well-known *adjective* FAMOUS, celebrated, familiar, noted, popular, renowned

well-off *adjective* RICH, affluent, comfortable (*informal*), moneyed, prosperous, wealthy, well-heeled (*informal*), well-to-do

well-to-do *adjective* RICH, affluent, comfortable (*informal*), moneyed, prosperous, wealthy, well-heeled (*informal*), well-off

well-worn *adjective* STALE, banal, commonplace, hackneyed, overused, stereotyped, trite

welt *noun* MARK, contusion, streak, stripe, wale, weal

welter *noun* JUMBLE, confusion, mess, muddle, tangle, web

wet *adjective* **1** DAMP, dank, moist, saturated, soaking, sodden, soggy, sopping, waterlogged, watery 2 RAINY, drizzling, pouring, raining, showery, teeming ▸noun 3 RAIN, drizzle 4 MOISTURE, condensation, damp, dampness, humidity, liquid, water, wetness ▸verb 5 MOISTEN, dampen, douse, irrigate, saturate, soak, spray, water

whack verb 1 STRIKE, bang, belt (informal), clobber (slang), hit, smack, thrash, thump, thwack, wallop (informal) ▸noun 2 BLOW, bang, belt (informal), hit, smack, stroke, thump, thwack, wallop (informal) 3 Informal SHARE, bit, cut (informal), part, portion, quota 4 As in **have a whack** ATTEMPT, bash (informal), crack (informal), go (informal), shot (informal), stab (informal), try, turn

wharf noun DOCK, jetty, landing stage, pier, quay

wheedle verb COAX, cajole, entice, inveigle, persuade

wheel noun 1 CIRCLE, gyration, pivot, revolution, rotation, spin, turn ▸verb 2 TURN, gyrate, pirouette, revolve, rotate, spin, swing, swivel, twirl, whirl

wheeze verb 1 GASP, cough, hiss, rasp, whistle ▸noun 2 GASP, cough, hiss, rasp, whistle 3 Brit. slang TRICK, idea, plan, ploy, ruse, scheme, stunt

whereabouts noun POSITION, location, site, situation

wherewithal noun RESOURCES, capital, funds, means, money, supplies

whet verb 1 As in **whet someone's appetite** STIMULATE,

arouse, awaken, enhance, excite, kindle, quicken, rouse, stir 2 SHARPEN, hone

whiff noun SMELL, aroma, hint, odor, scent, sniff

whim noun IMPULSE, caprice, fancy, notion, urge

whimper verb 1 CRY, moan, snivel, sob, weep, whine ▸noun 2 SOB, moan, snivel, whine

whimsical adjective FANCIFUL, curious, eccentric, freakish, funny, odd, playful, quaint, unusual

whine noun 1 CRY, moan, sob, wail, whimper 2 COMPLAINT, gripe (informal), grouch (informal), grouse, grumble, moan

whip noun 1 LASH, birch, cane, cat-o'-nine-tails, crop, scourge ▸verb 2 LASH, beat, birch, cane, flagellate, flog, paddle (U.S. & Canad.), scourge, spank, strap, thrash 3 Informal DASH, dart, dive, fly, rush, shoot, tear, whisk 4 BEAT, whisk 5 INCITE, agitate, drive, foment, goad, spur, stir, work up

whirl verb 1 SPIN, pirouette, revolve, roll, rotate, swirl, turn, twirl, twist 2 FEEL DIZZY, reel, spin ▸noun 3 REVOLUTION, pirouette, roll, rotation, spin, swirl, turn, twirl, twist 4 BUSTLE, flurry, merry-go-round, round, series, succession 5 CONFUSION, daze, dither, giddiness, spin

whirlwind noun 1 TORNADO, waterspout ▸adjective 2 RAPID, hasty, quick, short, speedy, swift

whisk verb 1 FLICK, brush, sweep, whip 2 BEAT, fluff up, whip ▸noun 3 FLICK, brush, sweep, whip **4** BEATER

whisper verb **1** MURMUR, breathe **2** RUSTLE, hiss, sigh, swish ▶ noun **3** MURMUR, undertone **4** RUSTLE, hiss, sigh, swish

white adjective PALE, ashen, pallid, pasty, wan

white-collar adjective CLERICAL, nonmanual, professional, salaried

whiten verb PALE, blanch, bleach, fade

whitewash noun **1** COVER-UP, camouflage, concealment, deception ▶ verb **2** COVER UP, camouflage, conceal, gloss over, suppress

whittle verb **1** CARVE, cut, hew, pare, shape, shave, trim **2 whittle down** or **away** REDUCE, consume, eat away, erode, wear away

whole adjective **1** COMPLETE, entire, full, total, unabridged, uncut, undivided **2** UNDAMAGED, in one piece, intact, unbroken, unharmed, unscathed, untouched ▶ noun **3** TOTALITY, ensemble, entirety **4 on the whole: a** ALL IN ALL, all things considered, by and large **b** GENERALLY, as a rule, in general, in the main, mostly, predominantly

wholehearted adjective SINCERE, committed, dedicated, determined, devoted, enthusiastic, unstinting, zealous

wholesale adjective **1** EXTENSIVE, broad, comprehensive, far-reaching, indiscriminate, mass, sweeping, wide-ranging ▶ adverb **2** EXTENSIVELY, comprehensively, indiscriminately

wholesome adjective **1** BENEFICIAL, good, healthy, nourishing, nutritious, salubrious **2** MORAL, decent, edifying, improving, respectable

wholly adverb COMPLETELY, altogether, entirely, fully, in every respect, perfectly, thoroughly, totally, utterly

whopper noun **1** GIANT, colossus, crackerjack (informal), jumbo (informal), leviathan, mammoth, monster **2** BIG LIE, fabrication, falsehood, tall tale (informal), untruth

whopping adjective GIGANTIC, big, enormous, giant, great, huge, mammoth, massive

whore noun PROSTITUTE, call girl, ho (slang), streetwalker, tart (informal)

wicked adjective **1** BAD, corrupt, depraved, devilish, evil, fiendish, immoral, sinful, vicious, villainous **2** MISCHIEVOUS, impish, incorrigible, naughty, rascally, roguish

wide adjective **1** BROAD, expansive, extensive, far-reaching, immense, large, sweeping, vast **2** SPACIOUS, baggy, capacious, commodious, full, loose, roomy **3** EXPANDED, dilated, distended, outspread, outstretched **4** DISTANT, off course, off target, remote ▶ adverb **5** FULLY, completely **6** OFF TARGET, astray, off course, off the mark, out

widen verb BROADEN, dilate, enlarge, expand, extend, spread, stretch

widespread adjective COMMON, broad, extensive, far-reaching, general, pervasive, popular, universal

width noun BREADTH, compass, diameter, extent, girth, scope, span, thickness

wield verb 1 BRANDISH, employ, flourish, handle, manage, manipulate, ply, swing, use 2 As in **wield power** EXERT, exercise, have, maintain, possess

wife noun SPOUSE, better half (humorous), bride, mate, partner

wiggle verb, noun JERK, flutter, jiggle, oscillate, shake, shimmy, squirm, twitch, wag, wave, writhe

wild adjective 1 UNTAMED, feral, ferocious, fierce, savage, unbroken, undomesticated 2 UNCULTIVATED, free, natural 3 UNCIVILIZED, barbaric, barbarous, brutish, ferocious, fierce, primitive, savage 4 UNCONTROLLED, disorderly, riotous, rowdy, turbulent, undisciplined, unfettered, unmanageable, unrestrained, unruly, wayward 5 STORMY, blustery, choppy, raging, rough, tempestuous, violent 6 EXCITED, crazy (informal), enthusiastic, hysterical, raving, wired (slang) ▶noun 7 **wilds** WILDERNESS, back of beyond (informal), desert, middle of nowhere (informal), wasteland

wilderness noun DESERT, jungle, wasteland, wilds

wiles plural noun TRICKERY, artfulness, chicanery, craftiness, cunning, guile, slyness

will noun 1 DETERMINATION, purpose, resolution, resolve, willpower 2 WISH, desire, fancy,

inclination, mind, preference, volition 3 TESTAMENT, last wishes ▶verb 4 WISH, desire, prefer, see fit, want 5 BEQUEATH, confer, give, leave, pass on, transfer

willful adjective 1 OBSTINATE, determined, headstrong, inflexible, intransigent, obdurate, perverse, pig-headed, stubborn, uncompromising 2 INTENTIONAL, conscious, deliberate, intended, purposeful, voluntary

willing adjective READY, agreeable, amenable, compliant, consenting, game (informal), inclined, prepared

willingly adverb READILY, by choice, cheerfully, eagerly, freely, gladly, happily, of one's own accord, voluntarily

willingness noun INCLINATION, agreement, consent, volition, will, wish

willowy adjective SLENDER, graceful, lithe, slim, supple, svelte, sylphlike

willpower noun SELF-CONTROL, determination, drive, grit, resolution, resolve, self-discipline, single-mindedness

wilt verb 1 DROOP, sag, shrivel, wither 2 WEAKEN, fade, flag, languish, wane

wily adjective CUNNING, artful, astute, crafty, guileful, sharp, shrewd, sly, tricky

wimp noun Informal WEAKLING, coward, drip (informal), loser (slang), mouse, sissy, softy or softie

wimpy adjective Informal FEEBLE, effete, ineffectual, soft, spineless, timorous, weak, weedy (*informal*)

win *verb* **1** TRIUMPH, come first, conquer, overcome, prevail, succeed, sweep the board **2** GAIN, achieve, acquire, attain, earn, get, land, obtain, procure, secure ▸ *noun* **3** VICTORY, conquest, success, triumph

wince *verb* **1** FLINCH, blench, cower, cringe, draw back, quail, recoil, shrink, start ▸ *noun* **2** FLINCH, cringe, start

wind¹ *noun* **1** AIR, blast, breeze, draft, gust, zephyr **2** BREATH, puff, respiration **3** FLATULENCE, gas **4** TALK, babble, blather, bluster, boasting, hot air, humbug **5** *As in* **get wind of** HINT, inkling, notice, report, rumor, suggestion, warning, whisper

wind² *verb* **1** COIL, curl, encircle, loop, reel, roll, spiral, twist **2** MEANDER, bend, curve, ramble, snake, turn, twist, zigzag

windfall *noun* GODSEND, bonanza, find, jackpot, manna from heaven

wind up *verb* **1** END, close, conclude, finalize, finish, settle, terminate, wrap up **2** END UP, be left, finish up

windy *adjective* BREEZY, blowy, blustery, gusty, squally, stormy, wild, windswept

wing *noun* **1** FACTION, arm, branch, group, section ▸ *verb* **2** FLY, glide, soar **3** WOUND, clip, hit

wink *verb* **1** BLINK, bat, flutter **2** TWINKLE, flash, gleam, glimmer, sparkle ▸ *noun* **3** BLINK, flutter

winner *noun* VICTOR, champ (*informal*), champion, conqueror, master

winning *adjective* **1** VICTORIOUS, conquering, successful, triumphant **2** CHARMING, alluring, attractive, cute, disarming, enchanting, endearing, engaging, likable *or* likeable, pleasing

winnings *plural noun* SPOILS, gains, prize, proceeds, profits, takings

winnow *verb* SEPARATE, divide, select, sift, sort out

win over *verb* CONVINCE, bring *or* talk round, convert, influence, persuade, prevail upon, sway

wintry *adjective* COLD, chilly, freezing, frosty, frozen, icy, snowy

wipe *verb* **1** CLEAN, brush, mop, rub, sponge, swab **2** ERASE, remove ▸ *noun* **3** RUB, brush

wipe out *verb* DESTROY, annihilate, eradicate, erase, expunge, exterminate, massacre, obliterate

wiry *adjective* LEAN, sinewy, strong, tough

wisdom *noun* UNDERSTANDING, discernment, enlightenment, erudition, insight, intelligence, judgment, knowledge, learning, sense

wise *adjective* SENSIBLE, clever, discerning, enlightened, erudite, intelligent, judicious, perceptive, prudent, sage

wisecrack *noun* *Informal* **1** JOKE, jest, jibe, quip, witticism ▸ *verb* **2** JOKE, jest, jibe, quip

wish *verb* **1** WANT, aspire, crave, desire, hanker, hope, long, yearn ▸ *noun* 2 DESIRE, aspiration, hope, intention, urge, want, whim, will

wispy *adjective* THIN, attenuated, delicate, fine, flimsy, fragile, frail

wistful *adjective* MELANCHOLY, contemplative, dreamy, longing, meditative, pensive, reflective, thoughtful

wit *noun* 1 HUMOR, badinage, banter, drollery, jocularity, raillery, repartee, wordplay 2 HUMORIST, card (*informal*), comedian, joker, wag 3 CLEVERNESS, acumen, brains, common sense, ingenuity, intellect, sense, wisdom

witch *noun* ENCHANTRESS, crone, hag, magician, sorceress

witchcraft *noun* MAGIC, enchantment, necromancy, occultism, sorcery, the black art, voodoo, wizardry

withdraw *verb* REMOVE, draw back, extract, pull out, take away, take off

withdrawal *noun* REMOVAL, extraction

withdrawn *adjective* UNCOMMUNICATIVE, distant, introverted, reserved, retiring, shy, taciturn, unforthcoming

wither *verb* WILT, decay, decline, disintegrate, fade, perish, shrivel, waste

withering *adjective* SCORNFUL, devastating, humiliating, hurtful, mortifying, snubbing

withhold *verb* KEEP BACK, conceal, hide, hold back, refuse, reserve, retain, suppress

withstand *verb* RESIST, bear, cope with, endure, hold off, oppose, stand up to, suffer, tolerate

witless *adjective* FOOLISH, halfwitted, idiotic, inane, moronic, senseless, silly, stupid

witness *noun* 1 OBSERVER, beholder, bystander, eyewitness, looker-on, onlooker, spectator, viewer, watcher 2 TESTIFIER, corroborator ▸ *verb* 3 SEE, note, notice, observe, perceive, view, watch 4 SIGN, countersign, endorse

wits *plural noun* INTELLIGENCE, acumen, brains (*informal*), cleverness, comprehension, faculties, ingenuity, reason, sense, understanding

witticism *noun* QUIP, bon mot, one-liner (*slang*), pun, riposte

witty *adjective* HUMOROUS, amusing, clever, droll, funny, piquant, sparkling, waggish, whimsical

wizard *noun* MAGICIAN, conjurer, magus, necromancer, occultist, shaman, sorcerer, warlock, witch

wizardry *noun* MAGIC, sorcery, voodoo, witchcraft

wizened *adjective* WRINKLED, dried up, gnarled, lined, shriveled, shrunken, withered

wobble *verb* 1 SHAKE, rock, sway, teeter, totter, tremble ▸ *noun* 2 UNSTEADINESS, shake, tremble, tremor

wobbly *adjective* UNSTEADY, rickety, shaky, teetering, tottering, uneven

woe *noun* GRIEF, agony, anguish, distress, gloom, misery, sadness, sorrow, unhappiness, wretchedness

woeful *adjective* 1 SAD, deplorable, dismal, distressing, grievous, lamentable, miserable, pathetic, tragic, wretched 2 PITIFUL, abysmal, appalling, bad, deplorable, dreadful, feeble, pathetic, poor, sorry

woman noun LADY, female, girl

womanizer noun PHILANDERER, Casanova, Don Juan, lecher, seducer

womanly adjective FEMININE, female, ladylike, matronly, motherly, tender, warm

wonder verb 1 THINK, conjecture, meditate, ponder, puzzle, query, question, speculate 2 BE AMAZED, be astonished, gape, marvel, stare ▶ noun 3 PHENOMENON, curiosity, marvel, miracle, prodigy, rarity, sight, spectacle 4 AMAZEMENT, admiration, astonishment, awe, bewilderment, fascination, surprise, wonderment

wonderful adjective 1 EXCELLENT, brilliant, fabulous (informal), fantastic (informal), great (informal), magnificent, marvelous, outstanding, superb, terrific (informal), tremendous 2 REMARKABLE, amazing, astonishing, extraordinary, incredible, miraculous, phenomenal, staggering, startling, unheard-of

woo verb COURT, cultivate, pursue

wood noun 1 TIMBER 2 WOODLAND, coppice, copse, forest, grove, thicket

wooded adjective TREE-COVERED, forested, sylvan (poetic), timbered, tree-clad

wooden adjective 1 WOODY, ligneous, timber 2 EXPRESSIONLESS, deadpan, lifeless, unresponsive

wool noun FLEECE, hair, yarn

woolly adjective 1 FLEECY, hairy, shaggy, woollen 2 VAGUE, confused, hazy, ill-defined, indefinite, indistinct, muddled, unclear

word noun 1 TERM, expression, name 2 CHAT, confab (informal), consultation, discussion, talk, tête-à-tête 3 REMARK, comment, utterance 4 MESSAGE, communiqué, dispatch, information, intelligence, news, notice, report 5 PROMISE, assurance, guarantee, oath, pledge, vow 6 COMMAND, bidding, decree, mandate, order ▶ verb 7 EXPRESS, couch, phrase, put, say, state, utter

wording noun PHRASEOLOGY, language, phrasing, terminology, words

wordy adjective LONG-WINDED, diffuse, prolix, rambling, verbose, windy

work noun 1 EFFORT, drudgery, elbow grease (facetious), exertion, industry, labor, sweat, toil 2 EMPLOYMENT, business, duty, job, livelihood, occupation, profession, trade 3 TASK, assignment, chore, commission, duty, job, stint, undertaking 4 CREATION, achievement, composition, handiwork, opus, piece, production ▶ verb 5 LABOR, drudge, exert oneself, peg away, slave, slog (away), sweat, toil 6 BE EMPLOYED, be in work 7 OPERATE, control, drive, handle, manage, manipulate, move, use 8 FUNCTION, go, operate, run 9 CULTIVATE, dig, farm, till 10 MANIPULATE, fashion, form, knead, mold, shape

workable *adjective* VIABLE, doable, feasible, possible, practicable, practical

worker *noun* EMPLOYEE, artisan, craftsman, hand, laborer, tradesman, workman

working *adjective* 1 EMPLOYED, active, in work 2 FUNCTIONING, going, operative, running

workman *noun* LABORER, artisan, craftsman, employee, hand, journeyman, mechanic, operative, tradesman, worker

workmanship *noun* SKILL, artistry, craftsmanship, expertise, handiwork, technique

work out *verb* 1 SOLVE, calculate, figure out, find out 2 HAPPEN, develop, evolve, result, turn out 3 EXERCISE, practice, train, warm up

works *plural noun* 1 FACTORY, mill, plant, workshop 2 WRITINGS, canon, *oeuvre*, output 3 MECHANISM, action, machinery, movement, parts, workings

workshop *noun* STUDIO, factory, mill, plant, workroom

world *noun* 1 EARTH, globe 2 MANKIND, everybody, everyone, humanity, humankind, man, the public 3 SPHERE, area, domain, environment, field, realm

worldly *adjective* 1 EARTHLY, physical, profane, secular, temporal, terrestrial 2 MATERIALISTIC, grasping, greedy, selfish 3 WORLDLY-WISE, blasé, cosmopolitan, experienced, knowing, sophisticated, urbane

worldwide *adjective* GLOBAL, general, international, omnipresent, pandemic, ubiquitous, universal

worn *adjective* RAGGED, frayed, shabby, tattered, tatty, the worse for wear, threadbare

worn-out *adjective* 1 RUN-DOWN, on its last legs, ragged, shabby, threadbare, used-up, useless, worn 2 EXHAUSTED, dead-tired, done in (*informal*), fatigued, ready to drop, spent, tired out, weary

worried *adjective* ANXIOUS, afraid, apprehensive, concerned, fearful, frightened, nervous, perturbed, tense, troubled, uneasy, wired (*slang*)

worry *verb* 1 BE ANXIOUS, agonize, brood, fret 2 TROUBLE, annoy, bother, disturb, perturb, pester, unsettle, upset, vex ▶ *noun* 3 ANXIETY, apprehension, concern, fear, misgiving, trepidation, trouble, unease 4 PROBLEM, bother, care, hassle (*informal*), trouble

worsen *verb* 1 AGGRAVATE, damage, exacerbate 2 DETERIORATE, decay, decline, degenerate, get worse, go downhill (*informal*), sink

worship *verb* 1 PRAISE, adore, exalt, glorify, honor, pray to, revere, venerate 2 LOVE, adore, idolize, put on a pedestal ▶ *noun* 3 PRAISE, adoration, adulation, devotion, glory, honor, kudos, regard, respect, reverence

worth *noun* 1 VALUE, cost, price, rate, valuation 2 EXCELLENCE, goodness, importance, merit, quality, usefulness, value, worthiness

worthless *adjective* **1** USELESS, ineffectual, rubbishy, unimportant, valueless **2** GOOD-FOR-NOTHING, contemptible, despicable, lousy (*slang*), scuzzy (*slang*), vile

worthwhile *adjective* USEFUL, beneficial, constructive, expedient, helpful, productive, profitable, valuable

worthy *adjective* PRAISEWORTHY, admirable, creditable, deserving, laudable, meritorious, valuable, virtuous, worthwhile

would-be *adjective* BUDDING, self-appointed, self-styled, unfulfilled, wannabe (*informal*)

wound *noun* **1** INJURY, cut, gash, hurt, laceration, lesion, trauma (*Pathology*) **2** INSULT, offense, slight ▶ *verb* **3** INJURE, cut, gash, hurt, lacerate, pierce, wing **4** OFFEND, annoy, cut (someone) to the quick, hurt, mortify, sting

wrangle *verb* **1** ARGUE, bicker, contend, disagree, dispute, fight, quarrel, row, squabble ▶ *noun* **2** ARGUMENT, altercation, bickering, dispute, quarrel, row, squabble, tiff

wrap *verb* **1** COVER, bind, bundle up, encase, enclose, enfold, pack, package, shroud, swathe ▶ *noun* **2** CLOAK, cape, mantle, shawl, stole

wrapper *noun* COVER, case, envelope, jacket, packaging, wrapping

wrap up *verb* **1** GIFTWRAP, bundle up, pack, package **2** *Informal* END, conclude, finish off, polish off, round off, terminate, wind up

wrath *noun* ANGER, displeasure, fury, indignation, ire, rage, resentment, temper

wreath *noun* GARLAND, band, chaplet, crown, festoon, ring

wreck *verb* **1** DESTROY, break, demolish, devastate, ruin, shatter, smash, spoil ▶ *noun* **2** SHIPWRECK, hulk

wreckage *noun* REMAINS, debris, fragments, pieces, rubble, ruin

wrench *verb* **1** TWIST, force, jerk, pull, rip, tear, tug, yank **2** SPRAIN, rick, strain ▶ *noun* **3** TWIST, jerk, pull, rip, tug, yank **4** SPRAIN, strain, twist **5** BLOW, pang, shock, upheaval **6** SPANNER, adjustable spanner

wrest *verb* SEIZE, extract, force, take, win, wrench

wrestle *verb* FIGHT, battle, combat, grapple, scuffle, struggle, tussle

wretch *noun* SCOUNDREL, good-for-nothing, miscreant, rascal, rogue, swine, worm

wretched *adjective* **1** UNHAPPY, dejected, depressed, disconsolate, downcast, forlorn, hapless, miserable, woebegone **2** WORTHLESS, inferior, miserable, paltry, pathetic, poor, sorry

wriggle *verb* **1** TWIST, jerk, jiggle, squirm, turn, wiggle, writhe **2** CRAWL, slink, snake, worm, zigzag **3** As in **wriggle out of** MANEUVER, dodge, extricate oneself ▶ *noun* **4** TWIST, jerk, jiggle, squirm, turn, wiggle

wring *verb* TWIST, extract, force, screw, squeeze

wrinkle *noun* **1** CREASE, corrugation, crinkle, crow's-foot, crumple, fold,

furrow, line ▶*verb* **2** CREASE,
corrugate, crumple, fold,
furrow, gather, pucker, rumple

writ *noun* SUMMONS, court order,
decree, document

write *verb* RECORD, draft, draw
up, inscribe, jot down, pen,
scribble, set down

writer *noun* AUTHOR, hack,
novelist, penpusher, scribbler,
scribe, wordsmith

writhe *verb* SQUIRM, jerk,
struggle, thrash, thresh, toss,
twist, wiggle, wriggle

writing *noun* **1** SCRIPT,
calligraphy, hand, handwriting,
penmanship, scrawl, scribble
2 DOCUMENT, book,
composition, opus, publication,
work

wrong *adjective* **1** INCORRECT,
erroneous, fallacious, false,
inaccurate, mistaken, untrue,
wide of the mark **2** BAD,
criminal, dishonest, evil, illegal,
immoral, sinful, unjust,
unlawful, wicked, wrongful
3 INAPPROPRIATE, incongruous,
incorrect, unacceptable,
unbecoming, undesirable,
unseemly, unsuitable
4 DEFECTIVE, amiss, askew, awry,
faulty ▶*adverb* **5** INCORRECTLY,
badly, erroneously,
inaccurately, mistakenly,
wrongly **6** AMISS, askew, astray,
awry ▶*noun* **7** OFFENSE, crime,
error, injury, injustice, misdeed,
sin, transgression, wickedness
▶*verb* **8** MISTREAT, abuse, cheat,
dishonor, harm, hurt, malign,
oppress, take advantage of

wrongdoer *noun* OFFENDER,
criminal, culprit, delinquent,
evildoer, lawbreaker, miscreant,
sinner, villain

wrongful *adjective* IMPROPER,
criminal, evil, illegal,
illegitimate, immoral,
unethical, unjust, unlawful,
wicked

wry *adjective* **1** IRONIC, droll, dry,
mocking, sarcastic, sardonic
2 CONTORTED, crooked, twisted,
uneven

X x

Xmas *noun* CHRISTMAS, festive
season, Noel, Yule, Yuletide

X-rated *adjective* PORNOGRAPHIC,
adult, dirty, graphic, hardcore
(*slang*), obscene, scuzzy (*slang*)

X-rays *plural noun* RÖNTGEN RAYS
(*old name*)

Y y

yank *verb, noun* PULL, hitch, jerk,
snatch, tug, wrench

yardstick *noun* STANDARD,
benchmark, criterion, gauge,
measure, par, touchstone

yarn *noun* **1** THREAD, fiber
2 *Old-fashioned, informal* STORY,
anecdote, cock-and-bull story
(*informal*), fable, tale, tall tale
(*informal*)

yawning *adjective* GAPING,
cavernous, vast, wide

yearly *adjective* **1** ANNUAL
▶*adverb* **2** ANNUALLY, every year,
once a year, per annum

yearn *verb* LONG, ache, covet,

yell verb 1 SCREAM, bawl, holler (*informal*), howl, screech, shout, shriek, squeal ▸ *noun* 2 SCREAM, cry, howl, screech, shriek, whoop

yell at verb Informal CRITICIZE, censure, rebuke, scold, tear into (*informal*)

yelp verb CRY, yap, yowl

yen noun LONGING, ache, craving, desire, hankering, hunger, itch, passion, thirst, yearning

yes man noun SYCOPHANT, brown-noser (*slang*), minion, timeserver, toady

yet conjunction 1 NEVERTHELESS, however, notwithstanding, still ▸ *adverb* 2 SO FAR, as yet, thus far, until now, up to now 3 STILL, besides, in addition, into the bargain, to boot 4 NOW, just now, right now, so soon

yield verb 1 PRODUCE, bear, bring forth, earn, generate, give, net, provide, return, supply 2 SURRENDER, bow, capitulate, give in, relinquish, resign, submit, succumb ▸ *noun* 3 PROFIT, crop, earnings, harvest, income, output, produce, return, revenue, takings

yielding adjective 1 SUBMISSIVE, accommodating, acquiescent, biddable, compliant, docile, flexible, obedient, pliant 2 SOFT, elastic, pliable, spongy, springy, supple, unresisting

yoke verb BURDEN, encumber, land, load, saddle

yokel noun PEASANT, (country)

crave, desire, hanker, hunger, itch

bumpkin, countryman, hick (*informal, chiefly U.S. & Canad.*), hillbilly, redneck (*slang*), rustic

young adjective 1 IMMATURE, adolescent, callow, green, infant, junior, juvenile, little, youthful 2 NEW, early, fledgling, recent, undeveloped ▸ *plural noun* 3 OFFSPRING, babies, brood, family, issue, litter, progeny

youngster noun YOUTH, boy, girl, juvenile, kid (*informal*), lad, lass, teenager

youth noun 1 IMMATURITY, adolescence, boyhood, girlhood, salad days 2 BOY, adolescent, kid (*informal*), lad, stripling, teenager, young man, youngster

youthful adjective YOUNG, boyish, childish, fresh-faced, girlish, immature, inexperienced, juvenile, rosy-cheeked

Z z

zany adjective COMICAL, clownish, crazy, eccentric, goofy (*informal*), wacky (*slang*)

zeal noun ENTHUSIASM, ardor, eagerness, fanaticism, fervor, gusto, keenness, passion, spirit, verve, zest

zealot noun FANATIC, bigot, enthusiast, extremist, militant

zealous adjective ENTHUSIASTIC, ardent, devoted, eager, fanatical, fervent, impassioned, keen, passionate

zenith noun HEIGHT, acme, apex,

apogee, climax, crest, high point, peak, pinnacle, summit, top

zero *noun* 1 NOTHING, nada (*informal*), nil, nought, zilch (*informal*) 2 BOTTOM, nadir, rock bottom

zest *noun* 1 ENJOYMENT, appetite, gusto, keenness, relish, zeal 2 FLAVOR, charm, interest, piquancy, pungency, relish, spice, tang, taste

zip *noun* 1 *Informal* ENERGY, drive, gusto, liveliness, verve, vigor, zest ▶ *verb* 2 SPEED, flash, fly, shoot, whizz (*informal*), zoom

zone *noun* AREA, belt, district, region, section, sector, sphere

zoom *verb* SPEED, dash, flash, fly, hurtle, pelt, rush, shoot, whizz (*informal*)